CREEK (MUSKOGEE) TEXTS

CREEK (MUSKOGEE) TEXTS

Mary R. Haas

and

James H. Hill

Edited and translated by

Jack B. Martin, Margaret McKane Mauldin, and Juanita McGirt

University of California Press

UNIVERSITY OF CALIFORNIA PRESS, one of the most distinguished university presses in the United States, enriches lives around the world by advancing scholarship in the humanities, social sciences, and natural sciences. Its activities are supported by the UC Press Foundation and philanthropic contributions from individuals and institutions. For more information, visit http://ucpress.edu

University of California Press
Oakland, California

Volume 150

Creek (Muskogee) Texts
by Mary R. Haas and James H. Hill

© 2015 by The Regents of the University of California
All rights reserved. Published 2015
20 19 18 17 16 15 14 13 12 11 10   1 2 3 4 5

ISBN 978-0-520-28642-9

Library of Congress Control Number : 2014956251

v

Table of Contents

vi

List of Illustrations

Foreword

This book is an important reference for anyone interested in Oklahoma history, Muscogee (Creek) history, or for those who are descendants of the Muscogee (Creek) Tribe. Martin, Mauldin, and McGirt are experienced translators and editors of Creek documents and have spent years working on this project. While I am completely biased, I believe that this is their best work and an important account of Creek history and of the removal and relocation of the Creek Nation to what is now Oklahoma.

I first met Dr. Jack Martin in 2004. He was returning home to Williamsburg, Virginia from Philadelphia, Pennsylvania and had been searching for several years for descendants of James Hill. Since I worked in Washington, D.C. then, we agreed to meet in Bethesda. He had just spent a month researching and copying the Creek manuscripts of Mary Haas, my great-grandfather James Hill, and my grandparents Fanny Hill Sulphur and Alex Sulphur. Seeing documents written by my great-grandfather was incredibly emotional for me. I was in awe. I was so impressed that someone of Dr. Martin's experience and credentials would be interested in editing these Creek writings. I knew that this would be a daunting task. You see, all of the writings, stories, and personal history of James Hill, a full-blood Creek, were written in Creek. Therefore, you would need to find someone who could read Creek and understand the "old" Creek language. That person would have to interpret the writings and then be able to express them in English. This seemed so very difficult since our Creek language has changed so much even in my own lifetime. I am one of those American Indian children who was rounded up and sent to a federal boarding school. They had done their job well. They forbade us from speaking Creek and took my language away from me. It is hard for me to speak and read, but I understand it clearly.

So when we had our first meeting in 2004 in my favorite cafe in Bethesda, I was skeptical of his motives. When he arrived and addressed me, *hen'sci* in Creek, I greeted him back in English. We introduced ourselves and he began to tell me how he became interested in the Haas/Hill project. I was further intrigued when he told me that the manuscripts were housed in the American Philosophical Society Library in Philadelphia. I had not heard of the collaboration between Haas and my grandmother and great-grandfather. I was so very impressed that I immediately called my mother Billie Scott and my close friends about my meeting and the pending book. I told my mother, "Do you know how weird it was to have a white man, a PhD, speak Creek to me in this fancy cafe in Washington, D.C.?"

You see, I am Robyn Sulphur York of Eufaula, Oklahoma. I am the great-granddaughter of James Hill and the granddaughter of Fanny Hill Sulphur. I am a descendant of wise, resourceful and literary Creeks. My people could read and write in both English and Creek. I have always been proud of being Creek and a Hill-Sulphur. If you know even a little about Creek history, you know that there has been a fine line drawn by missionaries for our Tribe and tribal members even before the Removal. You were a good Creek if you attended a Protestant church and a bad Creek if you practiced the old ways, our ceremonial grounds or "Stomp Dance" ways. But I was truly lucky growing up in the late 1950's and 1960's. My grandmother Fanny took care of my sisters Ruth, Alexis, and me while my mother went to school and worked as far away as Seattle, Washington. As she said, it was no place for children and kept us home in Eufaula, Oklahoma.

My grandmother Fanny was a child of a preacher (James Hill) but was raised without a mother and taught herself to read and write English. She met and married Alex Sulphur, a traditionalist and medicine man. So their children and her grandchildren were brought up believing that both Christians and traditional people worshipped a higher being responsible for the earth and life. We were taught that we could be both Protestant and traditional. We were taught to appreciate both expressions of Creek life, and my grandmother would fiercely defend our family's right to practice both. My grandmother Fanny was well educated and well traveled. She could read and write in English and Creek. She was a Creek interpreter for families and friends in federal court and in oil, gas, and land dealings with the federal government. She could translate federal laws, court proceedings and procedures, and read and interpret legal documents such as leases, contracts, title, and business papers to her clients. My mother told me that there would be months and months when she had to a maintain the home while grandmother was back east helping her clients. I also recall helping my grandmother Fanny clean her house as she aged. I found pictures of a group of people in front of the U.S. Capitol and the Supreme Court Building. The people were Anne Walker, a friend, an unknown man, grandfather Alex Sulphur, and her. When I asked her, were you really in D.C.? She matter-of-factly said, yes, helping people fight with the BIA.

One mystifying point here is the family history of my great-grandfather. You see the family tradition about James Hill is that he made the walk on the Trail of Tears as a child of 8 to 10 years of age. His true age was unknown to his family. I have a memory of sitting at his feet and looking up at him and Uncle Jeff Hill, my grandmother's brother. I remember the smell of joint ointment like Ben Gay, and the rough feel of his gray wool pants with suspenders. I strongly recall his beautiful white hair and him talking to me in Creek. My size then was quite small, as I was sitting on his lap. I remember the lace curtains in the long, old-fashioned windows. My mother confirms the house as one where my great-aunt Mandy Hill Phillips lived in McAlester, Oklahoma. My grandmother, Uncle Jeff, and Grandpa Hill, as he was called, would often visit.

I hope that you enjoy this book. We are most grateful to Jack B. Martin, Margaret McKane Mauldin, and Juanita McGirt for bringing it to a larger audience. Our family is very proud of our history and our family members, who have left an enduring legacy for us and our children.

Robyn Sulphur York
Glenpool, Oklahoma

Preface

When Mary R. Haas died in 1996, she left behind several thousand pages of notes and texts in the Creek (Muskogee) language. She had collected these materials in eastern Oklahoma between 1936 and 1940, shortly after completing her doctorate in linguistics at Yale University. The majority of the texts in the collection came from the unpublished writings of James H. Hill of Eufaula, an especially knowledgeable elder who composed texts for Haas using the traditional Creek alphabet. Twelve other speakers, including one Seminole and one Creek freedman, served as sources for dictated texts. The texts cover traditional folktales, descriptions of ball-games and traditional activities, autobiography, history, sermons, and prayers.

Haas likely would have revised and published her collection had it not been for the outbreak of war in 1941. This volume represents a completion of her ambitious project to survey and document Creek literature. All the texts have been checked, transcribed, organized, and translated in a way that is consistent with Haas's final practices and current standards. Traditional Creek spellings for the texts have been added to make the work accessible to a larger audience.

Mary R. Haas was a gifted linguist whose studies of Tunica, Natchez, Creek, and Thai show a remarkable talent for phonetic detail, rigorous analysis, and careful regard for language in context. The Creek texts she gathered with James H. Hill and others are an important record of the traditional languages and literatures of the American South.

Acknowledgments

The editors would like to thank Mary R. Haas for opening her notebooks to us. Leanne Hinton helped facilitate the photocopying of her manuscripts. Sally McLendon, Catherine Callahan, and Victor Golla offered advice on format. Robyn York provided family history on her great-grandfather James Hill. Two reviewers provided helpful comments. The National Endowment for the Humanities (RT-21566-94) and the National Science Foundation (SBR-9809819) funded a dictionary and reference grammar that allowed us to begin our study. A grant from the American Philosophical Society (Phillips Fund) funded an initial set of translations. A subsequent Resident Library Fellowship from the same institution allowed Martin to examine Haas's original notebooks and papers. The bulk of the research was supported by the National Endowment for the Humanities.

Had she lived to see the publication of these texts, Haas would have noted that her field work in Oklahoma between 1936 and 1940 was conducted under the auspices of the Department of Anthropology, Yale University, the American Council of Learned Societies' Committee on Research in American Native Languages, and the American Philosophical Society (Penrose Fund). Several students, including William Shipley and Harvey Pitkin, provided clerical assistance funded by the Committee on Research, University of California, Berkeley.

Introduction

In 1936, at the age of just 26, Mary R. Haas moved from New Haven, Connecticut to Eufaula, Oklahoma to begin a study of the Creek (Muskogee) language. It was the height of the Great Depression and Dust Bowl, and jobs were scarce, but with help from former teachers Haas found meager support for her research until the threat of war in 1941. The texts in this volume are a result of that project.

About Mary R. Haas

Mary R. Haas was born January 23, 1910 in Richmond, Indiana to Robert Jeremiah Haas and Leona Crowe Haas.[1] She received three years of tuition scholarships at Earlham College, where she studied English.[2] She also received a scholarship in music during her final year and graduated at the head of her class in 1930.[3] She entered graduate school in the Department of Comparative Philology at the University of Chicago the same year. There she studied Gothic, Old High German with Leonard Bloomfield, Sanskrit, and Psychology of Language with Edward Sapir.[4] She also met and married her fellow student Morris Swadesh. The two traveled to British Columbia after their first year to work on Nitinat, and then followed Sapir to Yale University's Department of Linguistics in 1931. She continued her studies there of Latin, Greek, and Sanskrit and took two courses in Primitive Music.[5] Haas worked as Sapir's research assistant from 1931 to 1933.[6] In the summer of 1933, she received funding to conduct field work in Louisiana with the last speaker of Tunica, close to where Swadesh was working on Chitimacha.[7]

Haas's next project was the Natchez language of eastern Oklahoma. A fellow graduate student at Chicago named Victor E. Riste had been sent to work on Natchez in 1931. The field situation was difficult, however, because the last two speakers knew some Creek and Cherokee but spoke no English. Research on Natchez was thus conducted with Creek-speaking interpreters. In 1934, Franz Boas wrote to Haas that Riste had "fallen down completely on his Natchez work" and so, after consultation with Edward Sapir, Boas asked whether Haas would consider revising Riste's work by conducting field work of her own.[8] After Haas agreed, Boas had Harry Hoijer send Riste's Creek and Natchez field notes to her.[9]

Haas made her first field trip to Oklahoma in the fall of 1934.[10] Her work required that she learn some Creek while she worked on Natchez, and she elicited two Creek texts from Nancy Raven, one of her two Natchez consultants. She then returned to New Haven to complete a grammar of Tunica, for which she was awarded a doctorate in 1935. In 1936, Haas returned to Oklahoma to work on Creek.[11] Unlike Tunica and Natchez, Creek was then very much a living language, with monolingual speakers of all ages. Her notes indicate that she contacted a number of older individuals—mostly men—in the Creek and Seminole nations. She gathered vocabulary, texts, and grammatical paradigms, as well as information on kinship, naming, town relations, and ball-games. When possible, she hired literate native speakers to write texts for her. James H. Hill was Haas's primary source. She then had other speakers read his writings to her while she made phonemic transcriptions.

The four years between 1936 and 1940 were lean ones for Haas. Jobs for academics were difficult to find, and linguists were usually forced to choose between teaching anthropology or languages. Haas chose instead to continue field work.[12]

In May, 1937, Haas wrote to Swadesh about getting a divorce.[13] They had lived separately for some time, and Haas felt it might be hard to get a teaching job as a married woman. Swadesh agreed and accepted a two-year position the same year at the University of Wisconsin.[14]

Haas's and Swadesh's much-admired teacher Edward Sapir died in 1939. This must have made it more difficult to find jobs, but Sapir's students persevered and planned several collections of papers. Leonard Bloomfield advised Haas to publish more articles, advice which she readily took to heart.[15] She published an article on Natchez and Chitimacha clans and kinship in *American Anthropologist*.[16] The following year she published an article on Creek aspect in *Language*.[17] She published a grammatical description of Tunica the same year, managing, after much wrangling with Boas, to shorten her dissertation from some 650 pages to 143.[18] In 1941, in a volume dedicated to the memory of Edward Sapir, she published an influential classification of the Muskogean languages.[19]

While the 1930's were difficult years for Haas, she clearly enjoyed field work. She wrote to Alexander Spoehr in 1940,

> I have received a letter from Boas telling me that the Committee has awarded me a new grant for the continuance of my work. So my worries on that score are over for a while. This means that I shall get to do some work on Yuchi. I am glad of this for I seem to have a natural affinity for field work. I shall also have to go ahead and do what I can toward producing a Natchez grammar, though I have only recently finished up my large Tunica grammar. If this keeps up I'll soon have the world's record for putting out grammars.[20]

By this time Haas was in danger of accumulating more data than she could process. She had a Tunica dictionary and text collection to complete. She had copious notes on Natchez and Creek, and she had conducted, or was planning work on, Hitchiti, Yuchi, Koasati, Alabama, Choctaw—almost any language she could find. As she wrote to Swadesh, "the harder I work the more material I pile up to work on."[21] She still had not published anything substantial on Natchez though, and by the spring of 1941, with war fast approaching, her funding ran out.

It was at this critical juncture that Haas's former Sanskrit professor Franklin Edgerton stepped in. He wrote describing how the American Council of Learned Societies, with funding from the Rockefeller Foundation, was seeking to develop teaching materials in "living oriental languages."[22] Haas was offered a position to produce materials on Thai in

Washington, D.C., and through this work came to meet a second husband (Heng Ritt Subhanka) and a teaching position at the University of California, Berkeley. She taught there in the Department of Oriental Languages and then in the Department of Linguistics until her retirement in 1975.

Haas returned to Oklahoma for several brief trips in the 1970's. Most of her consultants had died by then, but James Hill's daughter Fannie Hill Sulphur was still alive. Haas worked with her on Creek accent patterns. She also assisted Susannah Factor and others in producing elementary school reading materials in Creek.[23]

By the 1980's, Haas's eyesight had weakened. A conference was held in her honor in 1986.[24] She died in 1996. Although only a small portion of her work has appeared in print, Haas is widely recognized as one of the great descriptive linguists of the twentieth century. Among her many publications are a Tunica grammar, text collection, and dictionary, a Thai student dictionary and teaching materials, a monograph on language pre-history, and a large number of essays.[25] Haas was a Guggenheim Fellow, president of the Linguistic Society of America, a member of the National Academy of Sciences, and chair of the Department of Linguistics at the University of California at Berkeley. The twenty-two doctoral students she supervised at Berkeley were crucial in shaping twentieth-century work on American languages and linguistics.

About James H. Hill

James H. Hill (1861–ca. 1953) was the source of 106 of the 156 texts in the Haas collection. He wrote the texts in Creek on loose sheets of lined paper, a writing pad, and three composition notebooks. Hill's originals are preserved in the Mary R. Haas Papers at the American Philosophical Society. As far as we know, these are the only writings he left.[26]

James Hill was Aktayahchi clan and a member of Hilabi (or Hillabee) Canadian tribal town, where he was known as Katcha Homahti (*ka·ccahomáhti*).[27] He was also a member by marriage of Kialegee and Arbeka tribal towns, where he was called Aktayahchochi (*aktayahcoci*).[28] We learn from his autobiography that he was born in July 1861 near Greenleaf tribal town, Creek Nation, Indian Territory.[29] His father's name was Hilly, nephew of Sikomaha. During the U.S. Civil War, his family fled south toward Denison, Texas. After the war they settled in the area of Shell Creek, west of Eufaula in present Burton township, McIntosh County. Hill never attended school, but he learned English and taught himself how to read and write Creek.

During Isparhecher's rebellion, Hill sided with the Muscogee Nation and helped arrest followers of Isparhecher. He participated actively in traditional ball-games and dances, and in 1895 was elected to represent Hilabi Canadian tribal town in the House of Kings (analogous to the U.S. Senate). He held that position until Oklahoma statehood, when he began attending Thlewahle Baptist Church near Hanna. In 1915 he was made Head Deacon and in 1921 became a preacher. In 1938 he was, along with Arthur E. Raiford, one of five candidates for Principal Chief.[30] He died about 1953.[31]

It is important to realize that Hill converted to Christianity following Oklahoma statehood, and that his descriptions of traditional practices are based on memories of an earlier era. His descriptions are thus placed in the remote past, but others were continuing those practices at the time of his writing and are still practicing them in 2014.

James Hill is listed as No. 6373 on the Dawes Final Rolls. His first wife was named Louisa.[32] His second wife was named Polly.[33] His children's names were Luella, Katie, Leah, Fannie, Jefferson, Lucy, Amanda, and Eugene. Fannie (Hill) Sulphur assisted Haas in checking and interpreting her father's texts, and her husband Alex Sulphur was a source for several texts.

The Hill family remembers a few stories about Haas, then a young woman. Robyn York, who was raised by her grandparents Fannie and Alex Sulphur, heard that Haas would sometimes walk miles from Eufaula to their home to work. She would write all day, and then they would feed her. They liked feeding her. One time, when first working with Jim Hill and Fannie, she turned to Fannie and said, "Ask him to say that again." Fannie said, "You ask him—he speaks English!"

Haas's methods

Haas's aim in her field work was to obtain a diverse collection of texts, to determine the contrastive sounds (phonemes) in the language, to compile a vocabulary, and to study the grammar of the language. She was also obligated to complete the work promised in her grant applications: from 1936 to 1938 she received funding from the Department of Anthropology at Yale and was free to collect a wide sample of texts; from 1938 to 1939 her work was funded by a research grant from the American Philosophical Society (Penrose Fund) to examine the history and organization of Creek tribal towns.

Haas took field notes on lined paper and then copied these in bound composition books. She completed twenty-two notebooks on Creek, each about 190 pages in length. Most of her transcriptions from the fall of 1936 to about May of 1937 were phonetic, after which she used phonemic transcriptions.

Haas began by eliciting verbal paradigms for person and tense. She then moved on to possession, infinitives and nouns, plural forms of verbs, and agent nominalizations. By page 25, she felt ready to collect her first text, the story of Rabbit and the Tar-Baby. She did this by asking a speaker to read or dictate a text, which she transcribed in her own orthography. She would then have the text interpreted, usually with another speaker. She would transcribe the text again in this second session along with word for word translations below each word. She would make a note of any corrections or alternate pronunciations offered by the second speaker. When a correction was made, she would write "orig.: ..." on the opposite page, or if a correction might be made, "read: ..." For an alternative pronunciation, she would write "or:

..." on the opposite page. Less accurate transcriptions made in the fall of 1936 were checked again in May of 1937.

Before the advent of computers, linguists made extensive use of file slips. Every word in a text was copied on a piece of paper along with the phrase it occurred in so that the linguist would have an index of every word in context. These slips allowed vocabularies to be compiled and helped identify inconsistent transcriptions or speaker variation. Slips were also made of grammatical topics or specific affixes. Haas had students help her copy her file slips, just as she had helped Sapir at Yale.

As part of the next stage, Haas had the texts in her notebooks typed. The typist would type the Creek and the English glosses on separate pages, drawing a vertical line in the notebook at the end of a line. Slashes were used in glosses to align Creek and English equivalents. Haas would then have planned to translate the texts using the glosses, but she only drafted a few translations this way.

Haas made almost no use of sound recordings. In many cases she relied on dictation, but when speakers were literate in their language, it was faster and more accurate to have them write texts for her. Jim Hill made lists of topics to write about in his notebook, and she or he would sometimes add further details. In one place she notes: "Tobacco was also used for medicine, e.g., for toothache, but H[ill] will write this out later as it is quite long."[34] Punctuation proved difficult for her: in more than one place she notes, "Punctuation marked as written by informant."[35]

Haas's other sources

Haas generally worked with older individuals who were knowledgeable about traditional practices. She elicited texts from 13 people, all men. Of these, one was Seminole (Wesley Tanyan), one was a Creek freedman (A. Grayson), and the rest were Creek. They represent several different tribal towns (Hilabi, Arbeka Talladega, Coweta, Kasihta, Hickory Ground, Eufaula, Thlopthucco). The majority of the texts were by James Hill, and the majority of the checking was done with Arthur E. Raiford or Fannie (Hill) Sulphur.

The following list of consultants is based on information in Haas's notes, supplemented by genealogy and family history.

Jasper Bell was a member of Cussetah tribal town, Bear Clan, a resident of Okmulgee, and a medicine maker.[36] He was introduced to Haas by Morris and Catherine Opler, and Haas in turn recommended him to Sigmund Sameth.[37] He was born six miles southeast of Okmulgee in 1874.[38] His name at Cussetah was Micco Hutke (*mi·kkohátki* or White King).[39] His mother Yana (*yá·na*) was Creek, and his father George Bell was half-Irish and half-Creek.[40] His father was a Lighthorse Captain until his death.[41] His older brother was named Jim Bell.[42] Jasper Bell used to do cattle ranch work for D. H. Middleton.[43] He served as an interpreter for the Creek Council.[44] He is listed as No. 3062 on the Dawes Final Rolls.

Jim Bullet was a member of Hilabi tribal town. He is listed as No. 589 on the Dawes Final Rolls.

Daniel Cook was a member of Thlopthucco tribal town, Bird clan.[45] His father was Tukabahchee town, Raccoon clan and was a nephew of Tukabahchee Harjo, one of Opothleyahola's captains during the Civil War.[46] He lived near Holdenville and was born about 1870. He is listed as No. 2283 on the Dawes Final Rolls.

Earnest (or Ernest) Gouge was a member of Hickory Ground tribal town, Beaver clan.[47] His father was Tukabahchee tribal town, Raccoon clan.[48] His wife Nicey was a member of Hilabi Canadian tribal town, which he joined. He lived west of Eufaula and was born about 1865. He is listed as No. 8497 on the Dawes Final Rolls. Gouge and his younger brother, "Big Jack," had previously worked with John Swanton.[49] Gouge is best known for a collection of 29 Creek stories he wrote for Swanton in 1915.[50] He died on September 4, 1955.

Adam Grayson was a Creek freedman who was bilingual in Creek and English. He was introduced to Haas through Sigmund Sameth, who had been conducting research in Okemah for a master's thesis on race relations.[51] He was also interviewed for the Indian-Pioneer History, where he describes how prophets were traditionally trained.[52]

I[som] Field is listed as No. 7072 on the Dawes Final Rolls.

Tucker Marshall was a member of Arbeka Talladega tribal town, Raccoon clan.[53] He is listed as No. 6561 on the Dawes Final Rolls. His mother Betty Tullamassee (*talamá·si*) was part Natchez, and his mother's mother spoke Natchez.[54] He lived in Burton township, McIntosh county, with a wife Minnie and twelve children.[55] He was a minister at Tuskegee Indian Baptist Church.[56] He died April 5, 1939 at the age of 75.[57]

Paskofa, or Johnson Late, was a member of Tukabahchee tribal town, Raccoon clan, born about 1851.[58] His father was a member of Hilabi tribal town, Ahalakalki clan.[59] He lived near Holdenville.[60]

Arthur E. Raiford (1878–1964) was a member of Coweta tribal town, Beaver clan.[61] He is listed as No. 5691 on the Dawes Final Rolls. As he describes in one story, his father Philip Raiford was captured by the Comanches. Raiford lived in Eufaula, McIntosh County.[62] He had a wife Tookah Raiford, a daughter Alice E. Raiford, and sons William A. Raiford and Felix E. Raiford.[63] Raiford told a few stories he knew and assisted in checking stories told by others.

Daniel Starr was a member of Arbeka Talladega tribal town, Alligator clan.[64] He was born July 4, 1857.[65] His father Ben Starr (Tu-sek-a-ya Hut-ke) was Bear clan.[66] Chitto Harjo was his uncle.[67] He lived near Arbeka ceremonial ground.[68] He is listed as No. 5672 on the Dawes Final Rolls.

Alex Sulphur was a medicine maker, a member of Eufaula tribal town, and a "lost" member of Little Tullahassee.[69] His father was a member of Hickory Ground.[70] He was married to James H. Hill's daughter Fannie.[71] He is listed as No. 9621 on the Dawes Final Rolls.

Wesley Tanyan was a Seminole, Hitchiti band, Deer Clan.[72] He was introduced to Haas through Alexander Spoehr, who had employed him as an interpreter.[73] Tanyan was only 35 when Haas met him. His father was Nina Tanyan and his father's father was Waxie Tanyan.[74] His great-grandfather A-ha-lak E-math-la was a medicine maker who assisted Wild Cat.[75] He is listed as No. 152 on the Dawes Final Rolls.

In addition to the above primary sources, Haas attempted to check and correct Creek texts gathered by Victor E. Riste. Riste transcribed texts that had been dictated phonetically.

Victor Emerson Riste was born 14 November 1897 in Oberlin, Kansas, the fifth of seven children.[76] In 1929, as a student at the University of Washington, he was awarded a field-training scholarship from the Laboratory of Anthropology at Santa Fe. There he and his fellow students (including Harry Hoijer) learned linguistic field techniques from Edward Sapir.[77] He subsequently joined Sapir and Hoijer at the University of Chicago. In July, 1931, he traveled to Oklahoma to conduct field work on Natchez and Creek, supported by the Committee on Research in American Native Languages. He managed, in a short period, to fill five writing pads with Natchez notes and four more on Creek.[78] After World War II, he worked for the State of Illinois in the Unemployment Division, where he worked as a manager over a large section of that department.[79] He died of a heart attack on 28 February, 1958.[80]

Riste worked with several Creek speakers, but did not always indicate who dictated a text. **John Toney** dictated the text "Curing the Back-ache." We know only that he was from Braggs, Oklahoma. **Peter Ewing** (1860–1932) dictated the text "The Singing River." Haas's notes indicate that Ewing was from Hitchiti tribal town, Wind clan. He served for many years as a Baptist minister and was elected Chief of the Muscogee (Creek) Nation in 1931.[81]

Haas spent considerable time forming her own opinions about Creek and Natchez before checking Riste's texts. She clearly intended to include them in her own collection, but never finished correcting them. Riste's Creek and Natchez notebooks are housed with Haas's papers at the American Philosophical Society.

Editorial methods and conventions

Editing this text collection was challenging because of its size and because there were often different versions of the same text. We knew from speaking with Haas that she wanted the texts to be checked and corrected. She also left instructions among her papers:

> The work that remains to be done is as follows: (1) The texts should be rechecked with native speakers in order to eliminate all possibility of phonetic error. (2) It will be necessary to provide finished translations which reflect as nearly as possible the spirit and mood of the original texts. (3) It would also be desirable to annotate the tales with a view to pointing out any similarities that exist between them and tales told by other tribes.[82]

We approached the editing of the manuscript with the idea of completing the texts the way Haas had intended. We leave to others the task of pointing out similarities with other tribes, however.

Most of the texts by James Hill were first written by him in one of his notebooks. These are fairly easy to read, but have very little punctuation and are open to different interpretations.

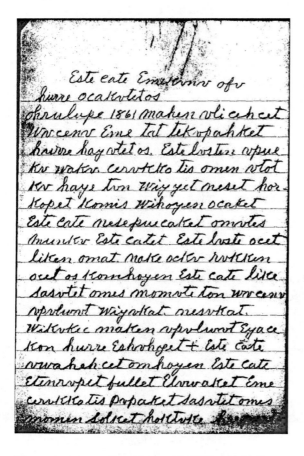

Figure 1: A page from James H. Hill's original.

As an example, the text in Figure 1 begins this way:

Este cate emekvnv ofv
hurre ocakvtetos
ohrulupe 1861 mahen vlicehcet

Haas's practice was to have another speaker interpret Hill's written texts. That speaker would read the text slowly, while she transcribed it phonetically. The speaker would then give English translations of each word.

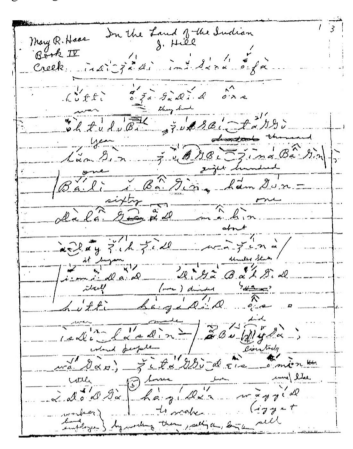

Figure 2: Mary Haas's phonetic transcription of the Hill text.

The three lines Hill wrote above thus appear as follows in Haas's notebook (Figure 2):

> In the Land of the Indian
> J. Hill

ɪsDɪ̌ža·tɪ ɪmi·Gɑnɑ ó·fɑ

húłɪ   ó·ža·GɑDí·D ô·ns
war   they had

ʋhɪʋlʋBíꞏ   ẓʋGBɪɫɑ́kkʋ
year   thousand

hɑ́mGɪn   ẓʋGBɪẓɪnɑBâꞏGɪn
one   eight hundred

Báꞏlɪ   iꞏBâꞏGɪn   hɑmGʋn-
sixty   one

DɑlâꞏGaꞏD   mâꞏhɪn
             about

ɑlɑyẓíhẓɪD
it began

Haas's transcription here is a phonetic transcription (meant to capture all the details of pronunciation). There are two layers of accent marks: an early one with smaller marks and a later one with larger, more definite marks. After several months, she began using a phonemic transcription (meant to abstract away from detail and to capture just the distinctions that were important in the language). She continued to revise her phonemic system of transcription until 1977.

In editing the texts for publication, we adopted a four-line format:

[The Civil War]   ← **added title**
J. Hill (Haas IV:1–25)   ← **author and source**

Este-cate	em ēkvnv	ofv	horre	ocakvtēt os.	←**traditional spelling**
isticá·ti	*imi·kana*	*ó·fa*	*hólli*	*ó·ca·katí·t ô·ⁿs*	← **phonemic**
[Indian	their land	in]	war	they had	← **word-for-word**
They had a war in Indian Territory.					← **free translation**

Ohrolopē	cokperakko	hvmken	cokpe cenvpaken
ohłolopi·	*cokpiłákko*	*hámkin*	*cokpicinapâ·kin*
year	thousand	one	eight hundred
It began in about the year eighteen hundred			

pale ēpaken	hvmkontvlakat	mahen	vlicehcet,
pá·li i·pá·kin	*hamkontalâ·ka·t*	*mà·hin*	*aleycíhcit*
sixty	one	about	it began
and sixty-one [1861].			

The first line of the text is the traditional Creek spelling. The spelling used is consistent with most standard sources on the language and what is familiar to most Creek speakers. The second line (in italics) is a normalized phonemic transcription based on Haas's notes. If we depart from Haas, we add an endnote. If Haas herself had a note, that is presented as a footnote. Footnotes reflect Haas's casual observations and sometimes use non-standard English. If an element appears in Hill's manuscript that was omitted in Haas's manuscript, we include that in angle brackets (< >). The third line is the word-for-word translation as it appears in Haas's notes. If she does not include a word-for-word translation, we omit this line. We have not attempted to systematically add word-for-word translations or to make them consistent, preferring to let Haas's notes speak for themselves. If we do make a change or addition, we indicate that in square brackets ([ ]). The fourth line is our free translation.

We chose the passage above, because it demonstrates some of the decisions we made in editing texts. As noted above, Hill's original has very little punctuation, and it is sometimes difficult to know where sentences begin and end. Haas interpreted the first line of Hill's manuscript as a title: "In the Land of the Indian." This meant that the second line would be translated as "They had a war." We disagreed with that interpretation. This particular text is about the effects of the Civil War, so it was hard for us to see how "In the Land of the Indian" would be an appropriate title. Instead, we interpreted the first and second lines of Hill's manuscript as part of one sentence. We thus created a new title, "[The Civil War]" and translated the first and second lines as "They had a war in Indian Territory."

Scope of the collection. The editors had several discussions among themselves and with the Hill family about what to include in this collection. We did not want to include culturally sensitive information. On the other hand, we did want to recognize the important work that Hill and others did and to make it accessible to others. In the end, we included all of the texts from Haas's Creek notebooks and papers except the following:

a. A "prayer" obtained from a Koasati medicine man in Elton, Louisiana. In 1937, Lyda Averill Paz (later Taylor) sent Haas this brief text.[83] Haas went over the prayer with A. E. Raiford and established that it was Creek.[84] The poor original transcription and source make the analysis questionable, however.

b. Two Creek texts obtained from Haas's Natchez consultant Nancy Raven and included in her Natchez notebooks.

c. A transcription of a recording ("The Discovery of Oil in the Creek Nation"). In the summer of 1941, Mr. C. A. Border lent Haas a record made by the Tulsa Chamber of Commerce containing a sample of Creek.[85] Haas sent Border a transcription and translation of the recording. These are preserved in her correspondence files.

d. Texts originally collected by Frank Speck. Haas attempted to reelicit some of Speck's texts but decided against including them with her own.

Haas did not check all of Victor Riste's texts. We have only included the texts that she checked and intended to include in her collection.

Order of texts. Haas left two sets of plans for organizing the Creek texts. In both plans, as with her *Tunica Texts*, she grouped texts by genre into myths, animal stories, etc. We modified this approach by grouping texts first according to author. We then grouped them loosely according to topic: history, culture, folktales, and stories.

Editors' additions or substitutions. Square brackets ([ ]) indicate material added by the editors.

Notes. Haas included notes related to the texts. These are presented here as footnotes and use Roman numerals. The editors also have notes, which are numbered with Arabic numerals and appear as endnotes.

Haas's practice was to add a note every time there was a difference in usage between her interpreter and the original text. We continued this basic approach: Martin recorded Margaret Mauldin and Juanita McGirt reading the texts. When they pronounced a word differently, he would add a note indicating either that a correction had been made or that an alternative pronunciation was possible.

Multiple versions of texts. In editing the collection, we had access to Hill's original manuscripts in the Creek alphabet, Haas's phonetic and phonemic transcriptions from her notebooks (sometimes with several versions), and later, typed phonemic versions of some texts. The typed versions were based on her phonemic transcriptions, but were never checked carefully. Given the existence of multiple versions of texts, we generally took the most recent phonemic transcriptions in her notebooks as a starting point.

Haas's early texts are particularly challenging to edit. The first versions are written phonetically with word-for-word glosses. The second versions are written phonemically (sometimes in an early form) and, in a few cases, have certain passages reworded. In this case we have used both versions to arrive at a final version.

Phonemic transcription. Haas used phonetic transcription from the fall of 1936 to May of 1937. This amounts to about 60 stories out of 155. She then switched to a phonemic transcription.[86] She made small revisions to her phonemic analysis until 1977.[87] We have attempted to normalize the transcriptions so that they are internally consistent and so they match her final system.

•*Tonal accent.* Creek has a complex and subtle system of pitch-related phenomena.[88] In editing the texts, we have used a slightly heavier hand in the early texts, and a lighter hand in editing the final texts (which come close to her 1977 practices).

In her notebooks, nouns consisting of two light syllables are transcribed phonemically with accent on the first syllable: *lóca* 'turtle', *íto* 'wood'. To be consistent with Haas's final (1977) practice, these are transcribed here with final accent (*locá, itó*). Exceptions are words like *háci* (shortened from *iháci* 'its tail'), which have accent on the penult. Following her later practice, the demonstratives *ma* 'that' and *ya* 'this' are written without accent; the longer forms *yamá* 'this' and *hiyá* 'this' are accented.

Tonal accent is one of the most challenging aspects of editing these texts. Creek uses tone to distinguish whether an action is ongoing or completed. Consider the following passage:

"Yvmv tat kvsvppē   hakēpet   omen,
yamáta·t   kasáppi·   há·ki·pít   o·mín
right here   cold   it is turning   it is
[and they talked to the bullfrog, saying,] "It's getting cold here, ...

The word <hakēpet> above can be read as *há·ki·pít* 'it is turning' or as *ha·kî·pit* 'it has turned'. This leads to two possible translations: "It's getting cold here" or "It has gotten cold here." The traditional alphabet does not make this distinction, so we have no way of knowing what Hill's intention was. In this case, Haas's interpreter read it one way (*há·ki·pít*), and McGirt read it the other way (*ha·kî·pit*). In instances like this we add an endnote giving the alternative reading. The patterns are fairly regular, however: forms like *há·ki·pít* are imperfective (translated as 'is doing', 'was doing', or 'would do'); forms with falling tone like *ha·kî·pit* are perfective and translated as 'did', 'had done', or 'has done').

•*Nasalized vowels.* When she was transcribing most of the texts, Haas believed nasal vowels could be derived from nasal consonants. She thus represented nasal vowels in the texts using *n* or *m* at the end of a syllable following a long vowel or vowel+sonorant: *hĭ·nlit* 'very much'; *fŏlnlit* 'keep going around'; *hămmkósi·* 'just one of a kind'. In later work, she decided nasal vowels needed to be distingiushed and used a raised *n* or *m* instead: *hĭ·ⁿlit*; *fŏlⁿlit*; *hămᵐkósi·*.[89] We have used a raised *n* in this edition: *hĭ·ⁿlit*; *fŏlⁿlit* 'keep going around'; *hămⁿkósi·*.

•*Phrase-final melodies.* Haas used accents ´ (level), ^ (falling), and ˘ (extra high or rising) for both tonal accent and phrase-final melodies (different intonation patterns used for questions, calling to someone, etc.). We place tonal accent over vowels: *cálki* 'my father', *o·kâ·t* 'saying'. We place phrase-final melodies immediately after a word: *calki·^* 'father!'.

•*The diphthong ay~ey.* Creek has a diphthong *ay* ranging from [ɑɪ] to [ɛɪ] and [eɪ]. Haas felt that this variation was dialectal or idiolectal (Haas 1977a:202, f.n. 2) and wrote *ay* for [ɑɪ] and *ey* for [ɛɪ], [eɪ], or [ɛ·]. We have maintained her practice of distinguishing *ay* and *ey*.

•*The suffix -w′ 'also, too'.* Creek expresses 'too' or 'also' with a suffix. Haas initially transcribed this suffix phonetically as *-ow*, as in *maow* 'that, too'. Her final phonemic transcription used *-w* after vowels and *-ow* after consonants: *maw* 'that, too', *ponsâ·sa·tow* 'those who are here with us, too'. We have followed her final conventions, except that we have added a prime (′) to show that the voice goes up on the last syllable of these forms.

•*The vowels o (u) and o· (u·).* When Haas transcribed Creek in her notebooks, she used the phonemic symbols *o* and *o·*. From 1946 to 1969, she used the symbols *u* and *u·* instead, and these symbols were used when she had the texts typed. During the 1970's she switched back to *o* and *o·*. We have used *o* and *o·* in this edition.

•*Word spacing.* Creek has liaison applying between some combinations of words. This can make it difficult to determine word boundaries. Following Haas's later practice, a verb form in *-i·* + *tâ·y-* 'can' is written as two words: *impo·yiyí· tâ·yi·s* 'we can beat them'. *-i* + *ma·h-* is written as one word: *'lisinlitkima·hatí·s* 'ran away from him entirely'.

•*Haas's additions and deletions.* When Haas intended for words or phrases to be inserted, moved, or struck out, we have made the changes without comment.

•*English spelling of Creek words and names.* There is a great deal of variation in how Creek words are spelled in English. We use the spelling Muscogee in free translations when referring to the Muscogee (Creek) Nation or a member of that tribe. We follow Haas in using the spelling Muskogee (or Creek) for the language.

In free translations, we generally favor spellings for personal names and place-names that are widely used. We use the spelling Hilabi instead of the more common Hillabee, however, because Haas used that spelling in titles.

The spelling used in word-for-word glosses differs from the spelling used in free translations, because glosses directly reflect Haas's notes. For this reason, the spelling Kayleidji appears in Haas's glosses, while Kialegee is used in the editors' free translation.

For names that are not well known, we adopted a system of representing Creek pronunciation in English. In the following list, the Creek spelling is in italics, and the English transliteration is in parentheses: *a* (a), *c*, (ch), *cc* (tch), *e* (i), *ē* (i), *f* (f), *h* (h), *i* (ay), *k* (k), *l* (l), *m* (m), *n* (n), *o* (o), *p* (p), *r* (thl), *s* (s), *t* (t), *v* (a), *w* (w), *y* (y).

Orthography

Two different orthographic systems are used in this edition. Creek forms that are not italicized are in the standard Creek spelling used in the nineteenth century.[90] Italicized Creek forms reflect the phonemic orthography developed by Haas.[91] These follow the Americanist guidelines advocated in Haas and others in 1934.[92]

Traditional	Haas's phonemic	Haas's phonetic	International Phonetic Alphabet
p	*p*	[B]	[p]
t	*t*	[D]	[t]
c	*c*	[ǯ]	[tʃ]
k	*k*	[G]	[k]
f	*f*	[f]~[φ]	[f]~[ɸ]
r	*ł*	[ɫ]	[ɬ]
s	*s*	[s]	[s]
h	*h*	[h]	[h]
m	*m*	[m]	[m]
n	*n*	[n]	[n]
n	*ŋ*	[ŋ]	[ŋ]
w	*w*	[w]	[w]
y	*y*	[y]	[j]
l	*l*	[l]	[l]
v	*a*	[α]	[ɐ]
a	*a·*	[a·]	[ɑː]
e	*i*	[ɪ]	[ɪ]
ē	*i·*	[i·]	[iː]
u	*o*	[ʋ]	[ʋ]
o	*o·*	[o·]	[oː]
i	*ey~ay*	[ɛɪ, eɪ]~[ɑɪ]	[ɛɪ, eɪ]~[ɐɪ]
ue	*oy*	[ʋɪ]	[ʋɪ]
vo	*aw*	[αw]	[ɐʋ]
eu	*iw*	[iow]~[iu·]	[ioʋ]~[iuː]

Before she developed her phonemic orthography, Haas used a phonetic system. Her phonetic symbols are enclosed in square brackets below, but are otherwise not used in this volume.

The plosives *p*, *t*, *c*, *k* are voiceless and unaspirated. *c* is a voiceless unaspirated palatal affricate (as in English *ea*ch). The plosives *p*, *t*, *c*, and *k* may be voiced between vowels or before a vowel and after a sonorant.

The fricatives *f*, *ł*, *s*, and *h* are voiceless. Haas described *f* as varying between labiodental and bilabial articulations. *ł* is a voiceless lateral fricative.

The sonorants *m*, *n*, *ŋ*, *w*, *y*, *l* are generally voiced. They are devoiced before *h* at the end of a syllable. *ŋ* is what Haas called a "defective" phoneme occurring only before *k* or *hk* and contrasting with *m* and *n* in that position in the speech of Haas's consultants. Modern speakers have lost any distinction between *nk* and *ŋk* (having only the latter). Since Haas herself overlooked this contrast for several years, we have had to examine her later practices to edit her earlier transcriptions.

Haas sometimes also recorded a glottal stop (ʔ) at certain boundaries.

The vowels are short and long *a*, *a·*, *i*, *i·*, *o*, *o·*. Short vowels are often centralized. Nasal vowels also occur, and are then usually long. A nasal vowel is indicated with a hook under the vowel in Haas's traditional and phonetic orthographies, and with a raised *n* in the phonemic orthography.

The diphthongs are *ay*, *oy*, *aw*, and *iw*. The first has a dialectal or idiolectal variant *ey*. The last arises by suffixing -*w* 'also' to the ends of words, as in *aniw* 'I also'.

Haas also recognized three phonemic tonal accents: ´ (level), ^ (falling), and ˘ (extra high or rising). When marked over vowels, these indicate word prosody (tonal accent); when following a word, they indicate intonation.[93] An apostrophe (') at the beginning of a phonemic form indicates that the following (usually light) syllable has mid pitch rather than low pitch. Parentheses in phonemic transcriptions indicate optional elements (elements that were pronounced or not pronounced on different repetitions). Haas used additional signs (including the sharp and flat signs) in her notebooks, but her presentation has been simplified here.

Abbreviations

FS	Fannie (Hill) Sulphur
H, JH, JHH	James Hill
[ ]	material added by the editors
< >	spelling in traditional Creek alphabet; an addition based on Hill's notes
italics	phonemic transcription
^{i}, ^{ii}, etc.	notes that Haas made in her notebook and formatted here as footnotes
^{1}, ^{2}, etc.	notes added by the editors and formatted as endnotes
(II), (III), etc.	Haas occasionally distinguishes Past II, Past III, etc. in glosses

Bibliography

Primary Sources

Haas, Mary R. [Creek notebooks.] Mary R. Haas Papers, American Philosophical Society. Philadelphia, Pennsylvania.

Hill, James H. [Creek notebooks.] Mary R. Haas Papers, American Philosophical Society. Philadelphia, Pennsylvania.

Riste, Victor E. [Creek notebooks.] Mary R. Haas Papers, American Philosophical Society. Philadelphia, Pennsylvania.

Secondary Sources

Berryhill, Jefferson. "Interview with Mr. Jasper Bell." Indian Pioneer Papers, vol. 7, interview 7077, 3 August 1937. University of Oklahoma Western History Collections. Norman, Oklahoma.

Byrd, Billie. "Interview with Adam Grayson." Indian-Pioneer Papers, vol. 35, interview 7812, 10 October 1937. University of Oklahoma Western History Collections.

Byrd, Billie. "Interview with Wesley Tanyan." Indian-Pioneer Papers, vol. 89, interview 1247, 22 December 1937. University of Oklahoma Western History Collections.

Cole, Fay-Cooper, R. B. Dixon, and A.V. Kidder. "Anthropological Notes and News: Anthropological Scholarships." *American Anthropologist, New Series*, 31.3 (July–Sep 1929), 571–572.

Creek Nation Census, 1900.

Davis, Lorene, Susannah Factor, and Mary R. Haas. *Nak-cokv Yvlunkv Enhake (Seminole Phonics I)*. Ada: Seminole Bilingual Education Project, ca. 1977.

Emmons, Jerome M. "Interview with Daniel Starr." Indian-Pioneer Papers, vol. 87, interview 6781, 20 July 1937. University of Oklahoma Western History Collections.

Final Rolls of the Citizens and Freedmen of the Five Civilized Tribes in Indian Territory.

Gouge, Earnest. *Totkv Mocvse / New Fire: Creek Folktales*, ed. and trans. Jack B. Martin, Margaret McKane Mauldin, and Juanita McGirt. Norman: University of Oklahoma Press, 2004.

Haas, Mary R. "Ablaut and Its Function in Muskogee." *Language* 16 (1940): 141–50.

Haas, Mary R. "Nasals and Nasalization in Creek." In *Proceedings of the Third Annual Meeting of the Berkeley Linguistics Society*. Edited by Kenneth Whistler et al., 194–203 Berkeley: Berkeley Linguistics Society, University of California, Berkeley, 1977.

Haas, Mary R. "Natchez and Chitimacha Clans and Kinship Terminology." *American Anthropologist* 41 (1939): 597–610.

Haas, Mary R. "The Classification of the Muskogean Languages." In *Language, Culture, and Personality: Essays in Memory of Edward Sapir*, edited by Leslie Spier et al., 41–56. Menasha, Wisc.: Banta Publishing Company, 1941.

Haas, Mary R. "Tonal Accent in Creek." In *Studies in Stress and Accent*. Edited by Larry M. Hyman. *Southern California Occasional Papers in Linguistics* 4, 195–208. Los Angeles: University of Southern California, 1977.

Haas, Mary R. "Tunica." In *Handbook of American Indian Languages*, vol. 4, edited by Franz Boas, 1–143. New York: J. J. Augustin, 1940.

Haas, Mary R. *Language, Culture, and History: Essays*. Edited by Anwar S. Dil. Stanford: Stanford University Press, 1978.

Haas, Mary R. *Thai Reader*. Washington: American Council of Learned Societies, 1954.

Haas, Mary R. *Thai-English Student's Dictionary*. Stanford: Stanford University Press, 1964.

Haas, Mary R. *The Prehistory of Languages*. Janua Linguarum, Series Minor 57. The Hague: Mouton, 1969.

Haas, Mary R. *The Thai System of Writing*. Washington: American Council of Learned Societies, 1954.

Haas, Mary R. *Tunica Dictionary. University of California Publications in Linguistics* 6. Berkeley: University of California Press, 1953.

Haas, Mary R. *Tunica Texts. University of California Publications in Linguistics* 6. Berkeley: University of California Press, 1950.

Haas, Mary R., and Heng R. Subhanka. *Spoken Thai*. 2 vols. New York: H. Hold and Co., 1945.

Herzog, George, Stanley S. Newman, Edward Sapir, Mary Haas Swadesh, Morris Swadesh, and Charles F. Voegelin. "Some Orthographic Recommendations." *American Anthropologist* 36, no. 4 (1934): 629–631.

"Kelley Funeral Home Records 1 Aug 1937 - 31 Dec 1984," last accessed 17 May 2004, http://www.rootsweb.com/~okmcinto/Kelley.txt.

Loughridge, Robert N. and David M. Hodge. *English and Muskokee Dictionary Collected from Various Sources and Revised* and *Dictionary of the Muskokee or Creek Language in Creek and English*. St. Louis: J. T. Smith, 1890.

Martin, Jack B. *A Grammar of Creek (Muskogee)*. Lincoln: University of Nebraska Press, 2011.

Sameth, Sigmund. "Creek Negroes: A Study of Race Relations." MA thesis, University of Oklahoma, 1940.

Sapir, Edward S., and Morris Swadesh. *Yana Dictionary*. Edited by Mary R. Haas. Berkeley: University of California Press, 1960.

Shipley, William, ed. *In Honor of Mary R. Haas*. Berlin: Mouton de Gruyter, 1988.

"Tuskegee Indian Baptist Church," last accessed 17 May 2004, http://www.rootsweb.com/~okmcinto/TuskHist.htm.

U.S. Federal Census, 1910.
U.S. Federal Census, 1920.
U.S. Federal Census, 1930.

TEXTS BY J. HILL

Autobiography

J. Hill (Hill II:14–20; Haas XVII:1–79)

Etvlwv	Vsselanvpe	hocefkē	este	vpopokat	ofvn	neskv-cukot	ocvtēs.
itálwa	*assila·napí*	*hocífki·*	*ísti*	*apo·pô·ka·t*[1]	*ó·fan*	*niskacókot*	*o·catí·s.*
a town	Greenleaf	named	people	living	in it	store	there was

Where people lived in a town by the name of Greenleaf, there was a store.

Horre	seko	monkof	Sekomahv	(James McHenry)	hocefkēt
hółłi	*siko·*	*móŋko·f*	*'sikomá·ha*[1]	*(James McHenry)*	*hocífki·t*
war	(before) not	before	man's name		named

Before the [Civil] War, [a man] named Sikomaha [Nothing-at-all or James McHenry]

neskv-cuko	hayēt	omvtēs.	Mv	neskv-cuko	tempusan	cvhēcket	omvtēs.
niskacóko	*há·yi·t*	*o·matí·s.*	*ma*	*niskacóko*	*tímposa·n*	*cahi·ckit*	*o·matí·s*
store	he had	it was	that	store	close to	I was born	it was

operated a store. I was born near that store.

Mohmen	este-lvste	hoktēt	cvhocēfvtēs,	"Ceme"	maket,
móhmin	*istilásti*	*hoktí·t*	*cahóci·fatí·s*	*cími*	*ma·kít*
And then	colored	woman	she named me	Jimmy	she said

And a black lady named me. "Jimmy," she said,

---

[1] *'sikomá·ha* = almost nothing at all. There is an old man over at Hanna named this. He was a seven month's baby and was so small they didn't expect him to live. Hence his name.

cvrke tat   Helle   hocefkvt   omvtēs.   Sekomahv   ēwvnwv   echuswvt
cálkita·t   hillí[2]   hocífkat   ô·mati·s   'sikomá·ha   i·wánwa   ichóswat
my father   Hilly   his name   it was   James McH.   his sister   her child
and my father's name was Hilly.

cvrket   omvtēs.   Hvyuce   enhvse   ohrolopē   cokpe-rakko   hvmken
cálkit   ô·mati·s.   hayóci   inhasí   ohłolopí·   cokpiłákko   hámkin
my father   he was   July   its month   the year   thousand   one
My father was Sikomaha's sister's son. I was born in July in the year

cokpe   cenvpaken   palē   ēpaken   hvmkontvlakat   omof,   cvhēcket   omvtēs.
cókpi   cinapâ·kin   pá·li·   i·pâ·kin   hamkontalâ·ka·t   ô·mo·f   cahi·ckit   o·matí·s
hundreds   eight   sixty   one (1861)   when it was   I was born   it was
eighteen hundred and sixty-one [1861].

Momof   Wvcenv   Kvsappv,   Lekothv   horre   etenhayē
mo·mô·f   wacína   kasá·ppa   likó·tha   hółli   itínha·yí·
At that time   the United States   the North   the South   war   they making on each other
At that time the United States, North and South, were engaged in war,

em oketvn   mv   horre   este-catvke   em ēkvnvn   yohcēyvranof,
imokitán   ma   hółli   istica·takí   imi·kanán   yohcí·yała·nô·f
during that time   that   war   the Indians   their land   when they were entering it
and when the war was coming into Indian Territory,

este-catvke   tekvpakvtēs.   Honvntake   vpvlwvt
istica·takí   tíkapa·katí·s   honantá·ki   apálwat
the Indians   they separated.   The men   some of them
the Indians divided. Some men

Kvsappv   ensuletawv   haken,   vpvlwvt   Lekothv   ensuletawv   haken,
kasá·ppa   insolitá·wa   ha·kín   apálwat   likó·tha   insolitá·wa   ha·kín
the North   its soldiers   they become   others   the South   its soldiers   they became
became soldiers for the North, and some became soldiers for the South.

momen   este-honvntake   vculakat,   hoktvke,   hoktvlvke,   hopuetakuce   esyomat
mo·mín   istihonantá·ki   acolâ·ka·t   hoktakí   hoktaláki   hopoyta·kocí   isyô·ma·t
Then   the men   old ones   women   old women   little children   them together
And of the old men, women, elderly women, and small children,

vpvlwvt Kvsvppof fvccvn vpēyen, vpvlwvt Lekothof fvccvn vpēyen
apálwat kasappo·ffácca\<n\> api·yín apálwat likotho·ffáccan api·yín
some up north they went some down south they went
some went to the North, and some went to the South,

cuko nake vtēhkat sulkēn wiket,
cokó nâ·ki atî·hka·t sólki·n weykít
house things that were in the house much they left it
leaving many things in their homes,

em vpuekvo wikahket pefatket omvtēs.
imapóykaw weykáhkit pifa·tkít o·matí·s
their livestock, too, they left them running they were
and leaving their livestock too, they ran.

Cvpvwv 'svculat Lekothv ensuletawv hakvtēs.
capáwa[i] 'sacô·la·t likó·tha insolitá·wa ha·katí·s.
My mat. uncle older one South's soldier he became.
My mother's eldest brother became a soldier for the South.

Momen Lekothof fvccvn 'svcvpēhoyvtēs,
mo·mín likotho·ffáccan 'sacapí·ho·yati·s
Then down south they went and took me along
So they took me toward the South,

em enak-ockv vpvlwv wihket. Este sulkē tohkvlkēt vpēyen,
iminâ·k ó·cka apálwa wéyhkit ísti sólki· tohkálki·t api·yín[3]
their belongings the rest of they left them people a lot together were going
leaving some of their belongings behind. Many people traveled together,

este sulkat fekhoniyet vpoken, cvpuse tatēt
ísti sólka·t fikhonêyyit apô·kin capósitá·ti·t
people a lot when they stopped they camped my grandmother (now deceased)
[but] many people stopped and camped, and my late grandmother,

---

[i] Mother's brother's name was *ayíkca* (boyhood), *yaholi·má·la* (town-name).

echuswv   cēpvnē   hvmken   ēyvpvyēt   rasfuliket
ichóswa   *ci·paní·* *hámkin* *i·yapáyi·t*[4]   *ła·sfolêykit*
her child   boy   one   she brought   when she returned
taking one of her sons with her,

wakvn   yesfulkvtēt   omēs.   Wakv   'nvcomusēt   omvtēs.
wá·kan   *yísfolkatí·t* *ô·mi·s.* *wá·ka* *'nacŏ·ⁿmosi·t* *<ô·mati·s>*
cattle   she took back   did.   cattle   not many, a few they were
returned and got the cattle. It was just a few cattle.

Momen   horre   ofv   penkvlkē   em oketvt   onkv,
mo·mín   *hółli* *ó·fa* *pinkálki·*   *imokitát* *òŋka*
Then   war   in   frightening, scary   during   it was
It was during the frightening time of war, so

Kvsappv   suletawv   estvn   vpoket   monkat   fullēpis   ohmēs   komat,
kasá·ppa *solitá·wa* *ístan* *apo·kit*   *móŋka·t* *fólli·pêys* *óhmi·s* *ko·mâ·t*
North   soldiers   where   they camped or   around   might be   they thought
thinking there might be Northern soldiers in the area,

cvrken   honvntake   ētv   hokkolet   vpaken
cálkin   *honantá·ki*   *í·ta* *hokkô·lit*   *apâ·kin*[5]
my father and the men   other   two (other men)   being with him
my father and two other men

vketēckvn   vtothoyvtēs.   Momen   estehvpo-rakko   enkvpahket
akiti·ckan   *atótho·yatí·s.* *mo·mín*   *istihapo·lákko* *iŋkapáhkit*
as guards   they were sent   Then   big camp   got away from
were appointed to scout around. And leaving the main camp,

hopvyēn   vpēyet   fullvtēs.
hopáyi·n *api·yit*   *follatí·s.*
away off   they went   and were around
they went far off.

Momen   honvntake   hokkoluset   'rvlahohket   okat,
mo·mín   *honantá·ki*   *hokkô·losit*   *'łala·hóhkit* *o·ká·t*
Then   men   two of them   came back   and said
Then only two men came back, saying,

"Ēkvnv cefahlakan fulleyof, Helle yopot encaten,
i·kaná cifahlâ·ka·n folliyô·f hilliᵋ yopó·t inca·tín
"Land rocky, rugged when we were about Hilly's nose bleeding
"When we were in rugged country, Hilly's nose started bleeding.

fekhonnet vpokēn, somkehpen, matan hopēleyvnks"
fikhônnit apô·ki·n somkíhpin ma·tá·n hopi·liyáŋks
we stopped and we camped he died right there we buried him"
We stopped and stayed there, and he died, and we buried him there,"

maket onvyakvtēt omēs.
ma·kít onáya·katí·t ô·mi·s.
they said they told it did
they said.

Ēkvnv estvmvn cvrke ēlet omvtē kerrvkot os.
i·kaná istaman cálki i·lít o·matí· kíłłako·t ô·ⁿs.
Land, place where my father died did know not I do
I don't know the land where my father died.

Momis Cahtv ēkvnvt omē witvtēs.
mo·mèys cá·hta i·kanát o·mí· wêytati·s.
but Choctaw Nation it is it might be
But it might be Choctaw country.

Monkv cvrke kerrvko monken elēpvtēt omēs.
môŋka cálki kíłłako· mònkin ili·patí·t ô·mi·s
Therefore, so my father not know I did he died did
So my father died before I knew him.

Horre oketv ofvn momvtēton, nake mahokat kerrvyē hakē ayof,
hółłi okíta ó·fan mo·matí·ton nâ·ki má·ho·kâ·t kíłłayi· ha·kí· a·yô·f
It happened during wartime, and I began to understand things that were said, and as time

"Hvcce Uecate-Rakko tempen vpokēt omēs" mahokēn: kērrvyvntvs.
hácci oyca·tiłákko tímpin apô·ki·t o·mí·s má·ho·ki·n ki·łłayántas
went on, people said, "We live near the Red River": I figured that out.

Tinesen Tikses tempet omvtēs. Coko 'tewǫlicusē vpokeyate
teynisín[7] téyksis tímpit o·matí·s. cokó 'tiwŏⁿlêycosi· apo·kiyâ·ti[8]
It was near Denison, Texas. We lived in houses close together—

Paskofv, Mēkkēmarv, Tvlwvyvholv, Tewvwihke, Konoyvholv
pa·skó·fa mi·kki·má·la talwayahóla tiwawéyhki konoyahóla
Paskofa, Mikkimathla, Talwayahola, Tiwawayhki, Konoyahola—

yv estvlket em estvlke ocvkēt vpokaken vpoket omeyvntvs.
ya istâlkit imistâlki o·cakí·t apo·kâ·kin apo·kít o·miyántas
these men lived with their families, and we lived there too.

Vhopvyēcusat cuko sulkēt omvtēs.
ahopayî·cosa·t cokó sólki·t o·matí·s.
Not too far away there were many houses.

Etopolokē cuko eshayvkvtē cuko hǫlwahokusēn vpoket omeyvntvs.
itopoló·ki· cokó ishá·yakáti· cokó hŏlⁿwa·hô·kosi·n apo·kít o·miyántas
We used to live in houses made of logs, ugly little houses.

Momen mv oketv este estemerkvkēt fullet omeyvntvs.
mo·mín ma okíta ísti istimiɫkakí·t follít o·miyántas.
At that time we were suffering.

Monkv cufe-comottv ehvrpen neshoyēt omvcoken,
môŋka coficomó·tta iháɫpin nísho·yi·t o·macókin[9]
Now rabbit skins were being bought,

cēpvnvke este vculvkē stomis cufe hopoyet pvsatat
ci·panáki ísti acolakí· stô·meys cofî hopo·yít pasa·tâ·t
and young men and even older men hunted rabbits and, killing them,

hvrpen encawet em vpeswv tat vpvlvthoyvntvs.
háɫpin ínca·wít imapíswata·t apalátho·yántas
took the skins and threw away the meat.

Mv omof, este-cate tat cufe vpeswv pvpetv tokot omēs makakēt onkv,
ma ô·mo·f isticá·tita·t cofî apíswa papíta tó·ko·t ô·mi·s. má·ka·kí·t ôŋka
At that time, Indians were not to eat rabbit meat, they said,

pvphoyekot omvntvs. Ohrolopē ostat senhoyvnusēn, hompetv sekon, accvkē tateu sekon,
paphoyíkot o·mántas[10] *ohłolopí· ô·sta·t sinhoyánosi·n*[11] *hompitá síkon a·ccakí·tá·tiw síkon*
and so it was not eaten. For a little over four years, there was no food, there were no clothes,

cēpvnvke em vculkv ohrolopē palē kolvpohkakat mahē em elecv ayat
ci·panáki imacólka ohłolopí· pâ·li· kolapohkâ·ka·t mâ·hi· imilicá â·ya·t
and boys about the age of seventeen and under

enatylkakuset fulleyvntvs.
ina·tănlkâ·kosit folliyántas
went around naked.

Momen mv horre herkv hahkof, pum ēkvnv raohfolēcēt eryiceyat
mo·mín ma hółli hílka háhko·f pomi·kaná ła·ohfolî·ci·t íłyeyciyâ·t
After the war became peace, we returned to our lands and lived along

Kvnēte vfopken vpoket omeyis, hompetv seko accvkē sekat emonken,
kaní·ti[12] *afó·pkin apô·kit o·miyêys. hompitá sikó· a·ccaki· siká·t imôⁿkin*
the edge of the Canadian [River], but we were still without food, without clothes

ohrolopē toccēnat mahe orvtēs. Vce tat lokcen hocet, taklike hayet,
ohłolopí· toccî·na·t mâ·hi o·łati·s. acíta·t lo·kcín ho·cít takléyki ha·yít
for about three years. Pounding ripe corn, making bread,

osafkeu hayet mvn hompet fullat,
osá·fkiw ha·yít man hompít follâ·t
making sofkee too, and eating it,

"Elvoko tat etehoyvnēcēs" komhoyvtēs. Vpeswv neha omakat seko estomis.
iláwkota·t[13] *itihoyanî·ci·s kómho·yatí·s apíswa nihá· o·mâ·ka·t sikó· istô·meys*
they thought, "We have come through starvation." Without even any fat, grease, and such.

Momen wakv tis elēhocewitat vpeswv wakvnehat hēckvtēs.
mo·mín wá·kateys ili·ho·ciwêyta·t apíswa wa·kanihá·t hi·ckatí·s
And when a cow was butchered, we had meat and beef fat.

Oketv kocǫknusat vpeswv hompvkē tayat eco, penwv omakat tąyet omis,
okíta kocŏ·ⁿknosa·t apíswa hómpaki· tâ·ya·t icó pínwa o·mâ·ka·t tă·ⁿyit o·mêys
For a short time meat was available for eating: deer, turkey, and such in abundance,

eccv enrē, tohottowv, cvtolanuce omakat sasēsekok
ícca inli· toho·ttowá catola·nocí o·mâ·ka·t sä·ⁿsi·siko·k
but without bullets, gunpowder, caps, and such,

estohmet ponvttv honecakat pvsatet homhopeko tayē oketvt omvtēt os.
istóhmit ponátta honicâ·ka·t pasa·tít homhopíko· tâ·yi· okítat o·matí·t ô·ⁿs
it was a time when we could not kill and eat wild game.

Momen fvllēckv maket ēkvnv cotkus mahen vhocet, lokcicet, vyocet,
mo·mín fallí·cka ma·kít i·kaná cò·ⁿtkos mâ·hin aho·cít lókceycít ayo·cít
Now they planted cotton on a small piece of land, raised it, gathered it,

enken nērkv sencawet 'setekaskv esfvllēckv estarkv hēckekv,
íŋkin ni·łka[14] sínca·wít 'sitiká·ska isfallí·cka istá·łka hi·ckika
and removed the seeds by hand, and having obtained a card, spinning wheel, and loom,

fvllēckv 'telekmicet polopokusēn hayet cvpuse tatēt fvllēcet
fallí·cka 'tilíkmeycít polo·pokósi·n ha·yít capósitá·ti·t[15] fálli·cít
my late grandmother would draw out the cotton and spin it into rolls

vfoshonoke hayet solēcof. Estarkv tat Tvfforakko hocefkēt este
afoshonóki ha·yít soli·cô·f istá·łkata·t taffołá·kko hocífki·<t> isti
when she had a large amount of thread. The loom was located in the house

likat encuko ofvn ocekv, mvn mv estarkv 'tvlemet omewitvtēs.
lêyka·t incokó ó·fan ô·cika man ma istá·łka 'talimít o·miwêytati·s
of a man named Taffothlakko [Big Grasshopper], so it was probably a public loom.

Mvn vfoshonoke hayvtē cvcke tatēt tvrepuecen, totkvfvlkv-cēkfv omēn hayof,
man afoshonóki ha·yatí· cáckitá·ti·t talípoycín to·tkafalkací·kfa ó·mi·n ha·yô·f
My late mother would weave with the thread she had made, and when she made a thick

<u>tarkv</u> makēt yokkofketv capkēn vnhahoyen accet arvyvntvs.
tá·łka ma·kí·t yokko·fkitá cá·pki·n anha·hô·yin â·ccit a·łayántas.
material, <u>tarkv</u> ['weaving'] they called it, a long shirt was made for me, and I wore it.

Momen mv Kvnēte vfopken vpokēn ohrolopē 'svtoccēnat mahe tis omvtēs.
mo·mín ma kani·ti afò·pkin apò·ki·n ohlolopí· 'satócci·nâ·t mâ·hiteys o·matí·s
And we lived about three years next to the Canadian River.

Ēkvnv vpuekv enfulletv hēran mahoken coneciket,
i·kaná apóyka infollitá hi·ⁿta·n má·ho·kin conicêyki·t
They talked of good land for livestock, so we moved.

hvcce cutkusē Folahpv Hvcce kihocēn hvccet wakken,
hácci cótkosi· folahpahácci kéyho·cí·n[16] háccit wâ·kkin
There was a small creek called Shell Creek,

mv tempen cuko holwakusēn hahoyen vpokeyvntvs.
ma tímpin cokó hôlⁿwâ·kosi·<n> ha·hô·yin apo·kiyántas.
and we lived in an ugly house they built near that.

Mv liketv vcule Folahpv Hvcce tempusat ētan cuko ocit likvyēt os.
ma leykitá acóli folahpahácci tímposa·t i·tá·n cokó ô·ceyt leykayi·t ô·ⁿs[17]
Also near the old place by Shell Creek is a house I have, and I live there.

Mv liketv mocvsē vpokeyat 'cvpofvt sekok
ma leykitá mocási· apô·kiya·t 'capó·fat síko·k
At the new place where we were living there were no fields,

Kvnite vfopkē ētan vce vhocet lokcicet omhoyen,
kanéyti afó·pki· i·tá·n aci aho·cít lókceycít ómho·yin
so corn was planted and raised along the Canadian River too.

este vculēt Semmvtmvye hocefket sokhv ocēpet omen,
ísti acóli·t simmatmayí hocífki·t sókha oci·pít[18] o·mín
An old man named Simmatmayi had hogs

cvpuse tatē vcen senyoposiken,
capósitá·ti· acín sinyoposêykin
and my late grandmother traded corn with him [for hogs].

mvt honapsen sokhv tat rakraken pvsvthoyekv,
mat hona·psín sókhata·t lákła·kin pasátho·yiká
Those [hogs] multiplied, and they were butchered when grown,

vpeswv neha hēckēhaken, wakv-tēhvkeu avculakekv wakv-vtotkvlken hayet
apiswa nihá· hi·cki·hâ·kin wa·kati·hakíw a·acóla·kiká wa·kaato·tkâlkin ha·yít
so we began to get pork grease. As the steers grew, we made them into oxen

mvn hvlvtepuecet, vce tat estvn neshoyen omat erwiyet
man halátipoycít acíta·t ístan nísho·yín o·mâ·t ílweyyít
and hitched them, and if corn was being bought somewhere, they'd go sell it

hockvtē-hvtke kafe okcvnwv neshoyē hakvtēt os. Momen mv vce wiyēpat,
hockati·hátki ká·fi okcánwa nísho·yí· ha·katí·t ô·ⁿs mo·mín ma ací wéyyi·pâ·t
and began to buy white flour, coffee, and salt. And as they sold corn,

vccusvkē tayat esnesephoyet omis, totkvfvlkv-cēkfv neshoyewiten omat,
áccosáki· tâ·ya·t isnisípho·yít o·mêys to·tkafalkací·kfa nísho·yiwêytin o·mâ·t
they began to buy clothing, but even when they bought the thick material,

yokkofketv-cvpko accvyē monket avrvyvntvs.
yokko·fkitacápko a·ccayí· môŋkit a·ałayántas
I continued to wear the long shirt.

Vm vculkv ohrolopē palē ostohkakē mahe orat momen mv oketv mahe omof
amacólka ohłolopí· pâ·li· ostohkâ·ki· mâ·hi ô·ła·t mo·mín ma okíta mâ·hi ô·mo·f
My age was about fourteen years, and about that time,

nakcokv este-Maskoke em opunvkv eshoccat ohhonvyetv cvkerrē haket arvyvntvs.
nâ·kcó·ka istima·skó·ki imoponáka ishô·cca·t ohhonayitá cakíłłi· hâ·kit a·łayántas
I had learned to read books written in the Muskogee language.

Vmvhahoyē tokon, ētv etemvhayephoyan astem apohicvyat tvlkusēt kērrvyvtēt os.
amahá·ho·yí· tó·ko·n í·ta itimaha·yípho·yâ·n a·stimá·poheycayâ·t tâlkosi·t ki·łłayáti·t ô·ⁿs
No one taught me: I learned by listening while others were being taught.

Momen cokv-mvhakv-coko vwolusmahat vkērkv cahkēpat tatēs.
mo·mín co·kamaha·kacóko awolosmâ·ha·t akí·lka cahkî·pa·t tá·ti·s
The nearest school was five miles away.

Momen cokvheckv vyarē vcohyekcicvrē este sekon,
mo·mín co·kahícka ayá·li· acohyikcéycáli· ísti síkon
And there was no one to encourage me to go to school;

cvrkeu sekon, cvpuse tat cokvheckv vyarē eyacekot onkv,
cálkiw síkon capósita·t co·kahícka ayá·li· iyá·ciko·t ôŋka
my father was gone, and my grandmother didn't want me to go to school,

hvse-vkērkv hvmkusis cokv vmvhahoyvtē sekot os, accvkē ocvkat omēcicēn.
hasiʔaki·łka hâmkoseys có·ka amaha·hoyáti· síko·t ô·ⁿs. a·ccakí· ó·caka·t omi·céyci·n
so I was never taught for even one hour, because I had no clothes.

Vm vculkv ohrolopē palē kolvpohkakē orvranē tasahcan,
amacólka ohłolopí· pâ·li· kolapohkâ·ki· olála·ní· tá·sa·hcâ·n
The spring just before I was seventeen,

vcvrahkvt ēkvnv satkē hokkolosēn 'cvpofvn hahyit,
acałáhkat i·kaná sa·tkí· hokkô·losi·n 'capó·fan háhyeyt
I made a field for myself on two acres of land,

pakpvkē-hvtke vhohcin lokcen mvyocit wiyit ohmē tvlket
pakpaki·hátki ahóhceyn[19] lo·kcín máyo·céyt weyyéyt óhmi· tâlkit
planted cotton, and when it was ripe, I picked it and sold it, and only then

mv oketv accvkē esfulhoyate omat accvyē hakvtēt os.
ma okíta a·ccakí· isfólho·yâ·ti[20] ô·ma·t a·ccayí· ha·katí·t ô·ⁿs.
did I begin to wear clothes as others did.

Momen ohrolopē toccēnat mahe orat Espahehcv hocefkēt este
mo·mín ohłolopí· toccî·na·t mâ·hi o·lâ·t ispa·híhca hocífki·t ísti
Then within about three years, a man named Isparhecher

este-Maskoke em vhakv empvtakvn vnrahpet, em esteu solehcet
istima·skó·ki[21] imahá·ka impatá·kan anłáhpit imístiw solíhcit
opposed the Muscogee constitution, gathered many of his people,

vhakv empvtakv vsvpaklvlken vnrvpēt horren hayet
ahá·ka impatá·ka asapa·klâlkin anłapí·t hółlin ha·yít
made war against the supporters of the constitution,

este-Maskoke etvlwv etekvpvyēcicvtēt os. Este-cate mahhe vculvkē mahat omvlkvt
istima·skó·ki itálwa itikapayí·ceycatí·t ô·ⁿs isticá·ti máhhi acolakí· mâ·ha·t omálkat
and divided the Muscogee Nation. All the old full-bloods

Espahehcvn em vnicēt fullvtēt os.
ispa·híhcan imanéyci·t follatí·t ô·ⁿs.
supported Isparhecher.

Vhakv empvtakv vsvpaklvlken vpakit arvyvtēt os.
ahá·ka impatá·ka²² asapa·klâlkin apâ·keyt a·łayáti·t ô·ⁿs.
I was with the supporters of the constitution.

Vhvmkv este sulkat Okmvlken vpokat
ahámka ísti sólka·t okmálkin[i] apô·ka·t²³
One time many people were in Okmulgee,

vketēcvlke este nvcomusēn vpēyecihocen fullof,
akiti·câlki ísti nacómosi·n api·yiceyhô·cin follô·f
and when a few men were sent out as scouts,

Espahehcv em esteu vketēcvlke nvcomusē ētat fullvten,
ispa·híhca imístiw akiti·câlki nacómosi· i·tá·t follatín
Isparhecher's people also had a few scouts about,

etefvciyet etēchet esfullen;
itifacêyyit iti·chít ísfollín
and they came upon each other and began shooting at each other;

vhakv em vnicē fullvtēt pefatken, este kolvpakat pvsahtet sulkat omvlkvt pefatkvtēs.
ahá·ka imanéyci· follati·t pifa·tkín ísti kolapâ·ka·t pasáhtit sólka·t²⁴ omálkat pifa·tkatí·s
those in favor of the constitution ran, the [others] killed seven men, and they all ran.

Momen Yofalv Kvntvckv Tamvs Pok vhakv 'mvnicvt omen,
mo·mín yofá·la kantácka tá·mas pô·k ahá·ka 'manéycat ô·min
In Eufaula District, Thomas Polk was the prosecuting attorney,

Sam Smith fvccēcvt omet,
Sam Smith[ii] faccí·cat ô·mit
and Sam Smith was the judge,

"Este vculvke vhakv vnrapv herkv vnrapvt omaket os" maket senkērkvn enhahyet,
ísti acolakí ahá·ka anłá·pa hílka anłá·pat omâ·kit ó·ⁿs ma·kit siŋki·łkan inháhyit
and he said, "The elders opposing the law are against peace."

---

[i] Used to say *okmólki*. Now say *okmálki*.
[ii] *séym smí·t* in Creek.

em ecerakkohkakvn yekcetvn ēmof, rakkohkakv este svlvfkueckv yekcetv ocat
imicilakkohká·kan yikcitán i·mô·f łakkohká·ka ísti salafkóycka yikcitá ô·ca·t
When he gave his lighthorsemen [or sheriffs] authority, only five lighthorsemen

este cahkēpusēt onkv, em vnicvranat, "Este palet ohhvpvkekvs" mahket,
ísti cahki·posi·t òŋka imanéycala·nâ·t ísti pâ·lit ohhapákikas máhkit
had the authority to arrest people, so to help them he said, "Let ten people join,"

este enhopoyat vcvpahyet,
ísti ínhopo·yâ·t acapáhyit
and included me in the search [i.e., the posse]:

"Este vculvke mahe Yofalv Kvntvckv vtehkan svlvfkvkuecaks" mahket,
ísti acolakí mâ·hi yofá·la kantácka atíhka·n salafkakóycaks máhkit
"Arrest all of the oldest people in Eufaula District," he said,

hocefhokv pumhohyen fullēkv, este vculvke sulkēn svlvfkvkuehcēt
hocifhoká pomhóhyin follí·ka ísti acolakí sólki·n salafkakóyhci·t
and gave us names and we went. So we arrested many old people

vpoyet vhecicēn; fvccēcv colvlke enhohiken
apô·yit ahiceycí·n faccí·ca co·lâlki[i] inho·hâykin
and kept them and watched over them. The judge called for a jury,

nvkvfitet em vfastat "Yv vculvke tat omvlkvt rokafkvkekvs,
nakafêŷit imáfa·stâ·t ya acolakíta·t omálkat[25] loka·fkakíkas
and after meeting and trying them, they said, "Let all these old ones be whipped,

vhakv vcakkvyēn" maket, enfvccēhohcen vpoket,
ahá·ka acakkayí·n ma·kít infaccí·hóhcin apô·kit
according to the law." After being sentenced,

"Pum vhakvhayvt ahyet mēkkot pum merrvrēn pum empohekvs" makaken,
pomaha·kahá·yat áhyit mi·kkot pommíłłáli·n pomimpohíkas má·ka·kín
[the old people] said, "Our lawyer should go and ask the chief for a pardon,"

---

[i] *co·l-* in *co·lâlki* from English *jury*.

fvccēcv vhakv-mvnicv em vkvsvmahket okat,
faccí·ca aha·kamanéyca imakasamáhkit o·kâ·t
and the judge and the prosecuting attorney agreed.

"Mucvnettv ayē netta 'svtuccēnat fvccvlike hoyanat
mocanítta a·yí·[26] nittá· 'satócci·nâ·t faccalêyki hoyâ·na·t
"I will wait three days from today,

hvse-vkērkv hokkolat vtēkusēn em ehakarēs" fvccēcv mahken, vhakvhayv
hasiʔakí·lka hokkô·la·t atî·kosi·n imihá·ká·li·s facci·ca máhkin aha·kahá·ya
until exactly two o'clock," the judge said. So the lawyer

este hokkolet vpaken vpehyen, mv este vculvke tat vpoken vhecicet fulleyvntvs.
ísti hokkô·lit apâ·kin apíhyin ma ísti acolakíta·t apô·kin ahíceycít folliyántas.
went, accompanied by two people, and we guarded the old people that were there.

Momen mv este vculvke vhecicetv em penkvlvkateu sulkētot omis
mo·mín ma ísti acolakí ahiceycitá impiŋkaláka·tiw[27] sólki·tot o·mêys
And though many were afraid to guard the old people,

estomvkeko tayekv fullemvts. Hofonē vculvke tatē ohhonvkv pohakvtēt omēcicen,
isto·makiko· tâ·yika follimác hofóni· acolakítá·ti· ohhonáka poha·katí·t omi·ceycín
they could not do anything. Because they had heard stories from long ago about the old

empenkvlaket omakemvts. Momen merkv vpohv rehyicekon,
impiŋkál<a·k>ít oma·kimác. mo·mín mílka apó·ha lihyéycikon
ones, [the guards] were afraid. Now those who had gone to ask for clemency

netta hvse-vkērkvo vnakuecusē hakēpof,
nittá· hasiʔakí·lkaw ană·ⁿkôycosi· há·ki·pô·f
had not returned and as the day and hour were drawing near,

rokafhoyvranē vpokat este rokafvranē fullat,
łoka·fhoyáła·ní· apô·ka·t ísti loká·fała·ní·[28] follâ·t
those who were to be whipped and those who were to do the whipping

omvlkvt feksumkvkē oketvt ocemvts.
omálkat fiksomkakí· okítat o·cimác
all felt panic at that time.

Hvse-vkērkv orēpekv hvse-vkērkuce palehokkolen 'mehahkit
hasiʔaki·łka oli·piká hasiʔaki·łkoci pa·lihokkô·lin 'miháhkeyt
"It is time, but I will wait twenty minutes,

estomvranat makarēs fvccēcv makof ohhvtvlvkusē feksumketv hakemvts.
istó·mała·nâ·t má·ká·li·s facci·ca ma·kô·f ohhatalakósi·[29] fiksomkitá ha·kimác
and then I will say what is to happen," the judge said, and the fear grew even more.

"Estomvrē tē?" maket etem pohet esterokafvlke taranat fullemvts.
istó·mali· ti·ⁿ^[i] ma·kít[30] itímpo·hít istiłoka·fâlki tá·la·nâ·t follimác.
"What's going to happen?" the floggers went around asking one another.

Momen fvccēcv oketv mellat orē mahusan, merkv vpohv eryihcen enhuehhohken,
mo·mín facci·ca okíta mílla·t o·lí· mă·ⁿhosa·n miłka apó·ha iłyéyhcin inhoyhhóhkin[31]
And right at the time the judge had set, those seeking clemency returned,

fvccēcv ehomvn vculvke tat vpohken,
facci·ca ihóman acolakíta·t apóhkin
and the old ones came and sat before the judge.

mēkko tat "Mv vculvke em mērris makēt on cenkērkuecis" fvccēcvn kihocof,
mí·kkota·t ma acolakí immi·łłéys ma·kí·t ô·n cinki·łkoycéys facci·can kéyho·cô·f
When the judge was told that the chief had pardoned the old ones,

este omvlkvt afvckakemvts. Monkv vculvke em etektvnkat
ísti omálkat a·fácka·kimác môŋka acolakí imitíktankâ·t
everyone rejoiced. So when the old ones were freed,

"Cehutetaken vpeyepaks. 'Svnvcomv herkv vyvmahkē
cihótitá·kin apiyipáks 'sanacóma hiłka ayáma·hkí·
the judge told them, "Return to your homes. Never again disturb the peace

vhakv vnrvpē vkerricē nvkaftē fuliyatskvs" kicet,
ahá·ka anłapí· akíłleyci· naka·ftí· folêyyá·ckas[32] keycít
or conduct meetings opposing the law."

---

[i] Fannie Sulphur: *stó·mahí·ti·ⁿ^.*

fvccēcv empunahyen, vwahemvts.
faccí·ca imponáhyin awa·himác
Thus the judge warned them, and they dispersed.

Ohrolopē palecahkēpvnkē mahet omvtēs.
ohłolopí· pa·licahkî·paŋkí· mâ·hit o·matí·s
That was about fifty years ago.

Espahehcv enhorre ohrolopē hokkolat oren herkv hakof
ispa·híhca inhólli ohłolopí· hokkô·la·t ô·lin híłka ha·kô·f
Isparhecher's war lasted two years and when peace was declared,

ohrolopē cokperakko hvmken cokpe cenvpaken palecenvpaken hokkolohkakan omvtēs.
ohłolopí· cokpiłákko hámkin cókpi cinapâ·kin pa·licinapâ·kin hokkolohkâ·ka·n o·matí·s
it was the year eighteen hundred and eighty-two [1882].

Momof vm vculkv ohrolopē palehokkolē hvmkontvlakat orētatēs.
mo·mô·f amacólka ohłolopí· pa·lihokkô·li· hamkontalá·ka·t ołí·tá·ti·s
At that time my age was twenty-one years.

Momen mv vtēkē atē ohrolopē cokperakko hvmkē cokpe ostvpakē palē vpakat
mo·mín ma atî·ki· a·tí· ohłolopí· cokpiłakkohámki· cókpi ostapâ·ki· pâ·li· apâ·ka·t
And from that year to the year nineteen hundred and ten [1910],

vlakat vm vretv opvnkvhaco hayēckvpvnkv uehomē esketv 'tekvpakusē
ałá·ka·t amałitá opankahá·co ha·yi·ckapánka oyhomí· iskitá[33] 'tikapa·kosí·
I went to crazy dances, fiddle dances, drank whisky,

pokkechetv hoktvke empokkechetv ocakē etvlwv like tayat
pokkichitá hoktakí impokkichitá ó·ca·ki· itálwa léyki tâ·ya·t
played [men's] ball-games, women's ball-games, and whatever a tribal town did.

nake hēren momēcaket etvlwv lilaket os komēt vkerricit omvko estomis
ná·ki hi·ⁿlin[34] momí·ca·kít itálwa leylá·kit ó·ⁿs kó·mi·t akiłłeycéyt omáko· istô·meys
In good activities I did not favor one tribal town over another,

nvkvftetv estvmvt estofvn fulhoyvranat kerrvyēt on omat erorvyē vlkēt omvtēt os.
nakaftitá ístamat istô·fan folhoyáła·nâ·t kíłłayi·t ô·n o·mâ·t iłólayi· álki·t o·matí·t ô·ⁿs.
whenever there was something going on and I heard about it, I always went.

Momis vm vculkv momēpē estomis cvcke vmpunayat em apohicvyēt
mo·mèys amacólka mo·mî·pi· istô·meys cácki ámpona·yâ·t ima·pohéycayi·t
Even though I was grown, my mother talked to me and I obeyed,

nake makat momvranin okēs enkomvyē arvyat omēcicēt
ná·ki ma·kâ·t mó·mała·néyn o·kí·s iŋkó·mayi· a·łayâ·t omi·céyci·t
and because I knew I must do as I was told,

vretv holwahokat enkvpvkēt arvyvtēt os.
ałíta holwa·hò·ka·t iŋkapáki·t a·łayáti·t ô·ⁿs.
I was not involved in anything bad.

Ohrolopē cokperakko hvmken cokpe cenvpaken pale-ostvpaken cahkepohkakat
ohłolopí· cokpilákko hámkin cókpi cinapâ·kin pa·liʔostapâ·kin cahkipohkâ·ka·t
In the year eighteen hundred and ninety-five [1895],

Otvwoskuce enhvse omof,
otawo·skocí inhasí ô·mo·f
in the month of September,

este-Maskoke etvlwv em vhakv vcakkvyēn 'temvrkvt ocen,
istima·skó·ki itálwa imahá·ka acakkayí·n 'timáłkat o·cín
the Muscogee Nation held an election according to the constitution,

Helvpe-Kvnēte etvlwv Mēkko cokopikvn cvhahoyvtēt os.
hilapikaní·ti itálwa mí·kko cokopéykan cahá·ho·yati·t ô·ⁿs
and I was made a representative to the [House of] Kings for Hilabi Canadian.

Mohmen ayen ohrolopē cokperakkohvmkē cokpe cenvpake pale ostvpake ostvpohkake
móhmin a·yín ohłolopí· cokpilakkohámki· cókpi cinapâ·ki pá·li ostapâ·ki ostapohkâ·ki
As time passed, in the year eighteen hundred and ninety-nine [1899],

otvwoskuce hvse hvtvm 'temvrkv ocen,
otawo·skocí hasí hatâm 'timáłka o·cín
in the month of September, another election was held,

vne ētan Mēkko cukopikv cvhahoyvtēt os.
aní i·tá·n mí·kko cokopéyka cahá·ho·yati·t ô·ⁿs
and I was again elected representative to the [House of] Kings.

Momen mv vhakv etvlwv em mēkketv ocē 'temvrkv ocvtē
mo·mín ma ahá·ka itálwa immi·kkitá ó·ci· 'timáłka o·catí·
As elected tribal leaders, our terms ended

tasahcuce netta sostat ohrolopē cokperakko hvmken cokpe ostvpaken ēpakat omof
ta·sahcocí nittá· sô·sta·t ohłolopí· cokpiłákko hâmkin cókpi ostapâ·kin i·pâ·ka·t ô·mo·f
on March 4, nineteen hundred

pum eyoksēpvtēt os.
pomiyóksi·patí·t ô·[n]s
and six [1906].

Mohmen Wvcenv em ohmēkketv em elecv min vtēhkeyvtēt os.
móhmin wacína imohmi·kkitá imilicamêyn ati·hkiyáti·t ô·[n]s.
We were then under the jurisdiction of the United States.

Mohmen ohrolopē cokperakko hvmkē cokpe ostvpakē cenvpakē vpakat omof
móhmin ohłolopí· cokpiłákko hâmki· cókpi ostapâ·ki· cinapâ·ki· apâ·ka·t ô·mo·f
Then in the year nineteen hundred and eight [1908],

pvnkv pokkechetv uehomē esketv omakat omvlkvn wihkit arin
pánka pokkichitá[35] oyhomí· iskitá o·mâ·ka·t omálkan wéyhkeyt a·łéyn
I quit all dancing, ball-playing, and whisky-drinking,

ayen vm vkerrickv 'mvrahken arit omikv,
a·yín amakiłłéycka 'małâ·hkin a·łéyt o·máyka
and as time passed my thinking changed.

Hesaketvmesē emvhakv em elecv vretv mit vkvsvmkv vnhēckekv,
hisa·kitamisí· imahá·ka imilicá ałíta mêyt akasámka anhî·ckika[36]
I found the faith to live under God's law instead

mēkusapvlke kihocē este fullat min vpvketvn kohmit,
mi·kosa·pâlki kéyho·cí· ísti follâ·t mêyn apakitán kóhmeyt
and wanted to be a member of the group called Christians instead.

Cēsvs Klist aksomecihocvrē vpohvtē vcakkvyēn
cí·sas kláyst[37] aksomiceyhocáłi· apo·hatí· acakkayí·n
And as Jesus Christ asked to be baptised

Ue-aksomkvlke em mēkusvpkv-cuko 'Rewahle Este-cate em Mēkusvpkv-cokon arit
oyaksomkâlki[38] *immi·kosapkacóko 'liwáhli isticá·ti immi·kosapkacókon a·léyt*
I went to a Baptist church, Thlewahle Indian Church,

uewv aksomketv vhakv vkvsvmvyēt onkv ēyohkērkuecin;
óywa aksomkitá ahá·ka akasamáyi·t óŋka i·yohkí·lkoycéyn
and confessed that I believed in the requirement of baptism;

ohrolopē cokperakkohvmke cokpe ostvpake palen vpakat eholē-hvse omof
ohłolopí· cokpiłakkohámki cókpi ostapâ·ki pâ·lin apâ·ka·t iholi·hasí ô·mo·f
in November of the year nineteen hundred and ten [1910],

erkenvkv Svnte Fif hocefkēt erke eppuce puyvfekcv vcakat
iłkináka sánti fâyf hocífki·t ílki ippocí poyafíkca acâ·ka·t
a preacher named Sandy Fife baptised me in the name of the Father, the Son

enhocefkv ofv uewv svcaksomecihcen mēkusapvlke vpvkē hakvyvtēt os.
inhocífka ó·fa óywa 'sacaksomicéyhcin[39] *mi·kosa·pâlki apakí· ha·kayáti·t ô·ⁿs*
and the Holy Ghost, and I became a member with these Christians.

Mēkusvpkv-cuko sulkē eteliketv hahoyvtē
mi·kosapkacóko sólki· itileykitá ha·ho·yati·[40]
Many churches were established by

Maskoke, Semvnole, Wecetv em eteliketv hocefkēt omēs.
ma·skó·ki simanó·li wicíta imi<ti>leykitá hocífki·t ô·mi·s
an organization named the Muscogee, Seminole, and Wichita [Baptist Association].

Mv ennvkvftetv ohrolopē cokperakko hvmke cokpe ostvpake
ma innakaftitá ohłolopí· cokpiłákko hámki cókpi ostapâ·ki
At their meeting in the year nineteen hundred

palen hokkolohkakat omof, Minecen Pot este kolvpake enwiketv hayat
pá·lin[41] *hokkolohkâ·ka·t ô·mo·f meynicín pô·t ísti kolapâ·ki inweykitá ha·yâ·t*
and twelve [1912], the Managing Board appointed seven people,

vcvpahoyēn arin, cvfekhonnihocekon ohrolopē kolvpakat orvtēs.
acapa·hô·yi·n[42] *a·léyn cafikhonneyhocíkon ohłolopí· kolapâ·ka·t o·latí·s*
and I was one of them and served for seven years without disruption.

Momen ohrolopē cokperakko hvmke cokpe ostvpake palen cahkepohkakat omof
mo·mín ohłolopí· cokpiłákko hámki cókpi ostapâ·ki pâ·lin cahkipohkâ·ka·t ô·mo·f
And in the year nineteen hundred and fifteen [1915],

mēkusvpkv-cukot cukovfastv yekcetv esfvckan vtotkv cvhahoyvtēt os.
mi·kosapkacókot cokoafá·sta yikcitá isfácka·n atá·ho·yatí·t ô·ⁿs
the church made me head deacon with full credentials.

Mohmen ohrolopē cokperakko hvmke cokpe ostvpake palen kolvpohkakat omof,
<móhmin ohłolopí·> cokpiłákko hámki cókpi ostapâ·ki pâ·lin kolapohkâ·ka·t <ô·mo·f>
Then in the year nineteen hundred and seventeen [1917],

mēkusvpkv-cuko em vcahnvn mahket,
mi·kosapkacóko imacá·hnan máhkit
they appointed me exhorter in the church,

erkenvkv em vtotketvt omēn mēkusvpkv-cukot vtotkv cvhayvtēt os.
ilkináka imatótkita·t ó·mi·n⁴³ mi·kosapkacókot atá·tka caha·yatí·t ô·ⁿs.
similar to the work of a preacher, and the church made me a worker.

Momen arin ohrolopē cokperakko hvmke cokpe ostvpake palehokkole hvmkontvlakat
mo·mín a·léyn ohłolopí· cokpiłákko hámki cókpi ostapâ·ki pa·lihokkô·li hamkontalâ·ka·t
Time passed, and in the year nineteen hundred and twenty-one [1921]

hvyorakko netta palehokkole cenvpohkakat omof,
hayołákko nittá· pa·lihokkô·li cinapohkâ·ka·t ô·mo·f
on August 28,

erkenvketv yekcetv esfvckan vtotkv cvhahoyvtēt os.
iłkinakitá yikcitá isfácka·n atá·tka caha·hoyáti·t ô·ⁿs.
I was given full authority to preach.

Erkenvkvlke Mase Haco, James McCombs, Joe Kvlpvt yv toccēnat
iłkinakâlki ma·sihá·co, James McCombs, Joe kálpat ya toccî·na·t
Ministers Marsey Harjo, James McCombs, Joe Colbert: these three

enke vcohwvkēcet emēkusvpahken hoyanof,
iŋki acohwakî·cit imi·kosapáhkin hoya·nô·f
laid hands on me and prayed, and afterwards,

estvmv estomis arat "Erkenvkekvs" komhoyen omat
ístama istô·meys a·lâ·t iłkinákikas kómho·yín o·mâ·t
wherever I went, I could preach when asked

Hesaketvmesē em opunvkvn este em onayet,
hisa·kitamisí· imoponákan ísti imóna·yít
to tell the word of God to all people.

serkenakē arvranat yekcetv enhēcket os komhoyvtēt omēs.
siłkina·kí· á·łała·nâ·t yikcitá inhî·ckit ó·ⁿs kómho·yatí·t ô·mi·s
They believed that this authority gave me the power to go and preach.

Momen mv vtotketv hvlatvyē monken mucvnettv vlakis,
mo·mín ma atotkitá hałâ·tayi· môŋkin mocanítta ałâ·keys
I have been in that work to this day,

Hvyorakko netta paletuccēnat ohrolopē cokperakko hvmken
hayołákko nittá· pa·litocci·na·t ohłolopí· cokpiłákko hámkin
August 30, nineteen hundred

cokpe ostvpaken paletuccēnen ostvpohkakat, Ceme (James Hill).
cókpi ostapâ·kin pa·litoccî·nin ostapohkâ·ka·t cími. (James Hill).
and thirty-nine [1939]. Jim (James Hill)

[The Civil War]⁴⁴

J. Hill (Haas IV:1–25)

Este-cate	em ēkvnv	ofv	horre	ocakvtēt os.
isticá·ti	*imi·kaná*	*ó·fa*	*hółli*	*ó·ca·katí·t ô·ⁿs*[i]
[Indian	their land	in]	war	they had

They had a war in Indian Territory.

Ohrolopē	cokperakko	hvmken	cokpe cenvpaken
ohłolopí·	*cokpiłákko*	*hámkin*	*cokpicinapâ·kin*
year	thousand	one	eight hundred

It began around the year eighteen hundred

---

[i] Raiford says *ô·s*.

pale ēpaken   hvmkontvlakat   mahen   vlicehcet,   Wvcenv   ēmētat   'tekvpahket,
pá·li i·pá·kin   hamkontalâ·ka·t   mâ·hin   aleycíhcit   wacína   i·mi·tá·t   'tikapáhkit
sixty   one   about   it began   United States   itself   (was) divided
and sixty-one [1861]. The United States itself divided

horre   hayvtēt   os.   Este-lvsten —   vpuekv,   wakv,   cerakko tis   omēn
hólli   ha·yatí·t   ô·ⁿs   istilástin —   apóyka,   wá·ka,   'cilákkoteys   ó·mi·n
war   made   did   colored people   livestock   cattle   horses even   were like
and made war. Colored people, like livestock, cattle, even horses,

vtotkv   hayetvn   wiyet   nēset   horkopet   komis   wihoyēn   ocaket
ató·tka   ha·yitán   wayyít   ni·sít   hólko·pít   kô·meys   wáyho·yí·n[45]   o·câ·kit
worker   to make   sell   bought   stole   did   sold   had
were bought, sold, and stolen to make workers; they were sold,

este-caten   nesepuecaket omvtēs.   Monkv   este-catet,
isticá·tin   nisipóyca·kít o·matí·s   móŋka   isticá·tit
Indian   made buy   for that reason   Indians
and they made Indians buy them. For that reason, if an Indian

este-lvste   ocēt   liken   omat,   nake ockv   rakkēn   ocēt   os
istilásti   ó·ci·t   lâykin   o·mâ·t   nâ·ki ó·cka   łákki·n   ó·ci·t   ô·ⁿs
negroes   owned   living   were   estate, property   big   had (was)   did
owned Negroes, some Indians

komhoyēn   este-cate   likē   sasvtēt omēs.   Momvtētan
komhoyí·n   isticá·ti   laykí·   sa·satí·t ô·mi·s   mo·matí·ta·n
recognized   Indian   lived   was   where it was
were recognized as having large estates. So it was that

Wvcenv   vpvlwvt   wiyvkat   "Nēsvkat   wikvkēts"   maken
wacína   apálwat   wayyakâ·t[46]   ni·sakâ·t   wáykakí·c   ma·kín
United States   part of them/the rest   selling   buying   let's quit did   say
when part of the United States was selling Negroes, some said, "Let's quit buying them."

vpvlwvt   eyacekon,   horre   eshahyet   este-cate   awahehcet   omhoyen;
apálwat   iyá·cikon   hólli   isháhyit   isticá·ti   awa·híhcit   omhô·yin
the rest   didn't want it   war   made   Indians   scattered   they did
And others didn't agree, so they made war, and the Indians were scattered.

este-cate	etenrvpēt	fullet	elvwaket	em ecerakko tis	pvpaket
isticá·ti	*itinɬapi·t*	*follít*	*iɬáwa·kít*	*imiciɬákkoteys*	*papa·kít*
Indians	disagreed	were about	hungered	their horses, even	they ate

The Indians disagreed and were so hungry that some ate

sasvtēt		omēs.	Momen	sulkēt
sa·satí·t		*ô·mi·s*	*mo·mín*	*sólki·t*
were some (people ate their own horses)		did	then	a lot of them

their own horses. Then many of them,

hoktvke	hopuetakuce	esyomat	vnrvwvn	fullvtēs.
hoktakí	*hopoyta·kocí*	*isyô·ma·t*	*ânɬawán*	*follatí·s*
women	children	together	anywhere	wandered about

women and children, wandered in the wilderness.

Estemerkv	rakkēn	hecaket	momet	hvcce	Wvsetv	hocefkē	vnakvn,
istimíɬka	*ɬákki·n*	*hica·kít*	*mo·mít*	*hácci*	*wasíta*	*hocífki·*	*aná·kan*
suffering	great	saw	then	stream	Washita	named	near by

They saw great suffering, and near the river named Washita,

hapo-rakko	hayet	vpoken
hapo·ɬákko	*hâ·yit*	*apô·kin*
a big camp	made	stayed

they made a big camp.

lecekakv	enokketvt	heciken,	sulkēt	pvsatken
licíká·ka	*inokkitát*	*hicâykin*	*sólki·t*	*pasa·tkín*
small-pox	disease	caught	several	died

Many caught small pox and died,

ena	vrvnakat	vtēkusēn,	fakke	ohranet	wihokvtēt	omēs.
iná·	*aɬanâ·ka·t*	*atĭ·ⁿkosi·n*	*fákki*	*óhɬa·nít*	*wáyho·katí·t*	*ô·mi·s*
body	out of view	only	dirt	covered	quit	[did]

and just to get them out of sight, they covered them with dirt and left.

Estemerkv	sulkēn	este-catehkvn	etehoyvnehcen,	herkv	hakvtēt	omēs.
istimíɬka	*sólki·n*	*istica·tíhkan*	*itihoyaníhcin*	*híɬka*	*ha·katí·t*	*ô·mi·s*
suffering	lots of	Indians	went through	peace	was made	[did]

The Indians endured great suffering before peace was made.

Cokperakko hvmken cokpe cenvpaken pale ēpaken cahkepohkakat mahen
cokpiłákko hámkin cokpicinapâ·kin pá·li i·pâ·kin cahkipohkâ·ka·t mâ·hin
[thousand one eight hundred sixty- five about]
In about eighteen hundred and sixty-five [1865],

mv horre omēcicē este-cate vwahetv enhakvtē vkerrickv
ma hólli omi·cáyci· isticá·ti awa·hitá ínha·katí· akiłłéycka
that war was the cause Indians to scatter started ideas
because of the war, the Indians had become scattered about, and their thoughts

vwahē monken mucvnettv oret os, cokperakko hvmken
awá·hi· mônkin mocanítta ô·lit ó·ⁿs cokpiłákko hámkin
not together during today still/continues [thousand one
are still not unified to this day,

cokpe ostvpaken pale tuccēnen kolvpohkaken.
cókpi ostapâ·kin pá·li toccî·nin kolapohkâ·kin
hundred nine thirty- seven]
nineteen hundred and thirty-seven [1937].

The Effect of the Civil War on the Indians

J. Hill (Haas IV:127–141)

Wvcenv Lepvpleken este-lvste pucas-seko hayetv eyacen,
wacína lipáplikin istilásti pocá·ssiko· ha·yitá iyâ·cin
U.S. the Republican party negroes with no owners to make they wanted
The United States Republicans wanted to free the Negroes, made war,

horre eshayē esfullvtē herkv hahkof, Wvcenvt etenfvccetvn
hólli isha·yí· ísfollatí· hílka háhko·f wacínat itinfaccitán
war made were around peace after it was made the U.S.'s agreement
and when peace came, the United States

este-caten enhayet omat, este-catet etvlwvt fvccehcet,
isticá·tin ínha·yít o·mâ·t isticá·ti itálwat faccíhcit
Indians making with did the Indian nation decided
was making treaties with the Indians, and the Indian [i.e. Muscogee] Nation decided:

"Este-lvste nēseyvtē vhonvpse esyomat,
istilásti ni·siyáti· ahonápsi isyô·ma·t
negroes that we bought descendants of together (with)
"Though they are not asking for it, we want the Negroes that we bought,

etvlwv tvsekvyv toyeyat, ētvpomēn
itálwa tasikayá tó·yiya·t i·tapó·mi·n
nation citizens (of the nation) we who were (citizens of the nation) just the same
together with their descendants, to be citizens just like those of us

tvsekvyvt omvrēn, vpohē tokon este-lvste puyacēs" maket,[47]
tasikayát omáłi·n apô·hi·[48] tó·ko·n istilásti poyá·ci·s ma·kít
the citizens to be we did not ask for negroes we want them said
who are citizens of the nation," they said.

Este-Maskoke Etvlwvt ēyem opunvyēpan em oh-vkvsahmet,
ísti ma·skó·ki itálwat i·yimopónayi·pâ·n imohhakasáhmit
the Muscogee Nation because they talked for themselves they approved for them
And the Muscogee Nation discussed the matter and approved it,

este-lvsten este-maskoke entvsekvyvn Wvcenvt hayvtēt omēs.
istilástin istima·skó·ki intasikayán wacinat ha·yati·t ô·mi·s
the negroes the Creeks their citizens the U.S. made them did
and the U.S. made the Negroes Muscogee citizens.

Ohrolopē cokperakko hvmken cokpe cenvpaken pale ēpaken ēpohkakat ofvn
ohłolopi· cokpilákko hámkin cókpi cinapâ·kin pá·li i·pâ·kin i·pohká·ka·t ó·fan
year thousand one hundred eight sixty- six in
The United States government understood the issue very well in the year eighteen hundred

Wvcenv etvlwv kērrusvtēs. Estvmv vtēn este-lvstehkvn
wacina itálwa ki·ⁿłłosáti·s ístama ati·n[49] istilastíhkan
U.S. Gov't it knew it very well whereabouts came from the negro
and sixty-six [1866]. It understood where it came from, and how the Negro

ēyvpvkē hayvtēt omat, este-cate entvsekvyv hakē tayē
i·yapáki· ha·yati·t ô·ma·t isticá·ti intasikayá há·ki· tâ·yi·
(made them) apart (of itself) made did Indian citizens can, could (not) become
was made to be a part of [the Muscogee Nation], but that Negroes

tokot omat kērrvtēs. Lepvpleken, Temoklit em etenrvwvn
tó·ko·t ô·ma·t kî·łłati·s lipáplikin tɛmɑklä·t imitînławan
not did knew that Republic[an] Democrat between (them)
were not entitled to become Indian citizens. [The Indians] were split between

vtēhkvtēs. Horre ofv este-lvste tat mohmen
ati·hkati·s[50] *hółli ó·fa istilástita·t móhmin*
they (the Ind.) were (between the 2 parties) war- time the negro then
the Republicans and the Democrats. In the war, the Negro won

Lepvpleken em eyackvn epoyekv
lipáplikin imiyá·ckan ipô·yika
the Republican's wants, desires for they won (their desires)
in the Republican victory,

este-lvste estēmē mont wihoyan
istilásti ísti·mí· mónt wáyho·yâ·n
the negro that were being traded were and were sold
because they didn't want trading and selling of Negroes.

eyacekat vrahkvt, horre eshahyet
iyá·cika·t ałáhkat hółli isháhyit
because they didn't want that for that reason war they made about
And for that reason they made war over it,

este-cate naken akerrēt omekot oman, etekvpvyēcihcē etepoyicet,
isticá·ti nâ·kin a·kíłłi·t omíkot o·mâ·n itikapayi·céyhci[i] *itípoyeycít*
Indians anything knew about didn't (did) they divided them they made them fight
and the Indians, not having anything to do with it, were divided and made to fight,

estemerkv honnēn este-caten ohwvkēcet, em enak-ockv,
istimílka honnî·n[51] *isticá·tin ohwakî·cit iminâ·kó·cka*
suffering great Indians caused upon their estate
and great hardships were imposed on the Indians. All their possessions,

---

[i] Raiford: *itikapayicéyhcit.*

ehute omvlkvn mont em ēkvnv tis enkvpvyecicen
ihóti omálkan mónt imi·kanáteys iŋkapayicêycin
their houses all then their land, even separated from them
and their houses, and even their lands were taken from them

ohrolopē ēpakat orvtēs. Cerakko tis wihkē pefathokvtē
ohłolopí· i·pâ·ka·t o·latí·s 'ciłákkoteys wáyhki· pifá·tho·katí·
years six got to be horses, even that were left ran away
for six years. Horses that were left when they ran away

honecvkēpekv, estimvt enaket omat estit kerrē tayat
honicakî·pika istêymat inâ·kit ô·ma·t istêyt kíłli· tâ·ya·t
they had gotten wild whose it is, who it belongs to is anyone that could know
had become wild, so nobody knew whose they were,

sekot tvleme hakēpekv,
siko·t 'talimí ha·kî·pika
there wasn't (anyone) public (property) it has become
and they became public property.

cerakko-honēce tat este estomis assēcet
'ciłakkohoní·cita·t ísti istô·meys á·ssi·cít
the horses wild person, any (person) that runs after them
So anyone who chased after a wild horse

hvlvtēpat ēyvnakuecet pohoyvtēt os.
haláti·pâ·t[52] i·yaná·koycít[53] pó·hoyatí·t[54] ô·ⁿs
and if they catch them claims it is his and got them all (in that way) did
and caught it, could claim it for himself until all were gone.

"Nake yvmahkvtē fēkarēs" Wvcenv makvtēs.
nâ·ki yamahkatí· fí·ká·li·s wacína ma·katí·s
that that was destroyed I will pay the U.S. said
The U.S. said, "I will pay for losses,"

Lepvpleken em vnicvtē tvlkusēn. Democrat em vnicvtē
lipáplikin imáneycatí· tâlkosi·n témakrät imáneycatí·
the Republicans those that helped the Rep. only (those) the Democrats that helped
but only to those who helped the Republicans. Those who helped the Democrats,

Wvcenv   ētat   estemerrvkuecvtēt   ont omat
wacína   *i·tá·t*[55] *istimiłłákoycatí·t*   *ônt o·mâ·t*
the U.S.   itself   caused with suffering with them (the Dem.) did
the U.S. itself made suffer,

"Fēkarēs"   makvtē   ohrolopē   pale kolvpakat   hoyanet   omētan
fi·ká·li·s *ma·katí·* *ohlolopi·* *pá·li kolapâ·ka·t* *hoyâ·nit* *o·mí·ta·n*
I will pay   it said   years   seventy   passed   have (passed)
and seventy years have passed since they said "I will pay,"

fēketv   eyacēsekon   mocvnettv   oret   os.   Nake   hiyomvkēn
fi·kitá   *iyà·ⁿci·sikon*[56]   *mocanítta* *o·lít*[57] *ô·ⁿs* *nâ·ki* *hayyo·maki·n*
to pay   it doesn't want to   to this day it has come   things   like this
with no intention of paying to this day. Through these sorts of actions,

este-cate   'sestemerrvkuehcet   este-lvste   pucassekon   hayekv,
isticá·ti   *sistimiłłakóyhcit*   *istilásti*   *poca·ssikón* *hâ·yika*
the Indian   made them suffer   negroes   no owners   have made, therefore,
they made the Indians suffer and freed the Negroes,

omvlkvn   Wvcenvt   entvsekvyvn   hayvten   omat   fvccvt   omvranvtēs.
omálkan   *wacinát*   *intasikayán*   *ha·yatín* *o·mâ·t* *fáccat* *omáła·natí·s*
all of them U.S.   its own citizens to make   (if)   right   it would have been
so it would have been right if the U.S. had made all of them its own citizens.

Mont oman   ohhvtvlakat,   este-lvste   pucasseko   hayvtēt
mònt o·mâ·n *ohhatalâ·ka·t*   *istilásti*   *poca·ssikó·* *ha·yatí·t*
therefore   further on   negroes   no-owners   made them (freedmen)
And on top of that, they freed the Negroes,

ēkvnv   este-maskoke   etvlwv   enaken   etewahlet
i·kaná   *istima·skó·ki*   *itálwa*   *inâ·kin*   *itíwa·hlít*
the land (of the) Muskogee Nation   belonging to they divided
divided the land belonging to the Muscogee Nation,

este-lvsten   ēmvtēt   os.   Este-cate nēsvtē   vhonvpse
istilástin   *i·matí·t*   *ô·ⁿs* *isticá·ti* *ni·satí·*   *ahonápsi*
negroes   did give (to the negroes) did   Indians   that bought them descendants
and gave it to the Negroes. They gave it not just to the descendants of those bought

tvlkekon Wvcenv entvsekvyv   mạhusan   sulkēn vpahyet,
tálkiko·n wacina intasikayá   mǎ·ⁿhosa·n   sólki·n apáhyit
not only   U.S.   its (own) citizens   own   many   put with
by Indians, but they also added many of the United States' own citizens.

nake   fvccekon celayet   omakvtē   eskērkv   este vhonkvtkv   enrahmet,
ná·ki   fácciko·n cila·yít   oma·katí·   iskí·łka   ísti ahoŋkátka   inláhmit
something unjust   handled it they did   the proof the roll of people   opened it
They fraudulently fixed the rolls of the Creek people,

este-maskoke   etvlwv   heciceko   tạyusēt   omvtēt os.
istima·skó·ki   itálwa   hicéyciko·   tǎ·ⁿyosi·t   o·mati·t ô·ⁿs
The Muskogee   Nation   to show them (not)   could not
and the Muscogee Nation was not allowed to see them.

Neklo Wa.   Herkv   hahken   hoyvnēpvtētan   ohrolopē   ēpakat   mahe   oren
níklu wá·   híłka   háhkin   hoɣáni·pati·ta·n   ohłolopí·   i·pâ·ka·t mâ·hi   ô·łin
           peace   made   afterwards   year   six   about   time
Negro War. After peace was made, about six years later,

este-cate   'ti-maskoke   etvlwv   etekvpahket eccv   as etencawet
isticá·ti   'tima·skó·ki   itálwa   itikapáhkit ícca   a·sitincá·wit
Indians   Creek   Nation   divided   guns   got
the Creek Indian Nation divided, and people took their guns

esfullē   ocvtēt os.   Momis   tohottowv   nēkren
isfolli·   o·catí·t ô·ⁿs   mo·mâɣs   toho·ttowá   ni·klín
being around   happened   But   gun-powder   burnt (powder)
around. But the gun-powder burnt,

rē   eteyoposkē   ocekon   este   ecatv   pvlvtkekon
lí·   itiɣopóski·   ó·cikon   ísti   icá·ta   palátkikon
bullets   exchanged   didn't happen   people's   blood   did not waste
there was no exchange of bullets, human blood was not spilled,

fekhonnēpvtēt os.   Nake vrahkvn omvtē   kērrat   este   sahsekos.
fikhónni·pati·t ô·ⁿs   ná·ki ałáhkan o·mati· kỉ·łla·t   ísti   sáhsiko·s
was quieted/stopped   what reason   was   (no person) knows   (no) person no
and it stopped. Nobody knows the reason it happened.

Mohmen mv hoyanat, ohrolopē kolvpakat mahe oren
móhmin ma hoya·nâ·t ohłolopí· kolapâ·ka·t mâ·hi ô·lin
then that after, further year seven (yrs.) about had elapsed
Then after that, about seven years later,

hvtvm este-cate maskoke etvlwv etekvpahket
hatâm isticá·ti ma·skó·ki itálwa itikapáhkit
again Indians Creek Nation divided
again the Creek Indian Nation divided,

horre hayē ocvtēt os. Neklo Wa rem ehomv
hółłi ha·yi· o·catí·t ô·ⁿs níkla wá· 'limihomá
war made there was a time that negro war before
and there was a time when they made war. Before the Negro War

este-cate mēkko hokkolen ocēt omvtēs. Mēkko hvmket
isticá·ti mí·kko hokkó·lin ó·ci·t o·matí·s mí·kko hámkit
Indian chiefs two had did chief one
the Indians had two chiefs. One chief

Kvnēte mēkkon kihocen hvmken Uecate mēkkon kihocen
kaní·ti mí·kkon kéyho·cín hámkin oycá·ti mí·kkon kéyho·cín
Canadian chief (was) called (him) (the other) one Arkansas chief (was) called
was called the Canadian [river] chief, and one was called the Arkansas [river] chief.

herkv hahkof Wvcenv, este-cate etenfvccetv ohrolopē cokperakko hvmken
hílka háhko·f wacína isticá·ti itinfaccitá ohłolopí· cokpiłákko hámkin
peace afterwards U.S. Indians agreement, treaty year [thousand one
And when peace returned, after the United States and the Indians

cokpe cenvpaken pale ēpaken ēpohkaken etenhahyof, este-cate
cókpi cinapâ·kin pá·li i·pâ·kin i·pohkâ·kin itinháhyo·f isticá·ti
hundred eight sixty-six] made (with each other) Indian
made a treaty in the year eighteen hundred and sixty-six [1866], the Indians

vhakv empvtakvn hayet omat mēkko hvmkusēt omvrēs makēt omen
ahá·ka impatá·kan ha·yit o·mâ·t mí·kko hámkosi·t omáli·s ma·kí·t ô·min
law foundation made did chief one will be provides, says
made a constitution providing for just one chief,

mvn	vnrvpēt	fullet	omvtēs.	Mēkko	hokkolan	eyacēt
man	*anłapi·t*	*follít*	*o·matí·s*	*mí·kko*	*hokkô·la·n*	*iyá·ci·t*
that	opposed	were about	did	chiefs	two	wanted

and some were opposed to that. They wanted two chiefs;

Kaccēmarv,	Espahehcv		hocefkēn
ka·cci·má·ła	*ispa·híhca*		*hocífki·n*
(town name)	(boyhood name)="several to whoop"	named

they were named Katcha Emathla and Isparhecher,

enhomahtv	hahken	fullet	omvtēs.
inhomá·hta	*háhkin*	*follít*	*o·matí·s*
leader	became	were about	did, was

and they became leaders.

Vhakv	vnrapat	nvcomēt	fullet	omvtēs.
ahá·ka	*anlâ·pa·t*	*nacómi·t*	*follít*	*o·matí·s*
law	against	few	were about	were/did

There were a few who were against the law.

Okēmv	tempen	tepohyet	este	nvcomusēn	pvsahtet	pefatkat
o·kí·ma	*tímpin*	*'tipóhyit*	*ísti*	*nacómosi·n*	*pasáhtit*	*pifâ·tka·t*
Okemah	near	fought	people	few	killed	fled

They fought near Okemah, killed a few people, and when they fled,

Wvsase	ēkvnv	rescehyet	vpoken	hofonemahekon	Wvcenvt
wasá·si	*i·kaná*	*liscíhyit*	*apô·kin*	*hofonimá·hikon*	*wacínat*
Osage	land	went into	stayed	long ago not very	U.S.

they entered the Osage Nation and stayed.[i] And before long, the U.S.

"Eckemelen	ēmēt	omēs"	maket	cvtoknawvn	este-caten	ēmēt	omen;
ickimílin	*i·mí·t*	*o·mí·s*	*ma·kít*	*catokná·wan*	*isticá·tin*	*i·mí·t*	*o·min*
orphan	gave	did	said	money	Indian	gave	was, did

said, "We are giving this for orphans," and gave the Indians money;

---

[i] Raiford: The Osage call themselves *wâ·sa·si* (Creek *wasá·si).*

"Punakeu vpvkēt omēs makēt
ponákiw' apáki·t ô·mi·s ma·kí·t
ours, too to be with (our money was with) was said
"Our part is included in that," they said,

Wvsase enkvpahket rapefatket ēwikēs maket eryicvtēt
wasá·si inkapáhkit ɫa·pifá·tkit i·wâyki·s ma·kít iɫyaycati·t
Osage separated from (Osage) run back gave up said came back
and they left the Osage and ran back,

mv vtēken herkv hakvtē mucvnettv oren herkvt os.
ma atî·kin híɫka ha·katí· mocanítta ô·lin híɫkat ô·ⁿs
then ever since (then) peace had today until (today) peace is
gave themselves up, and peace was made up to today.

Wvsase ohpefatkeko monkof hvpo hayet
wasá·si ohpifá·tkiko· môŋko·f hapó· ha·yít
Osage (before) they went (there to Osage country) before camp made
Before they ran off to the Osage, they made camp

estvcako hute-leskv enkvsvppofvn vpoken vhakv empvtakv em vnicvlket
istacá·ko hotilíska iŋkasappó·fan apô·kin ahá·ka impatá·ka imaneycâlkit
old agency north stayed constitution those in favor of
and stayed north of the Old Agency, and those who supported the constitution

oh-vpēyen keriyet pefatkat tvlofuce Hvfmvn tempen
óhhapi·yín kiɫêyyit pifâ·tka·t 'talo·focí háfman tímpin
were going upon found out ran, fled little town Hoffman near
were going to them. They found out and fled, and a man named Peter Larney

este hvmket Pētv Lane hocefkēt liken,
isti hámkit pi·talá·ni hocífki·t lêykin
person one Peter Lani by the name of living
was living near the little town of Hoffman,

pvkanv lokcekon wvsiket sem pefatkvtēt omen okat
paká·na lókciko·n wasêykit simpifa·tkatí·t ô·min o·ká·t
Green Peach thrashed and ran away with them did meant
and they thrashed [his] unripe peaches and fled with them,

Pvkanv	Lokceko	enhorren	kihocēn		mucvnettv	orēt os.
paká·na	*lókciko·*	*inhółlin*	*kéyho·cí·n*		*mocanítta*	*olí·t ô·ⁿs*
Peaches	Green	(its) war	they call it/it was called		today	to (this day)

so it's called the Green Peach war to this day.

Maskoke	etvlwv	hoporrenēt		omakis	onkv,
ma·skó·ki	*itálwa*	*hopołliní·t*		*omâ·kays*	*oŋká*
Creek	Nation	intelligent, sensible		they are	for

The Creek Nation is sensible:

Pvkanv lokcekan		horre	enhayeko	tayēt	omētis
paká·na lókcika·n		*hółli*	*inhá·yiko·*	*tâ·yi·t*	*ô·mi·teys*
Green Peach		war	not make	should	is

they did not make war over green peaches,

este-cate	hoporreneko		omēn	hayetvn	okakēs
isticá·ti	*hopołliniko·*		*ô·mi·n*	*ha·yitán*	*oka·ki·s*
Indians	with no sense, intelligence		like	to make	intention

but they aimed to make the Indians look stupid,

este-hvtket	okakekv.	Kaccēmarv	enhorre,
istihátkit	*oka·kiká*	*ka·cci·má·ła*	*inhółli*
white people	that's what they mean	[Katchimathla's	war]

because it was white people who called it that. Katchimathla's War,

Espahehcv	enhorre,	Pvkanv Lokceko	enhorre	horre	hvmkusēt	omēs.
ispa·híhca[i]	*inhółli*	*paká·na lókciko·*	*inhółli*	*hółli*	*hámkosi·t*	*ô·mi·s*
[Isparhecher's war]		Green Peach	[its war]	war	one	is

Isparhecher's War, and Green Peach War are the same war.

'Ste-lvste tat —	vpuekv,	wakv,	cerakko,	omakat tis	omen,
stilástita·t —	*apóyka*	*wá·ka*	*'ciłákko,*	*omâ·ka·tteys*	*ô·min*
[colored people	livestock	cattle	horses	and such	it is]

Colored people, like livestock, cattle, horses,

---

[i] Or: *ispa·yíhca.*

vtotkv   hayetv   komat   nēset   wiyet   horkopet   omhoyvtēt   omēs.
ató·tka   ha·yitá   kô·ma·t   ni·sít,   wayyít   hółko·pít   ómho·yatí·t   ô·mi·s
[worker   to make   wanting   bought   sold   stolen   they were   it is]
and such, were bought, sold, and stolen to use as workers.

The Coming of the White Man

J. Hill (Haas XV:79–89)

Hofonof este-cate tat este enaheckv 'mvrahkē sekon fullēpet omvtēs.
hofó·no·f isticá·tita·t ísti ina·hícka[58] 'małáhki· síko·n fólli·pít o·matí·s[59]
Long ago the Indians went about with no difference in the appearance of people's bodies.

Momvtētan este ena hvthvkēt enyihcen, hecaket fullvtēs.
mo·matí·ta·n ísti iná· hathakí·t inyéyhcin hica·kít follatí·s
But then people with white bodies came, and [the Indians] saw them there.

Momet vkerricet opunvyēcaket fullvtēs.
mo·mít akíłłeycít oponayí·ca·kít follatí·s
Then [the Indians] went around thinking about it and talking about it.

Estvmvn monkat estvmi awet enyicet omat kerrạke sekot onkv,
ístaman móŋka·t ístamêy a·wit[60] inyêycit o·mâ·t kiłłắ·ⁿki síkot oŋká
They didn't know where or which way [the white people] had come from to get there:

ēkvnvt estvn liken, este vpoke taye onkot, enrenakv orat vtēkusat,
i·kanát ístan lêykin ísti apó·ki tâ·yi óŋkot[61] inliná·ka ô·la·t atî·kosa·t
where was this land? It's an unlikely place for people to live. As far as their eyes could

uewvt sotvn 'tepvkvranosis omēn enheckvt omen hēcet fullvtēt onkv,
óywat sotán 'tipakałá·noseys[62] ô·mi·n inhíckat ô·min hi·cít follatí·t ôŋka
reach, they saw that the water appeared to come together with the sky, so

momaten estet ēkvnv encokfvlvwv yvpahwet, ēkvnv aem ohcemēcet fullet omen
mo·mâ·tin ístit i·kaná incokfaláwa yapáhwit i·kaná a·imohcimî·cit follít o·mín
then the people came to the edge of the land, when they saw [the white people] climb up

hecakat vkerricet opunvyēcaket omvtēs.
hica·kâ·t akíłłeycít oponayí·ca·kít o·matí·s[63]
onto their land and roam around on it, they thought about it and talked about it.

Uewv tylkuset tvlaket onkv naket ena haket,
óywa tăl^nkosit talâ·kit oŋká nâ·kit iná· ha·kít
There was only water there, but what made up their bodies?

vpeswv hakē tayat sekot, onkv uehvtkv akpakpvkē
apíswa há·ki· tâ·ya·t sikot oŋká oyhátka akpakpakí·
There was nothing from which flesh could be made. Or perhaps ocean foam

ena hakvtēt ont, hvthvkēt fullet omēs maket,
iná· há·kati·t ônt hathakí·t follít o·mí·s ma·kít
made up their bodies, because they go around white, they said.

momet este-hopueket omakēs, maket okakvtēs.
mo·mít istihopóykit omâ·ki·s ma·kít oka·katí·s
Then they must be <u>este-hopueke</u>, they said.

Este-hopueke este ena lokceko, hopuewusē vculeko maketvt omēs.
istihopóyki ísti iná· lókciko· hopóywosi· acóliko· ma·kitát ô·mi·s
<u>Este-hopueke</u> means a person with an unripe body, a baby not yet grown.

Hofonē ena hakvtē estet ohmekos komēt okakvtēs.
hofó·ni· iná· há·kati· ístit óhmiko·s kó·mi·t oka·katí·s
They are not people whose bodies have been made long, they thought.

Mohmen em ēkvnv ohfullen, hecaket fullekv,
móhmin imi·kaná óhfollín hica·kít folliká
Then they roamed about on their land, they went about looking, and so

etekerrvkē haken, ayof, este-hopueke estont fullat
itikiłłakí· ha·kín a·yô·f istihopóyki ístónt follâ·t
they got to know each other. As time went on, whatever it was the infants [<u>este-hopueke</u>]

vpaket fullat svsē hakvtēs.
apa·kít[64] follâ·t sási· ha·katí·s
were doing, some began to intermix with them.

Este-cate tat moman este-hopueke tat uewv homēn ocēt ēsket fullēt omen,
isticá·tita·t mo·mâ·n istihopóykita·t óywa homí·n ó·ci·t i·skít follí·t ô·min
The infants had bitter water and were going about drinking it,

kerrakvtēs. Mv uewv <u>weske</u> makēt hocēfēt, ēsket omaken
kiłła·katí·s ma óywa wíski ma·kí·t hoci·fí·t i·skit oma·kin
and the Indians found out about it. They called that water "whisky." They would drink it,

astem ēskat sasē hakvtēs.
á·stimi·ská·t sá·si· ha·katí·s[65]
and there got to be some who drank it with people.

Momen mv uewv homat este-hopueke em uewvt os makaket omis,
mo·mín ma óywa hô·ma·t istihopóyki imóywat ô·ⁿs má·ka·kít o·mèys
And that bitter water is the infant's [<u>este-hopueke</u>'s] water, they would say, but

este-cate ēme hocefēpat, <u>weske</u> kicakvtēs.
isticá·ti í·mi hocífi·pâ·t wíski kéyca·katí·s
when the Indians were naming it themselves, they would call it "whisky."

Momvtēton este-cate etvlwv maskoke hocefkat
mo·matí·ton isticá·ti itálwa ma·skó·ki hocífka·t
The Indian nation was called Maskoke then,

sulkemahat <u>weske</u> kicakē monken.
solkimâ·ha·t wíski kéyca·ki· móŋkin
and large numbers still called it "whisky."

Ohrolopē pale cahkēpvnkē mahe <u>weske</u> makakē emonkvt omvtēt os.
ohłolopí· pá·li cahkí·paŋkí· má·hi[66] *wíski má·ka·kí· imóŋkat o·matí·t*[67] *ô·ⁿs*
They still used to call it "whisky" about fifty years ago.

Momis hiyomat <u>uehomē</u> kihocē os.
mo·mèys hayyô·ma·t oyhomí· kéyho·cí· ô·ⁿs
Now, however, they call it <u>uehomē</u> ['bitter water'].

Momen hofonē este-cate weske ēskē fullat,
mo·mín hofó·ni· isticá·ti wíski i·skí· follâ·t
And long ago, when the Indians were roaming about drinking whisky,

este coknahusē tis arvtet vpaket, aren omat,
ísti coknáhosi·teys a·latít apâ·kit[68] *a·lín o·mâ·t*
a foolish person would be about and join them. And if he was about,

vpakē fulletv eyacekat,

apá·ki· follitá iyá·cika·t

and they didn't want to roam around with him,

este-hopueke em uewv 'svyvhiket, wesken akpofket

istihopóyki imóywa sáyaheykít[i] wiskin ákpo·fkit

they would sing with the <u>este-hopueke</u>'s water. When they would blow into the whisky

eskuecakan, hofonekon hahcet, mv este coknahat wakken,

iskóyca·ká·n hofónikon háhcit ma isti cokná·ha·t wâ·kkin

and make him drink it, he'd get drunk in no time, and the foolish person would lie

Vpokēpet monkat fullēpet, weske tat eskvkēpen,

apo·kî·pit móŋka·t fólli·pít wiskita·t iskaki·pín[ii]

down. The others would sit around or go around, and they would drink the whisky.

Netta hvmkis monkat nerē hvmkis fullēpvtēt omēs, maket

nittá· hámkeys moŋkâ·t nili· hámkeys fólli·pati·t ô·mi·s ma·kít

All day or all night they would do this, they say.

vculvke tatē onvyakvntvs. Monkv hiyomē oketv ofv tis,

acolakitá·ti· onáya·kántas móŋka hayyô·mi· okíta ó·fateys

The old people who are long gone used to say that. And now, even in this time,

este-hopueke em uewv 'svyēpis omēs.

istihopóyki imóywa sáyaheykâ·t sasî·peys o·mí·s

there might be some singing with the <u>este-hopueke</u>'s water.

---

[i] Or: *isyaheykít* for *sáyaheykít*.

[ii] They'd sing a song and blow in whisky and make one drunk.

Creek Chiefs Known by J. Hill (Mēkkvlke tatē)[i, 69]

J. Hill (Haas XXI:119–147)[ii]

Este-Maskoke etvlwv Wvcenv etenfvccetvn hayof,
istima·skó·ki itálwa wacína itinfaccitán ha·yô·f
The Muscogee Nation made a treaty with the United States

ohrolopē cokpe-rakko hvmken cokpe cenvpaken
ohłolopí· cokpiłákko hámkin cókpi cinapâ·kin
in July of the year eighteen hundred

pale ēpaken ēpohkakat hvyuce em ofv tatēs.
pá·li i·pá·kin i·pohkâ·ka·t hayóci imó·fa tá·ti·s
and sixty-six [1866].

Mohmen mv em elecv este-Maskoke etvlwv em mēkko hahoyē este fullvtē
móhmin ma imilicá istima·skó·ki itálwa immí·kko há·ho·yí· ísti follatí·
And under that [treaty], the names of the chiefs of the Muscogee Nation

hocefhokv heyvt omakēs.
hocifhoká hiyát omâ·ki·s
are these.

Enhvteceskv Same Cokote mēkken vpoktv Mēkko Hvtke
inhaticíska sa·micokó·ti mi·kkín apó·kta mi·kkohátki
In the beginning, Sam Checote, chief, and second chief Micco Hatki

ohrolope cokpe-rakko hvmken cokpe cenvpaken
ohłolopí· cokpiłakkohámkin cókpi cinapâ·kin
became chiefs in the year eighteen hundred

pale ēpaken kolvpohkakof mēkkaket omvtēs.
pá·li i·pâ·kin kolapohkâ·ko·f mí·kka·kít o·mati·s
and sixty-seven [1867].

---

[i] Title: *mi·kkâlki tá·ti·* 'former chiefs'.
[ii] Of this list of chiefs, J. Hill knew every one of them. In the case of the earlier list, he did not know them since they were before his time.

'Svhokkolat. Oktahvsas Haco vpoktv Lucv Haco
'sahókko·lâ·t. okta·hasâ·shá·co apó·kta lo·cahá·co
Second, Oktahasas Harjo and second chief Locher Harjo

ohrolopē cokpe-rakko hvmken cokpe cenvpaken
ohłolopí· cokpiłakkohámkin cókpi cinapâ·kin
became chiefs in the year eighteen hundred

pale kolvpakē cahkepohkakof mēkkaket omvtēs.
pá·li kolapâ·ki· cahkipohkâ·ko·f mí·kka·kít o·matí·s
and seventy-five [1875].

Pvsvtkehpof, 'svtoccēnat Wate Kocmv ohrolopē cokpe-rakko hvmken cokpe cenvpaken
pasatkihpo·f 'satócci·nâ·t wa·ti kó·cma ohłolopí· cokpiłakkohámkin cókpi cinapâ·kin
After they died, the third was Ward Coachman, becoming chief in the year

pale kolvpakē ēpohkakof mēkket omvtēs
pá·li kolapâ·ki· i·pohkâ·ko·f mi·kkít o·matí·s
eighteen hundred and seventy-six [1876].

Esostat (Joe M. Perryman) Cohkv Pilmv ohrolopē cokpe-rakko hvmken
iso·stâ·t (Joe M. Perryman) co·hkapéylma ohłolopí· cokpiłakkohámkin
The fourth was Joe M. Perryman, becoming chief in the year eighteen hundred

cokpe cenvpaken pale cenvpaken cahkepohkakof mēkket omvtēs.
cókpi cinapâ·kin pá·li cinapâ·kin cahkipohkâ·ko·f mi·kkít o·matí·s
and eighty-five [1885].

'Svcahkēpat Lēkvs Pilmvn mēkken vpoktv Hotvlk Ēmarv
'sacáhki·pâ·t li·kaspéylman mi·kkín apó·kta hotalki·má·ła
The fifth was Legus Perryman, chief, and second chief Hotalk Emathla,

ohrolopē cokpe-rakko hvmken cokpe cenvpaken
ohłolopí· cokpiłakkohámkin cokpicinapâ·kin
becoming chiefs in the year eighteen hundred

pale ostvpakē cahkepohkakof mēkket omvtēs.
pá·li ostapâ·ki· cahkipohkâ·ko·f mi·kkít o·matí·s
and ninety-five [1895].

Mohmen Lēkvs Pilmvn vnrvpkv enhahyet ossihohcen
móhmin li·kaspéylman anlápka inháhyit osseyhóhcin
Then Legus Perryman was politically scandalized and thrown out of office;

Hotvlk Ēmarv mēkkof ohrolopē cokpe-rakko hvmken cokpe cenvpaken
hotalki·má·la mi·kkô·f ohlolopí· cokpilakkohámkin cokpicinapâ·kin
Hotalk Emathla became chief in the year eighteen hundred

pale ostvpakē kolvpohkakof Hotvlk Ēmarv mēkko hakof
pá·li ostapâ·ki· kolapohkâ·ko·f hotalki·má·la mi·kko ha·kô·f
and ninety-seven [1897], and when Hotalk Emathla became chief,

Edward Bullette hocefhoyvtēt os. Mēkko sēpakat tatēs.
Edward Bullette hocífhoyatí·t ô·^{n}s^{70} mi·kko sí·pa·kâ·t tá·ti·s
he was named Edward Bullette. He was the sixth chief.

Eskolvpakat Espahehcv mēkken, vpoktv Lole Mvkentase
iskolápa·kâ·t ispa·híhca mi·kkín apó·kta lo·limakintá·si
The seventh chief, Isparhecher, and second chief Roley McIntosh

ohrolopē cokpe-rakko hvmken cokpe cenvpaken pale ostvpaken ēpohkakof mēkket omvtēs.
ohlolopí· cokpilakkohámkin cokpicinapâ·kin^{71} pá·li ostapâ·kin i·pohká·ko·f mi·kkit o·matí·s
became chiefs in eighteen hundred and ninety-six [1896].

Escenvpakat Pleasant Porter ('Tvlof Haco), vpoktv Mote Tikv
iscinápa·kâ·t Pleasant Porter ('talo·fhá·co) apó·kta mo·titáyka
The eighth, Pleasant Porter (Talof Harjo) and second chief Moty Tiger

ohrolopē cokpe-rakko hvmken cokpe cenvpaken
ohlolopí· cokpilakkohámkin cokpicinapâ·kin
became chiefs in the year eighteen hundred

pale ostvpakē ostvpohkakof Potv mēkket omvtēs.
pá·li ostapâ·ki· ostapohkâ·ko·f pó·ta mi·kkít o·mati·s
and ninety-nine [1899].

Elehpof Mote Tikv mēkkof ohrolopē cokpe-rakko hvmken cokpe ostvpaken
ilíhpo·f mo·titáyka mi·kkô·f ohlolopí· cokpilakkohámkin cókpi ostapâ·kin
After [Porter] died, Moty Tiger became chief in the year nineteen hundred

kolvpakat omof Mote Tikv mēkket omvtēs.
kolapâ·ka·t ô·mo·f[72] mo·titáyka mi·kkít o·matí·s
and seven [1907].

Esostvpakat Wasentvn Klisvn ohrolopē cokpe-rakko hvmken cokpe ostvpake
isostápa·kâ·t wa·sintán kléysan ohɫolopí· cokpilakkohámkin cókpi ostapâ·ki
The ninth, [George] Washington Grayson, was appointed by the president of the U.S.

pale kolvpohkakof Wvcenv mēkkot ohmellēn mēkket omvtēs.
pá·li kolapohkâ·ko·f wacína mi·kkot ohmílli·n mi·kkít o·matí·s
in the year nineteen hundred and seventeen [1917] and became chief.

Espalat Wase Klisvn (son of Washington Grayson) mēkko
íspa·lâ·t wa·sikléysan (son of Washington Grayson) mi·kko
The tenth chief, Wasi Grayson (son of Washington Grayson),

ohrolopē cokpe-rakko hvmken cokpe ostvpaken pale hokkolē hvmkontvlakat
ohɫolopí· cokpilakkohámkin cókpi ostapâ·kin pá·li hokkô·li· hamkontalâ·ka·t
was appointed by the president of the U.S. in the year nineteen hundred

Wvcenv mēkkot ohmellen mēkket omvtēs. Hiyomat wenakēt os.
wacína mi·kkót óhmillín mi·kkit o·matí·s hayyò·ma·t wina·kí·t ô·[n]s.
and twenty-one [1921] and became chief. He is living now.

Pale eshvmkontvlakat Cace Hel
pá·li ishamkontála·kâ·t ca·ci hil
The eleventh, George Hill,

ohrolopē cokpe-rakko hvmken cokpe ostvpaken pale hokkolen tuccenohkakan
ohɫolopí· cokpilakkohámkin cókpi ostapâ·kin pá·li hokkô·lin toccinohkâ·ka·n
was appointed by the president of the U.S. in the year nineteen hundred

Wvcenv mēkkot ohmellen mēkket omvtēs.
wacína mi·kkot óhmillín mi·kkít o·matí·s
and twenty-three [1923] and became chief.

Pale eshokkolohkakat Lole Kvnat mēkko. Ohrolopē cokpe-rakko hvmken cokpe ostvpake
pá·li ishokkolóhka·ka·t lo·li kanâ·t mí·kko ohɫolopi· cokpilakkohámkin cókpi ostapâ·ki
The twelfth [was] Chief Roley Canard. In the year nineteen hundred and

pale tuccēne ostohkakan mēkko hakvrē 'temvrkvt ohcen sulkat Lole Kvnat ensatahken
pá·li toccî·ni ostohkâ·ka·n mí·kko ha·káli· 'timálkat óhcin sólka·t lo·likanâ·t insa·táhkin
thirty-four [1934], there was a race to become chief. Many people voted for Roley Canard,

Wvcenv mēkkot ohhvkvsahmet yekcetv ehmen mēkket omvtēs.
wacína mí·kkot ohhakasáhmit yikcitá íhmin mi·kkít o·matí·s
and the president of the U.S. approved, gave him authority, and he became chief.

Pale estuccenohkakat Alec Noon (Vleke Fvccvlihke) mēkko
pá·li istoccinóhka·kâ·t Alec Noon (alíki faccaléyhki) mí·kko
The thirteenth was Chief Alec Noon (Aleki Fatchalayhki):

ohrolopē cokpe-rakko hvmken cokpe ostvpake
ohłolopí· cokpiłakkohámkin cókpi ostapâ·ki
in the year nineteen hundred and

pale tuccēnen cenvpohkakof mēkko hakvrē 'temvrkv ohcen sulkat Alec Noon ensatahken
pá·li toccî·nin cinapohkâ·ko·f mí·kko há·káli· 'timálka óhcin sólka·t Alec Noon insa·táhkin
thirty-eight [1938] there was a race to become chief; many voted for Alec Noon,

Wvcenv mēkkot ohhvkvsahmet yekcetv ehmen mēkket omvtēs.
wacína mí·kkot ohhakasáhmit yikcitá íhmin mi·kkít o·matí·s
and the president of the U.S. approved, gave him authority, and he became chief.

Hiyomat Vlike Fvccvlihket mēkkot os.
hayyô·ma·t alíki faccaléyhkit mí·kkot ô·ⁿs.
Alec Noon is chief at the present time.

Momen Espahehcv mēkkeko arofvt, este-Maskoke, Wvcenv em etenfvccetv
mo·mín ispa·híhca mí·kkiko· a·lô·fat istima·skó·ki wacína imitinfaccitá
Now before Isparhecher was chief, he opposed the treaty

momet em etvlwv em vhakv em pvtakvn vnrvpēn, este sulkēn
mo·mít imitálwa imahá·ka impatá·kan anłapí·n ísti sólki·n
between the Muscogees and the U.S. and the tribe's constitution, and he divided

kvpvyēcihcet vhakv em pvtakv ofv mēkketvn vnrvpēt horren hayvtēt os.
kapayi·céyhcit ahá·ka impatá·ka ó·fa mi·kkitán anłapí·t hóllin ha·yatí·t ô·ⁿs
many people and made war against them, serving as chief under the constitution.

Momen Wvcenv ensuletawv atoken nvcomusē Okmvlken vpokvntvs.
mo·mín wacína insolitá·wa a·tô·kin[73] nacómosi· okmálkin apo·kántas
And he drove out the American soldiers and only a few stayed in Okmulgee.

Etenfvccetv momet vhakv em pvtakv vcakkvyē este fullan em vnicēt
itinfaccitá mo·mít ahá·ka impatá·ka acakkayí· ísti follâ·n imanéyci·t
We wanted to help the people who followed the agreement and the constitution

herkvn hayvranet Espahehcv em este 'tepoyetv komē hopoyē fulleyat
hílkan ha·yála·nít ispa·híhca imísti 'tipoyíta kó·mi· hopo·yí· folliyâ·t
and bring about peace, and we went looking for Isparhecher's people planning to fight them,

este-catvke em estvcako respuhēcet "'Tepohyatskvs. 'Tepoyvranatskat tokot os.
istica·takí imistacá·ko lispóhi·cít 'tipóhyá·ckas 'tipoyála·ná·cka·t tó·ko·t ô·"s
and the Indian Agent found us and said, "Do not fight. It is not for you to fight.

Etvlwv hvmkusēt omatskes" maket,
itálwa hámkosi·t ô·má·ckis ma·kít
You are all one tribe."

opunvkv ētv sulkēn espumpunayet 'tepoyetv komeyat pum vsēhvntvs.
oponaká í·ta sólki·n ispómpona·yít 'tipoyíta kó·miya·t pomási·hántas
And he said many other things and warned those of us who wanted to fight against it.

Estvcako momē estomis vretv oketv sulkēn pufullicvntvs.
istacá·ko mo·mí· (i)stô·meys alíta okíta sólki·n pofólleycántas
Even so, the agent sent us many places many times.

Momen punfēketv tat toknawv tokon,
mo·mín ponfì·kitáta·t tokná·wa tó·ko·n
And our reward was not money:

elvokon, etkulkvn, hotoskvn, oskē, uelvokē teklvtketv sulkēn espunfēket
iláwkon[74] itkólkan hotóskan oskí· oylawkí· tiklatkitá sólki·n ispónfì·kít
while Isparhecher sat [as chief], he repaid us with hunger, cold, exhaustion,

Espahehcv liken fullet omeyvtēs.
ispa·híhca lêykin follít o·miyáti·s
and struggles against rain and floods.

Ohrolopē cokpe-rakko hvmkē cokpe cenvpaken pale cenvpakē tuccenohkakat mahen
ohłolopí· cokpiłakkohámki· cokpicinapá·kin pá·li cinapâ·ki· toccinohkâ·ka·t mâ·hin
About the year eighteen hundred and ninety-three [1893],

Espahehcv enhorre em eyoksvtēs, herkv hahken.
ispa·híhca inhólli imíyo·ksati·s hílka háhkin.
Isparhecher's war came to an end, and peace was made.

Mohmen hvtvm etenfvccetv ohrolopē cokpe-rakko hvmken
móhmin hatâm itinfaccitá ohłolopí· cokpiłakkohámkin
Then another agreement came, in the year nineteen hundred

cokpe-ostvpakē hvmkē vpakof Wvcenv Maskoke etenfaccan vnrvpēt Cetto Haco hocefkēt
cokpiʔostapâ·ki· hámki· apâ·ko·f wacína ma·skó·ki itinfâ·cca·n anłapí·t cittohá·co hocífki·t
and one [1901]. Chitto Harjo opposed the agreement between the U.S. and the Muscogees.

em este sulkēn nvkvftēcet,
imísti sólki·n nakáfti·cít
He held meetings with many of his people, going around saying,

"Etenfvccetv vculakan vsvpaklvkan hērēs.
itinfaccitá acolâ·ka·n asapáklaka·n hĭ·ⁿłi·s
"It would be better to stand by the old treaties.

Heyv etenfvccetv mocvsat pustemerrvkuecvranēt os" maket em aren,
hiyá itinfaccitá mocása·t postimiłłakóycała·ní·t ô·ⁿs ma·kít ima·lín
This new treaty is going to make us suffer."

este-cate tat sulkemahet ennvkaften vpakit arimvts.
isticá·tita·t solkimá·hit ínnaka·ftin apa·kéyt a·łéymac
Many Indians met with him, and I went about with them.

Momet opunvkv hervkemahēn opunayet okis.
mo·mít oponaká hiłakimá·hi·n opóna·yit o·kêys
I mean that he spoke in a most persuasive manner.

Vkerrickv mv omat este esnvkvftēcē 'svretv oketv hoyvnepēn arēt okekv,
akiłłéycka ma ô·ma·t ísti isnakáfti·cí· 'sałitá okíta hoyanipí·n a·łí·t o·kiká
It was too late to gather support for ideas of opposition,

em estvlke tat sulkēn svlvfkvkuecet vtotketv cokon vtothoyemvts.
imistâlkita·t sólki·n saláfkakoycít atotkitá cokón atótho·yimác
so many of his people were arrested and sent to the penitentiary.

Momen Cetto Haco tat estewvnayvlket hopoyet fullet
mo·mín cittohá·cota·t istiwana·yâlkit hopo·yít follít
Thus many lawmen were looking for Chitto Harjo.

encukon liken 'rem orihcet cukon em ēchet esfullen
incokón lêykin 'łimołéyhcit cokón imi·chít ísfollín
They went to his house and took shots at his house,

ēmeu mv este wvnayvlke a-ēchen etechaken
i·miw ma ʔísti wana·yâlki á-ʔi·chin iticha·kín[75]
and he too shot back at the lawmen, so they were shooting at each other.

Cetto Haco tat rahohet omis letiket aret Cahtv em ēkvnvn ahyet erēlvtēt omēs.
cittohá·cota·t la·hô·hit o·mêys litèykit a·lít cá·hta imi·kanán áhyit iłi·latí·t ô·mi·s
Chitto Harjo was shot, but ran and went to Choctaw country, where he died.

Mohmen ohrolopē cokpe-rakkohvmkē cokpe-ostvpakē kolvpakē vpakat mahen
móhmin ohłolopí· cokpiłakkohámki· cokpi ʔostapâ·ki· kolapâ·ki· apâ·ka·t mâ·hin
About nineteen hundred and seven [1907].

Cetto 'meste kihocē fullvtē tat fekhonnakvtēt omēs.
cittomísti kéyho·cí· follatí·ta·t fikhónna·katí·t ô·mi·s
Chitto's people, as they were called. stopped their activity.

The Town of Hilabi (Etvlwuce Helvpe-Kvnite Hocefkēt Vm Etvlwvt Omēs)[i]

J. Hill (Haas XXI:149–165)

Ohrolopē cokpe-rakko hvmkē cokpe cenvpakē
ohłolopí· cokpiłakkohámki· cokpicinapâ·ki·
From the year eighteen hundred

---

[i] Title: *italwocí hilapikanéyti hocífki·t amitálwat ô·mi·s* 'The little town named Hilabi Canadian is my tribal town'.

pale-ēpakē kolvpohkakat atē mucvnettv vlakat
pá·li ʔi·pâ·ki· kolapohkâ·ka·t a·tí· mocanitta alâ·ka·t
and sixty-seven [1867] to this day,

Helvpe cuko-rakko mēkko hahoyē este fullvtē heyvt omakēs.
hilápi cokołákko mí·kko há·ho·yí· isti follatí· hiyát omâ·ki·s
the people who were made Hilabi tribal town leaders are these.

Taskēke-mēkko enhenehv Heles-haco.
ta·ski·kimí·kko inhiníha 'hilishá·co.
Chief Taskiki and his second chief [henehv] Hilis Harjo.

Heles-haco elehpen Okēlosv henehv hahoyen welaket
'hilishá·co ilíhpin oki·losá hiníha ha·hô·yin wila·kít
Hilis Harjo died, and Okilosa was made second chief,

hokkolvt mēkusapvlke vpvkē hakvkehpen
hokkó·lat mi·kosa·mâlki apakí· ha·kakíhpin
[but] both became Christians.

'svhokkolat Mate mēkkoton enhenehv Cohkv 'cototoket omen welaket
'sahókko·lâ·t má·ti mí·kkoton inhiníha có·hka 'cototó·kit[76] ô·min wila·kít
The second [chief] was Chief Mati and his second chief Joe Chototoki.

hokkolvt pvsvtkehpof mēkkvlke sekon cukorakko nvkaftet fulhoyekon,
hokkó·lat pasatkíhpo·f mi·kkâlki síkon cokołákko naka·ftít[77] folhoyíkon
After both died, there were no leaders, and meetings at the square ground ceased.

ohrolopē sulkēt ohhoyahnen,
ohłolopí· sólki·t ohhoyáhnin
Many years passed,

cuko-rakko vpēttē encukeletot ohliketv tis omvlkvt lekwvkēpē oketv ocvtēt os.
cokołákko api·ttí· incokílitot ohleykitáteys omálkat líkwaki·pí· okíta o·catí·t ô·ⁿs
and the posts of the square ground arbors and benches all rotted during this time.

Mohmen 'svtuccēnat Kosv-haco mēkko hahoyekot omis
móhmin 'satóci·nâ·t ko·sahá·co mí·kko ha·hoyíkot o·mêys
Then the third [chief], Kosa Harjo, had not yet been made chief,

netta huerihcet "Yv nettvn nvkvftaks" mahken cuko-rakko tatē ēkvnv nvkvfhohten
nitta· hoyléyhcit ya níttan nakáftaks máhkin cokołakkotá·ti· i·kaná nakafhóhtin
but he set a day, saying "Meet on this day." So they met at the old square ground:

heyv cuko-rakko rakvwvpvkē tayēt on omat
hiyá cokołákko ła·kawápaki· tá·yi·t ô·n o·mâ·t
"The call was to discuss whether this square ground can be started back up,

mv opunvyēckv vrahkvt huehketvt omen nvkaftet omatskes" maket,
ma oponayí·cka ałáhkat hoyhkitát ô·min nakâ·ftit o·má·ckis ma·kít
and that is why you are meeting," he said.

Kosv-haco mēkkēt liken vpoket
ko·sahá·co mí·kki·t lêykin apô·kit
Thus Kosa Harjo was acting as chief.

cuko-rakko tat akvwvkepekvs maketvt fvciyen, ennettvkahcet vwvhvtet
cokołákkota·t a·kawakipíkas ma·kitát facêyyin innittakáhcit awáhatit
It was decided to start up the square ground, so they set a date and dismissed.

mv nettv ennvkvfitet cukorakko akvwvphoyvtēt os.
ma nítta innakafêytit cokołákko a·kawápho·yatí·t ô·ⁿs
They met that day, and the square ground was started up again.

Mohmen esostat Fus-yvholvn mēkko hahoyen aret omis
móhmin iso·stâ·t fosyahólan mí·kko ha·hô·yin a·lít o·mêys
And the fourth [chief], Fus Yahola, was made chief

encuko-rakko vrakkueceko ont aret mēkusapv hakehpet,
incokołákko ałakkóyciko· ônt a·lít mi·kosá·pa ha·kíhpit
but went about without showing respect for his square ground and became a Christian

"Mēkko toyaks" maket vrēpvcoken fullēt, Kvntvlēmarv Wakse-yvholucen etohkvlkēt
mí·kko tó·yaks ma·kít ali·pacókin follí·t kantali·má·la waksiyaholocín itohkálki·t
and went about saying, "I'm not chief." Kantal Emathla got together with Waksi Yaholochi:

"Cukorakko nvkaftet fullēpvkēs" maket,
cokołákko naka·ftít folli·pakí·s ma·kít
"Let's meet at the square ground," they said.

"Nettv huericeyat mvnettvlke hoktvke tis punnvkaften pokkēchet fullēkv
nítta hóyłeyciyâ·t manittâlki hoktakíteys pónnaka·ftín pókki·chít follí·ka
"When we set a date, young people and women will meet with us, we'll play ball,

'pvnkvo ocen fullet omvkan hērēs" kont,
pánkaw o·cin follít o·makâ·n hī·ⁿłi·s kónt
we'll have dances too, and that will be good," we thought.

Fus-yvholv-mēkko enhuehkeyat,
fosyaholamí·kko ínhoyhkiyâ·t
But when we called on Chief Fus Yahola,

a-epohhvtekon momē stomis eswikēkon
a·ʔipohhatikon mo·mí· stô·meys ísweykí·kon
he would not join us, but even so we did not stop,

pum vkvsamat nettvkvckv punhayen panēn hvyatken fulleyof
pomákasa·mâ·t nittakácka pónha·yín pa·ní·n haya·tkín folliyô·f
so he gave us permission and set a date for us and we began all night dances.

Helvpvlke 'svculvke tat a-epohhvweko tayet
hilapâlki 'sacolákita·t a·ʔipohhawiko· tâ·yit
But the Hilabi elders would not join us;

"Hoporrenkv tokon esfullvcoks" makaket fullēpvcoken
hopołłínka to·kô·n ísfollacoks má·ka·kít fólli·pacókin
they said, "They are going about doing things without wisdom,"

cuko-rakko vfulleyvtē wikēpeyvtēt os. Mohmen Fus-yvholv-mēkko tat elehpen.
cokołákko afolliyáti· weyki·piyáti·t ô·ⁿs móhmin fosyaholamí·kkota·t ilíhpin.
so we stopped activities at the square ground. Then Chief Fus Yahola died.

'Svcahkēpat Lahtvmvtahvn mēkko hahoyet omis,
'sacáhki·pâ·t lahtamatá·han[78] mí·kko ha·hô·yit o·mêys
The fifth [chief], Lahtamataha was made chief,

entvsekvyv em ēleskē omē arvcokat onvkv ocen arvtēt os.
intasikayá imi·líski· ó·mi· a·łacóka·t onáka o·cín a·latí·t ô·ⁿs
but he was sullen with his citizens, it was heard as he went about.

Mvo mēkusapvt omēpvtēt onkv,
maw' mi·kosá·pat omi·patí·t óŋka
He too had been a Christian,

momis vkerrickv hvmkusē enhakat cuko-rakko-mēkko hueretvt
mo·mêys akiłłéycka hámkosi· ínha·kâ·t cokołakkomí·kko hoyłitát
but he believed until his death

nake rakkemahat os komē aret elēpvtēt os.
nâ·ki łakkimâ·ha·t ô·ⁿs kó·mi· a·łít ili·patí·t ô·ⁿs.
that serving as square ground chief was a great honor.

Mohmen sēpakat 'Sekomahvn mēkko hahoyvtēt os.
nóhmin si·pa·kâ·t 'sikomá·han mí·kko há·ho·yatí·t ô·ⁿs.
Then the sixth [chief]. Sikomaha ['Nothing-at-all'], was made chief.

Este enhecketv oketv oreko heckvtēt,
ísti inhickitá okíta ołíko· híckati·t
He was born prematurely,

momis mvt Helvpe cuko-rakko-mēkkot hueret omēs, mucvnettv.
mo·mêys mat hilápi cokołakkomí·kkot hôyłit o·mí·s mocanítta.
but he is chief of Hilabi square ground to this day.

Momen cuko-rakko-mēkko oketv encvpkē estomusen mēkkēt huervranat
mo·mín cokołakkomí·kko okíta incapkí· istô·mosin mí·kki·t hôyłała·nâ·t
Now the length of a square ground chief's term

eskērkv sekon mēkihocēt omēs.
iski·łka síko·n mi·kéyho·cí·t ô·mi·s
is not set.

Ehlē tvlken monkat wikēpis maken em vkvsvmaken omat
íhli· tálkin móŋka·t wéyki·péys ma·kín imakasáma·kin o·mâ·t
He served until he died, or he could announce his resignation and be approved,

monkat mēkko heremahekot os komaken omat,
móŋka·t mí·kko hilimâ·hikot ó·ⁿs kó·ma·kín o·mâ·t
or if they thought he was not a very effective chief,

ossicet ētvn mēkkihocēt,
ósseycít i·tan mi·kkéyho·cí·t
he would be removed and another would be appointed chief:

vculvke tat "Tvlwv-mēkko huericetv rvkvpv honteko monken ometvt omēs"
acolakíta·t talwamí·kko hoyɬeycitá ɬakápa[79] *hóntiko· môŋkin omítat ô·mi·s*
"A tribal town chief should be chosen before the herbs grow,"

makaket omvtēs, vtakrv em vheleswv honteko monken.
má·ka·kít o·matí·s atákɬa imahilíswa hontíko· môŋkin
the elders said, before the medicine weeds grow.

Vncuko-rakko pvnhoyat
ancokoɬákko pánho·yâ·t
I did not attend my own square ground's dances

momet ētv to estomis vrvyvtē sekon ohrolopē pale tuccēnen tuccenohkakēs.
mo·mít í·ta tô· istô·meys aɬáyati· síkon ohɬolopí· pá·li toccî·nin toccinóhka·kí·s
and other [grounds] for thirty-three years.

Pvnkv arē wihkvyvtē hiyomē orat pvnkv hecetv yackv vkerrickv vnheckvtē sekot os.
pánka a·ɬí· wéyhkayáti· hayyô·mi· ô·ɬa·t pánka hicíta yá·cka akiɬɬéycka anhíckati· síko·t ô·ⁿs.
I quit going dancing; up to now I have not had a desire or thought to see a dance.

Helvpe etvlwv este nvcomēt omvtēt onkv, hiyomat pale ēpakat orepekis omēs.
hilápi itálwa ísti nacómi·t o·matí·t óŋka hayyô·ma·t pá·li i·pâ·ka·t olípikeys ô·mi·s
The people of Hilabi were few, and now there may not be as many as sixty.

Description of Hilabi Round House (Helvpe Cukorakko Oh-onvkv)[i, 80]

J. Hill (Haas IV:171–189, V:1–57)

Ohrolopē	cokperakko hvmken cokpe cenvpaken pale tuccēnat	mahe	atē
ohɬolopí·	*cokpilákko hámkin cókpi cinapâ·kin pá·li toccî·na·t*	*mâ·hi*	*a·tí·*[ii]
year	1830	about	has been coming

From about the year eighteen hundred and thirty [1830]

---

[i] Title: *hilápi cokoɬákko ohhonáka* 'Hilapi square-ground story'.
[ii] *a·tí·:* 'has been coming (said about from that time on up to now).

hiyomē   vlakat   oketv etehopvyvkē   nake   momakvtē
hayyô·mi·   alâ·ka·t   okíta itihopayakí·[81] *nâ·ki   mó·ma·kati·*
up to now that has come, arrived times far apart   things that were done in the past
until now there were events that happened far apart,

ocakat   ēkvntvckv Vlepamv hocefkat   seko   monkof,
o·câ·ka·t   i·kantácka alipá·ma hocífka·t   siko·   môŋko·f
that which was district   Alabama   called, named wasn't any before that time
before there was a state known as Alabama,

mv ēkvnv ofvn   Helvpe cukorakko-fvsket   likvtēs.
ma i·kaná ó·fan hilápi   cokołakkofáskit[82]   *leykati·s.*
that land   in   Hilabi   buskground house sharp-topped was sitting, was
and in that land was the Hilabi round house.

Este-cate enhocefkv Rvnvcelecv   hocefkē ēkvnvn   ohliket
isticá·ti   inhocífka łanacilíca[i]   *hocífki· i·kanán   ohlêykit*
an Indian his name   at the foot of the mountain named the ground on it was sitting
Rvnvcelecv was the Indian name of the ground

omvtēs. Cukorakko mēkkvke, tvsekvyv sehoyat   mv   etvlwv
o·matí·s cokołákko mi·kkakí tasikayá sihô·ya·t   ma   itálwa
was   buskground chiefs   members that they have that town
it sat on. The council house chiefs and members of that town

yvmạskusēt   ont, fvccetv ofvn   em vpoketv
yamă·ⁿskosi·t   ônt faccitá ó·fan imapo·kitá[ii]   (was) very peaceful
        was   justice   inside the place of sitting, living
were very peaceful and designed their living place with justice

hayvtēt   vpokēpet,   etvlwv estomēn
ha·yatí·t   apo·kî·pit   itálwa istó·mi·n
they made it (that their living place) and they lived there town nothing, in no way
and lived there

---

[i] Not known to Raiford. Cf. *łaní* 'mount'.
[ii] Raiford: *-itán.*

vnrvpkv   em ocvtē seko,
anłápka   *imó·cati· siko·*
(opposition(?)) against (any other town)   never did have (not)
without malice toward any other town.

etvlwv	encukorakkot	liket	omvtētan	Wvcenvt	vhakvn	eshahyet
itálwa	*incokołákkot*	*łâykit*	*o·matí·ta·n*	*wacínat*	*ahá·kan*	*isháhyit*
town's	buskground house	sitting	had been	U.S.	laws	made them

The town's round house was there until the U.S. made laws [and said],

"Akensv-hvcce	eteropottē	ēkvnv	likēn	cēmit	omikv,
a·kinsahácci	*itiłopó·tti·*	*i·kaná*	*léyki·n*	*cî·meyt*	*o·méyka*
Arkansas River	through (the Ar. R.)	land	that is	I have given you	have

"I have given you land with the Arkansas River running through it,

lvpkēn	ohcuneckaks.	Mv	ēkvnv	erohret	nokosen	elēcetskat
lápki·n	*ohconíckaks*	*ma*	*i·kaná*	*iłóhłit*	*nokósin*	*ili·cícka·t*
fast, quickly	(you-all) move on it	that	land	getting to it	bear	when you kill it

so you must must move there quickly. When you reach that land and kill a bear

eratakliket	oh-vpokēt	omen	fo encvmpē	ohfihhonē	ēkvnv	likēn
iła·taklêykit[83]	*ohhapó·ki·t*	*ô·min*[84]	*fó· incampí·*	*ohféyhho·ní·*	*i·kaná*	*léyki·n*
go and live on it	several live on it	do	the honey	flows over	the land	(that is)

you will live on it; I am giving you land

cēmvkit	omikv	mvn	cenhompetv	heraken	hompēpet
cî·makeyt	*o·méyka*	*man*	*cinhompitá*	*hiłă·ⁿkin*	*hómpi·pít*
that I've given you-all	have	there	your food	very good	(you) can eat

where honey flows, so you will eat well there,

estofis	vpokvranatskēt	os.	Ēkvnv	cem eyacēt
istô·feys	*apô·kala·ná·cki·t*	*ô·ⁿs*	*i·kaná*	*cimiyá·ci·t*
forever	you-all shall live (there)		land	if anyone wants it from you

and you shall live there forever.

cem pohēt	este	ena-hvtkēt	cehomv	hueren	hēcet
címpo·hí·t	*ísti*	*ina·hátkit*[85]	*cihóma*	*hôylin*	*hi·cít*
and they ask you for it	person	(with) body white	before you	standing	(you) see him

If you find yourself face to face with a white man wanting your land

vhueretskat   vnet   ohkvkos!
ahôylíckaˑt   *anít*   *óhkákoˑs*
when you stand up to him   I, me   it won't be
and asking for it, it will not be me!

Sutv   min   alvtkēt   ecehueret
sotá   *mèyn*   *aˑlátkiˑt*   *icihôylit*
sky   from   have fallen down   will come in contact with you
It will have to be a being fallen from the sky

ēkvnv   cem pohet   okvrēs" makakēt,   "Este-hvtke   ecetefullat
iˑkaná   *címpoˑhit*   *okáliˑs* *máˑkaˑkíˑt* *istihátki*   *icítifollâˑt*
land   will ask you for it will be they said   white people   that are amongst you
asking for your land." They said, "[It is having] white people among you

naorkv   hayekv."   Akensv-hvcce enlekothv   mont   enkvsappv
naˑólka   *hâˑyika*   *aˑkinsahácci* *inlikóˑtha*   *mónt*   *inkasáˑppa*
trouble   have made   Arkansas R. south of (the Ark. R.) and then   north (of it)
that has made trouble." The time came for [Hilabi] to move

aohcuneckvranat   oketv   ohren, mēkkvke tat
aˑohconíckalaˑnâˑt   *okíta*   *óhlin* *miˑkkakítaˑt*
(the time) when they are to move there the time came   the chiefs'
south and then north of the Arkansas River, and there was a day

entvsekvyv,   encukolice,   hopuetak-lopocke omvlkvn
intasikayá   *incokoléyci*   *hopoytaˑklopócki* *omálkan*
their citizens, members the family, household the children small all
when the chiefs gathered all their citizens, their families,

etohkalet   mēkkvke   kakē   nettv   ocvtēt os.
itohkâˑlit   *miˑkkakí*   *kâˑkiˑ*   *nítta*   *oˑcatíˑt ôˑⁿs*
put them together (where) the chiefs were sitting, living a day (once like that) there was
and small children.

Mv   cukorakko-fvske   cukele   rakrakē   svpaklēcvkvtēt   omvtēs.
ma   *cokolakkofáski*   *cokíli* *laklakíˑ* *sapaklíˑcakátiˑt* *oˑmatíˑs*
that   buskground house sharp-pointed posts   big ones   that had been put up it was
That round house had been put up with big posts.

Mv   cukorakko-fvskē   hahoyof
ma   cokołakkofáski·   *há·ho·yô·f*
that   buskground house sharp-topped   when they were making it
When [people] were making the round house,

mēkkvlke tat   hompekot   em ohliketv   ohkaken
mi·kkâlkita·t   hómpiko·t   *imohleykitá   ohkâ·kin*
the chiefs   not eating (the chiefs)   benches   they (chiefs) sitting on
the chiefs did not eat; they sat on their benches

omvlkvn   pohyet   'senhvyvtiket,
omálkan   póhyit   sinhayatêykit
all   finished it   they stayed up all night
until the work was finished and sat through the night,

uewvn   aklohpet,   homhopof,   hompakvtēs.
óywan   aklóhpit   *hómho·pô·f*   *hómpa·katí·s*
water   they bathed in   when they were eating   they (the chiefs) ate
bathed in water, and once all were eating, [then the chiefs] ate.

Mv   cuko tat   cule-hvrpe   vhopvkvtēt   omet   matat   esohrvnkēt,
ma   cokóta·t   coliháłpi   ahópa·katí·t[86]   *ô·mit   ma·tá·t   isohłáŋki·t*
that   house   pine-bark   (doesn't know)   [was]   the same   covered with
That house was covered with pine-bark of equal measurements, and the same on the roof.

poloksēt   cufoknēt   omen,   cukorakko-fvske   kicet   okakvtēs.
polóksi·t   cofókni·t   *ô·min   cokołakkofáski*   *keycít   oka·katí·s*
(it was) round   sharp-pointed   was   the house-big sharp   called it   they did
It was round and pointed, and they called it the <u>cukorakko-fvske</u> ['sharp big house'].

Mv ofv   taknvrkvpvn   totkv   etēcet   vfulutēcēt
ma ó·fa   taknałkapán   *tó·tka   itî·cit*[87]   *afóloti·cí·t*
inside that   right in the center   fire   they built (a fire)   they went around it
Inside that, right in the center, they built a fire, circled around it,

'pvnakvtēs.   Momvtēt on   vnokecakuset   omis,   wihket
pána·katí·s   mo·matí·ton[88]   *anokică·ⁿkosit*   *o·mêys*   *wéyhkit*
they danced   it had been   they loved it very much,   but   they left it
and danced. They loved it very much as it had been, but leaving it behind

momet ohrolopē cokperakko hvmkē cokpe cenvpakē pale tuccēnen hokkolohkakat
mo·mít ohłolopí· cokpiłákko hámki· cókpi cinapâ·ki· pá·li toccî·nin hokkolohkâ·ka·t
then the year 1832
in about the year eighteen hundred and thirty-two [1832],

mahen enkvpahkē ayē Akensv-hvcce vpvtvtapvkē
mâ·hin iŋkapáhki· a·yí· a·kinsahácci apatata·pakí·
about they separated from it going Arkansas R. up and down
going forward to reach

ēkvnv ocakat eroretv estemerkv estomvkēn etehoyahnet
i·kaná o·câ·ka·t iłolitá istimíłka isto·makí·n itihoyáhnit
land where there is to get there suffering what kind, how much they went through
those lands bordering the Arkansas River, they would survive terrible suffering

ohfēkvpetv eshehcet, hopuetake ohmahēcvranat kerrakēsekot
ohfi·kapíta ishíhcit hopoytá·ki ohma·hí·cała·nâ·t kiłłă·ⁿkî·siko·t
to rest upon they found it the children to grow them upon they did not know
to find rest. They didn't know if they would get to raise their children there,

yvkvpvranet sapokv em etetahket, Helvpe etvlwv likvtēt os.
yakápała·nít sa·poká imititáhkit hilápi itálwa leykatí·t ô·ⁿs
they were to walk their packs they got ready Hilabi town that's where it was
but they got their bundles ready to start the walk; this was the town of Hilabi.

Encukorakko-fvske vrakkueckv rakkemahēn em ocet
incokołakkofáski ałakkóycka łakkimă·ⁿhi·n imô·cit
their big sharp-pointed house honor, appreciation very much had for it
They had the utmost respect for their round house,

hopuetake etekērrusē etenokecvkē mahēckv ēkvnvn
hopoytá·ki itikǐ·ⁿłłosi· itinokicakí· ma·hí·cka i·kanán
children know each other very well loved each other raising of them land
for it was the ground where they raised children

licet omvtētok. Opanet eshvyvtketv
lêycit o·matí·to·k opa·nít ishayatkitá
they had it did have it, because/for danced staying up all night
who knew each other and loved one another. They danced and stayed up

osten   eshvyvtiket,   cukorakko   ofv   poskē
ô·stin   *ishayatêykit*   *cokolákko*   *ó·fa*   *po·skí·*
four times   they stayed up all night   the big house   inside of   busking
for four nights, sitting, fasting

vpokvranē   hvthvyvtke   em vheleswv
apó·kała·ní·   *hathayátki*   *imahilíswa*[i]
where they are to be sitting (in the) morning's medicine (of the morning)
in the round house; they took

vcakēn   vfastet,   totkv   etēcvntot
acá·ki·n   *afa·stít*   *tó·tka*   *iti·cántot*[89]
sacred (medicine) they used, took it fire   they would build it, kindle it
the sacred morning medicine, built a fire,

hompekot   vpoken,   yafkēt   omvtētok.
hómpiko·t   *apô·kin*   *ya·fkí·t*   *o·matí·to·k*
not eating   sitting   got evening   that's the way it was
and sat about without eating into the evening.

Mv   totkv   ētkvtē   em ēsso   nvcumusēn   esawvtē
ma   *tó·tka* *i·tkatí·*   *imí·sso*   *nacómosi·n*   *isa·watí·*
that   fire   that used to burn its ashes   a little bit of   they brought it
They took a few ashes

esfullet   yvmv   esyihcet   tvlofuce   Hanna, Oklahoma
*isfǒl*ⁿ*lit*[90]   *yamá* *isyéyhcit*   *'talo·foci*   *hä·na*   *oklahóma*
they were around with it   here   they brought   the little town of Hanna, Okla.
from that fire and brought them here,

enkvsvppofv   hvsossv   vkērkv   hvmkē   nvrkvpv   vpakat   mahet   omēs.
iŋkasappó·fa *hasó·ssa*   *akí·łka* *hámki·*   *nalkapá*   *apâ·ka·t* *mâ·hit* *o·mí·s*
north of   east (NE of it) miles   one   and a half and   about   it is
about a mile and a half north and east of the little town of Hanna, Oklahoma.

---

[i] *inhilíswa* is different — means 'its medicine'.

Rvnvcelecv	cukorakko-fvske	ofv	ēsso	esawvtē
łanacilíca	*cokołakkofáski*	*ófa*	*ísso*	*isawatí·*
(doesn't know)	the big house sharp-pointed	in	ashes	that they had brought

They placed there the ashes from inside the <u>Rvnvcelecv</u> round house,

mvn	vpohyet,	totkv	oh-etēcet,	opvnkv ēkvnv	hayakvtēs.
man	*apóhyit*	*tó·tka*	*óhhiti·cít*	*opánka i·kaná*	*há·ya·katí·s*
there	they put them	fire	built a fire on them	a dance- ground	they made it

built a fire on them, and established a dance-ground.

Momis	cukorakko-fvsket	sekatēs.
mo·mêys	*cokołakkofáskit*	*siká·ti·s*
But	(there was no) big sharp-topped house	there was no.

But there was no round house.

Heyv	onvpv	ocat	ohrolopē	pale cahkēpvnkē	mahen
hiyá	*onápa*	*ô·ca·t*	*ohłolopí·*	*pá·li cahkí·paŋkí·*	*mâ·hin*
here	that that's (here) on top	that is	years about	fifty (years) ago	about

The above was told about fifty years ago

Calohacot	onayvtēt	os.	Em vculkv	ohrolopē	palen kolvpohkakat
ca·lohá·cot	*ona·yatí·t*	*ô·ⁿs*	*imacólka*	*ohłolopí·*	*pá·lin kolapohká·ka·t*
Chaloharjo	told about it	did	(when) his age (was)	years	seventeen

by Chalo Harjo. His age

mahet	Rvnvcelecv	cukorakko-fvske	osiyet	vtvtēt	omvtēs.
mâ·hit	*łanacilíca*	*cokołakkofáski*	*osêyyit*	*atáti·t*	*ô·mati·s*
about	('under the roof')	of the big sharp-topped house	got out	came from	did

was about seventeen, when he came from the <u>Rvnvcelecv</u> round house.

Cukorakko-fvske	sekon	omis	opvnkv ēkvnv	mvn	hayekv,
cokołakkofáski	*sikon*	*o·mêys*	*opánka[91] i·kaná*	*man*	*há·yika*
the sharp-pointed house	there wasn't any,	but	dance-ground	there	made it

Although there was no round house, they made a dance ground there

em vyē	estomēn	posketv	ocet,	opvnkv	ocet
imayí·	*istó·mi·n*	*poskitá*	*o·cít*	*opánka*	*o·cít*
its ways, custom	what with	a busk	they had it	dances	they had

and, according to their customs, had fasts and

fullvten   omat   emonkusen   fullvtēs,
follatín   *o·mâ·t*   *imóŋkosin* *follatí·s*
were around   had been   the same as they had been about (long ago)
the same dances they used to have

ohrolopē   sulkēn   ohrolopē   cokperakko   hvmkē   cokpe   cenvpakē
ohłolopí·   *sólki·n*   *ohłolopí·* *cokpiłákko*   *hámki·*   *cókpi*   *cinapâ·ki·*
years   many   year   [thousand   one   hundred   eight
for many years, up until the year eighteen hundred

pale ēpakē hvmkontvlakat   oren   mv   oketv   omof,   Wvcenv   etekvlkēt
pá·li i·pâ·ki· hamkontalâ·ka·t *ô·lin*   *ma*   *okíta*   *ô·mo·f*   *wacína*   *itikálki·t*
sixty-one]   up to   (at) that time   at   The U.S.   was divided
and sixty-one [1861], at which time the United States divided

horren   hayet   este maskoke   herkv   ocē   kakēpvtē
hółłin   *hâ·yit*[92] *istima·skó·ki*   *hiłka*   *ó·ci·*   *ká·ki·patí·*[93]
and war   it made   The Muskogee Ind. peace   having they were living (in peace)
and made war, destroyed the peaceful existence of the Muscogees,

em vyvmahiket   vwahēcekv.
imayama·hêykit   *awa·hî·cika*
they destroyed it for them   have scattered them now
and scattered them.

Opvnkv   ēkvnv   momet   ehute take   em ēkvnv tis   omvlkvn
opánka   *i·kaná* *mo·mít*   *ihóti tá·ki*   *imi·kanáteys*   *omálkan*
dance-   ground   Then   their homes   their land, even   all
They left their dance-grounds, their homes, their land,

wihket   pefatiket,   Uecate-rakko   vnakusan
wéyhkit   *pifa·têykit*   *oyca·tiłákko*   *aná·kosa·n*
they quit it (left it)   they ran   the Red R.   near (the Red R.)
and ran, and stayed near the Red River

Tenesen, Tikses   atvpalvn   Cekvsv   em ēkvnvn
tinisín   *téksis*   *a·tapá·lan*   *cikása*   *imi·kanán*
Denison, Texas   on the side (of the river from)   Chickasaw   their country
on this side of Denison, Texas,

vpoken, | ohrolopē cahkēpat | hoyanen
apô·kin | *ohłolopí· cahkî·pa·t* | *hoyâ·nin*[94]
they were living in (the Ch. country) | years | five | (when) had passed
in Chickasaw country. And after five years,

eryicof, | nak omvlkvt | yvmahkēpen,
iłyeycô·f | *nâ·k omálkat* | *yamahkî·pin*
when they came back here | everything | had been destroyed
when they came back here, everything had been destroyed;

eto-pokhe | rakrvkēpen | hvfvpē | hērē | hakēpen
itopókhi | *łakłakî·pin* | *hafápi·* | *hĭ·ⁿłi·* | *ha·kî·pin*
bushes, brush | (had gotten) big | brushy | very | got to be
the brush had grown tall, it had gotten very weedy

eryicvtēt | omēs. | Mohmet | ētvn | hopoyet,
iłyeycatí·t | *ô·mi·s* | *móhmit* | *í·tan* | *hopo·yít*
they came back | here then | Then | some other | they were hunting
when they returned. Then they looked for another [place]

opvnkv ēkvnv | hērat | vkērkv nvrkvpv ennvrkvpv
opánka i·kaná | *hĭ·ⁿla·t* | *akí·lka nałkapá innałkapá*
dance-ground | the good one | mile | half's | half
that would be perfect for a dance-ground and moved it about one-quarter mile.

enhopvyē | omusēn | vkuyiyet | hvtvm heleswv enhayē
inhopayí· | *ô·mosi·n* | *akoyêyyit* | *hatâm 'hilíswa ínha·yí·*
the distance | about | they moved it | again medicine they made for
So again they took the coals from the fire that had originally been lit,

totkv techoyvtē | em ēsso ercahwet | vpohyet
tó·tka tícho·yatí· | *imi·sso iłcáhwit* | *apóhyit*
fire (which) they had made | its ashes they went and got them | and put [them] down
acccompanied by medicine ritual, and set them down,

totkv	oh-etēcet	opvnkv ēkvnv	hahoyvtēt os.
tó·tka	óhhiti·cít	opánka i·kaná[i]	ha·hoyáti·t[95] ô·ⁿs
fire	built it on	dance-ground	they have made it

built the fire on them, and made a dance-ground.

Monkv	mvn	posket	opvnhoyen	ēkvnv	liken
mòŋka	man	po·skít	opánho·yín	i·kaná	lêykin
Therefore	there	where they busk	they dance	the ground	is (there)

So that's the place where they fasted and danced

ohrolopē	cokperakko hvmken cokpe ostvpakat	orvtēt	os.
ohłolopí·	cokpilákko hámkin cókpi ostapâ·ka·t	o·łati·t	ô·ⁿs
(up to) the year	1900	up to	did

until the year nineteen hundred [1900].

Mv ofv	posketv	ocvranat,
ma ó·fa	poskitá	ó·cala·nâ·t
in that (year)	busk	they were going to have

In order to fast in that place,

enhvteceskv	mēkkvlke	netta	meliyet,
inhaticíska	mi·kkâlki	nittá·	milêyyit
the beginning	the town-kings	day	they set

at the very beginning, the town kings [mēkkvlke] set a day

"Mv	nettv	hompeko	nvkvftatskvrēs"	mahket,
ma	nítta	hómpiko·	nakáftá·ckáli·s	máhkit
that	day	not eating	you-all must meet (without eating)	they said

and said, "You must meet without eating that day,"

este	sulkat	enkērkuecen,
ísti	sólka·t	iŋkí·łkoycín
people	most of the (townspeople)	they gave them notice about it, informed them

and informed everyone,

---

[i] Raiford: *i·kanán.*

mv	nettv	hvthvyvtkē	hompekot	nvkvfiten
ma	*nítta*	*hathayátki·*	*hómpiko·t*	*nakafêytin*
that	day	in the morning	without eating	they met

and they met without eating on the morning of that day.

mēkkvlke	kakēpet	vkerrickv	hayet,	etem punahoyet
mi·kkâlki	*ka·kî·pit*	*akiłłéycka*	*ha·yít*	*itimponá·ho·yít*
the chiefs	they sat there	ideas	make	they talked to each other

And the chiefs met and put ideas forward and talked with each other

kaket	entvsekvyv tat	estofv	mahen
kâ·kit	*intasikayáta·t*	*istô·fa*	*mâ·hin*
they sat	their townsmen	when	about

when their townsmen

tektvnkē	ocen.		Mont
tiktanki·[96]	*ô·cin*		*mònt*
opportunity	(when they have the opportunity) presents itself		Then

had the opportunity. Then

mv etvlwv	tvsekvyv	vtēkat	enokketv	ensemahekon	kerraken	omat,
ma itálwa	*tasikayá*	*atî·ka·t*	*inokkitá*	*insimá·hikon*	*kiłła·kín*	*o·mâ·t*
that town's	members	every one	sickness	not very much	(if) they find	if do

if they found that all their town's members were in good health,

momusen	"Tekueketv	ocvrēs"	mahket,
mô·mosin	*'tikoykitá*	*ó·cáli·s*	*máhkit*
Then	to get together	they shall	they said

then they said, "There will be a get-together."

netta	meliyet	kakof,		em opunayvn	ocēt	onkv
nittá·	*milêyyit*	*ka·kô·f*[97]		*imoponá·yan*	*ó·ci·t*	*ôŋka*
day	they set	and when they assemble (lit. sit)		their spokesman		they have do

When they set a day, they had a spokesman,

enhuehiket   "Hiyomēn   pum ohkērkuecvs.
inho·hêykit[i]   *hayyó·mi·n*   *pomohki·lkóycas*
they called him   this way   (you) explain it to us!
so they called him and said, "Make this announcement.

Vkerrickv   pum etetakekv,
akilléycka   *pomititâ·kika*
ideas   we are ready with (our ideas)
We have made the decision, so

este   ena   cvfeknusē   vtēkat   omvlkuset
ísti   *iná·*   *cafíknosi·*   *atî·ka·t*   *omálkosit*
person   body   somewhat well, active   every one (who)   everybody, all those
all those who are of sound body,

heyv   fettv-rakko   likat   pum ohyicvrēn   puyacēt,
hiyá   *fìttalákko*   *lêyka·t*   *pomohyéycáli·n*   *poyâ·ci·t*
here, this   big yard   (where) it is   (we want) them to come upon   we want
we want them to come to our grounds,

nettv-kvckv   enhayēpēt   omēkv"   kihcet,
nittakácka   *inha·yî·pi·t*   *o·mí·ka*   *kéyhcit*
the appointed day   we made for them   we have   they said
as we have set a day for them," they said.

em opunayv   em onayat   "Tvsekvyv,   eppucetake,
imoponá·ya   *imóna·yâ·t*   *tasikayá*   *ippocitá·ki*
their spokesman   telling them   citizens', members of the town's[98]   sons
And their spokesman told them, "Citizens, their sons,

tvlhvtesvke   tvsekvyv   hayeyvtē
talhatisakí[ii]   *tasikayá*   *ha·yiyáti·*
intermarried ones (of the town)   members   that we have made (members of the town)
those married into the town, those we have made citizens,

---

[i] Raiford: *inhoyhêykit.* [Note: Some speakers pronounce *oy* as [u·] which Haas transcribed as *o·*. -JM.]

[ii] If they include women, they say *talhatisâlki* or *ohhatisâlki.* If only men are meant, they say *ohhiheysâlki.*

cukolice	vtēken	opunvkv	em vrēcet		vtotketv	ocusēt
cokolêyci[99]	atî·kin	oponaká	imáli·cít		atotkitá	ó·cosi·t
women	to	the word	tell it around about		work	with little (work)

and all housewives, spread the word to them,

omvrētok;		pocuswv tis,	esluekv tis,	ēhopakēpet
omáli·to·k		pocóswateys	islóykateys	i·hopa·kî·pit
will be, because (it will be)		ax, even	hoe, even	be prepared with

for there is to be some work; be prepared with an ax, a hoe,

yepunnvkaftet		omvrēn	okekv,		hiyomē
yipónnaka·ftít		omáli·n	o·kiká		hayyô·mi·
we want them to meet with us		that way	that's what we mean		this way

for we mean for them to come be with us,

afulluseko		punsasateu
a·fóllosiko·		ponsâ·sa·tiw'[100]
(those that are) not around about (with us)		those of them that are (not) with us, too

so those who aren't always with us,

etem onvyēpet		punfullet
itimonáyi·pít		pónfollít[i]
(you-all) tell each other		(we intend for them) to be around with us

let them tell one another

omvrēn	okēs"		kihcofvn,
omáli·n	o·ki·s		kéyhco·fan
that way	we mean, intend		after he told them

that we want them to be here," he told them.

aenpunayv tat		heyv	nake makat	omvlkvn
a·inponá·yata·t[ii]		hiyá	nâ·ki ma·kâ·t	omálkan
their spokesman (the one that speaks for him)		here	that what he's saying	all of it

And after their spokesman announced

---

[i] Raiford: *pómfollít.*

[ii] Or: *inponá·yata·t.*

kērkuehcof,   encuko   hopvyvkē   sasat
ki·lkóyhco·f   *incokó*   *hopayakí·*   *sâ·sa·t*
after he has told them   their homes   far away   those (whose homes are far away)
all of this,

em onvyvrē   vtotet   okat.   "Vhakuce   ocusat   omvntokv,
imonayáli·   *ato·tít*   *o·kâ·t*   *aha·kocí*   *ó·cosa·t o·mánto·ka*
to tell them   they send them   mean, intend   little laws   to have   generally do
he sent them to tell those whose homes were far away: "There are little restrictions,

mvo   punkērrakuset   omvrēs"   maket
maw'   *poŋkĭ·ⁿlla·kosit*   *omáli·s*   *ma·kít*
That, too   understanding us thoroughly   they must   they/he said
so they must understand those thoroughly," he said,

'svtuthoyen   onvyaket
'satótho·yín[101]   *onáya·kít*
they sent by them (sent the message) by them   they told it
and they were sent

fullvtēt omēs.   'Tekueketv   nettv
follati·t ô·mi·s   *'tikoykitá*   *nítta*
they were around (doing that) long ago.   to move over (to be together)   day
to spread the word. The day

ohkērkuehocvtē   oketv   ohren,
ohki·lkóyho·catí·   *okíta*   *óhłin*
that was given out (as the appointed one) by someone   the time   arrived
that had been announced for the get-together arrived,

este   yvnvkvfitet   mv   nerē   'panet
ísti   *'yanakafêytit*   *ma*   *nilí·*   *pa·nit*
the people   gathered there   that   night   they danced
and the people gathered. They danced that night,

hofonusekon   wihket   nocicen   ohhvyvtiken,
hofónosikon   *wéyhkit*   *nocêycin*[102]   *ohhayatêykin*
(in) not very long   they stopped, quit   they slept   it got morning
quit before long, and slept until morning.

hvthvyvtke	huehketv	hakof,		honvntake	omvlkvt
hathayátki	*hoýhkitá*	*ha·kô·f*		*honantá·ki*	*omálkat*
morning	to call	it got (to be time)		the men	all

And when the morning call was made, all of the men

estvt	em ohliketv	omat	kērrakusē	vlkēt	onkv,
ístat	*imohleykitát*	*ô·ma·t*	*kĭ·ⁿłła·kosi·*	*álki·t*	*òŋka*
where	they were to sit	(wherever)	knew very well	each one (knew)	for

knew very well where to sit,

omvlkvt	oh-vpokof,
omálkat	*óhhapo·kô·f*
all of them	when they sat down (on the benches)

so when everyone was sitting down,

mv	ohliketv	eto-poloket	omaken	oh-vpētticat
ma	*ohleykitá*	*itopoló·kit*	*omâ·kin*	*ohhapí·tteycâ·t*
that, those	seats	round logs	they are	that that gives shade for them

their seats were round logs, and for shade

eto	yakyvpē	cakcvhehcē
itó	*yakyapí·*	*cakcahíhci·*
logs, pole	forked	they stand them up (in the ground)

forked posts were stuck in the ground

eto-polokē	cvpcvkēn	ohlumhicē	fulutecihcē
itopoló·ki·	*capcaki·n*	*ohlómheycí·*	*foloticéyhci·*
round poles, logs	long ones	they laid them upon (...)	clear around

with long poles laid on them around all sides,

mont	eto-polokē	lopockusēn	er ohtvlvlihcet
mónt	*itopoló·ki·*	*lopóckosi·n*	*iłoltalaléyhcit*
Then	the round poles	small ones	they put them crosswise

and small poles laid down crosswise,

eto-pokhv	esse	ocakan	'sohwikvkvtēt	omaken,
itopó·kha	*íssi*	*o·câ·ka·n*	*sohwéykakáti·t*	*omâ·kin*
brush	(with) leaves	that has	they throw them upon...	they are

and leafy brush thrown on top,

mvn	cukucen	kicet,	este	em vliketv
man	*cokócin*	*kaycít*	*ísti*	*imaleykitá*
that	the little house	they called it	people	(of certain) their (respective) clans

and they called that a <u>cukuce</u> ['little house'],

kerkvkēt	vpopokēt	omēs.	Mvt	eto	lekwaket
kiłkakí·t	*apó·po·kí·t*	*ô·mi·s*	*mat*	*itó*	*likwâ·kit*
are known	they sit there together	do	(if) those	logs	are rotted

and people of the same clan sit together. If the logs have rotted

cukuce	vhopvnhokepētis	on	omat
cokóci	*ahopanhokipí·teys*	*ô·n*	*o·mâ·t*[103]
little houses	if they should happen to be ruined	if	

or the little houses have come apart,

mv	em vhericetv	vrahkvn	nettv	mellat	okēs.
ma	*imahiłeycitá*	*aláhkan*	*nítta*	*millâ·t*	*ô·ki·s*[104]
those	to repair them	for that purpose	a day	they set	do

they set a day to repair them.

'Tekueketv	monkv	em ohliketv	oh-vpokof,
'tikoykitá	*môŋka*	*imohleykitá*	*óhhapo·kô·f*
to [meet] there	therefore	their sitting-place, seat	when they sit on them

As they sat on their benches at their get-together,

este	hocefhuecet	vtotketv	estomēn	vtotkvranat,
ísti	*hocífhoycít*	*atotkitá*	*istó·mi·n*	*atótkała·nâ·t*
people	they name	(of) work	of whatever kind	they are going to work

they named the people and the job they were to do.

hokkolē	vlkēn	vtotet	omvlkvranusēt	vtotkihocēt	omēs.
hokkô·li·	*álki·n*	*ato·tít*	*omalkałă·ⁿnosi·t*[i]	*atotkéyho·cí·t*	*ô·mi·s*
two	(at) each time	they sent them	nearly all of them	they work them	do

They would assign them in pairs and would work nearly everyone.

---

[i] Or: *omalkahă·ⁿnosi·t.*

Topv	'mvwetēnv	kicēt	enhopohoyē
topá[105]	*'mawití·na*	*keycí·t*	*inhopohoyí·*[106]
bed	ones that hold it down	they called him, them	have selected from

Those selected to be what are called <u>topv 'mvwetēnv</u> ['bed/arbor pressers']

mvt	vtotkekot	vpokēt	omēs.
mat	*atótkikot*	*apo·kí·t*	*ô·mi·s*
those	don't work	they remain sitting	do.

do not work and remain sitting.

Heyv	vtotkē	fullvtēt
hiyá	*ato·tkí·*	*follatí·t*
these	that are working	being about, have been about (working)

When these who have been working

poyvkēpen	omat,	"Entopvn	vtehkekvs"
pó·yaki·pín	*o·mâ·t*	*intopán*	*atíhkikas*
(if) they should finish	if they should	their benches	be seated (in their places)

are finished, the chief says, "Have them get in their places."

mēkko	mahken	vtēhkof,	opanē	takhvyayicetvn
mí·kko	*máhkin*	*ati·hkô·f*	*opa·ní·*	*takhaya·yeycitán*
the king	says	when they get in their places	dancing	to make light

And when they get in [their places], in order to light up the dancing,

"'To-talucen	res vlaketv	hokkolen	hopoyekvs"	mēkko	makof,
'tota·locín	*'lisalakíta*	*hokkô·lin*	*hopóyikas*	*mí·kko*	*ma·kô·f*
little dry brush	to bring it	two (trips)	hunt	the king	says

the chief says, "Make about two trips searching for dead wood,"

asenpunayet	kērkuecen,
a·sínpona·yít	*kí·łkoycín*
makes a talk to them	he makes it known, a statement (by talking to them)

and [the speaker] announces it,

omvlkvranuset	fullet	eto tat	hopoyaken,	vhokkolv tis
omalkałâ·nosit[107]	*follít*	*itóta·t*	*hopóya·kin*	*ahokkoláteys*
nearly all of them	being about	the wood	they hunt for it	sometimes twice

and almost all of them go look for wood, sometimes twice.

Momēn   eto   hopoyepuehcet,
mó·mi·n   *itó*   *hopoyipóyhcit*
In that way   wood   they make them hunt
They have them look for wood like that [i.e., as he ordered],

omvlkvt   ohliketv   ohtēhkof,   omvlkuset   es osiyet,
omálkat   *ohleykitá*   *óhti·hkò·f*   *omálkosit*   *isosêyyit*
all of them   their seats   when they get in them   all   they go out
and when all of them are in their seats, they all go out.

"Uewvn   aklopekvs"   mēkko   mahkof,   omvlkvt   vpehyet
óywan   *aklopíkas*   *mí·kko* *máhko·f*   *omálkat*   *apíhyit*
water   must bathe in   the king   when he says   all of them   go
And after the chief says, "Let them bathe in the water," they all go,

uewv   aklopet   eryihcet   entopv   yvtehiket
óywa   *aklô·pit*[108] *iłyéyhcit*   *intopá*   *'yatihêykit*
water   they bathe in   and they come back   their benches   they get in them
bathe in the water, come back, and after they get in their arbor

vpokof,   "Nake tat   hiyomvkēn   momēcvrēn
apo·kó·f[109]   *nâ·kita·t* *hayyo·makí·n*   *momí·cáłi·n*
and when they sit down   something   that is to be this way   want it to be done
and are sitting, [the chief says] "We made the call for things

huehketv   enhayet
hoyhkitá   *ínha·yít*
the call (for it to be done this way?)   it was made for them
to be done this way,

okeyvnken   ohyicet
o·kiyáŋkin   *ohyêycit*
we were intending ("meaning")   they have come to
and they have come

vtotketv   momēcet   sehoken   hiyomat   oren
atotkitá   *momi·cít*   *sihô·kin*   *hayyô·ma·t*   *ô·łin*
(to) work   they have done   they did do   (up to) this time   up to
and have done the work up to this time,

nake tat   etetakuehcet   kakatsken
nâ·kita·t   itita·kóyhcit   *kâ·ká·ckin*[i]
things   getting things ready, in readiness   you-all must remain
so after you have made everything ready, be seated,

momen   yomockē   vlakat   omvlkuset   erascehyet
mo·mín   *yomockí.*[110]   *ala·kâ·t*   *omálkosit*   *iła·scíhyit*
Then   darkness, night   when it has come all together come back in
and then when darkness comes, all of you come back in.

afvcketv   momēcet   taksehokatsken   ecohhvyvtkvranvkēt   omēs.
a·fackitá   *momi·cít*   *taksihô·ká·ckin*   *icohhayátkala·naki·t*   *ô·mi·s*
enjoyment   (you) must do   you-all stay together it's going to come day on you is
You are to perform your duty, celebrating until daylight.

Etehēricet   sehoket   omatskvrēs.
itihĭ·ⁿlêycit[111]   *sihô·kit*   *omá·ckáli·s*
be careful of each other   remain together   you-all must do, be
You must all take care of one another.

Monkv   hiyomusēn   es osiyet   estem ēhvlwicēpet   etefullekvs"
môŋka   *hayyô·mosi·n*[112] *isosâyyit*   *istimi·halwéyci·pít*   *itifóllikas*
Therefore right now   you-all go out   you-all eat your meals   be around about
So go out now and eat your meals with one another,"

mēkkvke   makof,   enyvtekvt
mi·kkakí   *ma·kò·f*   *inyatíkat*
the kings   when they say   their interpreter, spokesman
the chiefs say, and when their interpreter

em ohkērkuecof,   vwahhet   hompakēt   omēs.
imohkí·lkoycô·f   *awáhhit*   *hómpa·kí·t*   *ô·mi·s*
interprets it to them, announces, tell it to them they scatter   and then they eat do
announces this to them, they dismiss and eat.

---

[i] Here refers to more than two.

Momen yomociken mēkkvke em ohliketv ohkahkof,
mo·mín yomocâykin mi·kkakí imohleykitá ohkáhko·f
Then when it gets dark the kings their seats when they take them
Then when it gets dark, and the chiefs have taken their seats,

enhuehkv ocēt onkv, "Centopvtaken vtehkaks"
inhóyhka ó·ci·t ôŋka cintopatá·kin atíhkaks
caller they have got do you-all's benches get them
they have a caller.

maket huehken, vtehkepokof,
ma·kít hoyhkín atíhkipo·kô·f
they say they called, call them when they all occupy their benches
So he calls, "Get in your arbors," and when they're all in them,

opvnkv 'senhomahtv enhopoyē opvnēcvranat
opánka sinhomá·hta ínhopo·yí· opaní·caɫa·nâ·t
the dance- leader hunt for him to make them dance
he selects a person to choose

este enhopohyet
ísti inhopóhyit
the people, person they select
the leaders for the people to dance and announces to them,

"Heyv estet cem punayvken omat,
hiyá ístit címpona·yakín o·mâ·t
this person when he talks to you-all when does
"When this person makes his selection

momvranen okēs enkomatskvrēs" maket
mó·maɫa·nín o·kí·s iŋkó·má·ckáli·s ma·kít
it is going to be done that way he means, intends you-all must think so they said
and speaks to you, you must expect things

em ohkērkuehcen, mv estet opvnkv 'senhomahtv enhopoyen
imohki·ɫkóyhcin ma ístit opánka sinhomá·hta ínhopo·yín
he announces it to them that person (who) is dance-leader they select him
to take place as he says." And that person selects dance-leaders,

pvnhoyen   hvyatkēt   omēs.
pánho·yín   *haya·tkí·t*   *ô·mi·s*
they dance   till day comes does
and they dance until morning.

Hvyayakan   vpakusen,   "Esluekv   hopoyaks"   mahohken
hayá·ya·kâ·n   *apǎⁿkosin*   *islóyka* *hopóyaks*   *ma·hóhkin*
when it gets light immediately   the hoe   you-all look for it when they say
As soon as it gets light they say, "Look for hoes."

hoktvke tis   esluekv   ocvkēpat   sasēt onkv
hoktakíteys   *islóyka*   *o·cakî·pa·t* *sá·si·t ôŋka*
even those of the women   (that) hoes they have   for there are (women that have hoes)
There are women too, who have hoes,

vrahkvn   ēkvnv   'senkērkuehohcen
aláhkan   *i·kaná*   *siŋki·lkoyhóhcin*
to themselves   ground   they designate (the ground) for them
so just for them they designate ground,

lueyaket   omvnts.
lóyya·kít   *o·mánc*
they hoe   (generally) do (that's the way they do)
and they hoed that.

Poyvkekon   honvntake   poyaken omat,
pó·yakíkon   *honantá·ki*   *pó·ya·kín o·mâ·t*
if they don't finish the men   if they do finish
If they don't finish before the men finish,

hoktvken   em vnicen,   hoktvket   poyvkēpen   omat,
hoktakín   *imáneycín*   *hoktakít*   *pó·yaki·pín* *o·mâ·t*
the women (obj.)   they help them   the women   if they finish (if)
they help the women, and when the women finish

honvntake em vnicen   poyahkē   tvlket   omvnts.
honantá·ki *imáneycín*   *po·yáhki·*   *tâlkit*   *o·mánc*
the men   they help (them) after they finish always (work until they do finish) do
with the men helping them, they finish completely.

Mohmen   "Vteloyaks"   mahohken,
móhmin   atiló·yaks   ma·hóhkin
Then   gather them!   they say
Then they say, "Gather it up,"

enhomv   vpohoyvtē   ocakat   ētan
inhomá   apó·ho·yatí·   o·câ·ka·t   i·tá·n
before, previously where they piled them (before) the places   the same (places)
and where they piled it before,

eroh-vpoyet   pvhe   vtakrv   eto-esse tale tis
iłóhhapo·yít   pahí   atákla   itoissitá·liteys[i]
they piled them on   grass   and weeds   and leaves even dry ones
they pile it in the same place and rake grass, weeds, dry leaves,

nake   estomis   omvlkvn   pashoyēt   omvnts.
nâ·ki   istô·meys   omálkan   pá·sho·yi·t   o·mánc
something   everything   all   they clear it all off they generally do
and everything else.

Mv   ēkvnv   luyiyē   pashohyē   likat   ofvn
ma   i·kaná   loyèyyi·   pa·shóhyi·   leykâ·t   ó·fan
that   ground   which is hoed cleared off   it remains   inside
There are three arbors ['little houses']

cukuce   tuccēnet   ocēt   omen,   mv   nvrkvpv   hēran
cokóci   tocci·nit   ó·ci·t   ô·min   ma   nalkapá   hǐ·ⁿla·n
little houses   three   are there   do   the   middle   right in
where the ground is hoed and cleared off, and right in the middle,

totkvn   etechoyēt   omen   mvn   vfulutēcēt   'pvnhoyēt   omen
tó·tkan   itícho·yí·t   ô·min   man   afóloti·cí·t   pánho·yí·t   ô·min
a fire   they build   do   that   they go around (that)   they dance   do
they build a fire and go around that and dance,

---

[i] Separates it [into] *tá·li teys* in lento speech.

cukuce	ocakat	em vhopvyusēn
cokóci	*o·câ·ka·t*	*(i)mahopayósi·n*
little houses	that are	a little ways off

and a little further out from where the houses are,

vfulutkēn	lueyet	paset	omhoyvnts.
afolótki·n	*loyyít*	*pa·sít*	*ómho·yánc*
around (them)	hoe	and clean off	they do

they would hoe and clean off around them.

Mv	vtotketv	<u>tvco-paskvn</u>	kihocēt	omēs.
ma	*atotkitá*	*tacopá·skan*	*kéyho·cí·t*	*ô·mi·s*
that	work	buskground cleaning off	that's what they call it.	

That work is called <u>tvco-paskv</u> ['ring-sweeping'].

Momen	mvn	vtotket	fulhoyof,
mo·mín	*man*	*ato·tkít*	*fólho·yô·f*
Then	there	working (there)	when they are about

While they are working,

mēkkvke	kohv-rakkon	vhopakuce	tuccēnusē	tayēn	tacet,
mi·kkakí	*kohalákkon*	*ahopa·kocí*	*tocci·nosi·*	*tâ·yi·n*	*tâ·cit*
the kings	big cane	(measure) inches	three	about	cut them

the kings cut big canes into about three-inch lengths,

lopockusē	eteselsēcet
lopŏ·⁽ⁿ⁾ckosi·	*itisílsi·cít*
very small	they split them up

then split them up [lengthwise] very small

kolvpakusēn	wvnawicet	kakēpēt	omēs.
kolapá·kosi·n[113]	*waná·weycít*	*ká·ki·pí·t*	*ô·mi·s*
only seven	tie them	and they sit (tying them together)	do

and sit, tying them into [bundles of] seven.

Mv	kohv-fvlahluce	kolvpakat
ma	*kohafalahlocí*	*kolapâ·ka·t*
that	split cane	seven

Those seven split canes

nettv   estofvt   posketvtaranat   eskērkvt   omēn
nítta   istô·fat   poskitatá·la·nâ·t[114]   *iski·lkat*   *ô·mi·n*
day   when it will be busk when it's going to be the signification is
are a count of how many days until the posketv ['fast']

nettv kvckv   kicēt   okakvnts.
nittakácka   *keycí·t*   *oka·kánc*
broken-days   they call it that's what they mean
and were called nettv kvckv ['broken days'].

Etvlwv   ētv   enhesse   sasan   ohtotaken,
itálwaʔ *i·taʔ*   *inhíssi*   *sâ·sa·n*   *óhtota·kín*
town   some other   its friend   that is   they send them to
They send them to other towns who are friends,

encukopericen   etohkvlkēpet   opanet
incokópiɫeycín   *itohkalkî·pit*[115]   *opa·nít*
they visit them   they're/get all together they dance
so that they might come to visit them, get together, and dance;

fullepvranat   huehketv   enhayat   omakēs.
follipáɫa·nâ·t   *hoyhkitá*   *ínha·yâ·t*   *oma·kí·s*
where they should be about (and dance) the call is made   that's why
that is how they make their invitation ['call'].

Ēyafvcecicē   vretv   netta   rakkēn   omēn
i·ya·facíceycí·[116] *aɫitaʔ*   *nittá·*   *ɫákki·n* *ó·mi·n*
to enjoy themselves   to be about   (a) day   big   like
It is a big day to be glad

'sem afvcketvt   onkv
'sima·fackitát   *ôŋka*
for that is their enjoyment it is
and to celebrate,

este   enhopoyet   kohv-fvlahluce   es vtotet
ísti   *ínhopo·yít*   *kohafalahlocí*   *isáto·tít*
people   they select them   little split cane   they sent them by (selected persons)
so they select people and send them with the split canes,

res empokat		vwahēcet	omvnts.
'lisímpo·kâ·t		*awá·hi·cít*	*o·mánc*
when they're exhausted (the canes)		scatter them	they do

and when they run out of them, they would scatter them about.

Estofvt	posketvtaranet	omat	kerrakekv,
istô·fat	*poskitatá·ła·nít*[i]	*o·mâ·t*	*kiłłâ·kika*
when	busk is to be	(if, when)	(for) they generally know, therefore

Since they know when the busk is to be,

ehvpo tis	paset	em vhericet	fulhoyēt	omvnts.
ihapó·teys	*pa·sít*	*imáhiłeycít*	*fólho·yí·t*	*o·mánc*
camp	they clear off (the ground)	they fix it up	that's the way	they do

they sweep the camp and fix it up.

Mohmen	netta	cahkēpē	oran,
móhmin	*nittá·*	*cahkî·pi·*	*o·łâ·n*
Then	days	five	at the end of (5 days)

Then in five days

hvtvm	yvnvkvfhotēt	omēs.
hatâm	*'yanakáfho·tí·t*[ii]	*ô·mi·s*
again	they meet back (in the same place)	do

they come together again.

Mv	nerē	'panet	hofonekon	wihket	nocicen	hvyvtiken,
ma	*nili·*	*pa·nít*	*hofónikon*	*wéyhkit*	*nocêycin*[117]	*hayatêykin*
that	night	they dance	(in) not very long	they quit	they go to sleep	when it gets day

They dance that night, and before long they quit and sleep until dawn,

hoktvke	'pvnvranat	ohyekcicvrē
hoktakí	*pánala·nâ·t*	*ohyikcéycáłi·*
the women	those that are to dance (going to dance)	to exact upon them

and the kings appoint two men to urge

---

[i] Or: *-tá·ha·nít.*

[ii] Raiford: *yinakáfho·tí·t* (either way is okay).

honvntake	hokkolen	mēkkvlket	enwiketv	hayēn,
honantá·ki	*hokkó·lin*	*mi·kkâlkit*	*inweykitá*	*há·yi·n*
men	two	the chiefs	appoint them	generally do

the women to dance,

mvt	'senhomahtv,	vwihēkv
mat	*sinhomá·hta*[i]	*aweyhí·ka*
the	the leader and	(the one) following (the leader) = the second

and they make arrangements for a leader and one to follow directly behind him,

'tepaken	em etetakuecet,	"Em etetakaks"	kicet,
'tipâ·kin	*imititá·koycít*	*imititá·kaks*	*keycít*
both together	get things ready for them	you-all get ready	they tell them

and tell [the women], "Get ready."

estehvpo	omvlkvn	'sencukopericet	welakvntot	fekhonnet,
istihapó·	*omálkan*	*sincokópiłeycít*	*wila·kántot*	*fíkhonnít*
camps	all of them	they visit them	once in a while they're about	they stop

And they go about together visiting all the camps [four times], resting each time around,

welakē	es osticat	"Lvpecicēt	a vwaks"	kicet
wila·ki·	*isósteycâ·t*	*lapicéyci·t*	*a·awáks*	*keycít*
and being about	the fourth time	(you-all) hurry up	and go in	they say

and the fourth time around they say, "Hurry up and come,"

opvnkv	ēkvnvn	ra enhuehken	oh-vpēyat,
opánka	*i·kanán*	*la·ínhoyhkín*	*óhhapi·yâ·t*
dance-	ground	they call from (the dance-ground)	while going towards it

and call from the dance-ground. So they all go to it

takfulwv	es ēwvnaket	encvpkē	ēkvnv	tekkekvranusen,
takfólwa	*isi·wanâ·kit*	*incapkí·*	*i·kaná*	*tikkikałă·ⁿnosin*
ribbons	they tie around them	(in) their length	the ground	nearly touching (the ground)

with ribbons tied around them almost long enough to touch the ground,

---

[i] Raiford would prefer: *ma sinhomá·hta*.

entvphē   estomēn   eyacat,
intaphí·   *istó·mi·n*   *iyâ·ca·t*
(in) their width   (they are) whatever (width)   they want
of whatever width they want,

mohmet   'kvwelēpkvn   takfulwv   cahmelikv
móhmit   *'kawilí·pkan*[i] *takfólwa*   *cahmiléyka*
Then   head-decoration   ribbon   of different colors
and they tie ribbons of many colors to their head-pieces,

mont   encvpkē   estomēn   eyacat,   'svwvnawicet
mónt   *incapkí·*   *istó·mi·n*   *iyâ·ca·t*   *'sawana·wêycit*[118]
Then   the length is   whatever (kind)   they want   they tie it on
of whatever length they want, and tie them

'sekvwelēpet   ascehyet   vpokof,
'sikawilí·pit   *a·scíhyit*   *apo·kô·f*[119]
they put it over (their backs)   and when they come in   and sit down
all over their dresses and head-pieces. And when they have all come in and sat down,

"'Tetaket   os.   Opvnaks!"   empohattv   kicof,
'titâ·kit   *ó·ⁿs* *opánaks*   *impohá·tta*[ii] *keycô·f*
ready for them   it is   dance (pl.)!   [the coach]   when he tells them
the empohattv ['inviter'] tells them, "It's ready. Dance!"

asvpvkilet   takhaket   svpaklof,
a·sapakêylit   *takhâ·kit*   *sapa·klô·f*
they stand up   they get in line (side by side)   when standing
And when they all stand up and stand in line [side by side],

empohattv   hvmket   enhomahtet,
impohá·tta   *hámkit*   *inhoma·htit*[120]
the coach   one, a certain   (he) leads her (the leader)
one empohattv leads them,

---

[i] Literally, 'something that goes over the head'.
[ii] *sinhomá·hta* = the leader (a woman in this case); *impohá·tta* = the coach (a man); *inyahéyka* = singers (two men). There is only one coach.

totkv-hvpo   'svfulotket,
to·tkahapó·   *sáfolo·tkít*
(around) fire-place (refers to center fire)   he goes around it
around the center fire [totkv-hapo],

'senhomahtv   enyvhikv   kakat   ehomvn
sinhomá·hta   *inyahéyka*   *kâ·ka·t*   *ihóman*
the leader   (where) the singers   (two) are sitting   in front of them
and he leads them to where the singers are seated and stops there,

ersehohyen   enyvhihoken   'panēt   omvnts.
iɬsihóhyin   *inyaháyho·kín*   *pa·ní·t*   *o·mánc*
stands them up (in front)   (while) they sing for them   they dance   that is the way
and they sing for them, and [the women] dance.

Vfulutketv   osten   pahnof,
afolotkitá   *ô·stin*   *páhno·f*
going around   four times   while dancing
After they dance four times around,

fēkapet   fēkvpetv   osten   pahnen   hoyanof,   wikēt   omvnts.
fì·ka·pít   *fì·kapíta*   *ô·stin*   *páhnin*   *hoya·nô·f*   *waykí·t*   *o·mánc*
resting   resting   four times   dancing   after   they quit   (generally do)
they rest, and after dancing and resting four times, they quit.

Mv   yomockat   panet   hofonekon   wihket,
ma   *yomo·ckâ·t*   *pa·nít*   *hofónikon*   *wéyhkit*
that   night   they dance   in not long   they quit
That night they dance and quit before long

nocicen   hvyvtiken   mv   opvnkv   ēkvnv   likan
noceycín   *hayatêykin*   *ma*   *opánka*   *i·kaná*   *lêyka·n*
they sleep   till morning   that   dance-   ground   (which is)
and sleep until dawn, and the place where the dance-ground is located

cukorakkon   kicet   okvnts.
cokoɬákkon   *keycít*   *o·kánc*
"big-house"; buskground   call it   they generally do
is called the cukorakko ['big house'].

Mv	ohliketv	ocat	omvlkvt	oh-vpokvrēn	eyacēt
ma	*ohleykitá*	*ô·ca·t*	*omálkat*	*ohhapó·káłi·n*[121]	*iyá·ci·t*
that	sitting-place	where (it is)	all of them	want them to sit there	they want

The mekkos sit, wanting everyone to be on the benches there,

mēkkvlke	kaken,		huehhoken
mi·kkâlki	*kâ·kin*		*hóyhho·kín*
the chiefs	(2 or more) are sitting		they do call

and call.

a awet	pokof,		totkvn	tehcet	vpoket
á·a·wit	*po·kô·f*		*tó·tkan*	*tíhcit*	*apô·kit*
they begin coming in	when the last one is in		fire	they make	and sit down

And when all have come, they light the fire and sit,

tafv 'mvpe	hopoyvranat	vtothohyen
ta·famápi	*hopóyała·nâ·t*	*atothóhyin*
feather-handle	to hunt for	someone sends them

sending some to search for feather sticks,

res yicof,		tafv-hvtken	'mvtvrtihcet,
łisyeycô·f		*ta·fahátkin*	*'matałtéyhcit*
when they get back with it		white feathers	they hang them to (something)

and when they come back with them they hang white feathers on each one,

cukuce	ehomv	cukele	ocakat,
cokóci	*ihóma*	*cokíli*	*o·câ·ka·t*
little house	in front of	the posts	where they are

and where there are posts in front of the arbors

omvlkvn	eceskv	tafv-hvtken	escakcvhēcet	vpoken,
omálkan	*icíska*	*ta·fahátkin*	*iscakcahî·cit*[122]	*apô·kin*
all of them	at the foot of the (post)	the white feathers	they stick them up	they sit there

they sit with all of the sticks with white feathers in the ground at the base of every post,

heleswv	hahoyan	ēsket
'hilíswa	*ha·hô·ya·n*	*i·skít*
medicine	that is made	they drink

and without eating, they sit drinking the medicine that has been prepared

vwotet	vpokat	hompekot	vpoket	onkv,
awo·tít	*apo·kâ·t*[123]	*hómpíko·t*	*apo·kít*[124]	*oŋká*[125]
they vomit	while sitting	not eating	they remain	(for)

and purge themselves.

mvt	posketvt	omēs.
mat	*poskitát*	*ô·mi·s*
that (is)	busking[126]	is

So that is <u>posketv</u> ['fasting'].

Ēelvwēcat	vtēkat
i·ílawi·câ·t	*atî·ka·t*
those that are fasting (one or more)	every one (that is fasting)

All those who go without eating,

poskēn	kihocēt	omvnts.	Monkv	poskof,
po·ski·n	*kéyho·cí·t*	*o·mánc*	*môŋka*	*po·skô·f*
busking	they call that	do	Therefore	when they busk

they call it <u>poskē</u> ['fasting']. So when they fast,

tafv-hvtke	es esē	vlkēt	es opanet,
ta·fahátki	*isísi·*	*álki·t*	*isópa·nít*
white feather	holding	each one	dancing with

each one dances holding a white feather.

pvnkv	cahmelikēn	opanet,	heleswv	ēsket	vwotet,
pánka	*cahmiléyki·n*	*opa·nít*	*'hilíswa*	*i·skít*	*awo·tít*
dances	of different kinds	they dance	medicine	they drink	they vomit

They dance different dances, drink medicine and vomit,

kulkē	eshayetv	eto-taluceu	hopoyvntot	vpoken
kolkí·	*isha·yitá*	*itota·locíw'*	*hopo·yántot*	*apô·kin*
light	something to make it with	dry brush, too	sometimes they hunt	they sit

gather dry brush to furnish light, and sit. And when it gets to be evening,

yafkof,	uewvn	aklohpet	eryihcet	vwahhet,
ya·fkô·f	*óywan*	*aklóhpit*	*iɫyéyhcit*	*awáhhit*
when it gets to be evening	water	they bathe in	they return	they disperse, scatter

they bathe in the water, come back, disperse,

hompakēt	omvnts.	Mv	yomockan	pvnąken	hvyvtiken
hómpa·ki·t	*o·mánc*	*ma*	*yomo·ckâ·n*	*panǎ·ʷkin*	*hayatêykin*
eat	they do	that	night	they dance	till day comes

and eat. That night they dance till daylight comes,

vwahen omat,		etvlwv hvmēcat	posketv	enhoyanēt omēs.
awa·hín o·mâ·t		*itálwa hami·ca·t*	*poskitá*	*ínhoya·ní·t ô·mi·s*
and if they scatter		(all of) one town	the busk	is generally over (for that town)

and when they dismiss, the whole town is generally finished with the <u>posketv</u> ['fast'].

Ohrolopē	hvmkat	vrahkv	ohrolopē	omvlkvn
ohłolopí·	*hámka·t*	*ałáhka*	*ohłolopí·*	*omálkan*
year	(for) one (year)	for	year	all of it

For the whole year, every year,

Hvyuce,	Hvyo-rakko	'tepakat	posketv	enhvset	omakēs.
hayóci	*hayolákko*	*'tipâ·ka·t*	*poskitá*	*inhasít*	*omâ·ki·s*
July (and)	August	together	the busking	month	they are

July and August are the fasting months.

Etvlwv	encukorakko	ocēsasat	omvlkvt
itálwa	*incokołákko*	*ó·ci·sâ·sa·t*	*omálkat*
towns	(their) buskgrounds	(those) that have	all of them (that)

All those towns who have grounds

heyv	onvkv	ocat,	encukorakko	ocēsasat
hiyá	*onáka*	*ò·ca·t*	*incokołákko*	*ó·ci·sâ·sa·t*
this	saying	have	buskground	that have

have this understanding. Every town that has a ground,

vtēkat	omvlkvt	enfulletv	momvkē	vlkēt	omēs.
atî·ka·t	*omálkat*	*infollitá*	*mo·makí·*	*álki·t*	*ô·mi·s*
every one	all of them	their ways, custom	that is	(for) each one	it is

their ways are each like this.

Momis	Tokepahce,	Kilice	'tepakat
mò·meys	*tokipáhci*	*kaylêyci*	*'tipâ·ka·t*
But	the Tukabahchee	Kayleidji	together, both of them together

But Tukabahchee's and Kialegee's customs

enfulletv	mvrahkusēn	fullēt	poskēt	omakēs.
infollitá	*'małáhkosi·n*	*folli·t*	*po·ski·t*	*omâ·ki·s*
their ways	a little different	being around	busking	they are

are a little different when they fast.

Momet	cukorakko	yvmahken	oketv	ocakvtēs
mo·mít	*cokołákko*	*yama·hkín*	*okíta*	*ó·ca·katí·s*
Then	buskground, big house	became [wasted]	the time	there once was

There's a story that the grounds

maketv	ocat	cukorakko	ocakat
ma·kitá	*ô·ca·t*	*cokołákko*	*o·câ·ka·t*
that saying	that is	big house (buskgrounds)	those that have

were once destroyed, but all the grounds

omvlkvt	yvmahkvtē	vlkēt	omēs.
omálkat	*yama·hkatí·*	*álki·t*	*ô·mi·s*
all of them	have been destroyed	each one	has been

have been destroyed.

Momen	hiyomat	etvlwv	encukorakko	wikvtē	sulkēt	omēs.
mo·mín	*hayyô·ma·t*	*itálwa*	*incokołákko*	*weykatí·*	*sólki·t*	*ô·mi·s*
Then	at this time	towns (several)	buskground	have quit	several	there are

And now many towns have abandoned their grounds.

All about the Names of the Towns

J. Hill (Haas XVII:83–185)[i]

1.	Apehkv Tvlvtēke	2.	Apehkv Oktah-hvcce
	a·píhka talatî·ki		*a·píhka okta·hácci*[127]
1.	Arbeka Talladega	2.	Arbeka North Fork
3.	Apehkuce	4.	Vlepamv
	a·pihkocí		*lipá·ma*
3.	Little Arbeka	4.	Alabama

---

[i] This material prepared at the suggestion of JH himself.

5. Atvse
   a·tasí
5. Artussee

6. Cēyahv
   ci·yá·ha
6. Cheyarha

7. Kilice
   keylêyci
7. Kialegee

8. Keco Pvtake
   kicopatâ·ki
8. Kicho Patake

9. Kowassate 'Mvhvmkvtkv Hvmkat
   kowa·ssá·ti 'mahamkátka hámka·t
9. Koasati No. 1

10. Kowassate 'Mvhvmkvtkv Hokkolat
    kowa·ssá·ti 'mahamkátka hokkô·la·t
10. Koasati No. 2

11. Kvncate
    kancá·ti
11. Kancharte

12. Kvwetv
    kawíta
12. Coweta

13. Kvsehtv
    kasíhta
13. Cusseta

14. Helvpe
    hilápi
14. Hilabi

15. Okcaye
    okcá·yi
15. Okchayi

16. Osuce
    o·socí
16. Osoche

17. Oce Vpofv
    ociapó·fa
17. Hickory Ground

18. Pvkvn-Tvlvhasse
    pakantalahá·ssi
18. Peach Ground

19. Raprakko
    la·płákko
19. Thlopthucco

20. Rvro-kvlkuce
    lałokalkocí
20. Fish Pond

21. Rvro-makwikv
    <*lalomakwéyka*>
21. Thlathlo Makwayka

22. Rē Kackv
    li·ká·cka
22. Broken Arrow

23. 'Rewahle
    'liwáhli
23. Thewahle

24. Tvlse Kvnēte
    talsikaní·ti
24. Tulsa Canadian

25. Tvlse Lucvpokv
    tálsi locapó·ka
25. Tulsa Lochaboga

26. Tvlse Oktahhvcce
    tálsi okta·hácci
26. Tulsa North Fork

27. Tokepahce
    tokipáhci
27. Tukabahchee

28. Taskēke
    ta·skí·ki
28. Tuskegee

29. Tvlmocvse
    talmocási
29. New Tulsa

30. Tokpafkv
    tokpá·fka
30. Tookparfka

31. Tvlvhassuce
    talaha·ssoci
31. Little Tullahassee

32. Tvlwv-Rakko
    talwalákko
32. Big Town

33. Ueki-Rakko
    oykeyłákko
33. Big Spring

34. Ue-Wohkv
    oywó·hka
34. Wewoka

35. Ue-Okofke
    oyʔokófki
35. Weogufkee [or Muddy Water]

36. Vsse Lanvpe
    assila·napí
36. Green Leaf

37. Akfvske Kvnēte
    akfaskikaní·ti
37. Okfuskee Canadian

38. Akfvske Hvcce Sufke
    akfaskihaccisófki
38. Okfuskee Deep Fork

39. Yocce
    yó·cci
39. Euchee

40. Yofalv Kvnēte
    yofa·lakaní·ti
40. Eufaula Canadian

41. Yofalv Hopaye
    yofa·lahopá·yi
41. Far-away Eufaula

42. Hecete
    hicíti
42. Hitchiti

43. Hvcce-Cvpv
    haccicápa
43. River's Edge

44. Apehkv Hvcce Sufke
    a·pihkahaccisófki
44. Arbeka Deep Fork

45. Noyakv
   no·yá·ka
45. Nuyaka

Heyv onvpv hocefkv ocakat este-Maskoke hocefkē etvlwv likat em ofv
hiyá onápa hocífka o·câ·ka·t ísti ma·skó·ki hocífki· itálwa lêyka·t imó·fa
The names above are the names of the small tribal towns

etvllopocke ocakat enhocefhokvt omakēs.
itallopócki o·câ·ka·t inhocifhokát omâ·ki·s.
in what is called the Muscogee Nation.

Ohrolopē cokperakko hvmken cokpe cenvpaken pale ēpaken hvmkontvlakat omof,
ohlolopí· cokpilákko hámkin cokpicinapâ·kin pá·li i·pâ·kin hamkontalâ·ka·t ô·mo·f
In the year eighteen hundred and sixty-one [1861],

horre hakē este-cate vwahvtē herkv hahken,
hólli ha·kí· isticá·ti awa·hatí· hílka háhkin
when war broke out, the Indians scattered and peace was made,

em ēkvnv raohfolēcet ehute hayetv vlicēcaken ayof,
imi·kaná la·óhfoli·cít ihóti ha·yitá aleycí·ca·kín a·yô·f
but when they returned to their lands and began to build homes,

ohrolopē cokperakko hvmken cokpe cenvpaken pale ēpaken ēpohkakat em ofv tatēs.
ohlolopí· cokpilakkohámkin cokpicinapâ·kin pá·li i·pâ·kin i·pohkâ·ka·t imó·fa tá·ti·s
it was in the year eighteen hundred and sixty-six [1866].

Momen mv omof etenfvccetv Wvcenvt este Maskoken enhayekv,
mo·mín ma ô·mo·f itinfaccitá wacínat ísti ma·skó·kin inhâ·yika
At that time the United States made an agreement with the Muscogee people,

momen este Maskoke vwahvtē em ēkvnv vtēhkē pokekv,
mo·mín istima·skó·ki awa·hatí· imi·kaná ati·hkí· po·kiká
and the Muscogee people that had scattered were settled back on their lands,

etvlwvn ēyem vhericvranet nvkaftet fullet, vhakv empvtakv ēenhayofvt,
itálwan[128] *i·yimahiłéycaɬa·nít naka·ftít follít ahá·ka impatá·ka i·ínha·yô·fat*[i]
so they met to make plans to restore the nation and, in making a constitution for themselves,

etvllopocke hocefkv enhayaket omvtēs.
itallopócki hocífka inhá·ya·kít o·matí·s
they gave names to the small tribal towns.

Etvlwv hocefkv mocvsvkē sasat hiyomēn etvlwv hocefkv mocvsakat heyvt omakēs:
itálwa hocífka mocasakí· sâ·sa·t hayyó·mi·n[129] *itálwa hocífka mocasâ·ka·t hiyát omâ·ki·s*
These are some of the new tribal town names:

Apehkv tvlvtēke hvmkuset omvtēs.
a·píhka talatî·ki hámkosit o·matí·s
Arbeka Talladega was one.

Hvcce Kvnēte hocefkat vnakvn 'tvlofv hayēt
hácci kaní·ti hocífka·t aná·kan 'taló·fa há·yi·t
They built their ʼtvlofv [ʻtownʼ] near the Canadian River

encukorakko ocēt vpoket omvtēs. 'Tvlofv makat cuko etewolicē vpokakan okēs.
incokolákko ó·ci·t apô·kit o·matí·s 'taló·fa ma·kâ·t cokó itiwoléyci· apó·ka·kâ·n o·kí·s
and had their own square ground. ʼTvlofv means the houses were very close to each other.

Horre ocvtē herkv hahkof, vpvlwvt Oktah-hvcce Hvccesofke etohfihnat tempen
hółli o·catí· hiłka háhko·f apálwat okta·hácci haccisófki itóhfeyhnâ·t tímpin·
After the war, when peace was made, others built homes and settled close to where

ehute hayaket vpokaken
ihóti ha·yâ·kit apo·kâ·kin
the Oktahatchi [North Fork] River and Deep Fork join,

Oktah-hvcce Apehkvn hocefhoyvtēt omēs.
okta·hácci a·píhkan hocífho·yatí·t ô·mi·s[130]
and they were named Oktahatchi Arbeka.

---

[i] Or you can say: *i·yínha·yô·fat.*

Vpvlwvt Hvccesofke yoksv fvccvn ehute hayēt vpokaket omen,
apálwat haccisófki yóksa fáccan ihóti há·yi·t apo·kâ·kit o·mín
Others built homes and settled toward the end of the Deep Fork,

Hvccesofke Apehkvn hocefhoyvtēt omēs.
haccisófki a·píhkan hocífho·yatí·t ô·mi·s.
and were named Deep Fork Arbeka.

Vpvlwvt Oktah-hvcce yoksv fvccvn ehute hayēt vpokaken,
apálwat okta·hácci yóksa fáccan ihóti há·yi·t apo·kâ·kin
Others built homes and settled toward the end of the Oktahatchi [North Fork]

Apehkucen hocefhoyvtēt omēs. Nvcǫmusat omēcicēn
a·pihkocín hocífho·yatí·t ô·mi·s. nacǒ·ⁿmosa·t omi·céyci·n
and were named Arbekochi ['Little Arbeka']. Because there were so few of them,

Apehkv Cutkusē maketvt omēs. Vpvlwvt Hvcce Uecate tempen ehute hayēt vpokaken
a·píhka cótkosi· ma·kitát ô·mi·s. apálwat hácci oycá·ti tímpin ihóti há·yi·t apo·kâ·kin
they named it Little Arbeka. Others built homes and settled near the Red River

Kvncatvlken hocefhoyvtēt omēs.
kanca·tâlkin hocífho·yatí·t ô·mi·s.
and were named Kanchartalki [Red Land People].

Kilice Tvlvtēke cukorakko vnakvn 'tvlofv hayet
keyléyci talatî·ki cokołákko aná·kan 'taló·fa há·yit
Some made a town near the Kialegee Talladega square ground

cukorakko ocēt vpoken, vpvlwvt Oktah-hvcce tempen ehute hayēt vpokaken
cokołákko ó·ci·t apô·kin apálwat okta·hácci tímpin ihóti há·yi·t apo·kâ·kin
and had their own square ground. Others built homes and settled near the North Fork

Hvccecvpvlken hocefhoyvtēt omēs.
haccicapâlkin hocífho·yatí·t ô·mi·s
and were named Hatchichapalgi [River's Edge People].

Kowassate Oktah-hvcce Hvccesofke etohcakhat vnakv
kowa·ssá·ti okta·hácci haccisófki itohcákha·t[i] aná·ka
The Koasati [or Quassartey] built a town and settled

'tvlofv hayēt vpoket omvtētan, Kowassate 'mvhvmkvtkv hvmkan hocefhoyvtēs.
'taló·fa há·yi·t apô·kit o·matí·ta·n kowa·ssá·ti 'mahamkátka hámka·n hocífho·yatí·s.
near where the North Fork and Deep Fork join, and were named Koasati No. 1.

Vpvlwvt Oktah-hvcce yoksv fvccvn ehute hayvkvtēt vpokaken
apálwat okta·hácci yóksa fáccan ihóti ha·yakáti·t apo·kâ·kin
Others built homes and settled toward the tip of the North Fork

Kowassate 'mvhvmkvtkv hokkolan hocefhoyvtēt omēs.
kowa·ssá·ti 'mahamkátka[ii] hokkô·la·n hocífho·yatí·t ô·mi·s.
and were named Koasati No. 2.

Okcaye Rvrokvlkv kihocēt Kvnēte vfopken 'tvlofv hayēt
okcá·yi lalokálka kéyho·cí·t kaní·ti afó·pkin 'taló·fa há·yi·t
The Okchayi called Thlathlokalka ['Fish Pond'] built a town along the Canadian [River]

cukorakko ocēt vpoken; vpvlwvt Oktah-hvcce yoksv fvccvn cukorakko ocēt
cokolákko ó·ci·t apô·kin apálwat okta·hácci yóksa fáccan cokolákko ó·ci·t
and had a square ground; others had a square ground toward the end of the Canadian

ehute ocvkēt vpoken Rvrokvlkucen hocefhoyvtēs.
ihóti o·caki·t apô·kin[131] lalokalkocín hocífho·yatí·s
and had homes and were named Thlathlokalkochi ['Little Fish Pond'].

Nvcomuset omis 'tvlofv hayet onkv,
nacô·ⁿmosit o·mêys 'taló·fa hâ·yit oŋká
Though they were few in number, they built a town,

Rvrokvlkv Cutkusē maketvt omen hocēfet omhoyvtēs.
lalokálka cótkosi· ma·kitát ô·nin hoci·fit ómho·yatí·s.
so they were called Little Thlathlokalka.

---

[i] *itohcákha·t* means about the same as *itohféyhna·t*.
[ii] Or you can say: *'mahaŋkátka*. [The word for 'number' may be pronounced *'mahamkátka, 'mahaŋkátka*, or *'mahoŋkátka*.]

Tvlse Lucvpokv hiyomē 'tvlofv Tvlse hocefkē likat ofv,
tálsi locapó·ka hayyô·mi· 'taló·fa tálsi hocífki· léyka·t ó·fa
Tulsa Lochaboga, where the city of Tulsa is now,

Uecate vfopket encukorakkot on,
oycá·ti afó·pkit incokolákkot ô·n
their square ground was along the Arkansas [River],

mv vnakvn ehute ocaket vpokakvtēt omis,
ma aná·kan ihóti o·câ·kit apó·ka·katí·t ô·meys
and they had homes in that vicinity and lived there,

vpvlwvt Hvccesofke vnakvn 'tvlofv hayēt vpokaken
apálwat haccisófki aná·kan 'taló·fa há·yi·t apo·ká·kin
but others built a town and settled near the Deep Fork [of the Canadian River]

Tvlse Kvnēten hocefhoyvtēs.
talsikaní·tin hocífho·yatí·s.
and were named Tulsa Canadian.

Momen vpvlwvt Vcenv Hvcce hocefkē hvcce wakkē vnakvn 'tvlofv hayēt
mo·mín apálwat acinahácci hocífki· hácci wákki· aná·kan 'taló·fa há·yi·t
And others built a town in the vicinity of a river named Cedar River

cukorakko ocēt vpokaken Vcenv Hvcce Tvlsen hocefhoyvtēt omēs.
cokolákko ó·ci·t apo·kà·kin acinahaccitálsin hocífho·yatí·t ô·mi·s.
and had a square ground and were named Cedar River Tulsa.

Akfvske Kvnēte Cvtaksohkv hocefhoyēt omvtēs.
akfaskikaní·ti cataksó·hka[i] hocífho·yi·t ô·mati·s.
Okfuskee Canadian was named Chataksohka.

Kvnēte Oktah-hvcce 'tekacat tempen 'tvlofv hayet
kaní·ti okta·hácci 'tikâ·ca·t[ii] tímpin 'taló·fa há·yit
They built a town close to where the Canadian and Deep Fork divide,

---

[i] The first time JH heard mention of *akfáski*, it was called *cataksó·hka*. Later was called *akfaskikaní·ti*.

[ii] *'tikâ·ca·t* is the same as *'tohcákha·t*.

cukorakko ocēt vpoken,
cokołákko ó·ci·t apô·kin[132]
and they had a square ground;

vpvlwvt Hvccesofke yoksv fvccvn ehute hayahket vpoken
apálwat haccisófki yóksa fáccan ihóti ha·yáhkit apô·kin
others built homes and settled toward the end of the Deep Fork

Akfvske Hvccesofken hocefhoyvtēt omēs. Yofalv Cvtaksohkv enhvsaklatkvn
akfáski haccisófkin hocífho·yatí·t ô·mi·s. yofa·la cataksó·hka inhasaklá·tkan
and were named Okfuskee Deep Fork. Eufaula built a town west of Chataksohka

Kvnēte vnakvn 'tvlofv hayet vpoken, hiyoman Yofalv Kvnēten hocefhoyēt os.
kaní·ti aná·kan 'taló·fa há·yit apô·kin hayyô·ma·n[133] *yofa·lakaní·tin hocífho·yí·t ô·ⁿs.*
and settled near the Canadian and are now called Eufaula Canadian.

Momen vpvlwvt Hvccesofke yoksv fvccvn ehute hayet vpokaken
mo·mín apálwat haccisófki yóksa fáccan ihóti há·yit apo·kâ·kin
Then others made homes and settled toward the end of the Deep Fork

Yofalv Hopayvlken hocefhoyvtēs. Hiyoman Hvccesofke Yofalvn hocefhoyēt os.
yofa·lahopa·yâlkin hocífho·yatí·s hayyô·ma·n haccisofkiyofá·lan hocífho·yí·t ô·ⁿs.
and were named Far-away Eufaula. At the present time they are called Deep Fork Eufaula.

Apehkv-tvlvtēke, Vlepamv, Atvse, Cēyahv, Kilice, Kecopvtake, Kowassate, Kvwetv,
a·pihkatalatî·ki alipá·ma a·tasí ci·yá·ha keyléyci kicopatâ·ki kowa·ssá·ti kawíta
Arbeka Talladega, Alabama, Artussee, Cheyarha, Kialegee, Kicho Pataki, Koasati, Coweta,

Kvsehtv, Helvpe, Noyakv, Osuce, Ocēvpofv, Pvkvntvlvhasse, Raprakko,
kasíhta hilápi <noyá·ka> o·socí oci·apó·fa pakantalahá·ssi ła·plákko
Cusseta, Hilabi, Nuyaka, Osochi, Hickory Ground, Peach Ground, Thlopthucco,

'Rewahle, Tvlse, Tokepahce, Tokpafkv, Tvlvhassuce, Tvlwvrakko, Uewohkv,
'liwáhli tálsi tokipáhci tokpá·fka talaha·ssocí talwałákko oywó·hka
Thewahle, Tulsa, Tukabahchee, Tookparfka, Little Tallahassee, Big Town, Wewoka,

Ueokofke, Vsselanvpe, Akfvske-cvtaksohkv, Yocce, Yofalv, Hecete, Okcaye,
oyokófki assila·napí akfaskicataksó·hka yó·cci yofá·la hicíti okcá·yi
Weogufkee, Green Leaf, Okfuskee Chataksohka, Euchee, Eufaula, Hitchiti, Okchayi,

Rvrokvlkv, Taskēke, Tvlmocvse: Heyvt etvlwv hocefkv vculvkēt omakēs.
łalokálka ta·skí·ki talmocási hiyát itálwa hocífka acolakí·t omâ·ki·s.
Thlathlokalka, Tuskegee, New Tulsa: these are the old town names.

Rēkackv, Uekirakko 'tepakat hēren kerrvkot omis,
li·ká·cka oykeyłákko 'tipâ·ka·t hĭ·ⁿlin kíłlakot o·mêys
I don't know much about Thlikachka ['Broken Arrow'] and Wikaythlakko ['Big Spring'],

mocvsvkē tis ohmēs.
mocasakí· teys óhmi·s
they may be new.

Eccvkotakse enrē hayetv hervkemahēt Ue-akroswv hocefkēt
iccakotáksi inłí· ha·yitá hiłakimá·hi·t oyakłó·swa hocífki·t
There was a place called Wiakthloswa [a shrub used for making arrows]

vfoswvt tayēt omen
afó·swat tă·ⁿyi·t ô·min
that had plenty of switches to make arrows of good quality

este eccvkotakse esfayvlket sulkēt rēhakvn hopoyvkemąhēn ēkvnvt liket oman
ísti iccakotáksi isfa·yâlkit sólki·t łi·há·kan hopoyakimă·ⁿhi·n i·kanát lêykit o·mâ·n
and many hunters who used bows to hunt would come to this land to look for arrow stock,

'tvlofv hayusēt este vpokvkēt omen,
'taló·fa há·yosi·t ísti apo·kakí·t ô·min
and some had made and settled in a little town,

Rēkvckv-tvlofvn hocefhoyvtēs, maketvt omvnts.
li·kackataló·fan hocífho·yatí·s. ma·kitát ô·mánc.
and it was named Broken Arrow town, it was told.

Mohmen mv vnakvranēn uekiwv liket omat uewv sulkemąhē ocēt omen
móhmin ma ana·kalâ·ni·n oykéywa lêykit o·mâ·t óywa solkimă·ⁿhi ó·ci·t ô·min
Now near there was a spring with so much water that

Uekirakko hocefkēt liket oman,
oykeyłákko hocífki·t lêykit o·mâ·n
it was called Wikaythlakko ['Big Spring'],

mv tempen 'tvlofv hayet este vpokaket omen
ma tímpin 'taló·fa há·yit ísti apo·kâ·kit o·mín
and near there people had built a town and settled,

Uekirakkvlken hocefhoyvtēs mahokvntok.
oykeylakkâlkin hocífho·yatí·s má·ho·kánto·k
so they were called Wikaythlakkalki ['Big Spring people'].

Este-cate etvlwv Maskoke hocefkat enake ēkvnv-tvleme likat ofv
isticá·ti itálwa ma·skó·ki hocífka·t iná·ki i·kanatalimí lêyka·t ó·fa
Within the public land owned by the Muscogee Nation

hvcce lomhakate vhocefhokē
hácci lomhâ·ka·ti ahocifhokí·
all the small towns named after

etvllopocke hocefhokv ocakat vtēkat mocvsvkēt omētok:
itallopócki hocifhoká o·câ·ka·t[134] atî·ka·t mocasaki·t ô·mi·to·k
rivers are new.

Mvn vpvkēt omēs, Rēkackv, Uekirakko 'tepakat komvyēt os.
man apáki·t o·mí·s łi·ká·cka oykeyłákko 'tipâ·ka·t kó·mayi·t ô·ⁿs.
I believe Broken Arrow and Big Spring are in that group.

Mohmen este-na-lvste vpuekv omē wihoyē oketv omof
móhmin istina·lásti[135] apóyka ó·mi· wéyho·yí· okíta ô·mo·f
Now during the time when black people were sold like livestock,

este-catvlket nesakēt sasvtēt omēs.
istica·tâlkit nisa·kí·t sa·satí·t ô·mi·s.
some Indians bought them.

Este-lvste nēsē horkopē wiyē esfolhoyaten horren eshahohyen,
istilásti ni·sí· hołko·pí· weyyí· isfólho·yâ·tin hółłin isha·hóhyin
Those who went around buying, stealing, and selling black people caused the war,

este em enak ockv vpuekv este tis sulkēt yvmvhikof
ísti iminâ·k ó·cka apóyka ístiteys sólki·t yamahêyko·f
and after people's belongings, livestock, and even many people were wasted,

herkv hahken este Maskoke, Wvcenv 'tepakat etenfvccetv etenhayof
hílka háhkin istima·skó·ki wacína 'tipâ·ka·t itinfaccitá itinha·yó·f
peace was made, and the Muscogee people and the United States made a treaty

ohrolopē cokperakko hvmken cokpe cenvpaken pale ēpaken ēpohkakat omof tatēs.
ohlolopí· cokpiłákko hámkin cókpi cinapâ·kin pá·li i·pâ·kin i·pohkâ·ka·t ô·mo·f tá·ti·s
in the year eighteen hundred and sixty-six [1866].

Momen ena-lvste pucasseko hakekv,
mo·mín ina·lásti poca·ssikó· há·kika
And the blacks no longer had owners,

este-cate em vpuekv tatē omvlkvt este Maskoke vpvkēt vhonkvtiken
isticá·ti imapóyka tá·ti· omálkat istima·skó·ki apáki·t akoŋkatêykin
those who had been the property of Indians were counted among the Muscogee people

este Maskoke entvsekvyv hahken, vhakv estomvkēn ēyenhayet
istima·skó·ki intasikayá háhkin ahá·ka isto·makí·n i·yínha·yít
and became Muscogee citizens, and made whatever laws for themselves,

este Maskoke etvlwv liken omat,
istima·skó·ki itálwa lêykin o·mâ·t
and if they lived in the Muscogee Nation,

mv em elecvn sehokvranēn etenfvccetv hahoyekv,
ma imilicán sihó·kała·ní·n itinfaccitá ha·hò·yika
it was agreed that we would live under those [laws],

este ena-lvste pucasseko hakvtē
ísti ina·lásti poca·ssikó· há·kati·
so all the black people who'd become freedmen

este-cate em este tatē omvlkvt ēyvhonkvtakvtēt omēs.
isticá·ti imísti tá·ti· omálkat i·yahóŋkata·katí·t ô·mi·s
and had belonged to Indians took a count of themselves.

Mohmet este Maskoke etvllopocke ocakvtē omēn,
móhmit istima·skó·ki itallopócki o·câ·kati· ó·mi·n
Then just as the Muscogees had small tribal towns,

etvlwv tuccēnē omēn enhocefhokv hayakvtēt omēs.
itálwa toccî·ni· ó·mi·n inhocifhoká há·ya·katí·t ô·mi·s.
they had three tribal towns and made names for them.

Hvmket Uecate este-lvste, hvmket Oktahvcce este-lvsteton,
hámkit oycá·ti istilásti hámkit okta·hácci istiléstiton
One was Arkansas Colored,[136] one was North Fork Colored,

hvmket Kvnēte este-lvstet omen, monkv yv tuccēnat vrahrvkvt 'temvrkv hayaket,
hámkit kaní·ti istilástit ô·min môŋka ya toccî·na·t alahłakát 'timáłka há·ya·kít
and one was Canadian Colored. So they held elections for each of these three,

este Maskoke vhakv hayē nvkaftat vpakvranat
istima·skó·ki ahá·ka ha·yí· naka·ftâ·t apá·kała·nâ·t
and to participate in Muscogee sessions to make laws,

Mēkko cukopikv hayet,
mí·kko cokopéyka há·yit
they elected a representative to the [House of] Kings

Tvstvnvke cukopikv maketvo hahicakvtēt omēs.
tastanáki cokopéyka ma·kitáw ha·háyca·katí·t ô·mi·s
and also what is called a representative to the [House of] Warriors.

Este Maskoke etvlwv em enak ockv vtēkat omvlkvt celayetv em etektvnkvtēt omen
istima·skó·ki itálwa iminâ·k ó·cka atî·ka·t omálkat cila·yitá[137] imitiktánkati·t ô·min
All the treaty rights of the Muscogee Nation were available for their use,

"Este Maskoke toyēs" ēkomē hēret fullet omis,
istima·skó·ki tô·yi·s i·kô·mi· hǐ·ⁿłit[138] follít o·mêys
and they really believed they were Muscogees,

mv etvlwv tuccenicat hvmkis 'pvnkv ēkvnv, cukorakko ēyenhayvkekatēt os.
ma itálwa toccinêyca·t hámkeys pánka i·kaná cokołákko i·yinha·yakíká·ti·t ô·ⁿs.
but not one of those three tribal towns made themselves a dance ground or square ground.

Eyacaken omat, cukorakko hayvkvranvtēs.
iyá·ca·kín o·mâ·t cokołákko ha·yakáła·natí·s
If they had wanted one, they could have made a square ground.

Ēkvnv 'tvlemen ocaket em etektvnkusekv,
i·kaná 'talimín o·câ·kit imitiktánkosíka
Public land was available to them,

'sem vnvcecēt fullēkis ohmēs kont omakewitvtēs.
'simanacíci·t[139] fólli·keys óhmi·s kônt oma·kiwêytati·s[140]
so they might have thought it would be unseemly.

Mv etvlwv ēnvkvftēcet ēyvhonkatē este ensulkē kērret
ma itálwa i·nakáfti·cít i·yahóŋka·tí· ísti insolki· ki·łłít
In order for the tribal towns to meet and take a count of their people,

vhakv hayē nvkaftē fullvranat
ahá·ka ha·yí· naka·ftí· fóllala·nâ·t
in the law-making sessions,

etvlwuce omvlkvt Mēkko cukopikv hvmkē vlkēn hayet
italwocí omálkat mí·kko cokopéyka hámki· álki·n ha·yít
all the tribal towns selected one representative each to the [House of] Kings

Tvstvnvke cukopikv 'tepakan hahicakvtēs.
tastanáki cokopéyka 'tipâ·ka·n ha·héyca·katí·s
and also elected one representative to the [House of] Warriors.

Momis Tvstvnvke cukopikv hvmkat senhoyvnē hayat sasvtēs,
mo·mêys tastanáki cokopéyka hámka·t sinhoyáni· ha·yâ·t sa·satí·s
But some elected more than one representative to the [House of] Warriors,

etvlwuce este ensulkē vcakkvyēn.
italwocí ísti insolkí· acakkayí·n
based on the tribal town's population.

Mohmet omvlkv em mēkko, vpoktv 'tepakan hahyen nvkaftet
móhmit omálka immí·kko apó·kta 'tipâ·ka·n háhyin naka·ftít
They elected a principal chief and vice-chief and convened

"Este Maskoke etvlwv toyēs" maket fullof, 'mvpvkvlken kihocvtēt os.
istima·skó·ki itálwa tô·yi·s ma·kít[141] follô·f 'mapakâlkin kéyho·cati·t ô·ⁿs
and said, "We are the Muscogee Nation," and they were called 'mvpvkvlke ['members'].

Momis etvlwuce vtēkusat em mēkko enhenehv makēt vpoktihocēt omvtēs.
mo·mêys italwocí atî·kosa·t immí·kko inhiníha ma·kí·t apokteyhocí·t o·matí·s
The chiefs of all the tribal towns were assisted by what are called <u>henehv</u> ['second chiefs'].

Momis mv tat opanē ēyafvcecicē fullēpatet mēkkvke hayēpet omakvtēs.
mô·meys máta·t opa·ní· i·ya·facíceyci· fólli·pâ·tit mi·kkaki há·yi·pít oma·katí·s.
However, they selected chiefs for the dances and celebrations.

Panē fulletv ēkvnv <u>cukorakko</u> kicēt ocvkēt
pa·ní· follitá i·kaná cokolákko keycí·t o·cakí·t[142]
They had land for dancing called <u>cukorakko</u> [literally, 'big house'],

mv ofv vretv sēyenfvyvtetv vhakuce ocvkēt mvn ohmēkkicet omhoyvtēs.
ma ó·fa alíta s<i·y>infayatitá aha·kocí o·cakí·t man ohmí·kkeycít ómho·yatí·s.
and they had rules to direct customs there that governed [all functions].

Momen mēkko hayat Aktvyahcvlke, Wotkvlke kihocēt estet fullēt omēs.
mo·mín mí·kko ha·yâ·t aktayahcâlki wo·tkâlki kéyho·cí·t ístit follí·t ô·mi·s
And in selecting a chief, there were people called Aktayahchi clan and Raccoon clan.

Mv mēkkicat etvlwuce omvlkvrạnusēt omēs.
ma mí·kkeycâ·t italwocí omalkală·ⁿnosi·t ô·mi·s
Almost all the tribal towns were led by [members of those clans].[i]

Mv mēkkvlket etvlwv hvmēcat "Estofvn nvkvftekvs" maken omat,
ma mi·kkâlkit itálwa hamî·ca·t istô·fan nakáftikas ma·kín o·mâ·t
Whenever those chiefs set a meeting date,

encukorakko ernvkaftet nerēn panen hvyatkēt omen,
incokolákko ilnaka·ftít nilí·n pa·nín haya·tkí·t ô·min
they met at their <u>cukorakko</u> and danced all night

<u>eshvyvtketvn</u> kicēt fullēt omēs.
ishayatkitán keycí·t follí·t ô·mi·s
and called it <u>eshvyvtketv</u> [literally, 'all-night [dance]'].

---

[i] "Town chief and town king is different. Town chief has charge of dancing and stomp ground activities. For this purpose every little town has a chief. Town king is council member, equal to senator. Didn't have town king before 1866."

Momen meskē nvrkvpv orē vtēkat mv 'pvnkv ēkvnv pvhe, vtakrv
mo·mín miskí· nalkapá o·lí· atî·ka·t ma pánka i·kaná pahí atákła
Now in the middle of every summer, they hoed and swept the dance ground

ohhontan lueyet paset hvthvyvtke hompekot vtotket omhoyvtēs.
óhhontâ·n loyyít pa·sít hathayátki hómpíko·t ato·tkít ómho·yatí·s
where grass and weeds had grown, working without eating breakfast.

Mv vtotketv <u>tvco-paskvn</u> kicakvtēs.
ma atotkitá tacopá·skan kéyca·katí·s
This work was called <u>tvco-paskv</u> ['ring-sweeping'].

Mv ēkvnv pashoyē likat <u>fettv-rakkon</u> kicet
ma i·kaná pa·shoyí· lêyka·t fittalákkon keycít
The ground that had been swept was called the <u>fettv-rakko</u> ['big yard'],

mv ofvn totkv etēcet mvn vfolotēcēt panet omakvtēs.
ma ó·fan[143] tó·tka iti·cít man afolóti·ci·t[144] pa·nít oma·katí·s.
and they would light a fire in that [circle] and dance around it.

<u>'Pvnkv-Haco</u> kicaket mv 'pvnetv,
pankahá·co[145] kéyca·kit ma 'panitá
To dance the one called <u>'Pvnkv-Haco</u> ['Crazy Dance'],

lucv-lopocke lvpvtke fullusan hopoyet, hvrpe-tvkvcwat vhopvnekot,
localopócki lapátki follosâ·n hopo·yít hałpitakácwa·t[146] ahopaníko·t
they hunted for small turtles in the woods, and without damaging the hard shells,

vpeswv aencawet, mv hvrpe-tvkvcwan kvrpēcet solēcofvt
apíswa a·inca·wít ma hałpitakácwa·n[147] kálpi·cít soli·cô·fat
they took out the flesh, dried the shells, and when they had quite a few,

lopockusēn rolahlēcet cvto-hvtkuce lopọckusan vtehtēcofvt,
lopóckosi·n lolahlî·cit catohatkoci lopŏ·ⁿckosa·n atihtí·co·fát
they made small holes in them and put little white pebbles in them,

eco-hvrpen monkat wakv-hvrpe tis ele empakko vfolotkusēn,
icohálpin móŋka·t wa·kahálpiteys ilí impá·kko afolô·tkosi·n
and using deer hide or cow hide [to wrap] around the calf,

entvphēn encvpkē matvpomusis omēs.
intaphí·n incapkí· ma·tapô·moseys o·mí·s
the width and the length should be about the same [i.e., square].

Wahret mv lucv-hvrpen cvtuce vtehtēkan escenvpakat mahe tis omēs.
wáhłit ma locahálpin catóci atihtî·ka·n iscinapâ·ka·t mâ·hiteys o·mí·s
They would cut it and have about eight turtle shells with pebbles in them.

Cusse-selkucen lucv-hvrpe rolahlusan eteropotecēn
cossisilkocín locahálpi łoláhlosa·n <i>tiłopo·ticí·n
They'd thread little strips of buckhide through the holes in the turtle shells

eco-hvrpen svwvnawihcet, eshokkolēn eshayvkvtēn ocvkēt hoktvket sasekv
icohálpin 'sawana·wéyhcit ishokkô·li·n ishá·yakáti·n o·caki·t hoktakít sâ·sika
and tie them onto the deer hide; women had two that they'd made,

momet mv nake hahokicē 'sopvnetv sēyemvhayē eskerrvkvtē hoktvke sasat
mo·mít ma nâ·ki há·hokeyci· 'sopaníta s<i·y>imáha·yí· iskiłłakáti· hoktakí sâ·sa·t
and by practicing, some women learned to dance with those noise-makers.

ele hackowvn 'svpvllvkēn 'svwvnawicet 'metetakēt liketayen
ilí ha·ckowán[148] *'sapallakí·n 'sawana·wêycit 'mititá·ki·t léykitâ·yin*
They wrapped and tied them to their lower legs and would sit waiting,

'Pvnkv-Haco pvnetv vlicēhohcen 'pvnkv senhomahtv heckuehcet
pankahá·co panitá aleyci·hóhcin pánka sinhomá·hta hickóyhcit
and when they began to dance the Crazy Dance, they chose a dance leader.

"Omvlkuset afvckatskvrēs" mahket senhomahtv enhuehhohken ayof
omálkosit a·facká·ckáli·s máhkit sinhomá·hta inhoyhhóhkin a·yô·f
"You all celebrate," she said, and when the leader was called and went [toward the fire],

honvntake ētv empohvthoyat sulkēt vcakkvpēyen
honantá·ki í·ta impohathô·ya·t sólki·t acákkapi·yín
many men who'd been invited followed,

totkv ētkan vfolotēcet pvnakof,
tó·tka i·tkâ·n afóloti·cít pána·kô·f
and as they danced around the burning fire,

mv hoktvke hackewv lucv-svokv 'svwvnawicē liketayvtē
ma hoktakí ha·ckiwá locasáwka 'sawana·wéyci· léykitâ·yati·
one of the women who'd been waiting here and there with the turtle shakers tied to her shins

hvmket senhomahtvn 'svcakkayet
hámkit sinhomá·htan 'sacákka·yít
followed directly behind the leader,

senhomahtv ele vwikat vcakkąyusen sopanet sayof,
sinhomá·hta ilí aweykâ·t acakkă·ⁿyosin sópa·nít sa·yô·f
and when she got in perfect step with the leader,

matvpomēt vpvltakeu yopvn lucv-sopanvlke vpvlwv sopvnaket omvnts.
ma·tapó·mi·t apaltá·kiw yópan locasopa·nâlki apálwa sópana·kít o·mánc
the others would dance behind her with their shakers.

Mvt 'panvlke enhomahtvt omakēs.
mat pa·nâlki inhomá·htat omâ·ki·s
Those [women] are the leaders for the dancers.

Hoktvket lucv-sopvnakat sekon omat 'pvnkv hẹre onkot omvnts.
hoktakít locasópana·kâ·t síkon o·mâ·t pánka hĭ·ⁿli ôŋko·t o·mánc
When there were no women with shakers, the dance was not very good.

Momen 'pvnkv senhomahtv honvnwv yvhikof,
mo·mín pánka sinhomá·hta honánwa yaheykô·f
And when the male dance leader would sing,

honvntake yopv fullat omvlkvt yvhikakēt 'panet omhoyvtēs.
honantá·ki yópa follâ·t omálkat yahéyka·kí·t pa·nít ómho·yatí·s
all the men followed behind, singing and dancing.

'Pvnkv-Haco 'panē yvhiketv kẹrkakusēt omēs.
pankahá·co pa·ní· yaheykitá kĭ·ⁿlká·kosi·t ô·mi·s.
Songs for the Crazy Dance are well known.

Senhomahtv fekhonnēpof,
sinhomá·hta fikhónni·pô·f
When the dance leader stopped,

omvlkvt vwahen, senhomahtv ētvn hopohoyēt omēs.
omálkat awa·hín sinhomá·hta i·tan hopó·ho·yí·t ô·mi·s.
as everyone would leave [the circle], another leader was chosen.

'Pvnk-eshomahtvlke este kẹrkakusēt onkv, mv senhomahtv hvmkē 'panē oketv ofv,
pankishoma·htâlki ísti kǐnłká·kosi·t ônka ma sinhomá·hta hámki· pa·ní· okita ó·fa
Men who were dance leaders were well known, so when one of those leaders was dancing,

este-honvntake cēpvnvke estomomuset 'pvnetvn eyacvkēton omat,
istihonantá·ki ci·panáki istô·mó·mosit 'panitán iya·caki·ton o·mâ·t[149]
if men and young boys wanted to dance,

omvlkvt 'metektvnkēt omēs. Momen hoktvkeu matvpọmuset em etektvnkēt omēs.
omálkat 'mitiktánki·t ô·mi·s mo·mín hoktakíw ma·tapồ·ⁿmosit imitiktánki·t ô·mi·s.
all were free to do so. And women too were in the same way free to do so.

Etvlwv hvmēcusat tokot etvlwv ētv assossē encukopericateu omvlkvt em etektvnkēt omēs.
itálwa hamî·cosa·t tó·ko·t itálwa i·ta a·ssóssi· incokopileycâ·tiw omálkat imitiktánki·t ô·mi·s
Not just the one town, but all the other visiting towns too were free to do so.

Mv senhomahtv hvmkē panē oketv este ensulkē estomvtēket 'pvnepvranis tektvnkēt omēs.
ma sinhomá·hta hámki· pa·ní· okíta ísti insolkí· istô·mati·kit 'panipála·nèys tiktánki·t ô·mi·s
When the one leader danced, it didn't matter how many people danced, it was open to all.

Mohmen opvnkvhaco 'pvnhoyē ennerē ofv tat
móhmin opankahá·co[150] *pánho·yí· innilí· ó·fata·t*
So the night the Crazy Dance was danced,

'pvnkv 'mvrahrvkv sulkēn nak 'pvnkuce kicet 'pvnhoyēt omvtēs.
pánka (?) 'malahłaká sólki·n nâ·k pankocí keycít pánho·yí·t o·mati·s
many different dances called nak pvnkuce ['little dances'] were performed.

Mv 'pvnkv enhocefhokv hiyomvkēt omēs:
ma (?) pánka inhocifhoká hayyo·maki·t ô·mi·s
The names of the dances were these:

'Tehvlvtkv-Pvnkv, Tvlak-Pvnkv, Estekene-Pvnkv, Fuco-Pvnkv,
'tihalatkapánka tala·kpánka istikinipánka focopánka
Round Dance ['holding hands dance'], Bean Dance, Horned Owl Dance, Duck Dance,

Wakv-Pvnkv, Yvnvsv-Pvnkv, Vce-Pvnkv, Osah-Pvnkv,
wa·kapánka yanasapánka acipánka osahpánka
Cow Dance, Buffalo Dance, Corn Dance, Crow Dance,

Sule-Pvnkv, Echas-Pvnkv, Wotko-Pvnkv, 'Cerakko-Pvnkv,
solipánka icha·spánka[151] *wo·tkopánka 'cilakkopánka*
Buzzard Dance, Beaver Dance, Raccoon Dance, Horse Dance,

Okyeha-Pvnkv, Cetto-Pvnkv, Ēsapv-Pvnkv, Okyvn-Pvnkv,
okyiha·pánka cittopánka i·sa·papánka okyanpánka
Mosquito Dance, Snake Dance, Gar Dance, Catfish Dance,

Ekv-hokkolv-Pvnkv, Akkvtvlas-Pvnkv, Haco-Pvnkv, Rvro-Pvnkv.
ikahokko·lapánka akkatala·spánka[i] *ha·copánka*[ii] *lalopánka*[iii]
Double-Header Dance, Spring Frog Dance, Crazy Dance, Fish Dance.

Heyv 'pvnkv hocefhokv ocat omvlkvranusēt
hiyá pánka hocifhoká ô·ca·t omalkalá·ⁿnosi·t
Dances with these names, almost all of them,

'pvnkv-haco 'panē ele vwiketv 'mvrahkvkusē vlkēt omēs.
pankahá·co pa·ni· ilí aweykitá 'malahkakósi· álki·t ô·mi·s
had different steps in the Crazy Dance.

Momet enyvhiketv 'mvrahkv vlkēt omen, enyvhihoken pvnhoyateu sulkēt omēs.
mo·mít inyaheykitá 'maláhka álki·t ô·min inyaháyho·kín pánho·yâ·tiw sólki·t ô·mi·s
And each had its own song, and there were many who sang them and danced.

'Pvnk-eshvyvtketv ocē vtēkat 'pvnhohoyvranē tvlkusē tokot omakēs.
pankishayatkitá o·cí· ati·ka·t panhóhyala·ni· tàlⁿkosi· tó·ko·t omá·ki·s
Not all these are danced at every 'pvnk-eshvyvtketv ['all-night dance'].

'Pvnhoyemahat 'Tehvlvtkv-Pvnkv tvlkusēt omvnts.
panhoyimá·ⁿha·t 'tihalatkapánka tàlⁿkosi·t o·mánc
The most danced one was the Round Dance ['holding hands dance'].

---

[i] *akkatalá·swa* = kind of small frog in the water.

[ii] *ha·copánka* is different from *pankahá·co*.

[iii] Never did see *solipánka* ['buzzard dance'], *cittopánka* ['snake dance'], and *lalopánka* ['fish dance'].

Momis hiyomat estomēt fulhoyēt omat kerrvkot os.
mo·mêys hayyô·ma·t istó·mi·t fólho·yi·t ô·ma·t kíłłako·t ô·ⁿs
But I don't know how they're doing it now.

Cukorakko vrvyvtē sekat ohrolopē paletuccēnen hokkolohkakat hoyanekv,
cokolákko ałáyati· sikâ·t ohlolopí· pa·litoccî·nin hokkolohkâ·ka·t hoyâ·nika[i]
I haven't been to the square ground in thirty-two years,

nake estomē fulhoyē hēcvyvtē sulkēt 'mvrahkvkēpewitēs.
nâ·ki ísto·mí· fólhoyi· hi·cayáti· sólki·t 'małahkakî·piwêyti·s.
so many of the things I've seen them do may be different.

Mv 'pvnetv ēkvnv <u>totkētkv</u> kicet
ma 'panitá i·kaná to·tkí·tka keycít
The dance area they called the <u>totkētkv</u> ['where the fire burns'],

<u>nvrkvpofv</u> tis kicēt hocefaket omvtēs. Momen tvco pahsof netta ostē orat,
nałkapó·fateys keycí·t hocífa·kít o·matí·s mo·mín tacó páhso·f nittá· ô·sti· o·lâ·t
or they called it <u>nvrkvpofv</u> ['middle area']. And four days after they swept the ring,

mv etvlwv tvsekvyv omvlkuset ernvkaftat
ma (?) itálwa (?) tasikayá omǎⁿkosit íłnaka·ftâ·t
when all the citizens of the tribe came together for a get-together,

<u>vnvkvftetv-nettvn</u> kicakēt omēs.
anakaftitaníttan kéyca·kí·t ô·mi·s
they called it <u>vnvkvftetv-nettv</u> ['coming together day'].

Momet ehvpo kerkvkēn ēkvnv ocē vlkēt onkv, mvn vpokaken netta tuccēnat orēs.
mo·mít ihapó· kiłkakí·n i·kaná ó·ci· áłki·t ôŋka man apo·kâ·kin nittá· toccî·na·t o·łi·s.
And each one had a spot for their camp, and they stayed there three days.

Vnvkvftetv-nettv yomockat panet hofonekon wihket
anakaftitanítta yomo·ckâ·t pa·nít hofónikon wéyhkit
On <u>vnvkvftetv-nettv</u>, at dark, they danced for a short time and stopped

---

[i] Or: *ô·łika* in place of *hoyâ·nika*.

nucicen hvyvtiken fvccvlike hoyanat, estofvn hoktvke 'metetakaken omat,

nocêycin hayatêykin faccaléyki hoya·nâ·t istô·fan hoktakí 'mititá·ka·kín o·mâ·t

and slept until daylight, and in the afternoon, whenever the women were ready,

pvnkv ēkvnv aohhvwvrēn enhuehhokof, omvlkvt aohhawof,

pánka i·kaná a·ohhawáli·n inhóyhho·kô·f omálkat a·óhha·wô·f

when they were called to come to the dance ground, when all came forward,

senhomahtv vwihekvranat enhopohoyēt onkv,

sinhomá·hta aweyhikála·nâ·t inhopo·hoyí·t óŋka

the leader and the one directly following her had already been chosen.

asehohken ētv hoktvlvkvranan vwihekēn,

a·sihóhkin[152] *í·ta hoktalakaɫâ·na·n aweyhikí·n*

So when they were in place, the older women were positioned next,

'svpaklēhohcen empohattvt enhomahtet,

'sapakli·hóhcin impohá·ttat inhomâ·htit[153]

and when all were in place, the [male] empohattv ['inviter'] took the lead,

ēkvnvn sētekkekvn essatet enhomahtet sayet, totkv ētkvtēn rasvfolotiket

i·kanán si·tikkikán íssa·tít inhomâ·htit sa·yít tó·tka i·tkatí·n la·safolotêykit

marking the ground with a cane as he led and circled the fireplace,

enyvhikvlke ehomvn senhomahtvt erfekhonnof,

inyaheykâlki ihóman sinhomá·htat iɫfíkhonnô·f

and when the [man] dance leader stopped in front of the singers,

enyvhihoken 'panet vpēyen,

inyaháyho·kín pa·nít api·yín

they continued to sing for them while [the women] danced forward

senhomahtv totkētkv vfolotiket,

sinhomá·hta[154] *to·tkí·tka afolotêykit*

and the [woman] leader circled the totkētkv ['fireplace'],

enyvhikvlke ehomvn rorat,

inyaheykâlki ihóman ɫo·ɫâ·t

and when she arrived in front of the singers,

fekhoniyen, hvtvm enyvhihokof, panēt omēs.
fikhonêyyin hatâm inyahéyho·kô·f pa·ní·t ô·mi·s.
she stopped, and when they sang again, she would dance.

Vlicehcē totkētkv vfolotehcē
aleycíhci· to·tkí·tka afolotíhci·[155]
After they circled the fireplace

senhomahtv enyvhikvlke ehomv rohrē 'panvtē fekhonnof,
sinhomá·hta inyaheykâlki ihóma lóhłi· pa·natí· fikhonnô·f
and she stopped in front of the singers,

honvntake entopv vtēhkat, 'svculvke 'mvnettvkē estomis,
honantá·ki intopá atî·hka·t 'sacoláki 'manittakí· istô·meys
the men in the arbor, old ones and young ones alike,

"Mvto-o-o" maket vpoket omvnts.
matô·[i] ma·kít apo·kít o·mánc.
would sit and say <u>Mvto-o-o!</u> ['Thank you!'].

Ohhvrakkuecē ohhafackat "Heremahēs cv" maketvt omēs.
ohhałakkóyci·[156] *ohhá·fa·ckâ·t hilimá·hi·s ca^ ma·kitát ô·mi·s*
To pay respect joyfully, "Heremahēs cv" ['very good!'] is what should be said.

Mv fēkvpkv sosticofvn, <u>ele-wiyv</u> makēt enyvhihoken,
ma (?) fi·kápka sósteycô·fan[157] *iliwéyya ma·ki·t inyahéyho·kín*
After four rest periods, they sang what is called <u>ele-wiyv</u> ['foot extended'],

mvo vfolotketv ostēn 'pvnkv yekcēn 'panof,
máw afolotkitá ô·sti·n pánka yíkci·n pa·nô·f
and for that one too, when he circled four times dancing hard,

'Pvnkv-Cule kicēt senhomahtv este-honvnwvn enhopohoyen,
pankacóli keycí·t sinhomá·hta istihonánwan inhopohó·yin
they selected a male leader for the Old Dance,

---

[i] The fall on *matô·* has a slide of an octave ‾_.

honvntaket 'pvnetv vlicecof, hoktvke 'pane fullateu asohcehyen,
honantá·kit 'panitá aléyci·cô·f hoktakí pa·ní· follá·tiw a·sohcíhyin
and when the men began to dance, the women dancers got in too,

mvo 'pvnkv yekcen 'pahnet wikakof, empohattvt okat,
máw pánka yíkci·n páhnit wéyka·kô·f impohá·ttat o·ká·t
and after they danced hard and stopped, when the underline empohattv /underline ['inviter'] said

"Mv-tv-li-ke-e!" makof, entopv vtehkat "Ya-ah!" mahken,
mataleyki·^i ma·kò·f intopá atíhka·t ya·^ máhkin
"Mv-tv-li-ke-e!" ['That's all!'], those in the arbor would reply "Ya!"

hoktvke tat ehvpon ohhvpeyepet omvnts.
hoktakíta·t ihapó·n ohhapí·yi·pí·t o·mánc[158]
and the women would return to their camps.

Momof etvlwv enhessetake estomuset ohyicat hoktvke omvlkvt em etektvniken,
mo·mô·f itálwa (?) inhissitá·ki istô·mosit ohyéyca·t hoktakí omálkat imitiktanêykin
Then of the friends who had come from other tribal towns, all the women were welcome,

'pvnetv eyacat vtekat 'panen hoktvkuceto estomis 'pvnvre em etektvnket omvnts.
'panitá iya·câ·t ati·ka·t pa·nín hoktakócito· istô·meys pánáli· imitiktánki·t o·mánc.
and all who wanted to dance would dance; even little girls were welcome to dance.

Momof este estomet hoyopetvn eyacen omat em etektvnkusen,
mo·mô·f ísti istó·mi·t hoyopitán iyá·cin o·mâ·t imitiktánkosin
At that time, anyone who wanted to watch was welcome,

hoyopet folhoyet omes. Momen mv nettvn takfulwv enheckv encahmeliketv estomuset ont
hoyo·pít fólho·yí·t ô·mi·s mo·mín ma níttan takfólwa inhícka incahmileykitá istô·mosit ónt
and there are some who just watch. And on that day many colors of ribbons,

entvptvhe estomaket omat mvn hechoyet omes.
intaptahi·[159] *isto·má·kit ô·ma·t man hicho·yí·t ô·mi·s.*
of many widths, could be seen there.

---

[i] *mataleyki·^* (with octave fall like *matò·*).

Momis hofonof takfulwv tvskucakvn sēnehicvkēt 'panet omhoyekatēs,
mo·mêys hofŏ·ⁿno·f takfólwa taskocá·kan si·niheycakí·t pa·nít omhoyíká·ti·s
But long ago they didn't decorate themselves and dance with thin ribbons,

sepekokv. Mv 'pvnkv Hoktvk-Panv,
sipíko·ka.[160] *ma pánka hoktakpá·na*[161]
since there were none. Those dances were called the Hoktvk-Panv ['Women Dancer'],

Netta-Pvnkv, Echv-Pvnkv kihocēt omvtēs, hofonof.
nitta·pánka ichapánka kéyho·ci·t o·matí·s. hofŏ·no·f
Netta-Pvnkv ['Day Dance'], or Echv-Pvnkv ['Gun Dance'] long ago.

Momis hiyomat este-hvtket okat Takful-Panvn kicakēt os.
mo·mêys hayyô·ma·t istihátkit o·kâ·t takfolpá·nan kéyca·kí·t ô·ⁿs.
But now the white people say, "Ribbon Dance."

Momen mv 'pvnetv totkētkv vfolotketv osten 'pahnet fēkapet vpoken
mo·mín ma 'panitá to·tkí·tka afolotkitá ô·stin páhnit fí·ka·pít apô·kin
And to dance that, they dance around the fire four times and sit resting,

enpohattvlke hvtvm "'Pvnaks!" kicof, 'panet fēkvpkv osten
inpoha·ttâlki hatâm pánaks keycô·f pa·nít fí·kápka ô·stin
and when the inviters again say, "Dance!" they dance and rest four times,

mv fēkvpkv ostan okat vfolotketv ostan kicakēt omvnts.
ma fi·kápka ô·sta·n o·kâ·t afolotkitá ô·sta·n kéyca·kí·t o·mánc.
and the four rests were called vfolotketv ostan ['four circlings'].

Mohmen mv nerē Pvnkv-Haco panet hofonekon wihket
móhmin ma nili· pankahá·co pa·nít hofónikon wéyhkit
And that night they would dance the Crazy Dance a short time and quit,

nocicen hvyatkof, mēkkvlke em ohliketvn ohkaket
noceycín haya·tkô·f mi·kkâlki imohleykitán ohkâ·kit
then sleep until morning, and the chiefs would sit in their seats and say:

"Yvmvn omylkuset avwekvs, honvntake vtēkat" makaken, enyvtekvn ocēt onkv,
yamán omǎlⁿkosit a·awíkas honantá·ki atî·ka·t má·ka·kín inyatíkan ó·ci·t óŋka
"Everyone must come here, all men," they said, and they had interpreters,

mvt enhuehken tvsekvyv vculkv ohrolopē palē kolvpohkicat mahē ayat
mat ínhoyhkín tasikayá acólka ohłolopí· pâ·li· kolapohkêyca·t mâ·hi· â·ya·t
so they would call, and their <u>tvsekvyv</u> ['citizens'] of about seventeen years on up

vculemahat somvlkvt em ohliketv kerrvkēt onkv ohhvpoken ayof
acolimâ·ha·t 'somálkat imohleykitá kiłłakí·t ôŋka óhhapo·kín a·yô·f
to the oldest were all seated in their special places,

etvlwv ētv tvsekvyvt omē estomis eppucetaket omaken omat enhuehket
itálwa i·ta tasikayát ô·mi· istô·meys ippocitá·kit omâ·kin o·mâ·t ínhoyhkít
and they'd even call sons of <u>tvsekvyv</u> from other tribal towns,

tvsekvyv hoktē ehet on omat, omvlkvn enhuehket vpoket omvnts.
tasikayá hoktí· ihít ô·n o·mâ·t omálkan ínhoyhkít apo·kít o·mánc.
the husband of a woman <u>tvsekvyv</u>, they'd call all of them and sit in a group.

Mv momē vpokat <u>nvrkvpofvn</u> vtēhket omēs.
ma (?) mó·mi· apo·kâ·t nałkapó·fan atî·hkit o·mí·s
The place where they sat was called the <u>nvrkvpofv</u> ['middle area'].

Mohmof este osten vtohten
móhmo·f ísti ô·stin atóhtin
Then four people were sent,

eto-lanakan osten est-ele vhopakv toccēnat mahē encvpcvkēn resyihcen,
itola·nâ·ka·n ô·stin istilí ahopá·ka toccî·na·t mâ·hi· incapcaki·n lisyéyhcin
and they returned with four green limbs about three feet long.

enheles-hayvt totkvn tehcet,
inhilishá·yat[162] tó·tkan tíhcit
The <u>heles-hayv</u> ['medicine maker'] would light the fire,

mvn vtekkekusēn hvsossv-fvccvn hvmken wvkehcet,
man atik<k>ikósi·n haso·ssafáccan hámkin wakíhcit
and he laid one [log] pointed toward the east at the edge [of the fire],

hvmken honerv-fvccvn wvkehcet, hvmken aklatkv-fvccvn wvkehcet,
hámkin honiłafáccan wakíhcit hámkin akla·tkafáccan wakíhcit
he laid one pointed toward the north, he laid one pointed toward the west,

hvmken wvhvlv-fvccvn wvkēcet omvnts.
hámkin wahalafáccan waki·cít o·mánc
and he would lay one pointed toward the south.

Momen mv eto-lane warkē ostē lomhicat <u>takhvce ostan</u> kicet okvnts.
mo·mín ma (?) itolá·ni wá·lki· ô·sti· lómheycâ·t takhací ô·sta·n keycít o·kánc
And the four green logs that he laid out were called <u>takhvce ostan</u> ['four ground-tails'].

Momet, "Yv takhvce ostatet 'svmēkērkvt os.
mo·mít ya takhací ô·sta·tit 'sami·kí·łkat ô·ⁿs
And he'd say, "These four logs are a symbol to me.

Hvsossv, honerv, hvsaklatkv, wvhvlv em etenrvwv vnherkv fvckēn likit omis" makatet,
hasó·ssa honiła hasaklá·tka wahála imitînława anhílka fácki·n lêykeyt o·méys ma·kâ·tit
Bounded by the east, north, west, and south, I am full of peace."

"Takhvce ostat taklomhicet, etvlwv liket omēs" mahokvnts.
takhací ô·sta·t taklómheycít itálwa leykít o·mí·s má·ho·kánc
"With the four fire logs laid down, the tribal town sits [in peace?]," it was said.

Vculvke tatēt makvnts, hofonof. Momen momē vpokat <u>poskē</u> kicēt omēs.
acolakitá·ti·t ma·kánc hofô·ⁿno·f mo·mín mó·mi· apo·kâ·t po·skí· keycí·t ô·mi·s
The old ones used to say that, long ago. And those who sat there would <u>poskē</u> ['fast'].

Hompekot vpoket omēs. Monkv <u>posketvn</u> kihocēt omēs.
hómpiko·t apo·kít o·mi·s. môŋka poskitán kéyho·cí·t ô·mi·s
They went without eating. So it's called <u>posketv</u> ['to fast'].

Ēelvwēcat okēs. <u>Poskē</u> kicat
i·iláwi·câ·t o·kí·s po·skí· keycâ·t
It means to make oneself hungry. They called it <u>poskē</u>,

mv takhvce ostat ohhetēcv este wiketv hahoyēt omen,
ma (?) takhací ô·sta·t ohhiti·ca ísti weykitá ha·hoyi·t ô·min
and one person was appointed to light the four fire logs;

mvt ohhetēcet, takhvce ostat yoksv nēkrof,
mat óhhiti·cít takhací ô·sta·t yóksa ni·kłô·f
he lights it, and when the ends of the four logs burn off,

etohsoloten omvlkvt nekirē tvlkvranēn vpoket omēs.

itóhsolo·tín omálkat nikêyli· tálkała·ni·n apo·kít o·mí·s

he slides the burning ends together, and they sit until all have burnt.

Mohmen hoktvke hompetv esnoricvkvranat, mv heles-hayvt totkv etēcat toko,

móhmin hoktakí hompitá isnołeycakála·nâ·t ma 'hilishá·yat tó·tka itî·ca·t tó·ko·

And the women did not cook food with it, not the fire that the <u>heles-hayv</u> lit.

ētvn tvco vtēkat mahe min totkv em etehcen, eto-talucet onkv vhētkusan sēset,

i·tan tacó atî·ka·t[163] *mâ·hi mêyn tó·tka imitíhcin itota·locít ôŋka ahi·tkosâ·n si·sít*

He lit a fire near the edge in the ring, and because it was dry wood, he carried a flaming stick

ehvpon sohhayet etēcet, hompetv esnoricaket omvnts.

ihapó·n sóhha·yít iti·cít hompitá isnołéyca·kít o·mánc

and took it to the camps and lit [their fires], and they cooked food with that.

Momen hopuetakuceu heleswv enhahoyekv, ekv, etorofv, ena hvmkv tis

mo·mín hopoyta·kocíw 'hilíswa inha·hô·yika iká itołó·fa iná· hámkateys

And they made medicine for the children too, so when they dampened their heads,

mv heleswvn eslvcpēcet esfolhoyof,

ma (?) 'hilíswan islácpi·cít isfólho·yô·f

their faces, or sometimes their whole bodies with the medicine,

cēpvnvkuce epvwv tis monkat em vculē tis sohhvpēhoyen, ensapet omakvnts.

ci·panakocí ipáwateys moŋkâ·t imacolí·teys sohhapí·ho·yín ínsa·pít oma·kánc

they took the boys to their maternal uncle or to a male elder, and he would scratch them.

Essapetv tat kvco-mvpen cokele ceskvn cakhēhocen,

issa·pitáta·t kaco·mapín cokili cískan cakhi·hô·cin

For the scratching instrument, a blackberry cane was stuck in the ground next to a post,

enfvskēn em ēset sapvranan aemhoyen,

infaski·n imi·sít sá·pała·nâ·n[164] *a·ímho·yín*

and they would take a thorn off and hand it to the one who would scratch them,

mv kvco enfvskēn sensapet omakvnts.

ma (?) kacó· infaskí·n sínsa·pít oma·kánc

and they were scratched with that blackberry thorn.

Monkv vncēpvnvke sasvcoken svnyihocen, ensapvyis likvyē ocvtēt os,
môŋka anci·panáki sa·sacókin sanyéyho·cín insa·payêys leykayi· o·catí·t ô·ⁿs
So some of my boys were brought to me, and I would scratch them

poskē likvyat.
po·skí· leykayâ·t
when I was fasting.

Momofv tat poskvlke tat heleswv celayvranat
mo·mô·fata·t po·skâlkita·t 'hilíswa cilá·yała·nâ·t
At that time, when those fasting were preparing to take the medicine,

'tetaken heleswv tat mēkko-hvnēcv 'yvlonkvn paccet,
'titâ·kin 'hilíswata·t mi·kkohaní·ca 'yalóŋkan pa·ccít
they would beat roots of red root [*Salix tristis*, a dwarf willow]

uewv sulkēn aktehkēn heles-hayvt kohv tvckēn ēset,
óywa sólki·n aktíhki·n 'hilishá·yat kohá tácki·n î·sit
and put it in lots of water, and the <u>heles-hayv</u> would take a cut piece of cane

yvhiket liket, mv uewv kohv-tvcken sakpofket wihkof
yaheykít lêykit ma óywa kohatáckin sákpo·fkít wéyhko·f
and sit singing, and when he quit blowing in the water with that cut cane,

mēkkvlke mont mv poskē vpokat eskaket asvwotet fullēt omēs.
mi·kkâlki mónt[165] ma po·skí· apô·ka·t íska·kít á·sawo·tít follí·t ô·mi·s.
the chiefs and the ones who sat fasting would drink it and vomit it back up.

Momof mv netta pvnvranat metetaket vpoket onkv,
mo·mô·f ma nittá·[166] pánała·nâ·t mítita·kít apô·kit oŋká
Then on that day they sat and prepared to dance,

<u>empohattv</u> kicet este hokkolen wiketv hahoyēn
impohá·tta keycít ísti hokkô·lin weykitá ha·hoyí·n
so two people were chosen to be what is called <u>empohattv</u> ['inviters'],

poskvlke pvnvranat Setahvyv-Pvnkv enyvhikvlke enhopoyakēt omēs.
po·skâlki pánała·nâ·t sita·hayapánka[167] inyaheykâlki inhopóya·ki·t ô·mi·s
and for those fasting who were to dance, singers were chosen for the Feather Dance.

Foshvtkv etvrpv tafvn sese vlkēt sopvnvranet onkv
foshátka itáłpa tá·fan sísi álki·t 'sopanáła·nít oŋká
Because they would always dance carrying feathers from the wing of a white crane,

tafv-mvpe hopoyvranat vtothoyen,
ta·famapí hopóyała·nâ·t atothô·yin
they were sent to look for poles for the feathers,

vfoswv estele vhopakv cahkēpē monkat senhoyvnvkusē tis omēs.
afó·swa istilí ahopá·ka cahkî·pi· móŋka·t sinhoyanakósi·téys o·mí·s
and they also brought five feet or more of thread.

Sulkē resyihcof tafv-hvtke sulkē pvkvfkēn
sólki· lisyéyhco·f ta·fahátki[168] *sólki· pakáfki·n*
After they brought those things, they threaded lots of white feathers,

etuce yoksvn sem vwvnawihcof, vpēttē encukele homv svpaklan
itóci yóksan 'simawana·wéyhco·f api·ttí· incokíli hóma sapákla·n
and after tying them to the end of a stick, they stood in front of the arbor posts,

omvlkv setetayen cukele ceskvn escakcvhēcet vpoket omvnts.
omálka 'sititá·yin cokíli cískan iscakcahî·cit apo·kít o·mánc
and they would stick them in the ground at the base of each pillar where they sat.

Em vliketv Fuswvlke, eppucetake esyomatet tafv sopvnhoyvranat 'tetakuecakēt omēs.
imaleykitá foswâlki ippocitá·ki[i] *isyô·ma·tit tá·fa 'sopanhoyáła·nâ·t 'tita·kóyca·ki·t ô·mi·s*
The Bird clan and their sons prepared the feathers to be used in the dance.

Omvlkvn mvherice poyof,
omálkan 'mahiłéyci pó·yo·f
When they were finished fixing all of them,

'sopvnvkvranat este em vliketv vcakkvyēt tafv epucasvkuecēt omēs.
'sopanakáła·nâ·t ísti imaleykitá acakkayí·t tá·fa ipocá·sakoyci·t ô·mi·s
the feathers were given to the dancers according to their clan.

---

[i] Or: *i·ppocitá·ki* (same thing; can say either way).

Nokosvlket ēppucetaken enhuehken aohhatof,
nokosâlkit i·ppocitá·kin ínhoyhkín a·óhha·tô·f
When the Bear clan called their sons, and they came forward,

"Tafv heyv eshueran sēset, safvcketskvrēs," kicet,
tá·fa hiyá ishôyla·n sî·sit sá·fackíckáli·s keycít
they were told, "Take the feather [stick] standing here and enjoy yourself,"

momen Kaccvlkeu ēppucetake enhuehken aohhatan,
mo·mín ka·ccâlkiw i·ppocitá·ki ínhoyhkín a·óhha·tâ·n
and the Tiger clan also called their sons, and they came forward,

Tafv tat sēsē sopanē svrvranat epucasēcēt omēs.
tá·fata·t sî·si·[169] sópa·ní· sálala·nâ·t[170] ipocá·si·cí·t[171] ô·mi·s
and he instructed them to take the feathers they were going to use in dancing.

Monkv emvliketv maketv 'mvrahrvkv estomuset posket vpoket omat
mônka imaleykitá[172] ma·kitá 'małahłaká istô·mosit po·skít apô·kit o·mâ·t
So when all the different clans who take part in the fast

omvlkvt ēppucetaken tafv epucasvkuecē poyof, 'pvnhoyvranate 'tetaket omēs.
omálkat i·ppocitá·kin tá·fa ipoca·sakóyci· po·yô·f panhoyála·nâ·ti títa·kít o·mí·s
had made their sons take their feathers, it was time to dance.

Monkv mv 'pvnkv tat Tafv 'Sopvnkv kicet
mônka[173] ma (?) pánkata·t tá·fa 'sopánka keycít
So that dance was called Tafv 'Sopvnkv ['feather dance'],

Setahvyv-Pvnkv tis hocēfet 'panet omhoyvnts.
sita·hayapánkateys hoci·fít pa·nít ómho·yánc
or it was called Setahvyv-Pvnkv.

'Panē fulletv 'mvrahrvkv vnvcomēn 'pvnhoyēt omēs.
pa·ní· follitá 'małahłaká anacomí·n pánho·yí·t ô·mi·s
Many different dances are danced.

Mv nettv mv 'panat ele-vwiketv 'mvrahkusē vlkēt omēs.
ma (?) nítta ma (?) pa·nâ·t iliaweyki<tá> 'małáhkosi· álki·t ô·mi·s.
The day they dance them, the dance steps are always a little different.

Mohmen mv nettv este hocefkv etvlwv vrahkusē
móhmin ma (?) nitta (?) ísti (?) hocífka (?) itálwa (?) ală̆ⁿhkosi.[174]
And on that day, names were given to people

hocefetvn hocefhuecvkvranat <u>tvsekvyv hocefkvn</u> kicet,
hocifitán hocifhoycakála·nâ·t tasikayá hocífkan keycít[175]
by their tribal towns called <u>tvsekvyv hocefkv</u> ['citizen names'];

cēpvnvke nak vtotkv em vculkv orakof, hocefhuecakēt omvnts.
ci·panáki nâ·k atótka imacólka ola·kô·f hocifhóyca·kí·t o·mánc
when young boys reached the age of doing chores, they would name them.

Mv etvlwv hoktē ehet on, momet echuste ehe, momen ēppucetake esyoman
ma itálwa hoktí· ihít ô·n mo·mít ichósti ihí mo·mín i·ppocitá·ki isyô·ma·n
They name the husbands of women belonging to that town and their daughters' husbands

hocefhuecakēt omēs. Momvranat tektvnkēn ēmet mēkkvlket makakof,
hocifhóyca·kí·t ô·mi·s[176] *mó·mala·nâ·t tíktanki·n i·mít mi·kkâlkit má·ka·kô·f*
and their own sons. When the chiefs gave permission

sulkat enkērkuehohcen vpoket,
sólka·t inki·lkoyhóhcin[177] *apô·kit*
it was announced to everyone,

<u>em vliketv</u> maketv vtēkat vrahrvkvt etohkvlkahket vpokaket
imaleykitá ma·kitá atî·ka·t alahlakát itohkalkáhkit apo·kâ·kit
and they sat in separate groups according to what are called <u>em vliketv</u> ['clans'],

mv em vliketv hvmēcat ēppucetaket poskat liken,
ma (?) imaleykitá (?) hamî·ca·t i·ppocitá·kit po·skâ·t[178] *lèykin*
and the sons of the whole <u>em vliketv</u> would sit fasting,

monkat vpokaken omat, naken vhocefē tayat vkerricet,
móŋka·t apo·kâ·kin o·mâ·t nâ·kin ahocifi·[179] *tá·ya·t akílleycít*
or while they sat, they thought about things they could name them after

'tem opunvyēcet vpoket, hocefkv "Yvt senhērēs" komēt
'timoponáyi·cít apô·kit hocífka yat sinhĭ̆·ⁿli·s kó·mi·t
and sat about discussing them, trying to come up with fitting names,

etem vkvsvmaken omat, ēyvpahyet,
itimakasáma·kín o·mâ·t i·yapáhyit
and if they agreed, they took [the person to be named]

totkētkv pvlhvmke cukuce ofv ohliketv ocan erlihcet,
to·tkí·tka palhámki cokóci ó·fa ohleykitá ô·ca·n iłłéyhcit
to where they kept a chair in a little house on the other side of the central fireplace,

hocefvranē 'tem vkvsamatet hocēfet enhuehhokof,
hocífała·ní· 'timakasâ·ma·tit hoci·fít inhóyho·kô·f[180]
and after they called out the name agreed upon,

"Vyvs. Cēmen cenhuehket okhos" kihohcen,
ayás cí·min cínhoyhkít ókho·s keyhóhcin[181]
he was told, "Go. They're calling your [new name]."

ayet enhuehkē huerat ehomvn rorof,
a·yít ínhoyhkí· hôyła·t ihóman lo·lô·f
And when he arrived in front of the person who had stood calling his name,

hece emhoyof, hocēfē vpokat ehomvn huerekv,
hicí[182] *ímho·yô·f*[183] *hoci·fí· apô·ka·t*[184] *ihóman hôyłika*
when he was given the tobacco, as he stood in front of the naming people,

"Yoh, yoh!" maket esakpvn ohwiyof, omvlkvt "Ya-ah!" kicahken,
yoh yoh ma·kít isákpan óhweyyô·f omálkat ya·h^ keycáhkin
he said, "Yoh, yoh!" and when he held out his arm [or arms], all the others said "Ya-ah!"

"Hayeyvtē hocefkv svsekot punhuervtēn, hocefkv enhayēpet omēkv."
ha·yiyáti· hocífka sasíko·t[185] *ponhôyłati·n*[186] *hocífka inhá·yi·pít*[187] *o·mí·ka*
"He [the young man] stood with no name, so we have made a name for him."

Mēkkvke, tvsekvyv etohkalet kakat
mi·kkakí tasikayá itohkâ·lit ka·kâ·t
The chiefs and the <u>tvsekvyv</u> ['citizens'] sitting together

este-mocvse sulkēn nake vtotetv eyacēt kaket omvntok:
istimocási sólki·n nâ·ki atotitá iyá·ci·t ka·kít o·mánto·k
wanted to assign the new people to do many chores:

"Yvn punhocefēpet, nake pum vtotephoyen punhuervrēs" komēt,

yan ponhocífi·pít nâ·ki pomatotípho·yín ponhôyłáłi·s kô·mi·t

"They have named him for us, now he'll be asked to do things for us," we thought,

"Hocefkv vlicēpēt omēkv, pum enkērkuecvs" makaken,

hocífka aléyci·pí·t o·mí·ka pomiŋki·łkóycas má·ka·kín

"Because we have set the name, announce it to us," they said,

"Kērkuecin mapohicet pvlatket omatskes ca!" makof,

ki·łkoycéyn <m>á·poheycít palâ·tkit o·má·ckis ca^ ma·kô·f

and when he said, "All of you here have heard what I announced,"

poskē vpokat omvlkvt "Ya-ah!" maket vpoket omvnts.

po·ski· apô·ka·t omálkat ya·h^ ma·kít apo·kít o·mánc[188]

all those fasting there would sit saying "Yah!"

Mohmof mv cukorakko nvkvfhotēn arē vtēkat mvn liket,

móhmo·f ma cokolákko nakáfho·tí·n[189] *a·li· atî·ka·t man leykít*

After that time, whenever that square ground came together and he was there,

estofis vrēpvranan licet omhoyēs.

istô·feys ali·pála·nâ·n leycít ómho·yí·s.

they seated him so he was to be included in the functions.

Resolutions Presented at Henryetta February 27, 1941

J. Hill (Haas XVIII:163–181)

Creek Nation ennvkvftetv rakkan nvkvftēt vpoket vkerrickuce 'tetakuecat

Creek Nation innakaftitá łákka·n nakáfti·t apô·kit akiłłeyckocí 'titá·koycâ·t

The Creek National Council was in session preparing resolutions,

vhakvhayv Van Court Court-of-Claims 'tehoyvnē epoyvtē toknawv

aha·kahá·ya Van Court Court-of-Claims 'tihoyaní· ipó·yati· tokná·wa

and the attorney Van Court said to withdraw the money that was in the bank

Wvcenv entoknaphute ofv toknawv likan ossihcet

wacína intokna·photí ó·fa tokná·wa lêyka·n osséyhcit[190]

in the U.S. won through the Court-of-Claims

este ekv vrahkvn epuwahholekvs maket fvccēcvtēt ohhvrepekvs.
ísti iká ałáhkan ipowahholíkas ma·kít fácci·catí·t ohhalipíkas
and to distribute it per capita, ['Let the judgment be sent out?']

Feb. 27, 1941. Creek Nation ennvkvftetv rakkan nvkaftet vpoket
Feb. 27, 1941. Creek Nation innakaftitá lákka·n naká·ftit apô·kit
Feb. 27, 1941. The Creek National Council was in session

vkerrickuce hayat toknawv Court-of-Claims etehoyvnē
akiłłeyckocí ha·yâ·t tokná·wa Court-of-Claims itihoyáni·
preparing resolutions for the money now in the U.S. Treasury

Creek Nation enake hakvtē toknawv Wvcenv entoknaphute vtehkat
Creek Nation inâ·ki há·kati· tokná·wa wacína intokna·photí atíhka·t
which, through the Court-of Claims, had become Creek Nation's;

estomēcvkatet etvlwv safvcecicvkē tayat, vkerrickv hiyomēt 'tetakēt os.
istomî·caka·tít itálwa sa·facicéycaki· tâ·ya·t akiłłéycka hayyó·mi·t títa·kí·t ô·ⁿs
and on what they could do with it to satisfy the nation, this is what they decided.

Court-of-Claims etehoyvnē vhakvhayv Van Court epoyvtē
Court-of-Claims itihoyáni· aha·kahá·ya Van Court ipo·yatí·
Through the Court-of-Claims, the attorney Van Court had won

toknawv Wvcenv entoknaphute vtehkan, one-third fekhonnihcet,
tokná·wa wacína intokna·photí atíhka·n one-third fikhonnéyhcit
monies now in the U.S. Treasury: one-third was to be retained

two-third ohhontv vpvkēn ossihcet,
two-third ohhónta apáki·n osséyhcit
and two-thirds plus interest was to be withdrawn,

vhakvhayv Niebel epoyvtē toknawv likat omvlkvn ohhontv vpvkēn fvyēcihcet
aha·kahá·ya Niebel (nepil) ipo·yatí· tokná·wa lêyka·t omálkan ohhónta apáki·n fayi·céyhcit
and all the monies that the attorney Niebel had won plus interest were to be set aside

ekv fēketvn punhahoyekvs momat hiyomēt omvrēs.
iká fi·kitán ponha·hoyíkas mo·mâ·t hayyó·mi·t omáli·s
with payments made to us per capita, and this is the way it will be.

Creek Nation este vhonkvtkv hayof,
Creek Nation ísti ahoŋkátka ha·yô·f
When Creek Nation conducted a census,

April 1, 1899 omof este wenakēt omvten omat,
April 1, 1899 ó·mo·f ísti wina·kí·t ó·matin o·má·t
the Dawes commissioner was given the authority that if a person was alive on April 1, 1899,

elēpvtētis vhonkvtkvrēs makē Dawes Commissioner yekcetv emhohyē
ili·patí·teys ahoŋkátkáli·s ma·ki· Dawes Commissioner yikcitá imhóhyi·
even if he had died since, he would be counted;

vhonkvtakvtē elēpvtē estomis catv vwolicvt cvwepvrēs.
ahóŋkata·katí· ili·patí· istô·meys cá·ta awoléycat cawípáli·s
and for those counted who had since died the next of kin would claim it.

Momis hiyomēt omvrēs. Dawes Commissioner este vhvnkatat
mo·mêys hayyó·mi·t omáli·s Dawes Commissioner ísti aháŋka·tâ·t[191]
But it will be like this. Before the Dawes Commissioner Census

April 1, 1899 oreko monkv este pvsatkvtē sulke vhonkvtkv vpahyet
April 1, 1899 oliko· móŋka ísti pasa·tkatí· sólki ahoŋkátka apáhyit
of April 1, 1899, many dead people were included in the count,

ēkvnv 160 acres epucasēcahket este hvmkusis este hokkolē omēn hahyet,
i·kaná 160 acres ipoca·si·cáhkit[192] *ísti hámkoseys ísti hokkô·li*[i] *ó·mi·n háhyit*
and received 160 acres of land, a single person was counted as two,

ēkvnv 160 acres likē hokkolen pucasehcet, este tuccēnē omētis
i·kaná 160 acres léyki· hokkò·lin poca·sihcit[193] *ísti toccî·ni· ó·mi·téys*
receiving two sections of 160 acres, and there were even ones

vhonkahtet este hvmkusat ēkvnv 160 acres likē tuccēnis pucasēcet
ahoŋkáhtit ísti hámkosa·t i·kaná 160 acres léyki· toccî·neys pocá·si·cít
counted as three people, with a single person receiving three sections of 160 acres;

---

[i] Or: *hokkolí·*.

Creek Nation tvsekvyv tokis sulkēn vhonkahtet
Creek Nation tasikayá tó·keys sólki·n ahoŋkáhtit
we knew that many non-citizens of the Creek Nation were counted

ēkvnv 160 acres epucasēcvtēt omat kērrēkv,
i·kaná 160 acres ipoca·sí·cati·t ô·ma·t kî·łłi·ka
and received 160 acres of land,

mvt vpvkekon este ekv vrahkv 'metekvpicet omhoyvrēs.
mat apákiko·n ísti iká ałáhka 'mitikápeycít omhoyáli·s
so excluding those, [the funds] will be divided per capita.

Ēkvnv enrahkv asetetayēckvn afēkē estomis fvcceko
i·kaná inláhka a·sitita·yi·ckan á·fi·kí· istô·meys fácciko·
This was to make up for land claimed by [non-citizens]

este vhvnkvthoyvtēt vpvkekon afēket omhoyvrēs makeyēt os.
ísti ahaŋkathoyáti·t apákiko·n á·fi·kít omhoyáli·s ma·kiyí·t ô·ⁿs
in the count. They must not be in the group receiving compensation, the Council said.

Cokvhayv-rakko, este-cate enkvmesenv, mont enwiketv 'rem ētv estomis ohtoteyēt os.
co·kaha·yałákko isticá·ti iŋkamisiná mónt inweykitá 'limí·ta[194] istô·meys óhto·tiyi·t ô·ⁿs
To the Secretary General, the Indian Commissioner, and all other officers, we so order.

James Hill

Feb. 27, 1941. Creek Nation ennvkvftetv rakkan nvkaftet vkerrickuce hayat
Feb. 27, 1941. Creek Nation innakaftitá łákka·n nakâ·ftit akiłłeyckocí ha·yá·t
Feb. 27, 1941. The Creek National Council was meeting making resolutions,

cokvhayv-rakko, este-cate enkvmesenv, mont enwiketv ētvo Wasentv vpokan
co·kaha·yałákko isticá·ti iŋkamisiná mónt inweykitá í·taw wa·sínta[195] apô·ka·n
and to the Secretary General, the Indian Commissioner, and other officers in Washington,

ohtotēt os. Este na-lvste pucase seko hakof,
óhto·tí·t ô·ⁿs ísti na·lásti 'pocá·si síko· ha·kô·f
we send orders. When the black people became freedmen,

Creek Nation vpvkvrēn July 1866 omof tenfvccetv eshahoyvtē
Creek Nation apákáli·n July 1866 ô·mo·f tinfaccitá ishá·ho·yatí·
an agreement was made in July, 1866 that they would become part of the Creek Nation,

Creek Nation esten Dawes kvmesenvt vhvnkatof,
Creek Nation ístin Dawes kamisinát aháŋka·tô·f
and when the Dawes Commission took a count of the Creek Nation,

ena-lvste vpvkēn vhonkvtvtēt omen, mv vrahkv ohhvkerrickv hakat hiyomēt:
ina·lásti apáki·n ahoŋkatáti·t ô·min ma aláhka ohhakiłłéycka ha·kâ·t hayyó·mi·t
the black people were included in the count, and for them the plans were like this:

Court-of-Claims etehoyvnē vhakv-hayv Van Court ēpoyvtē toknawv likan
Court-of-Claims itihoyáni· aha·kahá·ya Van Court i·pó·yati· tokná·wa lêyka·n
of the monies that the attorney Van Court won through the Court-of-Claims,

one-third enwikeyēt os, estomēceyan hērēs komat ēmet celayvkepvrēn,
one-third ínweykiyí·t ô·ⁿs istomî·ciya·n hĭ·ⁿli·s ko·mâ·t í·mit cila·yakípáli·n
we give one third to do whatever they decide is best with it,

mohmen vhakv-hayv Niebel epoyvtē toknawv
móhmin aha·kahá·ya Niebel ipó·yati· tokná·wa
and the money that the attorney Niebel won,

Wvcenv entoknaphute ofv likat apunkerreko tayēs makeyēt os.
wacína intokna·photí ó·fa lêyka·t a·ponkíłłiko· tâ·yi·s ma·kiyí·t ô·ⁿs
which is in the United States Treasury, they will not have any part in that, we state.

July, 1866 etenfvccetv hahkofvn, ena-lvste tat Creek Nation entvsekvyv hakvtēt onkv,
July, 1866 itinfaccitá háhko·fán ina·lástita·t[196] Creek Nation intasikayá há·kati·t ôŋka
After the agreement of July, 1866, black people became Creek Nation citizens,

etenfvccetv 1866 hahoyeko monken, ēkvnv etemkv hakvtē ocan vpvkēt omen,
itinfaccitá 1866 ha·hoyíko·[197] môŋkin i·kaná itímka ha·kati· ô·ca·n apáki·t ô·min
so before the 1866 agreement, the land allotments included them,

ēkvnv vhopayē Wvcenv esfullof,
i·kaná ahópa·yí· wacína ísfollô·f
and when the United States was surveying the land,

mv ēkvnv Sakeyv vpvkekon vhopahyet ēkvnv 160 acres pum etekvpihocvtēt
ma i·kaná sa·kiyá apákiko·n ahopáhyit i·kaná 160 acres pomitikapeyhocáti·t
not including the Sauk and Fox land, 160 acres was allotted to each of us;

mohmof mv Sakeyv em ēkvnv omē likvtē
móhmo·f ma sa·kiyá imi·kaná ó·mi· leykatí·
after that, the land where the Sauk and Fox were living

Court-of-Claims ehomv akvwahpet fvccēcvlke fvccēcat
Court-of-Claims ihóma a·kawáhpit facci·câlki fácci·câ·t
was brought before the Court-of-Claims, and the judges ruled

Creek Nation em ēkvnv fvccvt os makēt fvccēcakof,
Creek Nation imi·kaná fáccat ò·ⁿs ma·kí·t facci·ca·kô·f
that it was properly Creek Nation's land; after so ruling,

ēkvnv enrahkv yvt 'tetayēs makof,
i·kaná inɫáhka yat 'titâ·yi·s ma·kô·f
they set a price for the land,

Wvcenvt fēkvrēn fvccēhocvtē toknawv likat
wacínat fi·káɫi·n facci·ho·catí· tokná·wa lèyka·t
and the money being held that the United States was to pay from the judgment,

pucaseko hakvtē honvpse apunkerreko tayēs.
'poca·sikó· há·kati·[198] honápsi a·ponkíɫlikŏ· tâ·yi·s.
the freedmen and their offspring should have no part in.

    James Hill

Notes on the Ball Game

J. Hill (Haas XIV:169–173)

Etvlwv tvleporv etem afackat pokkechetv etenfaccof,
itálwa 'talipóɫa itimá·fa·ckâ·t pokkichitá itínfa·ccô·f
When they agreed to play a game with a foreign town,

afvcketv tuccēnen monkat ostis etem afvckvranet etenfvciyen etem afackof,
a·fackitá tocci·nin móŋka·t ô·steys itima·fáckala·nit itinfacêyyin itimá·fa·ckô·f
a contract was made to play three or four games, and when they play,

etvlwv hvmkatet hokkolen vnrapv em poyen, hvmkusen pvlhvmket epoyen omat,
itálwa hámka·tit hokkò·lin anlá·pa ímpo·yín hámkosin palhámkit[199] *ipo·yín o·mâ·t*
if one town defeats an opponent two times, and the other side wins just one,

hokkolē epoyaten, mv etvlwvn enhesse monkat oh-vpvkē hakēt omēs.
hokkò·li· ipò·ya·tin ma itálwan inhíssi móŋka·t ohhapakí· ha·kí·t ô·mi·s
they become friends or members of the town winning twice.

Osten 'tenfaccvten omat, etvlwv hvmkat tuccēnen epoyen,
ô·stin tínfa·ccatin o·mâ·t itálwa hámka·t[200] *tocci·nin ipò·yin*
If they agree to four [games], and one town wins three,

vnrapv hvmkusen epoyen omat, tuccēnē epoyan enhesse monkat oh-vpvkē hakēt omēs.
anlá·pa hámkosin[201] *ipo·yín o·mâ·t tocci·ni· ipò·ya·n inhíssi móŋka·t ohhapakí·*[i] *ha·kí·t ô·mi·s*[ii]
and the opponent wins one, they become friends or members of the one winning three.

Mv entotkētkv hvmke entotkētkv maketv poskē vpokē enhvthvyvtke totkv etēcat,
ma into·tkí·tka hámki into·tkí·tka ma·kitá po·skí· apo·kí·[202] *inhathayátki tó·tka iti·câ·t*
Entotkētkv hvmke ['same fire'] means they sit fasting having [the same] fire lit all night,

enheleswv ocēn omekv, mata heleshakv ētvpomē etvlwv enheleswv sēyvfastēt
inhilíswa ó·ci·n ô·mika ma·tá· 'hilishá·ka i·tapó·mi· itálwa inhilíswa sí·yafa·stí·t
and have their [same] medicine. They're a town that uses the same preparation of medicines

poskēt etvlwvt likan mvn entotkētkv hvmke maket okhoyēt omēs.
po·skí·t itálwat leykâ·n[203] *man into·tkí·tka hámki ma·kít ókho·yí·t ô·mi·s*[iii]
when they fast. That is what they mean by entotkētkv hvmke ['same fire'].

---

[i] *ohhapakí·* = *iyohhapakí·* same as 'friend'.
[ii] Okchayi now "friends" with Hilabi, Tuka. Oyokofki same town as Hilabi + Tukpafka —
friends with Tuk. now. If Hilabi + Okchayi played, Okchayi might win first game + Hilabi
the next two; or Hilabi might win first game, Okchayi second, + Hilabi third; or Hilabi win
first two games + Okchayi win last — in any event, Hilabi would be the winner of the "set"
— the most games is what counts.
[iii] Members of town that got beat would not be *into·tkí·tka hámki* — they would keep their
own ways.

The Inter-Town Ball Game

J. Hill (Haas V:159–177)

Etvlwv	hokkolē	etenrvpē	pokkechvranat
itálwa	*hokkô·li·*	*itinłapí·*	*pokkíchała·nâ·t*[204]
towns	two	opposing each other	going to play ball

When two opposing towns are going to play ball,

encukorakkon	nvkaftet	pokkechetv	opunvyēcet
incokolákkon	*naka·ftít*	*pokkichitán*	*opónayi·cít*
its buskground	meeting (there)	to play ball	talk about

they meet at their grounds to talk about the ballgame,

sulkat	eyacvkēton	omat
sôlka·t	*iya·cakí·ton*	*o·mâ·t*
the majority	if they (the majority) want (to play ball)	if they do

and if the majority agree,

keriyet	etvlwv	estomatet	em afackat	komakat	kerrvkēt
kiłâyyit	*itálwa*	*istô·ma·tit*	*imá·fa·ckâ·t*	*ko·mâ·ka·t*	*kiłłaki·t*[i]
find out	towns	whichever (towns)	to make joy with	they want	they know

they find out which towns want to play stickball,

fullet	okakekv	enhopohyet
follít	*oka·kiká*	*inhopóhyit*
being about	they have decided	select from (other towns)

and they know which teams they play, so they select them and say,

"Heyv	etvlwvn	em pokkechēpvkēs,	pum vkvsamen	omat"
hiyá	*itálwan*	*impokkíchi·paki·s*	*pomákasa·mín*	*o·mâ·t*
and this	town	we can play ball with (this town)	if they agree with us	if

"We can play [that] town if they agree with us."

mahket	este	hokkolen	vtuthoyen
máhkit	*ísti*	*hokkô·lin*	*atothô·yin*
said	people	two	they send

They send two people,

---

[i] Raiford says the first word should be *ima·fackitá kô·ma·t kiłłaki·t.*

mv   etvlwv   ehomahtvn   erem onayet   okat   "'Este   mvnettvlket
ma   itálwa   ihomá·htan   ilímona·yít   o·kâ·t   ísti   manittâlkit
that   town   its leader   go and tell   say   people   the young (people)
and they tell that town's leader, saying, "We have been sent

pokko   hvlwēcet   etem assen   hoyopēpvkēs'   maket
pókko   hálwi·cít   itíma·ssín[205]   *hoyópi·paki·s   ma·kít*
ball   they throw up   run after   we can look on   they say
with the message that they wish to watch the young people

opunvkv   as pututhoyēt   os"   kicof,   vyoposket   okat,
oponaká   a·spotothoyí·t   ô·ⁿs   kaycô·f   ayópo·skít   o·kâ·t
talk   news they have sent by us   it is   when they say   in reply   they say
throw the ball up and run." They answer back,

"Mvnettvlke tat   nvcọmusēt   ont   'to-kun-celakv tis   kerrvkekotot   omis,
manittâlkita·t   nacŏ·ⁿmosi·t   ônt   tokoncilá·kateys[206]   *kiłłakíko·toⁱ*[207]   *o·mêys*
the young people   just a few   are   even to handle ball-sticks   they don't know   but
"There are only a few young people, and they do not know how to handle the ball-sticks,

enkērkuecin   ēmet   estomēn   makaken   omat   kerratskvrēs"
iŋkí·łkoycéyn   í·mit   istó·mi·n   má·ka·kín   o·mâ·t   kíłłá·ckáłi·s
I will tell them about it   themselves   whatever   they say   (if)   you-all will know
but I will tell them, and you will know what they say."

kihcen,   yefulhokēpēt omēs.
kéyhcin   'yifólhoki·pí·t[i] *ô·mi·s*
he told them   and they (2) generally go back.
So he tells them, and they go back.

Mohmen   mv   etvlwv   encukorakko   nvkvfiten
móhmin   ma   itálwa   incokołákko   nakafêytin
Then   that   town (at)   its buskground   they assemble
Then they meet at that town's buskground

---

[i] Raiford: *yọfólhoki·pí·t.*

"Afvcketvn   cem eyahocvket   onkv,   vhēricet   ēyvkerrihcet
aˑfackitán   *cimiyaˑhôˑcakit*[208]   *oŋká*   *ahiˑⁿɬeycit*   *iˑyakiɬɬéyhcit*
to have fun   with you-all they want   do   be careful   and [consider it]
and say, "We'd like to play ball with you, so consider it carefully

opunvkv   estenfulecicaks"   kihcen,   vpoket
oponaká   *istinfolicéycaks*   *kéyhcin*   *apôˑkit*
talk, news   return the (news, word)   he said   they stayed, sat (there) in assemblage
and send word back." They meet

opunvkv   fulecicet   okat,   "Etvlwv   hvmkusis   etekvpakē
oponaká   *folíceycít*   *oˑkâˑt*   *itálwa*   *hâmkoseys*   *itíkapaˑkiˑ*
word   returning   said   town   only one   divide
and send word back. "We are only one town divided,

fulhoyvnto   omuset   omēto   estomis
fólhoˑyánto·   *ôˑmosit*   *oˑmíˑto·*   *istôˑmeys*
like they generally do   generally do   (being if) they do that   being if
but whatever happens

pokkēchet   fullvranvkan   okhoyēs"   maket,
pókkiˑchit   *fóllaɬaˑnakâˑn*   *ókhoˑyíˑs*   *maˑkít*
we to play ball   will be around   as, like they say   they said
we will go and play ball as they say," they say.

vkvsvmaken   omat   opunvkv   fulecicahken
akasámaˑkín   *oˑmâˑt*   *oponaká*   *foliceycáhkin*
if they agree   if   word   they return (the word)
And if they agree and send word back,

vpohē   fullvtē   puhakof,
apoˑhíˑ   *follatiˑ*   *pohaˑkôˑf*
they've asked for   those that being around (asked for it)   when they heard it
when those who had gone around asking for it hear it,

nvkvfitet,   este   opunahoyat   herakemahan
nakafêytit[209]   *ísti*   *oponáˑhoˑyâˑt*   *hiɬâˑⁿkimâˑhaˑn*[210]
they meet   people   that talk   very good (speakers)
they meet and

ostē 'senhoyvnētis enhopohyen,
ô·sti· sinhoyáni·teys inhopóhyin
four even more than (four) they picked out, selected
select four or more very good speakers,

estofvn mont ēkvnv estvmvn etehecvranat enkērkuecēt omēs.
istó·fan mónt i·kaná ístaman itihicála·ná·t[211] iŋkí·lkoycí·t ô·mi·s
whenever then the ground wherever to see each other they are told are
and they are informed when and at what ground they are to see each other.

Mv etvlwv afvcketv enpohohvtēt mohmen mvo nvkvfitet,
ma itálwa a·fackitá inpó·ho·hati·t móhmin maw' nakafëytit
That town to have fun with they have asked Then that, too they meet
The town that asked to play meets too

este opunayv herakemahakētan nvcomen komēpat
isti oponá·ya hiłǎ·ⁿkima·hâ·ki·tá·n[212] nacô·min ko·mi·pa·t
spokesman very good ones, too however many they want
and selects as many good speakers as they want,

enhopohyen mv etoh-vpehyet etenpunahoyet,
inhopóhyin mat itohhapíhyit itinponá·ho·yít
they select that they go together (both towns) they talk to each other
and they go to one another and talk.

opunvkv yekcvkētis sulkēn es opunahoyet komēpat 'svpoket,
oponaká yikcakí·teys sólki·n isoponá·ho·yít ko·mi·pa·t 'sapô·kit
speech, words harsh, even several, lots they talk, say if they wish they stay (talking)
They remain discussing what they want in harsh words even

netta nvrkvpv 'senhoyanis vpohket,
nittá·[213] nałkapá sinhoyâ·neys apóhkit
day a half (-day) even more (than half a day) they stay, remain (in conference)
and stay half a day or more.

pokkechvranet etem vkvsamen omat,
pokkichala·nít itimakása·mín o·mâ·t
(if they're going) to play ball if they agree if
If they agree to play ball,

etenfvccetv yekcēn etenfaccēt   omēs komēt vpoket
itinfaccitá[i] *yíkci·n* *itinfâ·cci·t*[ii]   *o·mí·s* *kó·mi·t* *apô·kit*
agreement binding if we agree to, have made do if you think they stay
they feel they have made a binding agreement.

netta estofvn pokko hvlwvranatu   hvyakpotatu
nittá· *istô·fan* *pókko* *hálwała·nâ·tów*[214]   *hayakpó·ta·tów*[215]
day whatever ball to be tossed up, hoisted too prairie, too
They have an understanding about what day the ball will be thrown up

estvmvt omvranat etenkerrahket   'tekvpahket fulēcat
ístamat *omáła·nâ·t* *itiŋkiłłáhkit*   *'tikapáhkit* *foli·câ·t*
wherever it is to be they have an understanding they separate going back
and which stickball field it will be too, and they separate and go back

encukorakkon nvkvftēt vpokaken fullet onkv
incokołákkon *nakáfti·t* *apo·kâ·kin* *follít ôŋka*
to their buskground in assemblage still remain being around are
and meet in their buskground and still remain.

etenfvccetv estomēn hayakat
itinfaccitá *istó·mi·n* *ha·yâ·ka·t*
their agreement the kind they have made
The kind of agreement they made

este sulkan enkērkuecakēt omēs.
ísti sôlka·n *iŋki·łkóyca·kí·t ô·mi·s*
the majority convey the agreement to (them)
is conveyed to the majority.

Mohmofvn etvlwvt vrahkusat ēyvkerricaket fullēpēt omēs.
móhmo·fan *itálwat* *ală·ⁿhkosa·t* *i·akiłłéyca·kít* *fólli·pí·t* *ô·mi·s*
after that the town itself considers it being around are
Then the town takes special consideration of itself.

---

[i] Or: *itim͟faccitá*.
[ii] Or: *itinfâ·cci·t*.

Estomēt fulleyat   em poyeyē   tayēs   komat,
istó·mi·t folliyâ·t   *impó·yiyi·*   *tâ·yi·s*   *kô·ma·t*
in what way (whatever way we do)   we can beat them   can   they consider
They use their own judgment and consider how can we beat them

ēem vhoporrenket   etvlwv   enhesse   ensulkē tis
i·imahopółłinkít[216]   *itálwa*   *inhíssi*   *insolkí·teys*
they use their own judgment   town   its friends   the most, majority
and try to come out ahead

es etohfvnketv   komēt   fullēt   omēs.
isitohfankitá   *kó·mi·t*   *follí·t*   *ô·mi·s*
to have (more friends)   tries
in having more town friends.

Eto-lanofv   estvt   fulletv   hērvrēs   komen omat
itola·nó·fa   *ístat*   *follitá*   *hĭ·ⁿłáli·s*   *ko·mín o·mâ·t*
in the green woods   wherever   to be around   will be the best place   think   if they do
They consider where in the forest would be the best place

pokkechetv   hvyakpo   'tempvranēn   ehvpo hahyet   vpokēs.
pokkichitá   *hayakpó·*   *timpałâ·ni·n*   *ihapó· háhyit*   *apó·ki·s*
to play ball   prairie   near (will be near)   they make camp   stay there
to make a camp near the ball field and stay.

Pokkvnockvn   kicet   mv   nerē   este   sulkēt   nvkaften
pokkanóckan   *keycít*   *ma*   *nilí·*   *ísti*   *sólki·t*   *nakâ·ftin*
ball-dance   called   that   night   people   a lot   meet
It's called pokkvnockvn ['ball sleep'], and many people meet that night;

etvlwv   hvmkē   fullvcokat   fvccv   vhecēn
itálwa   *hámki·*   *follacóka·t*   *fácca*   *ahíci·n*
town   one   seem to be about   direction   looking (towards), facing
they set chairs up

ohliketv   etetakuecet,
ohleykitá   *itita·kôycit*
chairs   they prepare (chairs facing that way)
facing the other town,

<u>paskofv</u>   kicet   eto-wakkvn   hayet,
pa·skó·fa   *kaycít*   *itowákkan*   *ha·yít*
inside of the cleared ball-dance ground   called   benches   they make
and they make benches in the <u>paskofv</u> ['swept area'];

mv   ehomvn   'to-yakpe   hokkolen   cakcvhēcē
ma   *ihóman*   *'toyákpi*   *hokkô·lin* *cakcahí·ci·*
that   in front of   forked poles   two   they stand them up
they stick two forked poles in the ground in front of that,

eto-polokē   cutkusēn   cvpkēn   ohtakhayet,
itopoló·ki·   *cótkosi·n*   *cápki·n*   *ohtakhâ·yit*
round poles   small ones   long one   put across
put a small, long pole across,

mvn   'to-kunhe   ensulkē   estomusen   esyihocat,
man   *'tokónhi*   *insolkí·*   *istô·mosin*   *isyeyhô·ca·t*
there   ball-sticks   number   whatever there is   have been brought
and however many ball-sticks have been brought there,

omvlkvn   pokkēchē   'svretv   naket   omat
omálkan   *pókki·chi·*   *'salitá*   *nâ·kit*   *ò·ma·t*
all   playing ball   to have (while playing ball)   whatever   it is
and whatever will be used for playing ball,

omvlkvn oh-ocet,   mv elecvn   honvntake   hokkolet kaket
omálkan *ohhô·cit*   *ma ilícan*   *honantá·ki*   *hokkô·lit* *kâ·kit*
all of it   they put on it under that   men   two   sitting
they put all on top of it. Below that sit two men,

hvmket   vrkvshakucen nafket   hayēcen,
hámkit   *ałkasha·kocín na·fkít*   *há·yi·cín*
one of them   little drum   beating on making it sound
one beating on a small drum and making it sound

hvmket   svokvn ēset   mvyatet   hayēcen   yvhiket   kaken
hámkit   *sáwkan* *i·sit*   *maya·tít*   *há·yi·cín*   *yahaykít* *kâ·kin*
the other one a rattle taking motion making making it sound they 2 sing sitting
and one shaking a rattle while they sit singing.

era topvrvn   hoktvket   svpaklet yvhikakvtēton
ilá· topáłan   hoktakít   sapá·klit yaháyka·katí·ton
to their backs the women stand   from singing
Behind them the women are standing;

fekhonnihcet   este honvntake   eto-wakkv oh-vpokvtē   omvlkvt pahēcet,
fikhonnéyhcit   ísti honantá·ki   itowákka   ohhapô·kati·   omálkat pá·hi·cít
they stop them the men   benches   that sit on (benches) all   they whoop
they stop them from singing, and the men sitting on the benches all whoop,

ohpefatiket   'to-kunhen   omvlkvn   cahwet   pefatket yahket
ohpifa·têykit   'tokónhin   omálkan[217]   *cáhwit   pifa·tkit ya·hkit*
they run towards ball-sticks all of them   get, take running   they whoop
run toward them, take all the ball-sticks, and run and yell

fulutēcet   fullvtētot   wihket   vpokēt omēs.
folóti·cít   follatí·tot   wéyhkit   apo·kí·t ò·mi·s
they circle around they do that for a while they quit   and sit down
and circle around. They do that for a while, quit, and sit down.

Momakēt   fullet   omēs.   Roricat
mó·ma·kí·t   follít   o·mi·s   łółeycâ·t
that's the way they do being around are   when they get there
That's the way they go around. When they get there,

nocicen   hvyvtiken   vpēyat   hvyakpo   tempen   ervpohket,
noceycín   hayatêykin   api·yá·t   hayakpó·   tímpin   iłapóhkit
they sleep   till day   they go   prairie   near   they stop there
they sleep till daylight, and when they go, they stop near the field.

este   nvcomaket   omvranat   etenkeriyē
ísti   nacomá·kit   omála·nâ·t   itiŋkiłêyyi·
people how many   there will be (who will play)   there is an understanding
There is an understanding about how many people there will be,

vhonkvthohyen   ēkayahket   takhvkvn   takhvyahket
ahoŋkathóhyin[218]   *i·ka·yáhkit   takhakán   takhayáhkit*
they are counted by somebody they strip flaps   they put on
so they count them, they strip, put on breechcloths,

ensulkē	momᵥlkuset	yakyapv	sēhokat
insolkí·	*mô·mǎⁿlkosit*	*yakyá·pa*	*si·hô·ka·t*
many	just now (many)	ball-poles	where they stand

and equal numbers meet

em eto nvrkvpvn		etenrahpet
imíto nalkapán		*itinláhpit*
half-way between, midway (between the two poles)		they meet there

half-way between the goalposts.

ensulkē	etekeriyet	vpokē	cahkepicēt	etekvpahket	onkv
insolkí·	*itikiłêyyit*	*apo·kí·*	*cahkipêyci·t*	*itikapáhkit*	*ôŋka*
just how many	they agree on	bunches	five	they are divided	are

Having agreed on the number, they separate into groups of five,

enkẹrkakusēt	ensvpakletvn	ohpefatiket
iŋkĭ·ⁿlka·kosi·t	*insapaklitán*	*ohpifa·têykit*
they understand	where they are to stand	they run to (their position)

so they understand well, and when they've run to their positions

ersvpaklēpof,	pokko	hvlwēn	em vwihohken
ilsapákli·pô·f	*pókko*	*hálwi·n*	*imaweyhóhkin*
when they get there and stand	ball	up high	is thrown for them

and are standing there, the ball is thrown up high for them,

ralatkof,	etem asset	pokko	vwikekon
lá·la·tkô·f	*itíma·ssít*	*pókko*	*awéykikon*
when it comes down	they run after it	ball	from throwing

and when it comes down, they give chase, earnestly trying to prevent

etekomē	hẹret	etem vnvttēcat
itikó·mi·	*hǐ·ⁿlit*	*itimanátti·câ·t*
(preventing) each other	earnestly	they try to prevent, hinder one another

each other from throwing the ball.

'to-kunhen	'seterokafet	etenwaret
'tokónhin	*'sitíłoka·fit*	*itínwa·lít*[219]
(with) ball-sticks	one another they pound, hit (thrash)	cut one another

They whip each other with ball-sticks, cut each other,

catv	'svfihhonicuset	fullan		afvcketvn	kicet	okvnts.
cá·ta	*'safeyhhonêycosit*	*follâ·n*		*a·fackitán*	*keycít*	*o·kánc*
blood	streaming down	going about that way		fun	call it	they do

and go about with blood streaming down. And they called it fun.[i]

Match-Game Between Hilabi and Okfuskee, about 1876 (Cvtaksohkv monkat Akfvske Etvlwv espokē Helvpe Etvlwv emafackat, Ohrolopē 1876)[ii]

J. Hill (Haas XIV:11–45)

Akfvske	Etvlwv	emmēkko	Cesse Mēkko	este	hvmket	vpvkēn
akfáski	*itálwa*	*immí·kko*	*cissimí·kko*	*ísti*	*hámkit*	*apáki·n*[220]
Okfuskee	town's	chief	Tcissimeeko	man	one	with him (the Chief)

The Akfvske town chief Chissi Micco, joined by another person,

Helvpe	Etvlwv	emmēkko	Kosv Haco	hocefkēt	liken,
hilápi	*itálwa*	*immí·kko*	*ko·sahá·co*	*hocífki·t*	*lêykin*
Hilabi	town's	chief	Kosahajo	named	(where) living

came to where the Hilabi town chief named Coosa Harjo lived,

emvlahoket	etemafackēt	fullēn,
imala·hô·kit	*itimá·fa·ckí·t*	*follí·n*[221]
they 2 came to	playing ball	were around

and they were around playing ball:

"'Epupvlhvmkvtēt	ont	omis,	hvtvm	empohhatsken	emafackeyēs,'
ipopalhámkati·t	*ônt*	*o·mêys*	*hatâm*	*impohhá·ckin*[222]	*imá·fa·ckiyí·s*
(we) got beat	did	it was	another (game)	asking for	we (went) to play

"The young ones said, 'Although we were beat, ask for another [game],

---

[i] The Kaylêychis used to play against each other — those living near the buskground against those living far away. H. used to play with them. He wasn't afraid, because he was well guarded by the other players (V:176).

[ii] Title: *cataksó·hka móŋka·t akfáski itálwa ispo·ki· hilápi itálwa imá·fa·ckâ·t ohłolopí· cokpiłákko hámkin cókpi 'cinapâ·kin pá·li 'kolapâ·kin i·pohkâ·ka·t má·hitá·ti·s* 'The last time Chataksohka or Okfuskee Town played Hilabi Town was about eighteen hundred and seventy-six [1876].'

'mvnettvlket makaken, welakēs," maken,
'manittálkit má·ka·kín wila·kí·s ma·kín
[the young ones] said we have come he said
and we can play,' so we have come," [Chissi Micco] said.

Kosv Haco vyoposket okat:
ko·sahá·co ayópo·skít o·kâ·t
Kosahajo answered and said
Coosa Harjo answered and said:

"Cēpvnvke vwąhuset omētis kerrvkuecin estomēn makaken omat
ci·panáki awǎ·ⁿhosit[223] ô·mi·teys kiłłakoycéyn istó·mi·n má·ka·kín o·mâ·t
my boys scattered are, but I finding out what they say when I do
"My boys are scattered, but when I find out what they say,

vyoposkē 'ponvkv vnhecetskvrēs," kihcen, Cesse Mēkko folkehpen,
ayoposki· 'ponaká anhicíckáli·s" *kéyhcin cissimí·kko folkihpin*
answer word you will hear from me he said Tcissimeeko went back
you will hear word from me," he said, and Chissi Micco went back.

Kosv Haco, "Entvsekvyv Helvpe Etvlwv toyetskat
ko·sahá·co intasikayá hilápi itálwa tô·yícka·t
Kosahajo its citizens (of) Hilabi town you who
Coosa Harjo said, "Citizens of Hilabi Town,

cenkepayv pihketv ecohhayekv nvkvftaks," kihcen, ennvkaftof,
ciŋkipá·ya payhkitá icohhá·yika nakáftaks kéyhcin innaka·ftô·f
your enemy a whoop made on you get together he said when they got together
your enemy has made a whoop on you, so get together." When they got together, he said,

"Cemahkopvnetv yahocekv, ēyvkerrihcet
cimahkopanitá ya·hô·cika i·yakiłłéyhcit
to play with you they want think of yourselves (as a town)
"They want to play with you, so think of yourselves [as a town]

estomvrēn makatskat, 'ponvkv estenfolecicarēs," kihcen,
istó·máli·n ma·ká·cka·t 'ponaká istinfolicéycá·li·s kéyhcin
what we shall do you must decide word I will return he said
and when you decide what to do, I will send word back."

vpoket   afvcketv   eyacēt   makat:
apó·kit   *a·fackitá*   *iyá·ci·t*[224]   *ma·kâ·t*
all seated   to play   they wanted   saying
All those seated wanted to play and said:

"Emafackēt fulleyvtēt on okakekv emafvckeyvrēs ci!"   maket,
imá·fa·cki·t folliyáti·t ô·n oka·kiká *ima·fáckiyáli·s cay^*   *ma·kit*
we played with them before   and we shall play with them again they said
"We played with them before, so we shall play with them again!" they said

mēkkotat   'ponvkv   enwikahken.   Kosv Haco tat,
mí·kkota·t   *'ponaká*   *inweykáhkin*   *ko·sahá·cota·t*
the chief   word   they left   Kosahajo
and left word with the chief. Kosv Haco said:

"Cesse Mēkko   toyetskat,   hiyomat   afvcketv   maketskvnkē
cissimí·kko   *tô·yícka·t*   *hayyô·ma·t*   *a·fackitá*   *ma·kíckaŋkí·*
Tcissimeeko   you who are   now   to play, game   you have asked
"Chissi Micco, you have asked to play now, and

'ponvkv   cemēyenakuecaket onkv, estofvn estvmvn 'teheckv   tarēs
'ponaká   *cimi·yina·koycâ·kit* *oŋká* *istô·fan* *ístaman* *'tihícka*   *tá·li·s*
word   we accepted   when   and where to meet each other it will be
we have accepted, so if you announce when and where it will be,

maketsken   omat,   cetehechoyvrēs,"   kihcen,
ma·kíckin   *o·mâ·t*   *citihichoyáli·s*   *kéyhcin*
(when) you announce when   we will meet with you he said
we shall meet with you."

Cesse Mēkko pohat,   netta ēkvnv estvmvt omvranat   kērkuehcen,
cissimí·kko *po·hâ·t*   *nittá·* *i·kaná* *ístamat* *omála·nâ·t* *ki·lkóyhcin,*
Tcissimeeko heard it day place what   it should be announced
Chissi Micco heard it and announced what day and ground it would be.

mv   nettv orat,   etenfvccetvhayv   mēkko   Kosv Hacot on
ma   *nítta* *o·lâ·t*   *itinfaccitahá·ya*   *mí·kko*   *ko·sahá·coton*
that   day when it came the contract-makers the chief Kosahajo
When that day came, the contract-makers, Chief Coosa Harjo

Yvhole-ēmarvn 'tepaket vhohyen, Helvpe nvkvftēt vpoken,
yaholiʔi·má·lan[225] *'tipâ·kit* *ahóhyin* *hilápi* *nakáfti·ɫ*[226] *apô·kin*
and Yaholeemaala together (they 2) went off the Hilabi gathered together
and Yaholi Emathla, both went off together. Hilabi sat gathered together, and

'rvlahokat enkērkuecet okat
'lalá·ho·kâ·t *iŋkí·łkoycíɫ*[227] *o·kâ·t*
and when they 2 came back announced and said
when they both came back, [the chief] announced and said,

"'Pokko tat hvliwē tąlkosē eyackvt on okvyvnkekv,
pókkota·t *halêywi·*[228] *tălⁿkosi·* *iyá·ckat ô·n* *o·kayáŋkika*
the ball going up for certain he wants he has said
"Chissi Micco says he wants the ball to go up for certain, so

mvt mohmē tvlkvrēs, Cesse Mēkkotat maken,
mat *móhmi·* *tálkáɫi·s* *cissimí·kkota·t* *ma·kín*
so I (want that to be sure to take place) Tcissimeeko said
it will be just like that.

etemvkvsahmēt enkvpahkēs" maket kērkuecaken,
itimakasáhmi·t *iŋkapáhki·s* *ma·kít* *ki·łkóyca·kín*
agreed and left him he said and made the announcement
We agreed and left him," [the chief] said and made the announcement,

pohakof, afvckvkēt pahēcet cvhoket
poha·kô·f *a·fackakí·t* *pá·hi·cít* *caho·kít*
when they heard it they were glad and they whooped and gobbled
and when they heard, the Hilabis were glad and whooped and gobbled

Helvpe fullvntvs. Momen estofvn pokko hvlwvranet omat,
hilápi *folvántas* *mo·mín* *istô·fan* *pókko* *hálwała·nít*[229] *o·mâ·t*
the Hilabi gathered around Then when ball goes up
around. Then [Chissi Micco] had announced when the ball was to go up,

kērkuecakekv, mēkko tvsekvyv empunayet okat,
ki·lkoycâ·kika mí·kko tasikayá ímpona·yít o·kâ·t[i]
announced chief citizens talked to and said
so the chief [Coosa Harjo] talked to his citizens and said:

"Hiyomē tvsekvyv vhonkạtkusē hahkē etvlwv liketskat,
hayyô·mi· tasikayá ahoŋkă·ⁿtkosi·[230] *háhki· itálwa lêykícka·t*
Now citizens so very few being town you who are
"Town residents, the citizens have now become few in number,

cenkepayv pihketv ecohhayen kaket,
ciŋkipá·ya payhkitá icóhha·yín[ii] *kâ·kit*
your opponent a whoop has made on you sat, lived
your opponent has made a whoop on you,

opunvkv estemehset kaketskat nekēkv sekon takkakēpvranetskēt onhkos.
oponaká istimíhsit kâ·kícka·t niki·ka síko·n takka·kî·pala·nicki·t[231] *ónhko·s*
word took, accepted you sat, lived moving not you must (not) sit there
you have accepted their offer, you will not sit idly.

Cenkepayvtat encukolicen vpvtvtapaket takkaket,
ciŋkipá·yata·t incokolêycin apatata·pâ·kit[232] *takkâ·kit*
your opponents their women sitting beside sitting
Your opponents are not sitting around next to their women,

pihketv ecohhayet kaket ohkekos. Entokvrpe to estomis
payhkitá icóhha·yít kâ·kit óhkiko·s[iii] *intokálpito·*[iv] *istô·meys*
whoop made on you sitting not ball-sticks even
they are not sitting around making a whoop on you. I even have their ball-sticks

---

[i] He is adressing his citizens as though he thought they would not be able to play. Presumably he is making an intentionally disparaging speech.

[ii] "made a whoop on you" – a metaphorical expression.

[iii] I.e., Your opponents, having made a whoop on you, are not just sitting idly around with their women. (The chief is always encouraging + exhorting his men to greater activity + interest in respect to the forthcoming game.)

[iv] *intokálpi = intokónhi.*

yvn   cvnke   vtēhit,   'Hvyakpohvtke huerarēs'   kont,
yan   *cáŋki*   *atî·heyt*   *hayakpohátki* *hóylá·li·s*[233] *kônt*[i]
them   my hands   I have them in   ball-ground   right at
in my hand, and thinking 'I will stand at the ball-ground,'

emetetakvtē   hēret   asehoket   okētok.   Cēmeu   'Eto-kvrpetat yvt vmetetayvrēs,'
imititá·kati· *hǐ·ⁿlit*   *a·sihô·kit* *o·ki·to·k*   *ci·miw*   *itokálpita·t*   *yat amititâ·yáli·s*
prepared   well   to meet us   you, too   ball-sticks   suitable
they stand well prepared. You too are thinking, 'My ball-sticks are ready.'

kont,   ēyetetaketv   ohyekcēt   sehokatskvrēs,
kônt   *i·yitita·kitá*   *ohyíkci·t*   *sihó·ká·ckáli·s*[ii]
           to get yourselves ready   make sure   you shall stand
You must stand and make sure you have readied yourselves,

'Vnen   cvhēcat   okhoyēs'   kont.
anín   *cahi·câ·t*   *ókho·yi·s*   *kônt*[iii]
me   did see me   they are saying that
thinking, 'The ones who saw me are saying that.'

Cena   lowaketv   momēto   estomis,
ciná·   *lowa·kitá*   *mó·mi·to·*   *istô·meys*
your body   young and supple   [it is so]   even if
Even if you think your body is young and supple,

ēnekēyicvtē   hēricet   sehokatskvrēs,"   kihcet
i·niki·yéycati·[234]   *hǐ·ⁿleycit*[235]   *sihó·ká·ckáli·s*"   *kéyhcit*
move yourselves and take part   be sure to do that   you shall stand   he said
be careful to move yourself to take part, and you shall stand," he said

---

[i] The other side are saying "We have our ball-sticks prepared and are well-prepared to meet you at the ball-ground."

[ii] He (the chief) was encouraging them to have their ball-sticks prepared. (Each man has to have the right size for his own hands.)

[iii] They were always outwardly polite to the enemy, but at the same time they were making fun of them, saying, we know we can handle them just the way we want. We must be much better prepared than they are. Always town asking for game claims to be superior to the other side, but usually the other side gets so well prepared, they beat them. JH. says, we asked for it + got beat.

vwahēcvntvs.	Nettvkvckvo	este	vhopvyēcakat
awa·hi·cántas[236]	*nittakáckaw*	*isti*	*ahopayi·câ·ka·t*
and dismissed them	the day they set	the people	that live out from town

and dismissed them. They also notified the people that live out from town

Helvpe	tvsekvyv	vtēkat	omvlkvn	ohtohtet,	mohmen
hilápi	*tasikayá*	*ati·ka·t*	*omálkan*	*ohtóhtit*	*móhmin*
Hilabi	citizens	every, all together	all	notified	then

and all Hilabi citizens of the date set and

pokkvnockv	taranat,	nettv	fvccvlikē	hoyanat	sulkēt nvkvfitet
pokkanócka	*tá·lanâ·t*[237]	*nítta*	*faccaléyki·*	*hoya·nâ·t*	*sólki·t nakaféytit*
Ball-sleep	[it will be]	day	noon	when it passes	many gather together

where the Ball-sleep would be. In the afternoon many gathered together;

paskofv	'towakkv	vtotketv	'remētv	vtēkat	pohyet
pa·skó·fa	*'towákka*	*atotkitá*	*'limi·ta*	*ati·ka·t*	*póhyit*
cleared camping place	benches	work	other	all together	and finished

they all finished clearing the ground, the benches, and other work.

nerē	eshvyayicetv	etotaloceu	vtelohyet	vpoken	yomockof,
nili·	*ishaya·yeycitá*	*itota·lociw*	*atilóhyit*	*apô·kin*	*yomo·ckô·f*
at night	to make a light	dead timber	they gather	they sit	at night

To make a light at night, they gathered dead timber and sat, and when it got dark,

yahiket	'to-konhe ohhvpokvn	ohhvpohyet,
ya·hêykit	*'tokónhi ohhapó·kan*[238]	*ohhapóhyit*[i]

they whooped, they set their ball sticks in place, and

hoktvke	enyvhiket	yvhikepuecet
hoktakí	*inyaheykít*	*yahéykipoycít*

[the two men] sang for the women and made [the women] sing,

enyvhikv	vyoposhuecet	osticof,	fekhonnihcet vpoken,
inyahéyka	*ayopóshoycít*[239]	*ósteycô·f*	*fikhonnéyhcit apô·kin*

and when they had changed the [two men] singers four times, they stopped and sat down.

---

[i] There are more details in the Pakantalahassee story.

yekcetv sempunayvt okat: "Ta! Entokis ci!
yikcitasimponá·yat[240] *o·kâ·t*[i] *ta(?)*[ii] *into·kays cay*^[iii]
To strengthen them the speaker said, "Ta! Entokis ci!

Hiyomatē etolanofv paskofv 'metetahkē vtēhkofv,
hayyô·ma·ti·[241] *itola·nó·fa pa·skó·fa 'mititáhki· ati·hkó·fa*[242]
Now sitting within the forest and clearing that have been made ready,

tvsekvyv ena lowalokosē yvn kaken hēcvyē momēto estomis,
tasikayá iná· lowă·ⁿlo·kosi· yan kâ·kin hî·cayi· mô·mi·to· istô·meys
even though I see the citizen's young and supple bodies seated,

pum vculvke tatē em ahkopvnkv yvt omētes cē! Tvh! Mvtarētes cē!
pomacoláki tá·ti· imahkopánka[iv] *yat ô·mi·tis ci^ tah matá·li·tis ci^*
our forefathers mean for this to be a game! Thus it shall be.

Tvsekvyv ena lokcusē vnsekon ena lowalokusē estomis,
tasikayá iná· lókcosi·[243] *ánsikon iná· lowă·ⁿlo·kosi· istô·meys*
Though the citizen's bodies are immature and their bodies supple,

vhonkatkusē estenke vpvlhvmkusis fvckeko tayusē vntakkaken yvn hēcekv,
ahoŋkă·ⁿtkosi·[244] *istíŋki apalhámkoseys fáckiko· tă·ⁿyosi· antakkâ·kin yan hî·cika;*
because he sees I could get very few [players], not even a handful,

vnkepayv pihketv vcohhayen, opunvkv estemesvko vyosvmmvliken
aŋkipá·ya payhkitá acóhha·yín oponaká istimísako· ayosammalêykin[245]
my opponent has made a whoop on me. I didn't accept the challenge for a long time,

opunvkv enhervketv omēcicēn, opunvkv estemēsit omvyvnkes ce.
oponaká inhiłakitá omi·céyci·n oponaká istimi·séyt[246] *o·mayáŋkis ci^*
but because of such good talk, I accepted.

---

[i] Some men are gifted to talk this way + so they call on a gifted person — they don't call on just anyone.
[ii] Phonetically: [ɔ].
[iii] Or: *hinto·kays cay^*.
[iv] Fannie uses *-ŋ-*.

Tvh! Mvtarētes ce. Etolanofv etotketkv enlicit
tah matá·li·tis ci^ itola·nó·fa ito·tkítka inlêyceyt
Thus it shall be. I have set down the fire in the forest;

tvsekvyv cēpvnạkosē yekcetv empunayit,
tasikayá ci·pană·ⁿkosi· yikcitá ímpona·yéyt
I spoke forcefully to the youngest citizens,

yvn eskakvyate nak fvske awiyen ohhecvkuecit ohkvkotes ce.
*yan iskâ·kaya·ti[247] nâ·k fáski a·wêyyin ohhicákoycéyt óhkako·tis[248] ci^*
not just because they are pointing something sharp where we are.[249]

Pum vculvke tatē em ahkopvnkv yvt omētes ce. Vnkepayv vcvpvlhvmēcēto estomis,
pomacoláki tá·ti· imahkopánka yat ó·mi·tis ci^ aŋkipá·ya acapálhami·ci·to· istô·meys
This was always our forefathers' game. Though my opponents defeat me,

tvsekvyv, cukolice, hopuetaklopocke esomvlkvn cvkonahet ohmekotes ce.
*tasikayá cokolêyci hopoyta·klopócki isomálkan cakóna·hít óhmiko·tis ci^*
they will not take the citizens, womenfolk, and little children away from me.

Tvh! Mvtarētes ce! Pum vculvke tatē
tah matá·li·tis ci^ pomacoláki tá·ti·
Thus it shall be. Our forefathers

afackē semvnvcecē hvyakpohvtke sehokvnkē,
a·fa·ckí· simanacíci·[250] hayakpohátki siho·káŋki·
who used to go out in the ball-field and play an interesting game

yv ēkvnlvste pvtakaten vccepohiken.
ya (?) i·kanlásti patâ·ka·tin áccipohêykin[251]
are now all covered over with black dirt,

emohhonvpv tvsekvyv cēpvnạkosēt vntakkaken vnhēcekv,
imohhonápa tasikayá ci·pană·ⁿkosi·t antakkâ·kin anhî·cika
and above them, seeing I have only very young citizens left,

kepayv pihketv vcohhayē sehokofv mvtarēs. 'Yvn komis,' maket omes cē.
*kipá·ya payhkitá acóhha·yí· siho·kó·fa[252] matá·li·s yan kô·meys ma·kít ô·mis ci^*
the opponent will stand making a whoop on me. 'I want this,' he says.

Vpakse nettv hvse fvccvlikē, estvmv likē arofv, tvsekvyv nehickv 'metetahkē,
apáksi nítta hasí faccaléyki· ístama léyki· a·lô·fa tasikayá nihéycka 'mititáhki·
Tomorrow about noon, as the sun goes on, with the citizen's paraphernalia at the ready,

hvyakpohvtke vtehikofv, pokko hvtke cvllē emarofv,
hayakpohátki atihêyko·fa²⁵³ pókko hátki callí· ima·lô·fa²⁵⁴
when they get in the ball-field, when the white ball is rolling,

enkepayv ena estomēt huerēpis, 'Enan omēpēs' yvn komet,
iŋkipá·ya iná· istó·mi·t hoyli·peys²⁵⁵ iná·n omî·pi·s²⁵⁶ yan kô·mit
no matter how his opponent's body stands, 'It is his body,' you must think,

entvhopketv emokhackv empokko assetv omvlēcuset,
intahopkitá imokhá·cka impókko a·ssitá omali·ⁿcosit
with agility, full of fun, chasing the ball with all one's might.

hvyakpohvtke etewvlvpkēn este hvmkusē arvnto omen,
hayakpohátki itiwalápki·n²⁵⁷ ísti hámkosi·²⁵⁸ a·lánto· ô·min
Let it be as if you were a single person going clear across the ball-field.

vnsehokvrēn enkomikv yahketv yekcēn yahkekvs maken
ansihó·káli·n²⁵⁹ iŋkô·meyka²⁶⁰ ya·hkitá yíkci·n ya·hkíkas²⁶¹ ma·kín
I want them to stand for me, let them yell a strong yell," [the chief] said,

cenkērkuecvkin apohicet 'pvlatket ometskes ci."
ciŋkí·lkoycakéyn a·pohêycir²⁶² 'palâ·tkit o·míckis cay^ⁱ
"And I am announcing to you while you sit listening."

Makēt empunahyen yahiket vpokof,
ma·kí·t imponáhyin ya·hêykit apo·kô·f
So saying, he talked to them, and when [the men] yelled and sat down,

hvtvm hoktvke pokko 'mopanvlke enhuehiket svpaklēcen,
hatâm hoktakí pókko 'mopa·nâlki inhoyhêykit²⁶³ sapakli·cin
they called for the women ball-dancers and made them stand,

ⁱ All jump up and yell before he finishes talking. Only men make the *ya·hkitá.*

enyvhikvlke empohvthoyen, enyvhikaken, hoktvkeu yvhikaken,
inyaheykâlki impohátho·yín[264] *inyahéyka·kín hoktakíw yahéyka·kín*[265]
and the [male] singers invited them, they sang, and the women sang too,

yvhikv vyoposecicē osticat vtēkat fekhonnicet,
yahéyka ayoposíceyci· ósteycâ·t ati·ka·t fikhónneycít
and every fourth time the song changed, they stopped,

estomēn empunayen estomēt fullet yahket omat, momē vlkēn yahket esosticakof,
istó·mi·n impóna·yín[266] *istó·mi·t follít ya·hkít ô·ma·t*[267] *mó·mi· álki·n ya·hkít isostéyca·kô·f*
and however he spoke, however they yelled, they yelled the same way until the fourth time,

"Fēkvpkvn hopoyaks!" mēkkot kihcen, lomhet, nocicen,
fi·kápkan hopóyaks mí·kkot kéyhcin lomhít[268] *noceycín*
when the chief said, "Look for rest!" and they lay down and slept;

hvyvtiken hompahket, fullet 'metetahket yahiket vpēyat,
hayatêykin hompáhkit follít 'mititáhkit ya·hêykit apî·ya·t[269]
and in the morning they ate, and after getting ready, they yelled and went off,

vkērkv ēpakē enhopvyēn vpehyet, pokkechetv ēkvnv tempusan erfekhoniyet vpoket,
aki·łka i·pá·ki·[270] *inhopayí·n apíhyit pokkichitá i·kaná tímposa·n iłfikhonâyyit apô·kit*
and went a distance of six miles, stopped near the ball-ground, and camped.

afvckvranat enhopoyet, enwiketv hahyet, yakyapvo cakcvhehcet, 'metetahket, yahiket,
a·fáckała·nâ·t ínhopo·yít inweykitá háhyit yakyá·paw cakcahíhcit 'mititáhkit ya·hêykit
They selected who would play, assigned positions, stuck the goal-posts in, got ready, yelled,

emeto-sehokvn ohhvpēyet 'roricet svpaklen, Akfvskvlkeu emeto-sehokv yicet asvpaklet,
imitosihó·kan ohhápi·yít 'łoléycit[271] *sapâ·klin akfaskâlkiw imitosihó·ka yêycit a·sapâ·klit*
and went to their pole and stood. Okfuskee too got to their pole and stood there,

'metetahket yahiken Helvpeu yahiken etohhvpēyen,
'mititáhkit ya·hêykin hilápiw ya·hêykin itóhhapi·yín[272]
got ready, and yelled, and Hilabi too yelled, and they went toward each other,

Akfvskvlke yicat sulkēt etvlwv ētvt vpvkvkēn yicvntvs. Akfvskvlke, Okcaye,
akfaskâlki yeycâ·t sólki·t itálwa í·tat apakaki·n yeycántas. akfaskâlki okcá·yi
and when Okfuskee came, they came with many other towns. The Okfuskee, Okchayi,

Oyokofke, Tvlwv-Rakko, Kvsehtv esyomet etohkvlkēt yicet omis,
oyokófki talwałákko kasíhta isyô·mit itohkálki·t yêycit[273] o·mêys
Oyokofki, Big Town, and Cusseta came together,

vnrvpkv yekcat hayekot Helvpe emvkvsahmen, Akfvske tat pokko hvlwehcen
anłápka yíkca·t há·yikot hilápi imakasáhmin akfáskita·t pókko halwíhcin
but Hilabi accepted without strong objection. Okfuskee threw the ball up,

esfullet, Helvpet epohyet yahiket, rafolēcvntvs.
ísfollít hilápit ipóhyit ya·hêykit łá·foli·cántas
and they were around with it, and Hilabi won and yelled and came back.

Etvlwv vtēkat enkepayvn emafacken omat, epoyate vtēkat emeto-sehokvn
itálwa atî·ka·t iŋkipá·yan imá·fa·ckín o·mâ·t ipo·yâ·ti atî·ka·t imitosihó·kan
Every town, when playing their opponent, whenever they won, it was their

aohpefatiket vfolotēcet yahkvntot vwahēt 'semvpeyetvt omēs.
a·ʔohpifa·têykit afolóti·cít[274] ya·hkántot awa·hí·t 'simapiyítat ô·mi·s
custom to run up to their [own] crossed poles, go around them, yell, and disperse.

A Match-Game Between Hilabi and Pakantalahasi (1905)

J. Hill (Haas XIV:47–149)

Helvpe Pvkvntvlvhasse espokē etemafackof,
hilápi pakantalahá·ssi ispo·kí· itimá·fa·ckô·f
The last time Hilabi and Pakantalahasi [or Peach Ground] played

Hvyo-rakko netta palehokkolen cenvpohkaken,
hayołákko nittá· pa·lihokkô·lin cinapohká·kin
was on August the twenty-eighth

ohrolopē cokperakko hvmken cokpe ostvpaken cahkēpē vpakof,
ohłolopí· cokpiłákko hámkin cókpi ostapâ·kin cahkî·pi· apâ·ko·f
in the year nineteen hundred and five [1905].

Pvkvntvlvhasse etvlwv enkepayv emafvcketv eyacēt fullvcokat pohēt fullēn
pakantalahá·ssi itálwa iŋkipá·ya ima·fackitá iyá·ci·t follacóka·t po·hí·t follí·n
We had been hearing for a long time that Pakantalahassi town wanted to play against their

hofonē haken Helvpe etvlwv vkerricat,
hofóni· hâ·kin hilápi itálwa akíɬeycâ·t
opponent, and after a long time the town of Hilabi had been thinking,

"Punvcǫmuset omis, etvlwv cǫtkuse ētat fullet okekv,
ponacŏ·ⁿmosit o·mêys. itálwa cŏ·ⁿtkosi i·tá·t follít o·kiká
"There are very few of us, but they are a small town too,

afvcketv eyacēt fullet oken omat, empohēn pumvkvsamen omat etenfvciyet
a·fackitá iyá·ci·t follít o·kín o·mâ·t impo·hí·n pomákasa·mín o·mâ·t itinfacêyyit
and if they want to play, we'll ask them, and if they're willing, we'll decide

pokko tat enhvlwēcvkēton os makat saset ohmen, mv vrahkv huehketv hahken,
pókkota·t inhálwi·cakí·ton ó·ⁿs[i] ma·kâ·t sa·sít óhmin ma (?) aɬáhka hoyhkitá háhkin
and send the ball up," some said. For that purpose they made a call,

sulkat nvkvfitet, Helvpe etvlwv ēyvkerricet,
sólka·t nakafêytit hilápi itálwa i·yakíɬeycít
many gathered, and Hilabi reflected

este-mvnette afvckē tayusat vhonkatet vpoket, opunvyēcet etemvkvsamat
istimanítti a·fácki·tâ·yosa·t ahóŋka·tít apô·kit opónayi·cít itimakása·mâ·t
and discussed how many young men could play and when they agreed,

Pvkvntvlvhasse etvlwv afvcketvn empohvranet 'temvkvsvmakvntvs.
pakantalahá·ssi itálwa a·fackitán impohála·nít 'timakasáma·kántas.
they agreed to ask the town of Pakantalahassi to play.

Ofvp pohahoyē estomis vlesketv elkv vpvkēt omekis onkv,
o·fáp pohá·ho·yi· istô·meys aliskitá ílka apáki·t omíkeys oŋká
Even though we did get beat, there was no disgrace or death with it:

"Pokko enhvlwehcēn 'svfvllēpet yahket fullen enhesse hoyopkv hayvkepekvs"
pókko inhalwíhci·n 'safálli·pít ya·hkít follín inhíssi hoyópka ha·yakípikas
"Send up the ball and let them throw it and yell and make their friends watch,"

---

[i] Short way: *inhálwi·cakí·tnó·ⁿs.*

maket 'temvkvsahmet Helvpe etvlwv tat opunvkv ohtotvntvs,
ma·kít 'timakasáhmit hilápi itálwata·t oponaká óhto·tántas.
they agreed, and Hilabi sent word

etvlwv enkepayv. Mohmen Pvkvntvlvhasse etvlwv ēnvkvftēcet fullet,
itálwa iŋkipá·ya móhmin pakantalahá·ssi itálwa i·nakáfti·cít follít
to their enemy town. And Pakantalahassi town gathered themselves

afvcketv eyacet okakvtētok: opunvkv vyoposkat,
a·fackitá iya·cít oka·katí·to·k oponaká ayópo·ská·t
and wanted to play a game: and in reply said,

"Estofvn estvmvt ēkvnv eteheckvt omvranen omat pokerricatsken
istô·fan ístamat i·kaná itihíckat omála·nín o·mâ·t pokiłłêycá·ckin
"Let us know when and where to meet,

'tehēcet tempunahoyeyvrēs" maken, pohhēt
tíhi·cít timpona·hoyíyáli·s[i] ma·kín póhhi·t
and we will meet and talk it over," we heard,

ēkvnv netta estvmvt omvranat enkērkuecēn, mv nettv Helvpe etvlwv nvkvftēt vpoket
i·kaná nittá· ístamat omála·nâ·t[ii] iŋki·łkóyci·n ma nítta hilápi itálwa nakáfti·t apô·kit
and they announced the place and day it would be, and that day Hilabi town met

etenfvccetv-hayvlke este tuccēnen enwiketv hayet, mvt emopunahoyet omen,
itinfaccitaha·yâlki ísti toccî·nin inweykitá ha·yít mat imoponá·ho·yít o·mín
and appointed three agreement-makers and talked to them, [to serve] clear through

afvcketv 'remeyoksicvranan, Lahtvmvtahv,
a·fackitá 'limiyokséycała·nâ·n lahtamatá·ha
to the end of the game: Lahtamataha [Big Jack],

Kaccv Homahte, Solomon Bullet.
ka·ccahomáhti Solomon Bullet[iii]
Kacca Homahti [Jim Hill himself], and Solomon Bullet.

---

[i] Or: *timpona·hoyákáli·s.*
[ii] FS: *omáha·nâ·t.*
[iii] "Can't remember town-name, which should be used here."

Matvpomēn Pvkvntvlvhasse enwiketv hayat, Hopayuce,
ma·tapó·mi·n pakantalahá·ssi inweykitá ha·yá·t hopa·yocí
Pakantalahassi made appointments in the same way: Hopayochi [Hopayi Proctor],

'Cohacuce, Kelly Proctor.
'coha·cocí Kelly Proctor[i]
Choharjochi [Little Crazy Deer], and Kelly Proctor.

Yofalv Hacot esyomat yicen afvcketv etemopunvyēcet,
yofa·lahá·cot isyô·ma·t yêycin a·fackitá itimopónayi·cít
Eufaula Harjo [Lewis Proctor] came, and they talked about the game,

nake sulkēn etemvnrapet oketv cvpkēn vpoket etenfvccakvtēt os.
nâ·ki sólki·n itimánla·pít okíta cápki·n apô·kit itinfácca·katí·t ô·ⁿs.
and they opposed each other on many points, sat a long time, and came to an agreement.

Hiyomēn etvlwv tvsekvyv mahusatton, eppucetake, ohhehisvlke faccusan vtēkusēn,
hayyó·mi·n itálwa tasikayá mă·ⁿhosa·tton ippocitá·ki ohhiheysâlki[ii] fă·ⁿccosa·n atî·kosi·n
In this way just the town's true citizens, their sons and real son-in-laws only,

nehickv hahyen hvyakpo-hvtke etemvtēhet omeyvrēs makēt etenfvciyet etekvpakvntvs.
nihéycka háhyin hayakpohátki itimati·hit omíyáli·s ma·ki·t itinfacêyyit itíkapa·kántas.
we will decorate ourselves and go into the ball-ground; they agreed and parted.

Mohmen afvcketv orat eto-lanofvn tvsekvyv vtēkat,
móhmin a·fackitá o·lâ·t itola·nó·fan tasikayá atî·ka·t
Then when the [time for] the game arrived, all the citizens,

cokolice, hopuetak-lopocke ena cvfeknusē vtēkat vtelokvtēt os.
cokolêyci hopoyta·klopócki iná· cafíknosi· atî·ka·t atílo·katí·t ô·ⁿs.
all the women and children of sound body, gathered in the forest.

Vkērkv pale ostat senhopvyēn awat sasen, sulkēt vtelokof,
aki·lka pá·li ô·sta·t sinhopáyi·n a·wâ·t sâ·sin sólki·t atílo·kô·f
Some came more than forty miles, and when a bunch had gathered,

[i] "Should use town-name."
[ii] For *ohhiheysâlki* could say *ohhatisâlki*, but latter could include women and since women don't play, the other term is used.

ēkvnv enhopohyet "Yvn paskofv etetakuecaks," mēkkot mahken,
i·kaná inhopóhyit "yan pa·skó·fa itita·kóycaks," mí·kkot máhkin
they picked a place, and the chief said, "Get things ready here in this cleared place,"

este sulkat vtotket "Paskofv etowakkv 'tetakuecen
ísti sólka·t ato·tkít pa·skó·fa itowákka 'tita·kóycin
and many people worked, and the chief said, "Get the benches ready in the clearing

'to-konhen ohkakvn hayaks," mēkkot maken,
'tokónhin ohká·kan há·yaks mí·kkot ma·kín
and make a rack for the ball-sticks,"

eto-poloke cvpkēn yoksv lvcce esseu ocēn tacet, paskofv rasoh-awen,
itopoló·ki cápki·n yóksa lácci íssiw ó·ci·n tâ·cit, pa·skó·fa la·sóhha·wín
and they cut a long pole with branches and leaves at the end and brought it to the clearing.

eto yakyvposē hokkolen warateu resyicen, estele vhopakv pale-ostohkakat mahen
itó yakyapósi· hokkô·lin wâ·la·tiw lísyeycín istilí ahopá·ka pá·liostohkâ·ka·t má·hin
They brought two forked posts that they cut too, and about fourteen feet

'metehopvyēn ēkvnvn koriyet 'toyakpe cakcvhehcet,
'mitihopayí·n i·kanán kolêyyit 'toyákpi cakcahíhcit
apart, they dug in the ground and stuck the forked posts in

'to-poloke cvpkan ohtakhahyet, 'to-konhe ohkakv 'tetakuehcof,
'topoló·ki cápka·n ohtakháhyit 'tokónhi ohká·ka 'tita·kóyhco·f
and laid a long pole across, and after the ball-stick rack was prepared,

paskofv nvrkvpvn totkvn tehcet, honvntake sulkat fekhoniyet vpokof,
pa·skó·fa nalkapán tó·tkan tíhcit honantá·ki sôlka·t fikhonêyyit apo·kô·f
they built a fire in the center of the clearing, and all the men stopped and sat down.

nerē pefatkē yahkē fullvranat totkvn eshvyayicēt omvranekv,
nilí· pifa·tkí· ya·hkí· fóllala·nâ·t tó·tkan ishayá·yeyci·t omála·niká
Those who were going to run and yell at night would have to have firelight,

"To-talucen vlvkuecekvs," mēkkot maken, asempunayvt emohkērkuehcen,
'tota·locín alakóycikas mí·kkot ma·kín a·simponá·yat imohki·lkóyhcin
so the chief said, "Bring dry branches," and the spokesman announced it to them.

honvntake sulkat omvlkvt vpēyet, 'to-taluce sulkēn 'towakkv tempen cekhihcet,
honantá·ki sôlka·t omálkat api·yít 'tota·locí sólki·n 'towákka tímpin cikhéyhcit
All the men who were present went and piled lots of dry branches near the benches,

sulkat fekhoniyet vpokof, yafkekv cokolice hvlewv esfullvtē homhopvranat
sôlka·t fikhonêyyit apo·kô·f yâ·fkika cokolêyci halíwa[275] isfollatí· homhopála·nâ·t
and when all present had stopped and sat down, it was evening, and when the chief learned

'tetakuecakat mēkkot kērrof,
'tita·koycâ·ka·t mí·kkot ki·llô·f
that the provisions that the women had brought to eat were ready,

"Estehvpo ocakan oh-vpēyet homhopekvs" mēkkot maken,
istihapó· o·câ·ka·n óhhapi·yít homhopíkas mí·kkot ma·kín
he said, "Let them go to where the camps are and eat,"

asempunayvt emohkērkuehcen homipet fullof,
a·simponá·yat imohki·lkóyhcin homêypit follô·f
and the spokesman announced it to them. After they had eaten

"Cerakko esfullatskvtē vfvstepaks," mēkkot maken,
'ciłákko ísfollá·ckati· afastipáks mí·kkot ma·kín
the chief said, "Those of you who brought horses, attend to them,"

asempunayvt emohkērkuecof, omvlkvt honvntake vwahhet,
a·simponá·yat imohki·lkoycô·f omálkat honantá·ki awáhhit
and when the spokesman announced it, the men all scattered

cerakko pvhe-lane herakē ocan eshopoyet,
'ciłákko pahilá·ni hiłă·ⁿki· o·câ·n íshopo·yít
and picked out a spot with their horses where there was good green grass

eswvnakv cvpcvkēn eto hueretayan vwvnawicet fullet,
iswaná·ka capcakí·n itó hoylitâ·ya·n awána·weycít follít
and tied them with long ropes to the trees standing here and there,

'metetahket eryicē pokof
'mititáhkit íłyeycí· po·kô·f
and when they were ready and were all back,

"Yomockekv hiyomat nettv-kvckv emvrēcvyvtē
yomo·ckiká hayyô·ma·t nittakácka imáli·cayáti·
the chief said, "It's getting dark, so now the broken sticks I have sent you,

ena cvfeknusē vtēkat omvlkuset yvn vteloket omētok
iná· cafíknosi· atî·ka·t omä^ulkosit yan atilô·kit o·mí·to·k
everyone that is healthy has gathered here:

vnhesse tis omvlkuset empaskofv vtehkekvs," mēkko mahkof,
anhíssiteys omǎnlkosit impa·skó·fa atíhkikas," mí·kko máhko·f
let all my friends, too, enter the clearing," and after that

asempunayvt emohkērkuehcen, honvntake omvlkvt
a·simponá·yat imohki·lkóyhcin honantá·ki omálkat
the spokesman announced it to them. When all the men

eto-wakkvn ohhvpohket vpokof, honvntake hokkolen mēkkot enhohiken
itowákkan ohhapóhkit apo·kô·f honantá·ki hokkô·lin mí·kkot inho·hêykin
had sat down on benches and were sitting, the chief called on two men,

aoh-vthohyen empunayet okat,
a·ʔohhathóhyin ímpona·yít o·kâ·t,
and they came up, and he spoke to them, saying,

"Pokko 'mvyvhikusē tayat cokolice huerusen omat hopoyet,
pókko 'mayahéykosi· tâ·ya·t cokolêyci hoylosin o·mâ·t hopo·yít
"See if there is a woman here and there who can sing for the ball

homv svpaklēcet, emvcohkēpuset,
hóma sapaklî·cit imacóhki·posít
and stand them in front, prompting them to do their best,

honvntakeu enyvhikv empohvttēpuset welakatsken,
honantá·kiw inyahéyka impohátti·posít wila·ká·ckin
and go around and invite the men singers too.

yv fulletv hoyvnvrēn komit cenhuehkvkit okikv,
ya (?) follitá hoyánáli·n kô·meyt cínhoyhkakéyt o·kéyka
I am calling on you till this meeting has passed,

'tetaken omat empohvttepatskvrēs," kihcet enkērkuehcof,
tita·kín o·mâ·t impóhattipá·ckáli·s^i kéyhcit iŋki·lkóyhco·f
so if ready, you all invite them," he said, and after they announced it,

honvntake sulkat mēkkot enkērkuecet okat,
honantá·ki sôlka·t mí·kkot iŋki·lkoycít o·kâ·t
the chief announced to the men present,

"Eto-kvrpe ēhopakusēt yicet omatskētok ēyvnakuecepaks," maken,
"itokálpi i·hopá·kosi·t yêycit o·má·cki·to·k i·yana·koycipáks^{276} ma·kín^{ii}
"Come with the ball-sticks you have with you: bring yourselves near!"

eto-kvrpe ocat vtēkat cawet 'metetaket
itokálpi ô·ca·t atí·ka·t câ·wit 'mititá·kit
And everyone who had ball-sticks had them and had gotten ready

etowakkvn ohhvpoken, "Hiyomat este-mocvse vhonkatkusē
itowákkan ohhapô·kin hayyô·ma·t istimocási ahoŋkă·^{n}tkosi·
and had sat on the benches, and the chief said, "Now those few young people

etohkvlikē eto-lanofv empaskofv 'tetakuehcēn,
itohkalêyki· itola·nó·fa impa·skó·fa 'tita·kóyhci·n^{iii}
who have gotten together in the clearing in the forest

pvlatketskat cenkepayv aecohhēcet acensehokēton pvlatket ometskekv,
palâ·tkícka·t^{iv} ciŋkipá·ya a·ʔicohhí·cit a·cinsihô·ki·ton palâ·tkit o·míckika
spread out ready, your opponent is standing facing you and you are spread here, so

yahketv yekcē hērēn yahiket eto-kvrpen ohkayekvs!" mēkkot maken,
ya·hkitá yíkci· hĭ·^{n}li·n ya·hèykit itokálpin^{277} ohká·yikas," mí·kkot ma·kín
yell a really strong yell and put the ball-sticks on!"

---

^{i} The man-singers keep telling the women: *yahéykaks ci^, yahéykaks ci^* 'Sing! Sing!'
^{ii} When they first got there, they did not bring their ball-sticks, but here he tells them to come with their ball-sticks.
^{iii} Just their way of talking. They are all within the *pa·skó·fa*.
^{iv} When he is talking to those in front of him, he says *palâ·tícka·t*.

asempunayvt emohkērkuecet respoyan sulkat omvlkvt pahēcet pefatket,
a·simponá·yat imohki·łkoycít líspo·yâ·n sôlka·t omálkat pá·hi·cít pifa·tkít
And when the spokesman had finished announcing it, all those present whooped and ran.

'to-konhe ohkakv pvlhvmken eto cǫtkusē yoksv lvcce
'tokónhi ohká·ka palhámkin itó cǒⁿtkosi· yóksa lácci
At the other side of the ball-stick rack, they had stuck a small tree with branches

esseu ocēn cakhēcēt ont, mvn vfolotēcēt pefatket yahket fullvtētot rapefatiket,
íssiw ó·ci·n cakhí·ci·t ônt man afolóti·ci·t pifa·tkít ya·hkít follatí·tot ła·pifa·têykit
and leaves at the end in the ground, and they ran around [the small tree] yelling and ran

totkv ētkan eryihcet yahket totkv ētkan vfolotēcet fullvtētot
tó·tka i·tkâ·n ilyéyhcit ya·hkít tó·tka i·tkâ·n afolóti·cít follatí·tot
back, and they came back to where the fire was burning and circled the fire yelling,

'to-konhe ohkakvn 'rvsvpvkilet yahket wihket,
'tokónhi ohká·kan 'łasapakêylit ya·hkít wéyhkit
and stood at the ball-stick rack and yelled and stopped,

omvlkvt 'to-konhe, ēkofkv, kaccvhce, 'senockv esyomet
omálkat 'tokónhi i·kó·fka ka·ccaháci 'sinó·cka isyô·mit
and each man had his ball-sticks, breechcloth, tiger-tail, and necklace tied together

sēwvnaketvt eswvnvkēn omakekv, 'to-konhe ohkakvn 'to-poloke ohtakhakan
si·wana·kitát iswanáki·n o·má·kika 'tokónhi ohká·kan 'topoló·ki ohtakhâ·ka·n
with a belt, so they hung this on the pole that lays across the ball-stick rack,

ohtvrtihcet fekhonnat,
ohtałtéyhcit fíkhonnâ·t
and when they stopped,

fvccvlikē hoyanusē 'metetaketv vlicēcvtē 'metetahkē vpokat omēs.[278]
faccaléyki· hoya·nosí· 'mitita·kitá aleycí·cati· 'mititáhki· apo·kâ·t ô·mi·s
they started to get ready a little past noon and sat ready.

Mohmen mēkko okat, "Empohattvlke acensehoyit omikv,
móhmin mí·kko o·kâ·t "impoha·ttâlki^i a·cinsihô·yeyt o·méyka
Then the chief said, "I have appointed the inviters,

estomvrēn komet vsehoket enwelaken omat, 'Momvranin okēs' enkomē hēret
istó·máłi·n kô·mit asího·kít ínwila·kín o·mâ·t mó·mała·néyn o·kí·s iŋkó·mi· hĭ·ⁿłit
so whatever they want, when they get up, you must assume, 'This is what I am to do.'

tvsekvyv, cokolice yvn vnkaket omvrēs," maken asempunayvt
tasikayá cokolêyci yan aŋkâ·kit omáłi·s," ma·kín a·simponá·yat
I want my citizens and women to sit here with me," he said, and after the spokesman

enkērkuehcen hoyanof, empohattvlke cokolice yvhikvlke osten hopohyet,
iŋki·lkóyhcin hoya·nô·f impoha·ttâlki cokolêyci yaheykâlki ô·stin hopóhyit
announced it, the inviters picked out four women and singers,

yvhiketv emvlicēcvranateu este honvntake hokkolen enhopohyet,
yaheykitá imaleycí·cała·nâ·tiw ísti honantá·ki hokkô·lin inhopóhyit
and they picked out two men to begin the song,

ohliketv hokkolen 'metetakuehcet vskvsvtolkv, svokv 'tepakan
ohleykitá hokkô·lin 'mitita·kóyhcit askasatólka sáwka 'tipâ·ka·n
and they prepared two seats for them and set a drum and a rattle

ohliketv ehomvn emohcet, "Yvhikvlke cempohattvkeyat 'yemohkakepaks," kicen,
ohleykitá ihóman imóhcit yaheykâlki cimpohâ·ttakíya·t 'yimohka·kipáks," keycín
in front of their seats, and they said, "Let those of you singers we have invited come and

honvntake ohliketvn ohkakof, eratopvrvn hoktvke pokko 'mopanvlke 'svpvkilen
honantá·ki ohleykitán óhka·kô·f iła·topáłan hoktakí pókko 'mopa·nâlki 'sapakêylin
sit," and when the two men took their seats, the women ball dancers stood behind them,

vskvsvtolkvn nafket hayēcet yvhiken hvmket svwkvn ēset, 'mvyatet hayēcet
askasatólkan na·fkít há·yi·cít yaheykín hámkit sáwkan î·sit 'maya·tít há·yi·cít
and [the two men] played the drum and sang, and one had a rattle in hand and shook it up

---

^i *impoha·ttâlki* is the same as *tahpa·lâlki.*

aenyvhikof hoktvkew yvhiket svpaklet pvnaket omvtēs.
a·ʔínyaheykô·f hoktakíw yaheykít sapâ·klit pána·kít o·matí·s
and down, and when they sang out for them, the women too stood and sang and danced.

Hvmmakēt yvhiket,
hámma·kí·t yaheykít
They sang this way,

>   Yo-owē tonahē, yo-owē tonahē,
>   *(yoʔowi·) to·ná·hi· (yoʔowi·) to·ná·hi·*
>   Yo-owi tonahi, yo-owi tonahi,
>
>   Yowē tonahē, yowē tonahē,
>   *yo·wi· to·ná·hi· yo·wi· to·ná·hi·*
>   Yowi tonahi, yowi tonahi,
>
>   A awē maho-okē, a awē maho-okē
>   *á· a·wí· má·hooki· á· a·wí· má·hooki·*
>   They're coming, they're saying, they're coming, they're saying,
>
>   A awē maho-okē, a awē maho-okē,
>   *á· a·wí· má·hookí· á· a·wí· má·hooki·*
>   They're coming, they say, they're coming, they say,
>
>   Awepekvno-o mahokē,
>   *a·wipikáno·ʔo má·ho·ki·*
>   Let them come, they say,
>
>   Yowelēha, yowelēha,
>   *yo·wilí·ha· yo·wilí·ha·*
>   Yowiliha, yowiliha,
>
>   Hayowelēha, yowele-eha,
>   *ha·yo·wili·ha· yo·wilíʔiha·*
>   Hayowiliha, yowili-iha,
>
>   Pumetohkuekat okvnto,
>   *pomitohkóyka·t o·kánto·*
>   They've gathered together against us,

Pumetohkuekat okvnto,
pomitohkóyka·t o·kánto·
They've gathered together against us,

Yahiyakatē,
ya·heyya·ká·ti·
they are yelling (song form)
Those who are yelling,

Pumetohkuekat okvnto,
pomitohkóyka·t o·kánto·
They've gathered together against us,

Pumetohkuekat okvnto,
pomitohkóyka·t o·kánto·
They've gathered together against us,

Hiyoyvlē yahvnē, hiyoyvlē yahvnē
hayyo·yalí· ya·háni· hayyo·yalí· ya·háni·
Hayyoyali yahani, hayyoyali yahani,

Hiyoyvlē yahvnē, hiyoyvlē yahvnē
hayyo·yalí· ya·háni· hayyo·yalí· ya·háni·[i]
Hayyoyali yahani, hayyoyali yahani

'to-konhe ohhocat ehomvn panet svpaklet yvhiket okemvts.
'tokónhi ohhò·ca·t ihóman pa·nít sapâ·klit[ii] *yaheykít o·kimác*
They would sing, dancing and standing in front of where the ball-sticks were placed.

Yvhikvtē fekhonnihcet yahkvranof,
yaheykatí· fikhonnéyhcit yá·hkała·nô·f
When the singing stopped and they were about to yell,

---

[i] Or: *ya·ha·ni·*, or *ya·ha·li·*. Whole song is repeated four times.
[ii] They danced up and down in place.

yekcetv sempunayv hvmmakēt empunayvtēs:
yikcitá simponá·ya hámma·kí·t ímpona·yatí·s[i]
the spokesman talked to them about strength like this:

"Tah, entokis ci! Yvn momēt omvrēs.
ta[ii] *into·káys cay*^[iii] *yan mó·mi·t omáli·s*
"Tah, intokays chay! [a ritualistic introduction] I wanted it to be here

Yvn enkomit tvsekvyv nettv-kvcēkv em vrēcit omvyvtētes ce.
yan iŋkô·meyt tasikayá nittakací·ka[iv] *imáli·céyt o·mayáti·tis ci*^
and sent out broken sticks to citizens.

Pum vculvke tatē em ahkopvnkv yvt mvtarētes ce.
pomacolakítá·ti· imahkopánka yat matá·li·tis ci^.
This will be a game for our forefathers.

Pum vculvke tatē nehickv vnvckē 'metetahkē hvyakpo-hvtke vtēhkē sehokvnkē
pomacoláki tá·ti· nihéycka anácki· 'mititáhki· hayakpohátki ati·hki· siho·káŋki·
Our forefathers who used to stand ready in the ball-ground with beautiful ornamentation

yv ēkvn-lvste pvtakatet em vccetv haken,
ya i·kanlásti patá·ka·tit imaccitá ha·kín
[now] have this black ground spread out as their covering,

vccepohikē oh-onvpv tvsekvyv ena lowạlokusē rvhosikē
áccipohêyki· ohhonápa tasikayá iná· lowă·ⁿlo·kosi· 'lahosêyki·
all covered up, and above, the citizens who are left are very young, and when they stand

---

[i] If the Hilabi do not have a man who can make a speech in this manner, they must ask someone from a friendly town to do it for them. If the man's voice is good, the speech can be heard for about a quarter of a mile.

[ii] Beginning of speech given in special voice characteristic of speech style. This is a special ball-game speech. Final *a* approaches *ɔ* in speech-style.

[iii] *ta´ into·káys cay*^ is the formulaic introduction for a ball-game (*pokkichitá*) speech. *hayyo·ma·tí·* is formulaic introduction for any speech at a special meeting at square-ground (*cokolákko*).

[iv] Have to say that in speech – same as *nittakácka*.

pohyvketv enhakusē sehokofv, pum vculvke tatē em ahkopvnkv
pohyakíta inhă·ⁿkosi· siho·kó·fa pomacoláki tá·ti· imahkopánka
with loneliness coming upon them, I wanted the game of our forefathers

yvn mvtarēs enkomit, nettv-kvcēkv emvrēcit omvyvtēs ce.
yan matá·li·s iŋkô·meyt nittakací·ka imáli·céyt o·mayáti·s ci^i
to be here, and so have sent out the broken sticks.

Yvn makēt omes ce. Tv momvntes ce.
*yan ma·kí·t ó·mis ci^ ta mo·mántis ci^*
This is what [the chief] said. Ta momantis ci [another formulaic beginning].

Tvsekvyv ena lowalokusē cokolice etohkalit, eto-lanofv etotketkv enlicit,
tasikayá iná· lowă·ⁿlo·kosi· cokolêyci itohká·leyt itola·nó·fa ito·tkítka^ii inlêyceyt
I brought the citizens with young bodies and women together, I have put a burning fire here,

yekcetv empunayit yvn eskakvyate nak fvske awiyen ohhecvkuecit
yikcitá impóna·yéyt yan iskâ·kaya·ti nâ·k fáski^iii a·wêyyin ohhicákoycéyt
I exhort you, I, who am sitting here with [the chief], do not mean to point something sharp

yekcetv empunayit ohkvkotes ce. Pum vculvke tatē em ahkopvnkv yvt omētes ce.
yikcitá impóna·yéyt óhkako·tis ci^. pomacoláki tá·ti· imahkopánka yat ô·mi·tis ci^.
at you, I exhort you. This used to be the game of our forefathers.

Tvh! Mvtarētes ce. Vpakse nettv hvse fvccvlikē estvmv likē arofv,
tah matá·li·tis ci^. apáksi nítta hasí²⁷⁹ faccaléyki· ístama leykí· a·lô·fa
Thus it shall be. Tomorrow when the sun is directly above,

tvsekvyv ena lowalokusē vhvnkahtit, vlesketv enhakusē nehickv enhahyit,
tasikayá iná· lowă·ⁿlo·kosi· ahaŋkáhteyt aliskitá inhă·ⁿkosi· nihéyck a inháhyeyt
I have counted the citizens with young bodies, I have made disgraceful ornamentation for

hvyakpo-hvtke estemvtēhin sehokofv,
hayakpohátki istimatî·heyn 'sihô·ko·fa^iv
them, I have put them in the ball-ground, and as we stand,

---

i = *o·mayáti·tis ci^*.

ii Or: *ito·tkí·tka*.

iii *nâ·k fáski* refers to an implement of war.

iv Phonetically: [ɔʔ].

cvna momusē estomis, vnkepayv enan omēpēs enkomet,
caná· mô·mosi· istô·meys aŋkipá·ya iná·n omí·pi·s iŋkô·mit
even though my body is like that, my opponent thinks his body is that way,

'co-esse cvllē ehomv emarofv, vnet omarēs.
'coʔíssi callí· ihóma ima·ló·fa anít omá·li·s[i]
and as the rolling deer-hair [ball] is going about, it will be I [who does it].

'Vnpokko hoten vnet ohkueyarēs' yvn komet, este hvmkusē arvnto omēt,
anpókko[ii] *hótin anít ohkóyyá·li·s yan kò·mit ísti hámkosi· a·lánto· ô·mi·t*
Thinking, 'I will move my ball to its home,' we must move as one man going about,

ena lowalokusē estomis, emokhackv, entvhopketv omvlēcet,
iná· lowă·ⁿlo·kosi· istô·meys imokhá·cka intahopkitá omáli·cít
and even though his body is young, using all vigor and nimbleness,

pokk-vnvttēckv ēkvn-lvtketv momēto estomis,
pokkanattí·cka i·kanlatkitá mo·mí·to· istô·meys
even though blocking the ball and falling on the ground do occur,

ēkvnvt apvtakēs komvtē hēret,
i·kanát a·patà·ki·s kó·mati· hǐ·ⁿlit
think carefully about the ground spread out;

renakv sulkē emelecv yvn vnsehokvrēn enkomis. Yvn makēt omes ce.
'liná·ka sólki· imilicá yan ansihô·káli·n iŋkô·meys yan ma·kí·t ó·mis ciˆ
I want them to stand for me under the sight of many. [The chief] has said this.

'Opunvkv yomakusis, vm enkērkuehcetsken,
oponaká yo·mâ·koseys amiŋki·łkóyhcíckin
'Even if the words are just this, I want you to announce it for me:

Yahketv yekcē hēren yahkekvs' yvn maken,
ya·hkitá yíkci· hǐ·ⁿlin yá·hkikas yan ma·kín
Let them yell a strong yell,' he said,

---

[i] "Most of them use squirrel hide (rawhide) for ball. Long time ago they always used deerhide. Took hair off — put inside part on outside of ball. Never did see it, but sometimes used hide of loggerhead turtle."
[ii] Or: *ampókko*.

cenkĕrkuecvkin apohicet pvlatket ometskes ci."
*ciŋki·łkoycakéyn á·poheycít palâ·tkit o·mickis cey^*
and I announce to you all, and you have heard as you are spread out."

Makē wikan vpaken, honvntake omvlkvt yahket pefatiket,
ma·kí· weykâ·n apâ·kin honantá·ki omálkat ya·hkít pifa·têykit
Right after he stopped speaking, all the men ran around yelling,

'to-konhe 'to-poloke ohhocvtēn cvwaket, espefatket
'tokónhi 'topoló·ki ohhô·cati·n cawa·kit íspifa·tkít
and they took the ball-sticks they had on the pole and ran with them

eto cǫtkusē cakhēcakat pefatkēt vfolotēcet,
itó cǫ̆ⁿtkosi· cákhi·câ·ka·t pifa·tki·t afolóti·cít
and ran around the little tree they had stuck in the ground,

hvmket pokko etuce yoksv vtvrkusē sesēt makvranat
hámkit pókko itóci yóksa atálkosi· sísi·t má·kała·nâ·t
and one holding the ball hanging from the end of a stick was to say,

yekcetv emhoyēt onkv, "Yaaaaahaaaaa" makof "Wih" makof,
yikcitá imhoyí·t óŋka "ya····hâ····" ma·kô·f "wâyh" ma·kô·f
because he was given authority, "Yaaaaahaaaaa," and when they say "Wayh,"

hvmket enwiketv hahoyēn "Kvooooooo" makof,
hámkit inweykitá ha·hoyí·n "kâw·······" ma·kô·f
the one who was appointed said, "Kawwwwwww aw aw,"

"Wih wih wih" makēt yahkof, pokko sēsat "Yvkotvlē yvh" makof,
"wayh wayh wayh^" ma·kí·t ya·hkô·f pókko sî·sa·t yakotalí· yah[i] ma·kô·f
and when they say, "Wayh wayh wayh," and yell, the one with the ball says, "Yakotali yah,"

sulkat "Yvh" makateu fullē estomis, sulkēt pahēcet pefatkēt,
sólka·t "yah" ma·kâ·tiw folli· istô·meys sólki·t pá·hi·cit pifa·tki·t
and though many of them say, "Yah," many whoop and run;

---

[i] Or: *yakotali· hah* [pronounced as three eighth notes, a dotted quarter note, and an eighth note with a fall] very fast.

etucen vfolotēcēt fullvtet rapefatkat, totkv ētkan pefatkēt vfolotēcet
itócin afolóti·cí·t follatít la·pifâ·tka·t tó·tka i·tkâ·n pifa·tkí·t afolóti·cít
and when they circle the little tree and run back, they run to the burning fire, circle it,

"Yvkotvlē" makof, "Yvh" makvntot, "Yah hah" makvnton, "Wih" makof,
"yakotalí·" ma·kô·f "yah" ma·kántot "ya·h ha·h" ma·kánton "wayh" ma·kô·f
and when he said, "Yakotali," they said, "Yah," and, "Yah hah," and when they said,

"Kvo vo vo" maken "Wih wih wih" maket yahket
"kaw aw aw" ma·kín "wayh wayh wayh" ma·kít ya·hkít
"Wayh," he said, "Kaw aw aw," and they say, "Wayh wayh wayh," and yell,

vcewusēn foliyet pefatkat,
acíwosi·n folêyyit pifâ·tka·t
and when they went about and ran a good while,

'to-konhe ohkakvn 'to-poloke ohtakhakan ervsvpaklet,
'tokónhi ohká·kan 'topoló·ki ohtakhâ·ka·n ilasapâ·klit
they went and stood at the pole crossing the ball-stick rack.

yahket wikof, 'to-konhe ohkahyet vwahhet
yá·hkit weykô·f 'tokónhi ohkáhyit awáhhit
When they stopped yelling, they put the ball-sticks on it and dispersed,

eto-wakkvn estvmvn likvten omat, mv mahusan oh-vpokēt omet omvnts.
itowákkan ístaman leykatín o·mâ·t ma má·hosa·n óhhapo·kí·t ô·mit o·mánc
and wherever they had sat earlier on the bench, they sat in the same order.

Mohmet hvtvm hoktvke yvhikepueckvn vlicēcet omvnts.
móhmit hatâm hoktakí yaheykipóyckan aléyci·cít o·mánc
Then once more they began to make the women sing.

Enyvhikvlke honvntake eteyoposhuecē ostē oricē vtēkat
inyaheykâlki honantá·ki itiyopóshoycí· ô·sti· oleyci· atî·ka·t
Every four times the singers and men changed about,

heyv onvpv onvkv ocat omē vlkēn fullet,
hiyá (?) onápa (?) onáka (?) ô·ca·t ó·mi· álki·n follít
and went about each time like the description above,

yahketv osticat momusen mēkkot enkērkuecet okat,
ya·hkitá ósteycâ·t mô·mosin mí·kkot iŋki·łkoycít o·kâ·t
and when they yelled four times, the chief announced to them saying,

"Hiyomusen fekhoniyet fēkvpkvn hopoyekvs," makof, asempunayvt aenkērkuehcen,
"hayyô·mosin fikhonêyyit fi·kápkan hopóyikas," ma:kô:f, a·simponá·yat a·ʔiŋki·łkóyhcin
"Now let them stop and seek rest," and the spokesman announced it,

nocicēt omvnts. Afvckvranē enhuehhokvtē vtēkat omvlkvt
noceycí·t o·mánc[i] a·fáckała·ní· inhoyhhokáti· atî·ka·t omálkat
and they slept. Everyone that was called to play ball

ehitake enkvpvkē vlkēt nocicēt omvnts.
iheytá·ki iŋkapáki· álki·t noceycí·t o·mánc
always slept apart from their wives.

Em paskofv ofv tan pokkechvranat
impa·skó·fa ó·fa·tá·n pokkíchała·nâ·t
It is their rule that inside the clearing those who are to play

ehiwv enkvpvkēt nocicvranēt em vhakvt omēs.
ihéywa iŋkapáki·t nocéycała·ní·t imahá·kat ô·mi·s
must sleep apart from their wives.

Hoktē aenwakkēt aret afacken omat, nvfhohkewiten, tacken omat,
hokti· a·ʔínwa·kkí·t a·lít á·fa·ckín o·mâ·t nafhóhkiwêytin ta·ckín o·mâ·t
If someone sleeps with a woman and plays ball, he might get hit and if cut,

catvt tąyen pvlatkēs, hoktē catvt fihnēt onkv maket,
cá·tat tă·ⁿyin pala·tkí·s hokti· cá·tat feyhní·t óŋka ma·kít
blood would spill profusely, as it does when a woman's blood flows, they say,

vculvket vsēhēt omvnts. Mohmen nocicen hvyatkof,
acolakít asi·hí·t o·mánc. móhmin noceycín haya·tkô·f
and old folks cautioned them [not to do that]. Then they slept, and in the morning,

---

[i] Some towns, if they want, can do it all night.

avpohket fullof, "Uewvn aklopaks" mēkko makof,
a·ʔapóhkit follô·f "óywan aklopaks" mí·kko makô·f,
when they got up and were around, when the chief said, "Bathe in the water,"

hvccen vpehyet, ēnakayet, etem ehaket,
háccin apíhyit i·ná·ka·yít itimihâ·kit
they went to the creek, stripped down, and waited for each other;

omvlkvt ēnakvyahkēn tvlken, "Tokvs!" kihocof,
omálkat i·na·kayáhki·n tálkin "tókas" kéyho·cô·f
and all must [wait until] they undressed, then when they were told, "Now!"

honvntake enhuehhokvtē uewv aktasehcet aksomket osticat,
honantá·ki inhoyhhokáti· óywa akta·síhcit áksomkít ósteycâ·t
the men who were called upon jumped into the water and went under four times,

uewv asak-osset omvnts. Mohmet ēyvccehcet, em paskofv erohyicof,
óywa a·sákko·ssít[280] *o·mánc. móhmit i·yaccíhcit impa·skó·fa iłóhyeycô·f,*
and then got out of the water. Then they dressed and, when they got back to the clearing,

cukolice hvlewv ocakat
cokolêyci halíwa[281] *o·câ·ka·t*
when the chief knew that they were ready to eat

hvpo vrahrvkvt homhopvranat ʼmetetakaken mēkkot kērrat,
hapó· alahlakát homhopáła·nâ·t ʼmitita·kâ·kin mí·kkot ki·łâ·t
at each camp where the women had provisions,

este cukopericv afvcketv hoyopvranē yicat omvlkvt "Lvpecicēt hompvkekvs" mahken,
ísti cokopiléyca a·fackitá hoyópala·ní· yêyca·t omálkat "lapicéyci·t hompakikas" máhkin
to all the visitors who had come to watch the game, he said, "Hurry and let them eat,"

hompahket fullof, "Hiyomat lvpecicēt em etetakekvs," mēkko maken,
hompáhkit follô·f, "hayyô·ma·t lapicéyci·t imititá·kikas," mí·kko ma·kín
and when they had eaten, the chief said, "Now let them hurry and get ready,"

aem ohkērkuehohcen ʼmetetahket, yahiket, cerakkon oh-vpohket
a·ʔimohki·lkoyhóhcin ʼmititáhkit ya·hêykit ʼcilákkon ohhapóhkit
and it was announced to them, and they got ready and yelled, got on their horses,

mēkkot homvn ayof, entvsekvyv vcak-vpēyen, yopvn hoktvke, hopuetake
mí·kkot hóman a·yò·f intasikayá acákkapi·yín yópan hoktakí hopoytá·ki
and while the chief went in front, his citizens followed, and women, children,

mont cukopericvlkeu yopvn awen, este omvlkvt vpēyet,
mónt cokopiłeycâlkiw yópan a·wín ísti omálkat api·yít
and visitors too came behind, and everyone went

pokkechetv ēkvnv hvyakpo tempen erfekhoniyet vpokēt omvnts.
pokkichitá i·kaná hayakpó· tímpin iłfikhonâyyit apo·kí·t o·mánc.
and stopped near the ball-ground prairie and camped.

Momof lvpecicēt 'metetahket, etenfvccetv-hayvlke tat vpēyet
mo·mô·f lapicéyci·t 'mititáhkit itinfaccitaha·yâlkita·t[i] api·yít
Then they hurried and got ready, and the contract makers went

enkepayv etenfvccetv-hayvlken etehecaket,
iŋkipá·ya itinfaccitaha·yâlkin itihíca·kít
and met together with their opponent's contract makers,

afvckvranē hēret 'metetakē vlkēt on omat, etekērret,
a·fáckala·ní· hĭ·ⁿłit 'mititá·ki· álki·t ó·n o·má·t itíki·łłit
and if both sides are prepared to play, they should get acquainted:

"Vkerretv vpvkētis oken, em vkvsahmin enhessetake tis sēyvnihcēt,
akillitá apáki·teys o·kín imakasáhmeyn inhissitá·kiteys si·yanéyhci·t
"There may be trickery intended, after we agree, they may use their friends to defeat us,"

ofvp cvhahyēs" etekomēt, etem ēyvketēckv rakkē ocēt etem punahoyet
o·fáp caháhyi·s itikó·mi·t itimi·yakití·cka łákki· ó·ci·t itimponá·ho·yít
[each opponent] thought, and they talked to one another with great watchfulness of one

opunvkv etem vnrvpkv sulkēn nanvke opunvyēcet,
oponaká itimanłápka sólki·n ná·naki opónayi·cít
another, and they talked about many words of disagreement and things,

---

[i] *itinfaccitahá·ya* is the same as *páyhki·*; *imma·kâlki* ("talkers for") is an old time word for *itinfaccitaha·yâlki*.

tvhiketv opunvkv tis vpakvnton vpoket,
taheykitá oponakáteys apa·kánton apô·kit
and even quarrelsome talks would sometimes happen when they met

etenfvccetv hayakēt omvnts.
itinfaccitá há·ya·kí·t o·mánc.
and made the agreement.

"Hiyomen tvsekvyv tat cenkẹrhoyusin sehoyet oketskekv mv vtẹkusēn
"hayyô·min tasikayáta·t ciŋkï·ⁿłhô·yoseyn sihô·yit o·kíckika ma atï·ⁿkosi·n
"Now citizens, I know you well, you who are standing,

hvyakpo tat asossicetskvrēs.
*hayakpó·ta·t a·sosséycíckáli·s*²⁸²
so you must send just those to the prairie [i.e., the ball field].

Este kerkeko mahis vpayetsken hēcin omat, 'Ossicvs' cekicin omat, ossicetskvrēs.
isti kiłkikó· mâ·heys apa·yíckin hi·céyn o·mâ·t 'osséycas' cikeycéyn o·mâ·t osséycíckáli·s
If I see you put an unknown man in, if I say, 'Put him out,' you must put him out.

Vne tat tvsekvyv vhonkạtkusēn cēpvnạkusēn omēpikv,
aníta·t tasikayá ahoŋkă·ⁿtkosi·n ci·pană·ⁿkosi·n omî·péyka
On my part I have only a few very young citizens,

etvlwv cahmelikv em afvckē tayē tokon omikv,
itálwa cahmiléyka ima·fácki· tâ·yi· tó·ko·n ô·méyka
there is no way they can play a mixed town,

este kerkvkekat sossicetskekon omat,
isti kiłkakíka·t sosséycíckikon o·mâ·t
so if you don't expel the unknown people,

pokko tat hvlwekon cēpvnvkuce tat ravcekelhueceparēs,"
pókkota·t halwíkon ci·panakocíta·t la·ʔacikilhoycipá·li·s,"
I'll pull the boys back [i.e., call the game off] before the ball goes up,"

Helvpe maken, Pvkvntvlvhasse em vkvsahmen,
hilápi ma·kín pakantalahá·ssi imakasáhmin
Hilabi said, and Pakantalahassi agreed.

"Ensulkē tat pale-tuccēnen hvyakpo-hvtke tat vtēhet omeyvrēs," Helvpe makof,
"insolkí·ta·t pá·li toccî·nin hayakpohátkita·t ati·hít omíyáli·s," hilápi ma·kô·f
"The total number [of players] that we put in will be thirty players," Hilabi said,

Pvkvntvlvhasset okat, "Estohmit estvn vnheciken pale-tuccēnat orihcvkos.
pakantalahá·ssit o·kâ·t "istóhmeyt ístan anhicêykin pá·li toccî·na·t ołéyhcako·s
and Pakantalahassi said, "There's no way I can find thirty anywhere.

Cukolicen vpayin omateu 'sem vnvcikekotan onkv,
cokolêycin apa·yéyn o·mâ·tiw 'simanacêykiko·ta·n óŋka
If I add women too it won't seem right,

pale-hokkolen ēpohkakusen vhvmkvtepvyēt ont os" maken,
pá·li hokkô·lin i·pohkâ·kosin ahamkatípayi·t ônt ó·ⁿs," ma·kín
so I have counted just twenty-six."

etem opunvyēckv sulkēt hoyahnen pale-hokkolēn ēpohkakan
itimoponayí·cka sólki·t hoyáhnin pá·li hokkô·li·n i·pohkâ·ka·n
After much discussion, Hilabi agreed to twenty-six,

Helvpe vkvsahmen sulkat yohfulehcet, heyv etenfvccetv etenhayat
hilápi akasáhmin sôlka·t yohfolíhcit hiyá(?) itinfaccitá itinhâ·ya·t
and they returned to their members and announced this agreement

omvlkvn enkērkuecakvtēt os. Fvccvlikekv, hompetvn eshuehiken[283]
omálkan iŋki·łkóyca·katí·t ô·ⁿs. faccalêykika hompitán ishoyhêykin[283]
they made together to everyone. It was noontime, so he made a call for food,

em vtelohohyen, hompet este sulkat hompahkof,
imatilo·hóhyin hompít ísti sôlka·t hompáhko·f
and they gathered, and after all the people had eaten

mohmofvt pokkechvranat enhopoyetv vlicēcat,
móhmo·fat pokkíchała·nâ·t inhopoyitá aléyci·câ·t
after that, when they began to pick who would play ball,

este sulkē vpokvtē nvrkvpvn tektvnkvrēn mēkkot maken,
ísti sólki· apô·kati· nałkapán tiktánkáli·n mí·kkot ma·kín
the chief called for a space to be made in the middle of where everyone was sitting.

este vkueyēcen tektvnkē est'ele vhopakv palat hoyvnēt
ísti akóyyi·cín tíktanki· istilí ahopá·ka pâ·la·t hoyáni·t
He moved people, and a space of ten feet or more

encvpkēt pale-ostat mahet tektvniken, este enhopoyat
incapkí·t pá·li ô·sta·t mâ·hit tiktanêykin ísti ínhopo·yá·t
and about forty feet long opened up. To pick people,

mékkoton este hokkolet vpaken asempunayvo vpakekv,
mí·kkoton ísti hokkô·lit apâ·kin a·simponá·yaw apâ·kika
the chief had two others and the spokesman too,

enhocēfet "Yvn enhuehkvs," mēkkot kicof,
ínhoci·fít "yan inhóyhkas," mí·kkot keycô·f
so he named them, and when the chief said, "Call him here,"

hocefhuecet, "'Yvmvn vthuekvs' maks ci," kihcen,
hocífhoycít "'yamán athóykas' má·ks cay^," kéyhcin
[the spokesman] named them, and told them, "He says, 'Let him come here.'"

avthoyof, wvsketv taranan ēkvnvn takkahyet,
a·ʔátho·yô·f waskitá tá·la·nâ·n i·kanán takkáhyit[i]
And when they came, they seated the ones to be in center position on the ground,

fulecē taranan hokkolen hocefhuecet,
folici· tá·la·nâ·n hokkô·lin hocífhoycít
and he named two to be enemy side,

"'Yvmvn avthuekvs,' maks ci," kihcen,
yamán a·ʔathóykas,' má·ks cây kéyhcin
and [the spokesman] said, "He says, 'Let them come here,'"

---

[i] The Hilabi selected the players in this order: 1. *waskitá* (2 men); 2. *folici·* (2 men); 3. *'safallitá* (2 men); 4. *folici· naɬkaptakhá·ka* (2 men); 5. *'safallitá naɬkaptakhá·ka* (2 men); 6. *waskitá* (2 men); 7. *folici·* (2 men); 8. *'safallitá* (2 men); 9. *folici· naɬkaptakhá·ka* (2 men); 10. *'safallitá naɬkaptakhá·ka* (2 men); 11. *waskitá* (1 man) [not sure about order from here]; 12. *folici·* (1 man); 13. *'safallitá* (1 man); 14. three men left over placed in *waskitá*. Total men in each position: 1. *waskitá* (8 men); 2. *folici·* (5 men); 3. *'safallitá* (5 men); 4. *folici· naɬkaphá·ka* (4 men); 5. *'safallitá naɬkaphá·ka* (4 men). Jim Hill played in the *'safallitá* position.

lvpkē hēren rohhoyof, ēkvnv em meliyen takkahken,
lápki· hĭ·ⁿlin lóhho·yô·f i·kaná immilêyyin takkáhkin
and when they got there quickly, they pointed the ground out to them, and they sat down.

'svfvlletv taranateu
'safallitá tá·la·nâ·tiw
And to the two people who would be home base too,

este hokkole ētan "'Yvmvn avthuekvs,' maks ci," kicen,
ísti hokkô·li i·tá·n yamán a·ʔathóykas má·ks câγ keycín
he said in the same way, "He says, 'Let them come here,'"

lvpkē hēren rohhoyof, ēkvnv em meliyen takkakof,
lápki· hĭ·ⁿlin lóhho·yô·f i·kaná immilêyyin tákka·kô·f
and when they got there quickly, he pointed the ground out to them, and when they sat down

yefulehcet fulecē nvrkvptakhakv taranan rasvpaklet,
yifolíhcit folicí· nalkaptakhá·ka tá·la·nâ·n la·sapâ·klit
they went back, and those who would be the base next to the enemy side were standing,

hokkolen "'Yvmvn avthuekvs,' maks ci," kicen,
hokkô·lin yamán a·ʔathóykas má·ks caγ^ keycín
and he said to two, "He says, "Let them come here,'"

lvpecicēt rohhoyof, mvo takkahken hvtvm rawat
lapicéyci·t lohhô·yo·f maw takkáhkin hatâm lâ·wa·t[i]
and when they got there quickly, they too sat down, and again [the three men] came back,

'svfvlletv nvrkvptakhakv taranan svpaklet,
'safallitá nalkaptakhá·ka tá·la·nâ·n sapâ·klit
and to those standing to be the position next to home base

hokkole ētan "'Yvmvn avthuekvs,' maks ci," kicen, avthoyof,
hokkô·li i·tá·n yamán a·ʔathóykas,' má·ks caγ^ keycín a·ʔatho·yô·f[ii]
he told two in the same way, "He says, "Let them come here,'" and when they came,

---

[i] If they had had 30 players, they would have placed five men in each position (2, 2, + then 1) and then the remainder would have been placed in *waskitá*.

[ii] The ball usually goes over the men in the *nalkaphá·ka* position, so they need less men in these positions.

mvo takkahken vpokē cahkēpen vpohyet,
maw' takkáhkin apó·ki· cahkî·pin apóhyit
they sat down too, and he seated them in five groups and called them,

estomēt vpoyetv vlicēcatē vcakkąyusēn enhuehket oh-vpayet esfullet,
istó·mi·t apo·yitá aleycî·ca·ti· acakkă·ⁿyosi·n ínhoyhkít óhhapa·yít isfollít
following however the one who started seating them and went about putting them in.

este ensulkē eskerretv eto-kvckucen cvwēt omvtet enhuehkof,
ísti insolkí· iskiłłitá itokackocín cawí·t ô·matit ínhoyhkô·f
And to find out the number of men, he had little broken sticks, and after he called them,

este hvmken aēmen pokēpof,
ísti hámkin á·ʔi·mín pó·ki·pô·f
he handed one to another person, and when they were all gone,

este ensulkē eyacvtē tayēpat mēkkot kērrekv.
ísti insolkí· iyâ·cati· tá·yi·pâ·t mí·kkot ki·łłiká[i]
the chief knew there were enough of the desired men.

"Momusen esosiyet ēheromicekvs" makof, asem punayv
mô·mosin isosêyyit i·hiłoméycikas ma·kô·f a·simponá·ya
And when [the chief] said, "Now let them get out and decorate themselves," the spokesman

"'Sosiyet ēheromicekvs,' maks ci" kican vpaken,
sosêyyit i·hiłoméycikas má·ks câr̂y keycâ·n apâ·kin
said, "He says, 'Let them get out and decorate themselves,'" and as soon as he said that

pahēcet, pefatket fullet, tokunhe, esnehickv vpvkēn ocakvtētok cahwet
pá·hi·cít pifa·tkít follít 'tokónhi isnihéycka apáki·n o·câ·kati·to·k cáhwit
they whooped and ran around, they took the ball-sticks and decorations they had

---

[i] One part of the story he forgot to put in. Long time ago when two towns were playing against each other, the *mí·kko* would call for sticks — he did this to find out how many possible players he had on his side. Each man would break off a nearby stick and throw it down on a quilt that had been spread out for this purpose. Then the chief counted the sticks. They followed this procedure in this game, but JH forgot to put this part in. They did this right after they asked for the game.

pefatiket, este sulkan emvrvnakēt fullet, ēnakayet,
pifa·têykit ísti sôlka·n imałaná·ki·t follít i·ná·ka·yít[284]
and ran, and went out of sight from all the men present, pulled off their clothes,

ēkofkv sēkofaket, senockv ocakvtēn cufe-esse cate tis monkat lvslvtē tis enocaket,
i·kó·fka si·kó·fa·kít 'sinó·cka o·câ·kati·n cofiʔissi cá·titeys móŋka·t laslatí·teys inóca·kít
put on their breechcloths, put on handkerchiefs they had, of red or black flannel ['rabbit

fakke cate tis monkat torap-lvste tis cesapet, telekmicet etorofvn essiyet,
fákki cá·titeys móŋka·t 'tołapłástiteys cisa·pít tilíkmeycít itoló·fan íssayyít[i]
fur'], crushed red earth or charcoal, made it fine, and smeared it on the face,

ena tis essiyet holwvkē omēn ēhayet 'metetakahken,
iná·teys íssayyít holwakí· ó·mi·n i·ha·yít 'mitita·káhkin
smeared it on the body too, and by making themselves look ugly got ready

este sulkat ehomv svpvkilen, yekcetv em punayvt em punayof,
ísti sólka·t ihóma sapakêylin yikcitá imponá·yat ímpona·yô·f
and stood before the people present. When the exhorter spoke to them,

nekēhoyēsekot etenakuecuset svpaklen,
niki·hŏⁿyi·síkot itinăⁿkôycosit sapâ·klin[ii]
they didn't even move and stood close together,

---

[i] "They daubed it on the arms, then on legs, then on front of body. Then if they wanted some on their backs, they asked another player to daub it on their backs. It was daubed with palms of hands."

"It was put on sidewise with third finger on either cheek and above eyes, or it was smeared on with all fingers. Made as many stripes as they wanted."

[ii] "The chief can stay either with visitors or go off with players."

"In olden days they wouldn't even move even though they might be nervous. If anyone did seem fidgety, they would know he was afraid to play — hence all kept still."

"Ta! Entokis ce. 'Pum vculvke em ahkopvnkv yvt mvtarēs'
ta into·kéys ci^i pomacoláki imahkopánka yat matá·li·s
"Ta! Intokis chi! [a ritualistic introduction] The [two sides] are standing in the forest sending

enkomē tvsekvyv huehketv em vrēcvyvtē eto-lanofv sehoken,
iŋkômi· tasikayá hoyhkitá imáli·cayáti· itola·nó·fa sihô·kin
a call to the citizens with the hope, 'This is the game of our forefathers, thus it shall be.'

hvse enyvfketv hiyomē nehickv 'metetahkē estenrenakv sulkē em elecv yvn sehokofv,
hasí inyafkitá hayyô·mi· nihéycka 'mititáhki· istinliná·ka sólki· imilicá yan siho·kô·fa
And now standing here with the sun in the afternoon, the decorations ready, beneath the eyes

pum vculvke tatē em ahkopvnkv yvt mvtarēs ce.
*pomacolakitá·ti· imahkopánka yat matá·li·s ci^*
of the whole crowd that has gathered, this shall be a game for our forefathers.

Yvn makēt omes ce. Tv! Mvtarētes cē.
yan ma·kí·t ô·mis ci^. ta matá·li·tis ci^ii
Here [the chief] says it is. Ta! Thus it shall be.

Em pokko cvllē em arofv, ēyenhvlvtusēt tvlwv vlkēn enrenakv ehomv vnsehoket omekarēn
impókko callí· ima·lô·fa i·yinhalátosi·t tálwa álki·n inliná·ka ihóma ánsiho·kít omíká·li·n
When their ball is rolling, I do not want my town to hold back before the eyes of other

enkomikv, yvn vnkērret este hvmkusē arvnto omet em okhackv omvlēcet,
iŋkô·méyka yan aŋkì·llit ísti hámkosi· a·lánto· ô·mit imokhá·cka omali·cit
towns, so understand this, you must be as one man going about using all vigor

hvyakpo-hvtke vntaksehokof, mvtarēs.
hayakpohátki antáksiho·kô·f matá·li·s
when they stand on the ball-ground for me, it shall be.

---

[i] "These ball-speeches make you feel sad. That's what they're for — to remind you of your forefathers, old times, to remind you that things are not like they used to be though you are going to do your best. The whole town feels this way, the womenfolks, too. At the same time they're thrilled + proud of their town. "Our town's about all it." That lonesomeness sound comes on you when they talk of forefathers, then they get you all excited about the game, anxious to see it take place."

[ii] "Here they get excited and restless and anxious to get right in + play."

Yvn maket 'Yahketv yekcēn yahkekvs.' Yvn maken, cenkērkuecvkin,
yan ma·kít ya·hkitá yíkci·n yá·hkikas[i] *yan ma·kín ciŋki·lkoycakéyn*
This he said: 'Yell a strong yell!' He said this, and I announced it to you,

pvlatket ometskes ce" kicof,
palâ·tkit o·míckis ci^ keycô·f[ii]
and you have spread out here together," and when he said [that],

yahiket pefatket mēkkot enhueren vfolotēcet yahiket,
ya·hêykit pifa·tkit mí·kkot inhóylin afolóti·cit ya·hêykit
they yelled and ran, circled where the chief stood, and yelled,

yakyapv sehokan yvkapet vpēyof,
yakyá·pa sihô·ka·n yaka·pít api·yô·f
and when they walked to where the goal-posts stood,

hoyopvlke ensulkē estont fullvten omat,
hoyo·pâlki insolkí· istônt follatín o·mâ·t
however many spectators had gathered,

omvlkvt vcak-vpēyen, eto-sehokv rorihcet fekhonnēt omvnts.
omálkat acákkapi·yín itosihô·ka 'lołéyhcit fíkhonni·t o·mánc.
all of them followed, came to the support-poles and stopped.

Yakyapv eto warvranat enwiketv hahoyēn fullen,
yakyá·pa itó wa·lala·nâ·t inweykitá ha·hoyí·n follín[iii]
There were some who had been appointed to cut the goal-posts,

karonē ēkvnv soh-vpeyvranateu enwiketv hayēt,
ka·lô·ni· i·kaná sohhapíyala·nâ·tiw inweykitá há·yi·t
and [some] were appointed also to take them on their shoulders to the ground,

---

[i] After they got dressed, he talked to them, he's still talking to them.

[ii] He can say more if he wants to. It was not Big Jack who made this speech.

[iii] This part (according to JH) should be put in right after the part about where they circled the chief.

cakcvhēcvranateu enwiketv hahoyēt on, 'tetakuecvkēt omvnts.
cakcahí·cała·nâ·tiw inweykitá ha·hoyí·t ô·n[i] *'tita·koycakí·t o·mánc.*
and [others] were appointed to stick them in too and got them ready.

Em etehopvyē estomuset omvranat, etenkerrēt eto-sehokv cakcvhēcet omakvtēs.
imitihopayí· istô·mosit omáła·nâ·t itiŋkíłłi·t itosihó·ka cakcahî·cit oma·kati·s[ii]
Whatever the distance apart is to be, they let one another know and stick the support-poles

Eto-sehokv est'ele vhopakv tuccēnat mahet omēs.
itosihó·ka istilí ahopá·ka toccî·na·t mâ·hit o·mi·s
in. The support-poles are about three feet long.

Pokko vwihokat, mv eto-sehokat tenrvwvn ropotten, monkat mv eton esnvfhoken omat,
pókko awéyho·kâ·t ma itó sihô·ka·t tînławán łopo·ttín móŋka·t ma itón isnáfho·kín o·mâ·t
When they throw the ball, it goes between the support-poles, or if the pole is hit,

satkv hvmkēt omēs.
sá·tka hámki·t ô·mi·s
it's one point.

Mvn rē-sehokv kicakēt omēs.
man łi·sihó·ka kéyca·kí·t ô·mi·s
They call it r̲ē̲-̲s̲e̲h̲o̲k̲v̲ ['standing arrows', referring to the score-counters or pegs].

Este rē-sehokv cakcvhēckvn enwiketv hahoyen omat,
ísti łi·sihó·ka cakcahí·ckan inweykitá há·ho·yín o·mâ·t
If someone is appointed to stick the pegs in,

---

[i] Four or more men are appointed to take charge of getting the pole + setting it up. Those that cut the pole, those that dig the hole, those that carry it in can all help one another.
[ii] Both sides are setting up their posts at the same time.

enwiketv rakkēn yekcēn ocēt ēkvnvn takkakēs.
inweykitá lákki·n yíkci·n ó·ci·t i·kanán tákka·kí·s[i]
they have a big, difficult job and sit down on the ground.

Etenrvpēt enrē-sehokvn vketēcē hēret, tektvnkē enhēcken omat,
itinlapí·t inli·sihó·kan akití·ci· hĭ·ⁿlit tiktankí· ínhi·ckín o·mâ·t
They are very watchful of their opponent's pegs, and if they see an opening,

rē-sehokv etenhorkopetv 'metetakusēt 'tenakuset tentakhvkēt kaken,
li·sihó·ka itinhołkopíta 'mitită·ⁿkosi·t 'tină·ⁿkosit tintakhakí·t kâ·kin
they were ready to steal a point and sat close together, side by side,

aenhēcvlkeu enwiketv hakvkēt
a·ʔinhi·câlkiw inweykitá ha·kaki·t
and watchers [of the score-keepers] too were appointed

rvsehoken hecaket vpokvtēs.
'łasihô·kin hicâ·kit apo·katí·s
and went and stood right by them watching.

Helvpe, Pvkvntvlvhasse tepakat vrahrvkvt enwiketv hayvkēt omvtēs.
hilápi pakantalahá·ssi 'tipâ·ka·t ałahlakát inweykitá ha·yakí·t o·matí·s[ii]
Hilabi and Pakantalahassi each made appointments.

Matvpomēn enwiketv hayvkēn, Helvpe em eto-sehokvt
ma·tapó·mi·n inweykitá ha·yaki·n hilápi imitosihó·kat
They made appointments in the same way, and it was their job

---

[i] The score-keepers (called *li·sihó·ka há·ya*) are seated close to *waskitá*. There are 2 or 3 more [score-keepers] on each side. The score-keepers never watch the game.

At each goal there is a man watching to see if a score is made. Sometimes they (the onlookers) think a score is made + yell (*ya·hkitá*); then these watchers tell the score-keeper it was a mistake. The reason the score-keepers are so watchful is that the opposite side may take one of your sticks away. He might even put it with his scores. The opposite town has a clever man there who may be capable of stealing one of your sticks even though you may be looking — so the score-keepers have to be very watchful and dare not look at the game.
[ii] Each town has watchers at each goal.

pokkot ropotten monkat nafken omat hecakvranat wiketv hakēton
pókkot lopo·ttín móŋka·t na·fkín o·mâ·t hicâ·kaɫa·nâ·t weykitá há·ki·ton[i]
to see if Hilabi's ball went through the support-posts or hit it,

Pvkvntvlvhasseu matvpomēn estvmi vlkis ǫrusen
pakantalahá·ssiw ma·tapó·mi·n istamêy âlkeys ŏ·ⁿɫosin
and Pakantalahassi too, when either side in the same way

etem vketēcēt svpaklvranen enwiketv hayahkof, nak omvlkvt 'tetaketv
itimakití·ci·t sapâ·kɫaɫa·nín inweykitá ha·yáhko·f[ii] *nâ·k omálkat 'tita·kitá*
appointed people to stand and watch carefully, when everything was ready,

Helvpe em eto-sehokvn pefatket vfolotēcet yahket wikof,
hilápi imitosihó·kan pifa·tkít afolóti·cít ya·hkít weykô·f
Hilabi ran to their goal, circled it, and yelled, and when they quit,

Pvkvntvlvhasseu matvpomet yahiken etoh-vpēyet
pakantalahá·ssiw ma·tapó·mit ya·héykin itóhhapi·yít
Pakantallahassee too yelled in the same way, and they went up to each other,

retesvpaklof,
'ɫitisapa·klô·f[iii]
and when they stood facing each other,

tokunhen tentakhvkēn omvlkvt ēkvnvn tak-vpoyof,
'tokónhin tintakhakí·n omálkat i·kanán tákkapo·yô·f[iv]
when everyone placed their ball-sticks side-by-side on the ground,

---

[i] Ball could go through or could hit cross-piece on either of posts — in any event it counted one point. Must be your own goal.

[ii] "When the men were lined up + appointed to their position, at this same time the pole-cutters + others connected with the pole, the score-keepers, + the goal-watchers were appointed, says JH. He forgot to put it in there so he put it in here."

[iii] "That's why the Ind. are so long about putting on anything — they have so many rules + regulations to go through." F.S. "They never set (precise) time to play."

[iv] *iti·si·* = taking each other (when they place ball-sticks opposite each other)

"All players are lined up facing opposite goals. They come toward center kinda bunched up, then spread out side by side, each man beside teammate + facing opposition player."

ensulkē momvlkusē omat kerrakēs.
insolkí· mô·mà·lⁿkosi· o·mâ·t kíɫa·ki·s
they found out if the number was exactly the same.

Mont naken tohkayetvn eyacen omat tohkayēs.
mónt nâ·kin tohka·yitán iyâ·cin o·mâ·t tóhka·yí·s
Then if they want to bet something, they bet it.

Toknawv, kapv, nockv, yokkofketv, hoktvke tat nockv,
tokná·wa ká·pa nó·cka yokko·fkitáⁱ hoktakíta·t nó·cka
They bet money, coats, pocket handkerchiefs, and shirts, and the women bet handkerchiefs,

takfulwv, homohpackv tis tohkayvkofvt, vhopayet
takfólwa homohpá·ckateys tohka·yakô·fatⁱⁱ ahopa·yít
ribbons, and aprons, and they measured

estvt nvrkvpv tat keriyet,
ístat naɫkapáta·t kilêyyit
and when they found out where the middle [of the field was],

mvn svpaklen pokko ēset,
man sapâ·klin pókko î·sitⁱⁱⁱ
they stood there [around the ball-thrower], and he held the ball [and said],

"Hiyomē hvyakpo-hvtke 'tem vtehikē sehokofv,
"hayyó·mi· hayakpohátki 'timatihâyki· siho·kó·fa
"Now standing together in the ball field,

---

vpvlwusēn vnokēcit ohmvkotes ce.
apálwosi·n anokî·ceyt óhmako·tis ci^i
it's not that I love only part of them.

Momekv entvhopketv em okhackv em pokkassetv yvn vtēkusen hoyopkv hahoyof,
mô·mika intahopkitá imokhá·cka impokka·ssitá^ii *yan atî·kosin hoyópka há·ho·yô·f*^iii
Therefore all there was to watch was their agility, their vigor and ball-chasing,

mvtarēs yvn komit 'tem vnvttēckv em ofv
matá·li·s yan kô·meyt 'timanattí·cka imó·fa^iv
[?]

arakpvliket mvyatot essehoket omekarēn makusēt,
a·łakpalêykit maya·tót issího·kít omíká·li·n ma·kosí·t
Do not turn around and stand swinging,

Vnkerrekvs maken,
aŋkíłłikas ma·kín^v
Let them understand me," [the chief] said,

cenkērkuecin, pvlatket ometskes ci.
ciŋkí·lkoycéyn palâ·tkit^285 *o·míckis cây.*
and I have announced it to you spread out here.

---

^i All are around him when he starts to speak, then before he finishes the players scatter out to their proper positions.

After they find their number is even, they pick up their ball-sticks + stand around ball-thrower as he begins to speak + before he is finished they are scattered out to their positions.

They did not necessarily line up side by side, but if they did they would stretch out crosswise + not lengthwise of the field (contrary to the drawing on p. 462, Am. Rep. 42). Each man faces his own home goal. After they start to play, the sides are not separated but are mixed together — "you have to look out for your opponent, in front of you, behind you or at the side of you.;" (FS) at the same time you must watch the ball.

^ii = *impókko a·ssitá.*

^iii "The Pakantallahassee face their own goal, the Hilabi face theirs."

^iv A warning not to fight.

^v "Those speeches are long — there's no ending to it — they're a lot longer than he (JH) put down — he just put down part of one."

"(Alec was always one who was full of fun, who talked back — even to the opponent's women.)"

'Rē-sehokv pale-hokkolat yvn escemaraks ci. 'Tem assaks ci' mahket,
li·sihó·ka pá·li hokkô·la·t yan íscima·láks cay^ 'timá·ssaks cay^," máhkit
'Here goes a ball for twenty stakes. Chase after it!' he said,

pokko enhvlwehcen, 'tem asset omvnts.
pókko inhalwíhcin[i] tíma·ssít o·mánc
and he threw up the ball, and they chased after it.[ii]

Mohmen fulletv ocē fulhoyvtē onvkv ocat omē vlkēn
móhmin follitá o·cí· fólho·yatí· onáka ô·ca·t ó·mi· álki·n
So they always used to talk of having that custom,

este-Maskokvlke enkepayv etem afacēto vtēkat momē vlkēt enfulletvt omēs.
ísti ma·sko·kâlki iŋkipá·ya itimá·fa·ckí·to· atî·ka·t mó·mi· álki·t infollitát ô·mi·s[iii]
and every time Creek people played their opponents, it was their habit like that.

Yekcetv em punvyetv opunvkv,
yikcitá imponayitá oponaká[286]
Speeches to exhort them,

pokko em vyvhiketv, monkat pokko 'mopanvlke enyvhiketv vtēkat
pókko imayahaykitá móŋka·t pókko 'mopa·nâlki inyahaykitá atî·ka·t
to sing for the ball, or all the songs for the ball dancers,

enhakē mv vlkēt ont omis,
ínha·kí· ma álki·t ônt o·mêys
their tunes are all like that, but

heyv onvpv opunvkv ocat sensulkēn mahokēt omēs.
hiyá onápa oponaká ô·ca·t sinsólki·n má·ho·kí·t ô·mi·s
a lot more was said than the words above.

---

[i] "After the ball went up + just one side had been scoring," [?]
[ii] The Pakantalahassee won this game (not put in story — says FS, "maybe even today he didn't want to tell who won"). Doesn't remember how many points they made — didn't think then he'd ever write a story about it.
    The men who were in the game at that time — there are just two living today, JH + Earnest Gouch [sic for Gouge] (Hilabi) — though poss. some others have moved away.
[iii] There is a lot more to the speeches beginning: *ta into·kays cây*, but he gave just a part of it.

Momen yvhiketvo sulkēn yvhihokēt omēs, mvrahrvkvn.
mo·mín yahaykitáw sólki·n yaháyho·kí·t ô·mi·s 'matahtakán.
And they sing many songs too, different ones.

Creek Clans and Kinship

J. Hill (Hill 27–30; Haas XVIII:1–25)

<u>Em vliketv</u> maketv hiyomēt omakēs. Este-cate etvlwv hvmēcat
imaleykitá ma·kitá hayyó·mi·t omâ·ki·s isticá·ti itálwa hamí·ca·t
What are called <u>em vliketv</u> ['clans'] are like this. Indians from one town,

este-cate mahhe hofonof, etena-hvmkē makē etekerrē fullēpvranatet
isticá·ti máhhi hofô·no·f itina·hámki· ma·kí· itikítti· folli·pala·nâ·tit
full-blood Indians long ago, so that they would know they were kin,

nake honecvkē ele oste sasat tis fuswv tis ēyvhocefakvtēt omēs.
nà·ki honicakí· ili ósti sâ·sa·tteys fóswateys i·yahocífa·katí·t ô·mi·s
named themselves after some wild animals with four legs, or birds.

Heyv nanvken: vlepvtv, echaswv, fuswv, nokose, kaccv, eco, penwv, hotvlē, kono, wotko,
hiyá nâ·nakin alipatá ichá·swa fóswa nokósi ká·cca icó pínwa hotalí· konó wó·tko
These things: alligator, beaver, bird, bear, tiger, deer, turkey, wind, skunk, raccoon,

aktvyahce, wakse, culv, cetto, vhv, 'kvpeccv, kohv ēhocēfat hvmmakēt okakvtēs.
aktayáhci wáksi colá cítto ahá 'kapícca kohá í·hoci·fâ·t hámma·ki·t oka·katí·s.
aktayahchi, waksi, fox, snake, sweet potato, kapitcha, cane, they named themselves like that.

Vlepvtvlke, Echaswvlke, Fuswvlke, Nokosvlke, Ecovlke, Penwvlke, Hotvlkvlke,
alipatâlki icha·swâlki foswâlki nokosâlki icoâlki pinwâlki hotalkâlki
Alligator clan, Beaver clan, Bird clan, Bear clan, Deer clan, Turkey clan, Wind clan,

Konepvlke, Wotkvlke, Aktvyahcvlke, Waksvlke, Culvlke, Cettvlke,
konipâlki wo·tkâlki aktayahcâlki waksâlki[287] colâlki cittâlki
Skunk clan, Raccoon clan, Aktayahchi clan, Waksi clan, Fox clan, Snake clan,

Vhvlvkvlke, Kvpeccvlke, Kohvsvlke, Kaccvlke.
ahalakâlki 'kapiccâlki[288] kohasâlki ka·ccâlki.
Sweet Potato clan, Kapitcha clan, Cane clan, Tiger clan.

Vlepvtvlke hoktē echustake omvlkvt Vlepvtvlket omēs, honvnwvtot hoktēto estomis.
alipatâlki[289] *hoktí· ichostá·ki omálkat alipatâlkit ô·mi·s honánwatot hoktí·to· istô·meys*[290]
The children of an Alligator clan woman were all Alligator clan, whether male or female.

Monkv mvn etena-hvmke maket okakvtēs.
mônka man itina·hámki ma·kít oka·katí·s
In this way they structured kinship.

Em vliketv makateu enhocefkv hvmkusē este honvpsen okēs.
imaleykitá ma·kâ·tiw[291] *inhocífka hámkosi·*[292] *ísti honápsin o·kí·s*
In reference to the clan, it means all those born into the same [clan] name.

Monkv heyv onvpv hocefkv ocakat honvpse omvlkvt momvkē vlkēt omēs.
mônka hiyá onápa hocífka o·câ·ka·t honápsi omálkat mo·makí· álki·t ô·mi·s
So the offspring of all the [clan] names above are like that.

Momis Nokosvlke honvnwvt Vlepvtvlke hoktēn ēpahyen, hopuetake heckaken omat,
mo·mêys nokosâlki honánwat alipatâlki hoktí·n i·páhyin hopoytá·ki hícka·kín o·mâ·t
Now when a Bear clan man marries an Alligator clan woman, if children are born,

omvlkvt Vlepvtvlket omakēs. Momis Nokosvlke honvnwv vtēkat erket omaken,
omálkat alipatâlkit omâ·ki·s mo·mêys nokosâlki honánwa atî·ka·t ílkit omâ·kin
they are all Alligator clan. So every Bear clan man is their father,

Nokosvlke hoktvke omvlkvt epusvlket omakēs. Monkv nokose tat "cvrken" kicakēs,
nokosâlki hoktakí omálkat iposâlkit omâ·ki·s mônka nokósita·t cálkin kéyca·kí·s
and all Bear clan women are their grandmothers. So they call Bear "my father,"

mv Vlepvtvlke hopuetake tat. Monkv momvkē vlkēt omakēs,
ma alipatâlki hopoytá·kita·t mônka mo·makí· álki·t omâ·ki·s
those Alligator clan children do. So all are like that,

'Mvliketv maketv honvpse vtēkat.
'maleykitá ma·kitá honápsi atî·ka·t
all the offspring of what are called 'mvliketv ['clans'].

Monkv poskē vpokē <u>tvsekvyv hocefkv</u> makē hocefhoyēcakat hiyomēt omakēs:
mônka po·skí· apô·ki· tasikayá hocífka ma·kí· hocífhoyi·ca·kâ·t hayyó·mi·t omâ·ki·s
So when they sit fasting and are giving <u>tvsekvyv hocefkv</u> ['citizen names'], they are these:

Echaswvlke, Fuswvlke, Vlepvtvlke—yv tuccēnat etena-hvmket omēs maket
icha·swâlki foswâlki alipatâlki ya toccî·na·t itina·hámkit ô·mi·s ma·kít
Beaver clan, Bird clan, Alligator clan—these three are kin, they said and

hiyomēn hocēfet omakēs.
hayyó·mi·n hoci·fít oma·kí·s
named them this way.

Vlepvtvlke hoktē echustake cēpvnvke, Nokosvlke ēppucetake hocefhokv:
alipatâlki hoktí· ichostá·ki ci·panáki nokosâlki i·ppocitá·ki hocifhoká
The sons of an Alligator clan woman and a Bear clan man [had these] names:[293]

Vlpvtv Haco, Vlpvtv Mēkko,
alpatahá·co alpatamí·kko
Alpata Harjo ['Crazy Alligator'], Alpata Micco ['Chief Alligator'],

Echas Haco, Echas Fēkseko,
icha·shá·co icha·sfi·ksikó
Itchas Harjo ['Crazy Beaver'], Itchas Fixico ['Heartless Beaver'],

Echaswuce, Echas Yvholv,
icha·swocí icha·syahóla
Itchaswochi ['Little Beaver'], Itchas Yahola ['Beaver Crier'],

Fus Yvholv, Fus Haco, Fus Fēkseko,
fosyahóla foshá·co fosfi·ksikó
Fus Yahola ['Bird Crier'], Fus Harjo ['Crazy Bird'], Fus Fixico ['Heartless Bird'],

Nokos Ēmarv, Nokos Fēkseko,
nokosi·má·ła nokosfi·ksikó
Nokos Emathla ['Bear Emathla'], Nokos Fixico ['Heartless Bear'],

Nokos Yvholv, Nokos Haco, Nokos-ele,
nokosyahóla nokoshá·co nokosilí
Nokos Yahola ['Bear Crier'], Nokos Harjo ['Crazy Bear'], Nokos-ili ['Bear Foot'],

Nokos-ekv, Nokos-hvce, Nokosuce,
nokosiká nokosháci nokosocí
Nokos-ika ['Bear Head'], Nokos Hachi ['Bear Tail'], Nokosochi ['Little Bear'];

Vlepvtvlke honvnwv ēppucetake, Nokosvlke hoktē echustake cēpvnvke
alipatâlki honánwa i·ppocitá·ki nokosâlki hoktí· ichostá·ki ci·panáki
the sons of an Alligator clan man and a Bear clan woman

heyv hocefhokv ocate vlkēt omakes.
<hi>yá hocifhoká ô·ca·ti álki·t oma·kís[294]
always had these names.

Kaccvlke hoktē echustake cēpvnvke, Ecovlke honvnwv ēppucetake hocefhokv:
ka·ccâlki hoktí· ichostá·ki ci·panáki icoâlki honánwa i·ppocitá·ki hocifhoká
The sons of a Tiger clan woman and a Deer clan man [had these] names:

Kaccv Homahte, Kaccv Mēkko,
ka·ccahomá·hti ka·ccamí·kko
Katcha Homahti ['Tiger Leader'], Katcha Micco ['Chief Tiger'],

Kaccv Yvholv, Kaccv Fēkseko,
ka·ccayahóla ka·ccafi·ksikó
Katcha Yahola ['Tiger Crier'], Katcha Fixico ['Heartless Tiger'],

Kacc Ēmarv, Kaccv Tvstvnvke,
ka·cci·má·la ka·ccatastanáki[295]
Katch Emathla ['Tiger Emathla'], Katcha Tastanaki ['Tiger Warrior'],

Eco Ēmarv, Eco Fēkseko, Eco Yvholv,
icoi·má·la icofi·ksikó icoyahóla
Icho Emathla ['Deer Emathla'], Icho Fixico ['Heartless Deer'], Icho Yahola ['Deer Crier'],

Eco-ekv Haco, Eco-yvpe,
icoikahá·co icoyapí
Icho-ika Harjo ['Crazy Deer Head'], Icho-yapi ['Deer Horn'],

Eco Haco, Eco-ele Haco,
icohá·co icoilihá·co
Icho Harjo ['Crazy Deer'], Icho-ili Harjo ['Crazy Deer Leg'];

Kaccvlke honvnwv ēppucetake, Ecovlke hoktē echustake cēpvnvke yvt hocefhokvt omakēs.
ka·ccâlki honánwa i·ppocitá·ki icoâlki hoktí· ichostá·ki ci·panáki yat hocifhokát omâ·ki·s.
the sons of a Tiger clan man and a Deer clan woman had these names.

"Hotvlkvlke, Konepvlke etena-hvmkēt omēs" mahokvnts.
hotalkâlki konipâlki itina·hámki·t ô·mi·s má·ho·kánc
"Wind clan and Skunk clan are kin," it was said.

Hotvlkvlke hoktvke echustake cēpvnvke Tvmvlke, Penwvlken okēs.
Hotalkâlki hoktakí[296] ichostá·ki ci·panáki tamâlki pinwâlkin[297] o·ki·s
A Wind clan woman's sons are Tami clan and Turkey clan.

Honvntake ēppucetake hocefhokv:
honantá·ki i·ppocitá·ki hocifhoká
Men's sons names [were]:

Hotvlk Ēmarv, Hotvlke Haco,
hotalki·má·la hotalkihá·co
Hotalk Emathla ['Wind Emathla'], Hotalki Harjo ['Crazy Wind'],

Hotvlke Fēkseko, Hotvlkuce,
hotalkifi·ksi<kó> hotalkocí
Hotalki Fixico ['Heartless Wind'], Hotalkochi ['Little Wind'],

Hotvlke Yvholv, Kono Haco,
hotalkiyahóla konohá·co
Hotalki Yahola ['Wind Crier'], Kono Harjo ['Crazy Skunk'],

Kono Yvholv, Konep Haco,
konoyahóla[298] koniphá·co
Kono Yahola ['Skunk Crier'], Konip Harjo ['Crazy Skunk'],

Konep Ēmarv, Konep Fēkseko,
konipi·má·la[299] konipfi·ksikó
Konip Emathla ['Skunk Emathla'], Konip Fixico ['Heartless Skunk'],

Pen Haco, Pen Ēmarv,
pinhá·co pini·má·la
Pin Harjo ['Crazy Turkey'], Pin Emathla ['Turkey Emathla'],

Pen Fēkseko, Tvm Ēmarv,
pinfi·ksikó tami·má·la
Pin Fixico ['Heartless Turkey'], Tam Emathla ['Tami Emathla'],

Tvme Yvholv, Tvme Mēkko, Tvme Fēkseko,
tamìyahóla tamimí·kko tamifì·ksikó
Tami Yahola ['Tami Crier'], Tami Micco ['Chief Tami'], Tami Fixico ['Heartless Tami'],

Tvme Haco, Pen Fēkseko,
tamihá·co pinfì·ksikó
Tami Harjo ['Crazy Tami'], Pin Fixico ['Heartless Turkey'],

Pen Haco, Pen Ēmarv,
pinhá·co pini·má·la
Pin Harjo ['Crazy Turkey'], Pin Emathla ['Turkey Emathla'];

Tvmvlke, Penwvlke honvntake ēppucetake
tamâlki pinwâlki honantá·ki i·ppocitá·ki
Tami or Turkey clan men's sons

Hotvlkvlke, Konepvlke hoktē echustake cēpvnvke hocefhokvt os.
hotalkâlki konipâlki hoktí· ichostá·ᵘki ci·panáki hocifhokát ò·ᵘs.
and a Wind or Skunk clan woman's sons had [those] names.

Wotkvlke, Culvlke, Cettvlke, Vhvlvkvlke, Kvpeecvlke, Kohvsvlke etena-hvmket omēs
wo·tkâlki colâlki cittâlki ahalakâlki kapiccâlki kohasâlki itina·hámkit ò·mi·s
The Raccoon, Fox, Snake, Sweet Potato, Kapitcha, and Cane clans are kin,

mahokvnts. Aktvyahcvlke, Waksvlkeu etena-hvmket omēs.
má·ho·kánc aktayahcâlki waksâlkiw[300] itina·hámkit ò·mi·s
it was said. Aktayahchi and Waksi clans are kin.

Momis Wotkvlke hoktvke echustake cēpvnvke
mo·mêys wo·tkâlki hoktakí ichostá·ki ci·panáki
But the sons of Raccoon clan women

Aktvyahcvlke honvntake ēppucetake hocefhokv
aktayahcâlki honantá·ki i·ppocitá·ki hocifhoká
and Aktayahchi clan men [had these] names:

Wotko Yvholv, Wotko Fēkseko,
wo·tkoyahóla wo·tkofì·ksikó
Wotko Yahola ['Raccoon Crier'], Wotko Fixico ['Heartless Raccoon'],

Wotko Haco, Wotko Mēkko,
wo·tkohá·co wo·tkomí·kko
Wotko Harjo ['Crazy Raccoon'], Wotko Micco ['Chief Raccoon']

Wotk-ele, Wotk-ekv,
wo·tkilí wo·tkiká
Wotk-ili ['Raccoon Leg'], Wotk-ika ['Raccoon Head'],

Wotkuce, Wotko Homahte,
wo·tkocí wo·tkohomá·hti
Wotkochi ['Little Raccoon'], Wotko Homahti ['Raccoon Leader']

Culv Yvholv, Culv Fēkseko,
colayahóla colafi·ksikó
Chola Yahola ['Fox Crier'], Chola Fixico ['Heartless Fox']

Culv Haco, Cetto Haco,
colahá·co cittohá·co
Chola Harjo ['Crazy Fox'], Chitto Harjo ['Crazy Snake']

Vhvlvk Haco, Vhvlvk Mēkko,
ahalakhá·co ahalakmí·kko
Ahalak Harjo ['Crazy Sweet Potato'], Ahalak Micco ['Chief Sweet Potato'],

Vhvl Ēmarv, Vhv Yvholv,
ahali·má·la ahayahóla
Ahal Emathla ['Sweet Potato Scout'], Aha Yahola ['Sweet Potato Crier'],

Kvpeccv Mēkko, Kvpeccv Haco,
kapiccamí·kko kapiccahá·co
Kapitcha Micco ['Chief Kapitcha'], Kapitcha Harjo ['Crazy Kapitcha'],

Kvpecc Ēmarv, Kvpeccv Yvholv,
kapicci·má·la kapiccayahóla
Kapitch Emathla ['Kapitcha Emathla'], Kapitcha Yahola ['Kapitcha Crier'],

Kvpeccuce, Kvpeccv Fēkseko,
kapiccocí kapiccafi·ksikó
Kapitchochi ['Little Kapitcha'], Kapitcha Fixico ['Heartless Kapitcha'],

Kohvs Ēmarv, Aktvyahce Fēkseko,
kohasi·má·la aktayahcifi·ksikó
Kohas Emathla ['Cane Emathla'], Aktayahchi Fixico ['Heartless Aktayaychi'],

Aktvyahce Haco, Aktvyahcuce,
aktayahcihá·co aktayahcocí[301]
Aktayahchi Harjo ['Crazy Aktayahchi'], Aktayahchochi ['Little Aktayahchi'],

Aktvyahce Yvholv, Aktvyahc Ēmarv,
aktayahciyahóla aktayahci·má·la
Aktayahchi Yahola ['Aktayahchi Crier'], Aktayahch Emathla ['Aktayahchi Emathla'],

Waks-ēmarv Haco, Wakse Yvholv,
waksi·ma·lahá·co waksiyahóla
Waks-emathla Harjo ['Crazy Waksi Emathla'], Waksi Yahola ['Waksi Crier'],

Wakse-holaht Ēmarv, Wakse Haco
waksiholahti·má·la waksihá·co
Waksi-holaht Emathla ['Waksi Holahti Emathla'], Waksi Harjo ['Crazy Waksi'];

Wotkvlke hoktvke echustake cēpvnvke
wo·tkâlki hoktakí[302] *ichostá·ki ci·panáki*
the sons of Raccoon clan women

Aktvyahcvlke honvntake ēppucetake hocefhokvt omakēs.
aktayahcâlki honantá·ki i·ppocitá·ki hocifhokát omâ·ki·s.
and Aktayahchi clan men [had those] names.

Momis Wotkvlke hoktvke Aktvyahcvlke honvntake tvlkusēt ēpayēt omekon
mo·mêys[303] *wo·tkâlki hoktakí aktayahcâlki honantá·ki tâlkosi·t i·pa·yí·t omíkon*
But Aktayahchi clan men alone did not marry Raccoon clan women,

momet Aktvyahcvlke hoktvke Wotkvlke honvntake tvlkusēt ēpayēt omekatēs.
mo·mít aktayahcâlki hoktakí wo·tkâlki honantá·ki tâlkosi·t i·pa·yí·t omíká·ti·s
and only Raccoon clan men did not marry Aktayahchi clan women.

Momen Vlepvtvlke hoktvkeu Nokosvlke honvntake tvlkusēt ēpayēt omekon
mo·mín alipatâlki[304] *hoktakíw nokosâlki honantá·ki tâlkosi·t i·pa·yí·t omíkon*
And only Bear clan men did not marry Alligator clan women,

momet Vlepvtvlke honvntake tvlkusēt Nokosvlke hoktvke ēpayēt omekatēs.
mo·mit alipatâlki honantá·ki tâlkosi·t nokosâlki hoktaki i·pa·yí·t omíká·ti·s.
and only Alligator clan men did not marry Bear clan women.

Momis Nokosvlke honvnwv tat Nokosvlke hoktēn ēpvyvranat tokot omvtēs.
mo·mêys nokosâlki honánwata·t nokosâlki hoktí·n i·payála·nâ·t tó·ko·t o·matí·s.
And a Bear clan man is not to marry a Bear clan woman.

Mohmen Vlepvtvlke honvnwv tateu Vlpvtvlke hoktēn ēpvyvranat tokot omvtēs.
móhmin alipatâlki[305] honánwata·tiw alpatâlki ho·ktí·n i·payála·nâ·t tó·ko·t o·matí·s
And an Alligator clan man is not to marry an Alligator clan woman.

Honvnwv, hoktē 'tepakat em vliketv hvmkusat etēpvyekatēt omēs.
honánwa hoktí· 'tipâ·ka·t imaleykitá hámkosa·t iti·payíká·ti·t ô·mi·s
A man and woman of the same clan did not marry.

"Etena-hvmke toyēs" makakekv, hoktē em vculkv oren omat,
itina·hámki tô·yi·s má·ka·kiká hoktí· imacólka o·lín o·mâ·t
"We are kin," they said, so when a woman came of age,

epvwvlket honvnwv enhopoyet etēpvyepuecēt omvtēs.
ipawâlkit honánwa ínhopo·yít iti·payípoyci·t o·matí·s
her maternal uncles would find a man and give her in marriage.

Etena-hvmke tokat kerrakekv, hoktē ehet ēlen omat,
itina·hámki[306] tó·ka·t kiłłâ·kíka hoktí· ihít i·lín o·mâ·t
They knew they were not kin, so when the woman's husband died,

honvnwv ena-hvmkētan enwihokvtēs, mv hoktē.
honánwa ina·hámki·ta·n inwéyho·katí·s ma (?) hoktí·
they left her to the man's kin, that woman.

Story of Aktayahchi and Wotko Clans[307]

J. Hill (Hill II:30; Haas XVIII:27–29)

Aktvyahcvlke, Wotkvlke etenahvmket omakvtēs.
aktayahcâlki wo·tkâlki itina·hámkit omâ·kati·s.
Aktayahchi clan and Raccoon clan were kin.

Uewvn rescvwvranet uekiwv likan vhoyvtēs. Nerē yomockēn welaket ont
óywan liscawála·nít[308] *oykéywa*[309] *lêyka·n aho·yati·s nili· yomócki·n wila·kit ónt*
They went down to the spring to get water. The night was dark when they went,

kolkēn ocahket 'svhoyet oman kolkēt em vslahken welaket,
kolki·n o·cáhkit 'sahô·yit o·má·n kolkí·t imasláhkin wila·kít
so they took a light, but the light kept going out along the way.

honvnwv hoktē 'tepvkēt welaket onkv, etenaorkahket etenahvmketv em vhakvn kvcahken,
honánwa hokti· 'tipakí·t wila·kít ônka itina·olkáhkit itina·hamkitá imahá·kan kacáhkin
It was a man and woman who were going around; they sinned and broke the law of kin,

vhakv mocvsēn enhayet okat
ahá·ka mocási·n ínha·yit o·kâ·t
and a new law was made, which said,

"Hvthvyvtke ayat hvse fvccvlikē roran vtēkusēn
hathayátki a·yâ·t hasí faccaléyki· lô·la·n atî·kosi·n
"In the morning as soon as the sun gets to the noon hour,

Aktvyahcvlke Wotkvlke etenahvmket omvrēs.
aktayahcâlki wo·tkâlki itiná·hamkít omáli·s.
the Aktayahchi clan and Raccoon clan will be kin.

Momis hvse fvccvlikē hoyahnē ayē nerē vtēkat, etenahvmkē tokarēs mahohken,
mo·mêys hasí (?) faccaléyki· hoyáhni· a·yí· nili· atî·ka·t itina·hámki· tó·ká·li·s ma·hóhkin
But from noon up until night, they will not be kin," it was said.

"Aktvyahcvlke Wotkvlke etēpvyetvt em etektvnkvtēt omēs" maket,
aktayahcâlki wo·tkâlki iti·payítat imitiktánkati·t ô·mi·s ma·kít
So "Aktayahchi clan and Raccoon clan were free to marry," it was said,

vculvket onvyakēt omvnts.
acolakít onáya·kí·t o·mánc.
the elders used to tell.

Ways of Preparing Corn (Este-cate Vce Enhompetv Noricat)[i]

J. Hill (Haas IV:89–125)

<u>Vce-lvste.</u>   Vce-lvste   taklike   omē   eshayat   hocefhokv
acilásti   *acilásti*   *takléyki* *ó·mi·* *ísha·yâ·t*   *hocifhoká*
[black corn]   blackcorn   bread   like   making out of   names
<u>Black Corn.</u> There are five names for breads made of

cahkēpet   omēs.   Vce-lvste   celahset,
cahkî·pit[310] *ô·mi·s*   *acilásti*   *ciláhsit*
five   are   black corn shelled
black corn. (You) shell black corn,

uewv   esmorecetvn   uewvn   vcahnet,   totkv   ētkan
óywa   *ismo·licítan* *óywan*   *acáhnit*   *tó·tka* *i·tkâ·n*
water   to boil it with water   put in it   fire   burning
put water in [a pot] to boil,

onvpvn   sohlihcet   ēsso-homvn   torvwv   vpvkekon
onápan   *sohléyhcit* *i·ssohó·man* *toláwa* *apákiko·n*
on top of, over (the fire) set it on   ashes strong charcoal(s) not any, without
set it over the fire, put in a small amount of strong ashes

nvcomusēn   aktehhen,   morkof,   mv   vce   celvsken   aktēhen,
nacómosi·n *aktíhhin*[311] *mo·lkô·f* *ma* *ací* *ciláskin* *aktî·hin*
a little bit   put it in   when it boils that corn that's shelled had put it in
without any charcoal, and when it boils, put in the shelled corn,

esmoriken,   vcen   akcahwet   okkosof
ismo·lêykin *acín*   *akcáhwit*   *ókko·sô·f*
boiled with   corn   took it out   while (somebody) is washing it
and after it boils, take out the corn, and wash it off

vce   ehvrpuce omvlkvt enhvsvtiken   kvrpē   hakof,
ací *ihalpocí* *omálkat* *inhasatêykin*   *kálpi·* *ha·kô·f*
corn   skin   all   (got) cleaned off dried   got
until all the corn skin is removed; and when it's dry,

---

[i] Title: *isticá·ti ací (in)hompitá noleycâ·t* 'cooking Indian corn dishes'.

kecon   vtehhet,   kecvpen   eshocofvt
kicón   atíhhit   kicápin   ísho·cô·fat
mortar   put it in   pestle   when pounding with
put it in a mortar, and when you pound it with the pestle,

tvlako hvrpe monkat talvpe nekricvkvtē   em ēsson
talá·ko hálpi mónka·t ta·lapí nikłeycakáti[312]   *imí·sson*
bean hull or cobs that had been burnt   its ashes
add fine ashes from bean hulls

nokricvkvtē   telēkmusēn   vpayet   hocet   lopohtet
nokłeycakáti[313]   *tilĭ·ⁿkmosi·n   apa·yít   ho·cít   lopóhtit*
been burnt   very fine   put with   pounded   made it fine
or burnt corn cobs, pound it fine,

svlahwvn   es enyoyet, telekman encahwet,   tvlakon horkē
saláhwan   isínyo·yít tilíkma·n incáhwit   talá·kon hółki·
(sifter) fanner fanned it fine part separated from beans boiled (beans)
sift it with a fanner, remove the fine portion, stir in some boiled beans

noricvkvtēn   'teyahmet, uewvn escvlahpet,
nołéycakáti·n   'tiyáhmit[314] *óywan iscaláhpit*
been cooked by someone stirred it water mixed with (water)
that have been cooked,

wvnhēn ont,   enke-tvpekse hvmkusat fackusē tayen
wánhi·n ônt   iŋkitapíksi hâmkosa·t fâ·ckosi· tâ·yin
hard   while it was (hard) handful one full about (a handful)
mix it with water, and when it's stiff, break off about one handful,

kalet,   wetēnet   pokko omē tis hayet,
ka·lít   witi·nít   pókko ó·mi·teys ha·yít
breaking off (like bread) to press it (or with your hand) ball even like making it
squeeze it, make it into a ball,

monkat   tvpeksē poloksē tis hayet,
mónka·t   tapíksi· polóksi·teys ha·yít
or   flat or round making it
or make it flat and round,

uewv   morkēn   aktēhohen   norof,
óywa   mo·lkí·n   aktí·ho·hín[315]   *no·lô·f*
water   boiling (water) somebody put it in   when it got done (cooked)
and when they've been placed in boiling water and have cooked,

cvtvhakv   kicet   hocefhoyēt   omēs.
catahá·ka   kaycít   hocífho·yí·t ô·mi·s
blue dumpling   called it named it   do (call it)
they call it cvtvhakv [blue corn dumpling].

Opuswv   esketv   hērēt   omēs.
opóswa   iskitá   hi·ⁿli·t   ô·mi·s
soup   to drink   it's good (to drink) is
It's good to drink the soupy juice.

Hvtvm   vcehocke   matan   vtotketvo   cvtvhakv   hayvranē
hatâm   acihócki   ma·tá·n atotkitáw'   catahá·ka   há·yala·ní·
again   pounded corn same   to work, too blue dumplings going to make
Then using the same ground corn worked

vtotketv   mahusat   ētan   vtotiket   omis,   uewv   morkē
atotkitá   mǎ·ⁿhosa·t   i·tá·n   atotêykit   o·mèys   óywa   mo·lkí·
to work   place   very same worked   did   water   boiling (water)
as if to make cvtvhakv, when just about

aktehvranofvt   vce   hvrpen   'svyokkofet   eshoret
aktihála·nô·fat   ací   hálpin   'sayókko·fít   ísho·lít
when being about to put it in corn   shucks   wrapped with   boiled with
to put them in the boiling water, you wrap them in corn shucks and boil them in that,

noricat   vssvtulke   kicet, monkat
noleycâ·t   assatólki[i]   *keycít móŋka·t*
when cooking it blue dumplings wrapped in shucks called or
and cook them, and they're called vssvtulkē, or

---

[i] Written once: *assatólki·*; Raiford: *assitólki.*

puyvfekcv- <u>hake</u> tis   kicēt   pvphoyēt   omēs.
poyafikca   *há·kiteys*[316]   *keycí·t*   *pápho·yí·t*   *ô·mi·s*
spirit   like   called it   they eat it   do
they're called <u>puyfekcv-hake</u> ['like a ghost'] and eaten.

Hvtvm   meskē   hakof,   eto   essen   tvptahan   hopoyet,
hatâm   *miskí·*   *ha·kô·f*   *itó*   *íssin*   *taptâ·ha·n*   *hopo·yít*
again   summer   getting (summer)   (tree) leaves   wide ones   hunted for
Then in the summertime, they gather wide leaves of trees,

mvn   hvtvm   svyokkofet   eshorat,
man   *hatâm*   *'sayókko·fit*   *ísho·lâ·t*
that   again   wrapped it with (those broad leaves)   boiled it with
and they used those as wraps and boil them in those,

mvo   vssvtulke   kihocēt   omēs.
maw'   *assatólki*   *kéyho·cí·t*   *ô·mi·s*
that too   wrapped blue dumplings   it was called   was
and those are called <u>vssvtulke</u> too.

Hvtvm   tvlako   vpvyekot   uewv   escvlvpkat   tvlkusēn
hatâm   *talá·ko*   *apáyiko·t*   *óywa*   *(i)scalápka·t*   *tâlkosi·n*
again   beans   didn't put with it   water   mixed with   only
Then if beans are not added and just water is used to mix,

totkv   ētkat   em vtēkēn   'staklihcet   ēsso   hiyen   'sohrahnet
tó·tka   *i·tkâ·t*   *imati·kí·n*   *(s)taklêyhcit*[i]   *í·sso*   *háyyin*   *(s)ohláhnit*[ii]
fire   burning   edge   put down (one)   ashes   hot   covered it
you set it at the edge of the fire and cover it with hot ashes

noricat,   <u>taklike takhopelke</u>   kicēt   hocēfet
nołeycâ·t   *taklêyki takhopilki*   *kaycí·t*   *hoci·fít*
cooked it   bread   (some kind of roasted bread)   called   named
and cook it, and it's called <u>taklike takhopelke</u> ['buried bread'],

---

[i] Original: *taklêyhcit*, corrected by Raiford to *staklêyhcit*.
[ii] Original: *ohláhnit*, corrected by Raiford to *sohláhnit*.

hompakvtēt   omēs.   Fakke-pvlaknv   tvpestvkusē tis   hayēt   ocet
hómpa·katí·t   *ô·mi·s*   *fakkipalákna*   *tapistakósi·teys*   *há·yi·t*   *ô·cit*
they eat it   do   clay-plate   some of them flat   (had) made   had
and they ate it. They had little clay plates,

mvn   vce-telekme   cvlvpkat   vlicet   noricat
man   *acitilíkmi*   *calápka·t*   *aleycít*   *noɬeycâ·t*
that   small grits   mixed   put ... in ... cooking
and they pressed grits in those and cooked it,

<u>vpvtvkv</u>   kicet   hocefakvtēs.
apataká   *keycít*   *hocífa·katí·s*
batter-cake   called it   they named it
and called it <u>vpvtvkv</u> ['pressed against'].

Heyv   nake   hocefhokv   cahkēpat   takliket   omvtēs.
hiyá   *nâ·ki*   *hocifhoká*   *cahkî·pa·t*   *takléykit*   *ô·matí·s*
here   something   their names   five   bread   were
These five names were breads.

Momen vce   telekmihocat   nērkuce   encahwet
mo·mín *ací*   *tilikmeyhô·ca·t*   *ni·ɬkocí*   *incáhwit*
Then   corn   that had been made fine, pulverized large grits   took from, separated out
Now they removed the grits from corn that had been ground fine,

cvtvhakv   vpvyvranē   tvlako   horate   opuswvn   eshohret
catahá·ka   *apáyaɬa·ní·*   *talá·ko*   *hô·la·ti*   *oposwán*   *ishóhɬit*
blue dumplings   going to put with beans   had boiled   soup   boiled with
boiled them in the juice of the beans boiled to be added to <u>cvtvhakv</u>,

nehan   vpayet   <u>afke-lvste</u>   kicet   homhopvtēt   os.
nihá·n   *apa·yít*   *a·fkilásti*   *keycít*   *hómho·patí·t* *ô·ⁿs*
grease   put with   black hominy   called it   they ate it   did.
added grease, and called it <u>afke-lvste</u> ['black mush'], and ate it.

Mv   vce   ētan   telekmickv   sekon   horret
ma   *ací*   *i·tá·n*   *tilikméycka*   *síko·n*   *ho·ɬít*
that   corn   same (corn) (without) making it fine without   boiled it
When the same corn was boiled and cooked without grinding,

norof,		nehan vpayet,	<u>sokv</u>	kicēt	hocēfet
no·lô·f		*nihá·n apa·yít*	*soká*[317]	*keycí·t*	*hoci·fít*
when it was cooked		grease put with	hominy	called it	named it

grease was added, and it was called <u>sokv</u> ['hominy']

homhopēt	omvtēs.		Vce-lvste	sekon omat,
hómho·pí·t	*o·matí·s*[318]		*acilásti*	*sikon o·mâ·t*
they used to eat it (nearly everybody)			(if) black corn	not any

and eaten. If there is no black corn,

hompetv	hocefhokv	kolvpakat	omvlkvn	vce-hvtken	eshahoyēt	omēs.
hompitá	*hocifhoká*	*kolapâ·ka·t*	*omálkan*	*acihátkin*[319]	*ishá·ho·yí·t*	*ô·mi·s*
food	names	seven	all	white corn	made it with	did

all seven of the foods named are [also] made with white corn.

Vce-hvtkē	taklike	eshayvranat,		vce-hvtkē	celahset,
acihátki·	*takléyki*	*ishá·yaɫa·nâ·t*		*acihátki·*	*ciláhsit*
white corn	bread	will make (bread) with (white corn)		white corn	shelled it

When bread is to be made of white corn, you shell the white corn,

uewvn	aktehhet	esmorehcet,	uewv	em pvlahtet,
óywan	*aktíhhit*	*ismo·líhcit*	*óywa*	*impaláhtit*
water	put it in	boiled it with	water	poured out from

put it in water, boil it, pour the water from it,

kecon	vtēhet,	kecvpen	eshocet	telēkmof,
kicón	*ati·hít*[i]	*kicápin*	*ísho·cít*	*tili·kmô·f*
mortar	put it in	pestle	pounded it with	when it gets to be fine

put it in a mortar, pound it with a pestle, and when it's fine,

svlahwvn	'senyoyet,	telekman	encawet,	sulehcet,
saláhwan	*sínyo·yít*	*tilíkma·n*	*ínca·wít*[320]	*solíhcit*
fanner	fanned it with	the fine part	took away, separated from	got enough

sift it with a fanner, take out the fine part, and after you have enough,

---

[i] Raiford: *atíhhit*. [MM also reads it as *atíhhit*.]

uewvn   escvlahpet,   taklike   esnorickvn   vlihcet   noricet,
óywan   iscaláhpit   takléyki   isnołéyckan   aléyhcit   noleycít
water   mixed it with   bread   [pan]   put it in   cooked it
you mix it with water, put it in a bread pan, and cook it,

okfvlke takliken   kicēt,   hvtvm   tvskọcusēn   tvpeksicet,
okfâlki takléykin[i]   keycí·t   hatâm   taskŏ·ⁿcosi·n   tapíkseycít
baked corn-bread   called it   again   very thin   flattened it out
and it's called okfvlke taklike; or when you flatten it out very thin,

nehan   akpiket   noricat,   vpvtvkv   'sakmorken   kihocēt   omēs.
nihá·n   ákpaykít   nołeycâ·t   apataká   sakmó·lkin   kéyho·ci·t   ô·mi·s
grease   put it in   when cooking batter-cake fried (batter-cakes) called it   did
put it in grease, and cook it, it's called vpvtvkv 'sakmorke.

Vce-cvlvtwe.   Vce-cvlvtwe celahset,
acicalátwi   acicalátwi   ciláhsit
flint corn   flint corn   shelled it
Flint Corn. They shelled flint corn,

ue-kvsvppen   aktēhet   eslicet   vce   akcawet,
oykasáppin   aktî·hit   isléycit   ací   ákca·wít[321]
cold water   put it in   set it down   corn   separated out
put it in cold water, set it aside, then removed the corn,

kecon   vtēhet   vhericusēt   hocet   vce-hvrpucen   encopahlēcat,
kicón   ati·hit   ahiłéycosi·t   ho·cít   acihałpocín   incopáhli·câ·t
mortar   (already) put it in easily   pounded it   corn-skins   to skin (the corn)
put it in a mortar, pounded it lightly, and peeling off the corn-skins,

vce   aktonken   kicēt,   entvlē   essen   enwehset,
ací   aktóŋkin   keycí·t   intalí·   íssin   inwíhsit
corn   pulverized (corn) called it   pounded corn husks   sifted from
they called it vce aktonke ['pulverized corn'] and sifted off the pounded corn husks,

---

[i] Corrected by Raiford from *okfâlki takléyki·n*.

uewv   esmorēckv   rakkēn   lehayv-rakko   kicet,   facken   uewvn   vcahnen,
óywa   ismo·lí·cka   lákki·n   'liha·yałákko   keycít   fâ·ckin   óywan   acáhnin
water   [kettle   big]   pot big   called it   full   water   pour it (water) in
filled a big water kettle called a <u>lehayv-rakko</u> with water,

hiyof,   vce   aktonken   aktehhet,   em vhetēcet
hayyô·f   ací   aktóŋkin   aktíhhit   imáhiti·cít[322]
when it got hot   corn   pulverized   put it in   keep the fire burning around it
and when it got hot, they put the <u>vce aktonke</u> in, lit a fire under it,

totkv   rakkekon   em vhetēcen,   hvlvlątkusēt   morken,
tó·tka   lákkiko·n   imáhiti·cín[323]   *halală·ⁿtkosi·t   mo·łkín*
fire   not big   make around, kindled around   slowly   boiled it
not a very big fire, and it slowly simmered,

vcewē   hakof,
acíwi·   ha·kô·f
a good while   when it gets
and after quite a while,

ēsso-homvn   halo-leskv   vcopv   esrolahlēcakvtēn   vtehhet,
i·ssohó·man[i]   ha·lolíska   acó·pa   islolahlí·cakáti·n   atíhhit
strong ashes   old can   nail   made holes (in the can) with (a nail)   put it in
they put strong ashes in an old can perforated with nail holes,

uewvn   ohcanen,   ēsson opuswv   cvfcakan,
óywan   óhca·nín[324]   *i·sso opóswa   cáfca·kâ·n*
water   poured it in   (juice of the ashes) lye   when dripping
poured water on [the ashes], and they called the liquid dripped from the ashes

<u>kvpe-cvfke</u>   kicet,   remhusēn   cahwet,
kapicáfki   keycít   límhosi·n   cáhwit
lye-drip   called it   weak, diluted   took it
<u>kvpe-cvfke</u> ['lye-drip'], took the very clear liquid,

---

[i] To make wood-lye, they saved the ashes from green wood.

uewv vce esmorkan akcanen, vce aktonket aknorof,
óywa *ací* *ísmo·łkâ·n* *ákca·nín* *ací* *aktóŋkit* *ákno·łô·f*
water corn boil with poured it in corn pulverized when it's cooked
poured [the lye] into the corn boiling in water, and when the <u>vce aktonke</u> is cooked

opuswv sulkē ocēn vrkvswvn vcvnhoyvnts.
opóswa *sólki·* *ó·ci·n* *ałkáswan* *acánho·yánc*
soup lots has sofkee jar someone, they put it in (a sofkee jar)
with lots of juice, they poured it in a sofkee jar.

<u>Osafken</u> kicet vfastē noricat <u>onēpē</u> maket okhoyvnts.
osá·fkin *keycít* *afa·stí·* *nołeycâ·t* *oni·pí·*[i,325] *ma·kít* *ókho·yánc*[326]
sofkee called it attending to it cooked it a cook saying what they meant, called it
It's called <u>osafke</u>, and the one attending to it and cooking it was called <u>onēpē</u>.

Osafke hakvtan ocet lopocecihcet,
osá·fki *há·kata·n*[327] *ô·cit*[328] *lopocicéyhcit*[329]
sofkee that has been made to have (sofkee that is made) make small
Having made the sofkee small,

esnorickv cutkusēn uewv vcahnet, aktēhet, vpeswvn vpayet,
isnołéycka *cótkosi·n* *óywa* *acáhnit* *ákti·hít*[330] *apíswan* *apa·yít*
[pan] small water poured in put it in it meat put in it
you pour water in a small pot, put the corn in, add meat,

noricat, <u>sakkonepken</u> kihocēt omēs.
nołêyca·t *sakkonípkin*[331] *kéyho·cí·t* *ô·mi·s*
after it's cooked (corn-grit boiled in water with fresh meat in it) they called it did.
cook it, and it's called <u>sakkonepke</u>.

Vce-cvlvtwe lokcat, kvrpeko emonken celaset,
acicalátwi *lo·kcâ·t* *kálpiko·* *imôŋkin* *cila·sít*
flint corn when it gets ripe not dry before shell it
When flint corn gets ripe, before it hardens, they shell it,

---

[i] Or: *oní·pa* 'a cook'.

lehayv-rakkon	ēsson	vtēhet,	vce-celvsken	tohkalet,	totkvn	ētkēn
'liha·yałákkon	*i·sson*	*atî·hit*	*aciciláskin*	*tohkâ·lit*	*tó·tkan*	*i·tkí·n*
pot big	ashes	put it in	shelled corn	put it together	fire	burning

put ashes in a big kettle, put it on the fire with the shelled corn,

'sohlicet,	vpaset,	hvsottan	em ocet,	kvrpēcēt
sóhleycít[332]	*apa·sít*	*hasô·tta·n*	*imo·cít*	*káłpi·cí·t*
put it on	parched it	where it's sunny	put it	and dried it

parch it, dry it in a sunny place,

sulkēn	hericēt	ocet,	fakv	vpēhoyof,
sólki·n	*hilêyci·t*	*ô·cit*	*fá·ka*	*api·ho·yô·f*
lots	stored, put it away	had it, kept it	(hunter)	hunting when they go (hunting)

and keep lots of it stored away, and when they went hunting,

mv	vce	hvtvm	vpahset	ocet,	telekmekon	sulkēn	hahyet,
ma	*ací*	*hatâm*	*apáhsit*	*ô·cit*	*tilíkmiko·n*	*sólki·n*	*háhyit*
that	corn	again	they parch it	keep it	not pulverized	lots	made it

they parched that corn again and kept it and made lots of it without grinding it

hockvtē	kihocēn	fakv	'svpēhoyēt	omvnts.
hockatí·	*kéyho·cí·n*	*fá·ka*	*'sapí·ho·yí·t*	*ô·manc*
flour	called it	hunting	when they go taking it with them	did

and called it hockvtē and took it with them hunting.

Mvn	osafken	hayofvt,	vpvsk-osafken	kicet
man	*osá·fkin*	*ha·yô·fat*	*apaskosá·fkin*	*keycít*
that	sofkee	when making it	parched corn sofkee	called it

When making that kind of sofkee, they called it vpvsk-osafke ['parched corn sofkee'],

hvtvm	tak-vpvsk-onepken	kicēt	homhopvtēt	os.
hatâm	*takkapaskonípkin*[i]	*keyci·t*	*hómho·patí·t*	*ô·ⁿs*
again	(coarse cold flour)	called	they ate it	used to

or tak-vpvsk-onepke and ate it.

---

[i] Hill says it: *apaskosá·fkin*.

Heyv   vce   vpvske   ētan   ocet   svlahwv   lopockusē   ropotēcan,
hiyá   ací   apáski   i·tá·n   ô·cit   saláhwa   lopŏ·ⁿckosi· lopóti·câ·n
here   corn   parched same   had   (fanner) sifter small   those that go through
They kept this same parched corn and when they passed it through a fine fanner,

sēyoyet,   telēkmusen   ocet,   uewv   escvlapet,
sí·yo·yít   tilĭ·ⁿkmosin   ô·cit   óywa   íscala·pít
sifted it   well very fine   kept it   water   mixed with it
they sifted it and kept it very fine, mixing in water,

vpvske   wvpaksv   hocēfēt,   opuswv   sulkēn   cvlapet,
apáski   wapá·ksa   hoci·fi·t   *opóswa   sólki·n   cala·pít*
parched corn   swollen   called it   soup   lots   mixed it
and called it vpvske wvpaksv ['swollen parched corn'], mixed in lots of liquid,

momēn   eyacen   omat,   fo encvmpēn   escvmpēcet,
mó·mi·n   iyâ·cin   o·mâ·t[i]   *fó· incampí·n iscámpi·cít*
that way   want it (that way) if they do (want) honey   sweetened it with
and if they liked it that way, they sweetened it with honey

eskaket   fullvtēt   os.   Mv   vpvske   telekmeko   vhoskan
íska·kít[333] *follatí·t ô·ⁿs*   *ma   apáski   tilíkmiko·   aho·ská·n*
drank it   went about   used to   that   parched corn not fine   left over
and drank it. With the coarse parched corn remaining

afken   eshayet,   neha   vpayet,   homhopēt   omvnts.
á·fkin   ísha·yít   nihá·   apa·yít   hómho·pí·t   ò·manc
hominy grits made with   grease   put with   ate it   used to
they made hominy grits, added grease, and ate it.

Hvtvm   vce   kvrpan   celaset,   ēsson   vpvkēn   mvo   vpaset   ocet,
hatâm   así   kálpa·n   cila·sít   í·sso   apáki·n   maw'   apa·sít   ô·cit
again   corn   dried   shelled it ashes   with it   that, too parched it kept it
Sometimes they would shell dried corn, parch that with ashes also, and stored it and

---

[i] Could also say *o·n o·mâ·t* for *o·mâ·t.*

mvo	safke	eshayet,	<u>tak-vpvsk-onepkē</u>	kicēt,		
maw'	*sá·fki*	*ísha·yít*	*takkapaskonípki·*	*keycí·t*		
that, too	sofkee	made it with	roasted-by-the-fire	called it		

made sofkee from that, and called it <u>tak-vpvsk-onepkē</u>,

monkat	afke tis	hayet,	wakvpesē-cvmpen	vpayet	homhopēt	omvtēs.
moŋkâ·t	*á·fkiteys*	*ha·yít*	*wa·kapisi·cámpin*	*apa·yít*	*hómho·pí·t*	*ô·mati·s*
or	hominy even	made	sweet milk	put with	they ate	did

or they would make mush too, add sweet milk, and eat it.

Mv	afke	hayvranē	hochoyan
ma	*á·fki*	*há·yała·ní·*	*hochô·ya·n*
that	hominy grits	going to make	that that's pounded

When pounding corn to make mush, they took

telēkmusē	vpakan	encawet	<u>vpvske-hvtke</u>	kicēt	uewv	escvlapet
tilĭ·ⁿkmosi·	*apa·kâ·n*	*inca·wít*[334]	*apaskihátki*	*keycí·t*	*óywa*	*iscala·pít*
fine parts	that is with	take from	parched corn white	called it	water	mixed with

the fine ground portion called <u>vpvske-hvtke</u> ['white parched corn'], mixed it with water,

eshoket	omis,	vpvske	wvpaksv	enherē
ísho·kít	*o·mêys*	*apáski*	*wapá·ksa*	*inhiłí·*
drank it	did	parched corn	swollen	that good (wasn't as good)

and drank it, but it wasn't as good as

em oricekot	omvnts.
imołéyciko·t	*o·mánc*
wasn't as (good)	(wasn't)

vpvske wvpaksv.

<u>Vce-lowvcke.</u>	Vce	lokcē	vpessvkē	hakof,
acilowácki[335]	*ací*	*lo·kcí·*	*apissakí·*[336]	*ha·kô·f*
roasting-ear corn	corn	(getting) ripe	(getting) fat	when getting

<u>Roasting Ears.</u> When the corn was getting ripe and fat,

fueyet	em vtoklopēn	encawet,	em vpvlahtet,
foyyít	*imatoklopí·n*	*inca·wít*	*imapaláhtit*
shuck it	its silk	take from it	and throw it away

they shucked it, removed the silk and threw it away,

eco   notakhv-funen   pvlhvmkusēn   enute   ocan
icó   *notakhafónin*   *palhâmkosi·n*   *inóti*   *ô·ca·n*
deer's   jaw-bone   just one side   (one) its teeth [that] has on it
scraped it with one side of a deer's jaw-bone

eskaset,   entalvpen   encawet,   takliken   hayat
íska·sít   *inta·lapín*   *ínca·wít*   *takléykin*   *ha·yâ·t*
scrape it with it its cobs   take from it   bread   making it
having teeth on it, removed it from the cob, and the bread made from that

akkaske taklike   kicēt   norihocvnts.   Hvtvm   vce-lowvcke sulkēn
akká·ski takléyki[i]   *keycí·t*   *noléyho·cánc*   *hatâm*   *acilowácki sólki·n*
grated bread   called   they used to cook it   again   roasting-ear corn lots
was called akkaske taklike ['scraped bread'] and cooked. Then they would shuck lots of

fuyiyet,   totkv   rakkēn   etēcet,   vfulutkēn   vce   entalvpe
foyêyyit   *tó·tka*   *lákki·n*   *itî·cit*   *afolótki·n*   *ací*   *inta·lapí*
shucked it   fire   big   made, built   clear around it   corn-   cobs (with corn on them)
roasting ears, build a big fire, stand whole ears of corn

'semonkvn   totkvn   vsvpaklēcēt,   hotohpet,   norakof,   celahset,
'simóŋkan   *tó·tkan*   *asapaklí·ci·t*   *hotóhpit*   *noła·kô·f*   *ciláhsit*[337]
whole   fire   standing up to it   roasted it   when it got done   they shelled it
all around the edge of the fire, roast them, and when they were done, they shelled them,

hvsottan   em ohocen,   karpof,   ēcko   kicēt   hocēfet,
hasô·tta·n   *imo·hô·cin*   *ka·łpô·f*   *í·cko*   *keycí·t*   *hoci·fít*
in the sun   they put it   when it got dry   dried corn   they called it   they named it
put them in the sun, and when they were dry, they called it ēcko

hericet   horet   rvfon   homhopvnts.   Heyv   hompetv   hayat
hiłêycit   *ho·lít*   *lafón*   *hómho·pánc*   *hiyá*   *hompitá*   *ha·yâ·t*
they kept it   boiled it   in winter   they usually ate it   this   food   they made it
and stored it, boiled it, and ate it in the winter. Preparing this food

---

[i] Raiford: *takléykin.*

hoktvke	em vtotketvt	omēs.	Momis	hiyomat	hoktvke	nvcǫmusēs
hoktakí	*imatotkitát*	*ô·mi·s*	*mo·mêys*	*hayyô·ma·t*	*hoktakí*	*nacŏ·ⁿmosi·s*
the women	their work	it is	But	now	the women	just a few

is women's work. But now only a few women

nake	momvkē	hompetv	hayē tayat	hoktvlvke	fullat
nâ·ki	*mo·makí·*	*hompitá*	*há·yi· tâ·ya·t*	*hoktalákí*	*follâ·t*
things	like that	food	that can prepare	old women	that are about

can prepare food like that, and old women

tvlkuset	kerrakat	sasēs.	Vce-lvste,	vce-hvtke,	vce-cvlvtwē,
tâlkosit	*kiłłâ·ka·t*	*sâ·si·s*	*acilásti*	*acihátki*	*acicalátwi*[i]
only	that know	there are	black corn	white corn	flint corn

are the only ones who would know. Black corn, white corn, flint corn —

heyv	vce	tuccēnat	este-cate	enhompetv	mahhet	omēs.
hiyá	*ací*	*toccî·na·t*	*isticá·ti*	*inhompitá*	*máhhit*	*ô·mi·s*
these	kinds of corn	three	Indians'	their food	regular	is

these three corns are the Indians' real food.

Mvt	enlokcekon		omat,	"Elvoko	rakkēt	vlaket os"
mat	*inlókcikon*		*o·mâ·t*	*iláwko*	*lákki·t*	*alâ·kit ô·ⁿs*
(if) that	doesn't get ripe for them		if	famine	great	has come

When it doesn't make for them, they used to say,

maket	fullvtēt		os.	Heyv	vcet	sekomahen	omat,
ma·kít	*follatí·t*		*ô·ⁿs*	*hiyá*	*acít*	*sikomá·hin*	*o·mâ·t*
they say	they used to be about		were	this	corn	not any at all	if there is (not)

"A great famine has come." If there was none of this corn,

vce	rem ētv tis	hompaket	omis,	hẹremahat	tokot	os
ací	*'limí·tateys*	*hómpa·kít*	*o·mêys*	*hĭ·ⁿłimâ·ha·t*	*tó·kot*	*ó·ⁿs*
[corn]	other [even]	if they do eat it	do	(not) very good		not

they did eat other corn,

---

[i] Or: *acicilátwi(·)*.

komhoyvtēt   os.
kómho·yatí·t   *ô·ⁿs*
they did think that
but it was not considered very good.

Preparation of Meat and Hunting and Meat Taboos (Vpeswv, Wakv Vpeswv)[i]

J. Hill, Jan. 15, 1938 (Haas VII:137–179, VIII:1–7)

Hofonof   este-cate   wakv vpeswv   hericat,
hofô·no·f   *isticá·ti*   *wá·ka apíswa*   *hiłeycâ·t*
Long time ago   the Indians   beef   when they were putting it away
Long ago when Indians were storing beef,

wakv   elehcet,   torofat,   hvrpe   ofv   hvsvtkēn   cahwet
wá·ka   *ilíhcit*   *toło·fâ·t*   *háłpi*   *ó·fa*   *hasátki·n*   *cáhwit*
a beef   they killed   they skinned it skin, hide inside   clean   took it off
they killed the cow, skinned it, took off the inside part of the hide cleanly,

vpeswv   osten   'tewahret   vpoyet,
apíswa   *ô·stin*   *'tiwáhlit*   *apô·yit*
meat   in four parts   they cut it up and put it down
cut up the carcass in four parts and put it aside,

ehvfe   vpeswvn   encawet   vhopakuce   hvmkē   oruseko
iháfi   *apíswan* *inca·wít*   *ahopa·kocí*   *hámki·*   *olósiko·*
ham-   meat   they took off[338] a measure, inch one   not quite
and they took the meat off the thigh in [slices] that were not quite

encekfēn   hayet,   eslafkvn   eslaffet   tvpesticet
incikfí·n   *ha·yít*   *islá·fkan*   *isla·ffít*   *tapísteycit*
in thickness   made it   knife   cut it with   into flat pieces (like a book)
an inch thick, and they cut it with a knife into flat pieces,

---

[i] Title: *apíswa, wá·ka apíswa* 'meat, beef'.

efuluwv   vpeswvo   matvpomēcet,
ifolowá   *apíswaw*   *ma·tapó·mi·cít*
shoulder   meat, too   fixed it the same way
doing the same to the shoulder meat,

entalvn   vpeswv   cekfē vlikan   entvskucihcet,
intá·lan *apíswa*   *cíkfi· aleykan*   *intaskocéyhcit*
rib-   meat   where it has thick pieces in it   they made thin
and where the meat is thick on the ribs, they thinned it the same way

efune   hokkolē   ocēn   eteselsehcet   pucus-leskvn   escasket,
ifóni *hokkò·li·* *ó·ci·n*   *itisilsíhcit*[339] *pocoslískan* *ísca·skít*
bones   two   that have   they slice them up   old ax   hack it up with
and sliced it so that [each part] had two bones and hacked it with an old ax.

entalv-fune   kvcēkē   tuccēnen   vlkēn
inta·lafóni *kací·ki·* *toccî·nin* *álki·n*
ribs   broken   three   each
After they prepared each piece with meat attached

vpeswv   'setehvlvtē   vlkēn   etetakuecofvt
apíswa   *'sitihaláti·*   *álki·n* *ititá·koycô·fat*
meat   having on them   each   after they prepare it
to three broken rib bones,

vpeswv   omvlkvn   okcvnwvn   vpayet,
apíswa   *omálkan*   *okcánwan*   *apa·yít*
meat   all of it   salt   put with it
they salted all the meat,

wakv   hvrpen   pvticet   oh-vpoyet,   poyofvt
wá·ka   *hálpin*   *patêycit*   *óhhapo·yít*   *po·yô·fat*
cow-   hide   spread it out   put (the meat) on it   after they had
set it on a spread cowhide, and when finished,

hēren   mv   wakv-hvrpen   'svyokkofet   eslicen   ohhvyvtiken,
hî·ⁿlin *ma (?)*   *wa·kahálpin*   *'sayokkô·fit*   *islêycin*   *ohhayatêykin*
good   that   cow-hide   wrap it up in it   they put it down   until morning
they wrapped it up well in the cowhide and left it till morning.

vpeswv tat   cuko-sohrvnkv   onvpvn   vwahēn   tvpestakēn   oh-vpoyet,
apíswata·t   coko(ʔ)-sohłánka   onápan   awá·hi·n   tapistaki·n   ohhapô·yit
the meat   house roof   on top   they scatter it on flattened out they put it on
They set the meat out on top of the roof scattered flat,

onvpvt   karpof,   rakpvlrihocen,   omvlkvn   hvset   kvrpehcen
onápat   ka·lpô·f   łakpałłéyho·cín   omálkan   hasít   kałpíhcin
the top   when it gets dry they turn it over all of it the sun dries
and when the topside was dry, they turned it over, and after the sun dried it all,

herihocen   omat,   vhopvnkē   tayē tokon   ocet
hiłéyho·cín   o·mâ·t   ahopánki· tâ·yi· tó·ko·n ô·cit
they put it away when   spoil   so it won't   they have it
if they were storing it, Indians used to keep it that way,

hompet   este-cate   fullvtēt os.
hompít   isticá·ti   follatí·t ô·ⁿs
eating   the Indians   that was their custom
so it wouldn't spoil and ate it.

Mohmen   era-fune,   enok-fune,   fuluwv-fune,   hvfe-fune
móhmin   iła·foní   (i)nokfoní   'folowafóni   'hafifóni
Then   backbone   neck-bone   shoulder-bone   ham-bone
Then if the backbone, neck-bone, shoulder-bone, or thigh-bone

vpeswv   ocē   vhoskan,
apíswa   ô·ci·   ahô·ska·n
meat   they had that was left on
still had meat on it,

eto-polokuce   yakyvpusē   osten   ēkvnvn   cakcvhehcet,
itopolo·kocí   yakyapósi·   ô·stin   i·kanán   cakcahíhcit
little round poles that were a little forked   four   ground   they stuck them in
they stuck four forked sticks in the ground,

estele-vhopakv   tuccēnat   mahe   enhvlwēn   eto-polokucen   ohtvlvlihcet,
istiliahopá·ka   toccî·na·t mâ·hi   inhalwí·n   itopolo·kocín   ohtalaléyhcit
person-foot-measure three   about   high   the poles   they laid across
about three feet high, and laid poles on top

mv	fune	vpeswv	ocakat	oh-vpoyet,	elecv	em etēcet,
ma	*fóni*	*apíswa*	*o·câ·ka·t*	*ohhapô·yit*	*ilíca*	*imíti·cít*
those	bone	meat	have on them	they place on	underneath	they kindle a fire

and set those bones with meat on them on top, lit a fire below,

noricet,	<u>wakv-hotopken</u>	kicēt	hompakvtēt	os.
nołeycít	*wa·kahotópkin*	*keycí·t*	*hómpa·katí·t*	*ô·ⁿsⁱ*
cook it	barbecued beef	they called it	they used to eat it	did

cooked them, called it <u>wakv-hotopke</u> ['barbecued beef'], and ate it.

Empassv	omvlkvn	okkoset,	hvsvthihcet,	horet,	hompaket,
impá·ssa	*omálkan*	*ókko·sít*	*hasathéyhcit*	*ho·łít*	*hómpa·kít*
tripe	all	they wash it	clean it	boil it	they eat it

They washed all the stomach, cleaned it, boiled it, and ate it,

efekceu	hvsvthicet,	horet,	kvrpēcēt	ocet,
ifíkciw	*hasathêycit*	*hô·łit*	*kałpí·ci·t*	*ô·cit*
the entrails, too	they clean it	boil it	dry it	and keep it

and the entrails too, they cleaned it, boiled it, and kept it dried,

rvfon	tvlakcvpko	tohkvlkēn	horet	hompakvtēt	os.
łafón	*tala·kcápko*	*tohkálki·n*	*ho·łít*	*hómpa·katí·t*	*ô·ⁿs.*
winter	long beans	together with	they boil it	and they eat it	[do]

and in the winter they boiled it with green beans and ate it.

Wakv	ele-fune	'tewaret	lopockusēn	hahyet,	hohret,
wá·k(a)	*ilifóni*	*tíwa·łít*	*lopóckosi·n*	*háhyit*	*hóhłit*
cow-	foot	they cut it up	small pieces	they make	boil it

They cut up the foot bones of a cow into small pieces, boiled it,

noṛusē	hakof,	nehan	ohcawet
nŏ·ⁿłosi·	*ha·kô·f*	*nihá·n*	*óhca·wít*
good and done	when it gets	fat, grease	skim off

and when it was good and done, they skimmed off the fat,

ⁱ They arranged the four forked poles thus (in a rectangle): [Haas has a drawing here of a scaffold]. Then put four poles across on the forks. Then other sticks are laid across. *táyhi* 'scaffold for drying anything; drying-rack'.

lehayv   cutkusan   esmorēcet,   'svkvrpehcet,
'lihá·ya   *cótkosa·n*   *ismó·li·cít*   *'sakaɫpíhcit*
pot   small one   they boil it in   stew it down
boiled [the fat] in a small kettle, and after stewing it down,

uewvn   enkvrpehcet,   vfēkvn   eshayakvtēt   os.
óywan   *iŋkaɫpíhcit*   *afi·kan*   *ishá·ya·katí·t*   *ô·ⁿs*
water   dried it from   hair-oil   they made   did
they dried the water from it and made hair-oil out of it.

Wakv-hvrpe tat   hēren   vcayēcēt   kvrpēcet   omakekv
wa·kahálpita·t   *hi·ⁿlin*   *aca·yi·ci·t*   *káɫpi·cít*   *oma·kiká*
cow-hide   good   keep it   dry it   they did
They would keep the cowhide good and dry

pvtakv tis   hayet   ohnocicet   omakvtēs,
patá·kateys   *ha·yít*   *óhnoceycít*   *oma·katí·s*
pallet, even   they made   slept on it   they did
and would even make a pallet out of it and sleep on it,

ēkvnvn   taklumhēt   nocicēt   fullet   onkv.
i·kanán   *taklómhi·t*   *noceycí·t*   *follít*   *onká*
ground   they lay down on   they slept   were about, that was their way   they did
because they slept on the ground [at that time].

Este-cate   vpeswv   hopoyvranat,   <u>fakvn</u>   maket
isticá·ti   *apíswa*   *hopóyala·nâ·t*   *fá·kan*   *ma·kít*
Indians   meat   are going to hunt   hunting   they said
When Indians were going to look for meat, they called it <u>fakv</u> ['hunting'],

etenakuecē   vpokat   monkat   cuko hvmkusis   hvmkē   senhoyvnēt
itina·kóyci·   *apô·ka·t*   *móŋka·t*   *cokó hámkoseys*   *hamki·*   *sinhoyáni·t*
those near each other   that lived   [or]   family one   one   more than
and those living near each other, or if there was more than one man

este honvntaket   vpoken   omat,   em etetaket,
ísti honantá·kit   *apô·kin*   *o·mâ·t*   *imítita·kít*
(the) men   living there   if there are   they get ready
in some households, they got ready,

eco vpeswv   eswvnvyē   res vwvranat,
icó apíswa   *iswanáyi·*   *'lisawáɬa·nâ·t*
deer-meat   something to tie it with   to bring it back
and whatever they were going to bring the deermeat tied with,

wakv-hvrpe tis   selsēcet,   esseu   enkaset,   lowvcluecet,
wa·kahálpiteys   *sílsi·cít*   *íssiw*   *ínka·sít*   *lowácloycít*
cow-hide, even   they cut into strips   hair, too   they scraped it off   softened it
a cowhide even, they cut it into strips, scraped off the hair too, and softened it,

rē tis   cerencēcet   tohottowv tis   nēset   fullof,
lí·teys   *cilínci·cít*   *toho·ttowáteys*   *ni·sít*   *folló·f*
bullets, even   they made them round   powder, even   buying   while they were about
made bullets, and while they were buying gun powder,

hoktvketateu   vce   hocet,   vssvtulke,   cvtvhakv,
hoktakíta·tiw   *ací*   *ho·cít*   *assatólki*[1]   *catahá·ka*
the women, too   corn   pounded   blue-dumplings (wrapped in husks) blue-dumplings
the women too, would pound corn and cook lots of <u>vssvtulke</u>, blue-dumplings,

takliktokset   sulkēn   noricet,   vce   vpaset,
takleyktóksit   *sólki·n*   *noɬeycít*   *ací*   *apa·sít*
soaked, sour corn-bread   lots   they cooked   corn   they parched it
and sour cornbread, and they'd roast corn

osafkehakvn   hocet,   sulkēn   <u>vpvske-nērkv</u>   <u>hockvtē</u> kicēt
osa·fkihá·kan   *ho·cít*   *sólki·n*   *apaskini·lka*   *hockatí· keycí·t*
sofki-grits   they pounded   lots   cold-flour grits   flour   they called it
and pound sofkee grits and prepared lots of what is called <u>vpvske-nērkv hockvtē</u> ['pounded

em etetakuecen   'svpēyet,   mvn   hompet   fullet   omvtēs.
imititá·koycín   *sápi·yít*   *man*   *hompít*   *follít*   *o·mati·s*
they prepared it for   they took it with them   that   eating it   were about   they used to be
roasted seed'] for them, and [the hunters] took it with them and would eat that.

---

[1] Raiford: *assitólki.*

Fayē fullat   eco   elēcen   omat,   hvrpe   encahwet,
fa·yi· follâ·t   *icó*   *ili·cín*   *o·mâ·t* *háɫpi*   *incáhwit*
those that were about hunting a deer   they killed if   the hide   they took off
If those who were out hunting killed a deer, they removed the hide,

em vpeswv tat   enhvteceskv   era-vpeswvn   encahwet,
imapíswata·t   *inhaticíska* *iɫa·apíswan*   *incáhwit*
its meat   first   back-meat, tenderloin   they took it off
took off the meat from its back first,

hvtvm   efuluwv funen   a emehset,   eco   ena   pvlhvmkat
hatâm   *ifolowá fónin*   *a·imíhsit*   *icó*   *iná·* *palhâmka·t*
then   the shoulder-blade   they take it out deer's   body   one side
next they took out the shoulder bone, and on one side of the deer's body,

ekv   vtēkē ehvfe-topvrv   erorēn
iká   *atî·ki· ihafitopáɫa*   *ilóɫi·n*
its head   from   to the end of its thigh (tail-bone) clear to
from its head clear to the end of its thigh [the tailbone],

hvfe-vpeswv   tvskọcusēn   laffet   copahket,
hafiapíswa   *taskŏ·ⁿcosi·n* *la·ffít*   *copáhkit*
ham   very thin   they cut, slice tear it off
they sliced the thigh meat off very thin, tore it off,

entalv-fune omvlkvn   encahwet   vpvlahtet,
inta·lafóni *omálkan* *incáhwit*   *apaláhtit*
ribs   all   they take out and throw them away
took out all the ribs, and threw them away.

eco   ena   pvlhvmkat   etem vpọkusen   efune   sạsēsekon
icó   *iná·* *palhâmka·t*   *itimapŏ·ⁿkosin* *ifóni* *să·ⁿsi·síko·n*
deer's   body   the other side   all together   bones   having no
This side of the deer's body has no connected bones,

tvpeksēn   tvskọcusen   encahwet,   vpvlhvmkateu   matvpomēn
tapíksi·n *taskŏ·ⁿcosin* *incáhwit*   *apalhâmka·tiw*   *ma·tapó·mi·n*
flat   very thin   they take from   the other side, too the same way
and they laid it flat and took the meat off in thin slices.

vpeswv	encahwet	okcvnwv	vpvkekon
apíswa	incáhwit	okcánwa	apákiko·n
the meat	they remove	salt	with no

They did the other side the same way, and without salting it,

ohhvsottan	vtvrticen	karpan	eco entorofkv	kicēt
óhhaso·ttâ·n	atálteycín	ka·lpâ·n	icó intolófka	keycí·t
in the sunshine	they hang it	when it dries	deer-strip (one from each deer)	they call it

they hung it in the sun, and when it was dry, they called it <u>eco entorofkv</u> ['skinned deer'],

hericet	hompakvtēt	omēs.
hileycít	hómpa·katí·t	ô·mi·s
they put it away	they eat it	used to

and having stored it away, they would eat it.

Mv	eco	hvfe-vpeswv	fune	vlikat	waret,	eton	espvkafet,
ma	icó	hafiapíswa	fóni	alêyka·t	wa·lít	itón	íspaka·fít
that	deer	[thigh-meat	bone]	that's on	they cut it	stick	they run through it

They would cut up the meat on the deer's thigh bone, run a stick through these,

hotopet	efunen,	era-fune,	ekv	omakat	tvlkusen
hoto·pít	ifónin	ila·foní	iká	o·mâ·ka·t	tâlkosin
they roasted it	its bone	its backbone	its head	also	only

roast it, and cook and eat only the bones, backbone, head, and such

noricet	hompet	fullet	fayaket omvtēs.
noleycít	hompít	follít	fá·ya·kit o·matí·s[i]
they cook it	eat it	and are about	while they were hunting

when they hunted.

Penwv tat	hericēt	ocēsko	tayēt	vhopvnkusēt	omen,
pínwata·t	hiléyci·t	ó·cí·sko	tâ·yi·t	(a)hópankosí·t	ô·min
the turkey	put away	[not keep]	could	it spoils easily	[does]

The turkey could not be stored, because it spoils easily,

---

[i] "While they are on the hunting trip they eat only the bones, backbone, + head. The boned part they took home. They didn't waste anything, because if they did they might lose their luck." (VII:156)

encuko   yohfulecetv   em vwolicof   tvlkusen
incokó   *yohfolicitá*   *imáwoleycô·f*   *tâlkosin*
their homes   to go back to   when it was getting time   only
and they used to kill turkey

penwv   pvsatet   fullvtēt   omēs.
pínwa   *pasa·tít*   *follatí·t*   *ô·mi·s*
turkeys   they killed them they being about   were that way
only when they were about to return to their homes.

Momis   eco tawvn   elēcetv   'sem etetayē tayē onkot omvtēs.
mô·meys   *icóta·wán*   *ili·citá*   *'simititá·yi· tâ·yi· óŋko·t ô·mati·s*
But   but that deer   to kill it   they never could get enough of
But nothing could equal killing a deer.

Ēkvnv   tvnkē   este   encuko   vwolē   sekaten
i·kaná   *tánki·*   *ísti*   *incokó*   *awóli·* *sikâ·tin*
[land   vacant]   person's   home   nearby   where there was no
They used to make camp on vacant land where no one's house

ehvpo   hayet   omakvtēs.
ihapó·   *ha·yít*   *oma·katí·s*
camp   made   they did
was near.

Eco elēckv   em vnvckekatu   vpakis   ocen
icó ili·cka *imanáckika·tow*   *apa·kêys*   *o·cín*
deer-killing   those that are not lucky being with them   sometimes with
Sometimes those with no luck at killing deer

fullet omvtēs.   Encukon   likēpē   estomis
follít o·mati·s   *incokón*   *leyki·pi·* *istô·meys*
they were about with them   his home   being at   even if he is
would be with them. Even from their homes

honvnwv tat eco, penwv 'tepakat hopoye mahēt fullvtēt omēs.
honánwata·t icó pínwa 'tipâ·ka·t hopoymǎ·ⁿhi·t follati·t ô·mi·sⁱ
a man deer turkey both he hunted a great deal being around he was
the men used to go around hunting deer and turkey a great deal.

Vculvke tat este-mvnettvlke hompvkvrē heyv nanvken em vsēhet omvtēs.
acolakíta·t istimanittâlki hompakáli· hiyá nâ·nakin imási·hít o·matí·s
The old folks the young folks to eat [these] things they forbade did
The old folks forbade the young people from eating these things.

Eco etucen pahpetskvs. Cele-wesakv enokwvt warkusē
*icó itócin páhpíckas ciliwisá·ka (i)nókwat*ⁱⁱ *wa·lkosi·*
deer kidneys you mustn't eat! your toes neck easily torn loose
"Do not eat deer kidneys. The undersides of your toes

cenhahkvrēs, papetsken omat, kicakvtēt os,
cinháhkáli·s pa·píckin o·mâ·t kéyca·katí·t ô·ⁿs
you might get that way you eat if they used to tell them [did]
might easily tear lose if you eat them," they used to tell them,

estelepikv ocekot fullet onkv okakvtēs.
istilipéyka ó·ciko·t follít oŋká oka·katí·s
shoes without around they were that's what they meant
because they went around without shoes.

Eco-hvce 'mvpeswv pahpetskvs. Hopvnkv ofvn huervtet
icohací 'mapíswa páhpíckas hopánka ó·fan hôylatit
Deer-tail-meat don't eat it! war in time of when you are in (battle)
"Do not eat the meat of a deer's tail. In time of war,

lētketskof, hēcket estemayetsken cerahohhvrēs
li·tkícko·f hî·ckit ístima·yíckin cila·hóhháli·s
when you're running can be seen away from you might get shot
when you run, you will be seen and might get shot running from people,"

ⁱ "Men who were good hunters in the old days would have wives picked out for them. If they were not good hunters, they were not given opportunity to marry. There was a law forbidding adultery. Could have only one wife at a time." (VII:160)

ⁱⁱ *ciliwisá·ka (i)nókwat* 'the underneath part of the toes'.

kicvtēt   os.   Eco   lētkat,   ehvce   hatket
keycatí·t[340]   *ô·ⁿs*   *icó*   *li·tkâ·t*   *iháci* *hǎ·ⁿtkit*
they told them   [did]   deer   that is running   its tail very white
they said. Because, when a deer runs, its tail is very white

hopvyēt   hēcken   ayēt   onkv   okakvtēs.
hopáyi·t   *hî·ckin*   *a·yí·t*   *ôŋka*   *oka·katí·s*
a long ways   is visible   while it is going might be   they meant
and visible from afar.

Eco etolaswv   pahpetskvs.   Hopvnkof,
icó itolá·swa   *páhpíckas*   *hópankô·f*
deer-tongue   don't eat!   when it's time of war
"Do not eat the tongue of a deer. In time of war,

ewvnhkvn   cehlvrēs   kicakvtēt   os.
iwánhkan   *cíhláli·s*   *kéyca·katí·t*   *ô·ⁿs*
(from) thirst   you might die   [they told them   did]
you might die of thirst," they used to say.

Eco   torkopohlikv   pahpetskvs.   Hopvnkof   cefekehkvrēs
icó *to·lkopohléyka*   *páhpíckas*   *hópankô·f*   *cifikíhkáli·s*
deer   knee-cap   don't eat   in time of war   you will tremble with fright
"Do not eat a deer's kneecap. In time of war, you will tremble with fright,"

kicakvtēt   os.
kéyca·katí·t   *ô·ⁿs*[ii]
they told them   [did]
they used to say.

Eco ele   hackewvn   okat   empapvkē   sulkvn   kicakēt   omvtēs.
icó ilí *ha·ckiwán*[iii341] *o·kâ·t* *impa·pakí·* *sôlkan* *kéyca·kí·t* *o·matí·s*
deer-leg   shanks (shins)   called it [they eat] many   they called it [did (long ago)]
For deer-shanks, they had many names of dishes [?].

---

[i] "*hópankô·f* = lit. "when it's spoiled" = in time of war. It has reference to the fact that everything is spoiled in time of war. Everything becomes spoiled in time of war." (VII:162)

[ii] Couldn't eat deer-kidneys, deer-tail, deer-tongue, deer-kneecap.

[iii] Also: *hackiwán*. Everybody ate deer-shank.

Horket   nǫrusē   hakat,
ho·lkít[342]   *nǒ·ⁿłosi·*   *ha·kâ·t*
they boiled it[343] good and done   when it got
When it boils and has gotten good and done,

acofvkv   ocakat   pvpetv   hēruset   fvmēcuset   omen,
a·cofáka   *o·câ·ka·t*   *papíta*   *hǐ·ⁿłosi·t*   *famǐ·ⁿcosi·t*   *ô·min*
sinews   that are on   to eat   it is good   and it smells good   does
the sinews are good to eat and smell good,

pvpaket   omvtēs.   Momet   noricat,
papa·kít   *o·matí·s*[344] *mo·mít*   *nołeycâ·t*
they used to eat it did   Then   when cooking
and they used to eat them. And when they cooked them,

lakcv   meskulowv   em ēttēn   kvrpēcet,   paccet   hvrpen   encahwet,
lákca   *miskolówa*   *imi·ttí·n*   *káłpi·cít*   *pa·ccít*   *háłpin*   *incáhwit*
acorns   water-oak   its fruit   dried them   pounded them hull   take from it
they dried the acorns of the water oak, crushed them, removed the hulls,

'mvpeswvn   hocet,   telekmihcet,
'mapíswan   *ho·cít*   *tilikméyhcit*
its meat   they pounded pulverized it
and pounded the meat [of the acorns], pulverized them,

eco ele   horat   aktēhat,
icó ilí   *ho·lâ·t*   *ákti·hâ·t*
deer-foot when they were boiling when they put it in
and added it when boiling deer-foot,

<u>lakcaklike</u>   kicēt   hompaket   omvtēs.
lakcakléyki[i]   *keycí·t*   *hómpa·kít*   *o·matí·s*[345]
(name of dish)   they called it   [they ate   used to do]
and called it <u>lakcaklike</u> and used to eat it.

---

[i] Literally, 'sediment of acorns.' It's like soup, a dish of deer-foot boiled with acorn-meal.

Eco-hvrpe tat   pvtakv tis   hayaket   omvtēs.
icohálpita·t   patá·kateys   há·ya·kit   o·matí·s[346]
deer-hide   bedding, pallet, even   they made   did
They even made bedding out of deerhides.

Este-cate enhompetv vpeswv.   Nokose vpeswv,   nokose-neha tis
isticá·ti   inhompitá   apíswa   nokósi apíswa   nokosinihá·teys
[Indian   their food   meat]   bear-meat   bear-fat, even
Meats the Indians used for Food. Bear meat or bear fat

hompetv   eyacē   hēṟēt   fullvtēs.
hompitá   iyá·ci·   hĭ·ⁿli·t   follatí·s
to eat it   they liked   very much   they went about
was what they really liked to eat.

Nokose   elehcof,   neha   vlikekon   hvrpe   entorohfet,
nokósi   ilíhco·f   nihá·   aléykiko·n   hálpi   intolóhfit
a bear   when they killed fat   without any   hide   they skinned off
After they killed a bear, they skinned it without leaving any fat,

nokose-hvrpe   yekcēn   senēpehcet,   entvphē   encvpkē
nokosihálpi   yíkci·n   sini·píhcit   intaphí·   incapkí·
bear-skin   tight   they stretched it its width   and its length
stretched the bear hide tightly, as wide and as long

estomuset   senēpkē tayen omat   omylkusen   senēpkēn   kvrpehcet
istò·mosit   siní·pki· tâ·yin o·mâ·t   omǎlⁿkosin   siní·pki·n   kaɫpíhcit
just how much   it can stretch   as much as it would stretch   and dried it
as it would stretch, and dried it stretched out

nokose-hvrpe tat   pvtakv   hayakvtēt   omēs.
nokosihálpita·t   patá·ka   há·ya·katí·t   ò·mi·s
the bear-skin   for bedding   they made it   did
and used the bear hide for bedding.

Momet wotko   nehakof,   pvsatet   hotopet   hompakvtēs.
mo·mít   wó·tko   niha·kò·f   *pasa·tít*   *hoto·pít*   *hómpa·katí·s*
Then   coons   when they are fat   they kill them   barbecue them   and ate
Then coons, when they are fat, they killed them, roasted them, and ate them.

Sukhvhatkv papat este-cate saset omis, sulkemahatet
sokhahá·tka pa·pá·t isticá·ti sa·sít o·mêys solkimá·ha·tit
possums who would eat Indians some but most of them
Some Indians would eat opossum, but most

pvpvkekatēs. Este elē hopelhoyan enwoset
papákiká·ti·s ísti ili· hopílho·yâ·n inwo·sít
they didn't eat it a person dead and buried they scratch
would not eat them. [Opossums] dig where a corpse has been buried

sohcēyet este ēlv em vpeswvn papēt omakēs
sóhci·yít ísti i·la imapiswan pa·pí·t omà·ki·s
they go into (grave) dead person's flesh they eat of it [do]
and go in and eat the dead person's flesh,

makakat sulkēt omet pvpvkekot omvtēs.
má·ka·kâ·t sólki·t ô·mit papákikot o·matí·s[i]
say that a lot of them do [they didn't eat it used to]
they say, and many would not eat it.

Momis kono-vpeswvn hompetv hēremahēt os komēt
mo·mêys konoapíswan hompitá hi·ⁿlimá·hi·t ô·ⁿs ko·mí·t
But skunk meat as food was very good they thought
But skunk meat is very good to eat, they thought,

este-cate sulkemahat kono-vpeswvn hompet fullvtēt omēs.
isticá·ti solkimâ·ha·t konoʔapíswan hompít follatí·t ô·mi·s[ii]
Indians most of them skunk meat eating they were about did
and many Indians used to eat skunk meat.

Hvnoleske enkorret yvlonkvn uewv lvokat em akpaccen,
hanolíski[iii] iŋko·llit yalónkan óywa láwka·t imákpa·ccín
Devil's shoestring they dig it the roots water deep pounded it
They used to dig devil's shoestring and pounded the roots in deep water,

---

[i] In old days, people were buried in open graves, not being put in caskets or boxes. In this way the possums could get into the graves and scratch into the flesh of the dead and eat of it.
[ii] "Insert part about Rabbit Meat (when it can be found)" (VII:172)
[iii] Also: *halonískí*. W. Tanyan said *hinolíska*.

rvrot   akhacakof,   eccvkotakse   momen   enrēn   esrahricet,
łałót   *akhá·ca·kô·f*   *iccakotáksi*   *mo·mín* *inłí·n*   *isłáhłeycít*
fish   when they get drunk   bow   and   the arrow they shoot them with
and when the fish got drunk, they would shoot at them with bows and arrows,

sulkēn   pvsatet,   hotopēt   ocet,   horet,   hompaket,
sólki·n   *pasa·tít*   *hotópi·t*   *ô·cit*   *ho·lít*   *hómpa·kít*
lots of them they kill them   roast them   and keep them   boil it   they eat it
kill lots of them, and keep them roasted and boil them and eat them

opuswv tis   ēsket   omakvtēs.   Kofuckvn aktēhet   esnoricat,
opóswateys   *i·skít*   *oma·katí·s*   *kofóckan ákti·hít*   *ísnołeycâ·t*
the soup, too they drink it they used to mint   put in with it they cook it with it
and even drink the soup. Adding mint and cooking it with that

rvro pvpetv   opuswv esketv   eresheremahē omēn,   hompaket   fullvtēt os.
łałó papíta   *opóswa iskitá*   *iłishiłimâ·hi· ô·mi·n*   *hómpa·kít*   *follatí·t ô·ⁿs*
to eat fish   and to drink soup it is mighty good   eating   they were about
makes eating fish and soup even better, and they used to eat that.

Rvro   vtēkat,   ēsapv,   vcvpa   omakat,   omvlkvn   hompet omakvtēs.
łałó   *atî·ka·t*   *i·sá·pa*   *acapá·*   *o·mâ·ka·t* *omálkan*   *hompít oma·katí·s*
fish   all kinds   garfish   eel   like that   all of them they would eat them
All fish, gar, eel, and such, they used to eat all of them.

Lucv Vpeswv.   Lucv   uewv   akfullate   vtēkat   pvpaket   omis,
locá apíswa   *locá(?)*   *óywa*   *ákfollâ·ti*   *atî·ka·t*   *papa·kít*   *o·mêys*
turtle-meat   turtle   water   that stay in   all kinds of they eat   but
Turtle Meat. They used to eat all the water turtles,

takokfvmpen   pvpvkekatēs.   Momet lucv   kayakat,
takô·kfámpin   *papákiká·ti·s*   *mo·mít locá*   *ká·ya·kâ·t*
the loggerhead turtle they didn't eat it Then turtle   when they lay (eggs)
but they did not eat the loggerhead turtle.[347] And when the turtles are laying,

echustake   enhopoyet   senhēcat,   horet   hompaket   onkv
ichostá·ki *ínhopo·yít*   *sínhi·câ·t*   *ho·lít*   *hómpa·kít*   *oŋká*
the eggs   they hunt for them when they find them they boil them they eat them   for
they looked for eggs, and when they found them, they boiled them and ate them,

lucv-kayv   em oketv   kerrvkētok:
locaká·ya   imokitá   kiłłaki·to·k
turtle-laying   time   they knew when it was
so they knew when it was turtle-laying time:

uewv   a ossē   echustake   vketēcē
óywa   á·o·ssí·   ichostá·ki   akíti·cí·
water   when it comes out of   its eggs   they look for
when it comes out of the water they checked for its eggs

hvcce-vfopke   ēkvnv   fullan   elentet
hacciafó·pki   i·kaná   follâ·n   ilintit[i]
edge of the stream   the ground   they are about   they track them
and tracked them on the land

echustake   senhecaket   papet omakvtēs.
ichostá·ki   sínhica·kít   pa·pít oma·katí·s[348]
their eggs   they find them   and eat them
at the edge of streams where they go, and they found the eggs and ate them.

Lucv-tokocke   lvpvtke   ēkvnv   fullateu   hopoyet   eshēcat,
locatokócki   lapátki   i·kaná   follâ·tiw   hopo·yít   íshi·câ·t
terrapin   dry (land)   land   that are about   they hunt for   when they find them
They looked for box turtles that travel on land too, and finding them,

ēset   sulēcen   omat,   horet   hompaket
i·sít   soli·cín   o·mâ·t   ho·lít   hómpa·kít
they catch them   they get lots of them   if   they boil them   they eat them
they caught them, and when they had lots of them, they boiled them and ate them.

hvmkusis   ēsen   omat,   totkv ētkan   nvtaksēn   taklicet
hámkoseys   i·sín   o·mâ·t   tó·tka i·tkâ·n   natáksi·n   taklêycit
just one   they catch   if   fire   where it is burning   on its back   they put it down
If they caught just one, they set it belly-up in the fire

---

[i] *ilintitá* 'to track', or *alintitá* (W. Tanyan).

eto-tvckēn   'sem vwetēnen   ēlof
itotácki·n   *'simawitî·nin*   *i·lô·f*
piece of stick   they weight it down   when it dies
and pinned it down with a stick, and when it died,

ēsso-hiyen   ohrahnen   norof   papet   omakvtēs.
i·ssoháyyin   *ohłáhnin*   *no·lô·f*   *pa·pít*   *oma·katí·s*
hot ashes   they cover it with   when it gets done   they ate it   they did
they covered it with hot ashes and would eat it when it was done.

Momet   lucv   estit   totkv   taklican   entaklētken   omat,
mo·mít   *locá*   *istêyt*   *tó·tka* *taklêyca·n*   *intákli·tkin*   *o·mâ·t*
Then   terrapin   whoever   fire   has got it in should start to run   if
And whoever has a turtle in the fire that gets away and runs from him,

mv   este   hoktarēs   makaket,   entakletkvrē   eyacekot
ma   *ísti*   *hóktá·li·s*[i]   *má·ka·kit*   *intaklítkáli·*   *iyá·cikot*
that   person   will be passionate   they say   to run from them   not wanting
that person will be passionate, they say, [so] not wanting it to run from them,

yekcēn   ohwetenken   lucv   ehlētvlkēt   omvtēs.
yíkci·n   *óhwitinkín*   *locá*   *íhli·tálki·t*   *o·matí·s*
pretty hard   they mash it down terrapin   finally die   it did
they pinned it down hard, and the turtle finally died.

Momet   kēstowv   pakpakof,
mo·mít   *ki·stowá*[ii]   *pákpa·kô·f*
Then   the red-root   when it blooms
Now when red-root blooms,

echustaken   ētehēt   omakēs   maket,
ichostá·kin   *i·tihí·t*   *omá·ki·s*[349]   *ma·kít*
eggs   have in their pockets, inside of body   they have   they say
they said they had eggs in their pockets,

---

[i] *hokta·li·s* will be passionate (said of man or woman).
[ii] Hill says *mi·kkohaní·ca* 'black-root'.

mv omof lucv eyacvkemạhēt omvtēs, echustake enpvpetvn.
ma ô·mo·f locá iya·cakimà·ⁿhi·t o·mati·s ichostá·ki inpapítan
at that time terrapins they like very much they do the eggs to eat of them
and at that time they liked eating turtle eggs very much.

Ero sulkēn pvsaten omat, horkēn noricet hompaket omis,
iłó sólki·n pasa·tín o·mâ·t hólki·n noleycít hómpa·kít o·mèys
squirrels lots they kill if by boiling it they cooked it they ate it but
If they kill a lot of squirrels, they cooked them by boiling and ate them,

hvmkusis omat essen ennekrihcet, totkv tempen takwvkēcēt,
hámkoseys o·mâ·t íssin innikléyhcit[350] *tó·tka tímpin takwakî·ci·t*
only one if they had its hair they singed off fire edge they had it laying down
but if it was just one, they singed off the hair by laying it near the fire

ēsso-hiyen ohrahnen norof,
i·ssoháyyin ohłáhnin[351] *no·łô·f*
hot ashes they covered it with when it got done
and covered it with hot ashes, and when it was done,

este hvmkē monkat hokkolusis pvpēpen fulhoyvtēt omēs.
ísti hámki· móŋka·t hokkô·loseys papi·pín fólho·yatí·t ô·mi·s
person one or else only two they ate it they were about [did]
one person or even two used to eat it.

Hiyomis ero tat pvphoyē hēremahēt emonkvt os.
hayyô·meys iłóta·t pápho·yí· hǐ·ⁿlimá·hi·t imóŋkat ô·ⁿs
even now the squirrel is eaten very much still [it is]
Even now the squirrel is still very much eaten.

Cufe. Cufe tat papvken omat, este-celelēkēn
cofí cofíta·t pa·pakín o·mâ·t isticílili·kí·n
[rabbit] the rabbit anyone ate it if it makes them jerk
Rabbit. If you eat rabbit, it makes you jerk,

estehayēs	maket	pvpvkekatēt omēs.
ístiha·yi·s[i]	*ma·kít*	*papákiká·ti·t ô·mi·s*[ii]
it makes them that way	they say	they didn't eat it

they said, and didn't eat it.

Fuswv-lopocke tat,	kowikucen,	hēspakwvn,	sakkelv,	cukkoloswucen,	fuco,
foswalopóckita·t	*kowwêykocin*	*hî·spákwan*	*sakkilá*	*cokkolo·swocín*	*focó*
the small birds	quail	robin	blackbird	snowbird	duck

The small birds, quail, robin, blackbird, snowbird, duck,

pvce,	pvcehowe,	kowike-rakko,	rvnrvcukwuce	esyomat	pvpetvt	omaken,
pací	*pacihó·wi*	*kowwêykiłákko*	*lânłacokwocí*	*isyô·ma·t*	*papítat*	*omá·kin*
pigeon	dove	prairie chicken	hummingbird	like those	to eat	they are

pigeon, dove, prairie chicken, hummingbird, and such are to be eaten,

fuswv	rem ētv	pvpetv	tokot	omēs	makakvtēt os.
fóswa	*'limí·ta*	*papíta*	*tó·ko·t*	*ô·mi·s*	*má·ka·katí·t ô·ⁿs*
birds	of other kinds	to eat	not	they are	they used to say

[but] other birds should not be eaten, they used to say.

Mv	lopockusat	hvmkusis	elēhocat,
ma	*lopŏ·ⁿckosa·t*	*hámkoseys*	*ilí·ho·câ·t*
Those	small ones	even one	when they killed it

Even when they only killed one of those small ones,

hopuetaket	eckopēt	pvpvkemạhēt	omvtēs.
hopoytá·kit	*ícko·pí·t*	*papakimă·ⁿhi·t*	*o·matí·s*
the children	they roasted them	they ate it very much, often	did

the children roasted them and ate them often.

---

[i] "it makes your lieders jerk if he eats rabbit" (VIII:2).

[ii] "T. W. says in old times did not eat dove because your children did not grow cause the dove just lay maybe two eggs. Dove also used in love medicine — then about sundown, dove will fly to woman's house and sing lonesomely + make the woman very lonesome. Also ate "fieldlark"" (VIII:4).

Wild Fruits

J. Hill (Haas VIII:9–17)

Pvrko	em ēttē	lopǫcusē	pelofv	aklokcan	vteloyet,
pálko	*imi·tti·*	*lopŏ·ⁿckosi·*	*'piló·fa*	*áklo·kcâ·n*	*atílo·yít*
grape	its fruit	the small ones	in the bottoms	get ripe	they gather them

They used to gather the small grapes that get ripe in the bottoms,

sulkēn	em vpucen	enwvnawicet	'kvlike	kicēt
sólki·n	*imapocín*	*inwana·wêycit*[352]	*'kaléyki*	*keycí·t*
lots	the stems	they tied them	bunches, clusters	they called them

and having tied lots of them up by the stems, they called them 'kvlike

hericēt	ocet	rvfo tat	<u>pvrko-afke</u>	kicēt	noricet,
hiłéyci·t	*ô·cit*	*lafóta·t*	*pałkoá·fki*	*keycí·t*[i]	*nołeycít*
put them away	kept them	the winter	grape mush	they called it	they cooked it

and kept them stored away, and in winter they cooked what is called <u>pvrko-afke</u>

hompakvtēt	omen,	hiyomis	pvrko	este-cate	sulkemahat
hómpa·katí·t	*ô·min*	*hayyô·meys*	*pálko*	*isticá·ti*	*solkimâ·ha·t*
and they ate it	they did	Even now	grapes	Indians	most of

and would eat that. Even now very many Indians

hompaket os.	Opvkv	em ēttē	lokcē	latkan,
hómpa·kít ô·ⁿs	*opáka*	*imi·tti·*	*lo·kci·*	*la·tkâ·n*
eat it even now	passionflower	its fruit	get ripe	and falls off

eat grapes. When passionflower fruit gets ripe and falls off,

vteloyet,	hvrpen	vpvlahtet,	uewvn	aktehhet,	esmorēcet,
atílo·yít	*háłpin*	*apaláhtit*	*óywan*	*aktíhhit*	*ismó·li·cít*[353]
they gather them	skin, hull	they throw away	water	put them in	they boil them

they gathered them, threw away the hulls, put them in water, and boiled them,

nērkvn	encahwet	vpvlahtet,	vce-hocke	telēkmusan	aktēhet
ní·łkan	*incáhwit*	*apaláhtit*	*acihócki*	*tili·ⁿkmosa·n*	*aktî·hit*[354]
seeds	they take out	and throw them away	pounded corn	real fine	put it in

removed the seeds and threw them out, and having put them in really fine pounded corn,

---

[i] Or: *keycít.*

esnoricet   <u>opvkv-afke</u>   kicet   hompakvtēs.
isnołeycít   *opakaá·fki*   *keycít*   *hómpa·katí·s*
and they cook it with it   passionflower-mush   they called it   and they ate it
they cooked it and called it <u>opvkv-afke</u> and ate it.

Momet   selvwv   em ēttē   lokcan,   pvpvkemạhet   ont   omis,
mo·mít   *siláwa*   *imi·ttí·*   *lo·kcâ·n*   *papakimà·ⁿhit*   *ônt*   *o·mêys*
Then   haw   its fruit   when it gets ripe   they eat it very much   do   but
And when haw fruits got ripe, they ate a lot of them,

hericētokot   mont   noricētokot   papet   omakvtēs.
hiléyci·tó·ko·t   *mónt*   *nołeyci·tó·ko·t*   *pa·pít*   *oma·katí·s*
they didn't put it away   and   they didn't cook it   they ate it   did
but they didn't store and didn't cook them.

Kepalv,   kvco-hvlkv,   kvco-huerv,   pvkanv-catuce   em ēttē   lokcakat,
kipá·la   *kaco·hálka*   *kaco·hóyła*   *paka·naca·tocí*   *imi·ttí·*   *lókca·kâ·t*
strawberry   dewberry   blackberry   plum   their fruit   when they get ripe
When strawberries, dewberries, blackberries, or plums got ripe,

papet   fullet   omis,   mvo   hericekot   noricekot
pa·pít   *follít*   *o·mêys*   *maw'*   *hiléyciko·t*   *nołéyciko·t*
they ate   being around   but   that, too   they didn't put them away   they didn't cook them
they ate them, but those too they ate

papēt   omakekv,   svheremahē   vrakkuecekv   em ocvkekot   omvtēs.
pa·pí·t   *o·ma·kiká*   *'sahiłimâ·hi·*   *ałakkóycka*   *imo·cakíko·t*   *o·matí·s*
ate them   but they (did eat them)   not so very much   appreciation   they didn't have   did
without storing or cooking, so they didn't have much appreciation for them.

Pvrkuce,   opvkv   'tepakat   em ēttē   tvlkusen
palkocí   *opáka*   *'tipâ·ka·t*   *imi·ttí·*   *tâlkosin*
Possum grape   maypop   the two together   their fruits   only
They only appreciated the fruit

vrakkuecemahēt   omakvtēs.   <u>Svtv-semvnole</u>   kicet   em ēttē
ałakkoycimá·hi·t   *oma·katí·s*   *satasimanó·li*   *keycít*   *imi·ttí·*
they appreciated very much, a lot   did   persimmon   called   its fruit
of the possum grape and passionflower. When the fruit of what is called <u>svtv-semvnole</u>

lokcusē   haket,   ohhetotē   hakofvn,   vteloyet   kvrpēcvkvtēn
lŏ·ⁿkcosi· ha·kít   óhhito·ti·   ha·kŏ·fan   atílo·yit   kalpi·cakáti·n
very ripe   when they get   frosts on them after it does they gather them dried
['persimmon'] gets very ripe after a frost,

ocet   monkat taklike   omē   hayēt   pvphoyvtēt   omēs.
ô·cit   móŋka·t takléyki ó·mi·   há·yi·t   pápho·yatí·t   ò·mi·s
keep them or   bread   sort of make it   and they ate it did
they would gather them and keep them dried or make a kind of bread and eat it.

Heyv   Oklvhomv   ēkvntvckv   ofv   tokot   Vlepamv   ēkvntvckv   ofv tat
hiyá   oklahóma   i·kantácka ó·fa tó·ko·t alipá·ma   i·kantácka ó·fata·t
here   Okla.   district   in   not   Alabama   district   in the
Not in this state of Oklahoma, but in the state of Alabama

eto   em ēttē   pvpetv   mvrahrvkv   sulkēt   omvtē tis   omēs.
itó   imi·tti· papíta   'maⱡahⱡaká   sólki·t   o·matí·teys o·mí·s
tree   fruit of to eat   different kinds several   there was
there may have been lots of different fruit to eat.

Momis   yvmv tat   nvcumēt   ont omēs.   Pvrko-rakko
mô·meys yamáta·t   nacómi·t   ônt o·mí·s paⱡkoⱡá·kko
but   here   only a few there are   big grapes
But here there are few. There are big grapes

ēkvnv   cvto   vlkat tis   sasen   papet   fullet   omis,
i·kaná cató   âlka·tteys   sá·sin   pa·pít   follít   o·mêys
ground   rocky   even where it's there is some   eating them   going about do, but
growing even where it's rocky, and they ate them,

hericēt   omekot   lokcusē   hakat   tvlkusēn
hiⱡeycí·t   omíko·t   lŏ·ⁿkcosi·   ha·kâ·t   tâlkosi·n
put them away   they don't   real ripe   when they get only
but they didn't store them, and only when they got really ripe

norekon   papet   omakvtēs.
nolíko·n   pa·pít   oma·katí·s
uncooked, raw   they eat them [they do]
would they eat them raw.

Pottery Making

J. Hill (Hill III:2–3; Haas XVIII:111–125)

Vrkvswv, locowv nake hvmkusēt omēs.
ałkáswa locówa nâ·ki hámkosi·t ô·mi·s[i]
A crock [vrkvswv] and clay jar [locowv] are the same thing.

Fakke-tvlaswv lvstan eshahoyvtēt
fakkitalá·swa[355] *lásta·n ishá·ho·yáti·t*[356]
They were made of hard, black clay;

rakkemahat elecv empvtakv vhopakuce kolvpakat mahet poloksēt,
łakkimá·ha·t ilicá (?) impatá·ka ahopa·kocí kolapâ·ka·t mâ·hit polóksi·t
the largest had a base about seven inches round,

emmahē vhopakuce palē cahkepohkakat mahet pakkēt,
imma·hí· ahopa·kocí pâ·li· cahkipohkâ·ka·t mâ·hit pá·kki·t
rising to a height of about fifteen inches;

nvrkvpv mahe tat vhopakuce palat mahet omen,
nałkapá mâ·hita·t ahopa·kocí pâ·la·t mâ·hit ô·min
it was about ten inches around the middle,

yoksvt vhopakuce kolvpakat mahet omakvtēs. 'Resenlopockusateu (vrkvcuce) hahicet,
yóksat ahopa·kocí kolapâ·ka·t mâ·hit oma·kati·s. 'lisinlopóckosa·tiw ałkacóci[357] *há·heycít*
and the top edge was about seven inches. Smaller ones (vrkvcuce) were also made,

motēsv enhakv omēt ont omis, enhvokēt monkat cokwvt rakkētot omvtēs.
motí·sa inhá·ka ó·mi·t ônt o·mêys inhawkí·t móŋka·t cókwat łákki·tot o·matí·s.
similar in shape to a sofkee crock [motēsv], but the opening, or mouth, was large.

Fakke tat polokusēn hayet, lvcpēcet, etohlicet, ohwetenket,
fákkita·t polô·kosi·n ha·yít lácpi·cít itóhleycít óhwitinkít
Making a rope of clay, they wet it, coiled it around on itself, and pressed down

---

[i] Maybe a little different shape, I don't know. JH

enken 'setewetēnet 'telokpicet hvlwēcet omakvtēs.
íŋkin 'sitíwiti·nít 'tilókpeycít hálwi·cít oma·katí·s
and squeezing with the hands, they stacked them together for height.

Yv nake hayvranof, "Fakke-mocvse tvlkat norof, tvkockēs" maket,
ya nâ·ki há·yała·nô·f fakkimocási tâlka·t no·lô·f tako·ckí·s ma·kít
When making these things, they said, "When you bake new clay alone, it cracks,"

fakke norvtē vrkvswv vhopvnkvtēn paccet telekmicet,
fákki nołáti· ałkáswa ahopánkati·n pa·ccít 'tilíkmeycít
so they pounded baked clay from a broken pot into a fine powder,

mv fakken vpayet cvlahpet, vrkvswv, locowv, fakke-pvlaknv hahicet omakvtēs.
ma (?) fákkin apa·yít caláhpit ałkáswa locówa fakkipalákna há·heycít oma·katí·s
added it to the clay and mixed it and made crocks, clay jars, and clay plates.

Pvlaknv tat motēsv pvlaknv kihocē ocakat enhakv omvkēt omvtēs.
paláknata·t motí·sa palákna kéyho·cí· ó·ca·kâ·t inhá·ka o·makí·t o·matí·s.
The plates were similar to what is now called pottery.

Yv nake hayepohyof, folahpv hvrpen eskaset ofv,
ya nâ·ki ha·yipóhyo·f[358] foláhpa hálpin íska·sít
When they were shaped, the shell of a mussel was used to scrape it,

onvpvo hērusen mvherihcet,
ó·fa onápaw hĭ·ⁿlosin 'mahi<léyh>cit
designing the inside and out very prettily;

cvto tvkvcwē tenēpusan esfofoyet tenēpihcet hvsottan licen,
cáto (?) takácwi· tinĭ·ⁿposa·n isfó·fo·yít[359] tini·péyhcit hasô·tta·n lêycin
they were sawed repeatedly with a hard, smooth rock, smoothed and set in the sun,

karpofvn, eto-talucen ohhvpohyet 'mvhetehcet, mv fakke noricet omhoyvtēs.
ka·łpô·fan itota·locín ohhapóhyit 'mahitíhcit ma fákki nołeycít ómho·yatí·s
and when dry, [the pots] were set upon dry wood and lit, and the clay was baked.

Vrkvswv locowv uewv esmorecetvt omet, vpeswv eshoretvt omet,
ałkáswa locówa óywa (?) ismo·licítat ô·mit apíswa (?) ishołítat ô·mit
Crocks [vrkvswv] and clay jars [locowv] were for boiling water, boiling meat,

opuswuce esnoricetvt omvtēs. Momen hompvranof, fakke pvlaknv vcanet,
oposwocí isnołeycitát ô·mati·s. mo·mín hómpała·nô·f fákki (?) palákna acâ·nit
and cooking soup. And when they were going to eat, they'd pour it into a clay plate,

eto-hakkvn monkat yvnvs-yvpe hakkvn hvmkusēn akpikēt,
itohákkan móŋka·t yanasyapí hákkan hâmkosi·n akpéyki·t
they'd put in just one wooden spoon or spoon made of buffalo horn,

opuswuce ēsket homhopvtēt omēs. Yv nake hahicat hoktvket omvtēs.
oposwocí i·skít hómho·pati·t[360] o·mi·s[361] ya nâ·ki há·heycâ·t hoktakít o·mati·s.
and eat the soup. It was the women who made these things.

Cvpuse tatē natarvt omet, pvlaknv hahicen hēcit arvyvtēt os.
capósi tá·ti·[362] na·tá·lat[363] ô·mit palákna há·heycín hi·céyt a·łayáti·t ô·ⁿs.
My late grandmother was a potter, and I used to see her making plates.

Vrkvs-wvnvkv hoktvke natarvlke hayvtēt omēs. Mv vrkvcuce enrakkē tat
ałkaswanáka hoktakí na·ta·łâlki ha·yati·t ô·mi·s ma ałkacóci[364] inlakkí·ta·t
The tom-tom [vrkvs-wvnvkv] was made by the women potters. The little tom-tom

vhopakuce ostat mahetis omēs. Momen enhvlwē vhopakuce kolvpakat
ahopa·kocí ô·sta·t mâ·hiteys o·mí·s mo·mín inhalwí· ahopa·kocí kolapâ·ka·t
was about four inches around. And its height was about

mahetis omvtēs. Mv vrkvswucen uewvn nvcomusēn vcahnet,
mâ·hiteys o·mati·s. ma (?) ałkaswocín óywan nacómosi·n acáhnit
seven inches. A little water was poured in a small pot,

ecuce hvrpen esse enkasvkvtēn sohrahnet,
icóci hálpin íssi iŋká·sakáti·n sohláhnit
it was covered with fawn hide that had been scraped

eco-hvrpe selkēn sem ohwvnahoyvtēt, mvt <u>vrkvs-wvnvkvt</u> omet, <u>vrkvs-vtulkvtot,</u>
icohálpi sílki·n 'simohwana·hoyáti·t mat ałkaswanákat ô·mit ałkasatólkatot
and tied down with a strip of deer hide, and that was an <u>vrkvs-wvnvkv</u>, <u>vrkvs-vtulkv,</u>

vrkvs-hakvtot nvfketucet omēs. Momen heyv nake hēren mvherihcet nvfhoken omat,
alkashá·katot nafkitóciⁱ ô·mi·s mo·mín hiyá (?) nâ·ki hĭ·ⁿlin 'mahiłéyhcit náfho·kín o·mâ·t
or vrkvs-hakv, a small drum. And if these things are well made, they have a sound

enhakē ocēt omēs. Enhopvyē vkērkv hvmkat senhoyvnētis pohkēs.
inha·kí· ó·ci·t ô·mi·s inhopayí· akí·lka hámka·t sinhoyáni·teys pô·hki·s[365]
when hit. They can be heard a mile or more away.

Momen esnvfketv tat enrakkē encvpkē cokv eshoccicetv omusen,
mo·mín isnafkitáta·t inlakki·[366] *incapkí· có·ka isho·cceycitá ô·mosin*
And the drumsticks were about the size and length of a pencil,

esnafket hayēcet omhoyēs.
ísna·fkít há·yi·cít ómho·yi·s
and they played by hitting the drum with them.

Momen este-cate encuko-rakkon nvkvftēt 'panēt fullet,
mo·mín isticá·ti incokolákkon nakáfti·t[367] *pa·ní·t follít*
Now when the Indians were at the square ground to dance,

monkat pokkechvranet fullen omat, vrkvswvnvkv tat wvnayet mēkkvke kaket,
mónjka·t pokkíchała·nít follín o·mâ·t alkaswanákata·t wanâ·yit mi·kkakí kâ·kit
or if they were going to play stick-ball, the chiefs would tie the tom-toms and sit,

estomēn tvsekvyv fullvrē komat ohyekcicet, nerē ofv enkaken,
istó·mi·n[368] *tasikayá folláli· kô·ma·t ohyíkceycít nili· ó·fa injkâ·kin*
encouraging the citizens on how they were to act, sitting in the night,

totkvo 'to-tale sulkēn ohpvlvthoyen, hvyayvkē rakkēn ocet
tó·tkaw· 'totá·li sólki·n ohpalátho·yín haya·yakí· łákki·n ô·cit
and the fire would have much dry wood thrown onto it; and having a bright fire,

vrkvshakv nafket hayēcet este-cate vpoken omat, afvckvkēt vpoket onkv,
ałkashá·ka na·fki<t> ha·yĭ·ⁿcit isticá·ti apô·kin o·mâ·t a·fackakí·t apo·kít onjká
as the Indians sat pounding the tom-toms, they were enjoying themselves,

---

ⁱ *nafkitóci*, another name for *ałkaswanáka*, etc. Four names for the little drum.

vrkvshakv tat hạkē 'svmokhakēn vpoket omvnts. Momen mv vretv
ałkashá·kata·t hă·ⁿki· 'samo·khá·ki·n apo·kít o·mánc mo·mín ma ałíta
so the tom-tom played continuously as they sat. And being there

este omvlkvn ohcvfencicē omēt omen, nvfketucet hakekon omat,
ísti omálkan ohcafincéyci· ó·mi·t ô·min nafkitócit há·kikon o·mâ·t
makes everyone feel lively, and if the little drum doesn't sound,

vretv 'sem vnvckē onkon este-catet on omat vkerricēt omēs.
ałíta 'simanácki· óŋko·n isticá·tit ô·n o·mâ·t akiłłeyci·t ô·mi·s.
the Indian feels it is out of place to be there.

How to Make a Bow

J. Hill (Hill III:4; Haas XVIII:127–131)

Eccvkotakse hayetv eto kerkusēt omen,
iccakotáksi ha·yitá itó kíłkosi·t ô·min,
A special wood is used to make a bow;

eto eto-lane kihocat tvlkuset eccvkotakse hẹrēt omēs.
itó[369] itolá·ni kéyho·câ·t tâlkosit iccakotáksi hĭ·ⁿli·t ô·mi·s.
only a tree called eto-lane ['bois d'arc' or 'Osage orange'] makes a good bow.[i]

Entvphē vhopakuce hvmkē hoyanusēn,
intaphí· ahopa·kocí hâmki· hoyâ·nosi·n
The width is a little over one inch,

estele-vhopakv ostē nvrkvpv vpakē encvpkē tis ohmet,
istiliʔahopá·ka ô·sti· nałkapá apâ·ki· incapkí·teys óhmit
and the length is four and a half feet,

---

[i] JHH: Bois d'arc makes the very best bows but mulberry (*kíʻ*) and locust (*iccahá·hta*) can also be used. JHH made one out of mulberry one time.

Made arrows out of *oyʔakłóswa*. Old folks used to use cane (*kohá*) but there is none here. Make arrows any length you want. They must be straight. To check whether an arrow was straight, JHH sighted along it. To make it straight, hold it over or near a flame. When it gets hot bend it or rather straighten it the way you want it. Some of them bite on it + bend it while holding it between the teeth. JHH also tried to straighten an unheated one with his hands.

enlowaketv este esakpv enyekcvkē vcakkvyēt esfulhoyēt omēs.
inlowa·kitá ísti isákpa inyikcakí· acakkayí·t isfólho·yí·t ô·mi·s
and the strength of one's arm determined how limber it should be.

Momen eccvkotakse-fvkv hayetv ero-lane vculan elehcet, essen enlehmet torohfet,
mo·mín iccakotaksifáka ha·yitá iłolá·ni acóla·n ilíhcit íssin inlíhmit tołóhfit
To make the bow-string, kill an old fox squirrel, pick off all the fur, take the skin off,

senēpkēn poloksvranēn, etucvlken sentekkēyvken, kvripen,
siní·pki·n poloksałá·ni·n itocâlkin sintikkî·yakin kałêypin
stretch it as round as possible, support it with little sticks, and when dry,

eskotkvn eskotet poloksihcet, vhopakuce nvrkvpv ennvrkvpv orvhanen
iskó·tkan isko·tít polokséyhcit ahopa·kocí nałkapâ innałkapá ołahâ·nin
cut around it with scissors to be more circular, cut it into a strip with the scissors

entvphēn eskotkvn essēlet, poloksēn vfolotecicet pohyet,
intaphí·n iskó·tkan íssi·lít polóksi·n afolotíceycít póhyit
about a quarter inch wide in a continuous circle, and when finished cutting around it,

uelekhen aktēhvken netta hvmkvranen lowąckusē hakof, akcahwet, osten tepvkohlihcet,
oylíkhin aktî·hakin nittá· hamkałâ·nin lowǎ·ⁿckósi· ha·kô·f akcáhwit ô·stin 'tipakohléyhcit
put it in warm water for about a day, and when it gets soft, take it out, fold it four times,

yekcēn opvyiyet, senēpēcet, yekcēn yoksv vlkēn nake estomis vcokcorcuecvken,
yíkci·n opayêyyit sini·pî·cit[370] *yíkci·n yóksa álki·n nâ·ki istô·meys acokcołcôycakin*
twist it hard, then stretch it, and tie each end firmly to whatever there is;

kvripen, acawvken omat, enyekcē eston hvlatvkis tvcēsko tayēt omēs.
kałêypin a·câ·wakin o·mâ·t inyikcí· istô·n hala·takêys tací·sko· tâ·yi·t ô·mi·s.
take it off when dry, and no matter how hard you pull on it, it will not break.

Mvt eccvkotakse-fvkvt monkat eccv-fvkv kicēt okhoyvnts.
mat iccakotaksifákat móŋka·t iccafáka keycí·t ókho·yánc.
That is what they used to call eccvkotakse-fvkv or eccv-fvkv ['bowstring'].

Tanning Hide

J. Hill (Hill III:4; Haas XVIII:133–139)

Cusse makē hayat eco-hvrpen uewvn akkayet, netta vnvcomēn akkahken
cóssi ma·kí· ha·yâ·t icohálpin óywan akkâ·yit nittá· anacomí·n akkáhkin
To make buckskin, put a deerhide in water, and leave it in for several days.

esse enkasvranat 'topoloken conēkēn cakhēcet,
íssi iŋká·saɫa·nâ·t[371] 'topoló·kin coní·ki·n cakhî·cit
The hide to be scraped was draped over a small pole stuck in the ground

mvn ohpvticet, cusse-skaskv kicēt
man ohpatêycit cossiská·ska[i] keycí·t
in a leaning position, and there was what is called a <u>cusse-skaskv</u> ['leather scraper'],

eslafkv omēn faskusēn hayēt ocet, mvn eskaset, esse omvlkvn encahwet
islá·fka ó·mi·n fǎ·ⁿskosi·n há·yi·t ô·cit man íska·sít íssi omálkan incáhwit
like a knife and very sharp; you scrape it with that, removing all the fur,

eto lakcvpe hvrpen uewvn esmorēcet, mv eco-hvrpe aktēhet, poroyet,
itó lakcapi hálpin óywan ismo·lî·cit ma (?) icohálpi aktî·hit poɫǒ·ⁿyit
and you boil it in water with bark from an oak tree; the deerskin was rubbed in the water,

mv uewv svpvtehcet, etopoloken hokkolen cakcvhehcet
ma óywa sapatíhcit itopoló·kin hokkô·lin cakcahíhcit
and soaked until the oak was absorbed, two poles were stuck in the ground,

mv tenrvwvn yekcē senēpken vtvleksihcet,
ma (?) tînɫawan yíkci· siní·pkin ataliksêyhci<t>[372]
and in between them, you spread it out and stretch [the skin] tightly,

'to-selkv tvpeksē enfvsecvkvtēn eskaset kvrpēcofvt
'tosílka tapíksi· infasicakáti·n íska·sít kaɫpí·co·fát
scrape it with a flat board that's been sharpened, and when it's dried,

---

[i] *cossiská·ska* is something like a drawknife, but with a straight handle.

eco kvlpe hotopvkvtēn eto-kaske escvlvpkēn ocvtet
icó kálpi hotópakáti·n itoká·ski iscalápki·n ó·catit
put baked deer brains mixed with wood shavings

mvo uelekhen aktēhet poroyet, eto-kasken omvlkvn encahwet,
maw' oylikhin aktî·hit polo·yit itoká·skin omálkan incáhwit
in warm water too, and rub it, and take out all the wood shavings;

mv cusse taranat aktēhet poroyet, uewv svpvtehcet,
ma (?) cóssi tá·la·nâ·t aktî·hit polŏ·ⁿyit óywa sapatíhcit
what is to become buckskin is put in and rubbed and soaked in water,

'to-selkv fvskat enhomv eskasvtē ētvpomen eskasen, karpof,
'tosílka fáska·t inhomá (?) íska·satí· i·tapó·min iska·sín ka·lpô·f
the sharp board used earlier for scraping is used again the same way, and when it's dry,

lowackusē hakat mvt cusse-hvtketot omēs.
lowà·ⁿckosi· ha·kâ·t mat cossihátkitot o·mí·s.
when it's really soft, that's white buckskin.

Momen cusse-lane hayvranat, 'co-hvrpe enrakkē vcakkvyēn,
mo·mín cossilá·ni há·yala·nâ·t 'cohálpi inlakkí·[373] *acakkayí·n*
And to make gold buckskin, according to the size of the skin,

ēkvnvn poloksēn estele vhopakv hvmkē mahe ensofkēn koriyet,
i·kanán polóksi·n istilí ahopá·ka hámki· má·hi insofki·n koléyyit
dig a round hole about one foot deep,

'to-lopockucen 'co-hvrpe encvpkē vcakkvyēn osten
'tolopockocín 'cohálpi incapkí· acakkayí·n ô·stin
place four small poles about the length of the skin

ēkvnv korkat vnakusēn 'svfolotkēn ohsvpaklehcet,
i·kaná kólka·t anà·ⁿkosi·n 'safolótki·n ohsapaklíhcit
upright around the hole,

yoksvn vtelokēn wvnahyet 'metetahket,
yóksan atiló·ki·<n> wanáhyit 'mititáhkit
gather the ends, tie them together, and when ready,

cusse sukcv omēn vhohret, 'topolokuce svpaklan svyakkofet eshuericet,
cóssi sókca ó·mi·n ahóhłit[374] *'topolo·kocí sapákla·n sayakkô·fit* ishoyłêycit
sew the buckskin like a sack and wrap it around the poles and stand it up;

mv ēkvnv korkan eto-lekwen aktēhet 'mvhetēcen,
ma (?) i·kaná kółka·n itolíkwin aktî·hit 'mahíti·cín
put rotted wood in the dug out hole and light it;

ekkucē ētvn vpeyekot 'co-hvrpe sukcv ofvn fackofvt,
ikkocí· í·tan apíyikot 'cohálpi sókca ó·fan fa·ckô·fat
the smoke cannot go anywhere else, and when it fills the inside of the sack,

lanēcēt omen cusse hvtkē tat ont omis em ekkucihocvtēn,
lá·ni·cí·t ô·min cossihatki·tá·t ônt o·mêys imikkoceyhocáti·n
it makes it gold; it's white buckskin, but smoked,

cusse-lanen kicet okhoyvtēs.
cossilá·nin keycít ókho·yatí·s
and was called cusse-lane ['gold buckskin'].

Mv oman estelepikv eshayet, hvfvtehkv kicis eshahoyēt omvtēs.
ma ô·ma·n istilipéyka ísha·yit <h>afatíhka keycêys ishá·ho·yí·t o·matí·s.
Shoes and what are called hvfvtehkv ['leggings'] were made from it.

Creek Games (Este-cate em afvcketv ahkopvnkv)[i]

J. Hill (Haas VIII:19–69)

Pokkechetvt	omakēs.	Honvntake	'to-kunhen	cawet	pokkon	sēset
pokkichitát	*omâ·ki·s*	*honantá·ki*	*tokónhin*	*ca·wít*[375]	*pókkon*	*si·sít*[376]
Ball-games	there are	the men	ball-sticks	they have	ball	they catch with

There are ball games. The men had ball-sticks, and when they threw the ball

'svwiken	omat,	mvt	em afvcketv	omvtēs.
sáweykín	*o·mâ·t*	*mat*	*ima·fackitát*	*o·matí·s*[377]
they throw it	if, when	that	their enjoyment	it was

with them, it was their celebration.

---

[i] Title: *isticá·ti ima·fackitá ahkopánka* 'games that Indians enjoy'.

Etvlwv	hokkole	etenrvpē		etenpokkechetvt	sekon	omat,
itálwa(?)	*hokkô·li*	*itinlapí·*		*itinpokkichitát*	*sikó·n*	*o·mâ·t*
towns	two	opposition-towns		play ball with each other	they didn't	if

If two opposing towns hadn't played ball with each other,

etvlwv	etewolicakat		'tekvpvkaket,	'tesaksekon	kicēt
itálwa	*itiwoleycâ·ka·t*		*'tikapáka·kít*[378]	*'tisaksikón*[i]	*keycí·t*
towns	that were close together		they divided up	unmatched	they called it

towns that were close together were divided up, and they called it <u>'tesakseko</u> ("unmatched")

pokkēchet	fullvtēs.	Este	em vliketv	vcakkvyēn
pókki·chít	*follati·s*	*ísti*	*imaleykitá*	*acakkayí·n*
they played ball	that way	a person's	clan	according to

and played ball that way. According to a person's clan,

vpvlwvt	celokhokvn	ēhocēfen,
apálwat	*cilo·khó·kan*	*í·hoci·fín*
some of them	Different-language	they call themselves

some called themselves <u>celokhokv</u> ("ones who speak a different language"),

vpvlwvt	hvthakvn	ēhocēfen,
apálwat	*hathá·kan*	*í·hoci·fín*
the others	White-ones	they call themselves

the others called themselves <u>hvthakv</u> ("white ones"),

mvn	etenrvpēt		pokkechaket	omvtēs.
man	*itinlapí·t*		*pokkícha·kít*	*o·matí·s*
those	are the ones that oppose each other		and play ball	they do

and those played ball against each other.

Em vliketv	Kaccvlke,	Ecovlke,	Echaswvlke,	Wotkvlke,
imaleykitá	*ka·ccâlki*	*icoâlki*	*icha·swâlki*	*wo·tkâlki*
The clans:	Tiger	Deer	Beaver	Coon

The clans Tiger, Deer, Beaver, Coon,

---

[i] *'tisaksikó* 'unmatched (ball-game)': might be more on one side than on the other.

Aktvyahcvlke,   Vhvlvkvlke heyvt   <u>celokhokv</u>   ēhocefaken,
aktayahcâlki   *ahalakâlki*   *hiyát*   *cilo·khó·ka*   *i·hocífa·kín*
Aktayahchalki   Potato   these   Different-language clans   they call themselves
Aktayahchalki, Potato, these called themselves <u>celokhokv</u>,

Nokosvlke,   Vlpvtvlke,   Hotvlkvlke,   Fuswvlke,   Tvmvlke   esyomat
nokosâlki   *alpatâlki*   *hotalkâlki*   *foswâlki*   *tamâlki*   *isyô·ma·t*
Bear   Alligator   Wind   Bird   Tama   those like that
and Bear, Alligator, Wind, Bird, Tama, and those like that

hvthakvn   ēhocefaken   etenrvpēt   pokkechaket   omvtēs.
hathá·kan   *i·hocífa·kín*   *itinlapí·t*[379]   *pokkícha·kít*   *o·matí·s*
White-ones   they call themselves   against each other   they played ball   did
called themselves <u>hvthakv</u> and played against each other.

Pokkechetv-nettv   hvyvtkvranē   nerē tat   etekvpvkēt
pokkichitanítta   *hayátkala·ní·*   *nilí·ta·t*   *itikapáki·t*
the day that they play ball   when it's going to [dawn]   that night   they divided up
The day that they played ball, the night before, they divided up [to their respective sides]

ēkvnv   etem mellakvtē   tempen   nvkvftaket
i·kaná   *itimmílla·katí·*   *tímpin*   *nakaftâ·kit*
ground   that they had selected to themselves   near it   they met
and gathered near the ground they selected for each other,

hoktvken   svpaklēcet   enyvhiket   yvhikepuecet   opvnēcet,
hoktakín   *sapaklî·cit*   *inyahaykít*   *yaháykipoycít*   *opáni·cít*
the women   they stood them up   sang for them   made them sing   made them dance
and they had the women stand and would sing for them and made them sing and dance,

vpokvtet   fekhonnicvntot   yahket   fullvtētot
apô·katit   *fikhonneycántot*[380]   *ya·hkít*   *follatí·tot*
they stayed there   made them stop awhile   they whooped   and were around that way
and they sat awhile and made them stop awhile and whooped around

nocicen   hvyvtiken   este   vpvlwv   yicvranan   'mehaket   fullen,
noceycín   *hayatêykin*   *ísti*   *apálwa*   *yéycała·nâ·n*   *míha·kít*   *follín*
sleeping   (till) it got day   people   the rest   to come   waiting for   were around
and slept till day, and they waited around for the other people to get there.

fvccvlikē   hoyanof   em etetahket,   "Pokkechepvkets" maket
faccaléyki·   hoya·nô·f   imititáhkit   pokkichipáki·c   ma·kít
noon   after   they got ready   "let's play ball"   they said
After noon, they got ready and said, "Let's play ball,"

etem vkvsahmof,   celokhokvt   nvcomusen
itimakasáhmo·f   *cilo·khó·kat*   *nacô·mosin*[381]
after they had agreed   the Different-Lang.   were (only) a few
and after they agreed, whether the <u>celokhokv</u> only had a few,

hvthakvt   ensulkē   estomēpē   estomis
hathá·kat   *insolkí·*   *isto·mî·pi·*   *istô·meys*
the White-ones   their manyness   made no difference   [whatever]
and no matter how many <u>hvthakv</u>,

etem pokkechvranē   tvlkusēt   omēs.   Hvthakvt   nvcomusen
itimpokkíchaⱡa·ní·[382]   *tălⁿkosi·t*   *ô·mi·s*   *hathá·kat*   *nacô·mosin*[383]
to play ball with each other   they have to   do   The White-ones   only a few
they had to play ball with each other. Even if the <u>hvthakv</u> only had a few

celokhokvt   sulkē   hērēt   omēpē estomis
cilo·khó·kat   *sólki·*   *hĭ·ⁿⱡi·t*   *omi·pi· istô·meys*
the Different-Language ones   many   very   it made no difference
and the <u>celokhokv</u> had very many,

pokkechvranat   tvlkusēt   ont   celokhokv   hathakv
pokkíchaⱡa·nâ·t   *tălⁿkosi·t*   *ônt*   *cilo·khó·ka*   *ha·thá·ka*
to play ball   they have to anyway   do,   The Different-language   the White-ones
they had to play ball, and the <u>celokhakv</u> and <u>hvthakv</u>

'tepakat   estimvt   lvpkēn   em etetakēpet
'tipâ·ka·t   *istèymat*[384]   *lápki·n*   *imititá·ki·pít*
together   whichever   quickly   got ready
together, whichever one got ready sooner,

pokkechetv ēkvnv roricen omat, yahiket pokko tat hvlwēcet,
pokkichitá i·kaná łółeycín o·mâ·t ya·hâykit [i] *pókkota·t hálwi·cít*
and ball-ground if they get there if they whoop the ball throw it up
if they got to the ball-ground, they whooped, threw the ball up,

ahkopanet fullēpen, vpvlwvt yopvn yicē estomis,
áhkopa·nít fólli·pín apálwat yópan yeycí· istô·meys
they play be around that way the rest behind when they come if they did
and played around, and the rest, though they came after, [did the same,]

mvt emvhakvt omakēs.
mat imahá·kat omâ·ki·s [385]
that was their rule it was
that was the rule.

<u>Hoktvke em pokkechetv.</u> Celokhokv, hvthakv 'tepakat
hoktakí impokkichitá cilo·khó·ka hathá·ka 'tipâ·ka·t
[women their game] The Different-language the white-ones together
Women's Ball-Game. As in the game of the celokhakv

em ahkopvnkv vcakkvyē ētan,
imahkopánka acakkayí· i·tá·n
their game [following the same]
and hvthakv,

honvnwv, hoktēn etenfaccen,
honánwa hoktí·n itínfa·ccín
the men and women they enter into an agreement
the men and the women entered into an agreement with each other,

vhonkvtkv eskerkekon, honvntake 'to-kunhe pokko sēsēt on,
ahoŋkátka [386] *iskílkiko·n honantá·ki 'tokónhi pókko si·sí·t ô·n*
number not known men ball-sticks ball they catch [do]
and without knowing the number [?], the men caught the ball with the ball-sticks,

---

[i] *ya·hkitá* kind of a war-whoop; ball-game whoop. The Indians would run and whoop. They would run around the camp-fire + whoop before they go to the ballground.

hoktvken enke pokko sēsen etem pokkechaket omvtēs.
hoktakín iŋki pókko si·sín itimokkícha·kít o·matí·s[387]
the women hands ball catch with play ball with each other used to do
and the women caught the ball with their hands and played ball together.

Cukorakko nvkaftet omē estomis,
cokołákko naka·ftít o·mí· istô·meys
buskground they meet being if they do
If they met at the buskground,

vwolicē este vpokat fullvrē 'metektvnkēt omen,
awoléyci· ísti apô·ka·t fólláli· 'mitiktánki·t ô·min
nearby people living to be there they had opportunity was
people living nearby were free to be there,

etvlwv cahmelikēt nvkaftet omvtēs,
itálwa cahmiléyki·t naka·ftít o·matí·s[388]
towns different ones they met they did
and different towns met,

cukorakko em vhopvyēcēt este vpopoket omē estomis,
cokołákko imahopayí·ci·t ísti apo·pô·kit o·mí· istô·meys
the buskground far away people living like if they are
even people living far from the buskground,

ahkopvnkv eyacen omat.
ahkopánka iya·cín[389] *o·mâ·t*
the game they want if
if they wanted to play.

Honvntake vrahkv hvmket enhomahtat hahoyen hueren,
honantá·ki aláhka hámkit inhomáhta·t[390] *ha·hô·yin hôyłin*[391]
the men's side one at the head of it they appoint he being there
One stood as head of the men,

hoktvkeu hvmket enhomahtat hahoyēt enhueret omen,
hoktakíw hámkit inhomáhta·t[392] *ha·hoyí·t inhôyłit*[393] *o·mín*
the women, too one at the head of it they appoint and she is there is
and one stood as head of the women too,

mvt   etenfvccakof   pokkēchet   omakvtēs.
mat   itinfácca·kô·f   pókki·chít   oma·kati·s[394]
these   when they agree   play ball   they do
and when they agreed, they played ball.

Mv   este   vpokakat   tempe   ētan   <u>pokkvpe</u>   kicet
ma   ísti   apo·kâ·ka·t   tímpi   i·tá·n   pokkapí   keycít
those   people   are living   nearby   where they are   ball-pole   called it
Those same people living nearby [found] what is called a <u>pokkvpe</u> ['ball-pole'],

eto-poloke   estele   vhopakv   pale-tuccēnat   mahe tis   omvtēs.
itopoló·ki   istilí   ahopá·ka   pa·litocci·na·t   mâ·hiteys   o·mati·s[395]
pole   feet   measurement   thirty   [about], even   it is
a wooden pole of about thirty feet.

Huericet   estele vhopakv   ostvpake   mahe   enhvlwēn
hóyleycít[396]   *istilí ahopá·ka   ostapâ·ki   mâ·hi   inhalwí·n*
they stand it up   feet   nine   about   high
They stood it up, and about nine feet off the ground,

mv   'to-poloke   caske   vfulutkē   es enkērkv   enhayvkvtēt   omen,
ma   'topoló·ki   ca·ski·   afolótki·[397]   *isinki·lka   inhá·yakáti·t   ô·min*
that   pole   chop it   clear around   the mark   that has been made   is
a mark was made by chopping clear around the pole,

yoksvn   wakv   ekv-fune   kvrpen   monkat   cerakko   ekv-fune tis   em ohlicet,
yóksan   wá·ka   ikafóni   kálpin   mónka·t   'cilákko   ikafoníteys   imohlêycit
at the end   cow's   skull   dry   or else   horse's   skull, even   they set on the end
and at the top they set a dry cow skull or horse skull,

mv   eto-poloken   pokkon   'svfvllēt   ahkopanet   omakvtēs.
ma   itopoló·kin   pókkon   sáfalli·t   áhkopa·nit   oma·kati·s[398]
that   pole   the ball   they threw at   they play   that's the way
and they threw at the pole with the ball and played.

Momet   mv   es enkērkv   hakē   ocat   vtēkē   onvpv   ayat,
mo·mít   ma   isinki·lka   há·ki·   ô·ca·t   atî·ki·   onápa   â·ya·t
Then   that   mark   that has been made   (that is)   including   on the top   from there
And from that mark that was made to the top,

nake　　　　ekv-fune　elecvn　eton　　　pokkon　　es nafken　omat,
nâ·ki　　　*ikafoní*　*ilícan*　*itón*　　*pókkon*　　*ísna·fkín*　*o·mâ·t*
something's　[skull]　beneath　the pole　the ball　they hit it　if
below the skull, if they hit the pole with the ball,

vhonkvtkv　　　hvmken　hayēt　　omakvtēs.
ahoŋkátka[399]　*hámkin*　*há·yi·t*　*oma·katí·s*[i, 400]
count　　　　　one　　made　　they have
they made one point.

Mv　　ekv-fune　pokkon　es nafken　omat,　cahkēpen　vhonkatet　　omakvtēs.
ma　*ikafoní*　*pókkon*　*ísna·fkín*　*o·mâ·t*　*cahkî·pin*　*ahóŋka·tít*　*oma·katí·s*[401]
that　skull　　the ball　hit [with]　if　　five　　　it counted　did
If they hit the skull with the ball, it was five.

Hoktēt　　nafken　omat,　momen　　honvnwvo　nafkat o,　　matvpomen
hoktí·t　*na·fkín*　*o·mâ·t*　*mo·mín*　*honánwaw*　*na·fkâ·tow*　*ma·tapô·min*
a woman　she hit it　if　　then　　a man, too　he hit it, too　the same
Whether a woman hit it or a man hit it,

vhonkatet　　omakvtēs.　Ahkopvnvranet　　'metetakof,
ahóŋka·tít　*oma·katí·s*[402]　*ahkopánala·nit*　*'mitíta·kô·f*[403]
they counted it　they did　they are going to play　when they are getting ready
it was counted the same. When they were getting ready to play,

vhopakv　　　　pale-ostat　mahe tis　monkat　orusekis　　ēkvnvn　taksahtet,
ahopá·ka　　　*pa·liô·sta·t*　*mâ·hiteys*　*móŋka·t*　*olósikeys*　*i·kanán*　*taksáhtit*
a measure (=yards)　forty　about　or　　not quite　ground　they marked
they made a mark on the ground of about forty yards, or not quite,

mv　　satkvn　vtekkēkusēn　estele vhopakv　hokkolat　mahe　omusē
ma　*sá·tkan*　*atikkì·kosi·n*　*istilí ahopá·ka*　*hokkô·la·t*　*mâ·hi*　*ô·mosi·*
that　mark　up to　　feet　　　two　　about　(kinda like)
and up to that mark

---

[i] [Haas has a drawing of a ball-pole here, VIII:36]

'metehopvyēt   ensathoyēt   omvtēs.   Hoktēt   nafken   omat,
'mitihopayi·t   *insa·tho·yi·t*   *o·mati·s*[404]   *hokti·t*   *na·fkín*   *o·mâ·t*
that far apart   they marked it   did   woman   she hit it if
they made marks just about two feet apart.[i] If a woman hit it,

momen   honvnwvo   mata   yvtekkekēn   satkv   cvpkat   pvlhvmken
mo·mín   *honánwaw*   *ma·tá·*   *'yatikkiki·n*   *sá·tka*   *cápka·t*   *palhámkin*
and   a man, too   the same   adjoining   the mark   long   on the other side
or a man too, they made a long mark on the other side

ensathoyēt   omvtēs.   Hoktvke   ensathoyat,
insá·tho·yi·t   *o·mati·s*[ii, 405]   *hoktaki*   *insá·tho·yâ·t*[406]
they marked   they did   the women   where they mark
adjoining in the same place. Where they marked for the woman,

mv   satkv   cvpkan   res poyvkēpen   omat,
ma   *sá·tka*   *cápka·n*   *łispó·yaki·pín*   *o·mâ·t*
that   mark   that is long   they finish it out   if do
if they finished out that long mark,

hoktvket   epoyakēt   omvtēs.   Matvpomēn   honvntakeu   ensathoyat,
hoktakít   *ipó·ya·kí·t*   *o·mati·s*[407]   *ma·tapô·mi·n*   *honantá·kiw*   *insá·tho·yâ·t*
the women   won   they did   In the same way   the men, too   where they mark
the women won. In the same way where they marked for the men too,

mv   satkv   cvpkat   res pokēpen   omat,   honvntaket   poyat   omvtēs.
ma   *sá·tka*   *cápka·t*   *łispó·ki·pín*   *o·mâ·t*   *honantá·kit*   *po·yâ·t*   *o·mati·s*[408]
that   mark   that is long   they finish it out   if   the men   they win   do
if they finished out that long mark, the men won.

Mv   satkv   vhonkvtkv   vcakkvyekon   etem poyēt   ahkopvnaket
ma   *sá·tka*   *ahoŋkátka*[409]   *acakkayíko·n*   *itímpo·yí·t*   *ahkopána·kít*
That   mark   the count   not according   if they win   they play
They didn't win based on

---

[i] [Haas has a drawing here, VIII:38]
[ii] "I.e., the marks of the woman and the man join together, thus: (diagram)" (VIII:40).

fullet	omvtēs.	Mohmen	mv	afvcketv	hayē
follít	*o·matí·s*[i]	*móhmin*	*ma*	*a·fackitá*	*ha·yí·*
that is the way	they did	Then	that	pasttime	making

the number of points. Then when

ahkopanē	fulletv	oketv	tuccēnē	ostvtēkis	hoyanof
áhkopa·ní·	*follitá*	*okíta*	*toccî·ni·*	*ô·statî·keys*	*hoya·nô·f*
playing	to be about	times	three	or four	after they had

three or up to four times of playing and celebrating had passed,

mv	honvnwv	homahtē	arat	oket
ma	*honánwa*	*homáhti·*	*a·lâ·t*	*o·kít*
the	men's side's	leader	that is about	says:

the men's leader said,

"Afvcketv	hayē	ahkopanē	fulleyat
a·fackitá	*ha·yí·*	*áhkopa·ní·*	*folliyá·t*
fun-	making	and playing	we were about

"Let's hunt, so that we can play around

vrahkv	enfayvken,	naket	punhecken	omat,
ałáhka	*infâ·yakin*	*nâ·kit*	*pónhickín*	*o·mâ·t*
purpose	let's hunt	anything	we find	if

and celebrate, and if we find anything,

cukolice tat	opuswuce	es hayvkēpet	eskayvn	ayem eskēpēt
cokolêycita·t	*oposwocí*	*isha·yakí·pít*[410]	*íska·yán*	*a·yimíski·pí·t*[411]
the women	soup	they had made	they drank it	we drank with them

the women [cukolice] will make soup of it, drink it,

em ahkopanet	omeyvrēs"	mahket,
imáhkopa·nít	*omiyáli·s*	*máhkit*
and play with them	we will	he said

and we will drink it with them and play with them," he said.

---

[i] "The game was won not according to a set number of points to be made, but according to whoever finished out the length of the long line first." (VIII:42)

estofv   fakv   vpeyvranat   netta   em onahyet,
istô·fa   *fá·ka*   *apíyala·nâ·t*   *nittá·*   *imonáhyit*
when   hunting   they are going   day   they would tell them
He would tell them the day they were going hunting,

estitvket   fayē   tayēs   komat   este   hocefhuecen,
istêytakit   *fá·yi·*   *tá·yi·s*   *kô·ma·t*   *ísti*   *hocífhoycín*
who-all   hunt   could   they thought   persons   he named (them)
and he would name the people he thought could hunt,

estit   eyacēpat,   "Vneu   vyarēs"   maken,
istêyt   *iyá·ci·pâ·t*[412]   *aníw*   *ayá·li·s*   *ma·kín*
whoever   wants   me, too   I will go, too   he said
and anyone who wanted to said, "I'll go, too."

"Vncuko tempe tis   fayarēs"   makat o   sasen   fullet   fayaken,
ancokotímpi teys   *fá·yá·li·s*   *ma·kâ·tow*   *sâ·sin*   *follít*   *fá·ya·kín*
my house near   I will hunt   said, too   some   being around   hunting
There were some too who said, "I will hunt near my house," and they hunted,

eco tis   elēcet   monkat   penwa tis
icóteys   *ili·cít*   *mónka·t*   *pínwateys*
deer, even   they killed   or   turkey, even
and if they killed a deer or a turkey,

monkat   ero tvlkuset   enheckakē   estomis
mónka·t   *iłó tâlkosit*   *inhícka·ki·*   *istô·meys*
or   squirrels just   they got   anyhow
or if they only got a squirrel,

omvlkvn   mv   hoktvke   enhomahtē   aran   rem vpohoyof,
omálkan   *ma*   *hoktaki*   *inhomáhti·*   *a·lâ·n*   *'limapó·ho·yô·f*
all of them   that   women's side   head   that's about   they leave it
when they left all of it with the women's leader,

em vnvkuecv   hoktvken   enkērkuecet,
imanakóyca   *hoktakín*   *iŋkí·lkoycít*
her neighbor   women   she lets it be known to
she let it be known to her women neighbors:

"Em afackē   fullatskvtē   em omvlkuset   enhompvranatskat
imáfa·cki·   *follá·ckati·*   *imomălⁿkosit*   *inhómpala·ná·cka·t*
had fun with them   all those that   all together   you-all are going to eat with them
"They have found these things for you,

cenhopoyvket   onkv,
cinhopó·yakit   *oŋká*[413]
they have secured these things for you   have
so that all of you who celebrated with them could eat with them,

centakeu   matvpomen   'tetakuecaks.   Vce tat   hocet,
cintá·kiw   *ma·tapô·min*   *'tita·kóycaks* *acíta·t*   *ho·cit*
you-all, too   the same   get it ready   the corn   pound it
so all of you get ready too. Pound corn,

osafke,   taklik-tokse,   cvtvhakv,   sakkonepkhakv   omakat
osá·fki   *takleyktóksi*   *catahá·ka*   *sakkonipkihá·ka*   *o·mâ·ka·t*
sofkee   sourbread   blue-dumplings   hominy   like that
and prepare sofkee, sour cornbread, blue-dumplings, hominy, and such,"

'tetakuecaks"   kicen   omat,
'tita·kóycaks   *keycín*   *o·mâ·t*
(you-all) get it ready   she said to them   when
she told them.

em etetaket   fullet   pokkechetv ēkvnvn   res orihcet
imitíta·kit[414]   *follít*   *pokkichitá i·kanán*   *'lisoléyhcit*
they got ready   were around   the ball-ground   they took it to
They went around getting ready, took it to the ball-ground,

punvttv vpeswv tat   noricat   fullēpof,
ponattaapíswata·t   *noɬeycâ·t*   *fólli·pô·f*
game-meat   when they cooking it   while they were around
and while they were around cooking the game meat,

vpvlwvt   pokkēcat o   fullen   hompetv   'tetaken   omat,
apálwat   *pokki·châ·tow*   *follín*   *hompitá*   *títa·kín*[415]   *o·mâ·t*
the rest   were playing ball, too were about food   they get it ready   when
the others were around playing ball too, and when the food was ready,

pvlaknv   vtehtēcet,   ēkvnv   estak-vpohoyen,
palákna   *atíhti·cít*   *i·kaná*   *istakkapó·ho·yín*[416]
dishes   they put it in   ground   they set down
they put it in plates, set them down on the ground,

ēkvnvn   tak-vpokēt   hompaket,   fącficuset   hompahket,
i·kanán   *takkapó·ki·t*   *hómpa·kít*   *fă·ⁿcféycosit*[417]   *hompáhkit*
the ground   they sit down   they eat   they get real full   (after) they eat
and ate sitting on the ground, and they ate till they were really full.

pokko   etem asset   yahket   fullen   omat,
pókko   *itíma·ssít*   *ya·hkit*   *follín*   *o·mâ·t*
ball   they run after with each other   whooping   they are about (when)
And when they ran after the ball with each other and were whooping around,

"Heyvt   afvcketvtot   os"   komaket,   momet
hiyát   *a·fackitátot*   *ó·ⁿs*   *ko·mâ·kit*   *mo·mít*
this   enjoyment   it is   they thought   Then
they thought, "This is enjoyment," and,

"Heyvt   eterakkueckvtot,   etenokeckvtot,
hiyát   *itiɫakkóyckatot*   *itinokíckatot*
this   appreciation of each other   affection for each other
"This is mutual appreciation, it is mutual affection,

herkv   ocē   etekęrrusē   emahlvpvtkē   fulletvt
hílka   *ó·ci·*   *itikĭ·ⁿɫɫosi·*   *imahlapátki·*   *follitát*
peace   with   know each other very well   sober-minded   to be about that way
it is enjoyment itself to go about sober-minded, peacefully getting to know

afvcketvtot   os"   komēt   este-cate vculvke   enfulletv   tatēt   omēs.
a·fackitátot   *ó·ⁿs*   *kó·mi·t*   *isticá·ti* *acolakí*   *infollitá*   *tá·ti·t*   *ô·mi·s*
enjoyment   is   they think Indian-   old-timers   the habits of   was   it is like that
each other well," they thought, and these were the customs of the old-time Indians.

<u>Pokko-rakko.</u> Mohmen <u>pokko-rakko</u> kicēt
pokkołá·kko *móhmin* *pokkołá·kko*ⁱ *keyci·t*[418]
[big-ball] Now big-ball it is called
<u>Big-ball.</u> Now when they went around playing

sahkopvnaket fullet omat
sahkopána·kit *follít* *o·mâ·t*
they play with it being around when
what's called <u>pokko-rakko</u> ['big-ball'],

mvo etenfvccetv tat hoktvke, honvntake etenpokkechvranē
maw' *itinfaccitáta·t* *hoktakí* *honantá·ki* *itinpokkíchała·ní·*
that, too an agreement the women the men going to play ball together
that, too, as an agreement; they agreed on the same rules

fulletv em vyē ēta etenfaccet omakvtēs.
follitá *imayí·* *i·tá·* *itínfa·ccít* *oma·katí·s*
to be around the rules the same they agree they did
whereby the women and men are to play ball with each other.

Momis pokko ēsē vwikē etem assē em pvfnē
mo·mêys[419] *pókko* *i·sí·* *aweykí·* *itíma·ssí·* *impafní·*
But the ball they catch and throw and run after it in speed
But in catching the ball, throwing it, chasing after it together,

entvhopkē 'setemontvletv tokot omvtēs.
intahopkí· *'sitimontalíta* *tó·ko·t* *o·matí·s*[420]
and nimbleness, activity to outdo each other they were not it was
it was not to compete with each other in speed and agility.

Pokko tat estenke hvmkusē sesvkē tayan senrakkusēt omvtēs.
pókkota·t *istíŋki* *hámkosi·*[421] *sísaki·* *tâ·ya·n* *sinłákkosi·t* *o·matí·s*[422]
the ball hand one whichever they can too big it was
The ball was a little too big to catch with just one hand.

ⁱ *pokkołá·kko* was made of a hide-covering (from deer or cow). It was filled with cotton, rags, wool or yarn.

monkv	hoktvke	honvntakeu	enke	vlkēn	esēset	omakekv
môŋka	*hoktakí*	*honantá·kiw*	*iŋki*	*álki·n*	*isi·sít*	*oma·kiká*
Therefore	the women	and men, too	hands	only	caught it with	did

So women and men too caught it with both hands,

ehsē	eslētkan	vkonvhetv	estvmi-vlkis
íhsi·	*ísli·tká·n*	*akonahítan*	*istamey?âlkeys*
having caught it	and running with it	to take it away from	either side

and as they caught it and ran with it, each side

em omvlkusēt	etenceyvlhoyēt	onkv,
imomălⁿkosi·t	*itinciyálho·yí·t*	*oŋká*
their best	they scuffled	did

struggled with all their might to take it away.

pokko-rakko	sahkopanē	etenceyvlhoyetv	semontalat
pokkołá·kko	*sáhkopa·ní·*	*itinciyalhoyíta*	*'simontâ·la·t*
big-ball	playing with it	to scuffle with each other	any better

There might be no better Indian game than

ahkopvnkv	este-cate	em ahkopvnkv	seko witēs.
ahkopánka	*isticá·ti*	*imahkopánka*	*siko·wêyti·s*
play	Indian	game	there isn't any

to struggle with each other and play <u>pokko-rakko</u>.

Momen	mvo	hompetv	eshayet	hompet	fullet onkv,
mo·mín	*maw'*	*hompitá*	*ísha·yít*	*hompít*	*follít oŋká*
Then	that, too	food	they made	eating	were around

And for that one too they made food and went around eating:

"Afvcketv-rakkon	ocēt	omēs"	komvkēt	fullēpvtēt omēs.
a·fackitałákkon	*o·cí·t*	*o·mí·s*	*ko·makí·t*[423]	*fólli·patí·t ô·mi·s*
a big time	having	they were	they thought	being about

they went around thinking they were having a big celebration.

<u>Pvrko-fvkv</u>	<u>etenhvlvtetv.</u>	Etenfvccetv	em vyē	matan
pałkofáka	*itinhalatitá*	*itinfaccitá*	*imayí·*	*ma·tá·n*
[grapevine	pulling each other]	agreement	their rule, nature	the same

<u>Tug-of-War with a Grapevine.</u> The men and women decided

honvntake   hoktvke   etenfvciyet,
honantá·ki   hoktakí   itinfacêyyit
the men   the women   they agree
the same provisions of the agreement,

ahkopvnkv   hayet   afvcketv   ocvranat,
ahkopánka   ha·yít   a·fackitá   ó·cala·ná·t
a game   they make   pleasure   when they're going to have
and when they were going to play and have a contest,

este-honvntake   sulkē   nvkvftvrē   'tem vcahnen,
istihonantá·ki   sólki·   nakáftáli·   'timáca·hnín
men   many   to meet   they compel each other
they compelled many men to meet,

hoktvkeu   matvpomen   etenhuehket,
hoktakíw   ma·tapô·min   itínhoyhkít
the women, too   the same   they called each other together
and called on the women too, in the same way,

cukorakko   ernvkvfitet   vpoket,   em etetakat,
cokołákko   iłnakafêytit   apô·kit   imítita·kâ·t[424]
the buskground to meet there   and be there and they get ready
and they met at the buskground and sat, and when they were ready,

pvrko-fvkvn   cvpkēn   ratahcet,   ēkvnvn   taksahtet,
pałkofákan   cápki·n   ła·táhcit   i·kanán   taksáhtit
grape-vine   long   they go and cut it   ground   they mark
they went and cut a long grapevine and marked the ground

'tewvlvpkēn   pvrkofvkv   ohtakhahyet,
'tiwalápki·n   pałkofáka   ohtakháhyit
across   grapevine   they put across
and put the grapevine across it.

satkv   pvlhvmkan   hoktvket   svpaklen,   pvlhvmken   honvntake   svpvkilen,
sá·tka   palhámka·n   hoktakít   sapâ·klin[425] *palhámkin   honantá·ki   sapakêylin*
mark   on one side   the women   stand   on the other side the men   stand
The women stood one one side of the mark, and the men stood on the other side,

omvlkvt   pvrko-fvkv   etenhvlatet   'tenceyvlhoyet,
omálkat   pałkofáka   itínhala·tít[426]   *tinciyálho·yít*
all of them   grapevine   they pull it   they struggle with each other
and everyone pulled at the grapevine and struggled together,

ēkvnv   satkē   wakkan   etohtvlhoyēcetvn   kont,
i·kaná   sá·tki·   wákka·n   itohtalhoyi·citán[427]   *kônt*
ground   mark   is lying   to put one another over   they try
trying to pull each other over the marked ground.

hoktvken   'svpēhoyen   omat,   hoktvlemᴀhēt   alikēpvtē tis
hoktakín   'sapí·ho·yín   o·mâ·t   hoktalimă·ⁿhi·t   a·leykî·pati·teys
the women   they take   if   very old woman   there had been sitting by
If the women were being taken, a really old woman sitting there would

yohcēyen,   honvntaken   'svpehoyen   omat o,   este-honvn-culeu   alikvtētok:
yóhci·yín   honantá·kin   'sapího·yín[428]   *o·mâ·tow   istihonancolíw   a·lêykati·to·k*
she comes in   the men   they take   if, too   a real old man, too   was sitting by
come in, and if they were taking the men too, a really old man too would be sitting by:

mvo   yohcēyen,   etenceyvlhoyat,
maw'   yóhci·yín   itinciyálho·yâ·t
he, too   he comes in   when they are struggling with each other
he too would enter, and when they were struggling,

satkv   tohwvlvphuecet   esafacket   fullvtēt omēs.
sá·tka   tohwaláphoycít   isá·fa·ckít   follatí·t ô·mi·s
the mark   they put them across   for enjoyment   that's the way they did
when they put them across the mark, they enjoyed that.

Hoktvke   nvcumē tis   vtelokewitat,
hoktakí   nacómi·teys   atílo·kiwêyta·t
the women   even a few   if they should gather
If just a few women should gather,

em vnicvrē   honvnwv   enhopoyetv   em etetektvnkēt on,
imanéycáli·   honánwa   inhopoyitá[429]   *imititiktánki·t*[430] *ô·n*
want anyone to help them   men   to hunt   they have the privilege
they were free to look for men to help them,

enhopoyēpet	sēyvnicen	ahkopvnkv	hayet	omakvtēs.
inhopóyi·pít	*si·yáneycín*	*ahkopánka*	*ha·yít*	*oma·katí·s*
when they picked them out	they helped them	a game	was had	it was

and when they picked them out, they helped them, and a game was played.

Various Games

J. Hill (Haas XXII:73–105)

Mohmen este-cate em ahkopvnkv rē-ēhkv, vce-ēwēskv, etem ēhketv,
móhmin isticá·ti imahkopánka łi·ʔi·hka aciʔi·wí·ska itimi·hkitá
And Indian games are hide-the-bullet, corn-winnowing, hide-and-seek,

kowakke makē etēssēckv, sakyopv, hvlolo, etencvllēcetv,
kowá·kki[431] ma·kí· iti·ssí·cka sakyó·pa halólo itincalli·citá
[a game of] tag called wildcat, last one in, rolling deer bones to each other,

fakke-svkakv, wvnvkucē etem echetv, svtv-pvnēckv.
fakkisaká·ka wanakocí· itimichitá satapaní·cka.
dirt-sling, little-bundle shooting, and persimmon-dancing.

1. Rē-ēhkv tat nake estomis eco-hvrpe tis pvticet,
   łi·ʔi·hkata·t nâ·ki istô·meys icohálpiteys patêycit
1. For hide-the-bullet, you spread something out, maybe a deer-hide,

rē ohrvnkvranat nak leskv 'tepvkohlusēn este vrahrvkvn ocet,
łi· ohłánkała·nâ·t nâ·k líska 'tipakóhlosi·n ísti ałahlakán ô·cit
and each person has a folded piece of cloth to cover the bullet;

eccv enrē cereknusat hvmken ocet este hvmket ehset,
icca inłí· ciłíknosa·t hámkin ô·cit ísti hámkit íhsit
there's one little round bullet, and one person takes it,

nak leskuce elecvn enken vsēket espoyof,
nâ·k liskocí ilícan íŋkin asi·kít íspo·yô·f
and after sticking his hand under all the pieces of cloth,

estvn rē licēs kon omat enramat eshechoyekon omat, hvmken hayēpen
ístan łi· lêyci·s kó·n o·mâ·t ínła·mâ·t ishíchoyikon o·mâ·t hámkin há·yi·pín
they raise the cloth where they think the bullet is, and if it's not found, [the one hiding it]

eshecēpateu hvmken hayēpet ahkopanet omakvtēs
íshici·pâ·tiw hámkin há·yi·pít áhkopa·nít oma·kati·s
makes one [point], and someone who finds it also makes one, is how it was played.

Rē ehhē likat senhechoyekon omat, hvmken hayēpēt omēs.
łí· íhhi· lêyka·t sinhichoyíkon o·mâ·t hámkin há·yi·pí·t ô·mi·s
The one sitting there hiding the bullet makes one [point] if it is not found.

2.   Vce-ēwēskv. Vce-celvske tvptahan ostan cvto-hiyvn ohlicet
     aciłi·wí·ska. aciciláski taptâ·ha·n ô·sta·n catoháyyan óhleycít
2.   Corn-winnowing. Four wide [kernels] of shelled corn are placed on a hot stove;

pvlhvmken nekricet lvstēn hahyet svlahwvn vtēhet cēwēsen,
palhámkin níkłeycít lásti·n háhyit saláhwan atî·hit cí·wi·sín
one side is burned and made black and put in a corn riddle and winnowed;

vce rakpvlkat lvstat hokkolen omat, hvmken vhvmkatet,
ací łákpalkâ·t lásta·t hokko·lín o·mâ·t hámkin ahámka·tít
when the corn is turned over, if two are black, they count as one [point],

tuccēnen omat tuccēnen vhvmkatet, ostateu osten vhvmkatet,
toccî·nin o·mâ·t toccî·nin ahámka·tít ô·sta·tiw ò·stin ahámka·tít
if it's three, they count three, if four, they too are counted as four [points]:

ostet vpoket ahkopvnetvt omēs.
ô·stit apô·kit ahkopanitát ô·mi·s
the game is for four people.

3.   Etem ēhketv nerē ahkopvnetvt omēs. Cuko ofv tis vpoken hvmket osiyet,
     itimi·hkitá niłi· ahkopanitát ò·mi·s cokó ó·fateys apô·kin hámkit osêyyit
3.   Hide-and-seek is a night game. They sit inside even, and one goes out,

ēhketv enheckēpen omat, "kokkowē" makēt rahohiken
i·hkitá inhícki·pin o·mâ·t ko·kkò·wi·[i] ma·ki·t ła·ho·hêykin
and to find his hiding place, he calls out "kokkowē";

---

[i] Doesn't know meaning.

estvmvn ēhket okat hopoyet ahkopvnetvt omēs.
ístaman i·hkit o·kâ·t hopo·yít ahkopanitát ô·mi·s
it's a game where they search for his hiding place.

4.   Kowakkē ahkopvnvranat nvcomet on omat
     kowá·kki· ahkopánała·nà·t nacó·mit o·n o·mâ·t
4.   To play wildcat, however there are many [playing];

'setetayēn eto-kvckuce lopockusēn hvmket cawet,
'sititá·yi·n itokackocí lopõ·ⁿckosi·n¹ hámkit câ·wit
one person holds the same number of little sticks,

enke-tvpekse entvphē orakusēn onkv, yonot̄et,
íŋkitapíksi intaphí· olâ·kosi·n òŋka yonófi·t
and since they are about the width of one's palm, they are held tight;

hvmket cvpkē vpvkēn omvten, estit cvpkan ēsen omat,
hámkit cápki· apáki·n ô·matin istêyt cápka·n i·sín o·mâ·t
among them is one long one, and whoever draws the long one,

mvt kowakkuce hahket assēcet, hvmken vcelaken omat,
mat kowa·kkocí háhkit á·ssi·cít hámkin acíla·kín o·mâ·t
that [person] becomes the wildcat and chases all of them; if he tags someone,

mvo kowakke hahket 'mvnicen,
maw' kowá·kki háhkit 'máneycín
that [person] too becomes a wildcat and helps him,

vcelahokē vtēkat kowakke hakē ahkopvnkvt omēs.
acilá·ho·kí· atî·ka·t kowá·kki ha·kí· ahkopánkat ô·mi·s
and each person tagged becomes a wildcat; that's the game.

5.   Sakyopv hvcce uewv lvokē aklopvranof,
     sakyó·pa ⁱⁱ hácci óywa láwki· aklopála·nô·f
5.   For <u>sakyopv</u> ['last one in'], when people are bathing in deep water,

---

ⁱ Like match-sticks.
ⁱⁱ Doesn't know meaning of *sakyó·pa*.

yopv aklatkat sakyopvt omvrēs mahket
yópa ákla·tkâ·t sakyó·pat omáłi·s máhkit
the last one to fall in will be the <u>sakyopv</u>, they said.

ēkayaken hvmket em vcēwet espokēn uewv akhvtapken omat, mvt sakyopvtot
i·ká·ya·kín hámkit imáci·wít íspo·kí·n óywa ákhata·pkín o·mâ·t mat sakyó·patot
When they undress, if one takes longer and gets in the water last, that's the <u>sakyopv,</u>

omvlkvn vcelaketvn komē akkassēcen em pefatkē akfullat
omálkan acila·kitán kó·mi· akká·ssi·cín ímpifa·tkí· ákfollâ·t
and he tries to touch everyone and chases them in the water as they run from him.

mvt sakyopv ahkopvnkvt omēs.
mat sakyó·pa ahkopánkat ô·mi·s
That's the game of <u>sakyopv</u>.

6.   Hvlolo eco-funet monkat wakv-funet omēs.
     halólo icofónit móŋka·t wa·kafónit ô·mi·s
6.   <u>Hvlolo</u> is a deer bone or a cow bone.

Eco, wakv etorkowv funen lopockusēt vlomhēt omen,
icó wá·ka ito·łkowá fónin lopóckosi·t alómhi·t ô·min
They're small [bones] that lie on a deer's or cow's knee bone,

mvn hopoyet vteloyet mvhonkvtkv kerkvkēn hayvkvtēt omen,
man hopo·yít atilô·yit mahoŋkátka kiłkakí·n há·yakáti·t ô·min
and they search for those and gather them and each has a certain number of bones;

hokkolet etohhecēt kaket aetohcvllēcet,
hokkô·lit itohhicí·t kâ·kit a·itohcálli·cít
two sit facing each other and roll them toward each other,

ahkopvnetvt hvlolo sahkopvnkvt omēs.
ahkopanitát halólo sahkopánkat ô·mi·s
and that's how the game <u>hvlolo</u> is played.

7.   Fakke-svkakv eto eccv-kotakse enrē omusēn ocet,
     fakkisaká·ka itó iccakotáksi inłi· ô·mosi·n ô·cit
7.   For dirt-sling, you have a piece of wood just like an arrow,

fakkē tvlaswvn vlicet esmvyattēcvkat, hopvyēn vwikēt omen,
fakkí· 'talá·swan[432] *aleycít ismaya·tti·cakâ·t hopáyi·n aweyki·t ô·min*
attach a wad of clay, swing it, and it will throw it far;

eto tis 'svfvllet monkat 'setefvllet komat momēcē esfulletvt
itóteys sáfallít móŋka·t 'sitífallít kô·ma·t momi·cí· isfollitát
they are thrown at trees or at each other,

mvt <u>fakke-svkakv</u> ahkopvnkvt omēs.
mat fakkisaká·ka ahkopánkat ô·mi·s
and that's the game <u>fakke-svkakv</u> ['dirt-sling'].

8.   Wvnvkucē etem echetv 'tvfossucen ehvrpe vfehset 'tepvkohlicet,
     wanakocí· itimichitá 'tafo·ssocín ihálpi afíhsit 'tipakóhleycít
8.   To shoot each other's little bundle, they peel a piece of bark off a small elm and fold it,

vhopakuce cenvpakusē mahē encvpkēn vhopakuce hokkolusē encekfēn
ahopa·kocí cinapâ·kosi· má·hi· incapkí·n ahopa·kocí hokkô·losi· incikfi·n
about eight inches long and two inches wide, and tie it tightly

polokusēn yekcēn wvnayet, vhopvyusēn vwiket, eccvkotakse enrēn sēchē
poló·kosi·n yíkci·n wanâ·yit[433] *ahopayósi·n aweykít iccakotáksi inlí·n si·chí·*
in a little ball and throw [the bundle] a little ways off, and shooting arrows at it

esfulletvt wvnvkuce etem echetvt os. Rē-hutke tis tohkayet komat
isfollitát wanakocí itimichitát ô·ⁿs li·hótkiteys tóhka·yít kô·ma·t
is the way to shoot each other's little bundle. Betting feathered arrows,

wvnvkuce rvhekon omat rē em pohoyēt omvnts.
wanakocí łahíkon o·mâ·t lí· impó·ho·yi·t[i] *o·mánc.*
if they didn't shoot the little bundle, the arrow would be won [by the owner of the bundle].

9.   Svtv-pvnēckv. Svtv-honēcv em ēttēn hopoyet
     satapaní·cka. satahoni·ca imi·ttí·n hopó·yit
9.   Making persimmons dance: they look for the fruit of a wild persimmon and pierce

---

[i] Or (for *impó·ho·yí·t*): *imísho·yí·t* 'taken'.

eto tvkącwusan totkuce encvpkē, enrakkē omusē tayen svtv mēttē 'teropottēn espvkafet
itó takă·ⁿcwosa·n to·tkocí incapkí· inła·kkí· ô·mosi· tâ·yin sata? mi·tti· 'tilopó·tti·n ispakâ·fit
the persimmon with hard wood just about the length and size of a match-stick, sticking it all

eco-hvrpe tis monkat nake tvkvcwēn em pvticet ohhvpalofecicet,
icohálpiteys móŋka·t nâ·ki takácwi·n impatêycit ohhapa·ló·ficeycit[434]
the way through, and spread out a deer hide, or something solid, and spin it on it,

svtv pvnēcē sahkopvnkvt os.
satá páni·cí· sahkopánkat ô·ⁿs.
[and that's] the game of making a persimmon dance.

10. Rē 'tem ohwiketv etopohhucen monkat 'to-yvheklucen 'svpoyet
    li· 'timohweykitá itopohhocín móŋka·t 'toyahiklocín 'sapô·yit
10. For arrow [dropping?], they pile little shrubs or little bushes;

rē-hutke hokkolakusēn omaket,
li·hótki hokkolá·kosi·n omâ·kit
they have two feathered arrows each,

mv 'to-yvheklucen rē-hutken ohhvkvnrecopuetecicet sahkopvnetvt omēs.
ma? 'toyahiklocín li·hótkin ohhakanlicopóyticeycit sahkopanitát ô·mi·s
and it's a game to make the feathered arrows do somersaults on those little bushes.

Este em ahkopanvkat enake rē-hutket 'to-yvhekluce ofvn akhueren,
ísti imáhkopa·nakâ·t inâ·ki li·hótkit 'toyahiklocí ó·fan akhôylin
The feathered arrow of the person playing stands in the little bushes, and

rē este naken ohhvkvnrecopuetecicvkan, rē enhotkē tafvt
łi· ísti nâ·kin ohhakanlicopóyticeycakâ·n li· inhotkí· tá·fat
when someone makes a [second] arrow do a somersault over it, if a feather on the feathered

mv rēn vceelakēt ervccaken omat
ma? łí·n acilá·ki·t ilácca·kin o·mâ·t
arrow touches the arrow [standing in the bush] and leans against it,

em poyvkēt omēs. Rē-hutken tohkayet sahkopvnetvt omēs.
ímpo·yakí·t ô·mi·s li·hótkin tóhka·yit sahkopanitát ô·mi·s
he wins. It's a game to bet feathered arrows.

Monkv yv nake ahkopvnkvn este-cate 'sem afvcketvt omakvtēs.
mónka yaʔ nâ·kiʔ ahkopánkan isticá·ti 'sima·fackitát oma·kati·s
So these games were the Indians' recreation.

Rē ēhkv tat <u>este-celokke</u> maketv etvlwv este-maskoke tokatet ahkopanēt omaken,
li·ʔ i·hkata·t isticiló·kki ma·kitá itálwa istima·skó·ki tó·ka·tit áhkopa·ní·t omâ·kin
Hide-the-bullet was played by those called <u>este-celokke</u> — tribes who are not Muscogee,

mvn asenkerhohoyvtēt omēs mahokvnts.
man a·sinkílho·hoyáti·t ô·mi·s má·ho·kánc
and it was learned from them, it was said.

Ohrolopē pale ēpake cahkepohkakat mahe ore witēs.
ohłolopí· pá·li i·pâ·ki cahkipohkâ·ka·t má·hi ô·li wêyti·s
It might have been about sixty-five years ago.

Hiyomat este-hvtke hvmket pum vlaket netta sulkēn epupaket likvntvs.
hayyô·ma·t istihátki hámkit pomalâ·kit nittá· sólki·n ipopâ·kit leykántas
One white man came to us like this and would stay many days with us.

"Este-celokke fullan arvyvtēt os, ohrolopē sulkēn" makvntvs, este-hvtke vculēt.
isticiló·kki follâ·n a·layáti·t ô·ⁿs ohłolopí· sólki·n ma·kántas istihátki acóli·t
"I lived among the <u>este-celokke</u>, many years ago," he said, that old white man did.

Mv este-hvtk-vcule rē-ēhkv ahkopvnkvn eyacē hērēt omen,
maʔ istihatkacóli li·ʔi·hka ahkopánkan iyá·ci· hĭ·ⁿłi·t ô·min
That old white man really liked the hide-the-bullet game,

em ahkopvnusē hayet em enhorhohoyē hakvntvs.
imahkopanosí· hă·ⁿyit iminhołho·hoyí· ha·kántas
so they played it with him until they'd get bored.

Momen heyv ahkopvnkv 'mvrahrvkv cenvpakat nake tohkayē,
mo·mín hiyá ahkopánka 'małahłaká cinapá·ka·t nâ·kiʔ tóhka·yí·
And these eight different games were not to bet on things,

etem poyē, 'setenhomecetv, 'setem ēlesketv,
itímpo·yí· 'sitinhomicitá 'sitimi·liskitá
to lose to one another, to get mad at each other, to envy each other,

'setehvnetv tokon, etem ahkopanēt omhoyvtēs.
'sitihaníta tó·ko·n itimahkópa·ní·t ómho·yatí·s
or to quarrel with each other, but they were played with one another.

Vce-ēwēskv, rē-ēhkv ahkopanat svhvyatkis ahkopvnhoyvtēt omēs.
aci?i·wí·ska lí·?í·hka áhkopa·nâ·t sáhaya·tkêys ahkopánho·yatí·t ô·mi·s
Corn-winnowing and hide-the-bullet were sometimes played all night.

Vce-ēwēskv tat ahkopanvyat hvyatkē ocvtēt os.
aci?i·wí·skata·t áhkopa·nayâ·t haya·tkí· o·catí·t ô·ⁿs.
I've played corn-winnowing until dawn sometimes.

Fohfokv sahkopvnkvo ocēs. Estenhvmkusē svrēpē sahkopvnetvt omēs.
fo·hfó·ka sahkopánkaw ô·ci·s istinhámkosi· sáłi·pí· sahkopanitát ô·mi·s
There was also a game [called] <u>fohfokv</u> ['bull-roarer']. It's for someone to play alone.

The Customs of Hunters

J. Hill (Hill III:5–6; Haas XVIII:141–147)

Este-fayvlke sasvtē nake honecvkē pvpetv sasan elēcetv eyacē hopoyan okhoyvtēs.
istifa·yâlki sa·satí· nâ·ki honicakí· papíta sâ·sa·n ili·citá iyá·ci· hopó·ya·n ókho·yatí·s
This is about hunters who would hunt and kill wild game for food.

Este-fayv kicat fayvt on omat em etetakēt omēs.
istifá·ya keycâ·t fá·yat ô·n o·mâ·t imititá·ki·t ô·mi·s
What is called a hunter, if he's a hunter, is always prepared.

Eco elēcen omat, acokohyet 'resatēt onkv,
icó ili·cín o·mâ·t a·cokóhyit łísa·tí·t oŋka
When he kills a deer, he puts it on his back to bring it in;

eco elehcē eswvnvyetv vrahkusēn ocēt wakv-hvrpe selvkvtēn saret,
icó ilíhci· iswanayitá ałǎ·ⁿhkosi·n ó·ci·t wa·kaháłpi silákati·n sa·lít
he has special split cowhide strips to tie up the deer that's been killed;

hvyatkat yomockē monken ayet rvfotot meskēto estomis, momet yafkateu ayet
haya·tkâ·t yomócki· móŋkin a·yít łafótot miskí·to· istô·meys mo·mít ya·fkâ·tiw a·yít
he goes at dawn while still dark in winter, summer, whichever, and also in late evening,

eco elēcet 'resvlakat acokoyvtē yewvkēcan vpạkuset
icó ilî·cit lísala·kâ·t a·cokô·yati· yiwáki·câ·n apǎ·ⁿkosit
and killing a deer, returns with it on his back and immediately lays it down

enfolahpv kicēt nvrke ofvn likēt on aehset
infoláhpa keycí·t nálki ó·fan leykí·t ô·n a·íhsit
and takes out the <u>enfolahpv</u> ['mussel'], which is in the stomach,

totkv ētkan torvwvn ohlicet noricet papet omvnts.
tó·tka i·tkâ·n toláwan ohlêycit noleycít pa·pít o·mánc
setting it on coals in the fire, and cooks and eats it.

Este-fayv nake encakemahat mvt ocēt omēs. Cọtkusē estomis
istifá·ya nâ·ki inca·kimâ·ha·t mat ó·ci·t ô·mi·s cǒ·ⁿtkosi· istô·meys
That is the one thing a hunter is partial to. Even though it might be very small,

efv enlasvrē eyacekot omvnts. Momis ēmet pvpeko tayen omat,
ifá inlá·sáli· iyá·ciko·t o·mánc. mo·mêys í·mit papíko· tâ·yin o·mâ·t
he didn't want a dog to lick it. But if [the hunter] could not eat it,

mv eco enfolahpv hvmkvt totkvn takliket nēkren hēcen omat,
ma (?) icó infoláhpa hámkat tó·tkan takléykit ni·klín[435] *hi·cín o·mâ·t*
if he saw the whole deer <u>enfolahpv</u> sitting in the fire being totally burned,

'semahlvpvtkēt omvnts. Momen vculvke fayvlke vtēkat mome vlkēt omakvtēs.
'simahlapátki·t o·mánc. mo·mín acolakí fa·yâlki atî·ka·t mó·mi álki·t oma·katí·s.
he was satisfied. And all the old hunters were the same way.

Eco elēcvkat enfolahpv estet pvpekon, totkvn taknēkret omekon
icó (?) ili·cakâ·t infoláhpa ístit papíkon tó·tkan tákni·klít omíko·n
When those who killed the deer did not eat the <u>enfolahpv</u>, and it wasn't burned by the fire,

yvmahken omat, eco ētv rvhvkat ennokkihcēskos.
yamahkín o·mâ·t icó (?) í·ta lahakâ·t innokkeyhci·sko·s
it was wasted, so the next time a deer was shot at, it would not even be wounded.

Rahvkis estensumkēt omēs makakēt ont encakvkētot omvnts.
ła·hakêys istinsomkí·t ô·mi·s má·ka·kí·t ônt inca·kakí·tot o·mánc.
Though one shoots at it, it gets away, they said, so they didn't allow it.

Cvpvwvlke omvlkv sem vculat Ayekcv hocefkēt arēt omat
capawâlki omálka simacô·la·t a·yíkca hocífki·t a·lí·t ô·ma·t
When the oldest of all my uncles named Ayikcha was around,

fakv tvlkusē 'sem afvcketvt monkat 'sem ēnaorickvt ont omvntvs.
fá·ka tǎlⁿkosi· 'sima·fackitát móŋka·t 'simi·na·oɫéyckat ônt o·mántas.
hunting was his only pleasure or his only interest.

[Hunting a Turkey][436]

J. Hill (Hill IV:4–6; Haas XXI:29–53)

Ohrolopē cokpe-rakko hvmkē cokpe cenvpakē pale kolvpakē
ohɫolopí· cokpiɫákko hámki· cókpi cinapá·ki· pá·li kolapá·ki·
It was about the year eighteen hundred

ostvpohkakat mahe tis omvtēs,
ostapohkâ·ka·t má·hiteys o·matí·s
and seventy-nine [1879]

cvpvwvlke liketv monkat cuko hahyet vpokof.
capawâlki leykitá móŋka·t cokó háhyit apo·kô·f
when my mother's brothers built a dwelling or house and lived there.

Mvn vpakit likvyvtēt os. Folahpv-Hvcce hocefkē hvcce wakkē vnakusan
man apá·keyt leykayáti·t ô·ⁿs folahpahácci hocífki· hácci wákki· anǎ·ⁿkosa·n
I lived with them. There was a creek named Shell Creek very close

mv cvpvwvlke cuko licakvtē
ma capawâlki cokó léyca·katí·
to the house my uncles had built,

enhvsossv vkērkv nvrkvpv estomusē senhoyvnusē 'mvhopvyēn cvhute hayvyvtēt omet
inhasó·ssa aki·ɫka naɫkapá istǒ·ⁿmosi· sinhoyánosi· 'mahopayí·n cahóti há·yayáti·t ô·mit
and to the east, just a little over a half a mile in distance, I built my house,

mvn mucvnettv likis, Hvyuce netta pale eskolvpohkakat
man mocanítta lêykeys hayóci nittá· pá·li iskolapohkâ·ka·t
and I still live there today, July 17,

ohrolopē cokpe-rakko hvmkē cokpe ostvpake pale ostē hvmkontvlakate
ohlolopí· cokpiłákko hámki· cókpi ostapá·ki pá·li ô·sti· hamkontalâ·ka·ti
in the year nineteen hundred and forty-one [1941];

nettvn vm vculkv ohrolopē pale cenvpakes, yv hvse em ofvn.
níttan amacólka ohłolopí· pá·li cinapâ·kis ya hasí imó·fan[i]
that day my age was eighty years old, in this month.

Vyekcv, Yape, Mesv cvpvwv hocefhokvt omen,
ayikca yá·pi mísa capáwa hocífhokát ô·min
Ayikcha, Yapi, and Misa were the names of my uncles,

ecke Lose, cvcke Halēce.
ícki ló·si cácki ha·lî·ci.
and their mother Lucy, and my mother Halichi.

Este ētv encuko pum vnakuecat cuko hokkolusē omvntvs.
ísti í·ta incokó pomana·kóyca·t cokó hokkô·losi· ô·mantás
There were only two houses near us belonging to other people.

Konoyvholv ēppucetake Pahcēnv Tepse Vyaske enhvtese hoktē Nile,
konoyahóla i·ppocitá·ki pa·hcí·na típsi ayá·ski inhatísi hoktí· néyli
Kono Yahola's sons were Pahchina, Tipsi, Ayaski, and daughter-in-law Nellie;

yvt vwolusan vpoken, Mahtv echustaket Atvs-honvp-ēmarv Mēle
yat awŏ·ⁿlosa·n apô·kin má·hta ichostá·kit a·tashonapi·má·ła mí·li
these lived near by, and Mahta's children, Atas-honap-emathla and Mary,

vkērkv nvrkvpv mahen vpokvntvs.
akí·łka nalkapá mâ·hin apo·kántas
lived within about a half a mile.

Hvsossv fvccv, honerv fvccv, aklatkv fvccv vwolusē cuko sekot omvntvs.
hasó·ssa fácca honíla fácca aklá·tka fácca awólosi· cokó síkot o·mántas.
There were no houses close by toward the east, toward the north, or toward the west.

---

[i] Last Thurs., July 17, 1941.

Vpuekv tis naket sekot omen 'cerakko-honecakvt fullakēt os mahokvntvs.
apóykateys nâ·kit síkot o·mín 'ciłakkohonicá·kat fólla·kí·t ô·ⁿs má·ho·kántas
There were no livestock, but there were wild horses about, it was said.

Monkv ēkvnv honēcv likēt em oketv ofvn arit, este honēcv omēt vcvculepvtēt os.
môŋka i·kaná honí·ca léyki·t imokitá ó·fan a·łéyt ísti honí·ca ó·mi·t acacolípati·t ô·ⁿs
So it was a time that I lived in wild country, I went about like a wild person as I grew up.

Ēkvnv cvto vlkan arvyvntvs.
i·kaná cató álka·n a·layántas
I roamed about in rocky country.

Estelepikv tis cvle vtę̄hvyesekot meskē tot rvfo tis sulkēn etēhoyanvyvtēt os.
istilipéykateys calí atĭ·ⁿhayisíkot miskí·tot łafóteys sólki·n ití·hoya·nayáti·t ô·ⁿs.
I have come through many summers and winters without shoes on my feet.

Vm eccvkotaksen enrē-fvskē vpvkēn esyekēnin omat,
amiccakotáksin inłi·fáski· apáki·n isyikí·neyn o·mâ·t
I held my bow and arrow tightly

netta hihoyat netta kvsvphoyat kerrvkot arvyvtēt os.
nittá· hayhô·ya·t nittá· kasaphô·ya·t kíłłako·t⁴³⁷ a·łayáti·t ô·ⁿs
and didn't know hot days or cold days as I wandered about.

Momē arvyof, vm vculkv ohrolopē palē tuccenohkakat mahe tis omvtēs.
mó·mi· a·łayô·f amacólka ohłolopí· pá·li· toccinohkâ·ka·t mâ·hiteys o·mati·s
At that time, my age was about thirteen years.

Efv hokkolen ēyvpvyēt vnrvwvn arit,
ifá hokkô·lin i·yapáyi·t ânławan a·łeyt
I had two dogs with me out in the wilderness,

pen-vculet wakkvtet atasiket lētken
pinʔacólit wâ·kkatit a·ta·sêykit⁴³⁸ li·tkín
and an old turkey that had been lying down jumped up and ran,

efvt assehcet cakkaken, eton ohtvmiket ohhueren
ifát a·ssíhcit cákka·kín itón ohtamâykit ohhôyłin
and the dogs took chase and were catching up with it, so he flew into a tree and stood there,

rohrit rē-fvske sēchvyat,
łóhleyt łi·fáski sî·chaya·t[439]
and when I got there, I shot at him with an arrow;

rvhvkon tvmiket; ayen efv assehcet vhoyen,
łahákon tamêykit a·yín ifá a·ssíhcit aho·yín
I missed, and he flew off. The [two] dogs took off chasing,

arit rē tat sēchvyat 'resehpvyof,
a·łeyt łí·ta·t sî·chaya·t 'lisíhpayo·f
and when I went and got the arrow that I had shot,

efv tat vwohecakvcoken lētkit ayit rorvyan;
ifáta·t awóhica·kacókin li·tkéyt a·yéyt ło·layâ·n
the dogs were barking, so I took off running and got there.

eton rohtvmket ohhueren okaken
itón łohtâmkit ohhôyłin oka·kín
He had flown up in a tree and was standing up there,

rē-fvske sēchvyat, rvhepvkon,
łi·fáski si·chayâ·t łahípakon
and when I shot at him with the arrow, I missed,

pen-vcule tat ohhuerēpen arit ēchvyē monket,
pinʔacolíta·t ohhoylî·pin a·łéyt i·chayi·[440] *môŋkit*
and the old turkey just stood there as I kept shooting at him.

rē-fvske hvmken esrahhit vcakhēcet omvyan
łi·fáski hámkin isłáhheyt acakhî·cit o·mayâ·n
I shot one arrow into him,

aslvtkekot omen yafkusē hakēpan omen
a·slátkikot o·mín yă·ⁿfkosi· há·ki·pâ·n o·mín
but he didn't fall, and it was getting to be late evening,

mv eto vcemkit ayit penwv 'rvwolicin,
ma(ʔ) itó acimkéyt a·yéyt pínwa 'ławolêyceyn
so I climbed the tree. and as I was getting closer to the turkey,

eto-lvcce talēt vcakhen hvlatvyat, kahcit, ēsit, svcemkit, vnakusen rohrit,
itolácci tá·li·t acâ·khin halâ·taya·t káhceyt î·seyt sácimkéyt anä·ⁿkosin łóhleyt
I took hold of a dried limb that was sticking out, broke it off, took it, and climbed very close,

mv eto ēsvyvtē pen-vcule esnvfikin,
ma itó î·sayáti· pinʔacóli isnafêykeyn
and with the stick I was holding, I hit the old turkey,

tasiket ēkvnv erhuerof,
ta·sêykit i·kaná íłhoyłô·f
and when he jumped and landed on the ground,

efvt hvlvtaken ahvtvpikit penwv tat elehcit,
ifát halatâ·kin a·hatapêykeyt pínwata·t ilíhceyt
the dogs got hold of him, and I came down and killed the turkey

hompetv rakkēn heckuehcit
hompitá lákki·n hickóyhceyt
and provided a lot to eat.

afvcketvo rakkēn momet ēkvsvmkvo rakkēn heckuehcit arvyof
a·fackitáw lákki·n mo·mít i·kasámkaw lákki·n hickóyhceyt a·layô·f
As I was going around very happy and very proud of what I had supplied,

hvseu raklvtkepvranusen pen-vcule tat acokohyit rēsatvyvntvs.
hasíw łaklatkipalä·ⁿnosin pinʔacólita·t a·cokóhyeyt łí·sa·tayántas
it was almost sunset, so I put the turkey on my back and returned home.

Momen hiyomē kērrvyat vncuko 'mvhopiyē vkērkv tuccenvranusēn arit
mo·mín hayyô·mi· ki·llayâ·t ancokó 'mahopayyí· akí·lka toccinalä·ⁿnosi·n a·łéyt
Now I realize I was about three miles from my house

penwv elēcet omvyvtētot kērrvyetvnks. Mv ēkvnv tempusan arimvts.
pínwa ili·cít o·mayáti·tót ki·llayítaŋks ma i·kaná tímposa·n a·łéymác
when I killed the turkey. I was very near that land.

'Cerakko ohlikvyēt hofonē hakēpēn okis.
'ciłákko ohlêykayi·t hofóni· ha·kî·pi·n o·kéys
I mean a long time later I was riding a horse.

Pvne-rakkon 'tvyikit ēkvn-tvpekse rohrit ayvyof,
panilákkon 'tayêykeyt i·kantapíksi łóhłeyt a·yayô·f
I went across a big valley, and when I came to flat land,

cvyopvn pen-vculet cvhokvcoken, "Mvn ahoyanet ohmvyan oks" kont,
cayópan pin?acólit caho·kacókin man a·hoyá·nit óhmaya·n ó·ks kònt
behind me I heard an old turkey gobbling. "I just passed there," I thought,

hvyakpon 'rosiyit vyēpvyan
hayakpó·n 'losèyyeyt ayi·payâ·n
and when I came out on the prairie,

'tewolēn cvhoket oken ayit
'tiwolí·n caho·kít o·kín a·yéyt
the gobbling was getting more frequent. And I kept going,

tvpockucen ocvyēt omat vkerrihcit 'cerakkon wihkit raletikit
tapo·ckocín ó·cayi·t ô·ma·t akiłłéyhceyt 'cilákkon wéyhkeyt la·litêykeyt
and remembering I had a pistol, I left the horse, ran back,

eto 'tepoktvkēt tuccēnēt svpaklen mv ceskvn lihkit,
itó (?) 'tipoktakí·t toccî·ni·t sapâ·klin ma (?) cískan léyhkeyt
sat next to three trees standing next to each other,

pen-eckuce okit entaktakin
pin?ickocí ô·keyt[441] *intá·kta·kéyn*
and clucked like a little mother turkey.

cvhoket tenētkat pofken atvcoken
caho·kít tini·tkâ·t pô·fkin[442] *a·tacókin*
It came gobbling, making a thundering sound.

vm etetakēt likin ēkvnv tvpeksan yossat
amititâ·ki·t lêykeyn i·kaná tapiksa·n yo·ssâ·t
I sat there ready, and as it came out in the open,

vwolusen yehueren, eciyin, hvlwēn tasiket, nvtaksēt taklvtiket,
awŏ·ⁿlosin yihôylin icêyveyn[443] *hálwi·n ta·sêykit natáksi·t taklatêykit*
he stood really close, so I took a shot, and it jumped high and fell face up

nekēyekot takwakken, vwǫlusekv efēke tis enrahin omēs kont,
nikí·yikot takwâ·kkin awŏ·ⁿlosíka ifí·kiteys inłá·heyn o·mí·s kônt
and lay there without moving. Being so close, I thought I might have shot it in the heart.

eccv tvnecicvyat rēn espikehpit ayit
ícca tanicêycaya·t łi·n ispeykíhpeyt a·yéyt
I put a bullet in the gun I had emptied and went over,

rorvyan turwv tat cvfencakusen mesētticet takwakken
ło·layâ·n tółwata·t cafincâ·kosin misí·tteycít takwâ·kkin
and as I got there, its eyes looked alert, and it lay there blinking;

takkesvranit ohconēkvyof, atasiket vnlētkvntvs.
takkisáła·néyt óhconi·kayô·f a·ta·sêykit anlî·tkantás
and when I bent over to pick it up, it jumped up and ran from me.

Mohmen assēcit pvcēsset vm ayen esnvfketvo hopoyvyis,
móhmin á·ssi·céyt paci·ssít ama·yín isnafkitáw hopo·yayêys
So I chased it, and it darted in and out, and I looked for something to hit it with

naket vnheckeko tayen vnhopvyēcet vyēpet omis,
nâ·kit anhíckiko· tâ·yin anhopáyi·cít ayi·pít o·mêys
but couldn't find anything. It was getting further away from me, but

wikvko monken, ayet cvto-rakko ocvkēn raktasken,
wéykako· môŋkin a·yít catołá·kko o·cakí·n łákta·skín
I didn't quit, and it went where there were boulders and ran down among them:

"Vmontahletskes ce, mucv tan" kicit rohfvnkvyan,
amontáhlíckis ci^ mocáta·n keycéyt łóhfankayâ·n
"You have defeated me this time!" I said, and as I looked down over [a boulder],

a-aklatket ohmvtet nvtaksēt akwakken,
a·ʔákla·tkít óhmatit natáksi·t akwâ·kkin
it had fallen and was lying down there face up.

estele vhopakv kolvpakat mahet enhvlwēt omis,
istilí ahopá·ka kolapâ·ka·t mâ·hit inhalwí·t ô·meys
It was about seven feet high, but

a-ohtaskvyat, ekvn mohhuyirit, elēcvyvnts. Mv ēkvnv hēcvyat,
aʔohtâ·skaya·t ikán mohhoyêyłeyt ili·cayánc ma i·kaná hi·cayâ·t
I jumped down on it, landed on its head, and killed it. Later when I saw that place,

vne mit ēlēcvyē tayē ēkvnv enholwvketvt oman
animêyt i·lí·cayi· tâ·yi· i·kaná inholwakítat ô·ma·n
I realized I might have killed myself instead in that rugged country;

vm omvlkusēt lētkit aret omvyvtēt ont hēcimvts.
amomălⁿkosi·t li·tkéyt a·łit o·mayáti·t ônt hi·céymac
I saw that I had run with all my might.

Monkv ponvttv vnvttehcvkē eleko arē em oketv ofv tat
môŋka ponátta anattíhcaki· ilíko· a·łi· imokitá ó·fata·t
So when you wound an animal and it doesn't die and can still move about,

ēyestemerricvkē tayēt omēpvnts.
i·yistimillêycaki· tâ·yi·t omi·pánc
that is the time you could end up badly hurting yourself.

Hvtvm penvca hvmket tvmket vcvwvlapken ēchvyat,
hatâm pinacá·[444] *hámkit tamkít acawála·pkín î·chaya·t*[445]
Then a gobbler once flew over me, and when I took a shot,

rahhit elēcvyvntvs. Vcvculehpofvt okis.
łáhheyt ili·cayantás acacolíhpo·fat o·kéys.
I hit it and killed it. This is after I was old.

How to Tame a Fawn

J. Hill (Haas VI:45–53)[446]

Eco tat	nake	honecēt	omet	este	em vpvketv	tokot	ont	omis,
icóta·t	*nâ·ki*	*honíci·t*	*ô·mit*	*ísti*	*imapakíta*	*tó·ko·t*	*ônt*	*o·mêys*
The deer	something	wild	is	people	its associate	(is) not	is	but

The deer being something wild, it does not associate with people,

ecuce estet ehset vcayēcēt hompicen omat,
icóci ístit íhsit acá·yi·cí·t hómpeycín o·mâ·t
little deer person takes it takes care of it feeds it if he does
but if a person taking a baby deer [will] take care of it and feed it,

yvmạsusēt vcolēt omēs. Vpuekv yvmvsvkē em monkv sasat
yamă·ⁿsosi·t aco·lí·t ô·mi·s apóyka yamasaki· immóɳka sâ·sa·t
very gentle grows does stock gentle natural that are about
it will become very tame. It is even more gentle

res emontvlēt yvmvsēt omēs.
'lisimontalí·t yamási·t ô·mi·s
moreso gentle is
than stock that is gentle by nature.

Celahoyen netta hvmkusis ohyafken elạwusē haken
cilá·ho·yín nittá· hâmkoseys óhya·fkín ilă·ⁿwosi· ha·kín
they handle it day one, even till evening very hungry gets
If one handles it just one day until evening, and if, when it gets hungry,

wakv-pesē cvmpan emhoyen ēsket fvcēcusēt homipet
wa·kapisí· câmpa·n ímho·yín i·skít facĭ·ⁿcosi·t homêypit
milk sweet gives to drinks it gets very full eats
one gives it sweet milk to drink, it will eat and get full,

sumkē estomis elạwusē haken omat,
sómki· istô·meys ilă·ⁿwosi· ha·kín o·mâ·t
it goes away even if very hungry gets if they do
and then, even if it goes away, it's bound to come back

cukon ra oh-vtvranat tvlkusēt omēs. Estofvn sumikekos.
cokón la·ohhatála·nâ·t tàlⁿkosi·t ô·mi·s istó·fan somâykiko·s
house comes back bound to is [(not) ever it won't] go away
to the house when it gets hungry. It will never go astray.

Eco-honvnwvt on omat vcolof, holwvyēcē hakēt omēs.
icohonánwat ô·n o·mâ·t aco·lô·f holwayí·ci· ha·kí·t ô·mi·s
a buck [is] if when it's grown mean gets does
If it is a buck, it will become mean when it grows up.

Momis   enhoktēt   on   omat,   lopicusēt   ont
mo·mèys   inhoktí·t   ô·n   o·mâ·t   lopĕyⁿcosi·t   ônt
But   a doe   [is]   if   very cute   is
But if it is a doe, it is very cute,

hocefkvo   ēmetsken   omat,   kērrusēt   omēs.
hocífkaw   i·míckin   o·mâ·t   kĭ·ⁿłosi·t   ô·mi·s
name, too   you give it if   knowing it very well does
and if you give it a name, it knows it very well.

Nake   estomis   hompēs.
nâ·ki   istô·meys   hompí·s
anything   [whatever]   eats
It eats anything.

Vce tis,   tvlako tis,   vhv-cvmpv tis,   vpeswv tis,   hece tis   papēs
acíteys   talá·koteys   ahacámpateys   apíswateys   hicíteys   pa·pí·s
corn, even beans, even   sweet potatoes, even meat, even   tobacco, even   eats it
It will eat corn, beans, sweet potatoes, or even tobacco,

emhoyen   omat. Hopuetakucen   em enhērēt   ont
ímho·yín[447]   o·mâ·t hopoyta·kocín   iminhĭ·ⁿli·t[448] ônt
one gives it to it if   children   very fond of   is
if given it. It is very fond of children,

enfullen   omat,   vpaket   vrēpēt   omēs.
ínfollín   o·mâ·t   apâ·kit   ali·pí·t   ô·mi·s
they are around   if   with them   (it does) go about does
if they are about, and follows them around.

Cuko takfettvn   nocēpet   wakkvtētis,   ahuyiret
cokó takfíttan   noci·pít   wâ·kkati·teys   a·hoyêylit
(in the) yard   it sleeping even if it's lying it gets up
If it should be lying in the yard sleeping, if it gets up

ētvn   ayen   omat,   estet   vlvkvranan   omēs.
i·tan   a·yín   o·mâ·t   ístit   alákala·nâ·n   o·mí·s
somewhere else (if) it goes if does person   going to come   is
and goes somewhere else, someone will soon come.

Este   eton   caskēt   aren   omat,
ísti   *itón*   *ca·ski·t*[449]   *a·lín*   *o·mâ·t*
person   wood   chopping   is about   [if]

If somebody is around chopping wood,

erem oret   tẹmpusan   a arēt omēs.
ilimô·lit   *tĭm*^n*posa·n*   *á·a·lí·t ô·mi·s*
it (will) go where he is   right close to him   it (will) stay around

it will go close to where he is and hang about.

Kvsvppēton   omat,   totkvn   tvrretvn   eyacē   hẹrēt   omēs.
kasáppi·ton   *o·mâ·t*   *tó·tkan*   *taɫitán*   *iyá·ci·*   *hĭ·*^n*li·t*   *ô·mi·s*
cold   if it is   fire   to warm itself by   it wants   very much   does

If it is cold, it wants very much to warm itself by the fire.

Cuko   em vhopvyēcēt   arvtētok   estomis   oskēt   svlaken   omat,
cokó   *imahopáyi·ci·t*[450]   *a·latí·to·k*   *istô·meys*   *oskí·t*   *sála·kín*   *o·mâ·t*
house   far away from   it was around   even if   rain   is coming up   if

If a rain comes up, even if it is far away from the house,

em omvlkusēt   ra lētkat   soh-vpēttan   yohcemiket
imomăl^n*kosi·t*   *ɫa·lî·tka·t*   *sohhapí·ttan*   *yohcimâykit*
its best   comes running back   porch   gets up on

it comes running back with all its might, and it goes up on the porch,

cukot   hvokēton   omat,   ecehyet   wakkēpen   oskat   wikof,
cokót   *háwki·ton*   *o·mâ·t*   *icíhyit*   *wakkî·pin*[451]   *o·skâ·t*   *waykô·f*
house   open   if it is   it goes in   it lies down   raining   when it quits

and if the door is open, it goes inside and lies down, and then, when it quits raining,

osiyet   vrēpēt   omēs.   Mv   eco   epucase   em efv   tokot
osâyyit   *aɫi·pí·t*   *ô·mi·s*   *ma*   *icó*   *ipocá·si*   *imífa*   *tó·ko·t*
it goes out   it goes about   does   that   deer's   (his) master's   dog   (if it) isn't

it goes outside and wanders off. If there is a dog around

efv   kerrekon   em aren   omat,
ifá   *kíɫiko·n*   *ima·lín*   *o·mâ·t*
a dog   it doesn't know   being around   if

that is not his master's,

enhomecēt ont cuko ofv tis cēyen omat,
inhomíci·t ônt cokó ó·fateys ci·yín o·mâ·t
mad at it is house in, even (if) it goes in if
it is vexed with it, and if [the dog] goes into the house,

tēpket ohsicēt omēs.
ti·pkít óhseycí·t ô·mi·s
whips it makes it go out does
it whips it and makes it go outside.

Meskē tat cvpofuce ecēyet
miskí·ta·t 'capo·focí (i)ci·yít
In the summertime garden it goes in
In the summertime, it will get into the garden

tvlako nake estomis estennoksēt omēs,
talá·ko nâ·ki istô·meys istínno·ksí·t ô·mi·s
beans anything to destroy, eat up from does
and eat up the beans or anything,

nerēn arēt onkv. Eco vculicvyē svhokkolēt os,
nilí·n a·lí·t ôŋka icó acóleycayí· 'sahokkolí·t ô·^{n}s[452]
at night it goes about does deer I've grown, raised second time did
because it goes about at night. I have raised a deer twice,

oketv etehopiyēn.
okíta itihopáyyi·n
(at) times (that) were far apart
at times that were far apart.

Story About the Ancients in Olden Times (Hofonemahē Vculvke Ohhonvkv)[i]

J. Hill (Hill II:36–39; Haas XVIII:81–109)

<u>Hopayvke rakrakat</u> kihocēt 'sem ēkērkv ocēt fullvtēs.
hopa·yakí łakłâ·ka·t kéyho·cí·t 'simi·kí·lka ó·ci·t follatí·s
Once there were <u>hopayvke rakrakat</u> ['the big far-aways'] who had their own identity.

---

[i] Title: *hofonimá·hi· acolakí ohhonáka* 'story of elders from long ago'.

Hopayvke lopockusē kihocateu 'sem ēkērkv ocētat fullvtēs.
hopa·yakí lopóckosi· kéyho·câ·tiw 'simi·ki·łka ó·ci·tá·t follatí·s
There were also hopayvke lopockusē ['little far-aways'] who had their own identity.

Hopayvke lopockusmahē kihocateu
hopa·yakí lopockosmá·hi· kéyho·câ·tiw
There were also hopayvke lopockusmahē ['very little far-aways']

'sem ekērkv ocētat fullvtēs. 'Le-homahtvke kihocēt fullvtēs.
'simiki·łka ó·ci·ta·t follatí·s 'lihomahtaki kéyho·cí·t follatí·s.
who had their own identity. There were once 'le-homahtvke ['scouts'].

'Mvpvkvlke kihocateu fullvtēs.
'mapakâlki kéyho·câ·tiw follatí·s[i]
There were once 'mvpvkvlke ['joiners'] too.

Hopayvke rakrvkē kihocat
hopa·yakí łakłakí· kéyho·câ·t[ii]
The ones called hopayvke rakrvkē

este enokkat cvfeknicetv heleshakv ensulkē estomusēt ensulkēt omētat
ísti ino·kkâ·t cafikneycitá 'hilishá·ka insolkí· istô·mosi·t insolkí·t ô·mi·ta·t
were taught and learned all the many ways

omvlkvn emvhahoyat kerrvkvtēt, momet ēme vtēkusē sēyvnicē vrepvranateu
omálkan imahá·ho·yâ·t kiłłakáti·t mo·nít í·mi atî·kosi· sí·yaneycí· alípała·nâ·tiw
to make medicine to cure the sick and for personal use and health;

omvlkvn kerrvkvtēt, nake herekateu: este ele tis em vhopanet,
omálkan kiłłakáti·t[453] *nâ·ki hiłíka·tiw*[454] *ísti iłíteys imáhopa·nít*
they learned it all, bad things too: to cripple someone's foot,

este ena tis lekhowēn vlomhicet, este tat hompetv tis em vhopanet enokkicet,
ísti iná·teys likhowí·n alómheycít ístita·t hompitáteys imáhopa·nít inókkeycít
cause sores on someone's body, ruin someone's appetite to make them sick,

---

[i] JH says he has trouble getting the story started right.

[ii] It['s] that "Believe-it-or-not," but that's what the old folks said and they believed it, too.

este em opunvkv enhakē tis em vhopanet, heckekis ēhayet,
ísti imoponáka inha·kí·teys imáhopa·nít híckikeys i·ha·yít
ruin the sound of someone's voice, make themselves invisible sometimes,

este punvkv herąkē opunayv tis ehosicet,
ísti ponaká hilà·ⁿki· opona·yateys[455] ihóseycít[456]
make good speakers forget how to express themselves,

nerē oskē yomockē hĕrvntotis hopvyēn vfvnnaket,
nilí· o·ski· yomócki· hĭ·ⁿlantó·teys hopáyi·n afánna·kít
be able to see far away on very dark, rainy nights,

este elehvpo tis hēcet elentet, uewv lvokē hĕrat ofv tis nake tat hēcet,
ísti ilihapó·teys hî·cit ilintít óywa láwki· hĭ·ⁿla·t ó·fateys nâ·kita·t hi·cít
recognize people's footprints and track them, be able to see into very deep water,

rē tis vtvsennet rvheko tayēt ēhayet,
lí·teys atásinnít lahíko· tâ·yi·t i·ha·yít
make themselves so arrows ricochet and they can't be shot,

efvtot nake 'rem ētvo ēhayet, esteu vhoneceko tayēn nocicēcet,
ifátot nâ·ki 'limí·taw i·ha·yít ístiw ahonicíko· tâ·yi·n nocéyci·cít
turn themselves into dogs and other things, put people to sleep so they can't wake up,

nerē tvmkēt aret, cetto tis yvmvsēcet celayet, totkv tis kvsvppuecet,
nilí· tamkí·t a·lít cíttoteys yamási·cít cila·yít tó·tkateys kasáppoycít
fly around at night, tame and handle snakes, cool fire,

nake cǫtkusis rē hayet este esrahet enokkicet,
nâ·ki cŏ·ⁿtkoseys lí· ha·yít ísti isła·hít inókkeycít[457]
make the smallest things into arrows and shoot people with them and make them sick,

este em porretv, yvkapē hopvye vretv, este yvmvsēckv,
ísti impo·łlitá yaka·pi· hopáyi ałíta ísti yamasí·cka
to bewitch people, to have the ability to walk long distances, to make people docile,

elenhotis ocē tayat elehvpo vslēckv,
ilínho·têys ó·ci· tâ·ya·t ilihapó· aslí·cka
to erase footprints so they cannot be tracked,

ehiwv tis wihket vyēpat afulkvrē enhuehketv,
ihéywateys wéyhkit ayi·pâ·t a·fólkáłi· inhoyhkitá[458]
to call for the return of one who has abandoned his wife,

hoktē ēyvnokecickv, honvnwv ehiwv etewikepuecetv
hoktí· i·yanokicéycka honánwa (?) ihéywa (?) itiweykipoycitá
to make a woman love oneself, to make a man and his wife separate,

fayē vretv, heyv nanvke momēcetv enheleshakv yvhiketv vrahrvkv
fa·yí· ałíta hiyá nâ·naki momi·citá inhilishá·ka[459] *yaheykitá ałahłaká*
to have hunting abilities. They knew all the medicine songs

omvlkv emvhahoyē kerrvkvtēt, momet emvhayat honvnwv mvnettusof
omálka imahá·ho·yí· kiłłakáti·t mo·mít imáha·yâ·t honánwa maníttoso·f
taught them to do these things, so it was the elders who taught a man

em vculvket emvhayet omakvtēs.
imacolákit imáha·yít oma·katí·s
at a very young age.

Posecicet vnrvwv este vrē tayē onkan hompekon
posíceycít ânława ísti ałí· tâ·yi· óŋka·n hómpiko·n[460]
He was made to fast in the woods where no one would normally go without food;

wvkēcet heleswvn eskuecet, netta osten mont mv renhoyanat
wakî·cit 'hilíswan ískoycít nittá· ô·stin mónt ma łinhoyâ·na·t
they laid him down and gave him medicine to drink for four days, and after that,

netta cenvpakis elvwēcē posecicē yvhiketv emvhahoyat
nittá· cinapâ·keys iláwi·cí· posíceycí· yaheykitá imahá·ho·yâ·t
sometimes he would fast eight days and was taught all the songs;

omvlkv kerrvtēn 'sem ēkērkv ēmat
omálka kíłłati·n 'simi·ki·łka i·mâ·t
so as a sign to show all they had learned,

eyvpe hokkolen ekv ohcakcvhēn svrvrēn emhoyvtēt este sasvtēs.
iyápi[461] *hokkô·lin iká ohcakcahí·n sáłáłi·n imhoyáti·t ísti sa·sati·s*
some were given two horns which they wore on the head.

Mvt <u>hopayvke rakrakat</u> omvtēs.
mat hopa·yakí łakłâ·ka·t o·matí·s
Those were <u>hopayvke rakrakat</u> ['big far-aways'].

Mohmen este enokkat cvfeknicetv heleshakv yvhiketv
móhmin ísti ino·kkâ·t cafikneycitá 'hilishá·ka yaheykitá
And when almost finished learning medicine songs to cure the sick

momet nanvke 'rem ētv yvhiketv mvrahrvkv sulkat kerretv respoyvranē haken omat,
mo·mít nâ·naki 'limí·ta yaheykitá małahłaká sólka·t kiłłitá łispo·yałá·ni· ha·kín o·mâ·t
and many different songs for other things,

sem ēkērkv eyvpe hvmken ekv ohcakhēcēt vrvrēn yekcetv emhoyēt este sasvtēs.
'simi·kí·łka iyápi hámkin iká ohcakhí·ci·t ałáli·n yikcitá imhoyí·t ísti sa·satí·s
some were given the authority to go about with one horn on the head as a sign.

Mvt <u>hopayvke lopockusat</u> omvtēs.
mat hopa·yakí lopóckosa·t o·matí·s
Those were the <u>hopayvke lopockusat</u> ['little far-aways'].

Mohmet hvtvm este enokkv em vlekcetv yvhiketv,
móhmit hatâm ísti inó·kka imalikcitá yaheykitá
And when one began to learn the songs for doctoring the sick,

nake ētv heleshayetv yvhiketv omvlkv kerretvn emvhayetv vlicēhohcē este arat
nâ·ki í·ta 'hilisha·yitá yaheykitá omálka kiłłitán imaha·yitá[462] *aleyci·hóhci· ísti a·łâ·t*
the making of medicine, and all the songs for those, the beginning learner

'sem ēkērkv kakke ehokpe hvrpe tafv ocē
'simi·kí·łka ká·kki ihókpi háłpi tá·fa ó·ci·
would sometimes be given the authority to go about with the skin of a raven's breast,

estorofvkvtēn enokwvn vpvllayet vrvrēn yekcetv emhoyvtēt este sasvtēs.
istolófakáti·n inókwan apálla·yít ałáli·n yikcitá imhoyáti·t ísti sa·satí·s
skinned with the feathers on, wrapped around the neck as a sign [he was being taught].

Mvt <u>hopayvke lopockus-mahat</u> omakvtēs.
mat hopa·yakí lopockosmá·ha·t oma·katí·s
Those were <u>hopayvke lopockus-mahat</u> ['very little far-aways'].

Monkv mvt hiyome este cokv emvhahoyē kerretv respoyat
móŋka mat hayyô·mi ísti có·ka imahá·ho·yí· kiłlitá líspo·yâ·t
So that was much the same as now; when a person finishes a course,

eskērkv cokv emakhoyat omē tatēs.
iskí·łka có·ka (?) imákho·yâ·t ó·mi· tá·ti·s.
he is given a certificate as a sign [of completion].

'Le-homahtvke kihocat este enwiketvt omakvtēs. Mvt etvlwv ehomvn svpaklet
'lihomahtakí kéyho·câ·t ísti inweykitát oma·katí·s mat itálwa (?) ihóman sapâ·klit
Those called le-homahtvke were the people's officers. They stood before the tribe

herkv opunahoyvlket omakvranen, este hoporrenvke
hílka opona·ho·yâlkit[463] omâ·kała·nín ísti hopołłináki
and were the peace speakers, intelligent people

em etvlwv tvsekvyv sulkat vnokeckv emocvkēt. Etvlwv em etenrvwv
imitálwa tasikayá sólka·t anokícka imo·caki·t[464] itálwa imitînlawa
having love for their many tribal citizens. Between tribal towns

vkerrickv hervkekis kvwapken, etenrvpkv tis rakken ayof, horre tis hakē ohcēs.
akiłłéycka hiłákikeys kawa·pkín itinłápkateys la·kkín a·yô·f hółliteys ha·kí· óhci·s
bad thoughts may arise, and when strife became widespread, war might start.

Mēkkvke komakat etvlwv vcayēckv vrahkusē
mi·kkakí kó·ma·kâ·t itálwa (?) aca·yi·cka (?) ała·ⁿhkosi·
With the thought of keeping the town secure,

vfvnnakvlke enwiketv hayet omhoyvtēs.
afanna·kâlki inweykitá ha·yít ómho·yatí·s
the chiefs appointed people to be vfvnnakvlke ['scouts'].

Monkv estvmvn vkerrickv etenrvpkusē kvwapkvcoken pohaken omat
móŋka ístaman akiłłéycka itinłápkosi· kawa·pkacókin[465] poha·kín o·mâ·t
So whenever they heard of strife,

vpēyet mv etenrvpkv ocat, em etenrvwvn svpaklet herkv opunvkvn opunahoyet fullvtēs.
api·yít ma itinłápka o·câ·t imitînlawan sapâ·klit hílka oponakán opona·hŏ·ⁿyit follatí·s
they would go where the trouble was and go among them and talk peace.

Vculakusat, hoktvlvke, hopuetak-lopocke etolanofv erpvlvthohyen,
acolă·ⁿkosa·t hoktaláki hopoyta·klopócki itola·nó·fa iłpalathóhyin
Very elderly men, old ladies, and small children will be forced into the forest,

hopuetake em papvkē naket sekon hvkahēcen,
hopoytá·ki ímpa·pakí· nà·kit síkon haka·hĭ·ⁿcin
the children might cry without food,

hoktvlvke tis etoroposwv etorofvn ohfihhonen,
hoktalákiteys itołopóswa itoló·fan ohféyhho·nín
the old women will have tears streaming down their faces;

etolanofvn sehokē netta ocekarē vrahkvn
itola·nó·fan siho·kí· nittá· ó·ciká·li· ałáhkan
so that there would never be a day when they would be forced into the forest,

herkv hayvlket estofis sehokvranēn, este honvntake vkerrickv herakē vnokecvko ocvkēn,
híłka ha·yâlkit istô·feys sihó·kała·ni·n[i] isti honantá·ki akilléycka hiłă·ⁿki· anokíckaw o·cakí·n
peace makers would always be at work, men with good thoughts and love too.

etvlwv em vfvnnakvlke enwiketv hahoyvtē
itálwa (?) imafanna·kâlki inweykitá ha·hoyáti·
They were appointed to look out for the tribal towns

estvlken 'le-homahtvke kicet okhoyvtēs, vculvket makvnts.
istâlkin 'lihomahtakí keycít ókho·yatí·s acolakít ma·kánc.
and were called 'le-homahtvke, the old ones used to say.

'Mvpvkvlke kihocateu este em etvlwv vrahkv enwiketvt omakvtēs.
'mapakâlki kéyho·câ·tiw ísti imitálwa (?) ałáhka (?) inweykitát oma·katí·s.
Those called 'mvpvkvlke ['joiners'] were also officers for the people of the tribal town.

Etvllopocke omvlkvt nvkvftvrēn huehhokēt omen, mv nvkvfhotan estvpakvranan
itallopócki omálkat nakáftáłi·n hóyhho·kí·t ô·min ma nakáfho·tâ·n istapâ·kala·nâ·n
All the small towns were called to meet, and they were appointed to attend ['join']

---

[i] *'lihomahtakí* has charge of relations with other towns and other nations. Has charge of making peace between nations. Sort of peacemakers.

wiketv hayet omhoyvtēs. Etvlwv estont enliken aret omat onayet,
weykitá ha·yít ómho·yatí·s itálwa istónt inlêykin a·lít o·mâ·t ona·yít
those meetings. They reported on how their own town was doing,

naket estomvrēn eyacēt etvlwv enliket omateu onayet,
nâ·kit istó·máli·n iyá·ci·t itálwa inlêykit o·mâ·tiw ona·yít
they also reported on the needs of their town,

tvllopocke vpvltake nake em eyackv estomvkēt lomlohet omateu kērret,
tallopócki apaltá·ki nâ·ki imiyá·cka isto·makí·t lomlô·hit o·mâ·tiw ki·łłít
and they also should know of the needs of other small towns and how they were doing,

este nake estenhorkopvtē sasvten omateu ohfaccat
ísti (?) nâ·ki (?) istinhółko·patí· sa·satín o·mâ·tiw óhfa·ccâ·t
and if there were people who had been stealing and had been found guilty,

rokafet vhakv vfastet vpokvranet huehketv hayet omakvtēs.
loka·fít ahá·ka afa·stít apó·kała·nít hoyhkitá ha·yít oma·katí·s
they were whipped, and a meeting was called so they could carry out the law.

Monkv este esrokafhoyat, vfoswv hvmkē vlkēn etvlwv vrahrvkvt esvntot svwahet,
môŋka ísti (?) isłoká·fho·yâ·t afó·swa hámki· álki·n itálwa ałahłakát isántot sáwa·hít
So to lash people with, they distributed one cane [or "switch'] each to the different towns,

em etvlwvn empunayat mv vfoswvn ēset,
imitálwan ímpona·yâ·t ma afó·swan î·sit
and they spoke to their own towns and held the switch [saying,]

"Nake ocephoyat estem vyopkusē ahretskvs.
nâ·ki o·ciphô·ya·t istimayô·pkosi· áhłíckas
"Don't go sneaking around in search of other people's possessions.

Este-mvnette toyetskat ēyvcayēcet,
istimanítti tô·yícka·t i·yaca·yî·cit
You young people take care of yourselves:

nake cenake toko ohyopket vyomockusan hueret aretskat,
nâ·ki (?) cinâ·ki (?) tó·ko· óhyo·pkit⁴⁶⁶ ayomóckosa·n hoylít a·łícka·t
when you sneak around things that don't belong to you and lurk in the dark

vfoswv heyv omēt mahet cenhueren aret ometskvrēs.
afó·swa hiyá ó·mi·t ma·hít cinhôyłin a·lít omíckáli·s
you'll have a cane just like this waiting for you.

Yopkusēt cenake tokon nake ehsvtet hueretskat,
yó·pkosi·t cinâ·ki tó·ko·n nâ·ki íhsatit hôyłícka·t
When you sneak around and take something that doesn't belong to you,

vfoswv yv omat este-honvnwv esakpv enhonnē vpvkēt ceran ohwvkiket omekon omat,
afó·swa ya ô·ma·t istihonánwa isákpa inhonni· apáki·t cilá·n ohwakêykit omikon o·mâ·t
if a cane like this with the weight of a man's arm doesn't lie on your back,

cehvsvtkvrē tokon ēhuerihcetskēs.
cihasátkáli· tó·ko·n i·hoyłéyhcícki·s
you may put yourself in a position where your reputation cannot be cleansed.

Yv vfoswvt este hvsvtecvtēt wakket os" maket, etvlwv empunayet omvtēs.
ya afó·swat ísti hasaticáti·t wâ·kkit ó·ⁿs ma·kít itálwa impóna·yít o·matí·s
This cane lying here has cleansed others," he said and told [this] to his tribal town.

Nake mv omvkē makē em etvlwv vrahkv arvranē wiketv hahoyvtē este sasatet
nâ·ki ma o·makí· ma·kí· imitálwa[467] *(?) ałáhka á·lala·ní· weykitá ha·hoyáti· ísti sâ·sa·tit*
Those appointed to go before their tribal town informing them about such things

'mvpvkvlketot omvtēs.
'mapakâlkitot o·matí·s.
were 'mvpvkvlke ['joiners'].

The Stars (Hvlwē nake heckē ocakat este-cate-vculvke enhocefhueckv)[i]

J. Hill (Hill IV:1–3; Haas XXI:1–27)

Vholocē hvlwē fullat uehvtkv enhēfkēt omēs makakvnts, vholocē omusē tis
aholocí· hálwi· follâ·t oyhátka ínhi·fki·t ô·mi·s má·ka·kánc aholocí· ô·mosi·teys
Clouds way up high are ocean vapor, they used to say, somewhat like clouds

---

[i] Title: *hálwi· nâ·ki hícki· o·câ·ka·t isticá·ti acolakí inhocifhóycka* 'Old-Time Indians' names for things visible on high'.

monkat ēkkocē omusē tis. Sutv ceskvn asvpaklen hēcen omat,
móŋka·t i·kkocí·[468] *ô·mosi·teys sotá cískan a·sapâ·klin hica·kín*[469] *o·mâ·t*
or somewhat like smoke. If they saw them on the horizon like columns,

"Hvset uewvn acawet omēs. Oskvrēs" makakvnts, meskēt on omat.
hasít óywan á·ca·wít o·mí·s óskáli·s má·ka·kánc miskí·t ò·n o·mâ·t
they would say, "The sun is drawing water. It will rain," if it was summer.

Hvtvm rvfot on omat, "Kvstemvranet omēs" makakvnts.
hatâm ɬafót ô·n o·mâ·t kastimáɬa·nít[470] *o·mi·s má·ka·kánc.*
During winter they used to say, "It's going to get cold."

Momet 'holocē tat atet oskvranē hēret os komhoyof,
mo·mít 'holocí·ta·t a·tít óskaɬa·ní· hī·ⁿɬit ó·ⁿs komhô·yo·f
When the clouds come and they think it is surely going to rain

oskekot 'holocē-cate hahket somkēpē oketv vnvcomen omat,
óskikot 'holoci·cá·ti háhkit sómki·pí· okíta anáco·min o·mâ·t
but doesn't, and the clouds become red and disappear several times,

"Em pofhokvten omēs" 'holocē-catē hakē oskeko somkat makakvnts.
impo·fhò·katin[471] *o·mi·s 'holoci·cá·ti· ha·ki· óskiko· somkâ·t má·ka·kánc.*
it was said, "Medicine had been blown,"[472] when the clouds turned red and disappeared.

Em pofkē makat oskē honnē tis vlvkvranēt omē on hēcat
ímpo·fkí·[i] *ma·kâ·t oskí· hónni·teys alákaɬa·ní·t ô·mi· ô·n hi·cá·t*
Blowing means when someone saw that heavy rain might be coming,

estet mv 'holocē-lvste 'semēhonecketvn em penkalof,
ístit maʔ 'holoci·lásti 'simi·honickitán impiŋka·lô·f
when someone was afraid of awesome black clouds

fekhonnickvn komēt enyvhiket 'holocē atat vnrvpēn
fikhonnéyckan kó·mi·t inyáheykít 'holoci· a·tâ·t anɬapí·n
and wanting to stop it, he would sing against the oncoming clouds:

_____

[i] Or: *impó·fho·kí·.*

"Vpofket este hueret oskē fekhonnicēs" maket okakvnts.
apoꞏfkít ísti hoylít[473] *oskíꞏ fikhónneyciꞏs maꞏkít okaꞏkánc*
"A person who stands blowing at it [with a reed] can stop the rain," they used to say.

Hofonof oskē em pofkvlke este sulkē tatēs, honvntaketot, hoktvketo estomis.
hofõꞏnoꞏf oskíꞏ impoꞏfkâlki ísti sólkiꞏ táꞏtiꞏs honantáꞏkitot hoktakíto[474] *istõꞏmeys*
A long time ago there were many rain blowers, men and even women.

Oskē fekhonnickv yvhiketvn kerreko estomis estet oskē, hotvlē-rakko 'tepakat em penkalat,
oskíꞏ fikhonnéycka yaheykitán kílliko ꞏ istõꞏmeys ístit oskíꞏ hotaliꞏłákko 'tipâꞏkaꞏt impíŋkaꞏlâꞏt
When those who did not know the song to stop the rain were afraid of rain and tornadoes,

pocus-leskvn enfvskēt
pocoslískan infaskíꞏt
they would leave an old ax blade stuck in the ground

vholocē-lvste atat ohhecēn 'mvpe escakhēn enhuericakēt omvnts.
aholociꞏlásti aꞏtâꞏt[i] *ohhiciꞏn mápi iscákhiꞏn inhoyléycaꞏkíꞏt oꞏmánc*
with the handle upright, facing the direction from which the black cloud was coming.

Momēcat este sasēs, mucvnettv. Mv pocus-leskvt vholocēn 'tetahcen
momiꞏcâꞏt ísti sâꞏsiꞏs mocanítta ma(?) pocoslískat aholocíꞏn 'titáhcin
There are people who still do that today. The old ax cuts the cloud in half,

'tekvpahket oskekot somkēpēs maket omakvnts.
'tikapáhkit óskikot sómkiꞏpíꞏs maꞏkít omaꞏkánc.
and it splits; it doesn't rain, it disappears, it's said.

Oskē atat vlvkeko fekhonnicetv okcvnwvn nvcomusis totkvn takpvlatvken omat
oskíꞏ aꞏtâꞏt alákikoꞏ fikhonneycitá okcánwan nacŏⁿmoseys tóꞏtkan tákpalaꞏtakin oꞏmâꞏt
When rain is coming, to stop it before it arrives, pour a small amount of salt in the fire,

oskekot somkēs makateu sasēs.
óskikot somkiꞏs maꞏkâꞏtiw sâꞏsiꞏs
and it doesn't rain and goes away, some say.

---

[i] Or: *aꞏtâꞏn.*

Momen vculvke nake makat vkvsvmvyēt arvyvtēt onkv
mo·mín acolakí nâ·ki ma·kâ·t akasamáyi·t a·łayáti·t ôŋka
Now I went about believing the things the old ones said,

vhvmkv nerē hvmken ohhvyvtkvranēt 'tvlofv vnakvn puhvpo hayēt
ahámka nilí· hámkin ohhayátkała·ní·t 'taló·fa aná·kan pohapó· hâ·yi·t
so one time we were going to spend the night in a camp that we had made near town;

yafkē hvse-vkērkv ostat mahen welakeyof,
ya·fkí· hasiʔaki·łka ô·sta·t mâ·hin wila·kiyô·f[475]
in the evening about four o'clock, as we [two of us] went about,

vholocē-lvstet honerv fvccvn akvwvpiket omat, pvfnēt ahvlwēcen hēcet omeyis,
aholoci·lástit honiła fáccan a·kawapêykit o·mâ·t páfni·t a·hálwi·cín hî·cit[476] *o·miyêys*
a black cloud rose up from the north, and we could see it was quickly approaching,

estohmet oskē em vrvnakepvkē tayat vwolē naket sekon
istóhmit[477] *oskí· imałana·kipáki· tâ·ya·t awóli· nâ·kit síkon*
but there was no place to take shelter as there was nothing near;

oskē tat honnēt atet omat kērrēt fekhoniyet sehokēn;
oskí·ta·t hónni·t a·tít o·mâ·t kî·łłi·t fikhonêyyit sihô·ki·n
we knew that heavy rain was coming, so we stopped and just stood there;

hoktē 'tepakeyvtē eslafkvn vm pohen
hoktí· 'tipâ·kiyati· islá·fkan ámpo·hín
the lady that was with me asked me for a knife;

a-ehmin ehset yvkapet ayet vhopakv pale-ostat mahen ahyet
a·ʔíhmeyn íhsit yaka·pít a·yít ahopá·ka pa·liʔô·sta·t mâ·hin áhyit
I handed it to her, she took it and walked about forty yards away,

eto rakkēt hueren pvlhvmken erhuyiret ahueren
itó· łákki·t hôyłin palhámkin iłhoyêyłit a·hôyłin
and she was standing on the other side of where a large tree stood

hvse-vkērkuce palehokkolat mahe tis omvtēs. Osketv vlicēcet omat
hasiʔaki·łkocí pa·lihokkô·la·t[478] *mâ·hiteys o·matí·s oskitá aleycî·cit o·mâ·t*
for about twenty minutes. It started raining,

vholocē tat 'tekvpahket hvsossv-fvccvn ayen, hvsaklatkv fvccvo ayen,
aholocí·ta·t 'tikapáhkit haso·ssafáccan a·yín hasaklá·tka fáccaw a·yín
and the cloud parted, [one part] went east, and [one part] went west;

oskat estǫmusat pohken essomhokehpen, ra-atet 'rvlahket
oskâ·t istŏ·ⁿmosa·t pô·hkin[479] issomhokíhpin ła·ʔâ·tit 'laláhkit
the rain let up, and both [clouds] disappeared, and she came back and said,

"Oskē tat 'setekvpahket essomhokepeko" makemvts.
oskí·ta·t 'sitikapáhkit issomhokípiko·^ ma·kimác
"The rain parted and disappeared."

Ohrolopē pale-cahkēpē cahkepohkakat mahe tis omēs.
ohłolopí· pá·li cahkî·pi· cahkipohkâ·ka·t má·hiteys ô·mi·s
It might have been about fifty-five years ago.

Mvt "oskē sentvcketv" maketv cvnhonricusat vm ocvtēt os. Hofonē haken
mat oskí· sintackitá ma·kitá canhónłeycosá·t amo·catí·t ô·ⁿs hofóni· hâ·kin
It was then that I truly believed that expression, "to stop the rain." A long time later

em pohvyan vm onvyekvntvs, oskē sentacket, sentvckekatē.
impo·hayâ·n amonayíkantás oski· sínta·ckit sintáckiká·ti·
I asked her, and she wouldn't tell me whether she had stopped the rain or not.

Momen hvtvm oskē somkat,
mo·mín hatâm oskí· somkâ·t
And again, when rain disappears,

"Echus-elēcvt likan oskē asohhvtekot omēs" makakvnts.
ichosili·cat lêyka·n oski· a·sohhatíkot o·mi·s má·ka·kánc
they used to say, "Where a child-killer lives, it will not storm."

Nettahvse kvlaksē haket, monkat heckeko haken yomockat
nitta·hasí kaláksi· ha·kít mónka·t híckiko· ha·kín yomo·ckâ·t
When the sun becomes crescent shaped, or when it becomes invisible and it gets dark,

sopaktv-rakkot loken omēs, nerēhvseu matvpomē haket.
sopa·ktałákkot lo·kín[480] o·mí·s nili·hasíw ma·tapó·mi· ha·kít[481]
a big toad has swallowed it, and the moon is like that too, they say.

Hvrēssē vholocē omē sopakhvtkē vfolotkusē tis ocat,
hałi·ssí· aholocí· ó·mi· sopakhátki· afolótkosi·teys o·câ·t
When the moon has a whitish cloud-like circle around it,

"Oskvranen hvset ehuten hayet omēs" maket;
óskała·nín hasít ihótin ha·yít o·mi·s ma·kít
they say, "It's going to rain, and the moon is making itself a shelter."

hvse ehute ofvn 'kolaswvt heckvkēt on omat,
hasí ihóti ó·fan 'kolá·swat hickakí·t ô·n o·mâ·t
And if stars can be seen within the circle of the moon's shelter,

oskekon netta yvfyakēs: 'kolaswv hvmkat netta hvmkan vrahkvt omēs.
óskikon nittá· yáfya·kí·s 'kolá·swa hámka·t nittá· hámka·n ałáhkat ô·mi·s
it will not rain for several days: each star stands for one day.

Momen "Hvrēssē vnakusē 'kolaswv likan hvse ehiwvt omēs" maket okvnts.
mo·mín hałi·ssí· anǎⁿkosi· 'kolá·swa leykâ·n hasí (?) ihéywat ô·mi·s ma·kít o·kánc
And it was said, "The star nearest to the moon is the moon's wife."

'Kolaswv hokkolē etenakuecusē kakan Wotko-Turwvn hocēfet,
'kolá·swa hokkô·li· itinǎⁿkôycosi·[482] ka·kâ·n wo·tkotółwan hoci·fit
The two stars sitting right close together were called Raccoon's Eyes,

honerv fvccv 'kolaswv likan 'Kolas-Vyekon hocēfet;
honíła (?) fácca (?) 'kolá·swa leykâ·n 'kola·sʔayíkon hoci·fit
and the star toward the north was called the Star-Doesn't-Go;

hvyatkof a-ossē 'kolaswv likan 'Kolas-Rakkon hocēfet, Hvyvtēcv hocēfet,
haya·tkô·f á·ʔo·ssi· 'kolá·swa leykâ·n 'kola·słákkon hoci·fit hayatí·ca hoci·fit
the star that comes out at daybreak was called the Big Star or Morning Star,

momen 'kolaswv tuccenē etenakuecē vpokan 'Kolas-Senēcvn hocēfet,
mo·mín 'kolá·swa toccini·[483] itina·kóyci· apo·kâ·n[484] 'kola·ssini·can hoci·fit
and the three stars sitting near each other were called the Stretched Stars,

Ue-Sakcvokv tis 'Kolas-Perro tis kicakēt omvnts.
oysakcáwkateys[485] 'kola·spíłłoteys kéyca·kí·t o·mánc
and there was what they called the Water Dipper, or the Star Boat.

'Kolaswv kolvpake etenakusē vpokan 'Kolas-Coklofkvn kicet,
'kolá·swa kolapá·ki itinà·ⁿkosi· apo·kâ·n[486] *'kola·scokló·fkan*[487] *keycit*
The seven stars that sit really close to each other were called <u>Kolas-Coklofkv</u>.

mv 'kolaswv kolvpakat 'tvlvlvkēt hērusēn vpokēt omvtē tat,
ma 'kolá·swa kolapâ·ka·t 'talalakí·t hĭ·ⁿlosi·n[488] *apó·ki·t o·matí·ta·t*
Those seven stars were once neatly lined up.

nokosen entohket opelof-rakkon sakfullet,
nokósin ínto·hkít opilo·flákkon sákfollít
They went driving a bear in a big swamp

akkehosahket fullet 'yvtelokat estomis vpokvtēt on omēs.
akkihosáhkit follít yátilo·kâ·t[489] *istô·meys apo·katí·t ô·n o·mí·s*
and forgot their way and sat scattered about.

Momet vtotketvo enhorrvkēt ont tasahcof,
mo·mít atotkitáw inhołłakí·t ônt tá·sa·hcô·f
And they are too lazy to work, and in the spring

somēcvtet nak lokcē hakakofvn eryicēt omēs makakvnts.
somî·catit[490] *nâ·k lókci· há·ka·kô·fan ilyeycí·t ô·mi·s má·ka·kánc*
they disappear but return when the fruit ripens, they used to say.

'Kolaswv tis wecatiyet totkv ont cvpkē hakē somkan
'kolá·swateys wica·têyyit tó·tka ônt cápki· ha·kí· somkâ·n
When a star sparks like fire and becomes long and disappears,

'kolaswvt aholanet omēs kicakvnts.
'kolá·swat á·hola·nit o·mí·s kéyca·kánc
they used to say the star is defecating in this direction.

'Kolaswv wecattat ētvpomēt totkv ont hopvyēn ayet ersomkat
'kolá·swa wica·ttâ·t i·tapó·mi·t tó·tka ônt hopáyi·n a·yit íłsomkâ·t
Similar to the star that sparked, when [a star] goes out of sight a long distance like fire

tenētkē okēt pohkēt ocan "Mēkko-rakkot latket okēs" makakēt omvnts.
tini·tkí· ô·ki·t po·hkí·t o·câ·n mi·kkołákkot la·tkít o·ki·s má·ka·kí·t o·mánc
and what sounds like thunder is heard, they used to say, "The big king has fallen down."

Vholocē omusē cutkusē sutv 'tewvlvpkē wakkan,
aholoci· ó·mosi· cótkosi· sotá 'tiwalápki· wa·kkâ·n[491]
That which looks like a small cloud lying across the sky [i.e., the Milky Way]

"Este-ēlv ennene" monkat "Puyvfekcvlke ennene omēs" kicakvnts.
isti?í·la inniní moŋkâ·t poyafikcâlki inniní ô·mi·s kéyca·kánc
used to be called the "Path of the Dead" or the "Path of the Spirits."

Vtokyehattē vtokfenētkē vtoyehattē tenētkē 'tepakat
atókyiha·ttí· atókfini·tki· atóyiha·ttí·[492] *tini·tki· 'tipâ·ka·t*
Lightning that flashes, lightning and thunder together

naket estont okēs makakvtētis omēs. Momis mvtan kerraks.
nâ·kit ístónt o·kí·s má·ka·katí·teys o·mi·s mô·meys máta·n kíłłaks
mean something is happening, it was probably said. But I don't know that.

Ēkvnv ohfulleyat elecv encokele ocēn etohlikēt omēs.
i·kaná óhfolliyâ·t ilíca incokíli ó·ci·n itohléyki·t ô·mi·s
There are pillars underneath this earth we walk on, and the earth is sitting on them.

Mv cokele tat osa-rakkot omēs makēt vculvke 'punvyēcaken pohvyvntvs.
ma (?) cokílita·t osa·łákkot ô·mi·s ma·kí·t acolakí 'ponayí·ca·kín po·hayántas.
Those posts are great pokeweeds, I heard the old men tell.

Prophets

J. Hill (Hill II:39; Haas XVIII:155–161)

Owalv, kērrv emvhahoyvtē tokot, emmonkv esheckvtēt omēs.
owá·la ki·łła[i] *imaha·hoyáti· tó·ko·t immóŋka*[493] *ishíckati·t ô·mi·s*
A prophet [owalv] or knower [kērrv] was not taught by anyone; he was born with the gift.

Estuce hēckat, poktvt heckvkvtēt on omat,
istocí hi·ckâ·t póktat hickakáti·t[494] *ô·n o·mâ·t*
When a baby is born, if twins are born,

---

[i] *owá·la*, same as *kí·łła*.

yopv heckvtēt kērrv, owalv hakēt omēs, vculof.

yópa (?) híckati·t kí·łla owá·la ha·ki·t ô·mi·s, aco·lô·f.

the one born last becomes a knower or prophet when older.

Este enokkan enokketv estomēt monkat naket enokkicet omat onayēt omēs.

ísti ino·kkâ·n inokkitá istó·mi·t móŋka·t nâ·kit inokkéycit o·mâ·t ona·yí·t ô·mi·s

He can tell a sick person what his illness was or what is making him sick.

Este-cat-vculvke em maketv enokketv enhocefhokv hiyomvkēt omēs:

istica·tacolakí imma·kitá inokkitá inhocifhoká hayyo·makí·t ô·mi·s

These are the names the old Indian men had for the sicknesses:

Efv-vlicv, sokhvhatk-vlicv, cufe-vlicv, eco-vlicv, hvse-vlicv, cetto, ponvttv-lvste,

ifaaléyca sokhaha·tkaléyca cofialéyca icoaléyca hasialéyca cítto ponattalásti

Dog-cause, opossum-cause, rabbit-cause, deer-cause, sun-cause, snake, black-animal [bear],

oskentacv, nake 'remētv sulkēt omēs, enokketv hocefhokv tat.

o·skintá·ca nâ·ki 'limí·ta sólki·t ô·mi·s inokkitá hocifhokáta·t

rainbow, and there are many other names for sicknesses.

Estet enokiken heleswv enhahoyan, cvfekneko tayen omat,

ístit inokêykin 'hilíswa inhá·ho·yâ·n cafíkniko· tâ·yin o·mâ·t

When someone got sick and medicine was made for him, if he could not get well,

mv este enokkat accvtēn nake cutkusē tis sahyet

ma (?) ísti inókka·t a·ccati·n nâ·ki cótkosi·teys sáhyit

even just a tiny piece of clothing that the sick person wore was taken

mv kērrvn hecihocof, naket enokkicētot os maken omat,

ma (?) kí·łlan hicéyho·cô·f nâ·kit inokkéyci·tót ó·^{n}s ma·kín o·mâ·t

and shown to the knower, and if he says what is causing the illness,

mv vrahkusēn heleswv enhahoyen omat, mv este cvfēknēt omēs.

ma (?) ałă·^{n}hkosi·n 'hilíswa inhá·ho·yín o·mâ·t ma (?) ísti cafi·kní·t ô·mi·s

then medicine is made just for that, and the person gets well.

Este enokkat vrahkvn este sulkemahat

ísti (?) ino·kkâ·t ałáhkan ísti solkimâ·ha·t

Many people very often go to the knower

monkat oketv etewelēmahat kērrv vfulhoyēt omēs.
móŋka·t okíta (?) itiwili·mâ·ha·t ki·ƚƚa afólho·yí·t ô·mi·s
for an ill person and often make several trips.

Momen nake kerretv eyacet enpohohen omat onayēt omen,
mo·mín nâ·ki kiƚƚitá iya·cít[495] *inpóho·hín o·mâ·t ona·yí·t ô·min*
And they ask, wanting to know, and he tells them,

momen este-cate heles-hayv este enokkat hēcat, monkv enokketv ohhonvkv pohat,
mo·mín isticá·ti 'hilishá·ya ísti (?) inókka·t hi·câ·t móŋka inokkitá ohhonáka po·hâ·t[496]
and the Indian medicine man looks at a sick person, and when he hears the symptoms,

naket enokkicet omat hēcat enkerkē omēt, heleswv hayēt omēs.
nâ·kit inokkèycit o·mâ·t hi·câ·t inkíƚki· ó·mi·t 'hilíswa ha·yí·t ô·mi·s.
he can see what has made the person sick and makes the medicine.

Mv poktv yopv hēckvtē <u>fvccv-seko</u> kihocēt omēs.
ma (?) pókta yópa[497] *hi·ckatí· faccasíko· kéyho·cí·t ô·mi·s*
That twin that is born last is called <u>fvccv-seko</u> ['without truth'].

Mvt owalv haket omēs.
mat owá·la ha·kít o·mi·s
That one becomes a prophet [<u>owalv</u>].

Men and Women of Olden Times (Vculvke momet Hoktvlvke)[i, 498]

J. Hill (XXI:167–189)

Hiyomē cemvnēttē hueretskat ēyvcąyēcetskvrēs. Estit ececayehcekos.
hayyô·mi· cimanĭ·ⁿtti· hôylícka·t i·yacǎ·ⁿyi·cíckáli·s istêyt icica·yihciko·s
You who are now young, take care of yourself. No one will take care of you.

Hopuewusē hueretskof tawvn
hopóywosi· hôylícko·f ta·wán
When you were a little child,

---

ceckvlke nake tis ennokkihcēs monkat ēyennokkihcēs komatet,
cickálki ná·kiteys innokkéyhci·s moŋkâ·t i·yinnokkéyhci·s ko·mâ·tit
your parents, thinking something might harm you or that you might harm yourself,

setenhvlatet escewelakvnkis,
'sitinhalâ·tit isciwíla·káŋkeys
led you about between them holding you by the hand,

hiyomat cēmet ēyem vfvnnakvranetskē nettvn rosset hueretskekv,
hayyò·ma·t cí·mit i·yimafanná·kała·nícki· níttan lò·ssit hôylíckika
but now the day has come when you will stand up and look out for yourself;

Ohfvnkv nettv sulkē cemvtē tis ohmvrēs.
ohfánka nítta sólki· cimáti·teys óhmáli·s
it may be that the One Over All has given you many days.

Etvlwv encukelet huerepvranetskis omis kerretskekon estit keriyekos.
itálwa incokílit hoylipáła·níckeys ô·meys kíłłickikon istêyt kiłêyyiko·s
It may be that you will stand as the pillar of the nation, but you don't know, no one knows.

Cem ēyvkerrickvn, cem vretvn, cem opunvkvn cem vtetēhuecen huervranetskēt omekv,
cimi·yakilléyckan cimalitán cimoponákan cimatiti·hôycin hôylała·nícki·t ô·mika
Your personal thoughts, your actions, your language, He who gave you these will watch

cēmeu matan vketēcet hueretskvrēs.
cí·miw ma·tá·n akiti·cit hóylíckáli·s
as you live your life, and you too must watch the same things.

Este enfulletv cvpevkē tvhopkvkē fullēpat vhonkvtkē ahretskvs.
ísti iɲfollitá capcaki· tahopkakí· fólli·pâ·t ahoŋkátki· áhlickas
Do not be numbered among those whose ways are [long and agile??].

Opunvkv holwahokē tis ecohwvkechohyvrēs.
oponaká holwa·hokí·teys icohwakichóhyáli·s
Bad gossip will be laid on you.

Monkv "Opunvkv holwvkusēt cvcokwv osset omekarēs" kometskvrēs.
môŋka oponaká holwakósi·t cacókwa o·ssít omíká·łi·s kô·míckáli·s
Therefore you must think, "Bad words will not come out of my mouth."

Vnatoketv, nanvk-oketv, punvkvleckv, escoknahēt huyiretskvs.
ana·tokíta nâ·nakokitá 'ponakalícka iscokná·hi·t hoyêylíckas
Joking, gossip, blasphemy, do not talk idly.

Hoktạlusēt omet punvkvleckv nanvk-oketv escohcọket
hoktă·ⁿlosi·t ô·mit 'ponakalícka nâ·nakokitá íscohcŏ·ⁿkit
Like a whiny old woman spreading rumors, gossip, and talking nonsense,

cuko lihk-omvlkvn eshoyạnis maket
cokó layhkomálkan ishoyă·ⁿneys mâ·kit
going from one house to another,

nettv sulkēn svrvranēt ohkekos komet em apohihocekon eshoyạnet okvnts.
nítta sólki·n sáłała·ni·t óhkiko·s kô·mit ima·poheyhocikon íshoyă·ⁿnit o·kánc
they think she can't go on a long time, so no one listens as she goes about.

Momis este-honvnwv ena yekcē huerē em opunvkv hoktvlusē em punvkv onkot omēs.
mo·mêys istihonánwa iná· yíkci· hóyli· imoponáka hoktalósi· imponáka óŋko·t ô·mi·s
However, a strong-bodied man does not talk like an old woman.

Mohmet cehutvlke ehute ocē opokvkēpat enfettvn roret aretskat
móhmit cihotâlki ihóti ó·ci· opo·kakî·pa·t infíttan ło·lít a·lícka·t
Then when you go into the yards of those of your friends who own homes and live in them,

cokwakkvlke em ohhompetv tvlkusēn vkerricet aret ohmetskvs.
cokwakkâlki imohhompitá tálkosi·n akiłłeycít a·lít ohmíckas
do not go thinking only of your brother-in-law's table.

Cehutet onkv eto taluce kackusis karomet
cihótit ôŋka itó ta·locí kâ·ckoseys ka·lô·mit[499]
It is your house, so carry even a small, dried broken branch on your shoulder,

fettv resvlaket hueretskat cem afvchokēn vretskvrēs.
fítta łísala·kít hôylícka·t cima·fachokí·n ałíckáli·s
when returning to your yard, and they'll be pleased with you.

Mohmet estvn ayetskvtē rvlahkusēs kont,
móhmit ístan a·yíckati· 'łaláhkosi·s kônt
When you go somewhere and when they think you may return soon,

cennenehēcet, taklike secekerricet, cenlihocen roretskat,
cinninihî·cit takléyki 'sicikiɬêycit cinleyhô·cin ɬo·lícka·t
they will look for you, and save bread for you, and when you get there,

"Hompepvs" cekihocen hompet fettv estenhuerēpetskvrēs.
hompipás cikéyho·cín hompít fitta istinhoyɬí·píckáli·s
they will say to you "Please eat," and you will always eat like this within your own place.

Momis heromkv ǫcēsekot cehutvlke enfettv hueret aretsken omat,
mo·mays hiɬómka ǒ·ⁿci·siko·t cihotâlki infítta hoyɬít a·lickin o·mâ·t
But if you are not thoughtful within your family's yard,

este estomēckv tokat cekicet cem enherhoyeko hahken
ísti istomí·cka tó·ka·t cikeycít[500] ciminhiɬhoyíko· háhkin
they'll say, "That person is worthless," and will not like you,

fettvtēkē hueretskof, "Likepvs" cekicekot
fittatí·ki· hôylícko·f leykipás cikéycikot[501]
and when you come to the edge of the yard, they will not say, "Come and sit,"

cuko akhotiyet sumecephohyen,
cokó akhotêyyit[502] somiciphóhyin
they will close up the house, and they will disappear;

elawusēt potoket eto-ceskvn liketskis nettv ohcēs.
ilǎ·ⁿwosi·t potô·kit[503] itocískan lêykíckeys nítta óhci·s
hungry, head bowed, you might sit against a tree stump one day.

Monkv herǫmuset hueretskat, taklike kvlkusat acenwihoyen hompet vretskvrēs.
môŋka hiɬǒ·ⁿmosit hoyɬícka·t takléyki kálkosa·t a·cinwéyho·yin hompít alíckáli·s
So be considerate: a small piece of bread will be shared with you, and you will eat.

Mohmen cennettv vyētatēton vcǫlusē cehahkē hueretskof,
móhmin cinnítta ayi·tá·ti·ton[504] acǒ·ⁿlosi· ciháhki· hôylícko·f
Then as your days advance [?], when you grow very old,

escem ētekkekv cenhvlatet escefulhoyat,
iscimi·tikkiká cinhalâ·tit iscifólho·yâ·t
when they hold your cane and take you about,

cemvnettē heromē aretskvtē vrahkvn omhoyvrēs.
cimanítti· hilómi· a·líckati· ałáhkan omhoyáli·s
it will be because you were kind in your youth.

Mohmen cerkvlke kaken cem etecakketv vpaketskof,
móhmin cilkâlki kâ·kin cimiticakkitá apâ·kícko·f
When your parents were here and you were with your brothers,

nake cem vhḙrvrēn vrahkvn cem punvyakat, em ēcayē ahretskvs.
nâ·ki cimahi·ⁿłałi·n ałáhkan cimponáya·kâ·t imi·cá·yi· áhłíckas
they talked to you out of concern for your own good: do not be fretful.

Cuko vhopvniken fettv vsakwē tayē onkot liken
cokó ahopanâykin fítta asákwi· tâ·yi· óŋkot lêykin
It seemed the house could never be broken down and the yard overgrown

cerkvlke kakvnkis. Nettv vhonkatkusis kakvranēt omvtet,
cilkâlki ka·kánkeys nítta ahonkâ·tkoseys ká·kala·ní·t ô·matit
when your parents lived there. But their days were short,

momet mv fettv vtēhkvnkē estet omvlket pokephohyen
mo·mít ma (?) fítta ati·hkáŋki· ístit omálkit po·kiphóhyin
and all those who lived within that place have died;

ennvpa seko hahket aretskis nettv ohcēs. Monkv cem etecakketv emēleskē ahretskvs.
innapá· siko· háhkit a·líckeys nítta óhci·s môŋka cimiticakkitá imi·líski·[505] áhłíckas
you may find yourself with no one left one day. So do not be sullen with your brothers.

Fettv tvniken estvn ayat kḙrrēsekot,
fítta tanêykin ístan a·yâ·t kĭ·ⁿłłi·siko·t[506]
The place will be empty, and you will not know where to go;

mv fettv enkvpaketskvtē aret 'tvleporv tis rohcehyet hueretskat
ma fítta iŋkapa·kíckati· a·lít 'talipólateys łohcíhyit hoylícka·t
then when you leave that place and enter other territories as a stranger,

este cekerrē sekon hueret aretskof, hvse aklvtkvranusen,
ísti cikílli· síko·n hoylít a·lícko·f hasí aklátkalá·nosin
no one will know you as you travel, when the sun is about to set,

vhvoke restem vfvnkēpuset hueretskof este cekerrēkos,
aháwki listimafánki·posit hóylícko·f isti cikiłłi·kos
you will present yourself at doors, and no one will know you,

estvn atetskvten omat. "Mimatan yefulkvs" cekihocē hahken,
ístan a·tíckatin o·mâ·t mêyma·tá·n yifólkas cikéyho·cí· háhkin
or where you came from. They'll begin to tell you, "Go back where you came from,"

nettv cvpcvkē sulkēn ahret, mv 'tvleporv ossetskat,
nítta capcaki· sólki·n áhlit ma 'talipóła o·ssícka·t[507]
there will be many long days, and when you leave those strange places,

estvmin ayis konkot
ístamèyn a·yéys kóŋko·t
you won't think about where you are going,

ayetskvtē fettv enkvpaketskvtē vnakvn hueret vkerricetskat
a·yíckati· fítta (?) iŋkapa·kíckati· aná·kan hôylit akíłłeycícka·t
and when you stand near the yard you departed from and think about it,

"Cuko estomvten omat hehcvres" kont
cokó isto·matín o·mâ·t híhcalis kônt
you will think, "I will go and see what happened to the house."

aret rohret "Heyvn cuko likvntvs" kontskan,
ă·ⁿłit lóhłit hiyán cokó leykántas kônckâ·n
You will get there and think, "This is where the house used to be,"

osa-rakkot pokhen
osa·łákkot pò·khin
and there will be big clumps of pokeweed,

"Heyvt vhvoke homv fettvt omvntvs" kometskan
hiyát aháwki (?) hóma (?) fíttat o·mántas kô·mícka·n
and you will be thinking, "The yard used to be here in front of the door,"

pvkanv-catuce em vpet espvtaken hēcē hueretskof, hvse aklvtkvranusē hakēpen
paka·naca·tocí imápit ispatâ·kin hi·cí· hôylícko·f hasí aklátkalá·nosi· há·ki·pín
and as you stand looking at a patch of red plum trees, and as the sun is about to set,

censapokv eto wakkusē tis ohlihcet ohliketskat
cinsa·poká itó wákkosi·teys ohléyhcit ohlêykícka·t
you will set your bundle of clothing on a little log and sit down.

"Cuko liken vpohoken ạrvyvntvs" komet hvkihket
cokó lêykin apo·hô·kin á·ⁿłayantás kô·mit hakêyhkit[508]
"My family and I used to live in this house," you will think and cry,

estvmin vyvranat kẹrrēsekot liketskis nettv ohcē tis
istamêyn ayáła·nâ·t kĭ·ⁿlli·sikô·t[509] *lêykíckeys nítta óhci·teys*
and you will not know where to go one day.

cerkvlke, cem etecakketv em ēleskusē ahretskvs.
ciłkâlki cimiticakkitá imi·łískosi· áhłíckas.
So do not go acting sullen to your parents or brothers.

Heyv elecv 'punvkv ocat hoccicv em punvkvt os.
hiyá (?) ilíca (?) 'ponaká ô·ca·t ho·ccéyca imponákat ô·ⁿs[i]
The words below are the words of the writer.

Heyv onvpv opunvkv ocakat opunvkv vculvket omakēs.
hiyá (?) onápa (?) oponaká o·câ·ka·t oponaká acolakít omâ·ki·s
The words above are old words.

cvcēpvnē arvyof este vculạkusēt hoktvlạkusēt onvyaket okat
caci·paní· a·łayô·f ísti acolă·ⁿkosi·t hoktală·ⁿkosi·t onáya·kít o·kâ·t
When I was a very young boy, elderly men and women

yv opunvkvn este mvnette sem punayet
yaʔ oponakán ísti 'manítti simpóna·yít
would say these things to young people,

vculvkēt fullvtēs mahokvnts makaket onvyakvtēt omekv
acolakít follati·s má·ho·kánc má·ka·kít onáya·katí·t ô·mika
it is told, the old ones used to say.

[i] From here on — what JHH thinks about what is given above.

nake em vsēhē em punahohoyat vcakkvyē apohicē este mvnette vrēpat enhẹret vrēpen
nâ·ki imási·hí· impona·hó·ho·yâ·t acakkayi· a·pohéyci· ísti 'manítti ałi·pâ·t inhĩ·ⁿłit ałi·pín
So young people who heed the advice will be happy, and they have seen

nake em vhahoyat apohicekat ēyestemerricēt omen hēcvtēt onayet okakvtēs.
nâ·ki imahá·ho·yâ·t a·pohéycika·t i·yistimílleycí·t ô·min hi·catí·t ona·yít oka·katí·s
those who did not heed the teachings bring hardships upon themselves and told about it.

Monkv vkerricvyat ohrolopē cokpe toccēnat erpvlhvmke
môŋka akílleycayâ·t ohłolopí· cókpi toccî·na·t iłpalhámki
So as I think of times back beyond three hundred years ago,

este-cate fullvtē ohhonvkv opunvkv fvccvt omakēs makvyēt os.
isticá·ti follatí· ohhonaká oponaká fáccat omá·ki·s ma·kayí·t ô·ⁿs
I believe the ways of Indian life that are told to be true.

este mvnettē arē hēcvtēt arat ohhonvkv pohvtēt encēpvnvke em onayet okakvtēs.
ísti? 'manítti· a·lí· hi·catí·t a·lâ·t ohhonaká po·hatí·t inci·panáki imóna·yít oka·katí·s
They told the stories from those who saw young people going about and told their sons.

Este vcọlusē hahkof, estomēt arat hēcvtēt estomēt arat
ísti acŏ·ⁿlosi· háhko·f istó·mi·t a·lâ·t hi·catí·t istó·mi·t a·lâ·t
When a man became old, he had seen how some young men went about

ohhonvkv pohvtēt encēpvnvke em onayet okakvtēs.
ohhonaká po·hatí·t inci·panáki imóna·yít oka·katí·s
and heard stories about them and told their sons.

Enhvperkv cēpvnē penkvlēckv tokot,
inhapíłka ci·paní· piŋkalí·cka tó·ko·t
It was not to frighten young men needlessly,

cēpvnē huyir-omvlkvt nake em vhẹrē sehokepvrēn,
ci·paní· hoyêylomálkat nâ·ki imahĩ·ⁿłi· siho·kipáłi·n
but for the well-being of young men everywhere.

cēpvnē huyir-omvlkvn vnokẹcusēt em punayet okakvtēs makvyēt os.
ci·paní· hoyêylomálkan anokĩ·ⁿcosi·t ímpona·yít oka·katí·s ma·kayí·t ô·ⁿs.
They talked to them with love for young men everywhere, I affirm.

[A Rule for Eating]

J. Hill (Haas XXI:91–93)

"Hompetv nake pvlaknv vtehkat sēyohwvkecē homipetskvs.
hompitá nâ·ki (?) palákna atíhka·t si·yohwakíci· homêypíckas
"Do not eat with a plate of food on your lap.

Cenhopuetake tis 'svlohketskvrēs" maket,
cinhopoytá·kiteys 'salóhkíckáli·s ma·kít
You may eat your children along with [the food]," they said.

hoktvke-mvnettvlketot cēpvnvke tis nake sēyohwvkecē hompetv em vsehakēt omvnts.
hoktakimanittâlkitot ci·panákiteys nâ·ki si·yohwakíci· hompitá imasíha·ki·t o·mánc.
Young girls and boys were warned about eating food from a plate on their laps.

"Cenhopuetake 'svlohketskvrēs" makē hoktē-mvnette em punayat,
cinhopoytá·ki 'salóhkíckáli·s ma·kí· hokti·manítti impona·yâ·t
"You may eat your children," they told the young girls:

hopuewv heckuecetskat cem vculekot cem pokis ahretskēs makatet okvtēs,
hopóywa híckoycícka·t cimacolíkot címpo·kèys áhlícki·s ma·kâ·tit o·katí·s
children born to you may not grow up, and you may lose them, is what that means,

cēpvnvkeu matvpomēn sem punayet.
ci·panákiw ma·tapó·mi·n símpona·yít.
and [they] told the boys the same thing.

[Do not Stare at a Hawk]

J. Hill (Haas XXI:95–97)

Kēyakkv hvlwē folotkē hakē arat hoyohpetskvs.
ki·yá·kka hálwi· folo·tkí· ha·kí· ă·^{n}la·t hoyóhpíckas
Do not stare at a crying rabbit hawk circling up high.

hopuetaket em pokvtēt omen eshvkihket aret okētan,
hopoytá·kit impó·kati·t ô·min ishakày^{n}hkit ă·^{n}lit o·kí·ta·n
Her children are dead and that is why she is crying, so

eshoyopetskvtē hopuetaket cem poken ahretskēs maket,
ishoyŏ·ⁿpíckati· hopoytá·kit címpo·kin áhlícki·s ma·kít
if you stare at her, you might lose your children, they said.

hoktvkuce cēpvnvke esyomat keyakkv hakē arat hoyopetv em vsehakēt omvnts.
hoktakóci ci·panáki isyŏ·ma·t kiyá·kka ha·kí· a·lâ·t hoyopitá imásiha·kí·t o·mánc
Girls and boys both were warned against staring at crying rabbit hawks.

Hoktvlvket yv maketv fvccvt omen okakvtē tat kerraks.
hoktalákit ya ma·kitá fáccat ô·min oka·katí·ta·t kíłłaks.
The old ladies had this saying, and I do not know if it is true.

[When Someone's Ear Rings]

J. Hill (Haas XXI:99–101)

Este-hvcko ofvt svmamakken omat, este pvsvtkvtē em puyvfekcvt
istihácko ó·fat sama·mà·ⁿkkin o·mâ·t ísti pasátkati· impoyafíkcat
When someone's ear rings inside, it means it's the spirit of a dead person

estenhuehkan okēs maket, em vyoposkat,
istínhoyhkâ·n o·kí·s ma·kít imayópo·skâ·t
calling them, they say, and you are to answer, saying,

"Cvtvphvrakko vm pvtakat vnlekwan vtarēt o" maketvt omēs. Makakat sasen
cataphałákko ampatâ·ka·t anlíkwa·n atá·li·t ó· ma·kitát ô·mi·s má·ka·kâ·t sâ·sin
"When the big flat rock which is my bed decays, I will come." Some say,

"Cvto-wokocken oktahvt 'svm etekyvmken 'tekvpicēpin os.
catowokóckin oktá·hat 'samitikyâmkin 'tikapeyci·péyn ó·ⁿs
"Sand has mixed in with my small pebbles, and I'm separating them.

Mvn poyepvyat tat vtarēt o" maketvt omēs. Makakateu sasēt omvnts.
man po·yipáya·t tá·t atá·li·t ó· ma·kitát ô·mi·s má·ka·kâ·tiw sa·sí·t o·mánc.
When I finish, I will come," is what you say. There were some who said [that].

Cvtvphvrakko makat cvto-tvpekse-rakko pvtakan maketvt omēs.

cataphałákko[i] *ma·kâ·t catotapiksiłákko patâ·ka·n ma·kitát ô·mi·s*

To say cvtvphvrakko is to say a layer of big, flat rock.

Advice to Young Men (Cēpvnvke Lopockusat Este-honvnwv Ohrē Fullvranat)[ii]

J. Hill (Haas XXII:3–29)

1. Nake horkopē ahretskvs. Cvhechoyeks kontskis,
    nâ·ki hółko·pí· áhłíckas cahichoyíks kônckeys
1. Do not go around stealing things. You might think no one sees you,

renakv tis cenahhen nake epucase cehēcis
liná·kateys cináhhin nâ·ki ipocá·si cihî·ceys
but your eyesight may fail you, and the owner may see you.

estemehsetsken vhakv tis secefastet
istimíhsíckin[iii] *ahá·kateys sícifa·stít*[510]
When you take from someone, they might administer the law

este sulkē cehēcēn cerokafhoyis huyiretskēs.
ísti sólki· cihí·ci·n ciłoká·fho·yêys hoyêylícki·s
before many people watching you, as you stand and get whipped.

2. Hoktvlvke fullat em etenrvwv ēcvpakkuecusē okē opunayē ahretskvs.
    hoktaláki follâ·t imitînława i·capakkôycosi· ó·ki· opóna·yi· áhłíckas.
2. Do not go about talking angry-like among old women.

Este-honvnwvt aret ohketskekos. Ēposkelēcusēt ohketskēs.
istihonánwat a·łít óhkíckiko·s i·po·skilí·cosi·t óhkícki·s[511]
You will not be speaking as a man. You may get ēposkelēcusē.

---

[i] *catápha* = flat rock; concrete or rock pavement.

[ii] Title: *ci·panáki lopóckosa·t istihonánwa óhłi· fóllała·nâ·t* 'young boys who are almost men'.

[iii] Or: *istimî·síckin.*

3. Hvyatkē wakketskat hopvnkv ocof cem vfolothohyvrēs.
   hayâ·tki· wă·ⁿkícka·t hopánka o·cô·f[512] cimafolothóhyáli·s
3. If you stay in bed after daylight, they will surround you in time of war.

4. Eshuerēn homipetskvs. Hopvnkof cenvrken cem ohrahohhvrēs.
   ishóyli·n[513] homêypíckas hópankô·f cinálkin cimohla·hóhháli·s
4. Do not eat standing up. In time of war, they will shoot you in the stomach.

5. Sarēt homipetskvs. Cehiwvn ascenfullephuyis ahretskvrēs.
   sa·lí·t homêypíckas cihéywan a·scinfollípho·yêys áhlíckáli·s
5. Do not eat while moving about. Someone may keep company with your wife.

6. Eslafkv eswarē nake pahpetskvs. Cenutet ecenahhvrēs.
   islá·fka íswa·lí· nâ·ki páhpíckas cinótit icináhháli·s
6. Do not eat by cutting [your food] with a knife. You may lose your teeth.

Nake papetskat warkēt papet omvs akkē waran okēs.
nâ·ki pa·pícka·t wa·lkí·t pa·pít ómas a·kkí· wa·lâ·n o·kí·s
When you eat something, eat it cut up, cut by biting, it means.

7. Eswakkē homipetskvs. Cehiwv tis eslomhephoyen ahretskēs.
   iswákki· homêypíckas cihéywateys islomhiphô·yin áhlícki·s
7. Do not eat while lying down. Someone may lie with your wife.

8. Este ēnakayat hoyohpetskvs. Ceturhecekhahkvrēs.
   ísti i·na·kâ·ya·t hoyohpíckas citolhicikháhkáli·s
8. Do not look at a naked person. You may become blind.

9. Honvnwv, hoktē 'tepake estomakat eshoyohpetskvs.
   honánwa hoktí· 'tipâ·ki istó·ma·kâ·t ishoyóhpíckas
9. Do not look at a man and a woman having sexual intercourse.

Ceturwv tis escenhvmikvrēs.
citólwateys iscinhamêykáli·s
You may become one-eyed.

10. Este ena vhopvnkusē arat hoyohpetskvs. Enokketvt omvtētok
    ísti iná· aho·pánkosi· a·lâ·t hoyóhpíckas inokkitát o·matí·to·k
10. Do not look at a handicapped person. Because it is an illness,

cematvpohmvrēs. Monkat mv omē tis censihohcvrēs.
cima·tapóhmáli·s móŋka·t ma ó·mi·teys cinseyhóhcáli·s
the same may happen to you. Or you might father [a baby] just like that.

Monkat họlwakus kont vpelkv eshạyuset eshueretskat
*hŏl*ʰ*wa·kós kônt apílka ishǎ·*ⁿ*yosit ishôylícka·t*
Or if you think it's ugly and make a joke about it,

em vculvke hēcē vculvtēt ont nake ēyapohicē tis ohketsken escēhecehpvrēs.
imacoláki hi·cí· acólati·t ônt ná·ki i·ya·pohéyci·teys óhkíckin isci·hicíhpáli·s
he might grow up listening to his elders and may be very obedient and will find you out.

11. Cekv-esse cenkashoyē hvkihketskat,
     cika?íssi ciŋká·sho·yí· hakayhkícka·t
11. If you cry while your hair is being combed,

cewihoken estvhvkihkēt ahretskvrēs.
ciweyhô·kin istahákayhkí·t áhlíckáli·s
[your wife] may leave you, and you'll go about crying after her.

12. Este hompat escokhoyohpetskvs. Cemporhohyvrēs.
     ísti hompâ·t iscokhoyóhpíckas cimpo·lhóhyáli·s
12. Do not stare at the mouth of someone eating. They may do witchcraft on you.

13. Este turwv heceko aran vhayēt ahretskvs. Mv enokketv ecelihkvrēs.
     ísti tólwa hicíko· a·lâ·n aha·yí·t áhlíckas. ma inokkitá iciléyhkáli·s
13. Do not go about imitating a blind person. That disease may attack you.

Cēmeu heceko cehahkēs.
cí·miw hicíko· ciháhki·s
You too may become blind.

14. Este ele vhopvnkvtē enyvkvpkv vnvttusē aran vpelicēt yvkapan svhayēt ahretskvs.
     ísti ilí ahopánkati· inyakápka anáttosi· a·lâ·n apíleyci·t yaka·pâ·n sáha·yí·t áhlíckas
14. Do not go about imitating the walk and laughing about someone who's leg is crippled.

Cemomē hahkvrēs.
cimo·mí· háhkáli·s
You may become the same way.

15. Este hokcat vpelihcetskvs.
    ísti ho·kcâ·t apiléyhcíckas
15. Do not laugh when a person expels gas.

Nute seko cehahkēs, nute sekot okekv.
nóti síko· cihâhki·s nóti síko·t o·kiká.
You may become toothless, for [the one making the sound] has no teeth.

16. Cecēpvnusē hece cokpiket monkat mokkihcetskvs.
    cici·panósi· hicí cókpeykit mónka·t mo·kkéyhcíckas
16. While you're a very young boy, do not chew tobacco or smoke.

Ececulihcvrēs. Hece vculēt omēs.
icicoléyhcáli·s hicí acóli·t ô·mi·s
It may make you old. Tobacco is very old.

Cemvnettē emonkē este vcoluse omē cehahkēs.
cimanítti· imôŋki· ísti acŏ·ⁿlosi· ó·mi· cihâhki·s
Though you are young, you'll become like an old man.

17. Hece horkopetskvtē cettot ecehopahnvrēs. Monkv horkohpetskvs.
    hicí hołko·píckati· cíttot icihopáhnáli·s[514] môŋka holkóhpíckas
17. If you steal tobacco, a snake may ruin you. So don't steal.

18. Estuce lowạkusē monkē enkususowv enwarhoyvtē
    istocí lowà·ⁿkosi· môŋki· iŋkososowá inwá·łho·yatí·
18. If you cut the fingernails of a newborn baby,

horkopkvn tayē hakēs mahokvnts.
hołkópkan tǎ·ⁿyi· ha·ki·s má·ho·kánc.
it will grow up and steal things, they used to say.

19. Estuce lowạkusē pvnēhocat ele-hvckowv kotahēt vcolēs maket
    istocí lowà·ⁿkosi· 'pani·ho·câ·t ilihackowá kotá·hi·t aco·lí·s ma·kít
19. If newborn babies are made to dance, they will grow up bowlegged, it's said,

pvnēcetv vsēhohēt omvnts.
'pani·citá así·ho·hí·t o·mánc.
and they used to warn against making them dance.

20. Estuce nocē wakkat entvlkusē wihketskvs. Penkalēs mont enokkēs maket,
    istocí nóci· wâ·kka·t intâlkosi· wéyhkíckas píŋka·li·s[515] *mónt ino·kkí·s ma·kít*

20. Do not leave a sleeping baby by itself. It will get frightened and get sick, it's said:

"Yvt vhecicvrēs" mahket "Eslafkv tis monkat eskotkv tis eto-kvckuce tis aenwvkehcet
yat ahicêycáli·s máhkit islá·fkateys móŋka·t iskó·tkateys itokackocíteys a·inwakíhcit
"This will guard it," they said: "One should lay a knife or scissors or a little stick beside it

enkvpvketvt omēs" mahokvnts.
iŋkapakitát ô·mi·s má·ho·kánc.
and leave it," they used to say.

21. Estuce lowąkusēn estvn sayetsken omat, nene 'telacan rēsoretskat
    istocí lowǎ·ⁿkosi·n ístan sa·yíckin o·mâ·t niní 'tilâ·ca·n lí·so·lícka·t

21. If you take a newborn baby somewhere, when you get to where there is a crossroad,

eto-kvckucen nenen em ohwvkēcet, saret ometskekon omat
itokackocín ninín imóhwaki·cít sa·lít omíckikon o·mâ·t
place a little branch on the road, for if you do not,

nenen ehoset nerē tat tąyen hvkihkēs mahokēt omvnts.
ninín ihô·sit niłí·ta·t tǎ·ⁿyin hakayhkí·s má·ho·kí·t o·mánc.
it will forget [the path] and cry much at night, they used to say.

22. Cenak lēckv 'mvpeswv pvpētskat efune tat hopvyēn vwihketskvs.
    cinâ·k lí·cka 'mapíswa papí·cka·t[516] *ifónita·t hopáyi·n awéyhkíckas*

22. When you eat the meat of something you killed, do not throw its bones far.

Cem punvttv cenhopihcvrēs.
cimponátta cinhopáyhcáli·s
Your game may go far away from you.

Eco-fune penwv-fune tis vwikekot vhęricet wvkēcet omvs mahokvnts.
icofoní pinwafóniteys awéykikot ahǐ·ⁿłeycít waki·cít omás má·ho·kánc.
Do no throw deer bones or turkey bones away, but lay them down gently, they used to say.

23. Eco-tolaswv pahpetskvs. Hopvnkof ewvnhkvn cehlvrēs.
    icotolá·swa páhpíckas hópankô·f iwánhkan cíhláłi·s

23. Do not eat the tongue of a deer. In time of war, you may die of thirst.

24. Eco-torkop-ohlikv pahpetskvs. Hopvnkof cefekēkis huyiretskēs.
  icoto·łkopohléyka páhpíckas hópankô·f cifíki·kêys hoyêylícki·s
24. Do not eat the knee pan of a deer. In time of war, you may stand shaking.

Afvckvranetskēn yekcetvn cem punahohoyof,
a·fáckała·nícki·n yikcitán cimpona·hó·ho·yô·f
When you get ready to celebrate [i.e., play stick-ball] and they talk strictly to you,

fekēket huyiretskvrēs.
fíki·kít hoyêylíckáli·s
you may stand shaking.

25. Eco-hvce pahpetskvs. Hopvnkv ofvn huervtet lētketskat
  icoháci páhpíckas 'hopánka ó·fan hôyłatit li·tkícka·t
25. Do not eat the tail of a deer. In time of war, as you run,

hopvyēt hēcken ayetsken cerahohhvrēs.
hopáyi·t hî·ckin a·yíckin ciła·hóhháłi·s[517]
they will see you from afar and may shoot you.

26. Eco-hvsnērkv pahpetskvs. Poktvn cenkahohyvrēs.
  icohasní·lka páhpíckas póktan cinka·hóhyáłi·s
26. Do not eat deer testicles. Twins may be born to you.

27. Eco-falowa pahpetskvs. Hopvnkof, celotokikēs.
  icofa·lowá· páhpíckas hópankô·f cilotokêyki·s
27. Do not eat the marrow of a deer. In time of war, you may be unable to move.

28. Penwv encvkvspv pahpetskvs. Hopvnkof, ceholahnvrēs.
  pínwa incakáspa[ii] páhpíckas hópankô·f ciholáhnáłi·s
28. Do not eat turkey gizzards. In time of war, you may [accidentally] defecate.

29. Penwv esokso papetskvtē cemvnettē monket
  pínwa isókso pa·píckati· cimanítti· môŋkit
29. If you eat turkey hips [i.e., drumsticks] while you are still young,

---

[i] Or: *'hopánka ó·fan.*
[ii] Or any other kind of gizzard.

cesokso nokken hịhkēt ahretskēs.
cisókso no·kkín hǎyhnki·t áhlícki·s
your hips will hurt, and you'll go about groaning.

30. Nanvk-okusē ahretskvs. Nvpvt cem enhēren ahretskekos. Este naken makepekis,
    nâ·nakókosi· áhlickas napát ciminhĭ·ⁿlin áhlíckiko·s ísti nâ·kin ma·kipíkeys
30. Do not go around telling lies. No one will like you. It means the person who,

ohlaksē este aran okēs,
óhla·ksí· ísti a·lâ·n o·kí·s
although someone might not have said anything, goes about telling lies on others

etencvpakhokicetv komēn laksē opunvkv 'svretv.
itincapakhokeycitá kó·mi·n la·ksi· oponaká[518] *'salitá.*
and, in order to make people angry with one another, spreads lies.

31. Oyē aenhompetskat, cena yoksē hahkēs mahokvnts.
    oyí· a·inhompícka·t ciná· yóksi· háhki·s má·ho·kánc.
31. When you eat with a widow, your body becomes pointed, they used to say.

Hoktē ehe em ehlof, mv honvnwv ēlat ena-hvmke hoktvket vhecicēt estomis
hoktí· ihí imíhlo·f ma honánwa î·la·t ina·hámki hoktakít ahicéyci·t istô·meys
When a woman's husband dies, the dead man's female relatives would look after her,

vrekon licvranēt uewvn ekvn em ohkalet ostihcet
alíko·n léycała·ní·t óywan ikán imóhka·lít ostéyhcit
keeping her and not allowing her to go anywhere; they'd pour water on her head four times

ēkasekot hvse osten likvranēn em onahyet lihocēt omvtēs.
i·ká·siko·t hasí ô·stin léykała·ní·n imonáhyit léyho·cí·t o·matí·s
without combing it and tell her that she would stay there for four months.

Mvn oyē kicet okhoyvtēs. Mont "Mvn aenhomipetskvs" maket okhoyvtēs.
man oyí· keycít ókho·yatí·s mónt man a·inhomèypíckas ma·kít ókho·yatí·s
They told the widow that. And they said, "Do not eat with her."

Cena elusē omē hahken, cenke-wesakv tis cofuncokusē cehahkēs maketvt omēs,
ciná· ilósi· ó·mi· háhkin ciŋkiwisá·kateys cofoncokósi· ciháhki·s ma·kitát ô·mi·s
Your body may become numb and even your fingers may become sharply pointed, it's said;

cena yoksē makat. Momen mv oyē hakvtē hvse ostē orof,
ciná·yóksi· ma·kâ·t mo·mín ma oyi· há·kati· hasí ô·sti· o·łô·f
your body becomes pointed, they say. Then the widow, in four months,

ekv em akkesahyet, ekv enkahset, ēyvpayet esfullet pvnkvt ocen omat,
iká imakkisáhy·it iká iŋkáhsit i·yapâ·yit ísfollít pánkat o·cín o·mâ·t
they'll wash her hair, comb her head, and take her with them, and if there's a dance,

mvn 'resorihcet wihohken estomis vretv em etektvnkēt omvtēs, hofonof.
man 'lisoléyhcit[519] weyhóhkin istô·meys ałíta imitíktankí·t o·matí·s hofô·no·f
they'll take her there and leave her, and she was then free to go about, that was long ago.

Momen mv oyē ehe tate ena-hvmkē mahusat honvnwv ehiwv sekot aren omat,
mo·mín ma oyi· ihitá·ti ina·hámki· mă·ⁿhosa·t honánwa ihéywa síko·t a·łín o·mâ·t
And if a close male relative of the widow's former husband had no wife,

mv oyē epucaset omēn vkerrihocēt omvtēs.
ma oyí· ipocá·sit ó·mi·n akiłéyho·cí·t o·matí·s
it was thought that she belonged to him.

Momis mv honvnwv mv oyēn em enherepekon omat,
mo·mêys ma honánwa ma oyí·n iminhiłípikon o·mâ·t
But if that man did not like the widow,

honvnwv estoman komēpat ehiwv hakepvranat em etektvnket omvtēs.
honánwaʔ istô·ma·n ko·mî·pa·t ihéywaʔ ha·kipáła·nâ·t imitíktankít o·matí·s
she was free to have the one she liked and could become his wife.

Momen mv honvnwv tvlkēt oyē eyacekat tvlkēt omekon,
mo·mín ma honánwa tálki·t oyi· iyá·cika·t tálki·t omíkon
And if the man did not like the widow,

mv oyē tateu mv honvnwvn em enherekon omis, 'metektvnket omvtēs.
maʔ oyi·ta·tiw maʔ honánwan iminhilíkon o·mêys 'mitíktankít o·matí·s
or if that widow also didn't like the man, she was free.

Advice to Young Women (Vculvke, Hoktvlvke tis Emmvnette em Punvyakvtē)[i]

J. Hill (Haas XXII:31–47)

Hoktvke mvnettakat em vtotketv, ennak hakv heraken,
hoktakí 'manittâ·ka·t imatotkitá innâ·k há·ka hilă·ⁿkin
Even if young women do not do good work,

enhoporrenkv cvpcvkē sofsokēn ocet omeko estomis,
inhopołłínka capcakí· sofsokí·n ô·cit omíko· istô·meys
or have clear thinking and deep wisdom,

em ēyvcayēckv vcakkvyēn vrakkueckv em ohocen
imi·yaca·yí·cka acakkayí·n ałakkóycka imo·hô·cin
they will have total respect according to their self-esteem

fvccvkēt este omvlkv vrakkueckv em ocvkēt sehoket ennettv pokaket omvrēn
faccakí·t ísti omálka ałakkóycka imo·cakí·t sihô·kit innítta pó·ka·kít omáli·n
and be truly respectful of all people to the end of life,

enkusvpakuset em punayet okakvtēs.
iŋkosapă·ⁿkosit ímpona·yít oka·katí·s
they pleaded, talking.

Hvmmakēt cenhoktvlkv hoktē mvnettē ohrē aretskat
hámma·kí·t cinhoktálka hoktí· 'manítti· óhłi· a·łícka·t
Saying this, when you become a young woman,

este-honvnwv cem enhervranat huervtet ecefvciyen tem punayetskat,
istihonánwa ciminhiłáła·nâ·t hôyłatit icifacâyyin tímpona·yícka·t
when the man who will be good for you meets you, when you talk with him

mv honvnwv ohhvkerrickv hēren ohcet aretskof,
ma honánwa ohhakiłłéycka hĭ·ⁿlin óhcit a·łícko·f
and have good thoughts toward that man,

---

[i] Title: *acolakí hoktalákiteys immanítti imponáya·katí·* 'what men and women old-timers told the young'.

vkerrickv cem ēyvpayen ehiwv hahket liketskat,
akiłłéycka cimí·yapa·yín ihéywa háhkit leykícka·t
he will embrace your ideas, and you'll live as his wife;

cehute cenhahohyen liketskat nake hǫlwakusis hompvkē tayat entakcayet em onēpet
cihóti cinha·hóhyin lêykícka·t nâ·ki hŏlʰwâ·koseys hómpakí· tâ·ya·t intákca·yít imóni·pít[520]
you'll live in a home made for you, cooking meals that are lowly and scarce,

cehe vrakkuecē liketskat
cihí ałakkóyci· leykícka·t
[but] have respect for your husband;

cehe ehutvlke ecerakkuecvkēn hueretskat ecēfvckētarēs.
cihí ihotâlki iciłakkôycaki·n hoylícka·t ici·fácki·tá·li·s
your husband's family will respect you, and you'll be happy.

Momet cem vnakuecv monkat este estvmin vtēkē estomis cencukopericv cem vlakat
mo·mít cimana·kóyca móŋka·t ísti ístamêyn atî·ki· istô·meys cincokopiłéyca cimála·kâ·t
And when your neighbor or anyone at all comes to visit you,

vrakkuecē "Likepvs ce" kicet momet taklike kvlkusē estomis aenlicet
ałakkóyci· leykipás ci^ keycít mo·mít takléyki kálkosi· istô·meys a·ínleycít
politely say, "Have a seat," and place even a small piece of bread before them

"Vnhompvs" maket "Cennvthofv vpiketskvrēs."
anhómpas ma·kít cinnathó·fa apêykíckáłi·s
and say, "Eat my food. You will live this way in your home."

Stofis cennettv cvpkē tis omvtet,
stô·feys cinnítta cápki·teys ô·matit
When your days are long,

cehoktąlusē cehahket aliketv tot ahueretv tis omēseko cehahkof
cihoktă·ⁿlosi· ciháhkit a·leykitátot a·hoylitáteys ó·mi·siko·[521] *ciháhko·f*[522]
and you become old and unable to get up or stand up,

cehvlatet acelicet acehuericet cenekkēyuset
cihalâ·tit á·cileycít a·cihoyléycit cinikkî·yosit
they will take hold of you, get you up, stand you up, move you around a little;

vlekothusat monkat vpēttusat escehopohoyen cenhesaketv pokvrēs.
alikóthosa·t móŋka·t api·ttosa·t iscihopó·ho·yin cinhisa·kitá pó·káłi·s
they'll look for a warm place or a shady place until your life ends.

Momis cehe tot, cehe ehutvlke tis,
mo·mêys cihítot cihí ihotâlkiteys
But if you haven't the slightest respect for your husband, or your husband's family,

momet cem vnvkuecv, cencukopericv vrakkueckv cǫtkusis ocekot,
mo·mít cimanakóyca cincokopiłéyca ałakkóycka cŏ·ⁿtkoseys ó·ciko·t
your neighbors, or your visitors,

cenvthofv likēpetskvten omat cennettv cvpkē tis omvtet hoktaḷusē cehahkof,
cinathó·fa léyki·píckatin o·mâ·t cinnítta[523] *cápki·teys ô·matit hoktă·ⁿlosi· ciháhko·f*[524]
if you just sit in your house, when your days are long and you become very old,

ennvpa sekis omē cehahket ahueretv omeko cehahken,
innapá·[525] *sikêys ó·mi· ciháhkit a·hoylitá omiko· ciháhkin*[526]
there may be a day when there is no one around and you become unable to stand up,

ēsso mokkvt eceyvkofken, hvlkusēt sofotkē ēkvnvn takpvtaketskis nettv ohcēs.
i·sso mó·kkat iciyakô·fkin[527] *hăⁿkosi·t sofo·tkí· i·kanán takpata·kíckeys nítta óhci·s*
with dust blowing all around you, crawling and dragging yourself on the ground.

"Nettv momvkē hēcin omekarēs," ēkomet,
nítta mo·makí· hi·céyn omiká·łi·s i·kô·mit
"I will not see a day like this," you think to yourself.

cencukopericv hoktaḷuset, vcǫluset monkat este estvmvn vtēpis
cincokopiłéyca hoktă·ⁿlosit acŏ·ⁿlosit móŋka·t ísti ístaman atî·peys
Your visitors, whether an elderly woman, elderly man, or a [stranger] from anywhere,

vrakkuecē este vnokeckvn ocēt cenfettv hueretskvrēs.
ałakkóyci· ísti anokíckan ó·ci·t cinfítta hóyłíckáłi·s
show them respect and love, as you live in your home.

Vculaḳusat, hoktvlaḳusat vrakkuecēt cemvnettē aretskvtē
acolă·ⁿkosa·t hoktală·ⁿkosa·t ałakkóyci·t cimanítti· a·líckati·
Because you went about as a youth with respect for old men and women,

nake cem vhērēn nettv cvpkēn vretskvrēs kicakvtēt omēs.
nâ·ki cimahi·ⁿli·n nítta cápki·n alíckáli·s kéyca·kati·t ô·mi·s
you will live with things that are good for you and will have long days, they said to them.

Women's Rules (Hoktē ēposkat)[i]

J. Hill

Mohmen hoktē ēposkat ētv hompēn kihocēt omvtēs.
móhmin hokti· i·po·skâ·t í·ta hompi·n kéyho·cí·t o·matí·s
Now a woman who is menstruating should eat apart, it was said.

Cuko hoktvke honvntake tohkvlkēt vpoket omen hoktē hvmket ēposken omat,
cokó hoktakí honantá·ki tohkálki·t apô·kit o·mín hoktí· hámkit i·po·skín o·mâ·t
If women and men live together in a house, and if one woman was menstruating,

cuko osiyet, ehvpo hayusēt, fettvn liket,
cokó osèyyit ihapó· há·yosi·t fíttan lèykit
she left the house, made a little camp, and stayed outside,

sēyvrvhēcusē hompetv noricet hompēt onkv, mvn okhoyvtēs.
si·yalahî·cosi· hompitá nołeycít hompí·t oŋká man ókho·yatí·s
cooking and eating food only for herself, so that's what they meant.

Ētv hompē kicat, ehe tis aenwakkekot omvtēs.
í·ta hompí· keycâ·t ihíteys a·inwákkikot o·matí·s
Eating apart meant she didn't lie with her husband either.

Momet punvttv vpeswv pvpvrē em encahokē hērēt omvtēs.
mo·mít ponátta apíswa papáli· iminca·hokí· hǐ·ⁿli·t o·matí·s
And it was expressly forbidden to eat game meat.

Este honvntake mit hoktē ēposkē aenwakkvrē aenhompvrē
ísti honantá·ki mêyt hoktí· i·póski· a·inwákkáli· a·inhómpáli·
They did not want men to lie with or eat with

---

[i] Title: *hoktí· i·po·skâ·t* 'a woman who is menstruating'.

cuko ofv aentaklikvrē ēyacekot omakvtēs.
cokó ó·fa a·intakléykáłi· i·yá·cikot oma·kati·s
or to stay in the house with a menstruating woman.

Sennvthofv hoktē ētv hompēt acentakliket acenhompen omat,
sinnathó·fa hoktí· i·ta hómpi·t a·cintaklêykit a·cínhompín o·mâ·t
If a menstruating woman stays with you, eats with you,

cem punvttv vpeswv cem papēn, aret fayetskat,
cimponátta apíswa címpa·pí·n a·lít fa·yícka·t
and eats your game meat, when you go hunting,

cem punvttvt cem ēheckuehcekos kihocē vculvkvtēt onkv,
cimponáttat cimi·hickóyhciko·s kéyho·cí· acolakáti·t ôŋka
your game will not appear to you, they grew up being told, so

mvt omēcicen, ēposkvlke vpvkē hompekot este-honvntake fullet omvtēs.
mat omí·ceycín i·po·skâlki apáki· hómpikot istihonantá·ki follít o·matí·s
because of that, men did not eat with menstruating women.

Momen hoktvkeu honvntake sēyenfvyvtkv ocvkēpat
mo·mín ho·ktakíw honantá·ki si·yinfayátka o·cakî·pa·t
And women too considered the rules men had,

em vyvmahkēt omvkan hērēs komatet, enokkan vpakuset cuko osset omvtēs.
imayamáhki·t omáka·n[528] hĭⁿłi·s kô·ma·tit ino·kkâ·n apăⁿkosit cokó o·ssít o·matí·s
and believing it good not to break them, as soon as she had her period, she left the house.

Em enokketv nettv hoyanat em accakē omvlkvn okkohset,
iminokkitá nítta hoya·nâ·t ima·cca·kí· omálkan okkóhsit
When the days of her period had passed, she washed all her clothes,

uewvn aklohpet, coko-ofv racēyet omvtēs.
óywan aklóhpit cokoʔó·fa lá·ci·yít o·matí·s
bathed in water, and came back into the house.

Ētv hompē likvranat vrahkusē cuko enhahoyat sasvtēs.
i·ta hómpi· léykała·nâ·t ałăⁿhkosi·[529] cokó inha·hô·ya·t sa·satí·s
There were some who built houses for her to stay in and eat apart.

<u>Ēposkv-hute</u> kihocen mv cuko likvtēs.
i·poskahóti kéyho·cin ma cokó leykatí·s
That house was called <u>ēposkv-hute</u> ['menstruating house'].

Honvntake fayat heleswv ēyenhayēt
honantá·ki fa·yâ·t 'hilíswa i·yínha·yí·t
Men who were hunting made medicine for themselves,

monkat enhahoyēn esēyvfastēt fayet onkv,
moŋkâ·t inhá·ho·yí·n isí·yafa·stí·t fa·yít oŋká
or treated themselves with that which was made for them and hunted,

mv heleswv enyekcē kvckekarēn monkat topaksekarē vrahkv vhakucet omvtēs.
ma 'hilíswa inyikcí· káckiká·li·n móŋka·t topáksiká·li· ałáhka aha·kocít ô·matí·s
so it was a rule in order for medicine not to lose strength or become diluted.

Childbirth (Hoktē Sicat)[i]

J. Hill (Haas XXII:49–73)

Estucet heckvranēn hoktēt esenokken omat
istocít híckała·ní·n hoktí·t isíno·kkín o·mâ·t
If a baby was going to be born, and the woman went into labor

cuko ofv tokon cuko em vhopvyusēn hvfvpusan pvtakv enhayen
cokó ó·fa tó·ko·n cokó imahopáyosi·n hafáposa·n patá·ka inhâ·yin
not in the house, but a little ways from the house, they made a pallet for her in a thicket,

wakken hoktvlēt vhecicēt vpaket vfastet
wâ·kkin hoktalí·t ahicéyci·t apâ·kit afa·stít
and she lay down and an old lady with her watched over her and took care of her,

este heckekon vcewēpen omat heleswv enhayet svfastet,
ísti híckikon acíwi·pín o·mâ·t 'hilíswa ínha·yít sáfa·stít
and if the baby was not born for a long time, she made medicine for her and took care of her

---

[i] Title: *hoktí· seycâ·t* 'a woman who is giving birth'.

monkat mv hoktalat heleswv hayetv kerrekon omat,
móŋka·t ma hoktâ·la·t 'hilíswa ha·yitá kíłłikon o·mâ·t
with it, or if that old lady did not know how to make medicine,

"Heles-hayvn hopoyaks" maken omat, hopoyet heleswv enheckuehocen
'hilishá·yan hopóyaks ma·kín o·mâ·t hopo·yít 'hilíswa inhickóyho·cín
if she said, "Look for a medicine maker," they looked for one and found medicine for her,

svfastet omvtēs. Momet este etefullat vnąkvton omat
sáfa·stít o·matí·s mo·mít ísti itífollâ·t aną̆·ⁿkaton o·mâ·t
and she cared for her with that. And if people are going to and fro near by,

vlsēt ont lvpkēn este hecikekos maket
álsi·t ònt lápki·n ísti hicêykiko·s ma·kít
they say it will be embarrassed and won't be born quickly;

hvfvpan svpēyet omvtēs. Momen este hēckof,
hafápa·n sápi·yít o·matí·s mo·mín ísti hi·ckô·f
so they took her to the thicket. When the baby is born and they say,

"Honvnwvt hēcket os" mahoken colotkv pohen omat, tayepvtēs.
honánwat hî·ckit ó·ⁿs má·ho·kín coló·tka po·hín o·mâ·t ta·yipáti·s
"A boy is born," if a cricket hears [that], it is good enough.

"Cukon hayen aenlikēpit nettv-hvtken enyvhikeparēs" makakēs
cokón ha·yín a·inleykî·peyt nittahátkin[530] inyaheykípá·li·s ma·ka·kí·s
"He'll build a house, and I'll live with him and sing for him in the white day," [crickets] say,

mahokvnts. Hoktēt hēckes mahoken colotkv pohat,
má·ho·kánc hoktí·t hî·ckis má·ho·kín coló·tka po·hâ·t
it was said. If they say, "A girl is born," and a cricket hears, it says,

"Mv tawvts. Uewvn rescawet yesocen estakkelvranēt omēs" makēs mahokvnts.
matá·wac óywan lísca·wít yíso·cín istakkilála·ni·t ô·mi·s ma·kí·s má·ho·kánc
"My, my. She will draw water and set it down, and I'll drown in it," it was said.

Momen este hecikof, cuko 'rvsohhatē estomis
mo·mín ísti hicêyko·f cokó 'lasóhha·tí· istô·meys
And after the baby is born and she returns to the house,

nvthofv escēyihocekon hoktē ēposkat omēn vrahkusēn hompet liket
nathó·fa isci·yeyhocíkon hoktí· i·po·skâ·t ó·mi·n aláhkosi·n hompít lèykit
she is not allowed into the house, and she ate and stayed like a menstruating woman;

cvfekinet em accvkē omvlkvn okkohset aklohpē tvlkusen cuko ofv ecēyet arē hakēt omvtēs.
cafikêynit ima·ccaki· omálkan okkóhsit aklóhpi· tálkosin cokó ó·fa ici·yít a·lí· ha·kí·t o·matí·s
only after she had recovered, washed all her clothes, and bathed did she enter the house.

Momis ēhvsvteceko monkof tat
mo·mêys i·hasaticíko· mòŋko·fta·t
But before she cleaned herself,

eco vpeswv, penwv vpeswv, nokose vpeswv, momet nake este-honvnwv ennak lēckv,
icó apíswa pínwa apíswa nokósi apíswa mo·mít nâ·ki istihonánwa innâ·k lí·cka
deer meat, turkey meat, bear meat, and things men kill,

punvttv vpeswv vtēkat pvpvrē em encahokēt omvtēs.
ponátta apíswa atî·ka·t papáli· iminca·hokí·t o·matí·s
all game meat, she was forbidden to eat.

Este-honvnwv em punvttv hopoyat em puyafkekarēn,
istihonánwa imponátta hopo·yâ·t impoyá·fkiká·li·n
So that a man looking for his game will not fail,

momet enheleswv enyvmahkekarēn,
mo·mít inhilíswa inyamáhkiká·li·n[i]
and his medicine will not be ruined,

momen hoktvkeu ēyvcayēcē hēret omakvtēs.
mo·mín hoktakíw i·yaca·yí·ci· hĭ·ⁿlit oma·katí·s
the women took good care of themselves.

Honvntake em ēyvcayēckv ocē fullēpat em vyvmahketv eyacvkekot
honantá·ki imi·yaca·yí·cka ó·ci· fólli·pâ·t imayamahkitá iyá·cakíko·t
Men had rules to care for themselves, and [women] did not want to make it all useless;

---

[i] Or: *i·nyamáh-*.

nake tat momē hĕret omen okakēs komēt
nâ·kita·t mó·mi· hĭ·ⁿɫit o·mín oka·kí·s kó·mi·t
and believing such things were good,

nake em onayē em vsēhohat apohicē hĕret hoktvke fullēpvtēt omēs.
nâ·ki imóna·yi· imasí·ho·hâ·t a·pohéyci· hĭ·ⁿɫit hoktakí folli·patí·t ô·mi·s
[women] heeded well the things they told them and counseled them about.

"Vpeswv tis pvpvrē vm encaket cvstemerrihocētot os" kometv
apíswateys papáɫi· amínca·kít castimiɫɫeyhocí·tot ó·ⁿs ko·mitá
They did not go about thinking, "They're stingy and won't let me eat meat,

vkerricvkekot fullvtēt omēs. Honvntake 'sem vpeyetv tat vrakkuecvkē hĕrē
akíɫɫeycakíkot follatí·t ô·mi·s honantá·ki 'simapiyítata·t alakkoycakí· hĭ·ⁿɫi·
making me suffer." They respected men's ways,

ēposkv-huten enhahoyēt on omat, mv ofv min likēpet omvtēs.
i·po·skahótin inha·hoyí·t ô·n o·mâ·t ma ó·fa mêyn léyki·pít o·matí·s
so if a menstruation hut was built for her, she stayed in that instead.

Echuswv tvlkusē vpaken hoktvket encukopericat fullvtēt omvtēs.
ichóswa tálkosi· apâ·kin hoktakit incokopiɫeycâ·t fóllatí·t[531] o·matí·s
With only their children, the women would visit her.

Mohmen hoktvkuce momet hoktē enhoktvlkv oren omis,
móhmin hoktakóci mo·mít hoktí· inhoktálka[i] ô·lin o·mêys
Now little girls and even those who have reached womanhood

"Nake yv omakat momekot vretskvrēs" kicet, naket omakat em onayet
nâ·ki ya o·mâ·ka·t mô·mikot aɫickáɫi·s keycít nâ·kit omâ·ka·t imóna·yít
were told, "Do not do things like this," so they told them what these were,

em vsehaket vculvke hoktvlvke tis fullvtēs.
imásiha·kít acolakí hoktalákiteys follatí·s
and they instructed them about it, old men and women did.

---

[i] *inhoktálka* = grown girl (18 and up). "Nowadays 12, I guess."

1. Ēposkē aretskof honvntake fullat em etenrvwv ahretskvs.
   i·póski· a·lícko·f honantá·ki follâ·t imitînlawa áhlíckas.
1. When you are menstruating, do not go among men.

Ēposkvnahē cehahkvrēs kicakvtēt omēs. Ēposkvnahē makat
i·po·skaná·hi· ciháhkáli·s kéyca·katí·t ô·mi·s i·po·skaná·hi· ma·kâ·t
You may become ēposkvnahē, they said. Ēposkvnahē means

ēposkē cenwikeko 'svwoskē cehahkēs maketvn okakvtēs. Vretv estomepēto estomis
i·pó·ski· cinwéykiko· 'sawó·ski· ciháhki·s ma·kitán oka·katí·s alíta isto·mipí·to· istô·meys
your menstruation will never stop. They warned them

vrekot honvntake ayen hompet vrvranekon em vsēhet okakvtēt omēs.
álikot honantá·ki a·yín hompít alalá·niko·n imási·hít oka·katí·t ô·mi·s
not to go anywhere or to eat with men.

2. Pvtakv ohhvtakhvkē ohwvkiketskvs. Sicetskof,
   patá·ka ohhatakhaki· ohwakêykíckas seycícko·f
2. Do not lie across a bed. When you give birth,

cem vtakhahkvrēs kicakvtēs. Sicvranetskof,
cimatakháhkáli·s kéyca·katí·s séycala·nícko·f
[your baby] may be sideways, they said. That means that when you're going to give birth,

estuce vtakhvkēt ofvn wakkehpen escestemerikvrēs maketvn okakvtēs.
istocí atakhakí·t ó·fan wakkíhpin iscistimilêykáli·s ma·kitán oka·katí·s
the baby will lie sideways inside, and you'll suffer.

3. Eslafkv eswarē nake pahpetskvs. Sicetskof, escetvcikvrēs.
   islá·fka iswa·li· nâ·ki pahpíckas seycícko·f iscitacêykáli·s
3. Do not eat anything with a cutting knife. When you give birth, you may tear from it.

Warket hompet omvs kicakvtēs.
wa·lkít[532] hompít omás kéyca·katí·s
Eat it cut up, they said.

'Warkē' makat akket waret hompet omvs kicet escetvcikvrēs.
wa·lkí· ma·kâ·t a·kkít wa·lít hompít omás keycít iscitacêykáli·s
'Cut up' is to say bite it off and eat it, or you may tear from it.

Sēcehopvnikvrēs makat cenute tis cenahken
si·cihopanêykáli·s ma·kâ·t cinótiteys cináhkin
You may be ruined from it, they said, you may even lose your teeth,

vpelvranat cecukwv vtēpkis ahretskēs.
apílala·nâ·t cicókwa ati·pkêys áhlícki·s
and when you start to laugh, you may slap your hand in front of your mouth as you go about.

4.   Eco etolaswv pahpetskvs. Sicetskof ewvnhkvn escehlvrēs.
     icó itolá·swa páhpíckas seycícko·f iwánhkan iscíhláli·s
4.   Do not eat the tongue of a deer. When you give birth, you might die of thirst.

5.   Eco torkop-ohlikv pahpetskvs. Sicetskof escefekehkvrēs.
     icó to·lkopohléyka páhpíckas seycícko·f iscifikihkáli·s
5.   Do not eat the knee pan of a deer. When you give birth, you may tremble violently.

6.   Svyaklē huerē ahretskvs.
     sayá·kli· hoylí· áhlíckas
6.   Do not go about standing with your legs far apart.

Este sulkat ehomv hopuewv cenlvtikvrēs.
ísti sólka·t ihóma hopóywa cinlatêykáli·s
The baby might fall out in front of many people.

7.   Penwv esokso pahpetskvs. Cemvnettē monken
     pínwa isókso páhpíckas cimanítti·[533] *móŋkin*
7.   Do not eat turkey hips [drumsticks]. While you are still young,

cesokso cennokkē hahkis ahretskvrēs kicakvtēt omēs.
cisókso cínno·kkí· háhkeys áhlíckáli·s kéyca·katí·t ò·mi·s
your hips may become painful as you go about, they said.

8.   Nake encvkvspv pahpetskvs. Sicetskof, esceholahnvrēs.
     nâ·ki incakáspa páhpíckas seycícko·f isciholáhnáli·s
8.   Do not eat the gizzard of anything. When you give birth, you might defecate.

9.   Eco hvsnērkv papetsken omat estuce heckuecetskat cēpvnē vlkēn heckuecēt vretskvrēs.
     icó hasní·lka pa·píckin o·mâ·t istoci hickoycícka·t[534] *ci·pani· álki·n hickoyci·t alíckáli·s*
9.   If you eat a deer's testicle, the babies you have will only be boys.

10. Nake poktvn papetskvten omat, poktvn kayēt vretskvrēs.
    nâ·ki póktan[i] pa·píckatin o·mâ·t póktan ka·yí·t alickáli·s
10. If you eat something unnaturally double, you might give birth to twins only.

11. Hoktvke hoyvnakv vpakē ahretskvs. Ecohhokicvrēs kicakvtēs.
    hoktakí hoyaná·ka apâ·ki· áhłíckas icóhhokêycáli·s[535] kéyca·katí·s
11. Do not go around with adulterous [hoyvnakv] women. You might expel gas, they said.

Hoyvnakv hoktvke hoktarvken okēt omēs.
hoyaná·ka hoktakí hokta·łakín o·kí·t ô·mi·s
By hoyvnakv we mean adulterous women.

Mvn vpaket aretskat hoktarv em vretv ecohtvlikēs.
man apâ·kit a·lícka·t hoktá·la imalitá icohtalêyki·s
As you go about with them, the adulterer's ways may rub off on you.

Cesvpahtēs. Cehoktahrēs makatot okakvtēs.
cisapáhti·s cihoktáhłi·s ma·kâ·tot oka·katí·s
You might become conditioned to it. You may become an adulterer, they said.

12. Esarē homipetskvs. Ascenfullephohyvrēs.
    isa·li· homêypíckas a·scinfolliphóhyáli·s
12. Do not eat while walking around. Someone may have an affair with your [spouse].

Cehe tat hoktē ētvn ēyvpayet svrēpen aretskis ohcēs maketvt omēs.
cihita·t hoktí· i·tan i·yapa·yít sáli·pín a·líckeys óhci·s ma·kitát ô·mi·s
Your husband might go around with another woman, the saying means.

13. Eswakkē homipetskvs. Escenlomhephohyvrēs.
    iswákki· homêypíckas iscinlomhiphóhyáli·s
13. Do not eat while lying down. Someone might lie with your [spouse].

Cehe tat hoktē ētvt aenwakkēpen aretskētis ohcēs maketvn okakvtēs.
cihita·t hoktí· i·tat a·inwakkî·pin a·lícki·teys óhci·s ma·kitán oka·katí·s
Your husband might lie with another woman, they meant.

---

[i] Applies to eggs, potatoes, etc.

14. Este-honvntake taklēcētskat cehoktarēhohcvrēs
    istihonantá·ki takli·cí·cka·t cihokta·li·hóhcáli·s[536]
14. Men you ridicule might make you commit adultery.

Yvhiket heleswvn hayet hoktē hoktalēckvn kerrvkēt sasen okakvtēs.
yaheykít 'hilíswan ha·yít hoktí· hokta·lí·ckan kiłłaki·t sâ·sin oka·katí·s
They meant some knew how to sing and make medicine to make women adulterous.

Vculvke em punvkv tat hoktucen okat,
acolakí imponákata·t hoktocín o·kâ·t
In the old people's language, for hoktuce ['girl']

hoklosucen kicet, hoktvkucen okat hoklosvken kicakēt okakvtēs.
hoklosócin keycít hoktakócin o·kâ·t hoklosákin kéyca·kí·t oka·katí·s
they said hoklosuce, and for hoktvkuce ['little girls'], they said hoklosvke.

15. "Rē-hutke, eccvkotakse tat celahyetskvs. Cepesē tis cencvpcahkvrēs" kicet,
    li·hótki iccakotáksita·t ciláhyíckas cipisí·teys[537] *cincapcáhkáli·s keycít*
15. "Do not touch a feathered arrow or bow. Your breasts might get long," they said;

eccvkotakse enrē vpvkē celayetv em vsehakēt omvtēs, hoklosvke tat.
iccakotáksi inłí· apáki· cila·yitá imásiha·kí·t o·matí·s hoklosákita·t.
they were warned about touching a bow and arrow, little girls were.

A Short Saying (Nak Onvkv Koconcokusat)[i]

J. Hill (XXI:87)

Este-cate hoktvlvket okakat, "Hokoset hvkihket cokeko tayet,
isticá·ti hoktalákit oka·kâ·t 'hokosít hakeyhkít có·kiko· tâ·yit
Old Indian women used to say, "If an infant cries and can't nurse,

ecke epesē tis tepoyet noceko tayen omat,
ícki ipisí·teys típo·yít nocíko· tâ·yin o·mâ·t
fights his own mother's breast and can't sleep,

---

[i] Title: *nâ·k onáka koconcokósa·t* 'short stories'.

ohwikucet sahkopanen okēs maket,

ohweykocít[538] *sáhkopa·nín o·kí·s ma·kít*

it means the <u>ohwikuce</u> is playing with him," they said.

mv estuce ēyohhecēn ēset cukon svfolotket ostihcet esfekhonnvken omat

ma istocí i·yohhicí·n î·sit cokón sáfolo·tkít ostéyhcit isfikhônnakin o·mâ·t

If you hold the baby facing you and take him around the house four times and stop,

mv hokose hvkihkvtē wikēs makvnts.

ma 'hokosí hakeyhkatí·[539] *weykí·s ma·kánc.*

the infant will stop crying, they used to say.

[Signs of the Last Days][540]

J. Hill (Haas XXII:101–105)

Hofonē vculvke fullat okakat,

hofóni· acolakí follâ·t oka·kâ·t

The old people of long ago said

eto-esse vpēttē eshayvkvtē elecvn este vculạkuset, hoktvlạkusē estomis vpoket,

itoʔíssi api·ttí· isha·yakáti· ilícan ísti acolă·ⁿkosit hoktală·ⁿkosi· istô·meys apô·kit

old men and even old women will sit underneath arbors they had made with leaves,

Kelesto yvhiketvn yvhiket sakisạket vpokakē hakat

kilísto· yaheykitán yaheykít sá·keysă·ⁿkit apó·ka·kí· ha·kâ·t

singing <u>Kelesto</u> songs, shouting. And when this becomes common,

ēkvnv vculēpen este omvlkv ensumketvt vnakuecan omvrēs makakvtēs makakvnts.

i·kanáʔ acolî·pin ísti omálka insomkitát ana·kôyca·n omáłi·s má·ka·katí·s má·ka·kánc

the earth is getting old, the time is near when everyone passes away, they said, it was told.

<u>Kelesto</u> yvhiketv mēkosvpkv yvhiketv maketvt omēs.

kilísto· yaheykitá mi·kosápka yaheykitá ma·kitát ô·mi·s

<u>Kelesto</u> songs are said to be prayerful songs.

Ēkvnv vculēpat, eto tis casketskat catv fịhnen hēcetsken

i·kaná acolî·pa·t itóteys cá·skicka·t cá·ta féyⁿhnin hi·cíckin

When the world gets old, when you chop wood, you will see blood flow,

cvto tekvlikvtet catv fįhnen hvkįhket liken hechoyē hakat
cató tikalêykatit[541] *cá·ta féyⁿhnin hakàyⁿhkit lêykin hícho·yí· ha·kâ·t*
and when blood flows from a rock that is broken apart and is seen sitting there crying,

nettv espokē vnąkuecusan omvrēs makaket okvtēs.
nítta ispó·ki· anăⁿkoycósa·n omáli·s má·ka·kít o·katí·s
it will mean the final day is at hand.

"Hoktuce ˀpesē cokēn eshoyen hēcvyvnks, hvte vwǫlusat" kontskan,
hoktocí ˀpisí· co·ki·n ishô·yin hi·cayáŋks hatí awŏⁿlosa·t kônckâ·n
When you think, "I saw a little baby girl nursing just now,"

echuswv esēt eshueren hēcetsken omat,
ichóswa[542] *isí·t ishôylin hi·cíckin o·mâ·t*
then if you see her standing there holding her daughter,

nettv espokē vwulican omvrēs makakvtē mv mv tat onvkv sulkēn pohvyēt os.
nítta ispó·ki· awolêyca·n omáli·s má·ka·katí· ma matâ·t onáka sólki·n po·hayí·t ô·ⁿs.
the final day will be at hand, they said, and I have heard this many times.

[Dreams]

J. Hill (Haas XXII:107–109)

Wesken ēsket aret estvpuecat fon senhēcvkvnts makakvnts.
wískin i·skit a·lít ístapoycâ·t fó·n sínhi·cakánc má·ka·kánc.
When you dream of drinking whisky, you'll find bees, they used to say.

Hoktēn tem punayet estvpuecat punvttvn hehcēskos makakvnts.
hokti·n timpona·yít ístapoycâ·t ponáttan híhci·sko·s má·ka·kánc.
When you talk to a woman in a dream, you won't be able to find game, they used to say.

Econ sestvpuecat eco hehcēskos, fayē arvkat, makakvnts.
icón sístapoycâ·t icó híhci·sko·s fa·yi· a·lakâ·t má·ka·kánc
When you dream of deer, you won't find deer when you go hunting, they used to say.

Fakv arē totkv etēcvkan totkvt takyvhiken omat,
fá·ka a·lí· tó·tka itî·caka·n tó·tkat tákyaheykin o·mâ·t
If you go hunting and build a fire and the fire sings,

eco elēcet monkat penwv tis, nokose tis elēcvkēs makakvnts.
icó ili·cít móŋka·t pínwateys nokósiteys ili·cakí·s má·ka·kánc
you can kill deer or turkey or bear, they used to say.

Estet sukhv-yopon pvpemąhēt on omat 'cvpvkvn tąyēs makakvnts.
ístit sokhayopó·n papimā·ⁿhi·t ô·n o·mâ·t 'capakáⁿ[543] *tǎ·ⁿyi·s má·ka·kánc.*
If someone eats a lot of pig noses, he will plow a lot [?], they used to say.

Old Time Law

J. Hill (Hill III:6; Haas XVIII:149–153)

Vhakv empvtakv seko oketv omof, vhakvt ocvtēt omēs. Hoktēt ehe ocēt omat
ahá·ka impatá·ka síko· okíta ô·mo·f ahá·kat o·catí·t ô·mi·s[i] *hoktí·t ihí ó·ci·<t> ô·ma·t*
Before there was a constitution, there was a law. If a woman with a husband

honvnwv ētvn vcakkarēt omen, mv hoktē ehe enahvmkvlket kerraken omat,
honánwa í·tan acákka·li·t ô·min ma hoktí· ihi ina·hamkálkit kílla·kin o·mâ·t
was going with another man, and the woman's husband's kin found out,

hoktē honvnwv 'tepakvn vhonkvtkv sekon 'rokafruecakēt omvtēs.
hoktí· honánwa (?) 'tipǎ·ⁿkan[544] *ahoŋkátka síko·n 'loka·flóyca·kí·t*[545] *o·matí·s*
both the man and the woman would be whipped without count.

Mohmof wikekot 'setewelakē monken omat, 'svhokkolat ehvckon enwarakēt omvtēs.
móhmo·f wéykikot 'sitíwila·kí· môŋkin o·mâ·t 'sahókko·lâ·t iháckon inwá·la·ki·t o·matí·s[ii]
Then, if they didn't quit and kept going together, the second time they cut off an ear.

Mohmen wikekot 'setewelakē monkēpen omat, 'svtuccēnat eyopo yoksv lowvckan
móhmin wéykikot 'sitíwila·kí· moŋkî·pin o·mâ·t 'satócci·nâ·t iyopó· yóksa[546] *lowácka·n*
Then, if they didn't quit and kept going together, the third time they cut off

---

[i] The clan kinfolks had charge of morals. If there are not enough clan kin to hold the offender to whip him, then ask another clan member.

[ii] Used an old dull knife. If it happened to be sharp, knocked it against a rock to make it dull. I guess they gonna make him remember it.

When they cut off the ears, they throw them away so they can't find them any more. Otherwise, they might put them on again.

entvcakēt omvtēs. Momen honvnwv ehiwv ocēt omat
íntaca·kí·t o·matí·s mo·mín honánwa ihéywa ó·ci·t ô·ma·t
the tip of the nose, the soft part. And if a man had a wife

hoktē ētvn ehiwv hayēt 'svrēpen, hoktē enahvmkvlke kerraken omat,
hoktí· í·tan ihéywa há·yi·t sáłi·pín hoktí· ina·hamkâlki kíłła·kín o·mâ·t
but went with another woman as his wife, if the woman's kin found out,

mv vhakatan svfvshotēt omvtēs. Hofonē vculvketate em vhakvt omvtēs.
ma ahá·ka·tá·n[547] 'safásho·tí·t o·matí·s hofóni· acolakítá·ti imaha·kát ô·matí·s.
they applied that [same] law. This was the law of the old ones a long time ago.

Este rokvfhoyan hecvkot,
ísti łokáfho·yâ·n hicákot
Although I haven't seen anyone whipped,

yopo entvchoyvtē arateu hecvyvtē sekot omis,
'yopó· intachoyáti· a·lâ·tiw hicáyati· síkot o·mêys
and I haven't seen anyone going around with the tip of their nose cut off,

ehvcko enwarhoyvtēn hecakvyat sasvtēt os. Hoktvket vhakv sestvfastet omvtēs.
ihácko inwa·łhoyáti·n hica·kayâ·t sa·sati·t ô·ⁿs[i] hoktakít ahá·ka sístafa·stít o·matí·s
I have seen some with their ears cut off. The women applied the law.

Honvntakeu sēyvnicet hoktvke yekcvkē sasat tis ennake tokis,
honantá·kiw si·yáneycít hoktakí yikcakí· sa·sâ·tteys innâ·ki tó·keys[548]
They used men, and women who were very strong, and people who were not even kin;

em vnicv hopoyet este tat rokafaket omvtēs.
<im>anéyca hopo·yít ístita·t loká·fa·kít o·matí·s.
they looked for helpers and whipped the people.

---

[i] JH has seen man and his wife both with ears cut off (they cut off both ears). JH never saw anybody with nose cut off.

In old days don't hardly tell lies on each other — when asked whether they make mistake.

If those laws were enforced nowadays, there ain't nobody had ears on, only two yrs. old.

Scalp-Taking

J. Hill (Hill III:7; Haas XX:1–9)[i]

Hofonof este-cate horre etenhayē fullof, horre-ofv esten elēcat
hofôꞏnoꞏf isticáꞏti hółłi itínhaꞏyiꞏ follôꞏf hołłiʔóꞏfa isti\<n\> iliꞏcâꞏt
Long ago, when the Indians made war on each other, when a person was killed in battle,

ekvhvrpen encopaket, <u>tewv</u> kicet ocakvtēt omēs.
ikahálpin incopaꞏkít tiwá keycít óꞏcaꞏkatíꞏt ôꞏmiꞏs
they'd scalp the head, and that was called a <u>tewv</u> ['scalp or lock of hair'].

Este ekvhvrpe encopahkē ehvpo sohhayofvt, espihket sayet omvtēs.
ísti ikahálpi incopáhkiꞏ ihapóꞏ sóhhaꞏyôꞏfat[549] *íspeyhkít saꞏyít oꞏmatíꞏs.*
When the one who had scalped was taking it to his camp, he would whoop as he went.

Este ekvhvrpe ēsē espihketv kerkusēn espihket omakvtēt omēs.
ísti ikahálpi îꞏsiꞏ ispayhkitá kílkosiꞏn íspayhkít omaꞏkatíꞏt ôꞏmiꞏs
There was a special whoop to use when he had a scalp.

Este ekvhvrpe ehvpo 'resvlahkof, mv nerē nocekot senhvyatket omakvtēs.
ísti ikahálpi ihapóꞏ 'lisaláhkoꞏf ma niłíꞏ nocíkoꞏt sínhayaꞏtkít omaꞏkatíꞏs
When someone's scalp was brought back to camp, they would go all that night without

Momet cvtotvpeksen hiyēcet mv estekvhvrpen ohpvticet, hotopet,
moꞏmít catotapíksin háyyiꞏcít maʔ istikahálpin óhpateycít hotoꞏpít
sleep. Then a flat rock was heated, the scalp was spread out on it, baked,

tvpeksēn kvrpēcet omakvtēs. Momet ēlicet sopanet komis
tapíksiꞏn kálpiꞏcít omaꞏkatíꞏs. moꞏmít iꞏlêycit[550] *sópaꞏnít kôꞏmeys*
and they dried it flat. And they would dance with it,

---

[i] Written by J. Hill, Jan. 15, 1941. Read: June 24, 1941. J. Hill says this happened back in the East somewhere. "We never did have no war in this country beside that Civil War."

esfullvtēt omēs. Momen estuce hēckat cēpvnēt on omat,
ísfollatí·t ô·mi·s[i] mo·mín istocí hi·ckâ·t ci·paní·t ó·n o·mâ·t
wearing it [on the side over the hip]. And when a baby was born, if it was a boy,

mv cēpanat erke tis, monkat epuca tis, epvwv tis este ekvhvrpe encopaket omvten omat,
ma ci·pâ·na·t ílkiteys móŋka·t ipocá·teys ipáwateys ísti ikahátpi íncopa·kít o·matín o·mâ·t
that boy's father, or grandfather, or mother's brother, if they had taken a scalp,

mv estvlke honvpse cēpvnvke heckakat hocefhuecat
ma ʔistâlki honápsi ci·panáki hícka·kâ·t hocífhoycâ·t
the boys who were offspring of those people were named

Copahke, Tewvspihkv,
copáhki tiwaspáyhka
Copahke ['Peeled-it'], Tewvspihkv ['Whoops-with-scalp'],

Tewvlihce, Ēlihce.
tiwaléyhci i·léyhci.
Tewvlihce ['Set-down-the-scalp'], Ēlihce ['Set-it-on-himself'].

Copahke este elehce ekv encopakvtēn okēs.
copáhki ísti ilíhci iká incopa·katí·n o·kí·s
Copahke means the person who killed and took a scalp.

Tewv-espihkv este ekvhvrpe ēsē espihkē sayvtēn okēs.
tiwaʔispáyhka ísti ikahátpi î·si· íspayhkí· sa·yatí·n o·kí·s.
Tewv-espihkv means the person who took the scalp and went back whooping.

Ēlihce, Tewvlihce este ekvhvrpe ēlicē 'sopanvtēn okēs.
i·léyhci tiwaléyhci ísti ikahátpi i·lêyci·[551] sópa·natí·n o·kí·s
Ēlihce and Tewvlihce mean the person who put the scalp on [his hip] and danced with it.

---

[i] The scalp is always worn on the left side so that it will be next to the fire + can be seen. JHH never heard of a special scalp dance. Women danced, too, when the men wore scalps.

    They were very much afraid of a dead person. So after having taken a scalp, they stayed up that night to take medicine to keep that ghost from ever bothering them (didn't dance). Had special medicine + special medicine man. Their was a special song sung when they stretched and dried that scalp. The medicine man was the one that sang — if not, the one that took the scalp. Either one was all right, but the one that took the scalp did it only if he knew the proper song.

Este elehcof ekv encopvkekot wihkē lētkvtē este honvpse
ísti ilíhco·f iká incopákikot wéyhki· li·tkatí· ísti honápsi
The offspring of someone who killed without taking a scalp, who left it and ran,

Tewvwihke makēt hocefhuecakvtēt omēs.
tiwawéyhki ma·kí·t hocifhóyca·katí·t ô·mi·s
was named Tewvwihke ['Left the Scalp'].

Vhvlahte hocēfat este ekvhvrpe hotopat,
ahaláhti hoci·fâ·t ísti ikahálpi hoto·pâ·t
The name Vhvlahte means the offspring of the one who baked the scalp,

cvtohiyen ohpvticet, hvlatet, senēpēcet, tvpeksē kvrpēcvtēn honvpsen okēs:
catoháyyin ohpatêycit hala·tít siní·pi·cít tapíksi· kálpi·catí·n honápsin o·kí·s
spread it out on a hot rock, gripped it, stretched it, and dried it flat:

Vhvlahte, Hvlahte. Pihkelēcv horre-ofvn pihkē este aran elēcesasvten omat,
ahaláhti haláhti. payhkilí·ca holliʔó·fan payhkí· ísti a·lâ·n ili·cisâ·satin o·mâ·t
Vhvlahte, Hvlahte. Pihkelēcv: If the one who whoops in battle is killed by someone,

mv este elēcē arvtē este enahvmke honapsan Pihkelēcv kicet hocēfet omhoyvtēs.
ma ísti ili·cí· a·łatí· ísti ina·hámki hona·psâ·n payhkili·ca keycít hoci·fit ómho·yatí·s[552]
the offspring of the person doing the killing was named Pihkelēcv.

Hofonof este-cate vculvke 'sem vpeyetv encēpvnvken ensapēt omakvtēt omēs.
hofô·no·f[553] *isticá·ti acolakí 'simapiyíta inci·panákin insa·pí·t oma·katí·t ô·mi·s*[i]
In olden times, the custom of the old Indians was to scratch their boys.

Esakpv tis ensapet, ele-empakkon ensapaket omvtēs.
isákpateys ínsa·pít iliʔimpá·kkon insá·pa·kít o·matí·s.
They scratched their arms or the calves of their legs.

Ena yekcē taranan maket ensapet
iná· yíkci· tá·la·nâ·n ma·kít ínsa·pit
They were scratched so that their bodies would be strong,

---

[i] Grandfather (*ipocá·*) and uncle (*ipáwa*) scratched them.

ecke tis monkat erke tis nake hiyomēt aret omvs kicē emvhayakan
íckiteys móŋka·t íłkiteys nâ·ki hayyó·mi·t a·lít omás keycí· imahá·ya·kâ·n
and when their mother or their father taught them how to behave,

em apohicekot cēpvnvket fullen omat mv vrahkvo ensapet omakvtēs.
ima·poháyciko·t ci·panákit follín o·mâ·t ma ałáhkaw ínsa·pít oma·katí·s.
if the boys did not mind them, they scratched them for that too.

Momet "Tewvn yvmvn 'svlicvhanetskēt omēs kicet
mo·mít tiwán yamán[i] 'saléycaha·nícki·t ô·mi·s keycít
And saying, "You might wear a scalp here,"

empolokcon tohwelepkēn ensapet omakvtēs.
impolókcon[554] tohwilípki·n ínsa·pít oma·katí·s[ii]
they scratched a cross on their hip joints.

Mvt cēpvnvke apohicē fullicetv vrahkv ensapetvt mvt vhakucet omvtēs.
mat ci·panáki a·pohéyci· folleycitá ałáhka insa·pitát mat aha·kocít ô·mati·s[555]
To scratch the boys so they would be obedient, that was a rule.

The Comanches and the Creeks (Kvmince, Maskoken)[iii]

J. Hill (Hill III:8–10; Haas XX:11–29)

Kvmincvlket Maskokvlken horren enhayetvn eyacēton,
kamayncâlkit ma·sko·kâlkin hółlin inha·yitán iyá·ci·ton
The Comanche wanted to make war against the Muscogee,

este-Maskoke etvlwv kerrētot horre hakekan hē̄rēs komet
istima·skó·ki itálwa kíłłi·tot hółli há·kika·n hĭ·ⁿłi·s kô·mit
and the Muscogee Nation learned of it and thought it best

---

[i] Here *yamán* refers to the hip, because narrator indicates it.

[ii] They might put this cross on any disobedient boys. The cross was put only on boys, not on grown men. This threat was meant merely to make the boys obey. Once in a while they put a cross on them.

[iii] Title: *kamáynci ma·skó·kin* 'Comanche, Muscogee'.

este-Maskoke vkerricet omis. Etenherkē etvlwv kakvrēn komeyē estomis
istima·skó·ki akílleycít o·mêys itinhíłki· itálwa ká·káłi·n ko·miyí.[556] *istô·meys*
not to have war. We wanted the two nations to live in peace with each other,

este-Maskoke toyeyat pomet ohhvpēyēt etem punahoyetvn kohmēt
istima·skó·ki tô·yiya·t pó·mit óhhapi·yi·t itimpona·hoyítan kóhmi·t
and we, the Muscogee, wanted to go and talk with them,

'rem oricēn omat nake herekis ocē tayēs komaket fullet
'limółeycí·n o·mâ·t nâ·ki hiłíkeys ó·ci· tâ·yi·s kó·ma·kít follít
but they thought something bad might happen when we got there,

herkv hayvkvrēn este-Semvnolvlken ohtothoyvtēs.
híłka ha·yakáłi·n istisimano·lâlkin ohtótho·yatí·s
and to make peace, the Seminoles were sent to them.

Kvmincvlke 'rem orihcē tem punahoyvrēn
kamayncâlki 'limołéyhci· timpona·hoyáłi·n
The Muscogees and the Seminoles made an agreement,

este-Maskokvke Semvnolvke tenfaccat
istima·sko·kaki simano·laki tínfa·ccâ·t
so that they would go talk with the Comanches:

"Kvmince herkv yacekot acenholwvyēcaken omat,
kamáynci híłka yá·cikot a·cinholwayí·ca·kín[i] *o·mâ·t*
"If the Comanche do not want peace and become angry with you,

Maskoke toyeyat pomet tepoyeyvrēs" kicaken, este-Semvnole vkvsahmet vpēyat,
ma·skó·ki tô·yiya·t pó·mit 'tipoyíyáli·s kéyca·kín istisimanó·li akasáhmit apî·ya·t
we the Muscogees will fight with them," they said, and the Seminoles agreed and went.

Kvmince-mēkko 'rem oricet,
kamayncimí·kko 'limołêycit
They arrived before the Comanche chief

---

[i] Haas nb has *a·cinhólwayi·cakín*.

"Herkvn etem ocēt Kvmince, Maskoke 'tepakat
híɫkan itimóˑciˑt kaméynci maˑskóˑki 'tipâˑkaˑt
and said, "If both of you, the Comanche and the Muscogee,

kakatsken omat hērēs komeyatet
kâˑkáˑckin oˑmâˑt hìˑⁿliˑs kòˑmiyaˑtít
could live in peace with one another, it would be good, we believe,

cenyicet omēs" kicaket oman,
cinyêycit oˑmíˑs kéycaˑkít oˑmâˑn
and that is why we come to you," they told him.

Kvmince-mēkko tat "Herkv cvyaceks. 'Tepokv min cvyacēs" maket,
kameyncimíˑkkotaˑt híɫka cayáˑciks 'tipoˑkamêyn cayáˑciˑs maˑkít
But the Comanche chief said, "I do not want peace. I would rather fight," he said,

esakpv tat eccvkotakse enrē nake sechetv min 'svhopayet
isákpataˑt iccakotáksi inɫiˑ nâˑki sichitá mêyn[i] sáhopaˑyít
and using his arm like he was shooting something with a bow and arrow, he said,

hiyomēcetv min cvyacēs maket liket omen,
hayyomiˑcitá mêyn cayáˑciˑs maˑkít lêykit oˑmín[557]
"This is what I want to do," as he sat.

"Mon omat fulecvranēs. Momis opunvkv tat cenwikēkv, hērēn ohhvkerricet
móˑn oˑmâˑt folícalaˑníˑs moˑmêys oponakátaˑt cínweykíˑka[558] *hìˑⁿlin ohhakiɫéycit*
"Then we are going back. But we have left you word, so think about it well,

herkv tat vkvsametskan hērēs 'rehyiceyvrētok,
híɫkataˑt akasâˑmickaˑn[559] *hìˑⁿliˑs 'ɫihyéyciyáɫiˑtoˑk*
and if you agree to peace, it will be good. We will be back;

estomvranetskat fvccēcet liketsken yicēn omat,
istóˑmaɫaˑníckaˑt faccîˑcit lêykickin yeycíˑn oˑmâˑt
decide what you are going to do, and when we return,

---

[i] Haas nb has *siccihitamêyn*.

'tem punahokv espokētarēs kihcet 'rvwēpvtēs.
'timpona·hoká ispo·kí·tá·li·s kéyhcit láwi·patí·s
we will talk for the last time," they said and returned home.

'Svhokkolat Semvnolvke Kvmince-mēkko hecvranē vpeyvranof,
'sahókko·lâ·t simano·lakí[560] kamayncimí·kko hicála·ní· apíyala·nô·f
The second time the Seminoles were going to see the Comanche chief,

este-mvnettvlke yekcvkē ceyvlhoyē tayan sulkēn ēyvpahyet svpēyvtēs.
istimanittâlki yikcaki· ciyálho·yí· tâ·ya·n sólki·n i·yapáhyit sápi·yatí·s
they took with them many strong young men who could fight hard.

Momet yv mvnettvlke em punayet,
mo·mít ya 'manittâlki ímpona·yit
And they talked with the young men, [saying,]

"Puhvpon takkvpokatsken, Kvmince-mēkko tem punayeyan,
pohapó·n takkapô·ká·ckin kamayncimí·kko tímpona·yiyâ·n
"You will stay at the camp, and when we talk with the Comanche chief,

herkv pum vkvsvmeko tayen kērrēn omat, punken kvwapēn omat yahkatskvrēs.
hílka pomakasámiko· tâ·yin ki·llí·n o·mâ·t póŋkin kawa·pí·n o·mâ·t yá·hká·ckáli·s
if we find out he doesn't agree to peace, if we raise our hands, you will shout.

Mont yahket a-epuhpefatiket, Kvmince-mēkkon hvlvtatskvrēs"
mónt ya·hkít a·ʔipohpifa·têykit kamayncimí·kkon halatá·ckáli·s
And still shouting, you will run toward us and take hold of the Comanche chief,"

kicahken, este-mvnettvlke ehvpon fekhonnaken,
keycáhkin istimanittâlki ihapó·n fikhonnâ·kin
they ordered them. The young men stayed at their camp,

vculvke tat vpēyet Kvmince-mēkko ehomv 'rorihcet,
acolakíta·t apî·yit kamayncimí·kko ihóma 'lołéyhcit
and the old ones went before the Comanche chief, [saying.]

"Hiyomat hvtvm rehcenyicvkēt omēs. Herkv vkvsvmē tayet vkerricatsken omat,
hayyô·ma·t hatâm lihcinyêycaki·t o·mí·s hílka akasamí· tâ·yit akiłłêycá·ckin o·mâ·t
"Now again we come to you. We have come to you wanting to know

kerretvn puyacēt cenyicvkēt omēs" maket,
kiłłitán poyá·ci·t cinyêycaki·t o·mí·s ma·kít
if you have decided to agree to peace," they said.

Semvnolvke tat Kvmince-mēkkon em punvyaket oman,
simano·lakíta·t kamayncimí·kkon imponáya·kít o·mâ·n
The Seminoles talked with the Comanche chief, but he said,

"Herkv tat cvyaceks. Horre min cvyacēs" maket,
hiłkata·t cayá·ciks hółłi mêyn cayá·ci·s ma·kít
I do not want peace. I would rather have war," he said,

Kvmince-mēkko tat likēpen,
kamayncimí·kkota·t leykî·pin
and the Comanche chief sat undisturbed.

"Kos. Horre sekat mit hērētan oketskes kicaket omis,
kos hółłi sikâ·t mêyt hĭ·ⁿli·ta·n o·kíckis kéyca·kít o·mêys
"No. It would be good not to have war," they said,

vkvsvmeko tạyuset likēpen,
akasamíko· tǎ·ⁿyosit leykĭ·ⁿpin[561]
but he still would not agree, as he sat calmly.

vpokusỵmmvliket Semvnolvke herkv-hayv tat enken kvwvpaken,
apô·kosǎmⁿmalêykit simano·lakí hiłkahá·yata·t íŋkin kawápa·kín
After sitting a long time, the Seminole peace-makers raised their hands,

Semvnole este-mvnettvlke tat yahiket, yahket, ohpefatiket,
simanó·li istimanittâlkita·t ya·hâykit ya·hkít ohpifa·têykit
and the young Seminoles whooped and yelled and ran toward them,

'svculvke vpokan 'roricen, Kvmince mvnettvlkeu vpvkēt omvtētok:
'sacoláki apô·ka·n lółeycín kamáynci 'manittâlkiw apáki·t ô·mati·to·k
and as they got to where the old ones sat, the young Comanches were there:

em eccvkotakse cvwaket nēpket kotaksēcakof,
imiccakotáksi cawâ·kit ni·pkít[i] kotaksi·ca·kô·f
they took their bows, and when they pulled them back and bent them,

eccvkotakse enkvcēken rē tis enkvcēken, estomvkeko tayet fullen,
iccakotáksi íŋkaci·kín lí·teys íŋkaci·kín isto·makíko· tâ·yit follín
the bows broke, even the arrows broke, and they couldn't do anything.

Semvnolvke tat em mvnettvlken ohtohket,
simano·lakíta·t[562] immanittâlkin óhto·hkit
The Seminoles drove their young men forward:

"Kvmince-mēkkon hvlvtaks" kicahken, hvlvtakof,
kamayncimí·kkon halátáks keycáhkin haláta·kô·f
"Take hold of the Comanche chief," they ordered them, and when they got hold of him,

wenakē monken, ekvhvrpen encopahket, raspefatkehpen,
wina·kí· môŋkin ikahálpin incopáhkit la·spifa·tkíhpin
he was still alive, and they took his scalp and ran back with it,

Kvmince ēyvtelohyet a-assēcet fullof,
kamáynci i·yatilóhyit a·ʔá·ssi·cít follô·f
and when the Comanche gathered themselves and gave chase,

vnrvpēt hotvlē-rakkot oske-rakko vpvkēt ohhvlahken,
anlapí·t hotali·łákkot oskiłákko apáki·t ohhaláhkin
a strong wind with great rain came upon them,

uelvokē-rakko tis hakaken, estomvkeko tayet fekhonnahken,
oylawki·łákkoteys há·ka·kín isto·makíko· tâ·yit fikhonnáhkin
a lot of flooding took place, and they could do nothing and had to stop.

ayen netta vnvcomēt yvfyaken uelvokē hoyvnē poken,
a·yín nittá· anacomí·t yafyâ·kin oylawkí· hoyáni· pô·kin[563]
Many days passed, the flood waters all passed,

---

[i] *ni·pkitá* = to pull back on bow (old-time word). [MM doesn't know this word.]

Kvmince em opunayv tat ayet Semvnolvke 'rem oran
kaméynci imoponá·yata·t â·yit simano·lakí límo·lâ·n
and the speaker for the Comanche went to the Seminoles, and on arriving,

em mēkko ekvhvrpe tat senhvyatket encukorakkon nvkvftēt
immí·kko ikahálpita·t sinhayâ·tkit incokoɫákkon nakáfti·t
because of his chief's scalp, [the Seminoles] had stayed up all night, meeting at their square

Semvnolvke vpoken roret enkesmelkvn konkohicet 'tetakkayet
simano·lakí apô·kin lo·lít iŋkismílkan konkohêycit 'titakkà·yit
ground, and he reached the Seminoles and bending and hooking his forefingers together,

"Hiyomēn cvyacēs" maket vlakvtēs mahokvnts.
hayyó·mi·n cayá·ci·s ma·kít ala·katí·s má·ho·kánc
he came saying, "This is what I want," it was told.

"Kvmince toyvyat este-Maskoke etvlwv tat herkvn etem ocēt
kamáynci tô·yaya·t istima·skó·ki itálwata·t hílkan itimô·ci·t[564]
"I, who am Comanche, we want peace with the Muscogee Nation,

etehvlvtkvn ocetvn puyacēs" maketvn omvtēs, enkesmelkv 'tetakkayat.
itihalátkan o·citán poyá·ci·s ma·kitán o·matí·s iŋkismílka 'titákka·yâ·t
binding us together," he said, the forefingers joined together.

Monkv este-Maskoke etvlwv horre enhayetv eyacē
môŋka istima·skó·ki[565] *itálwa hóɫɫi inha·yitá iyá·ci·*
Therefore the Comanche Nation, who had wanted to wage war with the Muscogee Nation,

Kvmince etvlwv fullvtētat wikvtēt omēs makēt onahoyēt omvnts.
kaméynci itálwa follatí·ta·t weykatí·t ô·mi·s ma·kí·t oná·ho·yí·t o·mánc
ceased wanting it, it was told long ago.

About Creek and Cherokee Towns (Este-Maskoke Etvlwv, Cvlakke Etvlwv Ohhonvkv)[i]

J. Hill (Hill III:11–15; Haas XX:31–65)

Hofonē hvsosselecv este-cate etvlwv lilakof,
hofó·ni· haso·ssilíca isticá·ti itálwa leylâ·ko·f
Long ago when the Indian tribes [or nations] were in the Southeast,

este-Maskoke etvlwv, Cvlakke etvlwv horren etenhayēt omvtēs.
istima·skó·ki itálwa calá·kki itálwa hóllin itinha·yí·t ô·mati·s
the Muscogee Nation and the Cherokee Nation used to make war on each other.

Cvlakket este-Maskoken tepketvn eyacēt omvtēs.
calákkit[566] istima·skó·kin tipkitán iyá·ci·t[567] o·matí·s
The Cherokee wanted to whip the Muscogee.

'Tepokv tat ocet esfullusvmmvliket "Tenherkepvkēts" Cvlakket mahken,
'tipokáta·t o·cit isfollosammalêykit tinhiłkipákí·c calákkit máhkin
After a long period of battles, the Cherokee said, "Let us have peace."

este-Maskokeu em vkvsahmen etenherkahkof,
istima·skó·kiw imakasáhmin itinhiłkáhko·f
The Muscogee agreed, and after making peace with one another,

Cvlakket okat, "Este-Maskoke etvlwv toyetskat, cvrvhv toyetsken,
calá·kkit o·kâ·t istima·skó·ki itálwa tô·yicka·t caláha tô·yíckin
the Cherokee said, "You, the Muscogee Nation, will be my big brother,

Cvlakke etvlwv toyvyat, cecuse toyin kakēpvkvrēs.
calá·kki itálwa tô·yaya·t cicósi tô·yeyn ka·kî·pakáli·s
and I, who am Cherokee, we will be your little brother.

Nake yekcēn vcohhvlvkvranēt nettvt ocvtētot vcohhvlakis vcvhueretskvrēs.
nâ·ki yíkci·n acohhalákala·ní·t níttat ô·cati·tot acóhhala·kêys acahôylíckáli·s[568]
Should there be a day when hard times come upon me, you will stand by me.

---

[i] Title: *istima·skó·ki itálwa calá·kki itálwa ohhonáka* 'story of Creek towns and Cherokee towns'.

Cvrvhv toyetskat vneu cecuse toyvyat, vnyekcē omvlēcusit ecehuerarēs,
caláha tô·yícka·t aníw cicósi tô·yaya·t anyikcí· omalĭ·ⁿcoseyt icihóylá·li·s
You, my big brother, I also, as your little brother, will stand by you with all my strength,

este-cate vlkē toyēkv maket etenfvccvtēt omēs.
isticá·ti álki· tô·yi·ka ma·kít itinfáccati·t ô·mi·s
because we are both Indians," they said and made an agreement.

Cvlakke etvlwv, este-Maskoke etvlwv 'tepakat yv onvkv pohayvtēs, cvmvnettof.
calákki itálwa istima·skó·ki itálwa 'tipâ·ka·t ya? onáka po·hayáti·s⁵⁶⁹ camaníttoˑf
I heard the Cherokee Nation and the Muscogee Nation tell this story when I was young.

Momen ohrolopē pale ostvnkē mahen, Cvlakke este honvnwv hvmken tem punahoyēmvts.
mo·mín ohłolopí· pá·li ô·staŋkí· mâ·hin calákki ísti? honánwa? hámkin timponá·ho·yí·mac
And about forty years ago, a Cherokee man and I had a talk.

Este-hvtke opunvkv punayvt omen, vne este-hvtke em punvkv punayv toyvkok
istihátki oponaká 'poná·yat ô·min aní istihátki imponáka 'poná·ya tó·yako·k⁵⁷⁰
He could speak the white man's language, but because I was not an English speaker,

este Maskokvlke honvnwv Kvp Mikentvs hocefkēt punyvtēken,
ísti ma·sko·kâlki honánwa kap méykintas hocífki·t pónyati·kín
a Muscogee man named Cap McIntosh interpreted for us.

tem punahoyēt omēn okat,
timponá·ho·yí·t o·mí·n o·kâ·t
As we talked, [the Cherokee man] said,

"Hofonē vculvke tatē em etenfvccetv vcakkayat, cvrvhv toyetskēs" cvkicemvts.
hofóni· acolakítá·ti· imitinfaccitá acakkâ·ya·t caláha tô·yícki·s cakeycimác
"According to the agreement of the elders long ago, you are my big brother," he told me.

Momen "Mv toyin oketskes" kihcin,
mo·mín ma? tô·yeyn o·kíckis kéyhceyn
And I said, "I am."

"Momat estont omen vm vnicekot ometskvthaks, Wvcenv tenfvccetv vnhayof?
mo·mâ·t ístónt o·mín amanéycikot o·míckáthá·ks wacína? tinfaccitá ánha·yô·f
"Then why did you not help me, when the U.S. made a treaty with me?

Vm vnicetskvten omat, etenfvccetv hēris Wvcenv tat tenfvccvyē tayēt omvtēs.
amáneycíckatin o·mâ·t itinfaccitá hĭ·ⁿłeys wacínata·t tinfáccayi· tâ·yi·t o·matí·s
If you had helped me, I might have made a good treaty with the U.S.

Momis vm vnicetskekon, Wvcenv hoporrenkv svcohfᵧnkuset
mo·mêys amanéycíckikon wacína hopołłínka sacohfăⁿkosit[571]
But you did not help me, and the U.S. outsmarted me

ēme em eyackv vlkēn vcvkvsvmepuehcet
í·mi imiyá·cka álki·n acakasamipóyhcit[572]
and had me under their control, forcing me to agree to everything they wanted

vhakv tat hǫnhoyusen vcohlomhicet svm ohwetenkē monken huerit omis.
ahá·kata·t hŏnⁿhô·yosin[573] *acohlomhêycit 'samohwitĭnⁿki·*[574] *môŋkin hôyłeyt o·méys*
and laid heavy laws upon me, and they still press down on me as I stand here.

Cecuse toyvyat — hoporrenkv rakkē sofkēn ocetskēt onkv,
cicósi tô·yaya·t hopołłínka łákki· sófki·n ó·cícki·t ôŋka
I who am your little brother — because you have a great and deep wisdom,

mvn 'svm vnicetskvten omat, vnhērvnt os, cvrvhv toyetskat" makemvts.
man sámaneycíckatin o·mâ·t anhĭ·ⁿłant ó·ⁿs[575] *caláha tô·yícka·t ma·kimác*
if you had used these to help me, I might have been better off, my big brother," he said.

Momen em vyoposkvyat hiyomvkēn kicimvts:
mo·mín imáyopo·skayâ·t hayyo·makí·n keycéymác
And I answered him like this:

"Momēpet on oketskes. Purkvlke tatē erkvlke tatē tis seko monkē 'rem ehomvn
mo·mî·pit ó·n o·kíckis połkâlki tá·ti·[576] *iłkâlki tá·ti·teys síko·*[577] *môŋki· 'limihóman*[578]
"You are right. Before our fathers or their fathers existed,

yv etenfvccetv hahoyvtēt omēs. Vcayēcet yv tenfvccetv vsehokvkē tᵧyusēt omētan
ya itinfaccitá ha·hoyáti·t[579] *ô·mi·s aca·yi·cit ya tinfaccitá asihô·kaki· tă·ⁿyosi·t ô·mi·ta·n*
this agreement was made. We should stand by this agreement,

momēkot on oketskes. 'Cvcuse toyetskat,
mó·mi·kot ó·n o·kíckis cacósi tô·yícka·t
and you are right that we don't do this. The Cherokee Nation had said, 'My little brother,[580]

nake yekcēt vcohhvlvkvranē nettvt ocvtet vcohhvlakis, vcvhueretskvrēs,
nâ·ki yíkci·t acohhalákala·nî· níttat ô·catit acohhala·kêys acahóylíckáli·s
there will come a day when difficult times come upon me, but you must stand by me,

cvrvhv toyetskat' makē Cvlakke etvlwv sehokvtē nettvt cem vlaken arvtet oketskēs.
caláha tô·yícka·t ma·kí· calákki itálwa siho·kati·[581] *níttat cimalâ·kin a·latít o·kícki·s*
my older brother,' and that day has come for you.

Monkv cvrvhv toyetskat, nake momētis ocēs komvyvtē nettv vlakekv,
môŋka caláha tô·yícka·t nâ·ki mó·mi·teys o·cí·s ko·mayáti· nítta alâ·kika
So, my big brother, the day I had thought things might happen has arrived.

"Vcvhueretsken tenfvccetv cokv satvranis" maketskvten omat,
acahóylíckin tinfaccitá có·ka sá·tala·néys ma·kíckatin o·mâ·t
If you had said, "Stand by me as I sign the agreement,"

hoporrenkv ocvyat vm omvlkuset secehuervranvyvtē tis
hopollínka ô·caya·t amomăl^nkosit 'sicihóylała·nayáti·téys
I would have stood by you with all the wisdom I have,

cvrvhv huerēs cvkonkot,
caláha hòyli·s cakónkot
but you did not think of me, your big brother standing by,

cvkerricēsekot centawvt tenfvccetv estensatehpetsken,
cakiłłĕy^nci·síkot cintă·wat tinfaccitá istinsa·tíhpíckin
you did not let me know that you were the first to sign the agreement,

momusen vnyekcē kvckehpen huerit, estomvko ta̠yusē nettvt vcohcakkekv,
mô·mosin anyikcí· kackíhpin hôyłeyt istó·mako· tă·^nyosi· níttat acohcâ·kkika
and then I felt my strength was broken;[582] I could do nothing when the day was upon me,

tenfvccetv cokv satvyvtēt os" kicimvts. Momvtētan ohrolopē pale hokkolvnkē mahen,
tinfaccitá có·ka sa·tayáti·t ô·^ns keycéymác mo·mati·ta·n ohłolopi· pá·li hokkô·laŋkí· mâ·hin
so I signed the treaties," I said. After that, about twenty years ago,

mv este Cvlakke-honvnwv etehēcēn okat,
ma ísti calakkihonánwa itihi·ci·n o·kâ·t
that Cherokee man and I saw each other, and he asked,

"Hofonē Cvlakke este-Maskoke 'tepakat
hofóni· calákki istima·skó·ki 'tipâ·ka·t
"Do you remember when we discussed

em etenfvccetv tatē opunvyēcēma kērretskv?" maken,
imitinfaccitá tá·ti·[583] opónayi·cí·ma·[584] ki·łłícka^ ma·kín
the agreement between the Cherokee and the Muscogee?"

"Kērris" makit em vyoposkin okat,
kî·łłeys ma·kéyt imáyopo·skéyn o·kâ·t
"I remember," I answered, and he said,

"Nake momvkēn mahkēs cekomvkot okvyan vm vyoposket oketskemvts.
ná·ki mo·makí·n máhki·s cikó·makot o·kayâ·n amáyopo·skít o·kíckimác
"I did not think you would say those things, but you answered me.

Nake momvkēt ocen atvtēs komvkot okvyan
nâ·ki mo·makí·t o·cín[585] a·tatí·s kó·makot o·kayâ·n
I did not think of what you came through,

vm vyoposketskvtēt omen vkerricvyat, nake momaket omvtēt omen
amáyopo·skíckati·t[586] ô·min akílleycayâ·t nâ·ki mó·ma·kít o·mati·t ô·min
and when I think about how you answered me, how things took place,

fạccusen vm vyoposket oketskemvts" maken tem punahoyēmvts.
fằ·ⁿccosin amáyopo·skít[587] o·kíckimác ma·kín timponá·ho·yi·mác
your answer was the truth," he said as we talked.

Monkv Cvlakke etvlwv Maskoke 'tepakat etenfvccetv ocet,
mòŋka calákki itálwa ma·skó·ki 'tipâ·ka·t itinfaccitá ò·cit
So the Cherokee Nation and the Muscogee had an agreement with each other,

herkvn etem ocet, estofīs etvlwv kakēpvranēt emetenfvccetvt omēs.
híłkan itimô·cit istô·feys[588] itálwa ka·kí·pała·ni·t imitinfaccitát ô·mi·s
an agreement to always dwell with one another in peace.

Momen vculvke em maketv yvt omēs.
mo·mín acolakí imma·kitá yat ô·mi·s
And this is the saying of the old ones.

Etenfvccetv mv omat nene-hvtke hvmkusen wvkēcēt mvn etem ohsehoket
itinfaccitá ma ô·ma·t ninihátki hámkosin wakî·ci·t man itimohsihô·kit[589]
This agreement, we will lay down one white path and walk it with each other;

pvlaknv hvmkusen, hakkv hvmkusen setenhompēt kakeyvrēs.
palákna hámkosin hákka hámkosin 'sitínhompí·t ká·kiyáłi·s
we will dwell eating together with one plate, one spoon.

Etvlwv hokkoliceyat kakeyvrēs. Momet este mocvse puyopv amahat
itálwa hokkolêyciya·t ká·kiyáłi·s mo·mít isti mocási poyópa á·ma·hâ·t
The two nations will dwell with each other. And the newborns coming after us,

yv herkv etenfvccetv kerrvkēn mahēcet liketskvrēs.
ya hiłka itinfaccitá kiłłakí·n[590] *má·hi·cít léykíckáłi·s*
see that they learn of this peace agreement.

Cvcuse toyetskat, momen cervhv toyvyat,
cacósi tô·yícka·t mo·mín ciłáha tô·yaya·t
You are my little brother, and I am your big brother;

yv nene-hvtke vsakwekon
ya ninihátki asákwikon
this peace road will not be overgrown with weeds.

vm pvlaknv, hakkv 'tepakat cvcuse senhompetvt os komit kerrvkēn
ampalákna hákka 'tipâ·ka·t cacósi sinhompitát ô·ⁿs kô·meyt kiłłakí·n
I, as a Muscogee, will look out for the citizens and raise them

tvsekvyv mahēcit este-Maskoke toyvyat likarēs makvtēt omēs.
tasikayá má·hi·céyt istima·skó·ki tô·yaya·t lêyká·łi·s ma·katí·t ô·mi·s
knowing that I regard my plate and spoon both as my little brother's utensils.

Momis hiyomat estimvt opunvyēcē tayat sekon,
mo·mêys hayyô·ma·t istéymat oponayí·ci· tâ·ya·t síkon[591]
But now there is no one who can talk about it,

estimvt kērrat sekot omēs. Vculvke tatē yv opunvkvn sopunahoyet,
istéymat kî·łła·t síko·t[592] *ô·mi·s acolakítá·ti· ya oponakán 'soponá·ho·yít*
there is no one who knows about it. The elders spoke these words

herkv tenfvccetvn etenhayat opunvkv rakrvkēn vcacvkēn opunahoyēt okēs.
hiłka tinfaccitán itinha·yâ·t oponaká łakłaki·n aca·caki·n oponá·ho·yi·t o·ki·s
as they made a peace treaty between them; they used big, sacred words in their speeches.

Momet vnokeckv eterakkueckv rakkēn etem ocet etvlwv estofis kakeyvrēs
mo·mít anokícka[593] *itiłakkóycka łákki·n itimô·cit*[594]*itálwa istô·feys ká·kiyáli·s*
And with love and great respect, we two nations will live this way always,

komē hēret etem punahoyet fullvtēt omēs. Mv nettv
kó·mi· hĭ·ⁿlit itimponá·ho·yít follatí·t ô·mi·s ma nítta
they believed, and talked with one another. The day

Cvlakke Maskoke 'tepaket herkv tenfvccetv hayē kakof,
calákki ma·skó·ki 'tipâ·kit[595] *hiłka tinfaccitá ha·yí· kâ·ko·f*[596]
that the Cherokees and the Muscogees were making the peace agreement with one another,

Lole Mikentase	Tvkusv Fekseko
ló·li meykintá·si[597]	*takosafiksiko*
Rolly McIntosh	Ta-cosa-Fixico
Tokepahce Mēkko	Fekseko Haco
tokipahcimí·kko	*fiksikohá·co*
Tuckabatche Micco	Fixico Harjo
Pin Masvl	Ēspokok Yvholv
peyn má·sal	*i·spoko·kyahóla*
Ben Marshall	Spike-Oak-Yoholo
Eco Haco	Cosvpe Ka
icohá·co	*co·sapiká·*
E-cho-Hajo	Joseph Carr
Kowakkoce Ēmarv	Yvhv Tvstvnvke
kowa·kkoci·má·la	*yahatastanáki*
Co-war-coo-che Emathla	Yar-har Tustenugge
Celle Mikentase	Nokos Ēmarv
cílli meykintá·si	*nokosi·má·ła*[598]
Chilly McIntosh	Nokus Emathla

Hopēr-yvholv
hopi·lyahóla
Hopuethlyahola

Mēcv Melv
mí·ca míla
Major Miller

Tēfe Panv
ti·fi[599] *pá·na*
David Barnard

Cosvp Smētkv
có·sap smí·tka
Joseph Smith

Same Mellv
sá·mi mílla
Samuel Miller

Kvsehtv Haco
kasihtahá·co
Carsada Harjo

(He)nehv Rakko Cvpko
(hi)níha lakkocápko
Ne-har-locco-chopco

Ēmvs Patswēn
i·mas pa·cswí·n
Amos Boatswain

Cace Skate
cá·ci ska·ti·[600]
George Scott

Pvhos Yvholv
paho·syahóla
Powhose Yoholo

Okcvn Haco
okcanhá·co
Oak-chun-Harjo

Same Cokote
sá·mi cokó·ti
Samuel Checota

Cokatte Ēmarv
coka·tti·má·la
Cho-cotte-Emathla

yv estvlke mēkkvlket momen etvlwv enhomahhotvlke,
ya istâlki mi·kkâlki[601] *mo·mít itálwa inhoma·hho·tâlki*
these people were the chiefs and headmen of the Nation

mont em opunahoyvlket omakvtēs.
mónt imopona·ho·yâlkit oma·katí·s
and their speakers.

Este-Maskoke etvlwvn mv omof, etvlwv em vpoketv hokkolet omvtēs.
istima·skó·ki itálwan ma ô·mo·f itálwaʔ imapo·kitá hokkò·lit o·matí·s
The Muscogee Nation at that time had two groups.

Hocefkv Onvpvlke hvmkat omen hvmket Elecvlke maket hocefakvtēs.
hocífka onapâlki hámka·t ô·min hámkit ilicâlki ma·kit hocífa·kati·s
The name of one was the Upper Creeks, and they called one the Lower Creeks.

Caceyv ofv este-hvtke em vpoketv hakeko monkof,
ca·ciyá ó·fa istihátki imapo·kitá há·kiko·[602] *môŋko·f*
Before the white man settled in Georgia,[603]

Cvtohocce-Hvcce em vlvpvtke etvlwv em vpoketvt omaken,
catoho·ccihácci imalapátki itálwa imapo·kitát omâ·kin
they were settled in tribal towns along the banks of the Chattahoochee River,

Kvwetv, Kvsehtv 'tepakat etvlwv homahhotēt omvtēs.
kawíta kasíhta 'tipâ·ka·t itálwa homa·hhotí·t o·mati·s
and Kawita and Kasihta both were major tribal towns.

Mvt Elecvlke hocefkv tatēs.
mat ilicâlki hocífka tá·ti·s
Those were called Lower Creeks.

Kosv-Hvcce, Tvlvpos-Hvcce, Vlepamv-Hvcce 'mvlvpvtke
ko·sahácci talapo·shácci alipa·mahácci 'malapátki
On the banks of Coosa River, Tallapoosa River, Alabama River,

etvlwv sulkēt em vpoketvt on vpokaket omvtēs. Mvt Onvpvlket hocēfket omvtēs.
itálwa sólki·t imapo·kitát ô·n apó·ka·kít o·mati·s mat onapâlkit hoci·fkít o·mati·s
they lived in settlements of many tribal towns. Those were named Upper Creeks.

Heyv etvlwv em ēkvnv svpenkvlēcetv kohmē este-hvtke 'teyvmkē oketv omof,
hiyá itálwa imi·kaná sapiŋkali·citá kóhmi· istihátki tíyamkí· okíta ô·mo·f
At the time when white people were rushing around intent on stealing these tribes' lands,

mēkkvke tatēt omēs, yv mēkkvke tatē hocefhokv ocat.
mi·kkakí tá·ti·t ô·mi·s ya mi·kkakí tá·ti· hocifhoká[604] *ô·ca·t*
they were the chiefs, and these are the names of these chiefs.

Otvwoskv-rakko ohrolopē cokpe-rakko hvmken cokpe kolvpaken
otawo·skalákko ohłolopi· cokpilákko hámkin cókpi kolapâ·kin
In October of the year seventeen hundred

pale cenvpaken cahkepohkakat omof,
pá·li cinapâ·kin cahkipohkâ·ka·t ô·mo·f
and eight-five [1785],

Wvcenv, este-Maskoke etenfvccetv etenhayē oketvn mēkkēt fullet omvtēs.
wacína istima·skó·ki itinfaccitá itínha·yi·[605] *okítan mí·kki·t follít o·matí·s*
at the time the U.S. made a treaty with the Muscogee, they were serving as chiefs.

Momis Cvlakke, este-Maskoke etenhērkē etenfvccetv hayē kakē oketv ofv tat,
mo·mêys calákki istima·skó·ki itínhi·łkí· itinfaccitá ha·yí· kâ·ki· okíta ó·fata·t
But these chiefs were not serving [yet]

heyv este mēkkvke tat herkv hayet kaket omekatēs.
hiyá ísti mí·kkakíta·t híłka ha·yít ka·kít omíká·ti·s
when the Cherokee and the Muscogee made the peace agreement.

Ohrolopē cokpe-rakko hvmken cokpe kolvpake pale cenvpake cahkepohkakat
ohłolopí· cokpiłákko hâmkin cókpi kolapâ·ki pá·li cinapâ·ki cahkipohkâ·ka·t[606]
It was probably before the year seventeen hundred and eighty-five [1785]

'rem ehomvn Cvlakke, este-Maskoke etenherkvtētis omēs.
'limihomán[607] *calákki istima·skó·ki itínhiłkatí·teys ô·mi·s*
that the Cherokee and the Muscogee made peace.

Fiddle-Dance (Hayēckv-Pvnkv)[i,608]

J. Hill (Haas VIII:65–69)[ii]

Hayēckv-pvnkv	maket	nvkaftet,	nerē	'pvnhoyēn
ha·yi·ckapánka	*ma·kít*[iii]	*naka·ftít*	*nił·*	*pánho·yí·n*
Fiddle-dance	they called it	they gathered	night	they danced

They called it hayēckv-pvnkv ['fiddle dance'] and met and used to dance in the night

---

[i] Title: *ha·yi·ckapánka* 'fiddle-dance'.
[ii] Last fiddle-dance Hill heard of around here was in 1902.
[iii] Could say: *ha·yi·ckapánka keycít*.

hvyatket	omvtēs.	Este-cate	sulkēt	hayēckv-panvlket	omaket,
haya·tkit	*o·matí·s*[609]	*isticá·ti*	*sólki·t*	*ha·yi·ckapa·nâlkit*	*omâ·kit*
(till) day	they used to do	Indians	many	fiddle-dancers	they were

till daybreak. Many Indians were fiddle dancers

'pvnkv	vretv	em vlustvkē	hē.rēt	omvtēs.
pánka	*alíta*	*imalostakí·*	*hĭ·ⁿli·t*	*o·matí·s*[610]
dances	to be at	they enjoyed	very much	they used to

and very much enjoyed being at dances.

Rvfo tat	nerē	etewolēn	'panet,	'pvnkv-cuko	ocakat
lafóta·t	*nili·*	*itiwoli·n*	*pa·nít*	*pankacóko*	*o·câ·ka·t*
in winter	at night	often	they danced	dance-houses	that were

In winter they danced often at night, and the dance halls

etewolicvlke	'svhocefhokēt	omvtēs.	Nettvcako-Rakkon
itiwoleycâlki	*'sahocifhokí·t*	*o·matí·s*[611]	*nittaca·kolákkon*
neighbors	they were named after	it was	on Christmas (=Big Sunday)

were named after their neighbors [e.g., Arbeka dance, Eufaula dance, etc.]. On Christmas

hompetv-rakko	eshayet,	Ohrolopē-Mocvseu,
hompitalákko	*isha·yít*	*ohlolopi·mocásiw*[612]
big feast	they would give	on New Year's, too

they would make a big feast, and on New Year's too,

Vrakkueckv-Emkv-Nettv		hopuewv	enhecketv-nettv	omakat,
alakkoyckaimkanítta		*hopóywa*	*inhickitanítta*	*o·mâ·ka·t*
appreciation-giving-day (=Thanksgiving)		child's	birthday	like those

Thanksgiving, or on a child's birthday, and such.

hompetv	este	sulkat	entvlemicen,	esafackat,
hompitá	*ísti*	*sólka·t*	*intalímeycín*	*isá·fa·ckâ·t*[613]
food	people many		make public the news	have fun

Many people would publicize the food, and they'd have fun,

hayēckv	'panet	fulhoyvtēt omis,	hiyomat
ha·yí·cka	*pa·nít*	*fólho·yatí·t ô·meys*	*hayyô·ma·t*
a fiddle-dance	they dance	that's the way they used to do, but	now

and that's the way they used to dance the fiddle dance. But now

sekot	os.	Hofonē	este-cate	vculvke tatē	em afacketv
siko·t	*ô·ⁿs*	*hofóni·*	*isticá·ti*	*acolakitá·ti·*[614]	*ima·fackitá*
there aren't any	it is	Long time ago	Indians	used-to-be old-timers'	enjoyment

there are none. It was not the old time Indians'

tokot	omēs.	Em vlicēckv	kvsappv,	lekothv	horre	etenhayē
tó·ko·t	*ô·mi·s*	*imaleyci·cka*	*kasá·ppa*	*likó·tha*	*hólli*	*itínha·yi·*
it was not	like	The beginning	north	south	war	they made on each other

celebration. The fiddle dance had its beginning

ocvtē	mahetis	hayēckv-pvnkv	vlicēhocvtētis		omēs.
o·catí·	*mâ·hiteys*	*ha·yi·ckapánka*	*aleyci·ho·catí·teys*		*ô·mi·s*
they had	about that time	fiddle-dance	it might have been started		it was

at about the time the North and the South made war on each other.

About Supernatural Beings

J. Hill (Haas VIII:167–185)

Este-cate	vculvket	okakat,	"Este	omakēt	ēkvnv	eto-lane vlkan fullēs"
isticá·ti	*acolakít*	*oka·kâ·t*	*isti*	*o·ma·kí·t*[615]	*i·kaná*	*itolá·ni álka·n folli·s*
Ind.	old-people	(used to) say	humans	like		timber

"There are [beings] like humans roaming among the green trees," the old Indians used

makvnts:	este-cvpko	kicet,	ehosa,	momet	este-lopocke.
ma·kánc	*isticápko*	*keycít*	*ihosá·*	*mo·mít*	*istilopócki*

to say: este-cvpko ['tall person' or 'giant'], ehosa, and este-lopocke ['little people'].

Este-cvpko	este	omēt	esse ocēt		mahēt	omēs.
isticápko	*isti*	*ô·mi·t*	*íssi ó·ci·t*		*má·hi·t*	*ô·mi·s*
			having hair (all over)		tall	

The giant [este-cvpko] is a person who has hair [all over] and is tall.

Estet fayēt fullvtēs. Ehvpo hayēt vpoket
ístit fa·yi·t follatí·s ihapó· há·yi·t[616] *apô·kit*
Some people were once going about hunting. They were staying in a camp they had made

cēpvnē hvmken este-hvpo vhecicvn ocēt, fakv vpēyat eryicekon,
ci·paní· hámkin istihapó· ahicêycan[617] *ó·ci·t fá·ka apî·ya·t ilyéycikon*
and had a young boy to watch the camp. The hunters had not returned,

hvset raklvtkēpen, cēpanat tvlkēt takliket oman,
hasít łaklátki·pín ci·pâ·na·t tálki·t[618] *taklêykit o·mâ·n*
and the sun was going down. The boy was in the camp by himself

fotkēt efv tis enhuehkē okēt aresasvcoken pohet,
fo·tki·t[619] *ifáteys ínhoyhki· ó·ki·t a·łisâ·sacókin po·hít*
and heard someone going around whistling as if calling for a dog.

mv cēpanat takliken este-cvpkot aret oket em vlakvtēs.
ma ci·pâ·na·t taklêykin isticápkot a·lít ô·kit[620] *imála·katí·s*
It was the giant going around, and he came to where the boy was.

Wotko sulkēn ēyvpvyēt, mvn enfotket oket
wó·tko sólki·n i·yapáyi·t man ínfo·tkít ô·kit[621]
He had many raccoons with him and had been whistling for them,

wotko tat yvmasakusē ont, totkv ētkat eto taklumhat yoksv tis ohcemēcet hvtvpēcet
wó·tkota·t yamä·ⁿsa·kosi· ônt tó·tka i·tkâ·t itó taklómha·t yóksateys óhcimi·cít hatápi·cít
[for] the raccoons were very tame. They climbed up and down onto the edge of some wood

nake tis hopoyusē ont vwenayet,
nâ·kiteys hopo·yosí· ônt awína·yit
lying in the fire and sniffed as though they were looking for something.

enhonwusē ont takfullen hēcet takliken, este-cvpkot cēpanan em punayet
inhonwosí· ônt tákfollín hi·cit taklêykin isticápkot ci·pâ·na·n ímpona·yít
He sat and watched as they went around sniffing, and the giant asked the young boy,

"Estont aretskēt oma?" kicen,
istónt a·łícki·t ô·ma·[622] *keycín*
"What do you do?"

"Estomvkot os" maket em vyoposken,
istó·mako·t ô·ⁿs ma·kít imáyopo·skín
"I don't do anything," [the boy] replied.

"Estvn arētskēt oma?" kicen,
ístan a·łi·cki·t ô·ma·´ keycín
"Where do you go?" [the giant] asked.

"Estvn vrvkotvnks" kicen,
ístan ałáko·táŋks[623] *keycín*
"I don't go anywhere," he answered.

"Este kerrvkis vlaken omat,
ísti kíłłakeys ala·kín o·mâ·t
"When someone you don't know comes,

elēcvyēs kometskēt omeko?" kicen,
*ili·cayí·s ko·mícki·t omiko·^*[624] *keycín*
you have thoughts of killing them, don't you?" [the giant] asked.[625]

"Monkot os" kicof,
móŋko·t ô·ⁿs keycô·f
"It is not so," he said.

"Heyv takfullusat omis hēcin omat,
hiyá tákfollosâ·t ô·meys hi·céyn o·mâ·t
"When you see these little ones going about,

elēcvyēs kometskēt omeko?" kicen,
*ili·cayí·s ko·mícki·t omiko·^*[626] *keycín*
you think you might kill them, don't you?" he asked.

"Monkotvnks" kicof,
móŋko·táŋks keycô·f
"No, I never did," [the boy] answered,

fakv arvtē hvmket rvlakvcoken pohhet,
fá·ka a·latí· hámkit łála·kacókin póhhit
and then the giant heard one of the men who had gone hunting returning

este-cvpko tat enfotken, wotko tat a ohpefatiken,
isticápkota·t ínfo·tkín wó·tkota·t a·ʔohpifa·têykin
and whistled, and the raccoons ran to him,

enlētken saksaket em vfulohten 'svyēpvtēs mahokvnts.
ínli·tkín saksă·ⁿkit imafolóhtin sáyi·patí·s má·ho·kánc.
and as he ran, they yelped and surrounded him, and he left with them, it was told.

Hvtvm este ētvt fullvtēs. Fayvlke ētat mvo
hatâm ísti i·tat follati·s fa·yâlki i·tá·t maw'
Again there were other people going about. They were hunters too,

este-hvpo vhecicv cēpvnē oce ētat moman mvn este-cvpko aret omis,
istihapó· ahicéyca ci·paní· ó·ci i·tá·t mo·mâ·n[627] *man isticápko a·lít o·mêys*
and they also had a young boy to watch the camp. The giant was going about there,

eccv tvpocechoyan pohat penkvlē hḛrēt ont aret oman,
ícca tapo·cícho·yâ·n po·hâ·t[628] *piŋkalí· hĭ·ⁿlí·t ônt a·lít o·mâ·n*
and [the boy] heard someone shooting a gun and was going around very scared.

este-hvpo kohv vlkē tempusat ont omen, mv cēpanat kohv-lowaken rawaret
istihapó· kohá álki· tímposa·t ônt o·mín ma ci·pâ·na·t kohalowá·kin lá·wa·lít[629]
Right near the camp was a field of cane. The young boy cut some tender cane

ēsso hiyan tak-aseksēcen hihoyof, takcawet eton estēpkan
i·sso háyya·n takkasiksî·cin háyho·yô·f tákca·wít[630] *itón ísti·pkâ·n*
and stuck it into the hot ashes, and when it was very hot, he took the cane out and struck it

eccv oket tvpockēt omen, mvn sahkopanet vrḛpēt omvtēs.
ícca ô·kit tapo·ckí·t ô·min man sáhkopa·nít alĭ·ⁿpi·t o·matí·s
against the tree, and it popped like a gun going off, and he went around playing with that.

Este-cvpko em vlaket cēpanat em punayet,
isticápko imalâ·kit ci·pâ·na·t ímpona·yít
The giant came and spoke to the boy:

"Cent ometskētvnka, tvpocēcē cvletecicetskētvnkē?" kicen,
cínt o·mícki·taŋka·^[631] *tapó·ci·cí· caliticeycícki·taŋkí· keycín*
"Was that you doing that, shooting and making me run?"

"Monkotvnks. Eccv ohcvkos tvpocecetvo cvkeriyekos" kicet oman,
móŋko·taŋks[632] *ícca óhcako·s tapo·cicítaw cakilêyyiko·s keycít o·mâ·n*
"No, it was not. I do not have a gun, and I do not know how to shoot a gun," he said.

"Cent ontskētvnken okis" kicofvn, mv cēpanat kohv-lowake ēsso tak-vseksēcēt omen,
cínt óncki·taŋkín o·kéys keycô·fan ma ci·pâ·na·t kohalowá·ki i·sso takkasiksí·ci·t ô·min[633]
"It was you that was doing that," [the giant] said. The young boy still had the tender cane in

hihoyē hē̜rē hakofvn oken,
hayhoyí· hĭ·ⁿli· há·ko·fán[634] *o·kín*
the ashes, so when they were good and hot, he said,

"Tvpocecvkotvnket okis" kican vpaken, kohvt entaktvpocken,
tapo·cicáko·taŋkít o·kéys keycá·n apâ·kin kohát intáktapo·ckín
"I cannot shoot a gun, I said," and as soon as he said that, the cane popped.

"Cvhiyomēcetskēt omētvnken okis" mahket lētkof,
cahayyomî·cícki·t ô·mi·taŋkín o·kéys máhkit li·tkô·f
"This is what you were doing to me," he said, taking off running.

entvpocken kohv-rakko cekfan cehyet sumkvtēs mahokvnts.
intapo·ckín kohałákko cíkfa·n cíhyit somkatí·s má·ho·kánc.
And the popping continued, and he ran into the thick cane and disappeared, it was said.

Ehosa. Este hvmket fayet arofvn, oskēt honnēt aten hēcet ayet oman,
ihosá· ísti hámkit fa·yít a·lô·fan o·ski·t hónni·t a·tín hî·cit a·yít o·mâ·n
Ehosa. When a man was out hunting, he saw a heavy rain coming but continued on

eto rakkēt huervkis estetetayēt hvokēt hueren hehcet,
itó łákki·t hôyłakeys istititâ·yi·t háwki·t hôylin híhcit[635]
and came upon a large hollow tree, large enough for a man to stand inside,

mvn cēyet este huervtēs.
man cî·yit[636] *ísti hoylatí·s*
and he went in there and stood.

"Oskēt eshoyvnof, vyeparēs" komet, moman oskē honnē ayat,
oskí·t ishoyáno·f[637] *ayipá·li·s kô·mit mo·mâ·n oski· hónni· a·yâ·t*
"After the rain passes, I'll continue on," he thought. As the heavy rain was going over,

ehomvn ehosa lētkuset "Oskin, oskin" maket oskan,
ihóman ihosá· li·tkosit oskéyn oskéyn[638] *ma·kít o·skâ·n*
Ehosa was running along in front of [the rain], saying, "Rain, rain;"

yes ohfulotket hueret "Oskin, oskin" maket,
yisohfoló·tkit[639] *hoylít*[640] *oskéyn oskéyn ma·kít*
then turning around and standing toward [the rain] he said, "Rain, rain,"

mv eto-hvoken ecēyepvranet vrēpet okan, este huerēpvtet
ma itoháwkin ici·yipála·nít ałi·pít o·kâ·n ísti hoyli·patit
and was about to go into the hollow tree, when the man standing inside said,

"Nak maket 'saretska? Vsin 'saret okvs" kihcen
nâ·k ma·kít să·ⁿlícka·^[641] asêyn sa·lít okas kéyhcin[642]
"What are you going around saying? Go say it somewhere else," and the Ehosa

oskē-rakko wohkan cehyet, cunēkuset "Oskin, oskin" maket ayvtēs,
oski·łákko wö·ⁿhka·n cíhyit[643] *conî·kosit oskéyn oskéyn ma·kít a·yatí·s*
went out into the howling rain and stooping down really low, went saying, "Rain, rain,"

mv eto-hvoket ehutet omēpen:
ma itoháwkit ihótit omi·pin
because the hollow tree was his home.

"Mvn vpēttepvranekv oskēpis, cvlvcipekos" komēt aret
man api·ttipáła·niká óski·pêys calacêypiko·s kó·mi·t[644] *a·lít*
"I am going to take shelter there even when it rains, and I will not get wet," [Ehosa] thought,

oskin maket okvtēs mahokvnts.
oskéyn ma·kít o·katí·s má·ho·kánc
and that is why he said that, it was said.

Momen vnrvwvn arvken omat, ehosa hoyanan tohwvlvpkvken omat,
mo·mín ânławan a·łakín o·mâ·t ihosá· hoyá·na·n[645] *tohwalápkakin*[646] *o·mâ·t*
So if you go out in the forest, if you cross a path that Ehosa has made,

ēkvnvn kerrēsko hahket estehoset estesumkēs.
i·kanán kíłłi·sko· háhkit[647] *ístiho·sít ístisomki·s*
you will get lost not remembering the land.

Ēkvnv kērrusvkēt omvtēto estomis, eto tis cvto tis omvlkvt
i·kaná kĭ·ⁿłosáki·t o·matí·to·[648] *istô·meys itóteys catóteys omálkat*
Even if you know the land really well, the trees and rocks all

mvrahkv hakvkehpen estvmin ayvkat kerrēskot
małáhka ha·kakíhpin[649] *ístamêyn a·yakâ·t kíłłi·skot*
become different, and it could be you don't know where you are going

estvmi fvccvn atvkateu kerrēsko tayē hakēt omēs, mahokvnts.
istamêy fáccan á·taka·tíw kiłłi·sko· tâ·yi[650] *ha·kí·t ô·mi·s má·ho·kánc*
or which way you came, it was said.

Este-Lopocke.[651] Este-lopocke tvhopkvkusēt omaket esten sahkopanet
istilopócki[i] *istilopócki tahopkakósi·t omâ·kit ístin sáhkopa·nít*
The Little People. The little people are very agile and play tricks on people,

hacohakē omēn hayet, ēyvpayet esfullēt omēs.
ha·cohá·ki· ó·mi·n hâ·yit[652] *i·yapâ·yit ísfolli·t ô·mi·s*
drive them insane, and take a person with them wherever they go.

Ēkvnv vretv holwahokē hēran vyēcicet min vrēcicakēt omēs.
i·kaná alíta holwa·hokí· hĭ·ⁿła·n ayi·cêycit[653] *mêyn ali·céyca·kí·t ô·mi·s*
They send [people] to the rough part of the country and let them wander around there.

Momen este sulkēt onvyakvtēt omēs.
mo·mín ísti sólki·t onáya·katí·t ô·mi·s
Many people have told about this.

Este-lopocke vpakē arvtē nerē tis ēyvpayet esfullen,
istilopócki apâ·ki·[654] *a·latí· nili·teys i·yapâ·yit ísfollín*
They were taken by little people; even at night they take them around,

hvyatken netta tat cvto-rakko vlkan ēhkēn licaken,
haya·tkín nittá·ta·t catolákko álka·n i·hki·n leycâ·kin
and when it's daylight, they keep them hidden among the rocks.

yafken este-lopocke em vpoketv kerkvkēn ocvkēt ont,
ya·fkín istilopócki imapo·kitá kiłkaki·n o·caki·t ônt
The little people have special places where they live, and during the evening,

---

[i] Can't finish to tell it, there's so much to tell. About 9 or 10 years ago a little girl got lost. Looked for it many days, found it in a branch in some limbs. *istilopócki* caused this.

When Indians have twins, the second born (last one, says Bell) is known as *faccasiko*. No way of referring to the first one. Last-born is supposed to be different from other people, a kind of prophet. Get to be that way by themselves — they're that way when they're born. Some people are afraid of them when they're little children and some people love to play with them. *fácciko·* 'not true', *faccakíko·* (pl.)

etencukopericat, ēyvpayet esfullet
itincokópileycâ·t[655] *i·yapâ·yit ísfollít*
they visit one another. They take the person wherever they go and tell him,

"Accvkē tis vpoyetsken omvkēts" kicet, ēnakayepuecēt omakēs.
a·ccakí·teys apô·yíckin omáki·c keycít i·na·ká·yipoyci·t[656] *omâ·ki·s*
"Set your clothes aside," and strip him naked.

Eto cvpcvkētis vcemēcat "Vcemkvs" kihcet, vcemecicakēs.
itó capcakí·teys acími·câ·t acímkas[657] *kéyhcit acimicéyca·ki·s*
They climb tall trees and tell him, "Climb!" and [so] force him to climb.

Este mv vcak-ayvtē rvlvkekot vnrvwvn elēpat sasvtēt omēs.
ísti ma acákka·yatí· 'lalakíkot ânławán ili·pâ·t sa·satí·t ô·mi·s
Some of the people who went with them and didn't return died in the forest.

Este hvmket onayvtēs.
ísti hámkit ona·yatí·s
One man told [the following].

Este-lopocke vnsomecēpen vntvlkuset likit,
istilopócki ansomíci·pín[658] *antăl[n]kosit lêykeyt*
The little people had disappeared, and I was sitting there all by myself.

cvhoporrēnet omis ēkvnv kęrrvyē sekot omēpen fullet omeyētvnken,
cahopólli·nít o·mêys[659] *i·kaná kĭ·[n]łłayi· síko·t omi·pín follít o·miyí·taŋkín*
I was still in my right mind, but we went out, and I didn't even recognize the land.

"Yefulketv ceyacēt oma?" maket vm pohaken likit,
'yifolkitá ciya·cí·t ô·ma·^[660] *ma·kít ámpoha·kín lêykeyt*
I was sitting there, and they asked me, "Would you like to go back home?"

cvhoporrēnet omat ēkvnv kęrrvyē sekot omēpan okaken,
cahopołłî·nit o·mâ·t[661] *i·kaná kĭ·[n]łłayi· síko·t omî·pa·n oka·kín*
I was in my right mind, but I didn't know the land when they asked me.

"Fulkvyē tis, estvmin atvyvtē kerrępvyē sekot on os" kicin,
folkayí·teys istamêyn a·tayáti· kiłłĭ·[n]payi· síkot ó·n ó·[n]s keycéyn
"I would go back, but I do not know which direction I came from," I said.

"Mon omat ēkvnv kērhoyusan hopohyēn,
mo·n o·mâ·t i·kaná kĭ·ⁿɬho·yosa·n hopóhyi·n
"Then we will look for someone who knows a little about the land,

mvt cenhorkasen fulkepvccvs" cvkicaken, arit omvyat
mat cinhoɬkâ·sin folkipáccas cakáyca·kín a·ɬéyt o·mayâ·t
and he may go back as your companion," they told me. As I went about,

cvhoporrenēpet omat, cvnokkusēt ont cvle tis pvsvtkusēt
cahopollini·pit o·mâ·t⁶⁶² canókkosi·t⁶⁶³ ônt calíteys pasátkosi·t
I was of sound mind, but I was very sick, my feet were numb,

yvkvpkv vcǫmē sekot cvsumket omvtētat, cvcvf[ę]knusē cvhakēpet oman,
yakápka acǒ·ⁿmi· síko·t casomkít o·matí·ta·t cacafĭ·ⁿknosi· caha·kĭ·pit o·mâ·n
and not being able to walk, I got lost. As I began to feel better,

"Cem estonkot yvkapet roretskē tayēt oma?" cvkicaken,
cimistóŋkot yaka·pít 'loɬícki· tâ·yi·t ô·ma·^⁶⁶⁴ cakéyca·kín
they asked me, "Do you think you can walk and get there all right?"

"Naket vm estomē sekot onkv, rorēpvyēs" kicin,
nâ·kit amistó·mi· síkot oŋká lóɬi·payi·s keycéyn
"There is nothing wrong with me, so I can get there," I said.

"Mon omat, vyepvccvs. Cenhorkasv ēkvnv kērhoyusat cenheckuecēkv,
mô·n o·mâ·t ayipáccas cinhoɬká·sa i·kaná kĭ·ⁿɬho·yosa·t cinhickôyci·ka
"Well then, you may go. We have found you a companion who knows a little about the land,

vlaken omat vcak-vyepvccvs" cvkihcet sumecehpen likin,
ala·kín o·mâ·t acakkay[i]páccas cakéyhcit somicíhpin lêykeyn
so when he comes you may go with him," they said and disappeared leaving me sitting

wotkot vlaket okat,
wó·tkot alâ·kit⁶⁶⁵ o·kâ·t
there. A raccoon came and said,

"Cent cem vretvn vyetv ceyacēt oma? maken,
cínt cimalitán ayíta ciyá·ci·t ô·ma·^⁶⁶⁶ ma·kín
"You're the one who wants to return where you came from?"

"E̞he̞ vnet vyetv cvyacēt os" kihcin,
iⁿhí·ⁿ anít ayíta cayá·ci·t ô·ⁿs[667] *kéyhceyn*
"Yes, it's me who wants to go," I said.

"Mon omat, ayvyan vcvcak-a̞yetskvten, ēkvnv kērusetskan ercewikarēs" mahket,
mó·n o·mâ·t a·yayâ·n acacakkă·ⁿyíckatin i·kaná kĭⁿlosícka·n ilciwéyká·li·s máhkit
"Well then, I'll go and you keep following me, and I will take you to a place you recognize

vnhomvhiten vhoyet omeyan, pvnofv ocen omat min akhvtapket
anhomahèytin aho·yít o·miyâ·n panó·fa o·cín o·mâ·t[668] *mêyn akhatà·pkit*
and leave you," he said. He led me, and as we were going, he went into a steep ravine

a-ak-ayvntot kvnhvlwe onvpv entvpēksen omat,
a·Ɂakkă·ⁿyántot kanhálwi onápa íntapi·ksín o·mâ·t
and kept going on a rise until it evened out,

omvlkucvn koponhko̞yuset vnhomahten, pvne-yoksvn rorat min akhvtvpiket
omalkocán[669] *koponhkò·ⁿyosit anhomà·htin paniyóksan lo·lâ·t mèyn akhatapêykit*
leading me all hunched over. When he got to the end of the ravine

efekkomvt ak-vrepen vho̞yēn hvcce rakkē rohcakhētis pvnofv omēpen omat
ifikkó·mat[670] *ákkali·pín ahŏ·ⁿyi·n hácci lákki· lohcákhi·teys panó·fa omi·pin o·mâ·t*
he went around in it [?], and we continued on. A great river met the ravine,

aye monket aktaskvntot omiyet tikvntot,
ă·ⁿyi mòŋkit aktá·skantót[671] *omayyít teykántot*
and he kept going, jumped in, and swam across.

hvccen empicēcet ayat pvnofv yohcakhan rorat
háccin impéyci·cít â·ya·t panó·fa yohcákha·n lo·lâ·t
He went along the edge of the river reaching the place where the ravine met it,

mvn empicēcet aret pvne-yoksvn respoyen, rvne onvpv tat ēkvnv entvpēksen omat
man impéyci·cít a·lít paniyóksan líspo·yin laní onápata·t i·kaná íntapi·ksín o·mâ·t
hugging the edge until the ravine ended. And he went on top of a mound until it leveled out,

em omvlkvt koponhko̞yuset vwvlapket,
imomálkat[672] *koponhkŏ·ⁿyosit awála·pkít*
and with every ounce of strength he crossed all hunched over.

ēkvnv momvkē vlkēn ayen welaket omeyvnkan
i·kaná mo·maki· álki·n a·yín wilă·ⁿki·t o·miyáŋka·n
Any direction we took the land was all alike,

akhvsē likēn rakhvtvphoken
akhasí léyki·n łakhataphô·kin
and we went down and came to a place where there was a big lake.

"Sakcon ak-assēpvkvtēt vhoyvkvrēs" maket ont,
sákcon akká·ssi·pakáti·t[673] *ahóyakáłi·s*[674] *ma·kít ónt*
"Let's chase after some crawfish and then we'll go on," he said.

"Esti tat a-ak-esēpat a-ak-esekan nvfketvt omvrēs" maken,
istêytá·ⁿt akkísi·pâ·t[675] *akkisíka·n*[676] *nafkitát omáłi·s ma·kín*
"Whoever catches a crawfish may hit the one who didn't catch one," he said.

"Momepekvs" kihcin,
mo·mipíkas kéyhceyn
"So be it," I said.

sakco tis hecvko monken a-ak-esehpet cvnvfiken,
sákcoteys hicáko· môŋkin akkisíhpit[677] *canafêykin*
and before I had even seen a crawfish he caught one and hit me.

vhoyēn hvtvm akhasē tat liken akhvtvphoket omēn,
aho·yí·n hatâm akhasí·ta·t[i] *lêykin akhatápho·kít o·mí·n*
We kept going and came to a big lake and both got in.

"Hvtvm sakco a-ak-esepvkvrēs" maken,
hatâm sákco akka·ssipákáłi·s[678] *ma·kín*
"Again we will catch crawfish," he said.

"Henka" kicin, ak-vhoyēn rakhueren vneu akhuerin
hiŋka·^ keycéyn ákkaho·yí·n łakhôyłin aníw akhôyłeyn
"Okay," I said. We were going and he stopped and stood and I also stopped and stood:

---

[i] Or: *akhasí.*

"Tokvs" mahket kvskvnvn ue-ofvn akmvyattuecat ak-esehpet,
tókas máhkit kaskanán oyʔó·fan akmaya·ttôyca·t akkisíhpit
"Now," he said, and swinging his left paw in the water, he caught one

cvnvfiken vhoyeyat, hofonekvnton akhvsē liken omat,
canafêykin aho·yiyâ·t hofonikánton[679] *akhasí· leykín*[680] *o·mâ·t*
and hit me, and as we went on, before long there was a big lake,

sakco assetvn maket senhomvhakēsko tayēt omen, welạkēt omeyvnkan
sákco a·ssitán ma·kít sinhomaha·kí·sko·[681] *tâ·yi·t ô·min wilă·ⁿki·t o·miyáŋka·n*
and I couldn't surpass him in chasing crawfish. As we continued on

ēkvnv tat kẹrrusiyēn rorhoyēt vhoyet omeyisan,
i·kanáta·t kĭ·ⁿłosêyyi·n łołhó·yi·t aho·yít o·miyêysa·n
we came to a part of the country that I recognized, and as we kept going,

akhvsuce cọtkusēt liken rorhoyēn,
akhasóci cŏ·ⁿtkosi·t lêykin łołhô·yi·n
we came to a small lake,

"Yvn hvtvm sakco ak-assepvkēts" maken,
yan hatâm sákco akka·ssipáki·c ma·kín
and he said, "Let's chase crawfish here again,"

"Henka" kicin, ue-vfopken aksehohkēn
hiŋka·^ keycéyn oyʔafó·pkin aksihóhki·n
and I told him, "Okay." The two of us stood by the edge of the water,

"Tokvs!" mahken, eto-hvrpet ue-vfopkusan akwakken ak-ēsvyat
tó·kas[i] *máhkin itohálpit oyʔafó·pkosa·n akwâ·kkin akkî·saya·t*
and he said, "Now!" I had picked up a piece of tree bark laying at the edge of the water

sakco vpikēn sak-ehsit,
sákco apáyki·n sakkíhseyt
and it had a crawfish in it, and I caught it.

---

[i] There is a *tókas*.

"Vntạwvt sakco tat esēpis" kicin,
antà·ⁿwat sákcota·t isî·peys keycéyn
"I'm the first one to catch a crawfish," I told him.

"Momēcēpet okētskes" maken,
momi·cî·pit[682] okíckis[683] ma·kín
"You are," he said.

"Cenvfkvranvyat tvlket omēto" kicin,
cináfkala·nayâ·t tâlkit o·mí·to· keycéyn
"I will have to hit you," I said.

"Mvt omēs ca" mahken,
mato·mí·sca·^ máhkin
"It's a deal," he said.

"Vm ēfuliketsken ceran cennvfkvranis" kihcin,
ami·folêykíckin cilá·n cinnáfkala·néys kéyhceyn
"You turn around and I'll hit you on the back," I said,

vm ēfulken ekv-topvrvn ennvfikit sak-vwihkit,
amí·folkín ikatopálan innafêykeyt sakkawéyhkeyt
and with his back to me, I hit him on the back of the head; he fell over,

enlētkvyvnts makēt este hvmket onayvtēs mahokvnts.
inlî·tkayánc[684] ma·ki·t ísti hámkit ona·yati·s má·ho·kánc.
and I took off. One man told [this], it was said.

About the Little People (Este-Lopocke Ohhonvkv)[i]

J. Hill (XXII:75–85)

Este-cate vculvke okat, este-lopockucet fullēt omēs, eto-lanofvn.
isticá·ti acolaki o·kâ·t istilopockocít follí·t ô·mi·s itola·nó·fan
The old Indians said that there were little people in the green trees.

---

[i] Title: *istilopócki ohhonáka.*

Eto mahmvyēmahē sasan vcemēcet, hechoyeko tayēt fullēt omēs maket okakvnts.
itó ma·hmayi·má·hi· sâ·sa·n acími·cít hichoyiko· tâ·yi·t follí·t ô·mi·s ma·kít oka·kánc.
They climb up the tallest trees and go about unseen, they used to say.

Este hvmket fayet aret oman naket enheckekon,
ísti hámkit fa·yít a·lít o·mâ·n nâ·kit inhíckikon
One hunter went hunting and didn't get anything:

"Wakkit, fēkahpit, vyeparēs" kont wakkof,
wâ·kkeyt fi·káhpeyt ayípá·li·s kònt wâ·kko·f
"I'll lie down and rest and go," he thought, and as he lay there,

este-lopocke fullvcoket opunahoyen pohvtēs.
istilopócki follacókit oponá·ho·yín po·hati·s
he heard the little people going about and talking.

"Este elēhocēn wakkes" maket etem onayet okakvcoken,
ísti ili·hocí·n wâ·kkis ma·kít itímona·yít oka·kacókin
"Here lies someone who's been killed," they said to one another.

"Vne tis okahkēs" komē tatēs.
aníteys okáhki·s kó·mi· tá·ti·s
"They might mean me," he thought.

Mv este momis somēcat wakkē monken
ma ísti mo·mêys somî·ca·t wâ·kki· mônkin
The people who disappeared while he was still lying there

eryihcet fullvcokat pohvtē onayet fullet omvcoken, ētvo yicat
ilyéyhcit follacóka·t po·hati· ona·yít follít ô·macókin í·taw yeycâ·t
returned, and he heard them still talking about it, and when other [little people] came,

em onayet mv este ele wakkē eshēcat punvyēcet,
imóna·yit ma ísti ili wákki· ishî·ca·t pónayi·cít
they were told about the dead man they had found lying there:

"Estomehcēkotok yatan hericvraneyat tvlkēs" maket
istomihcí·ko·to·k ya·tá·n hiłéycała·niyâ·t tâlki·s ma·kít
"We can't do anything with him, so we'll have to bury him here," they said,

fullvcokof hvmket vlahkvcoken em onayet
follacóko·f hámkit aláhkacókin imóna·yít
and as they were going about, [another] one came and they told him:

"Nạken estonkot vrẹ̄pusē tvnkan elēcephoyen wakken eshēcēt
nǎ·ⁿkin istóŋko·t ałĭ·ⁿposi· tankâ·n ili·ciphô·yin wâ·kkin ishî·ci·t
"He wasn't doing anything to anyone, but he's been killed and we found him lying here,

onayēt foliyēkv pohet aret ontskēs kihocof,
ona·yi·t folêyyí·ka pô·hit a·łít óncki·s[685] *kéyho·cô·f*
and we've been going about telling people, so you've probably heard," they said.

"Hẹhhepat fvmẹ̄ts" maken, "Vsin wakkekv omēs" hvmket kicen,
hĭⁿhhipá·t famí·ⁿc ma·kín asêyn wâ·kkika o·mí·s hámkit keycín
"It smells like hẹhhepa," he said. "That's because there's one lying over there," one said.

"Mvt elēcēt omēs" maken, "Mv tat elehcekos" kihocvcoken,
mat ilí·ci·t ô·mi·s[686] *ma·kín máta·t ilíhciko·s kéyho·cacókin*
"That's what killed him," he said. "That wouldn't kill him," he was told.

"Wakkvranan ēkvnv etetakuecvkan hẹ̄rēs" mahket,
wákkała·nâ·n i·kaná itita·kôycaka·n hĭ·ⁿli·s máhkit
"It would be good if we prepare the ground where he is to lie," he said,

cvto rakpalē omēt esfullvcoken,
cató łákpa·lí· ô·mi·t ísfollacókin
and they could be heard going about turning over a rock.

"Wakkvranat tetaken omat,
wákkała·nâ·t títa·kín o·mâ·t
"When the place where he is to lie is ready,

takful-holattuce enocusēt wakkepvrēs" hvmket makvcoken,
takfolhola·ttocí inócosi·t wakkipáłi·s hámkit ma·kacókin
he'll wear a little blue ribbon around his neck as he lies there," one could be heard saying.

cvto rakpale omat esfuliyvcokat,
cató łákpa·lí ô·ma·t isfolêyyacóka·t[687]
After they had gone about turning over the rock, they said,

"'Tetaket os. Akhvtvpkepekvs" maket esfullvcoken, "Estont esfu̱llet okeha̱" kohmit
'titâ·kit ó·ⁿs akhatapkipíkas ma·kít ísfollacókin ístónt isfŏlⁿlit o·kiha·ⁿ^ kóhmeyt
"It's ready. Let him be lowered down." "What are they taking around?" I wondered,

ahuyirit ohhayvyan somecehpen,
a·hoyêyleyt óhha·yayâ·n somicíhpin
so I stood up and went toward them, but they had disappeared.

"Estomaket fullet okakeha̱" kont hopoyit arvyan,
istó·ma·kít follít oka·kíha·ⁿˋ kônt hopo·yéyt a·layâ·n
"What were they doing?" I wondered and went looking for them

taksvpulkuce sopakhvthvkusvntot elēt wakken
taksapolkocí sopakhathakósantó·t ili·t wâ·kkin
[and found] a little gray mountain boomer was lying there dead.

eshēcet esfullet ohmvtet
ishî·cit ísfollít óhmatit
That was what they had found and [were talking about],

takful-holattuce makat pvhe holattusē enocicēt
takfolhola·ttocí mâ·ka·t pahí hola·ttosi· inocéyci·t
and the little blue ribbon they had talked about was a blade of blue grass around his neck.

cvto cǫtkusē ēkvnv vsomkusē likvtēn rakpahlet
cató cŏ·ⁿtkosi· i·kaná asomkósi· leykatí·n lakpáhlit
I saw they had turned over a little rock that had been sunk in the ground,

mv sufkusan nvtaksē akwvkehcet somēcen hēcvyvntvs makēt
ma (?) sófkosa·n natáksi· akwakíhcit somî·cin hi·cayántas ma·kí·t
and in that little deep spot they had laid him face up and gone away,

este hvmket onayvtēs mahokvnts.
ísti hámkit ona·yatí·s má·ho·kánc.
someone once told, it was said.

The Origin of Corn (Vce hēckvtē oh-onvkv)[i]

J. Hill (Haas II:157–185, corrected, III:123–145)

Hoktạlusēt	omēs.		Hoktvke	hokkolet
hoktă·ⁿlosi·t	*ò·mi·s*		*hoktakí*	*hokkô·lit*
A very old woman	there was (once upon a time).		women	two

There once was a very old woman. Two women

welaket	omen	hoktvlusēt	mv	hoktvke	vhoyat
wilâ·kit	*o·min*	*hoktalósi·t*	*ma*	*hoktakí*	*ahô·ya·t*
they 2 going about	were	the old woman	those	women	(where) they 2 had gone

were going about, and an old woman followed the tracks

elehvpo	ocaken	mvn	vcakkayvtēs.
ilihapó·	*o·câ·kin*	*man*	*acákka·yatí·s*
their tracks	she saw (had?)	those (tracks)	she followed

where the women had gone.

Momen	catvt	eto-essen	vcvnkēt		esliken	eshēcvtēs.
mo·mín	*cá·tat*	*itoʔíssin*	*acánki·t*		*islêykin*	*ishi·catí·s*
Then	blood	tree-leaf	holding (liquid contents)		lying	she found

Then she found a leaf lying with blood in it.

Likvtēt	'svyēpet		totkv	tempen	'staklicvtēs.
leykatí·t	*'sayî·pit*		*tó·tka*	*tímpin*	*stákleycatí·s*
that which lay	she took it home		fire	near	she placed it down

She took that which lay there home and set it down near the fire.

Hofonē	haken	hēcan	cēpvnusēt	hocacket
hofóni·	*hâ·kin*	*hi·câ·n*	*ci·panósi·t*	*hocâ·ckit*
some time later	when it got to be	when she looked at it	a little boy	had been created

After a while when she looked at it, she saw a little boy

mv	catvn	akhocacket	omen	hēcvtēs.	Momen	mv	hoktalat	vfastet
ma	*cá·tan*	*akhocâ·ckit*	*o·mín*	*hi·catí·s*	*mo·mín*	*ma*	*hoktâ·la·t*	*afa·stít*
that	blood	created from	he was	she saw	Then	that	old woman	caring for him

had been created, created from the blood. Then the old woman cared for him

---

[i] Title: *ací hi·ckatí· ohhonáka* 'story of the origin of corn'.

mv   cēpvnusat   vculicvtēs.   Momen   mv   hoktalat   eccvkotaksen enhahyet
ma   *ci·panósa·t* *acóleycatí·s*   *mo·mín* *ma*   *hoktâ·la·t*   *iccakotáksin* *inháhyit*
that   little boy   she raised him. Then   that   old woman   a bow   she made for him
and raised the little boy. Then the old woman made a bow for him,

reu   enhayvtēs.   Mont "Fayvs"   kicen
łiw'   *ínha·yatí·s*   *mónt* *fá·yas*   *keycín*
an arrow, too   she made for him   Then   Go hunting! she told him
and she made an arrow too. "Go hunting!" she told him,

arē   hakvtēs.   "Fayat   naket   ele hokkolicēt
a·łí·   *ha·katí·s*   *fa·yâ·t* *nâ·kit*   *ilí hokkoléyci·t*[i]
and going around he got to be   hunting   something   two-footed
and he began to go around. "When hunting, I saw something two-footed

aren   hehcis.   cvpakkēt   aret   omen   encvpenkvlēt   rahtis"
a·łín   *híhceys*   *capákki·t*   *a·łít*   *o·mín* *incapinkalí·t*   *łáhteys*
going about I saw   angry, vicious going about it was becoming frightened I returned
going about. It was vicious, and I was frightened of it and returned,"

kicen,   "Penwvt omēs.   Mv oman   elēhocen   papvkvnts.
keycín   *pínwat* *ò·mi·s* *ma ô·ma·n*   *ilí·ho·cín*   *pa·pakánc*
he said   a turkey it was (anything) like that is usually killed and eaten
he said. "It was a turkey. [Things] like that are killed and eaten.

Hvtvm   hēcetskat   elēcetskvrēs"   kicvtēs.
hatâm   *hi·cícka·t*   *ilí·cíckáli·s*[ii] *keycatí·s*
another one when you see it you shall kill it she told him
When you see another one, you shall kill it," she told him.

Momen   hvtvm   ayat   aren   hehcet   elēcvtēs.
mo·mín *hatâm*   *â·ya·t*   *a·łín*   *híhcit*   *ilí·catí·s*
Then   once more   he went off   going about   he saw it   and killed it
Then when he went off again, he saw it going about and killed it.

---

[i] Or: *ilí hokkolí·t.*

[ii] Or: *ilí·cáccas.*

"Mvt omēton okvyvnkekv. Penwvt omes" kihcet ennoricen hompakvtēs.
mat ô·mi·ton o·kayáŋkika pínwat ô·mis kéyhcit ínnoɬeycín hómpa·kati·s
it was that kind (that) I referred to turkey it is she said cooked it for him and they ate
"That's the kind I meant. It is a turkey," she said and cooked it for them, and they ate.

Mont nake rem ētv punvttv hompetv herakat pvsaten
mónt nâ·ki 'limí·ta ponátta hompitá hiɬă·ⁿka·t pasa·tín
Then something different, else game to eat, food good kill
Then he killed different kinds of game, good food,

hompaket kakvtēs. Mv cēpanat mv hoktalan "Cvpuse"
hómpa·kít kâ·kati·s ma ci·pâ·na·t ma hoktâ·la·n capósi
and eat they 2 lived That boy that old woman my grandmother
and they would eat it. The boy started calling

kicē hakvtēs. Mont fakvn ayof, mv hoktalat
keycí· ha·katí·s mónt fá·kan a·yô·f ma hoktâ·la·t
calling her he started Then hunting when he was off that old woman
the old woman "Grandmother." While he was off hunting, the old woman

taklike, afke tis punvttv elēcat noricat opuswuce hayat
takléyki á·fkiteys ponátta ili·câ·t noɬeycâ·t oposwocí ha·yâ·t
bread mush, besides game which he killed she cooked soup she made
would cook bread and mush too and the game he had killed, and when she made soup,

vce aktehkēn ennoricen hompetv heremahēn hompēt arvtēs.
ací aktihki·n ínnoɬeycín hompitá hilimă·ⁿhi·n hompí·t a·lati·s
corn in it she cooked for him food very good eating he was about
she cooked it for him with corn in it, and he ate delicious food.

Mv cēpanat vce monkat nake rem ētv estomis taklike hayvkē tayat
ma ci·pâ·na·t ací móŋka·t nâ·ki 'limí·ta istô·meys takléykihá·yaki· tâ·ya·t
That boy corn or something else bread
That boy [noticed that] when there was no corn or anything else, no possible bread,

nake sekot omēpan hompetv heraken mv hoktalat noricen
nâ·kit síko·t omî·pa·n hompitá hiɬă·ⁿkin ma hoktâ·la·t noɬeycín
nothing else food good that old woman cooked
when there was nothing at all, the old woman cooked delicious food;

"Estvn naket enhēcken momēcet ǫhạ?" komēt
ístan nâ·kit ínhi·ckín momi·cít o·ⁿhá·(ⁿ)[i] kó·mi·t
where else something she could find did how he wondered
"Where is she finding these things?" he wondered

kerretvn eyacvtēs. Mv cēpanat "Fakvn ayis" kihcet ayat
kiłłitán iyâ·cati·s ma ci·pâ·na·t fá·kan a·yéys kéyhcit â·ya·t
to know he wanted That boy hunting I am going he told her and went off
and wanted to know. The boy told her, "I'm going hunting," and when he had gone

vrvnakat erorat fekhoniyet likvtēs.
alanâ·ka·t ilo·lâ·t fikhonêyyit lêykati·s
out of sight when he got he stopped and sat down.
and gotten out of sight, he stopped and sat down.

"Naken estomen omat hehcac" komēt epuse tat cepanat hecekon
nâ·kin ísto·mín o·mâ·t híhca·c[688] kó·mi·t[ii] ipósita·t ci·pâ·na·t hicíkon
what I'll see he thought his grandmother the boy not seeing
"I'll see what it is," he thought. Without his grandmother seeing him,

vyopket afke tat hayvranet aren cēpanat hēcet alikvtēs.
ayo·pkít á·fkita·t há·yała·nít a·lín ci·pâ·na·t hî·cit a·lêykati·s
[crept up] mush about to make she was around the boy watching he sat out
the boy crept up as she was about to make mush, and the boy sat there watching.

Totkv tat tehcet vrkvswvn takhuerihcet uewv vcahnet
tó·tkata·t tíhcit ałkáswan takhoyléyhcit óywa acáhnit
the fire she kindled a jar she placed water she poured it
She kindled the fire and set a crock on it, she poured water in it

em etetahket omet elehackowv lekhowēt vhvmkvt
imititáhkit o·mít iliha·ckowá likhowí·t ahámkat[iii]
and made everything ready [did] her shins, lower legs sore all over
and got everything ready, and the old lady had sores

---

[i] *o·ⁿhá· = o·mi·ti·^.*

[ii] Or: *hicá·li·s kó·mi·t.*

[iii] For *ahámkat*, one might say *alómhi·t* 'spotted'.

mv   hoktalat   omvtēs.   Momet   uewv   morēcē   estaklikan

ma   hoktâ·la·t   ô·mati·s   mo·mít   óywa   mó·li·cí·   istaklêyka·n

that   old woman   it was   Then   water   boiling   she put down (?)

all over her shins. Then she held her shins out

elehackowvn   erohwiyet   poroyet   mv   uewvn a aktosayet   omen

iliha·ckowán   iłohwêyyit   poło·yít   ma   óywan a·áktosa·yít   o·mín

her shins   held over it   rubbed them   that   water   she dusted them off into   did

over the boiling water and rubbed them, dropping [the sores] off into the water,

mvn   hehcet   cēpanat   vyēpvtēs.   ’Rvlakan

man   híhcit   ci·pâ·na·t   ayi·patí·s   łála·kâ·n

that   when he saw   the boy   went away.   When he came back

and the boy saw that and went away. When he came back,

afke   hēerusē   noricet   mv   vrkvswv   estaklicen   ’rvlakvtēs.

á·fki   hì·ⁿlosi·   nolêycit   ma   ałkáswa   istaklêycin   łála·katí·s

mush   very fine, good   she had cooked   that   jar   she placed   and came back

she had cooked very fine mush and placed it in the crock and then he came back.

“Hompvs”   kican,   cēpanat   mv   afke   pvpetv   em eyacekatēs.

hómpas   keycâ·n   ci·pâ·na·t   ma   á·fki   papíta   imiyá·ciká·ti·s

Eat   when she said   the boy   that   mush   to eat   he did not want for her

“Eat,” she said, but the boy didn’t want to eat the mush.

“Estomen   hompetv   vm eyaceko   cehaket   oḥa?”   kicof,

ísto·mín   hompitá   amiyá·ciko·   cihâ·kit   o·ⁿhá·(ⁿ)   keycô·f

Why   to eat   not wanting for me   you have become   is it?   she said

“Why have you come to dislike my food?” she asked;

“Estonkot   omis   os”   maket   em vyoposken   mv   hoktalat   okat

istóŋkot   o·mêys   ó·ⁿs   ma·kít   imáyopo·skín   ma   hoktâ·la·t   o·kâ·t

no reason   I have   it is   he said   answering her   that   old woman   spoke

“I have no reason,” he answered, and the old woman told him:

“Cvwēyet   ontsken   omat,   tohtucvlke hokkolen   hayetskvrēs”   kihcen

cawi·yit   ónckin   o·mâ·t   tohtocálki hokkô·lin   há·yíckáłi·s   kéyhcin

scorn me   you do   if   corn-cribs two   you are to build   she told him

“If you are repulsed by me, you are to build two corn-cribs,”

tohtucvlke vhvoke 'tefvnvnvkusēn hokkolen hayvtēs. Poyof,
tohtocâlki aháwki 'tifananakósi·n hokkô·lin ha·yatí·s po·yô·f
cribs openings facing each other two he made When he had finished,
and he made two corn-cribs with their doors facing each other. When he had finished,

"Yafkusos 'rvlaketskat, mv tohtucvlke hvmken vhvoken
yă·ⁿfkoso·s lála·kícka·t ma tohtocâlki hámkin aháwkin
Late in the evening when you return those corn-cribs one the door
she said, "When you come back late in the evening,

hvsossv-fvccv vhēcan 'rvcohlicvccvs" kicvtēs.
haso·ssafácca ahî·ca·n[689] 'lacohléycáccas keycatí·s
eastward that faces place me on it she said
place me on the one corn-crib with the door facing east."

Momen mv kicat vcakkvyēn rohlicvtēs.
mo·mín ma kêyca·t acakkayí·n lóhleycatí·s
Then that having said to him [following] he put her on
Then as she had said, he placed her on it.

"Vcvhepahket tohtuce ofvn acvwihket wakkepvccvs" kicen,
acahipáhkit tohtocí ó·fan a·cawéyhkit wakkipáccas keycín
shoving me the crib inside of throw me in and lie down she said
"Push me, throw me in the corn-crib, and go to bed," she said,

hvset raklatkof, vhepahket nvtaksēn awihket, cēpanat nocēpvtēs.
hasít lákla·tkô·f ahipáhkit natáksi·n a·wéyhkit ci·pâ·na·t noci·patí·s
sun when it went down shoving her backwards he threw her the boy he went to sleep
and when the sun set, he pushed her in, threw her in face-up, and the boy went to sleep.

Nerē tat naket estokemąhet omet mv tohtuce ofvn
nilí·ta·t nâ·kit isto·kimă·ⁿhit o·mit ma tohtocí ó·fan
during the night something unusual noise it was that crib in
During the night there was an unusual noise,

vrēpvcokē omen pohet omvtēs. Hecekatēs,
ali·ⁿpacoki· ô·min po·hít o·matí·s hicíká·ti·s
something kept going about in it was he heard did He did not see it
and he heard something going around in the crib. He didn't see it

mv	nerē tat.	Momis	hvyatkan	hvthvyvtken	vcet	tohtucvlke	hokkolvn
ma	*nilí·ta·t*	*mó·meys*	*hayâ·tka·n*	*hathayátkin*	*acít*	*tohtocâlki*	*hokkó·lan*
that	night	But	at daybreak	in the morning	corn	cribs	two

that night. But at daybreak the next day,

fącfakuset	vtēhken	mv	cēpanat	hēcvtēs.
fă·ⁿcfá·kosit	*atî·hkin*	*ma*	*ci·pâ·na·t*	*hi·catí·s*
completely	full	that	boy	saw

the boy saw that corn filled the two corn-cribs completely.

Monkv	vce tat	hoktąlusēt	omēs,	mahokvnts.
móŋka	*acíta·t*	*hoktă·ⁿlosi·t*	*ô·mi·s*	*má·ho·kánc*
Therefore	the corn	an old, old woman	is	That is what they say.

So corn is a very old woman, they used to say.

Mv	cēpanat	ēkvnv	hopotēcet	vhocen	hontet
ma	*ci·pâ·na·t*	*i·kaná*	*hopóti·cít*	*aho·cín*	*hontít*
the	boy	the ground	burned it off	planted (the corn)	when it sprouted

The boy burned off the ground, planted [the corn], it sprouted,

em ēttē	hayet	momēn	vce tat	hēcket omvtēs,	mahokvnts.
imi·ttí·	*ha·yít*	*mó·mi·n*	*acíta·t*	*hi·ckít o·matí·s*	*má·ho·kánc*
its seed	it made	In that way	corn	originated.	Thus it has been told

it set seed, and that's the way corn originated, it was told.

Vce tat	hoktąlusēt	onkv,	ēlesketv	enhērē
acíta·t	*hoktă·ⁿlosi·t*[690]	*ôŋka*	*i·liskitá*	*inhĭ·ⁿli·*
The corn	an old woman	for (still) is	to get vexed, surly	easy to get

Corn is an old woman,[691] so she gets pouty easily,

monkat	eyacēt	onkv,	hericat	hēren	vcayēcēt
móŋka·t	*iyá·ci·t*	*ôŋka*	*hiłeycâ·t*	*hĭ·ⁿlin*	*aca·yí·ci·t*
or else	likes to	for she does	when they put her away	good	carefully

or likes to, and when they put her away,

herihocekon	omat,	momet	hēren	em vtothokekon	omat
hiłeyhocíkon	*o·mâ·t*	*mo·mít*	*hĭ·ⁿlin*	*imatothokíkon*	*o·mâ·t*
if they don't put it away	if	Then	good	if they don't work it good	if

if they don't store her carefully, and if they don't work [the soil] well,

vce tat sumkēpēs, mahokvnts.
acíta·t sómki·pí·s má·ho·kánc
the corn disappears they say
the corn disappears, it was told.[i]

Origin of the Sapiya[ii, 692]

J. Hill (Haas II:143–147, corrected with H. III:97–105)

Honvnwv hoktē 'tepakat welakvtēs.   Yvhịkesasen
honánwa hoktí· 'tipâ·ka·t wila·katí·s   *yahăy[n]kisâ·sin*
a man a woman together they 2 were going about someone who kept singing
A man and a woman were going about together. They heard someone singing and singing

pohet esten hopoyakvtēs.   Yvhiketvn pohakis,
pô·hit ístin hopóya·katí·s   *yahaykitán poha·kêys*
they hearing a person they 2 were looking for the singing they heard but
and looked for the singer. They heard singing

este tat hecvkekatēs. Momen fekhonnet 'mapohicet
ístita·t hicákiká·ti·s mo·mín fikhônnit má·pohaycít
the person they did not see Then they stopped, listened,
but didn't see anyone. Then they stopped, listened,

vfvnnaket sehokvtēs. Vtakrvt fvnoket hueret oken
afánna·kit sihô·kati·s atáklat fanŏ·[n]kit hôylit o·kín
and looked around they 2 stood an herb swaying stood singing, saying
and stood looking around. They saw a plant standing [there], swaying back and forth,

hehcet ohtokoriket honvnwvt vtakrvn lēmetvn komis,
híhcit ohtokolêykit honánwat atáklan li·mitán ko·mêys
when they saw it they ran up to it the man the herb to pull it up he tried but
making a noise. When they saw it, they ran up to it, but when the man tried to pull up

---

[i] I.e., it rots or spoils if not put away carefully, and it doesn't "make" if it is not cultivated.
[ii] This story used to be told by Wakseholahtēmarv (*waksihola·hti·má·la*).

esse   tvlkusen   enrohfet   eshoyanvtēs.   Hoktēt   lēmvtēs.
íssi   *tălʰkosin*   *inłóhfit*   *íshoya·nati·s*   *hoktí·t*   *li·matí·s*
leaves   only, nothing but   slipped off   he went past   the woman   pulled it up
the plant, he only stripped off leaves and went past. The woman pulled it up.

Yvlonkvn   'svpeyv   vliken   ēsvtēs.   Monkv   hoktvke
'yalóŋkan   *'sapiyá*   *alêykin*   *i·satí·s*   *mòŋka*   *hoktakí*
root   sapiya   which was on (the root)   she took   therefore   women
The woman took the sapiya that was on the root. So it belongs

enaket   omēs.   'Svpeyv tat   hoktēt   pucaset   omēs.
inâ·kit   *ô·mi·s*   *'sapiyáta·t*   *hoktí·t*   *'pocá·sit*   *ô·mi·s*
their possession   it is.   The sapiya   a woman (i.e., women)   the owner   is
to women. A woman is the owner of the sapiya.

Monkv   hoktēt   'svpeyv   ocēt   aren   omat,
môŋka   *hoktí·t*   *'sapiyá*   *ó·ci·t*   *a·łín*   *o·mâ·t*
Therefore   a woman   a sapiya   who has   going about   if she does
So if a woman goes about with a sapiya,

este honvntaket   em afvckvkē   hēret   fullēt omēs.   Este honvnwv
istihonantá·kit   *ima·fackaki·*   *hì·ⁿlit*   *follí·t ô·mi·s*   *istihonánwa*
the men   having a liking for her   very   (when) they go about   a man
the men have a strong liking for her. Its power

'svpeyv   saran,   enyekcē   'semontvlēt   omēs.   Mahokvnts.
'sapiyá   *sa·lâ·n*   *inyikcí·*   *'simontalí·t*   *ô·mi·s*   *má·ho·kánc*
a sapiya   who has   its power (effect)   greater, more   is   That is what has been said.
is greater [when a woman carries it] than when a man carries a sapiya, it's been said.

Uses of the Sapiya

Addendum to "Origin of the Sapiya"[i]

J. Hill (Haas III:101–105)

Svpeyv	'svretv		heleswvt	omēs.	Punvttv	honecakat
'sapiyá	*'salitá*		*'hilíswat*	*ô·mi·s*	*ponátta*	*honicâ·ka·t*
The sapiya	to carry about (the use)		medicine	it is	game	that is wild

The sapiya is medicine to carry about. In order to overcome

'semontvletvt	omet,	mv	vrahkv	heleswv	hayēt
'simontalítat	*ô·mit*	*ma*	*aɬáhka*	*'hilíswa*	*há·yi·t*[ii]
to overcome (game)	in order to	that	[for][693]	medicine	made (medicine)

wild game, they have a song to use

'svretv	yvhiketv	ocaken,	honvnwv	hoktvke	em enhervkē
'salitá	*yaheykitá*	*o·câ·kin*	*honánwa*	*hoktakí*	*iminhiláki·*
to carry it	a song	they have	a man	(for) women	to have a liking for (him)

with the medicine; they have a song for

vrepetv	eyacateu,	em vyvhiketvo	vrahkvt	ocakēt	omēs.
alipitá	*iyâ·ca·tiw'*	*imayaheykitaw'*	*aɬáhkat*	*o·cakí·t*	*ô·mi·s*
to go around	if he wants	its song, too	[for]	[they have	do]

when a man wants to have women like him too.

Momen	em vhakuceu		yekcvkēt	ocvkēt	omēs.
mo·mín	*imaha·kociw'*		*yikcaki·t*	*o·caki·t*	*ô·mi·s*
[and]	[the rules for it, too]		strong	[they have	do]

And they have strong rules too [for the use of this herb].

---

[i] "They were not allowed to keep it in the house. Kept it outside somewhere. When you were about to take it, you had to sing the appropriate song (depending on what you wished to use it) and then just before you put it up you had to sing again." (III:102)

"You must know the song to get it out and you must know the song to put it away. If you do not know these two songs it is best not to use it. These had to be learned from some medicine-man." (III:102)

[ii] Or: *ha·yít*.

Mv	vhakuce	vcakkvyēn	honvnwv	svpeyvn	'saret	omekon	omat,
ma	*aha·kocí*	*acakkayí·n*	*honánwa*	*'sapiyán*	*sa·lít*	*omíkon*	*o·má·t*
[those]	the rules	follows (not)	a man	sapiya	[carrying]	doing not	if it is

If a man carrying a sapiya does not follow the rules,

enokketv tis	ēenhayēs,	enhopuetakuce tis	ehiwv tis.
inokkitáteys	*i·ínha·yi·s*[694]	*inhopoyta·kocíteys*	*ihéywateys*
his sickness	it makes for him	his children, even	his wife, even

he will make himself sick, or his children or his wife.

Monkat	mv honvnwv	eshoktarēs;
mónka·t	*ma honánwa*	*ishókta·lí·s*
Or else	the man	will become an adulterer

Or the man will become an adulterer,

monkat	ehiwv tis	enhoktarēs	makaket	vculvke tatē tat.
mónka·t	*ihéywateys*	*inhókta·lí·s*	*má·ka·kít*	*acolakítá·ti·ta·t*
or else	his wife	will become an adultress	they say	the old people

or his wife will become an adultress, the old people said.

Svpeyv	'svretv	vcayēcēt	hērēt	esfullet	omvtēs.
'sapiyá	*'saɫitá*	*aca·yĭ·ⁿci·t*[695]	*hĭ·ⁿɫi·t*	*isfollít*	*o·matí·s*
sapiya	to use	to take care of it	well	they carried it	did

They carried the sapiya around with great care.[i]

The Origin of Tobacco (Hece Eshechoyvtē Oh-onvkv)[ii, iii]

J. Hill (Haas II:149–155, corrected, III:107–111, addendum III:113–121)

Este-honvnwv	hoktē	'tepvkēt	vnrvwvn	nochoyvtēs.	Nerē	hvmkat	omvtēs.
istihonánwa	*hokti·*	*'tipaki·t*	*ânɫawan*	*nócho·yatí·s*	*niɫi·*	*hámka·t*	*o·matí·s*
man		woman	together	in the wilderness	they slept	night	one	it was

A man and a woman slept together out in the wilderness. They did it one night.

---

[i] "(These are all the usages that H. remembers for the sapiya.)" (III:105)

[ii] Title: *hicí ishícho·yatí· ohhonák*a 'story of the discovery of tobacco'.

[iii] Note written phonetically, II:150: "Jim says that an old Indian told him that this story about tobacco is true — that he (the old Indian) had slipped out into the woods several times with a woman and when he would go back to the place where they had slept he would find a weed growing there."

Hofǫnē haken mv ēkvnv hēcat,
hofǒ·ⁿni· hâ·kin ma i·kaná hi·câ·t
long time afterwards when it got to be that ground when he saw
After a long time, when he looked at the ground,

mv wakhokē nochoyvtē mǫhusat mv vtakrv tat hontvtet
ma wakhô·ki· nócho·yatí· mǎ·ⁿhosa·t ma atáklata·t hôntatit
there (where) they 2 had lain they 2 had slept exactly there that herb sprouting
right where they had lain and slept,

hueren eshehcet esse tat encahwet enfvmecē tat
hôylin ishíhcit íssita·t incáhwit infamicí·ta·t
stood when he found the leaves he gathered their odor
he found a weed had sprouted up, and he took leaves from it, and the smell

fvmḛcusēt ont omen, kvrpēcet hericet enfvmecē tat talofvt
famǐ·ⁿcosi·t[i] ônt o·mín kalpî·cit hilêycit infamicí·ta·t ta·lô·fat
very sweet was drying them he put them away the odor after they had dried
was good, and they dried it and stored it, and its fragrance, when dried,

enfvmecē yekcē hakvtēt omēs. Estomēcetvt omat
infamicí· yíkci· ha·katí·t ô·mi·s istomi·citát ô·ma·t
its odor strong became did what to do with them
grew strong. [The man] didn't know

kerrekot omis, hericēt ocet, hofonē haken
kíllikot o·mêys hilêyci·t ô·cit, hofóni· hâ·kin
not knowing he was put them away had them some time had expired
what to do with it, but he had it put away. After a long time,

enfvmecē hḛrusē ont omen celayemǫhvtēs.
infamicí·t hǐ·ⁿlosi· ônt o·mín cila·yimǎ·ⁿhati·s
the (sweet) odor very sweet was he handled them often
its fragrance was good, and he handled it often.

---

[i] Or: *hǐ·ⁿlosi·t.*

Mv	hece	enfvmecē	em enherēt	cokpiket		yvcakvtēs.
ma	*hicí*	*infamicí·*	*iminhilí·t*	*cókpaykít*		*yaca·katí·s*
that	tobacco	its odor	[he liked]	he put it in his mouth		and chewed it

He liked the smell of the tobacco and put it in his mouth and chewed it.

Mont	nekrican,	enfvmecē	heremahē	haket	omen
mónt[i]	*níkleycâ·n*	*infamicí·*	*hiłimă·ⁿhi·*	*ha·kít*	*o·mín*
Then	burning it	its odor	very good	became	did

And when he burned it, its odor was wonderful,

hvtvm		mv	hece	vhetēcet	mokkicē	hakvtēs.
hatâm		*ma*	*hicí*	*ahíti·cít*	*mó·kkeycí·*	*ha·katí·s*
some more (of)		that	tobacco	he lighted	and smoking it	he got to be

and he got in the habit of lighting the tobacco and smoking it.

Monkv	mv	hece tat	honvnwv	hoktē	'tepvkē
móŋka	*ma*	*hicíta·t*	*honánwa*	*hoktí·*	*'tipakí·*
Therefore	that	tobacco	a man	and a woman	together

So that tobacco grew where the man and woman

wakhokē	ohhvyatkvtē
wakhò·ki·	*óhhaya·tkatí·*
they two lay	where they slept all night

spent the night together,

mv	hece tat	hontet	os	komēt	mvt	omē	hḙret omē tvlkus,
ma	*hicíta·t*	*hôntit*	*ó·ⁿs*[696]	*kó·mi·t*	*mat*	*ô·mi·*	*hĭ·ⁿlit o·mí· tăⁿkos*[ii]
that	tobacco	came up	did	they thought that	like	it is bound to be (like that)

they thought, and it is surely so,

erem ētv	vtakrv	mv	omat	sekot	onkv.
ilimí·ta	*atákła*	*ma*	*ó·ma·t*	*síkot*	*oŋká*
no other	weed	that	being like	none	there is

because there was no other weed like that.

---

[i] *mónt = mo·mít.*

[ii] Or: *mat hôntit ô·matteys kó·mi· hĭ·ⁿlit akilléyca·katí·s.*

Momen	mv	este	eshēcē	arat	em ēttē	hayof,
mo·mín	*ma*	*ísti*	*íshi·cí·*	*a·lâ·t*	*imi·ttí·*	*ha·yô·f*
Now	that	man	(who) found it	was around	its seed	when it developed

Then where the man had found it, when it had begun to develop seeds,

hopotēcet	vhocen	mahof,
hopóti·cít	*aho·cín*	*ma·hô·f*
he burned it off	planted (the seed)	it grew

he set the fields on fire and planted it, and when it grew,

esse tat	kvrpēcet	ocet	cokpiket	mokkicet	hecakofvt
íssita·t	*kálpi·cít*[i]	*ô·cit*	*cókpeykít*	*mó·kkeycít*	*hica·kô·fat*
the leaves	dried		he put in the mouth	he smoked	when they saw

he dried the leaves, stored it, dried it, smoked it, and when they saw him,

este	sulkēt	celayakē	haket	omvtēs.	Mahokvnts.
ísti	*sólki·t*	*cilá·ya·ki·*	*ha·kít*	*o·matí·s*	*má·ho·kánc*
people	many	using it	started to	did	Thus it has been told

many people got into the habit of using it. That's what they used to say.

Addendum: Uses of Tobacco

Etvlwv	etenrvpē	essehokvtētis	herkvn	etenhayvranof,	hecen	ocaket
itálwa	*itinlapí·*	*íssiho·katí·teys*	*hílkan*	*itinhá·yala·nô·f*	*hicín*	*o·câ·kit*
nation			peace		tobacco	

When two opposing tribal towns were going to make peace, they had tobacco;

hecepakwv	hvmkusēn	vtēhet	vhetēcet	'setem palet
hicipákwa	*hámkosi·n*	*atî·hit*	*ahitî·cit*	*'sitímpa·lít*
pipe	a single one			

they filled only one pipe with it, lit it, passed it around to each one,

omvlkvt	mokkicēt	vpoket	etem punahoyet	herkv	etenhayet
omálkat	*mó·kkeycí·t*	*apô·kit*	*itimponá·ho·yít*	*hílka*	*itínha·yít*
all	smoking			peace	

and everyone sat and smoked, talked with one another, and made peace,

---

[i] Or: *kalpí·ci·t ô·cit.*

este-cate   vculvke tatē   fullet   omvtēs.
isticá·ti   *acolakítá·ti·*   *follít*   *o·matí·s*
Indian   ancestors   being around   were
and that is the way of the old ones.

'Meceskvculvke tatē   ennak onvkv:
'miciskacolakítá·ti·   *innâ·k onáka*
ancestors
A story of the ancestors long gone:

Hecet   totkvn   tepaket   estimvt   homahtēt   ēkvnv   monkat
hicít   *tó·tkan*   *'tipâ·kit*   *istêymat*   *homáhti·t*   *i·kaná*   *móŋka·t*
tobacco   fire   together   land
Tobacco and Fire wanted to know who would stand in the lead in the land

etvlwv em etenrvwv huervranat,   etekerretvn komet, netta osten, nerē   osten,
itálwa imitînlawa hóyłała·nâ·t itikiłłitán   kô·mit nittá· ô·stin nilí·   ô·stin
        between   days   four   nights four
or area between the tribal towns, and to test each other, they sat for four days

nockv   sekon   etehoyvnhoyvranet kakvtēs. Estomatet nocen omat,
nócka   síko·n   itihoyanhoyála·nít   ka·katí·s istô·ma·tit no·cín o·mâ·t
sleep   without
and four nights without sleep. Whoever went to sleep

mvt   yopvn   huervranen   etenfaccet   kaket omvtēs.
mat   yópan   hóyłała·nín   itinfâ·ccit   kâ·kit o·matí·s
        [behind] [would stand]   [they agreed]
would stand behind the other, they agreed, and sat.

Nerē   esostan   hvyvtkē vlakusen   totkvt nohcen hecet   homahtvtēt ont
nilí·   iso·stâ·n   hayatkí· ală·ⁿkosin   tó·tkat nóhcin hicít   homa·htatí·t ônt
night   the fourth   fire   tobacco
On the fourth night, just at daybreak, Fire fell asleep, and Tobacco became the leader,

herkvt   haken   omat,
híłkat   ha·kín   o·mâ·t
peace
and when peace is made,

mvn	hece	etvlwv	em etenrvwv	herkvn	hayet hueret omēs makakēt omet
man	*hicí*	*itálwa*	*imitînlawa*	*hílkan*	*ha·yít hôylit o·mí·s má·ka·kí·t ô·mit*
	tobacco			peace	making

Tobacco stands between the towns and makes peace, they have said;

hece tat	"Hece	Vculen"	kicet
hicíta·t	*hicí*	*acólin*	*keycít*
		[old]	

the Tobacco they called, "Old Man Tobacco,"

totkv tat	"Etotkv-mēkkon"	makēt	hocefhuecvtēs	makēt	vculvke tat	onayvnts.
tó·tkata·t	*ito·tkamí·kkon*	*ma·kí·t*	*hocífhoycatí·s*[i]	*ma·kí·t*	*acolakíta·t*	*ona·yánc*
the fire	fire-chief		they called it	saying	ancestors	

and the Fire was called, "King Fire," the old ones told.

Monkv	este	vtēkat	hecen	eyạcusen	omat,
móŋka	*ísti*	*atî·ka·t*	*hicín*	*iyă·ⁿcosin*	*o·mâ·t*
			tobacco		

So anyone who wants tobacco

estvn	este	kerkekot	hueren	hēcis	hece	em pohēs.
ístan	*ísti*	*kíłkiko·t*	*hôylin*	*hi·cêys*	*hicí*	*ímpo·hí·s*
					tobacco	

and sees an unknown person standing somewhere, asks him for tobacco.

Tvlofv	ofvtot	ēkvn-tvnke	penkvlkē	ofvto	estomis
'taló·fa	*ó·fatot*	*i·kantánki*	*piŋkálki·*	*ó·fatow*	*istô·meys*
[town]					

Whether in town or in dangerous open country,

enhẹ̄rkuset	enyvmạskuset	em pohēt	omēs.
inhĭ·ⁿlkosit	*inyamă·ⁿskosit*	*ímpo·hí·t*	*ô·mi·s*
	[meekly]		

humbly and meekly he asks him.[ii]

---

[i] *hocífho·yatí·s* would refer to one [fire]; the word in text refers to more than one.

[ii] Tobacco was also used for medicine, e.g., for toothache, but H. will write this out later as it is quite long. (III:120)

How Terrapin Got a Cracked Shell (Lucv, Kono)[i]

J. Hill (Haas VI:171–177)

Konucvlket	vpoken	Lucv-tokocket	rem oret		ont,
konocâlkit	*apô·kin*	*locatokóckit*[ii]	*'limô·lit*		*ónt*
little pole-cats	were living	terrapin	came up on them		did

Box Turtle came up to where some little skunks were living.

"Cecketake	estvn	aya?"		kicen,
cickitá·ki	*ístan*	*â·ya·^*[iii]		*keycín*
your (pl.) mother	where	has she gone?		he said

"Where has your mother gone?" he asked.

"Yatan	arētat	os"	kicaken,
ya·tá·n	*a·lí·ta·t*	*ó·ⁿs*	*kéyca·kín*
close, nearby	she is around	is	they told him

"She's close by," they said.

"Nakvlke	toyēs,	cecke	makētvnka?"	Lucvt	maken,
nâ·kâlki	*tô·yi·s*	*cícki*	*ma·kí·taŋka·^*	*locát*	*ma·kín*
what (relation, clan)	we are	your mother	does she say	the turtle	said

"Did your mother say what clan we are?" Turtle asked.

Konucvlket	okakat,	"Konepvlke	toyēs	makētvnks"	kicaken,
konocâlkit	*oka·kâ·t*	*konipâlki*[iv]	*tô·yi·s*	*ma·kí·taŋks*	*kéyca·kín*
the little pole-cats	said	Pole-cat clan	we are	she said	they told him

And the little skunks said, "She said we're Skunk clan."

"Mvtoyis"	makēt,
matô·yeys	*ma·kí·t*
I am that, the same	he said

"I am the same," he said.

---

[i] Title: *locá, konó* 'turtle, skunk'.

[ii] Raiford: *locatakóckit*.

[iii] For short: *tan â·ya·^*. Original: *â·ya·´* .

[iv] *konipâlki* 'Pole-cat (Skunk) clan'. According to Hill, this word is used instead of *konâlki* in referring to the clan. Raiford notes that the Wind clan goes with the Skunk clan, because the wind carries away the scent of the skunk.

"Rvcetokmusēn   'cēyet   vliken
lacitókmosi·n   *ci·yit*[697]   *alêykin*
a little round knoll in the side of a hill   it was going in   and was there
"She went into a little knoll and was there,

sem vkonokuehcit   ahoyahnit   okis"   kihcet,
'simakonô·kóyhceyt[i]   *a·hoyáhneyt*   *o·kéys*   *kéyhcit*
I had intercourse with her   and passed by   I mean   he said
and I skunked around with her and went on," he said.

vyēpen   konucvlke   hvkahēcet   vpoken,   ecke   rvlaket,
ayî·pin   *konocâlki*   *haka·hĭ·ⁿcit* *apô·kin*   *icki*   *'lalâ·kit*[698]
it had gone   the skunks   crying   were sitting   their mother   came back
After he'd gone, the little skunks sat there crying, and their mother came back

"Naket   eston   hvkahēcet   vpokatska?"   kicet   omen,
ná·kit   *istó·n*   *haka·hĭ·ⁿcit* *apô·ká·cka·(ⁿ)^*   *keycít*   *o·mín*
what   why   crying   are you-all sitting   said to them   did
and asked, "Why are you sitting there crying?"

"'Konepvlke toyis,'   maket,   'Rvcetokmusēn   cēyet
konipâlki   *tô·yeys,* *ma·kit* *lacitókmosi·n*   *ci·yit*
skunk (clan) I am   he said   [a little round knoll in the side of a hill   it was going in
"Someone said, 'I am Skunk clan.' He said, 'She went into a little knoll,

liken,   sem vkonokuehcit   ahtis'   mahket,
lêykin   *'simakonô·kóyhceyt*   *áhteys*   *máhkit*
and was there   I had intercourse with her]   I came   he said
and I skunked around with her and then came here,'

vyehpesasen   hvkahēcēt   omēs"   kicaken,
ayíhpisâ·sin   *haká·hi·cí·t* *o·mi·s* *kéyca·kín*
somebody went   we are crying   are   they said to her
and he left, and we're crying," they told her.

---

[i] This word is hard to interpret. It refers somehow to the fact that the terrapin has intercourse with the skunk — exact meaning unknown.

"Laksēs" mahket, kecvpen ehset assēcan,
lâ·ksi·s *máhkit* *kicápin* *íhsit* *a·ssî·ca·n*
he lied she said pestle she taking and ran after him
"He lied," she said and took her pounding stick and chased him.

sakco huten roret liken eshēcet ont
sákco *hótin* *lô·lit* *lêykin* *ishî·cit* *ónt*
crawfish den she got to and she sitting and found him did
Having reached a crawfish den, she found [Turtle] sitting there.

"'Sem vkonokuehcis' cvkicetskvcoken arit omvyē. Mahketska?"
simakonô·kóyhceys *cakâycíckacókin* *a·léyt* *o·mayi·^* *máhkícka·^699*
I had intercourse with her you said that about me I around I am did you say it?
"I'm here because you said 'I skunked around with her.' Did you say it?"

kicen, "Mạkvyēseks" Lucv maken,
keycín *mă·ⁿkayi·siks* *locá* *ma·kín*
[she said] I didn't say that turtle said
she asked. "I didn't say that," Turtle said.

"'Mahkis' makvs" kicē emonket omen,
máhkeys *má·kas* *keycí·* *imôŋkit* *o·mín*
I said that you say telling him she kept on did
"Admit you said it," she kept saying.

"Mahkis" makat Lucv 'Taskēpit' koman,
máhkeys *ma·kâ·t* *locá* *ta·skî·peyt*[700] *kô·ma·n*
I said that when he said turtle I will jump he thought
When he confessed, "I said it," Turtle thought he'd jump,

rēhotvwvt cuko tohtarkan em vtakkahken vliken,
ɬi·hotáwat *cokó* *tohtá·ɬkan*[701] *imatakkáhkin* *alêykin*
shot-pouch on the house- corner and he got hung and was hanging to
but he got caught on a shot pouch on the rafter of the house,

kecvpen esnvfiket cetakhoyvtēt omēs.
kicápin *isnafêykit* *citakhoyáti·t*[702] *ô·mi·s*
pestle she hit it with it had been mashed had been
and she hit him with her pounding stick, and he got mashed.

Mohmen   liket   huehket,   "Vtvkoca!   Cvtelih-lih,   cvtelih-lih!"
móhmin   *lêykit*   *hóyhkit*   *atakoca·^*   *catiléyhléyh*[i]   *catiléyhléyh*
Then   sitting   he called   ant   come put me together   [come put me together]
Then sitting, he called out, "Ants! Come put me together, come put me together!"

maket   liken,   vtvkocat   em vtelohket,
ma·kít   *lêykin*   *atakocá·t*[ii]   *imatilóhkit*
he said   and he was sitting   the ants   gathered together for it
he said, sitting there. The ants gathered together for him,

etelomhicet   mehcen,
itilomhĕyⁿcit   *míhcin*[703]
and they were putting him together   they did that
and they pieced him all back together,

enwikvtēt   ont   ehvrpe tat   etelumhēt   ont omēs.
ínweykatí·t   *ônt*   *ihálpita·t*   *itilómhi·t*   *ônt o·mí·s*
it had gotten well   had   its shell   is put together   in that way
and where it healed, his shell is still joined together that way.

Ball-Game between the Birds and the Animals

J. Hill (Haas VI:35–43)[iii]

Nake ele ostat   nake   etvrpv   ocat
nâ·ki ilí ô·sta·t   *nâ·ki*   *itálpa*   *ô·ca·t*
something that has four feet   something   that wings   has
The four-footed animals and the animals with wings

etem pokkechvranet   etenfaccet
itimpokkíchała·nít[704]   *itinfâ·ccit*[iv]
were going to play ball against each other   they had agreed with each other
had agreed to play ball together

---

[i] In ordinary language: *catiléycas*.

[ii] Original: *atakocát*. Raiford: *atakocá·*.

[iii] Swanton's "Story of the Bat."

[iv] Raiford: *itim-*.

fullvtēs.   Ele ostē   hvlēcat vtēkat omvlkvt
follati·s   *ilí ósti·*   *hali·câ·t*[705] *atî·ka·t* *omálkat*
they were around those with four feet that crawl every one all
and were about. Every one of the four-footed things that crawl

ēyvteloyen,   etvrpv ocē tvmēcateu omvlkvt
i·yatilô·yin   *itálpa* *ó·ci·* *tami·câ·tiw* *omálkat*
have gathered together wings (that) have that fly, too all
had gathered themselves together, and all the winged creatures that fly as well

ēyvteloyet vpoket   oman, Takfvlelēskvt sekatēs.
i·yatilô·yit *apô·kit* *o·mâ·n* *takfalilí·skat*[706] *siká·ti·s*
gathered together were sitting were the bat   wasn't there
had gathered and were sitting, [but] Bat was not there.

Emehaket omhoyan sepekon
imíha·kít *ómho·yâ·n* *sipíkon*
waiting for it they were it wasn't there
[The winged animals] were waiting for him, but he wasn't there,

hopoyvranat   vtothoyan
hopóyała·nâ·t *atothô·ya·n*
going to look for it they sent
and when they sent [people] to look for him,

ele ostvkē   vpokat   min vpvkēt likēpen eshecakvtēs.
ilí ostakí·[707] *apô·ka·t* *mêyn* *apáki·t* *leykî·pin* *íshica·katí·s*
those with four feet that were sitting those was with was sitting they found him
they found him sitting with the four-footed [animals].

"Pokkēchv hvmken punhorkopet   omatskes" maket
pokkí·cha *hámkin* *ponhołkô·pit* *o·má·ckis* *ma·kít*
ball player one you stole him from us you-all have said
"You have stolen a player from us,"

etvrpv ocakat   fullvtēs.
itálpa *o·câ·ka·t* *follati·s*
wings [those] having were about
the ones with wings said.

Momen   ele ostvkē   fullat   okakat
mo·mín   *ili ostaki·*   *follâ·t*   *oka·kâ·t*
then   those with four feet   that were about   saying
And the four-footed [animals] said,

"Faccusēn   enhuehkēpēt   omēs,   etenfacceyvtē   vcakkvyēn"   makaken,
fǎ·ⁿccosi·n[i] *inhoyhki·pi·t*   *o·mi·s*   *itinfa·cciyáti·* *acakkayí·n*   *má·ka·kín*
earnestly   we have called them we have   our agreement   according to   they said
"We have rightfully called him, in accordance with our agreement,"

etenfvccetv   hayē   fullvtēt   etem opunvyēcakvtēs.
itinfaccitá   *ha·yí·*   *follati·t*   *itimoponayí·ca·katí·s*
agreement   made   were around   they talked about it with each other
and those who had made the agreement discussed it with one another.

"Tvmket arēt   onkv, epukakvranē   tvlkusēn   eten faccet omeyvnks"
tamkít   a·lí·t   *ôŋka ipokà·kała·ni·*   *tǎlʰkosi·n*   *itinfà·ccit*[708] *ô·miyáŋks*
flying   going about do   they have to stand by [us] have to   we agreed   we did
"He flies about, so we agreed he must join us,"

etvrpv   ocē   fullat   makaken
itálpa *ó·ci·*   *follâ·t*   *má·ka·kín*
wings   having   were around they said
those there with wings said.

"Monkot   os.   Em accvkē tat   vchoyē   esfulleyaten   accēt   ont,
móŋkot   *ó·ⁿs* *ima·ccaki·ta·t*   *achô·yi·*[709]   *ísfolliyâ·tin* *a·ccí·t* *ônt*[710]
not that way   is   their clothes   what we wear   go about with   it wears does
"No. The clothes he wears are the same as the clothes we go about in,

enute   oceyat   ētvpomusēn   enute   ocēt   onkv,
inóti   *ó·ciya·t*   *i·tapô·mosi·n*   *inóti*   *ó·ci·t* *ôŋka*
its teeth like we have just the same   its teeth have   do
and he has teeth just like the teeth we have,

---

[i] Raiford: *fǎ·ⁿccosi·n* is the best; could also be *fǎ·ⁿccosin*.

mv   omakan   em pokkechvranēt   makatsken   etenfaccēt   omeyvnkekv,
ma   o·mâ·ka·n   impokkíchaɫa·ní·t   *ma·ká·ckin   itínfa·cci·t   ô·miyáŋkika*
that   kind   we're going to play ball with   you-all said   we agreed   we did
so you said you would play ball with that kind, and we agreed,

faccusēn   enhuehkepeyēt   os"   makakvtēs,   ele ostakat.
făⁿccosi·n   inhoyhkipíyi·t[711]   *ô·ⁿs*   *má·ka·katí·s*   *ilí ostâ·ka·t*
truthfully   we have called (them)   have   that's what they said   those with four feet
so we have rightfully called him," those with four feet said.

"Etvrpv   ocēt   ont   tvmket
itálpa   ó·ci·t   ônt   tamkít
those with wings   that have   do   flying
"It is our custom that those who have wings

hvlwēn   arēt   on   etohkvlkēt   punfulletvt   os.
hálwi·n   a·lí·t   ô·n   itohkálki·t   ponfollitát   *ô·ⁿs*
high up   going about   do   being together   that's our way of going about   is
fly high together.

Hvlket   ēkvnvn   oh-arat   hecatskvtē   sahsekos.
halkít   i·kanán   óhha·lâ·t   hicá·ckati·   sáhsiko·s
crawling   the ground   being on   that you saw   never did
None of you has ever seen [us] crawling on the ground.

'Tvmēcē   fullan   em pokkechetvn   puyac's'   makatskvnks"   makakvtēs.
tami·cí·   follâ·n   impokkichitán   poyâ·c   ma·ká·ckáŋks   *má·ka·katí·s*
those that fly   about   to play ball with we want   you-all were saying they said
You said you wanted to play ball with those that fly about," [the birds] said.

"Fuswvt   em accvkē tat   esfullatskat   omat   vccekot
fóswat   ima·ccakí·ta·t   ísfollá·cka·t   *ô·ma·t   ácciko·t*
birds   their clothes   like you-all go about with   like   haven't got on
"He doesn't wear bird clothes like you all wear;

tafvn   vchoyatskēt   os.
tá·fan   ácho·yá·cki·t   ô·ⁿs
feathers you-all wear   do
you all wear feathers.

Tvrpv	tafvn	estvmēcēt	omatsket	oman
tálpa	*tá·fan*	*ístami·cí·t*	*ô·má·ckit*	*o·mâ·n*
wing	feathers	they fly with	you-all do	like

You fly with feathered wings,

mv	omat	ocekot	omat	hēcuset	kērrusatskēt	os"	kihocvtēs.
ma	*ô·ma·t*	*ó·cíko·t*	*ô·ma·t*	*hǐ·ⁿcosit*	*kǐ·ⁿłłosá·cki·t*	*ô·ⁿs*	*kéyho·catí·s*
[that	like]	it doesn't have	like it	seeing it	you-all know it	do	they said

but he doesn't have ones like that, and looking closely, you realize [that]," they said.

Momen	fuswvt	okakat
mo·mín	*fóswat*	*oka·kâ·t*
then	the birds	they said

Then the birds said,

netta	nockv	tvlkēt	omis	okēkv		vrekvs"	kicahken,
nittá·	*nócka*	*tálki·t*	*ô·meys*	*o·kí·ka*		*alíkas*[712]	*keycáhkin*
(all) day	sleep	always	does	we are contending		let it be!	they said

"He sleeps all day anyway, so let him go," they said,

ele ostē		fullan	em vnicet	pokkēchvtēs.
ilí ô·sti·		*follâ·n*	*imáneycít*	*pókki·chatí·s*
those with four feet		were about	let him help	play ball

and he helped those with four feet and played ball.

The Owl and the Dog

J. Hill (Haas IV:31–37)

Efvt	aren	opvt	vnrapet	ont	em punayet	ont	este		enfulletv	estomēt
ifát	*a·lín*	*opát*	*anlâ·pit*	*ónt*	*impona·yít*	*ónt*	*ísti*		*infollitá*	*istó·mi·t*
Dog	was around	owl	met	did	talked	did	person, people		travelling	what way

Dog and Owl met, and Owl talked with him, and Owl asked Dog

omat	opvt	efvn	enpohvtēs.	"Pihkvyan	pohakat,
ô·ma·t	*opát*	*ifán*	*ínpo·hatí·s*	*payhkayâ·n*	*poha·kâ·t*
	owl	the dog	asked	when I whoop	(and) they heard it

about the ways of people. "When they hear me hoot ['whoop'],

naket oks   cvkicakvntē?"   maket   efvn   em pohen,
nâ·kit ó·ks   *cakáyca·kánti·^*   *ma·kít* *ifán* *ímpo·hín*
what is it   (that) they say about me   (he) said dog (of) he asked
what is it they say I am?" he said, asking Dog.

"'Pelof-cepanet   pihkvcoks'   makakvnts"   kicen,
pilo·fci·pá·nit   *payhkacóks*   *má·ka·kánc*   *kaycín*
Bottoms-boy   (is) whooping they said, say   said to
"They used to say, 'Bottoms Boy is whooping,'" he told him.

"Pihkvyē   pohakat   vm penkvlvkēt onkvntē?"   kicen,
payhkayí·   *poha·kâ·t* *ampiŋkaláki·t* *óŋkánti·^*   *kaycín*
(me) whooping they heard afraid of me   usually, generally told
"When they hear me hoot, are they afraid of me?" he asked.

"Monhkos.   Cem penkvlahkekos"   kihcofvt,
móŋhko·s   *cimpiŋkaláhkiko·s*   *káyhco·fat*
won't   they (won't) be afraid of you told
"No. They're not afraid of you," he said.

"Momis   hopuetakucen   espenkvlēcakvntis   okis"   kihcen,
mo·mâys *hopoyta·kocín* *ispiŋkalí·ca·kánteys*   *o·kéys* *kéyhcin*
but   children   to scare (the children) with I mean told
"But they do scare the children with your hooting," he said.

"O   tayēskomahet onko?"   opvt   makvtēs.
*o·'^*   *tá·yi·skomâ·hit óŋko·'*   *opát* *ma·katí·s*
well I don't amount to much did?   owl   said
"Well I don't amount to much, do I?" Owl said.

Hvtvm   opv   vpohet   okat,   "Naken   empenkvlvkēt
hatâm   *opá* *apo·hít* *o·kâ·t*   *nâ·kin*   *impiŋkaláki·t*[i]
again   owl   asked   said   what   are they afraid of
Again Owl asked, "What are people

---

[i] For the prefix *im-*, Hill uses *in-* before *p*, while Raiford uses *im-*.

este   fullet   omvntē?" kicen,   efvt   okat,
ísti   follít   o·mantí·^ keycín ifát   o·kâ·t
people   being around, go about usually   told   dog   said
usually afraid of?" and Dog said,

"Naken   em penkvlahkekos.   Este tokat   vtēkat   nvfkvntot
ná·kin   impiŋkaláhkiko·s   ísti tó·ka·t ati·ka·t   náfkantót
what   won't be afraid of anything if not a person as long as hit, strike
"They're not afraid of anything. As long as it's not a person, they hit it

elēcakēt   omēs" kihcofvt   "Momis   eto   lvtkētis
ilí·ca·kí·t   ô·mi·s káyhco·fat   mo·mâys itó   látki·teys
(and) killed it   do   after telling it   but   tree   fallen
and kill it," he told him, "But if a tree lies

tulkvtēt   wakken, hvtvm eto-yvhekle   sulkētis
tólkati·t   wâ·kkin hatâm itoyahíkli   sólki·teys
had fallen   lying   again   brush (pile of limbs) a lot of them
where it has fallen, or if there is a lot of brush

vpoken   omat, mvn em penkvlvkē hēṟēt   ont,
apô·kin   o·mâ·t man impiŋkaláki· hĭ·ⁿłi·t   ônt
together, (piled up) is   that afraid of   much (afraid), good (afraid of) is
piled up, they're very afraid of that

hopvyēn   vfulutēcēt   fullet   omvnts"
hopáyi·n   afóloti·cí·t   follít   o·mánc
quite a ways   go around it (brush pile) being around usually (go about that way)
and usually go quite a ways around it,"

efvt   kicen,   "Monkv eto-rakko wakkan ohlikin   cvhecaken   omat,
ifát   kaycín   móŋka itolá·kko wâkka·n ohlêykeyn   cahíca·kín   o·mâ·t
dog   said   If   big log   lying   sitting on   (if) they see me (if) do
Dog told him. "So if they see me sitting on a big fallen tree,

vm penkvlvkēt omēto?"   opvt maken,   "Cem penkvlahkekos.
ampiŋkaláki·t ó·mi·to·˙   opát ma·kín   cimpiŋkaláhkiko·s
afraid of me   would (they be)   owl   said   (wouldn't be) not afraid of you
they'd be afraid of me?" Owl asked. "They wouldn't be afraid of you.

Cenvfiket	acewikvkēs"	efvt	kicvtēs,	mahokvnts.
cinafêykit	*a·ciwéykaki·s[713]*	*ifát*	*keycatí·s*	*má·ho·kánc*
strike you	throw you off	dog	said, told	it has been said

They'd hit you and knock you off," Dog told him, it's been said.

A Catamount Gets Intoxicated (Kowakkuce)[i]

J. Hill (Haas IV:39–45)

Pvnkvn	ocet	este	sulkēt	fullet
pánkan	*o·cít*	*ísti*	*sólki·t*	*follít*
dance	having	people	lots	were there

They were having a dance and lots of people were there;

uehomē	eskakateu	sulkēton	hacakat	sulketot
oyhomí·	*íska·kâ·tiw'*	*sólki·ton*	*há·ca·kâ·t*	*sólki·tot*
whisky	drinking	several, many	getting drunk	several

there were many people drinking whisky and many getting drunk,

cvpakhokateu	mont	etehanateu	este tat	fullen
capákho·kâ·tiw'	*mónt*	*itíha·nâ·tiw'*	*ístita·t*	*fŏlⁿlin*
getting mad, too	and	were fussing, too	people	were going about

and there were people getting mad and arguing with each other

hvyatket	omētan	yafkusof	este	hvmket	aret
hayâ·tkit	*ô·mi·ta·n*	*yă·ⁿfkoso·f*	*ísti*	*hámkit*	*a·lít*
became day	it was	late in the evening	person	one	was about

until daylight, but late in the evening, a man was going

nenen	ayet	omaten	nene	tempen	hvfvpēt	ocet	oman
ninín	*a·yít*	*o·mâ·tin*	*niní*	*tímpin*	*hafápi·t*	*ô·cit*	*o·mâ·n*
road (on)	going	was	near	the road	brushy	was	was

down a road, and there was brush near the road,

mv	ofvn	estet	opunayet	okat,	"Honvnwv	toyis"	maket
ma	*ó·fan*	*ístit*	*opóna·yít*	*o·kâ·t*	*honánwa*	*tô·yeys*	*ma·kít*
[there	in]	person	talking	said	a man	I am	said

and someone was talking in there: "I am a man," he said,

---

[i] Title: *kowa·kkocí* 'bobcat'.

okēpen   herįcet   mapohican   "Honvnwv toyis"
okiˑpín   hiłĕyⁿcitⁱ   máˑpohaycâˑn honánwa   tôˑyeys
meant   [easily] quietly   did listen   man   I am
and the man listened carefully, "I am a man,"

etewolēn   maket oket oman este tat fullet
itiwolíˑn   *maˑkít o·kít o·mâ·n ístitaˑt follít*
close together, in succession said   meant did   people   were going about
he said right away again, and people had been going about,

este   elehvpo tat   etenceyvlhoyusē   omēt   fullvtet
ísti   ilihapóˑtaˑt   itinciyálhoˑyosíˑ ô·mi·t fŏłⁿlatit
person's   tracks   in a scuffle   [like] had been around
and their tracks looked like they had scuffled

sumechoyet   maket oken, "Este honvnwv toyis.
somichô·yit   *o·mâ·n o·kín ísti honánwa tô·yeys*
and had gone, disappeared had   meant man   I am
and disappeared. "I am a man.

Estimvn   em penkahlvkos"   hvfvpē hērat   ofvn   maket oken
istéyman impiŋkáhlakoˑs   hafápiˑ hĭ·ⁿla·t   ó·fan ma·kít o·kín
nobody   I'm afraid of   thicket very (brushy) in   said   meant
I'm not afraid of anyone," [the voice] said in the very thick brush,

hēren   mapohicet   vketēcan   fvlasko   tvnken
hĭ·ⁿlin máˑpohaycít   akítiˑcâ·n faláˑsko⁷¹⁴   tánkin
good   listened (good) noticed   bottle   empty
and when he listened carefully and checked around, he saw an empty bottle

hvfvpan   akwihoken   kowakkucet   eshēcet   ont   ensēfkepvntot
hafápa·n   akwayhô·kin   kowa·kkocít   ishî·cit ónt   insíˑfkiˑpántot
the thicket had been thrown in catamount   found it did   would smell it
had been thrown in the thicket, and a catamount had found it and had been smelling it

---

ⁱ Long way: *ahĭ·ⁿłeycit.*

hacēpet	akpvlpvkēpet	oken	hechoyvtēs	mahokvnts.
ha·cî·pit	*akpalpakī·ⁿpit*	*o·kín*	*hicho·yatí·s*	*má·ho·kánc*
got drunk	rolled about	(meant)	someone saw it	what they said

and had gotten drunk and was rolling about, it was said.

"Honvnwv	toyis	ca!"		maket	esakpv tat	tokohusēn
honánwa	*tó·yeys*	*ca·^ⁱ*		*ma·kít*	*isákpata·t*	*tokó·hosi·n*
man	I am	(boasting word)		said	its arm	(was) speckled

"I am a man!" he said, and it sat

akvwapet	aklikēpvten	okhoyvnts.
á·kawa·pít	*akleykī·ⁿpatin*	*ókho·yánc*
raised it	lived	they said, was said, someone did say

in the brush raising its speckled arm, someone said.

The Trading Snake

J. Hill [told by a man named Cook living close to Okemah] (Haas IV:47–53)

Este-cate	hvmket	"Rvron	'makwiyit		uewv	tempusan	aklikimvts"
isticá·ti	*hámkit*	*lałón*	*mákwayyéyt*		*óywa*	*timposa·n*	*aklêykeymac*
Indian	one	fish	I'm fishing for (fish)		water	near to	sitting (sometime ago)

Sometime back an Indian said, "I was sitting fishing

makemvts.	"Rvro enhompetv	a-akwikvyat	rvro tat	esēpet	omen
ma·kimác	*laló inhompitá*	*a·ákweykayâ·t*[715]	*lałóta·t*	*isi·pít*	*o·mín*
said	fish-bait	threw in (the water)	fish	get it (bite it)	did

down by the water. When I threw the bait in, the fish took it,

aswikēpit	omvyan	enhompetvt	vcvnahēpen
a·swéyki·péyt	*o·mayâ·n*	*inhompitát*	*acana·hî·pin*
I caught it	was (catching fish)	bait	gave out, was exhausted

and as I was catching fish, the bait ran out,

hopoyvranit	ahuervyan	cettot	wakket	omat
hopóyala·néyt	*á·hoyłayâ·n*	*cíttot*	*wâ·kkit*	*o·mâ·t*
I was going to hunt	when I stood up	snake	was lying	was

and when I stood up to look for some, I saw a snake was lying there

---

ⁱ *cah for Hill.*

vpvtvnvn cokpikepēt omen enheheit, rvro enhompetvn hayepetvn
apatanán cokpąykipí·t ó·min inhíhceyt łałó inhompitán ha·yipítan
bull-frog had in its mouth had I saw it fish-bait to make (fish-bait)
with a bullfrog in its mouth. I wanted

cvyahcet vpvtvnv svpenkvlehcit omvyan
cayáhcit apataná 'sapiŋkalíhceyt o·mayâ·n
I wanted, aimed to bull-frog I took it away from (the snake) I did
to make fish-bait and took the bullfrog from it, but

mv cetto wakken eto-kvckucen sem vwetēnvyan
ma cítto wâ·kkin itokackocín 'simáwiti·nayâ·n
that snake was lying stick broken I held it (the snake) down with (a broken stick)
when I pinned the snake down with a broken stick,

hvwaklet omen fvlaskon uehomē vcvnkēn sēpikvyēt omiset
hawâ·klit o·mín falá·skon oyhomí· acáŋki·n si·péykayi·t ô·meysit
opened its mouth did bottle whisky had in had it in my pocket did have
it opened its mouth, and as I had a bottle of whisky in my pocket,

cetto hvwaklof uehomēn em ohcanin nokmēlet ohmet
cítto hawa·klô·f oyhomí·n imóhca·néyn nókmi·lít óhmit
snake when it opened its mouth whisky poured in swallowed it did
when the snake opened its mouth, I poured some whisky in, and it swallowed some

wakken, vcewemahekon tulpoket rvtosket pvlpaket wakken
wâ·kkin aciwimá·hikon tólpo·kít lato·skít pálpa·kít wâ·kkin
lying not very long coiled up straightened out rolled lying
and lay there. Not very long after, it coiled up, straightened out, rolled around,

hēcvyvtē wihkit kute tat vpeswv tacit
hi·cayáti· wéyhkeyt kotíta·t apíswa ta·céyt
looking at it I quit (looking at it) frog meat I cut
and I quit looking at it and cut up the frog meat

cufokunhen 'mvlicit uewv sakwikvyan rvro tat vnturkēpen
cofokónhin máleycéyt óywa sákweykayâ·n łałóta·t antólki·pín
fish-hook I put on water when I threw it in fish bit for me
and put it on the hook, and when I put it in the water, the fish were biting for me.

aswikēpit　　　　svcafvckēt　　　aklikvyof　　　　　hofonemahekon
a·swéyki·péyt　　*'saca·fácki·t*　　*aklêykayo·f*　　　　*hofonimá·hikon*
I caught them　　I was pleased　　when [I was] sitting　not very long (after)
I caught them, and when I was happily sitting there, before long

naket　　　　　cvcefokkicen　　　ohfulutikit　　　　　hēcvyan
nâ·kit　　　　*cacifókkaycín*　　*ohfolotâykeyt*　　　*hi·cayâ·n*
something　　punched me　　　I turned around toward it　noticed it
something poked me, and when I turned around and looked,

mv　cetto　ētvwvt　vpvtvnv　ētvn　esepēt　　res vlaket
ma　*cítto*　*i·tawát*　*apataná*　*í·tan*　*isípi·t*　　*'lisalâ·kit*
that　snake　the same　bull-frog　another　had [caught]　brought it back
I saw that same snake had brought another bullfrog

escvrēfket　　　ohmvtēton　　hēcimvts.
iscali·fkít　　　*óhmati·ton*　*hî·caymac*
punched me　　did　　　　[I] did see
and had been poking me with it.

Momat　　mv　　vpvtvnucen　uehomēn　　svnyoposketvn　　eyacēt
mo·mâ·t　*ma*　*apatanócin*　*oyhomí·n*　*sanyoposkitán*　*iyá·ci·t*
then　　　that　little frog　　(for) whisky　to swap with me　wanted
So it wanted to swap that little frog for whisky

res vm vlaket　　　　ohmvthakemvts"　　maket　　onayemvts.
'lisamalâ·kit　　　*óhmátha·kimác*　　*ma·kít*　*ona·yimác*[716]
brought back to me　had (long time ago)　said　　he told
and had brought it back to me," [Cook] used to tell.

The Mice Plot Against the Cat (Cesse Oh-onvkv)[i]

J. Hill (Haas IV:55–61)[ii]

Cesse	sulkemahēt	nvkaftet	vpoket	omat	posen	em penkvlvkētot
císsi	*solkimá·hi·t*	*nakâ·ftit*	*apô·kit*	*o·mâ·t*	*pó·sin*	*impiŋkaláki·tot*
mice, rats	a lot of them	gathered	together	(were)	the cat	they [were] afraid of (the cat)

Many mice were gathered together, and being afraid of cats,

vnrvpēt		opunvyēcet	svpokvtēs.
anłapí·t		*opónayi·cít*	*sapô·kati·s*
to oppose, against		talked about	they were (together) in session

they were meeting to talk about opposing them.

"Pose	kihocē	fullat tat	vheremahen	pustemerrvkuecēt	os.
pó·si	*káyho·cí·*	*follâ·tta·t*	*ahilimă·ⁿhin*	*postimíłłakoycí·t*	*ô·ⁿs*
cats	are called	go about	awfully	punish us	do

"When the creatures called cats go about, they make us suffer terribly.

Pupvsatet	pupapēt	ont	hopuetakuce	punlokēpetonkv,
popása·tít	*popa·pí·t*	*ônt*	*hopoyta·kocí*	*pónloki·pít ôŋka*
kill us,	eat us	do	(our) little children	eat (ours) do

They kill us, eat us, and gobble up our little children;

omvlkeyan	pulokvranat	tvlkuset	onkv	estomēcvkē tayen	omat
omálkiya·n	*polókala·nâ·t*	*tălⁿkosit*	*oŋká*	*istomí·caki· tâ·yin*	*o·mâ·t*
all of us	will eat	(they're) sure to	is	whatever we can do with them	(can)

they're sure to gobble up all of us, so whatever we can do,

lvpkēn	estomēcvkan	hērēs"	maket	vkerricet	opunvyēcet
lápki·n	*(i)stomî·caka·n*	*hĭ·ⁿli·s*	*ma·kít*	*akíłłaycít*	*opónayi·cít*
quick	what can we do with it	good	said	thought about	talked about

it's best we do it quickly," they said and thought about it and discussed it

---

[i] Title: *císsi ohhonáka* 'story about mice'.
[ii] From Aesop's Fables : "Belling the Cat."

hofonēn　　　　svpoket　　　　"Nake　　rakrvkē tis　　cvmhcakvn
hofóni·n　　　　'sapô·kit　　　　nâ·ki　　łakłakí·teys　　camhcá·kan
for quite a while　(were in session)　something　big　　　　a bell
and met for quite a while. "Even big things

enocvkuehocē tat　hecēskis　　　pohken　　　fullēt　　　onkv,
inocakoyhocí·ta·t　hicí·skeys　　pò·hkin　　follí·t　　　ônka
around their necks　didn't see any　could be hear[d]　going about　was
you can't see can be heard when they have a bell around their neck,

mv　pose tat　omvlkvn　　cvmhcakucen　　enocvkuecvkan　　　hērēs,
má　pó·sita·t　omálkan　　camhca·kocín　inocakôycaka·n　　　hi·ⁿli·s
that　cat　　all of them　little bells　　put around their necks　is a good idea
so it would be good to put bells on all the cats,

arvcokat　　　pohkētok.　　Pefatkēpaken　estehecekot　　　　fullen
a·lacóka·t　　pô·hki·to·k　　pifa·tkí·pakin　istihícikot　　　follín
(hear) them about　could be heard　ran away　　they didn't see anybody　they were
so they could be heard going about. We could run and they couldn't find us

follēpvkan　　hērēs"　mahket, pose　omvlkvn
fólli·pakâ·n　hi·ⁿli·s　máhkit pó·si　omálkan
we go about　it's best　said　cat　all
and it would be good for us," they said, and they decided

cvmhcakucen　　enocvkuecvranet　　　　　fvccēcahket　　vpoken
camhca·kocín　inocakóycala·nít　　　　　facci·cáhkit　apô·kin
little bells　　will tie bells around their necks　they decided　sitting (were in session)
to put bells around the necks of all the cats.

cesse　vcǫlēt　　　cesse vpokat　　　　　rem vtēkē　　　mahhen
císsi　acǒ·ⁿli·t　　císsi apô·ka·t　　　　'limati·kí·　　máhhin
rat　　(very) old one　(where) the rats were sitting　on the outer edge　extreme (outer edge)
A very old mouse where the mice were meeting,

alikēpatet　vpohet　okat, "Mv　pose　cvmhcakv　enocvkuecatskof,
a·laykî·patit apo·hít　o·kâ·t ma　　pó·si　camhcá·ka　inócakoycá·cko·f
was sitting　asking　said　those　cats　bell　　　after you put the bells on
sitting on the outer edge asked, "When you put the bell on the cats' necks,

estit pose hvlvtvrētē?" maket vpohen, em vyoposkekot vwahvtēs. Mohmet
istêyt pó·si halátáłi·ti·˙ ma·kít apo·hín imayopóskikot awa·hatí·s móhmit
who cat will catch said asked didn't answer him adjourned [and]
who will hold the cat?" and without answering him they adjourned. So

pose tat cvmhcakv enocvkuecvkekon esmonkvtēt omēs.
pó·sita·t camhcá·ka inocakoycakíkon ísmoŋkatí·t ô·mi·s
cat bell didn't put around their necks never, (didn't) at any time (was)
they never did put bells on the cats' necks.

A Mouse Deceives a Cat

J. Hill (Haas IV:63–65)

Cessuce em vretv uewv escvokv vcvnkēt uewvt ocvten,
cissocí imałitá óywa iscáwka acánki·t óywat ô·catin[717]
the mouse's path water- bucket had (water) in it water was
A bucket of water was in a mouse's path,

cessucet a aklatket omiyet akhotosēpet ak-arof,
cissocít a·aklâ·tkit omayyít akhotosî·pit ákka·lô·f
mouse had fallen in swimming had become fatigued while in
and the mouse had fallen in, and when he had gotten very tired from swimming,

poset em vlaken, "A vcak-ēsvtet cvpvpepvccvs" cesset kicen,
pó·sit imalâ·kin a·acakkí·satit capapipáccas císsit kaycín
a cat came up take me out you can eat me the mouse said
a cat came up: "Take me out and you can eat me," the mouse said,

poset a ak-ēsen, "Cvlvcpē hḡret onkv, cvtakwvkēcetsken cvkarpof,
pó·sit a·akkî·sin calácpi· hĭ·ⁿłit oŋká catakwakî·cickin caka·łpô·f
cat took it out I'm very wet (is) lay me down when I get dry
and the cat took it out. "I'm very wet. Lay me down, and when I'm dry,

cvpvpepvccvs" kicen, takwvkēcet "Hompetv vnheckēs"
*capapipáccas kaycín takwakî·cit hompitá anhicki·s^*
eat me, you can eat me told it put it down to eat, food I have found for me
you can eat me," he said to him. And [the cat] lay him down thinking, "I've found food,"

komēt   pose tat   yvhikẹpet   takwakket   estaknohcen
kó·mi·t[718]   pó·sita·t   yahaykĭ·ⁿpit   takwâ·kkit istaknóhcin
thought   the cat   was singing, purring   was lying   went to sleep
and lying there purring, the cat went to sleep,

cessuce tat   vyēpvtēs.
cissocíta·t   ayi·patí·s
the mouse   went away.
and the mouse went away.

The Lion and the Frog

J. Hill (Haas IV:67–71)

Estepapvt   hvcce   wakkē   vfopken   aret   oman
istipá·pat   hácci   wákki·   afó·pkin   a·lít   o·mâ·n
lion, man-eater creek   was lying (near) bank   was about   was
Lion was going about along the bank of a stream

naket   hēhkẹpvcoken   pohvtēs.   "Nake   rakkē   hẹret   aret
nâ·kit   hi·hkĭ·ⁿpacókin po·hatí·s   nâ·ki   łákki·   hĭ·ⁿlit a·lít
something   (was) growling   he heard   something big   very   is around
and heard something growling. "Something very big is around making noise,"

okvcoks"   komēt   em penkalet   liket   vkerricet,
o·kacóks   kó·mi·t impiŋkâ·lit   lâykit   akiłłeycít
(is making this noise)   thought was afraid of it sitting thought about it
he thought, and frightened by it, he sat and thought about it:

"Naket   momvtēkē   rakkat   yvmv   arat   hecvyvtē sekot os.
nâ·kit   mó·matî·ki· łákka·t   yamá   a·lâ·t   hicáyati· síko·t ô·ⁿs
something   that great, big big   here   being about I never did see
"I've never seen anything that big around here.

Nake   estomēt   aret   oken   omat   hecarēs"
nâ·ki   istó·mi·t   a·lít   o·kín   o·mâ·t   hicá·li·s
something   what (kind of a thing)   is about is   can be   I will see
I will see whatever it is going about making the sound,"

mahket oh-ayvtēs.   Rvnakuecet   omacokat   naken   hecekot
máhkit óhha·yatí·s   *'laná·koycít*   *o·macóka·t*   *nâ·kin*   *hicíkot*
said   went up to it   got close to it   seemed to be   something   didn't see
he said and went toward it. He got close to it but didn't see anything

em penkalet   huervtētot   vyopket   ayet   roret   omat
impiŋkâ·lit   *hŏyⁿlati·tot*   *ayo·pkít*   *a·yít*   *lô·lit*   *o·mâ·t*
was afraid of it   was standing   slipping up on   was going   got there   (did) but
and stood there afraid. Then when he had crept up on it,

hecekot   pvhe   mahēt   ocē   ofvn   hēhket   oken,
hicíkot   *pahí*   *mă·ⁿhi·t*   *ó·ci·*   *ó·fan*   *hi·hkít*   *o·kín*
not seeing, didn't see it   grass   tall   was   in   was growling   (meant)
he didn't see anything, but it was growling in the tall grass;

pvhen   em peranan   kute-lanet   liket   oken,
pahín   *ímpila·nâ·n*   *kotilá·nit*   *lêykit*   *o·kín*
grass   near   green frog   was sitting   was
when he parted the grass a green frog was sitting there:

"Yih!"   kihcet   'mvwetēnit   kohmet   ohmvyatat   mvttecihcen,
yáyh   *káyhcit*   *máwiti·néyt*   *kóhmit*   *ohmayâ·ta·t*   *matticéyhcin*
pronounced slowly (lion) said   held it down   thought   struck at it   missed it
"Ya-ayh!" [Lion] said and tried to hold it down, struck at it, and missed;

"Cih!"   mahket   uewvn   akcēyvtēs   mahokvnts.
cáyh[i]   *máhkit*   *óywan*   *ákci·yatí·s*   *má·ho·kánc*
         (frog) said   water   jumped into   it was told
"Chayh!" [the frog] said and jumped into the water, it was told.

A Strange Catch

J. Hill (Haas IV:73–75)

Este-honvnwv   hvmket   aret   omat   cvmhcakv   wakv tis   cerakko tis
istihonánwa   *hámkit*   *a·lít*   *o·mâ·t*   *camhcá·ka*   *wá·kateys*   *'cilákkoteys*
man   one   going about   was   bell   even a cow   even a horse
A man was going about

---

[i] *cặh* high pitched.

enocihocē   vnrvwv   esfullē
inoceyhocí·   *ânława*   *ísfollí·*
was around the neck   on the range what they were
gathering lost bells that had been tied around the necks of

sumhuecakvtēn   vyocemahēt   aret   omvtētot
somhóyca·katí·n   *ayo·cimá·hi·t*[i]   *a·lít*   *o·matí·tot*
and lost   gathering them often he was around   had been
cattle and horses out on the range,

rvro   'makwikvn   ayet   aret   rvro   'makwiyat   aem esepē   hẹ̄rēt   on
laló   makwéykan   â·yit   a·lít   *laló   mákwayyá·t   a·imisipí·   hi·ⁿli·t   ô·n*
fish   fishing for   went   was going   fish   fishing for   biting   well   were
and he went fishing, and when he fished they were really taking his bait,

hofonekvnton   aswiket   akliket
hofónikánton   *á·sweykít*   *aklêykit*
not very long (apart)   caught   sat
and he caught one not long after,

enhompetv   mocvsēn   'mvlihcet   a-akwiken   raklatkan   vpakusen
inhompitá   *mocási·n*   *'maléyhcit*   *a·ákweykín*[719]   *lákla·tkâ·n*   *apă·ⁿkosin*
bait   new   put on   threw it in   as soon at it hits   immediately
put new bait on, and as soon as he threw it in, and it hit,

ehsvcoket   pvfnēt   sem vlētken   enhvlattuecat
íhsacókit   *páfni·t*   *símali·tkín*   *inhala·ttôyca·t*
got it   fast   was running with (his line)   when he jerked it
it took it and was running with it, so he jerked it

cvmhcakvn   aswikvtēs   mahokvnts.
camhcá·kan   *á·sweykatí·s*   *má·ho·kánc*
bell   he caught
and caught a bell, it was told.

---

[i] Or: *ishicimá·hi·t* 'found them often'.

The Fearless Terrapin

J. Hill (Haas IV:77–83)

Eto	rakkēt	tulkvtēt	hvokēt	wakket	oman
itó	*łákki·t*	*tolkatí·t*	*háwki·t*	*wâ·kkit*	*o·mâ·n*
tree	big	had fallen	hollow	lying	was

A big tree had fallen and was lying there hollowed out,

naket	ofvn	vpiket	on	hecaket
nâ·kit	*ó·fan*	*apêykit*	*ó·n*	*hicâ·kit*
something	inside	was inside	was	saw it

and they saw something was inside.

punvttv	holwvyēcakat	sulkēt	em vteloket	ossihcet
ponátta	*holwayi·câ·ka·t*	*sólki·t*	*imatilô·kit*	*osséyhcit*
animals	mean (animals)	many	had gathered	put it out

Many ferocious animals had gathered to drive it out,

naket	omat	hecetvn	eyacaket	omatet
nâ·kit	*ô·ma·t*	*hicítan*	*iya·câ·kit*	*o·mâ·tit*
whatever	it is	to see	wanted	(for that reason)

because they wanted to see what it was,

em penkvlaket	vpoken,	lucv-tokocket	vlaket,
impiŋkalâ·kit	*apó·kin*	*locatokóckit*	*alâ·kit*
they were afraid of it	were sitting	terrapin	came up

and were sitting there afraid. A box turtle came up:

"Estomen	vteloket	momēt	vpokatska?"	kicen,
ísto·mín	*atilô·kit*	*mó·mi·t*	*apô·ká·cka·ⁿ˘*	*kaycín*
for what reason	have gathered	that way	you all are sitting?	told

"Why are you gathered sitting like this?" he asked them.

"Heyv	eto	ofvn	naket	vpiket	omen	ossicetvn	puyacet	oman,
hiyá(?)	*itó*	*ó·fan*	*nâ·kit*	*apâykit*	*o·mín*	*osseycitá(n)*	*poyâ·cit*	*o·mâ·n*
this	log	inside	something	was [inside]	was	to get it out	we want	did

"Something is inside this log, and we want to drive it out,

a pum vkoslēt   likēpet   on   vpokēt   omēs"   kicaken
a·pomakósli·t   laykî·pit   ó·n   apô·ki·t   o·mí·s   káyca·kín
outdid us   still is sitting is   we were sitting we are   told it
but it's defeated us and is still in there, so we're just sitting here," they told him.

lucvt   okat   "Vnet   ossicarēs"   maken;
locát   o·kâ·t   aní t   osséycá·li·s   ma·kín
terrapin   said (as follows): I   will get it out said
Turtle said, "I will drive it out."

"Kos cē!   Ecehyetskvs!   Yekcē   ceyvllvr' tayēt   omakis
kosci·^   icíhyíckas   yíkci·   ciyállałtâ·yi·t   omâ·keys
no! Don't!   Don't go in there strong   able to resist   they were
"No! Don't go in there! It defeated even those who are able

a em vkoslēt   liket   onkv,   ecēyetsken   omat   celēcvrēs"
a·imakósli·t   lâykit   oŋká   icî·yíckin   o·mâ·t   cilí·cáli·s
they outdo it   sitting   is   if you go in there do   it will kill you
to put up a strong fight. If you go in there, it will kill you,"

kicaket   oman,   "Momis   naket   on   omat
káyca·kit   o·mâ·n   mô·mays   nâ·kit   ô·n   o·mâ·t
they told it   did   anyhow   (something) whatever   it is
they told him, but Turtle said, "Well I'm going to see

hecvranit   okis"   mahket,   lucvt   eto   hvokan   ecehyen
hicáła·néyt   o·kéys   máhkit   locát   itó   hâwka·n   icíhyin
I'm going to see   I'm saying   said   terrapin   log   hollow   went in
what it is," and went into the hollow log

em ehaket vpoken,   hofonē   hakēpet   on
imihâ·kit[720]   apô·kin   hofóni·   há·ki·pít   ó·n
waiting   sitting   long time   became, got to be   was
while they sat waiting. After quite awhile,

"Elēcephoyat   tvlkusēs"   maket   fullof   lucv-tokocke yossen
ili·ciphô·ya·t   tằl^kosi·s   ma·kít   follô·f   locatokócki[721] yo·ssín
it was killed by someone   bound to be   said   around   terrapin   came out
when they were saying, "He has surely been killed," they saw the box turtle

hecahket	oh-vpēyet,		"Naket	liket	oma?"	kicet
hicáhkit	*ohhapîˑyit*		*nâˑkit*	*lêykit*	*oˑmaˑˇ*	*keycít*
saw it	were going up to it		something	sitting	is	said

come out and went up to him. "What's in there?"

em pohaken	"Pvtot	liket	on	ohkatskvten	lohkit
ímpohaˑkín	*patót*	*lêykit*	*óˑn*	*óhkáˑckatin*	*lóhkeyt*
asked it, them	mushroom	sitting	was	you-all meant	I ate up

they asked him. "It was a mushroom you were talking about, and I ate it up

ra ossit	omis"	lucv-tokocket	maken	vhecakan,	naket	sekot on
láˑoˑsséyt	*oˑméys*	*locatokóckit*[i]	*maˑkín*	*ahícaˑkâˑn*	*nâˑkit*[722]	*síkot óˑn*
I came out	have	terrapin	said	they looked	nothing	wasn't there

and came out," the box turtle said, and when they looked, nothing was in there,

okēpen,	punvttv	rakrakē	holwvyēcat	nak	makekot	hvmkusvntot	ayet
okiˑpín	*ponátta*	*łakłakíˑ*	*holwayîˑcaˑt*	*nâˑk*	*máˑkikot*	*hâmkosántot*	*aˑyít*
meant	animals	big	mean	anything	didn't say	one at a time	went

just as he had said; and not saying anything, the big, ferocious animals

vwahvtēs	mahokvnts.
awaˑhatíˑs	*máˑhoˑkánc*
(they) went away	

went away one by one, it was said.

The Fawn and the Wolves

J. Hill (Haas V:179–185)[723]

Eco-tokohlucet	aret	oman
icó tokohlocít	*aˑlít*	*oˑmâˑn*
fawn ("speckled deer")	(was) around	was

A young fawn was about

yvhvt	ēlvtēton	efunet	vpoken	hēcet	ont	hueret
yahát	*iˑlatíˑton*	*ifónit*	*apôˑkin*	*hîˑcit*	*ónt*	*hôylit*
wolf	had died	its bones	lying	see (the bones)	did	and stood

and stood looking at some bones from a dead wolf sitting there:

---

[i] Raiford: *locatakócki.*

ya-há fŏ-ni ká·ł-ká·p   cá·-na-teys   sáyⁿ-sáyⁿ   so-lí-teys   mí·ł-mí·ł

"Yvhv   fune   karkap,
yahá   fóni   ká·łká·p
wolf   bones   dried up
"Wolf bones dry-drying,

Canv tis   si-si,
cá·nateys   sáyⁿsáyⁿ
flies, even   (buzzing)
Flies too buzz-buzzing,

Sule tis   mẹr-mẹr"
solíteys   mí·ⁿłmí·ⁿł
buzzards even   flapping
Buzzards too flap, flap,"

maket   vrẹpen   yvhvt   eshecaket
ma·kít   ałĭ·ⁿpin   yahát   ishicâ·kit
said   and was still about   wolves   found him (a fawn)/comes up on him
he said as he went about. The wolves found him,

"Naken   maket   oketska?"   kicen,   eco-lowakucet   okat,
nâ·kin   ma·kít   o·kícka·^   kaycín   icolowa·kocít   o·kâ·t
what   saying   are you?   said to it   young deer
and [one] asked, "What are you saying?" The fawn said,

"Naken   mahkēskos.   Est' ecke   kvco   hopoyēpusē
nâ·kin   máhki·sko·s   *istícki*   *kacó·*   *hopóyi·posí·*
what   anyone shouldn't say   anyone's mother (who) berries   while hunting for
"No one said anything. Someone's mother was killed

estem elehocvten,   eshvkihkẹpusēt   okaks"   kicen,
(i)stimilího·catín   *ishakayhkĭ·ⁿposi·t*   *o·káks*   *kaycín*
(somebody's) has been killed   I (or) we, are crying over it   are, am.   said
looking for berries, and I'm crying about that," he said.

"Hvkihkekot   ohketsken   okis"   yvhvt   kicen,
hakáyhkiko·t   *óhkíckin*   *o·káys*   *yahát*   *kaycín*
crying not   you did (not)   I mean   wolf   said to (the fawn)
"You weren't crying," [one] wolf said.

"Hvkihkit   ohkis"   kicen,
hakayhkéyt   *óhkays*   *keycín*
I crying   I did   told (the wolf)
"I was crying," [Fawn] said.

"Moman   hiyomen   mahkaki!"   yvhvt   kicen,
mô·ma·n   *hayyô·min*   *máhka·kêy*   *yahát*   *keycín*
well,   (right) now   say it!   wolf   said to (F.)
"Well let's hear you say it now!" the wolf told him,

eco-lowakucet   okat,
icolowa·kocít   *o·ká·t*
fawn   said to (W.)
and the fawn said,

'Fus-eka,   Fus-eka,   Fus-eka'   makvyēt ohkis"   kicen,
*fosika·^*   *fosika·^*   *fosika·^*   *ma·kayí·t óhkeys* *keycín*
bird head (?)   that's what I said told it
"Bird-head, Bird-head, Bird-head. That's what I said."

"Makekot   ohketskes"   yvhvt   kicen,
má·kiko·t   *óhkíckis*   *yahát*   *keycín*
did not say it that way you did (not)   wolf   told it
"You weren't saying that," the wolf said.

"Moman   ahyit   hvlwusan   ra ohhuerit   makin   pohvs"
mô·ma·n   *áhyeyt*   *hâlwosa·n*   *ła·ohhôyłeyt*   *ma·kéyn*   *pohás*
well,   I going to go (to) little knoll (go and) stand upon   I say   you [listen]
"Well I'm going to go stand on that little knoll and say it, and you listen,"

kicen   yvhvt   em vkvsahmen   ayat   ra ohhueret
keycín   *yahát*   *imakasáhmin*   *â·ya·t*   *ła·ohhôylit*
said the   wolf   consented   and (the F.) went   and stood (on the high place)
[Fawn] said, and the wolf consented, and Fawn went and stood up there.

Yvhv fune   karkap,
yahafoní   ká·łká·p
"Wolf bones dried up,

Canv tis   sị-sị,
cá·nateys   sáyⁿsáyⁿ
Flies too buzz, buzz,

Sule tis   mẹr-mẹr
solíteys   mí·ⁿłmí·ⁿł
Buzzards too flap, flap.

makit	ohkvyē!"	mahket	enletiken,
ma·kéyt	*óhkayi·*	*máhkit*	*inlitêykin*
I said	that's what (I said)	it said	and ran away from

That's what I said!" he said and ran away.

assēcaken	ayet	uewv	lvokēt	ocan
a·ssí·ca·kín	*a·yít*	*óywa*	*láwki·t*	*ô·ca·n*
they ran after it and	it was still going	water	deep	where (there was deep water)

They chased him, and at a place where there was deep water,

etot	akcunēkēt	ocvten	er ohtasiket
itót	*akconí·ki·t*	*ô·catin*[724]	*iłohta·sêykit*
tree	bending over	there was	it went and jumped upon

there happened to be a tree leaning over, and he jumped on top of that

uewv	nvrkvpv	onvpvn	raohhueren	yvhvt	yopvn	rorican
óywa	*nałkapá*	*onápan*	*la·ohhôylin*	*yahát*	*yópan*[725]	*'łołêyca·n*
water	middle	on top	stood upon	wolves	afterwards	they came

and stood over the middle of the water. The wolves got there afterwards

ecuce	em vpēttēt	uewv	ofvn	akhueren	hecahket
icóci	*imapi·ttí·t*	*óywa*	*ó·fan*	*akhôylin*	*hicáhkit*
fawn	its shadow	water	in	stood in	they saw it

and saw the fawn's reflection in the water:

"Akhvtvpikit   ra ossicvyof,   hvlvtatskvrēs"   kihcen,
akhatapâykeyt   ła·ósseycayô·f   hałátá·ckáłi·s   kéyhcin
I'll go down in   I will make it come out   you-all must catch it   told them
"I'll go down in the water and force him out, and you grab him," one said,

hvmket   tvpalvn   ra hueren,
hámkit   tapá·lan   ła·hôyłin
one   on the other side (of the stream)   was standing
and while the other one stood on the other side [of the water],

akhvtvpiket   omiyet   aksumket   ak-aret,
akhatapêykit   omayyít   áksomkit   ákka·łít
it went into   was swimming   was sinking   was around in it
[the first one] went in, swam, and kept diving in,

hecekomahhet   ra ossan,   uewv   melohlvtēt   wikan,
hicikomáhhit   łá·o·ssâ·n[726]   óywa   milo·hlatí·t   waykâ·n
didn't find it   when it came out   water   waving, rippling   when it (water) quit
but wasn't able to find him, and when he came out, when the water stopped rippling,

akhuerēpē   monken,
akhoyłî·pi·   môŋkin
it (F.) was still standing in   (still)
[Fawn] was still standing in it.

"Vne mit   omarēs"   hvmket   mahket, akhvtvpiket   aksumket
animêyt   omá·li·s   hámkit   máhkit   akhatapâykit   áksomkit
I (will)   will do it   one   said   went into   sank, went under
"I'll do it," another one said and went in, dove in,

uewv ofv ak-aret,   naken   hecekot   ra ossen,
óywa ó·fa ákka·łít   nâ·kin   hicíkot   łá·o·ssín
water in   was around   something, anything   didn't see, find   coming out
and went around in the water, but he didn't see anything and came out,

uewv nekēyekof,   akhuerēpē   monken hecaket
óywa niki·yiko·f   akhoyłî·pi·   môŋkin hica·kít
water while not moving about   it was still standing in   (still)   they saw it
and when the water was still, they saw he was still standing there,

etēyoposēcet   akfullet
iti·yopósi·cít   *akfŏlⁿlit*
they took it turn about   they were around in it
and the wolves took turns going around in the water,

yvhvt   akhotosahket   wikakvtēs   mahokvnts.
yahát   *akhotosáhkit* *wáyka·katí·s* *má·ho·kánc*
wolves   they got tired they quit   That's what is said.
got tired, and quit, it was said.

The Tasks of Rabbit

J. Hill (Haas VI:1–7)

Cufet   Hesaketvmesēn   rem oret   on:
cofit   *hisa·kitamisí·n* *'limô·lit* *ó·n*[727]
Rabbit   God   visited (God) did
Rabbit had gone to see God:

"Nake   ceyacet   aret   ontska?"   kicen;
nâ·ki *ciyâ·cit*   *a·lít*   *oncka·^*   *keycín*
what   do you want being around you for?   he said to him
"What are you going around wanting?" [God] asked;

"Cvhoporreneko mahēt   omet,
cahopołłinikomá·hi·t   *ô·mit*
I'm not very sensible   am (not)
"I don't have much sense,

centat   hoporrenemahēt   ontskekv,
cinta·t *hopołłinimá·hi·t*ⁱ   *ónckika*
you   very sensible, you have a great knowledge   you have
and you have great knowledge,

hoporrenēn   cvhayetskvrēn   cvyacēt os,"   Cufe   maket   omen,
hopołłiní·n   *cahá·yíckáli·n*   *cayá·ci·t ô·ⁿs* *cofí*   *ma·kít* *o·mín*
with knowledge   you will make me   I want   Rabbit   said   did
so I want you to make me smart," Rabbit said.

ⁱ Or might be *hopołłinitamá·hi·t*.

"Cetto cvpkemahēt likētok: mvn res vtetskvrēs,"   kihohcen,
cítto capkimá·hi·t lêyki·to·k man 'lisatíckáli·s   kayhóhcin
snake very long lying that you must bring it back he was told
"There is a very long snake: you must go and bring it back," he was told.

ayet eto-poloke cvpkēn esehpet sayet res oren,
a·yít itopolóki cápki·n isíhpit sa·yít líso·lín[728]
going pole long got it carried it getting there with it
After a while he got a long pole and took it there.

"Estomēcvranet   eto-poloken saretska?"   Cettot kicen,
*istomí·cala·nít   itopoló·kin sa·lícka·^*   *cíttot kaycín*
what are you going to do with (it) the pole you are carrying about? snake told him
"What are you going to do with that pole you are carrying about?" Snake asked.

"Heyv eto 'scencvpkēt omēs makaken, 'Monhkos' makat sasen,
hiyá itó scincápki·t ô·mi·s má·ka·kín mónhko·s ma·kâ·t sâ·sin
this stick longer than you is they said it's not some said some
"They said this stick is longer than you, but some said it was not,

'Er vhopayvs' mahoken sarit omis.
iłahopá·yas má·ho·kín sa·łéyt o·méys
go and measure it! they told me I'm going about with it I am
and I was told to come measure you.

Ohwakkvs" kicen, ohwakken, "Estomat cvpkē tat ent
ohwákkas keycín[729] *ohwâ·kkin istô·ma·t cápki·ta·t ínt*
lie on it he told it it lay on it which one is the longest itself (for themselves)
Lie on it," [Rabbit] said, and he lay on it. "They will see for themselves

hecvkepvrēs. Secēyin" kihcet,
hicakipáłi·s 'sicî·yeyn[730] *káyhcit*
they will see it I will take you told it
which one is longest. I will take you there," [Rabbit] said

soh-vwvnayet mehcet res vlaken,
sohhawána·yít míhcit 'lisalâ·kin
tied it on did got back with it
and tied him on [the stick] and brought him back.

Hvtvm "Eckvposwv sulkē hēṟēt vpokētok:
hatâm ickapó·swa sólki· hĭ·ⁿli·t apô·ki·to·k
again gnats a lot of them plenty there are there
Again [God said,] "There are many gnats:

mvn resvtetskvrēs" kihocen, sukcv hopoyet ayet eroren,
man 'lisatíckáli·s kéyho·cín[731] sókca hopo·yít a·yít ilo·lín[732]
them you are to get it was told sack he hunting for going getting there
you are to get them," he was told, so he looked for a sack and got there.

"Estomvranet aretska?" eckvposwvt kicaken,
istó·mala·nít a·lícka·^ ickapó·swat kéyca·kín
what are you going to do (you) going around? gnat(s) told him
"What are you going to do here?" the gnats asked,

"'Heyv sukcv fackēs' makat sasen,
hiyá sókca fâ·cki·s[733] ma·kâ·t sâ·sin
this sack it will get full some said
"Some said [there are so many of you that] this sack will get full,

'Fvcikekos' maket, 'setem vyekcet, 'svpoket,
facêykiko·s ma·kít 'sitimáyi·kcít 'sapô·kit[734]
will not get full said contending against each other were there
and [others] said it will not get full, and they sat contending with one another.

"Sukcv sem ahyetsken, vtēhken hehcet,
sókca 'simáhyíckin ati·hkín híhcit
sack take it to let them be put in let them see
"Take the sack to them, have them get in it and see,

ervtes" cvkihcahken arit omis.
iłátis cakaycáhkin a·łéyt o·méys
and come back they told me (so that's why) I'm around am
and then come back," they told me, and so I am here.

Vtehkaks, vhoskēsekot" kicen,
atíhkaks ahŏ·ⁿski·sikot keycín
(you-all) be put in, get in weren't any left told him
Get in, without any left," he said,

omvlkvt	vtehiken,	senwvnahyet,	"Ēmet	hecvkēpof
omálkat	*atihêykin*	*sinwanáhyit*	*í·mit*	*hicáki·pô·f*
all	got into	he tied it	(for) themselves	when they see

and all of them got in, and he tied it and said, "When they see,

ensulkē	estomuset	omatskat,	ēmet	hecvkepvrēs"	kihcet,
insolkí·	*istô·mosit*	*ô·má·cka·t*	*í·mit*	*hicakipáli·s*	*káyhcit*
how much	is it/it is	you-all are	(for) themselves	they will see	told them

they will see for themselves how many you are,"

res atet,		res vlahken,	"Mv	hoporrenkv	semontalat
'lisâ·tit		*'lisaláhkin*	*ma (?)*	*hopołłínka*[735]	*'simontâ·la·t*
brought them back		he got back	that	knowledge, sense	not any greater

and he brought them back. [Then God said,] "I can give

istimvn	emvko tayēt		onkv,	hoporrenkv	ocetskatet
istêyman	*imáko·tâ·yi·t*		*ôŋka*	*hopołłínka*	*ô·cícka·tit*
anybody	I can not give to (anyone)		is	knowledge	that you have

no one greater cunning than that, so you must use

sēyvnicet		hueretskvrēs"	kihohcen,	ratvtēt	omēs.
si·yaneycít		*hôyłíckáli·s*	*keyhóhcin*	*la·tatí·t*	*ô·mi·s*
that you use yourself	you must stay	he told him	he came back

the knowledge you have," he was told, and he came back.

Cow Makes a Request of God

J. Hill (Haas V:187–189)

Wakv hoktēt	Hesaketvmesēn		rem orvtēs.
wá·ka hoktí·t[736]	*hisa·kitamisí·n*		*límo·latí·s*
cow	(to where) God (is, was)		it went

A cow went to God.

"Naken	ceyacet	aret		ometska?"	kicen,
nâ·kin	*ciyâ·cit*	*a·lít*		*o·mícka·^*	*kaycín*
what	do you want?	(being) around		are you	said

"What do you want?" he asked.

"Hopuetake	sulkēn		ocetvn		cvacēt		os.
hopoytá·ki	*sólki·(n)*	*o·citán*	*cayá·ci·t*	*ô·ⁿs*[737]
children		several, many	to have		I want
"I want to have many children.

Sukhv tat	cutkusēt	oman		sulkē		ocēn		hayetskekv,
sókhata·t	*cŏ·ⁿtkosi·t*	*ô·ma·n*	*sólki·*	*o·cí·n*	*hâ·yickika*
the hog		small		is		many		it has		you have made
The hog is a very small thing, but you've made it where she can have many [children],

vne		mahvkvo		cvna		rakkēt		onkv"		maken,
aní		*mâ·hakaw'*	*caná·*		*łákki·t*	*ôŋka*		*ma·kín*
me		especially	my body		big		is		said
and my body is much bigger," she said.

"Hvthvyvtken	cem onvyarētok	Heyvn	ohhvyvtketskvrēs"			kihocen,
hathayátkin	*cimonayá·li·tô·k*	*hiyán*	*ohhayátkíckáli·s*			*kéyho·cín*
in the morning	I will tell you	here	you will stay all night (here)	it was told
"I will tell you in the morning. You will stay the night here," she was told,

essetapho	vhockvn		vpihokan
issitá·pho	*ahó·ckan*	*apayhô·ka·n*
cabbage		patch		put her in
and she was placed in a cabbage patch.

essetaphon	lokēpen			hvyvtiken,
issitá·phon	*lokî·pin*		*hayatèykin*
cabbage		had eaten it up		it became morning
By morning she had eaten all the cabbage.

"Cenhvmkusis	sulkēn		hompetskekv,
cinhâmkoseys	*sólki·n*	*hompíckika*
you alone	lots, much	you ate
[Then God said,] "You eat a great deal by yourself.

hopuetaken	sulkēn		ocetsken	omat,
hopoytá·kin	*sólki·n*	*o·cíckin*	*o·mâ·t*
children	many		you had		if (you had)
If you had many children,

hompetv	'setetayēckvt	yekcēt	omētok.
hompitá	*'sitita·yi·ckat*	*yíkci·t*	*ô·mi·to·k*
food	for everyone	difficult, hard	(because) it would be

it would be hard to have food for everyone.

Hvmkusis	cem etetayēs"		kihohcen	ratvtēt	omēs.
hâmkoseys	*cimititâ·yi·s*		*kayhóhcin*	*ła·tatí·t*	*ô·mi·s*
just one, even	would be enough for you		it was told	it came back	did

Just one is enough for you," she was told, and she came back.

Dog Makes a Request of God

J. Hill (Haas V:191–192)

Efvt	Hesaketvmesē	rem orvtēs.	"Naken	ceyacet	aretskisa?"	kicen
ifát	*hisa·kitamisí·(n)*	*límo·latí·s*	*nâ·kin*	*ciyâ·cit*	*a·líckeysa·^*	*kaycín*
[dog]	[God]	[went to]	what	do you want	being around?	he said

Dog went to God. "What do you want?" he asked.

efvt	okat,	"Nak	fvsken	cvyacēt	os.
ifát	*o·kâ·t*	*nâ·k*	*fáskin*	*cayá·ci·t*	*ô·ⁿs*
dog	did say, said	something	sharp	I want	do

Dog said, "I want a weapon.

Nake	holwvyēcvkē	rakrvkepē	estomis
nâ·ki	*holwayi·cakí·*	*łakłakipi·*	*istô·meys*
several somethings	mean, bad (pl.)	big (pl.)	if they are (bad)

You have told me to catch big bad things

hvlatit	'tepoyaren,
hala·téyt	*'tipoyá·lin*
to catch	and fight (the things that are big and mean)

and fight them,

'scvkicetskvtēt		omen	momvyēt	ont	omis,
scakaycíckati·t		*ô·min*	*mó·mayi·t*	*ônt*	*o·méys*
you have told me (to catch and fight)		did	that's what I do	(I) do	I do

and that is what I do,

cvnute	tvlkusēn	'sēyvnicvyat		vnyē̜kcusēt	ont,
canóti	*tâlkosi·n*	*sí·yaneycayâ·t*		*anyĭ·ⁿkcosi·t*	*ônt*
my teeth	only	I make use of to help myself with		very hard for me	is

but using just my teeth is hard for me,

nak	fvskēn	'sēyvnicin		omat	tvlkusan
nâ·k	*fáski·n*	*sí·yaneycéyn*		*o·mâ·t*	*tâlkosa·n*
something	sharp	(if) I help myself with (something sharp)		if	only

so I think it would be better for me if I could help myself with a weapon,"

vnhē̜rēs		komis"	maken,	"Hvthvyvtken	cem onvyarētok.
anhĭ·ⁿli·s		*kô·meys*	*ma·kín*	*hathayátkin*	*cimonayá·li·tô·k*
would be best for me		I think	it said	in the morning	I will tell you

he said. "I will tell you in the morning.

Heyvn	ohhvyvtketskvrēs"		kihocen,	ecēyat
hiyán	*ohhayátkíckáli·s*		*kéyho·cín*	*ici·yâ·t*
here	you will stay overnight (here)		it was told	when going in

You will spend the night here," he was told. When he went in,

wakv-hvrpe	tvkvcwēt	ocvten	est' enloken,		hvyvtiken
wa·kahálpi	*takácwi·t*	*ô·catin*	*istinlô·kin*		*hayatêykin*
cow-hide	hard	there was	it ate it up for, from		it got to be morning

he ate up everyone's cowhides that were there. In the morning

"Nak	fvskē	ocetskekis		cem etetạyuset
nâ·k	*fáski·*	*ó·cíckikeys*		*cimitită·ⁿyosit*
something	sharp	if it didn't have (anything sharp)		it would be enough for you

he was told, "It is enough for you to help yourself without

ēyvnicet	hueretskvrētis os"		kihohcen,	ratvtēt	omēs.
í·yaneycít	*hóylíckáli·teys ó·ⁿs*		*keyhóhcin*	*ła·tatí·t*	*ô·mi·s*
(you can) help yourself	you will stand, you will be, stay		it was told	it came back	did

a weapon," and he came back.

The Foolish Mule

J. Hill (Haas VI:9–13)[i]

Cerakko-pihkvt	epucasen	ensumket	aret	oman,
'ciłakkopáyhkat	*ipocá·sin*	*insômkit*	*a·lít*	*o·mâ·n*
mule	its master	it got lost from	was around	was

A mule got separated from its master and was about,

estepapv	ehvrpet	kaken	eshēcet	accet	arvtēs.
istipá·pa	*ihálpit*	*kâ·kin*	*ishî·cit*	*â·ccit*	*a·latí·s*
lion	hide	(was) lying	it found it	it put it on	he was around

and he found a lion's skin lying [there] and wore it around.

Momen	punvttv	honecakat	hēcat,
mo·mín	*ponátta*	*honicâ·ka·t*	*hi·câ·t*
Then	animals	wild	they saw it

Then when the wild animals saw him,

em penkvlvkē	hēret	em pefatket	omen	hēcat,
impinkaláki·	*hĭ·ⁿlit*	*ímpifa·tkít*[738]	*o·mín*	*hi·câ·t*
they were frightened	very much	they ran from it	did	it saw it

they were very frightened and ran from him, and seeing that,

vpelicēpet	esafvckē	hēret	svrēpvtēs.
apiléyci·pít	*isa·fácki·*	*hĭ·ⁿlit*	*sáli·patí·s*
laughed at (them)	it was happy	very	it was around with it (the hide)

he laughed at them and very happily wore it around.

Epucaseu	mv	cerakko-pihkv	hopoyat	arvtēton,
ipocá·siw	*ma*	*'ciłakkopáyhka*	*hopo·yâ·t*	*a·latí·ton*
its master, too	that	mule	he was looking for	had been around

His master too had been around looking for the mule,

cerakko-pihkvt	epucasen	hehcet,	"Mvo	penkvlehcit,
'ciłakkopáyhkat	*ipocá·sin*	*híhcit*	*maw'*	*piŋkalíhceyt*
mule	its master	saw	him, too	I will scare

and the mule saw his master and said, "I will scare him too

---

[i] From Aesop's Fables, "The Ass in the Lion's Skin."

vpeliceparēs"   mahket   oh-ayen,   epucaset   hehcet,
apileycipá·li·s   *máhkit*   *óhha·yín*   *ipocá·sit*   *híhcit*
and I will laugh at him   he said   going upon   its master   saw it
and have a laugh," and he went up to him, and his master saw him,

vheremahen   em penkahlofvt,
ahiłimă·ⁿhin   *impiŋkáhlo·fat*
after getting   scared of it
and after getting very scared,

hēren   vketēcan,   ehvcko   cvpcvkēt   omen   hēcan,
hi·ⁿlin   *akíti·câ·n*   *ihácko*   *capcakí·t*   *ô·min*   *hi·câ·n*
carefully   looking at it   its ears   long   were   saw it
when he looked carefully, he saw that his ears were long

em ecerakko-pihv-cule   ensumkvtet aret   ohmvtēton   keriyet,
imiciłakkopayhkacóli   *ínsomkatí·t a·lít*   *óhmati·ton*   *kiłêyyit*
his old mule   that had got lost from him it happened to be found it out
and realized it was his old mule that had gotten lost from him,

hvlatet   "Cerakko-pihkv-cule   cehoporrenekat,
halâ·tit   *'ciłakkopayhkacóli*   *cihopolliníka·t*
holding it   the old mule   you, that have no sense
and he grabbed him, [and said,] "You dumb old mule,

nake   sēhoneckē   ēhayetv   ceyacet   omis,
nâ·ki   *si·honícki·*[739]   *i·ha·yitá*   *ciyâ·cit*   *o·mêys*
something   very dangerous   to make yourself   you want to   but
you want to make yourself into something dangerous,

cehvcko   cvpcakan   ohranetskeko   tayekv,
cihácko   *capcâ·ka·n*   *ohla·níckíko·*   *tâ·yika*
your ears   are long   you to cover them over   are not able
but you can't cover your long ears.

mvt   cerakko-pihkvt   ometskat   ecohfvccēcet os"   kicet,
mat   *'ciłakkopáyhkat*   *ô·mícka·t*   *icohfácci·cít ó·ⁿs* *kaycít*
that   a mule   you are   it proves it on you told it
That proves you are a mule," he said to him,

epucaset	hvlatet	ehanet	nvfkvranet	sarvtēs.
ipocá·sit	*halá·tit*	*iha·nít*	*náfkala·nít*	*sa·łati·s*
its master	holding it	scolded it	was going to hit it	was around with it

and his master held him and scolded him and was going to hit him.

The Wise Cat

J. Hill (Haas VI:15–23)[i]

Poset	eto	rakkē	huerat	ceskvn	likēpen,	Culvt	eshēcet,
pó·sit	*itó*	*łákki·*	*hôⁿła·t*	*cískan*	*leykiˑⁿpin*	*colát*	*ishî·cit*
cat	tree	big	standing	at the butt	sitting	fox	found it

A cat was sitting at the base of a great tree, and Fox saw him.

"Naken	estont	liket	ometska?"	kicen,
nâ·kin	*ístónt*	*lêykit*	*o·mícka·^*	*keycín*
what	are you doing	sitting	you are?	told it

"What are you doing sitting there?" he asked.

"Naken	estomvkot	likit	omis"	kicof,
nâ·kin	*istó·mákot*	*lêykeyt*	*o·méys*	*kaycô·f*
nothing	I'm doing	I sitting	I am	when he told it

"I'm not doing anything," he told him,

efv-wohkvlket	fullvcoken	Poset	pohet	ont,
ifawo·hkâlkit	*follacókin*	*pó·sit*	*pô·hit*	*ónt*
the hounds	were around	cat	heard it	did

and then Cat heard hounds going around.

"Cehopoyaket	fullet	okahkekotē?"	Poset	kicen,
cihopóya·kit	*follít*	*okáhkiko·ti·^*	*pó·sit*	*keycín*
they're looking for you	they're around	don't you think they are?	the cat	told it

"Don't you think they're looking for you?" Cat asked.

"Cvhopoyakē tis,	cvhēcahkekos.
cahópoya·kí·teys	*cahi·cáhkiko·s*
they may be looking for me	they won't find me

"They may be looking for me, but they won't find me.

---

[i] From Aesop's Fables, "The Fox and the Cat."

Vkerretv	sukcv	fvckē	palen	ocvyēt	omēs"	Culvt	maket,
akiłlitá	*sókca*	*fácki·*	*pâ·lin*	*ô·cayi·t*	*ô·mi·s*	*colát*	*ma·kít*
scheme, cunning	sack	full	ten	I have	do	Fox	said

I have ten bags of tricks," Fox said.

"Centv?	Ecenrapv	esohfvnketv	vkerretv	ocetskēt
cínta'	*icinlá·pa*	*isohfankitá*[740]	*akiłlitá*	*ó·cícki·t*
how about you	your enemy	to overcome	the cunningness	have you

"How about you? Do you have enough cunning

omekvntē?"	maket	em pohen,
*omíkanti·^*	*ma·kít*	*ímpo·hín*
or haven't you?	said	and asked

to overcome your enemy?" he asked.

Poset	oket	"Naken	ohcvkos.
pó·sit	*o·kít*	*nâ·kin*	*óhcako·s*
cat	said	nothing	I have

Cat said, "I don't have anything,

Momis	vkerretv	estemẹrkusēn	hvmkusēn	ocvyēs"	kicen,
mo·mâys	*akiłlitá*	*istimĭ·ⁿlkosi·n*	*hámkosi·n*	*ô·cayi·s*	*kaycín*
but	scheme	very simple	one	I have	told it

except for one very simple trick," he said.

"Vne tat	sukcv	fvckē	palen	ocvyēs"	makof,
aníta·t	*sókca*	*fácki·*	*pâ·lin*	*ô·cayi·s*	*ma·kô·f*
I	sack	full	ten	I have	when it said

Now when [Fox had] said, "I have ten bags of tricks,"

efv-wohkvlke tat	vwulicvcoken,
ifawo·hkâlkita·t	*awóleycacókin*
the hounds	seemed to be getting closer

the hounds seemed to be getting closer.

"Ētvmạhen	vrēpin	hotosvkvrē tat	fullet	oks"
i·tamă·ⁿhin	*ali·péyn*	*hotosakáli·ta·t*	*follít*	*ó·ks*
[somewhere else] entirely	I'll be around	they will get tired	being around	are

"I'll be somewhere else completely, and they will get tired,"

mahket,   Culvt   letiket   ayof,
máhkit   *colát*   *litêykit*   *a·yô·f*
he said   fox   ran   and while it was going
he said, and Fox ran, and while he was going,

Poset   eto   rakkan   vcemket   ohliken,
pó·sit   *itó*   *łákka·n*   *acîmkit*   *ohlêykin*
cat   tree   big   climbed   and sat on it
Cat climbed the big tree and sat in it,

efv tat   hoyvnehcet   culv   ayan   vpehyen,   ohlikof,
ifáta·t   *hoyaníhcit*   *colá* *â·ya·n*   *apíhyin*   *ohlêyko·f*
the dogs   they passed   fox the way it went   they went   while sitting
and the dogs passed and went where Fox had gone, and while he was sitting,

Culvt   atvtē   ētat   fulket   lētket   hoyanen,
colát   *â·tati·*   *i·tá·t*   *folkít*   *lĭ·ⁿtkit*   *hoya·nín*
fox   the way it came   the same   came back   still running   passing by
Fox came back the same way he had gone and ran by.

hofonekan   efv-wohkvlke   hvtvm   culv   ayat   fvccvn
hofónika·n   *ifawo·hkâlki*   *hatâm*   *colá*   *â·ya·t*   *fáccan*
not long   the hounds   again   fox   (the way) it went   [toward]
Before long, he saw the hounds again going in the direction

vpēyen   hēcet   ohliken,   hofonē   haken,
api·yín   *hî·cit*   *ohlêykin*   *hofóni·*   *hâ·kin*
they went   (cat) saw them   sitting on   long time   got to be
the fox had gone, and sitting there after a long time,

hvtvm   Culv tat   enhvteceskv   atvtē ētat   lētket,
hatâm   *coláta·t*   *inhaticíska*   *â·tati· i·tá·t*[i]   *lĭ·ⁿtkit*
again   that fox   the first time   the same way it came   it was running
again Fox ran the same way he had first come,

---

[i] Raiford: *i·tá·n.*

etolaswv	capkē	hakēpen	hoyanen	hēcan,
itolá·swa	*că·pki·*	*ha·kî·pin*	*hoya·nín*	*hi·câ·n*
its tongue	very long	had become	passing by	when it saw it

and [Cat] saw as he passed that his tongue had grown long,

efv-wohkvlke	hēckusen	yopvn	fullen	hēcet	ohliket
ifawo·hkâlki	*hi·ckosin*[741]	*yópan*	*follín*	*hi·cit*	*ohlêykit*
the hounds	in sight	behind	were around	saw them	was sitting (on)

and he saw the hounds were in sight behind him, as he sat there.

Poset	okat,	"Vkerretv	sukcv	fvckē	palat
pó·sit	*o·kâ·t*	*akiłłitá*	*sókca*	*fácki·*	*pâ·la·t*
cat	said	cunningness	sack	full	ten

Cat said, "He sees ten bags of tricks

tąyen	estestemerricēt	omen	hēces.
tà·ⁿyin	*ististimiłłéyci·t*	*ô·min*	*hî·cis*
plenty	makes anyone suffer	does	saw

makes one suffer greatly.

Vkerretv	estemęrkusē	hvmkusatet	vkerretv	sukcv	fvckē	palan
akiłłitá	*istimi·ⁿlkosi·*	*hâmkosa·tit*	*akiłłitá*	*sókca*	*fácki·*	*pâ·la·n*
cunningness	very simple	just one	cunningness	sacks	full	ten

I've found that just one simple trick is far better

estvmąhen	senherēt	omvttis"	maket,
istamă·ⁿhin	*sinhiłi·t*	*ô·mátteys*	*ma·kít*
much more	very much better	I have found it	said

than ten bags of tricks," he said,

Pose	eton	ohlikvtēt	omēs.
pó·si	*itón*	*ohlêykati·t*	*ô·mi·s*
cat	tree	sitting on	was

and Cat just sat in the tree.

The Wise Rooster

J. Hill (Haas VI:25–33)[i]

Tottolose	enhonvnwvt	eto	huerē	elvccen	ohlikēpen,
tottolô·si	*inhonánwat*	*itó*	*hôyłi·*	*iláccin*	*ohleykì·pin*
rooster		tree	standing	branch	sitting on

A rooster was sitting on a tree branch,

Culvt	em vlaket,	"Vnhessē!
colát	*imalâ·kit*	*anhissi·^*
fox	came	my friend!

and Fox arrived. "My friend!

Estomen	ahvtvpkekot	ohliketska?"	kicen,
ísto·mín	*a·hatápkikot*	*ohlêykícka·^*	*keycín*
why	don't you come down	sitting up there	said

Why are you not down here instead of sitting up there?" he asked.

"Hvyatkof	ahvtvpkarēs.
haya·tkô·f	*a·hatápká·li·s*
when it gets morning	I will come down

"When morning comes I'll come down."

"Hiyomat	hvyayvkē	haket	onkv,
hayyô·ma·t	*haya·yakí·*	*hâ·kit*	*oŋká*
now	light	it has become	has

"It's light now.

ahvtvpiketsken	etem punahoyvken,
a·hatapâykíckin	*itimponá·ho·yakin*
you come on down	and we will talk to each other

Come down, and we'll talk:

opunvkv	hērēn	cem onvyetvn	ocet	okvyan	os"	Culvt	kicen,
oponaká	*hi·ⁿlin*[742]	*cimonayítan*	*ô·cit*	*o·kayá·n*	*ó·ⁿs*	*colát*	*kaycín*
[talk]	good	to tell you	I have	I mean		fox	said to (R.)

I have good news to tell you," Fox said.

---

[i] From Aesop's Fables, "The Fox, the Cock, and the Dog."

"Heyvn   ohlikvyis   pohikv,   vm onvyvs"   kicet,
hiyán   ohlêykayeys   pô·heyka   amonayás   keycít
here   I will sit   and hear it   tell me!   told him
"I will sit here and hear it, so tell me," he told him

aenhvtvpketvn   eyacekot   omen,
a·inhatapkitán   iyá·cikot   o·mín
to come down for him   didn't want   didn't
and didn't want to come down for him.

"Etvlwv vlke   omvlkv   nvkaftvtē   pohetskvnkv?"   Culvt   maken,
itálwa álki[743] *omálka   naka·ftatí·*   *pô·híckaŋka'*[744]   *colát   ma·kín*
nation   whole   they had a meeting   did you hear about it?   the fox   said
"Did you hear that the whole nation had a meeting?" Fox asked.

"Kerrvkos"   maket   em vyoposken,
kíłłakos[i]   *ma·kít*   *imáyopo·skín*
I don't know   said   answered him
"I didn't know," [Rooster] replied.

"Momepēt   os.   Nvkvftetv-rakko   ocet   oman   vretskekot   omen,
*mo·mipí·t   ô·*ⁿ*s   nakaftitalákkot   o·cít   o·mâ·n   alíckikot   o·mín*
it's that way   is   a meeting big   had   did   you weren't there   weren't
"It did indeed. There was a big meeting, and you weren't there,

'Vnhesse   eston   vreko   oha?'   komit   ecekerricvyvnket   ont,
*anhíssi   ísto·n   alíkot   ó·*ⁿ*ha·*[ii] *kô·meyt   icikíłłeycayáŋkit*   *ónt*
my friend   why   not here is   I thought   I was thinking about you then   was
and I wondered, 'Why is my friend not there?' and was thinking about you.

vhakv   hahoyvtēn   cem onvyvranis   ahvtvpiketsken"   kicen,
ahá·ka   há·ho·yatí·n   cimonayála·néys   *a·hatapâykíckin*   *keycín*
law   that was made   I'm going to tell you (about)   you come down   said to him
I'm going to tell you the law that was made after you come down," he said.

_____

[i] Or: *kíłłakot ó·s*; or: *kíłłaks.*
[ii] Hill: *ó·*ⁿ*ha·* ´; Raiford: *ómha·* ´.

Tottolose Enhonvnwvt okat, "Vhakv estomvkēn hayet omhoyvtē
tottolô·si inhonánwat o·kâ·t ahá·ka istó·maki·n ha·yít omhô·yati·[745]
rooster said law what kind was made they made
Rooster said, "Tell me what kind of law was made,

vm onahyetsken ahvtvpkarēs" kihcen, Culv onayet okat
amonáhyíckin a·hatápká·li·s kéyhcin colá ona·yít o·kâ·t
you tell me and I will come down he told him fox telling him said
and I'll come down" he said. Fox said,

"Mucvnettvn vtēkusen etem vkerrē etepvsatē
mocaníttan atî·kosin itímakiłłi·[746] itípasa·tí·
today only deceiving one another killing one another
"From today on, we will stop tricking each other, killing one another,

etepapē etestemerrvkuecē fullvkvtē wikēpet
itípa·pí· itistimíłłakoyci· follakáti· weykî·pit
eating one another harming one another like we used to be about doing quit
eating each other, and making one another suffer as we used to do,

etenokecạkusēt estofis punfulletvt omvrēs mahokēt os.
itinokică·ⁿkosi·t istô·feys ponfollitát ô·máłi·s ma·hokí·t ô·ⁿs
we shall love each other always [our way] shall be that's what was said did
and it shall be our custom to love one another always, it was said.

Mont vhakv yekcēn hahoyēt os.
mónt ahá·ka yíkci·n ha·hoyí·t ô·ⁿs
then the law strict they had made had
And they made a strict law.

Estimvt em vkerrusē omēt aret omekarēn
istêymat imakíłłosi· ô·mi·t a·lít omíká·li·n
whosoever in any way cunning is being around will not be
It was said that no one should be treacherous

mahokēt os" Culv makof,
ma·hokí·t[747] ô·ⁿs colá ma·kô·f
that's what they said did fox when he said
in any way," Fox said.

Tottolose Enhonvnwvt	oket	"Estitvket	fullet		vhakv	hayaket	omvnka?"
to·ttolô·si inhonánwat	*o·kít*	*istêytakit*	*follít*		*ahá·ka*	*há·ya·kít*	*o·máŋka·^*
rooster	said	[who]	were around		the law	made it	[did] then

Then Rooster asked, "Who all was there making the law?"

"Este omvlkvt	fullet		oman,	centvlkuset		vretskekot	omvnks.
ísti omálkat	*follít*		*o·má·n*	*cintǎlⁿkosit*		*alíckikot*	*ô·máŋks*
everybody	was around		was	you the only one		not there	was

"Everyone was there. You were the only one not there.

Monkv	heyv	vhakv	kerrekat		estit	ahrekos"	makofvn,
môŋka	*hiyá*	*ahá·ka*	*kíłłika·t*		*istêyt*	*áhliko·s*	*ma·kô·fan*
therefore	this	law	not knowing		anyone	[there isn't]	when saying

So there is no one who doesn't know this law," he said.

efv-wohkvlket	wohkaket	culv	atat		fvccvn	awvcoken
ifawo·hkâlkit	*wó·hka·kít*	*colá*	*â·ta·t*		*fáccan*	*a·wacókin*
hounds	barking	fox	(where) it came		the way	they seemed to be coming

Then hounds began barking and could be heard coming in the direction Fox had come.

Tottolose Enhonvnwvt	oket
to·ttolô·si inhonánwat	*o·kít*
the rooster	said

Rooster said,

"Mv	vhakv	kẹrrakusēt		fullet		omēto"		kicof,
ma	*ahá·ka*	*kĭⁿłła·kosi·t*		*follít*		*o·mí·to·*		*keycô·f*
that	law	they know well		being around		it's bound to be		when he said

"They are bound to know that law well," and when he said [that],

efv-wohkvlke	fullvcokan		pohhet,
ifawo·hkâlki	*follacóka·n*		*póhhit*
the hounds	seemed to be around		heard them

[Fox] heard the hounds going about and said,

"Mvtat		kerrahkekos,	fullekvnkekv!"		mahket
matâ·t		*kiłłáhkiko·s*	*fóllikáŋkika*		*máhkit*
that (the same)		they don't know	they weren't there		said

"They might not know about it, they weren't there!"

Culv   lētkvtēs   mahokvnts.
colá   *li·tkatí·s* *má·ho·kánc*
fox   ran   that's what was said
and ran away, it was said.

Crow Learns a Lesson

J. Hill (Haas VII:19–23)[748]

Lvmhet   arvtētot   yvpefikucet   aren   hehcet,   ehset,
lámhit   *a·latí·tot*   *yapifeykocít* *a·łín*   *híhcit*[749] *íhsit*
eagle   had been around lamb   was around   E. saw it caught it
An eagle had been going around and saw a lamb, caught it,

estvmken,   osahwvt   hēcvtētot   aret   oman
ístamkín   *osáhwat*   *hi·catí·tot*   *a·łít*   *o·mâ·n*
was flying with it   a crow   had seen him   was about   was
and was flying away with it, and a crow had seen him and was about,

yvpefikv   vculēt   aren   hehcet,
yapiféyka *acóli·t* *a·łín*   *híhcit*
ram   old   was about   saw it
and saw an old ram.

"Vneu   hvlatin   omat   estvmkvyēs,   lvmhe tat   estvmkvnkekv" mahket
aníw   *halâ·teyn*[750]   *o·mâ·t* *ístamkayí·s*   *lámhita·t*   *ístamkánkika* *máhkit*
me, too   I catch him   if   I can fly with him   the eagle   was flying with he said
"If I too catch him, I can fly with him, since the eagle flew with him," he said.

ohhuyiret   estvmketvn   koman,   honnēton,
ohhoyêylit   *istamkitán*   *ko·mâ·n*   *honnî·ton*[751]
he stood on it to fly with it he wanted   it was heavy
He stood on it and tried to fly with it, but it was heavy,

estomēceko mahhet   wiketvn   kont   oman,
istomi·ciko·máhhit   *weykitán*   *kònt*   *o·mâ·n*
couldn't do a thing with it   to quit it   tried   did
and he couldn't do a thing with it. He tried to leave it,

yvpefikv esset cvpcvkēt omēpvtet, ele-wesakvn enhvlahten,
yapiféyka íssit capcakí·t omî·patit iliwisá·kan inhaláhtin
the ram's wool long happened to be its toes caught
but the ram's wool happened to be long and caught his toes,

recopkeko tayet on, yvpefikvn osahwvt ohhuerēn
licópkiko· tâ·yit ó·n yapiféyka(n) osáhwat ohhóyłi·(n)
not loose could get the ram the crow standing on
and he couldn't get loose. The ram with the crow on top

cukon res vlaken yvpefikv pucaset oket
cokón 'lisála·kín yapiféyka (i)pocá·sit o·kít
the house it was coming to the ram's master said
was coming to the house, and the ram's master said,

"Osahwv toyetskat, cehoporrenusekot omat,
osáhwa tô·yícka·t cihopołłinósiko·t ô·ma·t[752]
crow you are you not very sensible are
"You crow, you're not very sensible;

mucv kērretskis omēs.
mocá ki·łłíckeys o·mí·s
now you are finding it out I suppose
maybe you're finding that out now.

Nake estomē fullephoyat omē momēcē vretskeko tayat" kihcet,
nâ·ki ísto·mí·[753] *follípho·yâ·t ó·mi· momi·cí· ałíckiko· tâ·ya·t kéyhcit*
whatever way others are about like do that you can't be about told him
You can't go around doing what everyone else does," he said.

hvlahtet elen enrecohpet ehsen,
haláhtit ilí(n) inłicóhpit íhsin
caught it feet loosened and took it
And he caught it, released its feet, and took it,

hopuetakucet	sahkopvnkvn		hayet	esfullvtēs.
hopoyta·kocít	*sahkopánkan*[i,754]		*ha·yít*	*ísfollatí·s*
and the children	plaything		made it	were about with it

and the children made it their pet.

"Nake	estomē	fullephoyat	ētvpomit	arvyēs"	komē	vretv
nâ·ki	*ísto·mí·*	*follípho·yâ·t*	*i·tapô·meyt*	*a·łayí·s*	*kó·mi·*	*ałíta*
whatever	others do	being about	the same as	I can do	he thought	to go about

The way of thinking, "Whatever others do, I can do the same,"

svlvfken	estehahoyē	tayēt omat,	osahwv-culet	pumvhayēt	omeko?
saláfkin[755]	*istiha·hoyí·*	*tâ·yi·t ô·ma·t*[756]	*osahwacólit*	*pomáha·yí·t*	*omíko·^*[757]
a prisoner	anyone	can be made	the old crow	teaches us	doesn't he?

can make people a prisoner, the old crow teaches us, doesn't he?

The Foolish Frog

J. Hill (Haas VI:141–149)[ii]

Fuswv	hokkolet	welakvtēs.	Ēkvnv	lekothan	vthoyēt
fóswa	*hokkô·lit*	*wila·katí·s*	*i·kaná*	*likótha·n*	*athoyí·t*
birds	two	were about	land	warm	(coming) from

Two birds were going about. They came from a warm land

akhvsēt	likēt	omen	mvn	welaket	omvtēs.
akhasí·t	*léyki·t*	*ô·min*	*man*	*wila·kít*	*o·matí·s*
ponds	were there	(were)	there	they were	about

where a pond was and went about there.

Uewv	vfopken	hompetv	hopoyvkēpēt		ont,
óywa	*afó·pkin*	*hompitá*	*hopóyaki·pí·t*		*ônt*
water's	edge	food	they had been hunting		(had)

They had been hunting for food at the water's edge,

---

[i] Or: *sakkopánkan*.

[ii] From the Panchatantra.

momen   vpvtvnvt   mata   akhvsēn   ak-arēt   omen,
mo·mín   *apatanát*   *ma·tá·*   *akhasí·n*   *ákka·li·t*   *ô·min*
Then   green frog[i]   that same pond   had been about in   (had)
and a bullfrog had been going about in that same pond.

etehēcet   etekẹrrakusē   haket   akfullēt   omvtēs.
itíhi·cít[758]   *itikĭ·ⁿɫâ·kosi·*   *hâ·kit*   *ákfolli·t*   *o·mati·s*
they saw each other   knowing each other very well got to   they were about in it were
They saw each other and got to know each other well as they went about in [the pond].

Meskēn   fullet   omvtēs.   Momvtētan   rvfo   hakēpet   omen,
miskí·n   *follít*   *o·mati·s*   *mo·matí·ta·n*[759]   *łafó*   *há·ki·pít*[760]   *o·mín*
summer   (were) about   were   they had been, but   winter   was coming   was
They went about in the summer. That's how it was, but winter was coming,

vpvtvnvn   em punvyaket   oket,   "Yvmv tat   kvsvppē   hakēpet   omen,
apatanán   *imponáya·kít*[ii]   *o·kít*   *yamáta·t*   *kasáppi·*   *há·ki·pít*[761]   *o·mín*
the frog   they were talking to   and said   right here   cold   it is turning   it is
and they talked to the bullfrog saying, "It's getting cold here,

ēkvnv   lekhothēn   welvkēpeyvtēt   ont   yefulhokepvranēs.
i·kaná   *likóthi·n*   *wiláki·piyáti·t*   *ônt*   *'yofolhokípała·ní·s*[762]
land   warm   we have been around in   have   we are going back
we've been in a warm land and are going back.

Etehēcet   heremahēn   akfullēpvkētvnkis,   vhoyepvranēs"
itíhi·cít   *hiłimá·hi·n*[763]   *akfollĭ·ⁿpaki·taŋkêys*   *ahoyipáła·ní·s*
seeing each other   very well   we used to be around in   we're going away
We've seen each other and gone around well together, but we're going,"

kicaket   omen,   vpvtvnvt   okat,   "Ececak-vyēpvkvyēs,
kéyca·kít   *o·mín*   *apatanát*   *o·kâ·t*   *icicákkayi·pakáyi·s*
they said to it did   the frog   said   I'll go with you-all
they said. The bullfrog said, "I will go with you,

---

[i] bull-frog?

[ii] Or: *timponáya·kít*.

vneu lekothan vretv cvyacēt onkv" maken,
aníw likótha·n alíta cayá·ci·t ôŋka ma·kín
me, too where it's warm to be around I like do he said
for I want to go where it's warm too," he said.

fuswvt okat, "Epucak-vyepetskvrēn puyacē hēret omis,
fóswat o·kâ·t ipocakkayípíckáli·(n) poyá·ci· hǐ·ⁿłit o·mêys
the birds said you to go with us we'd like very much but
The birds said, "We'd like very much for you to go with us,

estohmet epucak-ahyetskekos. Kvwvpikēt tvmhoket vhoyepvranēt okēkv
istóhmit ipocakkáhyíckiko·s kawapâyki·t támho·kít ahoyipáła·ní·t o·kí·ka
how, any way you can't go with us we will go up flying we will go we mean
but there is no way for you to go with us. We mean we'll go up and go by flying,

cetvrpvn ocetskekok estohmet pucak-ahyetskekos" kicaken,
citálpan ó·cíckiko·k istóhmit pocakkáhyíckiko·s kéyca·kín
your wings you have none how, in any way you cannot go with us they said to him
and you don't have wings; there is no way you can go with us," they said.

vpvtvnvt okat, "Eto-kvckucen eyoksv vlkēn akket omatsken,
apatanát o·kâ·t itokackocín iyóksa álki·n â·kkit o·má·ckin
the frog said a piece of stick the end each biting it you-all do
The bullfrog said, "Bite each end of a stick,

vneu nvrkvpvn akkit vtarkin, etentakhaket estvmhokatsken omat,
aníw nałkapán â·kkeyt atá·lkeyn itintakhâ·kit istámho·ká·ckin o·mâ·t
me, too in the middle I biting I hanging being side by side you-all flying if
and I too will bite it in the middle and hang, and if you fly with [the stick] side by side,

svcvhoyatskēs" maken, "Momēcēt es cetvmhokeyēs,
'sacáho·yá·cki·s ma·kín momí·ci·t iscitámho·kiyí·s
you-all can take me he saying in that way we can fly with you
you can take me," he said. "We can fly with you that way,

eto hopoyetsken omat" kicaken,
itó hopó·yíckin o·mâ·t káyca·kín
a stick you hunt if they said to him
if you find a stick," they said.

vpvtvnv tat   eto   etetakuecēpet   vtarken,
apatanáta·t   itó   itita·kóyci·pít   atâ·lkin
the frog   stick   was getting it ready was hanging
The bullfrog got the stick ready and hung on.

estvmhoket   svhoyof,
istámho·kít   *sáhho·yô·f*
they were flying with it while going with it
When they were flying with it,

estet   vtotkēt   cvpofvn   fullet   oman,
ístit   ato·tkí·t   'capó·fan   follít   o·mâ·n
people   who were working   in the field were around were
people were working in the field,

onvpvn   eshoyvnhoyen   hecahket,   estet   okat,
onápan   ishoyánho·yín   hicáhkit   ístit   o·kâ·t
above   they 2 were going by seeing   the people   said
and they saw them pass over with him. The people said,

"Estimvt   'Momēcaks'   kicen   svhoyet   eswelaket   omētē?"
*istêymat   momí·caks   kêycin   sáho·yít   íswila·kít   o·mí·ti·^*
who is it   you-all to do told   2 taking it they were about with it (I wonder)
"Wonder who told them to do that, taking him about with them?"

kicaken,   vpvtvnvt   pohhet,   "Vnet   ohkin!"   makat,
kéyca·kín   apatanát   póhhit   anít   óhkeyn   mâ·ka·t
they said   the frog   heard it   I   did   when saying
The bullfrog heard them and said, "I did!"

hvwvkilen   akkvtē   rocopiket   alatkvtēs.
hawakêylin   â·kkati·   locopâykit[i]   *á·la·tkati·s*
it opened its mouth   where it had bit it it became loose   and fell down
and opened his mouth, came loose from where he had been biting, and fell down.

---

[i] Originally: *licopâykit*.

Cricket and Mosquito (Colotkv, Okyeha)[i]

J. Hill (Haas VIII:113–115). Interpreted by J. Thompson (Haas VIII:112).

Colotkvt,	Okyehan	'tepaket	rvro	hopokvn	vhoyet	ohhvyatket,
coló·tkat	*okyihá·n*	*'tipâ·kit*	*laló*	*hopókan*	*aho·yít*	*ohhayâ·tkit*[ii,764]
cricket	and mosquito	together	fish	to hunt	they (2) went	overnight

Cricket went fishing with Mosquito overnight.

"Paksen	rvro tat	pvsvtvkvrēs,"	maket,
páksin	*lalóta·t*	*pasátakáli·s*[iii]	*ma·kít*
tomorrow	the fish	we'll kill	he said

"Tomorrow we'll kill fish," he said,

hvcce	tempen	hvpo	hayet	takkaken,
hácci	*tímpin*	*hapó·*	*hâ·yit*	*takkâ·kin*
river	next to	camp	they made	sat down there

and they made camp near a river and stayed there.

"Rvrot	akfullaken	omat,	vketēcvs"	Okyehan	kihcen,
lalót	*akfólla·kín*	*o·mâ·t*	*akití·cas*	*okyihá·n*	*kéyhcin*
fish	are in water	if	watch and see	to mosquito	(Cr.) said

"Check to see if there are fish," he told Mosquito,

akhvtapket	ra ak-arvtvtet	rvlaken,
akhatâ·pkit	*la·ʔákka·latít*	*lála·kín*[765]
going down to water	wandering around down there	coming back

and [Mosquito] went down, wandered around in the water, and came back.

"Akfullaka?"	Colotkvt	maken,
*akfólla·ká·^*	*coló·tkat*	*ma·kín*
are there any there	Cricket	asked

"Are there any?" Cricket asked,

---

[i] Title: *coló·tka okyihá·* 'cricket, mosquito'.

[ii] J. Thompson: *lohhayâ·tkit.*

[iii] Or (J.H.): *pasátiyáli·s.*

"Akfullaks,   este-hvckowv enrakkē omakusat"   Okyehat   mahken,
akfóllá·ks   *istihackowá inłakkí· o·mâ·kosa·t okyihá·t máhkin*[i]
there are some there   person's leg big   as (big) as mosquito said
"There are, as big as a person's calf," Mosquito said,

Colotkvt   vpelihcet,   estasket,   estak-aret,
coló·tkat apiléyhcit   ísta·skít   istákka·lít
cricket   laughed   jumped up and down   around on ground
and Cricket laughed at him and jumped up and down and around on the ground

totkvn   estaklvtiket,   nekiret,   lastusē   hakvtēt   omēs.
tó·tkan   istaklatêykit nikêylit   lă-ⁿstosi· ha·káti·t   ô·mi·s
fire   fell in   burned up   all black got to be   did
and fell into the fire and burned up, and he got to be all black.

Opossum and Raccoon Form a Friendship

J. Hill (Haas VI:129–139)

Sukhvhatkvt   Wotkot   aren   em punayet,
sokhahá·tkat   wó·tkot   a·łín   ímpona·yit
possum   coon   (who) was about was speaking to
Possum was speaking to Coon who was about:

"Etenhesse   hakēpet   welaket   omvkan   hērēs"   kicen,
itinhíssi   ha·kî·pit   wila·kít   o·makâ·n hi·ⁿli·s keycín
each other's friends let's be going about let's be it's good be saying
"It would be good if we became friends and went about together," he said.

Wotkot   okat,   "Hekos.   Vncvnrapvt   tayet   onkv,
wó·tkot o·kâ·t   híkos   acanlá·pat   tă·ⁿyi·t ôŋka
coon   said   No, sir   my enemies   many   are
Coon said, "No, sir. I have many enemies.

estofvn   vcvnrapvlke tat   es cvhecvkvranēt   omat   kērrvyesekot   onkv,
istô·fan   acanla·pâlkita·t[766] *iscahicakála·ní·t*[767] *ô·ma·t   *ki·ⁿłłayisiko·t* *ôŋka*
whenever   my enemies   going to find me   (when) are I don't know   (do)
I never know when my enemies will find me,

---

[i] I.e., mosquito's leg — that's the joke.

vnhesset   vcvpaketsken   puhechoyen   omat,
anhíssit   acapâ·kíckin   pohicho·yín   o·mâ·t
my friend   [you] being with me   they see [us]   if
so if they see you with me, my friend,

cestemerricētis   es cefulhoyē tayētok   vne tvlkuset   vrēpvyan   hērēs"
cistimiłłéyci·teys[768]   *iscifolhoyí· tâ·yi·to·k*   *anitâłkosit*   *ałi·payâ·n*   *hĭ·ⁿli·s*
they might punish you   and take you around   I alone   being about   is good
they might punish you and make you suffer; it is better if I go about alone,"

Wotko   maken,   "Ecenrapvt   sulkēt   on omat,
wó·tko   ma·kín   icinłá·pat   sólki·t   ô·n o·mâ·t
Coon   said   your enemies   many   if they are
Coon said. "If you have many enemies,

cenhesse   ceyacemahattot   os"   Sukhvhatkvt   makvtēs.
cinhíssi   ciya·cimâ·ha·ttot   ó·ⁿs   sokhahá·tkat   ma·katí·s
your friend   you need the most   are   Possum   said
you need a friend all the more," Possum said.

"Vnhesse   toyetsken   ecepakin   omat,   ecenrapv   es cehehcet
anhíssi   tô·yíckin   icipâ·keyn   o·mâ·t   icinłá·pa   iscihihcit
my friend   be!   If I am wth you   (if)   your enemy   they find you
"If I am with you, my friend, if your enemies find you

cestomēcvkvranen   omat,   vnet   homvn   huerit,
cistomi·cakáła·nín   *o·mâ·t   anít   hóman   hôyłeyt*
they're going to do anything to you   (if)   I   in front   will stand
and are going to do anything to you, I will stand in front;

ecenrapv tat   enyekcē   em etetayēcusit   enceyvllarēs.
icinłá·pata·t   inyikci·   imititâ·ⁿyi·coseyt   inciyáłłá·li·s
your enemy   his strength   I will equal   I will fight him back
I will fight with strength equal to your enemy.

Momet   cehēcin,   estomēt   em eyoksvranen   omis,
mo·mít   cihî·ceyn   istó·mi·t[769]   *imiyóksała·nín   o·mêys*
Then   I will see you   whatever (way)   it's going to end   going to, may
I will watch you, and however it might end,

ecehuerarēs"   makof,   efvt   wohkaket   fullvcoken,
icihôyłá·li·s   *ma·kô·f*   *ifát*   *wó·hka·kít*   *follacókin*[i]
I will stand by you   when he said   dogs   barking   were about
I will stand by you," [Coon] said. At that point dogs could be heard barking.

"Vcvnrapv tat   awē   hērvcoks   ce.
acanłá·pata·t[770]   *a·wí·*   *hĭ·ⁿłacoks*   *ci·^*[ii]
my enemy   coming   sure enough   are
"My enemies sure enough are coming.

Monkv   hiyomusen   vhoyvkis   hērēs"   Wotko   maket   oman,
môŋka   *hayyô·mosin*   *ahóyakeys*[771]   *hĭ·ⁿłi·s*   *wó·tko*   *ma·kít*   *o·mâ·n*
Therefore   right now   let's be going   it's good   Coon   said   (and) did
So it's best we be going now," Coon said,

Sukhvhatkvt   okat,   "Yicepekvs ca!"   maket   likvtēs.
sokhahá·tkat   *o·kâ·t*   *yeycipíkas cá*   *ma·kít*   *leykatí·s*[772]
the possum   said   let them come   said   and sat down
but Possum said, "Let them come!" and sat down.

Momis   Wotko tat   kērret   okekv,   vyēpen
mo·mêys   *wó·tkota·t*   *kî·łłit*   *o·kiká*   *ayi·pín*
But   Coon   knew   did   he was going
Coon knew what he was saying, though, so he left,

Sukhvhatkv   vcak-ayvtēs.   Tokorket   vhoyvtēs.
sokhahá·tka   *acákka·yatí·s*   *toko·lkít*   *aho·yatí·s*
possum   went with him   the 2 running   were going
and Possum went with him. The two went running.

Momen   efv tat   cakkof,   Sukhvhatkv   yopvn   arvtēton,
mo·mín   *ifáta·t*   *ca·kkô·f,*   *sokhahá·tka*   *yópan*   *a·latí·ton*
Then   the dog   when catching up   possum   behind   was going about
Then when the dogs were catching up, Possum was behind.

---

[i] Original: *-cókon*.

[ii] Original: *ci·^*.

efv vcule   hvmket   homvn   arvtētot,   alahket,   fekēyet,
ifá acóli   hámkit   hóman   a·latí·tot   aláhkit   fiki·yít
old dog   one   in front   had been about   came up   shook him
One old dog had been in front [of the pack], and he came up, shook [Possum],

vwihken,   tolpoket   liken   'yvcaket
awéyhkin   tolpô·kit   lêykin   yaca·kít
threw it down   (P.) coiled up   was sitting   (Dog) was chewing
and threw him down; [Possum] curled up, and [the dog] chewed on him,

entalvn   enwokohcet   wikvtēs.
intá·lan   inwokóhcit   weykatí·s
its ribs   broke them to pieces   and left it alone
crushed his ribs, and left him.

Wotko tat   efvt   hvlvtaket   omis,   aetepoyet   on   esfullen,
wó·tkota·t   ifát   halatâ·kit   o·mêys   a·itípo·yít   ó·n   ísfollín[i]
The Coon   dog   was holding   was   he was fighting it back   was   was about with it
The dogs caught the coon, but he was fighting back, and they were staying with him.

Wotkot   vkosilet   vyēpvtēs.
wó·tkot   akosêylit[773]   *ayi·patí·s*
Coon   got the best of it   he went away
Coon got the best of them and went away.

Momvtētan,   Wotko tat   aret   enhesse   eshēcet   ont
mô·mati·ta·n[774]   *wó·tkota·t   a·lít   inhíssi   ishî·cit   ónt*
after that   Coon   was about   his friend   found him   did
After that, Coon was about and found his friend,

"'Cem vnicin   estomēt   em eyoksen   omat,
cimáneycéyn   istó·mi·t   imiyo·ksín   o·mâ·t
I will help you   whatever way   it ends   (when it does)
"You said, 'I will help you. However it ends,

_____

[i] Original: *ísfollán*.

cehēcarēs'		maketskvnkat,				estvn		aretskvnka?
cihi·cá·li·s		*ma·kíckáŋkâ·t*				*ístan*		*a·líckáŋka·^*
I will see you		that's what you said (II)	where		were you?
I will look after you.' [So] where were you?

Cvlēhocvṛanusen				estenhesakēpvyvnks"		kicen,
cali·hocałà·ⁿnosin			*istinhisa·kî·payáŋks*[775]	*keycín*
they were about to kill me	I survived from them		he said
They were about to kill me, but I survived them," [Coon] said.

Sukhvhatkvt		okat,		"Etenkececērketvt			vpvkēt		omekon			omat,
sokhahá·tkat		*o·kâ·t*	*itinkicici·łkitái*[1776]	*apáki·t*	*omíkon*		*o·mà·t*
Possum			said		to tickle each other		with it		had not been	if
Possum said, "If it had not been for the tickling,

aem etetaỵēcusit			celayvkvranvyvtētis			hvmket		vnkececēriken
a·imititä·ⁿyi·coseyt		*cila·yakála·nayáti·teys*	*hámkit*	*aŋkicici·lêykin*[777]
I would have equalled them	I would have handled them	one			tickled me
I would have dealt with them in kind, but one tickled me,

vcvpelēpat			estohmit			ceyvllvko tayusmahen		omvnks."
acápili·pâ·t[778]	*istóhmeyt*			*ciỵállako· tä·ⁿyosmâ·hin*	*o·máŋks*[779]
I was laughing		I had no way		I couldn't resist			it was
and I was laughing so hard I couldn't resist them."

The Revenge of the Snakes

J. Hill (Haas VI:151–159)

Cetto	omvlkv	em mēkkon		em elēhocen			kerrahket,
cítto	*omálka*	*inmí·kkon*		*imili·hô·cin*			*kiłłáhkit*
snakes	all		their chief, king	someone had killed		they found out (I)
The chief of all the snakes was killed, and all the snakes found out

cetto	omvlkvt		nvkaftet		vpoket,			vketēckv		hayet		omat,
cítto	*omálkat*	*nakâ·ftit*		*apô·kit*		*akiti·cka*		*ha·yít*	*o·mà·t*
snakes	all			gathered		and were sitting	investigation	making		were
and gathered to conduct an investigation.

---

[i] Some say (including Raiford): *itincikici·lkitá*.

este hoktēt	elēcet	omen	kerraket		ont,
ísti hoktí·t	*ilî·cit*	*o·mín*	*kiɬâ·kit*		*ónt*
a woman	killed it	had	they found out		had

They found out a woman had killed him,

"Tohwakkvn	hayvkan		hērēs"	hvmket	maken,
tohwá·kkan[1780]	*hâ·yaka·n*		*hĭ·ⁿɬi·s*	*hámkit*	*ma·kín*
revenge	we had better get		good	one	said

and one said, "We had better get revenge,"

omvlkvt	etem vkvsahmet,		mv	hoktēn	elēcvranet	fvccēcakvtēs.
omálkat	*itimakasáhmit*		*ma*	*hoktí·n*	*ilî·caɬa·nít*	*facci·ca·kati·s*
all	agreed with each other		that	woman	to kill her	they decided

and all agreed, and they decided to kill the woman.

Mohmet	vpoket	estit	tohwakkv	hayē tayan
móhmit	*apô·kit*	*istêyt*	*tohwá·kka*	*há·yi· tâ·ya·n*
then	they were sitting	whoever	revenge	can take

Then they sat and were looking for someone

enhopoyaket	omis.
inhopóya·kít	*o·mêys*
they were hunting for	were

to get revenge.

"'Vnet	omarēs'	estit	komatskat	makepaks"	kihocen,
anít	*omá·li·s*	*istêyt*	*kó·má·cka·t*	*ma·kipáks*	*kéyho·cín*
I	will do it	whoever	you-all think	you-all say so	they told him

"Whoever thinks they will do it, say so," they said.

"Vnet	omarēs"	turlvpatkvt	maken,
anít	*omá·li·s,*	*tollapá·tkat*	*ma·kín*
I	will do it	the copperhead	said

"I will do it," the copperhead said.

---

[i] *tohwá·kka* 'revenge'. When one member of your family is killed, then you avenge his death by killing a member of the killer's family.

"Ecomekis   ohmēs. Enhvsvfēcat   tvlkusēt ontskvntok" kicaken,
icómikeys   óhmi·s inhasáfi·câ·t   tâlkosi·t ónckanto·k   kéyca·kín
you might not be able might   make it swell up for her only   you do   they told him
"You might not be able. You'll only make her swell up," they said.

"Vne mit omarēs"   apvyakvt   maken,
animêyt   omá·li·s   a·payá·kat   ma·kín
I, even   will do it   chicken snake said
"I will do it instead," the chicken snake said.

"O cēme mahvkvo   estohmetskekos.   Cenute tis   sekot ontskvntok"
ó· cí·mi mâ·hakaw'   istóhmíckiko·s   cinótiteys   siko·t ónckanto·k
oh   you   especially, too you can't do anything your teeth, even none   generally you have
"Oh, you especially can't do anything. You have no teeth,"

kicakvtēs. Tvstvnvkucet   tolpokuset   likēpvten,
kéyca·katí·s tastanakocít   tŏl^npô·kosit[781]   leykî·patin
they told it   the ground rattlesnake curled up   was lying ("sitting")
they said. The ground rattlesnake was sitting curled up,

"Cent omvccvs" kihocen,
cínt   omáccas   kéyho·cín
you   must do it they told him
and they said, "You must do it."

"Vcohmekos   ce. Ena   herakattis   tayet   oman   okatskes"
acóhmíko·s   ci^ iná·   hiłă·ⁿka·tteys tă·ⁿyit ô·ma·n o·ká·ckis
I'm not able to   bodies are better   several are   you-all said (for me to do it), but
"I am not able. You said for me to do it, but there are many whose bodies are better,"

maken, "Momis   em enhonrvkē tayat   centvlkēpuset os" kicaken   liket,
ma·kín mo·mêys iminhónłaki·tâ·ya·t   cintalkî·posit ó·ⁿs kéyca·kín   lêykit
he said But   one that anyone can depend on you only   are   they told it it lay
he said. "But you are the only one anyone can depend on," they said as he sat.

"Mvtarēs ci.   Pvhe-lvstvtēkusē   cvna   hakvtēt   os   kont
*matá·li·s cay^*   *pahilastatî·kosi·*   *caná·*   *ha·katí·t   ô·ⁿs   kônt*
that will be, indeed!   edge of the black grass[i]   my body   grew up   did   and thought
"That's it then, she'll think my body has become

huervkvns ca"   makvtēs.   Momē   mahkof,
hôylakansca·^[ii]   *ma·katí·s*   *mó·mi·*   *máhko·f*
anyone stands   he said   that (way)   after it spoke
the edge of the black grass [?]" he said. After he said that, [they said,]

"Estont   aren   omarēs   kontskat,   vce   hocof tis,
ístónt   *a·lín*   *omá·li·s*   *kôncka·t*[iii]   *así   ho·cô·fteys*
doing something   being about   I will do it   if you wish   corn   he's pounding, when, even
"However you wish it to be done: when she's pounding corn

fettv   pasof tis,   'to-taluce hopoyof tis   kontskat"
fítta   pa·sô·fteys   *'tota·loší hopo·yô·fteys*   *kôncka·t*
yard   while she's sweeping, even   brush   even while hunting   if you wish
or sweeping the yard or when she's gathering dried wood, if you wish,"

kicaken,   "Uewv   res cahwē   res atof   omarēs"
kéyca·kín   *óywa   liscáhwi·*[iv]   *lísa·tô·f*   *omá·li·s*
they told it   water   after she fetches   and is bringing it back   I will do it
they said. "I'll do it after she fetches water and is carrying it back,"

makvtēs.   Momēcvranet   okvtētok
ma·katí·s   momí·cala·nít   *o·katí·to·k*
he said   he's going to do her that way   that's what it meant
he said. He meant he was going to do it that way.

mv   hoktē tat   uewv   res cawet   saren,
ma   *hoktí·ta·t   óywa   liscâ·wit*   *sa·lín*
that   woman   water   when she had gotten it   going with it
When the woman had gotten water and was bringing it back,

---

[i] Meaning of *pahilasti* (lit., "black grass") might not be known to Raiford. Hill doesn't know whether this means black grass, burnt grass, or some kind of medicine made from herbs.
[ii] Raiford: *hôylakanscêy*.
[iii] Long way: *kô·mícka·t*.
[iv] Original: *liscâ·wi·*.

ele-toktoswvn   em vkiken,   atet   fettvtēkēn   'svlakuset   ehlen,
ilitoktóswan   imakâykin   a·tít   fittatí·ki·n[i]   *'sală·ⁿkosit íhlin*
her ankle   bit it   and was coming   edge of the yard   got to   she died
he bit her ankle as she got to the edge of the yard, and she died,

yetaklvtecicvtēs.   Monkv   tvstvnvkucet
'yitaklatíceycatí·s   *môŋka*   *tastanakocí(t)*
and threw her down   Therefore   the ground-rattlesnake
and he caused her to fall down in the yard. So the ground rattlesnake

cetto   holwvyēcemahat   omēs
cítto   holwayi·cimâ·ha·t   ô·mi·s
snake   the worst of all   is
is the the very worst snake.

The Bungling Host

J. Hill (Haas VI:105–127)

Nokoset   Cufen   em punayet,   "Vncukopericvs!"   kicvtēton
nokósit[ii] *cofín*   *ímpona·yít*   *ancokopiléycas*   *keycatí·ton*
bear   rabbit   was talking to   visit me!   had told him
Bear was talking with Rabbit and had told him, "[Come] visit me!"

ayet   rem oren,   Nokoset   "Tvlakon   horaks!"   mahken
a·yít[782]   *'limó·lin*   *nokósit*   *talá·kon*   *holáks*   *máhkin*
was going   got there   bear   beans   you-all boil he said
and when [Rabbit] got there, Bear said, "You all boil the beans!"

horet   omhoyan,   noret   oman,   "Nehat sepekot os"   kihocen,
hô·lit[783]   *ómho·yâ·n* *nô·lit*   *o·mâ·n nihá·t   sipíkot ó·ⁿs*   *kéyho·cín*
boiled them   they did   it got done did   grease (there) wasn't any they told him
And they boiled them, and when they were done, they told him, "There's no grease."

---

[i] Short for: *fítta ati·ki·n.*
[ii] Original: *nokósi.*

"Eslafkvn vnhopoyaks" Nokoset mahken, enhopohohyen,
islá·fkan *anhopóyaks* *nokósit* *máhkin* *inhopo·hóhyin*
knife hunt for me bear said they hunted it for him
"Find me a knife," Bear said, and they found one, and when he drew the knife

ele-ofvn 'mvsatet oman, neha sepekon,
ilió·fan *mása·tít* *o·mâ·n* *nihá·* *sipíkon*
foot-bottom cut (with a knife) did grease no (grease)
over the sole of his foot there was no fat,

envrken em vsahtet, ofvn neha ocan acahwen,
inátkin *imasáhtit* *ó·fan* *nihá·* *ô·ca·n* *a·cáhwin*
his belly he scratched upon inside grease where there was he took it out
and he drew the knife over his stomach and took out the fat that was inside,

mv neha tat tvlakon vpahohyen, hompahket kakvtēton
ma *nihá·ta·t* *talá·kon* *apa·hóhyin* *hompáhkit* *kâ·katí·ton*
that grease beans they put it with they ate they 2 were sitting
added that fat to the beans, and they sat and ate.

Cufet vyepvranet ont, "Cēmeu vncukopericvs" kihcet vyēpvtēton
cofít *ayípala·nít* *ónt* *ci·miw'* *ancokopitéycas* *kéyhcit* *ayi·pati·ton*[i]
Rabbit was fixing to go was you, too visit me! told him he went away
Rabbit was fixing to go and told him, "You visit me too," and left.

Nokose ayet, Cufen rem oren, kaket omen,
nokósi *a·yít*[784] *cofín* *'timô·tin* *kâ·kit* *o·mín*
bear going rabbit got to where (R.) was the 2 were sitting were
Bear went and got to Rabbit's [home], and they were sitting,

"Tvlakon horaks" Cufet maken, horhoyen noret oman,
talá·kon *holáks* *cofít* *ma·kín* *holhô·yin*[785] *nô·lit* *o·mâ·n*
beans (you-all) boil them! Rabbit saying they had them boiled it got done had
and Rabbit said, "You all boil the beans," and they boiled them, and when they were done

---

[i] *ayi·pati·ton* 'he had gone away'.

"Nehat sepekot os" kihocen, eslafkvn vpohen aemhohyen,
nihá·t sipíkot ó·ⁿs kéyho·cín islá·fkan apo·hín a·imhóhyin
grease there is no they told him knife he asked for they handed it to him
they told him, "There's no grease." He asked for a knife, and they handed it to him,

ele-ofvn 'mvsatet oman, neha sepekon,
ilió·fa(n) mása·tít[786] o·mâ·n nihá· sipíkon,
foot-sole he cut along did grease no (grease)
and when he drew the knife over the sole of his foot there was no fat,

envrken em vsatan tvskocusekv,
inálkin, imasâ·ta·n[787] taskŏ·ⁿcosika
his belly he cut along it being very thin
and when he cut along his belly, the skin being very thin,

efekce rorēn ohmet ēwehnen;
ifíkci lóli·n óhmit i·wíhnin
his intestines up to did he gutted himself
he reached his intestines and gutted himself.

"Tayen ēestemerrihcetskes ce. Vne tat omvyvnkan ometsken os"
tă·ⁿyin i·istimiłłéyhcíckis[788] ci^ aníta·t o·mayáŋka·n o·míckin ó·ⁿs,
very much you have punished yourself I, myself I did it myself you're doing that, but
"You have really injured yourself doing what I did,"

Nokoset mahket vyēpen, wakket on vlēkcvn hopoyet,
nokósit máhkit ayi·pín[789] wâ·kkit ó·n ali·kcan hopo·yít
bear said (B.) going he lying was a doctor he was hunting
Bear said and left. And as [Rabbit] lay there, [Bear] looked for a doctor

ayon eshēcet, "Em vlēkcetskēs. Vheremahen ēyvnvttēcēt
á·yon ishî·cit[790] imáli·kcícki·s ahiłimă·ⁿhin i·yanátti·cí·t
a hawk he found you can doctor him very much he has hurt himself
and found a hawk: "You can doctor him. He's hurt himself badly

wakket os" kihocan, "Vlekcetv cvkeriyekos" makēpen,
wâ·kkit ó·ⁿs kéyho·câ·n alikcitá cakiłêyyiko·s má·ki·pín
he's lying down is they told him to doctor I don't know (how) he was saying
and is lying down," he told him. "I don't know how to doctor," he was saying,

wihket,	ētvn	hopoyet,	Sulen	eshēcet,
wéyhkit	*í·tan*	*hopo·yít*	*solín*	*ishî·cit*[791]
he quit him	(someone) else	he was hunting	buzzard	he found

and [Bear] left him and looked for another and found Buzzard.

"Vlēkcetskēt	onkvntē?"	kihocen,	"Vlēkcvyēs"	mahken
ali·kcícki·t	*óŋkanti·^*	*kéyho·cín*	*ali·kcayi·s*	*máhkin*
you doctor	don't you?	he said	I can doctor	he said

"You doctor, don't you?" he asked. "I can doctor," he said,

ēvpahyet	svpēhoyen	liket	okat,
i·apáhyit	*'sapi·hô·yin*	*lêykit*	*o·kâ·t*
he got with him	and took him with him	sitting	said

and he got him and took him with him, and sitting, [Buzzard] said,

"Nake	mv	omē	vlekcetv tat	afken	hahyet,
nâ·ki	*ma*	*ó·mi·*	*alikcitáta·t*	*á·fkin*	*háhyit*
something	that	like	to doctor	mush	made it

"To doctor something like that, I usually have mush made

cuko	ofvn	aswvkechoyen	omvyvnts.
cokó	*ó·fan*	*a·swakichô·yin*	*o·mayánc*
the house	in	had it laying by	I usually do

and have it lying inside the house.

Mohmet	cuko-onvpv	ohrolahket	ohmatsken,	mvn	rosiyet,
móhmit	*cokó onápa*[792]	*ohłoláhkit*	*óhmá·ckin*[i]	*man*	*'losâyyeyt*
then	house on top	make a hole	you-all do	there	I'll get out

Then you should make a hole in the roof, and I'll go out there

hvlwēn	fulotkit	arit,	eto	talē	ahueran	erohhuervyof,
hálwi·n	*folo·tkéyt*	*a·léyt*	*itó*	*tá·li·*	*a·hôyła·n*	*iłóhhoyłayô·f*
up high	I'll go around	I'll be about	tree	dry	that's standing	when I stand

and circle around up high, and when I stand upon the dead tree standing there,

---

[i] Original: *ohłoláhki·n ô·má·ckin.*

cuko hvwehcet estomēcvyat hecatskvrēs" mahken,
cokó hawíhcit istomî·caya·t hicá·ckáli·s máhkin
house open it what I have done you[-all] will see he said
open the house and you will see what I have done," he said.

tetakuehcet afkeu rasenwvkechohyen, Sule tat cuko cehyen,
'tita·kóyhcit á·fkiw' ła·sinwakichóhyin[793] *solíta·t cokó cíhyin*
got him ready must, too laid it down for him buzzard house went in
And they got him ready and lay mush down for him, and Buzzard entered the house,

em akhothohyen, hofonemahekan, Cufe "Towēk" maken,
imakhothóhyin hofonimá·hika·n cofí towiⁿk ma·kín
they shut him up not very long Rabbit (exclam.) said
and they shut him in. Before very long, Rabbit said, "Toweek."

"Eston oka?" kihocen, "Tvckan em vcelakin oks" maken,
istó·n o·ka·^ kéyho·cín tácka·n[794] *imácila·kéyn ó·ks ma·kín*
what is he saying that for they said cut place I'm touching it is saying that
"Why is he saying that?" they asked. "I'm touching his cut," he said.

hofonekon hvtvm yekcicēt "Towēk" maken,
hofónikon hatâm yikcéyci·t towiⁿk ma·kín
not very long again loud (exclam.) saying
Before long he said again loudly, "Toweek."

"Eston oka?" kihocen, "Tvckan afken sem vlicvyan oks.
istó·n[i] o·ka·^ kéyho·cín tácka·n á·fkin símaleycayâ·n ó·ks
what does it mean they said cut place mush to apply to means
"Why is he saying that?" they asked. "I'm applying mush to his cut.

Hiyētacoken" maket, hofonē haken osiyet aret
háyyi·tá·cokin ma·kít hofóni· hâ·kin osâyyit a·lít
it must be hot saying a good while afterwards he went out going around
It must be hot," he said. After a long while he went out

---

[i] *istó·n* is short for *isto·mín* 'why'.

eto tale tat   rohhuyiren,   cuko   hvwechoyan
itó tá·lita·t   lohhoyêy̓in   cokó   hawichô·ya·n
a dead tree   stood upon   house   when open
and stood on the dead tree, and when the house was opened,

cufe   ena   em vpeswv   em papet,   afken   vpvkēt   omat   oket,
cofí   iná·   imapíswa   ímpa·pít   á·fkin   apáki·t[795] *ô·ma·t   o·kít*
rabbit's   body   flesh   was eating of   the mush   with   was   meant
they saw he'd been eating the rabbit's flesh with the mush.

lokehpet   ossēpet   omen   efune   tvlkusē taktohēksen hehcet,
lokíhpit   óssi·pít[796]   *ô·min   ifóni   tălⁿkosi· taktohî·ksin híhcit*
he ate it up   was going out   was   its bone only   were left saw
He ate it up and went out, and just Rabbit's bones were piled up.

hvtvm   mv   sulen   elēcetvn   eyahocvtēs.
hatâm   ma   solín   ili·citán   iyá·ho·catí·s[797]
again   that   buzzard   to kill him   it wanted to
Then they wanted to kill the buzzard.

Momet   elēcvranat   hopoyet   omhoyan,
mo·mít   ilí·cala·nâ·t   hopo·yít   ómho·yâ·n
Then   the one who is to kill it   looking for   they were
And they looked for someone to kill him

Lucvt   aren   eshēcet   Sule   elēcvrēn   kihocen,
locát   a·lín   ishî·cit   solí[i]   *ilí·cáli·n   kéyho·cín*
turtle   being around   found it   buzzard   to kill it   they told him
and found Turtle going around and told him to kill Buzzard.

"Mon omat   vmehakatsken"   maken,   hofonē hakēpen,
mó·n o·mâ·t   amihâ·ká·ckin   ma·kín   hofóni· há·ki·pín[798]
therefore   you-all wait for me   he said   quite a while had passed
"You all will have to wait for me then," he said, and after a long while,

---

[i] Better: *solín*.

"Cem etetaka?"   kihocan,
*cimititâ·ka·(ⁿ)^*   *kéyho·câ·n*
are you ready?   they said to him
they asked, "Are you ready?"

"Hvte   rēn   lvpotēpusis"   maken,
hatí   *lí·n*   *lapotĭ·ⁿposeys*[799]   *ma·kín*
just (now)   arrows   I'm straightening   he saying
"I'm just now straightening the arrows," he said,

vcewē   haken,   "Cem etetakis   oma?"   kihocat,
acíwi·   *hâ·kin*   *cimititâ·kays*   *o·ma·^*   *kéyho·câ·t*
a good while   elapsed   are you ready   are?   they told him
and after a good while, they asked, "Are you ready?"

"Hvte   rēn   fottēpusis"   maken...
hatí   *lí·n*   *fottĭ·ⁿposeys*[i]   *ma·kín*
just (now)   arrows   I'm feathering   he saying
"I'm just now feathering the arrows," he said.

Hofonēn   'mehahoken,   "Tokvs.   Vm etetaks"   mahket,
hofóni·n   *'miha·hô·kin*   *tókas,*   *amititâ·ks*   *máhkit*
for a good while   they waited for him   now!   I'm ready   he said
They waited for him a long while, and he said, "Now. I'm ready."

eccvkotakse   ehset   reu   cahwet   ayet
iccakotáksi   *íhsit*   *líw*   *cáhwit*   *a·yít*
bow   taking   arrows, too   taking   going
And he took his bow and picked up his arrows too

Sule   ohhuerat   rohret   ēchet   omat,
solí   *ohhôyla·t*   *lóhlit*   *i·chít*   *o·mâ·t*
buzzard   was standing   got there   he was shooting at him   was
and got to where Buzzard was standing and shot at him,

---

[i] Or: *isfottĭ·ⁿposeys.*

rvhekon	rēt	vnahēpen,	hueret	oman,
łahikon	*lí·t*	*ana·hî·pin*	*hôyłit*	*o·mâ·n*
didn't hit it	arrow	being out of	standing	was

but he didn't hit him and ran out of arrows. And as he stood there,

hofonē	rē-futke	sumecihocvtēt	cakhen	hehcet,
hofóni·	*łi·fótki*[i800]	*somicáyho·catí·t*	*câ·khin*	*híhcit*
a long time	feathered arrows	someone had lost	was sticking up	saw it

he saw a feathered arrow sticking up that someone had lost a long time before,

ehset,	lvpohtet,	sēchat,
íhsit	*lapóhtit*	*si·châ·t*
taking it	straightened it	shot at him with it

and he took it, straightened it, and shooting at him with that,

rahhet,	elehcen	tewahret	ehvfen	cemvranēs"
łáhhit	*ilíhcin*	*'tiwáhłit*[801]	*iháfin*	*cimála·ní·s*
hit it	killed it	cut it up	its thigh	we will give it to you

he hit him and killed him. Then they cut him up and told Turtle,

lucvn	kihocan,
locá(n)	*kéyho·câ·n*
turtle	they told

"We're giving you the thigh."

"Cvhvfe	nokihnoken	cvlēpusvnts"	maken,
caháfi	*nokâyhno·kín*[ii802]	*cali·posánc*	*ma·kín*
my thigh	hurt, hurt	I die easily	he said

"My thigh would ache and ache, and I'd surely die," he said.

"Efulowv	esepvs"	kihocen,
ifolowán	*isípas*	*kéyho·cín*
its shoulder	take	they told it

"Take the shoulder," they said.

---

[i] Originally: *hótki*.

[ii] Originally: *nokâyno·kín*.

"Cvfulowvo nokihnokusen cvlēpusvnts" maken,
cafolowáw *nokâyhno·kosin*[i] *cali·posánc* *ma·kín*
my shoulder, too hurts, hurts I die easily said
"My shoulder too would ache and ache, and I'd surely die," he said.

"Entalv tv?"   kihocan,
intá·lata   *kéyho·câ·n*
how about its ribs? they said to it
"How about the ribs?" they asked.

"Vntalv nokihnokusēn cvlēpusvnts" maken,
antá·la *nokâyhno·kosi·n*[ii] *cali·posánc* *ma·kín*
my ribs, too hurt, hurt I die easily saying
"My ribs would ache and ache, and I'd surely die," he said.

"Ekvn esepvs" kihocan,
ikán *isípas* *kéyho·câ·n*
its head take they told it
"Take the head," they said.

"Cvkv nokihnokusen cvlēpusvnts" mahken,
caká *nokèyhno·kosin* *cali·posánc* *máhkin*
my head hurts, hurts I die easily he said
"My head would ache and ache, and I'd surely die," he said.

"Vrekvs. Naken eyacekat okēs" kihcet,
alíkas *nâ·kin* *iyá·cika·t* *o·kí·s* *kéyhcit*
let him alone anything he doesn't want it must be told him
"Let him be. He doesn't want anything," [one] said,

omvlkvn cahwet svpeyephoyen,
omálkan *cáhwit* *'sapiyiphó·yin*
all of it he took they took it away
and they gathered everything up and took it away.

---

[i] Originally *nokâyno·kosín*.

[ii] *nokâyno·kosí·n*.

aret   catē-tolokfet   cǫtkusēt   liken   ehset,
a·lít   ca·ti·tolókfit[803]   *cŏ·ⁿtkosi·t   lêykin   íhsit*
going   blood-clot   very small   was lying   taking it
After a while [Turtle] saw a small blood clot and picked it up,

eto essen   svyokkohfet,   esrakkēn   hahyet   sayet,
itó íssin   'sayokkóhfit   islákki·n   háhyit   sâ·yit
a leaf   wrapped around it   big   made it   taking it
wrapped it in leaves to make it look bigger, and took it.

encuko   resorusen,   "Cē,   cvrke   fayēpa!"
incokó   liso·losín[804]   *ci·^   cálki   fá·yi·pa·^*
his house   just getting there with it   look   my father   been hunting
And just as he got to his house, his sons said, "Look, Father's been hunting!"

eppucetaket   makaken,   ehiwvt   enfuyan,   "Sekon."
ippocitá·kit   má·ka·kín   iháywat   ínfoyyâ·n[i]   síkon
his sons   they said   his wife   unwrapped it   nothing
His wife unwrapped it: "There's nothing here," [she said.]

"Ofusan"   maken,   eto-esse   encahwet   oman,   "Sekon."
ô·fosa·n"   ma·kín   itoíssi   incáhwit   o·mâ·n   síkon
just inside   she said   leaves   taking off   she was   [nothing]
"Way inside," he said, and as she was taking off the leaves, [she said,] "There's nothing."

"Ofusan"   makēpē monken   eshechoyan,
ô·fosa·n   má·ki·pi·mòŋkin   ishichô·ya·n
[just inside]   still saying that   when they found it
"Way inside," he kept saying, and when she found it,

catē-tolokfe   cǫtkusēt   vpiken   oken   ehset,
ca·ti·tolókfi   cŏ·ⁿtkosi·t   apâykin   ô·kin   íhsit
a clot of blood   very small   was in it   was meant   taking it
it was just a tiny blood clot in there, and she took it.

---

[i] Raiford: *im-*.

"'Cvppucetake momvtēkē sulkat setetayvrēs' komet
cappocitá·ki mô·matî·ki· sólka·t 'sititâ·yáli·s kô·mit
my sons that very many will have enough for each one thinking
"Did you think that would be enough

saretskisa?" kihcet eturwvn em ak-vretvchoyen,
sa·líckeysa·^ kéyhcit itólwan imakkałitácho·yín
you were about with it she said his eyes she threw it
for your sons?"[805] she asked and splattered it in his eyes.

eturwv akcatvkvtēt omet, hiyomis emonkvt ont omēs.
itólwa akca·takáti·t[806] *ô·mit hayyô·meys imóŋkat ônt ô·mi·s*
his eyes turned red did at this time, even the same is (is)
His eyes turned red, and they are the same way even now.

Rabbit Deceives Some Turkeys

J. Hill (Haas VI:161–169)

Penwvt fullen Cufet hehcet hoyahnet ayan,
pínwat follín cofít híhcit hoyáhnit a·yâ·n
turkeys which were about Rabbit saw them and passed by and was going on
Rabbit saw some turkeys as he passed by

kowakkucet aren reshēcet ont,
kowa·kkocít a·lín lishî·cit ónt
catamount who was about went and found him did
and then found a wildcat.

"Cencvmpvntot vsin fullis, penwv!" kicen,
cincâmpanto·t asêyn follêys pínwa keycín
that which you like yonder they were about turkeys he told him
"Some things you like were over there: turkeys!" he said.

"Esetv yēkcusēt omakēs" Kowakkucet maken,
isíta yĭ·ⁿkcosi·t omâ·ki·s kowa·kkocít ma·kín
to catch very difficult they are catamount said
"They're hard to catch," Wildcat said.

"Escem ēyvpayin omat, yekcekon ēsetskēs" kicet on,
iscimi·yapâ·yeyn[807] *o·mâ·t yíkcikon i·sícki·s*[i] *keycít ó·n*
I go and get them for you if not hard you (can) catch it he said did
"If I go and drive them to you, you can catch them easily," he told him.

"Moman res vtes" kihcen, Cufet okat,
mô·ma·n 'lisatís kéyhcin cofít o·kâ·t
well, then bring it, then! he said to him Rabbit said
"Well then, bring them," he said. Rabbit said,

"Heyvn wakkvccvs, elepvtē omēt" kicen,
hiyán wâ·kkáccas ilípati· ó·mi·t keycín
here lie down! as if you are dead are he said
"Lie down here like you were dead,"

wakken eto-lekwe hvtkan hopohyet
wâ·kkin ito-líkwi hátka·n hopóhyit
was lying rotten wood white kind he hunted for
and while he was lying down, [Rabbit] gathered rotten wood that was white

tofapet ohtosahyet ayat penwvn rem onayet okat,
tofa·pít ohtosáhyit â·ya·t pínwan 'limóna·yít o·kâ·t
crumbled it he scattered over him and went on turkeys he told them and said
and crumbled it, scattered it over him, and going on, he went and told the turkeys:

"Eceyopkē cepvsatē cestemē̠rrvkuecvkē
icíyo·pkí· cipása·tí· cistimǐ·ⁿłakôycaki·
(the one) slips up on you that kills you-all that makes you-all suffer very much
"The one who slipped up on you, killed you, and made you suffer

arē tvnkē elepvtēt wakkis. Erhecaks!" kicen,
a·lí·taŋkí· ilípati·t wâ·kkeys iłhicáks keycín
that is generally about is now dead and lying you-all go and see told them
is lying dead. Go see!" he told them.

---

[i] *ca·wícki·s* 'you can catch them'.

"Elekis ohketskēs" kicaken, "Elepēt cuntepvtēt omis.
ilíkeys óhkícki·s kéyca·kín ilípi·t contipáti·t ô·meys
not dead you might mean they said he's dead full of worms is, was
"He may not be dead as you say," they said. "He was dead and full of worms.

Hiyomof erhecaks. Cem ohhomahtvkarēs" kicen,
hayyô·mo·f iłhicáks cimohhomáhtaká·li·s keycín
now you-all go and see it I will lead the way for you-all he said
Go see him now. I'll lead the way for you all," he said.

vcak-vpēyet kowakkuce wakkan hecaket svpaklen,
acákkapi·yít[808] kowa·kkocí wâ·kka·n hica·kít[809] sapâ·klin
they went with him catamount who was lying they saw him they were standing
So they went with him and stood looking at the wildcat lying there.

"Em penkalusatskētvnkis elēpekv, hiyomof
impiŋkă·[n]losá·cki·taŋkêys ilî·pika hayyô·mo·f
you-all are usually afraid of him for he is dead right now
"You were afraid of him, but he's dead, so now

opanet vfulotēcatsken cenyvhikvkarēs" kicet,
opa·nít afóloti·cá·ckin cinyahéykaká·li·s keycít
dancing you-all go around and around him and I will sing for you-all he said
you dance around him, and I'll sing for you," he said.

vfulutēcet oman, pen-eckuce hvmket okat "Elekot onkv"
afóloti·cít o·mâ·n pinickocí hámkit o·kâ·t ilíko·t ôŋka
they were going around it were turkey hen one said not dead he is
And as they were going around him, one little turkey hen said, "He's not dead."

maken, "Elepvtēt os. Cuntv tis hatket omeko?" kicet
ma·kín ilípati·t ô·[n]s cóntateys hà·[n]tkit omíko·· keycít
she said it is dead is worms, even are white is it not? he told them
"He is dead. The worms are white everywhere, aren't they?" he said.

enyvhiket okat
ínyaheykít[810] o·kâ·t
he was singing for them and said
And singing for them, he said,

"Rakkan esv! Ekv catēcan esv!" kicen
lákka·n *isá*[i] *iká ca·tî·ca·n* *isá* *keycín*
the big one catch! the one with the red head catch! he told him
"Catch the big one! Catch the red-headed one!"

makēt okhoyekv maket pen-eckucet wikēpen,
ma·kí·t *ókho·yiká* *ma·kít* *pinickocít* *wéyki·pín*
saying they are he says turkey hen was quitting
And that being said, the little turkey hen quit:

"Kos. Cunte momat, estestomehcekos" kicet,
kós *cónti·* *mô·ma·t,* *ististomíhciko·s* *keycít*
No wormy like that couldn't do anything to anyone he said
"No. Wormy like that, he can't do anything to anyone," [Rabbit] said.

"Rakkan esv! Ekv catēcan esv!" maket,
lákka·n *isá* *iká ca·tî·ca·n* *isá* *ma·kít*
[the big one catch! the one with the red head catch!] he said
"Catch the big one! Catch the red-headed one!" he said.

"Ohrēfket omaks" kicen, ekv tis em ohrēfket,
óhli·fkít *omáks* *keycín* *ikáteys* *imóhli·fkít*
kick it you-all do he told him its head, even kicking it on
"Y'all kick it," he said, and they went about kicking its head,

ele em ohhueret vfulutēcet esfullen,
ilí *imóhhoylít* *afóloti·cít* *isfollin*
its feet standing on going around and around it they were about
standing on his feet, and circling around,

pen-vcule rakke-mahan kowakkucet ehsen vwahvtēs.
pinacóli *lakkimâ·ha·n* *kowa·kkocít* *ihsin* *awa·hatí·s*
old turkey big one the catamount caught and they scattered
and then the wildcat caught the biggest old turkey, and they scattered.

---

[i] In ordinary speech: *lákka·n isás* 'catch the big one!'.

Rabbit Deceives His Sister-in-Law

J. Hill (Haas VI:179–187)

Cufet	ehvcvwvn	eyacet	arvtēs.
cofĭt	*ihacawán*	*iyâ·cit*	*a·łatí·s*
rabbit	his sister-in-law	he wanting her	was going about

Rabbit once desired his sister-in-law.

"Fayvranis"	mahket	ayat	kvco	esse	catakan	hopohyet
fá·yała·néys	*máhkit*	*â·ya·t*	*kacó·*	*íssi*	*ca·tâ·ka·n*	*hopóhyit*
I'm going hunting	he said	he went	briars	leaves	red	he looked for

"I'm going hunting," he said and went and gathered briars with red leaves

pvhen	setehoret	etelumhihcet	accet
pahín	*'sitího·lít*[811]	*itilomhéyhcit*	*â·ccit*
grass	sewing it with	he put them together	and put it on

to sew together with grass. After he sewed them together and put it on,

cuko	tempe	hvfvpē	yvtēkan	vccetv	catē	vccēt	ahueret,
cokó	*tímpi*	*hafápi·*	*'yatî·ka·n*	*accitá*	*cá·ti·*	*ácci·t*	*a·hôylit*
house	near	the thicket-	edge	covering	red	had on	and was standing

he stood wearing the red wrap near the house, at the edge of a thicket;

"Pasokolvyv	lika?"		maken,	"Fakvn	ahyes"	kihocen,
pa·soko·layá	*lêyka·^*[812]		*ma·kín*	*fá·kan*	*áhyis*	*kéyho·cín*
(name of) Rabbit	is it at home?		he said	hunting	he went	he was told

"Is Pasokolaya there?" he asked. "He went hunting," he was told.

"Hopokv tarēs"	maket,
hopókatá·li·s[813]	*ma·kít*
There will be a hunt for him	he said

"There will be a search," he said.

"Ehvcvwvt	vrkvswv	rakkoman	acokohyen	avhoyvrēs.
ihacawát	*ałkáswa*	*ła·kkô·ma·n*[i]	*a·cokóhyin*	*a·ahóyáłi·s*
his sister-in-law	sofkee pot	kind of large one	shouldering	they 2 will go around

"His sister-in-law should shoulder a large crock, and they should go.

---

[i] Original: *ła·ⁿkkô·ma·n*.

Paksen	hvsossv	vyetv	nene	telacan
páksin	*hasó·ssa*	*ayíta*	*niní*	*'tilâ·ca·n*
tomorrow	east	the way to go	roads	(where) they come together

Tomorrow, where the roads going east cross,

tehecky tarēs"		mahoken,	"Aris"	maken
'tihíckatá·li·s		*ma·hô·kin*	*a·léys*	*ma·kín*
we will see one another		they said	I am around	he said

we will see one another," they said. "I am around," he said.

em onvyarēs	kihohcen	ahyet	vccetv	cate	ra kahyet
imonayá·li·s	*keyhóhcin*	*áhyit*	*accitá*	*cá·ti*	*ła·káhyit*
I will tell him	they told him	he went	covering, wrap	red	went and put it down

"I will tell him," he was told, and he went and lay his red wrap down

rvlaken	"Hopokv	vyetvn	cenhuehhokē"	ehiwvt	kicen,
'lalâ·kin	*hopóka*[814]	*ayítan*	*cinhoyhhô·ki·^[i, 815]*	*ihéywat*	*keycín*
came back	a hunt for	to go on	they were calling you	his wife	told him

and came back, and his wife told him, "They were calling you to go on a search."

"Estit	ohka?"	maken,
istêyt	*óhka·^*	*ma·kín*
who	was saying that	he said

"Who said that?" he asked.

"Vccetv	cate	vccēt	aret	okhohyē"	kihocen,
accitá	*cá·ti*	*ácci·t*	*a·lít*	*okhóhyi·^*	*kéyho·cín*
wrap	red	wearing	going about	they meant	they told him

"Someone wearing a red wrap," he was told.

"Naken	makis	fullēt	okhoyekon,	arvkētvnks"
nâ·kin[ii]	*ma·kêys*	*follí·t*	*okhoyíko·n*	*a·łakí·táŋks*
what	he says	when they are about	they don't mean it	anyone that's generally about

"When they say something they don't mean it,"

---

[i] Sic as to tone. Old-time old Indian women's words. Men didn't say it.

[ii] Original: *nâ·ki*.

maket omis, ehvcvwvt vrkvswv rakkoman acokoyen
ma·kít o·mêys ihacawát ałkáswa la·kkô·ma·n[i] *a·cokô·yin*
he said [did, but] his sister-in-law sofkee jar big kind of one shouldering it
he said, but his sister-in-law shouldered a big crock,

vhoyvtēs. Nene telacat rorhoyet omis, estit sepekon
aho·yatí·s niní 'tilâ·ca·t łołhô·yit[816] *o·mêys istêyt sipíkon*
and they 2 went roads where they meet they got to had anybody was not there
and they went. They got to where the roads meet, but nobody was there.

"Ayusvkan nene telacvnts. Min okhoyvten omēs"
ä·ⁿyosáka·n niní 'tilâ·canc mêyn okhô·yatin o·mí·s
a little ways you go roads where generally come together there that's what they meant
"You generally go a little ways when the roads meet. That's what they meant,"

mahken vhoyet rorhoyet omis,
máhkin aho·yít łołhô·yit o·mêys
he said they 2 went and got there did
he said, and they went and got there, but

"Estit sepekon ohhvyvtkvranvkat tvlkēs" mahket,
"istêyt sipíkon ohhayátkała·nakâ·t tâlki·s máhkit
anybody isn't there so we've got to stay all night have to he said
he said, "Nobody's here, so we'll have to stay all night,"

totkvn tehcet, eto-talen vteloyvtēs.
tó·tkan tihcit itotá·lin atílo·yatí·s
fire he built dry brush he gathered
and he built a fire and gathered dry brush.

Vtvkoca vtehtēkat vlkēn sulkēn yestak-vpohyet
atakocá· atihtî·ka·t álki·n sólki·n yistakkapóhyit
ants that had them each one (had) many he piled it up
He piled up many [branches] with ants on each one;

---

[i] Original: *ła·ⁿkkô·ma·n.*

"Heyvn atakwakket, a oh-etecēpet   ometskvrēs" kicet,
hiyán   a·takwâ·kkit   a·ohhitíci·pit   omíckáli·s   keycít
here   he lay by   keep it kindled you must   he said
"You might lie down and keep it burning," he said,

ehvcvwvn   emmeliyet,   totkv   pvlhvmken   wakkēpvtēs.
ihacawán   immilêyyit   tó·tka   palhâmkin   wákki·patí·s
his sister-in-law he directed[i] fire   the one side of he lay down
and he directed his sister-in-law and lay down on one side of the fire.

Ehvcvwvt   pvlhvmken   atakwakken   nochoyvranet   oman,
ihacawát   palhámkin   a·takwâ·kkin   nochoyála·nít   o·mâ·n
his sister-in-law the other side   was lying down   they were going to sleep were
His sister-in-law lay down on the other side, and as they were going to sleep,

vtvkocvt   vwahet   tayen   enan   em vfullen,
atakocá·t   awa·hít   tă·ⁿyin   iná·n   imáfollín
ants   were scattering very much her body were around on
the ants were scattering and were going all over her body.

"Naket   tayen   est vfulles"   ehvcvwvt   kicen,
nâ·kit   tă·ⁿyin   ístafollís   ihacawát   keycín
something   very much   are crawling on one his sister-in-law she said
"Something is crawling all over me," his sister-in-law said.

"Yvtat   naket sekos.   Ahtet   a vnwakkvs"   Cufe   maken,
yatâ·t[ii][817] *nâ·kit sikos*[818] *áhtit* *a·anwákkas*[iii] *cofi*[iv] *ma·kín*
here   there are none   come   and lie by me   rabbit   said
"There are none here. Come and lie down by me," Rabbit said,

---

[i] Literally, 'pointed to'.

[ii] Or: *hiyatâ·t*.

[iii] Raiford: *a·am-*.

[iv] Raiford: *cofĭt*.

ehvcvwv	a enwakken,	hvyvtiken	yefulhokvtēs,
ihacawá[i]	*a·inwâ·kkin*[ii]	*hayatêykin*	*'yifólho·katí·s*[iii]
his sister-in-law	lay beside him	when it got day	they 2 went back

and his sister-in-law lay beside him. When day came, they went back,

momvrē	eyacat	tvlkusēt	aret	okekv.
mó·máli·	*iyâ·ca·t*	*tâlkosi·t*	*a·lít*	*ô·kika*
in that way	he wanted her	the only (reason)	going around	he meant that

for he went around only wanting it that way.

Fox Gets Revenge on Wolf

J. Hill (Haas VII:1–9)[iv]

Estepapv	punvttv	ele oste	sasat	omvlkv	em mēkkot	omēs.
istipá·pa	*ponátta*	*ili ó·sti*	*sâ·sa·t*	*omálka*	*immí·kkot*	*ô·mi·s*
lion	animals	four-footed	that are	(of) all	the chief, king	is

Lion is the king of all the four-footed animals.

Momen	enokkēt	wakken	hēcet	vfullen	wakkvtēs.
mo·mín	*inókki·t*	*wâ·kkin*	*hi·cít*[819]	*afollín*	*wa·kkatí·s*[820]
Then	(when) sick	he lay	they saw	and they were about him	he was lying

He was lying sick, and all were about him as he was lying there.

Nake	ele oste	vtēkat	em mēkko tat	hēcet	fullet	oman,
nâ·ki	*ili ó·sti*	*atî·ka·t*	*immí·kkota·t*	*hi·cít*	*follít*	*o·mâ·n*
[thing]	four-footed	everyone	their king	they looking at him	were around	were

All the four-footed things were looking in on their king

Culvt	sekatēs.	Mont omen	yvhvt	enhomecētot,
colát	*siká·ti·s*	*mônt o·mín*	*yahát*	*inhomíci·tot*
fox	wasn't there	therefore	the wolf	was mad at it

except Fox. So Wolf was mad at him:

---

[i] Raiford: *ihacawát*.

[ii] Raiford: *a·im-*.

[iii] Raiford: *'yofol-*.

[iv] Based partly on "The Sick Lion" in Aesop's Fables.

"Estoman Culv atekot omētē?   Cenokkēt omat kę̄rruset ometat
ísto·mâ·n colá a·tíkot o·mí·ti·^821   cinókki·t ô·ma·t kĭ·ⁿłlosit o·mí·ta·t
why fox hasn't come is it?   you are sick are he knows does
"Why hasn't Fox come? He knows you're sick

a vtekot   os. Ēkvsamatet   'Momvyis' komēt
a·atíkot   ó·ⁿs. i·kasâ·ma·tit   mô·mayeys kó·mi·t
and he hasn't come here has he's proud (of himself) apurpose he thought
and hasn't come. He's proud of himself and thinks, 'I'll not go,'

cehecetv eyacekot aret   omēs.
cihicitá iyá·cikot a·łít   o·mí·s
to see you he didn't want being around he is
and doesn't want to see you.

'Elēpen omat, mēkko hakeparēs' komat a vtekot   aret   os.
ilî·pin^822 o·mâ·t mí·kko ha·kipá·li·s kô·ma·t a·atíkot   a·łít   ó·ⁿs
he dies if chief I will become he thinks not coming here being around is
He thinks if you die, he'll become king and doesn't come.

Mēkko toyetskekv, elēhocekvs   mahketsken elēhocan   hę̄rēs"
mí·kko tô·yíckika^i ili·hocíkas   máhkíckin ili·hô·ca·n^823   hĭ·ⁿli·s
chief you are let him be killed you say   and let him be killed would be good
You are king: if you say, 'Let him be killed,' then having him killed would be good,"

kicvtēs.   Momen Culv pohet   arvtētot,
kaycatí·s   mo·mín colá po·hít^824 a·łatí·tot
he told him Then fox hearing it and had been about
he said. Now Fox had been listening

mēkko wakkat rorvtēs.   Mont em punayet
mí·kko wâ·kka·t lo·latí·s   mónt ímpona·yít
chief was lying he got there Then he talked to him
and went to where the king was lying. And he said to him,

---

^i Raiford: *tô·yíccika.*

"Cenokkvcoken pohit arit cem enokketv estomēt omat
cinô·kkacókin po·héyt a·łéyt ciminokkitá istó·mi·t ô·ma·t
you're sick I heard and am around you sickness what kind it is
"I heard you were sick and am here;

omvlkvt keriyit vlēkcvn hopoyit arimvts.
omálkan kiłêyyeyt alí·kcan hopo·yéyt a·łéymac
all I was finding out doctor I was hunting I was around (III)
I found out all about your sickness and was looking for a doctor.

Cem enokketv wicēcē tayat vlēkcv sepekon arvyof,
ciminokkitá weycí·ci· tâ·ya·t[825] alí·kca sipíkon a·layô·f
your sickness one that can stop it doctor there is none while I was about
There is no doctor who can cure your sickness, [but] while I was about,

este hvmket vm onayet okat,
ísti hámkit amóna·yít o·kâ·t
a person one telling me said:
a man told me,

"Vlēkcv hvmket enokketv mv omat wicēcvranat tvlkusēt likvcoken"
alí·kca hámkit inokkitá ma ô·ma·t weycí·cala·nâ·t tăłⁿkosi·t lêykacókin
doctor one a disease that like that will cure it bound to is living
'There is one doctor who can cure a sickness like that.'

vm onahohyen, cecvfēknē tvlkusēn cvyahcet ayimvts.
amona·hóhyin cicafî·kni·[826] tăłⁿkosi·n cayáhcit a·yéymac[827]
he told me you get well to be sure I wanted you I went (III)
I went wanting to be sure you'd get well.

Nene cvpkē hērēt onkv, hotoskv momē estohmis
niní cápki· hĭⁿli·t ôŋka hotóska mo·mí· istóhmeys[i]
road long very is weariness like that somehow
The road is very long, but despite weariness

---

[i] Original: *istô·meys*.

cecvfeknvrēn   cvyacusekv,   arit   heleswv   keriyit,
cicafiknáli·n   *cayà·ⁿcosíka*   *a·léyt*   *'hilíswa*   *kiłêyyeyt*
you to get well   I wanted you   I was about   medicine   I found out
and wanting you to get well, I found medicine

rvlakit   omit,   cem onvyvranis.
'lalâ·keyt   *o·méyt*   *cimonayála·néys*
I have come back   have   I'm going to tell you
and have come back to tell you.

'Yvhvn   elehcet,   torohfet   hvrpe   hiyē   monken,
yahán   *ilíhcit*   *tolóhfit*   *háłpi*   *háyyi·*   *mòŋkin*
wolf   kill him   skin it   hide   warm   while
They told me, 'Kill the wolf, skin him, and while the hide is still warm,

accet   eswakken   omat,   cvfeknvranat   tvlkusēs'
â·ccit   *iswà·kkin*   *o·mâ·t*   *cafiknała·nâ·t*   *tǎlⁿkosi·s*
put it on   and lie down with it (on)   if   he will get well   be sure to
if he puts it on and lies down with it on, he is bound to get well.'

maket   vm onahoyet   onkv,   mēkko   toyetskekv,
ma·kit   *amona·hò·yit*   *ôŋka*   *mí·kko*   *tô·yickika*[i]
he said   they have told me this   have   chief   you are
My lord

'Yvhv tat   elēhocekvs'   mahketsken,   elēhocekvs   ehvrpe   accet
yahátat   *ili·hocíkas*   *máhkíckin*   *ili·hocíkas*   *iháłpi*   *â·ccit*
the wolf   let him be killed   you say   he will be killed   its hide   having it on
say, 'Let the wolf be killed,' and he will be killed, and having the skin on

cecvfēknan   hērētan os.
cicafí·kna·n   *hǐ·ⁿli·ta·n ó·ⁿs*
you'll get well   it would be good
you'll get well, and it would be good.

---

[i] Raiford: *tô·yíccika*.

Mēkko   cēme   omat   ētv   hehcēkos   komit,
mí·kko   *cí·mi*   *ô·ma·t*   *í·ta*   *híhcí·ko·s*   *kô·meyt*
chief   you   like   another   we can find (no other)   I think
I believe we will never find another king like you

cecvfeknē   tvlkusen   cvyacat,   hotoskv   rakkē   vpvkēn
cicafíkni·   *tălⁿkosin*   *cayâ·ca·t*   *hotóska*   *lákki·*   *apáki·n*
you to get well   sure to   I want   weariness   much   with
and want to be sure you get well. I say [this] with much weariness

heleswv   cenheckuecit   okikv"   Culv   maken,
'hilíswa   *cinhickôyceyt*   *o·kéyka*   *colá*   *ma·kín*
medicine   I have found for you   I am saying   fox   said
from finding medicine for you," Fox said.

mékkot   okat   "Yvhvn   elēhocekvs"   mahken   yvhv tat   elēhocvtēs.
mí·kkot   *o·kâ·t*   *yahán*   *ili·hocíkas*   *máhkin*   *yahátа·t*   *ilí·ho·catí·s*
chief   said   wolf   let someone kill him   he said   the wolf   they killed him
Then the king said, "Let the wolf be killed," and the wolf was killed.

Rabbit Deceives Alligator

J. Hill (Haas VII:11–17)[i828]

Vlepvtvt   pahcē-rakko   ofvn   wakken   Cufet   eshēcet   omen
alipatát[ii829]   *pahci·lákko*   *ó·fan*   *wâ·kkin*   *cofít*   *ishî·cit*   *o·mín*
alligator   big grass, tall grass   in   was lying   Rabbit   found him   did
Alligator was lying in tall grass, and Rabbit found him,

etem punahoyet   kaken,   Cufet   okat
itimponá·ho·yít   *kâ·kin*   *cofít*   *o·kâ·t*
and they were talking to each other   2 sitting   Rabbit   said
and they sat talking. Rabbit said,

---

[i]

[ii] *alipatá* 'alligator' ("old-folks used this") or *alpatá*.

"Hilfvyv kihocat honvnwvt omvnts" kicet omen
héylfaya kéyho·câ·t honánwat ô·mánc[i] keycít o·mín
Hell-fire they called him a man is much he said did
"That guy called Hell-Fire is a real man."

"Kerraks" Vlepvtvt maket,
kíłłáks alipatát ma·kít
I don't know him the alligator said
"I don't know him," Alligator said.

"Honvnwv vm ontalat estvmvn arēs komvkot omvnts.
honánwa amontâ·la·t ístaman a·lí·s kó·máko·t ô·mánc
a man overcome me anywhere being about I don't think
"He said, 'I don't think there's a man who can defeat me.

Vm ontvlē tayēt aren omat hecetv cvyacēs" maken,
amontali· tâ·yi·t a·lín o·mâ·t hicíta cayá·ci·s ma·kín
anyone overcome me can is about if to see him I want he said
If there's someone who can defeat me, I want to see him.'"

Cufet okat, "Honvnwvt omvnton kērrit okis.
cofit o·kâ·t honánwat ô·mantón kî·łłeyt o·kéys
Rabbit said man he generally is I knew him I say it
Rabbit said, "I know that he was a man.

Cēme omusē em vcekellē tayē tokot omēs" kicen,
cí·mi ô·mosi· imacikílli· tâ·yi· tó·ko·t ô·mi·s keycín
you like back away [can doesn't does] he said to him
He absolutely will not back away from the likes of you," he said.

Vlpvtv tat cvpakkēt "Estvn mv honvnwv aren omat,
alpatáta·t capákki·t[830] ístan ma honánwa a·lín o·mâ·t
the alligator was mad wherever that man is about if
Alligator said angrily, "If that man is around somewhere,

---

[i] By using *ô·mánc* instead of *má·ho·kánc*, it means Rabbit knew himself.

enlvpkē   estomusen   hecvyē   tayen   omat,   a vcoh-vtekvs"
inlapkí·   istô·mosin   hicáyi·   tâ·yin   o·mâ·t   a·acohhatíkas
how quick   shortest time I see him can   [if]   let him come to me
let him come to me as fast as I can see him,"

maket   omen,   "Vcekellicvyēs   komē   hēret   oketsken   omat,
ma·kít   o·mín   acikílleycayí·s   kó·mi·   hì·ⁿlit   o·kíckin   o·mâ·t
he said   did   [I] can make him back up   thinking honestly you [mean] if
he said. "If you honestly believe you can make him back away,

a ecoh-vtēcicvyēs"   Cufet   kicen,
a·icohhatí·ceycayí·s   *cofít   keycín*
I can make him come to you   rabbit   said to him
I can have him come to you," Rabbit said.

Vlpvtv   okat   "Vtepekvs   honvnwv   estomēn   em ēfulikit,
*alpatá*ⁱ   *o·kâ·t   atípikas   honánwa   istó·mi·n   imi·folèykeyt*
alligator   said thus: let him come man   any   I will turn my back on
Alligator said, "Let him come. You will not see me turn my back on any man

em vkuekit   arin   cvhehcetskekos"   kicen,
imákoykéyt   *a·léyn*   *cahíhcickíko·s*   *keycín*
I will move from   I being around   you will not see me   he said to him
or move away from him," he said.

"Mon omat   heyv tan   'mehaketsken,   a ecoh-vtecicarēs"   kihcet,
mó·n o·mâ·t   hiyáta·n   'mihâ·kíckin   a·icohhaticéycá·li·s   *kéyhcit*
if that's the case right here you wait for him I will make him come to you   he said to him
"Well then, you wait for him right here, and I'll have him come to you," he said,

ayat   totkvn   hopoyehpet   vlpvtv   wakkat   vfulutkēn
â·ya·t   tó·tkan   hopoyíhpit   alpatá   wâ·kka·t   afolótki·n
went   fire   he hunted for   alligator   where lying   around
and having gone, he looked for fire and set fire

ⁱ Raiford: *alpatát.*

pahcē-rakko tat   em vhethoyēcet   ˈsem vfulutecihcen,
pahci·łákkota·t   imahithoyi·cít   ˈsimafoloticéyhcin
the big grass   he set them afire   in a circle around him
to the tall grass around where Alligator lay, and it circled around him,

hopotkē-rakkot   a sohletiken   lētket   ayan
hopotki·łákkot   a·sohlitêykin   li·tkít   a·yá·n
the big woods fire   came running up on   while running   going
and a wildfire came rushing up on [Alligator], and he ran off;

totkv   vlvkēpen,   rvpvcēsset,   vrusvmmvliket,
tó·tka   aláki·pín   łápaci·ssít   ałosàmᵘmalêykit[i]
fire   was getting to him   dodging about   was around for quite a while
the fire was reaching him, and he was dodging it for quite a while.

tektvnkusat   enheciken,   ropotiyet
tiktànkosa·t   inhicêykin   lopo·têyyit
where there was a little opening   he found out   he went through it
He found where there was a little opening and went through it,

uewv   lvokēt   likan   mvn   vhēcet
óywa   láwki·t   lêyka·n   man   ahi·cít
water   deep   there was   that, there   he was looking towards
and he looked towards deep water,

estomuset   enletketvt   omētat   omvlēcus mahet   enhoyanen,
istô·mosit   inlitkitát   ô·mi·ta·t   omali·cosmâ·hit   ínhoya·nín
whatever   its running   has   it took all of it   he was passing by
and went with all the speed he had and was passing by [Rabbit]:

"Hiyomusē   aran   okēpvyvnts.
háyyo·mosí·   a·łâ·n   oki·payánc
this way   one that is about   is what I mean
"This is what I meant.

---

[i] Raiford: *alasàmᵘmalêykit.*

Honvnwv	em ēfulikē		lētkē	kicvyat,"	makvtēs.
honánwa	*imi·folêyki·*		*li·tkí*	*keycayâ·t*	*ma·katí·s*
man	turn the back from		running	I call it	R. said that

That's what I call turning the back on a man and running," [Rabbit] said.

Rabbit as a Successful Suitor (Cufe Oh-onvkv)[i]

J. Hill (Haas VIII:117–121)

Hoktvlēt	hoktē	mvnettē	ocēt	liket,
hoktalí·t	*hoktí·*	*'manítti·*[831]	*ó·ci·t*	*lêykit,*
old woman	[woman	young]	had	she lived

An old lady lived with a young woman and said,

"Enyvhiketv	hērēt	estit	vlaken	omat,	hoktē	mvnettat	ēpahyet
inyahaykitá	*hĭ·ⁿli·t*[ii]	*istêyt*	*ala·kín*	*o·mâ·t*	*hoktí·*	*'manítta·t*	*i·páhyit*
singing	well	somebody	would come	if	[woman	young]	marrying

"If anyone comes who can sing well, he can marry

likepvrēs"	maket omen,	pohakvtēt	Kowakkucet	"Vnt omarēs"	komet,
leykipáli·s	*ma·kít o·mín,*	*pohâ·kati·t*[832]	*kowa·kkocít*	*ánt omá·li·s*	*kô·mit*
would live	she said	they overheard	wildcat, bobcat	I'll be the one	he thought

the young woman." They overheard her, and Wildcat thought, "I will be the one."

yvhiketv	hērat	'metetakēpet	aret,	hoktalat	ehute	roret,
yahaykitá	*hĭ·ⁿla·t*	*'mitita·kî·pit*[833]	*a·lít*	*hoktâ·la·t*	*ihóti*	*lo·lít*[834]
song	good one	got ready	was around	old woman's	house	he got to

He prepared a good song and got to the old lady's home singing,[835]

ci·- to- tom   cí·- to- tom   cí·- to- tom

---

[i] Title: *cofí ohhonáka* 'rabbit story'.

[ii] Or: *hĭ·ⁿli·n*.

"Cētotom, cētotom, cētotom" maket yvhihket res oren,
cí·totom[i] *cí·totom* *cí·totom* *ma·kít* *yahaykít* *líso·lín*[836]
               he said   singing   came there
"Chee-to-tom, chee-to-tom, chee-to-tom," as he arrived.

"Mv oman okēskvnkē. Naken maket saret okēto?
ma ô·ma·n *okí·skáŋki·^* *nâ·kin* *mâ·kit*[837] *sa·lít* *o·ki·to·^*[ii]
like that   I didn't mean what   he's saying   around with it does he mean?
"I didn't mean like that. What is he going around saying?

Vsin sayet okeka!" hoktalat kihcen,
asêyn *sâ·yit* *okika·^*[iii] *hoktâ·la·t* *kéyhcin*
away   going with it   go away with it!   old woman   said
Let him take it over there!" the old lady said,

tehoyahnet ayvtēton, Cufet vrēpet 'metetahket,
'tihoyáhnit *â·yati·ton*[838] *cofít* *alĭ·ⁿpit* *'mititáhkit*
(W.) went past   when he had passed on   Rabbit   being around   got ready
and when Wildcat had passed on, Rabbit had been hanging around and got ready.

eco-hvce catēcvkvtēn kohcakhēcet,
icohací *ca·ti·cakáti·n*[839] *kohcakhî·cit*[840]
deer-tail   which had been made red   stuck on his head
He stuck a deer tail that had been painted red on his head

vrkvshakucen ēset nafket hayēcet
alkasha·kocín[841] *î·sit* *na·fkít* *há·yi·cít*
tom-tom   took   beat on drum   made a sound, noise
and held a tom-tom and played it, singing:

"Ya-vhossasē-ē hollo, hollo" makēt yvhiket,
ya·ʔahossâ·si·ʔí· hólló· hólló·[iv] *ma·kí·t* *yahaykít*
                he said   he sang
"Ya-ahossasee-ee hollo, hollo,"

---

[i] "Might be for *cíntotó·s* that's you" (VIII:116).

[ii] Women's speech *o·ki·to·^* = men's speech *okíkas*.

[iii] Old women used to say: *okika·^* (= men's speech *okíkas*).

[iv] notes crossed through, except la, la, la, la

'co-hvce-cate   fvnafaken   'sem vlaken,
'cohacicá·ti   *fanâ·fä·ⁿkin*   *símala·kín*
red deer-tail   waving (back and forth to music)   he was coming
and arrived waving the red deer tail.

"Enyvhiketv   hiyomē tis   honvnwv   sasēton   okvkvnkē.
inyahaykitá   *hayyó·mi·teys*   *honánwa*   *sâ·si·ton*   *o·kákáŋki·^ⁱ*
(his) song   that kind   a man   who has   I meant
"I meant a man who has that kind of song.

vpokephueka"   hoktalat   kihcen,
apo·kiphoyka·^ⁱⁱ,⁸⁴²   *hoktâ·la·t*   *kéyhcin*
let him live, stay   old woman   said to him
Let him stay," the old lady said,

Cufe tat   ehiset   likvtēs,   mahokvnts cē.
cofíta·t   *ihêysit*   *leykatí·s⁸⁴³*   *má·ho·kánc ci·^*
Rabbit   married her and   he lived   that's the saying
and Rabbit married her, it was said.

Rabbit Drives His Wife Away

J. Hill (Haas VIII:123)

Cufet   ehiwvn   ehanet   vtohken   vyēpen,
cofít   *ihéywan*   *iha·nít*   *ato·hkín*   *ayî·pin*
Rabbit   his wife   he scolded   he drove her off   she went away
Rabbit scolded his wife and drove her off, and when she was gone,

vkerricuset   liket   ont   "Tefok"   maket
akiłêycosit   *lěyⁿkit*   *ónt*   *tifók^ⁱⁱⁱ*   *ma·kít*
he got to thinking it over   he kept sitting   did   (sobbing sound)   he said
he got to thinking about it: "Sniff-sniff," he sobbed.

---

[i] Women's speech: *o·kákáŋki·^* (= men's speech *o·kákáŋks*).
[ii] Women's speech *apo·kiphoyka·^* = men's speech *apo·kiphóykas ci^*. Women did not use the particle *ci^*. Old women said *opa·ni·to·^* 'he's dancing' for men's speech *opa·ni·s*.
[iii] *tifók* sobbing like a child kinda mad, imitative of a single sob, hunh?

"Liken mont estenkvpakhoyat holwakēs mahokvnts komvkan
lêykin mônt istiŋkapakhô·ya·t[844] *holwâ·ki·s*[845] *má·ho·kánc kò·maka·n*
sitting when anyone departs from you it's bad they say thought, but
"When someone leaves you, it's bad," they used to say,

mvtat tvhiketskē tvnkekv,
matá·t[846] *'tahêykícki·*[847] *taŋkiká*
same thing, like that you've quarreled so much did
but you've quarreled so much,

estemerkēt liket oketskē" ecket kihcen,
istimíɬki·t[848] *lêykit o·kícki·*^[i] *íckit kéyhcin*
suffering sitting you are his mother said to him
you [will] sit and suffer," his mother told him.

"Tefofo" makēt hvkihkvtēs mahokvnts.
*tifô·fó·*ⁿ[hii] *ma·ki·t*[849] *hakayhkatí·s má·ho·kánc.*
(crying sound) he said and he cried That's the saying.
"Boo-hoo-hoo," he cried, they used to say.

Rabbit as a Rejected Suitor

J. Hill (Haas VIII:125–133)[iii]

Hoktvlēt emosuswv hoktē mvnettēn ocēt liket omen,
hoktalí·t imosóswa hoktí· manítti·n ó·ci·t lêykit o·mín
old woman her grandchild woman young had she was living
Once there lived an old woman who had a young granddaughter,

Cufet mv hoktēn estem eyacet aret, ecken vtotvtēs,
cofít ma hoktí·n istimiyá·cit a·lít íckin ato·tatí·s
Rabbit that girl, woman wanting her he was around his mother he sent her
and Rabbit wanted that girl and sent his mother

---

[i] Women's speech *o·kícki·*^ = men's speech *o·kíckis.*
[ii] eight, two eighths, half note; sol, la-sol, do
[iii] "Funny story." (VIII:132)

em vpohvrēn.   Momen   ecket   ahyofvn   yopvn   ēmeu   ayvtēs.
imapoháli·n   *mo·mín*   *íckit*   *áhyo·fan*[850]   *yópan*   *i·miw*   *a·yatí·s*
to ask for her for him   and   his mother   after she went   behind   he, too   went
to ask for her on his behalf. After his mother left, he went behind her.

Roret   fettv   totkv-hute   vkvnowvn   alikvtēs.
lô·lit   *fítta*   *to·tkahóti*   *akanowán*   *a·lêykati·s*
got there   outside   chimney   corner   he sat out there
When he got there, he sat outside at the corner of the chimney.

Nake   mahokan   em apohicet   mv   hoktalat   okat,
nâ·ki   *má·ho·kâ·n*   *ima·póheycit*[851]   *ma*   *hoktâ·la·t*   *o·kâ·t*
what   they (would) say   he listened   that   woman   said:
He was listening to what they were saying, and the old lady [grandmother] said,

"Yv   hoktē   mvnettat   naken   estomet   honvnwv   vfastet
ya   *hoktí·*   *manítta·t*   *nâ·kin*   *ísto·mít*   *honánwa*   *afa·stít*
this   [woman   young]   anything   does she do   man   to take care of
"I don't see how this young woman would know

likē   tayē   onkot   omat   kerrekatet   ecetothoyen
léyki·   *tâ·yi·*   *óŋko·t*   *ô·ma·t*   *kíllika·tit*   *icitothô·yin*[852]
             doesn't do   don't know   he sent you over
how to take care of a man, but you folks didn't know this,

vlaket   oketskētok: Mv   honvnwv tat   yv   hoktē   vpvkekis
alâ·kit   *o·kícki·to·k*   *ma*   *honánwata·t*   *ya*   *hoktí·*   *apákikeys*
came here   you have done   that   man   this   woman   to marry
and you were sent to find out: that man had better not marry this girl,"

estonhkos"   maken   pohet,   Cufe tat   letiket   kohv-motke   cvpkēn
istónhko·s[i]   *ma·kín*   *pô·hit*   *cofíta·t*   *litêykit*   *kohamótki*   *cápki·n*
had better not   she said   he heard   Rabbit   ran off   blowgun   long
he heard her say, and Rabbit ran

---

[i] Some say: *stóhko·s*.

esēpet	rvlahket,		totkv-hutet	rolakkēt	omvten
isî·pit	'laláhkit		to·tkahótit	łolákki·t	ô·matin
he got	and came back		chimney	hole in it	was

and got a long blowgun and brought it back. The chimney had a hole,

kohv-motken	a ropotticet,	mv	kohv-yoksvn	encokpiket,
kohamótkin	a·łopo·ttêycit[853]	ma	kohayóksan	incokpâykit[854]
blowgun	put down through	that	end of cane	he had in his mouth

and he put the blowgun in there and had the end of the cane in his mouth and said,

"Emosuswv	encakē	likat	ēlvn...to...h...h"	maken,
# imosóswa	incá·ki·	leykâ·t	i·lantó· #[i]	ma·kín
her granddaughter	stingy with	lives	will die (sing-song)	he said

"Anyone who is stingy with her granddaughter is sure to die."

enhakēt	totkv	ētkat	ofv min	rossen
ínha·kí·t	tó·tka	i·tkâ·t	o·famêyn	lo·ssín
making noise	fire	that was blazing	any	came out

The sound came out of the blazing fire,

mv	hoktalat	pohet	"Totkv tis	estokekv	em ahērat
ma	hoktâ·la·t	pô·hit	tó·tkateys	istô·kika	imá·hi·łá·t[855]
that	old woman	when she heard	fire, even	[talking to people]	(like) appealed to her

and the old lady heard it: "Even the fire is talking

okhoyētis	okikv,	hoktē tat	honvnwv	cem vpvkepvranan	omēs"
ókho·yí·teys	o·kéyka	hoktí·ta·t	honánwa	cimapakípała·nâ·n	o·mí·s
what is said	did	that woman	man	will have to (live) together	

about it, so the girl and your man will have to live together,"

maken,	Cufe tat	pohhet	afvciket	lētkat,	hopvyēcemahekot
ma·kín	cofíta·t	póhhit	a·facêykit	lî·tka·t	hopayi·cimá·hikot
said	Rabbit	heard it	got happy	ran	not very far away

she said, and Rabbit heard, rejoiced, ran off, and before he got very far,

---

[i] # to #. Hold thumb upside down in mouth while telling this part. Elvn.to..h..h Voice out of the fire do, do, re# (quarter, quarter, dotted half, sing-song.)

"Ķasosososot"   makēt   rapihken,   ecket   okat
kă·ⁿsosososot   *ma·ki·t*[856]   *lá·payhkín*   *íckit*   *o·kâ·t*
(a shout of joy)   said   got there and whooped   his mother   said
he whooped, "Kanh-so-so-so-sot!" [in joy]. His mother said,

"Mv   honvnwv   okvyat   pihket   okē"   mahken,
ma   *honánwa*   *o·kayâ·t*   *payhkít*   *o·ki·^*   *máhkin*[857]
that   man   talking about   whooped   now   she said
"That's the man I was talking about whooping now,"

"Mv   honvnwv tat   em vretv   kẽrusiyēt   onkv,   yv   hoktē tat   vpvkekis
ma   *honánwata·t*   *imałitá*   *kĭ·ⁿłosêyyi·t*   *óŋka*   *ya*   *hokti·ta·t*   *apákikeys*
that   man's   reputation   we know   do   this   girl   not to live together
and [the old lady] said, "We know all about that man's ways,

estonhkoto   rem onvya"   kihohcen,   ecke   yefulket   ehute   roren,
*istónhko·to·^*   *'łimonaya·^*   *keyhóhcin*   *ícki*   *yifólkit*[858]   *ihóti*   *lo·łín*
will be all right   tell him   they said   his mother   returned   her house   got there
so go tell him he is not to marry that woman," and his mother went back home.

"Nak   mahohka?"   Cufe   maken,   "Hoktē   vm vpvkekis   estonhkoto"
nâ·k   *ma·hóhka·^*   *cofí*   *ma·kín*   *hokti·*   *amapakíkeys*   *istónhko·to·^*
what   did they say   Rabbit   said   woman   to live together, marry   not to
"What did she say?" Rabbit asked. "She said, 'It won't do for him to marry my girl,'

makephohyen,   rarit omis"   kihcen,
ma·kiphóhyin[859]   *ła·łéyt o·méys*   *kéyhcin*[860]
they said   and I came back   she said
so I've come back," she told him.

"Vkvsvmhohyet   oman,   takļiketskis os.   Rvlakvkē tayis os"   maket,
akasamhóhyit[861]   *o·mâ·n*   *takłĕyⁿkickeys ó·ⁿs*   *'łalâ·kaki· tâ·yeys ó·ⁿs*   *ma·kít*
agreed, willing   are   you stay there   ought to have come back   he said
"She had agreed, but you kept staying there. You should have come back long ago," he said

ecken   ehanvtēs   mahokvnts cē.
íckin   *iha·natí·s*   *má·ho·kánc ci·^*
his mother   he fussed at   that's what they say
and scolded his mother, it was told.

Rabbit Makes Hunting-Medicine

J. Hill (Haas VIII:135–139)[i]

Cufe	"Fayit	omis"	maket	sumkvntot	rvlaket
cofí	*fa·yéyt*	*o·méys*	*ma·kít*	*sòmkántot*	*lála·kit*
Rabbit	hunting	I am	he said	disappeared	came back

Every now and then Rabbit would say, "I'm going hunting," and disappear and come back,

aret	eco	elvtēt	wakken	hehcet,	uewvn	akwvkehcet	ratet
a·lít	*icó*	*iláti·t*	*wà·kkin*	*híhcit*	*óywan*	*akwakíhcit*	*lâ·tit*[862]
and was around	deer	dead	lying	he saw	water	he put in in water	and came back

and [on one trip] he found a dead deer and put it in water and started back.

rvlahket	liket	heleswv	hayet	sēyvfastet	aret,
'laláhkit	*lèykit*	*'hilíswa*	*ha·yít*	*si·yáfa·stit*	*a·lít*
got there	sat down	medicine	he made	used the med.	was around

When he got back, he sat down and made medicine and went around using it:

"Eco	lēcet	omvkvntis	yvhikvkat,	estenhoktvlwv
icó	*li·cít*	*o·makánteys*	*yahaykakâ·t*	*istinhoktálwa*
deer	to kill	did	he sang	one's mother-in-law

"When one sings to kill deer, one's mother-in-law

ayvhikēn	omvkvntok	aret	omin os,"	maken,
á·yahayki·n[863]	*o·makánto·k*	*a·lít*	*o·méyn ó·ⁿs*	*ma·kín*
she was singing	is supposed to be	around	I am	he said

is supposed to sing too," he said.

"Estonhkoto	ayvhikvkēto"	enhoktvlwv	kihcen,
*istónhko·to·^*	*á·yahaykakí·to·^*[ii]	*inhoktálwa*	*kéyhcin*[864]
it's all right	I'll sing, too	his mother-in-law	she said

"Well if that's true, I can sing too," his mother-in-law told him,

---

[i] Omitted from written form: *móhmin hatâm* 'then another'. (VIII:134)

[ii] Women's speech *á·yaheykaki·to·^* = men's speech *á·yaheykakí·s cey^*.

heleswv	hayvranat	'metetahket	liket	"Hę̄cį,	hę̄cį,"	maken,
'hilíswa	*há·yala·nâ·t*	*'mititáhkit*	*lêykit*	*hí·ⁿceyⁿ*[i]	*hí·ⁿceyⁿ*	*ma·kín*
med.	he will make	got ready	sat down			he said

and when he was ready to make medicine, he sat down and said, "I see, I see,"

enhoktvlwvo		"Hę̄cį,	hę̄cį"	maken,
inhoktálwaw		*hí·ⁿcéyⁿ*[ii]	*hí·ⁿcéyⁿ*	*ma·kín*
his mother-in-law, too				she said

and his mother-in-law also said, "I see, I see,"

uewv	akpofiket	sēyokkohset,		nocen	hvyatkof,
óywa	*akpo·fáykit*	*si·yokkóhsit*		*nô·cin*	*haya·tkô·f*
water	he blew into (water)	washed his face with it		he slept	when day came

and he blew into the medicine, washed with it, and slept, and in the morning,

ayet	eco	enokkē	elvtē	rēset	res vlaket	torofen,
â·yit[865]	*icó*	*inókki·*	*iláti·*	*lî·sit*	*'lisalâ·kit*	*tolo·fín*[866]
he went	deer	sick	and dead	he got	came back with it	he skinned it

he went and got the sick dead deer and brought it back and was skinning it.

"Ecot	oklanē	os"	enhoktvlwvt	kicen,
icót	*oklá·ni·*	*ô·ⁿs*	*inhoktálwat*	*keycín*
deer	yellowish	is	his mother-in-law	she said

His mother-in-law told him, "The deer looks kind of yellow."

"Mahketskvs.	Vmmvtvlkvnts,		vmmvtvlkvnts"	makvtēs.
máhkíckas	*ámmatalkánc*		*ámmatalkánc*[867]	*ma·katí·s*
Don't say that	(if you do) I can't find any more			he said

"Don't say that! That's the best I could do," he said.

Mahokvnts.
má·ho·kánc.
That's what they say.
It was told.

---

[i] (do, la). Possibly = *hi·céyn* 'I see'.

[ii] Sung in falsetto to imitate the mother-in-law's singing.

Rabbit and Man-Eater Hold a Contest (Cufe Oh-onvkv)

J. Hill (Haas VIII:141–166)[i]

Estepapvt hvsossv-fvccvn atet omvcoken estet kerrakof,
istipá·pat haso·ssafáccan a·tít o·macókin ístit kíɬa·kô·f
Lion was coming from the east, and when people learned of it,

"Vlvkekan hēŗēs" komēt vkerricaket fullet,
alákika·n hĭ·ⁿli·s kó·mi·t[868] *akiɬléyca·kít follít*
they went about thinking, "It would be good if he didn't come."

em etetakat cufen enhuehiket "Nake maketv cem vnvckēt omvntok.
imítita·kâ·t[869] *cofin inho:hâykit*[870] *nâ·ki ma·kitá cimanácki·t ô·mantó·k*
In preparation, Rabbit was called: "You always had a way with what to say.

Estepapv atvcokat vlvkekon, ētvn vyēcicetskvrēn puyacēs"
istipá·pa a·tacóka·t alákikon í·tan ayi·céycíckáɬi·n poyá·ci·s
Lion is on his way but has not arrived: We want you to send him somewhere else,"

kicaket omen, ervnrvpvranet ayet arof, vrēpvcoken pohhet
kéyca·kít o·mín iɬanlapála·nít a·yit a·lô·f ali·pacókin póhhit
they told [Rabbit]. When he went to meet [Lion], he heard [Lion] going about,

hēŗen hēcet, vketēcan este-fune pvkvfvkvtē ētakkayet aret omen hehcet
hĭ·ⁿlin hi·cít akíti·câ·n istifóni pakafakáti· i·takkâ·yit a·lít o·mín híhcit[871]
and as he examined him carefully, he saw that he had human bones strung together attached

ētvn vletiket aret fune towet vpoket senheciken
í·tan alitêykit a·lít fóni tó·wit apô·kit sinhicêykin
to himself. [Rabbit] started running in a different direction, found some old bones,

pvkahfet ētakkayet, estepapv ervnrapet ont
pakáhfit i·takkâ·yit istipá·pa iɬanlâ·pit[872] *ónt*
strung them together, and attached them to himself. Then he met Lion:

---

[i] Title: *cofi ohhonáka* 'rabbit story'.

"Naket estont ocaken atet ometska?" kicen, Estepapvt okat,
nâ·kit ístónt o·câ·kin â·tit[873] *o·micka·^ keycín istipá·pat o·kâ·t*
"Why have you come?" [Rabbit] asked. Lion answered,

"Hvsossv-fvccv tat naket sekon hayit vtvyēt os.
haso·ssafáccata·t nâ·kit síkon ha·yéyt atáyi·t[874] *ô·ⁿs*
"I devoured everything to the east and have come.

Momis hoktąlusēt takliken wihkit atvyvnks" kicen,
mo·mêys hoktă·ⁿlosi·t taklêykin wéyhkeyt â·tayaŋks[875] *keycín*
But I left a little old lady there and came."

Cufet okat, "Vneu hvsaklatkv fvccv tat naket sekon hayit vtvyēt os.
cofit o·kâ·t aníw hasaklá·tka fáccata·t nâ·kit síkon ha·yéyt[876] *atáyi·t*[877] *ô·ⁿs*
Rabbit said, "I too devoured everything to the west and have come.

Momis hoktąlusēt takliken wihkit atvyvnks. Monkv naket sahsekos"
mo·mêys hoktă·ⁿlosi·t taklêykin wéyhkeyt â·tayaŋks[878] *môŋka nâ·kit sáhsiko·s*
But I left a little old lady there and came. So there is nothing at all,"

kihcen kaken, "Momis wvhvlv-fvccv tvlkusan nake hēckis omētok:
kéyhcin kâ·kin mo·mêys wahalafácca tálkosa·n nâ·ki hi·ckêys o·mí·to·k
he said, and they sat. "But it could be things could be found to the south:

Min vhoyvkvrēs" Cufet kicen kaket on okat,
mèyn ahóyakáli·s cofít keycín kâ·kit ó·n o·kâ·t
let's go there," Rabbit said, and as they sat, he said,

"Vhoyvranvkat tvlket omētis holvnehpet welaket omeyvrēs.
ahóyała·nakâ·t tâlkit o·mí·teys holaníhpit wila·kít omíyáli·s
"We really have to go, but let's relieve ourselves first.

Tentakhakuset mosolet kaket omeyvrēs" kihcen,
tintakhá·kosit[879] *mosô·lit kâ·kit omiyáli·s kéyhcin*
Let's sit side by side with our eyes closed tightly," he said,

Estepapv tat mosolet liken, "Vm etetakof, 'Tokvs' mahkin
istipá·pata·t mosô·lit lêykin amítita·kô·f[880] *tó·kas*[881] *máhkeyn*
and Lion sat with his eyes closed tightly. "When I'm ready, I'll say 'Now!'

tashokeyvrēs" kicet, estepapv enaken cawet
ta·shokiyáli·s keycít istipá·pa inâ·kin ca·wít
and we'll both jump," [Rabbit] said, and then he took the lion's waste

cufet likvtēt vpoyehpet enaken estepapvn likat elecvn em vpohyet
cofit leykati·t[882] *apo·yíhpit inâ·kin istipá·pan lêyka·t ilícan imapóhyit*
and put it where the rabbit had sat, and then he placed his own waste underneath where the

"Tokvs" kihcen tashohken, Estepapv renayan likvtē tat
tó·kas[883] *kéyhcin ta·shóhkin istipá·pa linâ·ya·n leykati·ta·t*[884]
lion was sitting and said, "Now!" and they jumped. When Lion opened his eyes,

pvhe telekmicvkvtē cerēhusēt vpoken hehcet "Cvmomuset omekvntis.
pahí tilikmeycakáti· cili·hosi·t apô·kin híhcit camô·mosit omíkantêys
where he'd been sitting he saw grass crushed up in little pellets: "I didn't used to be like

Vnnettv vwolacoks ci," Estepapvt maken,
annittawò·lacokscey[^885] *istipá·pat ma·kín*
that. My time is near," Lion said.

Cufe likvtēn estefune wokocke vpeswv neha 'seteyvmkē vpoken
cofi leykati·n[886] *istifóni wokócki apíswa nihá· 'sitiyámki·t apô·kin*
Where Rabbit had sat there were crushed human bones mixed with meat grease.

Cufe tat "Vntat hiyomēt estofis vm monkvt omēpvnts" makvtēs.
cofíta·t ánta·t hayyó·mi·t istô·feys ammóŋkat omi·panc ma·kati·s
"This is the way I've always been," Rabbit said.

Mohmen wvhvlv-fvccv vhoyet welaken
móhmin wahalafácca aho·yít wila·kín
Then as they were going to the south, [Rabbit] asked Lion,

"Cenocat, nak makēt cenocvntē?" kicet estepapvn em pohen
cino·câ·t nâ·k ma·kí·t cino·canti·[^887] *keycít istipá·pan impo·hín*
"What do you say when you sleep?"

"'Rvkvm' makin omat hērē cvnocat okvyvnts" kicen vhoyen,
łakám ma·kéyn o·mâ·t hĭⁿli· cano·câ·t o·kayánc keycín aho·yin
"If I say 'Tha-kam,' I am sleeping really well," he said, and they went.

"Eto Estohtulkv-hvccen nochoyeyvrēs" maket Cufe tat aren,
itó istohtolkaháccin nochoyiyáli·s ma·kít cofíta·t a·lín
"We will sleep at Tree-Falling-On-You Creek," Rabbit said, going about,

vhoyen yạfkusē haken, hvcce wakkēn rorhoyet oman,
aho·yín yă·ⁿfkosi· hâ·kin[888] *hácci wákki·n łółho·yít o·mâ·n*
and as they went, it was getting late. As they came to the river,

eto-talet tulkvranusēt hueren hehcet "Heyvn nochoyvkvrēs" kicen,
itotá·lit tolkałá·nosi·t hôyłin híhcit hiyán nochoyákáli·s keycín
they saw an unsteady dead tree standing there and said, "Let's sleep here,"

fekhonnaket omen, "Etot estohtulkē vlkē omēs mahokvnts cē.
fikhonnâ·kit[889] *o·mín itót istohtôlki· álki·t ô·mi·s má·ho·kánc ci·^*
and stopped. "They used to say a tree always falls on you [here].

Estomvrēs" kicet, "Eto-tale huerat tempen yvn nochoyepvkvrēs" kihcen,
istó·máłi·s keycít itotá·li hôyła·t tímpin yan nochoyípakáli·s kéyhcin
We'll see what happens," he said. "Let's sleep by the dead tree," he said.

wakhoken, Estepapv tat "Rvkvm" maket wakken, eto-tale vhepahket
wakhô·kin istipá·pata·t lakám ma·kít wâ·kkin itotá·li ahipáhkit
Lying there together, Lion [began] saying "Tha-kam!" and [Rabbit] pushed the dead tree,

ra ohtohlet, "Ạeh hvha, hiyomēt omēs mahokvnton okēpvyis os ci" maket
ła·ʔohtóhlit ăyⁿh haha·^ háyyo·mí·t ô·mi·s má·ho·kánton oki·payêys ó·ⁿscây ma·kít
making it fall on him: "Oh my, that's what I meant, that's the way they said it would be,"

cufe tat aret wvkiken hvyatken vhoyet omen,
cofíta·t a·łít wakêykin hayâ·tkin aho·yít o·mín
[Rabbit] said and went to bed. In the morning they started out:

"Estohfokakv-hvccen ernochoyeyvrēs" kicen vhoyen yạfkusē haken,
istohfoka·kaháccin iłnochoyiyáli·s keycín aho·yín yă·ⁿfkosi· hâ·kin[890]
"We will sleep at Dust-On-You Creek," he said, and in the late evening,

hvcce wakkēn rorhoyen, "Yvn nochoyvkvrēs" kicet fekhonnen,
hácci wákki·n łołhô·yin yan nochoyákáli·s keycít fikhônnin
they reached the river. "Let's sleep here," [Rabbit] said, and coming to a stop,

totkvo tēcet 'to-taluce tat sulkēn totkvn ohpvlaten, takkaken,
tó·tkaw tî·cit[891] *'tota·locíta·t sólki·n tó·tkan ohpalâ·tin*[892] *takkâ·kin*
he lit a fire and threw a bunch of little dried limbs on it. As they sat,

"Heyv hvcce vfopke nocvkat, estohfokake vlkēt omēs mahokvnts.
hiyá hácci afó·pki no·cakâ·t istohfoká·ki álki·t ô·mi·s má·ho·kánc
he said, "When you sleep here at the river's edge, you always get dusted, they used to say.

Estomepvranēs cē" kicen takkaket oman, eto-hvrpen hopoyet
isto·mipála·ní·s ci·^ keycín takkâ·kit o·mâ·n itohálpin hopô·yit[893]
I wonder what will happen," [Rabbit] said, and as they sat, he found some tree bark

'mvpe ocēn hayet omen, "Estomēcvranet ontska?" kicet estepapvt em pohen,
mápi ó·ci·n ha·yít o·mín istomí·cala·nít óncka·^ keycít istipá·pat ímpo·hín
and made a handle for it: "What are you going to do with it?" Lion asked him.

"Hvccet perron estiketvt oman, perro eskafkvt sekon arvkēt omētvnken
háccit píłłon isteykitát ô·ma·n píłło iská·fkat sikon a·laki·t o·mí·taŋkín
"You cross the river in a boat, but there have been times when there was no boat paddle,

hayit omis" kicen, wakhoken, Estepapv tat 'Rvkvm' maket entakwakken,
ha·yéyt o·méys keycín wakhô·kin[894] *istipá·pata·t łakám ma·kít intakwâ·kkin*
so I'm making one," he said. Lying there together, Lion [began] saying, "Tha-kam!"

cufet perro eskafkv hayē wvkēcvtē ra ehset, ēsson estakkehfet, estepapvn ohfokahyen,
cofit píłło iská·fka há·yi· wakî·cati· ła·ʔíhsit í·sson istakkíhfit istipá·pan ohfokáhyin
and Rabbit got the paddle he had made, scooped up some ashes, and threw them on the lion,

atasiket, "Cēmet cvmomēcet ometskes kont omis" kihcet, assēcen,
a·ta·sêykit cí·mit camómi·cít o·míckis[895] *kônt o·méys kéyhcit á·ssi·cín*
who jumped up: "I think you're the one who did this to me," he said and chased him.

hvccen em etohtasken a em etohtaskof,
háccin imitóhta·skín a·ʔimitóhta·skô·f
[Rabbit] jumped across the river, and when [Lion] jumped across,

rem pvcēsset ra em etohtasket em ayen 'svhoyen
łimpaci·ssít ła·ʔimitóhta·skít ima·yín sáho·yin
[Rabbit] dodged him and jumped back across, and as they went [back and forth],

Cufet okat, "Hvcce rakkvntǫ, Hvcce rakkvntǫ, Hvcce rakkvntǫ" maken
cofit o·kâ·t hácci ła·kkanto·ⁿʔ´ hácci ła·kkanto·ⁿʔ´ hácci ła·kkantó·ⁿʔ´ ma·kín
Rabbit would say, "Great River, Great River, Great River,"

ra etohtaskēpen, hvccet enrvkiken
ła·ʔitohta·skî·pin[896] *háccit inlakâykin*
and as he jumped back across, the river became very large,

estepapv hvccen ra tikeko mahvtēt ont,
istipá·pa háccin ła·teykiko·má·hati·t[897] *ònt*
and the lion could never cross back over.

yv otē ofv estepapv sekot omēs mahokvnts.
ya otí· ó·fa istipá·pa síkot o·mí·s má·ho·kánc.
So on this island [or this continent] there are no lions, it's been said.

Rabbit and the Tar-Baby

J. Hill (Haas XV:3–21)

Cufet aret omat, tvlako essetapho omakat vhockē ohocan ohcēyet
cofit a·łít o·mâ·t talá·ko issitá·pho o·mâ·ka·t ahócki· o·hô·ca·n óhci·yit
Rabbit was going around. He would go in where cabbage and beans were planted,

estempapet aret omat, nene hayēt omen,
istímpa·pít a·łít o·mâ·t niní há·yi·t ô·min
and as he went around eating people's things, he would make paths.

senhehcet estvhaken kolowvn eshahyet, ennenen emohhuerihocen,
sinhíhcit istahá·kin kolówan isháhyit inninín imohhoyleyhò·cin[898]
They discovered this, made a doll out of tar, and stood it in his path.

noksetv komē ayē arat, estvhaken 'rvhoyiret,
noksitá kó·mi· a·yi· a·lâ·t istahá·kin 'lahoyêylit
When he was going about trying to sneak in, he came upon the doll:

"Vmvkuekvs!" kican, nekēyekot omen,
amapóykas keycâ·n niki·yikot o·mín
"Move from me!" he said, but it didn't move.

"Vmvkuekvs! kont okis! Vkueketskekon omat, cenvfkarēs," kicet oman,
amakóykas kônt o·káys akóykíckikon o·mâ·t cináʃká·li·s keycít o·mâ·n
"Move from me, I say! If you don't move, I will hit you," he said,

nekēyepekon, nafkan, Cufe enket estvhaken vlokpehpen hueret,
niki·yipíkon nâ·fka·n[899] coʃí íŋkit istahá·kin alokpíhpin hôylit
but it didn't move. After he hit it, Rabbit stood there with his paw stuck to the doll.

"Cvwikvs!" kicet omis, hvlvtēpet omen,
cawéykas keycít o·mèys halatî·pit o·mín
"Let go of me!" he said, but it held on.

"Cvwiketskekon omat, cvnke hvmkan escenvfkarēs!" kicet oman, wikekon,
cawéykíckikon o·mâ·t cáŋki hámka·n iscináʃká·li·s keycít o·mâ·n wéykikon
"If you don't let go of me, I'll hit you with my other paw!" he said, but it didn't let go.

enke hvmkat esnafkan, enke tat estvhaken vlokpehpen,
íŋki hámka·t isnâ·fka·n[900] iŋkita·t[901] istahá·kin alokpíhpin
When he hit it with his other paw, that paw stuck to the doll.

"Cvhvlatat cvwikvs! Wiketskekon omat, cvlen ohmit ecohrefkarēs" kican,
cahalâ·ta·t cawéykas wéykíckikon o·mâ·t calin óhmeyt icohłíʃká·li·s keycâ·n
"Let go of me! If you don't quit, I'll kick you with my foot!" he said,

hvlatēpē monken, ohrēfkan, Cufe ele tat estvhaken vlokpehpen,
hala·tî·pi· móŋkin ohli·fka·n[902] coʃí ilíta·t istahá·kin alokpíhpin
but he still held him. After he kicked him, Rabbit's foot stuck to the doll.

"Cvwikvs!" kicet,
cawéykas keycít
"Let go of me!" he said.

"Cvwiketskeko tayen omat, cvle hvmken ohmit ecohrefkarēs" mahket,
cawéykíckiko· tà·yin o·mâ·t calí hámkin óhmeyt icohłíʃká·li·s máhkit
"If you don't let go of me, I'll kick you with my other foot!" he said.

Ohrēfkan mvo vlokipen vliket,
ohlî·fka·n maw' alokêypin alêykit
After he kicked him, that one stuck too, and he sat by it.

"Cvwikvs! Cvhvlatat wiketskekon omat,
cawéykas cahalâ·ta·t wéykíckikon o·mâ·t
"Let go of me! If you don't quit holding onto me,

cvkvn ohmit ececakharēs!" kihcet, vcakhan, mvo vlokipen,
cakán óhmeyt ìcicákhá·li·s kéyhcit acâ·kha·n[903] *maw' alokêypin*
I'll butt you with my head!" he said. After he butted him, that stuck too.

"Cvwiketskeko tayen omat, cvnuten ohmit ecekkarēs!" kihcet,
cawéykíckiko· tâ·yin o·mâ·t canótin óhmeyt icíkká·li·s kéyhcit
"If you won't let go of me, I'll bite you with my teeth!" he said.

Akkan, enuteu vlokpēpen vliken.
â·kka·n inótiw alokpî·pin alêykin
After he bit him, his teeth got stuck too, and he sat by it.

Hvthvyvtke rasehset, uelekhen ohkalet, copahket,
hathayátki ła·síhsit oylíkhin óhka·lít[904] *copáhkit*
In the morning they came to get him; they poured warm water on him, peeled him off,

vwvnayet, uemorken vkvlvranet kihocen,
awána·yít[905] *oymó·łkin akálała·nít kéyho·cín*
tied him up, and were going to pour boiling water on him, they said.

uewv morkvranē haken, Cufe likof, yvhvt hēcet ont
óywa mo·łkałá·ni· ha·kín[906] *cofí lêyko·f yahát hî·cit ónt*
The water was about to boil. While Rabbit was sitting, Wolf saw him.

"Kot! Vnhesse! Naket estomen cemvkerrickvt vhopvnkosē omen liketska?" yvhvt kicen,
kot anhíssi^ nâ·kit ísto·mín cimakiłłéyckat ahopánkosi· ô·min lêykícka·^ yahát keycín
"Oh, my friend! Why are you sitting there so wretchedly?" Wolf asked.

"'Vsi sokhvtēhvke vtehkan lokvs!' cvkihocet omen, mv omat vnhompetv tokepekok.
asêy sokhati·hakí atíhka·n[907] *lokás cakéyho·cít o·mín ma ô·ma·t anhompitá to·kipíko·k*
"They told me to eat up all those barrows in there, but that's not my kind of food, so

Vnhẹrē sekot likit omis," maket, Cufe liket:
anhĭ·ⁿłi· síkot lêykeyt o·méys ma·kít cofí lêykit
not feeling well, I'm sitting down," he said. Rabbit sat:

"Centawv? Mv omat cenhompetvt on omat, lokēpetskis omēs," yvhvn kicen,
cínta·wá^ ma ô·ma·t cinhompitát ô·n o·mâ·t loki·píckeys[908] *o·mí·s yahán keycín*
"What about you? If that is your kind of food, you can eat it up," he told the wolf.

Yvhvt okat, "Mv omat vnhompetvt onkv, lokvranvyat tvlkos," maket omen,
yahát o·kâ·t ma ô·ma·t anhompitát ôŋka[i] *lokála·nayâ·t tǎlⁿkos ma·kít o·mín*
Wolf said, "That is my kind of food, so it is certain that I will eat it up," he said.

"Mon omat, cvwvnakan vnrecohpetsken, cēmen ecewvnayin,
mô·n o·mâ·t cawanâ·ka·n anɬicóhpíckin cí·min iciwanâ·yeyn[909]
"Well if that's the case, you untie me where I'm tied up, and I'll tie you up.

Liketsken, vyēpin, "Tokvs" mahoken omat, hēren hompepvccvs," cufet kicen,
lêykíckin ayî·peyn tókas má·ho·kín o·mâ·t hĭ·ⁿlin hompipáccas cofít keycín
You sit down, and after I leave, when they say "Now!" you will eat really well," Rabbit said.

Yvhvt 'mvkvsahmet enrecohpen, Cufe vyēpof, uewv morket omen,
yahát 'makasáhmit inɬicóhpin cofí ayi·pô·f óywa mô·ɬkit[910] *o·mín*
Wolf agreed and untied him. When Rabbit left, the water was boiling.

Cufen vkvlvranet sohhvpēhoyan, yvhvt vwvnvkēt liken hehcet:
cofín akálaɬa·nít sohhapí·ho·yâ·n yahát awanakí·t lêykin híhcit
When they went up to pour it on Rabbit, they saw Wolf sitting there tied up:

"'Mvkerrēt omat, nerēn aret nokset omvnkekv, ēemvrahkuecēt
'makíɬɬi·t ô·ma·t niɬí·n a·ɬít no·ksít o·máŋkika i·imaɬahkóyci·t[911]
"Since he is so clever, and sneaks about stealing at night, he has transformed himself

likest" kihcet uemorken yvhvn vkvlhoyen,
léykíst kéyhcit oymó·ɬkin yahán akálho·yín
and is sitting there," they said and poured boiling water on Wolf.

tasket aret, eswvnakvn tahcet, lētkvtet, rofkē haket arvtētot.
ta·skít a·ɬít iswaná·kan táhcit lî·tkatit lo·fkí· hâ·kit a·latí·tot
He jumped about, broke the rope, ran off, and went about bald.

---

[i] *ôŋka = ô·mika.*

'Toceskvn wakkēpen, Cufe hehcet,
'tocískan wakkĭ·ⁿpin cofí híhcit
He was just lying for a long time at the foot of a tree when Rabbit saw him;

vyopiket, etokvckocen ēset, hvsnērkvn senhosken,
ayo·pâykit itokackocín î·sit[912] *hasní·łkan sínho·skín*
he slipped up on him, took a twig, and scratched his testicles with it.

ahēcan, Cufet ohmvtet, lētken
á·hi·câ·n cofít óhmatit li·tkín
When he looked around, [he saw] it was Rabbit. [Rabbit] ran:

"Cent vmvkērret omvnket aret ometskes" kihcet, yvhvt assehcen,
cínt amakî·łlit ô·maŋkit a·łít o·míckis[913] *kéyhcit yahát a·ssíhcin*
"You were the one who tricked me," Wolf said and chased him.

lētket, empvcēsset, emayen, sayosvmmvlken,
li·tkít ímpaci·ssít ima·yín sâ·yosámmálkin
[Rabbit] ran and dodged him and got away from him. This went on for some time. He went

eto hvokēt huervten cehyen: "Aossvs!" kican, aemosseko tayet omen,
itó háwki·t hòylatin cíhyin a·óssas keycâ·n a·imóssiko· tâ·yit o·mín
into a hollow tree standing there: "Come out!" Wolf said, but he wouldn't come out.

arof, Opvt ohliket omen,
a·lô·f opát ohlêykit o·mín
When he was going about, Owl was sitting there.

"Vm vhecicetsken, pocuswvn hopoyvranis," yvhvt kicen,
amahicêycíckin[914] *pocóswan hopóyała·néys yahát keycín*
"You watch him for me. I'm going to look for an axe," Wolf said.

"Cem vhecicarēs," Opv maken,
cimahicéycá·li·s opá[915] *ma·kín*
"I'll watch him for you," Owl said.

"Hēren vhecicet ometskvrēs. Cem vkeriyē osiyac," kicen,
hĭ·ⁿłin ahicêycit[916] *omíckáli·s cimakilèyyi· osâyyá·c keycín*
"You must watch him really well. He must not get out by tricking you," he said.

"Ossē estomis ahyekos. 'Yecēyicarēs" maken,
o·ssí· istô·meys áhyikos 'yici·yéycá·li·s ma·kín
"Even if he gets out, he won't get away. I'll make him go back in," he said.

Enwihket ayof, aatet:
inwéyhkit a·yô·f a·â·tit[917]
When [Wolf] had left him and gone, [Owl] came up:

"Avm vnvtakset, hēren cvhēcet liket ontsken, kaket omvkēts,"
a·amanatâ·ksit[918] *hǐ·ⁿlin cahi·cit lêykit ónckin kâ·kit omáki·c*
"Look up at me, and you'll be able to sit and see me really well. Let's sit down,"

kicen, Opv tat ohhayet, mvnvtakset liken,
keycín opáta·t ohhâ·yit[919] *'manatâ·ksit lêykin*
[Rabbit] said. Owl went up to him and sat looking up at him.

Cufe tat eto ofvn hosket, 'tolekwen tofapet,
cofíta·t itó ó·fan ho·skít 'tolíkwin tofa·pít[920]
Rabbit scratched inside the tree, crumbled up rotten wood bits,

opv eturwvn aemaktehhen, tasket, holanet,
opá itólwan a·imaktíhhin ta·skít hola·nit
and dropped them in Owl's eyes. [Owl] was jumping, pooping,

pvlpaket vrēpen, osiyet vyēpen, likof,
pálpa·kít ali·ⁿpin osêyyit ayî·pin lêyko·f
and rolling all over. [Rabbit] got out and left. While [Owl] was sitting there,

'rvlahket: "Lika?" kicen,
'laláhkit lêyka·^ keycín.
[Wolf] came back: "Is he there?" he asked.

"Likvcoks. Aosiyen, hvlahtin, hērē mahen tenceyvlhohyēn
lêykacóks a·osêyyin haláhteyn hǐ·ⁿli· mâ·hin tinciyalhóhyi·n
"He must be there. He came out, I grabbed him, and we struggled together really hard.

Yēcehyekv, likēs," maken.
yi·cíhyika lêyki·s ma·kín
He went back in there, so he's there," he said.

Eto tat casket, hvokat mohrolakan:
itóta·t ca·skít háwka·t mohłolâ·ka·n
[Wolf] chopped down the tree and opened up the hole:

"Sekon, vyepvtēn oketskes?!" kicen,
sikó·n ayípati·n o·kíckis keycín
"He's not there. You mean he's gone?!" he said.

"Aosiyen, hvlatin, vnceyvllen, tewikin,
a·osêyyin halâ·teyn[921] *ancíyallín tíweykéyn*
"He came out, I grabbed him, he was struggling against me, and I was wrestling him down,

holanet mont 'yecehyat os," Opvt maken.
holá·nit mônt 'yicíhya·t ó·ⁿs opát ma·kín
he pooped, then he went in there," Owl said.

"Heyv cufe holanat oma?" Yvhvt kicen,
hiyá cofî holâ·na·t ô·ma·^ yahát keycín
"Is this where Rabbit crapped?" Wolf asked.

"Mvt os," maken,
mat ô·ⁿs ma·kín
"That's it," he said.

"Tayēpēs. Welvnwv ennekricin omat, elepvrēs," kicen,
ta·yî·pi·s wilánwa inniklêyceyn[922] *o·mâ·t ilípáli·s keycín*
"That's enough. If I burn his droppings, he will die," he said.

"Vntis omvyis okin, cvlehcetskēt on..." maken,
ánteys ô·mayeys o·kéyn calíhcícki·t ó·n ma·kín
"It might even have been me, I mean. You might kill me..." [Owl] said.

"Holanet vr̨ecken vyēpēn oketskestv?!" kicen,
hola·nít ałı̆·ⁿckin ayî·pi·n o·kíckísta[923] *keycín*
"You mean to say you were crapping all over the place, and he got away?!" he asked.

"Q" makvtēs, mahokvnts.
ǒ`ⁿ· ma·katí·s má·ho·kánc
"Oooh," he said, they used to say.

Rabbit Deceives Some Gophers

J. Hill (Haas XV:23–29)

Hvcetekvt Cufen empunayet okat,
hacitikát[924] *cofín ímpona·yít o·kâ·t*
Gopher was talking to Rabbit saying:

"Vtotkē nake hayē ocēpeyat pum vhopvnhuecē arat,
ato·tkí· nâ·ki ha·yí· o·cî·piya·t pomahopánhoycí· a·lâ·t
"Those things which we have made by working are being destroyed in going about:

wikēpetskan hḛrēs. Cuko hayē ohranēpeyat,
weykî·pícka·n hĭ·ⁿłi·s cokó ha·yí· ohłá·ni·piyâ·t
it would be good if you ceased. When we are making a house and roofing it,

pum ohhahkopanet, punlekafet, pum ohhvholwvyēcē arat, wikepvccvs.
pomohháhkopa·nít ponlíka·fít[925] *pomohhahólwayi·cí· a·lâ·t weykipáccas*
you must cease going around playing on it, tearing it down, and spoiling it.

Yvn vtēkusen wiketskekon omat, cenherekis ohcētok.
yan atî·kosin |||wéykíckikon o·mâ·t|||[926] *cinhiłíkeys óhci·to·k*
If you don't cease right now, it might not be good for you.

Pum ohholanē aretskat, nake onko mḁhen puhayet ontskekv,
pomóhhola·ní· a·lícka·t nâ·ki oŋkomă·ⁿhin[927] *poha·yít ónckika*
When you go about defecating on it, you are making nothing of us, so

puyacekot os," kicen, Cufet okat,
|||poyá·cikot ó·ⁿs||| keycín cofít o·kâ·t
we don't want that," he said. Rabbit said,

"Mon omat sossepaks! Ētvn fullet, cuko hayēpet herḁkēn ocēt fullepaks.
mô·n o·mâ·t[928] *sossipáks í·tan follít cokó há·yi·pít hiłă·ⁿki·n*[929] *ó·ci·t follipáks*
"Well, you all get out! Go somewhere else, go about making your fine house.

Heyv ēkvnv tat cvnaken omēpis. 'Svyeparēs. Sossepaks!" kihcet, vyēpvtētot.
|||hiyá i·kanáta·t||| canâ·kin omî·peys[930] *'sayipá·li·s sossipáks kéyhcit ayî·pati·tot*
This land is mine. I will take it. You all get out!" he said and left.

Kowike entvlakfvkvn sulkēn opiyet, 'tecokcoret,
kowwêyki[i] intala·kfakán sólki·n opayyít[931] 'ticókco·lit[932]
[Then Rabbit] twisted lots of quail's bean vines, and after knotting them together

cvpkē hayet, wvkēcet,
cápki· hâ·yit wakî·cit
and making it long, he laid it out.

"Tokvs. Vmetetaks. Ēkvnv 'svyepvranis. Sossepaks! Sossatskekon omat,
tókas amititâ·ks i·kaná 'sayipála·néys sossipáks |||sóssá·ckikon o·mâ·t|||
"Now I'm ready. I'm going to take the land. You all get out! If you all don't get out,

nake herekis cemohcvkētok, yvn vtēkusen sossepaks!" kicet, hvcetekv tat empunahyet,
nâ·ki hilíkeys cimóhcaki·to·k yan atî·kosin sossipáks" keycít hacitikáta·t imponáhyit[933]
there might be unpleasant things for you, so get out now!" he said, speaking to the gophers.

Tvlakfvkv hvlahtet, hvlattēcet sarof, kowikucet tvmēcet
tala·kfaká haláhtit halá·tti·cít[934] sa·lô·f kowwêykocit tami·cít
He took hold of the bean-vine, and when he was jerking it around, quails were flying;

hopvyēn wemhēken,
hopáyi·n wîmhi·kin
far away they were going "Wim!"

"Tokvs cv! Ēkvnv 'rvtēkat a vnkuekvcoks cv!" maket, tvlakfvkv hvlattēcē monken,
tókas ca^ i·kaná 'lati·ka·t |||a·áŋkoykacóks ca^||| ma·kít tala·kfaká halá·tti·ci·[935] môŋkin
"Now! The end of the land is moving toward me!" he said, still jerking on the bean-vine.

hvtvm vwolēn kowwikuce tvmēcvcoken, wemhēken,
hatâm awóli·n kowwêykoci tami·cacókin wîmhi·kin
Again close-by, it seemed quails were flying, going "Wim!"

"Tokvs cv! Ekvn-yoksv yvwolicvcoks cv!" maket, hvlattēcē monken,
tókas ca^ i·kanyóksa[936] |||yáwoleycacóks[937] ca^ ma·kít halá·tti·ci· môŋkin
"Now! The end of the land is getting closer!" he said, still jerking it.

---

[i] *kowwêyki intala·kfaká* = a kind of weed that gets tangled up and kinda trips you when you walk in it.

Hvcetekvt okat, "Kos! Yvn vtēkusen ēkvnv tat fekhonnicvs!
hacitikát o·kâ·t kos yan ati·kosin i·kanáta·t fikhonnéycas
Gopher said, "No! Make the land stop now!

Sahyetskvs! Yvn likēpen, ofv tat fullēpēt naken hayeyis,
sáhyíckas |||yan leyki·pin||| ó·fata·t fólli·pí·t nâ·kin ha·yiyêys
Don't take it! Let it sit there. We'll go around inside, and whatever we make,

ohharet estont komat pum ohhvrēpvccvs" kicvtēt omen,
óhha·lít istónt[938] kô·ma·t pomóhhali·páccas[939] keycatí·t ò·min
you can go around on it and do whatever you want," he said to him.

Hvcetekv ēkvnv telekmē cekhican, ohhahkopanet, ohpvlpaket,
hacitiká i·kaná tilíkmi· cíkheycâ·n ohháhkopa·nít[940] ohpálpa·kít
Then as Gopher was piling up fine earth, Rabbit was playing on it, rolling on it,

tvpēksusēn hayet, ohholanēt, cufe tat vrēpet omēs, mahokvnts.
tapi·ⁿksosi·n ha·yit óhhola·ní·t cofíta·t ali·pit o·mí·s[941] má·ho·kánc[i]
making it really flat, and going around crapping on it, they used to say.

Opossum Deceives Rabbit

J. Hill (Haas XV:31–33)

Svtvt emēttē lokcēn eshueren, sokhvhatkvt eshēcet
satát imi·ttí· lókci·n[942] ishóylin sokhahá·tkat ishî·cit
A persimmon tree was standing with some ripe fruit on it, and a opossum found it and

pvpēt vrēpen, Cufet em vlaket:
papí·t ali·ⁿpin cofít imalâ·kit
was going about eating it. Rabbit came along:

"Svtv alatken papvka?" kicen,
satá á·la·tkin pa·paká·^[943] keycín
"You're eating the persimmons that have fallen?" he asks.

---

[i] That's what Rabbit does today.

"Alatkuset omen papit omis," kicen,
á·la·tkosít o·mín pa·péyt[944] *o·méys keycín*
"I'm eating a few of the ones that have fallen," he says.

"Estomēcvkan alatkisa?" kicen,
istomi·cakâ·n á·la·tkêysa·^ keycín
"How do you make them fall?" Rabbit asks.

"Vsv ahvlwusan onvpvn raohhoyiret, estem omvlkuset lētkēt
asá a·hálwosa·n[945] *onápan ła·ohhoyêylit istimomǎlⁿkosit li·tkí·t*
"You stand up there on top of that little hill and run with all your might back downhill

raaktasket, vhopvyusē monkētan tasiket,
ła·ákta·skít[946] *ahopayósi· môŋki·ta·n*[947] *ta·sêykit*
and jump; while you're still a short distance away, jump,

svtvpe hvlwan estekvn esrahvkan,
satápi hǎlⁿwa·n istikán isłâ·haka·n[948]
and when you hit your head a little ways up the persimmon tree,

sulkē hēret apvlatken papet omvkis," kihcen,
sólki· hǐ·ⁿłiť[949] *á·pala·tkín pa·piť*[950] *o·makêys kéyhcin*
a large number fall off, and you eat them," he said.

Cufe tat ahyet, hvlwat osiyet, raohhuervtet, em omvlkvt lētket aktasiket,
cofíta·t áhyit hálwa·ť[951] *osêyyit ła·ohhôylatiť*[952] *imomálkat li·tkít akta·sêykit*
Rabbit went and got up high, he stood awhile, then ran downhill with all his might;

svtvpe hueran vwolicat tasiket,
satápi hôyla·n awóleycâ·t ta·sêykit
he got close to where the persimmon tree stood and jumped,

svtvpen ekvn esrahhet, ralatkat wononotkuset elehpen,
satápin ikán isłáhhit ła·lâ·tka·t wononô·tkosit[953] *iłíhpin*
hit his head against the persimmon tree, fell back down, shivered a little, and died.

Sokhvhatkvt okat, "Estemomehpēs komakkv.
sokhahá·tkat o·kâ·t istimo·míhpi·s kô·mákka
Opossum said, "I was afraid that it might happen.

Vrēpusis encenkepvkat, rapvlvtepusat, pvpēpuset omvkisen os," mahket vyēpvtēs.
ali̵·ⁿposeys incinkipáka·t la·palátipósa·t[954] *papi·posít o·makêysin*[955] *ó·ⁿs máhkit ayi·patí·s*
I just climb after them, throw them down, and eat them," he said and went away.

Bluejay and Towhee Attempt to Kill Rabbit

J. Hill (Haas XV:35–37)

Cohawēskvt tvsen etenakuȩcusēt, echustaken vpoyvkēt omvtētan,
coha·wí·skat[i] *tasín itina·kŏyⁿcosi·t ichostá·kin apo·yakí·t ô·mati·ta·n*
Towhee and Bluejay were really close to each other. They had all their children together,

uelvokēt em pvsaten, eshvkihhoket okat: Cohawēskv "wis wis" maken,
oylawkí·t impasâ·tin ishakáyhho·kít o·kâ·t coha·wí·ska |||*ways ways*||| *ma·kín*
and a flood killed them, and they were grieving. The towhee said, "ways ways."

tvset "tvsekayv tins tins" maket, welakof,
tasít |||*tasiká·ya teyns teyns*||| *ma·kít wila·kô·f*
The bluejay said, "tasikaya teyns teyns." When they were going about,

Cufet likvtet lētken, "Mvt hopuetake pompvsatet ont lētket omēs!
cofít lêykatit li·tkín mat hopoytá·ki pom pasâ·tit ónt li·tkít o·mí·s
Rabbit was sitting there and ran. "That one killed our children and is running away!

Elēcvkēts!" mahket, assēcahken,
ili·cakí·c máhkit a·ssi·cáhkin
Let's kill him!" they said and chased him.

ayet, etohvokēt wakken cehyet tekrolakkēt omvten,
a·yít itoháwki·t wâ·kkin cíhyit[956] *tikłolákki·t ô·matin*
He was going on and went in where there was a hollow log [hollow] clear through.

'teropotiyet, vyēpan hecvkekot,
'tiłopo·tâyyit ayî·pa·n[957] *hicákikot*
He passed through and went on, and they didn't see him.

---

[i] Hasn't seen *coha·wí·ska* in long time, not sure how looks but thinks it looks like towhee.

"Estomēcvkat elēcvkē tayehạ," maket, yv 'tohvoken pikēs kont,
istomi·caka·t ili·cakí·[958] *tá·yiha·(ⁿ)˙ ma·kít ya 'toháwkin pâyki·s kónt*
"How can we kill him?" they asked. Thinking he was inside the hollow tree,

vhecicēt kaket oket: "Mvhvoken 'mvhetēcvken omat, nokiret elēpēs.
ahicéyci·t[959] *kâ·kit o·kít 'maháwkin 'mahitî·cakin o·mâ·t nokêylit ili·pí·s*
they sat watching and said: "If we start a fire in the entrance of the log, he will burn and die.

Elekot yossen omat, hvlvteyvrēs," mahket, 'mvhetēcet emēhaket kaken,
ilíkot yo·ssín o·mâ·t halátiyáłi·s máhkit[960] *'mahitî·cit*[961] *imi·hâ·kit kâ·kin*
If he comes out alive, we'll catch him," they said and set it on fire, and they sat waiting.

Vcẹ̄wē haken, lakcvt 'tohvoke ofvn likvtet nēkret totkv ētkat ofvn
acì·ⁿwi· hâ·kin lákcat 'toháwki ó·fan lêykatit ni·kłít tó·tka i·tkâ·t ó·fan
After a long time, an acorn sitting inside the hollow tree was burning in the fire

"tvf" maken, pohahket: "Turnērkvt okē.
táf ma·kin poháhkit tolní·łkat[962] *o·kí·*
and went "taf!" They heard it: "It's his eyeballs making that noise.

Hị hị!" mahket afvckvkēt, cohawēskv, tvse 'tepakat vhoyēpvtēs.
|||hêyⁿ hêyⁿ||| máhkit a·fackakí·t coha·wi·ska tasí 'tipâ·ka·t ahóyi·patí·s
Hah-hah!" they said and were happy, and the towhee and the bluejay went off together.

The Wise Old Dog

J. Hill (Haas XV:91–99)

Yvhvt aret oman, efv mvnettvlket fullen eshēcet,
yahát a·lít o·mâ·n ifá 'manittâłkit follín ishì·cit
A wolf was roaming about, and he found some young dogs going around

empunayet em vkeriyet, mv efv mvnettvlken tepketv eyacet omis,
ímpona·yít imakiłêyyit ma ifá 'manittâłkin tipkitá iya·cít[963] *o·mêys*
and deceived them by talking to them. He wanted to whip those young dogs, but

cukon ohpefatkētan kērret ont, estomēcekot,
cokón óhpifa·tkí·ta·n kì·łłit ónt isto·mí·cikot
he knew they would run to the house, so he didn't do anything.

'mvkerrēt celayetvn komēt,
'makílli·t cila·yitán kó·mi·t[964]
He wanted to trick them and get hold of them.

"Mvnettvlket nvkvftvranēt makaket ont, 'Puncukopericvkepvrēn puyacētan onkv,
'manittâlkit nakáftala·ní·t[965] *má·ka·kít*[966] *ónt poncokopiłeycakípáłi·n poyá·ci·ta·n oŋká*
"The young [wolves] say they will have a meeting. 'We want them to visit us,

'rem onvyvkvs!' cvkicaket on, arit omis," yvhv vcule maket,
'łimonáyakas[967] *cakéyca·kít*[968] *ó·n a·łéyt o·méys yahá acóli ma·kít*
so go tell them!' they told me, and that's why I am here," the old wolf said.

"'Roricatskē tvlkusan hērēs. Mvnettvlke toyatskat etohkvlket,
'loléycá·cki· tăl^ʰkosa·n hǐ·^ⁿłi·s 'manittâlki tò·yá·cka·t itóhkalkít
"You all should be sure to go there. You young ones should get together,

etekerrēt fullatskan hērētan fullekot omatskētvnks," kihcet vyēpvtēton,
itikílli·t[969] *follá·cka·n hǐ·^ⁿłi·ta·n follikot*[970] *o·má·cki·táŋks kéyhcit ayì·pati·ton*[971]
get acquainted, and roam about, but you don't usually go," he said and went on.

efv mvnette tat, "Cukopervn pum pohvthoyvmken vpeyvranēs," maket,
ifá 'manittita·t cokopilán pompohathó·yamkín apíyała·ní·s ma·kít
The young dogs said, "They invited us to visit, so we are going."

efv vcolēt toskēt wakken, em onvyaken,
ifá acŏ·^ⁿli·t tó·ski·t wâ·kkin imónaya·kín
An old, mangy dog was lying there, and they told him.

"Estit okvthaks?" maken,
istêyt ô·kátha·ks ma·kín
"Who was saying that?" he asked.

"Yvhvt pum onayet, 'Mvnettvlket cenhuehkvkēs,' pukicvnks," kicaken,
yahát pomóna·yít 'manittâlkit cinhóyhkaki·s[972] *pokéycáŋks*[973] *kéyca·kín*
"The wolf was telling us. He told us, 'The young ones are calling you,'" they said.

"Ececakkvyvkarēs" 'fv-vcule maken,
icicakkayáká·li·s 'faʔacóli[974] *ma·kín*
"I will go with you," the old dog said.

"Hekos! Likvccvs! Mvnettvlke tvlkusēn okhoyvnks" kihcet, vpēyēpen,
hikós lêykáccas, 'manittâlki tâlkosi·n okhô·yáŋks[975] *kéyhcit api·yi·pín*
"No! You must stay! They said it was to be the young ones only," they said and left.

yopvn ayan, ēkvnv em melhoyvtē 'roricēpen,
yópan â·ya·n[976] *i·kaná immilhô·yati· 'loleycî·pin*
He went behind, and they arrived at the place they had indicated.

yopvn roret aliken,
yópan lô·lit a·lêykin
He got there after and sat down.

"Tokvs! Ascēyaks!" kihocen, mvnettvlke tat escehyen,
tókas a·sci·yaks kéyho·cín 'manittâlkita·t iscíhyin
"Now come in!," they told them, and the young ones went in.

vpaket cehyen, em akhotiyet,
apâ·kit cíhyin imakhotêyyit
He went in with them, and they closed the door.

"Tokvs! Onvyaks! Fullēpeyat aepohpahēcet eposse fullatskētvnkē
tókas onáyaks fólli·piyâ·t a·ipohpá·hi·cít ipo·ssí· follá·cki·taŋkí·
"Now! Admit it! When we were going around, it was you all who would whoop at us

cent omatskvten omat hiyoman onvyaks" kicet, yvhv vculvket vpokēpen,
cínt o·má·ckatin o·mâ·t hayyô·ma·n onáyaks keycít yahá acolakít apo·kî·pin
and go around chasing us, admit it now!" he said. The old wolves were sitting there,

naken makekot, efv-mvnette tat vpoken,
nâ·kin má·kikot ifamaníttita·t apô·kin
not saying anything. The young dogs sat there.

'Tepiket 'yefulhuecetvn kont okaken, efv vculet
'tipêykit 'yifolhoycitán kônt oka·kín ifá acólit
[The wolves] wanted to whip them and send them back, they said. The old dog said,

"Vnet omvyētvnks. Yv tat mvnettvkēt os. Naken maket fuliyekos.
anít o·mayi·táŋks[977] *yatâ·t*[978] *'manittakí·t ô·ⁿs nâ·kin ma·kít folêyyiko·s*
"It was I. These are all young ones. They never go about saying anything.

Vnet ecohpihkit, ecēssēcvkit,
anít icóhpayhkéyt icí·ssi·cakéyt
I was the one who was whooping at you and chasing you.

cehvce tis centacvkit omvyētvnks. Heyvn wakkes cehvce take," kicet,
cihácíteys cínta·cakéyt o·mayí·táŋks hiyán wâ·kkis cihácitá·ki keycít
I even used to cut off your tails. Here they are, your tails," he said.

yvhv hvce entvcvkvtēn ocēpvtet, aenfvnvficet likēpen,
yahá háci intacákati·n o·cî·patit a·infanáfeycít leykî·pin
He had cut off the wolves' tails, and he waved them and sat there.

efv mvnette tat tepkekot wihohken rawvtēs.
ifá 'maníttita·t típkikot weyhóhkin ła·watí·s
The young dogs weren't whipped, and they left and came home.

Story About Alligator, Beaver, Bird Clans

J. Hill (Hill II:30–35; Haas XVIII:31–79)

Mohmen Vlepvtv, Echaswv, Fuswv esyomat ēmē tat 'tenahvmketv etenfvccakvtēs maket
móhmin alipatá ichá·swa fóswa isyô·ma·t i·mi·tá·t 'tina·hamkitá itinfácca·katí·s ma·kít
Now Alligator, Beaver, and Bird made an agreement among themselves to be kin, it is said:

"Este Vlepvtvlke, Echaswvlke, Fuswvlke esyomat etenahvmkē hakēt omakēs"
ísti alipatâlki icha·swâlki foswâlki isyô·ma·t itina·hámki· ha·kí·t omâ·ki·s
"The Alligator clan, Beaver clan, and Bird clan have became kin,"

maket okvnts, vculvke tat. Vlepvtv, Echaswv, Fuswv enahvmke etehayat hiyomēt omvtēs.
ma·kít o·kánc acolakíta·t alipatá ichá·swa fóswa ina·hámki (?) itíha·yâ·t hayyó·mi·t o·matí·s
they said, the elders said. This is how Alligator, Beaver, and Bird became kin.

Hvccet wakket oman uewv lvokēt ocēt omen
háccit wâ·kkit o·mâ·n óywa láwki·t ó·ci·t ô·min
There was a creek, and the water was very deep,

Echaswvt akliken Vlepvtvo matan akliken akkaket omvtētan
ichá·swat aklêykin alipatáw[979] *ma·tá·n aklêykin akkâ·kit o·matí·ta·n*
and Beaver and Alligator were both sitting in the same place, and after a while,

Vlepvtvt oket, "Vyepvs!" Echaswvn kicet omen,
alipatát o·kít ayípas ichá·swan keycít o·mín
Alligator told Beaver, "Leave!"

"Naket eston oketska?" kicen,
nâ·kit ístó·n o·kicka·^ keycín
"Why are you saying that?" [Beaver] asked,

"Naket estont omeko estomis vyepvs kont okis" Vlepvtvt maken,
nâ·kit ístónt omíko· istô·meys ayípas kônt o·kéys alipatát ma·kin
"Even if nothing's the matter, I just want you to go," Alligator said,

"Kos. Naken cekicvkot, naken cem vhopvnvkot,
kos nâ·kin cikéycako·t nâ·ki<n> cimahopánakot
"No. I've said nothing to you, I haven't damaged anything of yours,

cenaoricvkot oman oketskes" Echaswvt maken,
cina·ołêycakot o·mâ·n o·kíckis ichá·swat[980] ma·kín
and I haven't bothered you," Beaver said.

"Momēpē estomis vyepvs kont okis. Vyetskekon omat, nake herekis cemocē tayetok
mo·mí·pi· istô·meys ayípas kônt o·kêys ayíckikon o·mâ·t nâ·ki hiłíkeys cimo·ci· tâ·yito·k
"Even so, I want you to leave. If you don't go, something bad may happen to you:

Ossepvs. Uewv cvnaken omēpis estofis yvn aklikēparēs.
ossipás óywa canâ·kin omî·peys istô·feys yan akleykî·pá·li·s
get out, the water is mine, I will live here always.

Ahyet uewv ētvn hopoyepvs" kicof,
áhyit óywa (?) í·tan hopoyipás keycô·f
Go and find other water," he told him.

"Mon omat, cem ossarēs estofis yvn aklikēpvccvs" kihcet, Echaswv tat,
mo·n o·mâ·t cimóssá·li·s istô·feys[981] yan akleyki·páccas kéyhcit ichá·swata·t
"Well then, I'll get out, and you can stay in here forever," Beaver said,

uewv osiyet hvcce vrepv fvccvn ahyet, uewv sentackv-rakkon hahyen,
óywa osêyyit hácci alípa[982] fáccan áhyit óywa (?) sinta·ckałákkon háhyin
and he got out of the water and went upstream, built a big dam,

uewv tat lvokv-cvpkē estvmahet enheciken, mvn Echaswv tat aklikēpvtēs.
óywata·t lawkacápki· istamá·hit inhicêykin man ichá·swata·t akléyki·pati·s
obtained a great pool of water, and stayed there.

Mohmofvn fuswvt uewvn eyacaket Vlepvtvn rem oricet,
móhmo·fán fóswat óywan iya·câ·kit alipatán 'limołêycit
At that time the birds needed water and went to Alligator's [place]:

"Uewvn cem eskepetvn puyacēt fullēt omēs maket,
óywan cimiskipítan poyá·ci·t follí·t o·mí·s ma·kít
"We are here because we'd like to drink your water," they said,

em pohaket oman,
impóha·kít o·mâ·n
and when they asked him, [he said,]

"Uewv esketv cemvkvyē tayat ocaks. Ētvn hopoyēt ēsket fullēt omaks.
óywa (?) iskitá (?) cimákayi· tâ·ya·t ó·caks í·tan hopóyi i·skit follí·t omáks
"I do not have any drinking water I can give you. Go find somewhere else to drink.

Yv uewv tat cvnaken omēpis" maket, em encaken,
ya (?) óywata·t canâ·kin[983] *omî·peys ma·kít imínca·kin*
This water is mine," he said, being stingy toward them,

fuswv fullet Echaswvn 'rem oricet
fóswa follít ichá·swan 'limolêycit
and the birds went to Beaver's [place].

"Uewv esketvn Vlepvtvn empoheyan, pum encakēton fullēt omēs.
óywa iskitán alipatán ímpo·hiyâ·n pomincá·ki·ton follí·t o·mí·s
"We're here because we asked Alligator for a drink of water, and he was stingy with us.

Uewv tat cēmet ocēpetsket on hēcēt,
óywata·t cí·mit o·cî·píckit ó·n hi·cí·t
We see that you have water,

pum etektvnēcetsken cem eskēpēt fullet ometvn puyacēt cenyicēt omēs" kicaket ont,
pomitiktani·cícki<n>[984] *cimíski·pí·t follít omítan poyá·ci·t cinyêyci·t o·mí·s kéyca·kít ónt*
could you give us permission to drink? That is why we come to you," they said,

momet "Hiyomēn vkerricēt okēs. Pum vkvsahmetsken,
mo·mít hayyó·mi·n akiⱡⱡêyci·t o·kí·s pomakasáhmíckin
and, "This is what we are wondering. If you give us permission

uewvn cem eskēpēt fullēn omat, etenahvmkē toyēt vnokeckv, vrakkueckv etem ocet,
óywan cimíski·pi·t follí·n o·mâ·t itina·hámki· tô·yi·t[985] *anokícka aⱡakkóycka itimô·cit*
to drink your water any time, then we can be kin and have love and respect for one another,

fullēpvkan hēⱡrēs komeyēt fullēt omēs" fuswv tat makaken,
fólli·pakâ·n hĭ·ⁿli·s kó·miyi·t[986] *folli·t o·mí·s fóswata·t má·ka·kín*
and that is what we desire, that is the reason we're here," the birds said.

Echaswv vyoposket okat, "Mon omat hēⱡrē tis os.
ichá·swa ayópo·skít o·kâ·t mô·n o·mâ·t hĭ·ⁿli·teys ó·ⁿs
Beaver answered, saying, "Well then, that would be good.

Vnnvpasekot aklikin okatskekv, momen uewv sēyvnicvyē tayat senhoyvnusēn ocikv,
annapa·sikó·t aklêykeyn o·ká·ckika mo·mín óywa si·yanêycayi· tâ·ya·t sinhoyánosi·n ô·cáyka
I have no one and I stay here and I have more than enough water for my use,

estomomusen eskepatskē tayat ēsket fullepaks" maket, fuswvn etenfvciyen,
istô·mo·mosin iskipá·cki· tâ·ya·t i·skít follipáks ma·kít fóswan itinfacêyyin
so you may drink all you want," he said, and he made an agreement with the birds,

Echaswv, fuswv 'tepakat etenahvmken etehayakvtēs.
ichá·swa fóswa 'tipâ·ka·t <it>ina·hámkin itihá·ya·katí·s.
and Beaver and the birds became kin.

Mohmofvn Vlepvtv tat uewv emvkarpen aklikvtēs.
móhmo·fan alipatáta·t óywa imáka·ⱡpín[987] *ákleykatí·s*
Later Alligator's water began to dry up where he lived.

Aohfihnvtēn echaswvt sentvcēpekv, momē estomis Vlpvtv akkaren,
a·óhfeyhnatí·n ichá·swat sintacî·pika mo·mí· istô·meys alpatá ákka·lín
The beaver had blocked the water flow, but Alligator stayed there

uewv tat vkvrpemahēpen,
óywata·t akaⱡpimá·hi·pín[988]
until the water was almost completely dried up,

osiyet ahyet Echaswvn 'rem oret,
osêyyit[989] *áhyit ichá·swan 'limô·lit*
and then he got out and went to Beaver's [place]:

"Uewvt vm pokēpen ētv estomvko tayuset ont arit omis. Escemēyvnicēpit
óywat ampo·kî·pin í·ta istó·máko· tă·ⁿyosit ónt a·léyt o·méys iscimi·yanéyci·péyt
"My water is all gone, and I cannot do anything, so I've come. I would like to get in

aklikin akkakēpvkēs komvyēt arit omis" maket omen,
aklêykeyn akká·ki·pakí·s kó·mayi·t a·léyt o·méys ma·kít o·mín
and share your water and we can stay together is what I'm thinking," he said.

Echaswv vyoposket okat, "Hekos. Yefulkepvs. 'Estofis yvn aklikēparēs' maketsken,
ichá·swa ayópo·skít o·kâ·t híkos 'yifolkipás istô·feys yan akleykí·pá·li·s ma·kíckin
Beaver replied, "No. Go back. You said, 'I'll stay here forever,'

atvyvtēt onkv, matan akkvrēpvccvs. 'Estvn ahyvkos' maketskvtē kērretskētok vyepvs.
a·tayáti·t ôŋka ma·tá·n ákkali·páccas ístan áhyako·s ma·kíckati· kî·łłícki·to·k ayípas
so I came here, so stay in that water. Remember you said, 'I will not go anywhere,' so go.

Yvn akliket monkat akkaretsken omat,
yan aklêykit móŋka·t ákka·líckin o·mâ·t
If you stay in here,

nake herekis cem ocen ahretskētok: yefulkepvs" kicet oman,
nâ·ki hilíkeys cimo·cín áhłícki·to·k 'yifolkipás keycít o·mâ·n
something bad may happen to you; go back," he said.

"Kos. Naken cekihcvkos. Cenaorihcvkos.
kos nâ·kin cikéyhcako·s cina·oléyhcako·s
"No. I won't say anything to you. I won't bother you.

Momet naken cem vhopahnvkos" maket Vlpvtv tat ēyaskuset liken,
mo·mít nâ·kin cimahopáhnako·s ma·kít alpatáta·t i·yă·ⁿskosit lêykin
And I won't damage anything of yours," Alligator said humbly as he sat there.

"Momētot omis yefulkepvs kont okis kihcen,
mô·mi·tot o·mêys 'yifolkipás kônt o·kêys kéyhcin
"Even so, I want you to go back," he said.

"Echaswv toyetskat, este cehērēt omet, vnokeckv ocēt ont, heromkv rakkēn ocetskēt omat
ichá·swa tô·yícka·t ísti cihĭ·ⁿłi·t ô·mit anokícka ó·ci·t ônt hiłómka[990] *łákki·n ó·cícki·t ô·ma·t*
"You, Beaver, are a good person; I know you have love and

kērrit okis. Fuswv tat sulkemahēt ont omis,
ki·lleyt o·kéys fóswata·t solkimá·hi·t ônt o·mêys
great kindness. There are many birds,

omvlkvn vnokeckv em ocet enherǫmuset liketsken
omálkan anokícka imô·cit inhiłǒ·ⁿmosit lêykíckin
but you have love and kindness for all of them;

uewv tat escem ēyvnicēpet fullēpen akliket ometskat kērrit okis.
óywata·t iscimi·yanéyci·pít fólli·pín aklêykit o·mícka·t ki·lleyt o·kéys
I know that they use your water here where you live.

Vne mahvkvo vnhvmkusēt okis" kicen;
animá·hakaw anhâmkosi·t o·kéys keycín
Me, I am all by myself," he said.

"Fuswv tat etenfvciyet enahvmkē etehayeyvtēt ont, vnokeckv etem ocēt omēkv,
fóswata·t itinfacêyyit ina·hámki· itihá·yiyáti·t ônt anokícka itimô·ci·t o·mí·ka
"The birds and I made an agreement and became kin and have love for one another,

uewv estomusē ceyacat sēyvnicepaks kicvyvtēt on fullet omēt os" kihcof,
óywa istô·mosi· ciyâ·ca·t si·ⁿyaneycipáks kéycayáti·t ô·n follít o·mi·t ô·ⁿs kéyhco·f
so I told them they could use all the water they wanted," he said.

"Mon omat, vneu mata toyarēs. Vnokeckv ocit eyąskusit herǫmusarēs,
mó·n o·mâ·t aníw ma·tá· tô·yá·li·s anokícka ô·ceyt iyà·ⁿskoseyt hiłǒ·ⁿmosá·li·s
"Well then, I could do the same. I will have love and will be humble and kind,

uewvn escem ēyvnicēpit akkarin omat" mahken,
óywan iscimi·yanéyci·péyt ákka·léyn o·mâ·t máhkin
if I can stay in your water and make use of it," he said,

Echaswvt em vkvsahmen, Echaswv, Fuswv, Vlepvtv esyomat
ichá·swat imakasáhmin ichá·swa fóswa alipatá isyô·ma·t
and Beaver gave him permission. So Beaver, Bird, and Alligator

etenahvmkē hakvtēt omēs maket, este Echaswvlke, Fuswvlke, Vlepvtvlke
itina·hámki· há·kati·t ô·mi·s ma·kít ísti icha·swâlki foswâlki alipatâlki
became kin, they say, the people of Beaver clan, Bird clan, and Alligator clan,

yv toccēnat etenahvmkēt omakēs maket okakvnts, vculvke.
ya tocci·na·t itina·hámki·t omâ·ki·s ma·kit oka·kánc acolakí.
these three are kin, the old ones told.

Mohmen mv etenahvmkē monkat em vliketv maketv
móhmin ma (?) itina·hámki· mónka·t imaleykitá ma·kitá
And those kin, or what are called em vliketv ['clans'],

eterakkuecvkē hēŗēt mont etencakvkē hēŗēt omvtēt os. Hiyomēt omvtēs.
itilakkoycakí· hi·ⁿli·t mónt itinca·kaki· hi·ⁿli·t o·mati·t ô·ⁿs hayyó·mi·t o·matí·s
had much respect for each other and cared much for each other. This is how it was.

"Aktvyahcvlke, Wotkvlke, yv hokkolat etenahvmket omēs" maketvt onkv,
aktayahcâlki wo·tkâlki ya (?) hokkò·la·t itina·hámkit ô·mi·s ma·kitát ónka
"Aktayahchi clan and Raccoon clan, these two are kin," it is said,

hoktvke Wotkvlke echustvlke vtēkat,
hoktakí wo·tkâlki ichostâlki atî·ka·t
so all women who are daughters of Raccoon clan,

honvntake Wotkvlke ēppucetake vtēkat,
honantá·ki wo·tkâlki i·ppocitá·ki atî·ka·t
and all men who are sons of Raccoon clan,

momet Aktvyahcvlke ēppucetake momet echustvlke omvlkvt
mo·mít aktayahcâlki i·ppocitá·ki mo·mít ichostâlki omálkat
and all sons and daughters of Aktayahchi clan,

wotko tat "Cvrken" kicaket, vcayēcvkē hēŗēt este tat fullēpvtēt os.
wó·tkota·t cálkin kéyca·kít aca·yi·caki· hi·ⁿli·t ístita·t fólli·pati·t ô·ⁿs
call Raccoon, "My father," and people had great respect for him.

Wotko vpelihocvrē vrahkvn estet opunayen omat,
wó·tko apileyhocáli· aláhkan ístit opóna·yín o·mâ·t
If someone spoke jokingly about Raccoon,

pohetv eyacvkekot escvpakhokēt mv este wotko opunvyēcan,
pohíta iya·cakíkot iscapakhokí·t ma ísti wó·tko opónayi·câ·n
they did not want to hear it and were angry at the person joking about Raccoon,

enhomecvkemahēt este tat fullvtēt os.
inhomicakimá·hit ístita·t follatí·t ô·ⁿs
making some very angry.

Momen momēt omat kerrvyēt ont omis, wotko em vretv ohhonvkvn 'punvyēcit,
mo·mín mó·mi·t ô·ma·t kíłłayi·t ônt o·mêys wó·tko imalitá ohhonákan pónayi·céyt
Though I knew it was this way, I spoke of Raccoon's habits,

naket enhompetvt omakat, estont aret hompetv hopoyēt omētat,
nâ·kit inhompitát omâ·ka·t ístónt a·lít hompitá hopo·yí·t ô·mi·ta·t
about what his foods are, how he goes about hunting for food;

ohhonvkv pohvyvtēt onayvyvtēt on echustvlke pohvkēpvtētot
ohhonáka po·hayáti·t ona·yayáti·t ô·n ichostâlki poháki·patí·tot
I told what I had heard, and his daughters heard [what I had told]

svnrvpkv vnhayepēt fullēpofvn, cukorakko vnvkvfhotēn rorit arin,
sanłápka anha·yipí·t fólli·pô·fan cokolákko anakafhotí·n łô·leyt a·łéyn
and had planned trouble for me; at a square ground gathering where I had gone,

kvpotokvn vm esakvntvs. Toknawv ēpakē enrahkv nesvyvtēn
kapotókan amisâ·kantás tokná·wa i·pâ·ki· inłáhka nisáyati·n
they took my hat. I had bought it for six dollars,

mocvsēn vm esahkofvt, okakat,
mocási·n amisáhko·fát oka·kâ·t
it was new, and after they took it, they said,

"Wotko vpelihocekvs komē 'punvyetskvtē vrahkvn ēsēt omēs,
wó·tko apileyhocíkas kó·mi· pónayíckati·[991] ałáhkan î·si·t o·mí·s
"We took it, this hat, because you said things to make people laugh at Raccoon,"

yv kvpotokv tat" cvkicaket, "Fehketskē tvlkusen acemeyvrēs" cvkihcet esfullet,
ya 'kapotókata·t cakéyca·kít fíhkícki· tălⁿkosin a·cimíyáłi·s cakéyhcit ísfollít
they told me, "Only if you pay will we return it to you," they told me,

vm ēhvkēpen arit,
ami·hakî·pin a·téyt
and they hid it from me.

"Naken makit wotko 'punvyēcvyvtē kerrvkan okatskes" kicakvyan,
nâ·kin ma·keyt wó·tko pónayi·cayáti·[992] *kíłlaka·n*[993] *o·ká·ckis kéyca·kayâ·n*
"I don't know what I have said about the raccoon," I told them.

"Kērretskēs. Momis kerrekot oketsken omat, este hvmken fvccēcvn hahyēt,
kî·łlícki·s mo·mêys kíłlikot o·kíckin o·mâ·t ísti hámkin faccí·can háhyi·t
"You know. But if you don't know, we'll make one person the judge,

mv ehomvn onvyeyvrēs, nake maketskvtē
ma ihóman onáyiyáli·s nâ·ki ma·kíckati·[994]
and we will [go] before him and tell the things that you said,

momof cēmeu fvccēcv ehomvn ēyopunvyēcepvccvs.
mo·mô·f cí·miw faccí·ca ihóman i·yoponayi·cipáccas
then you will [go] before him and tell him your side.

Momis nake onayeyan makvyvtē seks maketsken omat,
mo·mêys nâ·ki ona·yiyâ·n má·kayáti· síks ma·kíckin o·mâ·t
But if you say you've never said the things we tell,[995]

akērrvlke ocēkv cehomv mont fvccēcv ehomv svpaklēceyvrēs" cvkicahket,
a·kí·łlâlki ô·cí·ka cihóma mont faccí·ca ihóma sapaklí·ciyáli·s cakeycáhkit
we have witnesses, so we'll stand them before you and before the judge," they told me

fvccēcv hayvranat vnkvpvkaket,
faccí·ca há·yała·nâ·t aŋkapáka·kít
and left me to appoint the judge.

"Pum ehaketsken, pum etetakof, cem onvyeyvrēs" cvkicahken,
pomihâ·kíckin[996] *pomítita·kô·f cimonayiyáli·s cakeycáhkin*
"Wait for us, and we'll tell you when we're ready," they told me.

likin hvmket 'rvlahket, "Tokvs. Yvmvn vtes" mahken,
lêykeyn hámkit 'laláhkit tókas yamán atís máhkin
I sat waiting and one returned: "Now. Come this way," she said,

ayit vpokat rorvyan, fvccēcv hayakat
a·yêyt apô·ka·t lo·layâ·n faccí·ca ha·yâ·ka·t
and I went, and when I got to where they were sitting, the judge they had chosen

hoktē hoktvlēn etenahvmkē maketv em vyē vhakuce ocē
hoktí· hoktalí·n itina·hámki· ma·kitá (?) imayí· aha·kocí (?) ó·ci·
was an elderly woman, their kin you could say, one who was familiar with the laws

este svculvke fullvtē kerrēn, fvccēcv hayet licaken,
ísti (?) sacoláki follatí· kíllí·n faccí·ca hâ·yit leycâ·kin
the elders used [for justice], and they had appointed her judge and seated her.

"Onvyaks, naket estont on okatskat" kicakof,
onáyaks[997] *nâ·kit istônt ó·n o·ká·cka·t kéyca·kô·f*
"Tell what happened," she told them:

kvpotokvn em ēsēt omēt fehkē tvlkusen aemeyvres kont omēt,
'kapotókan imi·si·t o·mí·t fíhki· tâlkosin a·imíyalis kònt o·mí·t
"We took his hat and will not return it until he pays, we decided,

fehkē tvlkē tayē tokon omat, punfvccēcetskvrēn puyacēt okēs" hvmket kihcen,
fíhki·[998] *tálki· tá·yi· tó·kon o·mâ·t ponfaccí·cickáli·n poyá·ci·t o·kí·s hámkit kéyhcin*
and if he shouldn't pay, we want you to judge this for us," one said.

"Naken maket monkat estomēt arvtet on fēkē tayēs kont okatskat onvyaks" kicahken,
nâ·kin ma·kít móŋka·t istó·mi·t â·latit ó·n fi·ki· tâ·yi·s kònt o·ká·cka·t onáyaks keycáhkin
"Tell what he said or what he's done that you want him to pay for," she told them.

"Este sulkēn vpvkēt liket wotko estomē arvtēn ohhonayen,
ísti (?) sólki·n apáki·t lêykit wó·tko (?) isto·mí· a·latí·n óhhona·yín
"In the midst of many people he sat and talked about how Raccoon does things,

este tat vpelhoyet sakkēpen likvten pum onahoyet omen,
ístita·t apílho·yít sa·kkĭ·ⁿpin lêykatin[999] *pomoná·ho·yít o·mín*
and people were roaring with laughter as he sat there pleased, we were told.

"Purke vpelkv pum ohhayvtēn puyacekot os.
półki apílka pomóhha·yatí·n poyá·cikot ó·ⁿs
We don't like him making fun of our father.

Estito estomis erke em vpelihocat esafvckēt ahrekotok: pomeu puyacekot okēs.
istêvto· istô·meys ilki imapiléyho·câ·t isa·fácki·t [1000]*áhliko·to·k pó·miw poyá·cikot o·kí·s*
No one would be happy about people laughing at their father: we don't like it either.

·Wotko tat vce lokcicēpvkan ahompet vcelowvcke tvlkekon
wó·tkota·t acǐ lokcéyci·pakà·n á·hompít acilowácki tálkiko·n
·The raccoon eats the corn that people raise, not only fresh corn,

vce kvripē hericēpvkattis papet, nerēn arēt onkv,
acǐ kałêvpi· hileycî·paka·tteys pa·pít niłí·n a·łí·t ôŋka
but also the dried corn that is stored away, and he goes about at night;

este nocicat eskerretv ocvkēt ont fullet omēs' mahokvntok:
ísti noceycâ·t iskiłłitá o·cakí·t ônt follit o·mí·s má·ho·kánto·k
they have a way of knowing when people are asleep,' it was told.

'Nocēpvkof ayopket noksakēt omēs' maket, okvten poheyēt os'' makaken,
noci·pakô·f á·yo·pkít nóksa·kí·t ô·mi·s ma·kit o·katín pohiyi·t ô·ⁿs má·ka·kín
'While you are asleep they creep up and steal,' he said, and we have heard it,'' they said.

fvccēcv tat "Maketskvtēt oma?" maket vmpohen, em vyoposkit makvyvtēt os.
faccí·cata·t má·kíckati·t ô·ma·^ ma·kit ámpo·hín imáyopo·skéyt ma·kayáti·t ô·ⁿs
The judge asked me, "Have you ever said this?" and I answered:

"Vpelihocvrē vrahkv tokon, wotko enfulletvn onayit okvyvtēt omēs" mahkin,
apileyhocáli· ałáhka tó·ko·n wó·tko (?) infollitán ona·yéyt o·kayáti·t ô·mi·s máhkeyn
"It was not to make people laugh at him, I told the ways of the Raccoon," I said.

"Mon omat estonkot omēs. Este enahvmke tat
mò·n o·mâ·t istóŋkot o·mí·s ísti ina·hámkita·t
"Well then, that is all right. People who are kin

nake etohhonayet fullet etepelicet komat
ná·ki itóhhona·yít follít itípileycit kô·ma·t
can go around telling things about each other, making fun of each other,

etem vnatoket fullet omvntok enhopuewvtok: em vretv onayet okvtētok:
itimaná·to·kít follít o·mánto·k inhopóywato·k imałitá ona·yít o·katí·to·k
joking with one another. He is [Raccoon's] nephew: he was just telling of his ways.

vpelkv eshayē estomis vculvke sem vpeyetv vcakkvyēn okvtētis onkv,
apílka ísha·yi· istô·meys acolakí (?) 'simapiyíta acakkayí·n o·katí·teys oŋká
Even though he made fun of him, he was following the ways of the old ones,

fēkekis, kvpotokv tat aematskē tayet os" mahkofvt okat,
fi·kikeys 'kapotókata·t a·imá·cki· tâ·yit ô·ⁿs máhko·fat o·kâ·t
so he shouldn't have to pay, and you should give the hat back to him," she said.

"Vne tat penwvlke toyikv, penwv tat ohtvhikit vpelihocvrē
aníta·t pinwâlki tô·yéyka pínwata·t óhtaheykéyt apileyhocáli·
"I am of the Turkey clan, I can complain about turkeys, so people laugh at him;

pen-vcule tat vm vculē tis kicit, em vretv onayit vrēpvyēt onkv,
pinacólita·t amacolí·teys keycéyt imalitá ona·yéyt ali·payí·t ôŋka
I call old gobblers, "my old man," and I tell of his ways wherever I go,

matvpomēn okvtētok: aemaks" mahken,
ma·tapó·mi·n o·katí·to·k a·imáks máhkin
so he has spoken in the same manner: give it back to him," she said,

'kvpotokv avmhoyvtēt os.
'kapotóka a·ámho·yatí·t ô·ⁿs.
and they returned the hat to me.

Momen este em vliketv makē punvttv vhocefkat
mo·mín ísti imaleykitá ma·kí· ponátta ahocífka·t
And the clans named after animals,

ēppucetake echustvlke momvkē vlkēt omēs.
i·ppocitá·ki ichostâ<l>ki mo·makí· álki·t ô·mi·s
their sons and daughters are each the same.

"Hotvlkvlke, Konepvlke 'tepakat etenahvmket omēs" mahokēt onkv,
hotalkâlki konipâlki 'tipâ·ka·t itina·hámkit ô·mi·s má·ho·kí·t ôŋka
"The Wind clan and the Skunk clan are kin," it is said,

Hotvlkvlke ēppucetake echustvlke omvlkvt konon "Cvrke" kicakēt onkv,
hotalkâlki i·ppocitá·ki ichostâlki omálkat konón cálki kéyca·kí·t ôŋka
so all the sons and daughters of Wind clan call skunk, "My father,"

konon opunvyēhocen omat, este tat escvpakhoketvt omvnts.
konón oponayí·ho·cín o·mâ·t ístita·t iscapakhokítat o·mánc
and if they hear someone talking about skunk, people would get very angry about it.

Este kono punvyēcan senhomecvkēt
ísti (?) konó (?) pónayi·câ·n sinhomicakí·t
They got mad at the one who talked about skunk,

momis hiyomat em vliketv, etenahvmke makē
mô·meys hayyô·ma·t imaleykitá itina·hámki ma·kí·
but now there is no one who knows the ways and rules about the clans and kinship

vculvke 'sem vpeyetv vhakuce ocakvtē kerrat este seko hakēpat omēcicēn,
acolakí 'simapiyíta aha·kocí ó·ca·katí· kíłła·t ísti siko· ha·kî·pa·t omi·céyci·n
that the old ones had, and for that reason,

em vliketv, enahvmke maketv naket omat kerhohoyeko omē hakepēt os.
imaleykitá ina·hámki ma·kitá nâ·kit ô·ma·t kiłho·hoyíko· ó·mi· ha·kipí·t ô·ⁿs
it's gotten so almost nothing is known about what clans and kinship are.

Mohmen vculvke hofonē fullvtēt okakat
móhmin[1001] *acolakí hofóni· follatí·t oka·kâ·t*
And the elders from long ago said,

"Nake ele oste sasat, em etenahvmketv kerkvkēt omēs" makakvtēt omēs.
nâ·ki ili ósti sâ·sa·t imitina·hamkitá kiłkakí· ô·mi·s má·ka·katí·t ô·mi·s
"Those with four feet know which ones are their relatives," they said.

Nokose, kono, yvhv yv toccēnat etenahvmken,
nokósi konó yahá ya toccî·na·t itiná·hamkín
Bear, skunk, wolf, these three are kin,

kaccv, kowakkuce, pose esyomat etenahvmkēt omakēs.
ká·cca kowa·kkocí pó·si isyô·ma·t itiná·hamkí·t omâ·ki·s.
and tiger, bobcat, and cat are kin.

Este ēlet omen hopelhoyet oman, tvlakon ocēt omvtēton,
ísti î·lit o·mín hopilhô·yit o·mâ·n talá·kon ó·ci·t ô·mati·ton
A man died and was being buried, and he had left [a field of] beans.

mv este elvtē Hotvlkvlket omvtēton, enahvmken hopohoyan,
ma (?) ísti iláti· hotalkâlkit ô·mati·ton ina·hámkin hopó·ho·yâ·n
The deceased was of the Wind clan, and they looked for kin,

Hotvlkvlke vwolusat sekot omēpen, tvlako-vhocke eslikēpet omen,
hotalkâlki awólosa·t síkot omi·pín tala·koahócki isleykí·pit o·mín
but no Wind clan [member] was in the area, and the field of beans remained.

"Estit enahvmket on omat, tvlako tat vcayēcēpan hērētan os" mahoket omen,
istêyt ina·hámkit ô·n o·mâ·t talá·kota·t aca·yi·cî·pa·n hĭ·ⁿlita·n ó·ⁿs má·ho·kít o·mín
"Whoever his kin is, if he would take care of the beans, it would be good," they said.

Cufet pohhet, "Vnet Hotvlkvlke toyis" mahket, tvlakon sepocasvtēs.
cofit póhhit anit hotalkâlki tô·yeys máhkit talá·kon sípoca·satí·s
Rabbit heard and said, "I am of the Wind clan," and became owner of the bean field.

Momis Hotvlkvlke tokot os komhoyēt omēs.
mô·meys hotalkâlki tó·ko·t ô·ⁿs komhoyí·t ô·mi·s.
But it's not believed that he is Wind clan.

The Indians Obtain a White Ball From God

J. Hill (Haas XV:39–45)

Hesaketvmesēt este-cate sahkopanvranan pokkon ēmvtēs.
hisa·kitamisí·t isticá·ti sáhkopa·nała·nâ·n[i,1002] pókkon i·matí·s
God gave the Indians a ball to play with.

Momat enhvteceskv, pokko-lanen aenhvtvpecicen, 'setem ahkopanet oman,
mo·mâ·t[1003] inhaticíska pokkolá·nin a·inhatapicêycin[1004] 'sitimáhkopa·nít o·mâ·n
In the beginning, he brought them down a yellow ball, and when they were playing with it,

rē-sehokv ostekon, este ehlen,
li·sihó·ka óstikon ísti íhlin
the score was not yet four, and someone died.

---

[i] Or (FS): *sáhkopa·naha·nâ·n.*

wahǫket este vwahen,
wa·hŏ·ⁿkit ísti awa·hin
Wailing and mourning, the people scattered.

'svhokkolat, pokko-caten aenhvtvpecicen, 'setem ahkopanat,
'sahókko·lâ·t[1005] *pokkocá·tin a·inhatapicêycin*[1006] *'sitimáhkopa·nâ·t*
The second time, he brought them down a red ball, and when they were playing together

mvo rē-sehokv ostekon, este ehlen,
maw' li·sihó·ka óstikon ísti íhlin
with it that time too, the score was not yet four, and someone died.

wahǫket este vwahen,
wa·hŏ·ⁿkit ísti awa·hin[1007]
Wailing and mourning, the people scattered.

'svtuccēnat, pokko-lvsten aenhvtvpecicen, 'setem ahkopanat,
'satócci·nâ·t[1008] *pokkolástin a·inhatapicêycin*[1009] *'sitimáhkopa·nâ·t*
The third time, he brought them down a black ball, and when they played together with it,

mvo rē-sehokv ostekon, este ehlen,
maw' li·sihó·ka óstikon ísti íhlin
that time too, the score was not yet four, and someone died.

wahǫket este vwahen,
wa·hŏ·ⁿkit ísti awa·hin[1010]
Wailing and mourning, the people scattered.

esostat, pokko-yocken aenhvtvpecicen, 'setem ahkopanat,
iso·stâ·t[1011] *pokkoyó·ckin a·inhatapicêycin*[1012] *'sitimáhkopa·nâ·t*
The fourth time, he brought them down a wrinkled ball, and when they played together

mvo rē-sehokv ostekon, este ehlen,
maw' li·sihó·ka óstikon ísti íhlin
with it that time too, the score was not yet four, and someone died.

wahǫket este vwahen,
wa·hŏ·ⁿkit ísti awa·hin
Wailing and mourning, the people scattered.

'svcahkēpan, pokko-hvtken aenhvtvpecicen, 'setem ahkopanat,
'sacáhki·pâ·n[1013] *pokkohátkin a·inhatapicêycin*[1014] *'sitimáhkopa·nâ·t*
The fifth time, he brought them down a white ball, and when they played together with it,

naket estomēsekon, rē-sehokv pale hokkolat ohren,
nâ·kit istó·mi· síkon li·sihó·ka pá·li hokkô·la·t óhlin
nothing happened. The score reached twenty,

este omvlkvt afvckvkē hḛret, este vwahen,
ísti omálkat a·fackakí· hĭ·ⁿlit ísti awa·hín[1015]
everyone was very happy, and the people scattered.

Hesaketvmesē hēcat: "Este-cate es em afvcketv tat pokko-hvtket omen,
hisa·kitamisí· hi·câ·t isticá·ti isima·fackitáta·t pokkohátkit ô·min
God saw this: "The white ball is for the Indian to have a good time.

Estofis yv pokkon esafacket, este-cate sehokvrēs," mahket,
istó·feys[1016] *ya pókkon isá·fa·ckít isticá·ti sihó·káli·s*[1017] *máhkit*
As long as they play with that ball, the Indians will live," he said.

"Hesaketvmesēt pokko-hvtken este-catvke ēmvtēs," makakēt onkv,
hisa·kitamisí·t pokkohátkin istica·takí i·matí·s má·ka·kí·t ôŋka
"God gave the white ball to the Indians," they say, so

hvyakpo-hvtke etem vtehikē, pokko-hvtke hvlwehcēn,
hayakpohátki itimatihêyki·[1018] *pokkohátki halwíhci·n*
when entering the ballfield, they send up a white ball.

etem assē esafvchokē, oketv ocakvtē opunvyēcetv vtḛkusis,
itíma·ssi· isa·fácho·ki·[1019] *okíta ó·ca·katí· oponayi·citá atĭ·ⁿkoseys*[1020]
They run after each other and are happy, just to take time to talk about the games they had;

eyacvkē hḛret esafac̣kakuset, opunvyēcet fullet omvnts.
iya·cakí· hĭ·ⁿlit isa·fă·ⁿcká·kosit[1021] *opónayi·cít follít o·mánc*
they liked it very much and were happy and went about talking about it.

Pokko-hvtke herkv pokko maketvt omen,
pokkohátki hílka pókko ma·kitát ô·min
The white ball means the ball of peace.

hvyakpo-hvtke maketv herkv hvyakpo maketvt omēs.
hayakpohátki ma·kitá hítka hayakpó· ma·kitát ô·mi·s
To say hvyakpo-hvtke [white prairie or ballfield] is to say the prairie of peace.

The Unbeliever

J. Hill (Haas XV:47–51)

Este-cate honvntake toccēnet fullet, cvto rakkē likēn 'roricet,
isticá·ti honantá·ki toccî·nit follít cató łákki· léyki·n[1022] 'łołêycit
Three Indian men were going about, and came to a big rock

mv cvton opunvyēcaket omen, hvmket okat,
ma catón oponayí·ca·kít o·mín hámkit o·kâ·t
and were talking about that rock. One said,

"Hesaketvmesēt hayvtēt omēs. Cvto ocakat mahokvnts," kicen, hvmket okat,
hisa·kitamisí·t há·yati·t[1023] ô·mi·s cató o·câ·ka·t má·ho·kánc keycín hámkit o·kâ·t
"God made that. Where there are rocks, they used to say," he said. One said,

"Naket hayekatēs. Emmonkv estofis ocēpvtēt omēs" maken,
nâ·kit há·yiká·ti·s immóŋka istô·feys ó·ci·patí·t ô·mi·s ma·kín
"Nothing made it. It's natural, it's always been here," he said.

hvmket "Hesaketvmesē tat likēt omēs. Naken momēcvrē eyacen omat,
hámkit hisa·kitamisí·ta·t léyki·t ô·mi·s nâ·kin momí·cáłi· iya·cín[1024] o·mâ·t
The other said, "God lives. If one wants him to do something,

ēelvwēcet empohohen omat, momēcēt omēs" kicof,
i·iláwi·cít impó·ho·hín o·mâ·t momi·cí·t ô·mi·s keycô·f
if he fasts and asks him for it, he does it," he said.

"Mon omat, ēelvwēcēt heyv cvto lowvckē hayvrēn empohatsken,
mô·n o·mâ·t i·ilawí·ci·t[1025] hiyá cató lowácki· há·yáłi·n ímpo·há·ckin
"All right then, you all fast and ask him to make this rock soft.

Lowvckēn hahyen hēcin omat, vkvsvmarēs" maken,
lowácki·n háhyin hi·céyn o·mâ·t akasamá·li·s ma·kín
If I see he has made it soft, I will believe," he said.

"Henka! Hiyomis em pohvkēs, hompēkok," maket,
hiŋka·^ hayyô·meys ímpo·hakí·s hompí·ko·k[1026] *ma·kít*
"All right! We can ask him right now, since we haven't eaten," he said.

hokkolat 'tem vkvsahmet, mv cvto tempen vpoket:
hokkô·la·t 'timakasáhmit ma cató tímpin apô·kit
The two of them agreed, and they all sat close to that rock:

"Hesaketvmesē toyetskat, heyv cvto hayetskvtē likan,
hisa·kitamisí· tô·yícka·t hiyá cató há·yickati·[1027] *lêyka·n*
"God, this rock you have made sitting here,

lowvckēn hayetsken hecetvn puyacēs. Pum momēcvs" makaket,
lowácki·n ha·yíckin hicítan poyá·ci·s pommomí·cas má·ka·kít
we want to see you make it soft. Do it for us," they said.

hokkolat kaken, vcēwemahekon,
hokkô·la·t kâ·kin aci·wimá·hikon
The two of them sat there. Before long they said,

"Hesaketvmesē nake vcewē momēcēt onhkotok, lowvcecēpis omēs," kicahken,
hisa·kitamisí· nâ·ki acíwi· momi·cî·t ónhko·to·k[i] *lowacicî·peys o·mí·s keycáhkin*
"God will not be long doing this. Maybe it has softened."

cvto naket hayekatēs makē aran vtotahken,
cató nâ·kit há·yiká·ti·s ma·kí· a·lâ·n atotáhkin
They sent the one there who had said nothing to the rock.

ahyet mv cvto celayan, lowackusēn celahyet, vhere-mahen feksumket aren
áhyit ma cató cila·yâ·n lowǎ·ⁿckosi·n ciláhyit ahilimà·ⁿhin fiksômkit[1028] *a·lín*
When he went and touched that rock, he felt it was really soft, and he was really startled.

fullvtēs, mahokvnts.
follatí·s má·ho·kánc
They went about long ago, they used to say.

---

[i] *ónhko·to·k = óhmiko·to·k.*

A Rattlesnake Saves a Law-Breaker

J. Hill (Haas XV:53–61)[i]

Cetto-mēkkot este-cate hvmken empunayvtēs, mahokvnts.
cittomí·kkot isticá·ti hámkin impona·yatí·s má·ho·kánc
Rattlesnake was talking to an Indian, they used to say.

Mv este vhakv-kacvt omen, rokafvranet enfvccēhocēt ont omis,
ma ísti aha·kaká·cat ô·min loká·fala·nít infacci·hocí·t ônt o·mêys
That person was a lawbreaker, and they had decided to whip him, but

kerrihocekon, aret omen, em onayet okvtēs:
killeyhocíko·n a·lít o·mín imóna·yít o·katí·s
they weren't going to let him know. He was going about, and [Rattlesnake] told him,

"Opanē eshvyvthokvranē, nerēn cerokafhoyvranēt os.
opa·ní· ishayathokála·ní· nili·n ciloka·fhoyála·ní·t ô·ⁿs
"They will stay up all night dancing, and at night they are going to whip you.

Momē estomis vyvccvs! Roret aretsken, vhakv 'secefvstvranateu
mô·mi·[1029] istô·meys ayáccas lò·lit[1030] a·líckin ahá·ka 'sicifástala·nâ·tiw
Anyway, you must go! Go there and be about. Those that are to apply the law to you

fullvrētok. Momen opvnhoyen ayvtēton,
follalí·to·k[1031] mo·mín opánho·yín a·yatí·ton
will be there, too. Then as the dance progresses,

hiyomat este hvmken vhakvn 'svfvshotvranēn mahokēt onkv, mvt hoyahnen,
hayyô·ma·t ísti hámkin ahá·kan 'safashotála·ní·n ma·hokí·t ôŋka mat hoyáhnin
they will apply the law to one person right then, they said, so after that

afvcketv ayet omvrēs, mahokof,
a·fackitá a·yít omáli·s má·ho·kô·f
the celebration will continue, they said.

---

[i] "Something like this story, the Indians kina believe it."

ahyet cuko-rakko vhvokē kulhen erhuervccvs.
áhyit cokołákko ahawkí· kólhin[1032] *ilhóyláccas*[i]
You must go and stand in the curve of the square-ground opening.

Momof este enwikvtvlke 'tetakēpet os.
mo·mô·f ísti inweykatâlki 'tita·kî·pit ó·ⁿs
Then the ones appointed for the people will be ready.

"Estvt mv tat hvlvtaks!" mahket hopoyet folhoyof, hvmken vkikin,
ístat matâ·t halátaks máhkit hopo·yít fólho·yô·f hámkin akêykeyn
When he says, "Hold that one!" and they are about looking for you, I will bite one.

"Naket vcakkes cē!" makof,
nâ·kit aca·kkís ci·^ ma·kô·f
When he says, "Something bit me!" they'll say,

"Este hvmken naket vhopanes cē!" mahket, min hopoyet fulhoyof,
ísti hámkin nâ·kit ahopâ·nis[1033] *ci·^*[ii] *máhkit mêyn hopo·yít fólho·yô·f*
"Something has destroyed one person!" When they are about looking for that one,

hospvfopken vpicēcit hueretskat 'rorarētok.
ho·spafó·pkin apéyci·céyt hôyłícka·t 'lólá·li·to·k
I will go along the wall and get to where you are standing.

Cahset 'svcayet hvfvpan rehcvlihcet vyepvccvs," kicvtēs.
cáhsit sáca·yít[1034] *hafápa·n łihcaléyhcit*[1035] *ayipáccas keycatí·s*
You must pick me up, take me, and go leave me in the bush and leave," he said.

Momen eshvyvtketv ocvranet on okekv, mv este vhakvkacv ayvtēs.
mo·mín ishayatkitá ó·cała·nít ó·n ô·kika ma ísti aha·kaká·ca a·yatí·s
Then there was an all-night celebration as he had said, so that lawbreaker person went.

Roret arvtēs. 'Pvnhoyan,
łô·łit[1036] *a·latí·s pánho·yâ·n*
He got there and was going around. Where they were dancing,

___

[i] They used to dance inside of the square-ground house.
[ii] The snake didn't like them to say he bit anybody, so they used *ahopâ·nis*.

momen vhakv vfastvlke fullen omat, lvpecicēt vhakv vfvstvkvrē ohyekcihocan pohhet,
mo·mín ahá·ka afa·stâlki follín o·mâ·t lapicéyci·t ahá·ka afastakáli· ohyikcéyho·câ·n póhhit
if the law enforcers were about, they insisted on enforcing the law quickly, he had heard.

Cetto-mēkko empunayvtē vkerrihcet ahyet,
cittomí·kko impóna·yatí· akiłłéyhcit áhyit
He remembered what Rattlesnake had told him and went

cuko-rakko-fvske em vhvoke kulhen erhuervtēs.
cokołakkofáski imaháwki kólhin iłhoyłatí·s
and stood in the curve of the opening of the sharp-pointed house.

Momof "Vhakv-kacv estvt mvton omat hvlvtaks!" mahokof,
mo·mô·f aha·kaká·ca ístat máton o·mâ·t halátaks má·ho·kô·f
Then when they said, "Hold whichever lawbreaker is here!"

este hvmket "Naket vcakkes" mahken,
ísti hámkit nâ·kit aca·kkís máhkin
one person said, "Something bit me!"

"Naket vhopanvcoks cē!" mahoken, min hopoyet folhoyvcoken,
nâ·kit aho·pâ·nacóks[1037] ci·^ má·ho·kín mêyn hopo·yít fólho·yacókin
They said, "Something must have destroyed him!" They went about looking for that one,

pohet hueren, Cetto-mēkko tat hospvfopken sololotket
pô·hit hôylin cittomi·kkóta·t ho·spafó·pkin sololŏ·ⁿtkit
and he stood there listening. The rattlesnake was crawling and crawling close to the wall,

em vlaken, ehset sayet, hvfvpan erlihcen,
imála·kin ihsit sa·yít hafápa·n iłłéyhcin[1038]
coming to him. He picked him up, and took him, and went and put him in the bush.

"Vyepvs!" kihcet okat: "Satēci satēci, satēci satēci sv!" maket,
ayípas kéyhcit o·kâ·t sa·tí·ⁿceyⁿ sa·ti·ceyⁿ sa·tí·ceyⁿ sa·tí·ceyⁿ sa^ ma·kít
"Go away!" [Rattlesnake] said, singing: "Satēci satēci, satēci satēci sv!

"Hueretskvrēs," kicvtēt omen, maket, mv este arvtēs.
hóyłíckáłi·s[1039] keycati·t ô·min ma·kít ma ísti a·łatí·s
You must stand," he told him, and that person went about.

Momen vhakv-kacv 'rokafvranvtē momēhocekon esmonkvtēt omēs.

mo·mín aha·kaká·ca 'łoká·fała·natí· momi·hocikon ismóŋkati·t[1040] *ó·mi·s*

And they still never have whipped the lawbreaker.

The Creation of Horned Owl

J. Hill (Haas XV:63–67)

Estekenet em paskofvn hayēt arvtēs.

istikínit[i] *impa·skó·fan há·yi·t a·latí·s*[ii]

Horned Owl was roaming around a cleared-off place he had made.

Momet "Vnnvkvftaks!" maken,

mo·mít annakáftaks ma·kín

Then he said, "Meet with me!"

ennvkvfhoten, estekene-pvnkvn senhomahten, 'panet fulhoyvtēs.

innakáfho·tín[1041] *istikinipánkan sínhoma·htín pa·nít fólho·yatí·s*

They met with him, he led them in the Horned Owl dance, and they danced about.

Momē pvnhoyvcokat pohakat, ohhvpēyet hoyopet fulhoyvtēs.

mó·mi· pánho·yacóka·t poha·kâ·t óhhapi·yít hoyo·pít fólho·yatí·s

When they heard them dancing like that, they all went and were watching them.

Momen sulkēt ennvkvfhotē haken, vrēpet on,

mo·mín sólki·t innakáfho·tí· hâ·kin ali·pít ó·n

Those gathering with him had grown in number, and he went about.

esem afvchokē hēren svrēpet onkv,

isima·fachokí· hĭ·ⁿlin sáli·pít oŋká

They were very pleased with him, and he was going about with them so

vwolvtēkusat hoktvke em etohkueken, esafvckē hēret,

awolati·kosa·t hoktakí imitóhkoykín isa·fácki· hĭ·ⁿłit

from the nearest places, women were coming to him. He was very pleased with it,

---

[i] Horned owl is kind of a chief.

[ii] That's a story, but that seems kind of real (FS).

vrēpet oman hoktvke ehe ocvlke sulkēt hoktarvke hakvkēpet omen,
ali·pít o·má·n hoktakí ihí o·câlki sólki·t hokta·lakí há·kaki·pít o·mín
and when he was about, many women who had husbands were becoming adulterous.

senhomehcet, nafket, elehcet, 'rvwihoken,
sinhomíhcit na·fkít ilíhcit 'laweyhô·kin
They got angry at him, hit him, killed him, and threw him away.

wakken este fvccvsekot eshehcet, raehset,
wâ·kkin ísti faccasíkot ishíhcit la·íhsit
A person with special power found him lying there, took him out,

hece-pakpvkēn efēken enhahyet, ahesayehcet empunayet:
hicipakpakí·n ifí·kin inháhyit a·hisa·yíhcit ímpona·yít
made a heart for him out of tobacco bloom, and brought him back to life, admonishing him:

"Yvn vtēkusen wikepetskvrēs.
yan atî·kosin weykipíckáli·s
"From now on you must stop this.

Cem paskofv yohfulkē 'Vnnvkvftaks!' makē huyiretskvs!
cimpa·skó·fa yohfólki· annakáftaks ma·kí· hoyêylíckas
Go back to your cleared place and and stop saying, 'Meet with me!'

Momet ēkvnv ētvto estomis cem paskofv lihcet 'Vnnvkvftaks' maket hueretskekarēs.
mo·mít i·kaná i·tato· istô·meys cimpa·skó·fa léyhcit annakáftaks ma·kít hoylíckiká·li·s
Do not put any other land in your cleared place and do not say, 'Meet with me!'

Yvn vtēkusen fekhonnepvccvs," kihocen,
yan atî·ⁿkosin fìkhonnipáccas kéyho·cin
From now on, you must stop this," he was told.

"Henkv! Mon omat, rvneyoksv pvnesofkē erpokakosat tis huerēparēs," makvtēt ont.
hiŋka^ mó·n[1042] o·mâ·t laniyóksa panisófki· ilpo·kâ·kosa·tteys hoylî·pá·li·s má·kati·t[1043] ônt
"All right! Then I will stay where the ravines at the foot of the mountains end," he said.

Pvnesofke ocakat min estekene tat hemokhehǫket okēs.
panisófki o·câ·ka·t mêyn istikínita·t[1044] himó·khihŏ·ⁿkiⁱ[i,1045] o·kí·s
Where there are ravines, there the horned owl hoots.

The Powers of Conjurers

J. Hill (Haas XV:69–77)

Este-catvlke tat porrakēt sasēs mahokēt omen,
istica·tâlkita·t pó·łła·kí·t sâ·si·s má·ho·kí·t ô·min
There are some Indians who conjure, they say,

momē hęrēt omēs monkat fvccvt os komat, este sulkēt vkvsvmvkēt omvnts.
mo·mí· hĭ·ⁿli·t[1046] ô·mi·s móŋka·t fáccat ô·ⁿs[ii] kô·ma·t ísti sólki·t akasamáki·t ô·mánc
and many people believed it was true and good.

porrē vretv enheleswv hayetv yvhiketvn kerrvkē saset omvtēs.
po·łłi· alíta inhilíswa ha·yitá yahaykitán kiłłakí· sâ·sit o·matí·s[1047]
There were some who knew the medicine songs to go around conjuring.

Momen mv porrv nerēn arēt omes.
mo·mín ma pó·łła niłí·n a·łí·t ô·mis
Now the conjurer goes about at night.

Tvmket komat, estekenen enhaketvn hakemǫhet aret;
tamkít kô·ma·t istikínin inha·kitán ha·kimá·ⁿhit a·łít
He flies when he wants and goes around making sounds just like the sound of a horned owl.

etorwv tis rakrvkēt, hopvyēt hēckis aret, heckekis ēhayet aret,
itółwateys łakłaki·t hopáyi·t hî·ckeys a·łít híckikeys i·ha·yít a·łít
His eyes are big, he is visible from far off, and he goes about making himself invisible,

este enǫkkusis wakkan, aohyopket enokkv vhecickvn em orihocekon omat,
ísti inŏ·ⁿkkoseys wa·kkâ·n[1048] a·óhyo·pkít[1049] inó·kka[1050] ahicéyckan imołeyhocíkon o·mâ·t
and where a really sick person is lying, he slips up, and if they don't watch the sick one

---

[i] Cf. *ha·hŏ·ⁿkit* 'they call (like that)': *'tolô·si ha·hŏ·ⁿkit* 'rooster crowing'.
[ii] *ô·ⁿs = ô·mis.*

ervlihket, enokkv efēken aem esehpet svyēpof,
iłaléyhkit[1051] *inó·kka*[1052] *ifí·kin a·imisíhpit sáyyi·pô·f*
enough, he goes and sits, takes the sick one's heart out, and then when he takes it away,

elēpēt omēs. Mohmet mv este efēke tat encukon 'resorepofvt,
ili·pí·t ô·mi·s móhmit ma ísti ifí·kita·t incokón łísoli·pô·fat[1053]
[the sick one] dies. Then when he arrives at his house with that person's heart,

hotopehpet hompēpēt omēs. Este efēke em ehsē elēcan,
hotopíhpit hómpi·pí·t ô·mi·s ísti ifí·ki imíhsi· ili·câ·n
he roasts it and eats it. The one who kills to take a person's heart,

mvn porrv kihocēt omēs. Hvtvm este cvfeknē tis enokkicvrēn yvhiket,
man pó·łla kéyho·cí·t ô·mi·s hatâm ísti cafíkni·teys inokkéycáli·n yahaykít
they call him or her a porrv [conjurer]. Or else he sings to make even a healthy person sick

hompetv em ohpofkēn, homipen este enokkican, porrē kihocēt omēs.
hompitá imohpó·fki·n[1054] *homêypin ísti inókkeycâ·n po·łłí· kéyho·cí·t ô·mi·s*
and blows on his food. When a person is made sick by eating, they call it porrē [conjuring].

Monkat enholacē kihocēt omēs. (Enholacē maketv enhomecē maketv omēt omēs.)
móŋka·t ínhola·cí· kéyho·cí·t ô·mi·s (ínhola·cí·[i] *ma·kitá inhomíci· ma·kitá ó·mi·t ô·mi·s)*
Or they call it enholacē. (Saying he is enholacē is like saying he is mad at him.)

Momen este efēke papē arat,
mo·mín ísti ifí·ki pa·pí· a·lâ·t
And one who goes around eating a person's heart,

elē tayēn rahohis encokon rorekat, ehlekos, mahokvnts.
ili·tâ·yi·n[1055] *łá·ho·hêys incokón łólika·t íhliko·s má·ho·kánc*
when he gets back to his home almost dying and shot, he won't die, they used to say.

Porrv hokkolet hoktēt ehe 'tepvkēt welaket omat tvmhokēt vhoyet
pó·łla hokkô·lit hoktí·t ihí 'tipakí·t wila·kít o·mâ·t támho·ki·t aho·yít
When two conjurers, a woman together with her husband were going about flying,

---

[i] *holácka* is about the same as *pó·łka* 'a conjuring, a bewitching'; *holacitá* 'to bewitch is about the same as *po·łłitá*.

hvcce rakkē 'tvpalvn vhoyet oman,
hácci lákki· 'tapá·lan aho·yít o·mâ·n
they were going to the other side of a big river,

hoktēt uewv onvpvn rorofvt,
hoktí·t óywa onápan lo·lô·fat
and just when the woman was getting there above the water,

elecvn uewvt ocen hehcet, aaklvtiken, ehet 'tvyiket,
ilícan óywat ò·cin híhcit a·aklatêykin ihít 'tayêykit
she saw the water there beneath her and fell in. Her husband got across.

etotalen yoksvn erohhueret, estekenen haketvn kohmet,
itotá·lin yóksan ilohhôylit istikinin ha·kitán kóhmit
He went and stood on the very top of a dead tree and tried to cry like a horned owl,

"Heⁿhheheⁿh hah hah hah!" maken pohohvtēs, mahokvnts.
hiⁿhhihíⁿh hah hah hah ma·kín pó·ho·hatí·s má·ho·kánc
saying, "Hinh-hi-hinh hah hah hah!" they heard him, they used to say.

Hoktē uewv aaklatkē hēcatet, vpēlet okvtēs.
hoktí· óywa a·ákla·tkí· hî·ca·tit api·lít o·katí·s
He had seen the woman falling into the water and was laughing.

Monkv porrvt tvmkē ayat, elecv ahecekot fullēt omēs.
móŋka pó·llat tamkí· a·yâ·t ilíca a·hicíko·t follí·t ô·mi·s
So when a conjurer goes flying, they go around without looking below them.

Elecvn ahēcen omat, alatkēt omēs.
ilícan á·hi·cín o·mâ·t á·la·tkí·t ô·mi·s
If they look below them, they fall down.

A Story About a Hunter

J. Hill (Haas XV:101–109)

Este hvmket fayē arvtēt, onayet okat...
ísti hámkit fa·yi· a·latí·t[1056] ona·yit o·kâ·t
One person used to go about hunting, and he would tell this...

Vnrvwvt omēpan,
ânlawat omî·pa·n
It was in the wilderness,

eto fvlahlēt tvskocvkē tvlvlicvkvtēt ocen hehcit,
itó faláhli·t taskocáki· talaleycakáti·t ò·cin híhceyt
a tree had cracked open, and I saw that strips had been laid out side by side.

vketēcvyan, vpescatet vtarken hehcit,
akíti·cayâ·n apiscá·tit atà·lkin híhceyt
When I was inspecting it, I noticed raw meat hanging there.

"Estomvranan momēcet omhoyeha̧" komit, ohhahyit,
istó·mała·nâ·n momî·cit omhò·yihä·ⁿ kô·meyt ohháhyeyt
"I wonder why they would do that?" I thought and went toward it.

Mv eto tvpeksen ohhuervyan—momvranēn hayephoyēt omvten—
ma itó tapíksin ohhôyłaya·n mó·mała·ní·n[1057] ha·yiphoyí·t ô·matin
When I stepped on those boards—they had made it so it would happen—

esvfvleniyen avcaklvtiket oman, ēkvnv sofkēn rakkēn korrephoyēt omvten,
isafalinâyyin[1058] a·acaklatêykit o·mâ·n i·kaná sófki·n łákki·n kołłiphoyí·t ô·matin
I tipped over and fell in. They had dug a big, deep hole,

estohmit ossvko tayet, aklikin, ya̧fkusē hakēpvcoken
istóhmeyt óssako· tâ·yit aklêykeyn yä·ⁿfkosi· há·ki·pacókin[1059]
and unable to get out, I sat down there. It seemed to be getting really late in the evening,

aklikvyof, nake tat arvcoken pohit,
aklêykayo·f nâ·kita·t a·łacókin pò·heyt[1060]
and as I was sitting down there, I heard something roaming around.

aklikvyof yvhvt aret ont, 'totvpekse yohcemiken,
aklêykayo·f yahát a·lít ônt[1061] 'totapíksi yohcimêykin
While I was sitting down there, a wolf was roaming around. He got up on a plank,

esfvleniyen, aaklvtiken, akkakēt omeyis,
isfalinêyyin[1062] a·aklatêykin akkâ·ki·t o·miyèys
it tipped him over, he fell down in there, and there we were sitting down there.

yvhv tat vnhomecē ont omis, cvstomēcekot,
yaháta·t anhomíci· ônt o·mêys castomí·cikot
The wolf was mad at me, but he didn't do anything to me.

Vnhopvyēcusēt akliken,
anhopayí·cosi·t aklêykin
He was sitting down in there some distance from me.

akkakēn hofonemahekon hvtvm nake tat nake yvcakē omēt
akkâ·ki·n hofonimá·hikon hatâm nâ·kita·t nâ·ki yaca·kí· ô·mi·t
We were sitting in there, and before long again, something sort of chewing, something

kvpotkicēt arvcoken pohēt, akkakeyof,
kapó·tkeycí·t[i] a·lacókin pô·hi·t[1063] *akkâ·kiyo·f*
going around crunching, we heard. While we were sitting down there,

mvo 'totvpekse ohhoyirvcoken esfvleniyen,
maw' 'totapíksi ohhoyêyłacókin isfalinêyyin[1064]
that one too stepped on the plank, and it tipped him over.

yaklatkat sokhv-hunvnwv vculēt vrēpet omvtet,
yaklâ·tka·t[1065] *sokhahonánwa acóli·t ałi·pít ô·matit*
When it came falling down, it turned out it had been an old boar going around,

yaklvtiket, enute tat cvpcvkē hēren ocēt,
yaklatêykit inótita·t capcakí· hǐ·ⁿlin ó·ci·t
and he had fallen down in. He had very long teeth

fvsficet akhuerēpen, yvhv 'tepakuseyof tat,
fásfeycít akhoyłî·pin yahá 'tipâ·kosíyo·ftá·t
and was standing down there sharpening them. When the wolf and I were together,

etehopvyēcusēt akkaket omeyiset omis,
itihopayí·cosi·t akkâ·kit o·miyêysit o·mêys
we'd been sitting some distance from each other, but

---

[i] FS never did hear *kapó·tkeycí·t.*

sokhv-honvnwvt estǫmusis nekēyen omat, yvhvt vcohkueken,
sokhahonánwat istŏ·ⁿmoseys niki·yín o·mâ·t yahát acóhkoykín[1066]
if the boar moved just a little, the wolf would move toward me.

Vneu estomusat em vkuekvyan, sokhvculet ennekēyat,
aníw istô·mosa·t imákoykayâ·n sokhacólit inníki·yâ·t[1067]
I also moved a little from him, and the old boar stirred around

avcohkuekē monken, akkvpokēn,
a·acóhkoykí· môŋkin akkapô·ki·n
and kept moving toward me. We were all sitting in there,

yvhv tat 'tenakuecē haken, hvyatkvcoken,
yaháta·t 'tina·kóyci· há·kin[1068] *haya·tkacókin*
the wolf and I getting closer together. When morning came,

este tat vlahket, kvnkorke enraman, akkvpokēn,
ístita·t aláhkit kankółki inlâ·ma·n akkapô·ki·n
someone arrived. When he opened the hole in the ground, we were all sitting down there.

"Estomatskạ?" mahokis, vyoposketv este kerrepekon,
ísto·má·cka·ⁿ^ má·ho·kêys ayoposkitá ísti killipíkon
"What are you all doing?" they said, but no one knew how to answer.

Yvhv tạwvn wvnahyet, aehset, nvfiket, elēcephohyvcoken,
yahá tă·ⁿwan wanáhyit a·ihsit nafêykit ili·ciphóhyacókin
He tied the wolf first, took him out, hit him, and killed him.

"Estomvrē tē̦?" komvkist omis, vcossihcet, sokhvculeu ossihcet,
istó·máli· ti·ⁿ^ kô·makeyst o·mêys[1069] *acosséyhcit*[1070] *sokhacóliw osséyhcit*[1071]
"What's going to happen?" I wondered. He let me out, and let out the old boar too.

Puwihokvntvs, makvtēs. Sukhv enfulletvt omen,
powéyho·kántas ma·katí·s sókha infollitát ô·min
We were free, he said. It was a place where hogs regularly came,

sokhucen yvhv estenpapen, mv esetvn kont, 'tetakuecēt omhoyvtēs.
sokhocín yahá istinpa·pín ma isítan kônt 'tita·kóyci·t[1072] *ómho·yatí·s*
and the wolf ate the people's pigs, and they wanted to catch him and had prepared it.

About Opossum

J. Hill (Hill III:16; Haas XX:67–73)

Este hvmket hayēckvn hayēcephoyan eyacetot
ísti hámkit[1073] *ha·yí·ckan ha·yi·cípho·yâ·n iyá·citot*
There was a man who heard music playing, and liking it,

eshayēckv heckuecet omis, hayēcetvn kerrekot omet
isha·yí·cka hickôycit o·mêys ha·yi·citán kíłłiko·t[1074] *ô·mit*
he got a fiddle but didn't know how to play it.

"Estohmit kērrvyatē" komet, hayēckv celayet omis
istóhmeyt kì·łłaya·ti·^ kò·mit ha·yí·cka cila·yít[1075] *o·mêys*
"I wish I could learn somehow," he thought, and though he tried to make music,

kērre sekot aret omvtētot vnrvwvn ayet
kì·ⁿłłi[1076] *síkot a·lít o·matí·tot ânławan â·yit*
he could not learn, so he went into the wilderness

ēkvnv cefahlē cvtorakko taᵧēn roret hueret vfvnnaket aret oman
i·kaná cifáhli·[1077] *catolákko tă·ⁿyi·n lô·lit hoylít afánna·kit a·lít o·mâ·n*
to a place with many rocks and boulders. As he stood looking all around,

hayēckvt haken pohhet estit hayēcet omat hecetvn eyacētot,
ha·yí·ckat ha·kín póhhit[1078] *istêyt há·yi·cít o·mâ·t hicítan iyá·ci·tot*
he heard music playing, and wanting to see who was playing,

hopoyet hueret vfvnnaket aret omat
hopo·yít hoylít afánna·kit a·lít o·mâ·t
he would search and then stand around looking.

esten hecekot aret em apohicet hueret omat
ístin hicíkot a·lít imá·poheycít hôylit o·mâ·t[1079]
He didn't see anyone, but as he stood listening,

cvto rakkēt likan mv pvlhvmken hayēckv tat haket oken vhēricet yvkapet,
cató łákki·t lêyka·n ma palhámkin ha·yí·ckata·t ha·kít o·kín ahǐ·ⁿleycít yaka·pít[1080]
the music was playing on the other side of a boulder. Walking very carefully,

cvtorakko vfolotket aret omat, este hecekot fekhoniyet hueren
catolákko afólo·tkít a·lit o·mâ·t isti hicíkot fikhonêyyit hóylin
he went around the boulder. Not seeing anyone, he stopped and stood,

hvtvm hayēckv tat haket omat cvto elecv min okēpen
hatâm ha·yí·ckata·t ha·kít o·mâ·t cató ilíca mèyn oki·pín
and the music played again but was coming from under the boulder.

cvtot tvheksēt omen, cunehket em vcvnēyan,
catót tahíksi·t ò·min coníhkit imácani·yâ·n
The boulder was tilted, and when he stooped down and peered under it,

sukhvhatkvt liket ont tottolose funen wvkēcet ont mvn em vkvlaket
sokhahá·tkat lêykit ónt to·ttoló·si fónin wakî·cit ónt man imakála·kít
there sat a opossum with a chicken bone on the ground, and by gnawing on that,

hayēckv mahusēn hayēcet omen, hehcet ayat encuko rohret
ha·yí·cka mă·ⁿhosi·n[1081] há·yi·cit o·mín híhcit â·ya·t incokó łóhlit
he made it sound just like music. After seeing that, he arrived back at his house

eshayēckv ra-ehset, efvkv 'sem vyekcvkuehcet, esfoyetv esfoyat
isha·yí·cka la·ʔihsit ifáka 'simayikcakóyhcit isfo·yitá isfô·ya·t
and took out his fiddle, tightened the strings, and as he moved the bow across the strings,

heremahēn yvhikepuecet hayehcet
hiłimá·hi·n yaheykípoycít ha·yihcit
he played it so that it sang beautifully,

mvn hayēckv hayēcetv mvnvcke here-mahē hakesasvtēs.
man ha·yí·cka ha·yi·citá 'manácki hiłimà·ⁿhi·[1082] ha·kisâ·sati·s
and he became an accomplished musician.

Birds (Fus-Lopocke Ēyopunvyēcet Fullvtēs)[i]

J. Hill (Haas XXI:55–73)

Fus-lopocke ēyopunvyēcet fullvtēs.
foslopócki i·yopónayi·cít follatí·s
The small birds were discussing their situation.

"Pum vfvnnakvrē ocēkot fullēkv,
pomafanná·káłi· ó·cí·kot follí·ka
"We go about with no one to look out for us,

puyvmahhoken fullet omēkv pum mēkkon hayet omvken
poyamáhho·kín follít o·mí·ka pommí·kkon hâ·yit o·makín
and they are destroying us, so we will make us a king,

mvt nake maken omat mvn em apohicēt fullvken omat hḛrēs" maket
mat nâ·ki ma·kín o·mâ·t man ima·pohêyci·t follakín o·mâ·t hĭ·ⁿłi·s ma·kít
and whatever he says we'll listen, and that will be good," they said,

etem vkvsahmet fullen mēkko-hakv oketv encvkikin vteloket vpoket
itimakasáhmit follín mi·kkohá·ka okíta incakáykeyn atilô·kit apô·kit
and all agreed, and the time came to choose a king, and they assembled together.

"Estvt mēkken omat hḛrēs komē
ístat mî·kkin o·mâ·t hĭ·ⁿłi·s kó·mi·
"Whichever one you think will make a good king

em enhǫnrusat enhopoyaks" maket vpoken
iminhŏⁿłosa·t inhopóyaks ma·kít apô·kin
and you have complete faith in, make your choice," they said.

tvset liket on hvmket okat, "Yv likat mēkken omat hḛrēs.
tasít lêykit ó·n hámkit o·kâ·t ya (?) lêyka·t mî·kkin o·mâ·t hĭ·ⁿłi·s[1083]
A jaybird was sitting there, and one said, "This one sitting here would be a good king.

---

[i] Title: *foslopócki i·yopónayi·cít follatí·s* 'the small birds were discussing their situation'.

Em accvkē em ēnehickv tis 'sem vnvckēt ont,
ima·ccakí· imi·nihéyckateys 'simanácki·t ônt
His clothes and decorations are handsome,

ena enrakkē 'sem eteṭayusē, em vretvo cvpkēt ont,
iná· inḷakkí· 'simitită·ⁿyosi· imalitáw cápki·t ônt
his body size is just right, his life is long,

enhakē tis hḗrē onkv, entvhopketv tis 'metetayusēt onkv,
inha·kí·teys hĭ·ⁿḷi· ôŋka intahopkitáteys 'mitită·ⁿyosi·t ôŋka
he has a good voice, his swiftness is just right,

mvt mēkkan hḗrēs" mahken, em vkvsahmet mēkkihocen aret,
mat mî·kka·n hĭ·ⁿḷi·s máhkin imakasáhmit mi·kkeyhô·cin a·lít
so he would make a good king," he said. They agreed and made him king.

naket estomusis ennekēyat "tins, tins" makof,
nâ·kit istŏ·ⁿmoseys inniki·ya·t têyns têyns ma·kô·f
For every little thing that moved, he would say, "tayns, tayns,"

hvfvpakan sakcēyet fullet oman naket vrepekan oken,
hafapâ·ka·n sákci·yít follít o·mâ·n nâ·kit alípika·n o·kín
and they would go into the thicket. But there would be nothing approaching,

Mēkko-Laksvn kicakvtēs. Momet "Mēkko tat epofvcecicekot onkv,
mi·kkolá·ksan kéyca·katí·s mo·mít mí·kkota·t ipo·facicéycikot oŋká
and they called him Liar King. "The king does not please us,

ossihcet, mēkko ētvn hayvkan hḗrēs" makvket fullet,
o·sséyhcit mí·kko í·tan hâ·yaka·n hĭ·ⁿḷi·s má·kakít follít
so we should oust him and choose another king," they said,

ennvkvfitet tvse-mēkko tat ossihcet vpoket,
innakafêytit tasimí·kkota·t osséyhcit apô·kit
and they held a meeting and ousted King Jaybird.

"Hiyomat mēkko ocēkok estit hḗrēs komat
hayyô·ma·t mí·kko ó·cí·ko·k istêyt hĭ·ⁿḷi·s kô·ma·t
"Now we do not have a king: whoever you think would be good,

enhopoyatsken mēkkekvs" hvmket maken vpoket oman,
inhopo·yá·ckin mí·kkikas hámkit ma·kín apó·kit o·mâ·n
choose him, and let him be king," one said as they sat.

fetokko-lanet liken, "Heyv likat mēkko hērēs" hvmket maket,
fitokkolá·nit lêykin hiyá lêyka·t mí·kko hĭ·ⁿli·s hámkit ma·kít
Yellowhammer was sitting there: "The one sitting here would be a good king," one said.

"Ēyąskusēt ont em enockv-lvste mēkko oceyvtē ētvpomēt omet
i·yă·ⁿskosi·t ônt imino·ckalásti mí·kko o·ciyáti· i·tapó·mi·t ô·mit
"He is humble, he has a black collar like our former king had,

ena enrakketvo 'sem etetayē ētat ont cvyąyakusēt em vretvt onkv
iná· inłakkitáw 'simititâ·yi· i·tá·t ônt caɣ̧ă·ⁿyá·kosi·t imałitát ôŋka
his body size is also just right, and it's his custom to go about quietly,

mvt mēkko hērēs" mahken, em ohhvkvsahmet,
mat mí·kko hĭ·ⁿli·s máhkin imohhakasáhmit
so he would be a good king," he said and [all] agreed,

fetokko-lanen mēkko hahoyen;
fitokkolá·nin mí·kko ha·hô·yin
and they made yellowhammer king.

aret omat, fuswv sulkat em vfvnnakekot mont vpvkekot,
a·lít o·mâ·t fóswa sólka·t imafanná·kikot mónt apákikot
But as he went about, he did not look out for all birds and did not mix with them;

enhvmkuset vrēpet eto-tale vlkan aret,
inhâmkosit ałi·pít itotá·li álka·n a·lít
he went about by himself, wandering through only dead trees;

eto-talen vliken omat, mvn vpotoket 'mvcvnēyet 'mvcvskēpusē omēt
itotá·lin ałêykin o·mâ·t man apotó·kit mácani·yít 'macáski·posi· ô·mi·t
he would sit at the side of a dead tree, with his face at the tree, peeking and pecking,

eto-talen vfolotkusēt vlikēpen;
itotá·lin afólo·tkosí·t aleykĭ·ⁿpin
and would circle around the dead tree.

yafkof, ahyet ehute 'mvhvoke tempen erlihket "Yafkes ci!" mahket
ya·fkò·f áyhit ihóti 'maháwki tímpin iɬléyhkit yá·fkis cey^ máhkit
When evening came, he would return to his home, sit near the opening and say, "It's late!"

ehuten cēyvntot nocēpet,
ihótin cí·yántot noci·pít
and then he would go in to his nest and sleep.

netta omvl ēmē vtēkusē hompvranat tvlkusēt
nittá· omál[1084] í·mi· atî·kosi· hómpala·nâ·t tálkosi·t
Every day most of the birds saw that he would go around

ēm vfvnnakēt vrēpet omen hecaket, fuswv sulkat,
i·mafánna·kí·t aɬi·pít o·mín hica·kít fóswa sólka·t
looking out for himself only and what only he could eat:

"Mēkko tat pum vfvnnakē pum vnicetv vkerricekot,
mí·kkota·t pomafánna·kí· pomaneycitá akilléycikot
"The King is not thinking about looking out for us and helping us.

naken pum onvyekot, putempunvyekot vrēpekv,
nâ·kin pomonayikot potimponáyikot[1085] aɬi·piká
Since he does not tell us anything and will not talk with us,

Fetokko-Mēkko tat puyacepēkot os" makaket,
fìtokkomí·kkota·t poya·cipí·kot ó·ⁿs má·ka·kít
we don't want King Yellowhammer," they said.

"Mvo ossihcet,
maw' osséyhcit
"It would be good if we ousted him

mēkko epupakē arē tayan hayēpvkan hērēs" makaket,
mí·kko ipopâ·ki· a·li· tâ·ya·n ha·yì·paka·n hǐ·ⁿli·s má·ka·kít
and chose a king who would go around with us," they said,

fus-lopocke sulkat fullet mvo ennvkvfitet,
foslopócki sólka·t follít maw' innakafěytit
so most small birds gathered,

mēkko em vretv opunvyēcet 'svpoket Fetokko-Mēkko ossihcet vpoken
mí·kko imaḷitá opónayi·cít 'sapô·kit fitokkomí·kko osséyhcit apô·kin
and sat talking about the king's ways and ousted King Yellowhammer and said,

"Hiyomat mēkko hḙrē tayat hopoyetvt epohcakken vpokēkv,
hayyô·ma·t mí·kko hĭ·ⁿli· tâ·ya·t hopoyitát ipohcâ·kkin apô·kí·ka
"Now here we are, the time is upon us to choose another leader,

mucv tat hḙren vkerrickv etohkahlet mēkko hayet omvkan hḙrēs" makaket omen,
mocáta·t hĭ·ⁿlin akiḷḷéycka itohkáhlit mí·kko ha·yít ô·maka·n hĭ·ⁿli·s má·ka·kít o·mín
so it would be good if this time we put our thoughts together well in appointing a king."

hvmket okat, "Mon omat cohawēskvn mēkko hayēpvkan hḙrēs.
hámkit o·kâ·t mó·n o·mâ·t coha·wí·skan mí·kko ha·yî·paka·n hĭ·ⁿli·s
One said, "It would be good if we made towhee the king.

Mv tat estofis epupakēt em vretvt onkv, momet ēkvnv cefahlakat tis aret,
matâ·t istô·feys ipopâ·ki·t imaḷitát ôŋka mo·mít i·kaná cifahlâ·ka·tteys a·lít
He is always with us and goes about in rugged country

ēkvnv hvfvpvkemahat tis yvkapēt eteropottet,
i·kaná hafapakimâ·ha·tteys yaka·pí·t itiłópo·ttít
and even walks through the most overgrown land.

ēkvnv hvyakyapateu aret,
i·kaná hayakyâ·pa·tiw a·lít
He goes about in open range too

eto mahmayat yoksvt o stomis estvmv to estomen fulleyis
itó ma·hmâ·ya·t yóksat ô· stô·meys ístama tô· istô·min folliyêys
and to the tops of the tall trees, and wherever we go

epupakē em vretvt onkv, cohawēskvt mēkken omat hḙren,
ipopâ·ki· imaḷitát ôŋka coha·wí·skat mí·kkin o·mâ·t hĭ·ⁿlin
he is always with us, so it would be good if the towhee is king:

pum vfvnnaken vpakēt fullēpvkētokv hḙrēs komvyēt os.
pomafánna·kín apâ·ki·t folli·pakí·to·ka hĭ·ⁿli·s kó·mayi·t ô·ⁿs
he would look out for us, and as we could all be together, it would be good, I think.

Mv 'resenhĕrat mēkko punhecikekos" mahken,
ma 'lisinhĭ·ⁿla·t mí·kko ponhicêykiko·s máhkin
We can find no better king," he said,

omvlkvt em ohhvkvsahmet mēkkicakvtēt omēs.
omálkat imohhakasáhmit mi·kkéyca·katí·t ô·mi·s
and they all agreed and made him the king.

Em vretv hiyomētarēs mahokvtē vcakkvyēn aret omen,
imalitá hayyó·mi·tá·li·s má·ho·katí· acakkayí·n a·lít o·mín
He went about in the way they had said he would,

em afvckvkēt fus-lopocke cahmelikv fullēt omēs,
ima·fackaki·t foslopócki cahmiléyka follí·t ô·mi·s
and all the varieties of small birds are happy with him,

este vculvke makvnts.
ísti acolakí ma·kánc
the old people used to say.

Monkv cohawēskvt fus-lopocke cahmelikv omvlkv em mēkkot omēs, mucvnettv.
môŋka coha·wí·skat foslopócki cahmiléyka omálka immi·kkot ô·mi·s mocanítta
So to this day the towhee is the king of all the different little birds.

Old-Time Hunters (Este-cate Vculvke Fakv Fullvtē Ennak Onvkvt Os)[i]

J. Hill (Hill III:31; Haas XX:75–85)

Yvhvt punvttv holwvyēcē mahat omēs maket,
yahát ponátta holwayí·ci·[1086] *má·ha·t*[1087] *ô·mi·s ma·kit*
The wolf is the meanest animal, they said,

em penkvlvkēt fayat fullēt omvtēs.
impiŋkaláki·t[1088] *fa·yâ·t follí·t*[1089] *o·matí·s*
and they were much afraid when they were

---

[i] Title: *isticá·ti acolakí fá·ka follatí· innâ·k onákat ó·ⁿs* 'it is a story of Indian elders going about hunting'.

Fayv hvmket okat, "Yvhv hokkolet welaket omat vcohhvthoyen enlētket omvyan
fá·ya hámkit o·kâ·t yahá hokkô·lit wila·kít o·mâ·t acohhátho·yín ínli·tkít o·mayâ·n
hunting. One hunter said, "Two wolves were coming toward me, and as I ran,

vcassēcaket cvwikvkepeko tayet on, eto huerēn encemket omvyan,
aca·ssí·ca·kít caweykakípiko· tâ·yit[1090] *ó·n itó hóyli·n incîmkit o·mayâ·n*
they chased me and wouldn't stop. I climbed a tree,

acemhoketv tis yacvkēton ohlikin, hvmket okat
a·cimhokítateys ya·cakí·ton ohlêykeyn hámkit o·kâ·t
and they wanted to climb up. As I was sitting there, one said,

"'Mvyvhihket awikvs" kicet omen, eswvnakvn eton sēyohhvwvnayit
'mayaháyhkit a·wéykas keycít o·mín iswaná·kan[1091] *itón si·yohhawanâ·yeyt*[1092]
'Sing the song to make him fall down!' but I tied myself to the tree with a rope

ohlikin, "Mvyvhihket awikvs" kicēpē monket omen,
ohlêykeyn 'mayaháyhkit a·wéykas kéyci·pí· môŋkit o·mín
and sat there. 'Sing the song and bring him down!' he kept saying.

"Awikvyētes" mahket,
á·weykayí·tis[1093] *máhkit*
'I will make him fall down,' [the other] said,

eto ohlikvyan yem ēfulkēt huyiret,
itó ohlêykaya·n 'yimi·fólki·t hoyêylit
and with his back to me he stood where I was sitting in the tree.

"Afken pahpit, matan pahpit lētkin" mahket, taskan
á·fkin páhpeyt ma·tá·n páhpeyt lî·tkeyn[1094] *máhkit ta·skâ·n*
'I ate mush, I ate the same, and I have run,' he sang, and as he jumped,

cvsolotiket omis ēyvwvnvyvyētok acvlvtkekon, cvwihket vhoyēpen,
casolo·têykit[1095] *o·mêys i·yawanaŋáyi·to·k a·calátkikon*[1096] *cawéyhkit ahóyi·pín*
I slid, but I had myself tied so I did not fall. Then they left me and went on,

atasiket letikis maket onayvtēt omēs.
a·ta·sêykit[1097] *litèykeys ma·kít ona·yatí·t ô·mi·s*[i]
and I jumped down and ran," he told.

Hvtvm este hvmket okat, "Fayit arvyan yvhvt cvcakket omen,
hatâm ísti hámkit o·kâ·t fa·yéyt a·layâ·n yahát caca·kkít o·mín
Another time one man said, "While I was out hunting, a wolf was catching up with me,

a-ohfolotkvyan ēmeu vcvfolotken sarin
a·ʔóhfolo·tkayâ·n í·miw acáfolo·tkín sa·léyn
so I turned to look at him, and he began circling around me too,

vcewēpen vculvke "'Pvnkv enyvhiketvn enyvhikvken omat,
aciwî·pin acolakí pánka inyaheykitán ínyaheykakin o·mâ·t
and after a while I remembered the elders used to say, 'If you sing a dance song,

este wihket vyēpēt omēs" mahoket omvnton,
ísti wéyhkit ayi·pí·t ô·mi·s má·ho·kít o·mánton
the wolf will go away.'

vkerrihcit culekoswvt ocvten hokkolen cvwehpit setenafkit,
akilléyhceyt[1098] *colikóswat ô·catin hokkô·lin cawíhpeyt sítina·fkéyt*
After I remembered that, I took two pine knots that were there and hit them together,

"Vculē tvmki, vculē tvmki" makin, vcvfolotkat
acolí· tamkey acolí· tamkey ma·kéyn acáfolo·tkâ·t
'Old one fly, old one fly, old one fly,' I said, and going around me

vnhopvyēcusēn ayen huerin hopvyusēn ra-ayē haken,
anhopayí·cosi·n a·yin hôyleyn hopáyosi·n lá·ʔa·yí· hâ·kin[1099]
[the wolf] went a little distance from me as I stood and began to circle farther away,

culekoswv lvpecicēt setenafkit,
colikóswa lapicéyci·t sítina·fkéyt
and I hurriedly hit the pine knots together and said,

---

[i] "End."

"Vculēt ayvnta, vculēt ayvnta" kicvyan,
acolí·t â·yánta· acolí·t â·yánta· keycayâ·n
'The old one went long ago, the old one went long ago, the old went gone long ago,'

reswihwayē hahket erlvpotehcet ahyen,
lìswéyhwa·yí·[1100] *háhkit illapotíhcit áhyin*
and he began to trot and left straightaway;

to-essvhasse tat cvscạken vyēpvcokvnts makvtēt omēs.
'toʔissahá·ssita·t[1101] *cască·ⁿkin ayî·pacókánc ma·katí·t ô·mi·s*[i]
he made dry leaves rattle as he went away," he said.

Monkv fayvlke yvhv opunvyēcē vretv eyacekot omakvnts.
môŋka fa·yâlki yahá opónayi·cí· alíta iyá·ciko·t oma·kánc
So hunters did not like to talk about the wolf when hunting.

Fayv tokot estomis ste-cate vtēkat Yvhv em penkvlēt omakvnts.
fá·ya tó·ko·t istô·meys sticá·ti atî·ka·t yahá impiŋkalí·t oma·kánc
Even those who are not hunters, all Indians were afraid of Wolf.

"Yvhv opunvyēcet, vpelihocvrē ecayēt opunvyēcet,
yahá opónayi·cít apileyhocáli· icá·yi·t[1102] *opónayi·cít*
"If someone talks about Wolf, makes fun of him so people will laugh,

monkat taklēcē omē opunvyēhocat, kerrēt omet,
móŋka·t taklí·ci· ó·mi· oponayí·ho·câ·t[1103] *kílli·t ô·mit*
or ridicules him, he knows of it

este enak ockv, vpuekv, sukhucvlke pvsatet stenlokēs" maket,
ísti inâ·k ó·cka apóyka sokhocâlki pasa·tít stínlo·ki·s[1104] *ma·kít*
and kills people's possessions, livestock, little pigs, and eats them," they said

opunvyēcetv yacvkekot omvnts. "Yvhvn rvhetvn komēt ēchvken omat,
oponayi·citá ya·cakíko·t o·mánc yahán lahítan kó·mi·t i·chakín o·mâ·t
and did not like to talk about him. "If you shoot at a wolf wanting to hit him,

---

[i] Here to end dictated.

eccv tis vhopanēt omēs" maket,
íccateys ahópa·ní·t ô·mi·s ma·kít
he can ruin your gun," they said,

em eccv tat yvhv sechetv eyacvkekot omvnts.
imíccata·t yahá sichitá iya·cakíko·t o·mánc.
so they did not like to shoot at the wolf with their guns.

A Song

J. Hill (Haas XXI:89)

Hvtvm estuce hvkihkat enyvhiket nocicēcetvt ocēt omēs maket
hatâm istocí hakeyhkâ·t inyáheykít noceyci·citát ó·ci·t ô·mi·s ma·kít
Another [way], when a baby cries, there is a song to sing to put it to sleep, they said

enyvhikakēt omvnts. Hvmmakēt,
inyahéyka·kí·t o·mánc. hámma·kí·t
and would sing it. Saying this,

> Ho-ocv, ho-ocv, ho-ocv,
> *hó· ʔo·ca hó· ʔo·ca hó· ʔo·ca*
> Ho-ocv, ho-ocv, ho-ocv,
>
> hokosucehkvn nocēpvrēt o
> *'hokosocíhkan noci·palí·t ô·*
> Little baby will go to sleep,
>
> mahket to
> *máhkittô·*
> she said.
>
> ceckehkvn lucvhopokvn
> *cíckíhkan locahopókan*
> Your mother went
>
> ayvnkē
> *á·yaŋkî·*
> turtle hunting.

nocepvs ce
*nocípas ci^*
Go to sleep.

Ho-ocv, ho-ocv, ho-ocv,
hó· ?o·ca hó· ?o·ca hó· ?o·ca
Ho-ocv, ho-ocv, ho-ocv,

maket enyvhikaket omvntvs.
ma·kít inyahéyka·kit o·mántas.
saying [these things], they would sing for [the baby].

Christian Songs

J. Hill (Hill III:17–18; Haas XX:87–95)

Este Maskokvlke, Este Semvnolvke mēkusapvlke heyvn yvhikvke mahēt omēs.[1105]
Muscogee and Seminole Christians continue to sing this.

Cēsvs mapohicat[1106]
cí·sas ma·pohéycat
Those who obey Jesus

Em afackakusēs.
ima·fäⁿckâ·kosi·s
are happy in him.

'Mvkerrickv hvlwēn em ocēs.
'makiɬéycka hálwi·n imô·ci·s
Their thoughts are about heaven.

Em afvcketahkvn
ima·fackitáhkan[1107]
The newly born joy

Hvtuse enhēckat tolaswv onvyeko tayēs.
hatósi[1108] *ínhi·ckâ·t 'tolá·swa*[1109] *onáyiko tâ·yi·s*
They have just received, their tongues cannot express

Heyv afvcketv cvnaken hayvyvnks.
hiyá a·fackitá canâ·kin ha·yayáŋks
This happiness I made mine.

Cēsvs ofvn eshēcvyofv,
cí·sas ó·fan íshi·cayô·fa
When in Jesus I found it,

Mont vkvsamvyof,
mónt akása·mayô·f
And when I believed,

Cēsvs enhocefkv
cí·sas inhocífka
In Jesus's name,

Ofvn vcafackusē hakvnks.
ó·fan aca·fǎ·ⁿckosi· ha·káŋks
How joyous I became.

Cēsvs kērrvyofv vcafackusvnkes.
cí·sas ki·łłayô·fa aca·fǎ·ⁿckosaŋkis[1110]
When I knew Jesus, I was so very happy.

Em estvlkeu afackakuset
imistâlkiw a·fǎ·ⁿckâ·kosit
And his people were happy too

Estonko ʾtetayet
istóŋko· ʾtitâ·yit
And could do nothing but

Homvn takpvlatket
hóman tákpala·tkít
Fall before him

Cēsvs emēkusvpakvnkes.
cí·sas imi·kosápa·káŋkis[1111]
And pray to him.

Cēsvs em afackit,
cí·sas imá·fa·ckéyt
I was happy with Jesus,

yvḥikin yafkvnkes.
yahĕyⁿkeyn ya·fkáŋkis
I sang all the day long.

Aẹha! Este omvl' kērrate!
ăyⁿha· ísti omál kî·lla·ti^[1112]
Alas! That all people might know!

Vcvnokēcvtēs.
acánoki·catí·s
He loved me.

Vm estemērkvtēs.
amístimi·lkatí·s[1113]
He has suffered.

Vnen cvnēsatet omvtēs.
anín cani·sâ·tit o·matí·s
It was for my redemption.

'Mvnokeckv tvrpvn
'manokícka tálpan
With wings of love

Escvkvwvpiken
iscakawapêykin
He lifted me

Na-orketv mv ofvn wikit;
na·ʔołkitá ma ó·fan wêykeyt
From sin;

Mont cvstemeriket,
mónt castimiłêykit
Then that I would suffer,

Cvfēke nokikēs.
cafi·ki nokêyki·s
That my heart would be in pain,

Komē vkvsvmkv ocvkvnks.
kó·mi· akasámka ó·cakáŋks
I did not believe.

Vm etektvniken,
amitiktanêykin
I was pardoned,

Vnhvyạyakusen,
anhayă·ⁿyâ·kosin
And my way was bright,

Elicv ayvtē omvyvnks.
iláyca a·yatí· ô·mayáŋks
Like Elijah's departure.

Vm poyvfekcahkvn
ampoyafìkcáhkan
My spirit

Mvn vkvwapkvnkes.
man akáwa·pkáŋkis
Arose.

Hvrēssē cvlecvn likvnkes.
hali·ssí· calícan leykánkis[1114]
The moon was beneath me.

Aẹha mv nak hẹrē vcakē ocate
ăyⁿha· ma nâ·k hĭ·ⁿli· acá·ki· ô·ca·ti
Alas! I learned the good and the sacred

Cēsvs a-ossēt on kērrvyvnks.
cí·sas a·ʔóssi·t ô·n[1115] *ki·llayáŋks*
Comes from Jesus.

Cēsvs vcvpakof vcafvcecicvnks enherkvt cvfvckēt ont omvnks.
cí·sas acapâ·ko·f aca·faciceycáŋks inhiłkat cafácki·t ónt[1116] o·máŋks
When Jesus was with me, he made me happy, his peace filled my being.

Cēsvs vcvpakof vcafvcecicvnks enherkvt cvfvckēt ont omvnks.
cí·sas acapâ·ko·f aca·faciceycáŋks inhiłkat cafácki·t ónt o·máŋks
When Jesus was with me, he made me happy, his peace filled my being.

Mēkusvpkv-cuko ofv etohkvlikē mēkusapē erkenvketv em apohicē
mi·kosapkacóko[1117] ó·fa itohkalêyki·[i] mí·kosa·pi· ilkinakitá imá·poheycí·
Coming together in the church house, praying and listening to preaching,

mont yvhiketv ētv sulkēn yvhikē vpokvtē vwahepvranof,
mónt yaheykitá í·ta sólki·n yaheykí· apô·kati· awa·hipáła·nô·f
singing many songs, when dismissal time comes,

heyvn yvhihket vwahēt omēs:
hiyán yahéyhkit awa·hí·t ô·mi·s[ii]
they sing this and dismiss:

> Cemēkusapeyvtē momusen tem vwahēs.[1118]
> *cimi·kosà·ⁿpiyáti·[1119] mô·mosin[1120] tímawa·hí·s*
> We have worshipped you, and now we dismiss.

> Cenherketvn puwahlvs.
> *cinhiłkitán powáhlas*
> Give to us your peace.

> Mohmet 'sepuwahēcvs.
> *móhmit 'sipowa·hí·cas[1121]*
> And dismiss us.

> Mohmen yvmv ēkvnv enkvpvkakeyofvt
> *móhmin yamá i·kaná inkapáka·kiyó·fat[1122]*
> Then when we leave this world

---

[i] All Indian church[es] (Baptists) — Creeks and Seminoles.
[ii] Old song — hasn't heard it in over 60 years.

Cenliketvn 'roricet fēkvpetvn puyacēs
cinleykitán 'lolêycit fi·kapitan poyá·ci·s[1123]
And arrive at your dwelling, we want rest.

Preacher's Prayer

J. Hill (Hill III:19–20; Haas XX:95–107)[i]

Hesaketvmesē, punhesaketvmesē mehenwv hvmkusetskat ecohhvkvsamēt
hisa·kitamisí· ponhisa·kitamisí· mihínwa hámkosícka·t icohhakása·mí·t
Lord, praising you, our one true God,

cemēkusvpvranet cehomvn yicēs, puhayetskat.
cimi·kosápala·nít[1124] *cihóman yêyci·s poha·yícka·t*[1125]
we come before you to offer our prayers to you who create us.

Ēkvnv emmokkēn puna-vpeswv eshahyet,
i·kaná immo·kki·n pona·ʔapíswa[1126] *ishá hyit*
You made our flesh from the dust of the earth,

wenakē hesakē vretv yekcetv cenake a-enkvpvkēn
wina·kí· hisa·kí· alíta yikcitá cinâ·ki a·ʔiŋkapáki·n
you put a portion of your strength for living and breathing

puyvfekcv cenaken puna-vpeswv ofvn vpiketskvtēt omekv,
poyafíkca cinâ·kin pona·ʔapíswa[1127] *ó·fan apeykíckati·t ômika*
and your spirit in our bodies of flesh;

purke toyetskat kērrēt vrakkueckv cēmeyat,
pólki tô·yícka·t[1128] *ki·lli·t*[1129] *alakkóycka ci·miyâ·t*
we know that you are our Father,

pufēke punpuyvfekcv puna-vpeswv punyekcē esomvlkusen ecekvsvmetvn komeyof,
pofí·ki ponpoyafíkca[1130] *pona·ʔapíswa ponyikcí· isomàlⁿkosin*[1131] *icikasamitán ko·miyô·f*
we honor you with our hearts, our spirits, our bodies, and all our strength, as we praise you

---

[i] Used by Creek or Seminole. The preacher's prayer will usually be something like this one.

"Momekvs" maket epupaketskvrēn komēt eyạskakuset cemēkusapēs.
mó·mikas ma·kít ipopâ·kíckáli·n kó·mi·t[1132] *iyă·ⁿskâ·kosit*[1133] *cimí·kosa·pí·s*
saying, "Let it be so," wanting you to be with us, we pray in all humbleness.

Purke toyetskat punhesaketvmesē purke hvlwē liketskat,
półki tô·yícka·t ponhisa·kitamisí· półki hálwi· lêykícka·t
Our Father, our God, our Father who art in heaven,

cēppuce yekcetv ēmetskvtē etehoyvnē
ci·ppocíˊ yikcitá i·míckati· itihoyáni·
because of the power you gave your son,

punnaorketv pum ohrvnkvtē ohrvnkē emonket omekvs.
ponna·ʔolkitá pomóhłankatí· ohłánki· imôŋkit omíkas
our sins have been covered, and may they stay covered.

Naken estomet cem ēmvtteciceyvten omat, omvlkvn espunwikvs.
nâ·kin ísto·mít cimi·mátticeyciyátin[1134] *o·mâ·t omálkan isponwéykas*[1135]
Whatever sin we have committed against you, forgive us for all.

Cem vhakv mehenwvkē hvsạthakusat ofvn vpẹ̄yet em eyoksiceyvrēn pum vnicvs.
cimahá·ka mihinwaki· hasă·ⁿthâ·kosa·t ó·fan apǐ·ⁿyit imiyokséyciyáli·n pomanéycas[1136]
Help us to live within your sacred, pure laws to the end.

Purke toyetskat pustemẹ̄rkakusē nettv vlvkvranat,
półki tô·yícka·t postimǐ·ⁿłkâ·kosi· nítta alákała·nâ·t
Our Father, there will come a day when we suffer,

vkerrịceyē sekot fulleyvten omis, mucvnettv epukerricepuecet,
akiłłěyⁿciyí· síko·t[1137] *folliyátin o·mêys mocanítta ipokiłłéycipoycít*
we have gone about with no thought of this, but help us to think about this today

epupaketskē monkvrēn cemēkusapēs, purke toyetskat.
ipopâ·kícki· móŋkáli·n cimí·kosa·pí·s[1138] *półki tô·yícka·t*
that you will continue to be with us, we pray, our Father.

---

[i] Or: *cippocí.*

Momet yv nettv hvse-vkērkv oketv cehomv etohkvlkeyat
mo·mít ya nítta hasiʔakí·lka okíta cihóma itohkâlkiya·t
And we gather before you this day and hour to hear

vhesaketv vhakv punwiketskvtēn ohmocvske opunvkvn pohvranēt
ahisa·kitá ahá·ka pónweykíckati·n ohmocáski[1139] *oponakán pohála·ní·t*[1140]
anew the life giving commandments in words you gave us,

nvkafteyof mv vhesaketv vhakv poheyat,
naka·ftiyô·f[1141] *ma ahisa·kitá ahá·ka po·hiyâ·t*[1142]
as we come together and hear the life-giving commandments,

pufēke ofvn fekhonnē tayē vkvsvmkvn ocēt,
pofí·ki ó·fan fikhónni· tâ·yi· akasámkan ó·ci·t
having faith that it may settle in our hearts,

momet punpuyvfekcv enfēkvpkv eshecetv yv vhakv ofvn ocēs komēt,
mo·mít ponpoyafíkca infí·kápka ishicíta ya ahá·ka ó·fan ô·ci·s kó·mi·t
hoping that our spirits will find rest in these commandments,

puyvfekcv vcakat punheckvrēs komēt opunvkv em apohicēt ometvn komeyof,
poyafíkca acâ·ka·t ponhíckáli·s[1143] *kó·mi·t oponaká imá·poheycí·t omitan*[1144] *ko·miyô·f*
hoping to receive the Holy Spirit as we strive to obey the word;

kerretv ohmocvskēt punheckvkvrēn pum vnicet,
kiłłitá ohmocáski·t[1145] *ponhickakáli·n pomaneycít*
help us that we might receive renewed knowledge;

epupaketskvrēn cemēkusapēs, purke toyetskat. Momet vtotkv cemvhakv opunvyēcvranat,
ipopâ·kíckáli·n cimí·kosa·pí·s półki tô·yícka·t mo·mít ató·tka cimahá·ka[1146] *oponayí·cała·nâ·t*
we pray you will be with us, our Father. And when the servant speaks of your law,

puyvfekcv mvhayv mehenwat enyekcē 'tem vpokēn ahvtvpiket,
poyafíkca mahá·ya mihínwa·t inyikci· 'timapó·ki·n a·hatapêykit
let the spirit teacher of truth descend with sound authority,

yv vtotkvn vpaket emvhayen em apohicet omeyvrēs komēt,
ya ató·tkan apâ·kit imáha·yín imá·poheycít omíyáłi·s kô·mi·t
hoping we listen to him; be with this servant and teach him,

vtotkv cenyekcē rakkat ofvn wiket, vpaketskvrē cemēkusapet,
atô·tka cinyikci· łákka·t ó·fan weykít apâ·kickáli· cimí·kosa·pít
leaving this worker in your higher power, we pray you will be with him,

cehocefkv rakkē vcakat ofvn, ēwikēt
cihocífka łákki· acâ·ka·t ó·fan i·wêyki·t[1147]
in your most holy name, we commit ourselves fully

vtotkvo cēmen cenwiket
atô·tkaw cí·min cinwêykit
and leave this dedicated worker too with you,

vpaketskvrēn mēkusapēt, yomusēn fekhonnēs.
apâ·kickáli·n mí·kosa·pí·t yô·mosi·n fíkhonní·s[i]
praying that you will be with him, and on this matter we conclude.

Mēkusapvlke mēkusvpkv-cuko nvkvfitē
mi·kosa·pâlki mi·kosapkacóko nakafêyti·[1148]
When Christians meet at the church house,

erkenvketv ocvranē erkenvkv enhopohkē likof, mēkusvpetvt omēs.
iłkinakitá ó·caɫa·ní· iłkináka inhopóhki· lêyko·f mi·kosapitát ô·mi·s[ii]
after a preacher is chosen for the preaching service, he should pray in this manner.

Prayer[iii]

J. Hill (Hill III:21–22; Haas XX:107–121)

Hesaketvmesē cvrke hvlwē liketskat, nettv herąkē sulkēn
hisa·kitamisi· cálki hálwi· lêykícka·t nítta hiłä-ⁿki· sólki·n
God our Father who lives on high, you have brought me through many good days

momet ohrolopē tis cvpcvkē herąkē sulkēn escvtehoyanetskes.
mo·mít ohlolopí·teys capcakí· hiłä-ⁿki· sólki·n iscatihoyâ·níckis
and many good years.

---

[i] End of Prayer
[ii] End.
[iii] This prayer is for one (a single person) to pray anywhere, any time he wants to, rain or shine.

Oketv encvpkē mომēto estomis, enokketv yekcakvo sulkēto estomis,
okíta incapkí· mô·mí·to· istô·meys inokkitá yikca·káw sólki·to[1149] *istô·meys*
Over a long period of time, even through serious illnesses,

omvlkvn enkvpvkēn cem vnokeckv escvhvlatetsken, yv nettv hueris, cvrke toyetskat.
omálkan inkapáki·n cimanokícka iscahalá·tíckin[1150] *ya nítta hôyleys cálki tô·yícka·t*
in all things you have held me in your love, and I stand this day, my Father.

Nettv enhervkē mv omat sulkēn hecvranvyat kērrvyesekot huerit
nítta inhiłakí· ma ô·ma·t sólki·n hicála·nayâ·t kĩ·ⁿłayisíkot[1151] *hôyleyt*[1152]
I did not know that I would see so many good days,

mucvnettvn vkerricis, cvrke toyetskat.
mocaníttan akílleycéys[1153] *cálki tô·yícka·t*
and I realize it this day, my Father.

Momis cēppuce cvhesayēcv etehoyvnē vm vhesaketv ecofvn ēhken vm ocetskēs.
mo·mêys ci·ppocí cahisa·yí·ca itihoyáni· amahisa·kitá icó·fan í·hkin amô·cícki·s
But through your son, my savior, you have my life hidden in you.

Monkv mv hesaketv eshecēpit ēyenakuecēpvyat komit.
môŋka ma hisa·kitá íshici·péyt[1154] *i·vina·koycî·paya·t kô·meyt*
So I want to find that life and make it mine;

fvccetv vm onayetskat mv vhakv ofvn hueretvn komvyis,
faccitá amóna·yícka·t maʔ ahá·ka ó·fan hoylitán ko·mayêys[1155]
I want to stand in the truth you tell me, in the commandments,

holwakateu cvfēke vpiken arikv, ecenrvpēn vkerricit,
holwá·ka·tiw cafî·ki apêykin a·léyka icinłapí·n akílleycéyt
but I go about with wickedness in my heart, my thoughts are against you,

ecenrvpēn opunayit, ecenrvpēt vrēpvyis omēs.
icinłapí·n opóna·yéyt icinłapí·t alĩ·ⁿpayeys o·mí·s[1156]
my talk is against you, I go about opposing you.

Aẹha, momē estomis cvwihketskvs, cvrke toyetskat.
àyⁿha· mó·mi· istô·meys cawéyhkíckas cálki tô·yícka·t
Alas, do not forsake me, my Father.

Cem vtotkv toyis. Puyvfekcv vcakat vcvpaken,
cimató·tka tô·yeys poyafíkca acâ·ka·t acapâ·kin
I am your servant. The Holy Spirit is with me,

naorketv ensulkē estomen esecenrapvyvtēto estomis, omvlkvn esvnwiket,
na·ʔołkitá insolkí· istô·min isicínła·payáti·to·[1157] *istô·meys omálkan*[1158] *isanwêykit*
and no matter how many sins I have sinned against you, forgive me for all of them,

omvlkvn vnkvpvyēcicvs, cvrke toyetskat.
omálkan aŋkapayi·céycas cáłki tô·yícka·t
remove them all from me, my Father.

Cem ēyaskusis vnrapuset huerin,
cimi·yă·ⁿskoseys anłă·ⁿposit hôyłeyn
I stand with humility toward you, and very much opposing [sin],

cvhēcvrēs cekomikv, ēkvnv enwahkv etetakuecat vpvkēn
cahî·całí·s ciko·máyka i·kaná inwáhka itità·koycâ·t apáki·n
and hope you will watch over me; at the same time you created the foundation of the earth,

vnrvpkv estomakat em afvcketskekot omat onvyetskvtēt onkv,
anłápka isto·mâ·ka·t ima·fáckíckiko·t ô·ma·t onayíckati·t ôŋka
you made it clear that you did not like evil,

cem vhakv fvccakat vnrvpvkot em eyoksicarēn vm vnicvs.
cimahá·ka faccâ·ka·t anłapákot imiyokséycá·li·n amanéycas
so help me that I will not go against your laws to the end of my life.

Momet hesaketv yoksv seko, afvcketv yoksv seko, fēkvpkvo yoksv seko,
mo·mít hisa·kitá yóksa síko· a·fackitá yóksa síko· fì·kápkaw yóksa síko·
And everlasting life, everlasting joy, everlasting rest too,

liketv etetakuecvtēt omet mv ofvn likarēn vnhuehketskvtēt omat
leykitá itità·koycati·t ô·mit ma ó·fan léyká·li·n ánhoyhkíckati·t ô·ma·t
you have prepared a place [for me], and you have called me that I might live there,

cēppuce em estemerketv eteropotiyet, mv liketv vcakat ecēyetv onvyvtēt onkv,
ci·ppocí imistimiłkitá itilopo·tâyyit maʔ leykitá acâ·ka·t ici·yitá onáyati·t ôŋka
and through the suffering of your Son, told how to enter that holy place,

mv ofvn likarē vm vnicvs, cvrke toyetskat.
ma ó·fan léyká·li· amanéycas cálki tô·yícka·t
so help me that I might live there, my Father.

Cem poyvfekcv vcakat enyekcetvn esvm vnicvs. Estofis cem vhakv ofvn ēyạskusit
cimpoyafikca[1159] *acâ·ka·t*[1160] *inyikcitán isamanéycas istô·feys cimahá·ka ó·fan i·yă·ⁿskoseyt*
Help me with the strength of your Holy Spirit. That I may always in humbleness

yv ēkvnv vretv em eyoksicarēt, cēmen ecohhvkvsamis,
ya i·kaná alíta imiyokseycá·li·t ci·min icohhakása·méys
respect your laws, as I live on this earth until the end of my time; I praise you

cvfēke, vm puyvfekcv, vm vkvsvmkv, vnyekcē 'somvlkvn.
cafi·ki ampoyafíkca amakasámka anyikcí· 'somálkan
with all my heart, my spirit, my faith, and my strength.

Vkvsvmvkekat vnfēkvpkv escēyekarēs maket
akasamákika·t anfi·kápka iscí·yiká·li·s ma·kít[1161]
Those who do not believe will not enter into my place of rest,

hocefhuecet fvccēcarēs maketskvtē
hocífhoycít faccí·cá·li·s[1162] *ma·kíckati·*
by name I will judge them, you said;

yv opunvkv ehosvranē tokot opunayet oketskvtēn kērrit, ecekvsamit okikv,
ya oponaká ihósala·ní· tó·ko·t opóna·yít o·kíckati·n kî·łłeyt icíkasa·méyt o·kéyka
I know you spoke these words and would not forget them, and I praise you,

cem vhakv omvlkv vcayēcetvn vm vnicvs. Cenyekcē cvfēke ofvn fekhonnicet,
cimahá·ka omálka aca·yi·citán amanéycas cinyikcí· cafi·ki ó·fan fikhonnêycit
help me to preserve all of your commandments. May your strength dwell in my heart,

holwakat vkerricē vcakkvyetv kometv cvfēke ecēyekarēn,
holwâ·ka·t akíłłeycí· acakkayíta ko·mitá cafi·ki icí·yiká·li·n
so that the thought of following evil desires will not enter my heart,

cvstemērkē nettv ocvranat enkvpvketv vkerricvyof,
castimĭ·ⁿłki· nítta ó·cala·nâ·t iŋkapakitá akíłłeycayô·f
for there will come a day when I will suffer; I think of how to avoid it,

vcvpaket vm vnicetsken cenfvccetv vcakkvyēn,
acapá·kit amáneycíckin cinfaccitá acakkayí·n
be with me and help me, according to your judgment.

emēkusapit em eyoksicvyatē komit, ēyaskusit vnickvn cem pohēpit,
imi·kosă·ⁿpeyt[1163] *imiyoksêycaya·ti·^ kô·meyt i·yă·ⁿskoseyt anéyckan címpohi·péyt*
I want to be in constant prayer until my days shall end, I humbly ask your help;

vm vnicvrēs kont cemekusapit, puyvfekcv vcakat ofvn ēwikit,
amanéycáli·s kònt cimikosă·ⁿpeyt poyafíkca acâ·ka·t ó·fan i·wêykeyt
I pray believing you will help me, leaving myself in the Holy Spirit,

yomusen fekhonnis, momatē.[1164]
*yô·mosin fíkhonnéys mô·ma·ti·^*
I now close that it might happen.

A Sermon (Erkenvketv)[i]

J. Hill (Hill III:23; Haas XX:123–193)

Oketv netta hĕrusē ofvn etohkvlkvkēt os, mucvnettv.
okíta nittá· hi·ⁿlosi·[1165] *ó·fan itóhkalkakí·t ô·ⁿs*[ii, iii] *mocanítta*
We come together at this time on a beautiful day today.

Momen pupucase Cēsvs Klist em vtotketv ofv, vm etecakkvlke mont cawvntake toyatskat
mo·mín popocá·si cí·sas kláyst imatotkitá ó·fa amiticakkâlki[1166] *mónt ca·wantá·ki tô·yá·cka·t*
And in the service of our lord Jesus Christ, my brothers and sisters,

momet punhessvlke tohkvlke nvkaftatskat
mo·mít ponhissâlki tohkálki nakâ·ftá·cka·t
and our friends you meet together.

---

[i] Title: *ilkinakitá* 'sermon'.

[ii] *hisa·kitamisí·* = God (< *hisa·kitá* 'breath, life' + *imisí·* 'controller'). *imisí·* = person picked out to make rules, to take care of a group of people — he was above all of them. This is the way this word was used by old people. He was elected by the majority.

[iii] *ohfánka* = old time word for God, what is above everything. *Real* old word. Didn't have Bible when they used this word.

cetem punvyvkarē vtotketv vnwihokan vlicēcetvn komit cehomv take ahuervyēt os.
citimponáyaká·li· atotkitá anᵂeyhô·ka·n aleyci·citán kô·meyt cihóma tá·ki á·hoylayi·t ô·ⁿs
I am going to begin the work given to me, to talk to you and stand up before you.

Monkv esvlicēckv Cokv-rakkon ohhonvyarēs.
mòŋka isaleyci·cka co·kalákkon ohhonáyá·li·s
So to start I will read the Bible.

'Punvkv svlicēckv tat cokv Hēplo-vlke ohtothoyvtē
'ponaká 'saleyci·ckata·t có·ka hi·plo?álki ohtótho·yatí·[1167]
The beginning words are the letters sent to the Hebrews,

'setentvckē 'svhokkolat lopockusat 'svhokkolat: Hiyomēt omekv
'sitintácki· 'sahokkô·la·t lopóckosa·t 'sahokkô·la·t[1168] *hayyó·mi·t ô·mika*
the second chapter, second verse:

"Opunvkv encelvlke opunahoyvtēt yekcēt omen,
oponaká incilâlki[1169] *oponá·ho·yatí·t yíkci·t ô·min*
"For if the word spoken by angels was steadfast,[1170]

vhakv-kackv momet mapohickv tokat vtēkat
aha·kaká·cka mo·mít ma·pohéycka to·kâ·t[1171] *atî·ka·t*
and every transgression and disobedience

fēketv fvccvt enheckakvten omat;
fi·kitá fáccat inhícka·katín o·mâ·t
received a just recompense of reward;

vhesaketv enrakkē momvtēkan vmoskomēkon omat
ahisa·kitá iṅłakki· mŏ·ⁿmati·ka·n[1172] *amŏ·ⁿsko·mí·kon o·mâ·t*
How shall we escape, if we neglect so great salvation;

estomēt mvnvttepeyvrhaks, enhvteceskvn 'Pucaset onvyetvn vlicehcen,
istó·mi·t 'manattipíyálhá·ks[1173] *inhaticískan 'pocá·sit onayitán aleycíhcin*
which at the first began to be spoken by the Lord,

pohakvtēt pum ohyekcicaken," makē hoccēn ohhonayis.
poha·katí·t pomohyikcéyca·kín ma·kí· hó·cci·n óhhona·yéys
and was confirmed unto us by them that heard him," it is written, I have read.

Hvlwē-este cuko-yekcvn hvwehcet, vpvstelvlken sossihcet,
halwi·ʔísti cokoyíkcan hawíhcit apastilâlkin sosséyhcit
The angel opened the prison, and let the apostles out, and said,

"Vpehyet, cuko-vcakat ofvn svpaklet,
apíhyit cokoʔacâ·ka·t ó·fan sapâ·klit
"Go, stand and speak in the temple[1174]

heyv hesaketv opunvkv omvlkvn este 'monvyaks" kicvtēs.
hiyá hisa·kitá oponaká omálkan ísti 'monayáks keycati·s
to the people all the words of this life."

"Fvccat vlvkvranat homv kērkuecakan pvsvtakvtēs.
fácca·t alákaɬa·nâ·t hóma ki·ɬkóyca·kâ·n pasáta·kati·s
"and they have slain them which shewed before of the coming of the Just One;

Mv cēme hiyomat wiyvlke, momet elēcvlke hakatskvtēt.
ma cí·mi hayyô·ma·t weyyâlki mo·mít ili·câlki ha·ká·ckati·t
of whom ye have been now the betrayers and murderers:[1175]

Cēmet encvlvlke wiyakat vhakv cenhēckvkvtēt omis,
cí·mit incalâlki[1176] wáyya·kâ·t ahá·ka cínhi·ckakáti·t[1177] ô·meys
Who have received the law by the disposition of angels,

vcayēcatskekat" makēt hoccvkēt os. Monkv hvlwē este vhakv este ēmvtēn
aca·yi·câ·ckika·t ma·kí·t ho·ccakí·t ô·ⁿs môŋka hálwi· ísti ahá·ka ísti i·matí·n
and have not kept it," it is written. So the laws the angel brought to man

mv vhakvn kacet, apohiceko este fullvtē senfēketv naket enheckakvten omat
ma ahá·kan ka·cít a·pohéyciko· ísti follatí· sinfî·kitá nâ·kit inhícka·katín o·mâ·t
were broken by people who wouldn't listen; therefore whatever rewards they received,

vkerricēt esteu eshocēfet 'punvyēcvkvrēs.
akiɬɬeyci·t ístiw íshoci·fit 'ponayi·cakáɬi·s
we will think about and name these people and talk about them.

Enhvteceskv, Hesaketvmesē hvlwē, ēkvnvn hahyof,
inhaticíska hisa·kitamisi· hálwi· i·kanán[1178] háhyo·f
In the beginning, after God created heaven and earth,

nake ēkvnv ohhocakat omvlkvn hahihcet etetakuehcof,
nâ·ki i·kaná ohho·câ·ka·t omálkan ha·héyhcit itita·kóyhco·f
after he made and prepared everything on the earth,

epucase taranat ēkvnv em mokkēn este honvnwvn eshahyet
ipocá·si tá·la·nâ·t i·kaná immo·kkí·n ísti honánwan isháhyit
he made a man, the one who would be its master, from the dust of the earth,

ēme enyekcē a-ossēn vhesaket, este honvnwv wenakēn hahyet,
i·mi inyikcí· a·ʔóssi·n ahísa·kit ísti honánwa wina·kí·n háhyit
from his own power he breathed into him, giving the breath of life to the man,

Atvmen hocehfet hompvranateu eto em ēttē em pvpē tayat vtēkat em etetakuehcet
a·tamín hocíhfit[1179] *hómpala·nâ·tiw itó imi·ttí· impapí·*[1180] *tâ·ya·t atî·ka·t imitita·kóyhcit*[1181]
named him Adam, and for food, he prepared all kinds of trees whose fruit he could eat,

mv 'cvpofucen vpikvtēs. Mohmet em punayet okat,
ma 'capo·focín apaykatí·s móhmit ímpona·yít o·kâ·t
and put him in the garden. Then talking with him he said,

"Yvn vfvstvs" kihcet, momet "Yv eto em ēttē etektvnkusen hompetskē tayēs.
yan afástas kéyhcit mo·mít yaʔ itó imi·ttí· itiktánkosin hómpícki· tâ·yi·s
"Take care of this place," and he said, "You are free to eat the fruit of these trees.

Momis eto hērē momet holwakat kerretv em ēttēn homipetskvs.
mo·mêys itó hĭ·ⁿɫi· mo·mít holwâ·ka·t killitá imi·ttí·n homêypíckas
But you shall not eat the fruit of the tree of the knowledge of good and evil.

Mv nettv hompetskan celvranat tvlkusekv" kicvtēs. "'Mv eto pahpetskvs'
ma nítta hompícka·n cilála·nâ·t tăɫⁿkosíka[1182] *keycatí·s ma itó páhpíckas*
The day you eat of it, you shall surely die," he said. "'Do not eat of that tree,'

cekicvyvtē papetskekv, ecerahkvn ēkvnv ohtvhikvrēt os.
cikeycayáti· pâ·píckika iciɫáhkan i·kaná ohtahéykáli·t[1183] *ô·ⁿs*
I told you, and you ate of it, so because of you the ground will be cursed.

Fēknokketv ofvn nake mv ohhontan hompetskvrēs.
fì·knokkitá ó·fan nâ·ki maʔ óhhontâ·n hómpíckáli·s
With heartache you will eat what grows from the ground.

Hesaketskē nettv vtēkat cetorofv em mēsken takliken hompetskēt,
hisa·kícki· nítta? atî·ka·t citoló·fa ímmi·skin takléykin hompícki·t
All the days of your life you will eat bread from the sweat of your brow

momet ēkvnvn ohfulketskvrēs'' kihocvtēt os.
mo·mít i·kanán ohfólkíckáli·s kéyho·cati·t ô·ⁿs[1184]
and to dust you shall return,'' it was said.

Monkv hvlwē-este em apohicekat feknokketvn senfēhokvten omat,
môŋka halwi·?ísti[1185] *ima·pohéycika·t fìknokkitán sinfi·ho·katín o·mâ·t*
So if those who did not obey the angel were rewarded with heartache,

vhakvn kacēn omat, fēknokketvn espunfēhokvrēs.
ahá·kan ka·cí·n[1186] *o·mâ·t fì·knokkitán isponfi·hokáli·s*
when we break a commandment, our reward will be heartache.

Mohmen Atvme hvlwē-este vhakv ēmvtē vcayēcekat omēcicēn,
móhmin a·tamí halwi·?ísti ahá·ka i·mati· aca·yí·cika·t omi·céyci·n
Because Adam did not obey the commandments given to him by the angel,

Hesaketvmesē ēkvnv ohtvhikvtē ofvn este honapset sulkē haken,
hisa·kitamisí· i·kaná óhtaheykatí· ó·fan ísti hona·psít sólki·[1187] *ha·kín*[1188]
people multiplied greatly in the land God cursed

etvlwv sulkē hakvtēs. Momof Lēmek eppucet hēckof, Novn hocēfvtēs.
itálwa sólki· ha·katí·s mo·mô·f lí·mik ippocít hi·ckô·f nó·wan hoci·fatí·s
and became many nations. Then when Lemech's son was born, he named him Noah.

Momen em vculkv ohrolopē cokpe cahkēpē orvtēs.
mo·mín imacólka ohłolopí· cókpi cahkî·pi·[1189] *o·latí·s*
And he reached the age of five hundred years.[1190]

Momen Hesaketvmesēt Novn kicvtēs: "Ēkvnv holwvyēckv esfvckēt omekv,
mo·mín hisa·kitamisí·t nó·wan keycatí·s i·kaná holwayi·cka isfácki·t ô·mika
And God said to Noah:[1191] "The earth is filled with evil,

vpeswv ēkvnv enkvpvkēn somecicarēs. Monkv perro-cokon ēyenhayvs.
apíswa i·kaná iŋkapáki·n somicéycá·li·s môŋka pillocókon i·yinhá·yas
so I will erase flesh from the earth. So make thee an ark.

Vnet vpeswv wenaketv hesaketv ocat hvlwat elecv omvlkv somecicarēt,
anit apíswa wina·kitá hisa·kitá ô·ca·t hâlwa·t ilíca omálka somicéycá·li·t
I shall destroy every living thing of flesh under heaven

uelvokē-rakkon ēkvnv ohhvlvkuecvranvyēt os.
oylawki·łákkon i·kaná ohhalakóycała·nayi·t ô·ⁿs.
and bring a great flood to the earth.

Nake ēkvnv ohfullat omvlkvt pvsvtkvrēs" Hesaketvmesē makvtēs.
nâ·ki i·kaná óhfollâ·t omálkat pasátkáli·s hisa·kitamisí· ma·katí·s
Everything that is on the earth shall die." God said.[1192]

Monkv nake ele-oste vtēkat fuswv enhonvnwv enhoktē tempvlsen cvwetskvrēs,
môŋka nâ·ki iliʔósti[1193] atî·ka·t[1194] fóswa inhonánwa inhoktí· timpálsin cawíckáli·s
So you will gather up all four-footed things and birds, male and female in pairs,

hesahokē vcayēckvn.
hisá·ho·kí· aca·yi·ckan
to keep them alive.

Monkv Novt Cehofv nak kicvtē vcakkvyēn omvlkvn momēcvtēs.
môŋka nó·wat cihó·fa nâ·k keycatí· acakkayi·n omálkan momi·catí·s
So Noah did everything Jehovah told him to do.

Mv omof este honvntake rakrvkemahēt ēkvnv ohfullvtēs.
ma ô·mo·f ísti honantá·ki łakłakimá·hi·t i·kaná óhfollati·s
In those times giants roamed the earth.

Este yekcvkēt hofonvlket este pohkvkēt fullet omvtēs.
ísti yikcaki·t hofonâlkit ísti pohkaki·t follít o·mati·s
They were mighty men of old who were well known.

Mv este enholwvyēckv rakkemahet omen, efēke em vkerrickv nake vkerricat vtēkat
ma isti inholwayí·cka łakkimá·hit o·mín ifî·ki imakiłłéycka nâ·ki akiłłeycâ·t atî·ka·t[1195]
Man's wickedness was great, the thoughts of his heart and everything he thought about

estofis holwvkē tvlkēt omen hēcvtēs.
istô·feys holwaki· tálki·t ô·min hi·cati·s
he saw were always evil.

Momet Cehofvt este ēkvnv ohhayvtē na-o̜rusēn hayet,
mo·mít cihó·fat ísti i·kaná óhha·yatí· na·ʔŏ·ⁿlósi·n ha·yít
And seeing the man he had made on the earth do sin

efēken enno̜kkicuset este fullen hēcet,
ifí·kin innŏ·ⁿkkêycosit[1196] ísti follín hi·cít
made Jehovah's heart grieve:

"Este mv hayvyvtē ēkvnv enkvpvkēn somecicarēs,
ísti ma ha·yayáti· i·kaná iŋkapáki·n somicéycá·li·s
"I shall destroy the man I have created from the earth,

este, momen nake ele ostvkē, hvlēcat, hvlwē-fuswv esyoman,
ísti mo·mín nâ·ki ilí ostakí· hali·câ·t halwi·fóswa isyô·ma·n
man, and the four-footed creeping things, and the birds of the air that I have made,

hahicvyvtēt sēyennokkicikv" maket, Cehofv likvtēn vkerriceyēt os.
há·heycayáti·t[1197] si·yinnókkeycéyka ma·kít cihó·fa leykatí·n akíɫleyciyí·t ô·ⁿs
for I am grieved that I have made them," he said,[1198] and we think about Jehovah's position.

Momis Nov Cehofv enrenakv ehomvn heromkvn eshēcvtēs.
mo·mêys nó·wa cihó·fa inliná·ka ihóman hiɫómkan íshi·catí·s
But Noah found grace before the eyes of Jehovah.[1199]

Monkv Nov Cehofv em punayan em vkvsa̜muset
môŋka nó·wa cihó·fa ímpona·yâ·n imakasă·ⁿmosit
Therefore if Noah willingly did what Jehovah told him to do

nake momēcatet heromkv eshēcvten omat, pomeu Cehofv em vhakv poheyat,
nâ·ki momi·câ·tit hiɫómka íshi·catín o·mâ·t pó·miw cihó·fa imahá·ka po·hiyâ·t
and found grace, then we too, who hear Jehovah's laws,

vkvsa̜muset fa̜ccusen Cehofv vkvsamēt em vtotkēt emekusapēn omat,
akasă·ⁿmosit fă·ⁿccosin cihó·fa akása·mí·t[1200] imáto·tkí·t imíkosa·pí·n o·mâ·t
if we willingly and truthfully praise Jehovah, serve him, and pray to him,

Cehofv enheromkv esheceyvrēs, ohfvccēckv-rakko netta omof.
cihó·fa inhiɫómka ishicíyáli·s ohfacci·ckaɫákko nittá· ô·mo·f
we will find Jehovah's grace on Judgment Day.

Nake ele-oste vtēkat, momet fuswv tis, este em opunvkv opunahoyekat tis,
nâ·ki ili?ósti atî·ka·t mo·mít fóswateys ísti imoponáka opona·hoyíka·tteys
All four-footed things and fowl and those not able to speak the language of man,

Cehofv em vtotkv Nov enhakē pohakat, vkvsamuset a-ohhawet
cihó·fa imató·tka nó·wa inha·kí· poha·kâ·t[1201] akasă·ⁿmosit a·?óhha·wít
when they heard the sound of Noah, Jehovah's servant's voice, they willingly came forward

perrocuko-rakko escēyet, vhesaketv ēyvnakuecvkēpvten omat
piłłocokołákko ísci·yít ahisa·kitá i·yana·kóycaki·patín[1202] o·mâ·t,
into the ark, and if they chose salvation for themselves,

pomeu pupucase Cēsvs Klist vhakv espum vlahkē
pó·miw popocá·si cí·sas kláyst ahá·ka ispomaláhki·[1203]
so we too, to whom our lord Jesus Christ brought the laws,

sēyestemerricē punhuehkvtēn vkvsamusēt a-ohhawēn omat,
si·yistimiłłéyci·[1204] pónhoyhkatí·n akasă·ⁿmosi·t a·?óhha·wí·n ó·ma·t
are called through his suffering, and if we willingly come forward,

cuko-vcakv-rakko enke eshayvkvtē tokon
coko?aca·kałákko íŋki ishá·yakáti· tó·ko·n
then we will enter the sacred mansion that is not made by hands,

cvtoknaplane eshake cuko hvlwē sutv ofv likat escēyeyvrēs.
caokna·plá·ni ishá·ki cokó hálwi· sotá ó·fa lêyka·t iscí·yiyáłi·s[1205]
[but] made of gold: the heavenly home in the sky.

Momis hvlwē-este Nov em punayat:
mo·mêys halwi·?ísti nó·wa? ímpona·yâ·t
But the angel spoke to Noah,

'Uelvokē-rakkon este essomecicarēs' kicvtē onayet omis,
oylawki·łákkon ísti issomicéycá·li·s keycatí· ona·yít o·mêys
and [Noah] said [God] said, 'I shall destroy people with a great flood,'

vkvsvmvkekat uewv ohlvwiken estemerkakvtēs.
akasamákika·t óywa ohlawêykin istimíłka·kati·s
but those who did not believe perished in the flood.

Vhakv kacē apohickv toko fullvtē estemerketvn senfēhokvtēt os.
ahá·ka ka·cí· a·pohéycka tó·ko· follatí· istimiɬkitán sinfí·ho·katí·t ô·ⁿs
Those breaking commandments without heed were rewarded with suffering.

Fēketv fvccvt enheckaket omvtēs. Este cenvpakuset hesahokvtēt onvkvt os.
fi·kitá fáccat inhícka·kít o·matí·s ísti cinapâ·kosit hisá·ho·katí·t onákat ô·ⁿs
They received their just reward. It is said that only eight people survived.

Mohmen 'tvlofv Satvme, Komalv 'tepakat hvlwē-este, Cehofvt somhuecvtēs,
móhmin 'taló·fa sa·tamí komá·la 'tipâ·ka·t halwi·ʔísti cihó·fat sómhoycatí·s
Then the angels and Jehovah destroyed the towns of Sodom and Gomorrah,

Satvme este honvntaket holwvyēckv svheremahēn Cehofv vna-orkakat omēcicēn.
sa·tamí ísti honantá·kit holwayí·cka 'sahiɬimä·ⁿhi·n[1206] cihó·fa ana·ʔóɬka·kâ·t omi·céyci·n
because the men of Sodom had become very evil and sinned against Jehovah.

Hvlwē-estvlke hokkolet Satvmen vlahokvtēs.
halwi·ʔistâlki hokkô·lit sa·tamín alá·ho·katí·s
Two angels came to Sodom.

Momen Lat vrakkuecet "Cem vtotkv encukon fekhonnatsken hvyvtkekvs" kicet omis,
mo·mín lâ·t aɬákkoycít cimató·tka[1207] incokón fikhônná·ckin hayátkikas[1208] keycít o·mèys
And Lot greeted them and said, "Stay here in your servant's house until morning."[1209]

"Monkos. Etehoyvnkvn fekhonnēn epohhvyvtkvrēs" kicakvtēs.
mónŋkos itihoyánkan fikhônni·n ipohhayátkáli·s kéyca·katí·s
"Nay," they said, "We will stay the night in the street."

Momof Satvme 'tvlofv honvntake mvnettakat vculakat tis omvlkvt 'tvlofv sosset
mo·mô·f sa·tamí 'taló·fa honantá·ki 'manittâ·ka·t acolâ·ka·tteys omálkat 'taló·fa sô·ssit[1210]
And the men of Sodom, both old and young, all came out of the town

hvlwē-estvlken vnrvpuecakvtēs.
halwi·ʔistâlkin anɬapóyca·katí·s
and did evil to the angels.

'Tecakkvyvtē toyatskat, momvtēken naorihcatskvs" maket Lat vsēhvtēs.
'ticákkayáti· tô·yá·cka·t mó·matî·kin[1211] na·ʔoɬéyhcá·ckas[1212] ma·kít lâ·t asi·hatí·s
"My brethren, do not be so wicked," Lot warned them.

Hvlwē estvlke Lat lvpecicakvtēs.
hálwi· istâlki lâ·t lapicéyca·katí·s
The angels hastened Lot.

"Ahuyiret cehiwv, cechustvlke yv kakan ēyvpvyvs,
a·hoyêylit cihéywa cichostâlki ya? kâ·ka·n i·yapáyas
"Rise up and take thy wife and thy daughters here,

'tvlofv enholwvyēckv ofvn cesomkekarēt" kicakvtēs.
'taló·fa inholwayí·cka ó·fan cisómkiká·li·t kéyca·katí·s
lest you be lost in the wickedness of the city," they said.

Momet hokkolvt Lat, ehiwv, echustvlke hokkolvt enken enhvlvthicakvtēs
mo·mit hokkó·lat lâ·t ihéywa ichostâlki hokkó·lat íŋkin inhalathéyca·katí·s
And the two laid hold of Lot's, and his wife's, and his daughter's hands.

Cehofvt em mērren 'tvlofvn eswolkvtēs.
cihó·fat ímmi·llín 'taló·fan íswolkatí·s
Jehovah was merciful, and they brought him out of the city.

Mohmet "Cenhesaketv vrahkvn letkvs, cetopvrvn ahecekot" kicakvtēs.
móhmit cinhisa·kitá aláhkan lítkas citopalán a·hicíkot kéyca·katí·s
Then they said, "Run for your life, looking not behind thee."

Momis Lat eratopvrvn ehiwvt eyopvn vhehcet okcvn-cokele hakvtēs.
mo·mêys lâ·t ila·topálan ihéywat iyópan ahíhcit okcancokíli ha·katí·s
But in back of Lot, his wife looked behind her and became a pillar of salt.

Momof Cehofvt hvlwē a-ossēn Cehofv a-enkvpvkēn tohottoplane totkv 'tepakan
mo·mo·f[1213] *cihó·fat hálwi· a·?óssi·n cihó·fa a·?iŋkapáki·n toho·ttoplá·ni tó·tka 'tipâ·ka·n*
Thenout of the heavens, Jehovah rained brimstone and fire

Satvme Komalv 'tepakan sohhoskolicvtēs.
sa·tamí komá·la 'tipâ·ka·n sohhoskó·leycatí·s[1214]
upon Sodom and Gomorrah.

Mv ēkvnv em ekkucē cvto-rekkickv-hute em ekkucē omet kvwapkvtēs.
ma i·kaná imikkocí· catołikkeyckahóti imikkocí· ò·mit kawa·pkatí·s
The smoke of that land rose like the the smoke of a furnace.

Mv 'tvlofv Lat likan somhuecof,
ma 'taló·fa lâ·t lêyka·n sómhoycô·f
When the towns where Lot lived were destroyed,

Lat somketv ennvrkvpv ossēn vyēcihocvtēt os.
lâ·t somkitá innałkapá óssi·n ayi·céyho·catí·t ô·ⁿs
Lot was sent out of the midst of the destruction.

'tvlofv Satvme Komalv ofv este vpokat em enak ockv sulkēn ocaket
'taló·fa sa·tamí komá·la ó·fa ísti apô·ka·t iminâ·k ó·cka sólki·n o·câ·kit
The people in the towns of Sodom and Gomorrah had much wealth;

toknaphvtke toknaplane ocaket, encuko herąken ocet, toknaplane sesketuce ocaket,
tokna·phátki tokna·plá·ni o·câ·kit incokó hiłǎ·ⁿkin ô·cit tokna·plá·ni siskitóci o·câ·kit
they had silver and gold, they had fine houses, they had cups of gold,

toknaphvtke eslafkvn eshompet, toknaplane hvckvtarkvn ehvckon vtvrticet
tokna·phátki islá·fkan íshompít tokna·plá·ni hackatá·łkan iháckon atałtêycit[1215]
they ate with knives of silver, they hung earrings of gold in their ears,

em accvkē hvsąthakusen vchoyet vfēkv-fvmēcvo sēfvmecicet
ima·ccakí· hasǎ·ⁿthâ·kosin achô·yit afi·kafami·caw si·famicêycit
they wore immaculate clothing, they scented themselves with perfumes,

helok-fvmēcvo cokwv vpiken, mv 'tvlofv rakkē vcakat ofv fullēpof,
hilokfami·caw cókwa apêykin ma 'taló·fa łákki· acâ·ka·t ó·fa fólli·pô·f
and had scented gum in their mouths, and when they were living in that fine, big town,

"Ēkvnv ohhonvpv hvse likat em etenrvwv,
i·kaná ohhonápa hasí lêyka·t imitînława
they thought, "There is nothing between sun and earth

naket cvstemerricē tayat sahsekos komaket fullvtēs."
nâ·kit castimilłéyci· tâ·ya·t sáhsiko·s ko·mâ·kit follatí·s
that can harm me."

Afąckakuset, momis honvntake holwvyēckv 'svheremahen Cehofv vna-orkakat
a·fǎ·ⁿckâ·kosit mo·mêys honantá·ki holwayí·cka 'sahiłimâ·hin cihó·fa ana·ʔółka·kâ·t
They were happy, but the men's wickedness grew worse, and they sinned against Jehovah,

hopuetakuce este vculakusat vtēken totkvn senfēhoken estemerkakvten omat,

hopoyta·kocí ísti acolă·ⁿkosa·t atî·kin tó·tkan sinfi·ho·kín istimiɬka·katín o·mâ·t

and if all from babies to old people were rewarded with fire and suffering,

senfēketv em onahyet oman, hvlwē-este em apohicvkekat,

sinfi·kitá imonáhyit o·mâ·n halwi·Ɂísti ima·poheycakíka·t

he had told them of their pending reward, but they paid no heed to the angels,

fēketv fvccvt enheckakan estemerkaket omvtēs.

fi·kitá fáccat inhícka·kâ·n istimiɬka·kít o·matí·s

so they received their just reward and suffered.

Monkv pomeu mv vhakv kacēt apohickv tokon fullēn omat, pustemerrvkuecvrēs.

môŋka pó·miw ma ahá·ka ka·cí·t a·pohéycka tó·ko·n follí·n o·mâ·t postimiɬlakóycáli·s

So if we too break those commandments without heed, he will make us suffer.

Cehofv Satvme Komalv ennettv omof, tohottoplane, totkv 'tepakat ocet

cihó·fa sa·tamí komá·la innítta ô·mo·f toho·ttoplá·ni tó·tka 'tipâ·ka·t[1216] *ô·cit*

In the days of Sodom and Gomorrah, Jehovah had brimstone and fire,

Cehofv likvten omat mucvnettv ocē monket Cehofv likēs.

cihó·fa leykatín o·mâ·t mocanítta ó·ci·[1217] *môŋkit cihó·fa lêyki·s*

and if Jehovah had them then, he still has them today where he dwells.

Momen ohrolopē cokpe-rakko ostet hoyanē estomis,

mo·mín ohɬolopí· cokpiɬákko ô·stit hoya·ní· istô·meys

Though four thousand years pass,

tohottoplane, totkv 'tepakat ocē monket Cehofv liken,

toho·ttoplá·ni tó·tka 'tipâ·ka·t[1218] *ó·ci· mônkit cihó·fa lêykin*[1219]

Jesus still has both brimstone and fire,

elkv rakvwvpketv mon ohfvccēckv nettv, nettv estomahat orvrēs.

ílka la·kawapkitá mó·n ohfaccí·cka nítta nítta[1220] *istŏ·ⁿma·ha·t*[1221] *oláli·s*

and when the dead arise, the Day of Judgment, that awful day will come.

Momen ponhopelkv asosseyof, Cehofv em vhakv kacet,

mo·mín ponhopílka á·so·ssiyô·f cihó·fa imahá·ka ka·cít

And when we come up out of our graves, if we who broke Jehovah's laws

apohickv ocekot fulleyvtē epohfaccen omat,
a·pohéycka ó·cikot[1222] *folliyáti· ipóhfa·ccín o·má·t*
and went about without heed are judged,

tohottoplane, totkv 'tepakat ofvn pustemerkvrēs,
toho·ttoplá·ni tó·tka 'tipâ·ka·t ó·fan postimílkáli·s
we will be tormented in brimstone and fire,

momvranēt omat Cēsvs Klist onayvtēt onkv. Mv em apohickv tokot
mó·mala·ni·t ô·ma·t ci·sas kláyst ona·yatí·t[1223] *ôŋka ma ima·pohéycka tó·ko·t*
for Jesus Christ told that this would happen. Because we did not listen,

vhakv kacē fulleyvtē omēcicēn, totkvn espunfēhoken,
ahá·ka ka·cí· folliyáti·[1224] *omi·céyci·n tó·tkan isponfi·ho·kín*
and went about breaking these commandments, we will be rewarded with fire,

mv ofvn pustemerkaket hvkahēceyvtet lopihcekos.
ma ó·fan postimílka·kít haka·hĭ·ⁿciyátit[1225] *lopéyhciko·s*
and in that, our suffering and crying will do no good.

Fēketv onahoyvtē fvccvt punhēcket omvrēs.
fi·kitá ona·hoyáti·[1226] *fáccat pónhi·ckít omáli·s*
We will receive the just reward spoken of.

Momen Cehofv em vhakv apohicakat,
mo·mín cihó·fa imahá·ka a·pohéyca·kâ·t
Now of those who obeyed Jehovah's commandments,

uelvokē-rakko onvpvn este cenvpaket perrocuko-rakko ofvn hesahokvtēt omen;
oylawki·lákko onápan ísti cinapâ·kit piłłocokołákko ó·fan hisá·ho·katí·t ô·min
eight people were saved in the ark above the flood;

Satvme, Komalv 'tepakat nēkrof,
sa·tamí komá·la 'tipâ·ka·t ni·klô·f
and when Sodom and Gomorrah both burned,

este tuccēnuset ēkvnhvlwe onvpvn ohpefatiket hesahokvtēs. Cehofvt em mērren,
ísti tocci·nosit i·kanhálwi onápan ohpifa·têykit hisá·ho·katí·s cihó·fat ímmi·łłín
just three people ran to the mountain and survived. Jehovah had mercy on them,

monkv etecakkeyvtē, cawvntake, momet vnhessvlke vnokecke toyatskat
mónka iticakkiyáti· ca·wantá·ki mo·mít anhissâlki anokícki[1227] *tô·yá·cka·t*
so my brothers, my sisters, and my beloved friends,

heyv ēkvnv vhētkof, Cehofvt pummērren,
hiyá i·kaná ahi·tkô·f cihó·fat pómmi·llin[1228]
when this earth is on fire, Jehovah will have mercy on us,

hvlwē 'tvlofv cuko-vcakv rakko ofvn,
hálwi· 'taló·fa coko?acá·ka lákko ó·fan
so that we might live in the big mansion in heaven

hesaketv, afvcketv, fēkvpkv yoksv sekan vpokēpeyvrē vrahkvn.
hisa·kitá a·fackitá fi·kápka yóksa sikâ·n apo·kî·piyáli·[1229] *aláhkan*
with life, happiness, and eternal rest.

Vheremahen Cehofv vna-orkēkot, em vhakv ofvn vtēhkēt em eyoksicēn omat,
ahilimǎ·ⁿhin cihó·fa ana?ólki·kot imahá·ka ó·fan atî·hki·t imiyókseycí·n o·mâ·t
If we do not sin so much against Jehovah, and stay within his laws until the end,

hesaketv yoksv sekon Cēsvs enherketvn vpaket,
hisa·kitá yóksa síko·n cí·sas inhilkitán apà·kit
we will live happily there with eternal life, in Jesus's peace,

epofackakuset hvlwē 'tvlofv min vpokeyvrēs. Monkv ēyvcayēcepetv vrahkvn
ipo·fǎ·ⁿckâ·kosit[1230] *hálwi· 'taló·fa mêyn apó·kiyáli·s mónka i·yaca·yi·cipíta*[1231] *aláhkan*
in that city on high. Therefore, in order to save yourselves,

Hesaketvmesēn vrakkueckv rakkēn ocēt, emēkusapet fullatsken,
hisa·kitamisí·n alakkóycka lákki·n ò·ci·t imí·kosa·pít[1232] *follá·ckin*
pray with great reverence for God

vkvsvmkv vkerrickv etohkalēt este hvmkusē em vkerrickv omen
akasámka akiłłéycka itohkâ·li·t ísti hâmkosi· imakiłłéycka ô·min
and go about together in faith and mind as of one person,

fullepvkē tayēt onkv ēyvkerricepvkvrēs, omvlkeyat. Momen Cēsvs Cutev ofv hēckof,
follipáki· tâ·yi·t ônka i·yakiłłeycipákáli·s omálkiya·t mo·mín cí·sas cúwtiya ó·fa hi·ckô·f
so let us examine ourselves, all of us. And when Jesus was born in Judea,

mēkko Hēlot hocefkēt likvtēs. Momen este hoporrēnvlket enyicet,
mí·kko hí·lot[1233] *hocífki·t leykatí·s mo·mín ísti hopołłi·nâlkit ínyeycít*
there lived a king named Herod. And wise men came to him and when they asked,

"Cosvlke em mēkko hēckat estvn likehaks?" maket, em pohakof,
co·sâlki immí·kko hí·cka·t ístan lêykihá·ks ma·kít ímpoha·kô·f
"Where is the one born king of the Jews?"

Hēlot Mēkko em etvlofvlke omvlkvt fekhervkekatēs.
hí·lot mí·kko imitalo·fâlki omálkat fikhilákiká·ti·s
all of King Herod's citizens were greatly troubled.

"Cutev em mēkkvlke vpaket cutkusmahat toyetskekos" kicaken likvtēs.
cúwtiya immí·kkâlki apâ·kit cŏ·ⁿtkosmâ·ha·t[1234] *tó·yíckikos kéyca·kín leykatí·s*
"But you are not the least among Judea's rulers," they said, it is written.

Momof 'pucase emencelvt Cēsvs erke-vhaken Cosen em ēheckuecet
mo·mô·f 'pocá·si imincilát[1235] *cí·sas iłkiʔahá·kin có·sin imi·híckoycít*
And then an angel of the Lord appeared to Jesus's step-father Joseph and said,

"Hopuewuce, ecke 'tepakan Ēcepsen sohletkvs,
hopoywocí ícki 'tipâ·ka·n i·cípsin sohlítkas
"Take the young child and his mother and flee into Egypt,

Hēlot hopuewucen elēcetvn komēt hopoyvranekv" kicvtēs. Momof Hēlot tayen cvpakkvtēs.
hí·lot hopoywocín ili·citán kó·mi·t hopóyala·niká keycatí·s mo·mô·f hí·lot tă·ⁿyin capa·kkatí·s
because Herod will seek to kill the child." Now Herod became very angry.

Momet este vtotet cēpvnvkuce ohrolopē hokkolicē em elecv ayat
mo·mít ísti ato·tít[1236] *ci·panakocí ohłolopí· hokkolêyci·*[1237] *imilicá â·ya·t*
And he gave orders and killed all the baby boys two years old and under

Pērehim vtēhkat omvlkvn pvsatvtēs,
pí·liheym atî·hka·t omálkan pasa·tatí·s
in Bethlehem,

"Cosvlke em mēkko hēckat estvn likehaks?" kihocvtē omēcicēn.
co·sâlki immí·kko hî·cka·t ístan lêykihá·ks kéyho·catí· omi·céyci·n
because it was asked, "Where is he who was born king of the Jews?"

Mv nettv take omof, Cane-Paptisvt Cutev ofvn erkenaket arvtēs.
ma nítta tá·ki[1238] *ô·mo·f ca·nipa·ptéysat cúwtiya ó·fan iɬkina·kít a·latí·s*
In those days, John the Baptist was preaching in Judea.

Momen Hēlot estvtoten svlvfkuehcet cukoyēkcvn vpihokvtēs.
mo·mín hí·lot istatô·tin salafkóyhcit cokoyí·kcan apéyho·katí·s
And Herod gave orders, and he was arrested and put in jail.

Mohmen Hēlot Mēkko hēckvtē nettvn vrakkuehocen likof,
móhmin hí·lot mí·kko hi·ckatí· níttan aɬakkóyho·cín lêyko·f
When King Herod was attending his birthday celebration,

ēchust-vhaket opanet ehomvn aret mēkkon afvcecicof,
i·chostahá·kit opa·nít ihóman a·lít mí·kkon a·facíceycô·f
his step-daughter danced before him, and when she had pleased the king,

"Naketo estomis vm pohetskis cemarēs,
nâ·kito· istô·meys[1239] *ámpo·híckeys cimá·li·s*
he said, "Whatsoever you ask of me I will give to you,

vm ohmēkketv ennvrkvpv orē estomis" kihcof,
amohmi·kkitá innaɬkapá ô·li· istô·meys kéyhco·f
even up to half of my kingdom," he said,

mv hoktē "Cane-Paptisv ekvn cvyacēs" kihcen, mēkko efēke nokkēt omis,
ma hoktí· ca·nipa·ptéysa ikán cayá·ci·s kéyhcin mí·kko ifí·ki nókki·t ot[1240] *o·mêys*
and the woman said, "I want the head of John the Baptist," and though it grieved the king,

"Emaks" maket, estvtohtet Cane cukoyēkcv ofv ekv entacvtēs.
imáks ma·kít istatóhtit cá·ni cokoyí·kca ó·fa iká ínta·catí·s
he said, "Give it to her," and gave orders to behead John in jail.

Momof Hēlot Mēkko enfēketv enhēckvtēt os. Momen momē ocvtēs,
mo·mô·f hí·lot mí·kko infi·kitá ínhi·ckatí·t ô·ⁿs mo·mín mo·mí· o·catí·s
And King Herod received his reward. There was a time

vpastelvlke ennettv omof, erkenaket fullof,
apa·stilâlki innítta ô·mo·f íɬkina·kít follô·f
in the days of the apostles, as they went about preaching

mēkusapvlke sulkē hakē ayof, mēkusvpkv-cukou ocaken,
mi·kosa·pâlki sólki· ha·ki· a·yô·f mi·kosapkacókow[1241] *o·câ·kin*
and as there began to be many Christians, when they had churches

cuko-vfastvlkeu, este honvntake vkvsvmkv yekcē ocakan enhopohyet,
coko?afa·stâlkiw isti honantá·ki akasámka yíkci· o·câ·ka·n inhopóhyit
and deacons too, and they chose men who had great faith

kolvpaken yekcetv emahket, 'pucase em opunvkv este em onvyetv kvwapket ayof,
kolapâ·kin yikcitá imáhkit 'pocá·si imoponáka isti imonayíta[1242] *kawa·pkít a·yô·f*
and gave seven authority, and when the Lord's word to people began to rise,

Hēlot Mēkko mēkusapvlke estemerrvkuecetvn vlicēcvtēs.
hí·lot mí·kko mi·kosa·pâlki istimiłłakoycitán aléyci·catí·s
King Herod began to punish the Christians.

Momet Cems, Cane etecakkan eslafkv-cvpkon eselēcvtēs. Pētvo esetvn komvtēs.
mo·mít cìms[1243] *cá·ni iticâ·kka·n isla·fkacápkon isíli·catí·s*[1244] *pí·taw isítan ko·matí·s*
And he killed James, the brother of John, with a sword. He wanted to capture Peter, too.

Momen ehsof cuko-yekcvn vpikvtēs. Momis moman vpakusen mēkusvpkv wikekot,
mo·mín íhso·f cokoyikcan apaykatí·s[1245] *mo·mêys mo·mâ·n apá·ⁿkosin mi·kosápka wéykikot*
And after he got him, he put him in jail. Immediately without ceasing,

Hesaketvmesēn emēkusapvtēs. Nerē Pētv cvto-tetakkakv hokkolen eswvnvkēn nocvtēs.
hisa·kitamisi·n imí·kosa·patí·s nili· pí·ta catotitakká·ka[1246] *hokkô·lin iswanáki·n no·catí·s*
he prayed to God. During the night Peter slept bound with two chains around him.

Vhecicvlke cuko-yēkcv vhvoken vhecicakvtēs.
ahiceycâlki cokoyí·kca aháwkin ahicéyca·katí·s
The guards guarded the jail door.

'Pucase em encel ohhvlahken, cuko-yēkcv ofvn hvyayakvtēs.
'pocá·si imíncil ohhaláhkin cokoyí·kca ó·fan hayá·ya·katí·s
The angel of the Lord came upon him, and there was light in the jail.

Mv encel Pētvn ahuericvtēs. Momof cvto-tetakkakvt enke enyorkvtēs.
ma íncil pí·tan a·hóyleycatí·s mo·mô·f catotitakká·kat iŋki inyo·łkatí·s
The angel helped Peter to stand up. And the chains fell from his hands.[1247]

Momen osiyet hvlwē-esten vcakkayvtēs.
mo·mín osâyyit halwi·ʔístin acákka·yatí·s
And he went out, following the angel.

Momen hvyatkat vpaken Pētv estvn estomat kerrekat
mo·mín haya·tkâ·t apâ·kin pí·ta ístan istó·ma·t kíllika·t
And at the break of dawn, because the soldiers had not known what had happened to Peter,

suletawvlke em eteyvmketv rakkē tatēs. Momen Hēlot hopoyet eshecekof,
solita·wâlki imitiyamkitá łákki· tá·ti·s mo·mín hí·lot hopo·yít ishiciko·f
there was a great commotion. And when Herod had looked for him and didn't find him,

vhecicvlken oh-vketēce poyat pvsvthoyvrēn makvtēs. Monkv Hēlot Mēkko vkerricat,
ahiceycâlkin ohhakití·cipo·yâ·t[1248] pasathoyáłi·n ma·katí·s môŋka hí·lot mí·kko akíłłeycâ·t
he examined the guards and commanded that they be put to death. So King Herod thought,

"Vhakv-vfastvlke vm elecv enwiketv sehokat vm vhakv vnrvpēt,
aha·kaʔafa·stâlki[1249] amilíca inweykitá sihô·ka·t amahá·ka ałłapí·t
"The law-keepers appointed beneath me have gone against my law

mēkusapvlke enhomahtv yekcē este aran hesayēcetvn komēt,
mi·kosa·pâlki inhomá·hta yíkci· ísti a·lâ·n hisa·yi·citán kó·mi·t
and wanting to save the strong leader of the Christians,

cuko-yēkcv vhvoke-vhecicvlket Pētvn ossicaket os" komēt,
cokoyí·kca ahawkiʔahiceycâlkit pí·tan osseycâ·kit ó·ⁿs kó·mi·t
the guards of the jail doors let Peter go free,"

mēkko cvpakkēt liket okvtēs. Momen Hēlod netta mellet mēkko em accvkēn accet
mí·kko capákki·t[1250] lêykit o·katí·s mo·mín hí·lot nittá· millít mí·kko ima·ccaki·n â·ccit
the king thought angrily. And Herod set a day, and wearing royal apparel,

em ohliketvn ohliket opunvkv-cvpkon enwvkecakvtēs.
imohleykitán ohlêykit oponakacápkon inwakíca·katí·s
he sat upon his throne and made a lengthy oration to them.

Momen vyakhvmkusen 'pucase em estet enokketvn vlicvtēs,
mo·mín ayakhàmⁿkosin 'pocá·si imístit inokkitán aleycatí·s
Immediately the angel of the Lord afflicted him with a sickness,

vkvsvmkv Hesaketvmesēn emekokv. Momen cuntvt pvpaken hesaketvn wikvtēs.
akasámka hisa·kitamisí·n imiko·ka mo·mín cóntat papa·kín hisa·kitán weykatí·s
for he did not give glory to God. And worms ate him, and he gave up life.

Momis Hesaketvmesē em opunvkv ohhvtvlaket ạye mahvtēs.
mo·mêys hisa·kitamisí· imoponáka ohhatála·kít[1251] ă·[n]yi mâ·hati·s
But the word of God grew and multiplied.

Monkv Cutev ofv nake estomēt ocaken,
môŋka cúwtiya ó·fa nâ·ki istó·mi·t ó·ca·kín
Therefore things that were to take place in Judea

Hēlod Mēkko estomēt vrvranat oketv oreko monken
hí·lot mí·kko istó·mi·t alála·nâ·t okítaʔ olíko· môŋkin
before the time when King Herod was going to do them

hvlwē este kerraket onvyakvtēt on kērreyēt os.
halwí· ísti kiłłâ·kit onáya·katí·t ô·n ki·łłiyí·t ô·[n]s
were known by the angels who revealed them, we now know.

Momen Hēlod mēkusapvlke estemerrvkueckv vlicēcat,
mo·mín hí·lot mi·kosa·pâlki istimiłłakóycka aléyci·câ·t
And Herod began to punish the Christians,

Hesaketvmesē vnrvpkv rakkē yekcēn esvnrapet vtotkvlke em pvsatet omvtēs.
hisa·kitamisí· anłápka łákki· yíkci·n isánła·pít ato·tkâlki ímpasa·tít o·mati·s
he had great animosity toward God and killed His servants.

'Pucase vtotkvlke em pvsatvtē senfēketv cuntvn ena-vpeswv ofvn em vtēhohen pvpaket
'pocá·si ato·tkâlki ímpasa·tatí· sinfi·kitá cóntan ina·ʔapíswa ó·fan imati·hô·hin papa·kít
As his payment for killing the Lord's servants, worms were put in his flesh, and they ate him

mēkko elēcaket omvtēs. Monkv vkerricvkat hiyomē mēkusvpkv-cuko liketayat,
mí·kko ilí·ca·kít o·mati·s môŋka akíłłeycakâ·t hayyô·mi· mi·kosapkacóko leykita·yâ·t[1252]
and killed the king. So as we think now of the churches here and there,

vtēhkvlke, mēkusapvlke, erkenvkvlke, cuko vfastvlke esyomat
ati·hkâlki mi·kosa·pâlki iłkinakâlki coko afa·stâlki isyô·ma·t
the members, Christians, preachers, deacons, all of these,

vnrvpē vretv Hesaketvmesē vnrvpetvt omēs komeyēt os.
anłapí· ałíta hisa·kitamisí· anłapítat ô·mi·s ko·miyí·t ô·ⁿs
we believe to despise them is to despise God.

Monkv etecakkeyvtē, cawvntake toyatskat, vhēricet vkerricepvkvrēs.
môŋka iticákkiyáti· ca·wantá·ki tô·yá·cka·t ahì·ⁿłeycit akíłłeycipákáłi·s
So, my brothers and sisters, let us think about this carefully.

Hēlot Mēkko Cane-Paptisv elēcat, mont Cems elēcat,
hí·lot mí·kko ca·nipa·ptéysa ili·câ·t mónt cîms ili·câ·t
King Herod, in killing John the Baptist, and in killing James,

momet Cēsvs enkerrēpvlke estemerrvkueckv vlicēcat
mo·mít cí·sas iŋkíłłi·pâlki istimíłłakóycka aléyci·câ·t
and in beginning to punish Jesus's disciples,

vheremahen Cehofv vna-orket omvtēs,
ahiłimă·ⁿhin cihó·fa aná·ʔo·lkít o·matí·s
sinned greatly against Jehovah,

Satvme, Komalv ennettv ofv Cehofv vna-orkakvtē ētvpomen.
sa·tamí komá·la innítta ó·fa cihó·fa ana·ʔółka·katí· i·tapô·min
just as they sinned against Jehovah in the days of Sodom and Gomorrah.

Vhesaketv-vhakv hvlwē-estet onvyakvtē apohickv tokon
ahisa·kitaʔahá·ka halwi·ʔístit onáya·katí· a·pohéycka tó·ko·n
In not heeding what the angels said about the law for everlasting life,

vhakv kacat fvccvt fēketv enhēckat, cuntvn emhoyen
ahá·ka ka·câ·t fáccat fi·kitá ínhi·ckâ·t cóntan imhô·yin
and breaking the law, [King Herod] received a just reward; he was given worms,

ena-vpeswv ofvn vtēhket pvpaken, Hēlot Mēkko tat estemērkuset ēlvtēs.
ina·ʔapíswa ó·fan atî·hkit papa·kín hí·lot mí·kkota·t istimĭ·ⁿłkosit i·latí·s
and they got in his flesh and ate him, and King Herod died pitifully.

Mēkko ēme enyekcē ēyohhvkvsamat vheremahen Cehofv vna-orket omvten hēceyēt os.
mí·kko í·miʔ inyikcí· i·yohhakása·mâ·t[1253] ahiłimă·ⁿhin cihó·fa aná·ʔo·lkít o·matín hi·ciyí·t ô·ⁿs
We can see that the king who was boastful about his power sinned greatly against Jehovah.

Monkv pomeu etvlwv 'sem vpeyetv vhakv ocēpeyat mit
môŋka pó·miw itálwaʔ 'simapiyíta ahá·ka o·cî·piya·t[1254] *mêyt*
So we too, when we stand firmly by customs and

yekcēn vsvpaklēn omat, Cehofv vna-orkeyēt os.
yíkci·n asápa·klí·n o·mâ·t cihó·fa aná·ʔo·łkiyí·t ô·ⁿs
laws of the tribal town instead, we sin against Jehovah.

Monkv hvlwē-este opunahoyat vhesaketv-vhakvn onayet okakvten kērreyēt os.
môŋka halwi·ʔísti oponá·ho·yâ·t ahisa·kitaʔahá·kan ona·yít o·ka·katín kî·łiyi·t ô·ⁿs
So when the angels spoke, we know they were telling about the law of everlasting life.

Momis vhesaketv enrakkē momvtēkan vmoskomēkon omat
mo·mêys ahisa·kitá inłakkí· mó·mati·ka·n amô·skó·mí·kon o·mâ·t
But if we do not care about the greatness of everlasting life,

estemerkv rakkē etvlwv omvlkv ohhvlakat, estohmet mvnvttepeyvrhaks,
istimíłka łákki· itálwaʔ omálkaʔ óhhala·kâ·t istóhmit 'manattipiyáłha·ks
when great suffering comes upon all the tribal towns, how will we escape it,

mv estemerketv? Monkv ēyohhvkerrickv hēren ocet vkerricvyat
ma istimilkitá môŋka i·yohhakiłłéycka hĭ·ⁿlin[1255] *ô·cit akíłłeycayâ·t*
that suffering? So let us examine ourselves,

senherąkēn vkerricet 'tecakkeyvtē fullet omēs komēt
sinhiłă·ⁿki·n akíłłeycít 'ticákkiyáti· follít o·mi·s kó·mi·t
in hope that our brothers and sisters are going about with even greater thoughts;

este enhvperkusē omē opunayē este taklēckv estomvkēt
ísti? inhapĭⁿłkosi·[1256] *ó·mi· opóna·yi· ísti taklí·cka isto·makí·t*
when people act like they can't help, blaspheming others,

opunvkv fullē estomis eyąskuset fullvkvrēs makit,
oponaká folli· istô·meys iyă·ⁿskosit fóllakáli·s ma·kéyt
no matter what kinds of rumors circulate, let us go about humbly, I say,

yomusen fekhonnēpis.
yò·mosin fikhónni·péys
and close here.

Ghosts

J. Hill (Haas XXI:103–109)

Este pvsvtkvtē enpuyvfekcvlket nerēn fullēt omēs. Ēkvnv vcelakekot,
ísti pasátkati· inpoyafikcâlkit nilí·n follí·t ô·mi·s i·kaná (?) acilá·kiko·t
The ghosts of dead people go about at night. They don't touch the ground,

estele vhopakv hokkolē mahē enhvlwēn kvwvpkusēt fullēt omēs vculvket makakvnts.
istilí ahopá·ka hokkô·li· má·hi· inhalwí·n kawápkosi·t follí·t ô·mi·s acolakít má·ka·kánc
they go around about two feet above the ground, the old ones used to say.

Mont em penkvlvkēt sasen svheremahē em penkalateu
mónt impiŋkaláki·t sâ·sin 'sahilimá·hi· impiŋkâ·la·tiw
And there are those who are afraid of them; there are Indians

este-catet ayēt omēs, hiyomē stomis.
isticá·tit ǎ·ⁿyi·t ô·mi·s hayyô·mi· stô·meys
who are very afraid, even now.

Momen hofonof erkenvkv yvkvpekot likvtēs.
mo·mín hofó·no·f iɫkináka yakápiko·t leykati·s
Now a long time ago there was a preacher who couldn't walk.

Puyvfekcvlke em penkvlē hērēt omvtēs. Yvkvpekok
poyafikcâlki impiŋkali· hĭ·ⁿli·t ô·mati·s yakápiko·k
He was terrified of ghosts. Because he couldn't walk,

erkenvkvranē ayat ēcokoyet esfulhoyet omvtēs.
iɫkinákaɫa·ní· a·yâ·t i·cóko·yít isfólho·yít ô·mati·s
they would carry him on someone's back to wherever he was to preach.

Mēkusvpkv-cuko vyetv nene tempen vhahwv etot huerēt omen,
mi·kosapkacóko ayíta niní tímpin ahá·hwa itót hóyli·t ô·min
Near the road leading to the church was a walnut tree,

tempusan este hopelhoyvtē sulkēt ocēt oman, cēpvnvke hokkolet vhahwv em ēttēn vteloyet
tímposa·n ísti hopilhoyáti· sólki·t ó·ci·t ô·ma·n ci·panáki hokkô·lit ahá·hwa imi·ttí·n atilô·yit
and close by were many graves. Two boys had gathered walnuts

este hopelkv ocakan eskaket 'tekvpicet ont,
ísti hopílka o·câ·ka·n iskâ·kit 'tíkapeycít ónt
and were sitting in the cemetery dividing them:

"Yvn esēpin" hvmket kicen,
yan isi·péyn hámkit keycín
"I'll take this one," one said,

"Vneu yvn esēpin" hvmkateu kicen eskakof,
aníw yan isi·péyn hámka·tiw keycín iskâ·ko·f
"And I'll take this one," the other said, and as they were sitting there,

erkenvkv acokoyēt svlaket
iłkináka a·cokóyi·t sála·kit
a man carrying the preacher on his back came close,

"Hesaketvmesēt estenekricen 'tepakat poyvfekcvlken 'tekvpicet okakvcoks ce" kicofvn,
hisa·kitamisí·t istinikłéycin 'tipâ·ka·t poyafikcâlkin 'tíkapeycít oka·kacóks ci^ keycô·fan
and [right when the man] said, "God and the devil are dividing the souls,"

vhahwv hvmkuset vhosken,
ahá·hwa hâmkosit aho·skín
only one walnut was left.

"Yvn esēpin, vsi alatkan esepvccvs" makof,
yan isi·péyn asêy á·la·tkâ·n isípáccas ma·kô·f
[One boy] said, "I'll take this one, and you can take the one that falls,"

erkenvkv acokoyat eshoyanen cēpvnē hvmkat hehcet,
iłkináka a·cokô·ya·t íshoya·nín ci·paní· hámka·t híhcit
and one boy saw the man passing with the preacher on his back

"Hi!" kihcen, erkenvkv awihket enlētken,
hey^ kéyhcin iłkináka a·wéyhkit ínli·tkín
and said "Hey!" and the man dropped the preacher and took off running,

erkenvkvo atvsiket,
iłkinákaw a·tasêykit
and the preacher, too, jumped up

ēcokoyvtē lētkat cakket
i·coko·yatí· li·tkâ·t câ·kkit
and was almost up with the running man who had carried him:

"Vm ehakvs!" kicen,
amihá·kas[1257] *keycín*
"Wait for me!" he said,

a-em penkalen cakkuset yopv hueret,
a·ʔimpíŋka·lín câ·kkosit yópa hôylit
and the man got even more scared with the preacher right behind him.

vkērkv hokkolat mahen vhoyet cuko rorhoyvtēs mahokvnts.
akí·łka hokkô·la·t mâ·hin ahô·yit cokó lółho·yatí·s má·ho·kánc.
They went about two miles and got back home, it was told.

When I Saw a Ghost

J. Hill (Haas XXI:111–117)

Momen vneu puyvfekcv hehcis komvyvtē ocēt os.
mo·mín aníw poyafíkca híhceys ko·mayáti· ó·ci·t ô·ⁿs
And there was a time I thought I might have seen a ghost.

Nettan yafkē hvse aklvtkvranē hvse-vkērkv hvmkat mahet vhosken,
nittá·n ya·fkí· hasí aklátkała·ní· hasiʔakí·łka hámka·t má·hit ahô·skin
Late one evening, about one hour before sundown,

hokkolēt escvllēckv ohkakēt nenen vhoyēn,
hokkô·li·t iscallí·cka ohká·ki·t ninín aho·yí·n
two of us were going down a road in a wagon,

nene-tempen esteherickv ēkvnvt ocēt omētan mvn hoyvnhoyeyof,
ninitímpin istihiłéycka i·kanát ó·ci·t ô·mi·ta·n man hoyánho·yiyô·f
and near the road was a graveyard, and as we were passing that,

mv esteherickv ocat fvccvn atet,
ma istihiłéycka ô·ca·t fáccan a·tít
I sat and watched a woman come from the direction of the graveyard

puhomvn hoktēt nenen tohwvlapken hēcit ohlikin,
pohóman hoktí·t ninín tóhwala·pkín hi·ceyt ohlêykeyn
and cross the road in front of us,

ayet, eto rakkēt hueran mvn rohret, somiken,
a·yít itó łákki·t hôyła·n man łóhlit somêykin
and as she got to a big tree, she disappeared.

"Mv eton vhueret omēs" komit,
ma itón ahôylit o·mi·s kô·meyt
"She's standing by the tree," I thought.

"Nene tempusattok hecarēs, estit aret omat" komvyvtē
niní tímposa·tto·k hicá·li·s¹²⁵⁸ istêyt a·lít o·mâ·t kó·mayáti·
"Since it is so near the road, I'll see who it is," I thought,

este sepekon ēkvnvo hvyakpēt onkv,
ísti sipíkon i·kanáw hayákpi·t óŋka
but there was nobody, and the area was clear [of brush and trees],

este tat hopvyēn hēcvken arē tayēt oman hecvkon somiken
ístita·t hopáyi·n hî·cakin a·lí· tâ·yi·t ò·ma·n hicákon somâykin
so you could see a person a long way, but she disappeared.

"Vne tvlkusen naket este vm vhaket ọha?
*aní tálkosin nâ·kit ísti amáha·kít o·ⁿha·ⁿ^*
"Am I the only one seeing this person?

Svyakletv pale cahkēpusē tayēn hēcet ohmvyan os komit ohlikin,
sayaklitá pá·li cahki·posi· tâ·yi·n hî·cit óhmaya·n o·ⁿs kô·meyt ohlêykeyn
I saw her just about fifty steps away," I thought as I sat there,

hoktē vcvpakat, "Hoktēt arv kohmvyat estohma?"
hokti· acapâ·ka·t hoktí·t á·la kóhmaya·t istóhma·˘
[and I said to] the woman with me, "I thought there was a woman. Where did she go?"

"Hēcēkisv?" cvkicen,
hi·ci·keysa˘ cakeycín
"Didn't we see her?" she asked me.

"Hēcvyis. Cēmeu hehcetskv?" kicvyan,
hîꞏcayeys ciꞏmiw híhcickaˊ keycayâꞏn
"I saw her. Did you see her, too?" I asked.

"Eto huerat rorat vtēkusēn hehcis" makemvts.
itohôyłaꞏt łoꞏlâꞏt atîꞏkosiꞏn híhceys maꞏkimác
"I just saw her get to that tree," she said.

Mv ēkvnv vnakv este vpokakat kerrvkot, estet arēs komvkon,
ma iꞏkaná anáꞏka ísti apoꞏkâꞏkaꞏt kíllakoꞏt ístit aꞏliꞏs kóꞏmakoꞏn
I didn't know anyone lived in that area, and I didn't expect anyone,

vcvpakvteu este kerrekat mv vnakv sekot oman kerrēkot aren,
acapâꞏkatiw ísti killikaꞏt ma anáꞏka síkoꞏt ôꞏmaꞏn killíꞏkoꞏt aꞏlín
and the person with me didn't know anyone near there, so we didn't recognize her.

oketv kocoknusēn hehcēn somkvtēt omat omēcicēn
okíta kocŏⁿknosiꞏn híhciꞏn somkatíꞏt ôꞏmaꞏt omiꞏcéyciꞏn
We saw her just a short time, and she disappeared, and that is why

este elvtē em puyvfekcv hēcet omeyvtēs komvyēt omēs.
ísti iláti· impoyafíkca hiꞏcít oꞏmiyátiꞏs kóꞏmayiꞏt ôꞏmiꞏs
I believe that we saw the ghost of a person long dead.

Mv hvse-vkērkv oketv ofv tat opunvyēcetv tis pufekhvmkvkekot omvntvs.
ma hasiʔakiꞏlka okíta óꞏfataꞏt oponayiꞏcitáteys pofikhamkakíkoꞏt óꞏmantás.
In that hour we weren't brave enough to discuss it.

TEXTS BY T. MARSHALL

The Origin of Corn

T. Marshall (Haas VI:57–63)

Hoktvlēt likvtēs.
hoktalí·t leykatí·s[1]
old woman was living
There once was an old woman.

Emosustake cēpvnvke hokkolen ocēt omvtēs.
imosostá·ki ci·panáki hokkô·lin ó·ci·t ô·mati·s
her grandchildren boys two she had did
She had two grandsons.

Momen netta omvlkvn fayakēt omvtēs.
mo·mín nittá· omálkan fá·ya·kí·t ô·mati·s
Then every day they hunted did
And they hunted every day.

Momen fayetvn welvkēpof,
mo·mín fa·yitán wiláki·pô·f
Then to hunt when they 2 were around
And when they were out hunting,

hoktalat osafken hayvlkēt omvtēs.
hoktâ·la·t osá·fkin ha·yăⁿki·t ô·mati·s
the old woman sofkee always made did
the old woman would always make sofkee.

Cepvnvke tat   eyacvkēt   em eskakēt   omvtēs.
ci·panákita·t   *iya·caki·t*   *imíska·ki·t*   *ô·mati·s*
the boys   they wanted   they drank it for her   did
The boys liked it and would drink it for her.

Momen   osafke   eshayetv   vce   ocekot   omatet   hayēt   ont   omvtēs.
mo·mín *osá·fki* *isha·yitá*   *ací* *ó·ciko·t*   *ô·ma·tit*   *ha·yi·ŕ²* *ônt*   *o·mati·s*
Then   sofkee   to make with corn didn't have did(n't)   made it   did   it was
And she made it without having the corn to make sofkee.

Momen   nettv hvmken   cēpvnvke   hokkolat   vketēcetvn   komakvtēs.
mo·mín *nítta hámkin* *ci·panáki*[i] *hokkô·la·t* *akiti·citán*   *kó·ma·kati·s*³
Then   one day   boys   two   to watch   wanted to
Then one day the two boys wanted to investigate.

Hvthvyvtke   hvmken   fayetvn   vhoyohmet   em ēhkakvtēs.
hathayátki   *hámkin*   *fa·yitán*   *aho·yóhmit*   *imí·hka·katí·s*
(one) morning   one   to hunt   pretended   and hid from (her)
One morning they pretended to go hunting and hid from her.

Osafke   naken   eshayet   omat   kerretvn   komakvtēs.
osá·fki *nâ·kin* *ísha·yít*   *o·mâ·t* *killitán*   *kó·ma·katí·s*⁴
sofkee   what   she making it with   (if) what to know   they wanted
They wanted to know what she was making the sofkee with.

Momen   cēpvnvke   vketēcaken,   lehayv   uewv   vcanvtēs.
mo·mín *ci·panáki*   *akiti·câ·kin*   *'lihá·ya* *óywa*   *aca·natí·s*
Then   boys   they watched   pot   water   she put in it
And as the boys watched, she poured water in a big iron kettle.

Momen   ēme   ena-vpeswvn   osafke   eshayet   omvtēton
mo·mín *í·mi*   *iná· apíswan*   *osá·fki* *ísha·yít*   *o·matí·ton*
Then   herself   her flesh   sofkee   she making it with she had been
Then when they found out she had been making sofkee out of her own flesh,

---

[i] Original: *ci·paní· hokkô·la·t.*

kerrakof,   osafke   em esketvn   eyacvkekatēs.
kílla·kô·f   *osá·fki*   *imiskitán*   *(i)ya·cakiká·ti·s*
when they found it out   sofkee   to drink it for (her)   didn't want to
they didn't want to drink it for her.

Em ēhkahket   hoktalat   osafke   hayat   kerrekatēs.
imi·hkáhkit   *hoktá·la·t*   *osá·fki*   *hâ·ya·t*   *kílliká·ti·s*[5]
they hid from (her)   the old woman   sofkee   that she made   she won't know
They hid from her, [so that] the old woman making sofkee would not find out.

Mont omis   em esketvn   yacvkekon   hēcof,
mônt o·mêys *imiskitán*   *ya·cakikon*   *hi·cô·f*
but   to drink for (her)   not wanting   when she saw it
But when she saw that they didn't want to drink it,

mont omat   kērrvtēs.   Momen   hoktalat   okat,
mônt o·má·t   *ki·łłati·s*   *mo·mín*   *hoktá·la·t*   *o·kâ·t*
that it was the way   she found (that)   Then   the old woman   said
she figured out why. And the old woman said,

"Osafke   naken   eshayit   omvyvtē   mucv tat   cvkerrēpet   omatskes.
osá·fki *nâ·kin*   *ísha·yéyt*   *o·mayáti·* *mocáta·t*   *cakillî·pit*   *ô·má·ckis*
sofkee   what   I made with   I did   now   found me out   you have
"Now you have found out what I make sofkee with.

Monkv   hiyomat   cukon   vm akhotiyet,   'mvhetehcet,   vcohnokricatskvrēs."
moŋká   *hayyô·ma·t*   *cokón*   *amakhotêyyit*   *'mahitíhc·it*   *acohnokłéycá·ckáłi·s*
therefore now   house   shut me up in   set it on fire   burn down over me
So shut me up in my house now, set it on fire, and burn it down on top of me."

Monkv   cēpvnvke tat   hoktalat   cukon   'makhotiyet,
môŋka   *ci·panákita·t*   *hoktá·la·t*   *cokón*   *makhotêyyit*
Therefore the boys   the old woman   house   shut it up on her
So the boys shut the woman up in her house,

'mvhetehcet,   nokricakvtēs.   Momen   tasahcat,
'mahitíhcit[i]   *nokłéyca·katí·s*   *mo·mín*   *tá·sa·hcâ·t*
set it afire   they burnt it   Then   in the spring
set it on fire, and burned it down. Then in the spring

mv   cuko   nokrvtē   vcet   orēn   hervkēt   hontvtēs.
ma   *cokó*   *no·kłatí·*   *acít*   *ołí·n*   *hiláki·t*   *hontatí·s*
that   house   where burned   corn   awful   very good   came up
corn sprouted vigorously where the house had burned.

Mohmet   vce   sulkēt   lokcvtēs.
móhmit   *ací*   *sólki·t*   *lo·kcatí·s*
then   corn   plenty   ripened
Then a great quantity of corn ripened.

Monkv   este-cate tat   vce tat   hoktvlusēt   omvtēt   omēs.
mônka   *(i)sticá·tita·t*   *acíta·t*   *hoktalósi·t*   *o·matí·t*   *ô·mi·s,*
Therefore   the Indians   corn   the old woman   had been   (was)
So [for] the Indians, corn had been an old woman

enhvteceskv   omof.   "Momēn   vce   hēckvtē   em vlicēckv
inhaticíska   *ô·mo·f*   *mó·mi·n*   *ací*   *hi·ckatí·*   *imaleycí·cka*
in the beginning   in   That's the way   corn   was created   its beginning
at first. "That's the way corn

hiyomēt   omvtēs"   makakēt   omvtēt   os   cē.
hayyó·mi·t   *ô·mati·s*   *má·ka·kí·t*   *o·mati·t*   *ô·s*   *cî·*[ii]
this way   was   that's what they said   about it
was created," they used to tell.

---

[i] Long way: *imahitíhcit.*
[ii] Raiford says *ci^*; some say *ci·^.*

The Lion and the Little Girl (Estepapvt Hoktucen Horkopvtēs)[i]

T. Marshall (Haas IV:143–159)

Estepapvt	hoktucen	horkohpet	ehuten	'sayvtēs.
istipá·pat	*hoktocín*	*hołkóhpit*	*ihótin*	*sa·yatí·s*
lion	a little girl	he stole (her)	to his home	he took her

A lion stole a little girl and took her to his den.

Momen	'stepapv hoktē	estepapv honvnwv	'tepakat	fakvn	vhoyvtēs.
mo·mín	*stipá·pa hoktí·*[6]	*istipá·pa honánwa*	*'tipá·ka·t*	*fá·kan*	*aho·yatí·s*
then	the female lion	and the male lion	both together	hunting	they went

Now the lioness went hunting with the lion.

Momen	hoktuce tat	estepapucvlken	vpvkēt	likvtēs.
mo·mín	*hoktocíta·t*	*istipa·pocâlkin*	*apáki·t*	*lêykati·s*
Then	the little girl	the lion cubs	with them	was sitting, living

And the little girl stayed with the lion cubs.

Momof	hoktuce tat	encukon	yefulkēpvtēs,	vyetv	yacehē̜rvtētok.
mo·mô·f	*hoktocíta·t*	*incokón*	*'yifólki·patí·s*	*ayíta*	*ya·cihĭ·ⁿlati·to·k*
Then	the little girl	her home	she returned to	to go	wanted (to go) very badly

During that time the little girl started back home, for she very badly wanted to go.

Momēpen		estepapv hoktē	rvlakvtēs.
mo·mî·pin		*istipá·pa hoktí·*	*łála·katí·s*
it happened (that she had gone)		the lioness	came back

But it happened that the lioness came back,

Momen	assēcvtēs.		Encuko	fvccvn	vyēpen
mo·mín	*á·ssi·catí·s*		*incokó*	*fáccan*	*ayî·pin*
Then	she ran after her, pursued her		(towards) her home	towards	she had gone

and she chased after her. [The girl] had gone toward her home, and [the lioness]

---

[i] Title: *(i)stipá·pat hoktocín hólko·patí·s* 'lion stole the girl'.

assēcetvn vlicēcvtēs. Nake assepueckv ocvtē raehset,
a·ssi·citán aléyci·catí·s nâ·ki a·ssipóycka[i] ô·cati· la·ihsit[7]
to run after her she began something to pursue her with she had she went and got it
began to run after her. [The lioness] took out something she had to chase her with,

elehvpon rohhuerihcof, mv nake letketvn
ilihapó·n łohhoyłéyhco·f ma nâ·ki litkitán
her foot-prints when she went and put it on (her foot-prints) that something running
and when she put it in her footprints, the thing

vlicēcvtēs. Mv nake hocefkv motvkv mvt omvtēs.
aléyci·catí·s ma nâ·ki hocífka, motáka mat ô·mati·s
it began that something name mutaka that was its (name)
began to run. The name of the thing was a <u>motvkv</u>.[8]

(Nake 'sencvllv omē enhakvt omvtēs.)
nâ·ki sincálla ó·mi· inhá·kat ô·mati·s
something's wheel like the make (of a wheel) was
(It had the shape of a wheel.)

Momen pvfnēt nake assēcēt omen,
mo·mín páfni·t nâ·ki á·ssi·cí·t ô·min,
Then fast (after) something it ran after did
It chases after things quickly,

mvn assepuecet omvtēs. Mont cakken omat,
man á·ssipoycít o·matí·s mónt ca·kkín o·mâ·t
(with) that she pursued her with (that) did Because catching up to it if
and she made it chase her. And if it catches up,

ohcvllet vwikēt omen, 'saret
óhcallit aweyki·t ô·min sa·lít
it rolls on it, over it and knocks it down does is (why) she takes it around with her
it rolls over on what it is chasing and knocks it down, and that is why

---

[i] Raiford: *a·ssipéycka.*

omvtēs.	Momen	assē	'svyēpat
o·matí·s	*mo·mín*	*a·ssí·*	*sáyi·pâ·t*
is why, is the reason why		she running after, pursuing	going along with it

she carried it around. And giving chase with it,

yopvn	lētket	estepapv-hoktē	arvtēs.
yópan	*li·tkít*	*istipa·pahoktí·*[i]	*a·latí·s*
behind	running (behind)	lioness	was around

the lioness ran behind.

Mv	nake	assepuecat	"Pvfnvs"	maket
ma	*nâ·ki*	*á·ssipoycâ·t*	*páfnas*	*ma·kít*
(with) that	thing	pursuing it with	get fast!	she said

To make it give chase, she said, "Be quick!"

'tewolusen		yopvn	'sayvtēs.
'tiwô·losin		*yópan*	*sa·yatí·s*
(she said) in succession, close together		behind	was going along

several times quickly as she followed behind.

Momen	hoktuce	ecke	ocēt	omvtēs.	Momen	cēpvnvke	hokkolen
mo·mín	*hoktocí*	*icki*	*ó·ci·t*	*ô·mati·s*	*mo·mín*	*ci·panáki*	*hokkô·lin*
Then	the girl	a mother	she had	did	Then	boys	two

Now the girl had a mother. And she had

ocēt	omvtēs.	Mvt	ecertaket	omvtēs.	Nettv	hvmken	cēpanat
ó·ci·t	*ô·mati·s*	*mat*	*iciltá·kit*	*ô·mati·s*	*nítta*	*hámkin*	*ci·pâ·na·t*
she had	did	those	her brothers	they were	(one) day	one	the boy

two boys. They were [the girl's] brothers. One day [one] boy

arvtēs.	Ēwvnwv	estomvten	omat	vkerricet,
a·latí·s	*i·wánwa*	*istô·matin*[ii]	*o·mâ·t*	*akílleycít*
was about	his sister	what became of her	had	he wondered (what —)

was about. He was wondering what had happened to his sister,

---

[i] Or (in his written version): *istipa·pahoktálwa* 'old lioness'.

[ii] Original: *istô·matit.*

sumkvtē		netta	yvfyvkēt	omekv.
somkatí·		*nittá·*	*yafyakí·t*	*o·miká*[9]
had gone away, gotten lost		days	several evenings (of days)	had (passed)

because it had been several days since she disappeared.

Momof	estomuset	pohken,	yvhikesasvcoken	pohvtēs.
mo·mô·f	*istô·mosit*[10]	*pô·hkin*	*yahaykisâ·sacókin*	*po·hatí·s*
then again	a little bit	he heard	somebody singing	he heard it

Then something faint could be heard; he heard somebody singing.

Momen	hēren	em apohicvtēs.	Moman	enhakētat	mv	hoktucet	okēpat
mo·mín	*hĭ·ⁿlin*	*(i)má·pohaycatí·s*	*mo·mâ·n*	*inha·ki·ta·t*	*ma*	*hoktocít*	*oki·pâ·t*
Then	good	he listened at it	Then,	her voice	that	little girl	it was her (voice)

Then he listened carefully. And the voice was the little girl's,

'satēt		okvcoken	lvpkēn	lētket	ahyet
sa·tí·t		*o·kacókin*	*lápki·n*	*li·tkít*	*áhyit*
and she coming toward (them)		seemed to be	fast	running	he went

coming toward him, and he ran fast

ecken	cēpanat	hvmket	'tepakan	'monayvtēs.
íckin	*ci·pâ·na·t*	*hámkit*	*'tipâ·ka·n*[11]	*móna·yatí·s*
mother	the boy	the other one	together	he told her and the other boy

and told his mother and the other boy.

Momis	vkvsvmvkekatēs.		"Naket	esēpet	omvtētok.
mo·mâys	*akasamákiká·ti·s*		*nâ·kit*	*isî·pit*[12]	*o·matí·to·k*
Then, But	they didn't think it was so, believe it		something	had caught her	because it had

But they didn't believe it. "Something caught her.

Svnvcumvn	rvlaken	heceyvrēs	komēks"	makakvtēs.
'sanácoman[13]	*lála·kín*	*hicíyáli·s*	*kó·mí·ks*	*má·ka·katí·s*
(never again) ever	her coming back	will we see her	we don't think	they said

We'll never see her come back again," they said.

Momen	cēpanat	ohyekcicen	hvmkat	'mapohicvtēs.
mo·mín	*ci·pâ·na·t*	*ohyíkcaycín*	*hámka·t*	*(i)má·pohaycatí·s*
then	the boy (the other)	was exacted upon	the other one	and he listened to him

Then the boy insisted, and the other [boy] paid attention to him.

Mvt	okēpen	kērrvtēs.	Momen	hoktuce	yvhikat
mat	*oki·pín*	*ki·ɬatí·s*[i]	*mo·mín*	*hoktocí*	*yahaykâ·t*
it	to be her	he found out	then	the girl	when singing

He knew it was her. And the girl sang,

"Cvcertake	kakat	orvkot
caciltá·ki	*kâ·ka·t*	*olákot*
my brothers	who are living	before I (don't) get there

"Before I reach where my brothers live,

cvlepvranis	omēpēs"
calípaɬa·néys	*omi·pí·s*
I will die, I may die	maybe

I may die,"

maket	yvhiket	omen,	pohakat	lētket	atēt	okvcoken
ma·kít	*yahaykít*	*o·mín*	*poha·kâ·t*	*li·tkít*	*a·tí·t*	*o·kacókin*
she said	as she singing	was	when they heard it	she running	coming	seemed to be

she was singing, and they heard her and when they figured out

kerrakof,	"Naket	aren	atet	omvcoks"	makakvtēs.
kíɬɬa·kô·f	*nâ·kit*	*a·lín*	*a·tít*	*o·macóks*	*má·ka·katí·s*
when they found it out	something	being about	coming	she is	

she was coming running, they said, "Something [else] is there as she's coming."

Mont	vhohyet	ecke tat	'monvyaket,	"Vnrvpvranēs"
mônt	*ahóhyit*	*íckita·t*	*mónaya·kít*	*anɬapáɬa·ní·s*
Then	they went	their mother	they told her, were telling her	we're going to meet her

Then they went and told their mother, "We're going to meet her,"

maket,	eccvkotakse	racvwahket	vhoyvtēs.
ma·kít	*iccakotáksi*	*ɬa·cawáhkit*	*aho·yatí·s*
they said	bows	they went and got and (then)	they 2 went on their way

they said, and they got their bows and went.

---

[i] Might also be *ki·ɬatí·s*.

Tokorket   momen   vwolusen   vlvkēpvcoken   pohaket,
toko·lkít   *mo·mín*   *awǒ·ⁿlosin* *aláki·pacókin*   *pohâ·kit*[14]
they 2 were running   then   close   she seemed to be coming   they heard
They were running and heard her coming closer,

naket   assēcē   hēret   omvcoken   kerrakat,
nâ·kit   *á·ssi·cí·* *hǐ·ⁿlit*   *o·macókin*   *kíɬa·kâ·t*
something   pursuing her sure was (pursuing) seemed to be   when they found it out
and when they figured out something was really chasing her,

fihohket   em ēhkēt   nenuce   vfopken   kaken,   hoktuce tat
fayhóhkit   *imí·hki·t*   *ninóci* *afó·pkin* *kà·kin*   *hoktocíta·t*
they turned off   and hid   a trail   nearby   they 2 sat   the little girl
they turned off and sat hiding near a trail, and the little girl

lētket   hoyahnet   ayvtēs.   Encuko   rvlvkēpet   omvtēs.
li·tkit   *hoyáhnit* *a·yatí·s* *incokó*   *ɬálaki·pít*[15] *o·matí·s*
running   passed by   and went   to her home coming back to   she was
ran past. She was coming back to her home.

Momof   mv   nak   'sencvllv   pvfne   hēret   aten   hecakvtēs.
mo·mô·f   *ma* *nâ·k* *sincálla* *páfni*   *hǐ·ⁿlit*   *a·tín*   *hica·katí·s*
Then   that thing wheel   fast   very   coming   they saw it.
Then they saw that wheel-thing coming really fast.

Mont   'mēhakaken   hvmket   ēccvtēs.   Mont   emmattvtēs.
mónt   *(i)mi·ha·kâ·kin* *hámkit*   *i·ccatí·s*[i] *mónt*   *ímma·ttatí·s*
Then   they waited for it one of them shot at it   he missed it
And they waited for it, and one shot at it. And he missed it.

Hvmkat   ēccat   rahhet   hopanvtēs.
hámka·t   *i·cca·t*[ii]   *ɬáhhit*   *hópa·natí·s*
The other one when he shot at it he hit it (and) spoiled it
When the other one shot at it, he hit it and broke it.

---

[i] Some say (including Raiford): *i·chatí·s* (IV:156).
[ii] Raiford: *î·cha·t*.

Estepapv hoktē yopvn arvtet   vlakof,
istipá·pa hoktí· yópan a·łatít   *ala·kô·f*
lioness   behind   had been around (behind)   when she was coming
When the lioness that had been behind it arrived,

rahhet   'lēcakvtēs.   Momen hoktuce tat   encukon   rvlvkēpvtēs.
łáhhit   *(i)li·ca·katí·s*   *mo·mín hoktocíta·t incokón*   *łálaki·patí·s*
he hit her (in shooting)   and killed her.   Then   the little girl to her home   returned to
they shot her and killed her. So the little girl returned to her home.

Cēpvnvke   'monvyahken estepapv hute   ocan   vhoyvtēs.
ci·panáki   *'monayáhkin istipá·pa hóti*   *ô·ca·n*   *aho·yatí·s*
The boys   she told them   the lion's   dwelling   where was
She told the boys, and they went to where the lion's den was.

Estepapv honvnwv sepekon   'mehakaken,   rvlahken,   'lēcahket
istipá·pa hoñánwa sipíkon   *'miha·kâ·kin*   *'laláhkin*   *li·cáhkit*
the lion   wasn't there   they waited for him   he returned   they killed him
The lion wasn't there, so they waited, and upon his return, they killed him,

estepapucvlke tat   cahwet   encukon   res vthoyēpvtēs.
istipa·pocâlkita·t   *cáhwit*   *incokón*   *'lisáthoyi·patí·s*
the lion cubs   they took   and home (their home)   they brought them back
took the lion cubs, and brought them home.

How Deer Fooled Rabbit (Eco ton momen Cufe)[i]

T. Marshall (Haas IV:161–169)

Ecot Cufen   'mvkērrvtēs.   Cufe tat hofonof   elaksvn ocēt omvtēs.
icót cofín   *máki·llatí·s*   *cofíta·t hofô·no·f*   *iláksan ó·ci·t ô·mati·s*
Deer   the Rabbit   he fooled (R.)   Rabbit   long time ago   hoofs   had   did
Deer fooled Rabbit. Long ago Rabbit had hoofs.

Momen Ecot   Cufe ele   hiyome   ocat   omēt   omvtēs.
mo·mín icót   *cofi ilí*   *hayyó·mi· ó·ca·t o·mí·t o·matí·s*
then   the deer   rabbits feet   like   had   did   it was (long ago)
And Deer had feet like Rabbit.

---

[i] Title: *icóton mo·mín cofí* 'deer and rabbit'.

Momen Ecot Cufe 　'mestelepikvn 　'svpenkvlēcetvn 　　　　komvtēs.
mo·mín icót cofí 　mistilipéykan 　'sapiŋkali·citán 　　　　kô·mati·s
Then 　Deer 　Rabbits shoes 　　　　to take away from, dispossess him of 　intended
Then Deer tried to steal Rabbit's shoes.

Mont 　"Estelepikv herakusēn 　ontskes. 　Vnpaletsken 　cem vtehēpit 　hecvranis"
mónt 　istilipéyka hilă·ⁿkosi·n 　ônckis 　anpâ·líckin[i] 　cimatihî·payt 　hicála·néys
Then 　shoes 　　　pretty ones 　you have 　you loan to me 　I'll put them on 　I will see
"You have such pretty shoes. Lend them to me, and I'll try them on,"

kihcen, 　　"Vnmehcewitēs" 　　　kont omis 　　'mvkvsahmen,
káyhcin 　anmíhciwâyti·s[ii] 　　kônt o·mêys 　'makasáhmin
he said 　he might do that for me 　he thought, but 　he consented
he said. [Rabbit] thought, "He might [take them] from me," but agreed,

vtehhet 　　　　eslētket 　　　　'sarvtēs.
atíhhit 　　　ísli·tkít 　　　sa·latí·s
he put them on 　he ran with them 　and was around with them
and [Deer] put them on and ran around with them.

Res kololuecet 　　　　　　'sarvtēs. 　　　　　Momen 　hvtvm
liskolóloycít 　　　　　sa·latí·s 　　　　　mo·mín 　hatâm
he went in a circle with them 　and was about with them 　Then 　again
He went around in circles. Then

res enhopvyusēn 　'sayet 　　　'saret
'lisinhopáyosi·n 　sa·yít 　　sa·lít
a little bit further 　he went with them 　he was around with them
he went around with them a bit further

res enletkemahvtēs. 　　　　　　Momen Cufe tat 　assēcet 　　ont omis
'lisinlítkima·hatí·s 　　　　　mo·mín cofíta·t 　á·ssi·cít 　ónt o·mêys
he ran away from him with them entirely 　Then 　Rabbit 　ran after him 　did, but
and finally ran away with them entirely. Though Rabbit chased him,

---

[i] Raiford: *ampâ·l-.*

[ii] Raiford: *ammíh-.*

cakkeko tayen   'sayet   'sensumkēpvtēs.
cákkiko· tâ·yin   *sa·yít*   *sinsómki·patí·s*
could not catch him   went away with them   he took them away from him
he couldn't catch him, and [Deer] disappeared.

Momen   Cufe tat   Eco   'mestelepikvn   vtehhet   yacekot ont   omis
mo·mín   *cofíta·t*   *icó*   *mistilipáykan*   *atíhhit*   *yá·cikot ónt*   *o·mêys*
Then   Rabbit   Deer's   shoes   put them on   he didn't want them,   but
Now Rabbit put on Deer's shoes and didn't like them,

'saret   'svmonkhakvtēt omēs.   Momvtēt   ont omen,
sa·lít   *'samoŋkha·katí·t ô·mi·s*   *mo·matí·t*   *ônt o·mín*
was around with them   he did get used to them   that's the way   it was
but he got used to them. That's the way it happened,

Cufe tat   enpvlecetvn   kont   arvtētot
cofíta·t   *inpalicitán*   *kônt*   *a·latí·tot*
Rabbit   to pay him back   thought, trying   he had been about
so Rabbit thought about getting revenge,

hvtvm   'tehecakvtēs.   Mont omis   'tem opunvyēcvkekatēs,
hatâm   *tíhica·katí·s*   *mónt o·mêys*   *'timoponayi·cakíká·ti·s*[16]
again   they saw each other   but then   we'll not talk about it to each other
and they saw each other again. But they didn't discuss it,

nake   'tem vkerrakvtē   ohfvccv tat.   Momen
nâ·ki   *'timakíłła·katí·*   *ohfáccata·t*[17]   *mo·mín*
that   that they had fooled each other with   about (that)   Then
the matter of fooling each other. Now

Cufet   eco-yvpen   'meyacētot   cufen   'mvkvsvmē tatēs.
cofít   *icoyapín*[18]   *'miyá·ci·tot*[19]   *cofín*   *'makasamí· tá·ti·s*
Rabbit   Deer's horns   wanted them   Rabbit   he consented for the R. (to do so)
Rabbit wanted Deer's antlers, and [Deer] was agreeable to Rabbit.

Mont   "'Svnpaletsken,   'sekohlicin   hecvkēs"   kihcen,
mónt   *sanpâ·líckin*   *'sikohlêyceyn*   *hicáki·s*[20]   *káyhcin*
Then   you loan them to me   I will put them on (my head)   and we can see   he said
"Lend them to me, and let's see me try them on my head," he said,

'senpalvtēs.　　　　　　Momen　Cufe tat　eco-yvpen　'sekohlicet
sínpa·latí·s　　　　　　*mo·mín*　*cofíta·t*　*icoyapin*　*sikohlêycit*
he loaned them to him　Then　　Rabbit　Deer-horns　had them on (his head)
and [Deer] lent them to him. So Rabbit put the deer antlers on his head

'sarvtēs.　　　　　　　　"Eslētkit　　　　　'sarin　　　　　hecvkēts"　kicen,
sa·latí·s　　　　　　　*ísli·tkáyt*　　　　*sa·léyn*　　　*hicáki·c*[i]　*kaycín*
and was around with them　I will run with these　around with them　let's see　he said
and went around with them. "Let's see me run around with them," he said.

"Enka"　　kihcen,　　Cufe tat　　'sekohlicet　eslētket　　'sarvtēs.
*iŋka·^*[ii]　*káyhcin*　*cofíta·t*　　*'sikohlêycit*　*ísli·tkít*　*sa·latí·s*
all right　he said　　the Rabbit　had them on　was running　around with them
"Okay," [Deer] said, and Rabbit put them on his head and ran around with them.

Mont　　　'senhopvyusēn　ēmeu　　'sayet　　　'saret　　　　　'sen lētkvtēs.
mónt　　*sinhopáyosi·n*　*i·miw'*　*sa·yít*　　*sa·lít*　　　*sínli·tkatí·s*
Then　　　a little further　he, too　going with it　was around with it　and ran away with it
Then he too went off a little further each time and ran off with them.

Momen　　'svyēpet　　　　　　omen　Eco　　kērrof,　　　　　assēcvtēs.
mo·mín　*'sayî·pit*[21]　　　　*o·mín*　*icó*　*ki·łô·f*　　　*á·ssi·catí·s*
Then　　　it had gone with them　had　　Deer　when he found it out　ran after him
And when Deer found out that he'd gone off with them, he chased him.

Momen　　Cufe tat　　esletkusēhayet,　　　　　　estonkomahhet
mo·mín　*cofíta·t*　　*íslitkosí·hâ·yit*[22]　　　　*istoŋkomáhhit*
then　　　Rabbit　　　was running pretty well with it　and he couldn't do anything
Now Rabbit was running pretty well with them, but unable to outrun him,

Ecot　　cakkēpen,　　　　eton　　res ohsehket　　　vyēpen,
icót　　*cákki·pín*　　　*itón*　　*'lisohsíhkit*　　*ayî·pin*
Deer　　was catching up to him　tree　　he hung them up on (a tree)　and had gone
Deer caught up with him. [Rabbit] hung them on a tree and took off,

---

[i] Original: *hicáki·s.*
[ii] Some say *hiŋka·^.*

Eco tat	eyvpe	resehpet	'sekohlicēpvtēs.
icóta·t	*iyápi*	*'lisíhpit*	*'sikohléyci·pati·s*
Deer	its horns	got them	and put them on his (own) head

and Deer got his antlers and put them back on his head.

Momen	Cufe tat	enpoyaʄkvtēs.
mo·mín	*cofíta·t*	*ínpoya·ʄkatí·s*
Then	Rabbit	got left

And Rabbit had failed to get them.

The Race of the Hummingbird and the Crane

T. Marshall (Haas V:135–139)

Rvnrvcokwvt	akcvohkon	'tem vretvn	komakvtēs,
łánłacókwat	*akcâwhkon*	*'timałítan*	*kó·ma·katí·s*[23]
hummingbird	and crane	to race one another	they tried

The hummingbird and the crane wanted to race each other,

momen	cahkē-rakko	uewv	rvro	ak-eccetv
mo·mín	*cahki·łákko*	*óywa*	*łałó*	*akkiccitá*
Then	big shoal	water	fish	to shoot at

[to see] which one could first get to the big shoal where

hēran		estvmi tawvt	rorepē tayen	omat
hĭ·ⁿla·n		*istamêytá·wat*	*'lolipí· tá·yin*	*o·mâ·t*
a good one, the best place		which one first	get there (first)	(if)

it's good to shoot at fish.

Monkv	'tem vpvlwusen	vhoyvtēs.
mônka	*'timapálwosin*	*aho·yatí·s*
therefore	at the same time	they 2 went

So they both took off at the same time.

Momen	rvnrvcokwvt	pvfnēt	vyēpvtēs.
mo·mín	*łánłacókwat*	*páfni·t*	*ayi·patí·s*
	the hummingbird	fast	he went

The hummingbird went fast.

Mon   vyēpen   yomockat   fekhoniyet   nocēpen
mô·n   ayi·pín   yomo·ckâ·t   fikhonâyyit   nocî·pin
           (one) going   at dark   he stopped   sleeping
He left, and when it got dark, he stopped and slept:

"Hvyatkof   vyarēs"   kohmet   nocēpvtēs.
haya·tkô·f   ayá·li·s   kóhmit   noci·patí·s
when it was morning   "I will go"   he thought   he went to sleep
"I'll go in the morning," he thought and went to sleep.

Momen   akcvohko tat   ayvtēs.   Hvlvlatkuset   vyēpen,   yomociken,
mo·mín   akcâwhkota·t   a·yatí·s   halalǎ·ⁿtkosit   ayi·pín   yomocêykin
            the crane   went   slow   going   it got dark
Then crane went. He went slowly, and it got dark;

nerē   vyēpen   hvyatkvtēs.
nilí·   ayi·pín   haya·tkatí·s
at night   going   it got daylight
he went by night, and morning came.

Momen   cahkē-rakko   rorepēt   hvse   aossat,
mo·mín   cahki·lákko   'lolipí·t[24] hasí   á·o·ssâ·t
Then   the big shoal   he got to   the sun   coming up
He got to the big shoal, and when the sun came up,

rvro   pvsvtēpet   akhuerēpen,   rvnrvcokwv tat   rohret   cvpakkvtēs,
laló   pasáti·pít   akhoylî·pin   lânlacókwata·t   lóhlit   capa·kkatí·s
fish   killing   he stood there   the hummingbird   got there   he got mad
he was standing there killing fish, and hummingbird arrived and got mad,

enpohoyen   hēcof.   Mon   okat   "Ohhvtvlakat
inpo·hô·yin   *hi·cô·f*   *mô·n*   *o·kâ·t*   *ohhatalâ·ka·t*
(when he saw) he had lost   when he saw   Then   said   from now on
seeing that he had lost. Then he said, "From now on,

pakpvkuce   omusis   enlasēpit   vreparēs   mahket
pakpakóci   ô·moseys   inlá·si·péyt   alipá·li·s   máhkit
a little flower   it was like   sucking (a little flower)   he said
I'll go around sucking on little flowers,"

ayvtēt omet	pakpvkucen	enlaset	fullēt		omēs	maketvt omēs.
a·yatí·t ô·mit	*pakpakócin*	*ínla·sít*	*follí·t*		*ô·mi·s*	*ma·kitát ô·mi·s*
and he went	flower	sucking	they go around		that way	that's the saying

and he left, and they do go around sucking flowers, the saying is.

Momen	akcvohkv	mvo	epoyvtēt	uewvn	akhuerē	svmokhaket	omvtēt
mo·mín	*akcâwhko*	*maw'*	*ipo·yatí·t*	*óywan*	*akhóyli·*	*samó·kha·kít*[25]	*o·matí·t*
Then	the crane	he, too	had won	water	standing in	in the habit of	it had been

And the crane who had won got used to standing in the water

uewvn	akhuerēt	ont	omēs	mahokvnts.
óywan	*akhóyli·t*	*ônt*	*o·mi·s*	*má·ho·kánc*
water	standing in		he always does.	That's what has been said.

and always stands in the water, it was said.

Raccoon Marries Goose

T. Marshall (Haas V:141–143)[26]

Lekothofvn	sasakwvt	aren	wotkot	ēpayvtēs.
likothó·fan	*sâ·sákwat*	*a·lín*	*wó·tkot*	*i·pa·yatí·s*
south	goose (subj.)	was about (obj.)	coon (subj.)	married her (of man)

A raccoon once married a goose in the south,[i]

Momen	hopuetake	vnvcumēn	ocakvtēs.	Momen	sasakwv tat
mo·mín	*hopoytá·ki*	*anacomí·n*	*o·câ·kati·s*	*mo·mín*	*sâ·sákwata·t*
then	children	several	they had	Then	those geese (his wife and children)

and they had several children. And those geese

---

[i] [Raiford notes that] Marshall is a Coon and can tell this story "on himself." However, if his "daddy" was a Coon, he couldn't tell this story or one about Coon or make fun of the coon in any way. Formerly, they would take something away from you or fine you for this. If you start to tell a story about Coon, and if anybody in the group's father is a Coon, he used to try to make you stop. Now, they usually listen to you, but when you finish they praise the Coon and point out its good qualities in defense.

You can tell a story on your own clan (e.g., Beaver), however, and if anyone whose father is of the same clan as yours is present, he can make objections, but he can't take anything away from you, because you're priveleged to tell jokes "on yourself." However, if you tell something on your father's clan, then another "son" can object and take something from you. Also, if you tell something on an unrelated clan.

kvsvppofvn   vpeyepetvn   komvtēs.   Momen 'metetaket   fullen
kasappó·fan   *apiyipítan*   *kô·matí·s*   *mo·mín nítita·kít*   *follín*
north   to go (north)   they wanted   Then   getting ready were about
wanted to go north. Now they were getting ready,

oketv   cvkiken   hvyatkat   vpeyēpvtēs.
okíta   *cakâykin*   *haya·tkâ·t*   *apíyi·patí·s*
the time   came (and)   in the morning they went
and when the time came, they started off in the morning.

Sasakwv tat   tvmecēpet   vpeyēpen   wotko tat   lētket   lecvn hueren   vpēyen
sà·sákwata·t   *tamíci·pít*   *apíyi·pín* *wó·tkota·t* *li·tkít* *lícan hòylin*   *api·yín*
those geese   flew   going   the coon   running   standing beneath they going
As the geese flew along [in the sky], the raccoon ran along beneath them,

hvcce rakkēt   ocen   tvyecehpet   vpeyephoyen   wotko tat   hvccen   tikeko tayet
hácci lákki·t *ô·cin* *'tayicíhpit* *apiyípho·yín* *wó·tkota·t* *háccin* *táykiko· tâ·yit*
big stream   was   they crossed   were going   coon   stream   couldn't cross
[but] when [the geese] crossed over a big river, the raccoon couldn't cross.

hvccen   vpicēcet   aret   estonkomahhet   fekhonnvtet   omet
háccin   *(a)páyci·cít*   *a·lít*   *istoŋkomáhhit*   *fíkhonnatít* *ô·mit*
stream   going up and down   was about   couldn't do anything stopped   did
He could do nothing but go up and down along the stream; finally he stopped,

hvccen   picēcē monket   omēs   maketvt omēs.
háccin   *páyci·cí· môŋkit*   *ô·mi·s* *ma·kitát ô·mi·s*
stream   still going up and down (the stream) is   that is the saying
and he still goes up and down the stream, it is said.

The White Man Who Used the Conjurers' Medicine (Este-hvtket Porrvlken Helēswvn Encelayvtēs)[i]

T. Marshall (Haas V:145–151)[27]

Este	vculēt	omen	ehiwv	hoktalusēt	omen	kakvtēs.
ísti	*acóli·t*	*ô·min,*	*iháywa*	*hoktă-ⁿlosi·t*	*ô·min*	*kâ·kati·s*
an old man			his wife	an old woman		were living

Once there was an old man and his wife, an old woman.

Momen	este-hvtke	vtotkvn	licvkēt	omvtēs.
mo·mín	*istihátki*	*ató·tkan*	*leycakí·t*	*ô·mati·s*
Then	a white person	as work-hand	they had	did

Now they had a white man as a hired hand.

Momen	cuko ofv	hvmkusen	nocicēt	omvtēs.
mo·mín	*cokó ó·fa*	*hámkosin*[28]	*noceycí·t*	*ô·mati·s*
Then	in (one) room, place, house	one	they (all) slept	did

And they all slept in one room.

Mon	este-hvtke	nocēpof	estvn	komat	vhoyēpet
mô·n	*istihátki*	*noci·pô·f*	*ístan*	*kô·ma·t*	*ahóyi·pít*
	the white man	when he was sleeping	where	they wanted to	they 2 went

Now [the old man and woman] would go off while the white man slept,

welvkēpen	hvyatken	rvlahoket	welakēt	omvtētot
wiláki·pín	*haya·tkín*	*'lalá·ho·kít*	*wila·ki·t*	*ô·mati·tot*
they 2 were around	it got day	they 2 came back	being around	they had been

and they would come back at day break.

nerē	hvmken	vhoyetvn	kont	kulkē	kulecahket
nilí·	*hámkin*	*ahoyitán*	*kònt*	*kolkí·*	*kolicáhkit*
night	one	they 2 to go	wanted	a lamp	they lighted

One night when they intended to leave, they lit a lamp

---

[i] Title: *istihátkit po·llálkin 'hili·swan íncila·yatí·s* 'white person used the conjurers' medicine'. *'hilíswa* 'medicine' is *'hilí·swa* in Marshall's dialect.

'metetaketvn	vlicēcakvtēs.	Mont	helēswv	haluce	vcvnkusēn
'mitita·kitán	*aleycí·ca·katí·s*	*mônt*	*'hilí·swa*[29]	*ha·locí*	*acáŋkosi·n*
to get ready	they started	Then	medicine	tin-cup	in (the tin-cup)

and began to get ready. Now they had medicine in a little cup,

eslicaket		sēsiyet		hvmkvn
isleycâ·kit		*sí·sayyít*		*hámkan*
had (medicine) sitting in (a tin-cup)		rubbing it on themselves		all over

and they rubbed it all over themselves,

poyakof		este vculat	tvmiket
pó·ya·kô·f		*ísti acóla·t*	*tamâykit*
when they were through		the old man	flew

and when they had finished, the old man flew out

totkv-huten	osiyet	vyehpen	hoktalateu	matan	osiyet
to·tkahótin	*osêyyit*	*ayíhpin*	*hoktâ·la·tiw'*	*ma·tá·n*	*osêyyit*
chimney	he went out at	went	[the old woman]	[the same way]	[she went out]

through the chimney and went off, and the old woman got out the same way

vyēpvtēs.	Momen	este-hvtke vtotkv tat	nocepekot omvtet
ayi·patí·s	*mo·mín*	*istihátki ató·tkata·t*	*nocípiko·t ô·matit*
		the white work hand	hadn't been asleep

and went off. Now the white hired hand had not been asleep

estomē	welakē	vhoyat	omvlkvn	hēcvtētot
ísto·mi·[30]	*wila·kí·*	*ahô·ya·t*	*omálkan*	*hî·cati·tot*
what they were doing,	being around	(before they) went	all of it	he saw

and had seen everything that they had done before leaving.

alihket	ēmeu	helēswv	sēyvfastvtēs.
a·léyhkit	*í·miw'*	*'hilí·swa*	*'siyáfa·statí·s*
he got up	and he, too	the medicine	he used on himself

He got up, and he also used the medicine.

Hvmkvn	sēsiyet	poyof
hámkan	*sí·sayyít*	*po·yô·f*
all over	rubbing it on himself	when he finished

When he had finished rubbing it all over himself,

tvmkē hayvtēs.   Mont   tvmket   cuko ofvn   aret
tamkí· ha·yatí·s   *mônt*   *tamkít*   *cokó ó·fan*   *a·lít*
he pretended to fly   Then   flying   in the house   he was about
he tried to fly. Now he flew about in the house,

cuko ofv   nake   ocakan   vcakhet   ataklatket
cokó ó·fa   *nâ·ki*   *o·câ·ka·n*   *aca·khít*   *a·tákla·tkít*
in-the-house   things   that are (in the house)   he ran into   and he fell down
bumped into the things in the room, fell down,

estont   fekhonneko   tayet   ehlvhokvtēs.
istônt   *fikhónniko·*   *tâ·yit*   *íhlaho·katí·s*
in any way   not stopping   he could   came mighty near dying
and unable to stop, he very nearly died.

Ekv tis   waret   ēennokkicet   wakken   vculvke   rvlahokvtēs.
ikáteys   *wâ·lit*[31]   *i·innokkêycit*   *wâ·kkin*   *acolakí*   *'lalá·ho·katí·s*
head, even   he cut   hurt himself   lying down   old people   came back
Having cut his head and hurt himself, he lay down [until] the old people returned.

Momen   enpohaken   "Cvnokkēpē ont omet
mo·mín   *ínpoha·kín*[32]   *canokkî·pi· ônt o·mít*
Then   they asked him   I'm sick
They asked him about it. "I am sick.

helēswv   sēsiyatskētvnkēn   sēsiyit   omvyan
'hilí·swa   *sí·sayyá·cki·taŋki·n*[33]   *sí·sayyéyt*   *o·mayâ·n*
medicine   you-all (usually) rub on usually   I rubbed it on myself   did
I used the medicine that you are in the habit of using,

cvkvwapet   nake   estomis   vcvcakhēcet
cakáwa·pít   *nâ·ki*   *istô·meys*   *acacákhi·cít*
it lifted me up   anything   any kind of thing   ran me into (anything)
and it lifted me up, bumped me into all sorts of things,

vnnokkicet   os"   maken
annokkêycit   *ó·s*[34]   *ma·kín*
it has hurt me   has   he said
and injured me," he said.

mv	vrahkv	heléswv	tokon	sēsiyetsket		ont on
ma	*aláhka*	*'hilí·swa*	*tó·ko·n*	*si·sayyíckit*		*ónt ó·n*
(for) that	purpose	medicine	[is] not	you have rubbed it on yourself		

"The medicine you used was not intended for that purpose

celehcahoket os	kicakvtēs cē.
cilíhcahô·kit ó·s	*kéyca·kati·s ci^*
it has come very near to killing you.	They told him that

and has come very near to killing you," they told him. So!

The Bear and the Alligator

T. Marshall (Haas V:153–157)   ·

Nokose	hompetv	hopoyat	eton	lomhakan	rakpvlpicet
nokósi	*hompitá*	*hopo·yâ·t*	*itón*	*lomhâ·ka·n*	*łakpálpeycit*[35]
bear	food	looking for	logs	were lying	turning them over

Bear was looking for food and would overturn logs that were lying around

nak wenahokv	sokso	mvo	makan	papēt	omvtēs.
nâ·k wina·hó·ka	*só·kso*	*maw'*	*ma·kâ·n*	*pa·pí·t*	*ô·mati·s*
bugs	black bugs	them, that, too	like those	eats	usually does

and eat bugs and betsy bug beetles.

Eto	hvmken	rakpalvtēs.	Vhvlwat	vfvccvn	rakpalof,
itó	*hámkin*	*lákpa·lati·s*	*ahálwa·t*[36]	*afáccan*	*łákpa·lô·f*
log	one	he turned over	up-hill	direction	when he turned it over

He turned one log over. When he turned it over uphill,

sokso	sulkēt	fullen	hēcet	cawet	pvpetvn	kont	omis,
só·kso	*sólki·t*	*follín*	*hî·cit*	*ca·wít*	*papítan*	*kònt*	*o·mêys*
black bugs	a lot	were about	he saw	catching them	to eat them	trying	did

he saw lots of betsy bugs and tried to catch them and eat them,

eto	hvlvteko tat	a ohtolonken
itó	*halátiko·tâ·t*	*a·óhtoloŋkín*[37]
log	couldn't hold it	it was rolling back on him

but he couldn't hold the log, and it rolled toward him.

enke	hvmkusat		eshvlvteko tat,		enke hvmkan	eshvlatof,
íŋki	*hámkosa·t*		*ishalátiko·tâ·t*		*íŋki hámka·n*	*íshala·tô·f*
hand	with only one (hand)		couldn't hold it with		the other hand	while holding it with

He couldn't hold it with just one paw, and when he held it with the other paw,

hompetv	estomehcet	cawet	hompeko tayvtēs.
hompitá	*istomíhcit*	*ca·wít*	*hómpíko· tâ·yati·s*
food	no way to	get, catch	he couldn't (catch) them and eat

there was no way to get the food, and he couldn't eat them.

Momen	nak wenahokv	omvlkvt	pefatkēpvtēs.
mo·mín	*nâ·k wina·hó·ka*	*omálkat*	*pifá·tki·patí·s*
Then	bugs	all	ran away.

Then the bugs all ran away.

Nokose	eton	hvlatet	vlikvtēs.	Wiken omat
nokósi	*itón*	*halâ·tit*	*alêykati·s*	*weykín o·mâ·t*
bear	log	holding	to it	if he quit (if turned it loose)

The bear sat holding the log. If he turned it loose,

mv	etot	nvfkē tayet	ont omen,	estometv	kerrekatēs.
ma	*itót*	*náfki· tâ·yit*	*ônt o·mín*	*isto·mitá*	*kíłłiká·ti·s*
that	log	could hit him	for the reason	what to do	didn't know

the log could hit him, so he didn't know what to do.

Momen	yopv-fvccv	hvccet	omvtēs.
mo·mín	*'yopafácca*	*háccit*	*ò·mati·s*
Then	behind it	a stream	there was

Now there was a stream behind him.

Uewv	lvokēt	ocēt omen,	mv onvpvn	'sohliket	omvtēs.
óywa	*láwki·t*	*ó·ci·t ô·min*	*ma onápan*	*sohlêykit*	*o·mati·s*
water	a deep place, hole	was there was	opposite that	sitting	he was

There was deep water there, and he was sitting above the water.

Momis	eto	wihket	uewvn	a akcēyvtēs.
mo·mèys	*itó*	*wéyhkit*	*óywan*	*a·ákci·yatí·s*
But	log	turning loose	water	he jumped into

But he let go of the log and went into the water.

Momen	'to-rakko	mvo	uewv	a aklatkvtēs.
mo·mín	*'tolákko*	*maw'*	*óywa*	*a·ákla·tkatí·s*
Then	the big log	that, too	water	it fell into

And the big log fell into the water too.

Nokose	rakcēyat		mahen	nokose tat	uewv	aksumiket,
nokósi	*łákci·yâ·t*		*mâ·hin*	*nokósita·t*	*óywa*	*aksomêykit*
bear	where he went in		about	the bear	water	went under

Right about where the bear went in, the bear went underwater,

uewv	aknvrkvpvn	rorof,
óywa	*aknałkapán*	*lo·lô·f*
water	middle	when he got to

and when he got to the middle of the water,

vlpvtvt	akwakkvtet	nokosen	'tepoyvtēs.
alpatát	*akwâ·kkatit*	*nokósin*	*típo·yatí·s*
alligator	lying there	bear	he (alligator) fought (the bear)

an alligator was lying there and fought the bear.

Tohyorket		uewv	ofvn	'sakwelaket,
tóhyo·lkít		*óywa*	*ó·fan*	*sákwila·kít*
they both contacted each other		water	in	they were scuffling

They scuffled around in the water,

nokoset	vlpvtv	yekcēn		otahket	elēcēpet,
nokósit	*alpatá*	*yíkci·n*		*otáhkit*	*ili·cî·pit*
Bear	alligator	strong, hard, tight		hugged him	and killed him

and the bear squeezed the alligator hard and killed him

lvpvtken	rvwikvtēs.
lapátkin	*łáweykatí·s*
on the shore	threw him

and threw him ashore.

Momen	nokose	yekcetv	'sēkvsamat	omvtēs	maketvt omēs.
mo·mín	*nokósi*	*yikcitá*	*si·kasa·mâ·t*	*o·matí·s*	*ma·kitát ô·mi·s*
Then	bear	his strength	he bragged on	did	that's the saying.

And the bear bragged about his strength, the saying is.

The Tasks of Rabbit (Cufe Hoporrenkvn Hesaketvmesēn em pohvtēs)[i]

T. Marshall (Haas VI:65–85)

Cufe tat	nak	kerretvn	komet	Hesaketvmesēn	em pohvtēt	omēs.
cofíta·t	*nâ·k*	*kiłłitán*	*kô·mit*	*hisa·kitamisí·n*	*ímpo·hatí·t*	*ô·mi·s*
Rabbit	something	to know	wanted	God		asked for	did

Rabbit wanted to know things and asked God for it.

"Cvhoporrenēt	omvrēn	cvyacēt	os"	maket	enpohet	omen,
cahopollíní·t	*omáli·n*	*cayá·ci·t*	*ô·s*	*ma·kít*	*ínpo·hít*	*o·mín*
I have sense	to have	I want		said	asked him	did

"I want to be knowledgeable," he said asking him,

Cufet	cetto-mēkkon	res vtvrēn	Hesaketvmesēt	kicvtēs.
cofít,	*cittomí·kkon*	*'lisatáli·n*	*hisa·kitamisí·t*	*keycatí·s*
rabbit	rattlesnake	to bring	God	told him

and God told Rabbit to bring a rattlesnake.

Mohmen	Cufe tat	orēn	vkerricet	arvtēt	omēs.
móhmin,	*cofíta·t*	*olí·n*	*akíłłeycít*	*a·latí·t*	*ô·mi·s*
Then	rabbit	hard	studied	was around	was

Then Rabbit went around thinking about that very hard.

Ohhoporrenket	estomēcēt	res vtē tayat	kerrekot	omvtē tis,
ohhopółłinkít[38]	*ístomi·cí·t*	*'lisatí· tâ·ya·t*	*kíłłikot*	*o·matí·teys*
thought it over	just how	to bring it back	didn't know	(did)

He thought it over, but he couldn't figure out how to bring him back;

vkerricat	sētekkekvn	tacvtēs,	estele	vhopakv	ēpakat	mahen.
akíłłeycâ·t	*si·tikkikán*	*ta·catí·s*	*istilí*	*ahopá·ka*	*i·pâ·ka·t*	*mâ·hin*
studied about it	walking-stick	he cut it	foot, feet	measure	six	about

he thought about it and cut a walking stick about six feet long.

Momet	yoksv-hvmken	enfvsēcvtēs.	Momet	ehset	ayvtēs.
mo·mít	*yoksahámkin*	*ínfasi·catí·s*	*mo·mít*	*íhsit*	*a·yatí·s*
Then	one end	he sharpened	Then	he took it	and went

Then he sharpened one end. Then he took it and went.

---

[i] Title: *cofí hopołłíŋkan hisa·kitamisí·n ímpo·hatí·s* 'Rabbit asked God for knowledge'

Cetto-mēkko tat　eshēcvtēs.　　En punayet　　okat,
cittomí·kkota·t　íshi·catí·s　　ínpona·yít　　o·kâ·t
the rattlesnake　　he found it　　he talked to it　and said
He found the rattlesnake. He talked with it, saying,

"'Heyv　eto　　ēsvyan　　sencvpketskēt　　　omēs' makvyan,
hiya　itó　　î·saya·n　　sincápkícki·t　　　ô·mi·s ma·kayâ·n
this　　stick　I have　　you are longer than　are　I said
"I said you're longer than this stick I'm holding,

'Monhkos,　eto mit　　cvpkēt　　omēs'　cvkihocen　　aret omis"　　maket,
mónhko·s,　itomêyt　　cápki·t　　ô·mi·s　cakáyho·cín　a·lít o·méys[i]　ma·kít
it's not　　the stick　long　　　is　　　they told me　I'm about　　said
but I was told, 'No, the stick is longer'," so [that's why] I'm here,"

cetto-mēkkon　　　'monayvtēs.　Cetto-mēkkot　　okat,
cittomí·kkon　　　móna·yatí·s[ii]　cittomí·kkot　　o·kâ·t
the rattlesnake　　R. told it　　the rattlesnake　said
he told the rattlesnake. Rattlesnake said,

"Mv　　eto　　omusat　　sencvpkvyēt　　omēs" makof,
ma　　itó　　ô·mosa·t　　sincápkayi·t　　ô·mi·s ma·kô·f
that　stick　like that　I'm longer than　am　　when he said
"I am longer than a stick like that," whereupon

"Mon omat,　　lvpotkuset　　wvkiketsken,
mò·n o·mâ·t　　lapŏ·ⁿtkosit　　wakêykíckin,
well, then　　very straight　lie down!
[Rabbit] said, "Well then, lie down very straight,

heyv　　eton　　cehopayvranis"　　　　kicen,
hiyá　　itón[iii]　　'cihopá·yała·néys[iv]　　kaycin
this　　stick　I'll measure you (with)　he said to it
and I'll measure you against this stick,"

---

[i] Marshall: *o·mêys.*

[ii] Long way: *imóna·yatí·s.*

[iii] Short: *ya itón.*

[iv] Long way: *ici-.*

wakkof,   Cufe tat   vhopayet
wâ·kko·f[39]   *cofíta·t,*   *ahópa·yíf*[40]
while lying   the rabbit   measured
and as he lay, Rabbit measured him,

mv   eto   fvskat   fvccvn   cetto-mēkko   ekvn   sensekehyet,   elēcvtēs.
ma   *itó*   *fáska·t*   *fáccan*   *cittomí·kko*   *ikán*   *sinsikíhyit*   *ili·catí·s*
that   stick   sharp   part, end   the rattlesnake's   head   stuck it with   and killed it
pierced the rattlesnake's head with the end of the sharp stick, and killed him.

Mont   cufe tat   sēkaronet   res vlakvtēs.
mónt   *cofíta·t*   *si·ka·lô·nit*[41]   *'lisála·katí·s*
Then   rabbit   shouldered it   brought back
Then Rabbit put him on his shoulder and brought him back.

Res vlahkof   "Cehoporrēnet   ont omis os"   kihocvtēs.
'lisaláhko·f   *cihopółti·nít*   *ónt o·mêys o·s*   *káyho·catí·s*
after he brought it back   you're getting sense   all right
After he brought him back, he was told, "You're getting smart, all right."

"Hvtvm   tvkoca-cate   sulkēn   res vtes"   kihocvtēs.
hatâm,   *'takocacá·ti*[i42]   *sólki·n*   *'lisatís*   *kéyho·catí·s*
again   red ants   lots   get, fetch
"This time bring lots of red ants," he was told.

Momen   ahyet,   'stomēcē   cvwetv   kerrekatēs.
mo·mín   *áhyit*   *stomí·ci·*   *cawíta*   *kíłłiká·ti·s*
Then   he went   just how   to get them   he didn't know
Then he went, [but] he didn't know how to get them.

Momis   nehē-cvmpv   res em orvtēs.
mo·mêys   *nihi·cámpa*[43]   *lisimo·łatí·s*
But   molasses   he took to them
But he took some molasses to them.

---

[i] *'takocá·* = ant(s); *'takoca-cá·ti* = 'red ant(s)'.

Tvkoca	hute	ocan	enpunayet
'*takocá·*	*hóti*	*ô·ca·n*	*ínpona·yít*
ant	home	where it is	he talked to them

He spoke with them where the ant home was:

"'Yv	nehē-cvmpv	lokakēs'	makvyan,
ya	*nihi·cámpa*	*loka·kí·s*	*ma·kayâ·n*
this	molasses	they can eat it up	I said

"I said they could finish off this molasses,

'Monhkos'	mahoken,	satit	omis"	makvtēs.
mónhko·s	*má·ho·kín*	*sa·téyt*	*o·méys*	*ma·katí·s*
No	they said	I brought it	did	he said

but I was told, 'No,' and have brought it here," he said.

Tvkocat	okakat,	"Lokvraneyat	tɪlkus"	makaken
'*takocá·t*	*oka·kâ·t*	*lokála·niyâ·t*	*tălⁿkos*	*má·ka·kín*
The ants	said	we're to eat it up	sure to	they said

The ants said, "We are sure to eat it up,"

"Mon omat,	lohkatsken	hecvranis"	Cufe tat	kihcen,
mó·n o·mâ·t	*lóhká·ckin*[44]	*hicála·néys*	*cofíta·t*	*káyhcin*
well, then	(you-all) eat it up	I want to see	Rabbit	said to them

"Well then, I want to see you eat it up," Rabbit told them,

pvpetv	vlicēcakvtēs.	Tvkoca	omvlkvt	halo	vtēhkvtēs.
papíta	*aleycí·ca·katí·s*	'*takocá·*	*omálkat,*	*há·lo*	*atî·hkatí·s*
to eat (it)	they began	the ants	all	(tin) bucket	got in

and they began to eat it. The ants all got into a tin bucket.

'Makhotiyet	'shvlahtet	res vlakvtēs.
makhotêyyit	*shaláhtit*[45]	*lísala·katí·s*
he shut them up	holding it	he took it back

He shut them up, and holding it, he brought it back.

Momen	"Cehoporrenē	hakis os"	kihocvtēs.
mo·mín	*cihopollíní·*	*ha·kêys ó·s*	*káyho·catí·s*
Then	knowledge	you're getting	he, they told him

Then he was told, "You're getting smart."

Momen hvtvm vtothoyvtēs, vlpvtv mvn res vtvrēn.
mo·mín hatâm atótho·yatí·s alpatá man[46] *'lisatáli·n*[i]
Then again he sent him alligator that to bring
Then he was sent again to bring an alligator back.

Momen ayvtēs. Hvccen akhvtapkvtēs.
mo·mín, a·yatí·s háccin ákhata·pkatí·s
Then he went creek he got down to
And he went. He went down to the creek.

Uewv lvokēt ocēt omen, vlpvtvt mvn akwakkvtēs.
óywa láwki·t ó·ci·t ô·min alpatá(t) man akwâ·kkati·s
the water deep [there] was (was) the alligator there it was lying
There was deep water, and the alligator was lying there.

Cufe tat rem orvtēs. Enhuehket
cofíta·t límo·latí·s ínhoyhkít
Rabbit got there where he was he called to it
Rabbit got to his [place there]. He called to it

"Vnhessē!" maket enhuehken, yak-vfvnkvtēs.
anhissi^[ii] *ma·kít ínhoyhkín yákkafankatí·s*[47]
my friend he said he called to it it peeped out from (the water)
saying, "My friend!" and it peeped out from the water.

"Naken ceyaca?" kicet enpohen,
nâ·kin ciyâ·ca·^ *kaycít ínpo·hín*
what do you want it said to him it asked him
"What do you want?" he asked.

"Vtotketvn vm vnicvs" kicvtēs.
atotkitán, amanéycas keycatí·s
(to) work help me! he said to it
"Help me work," he said.

---

[i] Correct way (according to Raiford): *alpatán 'lisatáli·n.*

[ii] Sic: *anhissi*^.

"Eto seletvn vm vnicetskvrēn mahoket omen arit omis"
(i)tó silítan amanéycíckáłi·n má·ho·kít o·mín a·léyt o·méys
wood to split you to help me they say [do] I am around I am
"I'm here because I was told you'd help me split wood,"

kicof, 'mvkvsamvtēs. Uewv a ak-osiyen vhoyvtēs.
kaycô·f mákasa·matí·s[i] óywa a·akkosêyyin aho·yatí·s
when he told it it consented water it came out of and they 2 went
he said, whereupon he agreed. He came up out of the water, and they went.

Eto vlkan eto herakēt ocaken hecaket vwelakvtēs.
itó âlka·n itó hiłă·ⁿki·t o·câ·kin, hica·kít awíla·katí·s
where there are trees wood good there were they saw they were about
In a forest they saw good wood and looked it over well.

Vlpvtv 'to-selkv hayetv hērē tayan hēcet
alpatá 'to-sílka ha·yitá hĭ·ⁿłi· tâ·ya·n hi·cít
alligator boards to make it would be good he was looking for
Alligator looked for [wood] that was good for making boards,

vharof, Cufet pucuswvn ekvn sennafkvtēs.
aha·lô·f cofít pocóswan ikán sínna·fkatí·s
while he was about Rabbit the ax its head he hit it on
and while he was looking it over, Rabbit hit him in the head with an ax.

Sennafkof, enlētkvtēs. Cakkeko tayen uewvn rakcēyēpvtēs.
sínna·fkô·f ínli·tkatí·s cákkiko· tâ·yin óywan łakcí·yi·patí·s
when he hit it it ran from he couldn't catch it water it went into
When he hit him, he ran from him. He couldn't catch him, and he went into the water.

Mohmof Cufe tat enholwvkē tatēs. Netta sulkēt hoyanen rem orvtēs.
móhmo·f cofíta·t inholwakí·ta·ti·s nittá· sólki·t hoyâ·nin limo·latí·s
afterwards Rabbit was grieved several days had passed he went back where it was
Afterwards Rabbit was grieved. Many days passed, and he went back.

---

[i] Long way: *imá-*.

Hvtvm   enhuehkvtēs: "Vnhessē!"   kicet,   "Estoma?"   Vlpvtvt   kicvtēs.
hatâm   ínhoyhkatí·s   anhissi^   keycít   istô·ma·^   alpatát   keycatí·s
again   he called it   my friend   he said to it   what is it? alligator said to him
Again he called him: "My friend!" he said. "What is it?" Alligator asked.

"'Hvtvm   vtotketvn   cem vnicekvs'   mahoken   arit   omis"   makvtēs.
hatâm   atotkitán   cimanéycikas   má·ho·kín   a·léyt   o·méys   ma·katí·s
again   to work   he must help you they said   I am around   am   he said
"I'm here because I was again told to have you help me work," he said.

"Momof   Vlpvtv   penkvlētatēs   mahoken:
mo·mô·f[48] *alpatá*   *piŋkalí·ta·ti·s* *má·ho·kín*
Then   alligator   was afraid   when they said
Then Alligator became frightened when he heard that:

"Arvkat,   tayen   estenafket   omhoyvnks"   makvtēs.
a·lakâ·t   tă·ⁿyin   istina·fkít   ómho·yánks   ma·katí·s
you go about   a lot   they hit anyone   did   it said
"Going about, a person can be hit pretty bad," he said.

Momof   Cufe tat   turnēkrv   a ak-ehset
mo·mò·f   cofíta·t   tolní·łka   a·akkíhsit
Then   Rabbit   eyeball   he took out
This time Rabbit had taken out an eyeball

turwv   hvmkusen   hayēt   aret   omvtēs.
tółwa   hâmkosin   há·yi·f[49] *a·lit*   *o·matí·s*
eyed   one   made   going around   was
and went about with just one eye.

Momen   Vlpvtv tat   penkvlētot   omis,   em vkvsamvtēs,
mo·mín   alpatáta·t   piŋkalí·tot   o·mêys   imákasa·matí·s
Then   alligator   afraid   was, but   he consented
And Alligator was afraid, but he consented

vtotketv   em vnicvranat.   Cufet   okat,   "Tecakkvyat   cenafket   omvtēs.
atotkitá   (i)manéycala·nâ·t   cofít   o·kâ·t   'ticâ·kkaya·t   cina·fkít   ô·matí·s[50]
to work   to help him   Rabbit   said   my brother   hit you   he did
to help him work. Rabbit said, "It was my brother who hit you.

Cenafkvtē   vm onayen,   ehanvyvnks"   makvtēs.
cina·fkatí·   *amóna·yín*   *ihâ·nayaŋks*[51]   *ma·katí·s*
the one that hit you   told me   I scolded him   he said
The one that hit you told me, and I scolded him," he said.

Momen   hvtvm,   eto tat   hopoyakvtēs,   'to-selkv   eshayetv tat.
mo·mín   *hatâm,*   *itóta·t*   *hopóya·katí·s,*   *'tosílka*   *isha·yitáta·t*
Then   again   wood   they hunted for   boards   to make with
Then again they hunted for wood to make boards with.

Momen   tentakhaket   vhoyen,   Cufet   enpohet,
mo·mín   *tintakhâ·kit*[52]   *aho·yín*   *cofít*   *ínpo·hít,*
Then   side by side   they 2 were going along   Rabbit   asked him
As they were going along side by side, Rabbit asked him,

"Tecakkeyat,   estvmvn   cennafkat   celēcvranvtētē?"   kicen,
'ticâ·kkiya·t   *ístaman,*   *cinnâ·fka·t*   *cilí·caɫa·natí·ti·^*   *kaycín*
my brother   where   should he have hit you   to kill you   he said to him
"Where should my brother have hit you in order to kill you?"

"Cvsokson   vnnafkvtē   cvlvhanvtēs"   Vlpvtv   kihcof,
casókson   *annâ·fkatí·*   *caláha·natí·s*   *alpatá*   *káyhco·f,*
my hip   had he hit me on   I would have died   alligator   when he said
"If he had hit me on my hip, I would have died," Alligator said,

eton   vketēcet   vharof,
itón[i]   *akíti·cít*   *aha·lô·f*
trees   looking at   while he was going round about
and while he was checking out a tree and going around it,

Cufet   pucuswvn   esokson   sennvfiket,   elēcvtēs.
cofít   *pocóswan*   *isókson*   *sinnafêykit*   *ili·catí·s*
Rabbit   ax   his hip   he hit him on   killed him
Rabbit hit him on his hip with the ax and killed him.

---

[i] Or: 'among the trees'.

Res vlakvtēs.   Momen   Hesaketvmesē   okat,
ɫisala·katí·s   *mo·mín*   *hisa·kitamisí·t*   *o·kâ·t*
took him back with him   Then   God   said
He brought him back. And God said,

"Hoporrenkv tat   rohhvtvlakat   naken   ceyacekot os"   kicvtēt   omen,
hopoɫínkata·t[53]   *lohhatalâ·ka·t*   *nâ·kin*   *ciyá·cikoto·s*   *keycatí·t*   *ô·min*
knowledge   any further   anything   you don't want   he said to him   did
"You have no need of any additional cleverness."

"Cufe tat   orēn   'mvkerrvkēt   ont   omēs"   maket   este-cate   onvyakvtēt   omēs cē.
cofíta·t   *oɫí·n*   *'makiɫlakí·t*   *ônt*   *o·mí·s*   *ma·kít*   *isticá·ti,*   *onáya·katí·t*   *ô·mi·s ci·^i*
the Rabbit   very   cunning   is   (is)   said   Indians   told about it   did
"Rabbits are very cunning," the Indians used to say.

Rabbit and the Tie-Snake

T. Marshall (Haas VI:87–95)

Cufet   cetto   yekcakan   "Escenyekcvyēt   omēs"   kihcen
cofit   *cítto*   *yikcâ·ka·n*   *iscinyíkcayi·t*   *ô·mi·s*   *káyhcin*
Rabbit   snakes   strong   I'm stronger than you are   I am   (R.) said
Rabbit told some strong snakes, "I am stronger than you,"

tenceyvlhoyvtēs.   Kvnhvlwet   likēt   omen,
tinciyálho·yatí·s[54]   *kanhálwit*   *léyki·t*   *ô·min*
they contested each other   a mountain   was (sitting)   was
and they contested with one another. There was a mountain

hvccet   vpvnrvnkeu   ocen,   uewv   lvolvkēt   omvtēs.
háccit   *apanɫâŋkiw*[ii55]   *ô·cin*   *óywa*   *lawlakí·t*   *ô·mati·s*
creeks   on the other side, too   was   waters   deep (holes in the creek)   were
with creeks on both sides, and the water [in them] was deep.

---

[i] Or (Raiford): *onáya·kít o·matí·s ci^*.

[ii] Raiford would say: *apaɫlâmki* or *apalhâmki*.

Momen cetto yekcakat uewv lvokat akkakē vlkēt omvtēs.
mo·mín cítto yikcâ·ka·t óywa lâwka·t ákka·ki·[56] álki·t ô·mati·s
Then snakes strong (pl.) water (the) deep (in) (2) stayed in always
And each strong snake stayed in its own deep water.

Cetto hvmken em punayet "Eswvnakvn tenhvlvteyvrēs" Cufet oket,
cítto hámkin ímpona·yít iswaná·kan tinhalátiyáli·s cofít o·kít
snake one talked to it rope we'll pull against each other rabbit said
Rabbit talked to one snake, saying, "Let's tug on a rope with each other.

"Uewv tat cekkossicarēs" kicvtēs. Momen hvmkateu
óywata·t cikkosséycá·li·s keycati·s mo·mín hámka·tiw'
the water I will take you out of (R.) told it Then the other one, too
I will pull you out of the water," he said. And he told the other one,

cetto hvcce hvmke aklikateu matvpomētan kicvtēs.
cítto hácci hámki aklêyka·tiw' ma·tapó·mi·ta·n keycatí·s
snake creek the other staying in, too in the same way he told him
the snake in the other creek, the same thing.

"Uewv tat cekkossicarēs" kicvtēs.
óywata·t cikkosséycá·li·s keycatí·s
the water I will take you out of he told him
"I will pull you out of the water," he said.

"Monhkos" cettot kicvtēs.
mónhko·s cíttot keycatí·s
no the snake told him
"It won't happen," the snake told him.

Momen Cufe tat nettv huericvtēs, 'swvnakv tenhvlvtvkvranat.
mo·mín cofíta·t nítta hóyleycatí·s swaná·ka tinhalatakála·nâ·t[57]
Then Rabbit day he set rope they are to pull against each other
Then Rabbit set a day to have a tug-of-war.

'Swvnakv cvpkēn takuehcet, hvcce hvmkat kvnhvlwe vwvlvpkēn
swaná·ka cápki·n ta·kóyhcit[i] hácci hámka·t kanhálwi awalápki·n
rope long he got ready creek the one mountain across, over
He prepared a long rope, from one creek over the mountain

hvcce hvmkateu rorēn takuecvtēs.
hácci hámka·tiw' łóli·n[58] tá·koycatí·s
creek the other one, too over to he got it ready
to the other creek, and got it ready.

Cufet oket, "'Tokvs!' makin omat,
cofít o·kít tókas ma·kéyn o·mâ·t
rabbit said Now, ready! when I say
Rabbit said to each of them, "When I say 'Now!'

hvlvtepetskvrēs" kicake vlkēt omvtēs.
halatipíckáłi·s kéyca·kí álki·t[59] ô·mati·s
you will pull he told them each one did
you pull."

Cufe tat ēkvnhvlwe onvpvn ohlikvtēs.
cofíta·t i·kanhálwi onápan ohlêykati·s
Rabbit mountain on top sat on
Rabbit sat on top of the mountain.

"Tokvs!" mahken, 'swvnakv cetto vlkēn tenhvlvtepuecvtēs.
tókas máhkin swaná·ka cítto álki·n tinhalátipoycatí·s[60]
Ready! he said rope snake each one he made them pull against each other
"Now!" he said and made each snake pull the rope against the other.

Cufe tat pihkat pohken kvnhvlwe onvpvn ohlikvtēs.
cofíta·t payhkâ·t pô·hkin kanhálwi onápan ohlêykati·s
Rabbit whooping was heard mountain on top he was sitting
Rabbit could be heard whooping as he sat on top of the mountain.

---

[i] Or: *(i)tita·kóyhcit.*

Tenhvlvtaket, hofonēn
tinhaláta·kít *hofóni·n*
they were pulling against each other for quite a while
They were pulling against each other and for quite a while

'testomēcvkeko tayet ont omet, cetto hvmket vketēcat
(i)tistomi·cakíko· tâ·yit ônt o·mít *cítto hámkit akitî·ca·t*[61]
they couldn't do anything with each other snake one noticed
were unable to do anything with each other, and then one snake investigated

emētat 'tenhvlatet omet kērrvtēs.
i·mí·ta·t tínhala·tít[62] *o·mít ki·łłatí·s*
each other they were pulling against each other were found out
and found out they were pulling against each other.

Momen Cufe tat letkēpvtēs. Momen cettot okakat,
mo·mín cofíta·t lítki·patí·s mo·mín cíttot oka·kâ·t
Then Rabbit ran away Then snakes said
Then Rabbit ran away. Then the snakes said,

"Orēn tenceyvlhoyet omēt,
ołi·n tinciyálho·yít[i] *o·mí·t*
mighty hard we were pulling against each other were
"We were really struggling with each other;

uewv tis orēn ak-vholwvhuecēt omēkv,
óywateys ołi·n akkaholwahóyci·t o·mí·ka
water, even very, badly druggy made we have
we have even fouled the water,

svnvcomvn Cufe tat uewv pum eskekot vrvrēs" makakvtēs.
'sanácoman[63] *cofíta·t óywa pomískikot aláłi·s má·ka·katí·s*
never again Rabbit water won't drink ours will be about they said
so Rabbit shall never drink our water again," they said.

---

[i] Marshall perhaps said *tincihálho·yít*.

Cufe tat	uewv	eskekot	netta	nvcomēn	aret,
cofíta·t	*óywa*	*ískikot*	*nittá·*	*nacómi·n*[64]	*a·lít*
Rabbit	water	not drinking	day	several	was around

Rabbit went several days without drinking water,

wvnhkv	elvranet,	eco-hvrpen	vciyet,
wánhka	*ilála·nít*	*icohálpin*	*acêyyit*
thirst	he will die of	deer-hide	he put on

and dying of thirst, he put on a deerhide,

eco	omēt	uewv	rakhvtvpiket	ēskvtēs.
icó	*ó·mi·t*	*óywa*	*lakhatapêykit*	*i·skatí·s*
a deer	like	water	he went down to	and he drank

and like a deer, he went down to the water and drank.

Cetto	kerrvkekon	uewv tat	em eskēpet	vrēpvtēt	omēs	maketvt os cē.
cítto	*kiłlakíkon*	*óywata·t*	*imíski·pít*	*ali·patí·t*	*ô·mi·s*	*ma·kitát ô·s ci^*
snakes	didn't know it	water	he drank of	was around		that's the saying

The snakes didn't know, and he went about drinking their water, the saying is.

How Rabbit Fooled a White Man (Cufet este-hvtken 'mvkērrvtēs)[i]

T. Marshall (Haas VI:97–103)

Cufet	hvccen	uewvn	ēsket	arvtētot	yossof,
cofít	*háccin*	*óywan*	*i·skít*	*a·łatí·tot*	*yo·ssô·f*
Rabbit	creek	water	drinking	had been about	when it came out

Rabbit had been drinking water in a creek, and when he came out,

este-hvtket	eccv	esēt	ohhueren	hēcvtēs.
istihátkit	*ícca*	*isí·t*	*ohhôylin*	*hi·catí·s*
a white person	gun	was carrying	standing on	(R.) saw him

he saw a white man standing holding a gun.

Este-hvtket	oket,	"Estvmin	ratetska?"	kicen,
istihátkit	*o·kít*	*istamêyn*	*ła·tícka^*	*keycín*
white man	said	where	are you coming from?	said to it

The white man said, "Where are you coming from?"

---

[i] Title: *cofít istihátkin máki·łłatí·s* 'rabbit fooled a white person'.

"Uewv lvokat roretvn tvlofv hĕrusēt
óywa lâwka·t 'loĺitán 'taló·fa hĭ·ⁿłosi·t
water the deep to get close town pretty
"There's a pretty town just before you get to deep water.

hoktvke tis herạkusēt vpokēt omēs.
hoktakíteys hiłă·ⁿkosi·t apó·ki·t ô·mi·s
women, even were pretty are living there are
The woman there are pretty, too.

Erhecēpvyēt omētvnket, mvn ratis" makvtēs.
iłhici·payí·t ô·mi·táŋkit man ła·téys ma·katí·s
I'll go to see them I generally do there coming from he said
I generally go see them and have come," he said.

Cufe tat 'lēhocvranen kērret onkv, penkvlētot
cofíta·t li·hocáła·nín ki·łlit oŋká piŋkali·tot
Rabbit he was going to kill him he knew it did he was afraid
Rabbit knew [the man] was going to kill him,

okvtēs. Momen 'ste-hvtken oket,
o·katí·s mo·mín stihátkin o·kít
that was the reason Then to the white person he said
so he spoke out of fear. Then to the white man he said,

"Mv tvlofvn vyetvn ceyacen omat, cem vnicarēs" kicvtēs.
ma 'taló·fan ayítan ciyâ·cin o·mâ·t cimanéycá·li·s keycatí·s
that town to go to you want if I will help you he told him
"If you want to go to that town, I'll help you."

Nettv enhuericvtēs, rvlvkvranat. "Tohahvwv ocepēt ometskvrēs" kicvtēs.
nítta inhóyłeycatí·s 'lalakáła·nâ·t toha·hawá o·cipí·t omickáli·s keycatí·s
day he set for him to come back box have you must he told him
He set the day for him to come back. "You must bring a box," [Rabbit] said.

"Momen 'ste-hvtke honvntake vpeyetvn 'yacen omat,
mo·mín stihátki honantá·ki apiyitán[65] yâ·cin o·mâ·t
Then white people men to go want if
"And if [other] white men want to go,

'monvyvkvccvs   tohahvwv   ocvke   vlkēt"   kihcen,
(i)monayákáccas   toha·hawá   o·caki   álki·t   kéyhcin
you must tell them   box   must have   each one   told him
you must tell them that each should have a box," he said,

mv   nettv   orat,   'ste-hvtke   mvnette   vnvcomēt
ma   nítta   o·lâ·t   stihátki   manítti   anacomí·t
that   day   when it came   white people   young   several
and when the day came, several young white men

tohahvwv   hahicvkvtēt   res orihcen,   Cufe tat   mv   este-hvtke
toha·hawá   ha·heycakáti·t   'lisoléyhcin   cofíta·t   ma   istihátki
boxes   that they had made   they got there with   Rabbit   those   white people
came with boxes they had made, and Rabbit

tohahvwvn   vtehtēcet,   vcopvn   sem ohcakcvhēcet
toha·hawán   atíhti·cít[66]   acó·pan   'simohcákcahi·cít[67]
box   he put (each one) in   nail   he nailed it up
put the white men in the boxes and nailed them in.

"Tvlofv   hērusat   mvn   ecetotvkis"   kicet,
'taló·fa   hĭ·ⁿlosa·t   man   icíto·takéys   kaycít
town   the pretty   that   I'm sending you-all to   he told them
"I'm sending you all to that beautiful town," he said

uewv   lvokan   omvlkvn   asakpvlatvtēs.
óywa   láwka·n   omálkan   a·sákpala·tatí·s
water   the deep   all   he threw them in
and threw them all down into the deep water.

Este-hvtke   vnvcomēn   pvsatvtēt   omēs,   'mvkeriyet.
istihátki   anacomí·n   pasa·tatí·t   ô·mi·s   'makiłêyyit
white people   several   he killed   did   (and) he fooled them
He killed quite a few white men, tricking them.

Monkv   cufe tat   nake vtēkis   omvlkvn   'mvkerretv   ohfvnkēt   omēs,
môŋka   cofíta·t   nâ·ki atî·keys   omálkan   'makillitá   ohfánki·t[68]   ô·mi·s
Therefore   Rabbit   everything   all   deception   it's ahead   is
So Rabbit surpasses everything else at deceit,

maketvt	omes ce.
ma·kitát	*ô·mis ci*^
the saying	is (thus)

is the saying.

TEXTS BY A. E. RAIFORD

The Story of Raiford's Father (Philip Raiford Horkophoyatē)[i]

A. E. Raiford, Dec.1936 (Haas II:5–15, corrected VII:63–79)

Cvrke tatē		Felvp	Lifvt	hocefkvt	omvtēs.	Momen	este-celokke
cálki tá·ti·		*filáp*	*léyfat*	*hocífkat*	*ô·mati·s*	*mo·mín*	*(i)sticiló·kki*
my former father		Philip	Raiford	his name	[was]	then	the Comanches

My late father's name was Philip Raiford. And the Comanches

horkopakvtēt	omēs.	Oketv	horkopakvtē	ohrolopē
hółkopa·katí·t	*ô·mi·s*	*okíta*	*hółkopa·katí·*	*ohłolopí·*
stole him	[did]	the time	he was stolen	the year

once kidnapped him. The year he was stolen

cokpe-rakko	hvmken	cokpe	cenvpaken	pale ostē	tuccenohkakat
cokpiłákko	*hámkin*	*cókpi*	*cinapâ·kin*	*pá·li ô·sti·*	*toccinohkâ·ka·t*
[thousand	one]	[hundred	eight]	forty	three

was about eighteen hundred

mahe	tatēs.	Hvte	cutkusof,	'mvculkv	ohrolopē	cahkepicat
mâ·hi	*tá·ti·s*	*hatí*	*cótkoso·f*	*'macólka*	*ohłolopí·*	*cahkipêyca·t*
about	it was	when	he was small	age	years	five years

and forty-three [1843]. It was when he was still small,

mahe to witvtēs.	Este ensulkē	tuccēn	vtēket	tohkvlkē tatēs.
mâ·hito wêytatí·s	*ísti insolkí·*	*toccî·n*	*atî·kit*	*tohkálki· tá·ti·s*
about	people	three	about	were together

about the age of five. About three people were together.

---

[i] Title: Philip Raiford *hołkópho·ya·tí·* 'the theft of Philip Raiford'.

Vnrvwvn fullen rvro 'makwiyis fullewitvtēs. Momen
ánławan *follín* *łałó* *mákweyyêys* *folliwêytati·s* *mo·mín*
out in the prairie they were fish fishing rambling about then
They were going about, maybe fishing out on the prairie. And

fullof, 'ste-celokke vnvcumēt rakko oh-vpokēt esyihcet ohmen
follô·f *(i)sticiló·kki* *anacomí·t* *łákko* *ohhapó·ki·t* *isyéyhcit óhmin*
while they were rambling Comanches several horses riding came
while they were there, several Comanches came on horseback

penkvlvkuehocvtēs. Cvrke tatēt lētkē hayvtēs. Momen lētkē hat omis,
piŋkalakóyho·catí·s *cáłki tá·ti·t* *li·tkí·ha·yatí·s* *mo·mín* *li·tkí·há·t*[1] *o·mêys*
they scared them my dead father tried to run then trying to run
and scared them. My late father tried to run. And though he tried to run,

vkeleftēn vcemkē hayen hvmket ehset rakkon a ohlihcet esletkēpvtēt omēs.
akiliftí·n *acimki·ha·yín* *hámkit* *íhsit*[2] *łákkon* *a·ohléyhcit* *islítki·patí·t ô·mi·s*
bluff tried to climb one got him horse put him on and ran off with him
he tried to climb a bluff, and one caught him, put him on a horse with him, and rode off.

Vsv hokkolat vcakwelakvtē estomakvtē kerrvtē sekatēs.
asá *hokkô·la·t* *acákwila·katí·* *istó·ma·katí·* *kíłłati· siká·ti·s*
[those two] that were with him what became of them he never knew again
What became of the two that were with him, he never found out.

Momen 'ste-celokke tat espefvtkēpvtēs. Momen vpēyen yvfiken
mo·mín (i)sticiló·kkita·t ispifátki·patí·s *mo·mín* *api·yín* *yafêykin*
[then] the Comanches went away [then] they travelled until it got evening
And the Comanches rode off. And they went and stopped at dusk

fekhonnahket, ehvpo hayakvtēs. Momen hvpo hahyof,
fikhonnáhkit *ihapó·* *há·ya·katí·s mo·mín* *hapó· háhyo·f*
when they stopped camp they made then after they camped
and made camp. And after making camp,

cerakkon elēcakvtēs. Momen torofakvtēs. Torofahkof, 'tewarwicakvtēs.
ciłákkon *ilí·ca·katí·s* *mo·mín* *tołófa·katí·s* *tolofáhko·f* *'tiwa·łwéyca·katí·s*
a horse they killed then they skinned it after they skinned it they cut it up
they killed a horse. And they skinned it. After they skinned it, they cut it up.

Momen   pvpakvtēs, norekon.   Momen   cvrke tate tat   cutkē tok
mo·mín   papa·katí·s nolíko·n.   mo·mín   cálki tá·tita·t   cótki·to·k
then   they ate it   raw   then   my father   was small
And they ate it raw. Now since my father was small,

mont   elvwē tok   papvtēt   omēs.   Hopuetake ētv 'stencvwvkē tatēs.
mónt   iláwi·to·k   pa·patí·t   ò·mi·s   hopoytá·ki í·ta stincawáki· tá·ti·s
too   he was hungry (too)   he ate it   [did]   other children   they had gotten from someone
and he was hungry, he ate it. They had taken other people's children.

Vculicakat   sasen   lopockvkusat cvrke omat   mvo   sasvtēs.
acoleycâ·ka·t   sâ·sin   lopockakósa·t cálki ô·ma·t   maw'   sâ·sati·s
older ones   with them   smaller ones   like my father   [those, too]   were with them
There were older ones and smaller ones too, like my father.

Momen   vculicvkē sasat   cerakko-vpeswv norekat pvpvkeko tayvtēs.
mo·mín   acoleycakí·[3] sâ·sa·t   cilakkoapíswa   nolíka·t papákiko· tâ·yati·s
then   the older ones   horse-meat   raw   they could not eat it
And some of the older ones could not eat raw horse meat.

Momen   pvpvkeko tayat   pvsvtakvtēt omēs.
mo·mín   papákiko· tâ·ya·t   pasáta·katí·t ô·mi·s
then   those that could not eat it   they killed them
And those that could not eat it, they killed.

Momen ohrolopē hokkolē tuccēnat   mahe   cvrke tatē tat   'ste-celokke
mo·mín ohłolopi· hokkò·li· toccî·na·t   mâ·hi   cálki tá·ti·ta·t   (i)sticiló·kki
then   years   two   or three   about   my father   Comanches
My father was with the Comanches

vpakvtēt omēs.   Momen vpakof,   'ste-celokke tat
apa·katí·t ô·mi·s   mo·mín apâ·ko·f   (i)sticilókkita·t
was with them   then   while he was with them   Comanches
about two or three years. And when he was with them,

cerakko vnvcumēn omvkēpekv,   sapokv omat   cerakkon sohwvnawicēt
cilákko anacomí·n omakî·pika   sa·poká ô·ma·t   'cilákkon sohwaná·weycí·t
horses   several   had   like packs   horse   tied them on
the Comanches had many horses, and they would tie [the children] on

omakvtēt omēs. Momen cvrke tateu sapokv mvo eshahoyen
omâ·kati·t ô·mi·s mo·mín cálki tá·tiw' sa·poká maw' isha·hô·yin
that's the way they did then my father, too pack [that, too] they made of
like pack bundles. And they made a pack bundle of my father too

cerakkon sohwvnvyēt esfullvtēt omēs. Punvttv honecakat
'cilákkon sohwanáyi·t ísfollatí·t ô·mi·s ponátta honicâ·ka·t
horse tied him [to] it they took him about [did] animal wild (ones)
and took him about tied on a horse. They would shoot wild animals

cvkotakse rē rakhe omat esrahet hvtvm nak fvske omat tis
'cakotáksi lí· łákhi ô·ma·t ísła·hít hatâm nâ·k fáski ô·ma·tteys
bow and speared arrow shot it again, also something sharp like
with a bow and speared arrow or pierce them

essekēyet pvsatet norekon papet fullvtēt omēs.
íssiki·yít pasa·tít nołíko·n pa·pít follatí·t ô·mi·s
they would stick them killed raw eating it that's the way they roamed about
with something sharp, kill them, eat them raw, and roam about.

Momen Yonv Mvkentase tatē Oklahomv em aklatkv fvccv
mo·mín yownamakintá·si tá·ti· oklahó·ma imakla·tkafácca
the[n] Yunah McIntosh (Colonel McIntosh) Oklahoma western
Now [Colonel] Yunah McIntosh[4] was out in western Oklahoma

enkvntvckv vfopke mahen arvtēs. Arof, 'ste-celokke
inkantácka afó·pki mâ·hin a·latí·s a·lô·f (i)sticiló·kki
near the (western Okla.) line he was (near) when he was over there Comanches
about near the state line. As he traveled, the Comanches

hvpo hayēt ak-vpoken rem orakvtēs. Rem orahkof,
hapó· há·yi·t akkapô·kin límoła·katí·s 'limołáhko·f
(in their) camp over there he came upon them after he came upon them
were camping, and he came upon them there. After he got to their camp,

cēpvnusēn vrēcicaken hēcvtēs. Mv cēpvnusat 'mvlostvtēs.
ci·panósi·n ałi·céyca·kín hi·catí·s ma ci·panósa·t (i)málo·statí·s
a little boy they had with them he saw (them) [that] little boy he took a liking to (him)
he saw they had a little boy with them. He took a liking to the little boy.

Momen "Mv cēpvnuse arat vmatskē taya?" kicet em pohvtēs.
mo·mín ma ci·panósi a·lâ·t amá·cki· tâ·ya·^ kaycít impo·hatí·s
then that little boy that was there can you give him to me he said in asking for him
And he asked them, "Can you give me that little boy there?"

"Cemeyē tayis os" kihcet emakvtēt omēs.
cimíyi· tâ·yeys o·s kéyhcit ima·katí·t ô·mi·s
we'll give him to you they told him they did give him to him
"We can give him to you," they said and gave him to him.

Momen emahkof, res ahtet encuko tat
mo·mín imáhko·f 'lisáhtit incokóta·t
then after they gave him to him he brought him back to his home
And after they gave him to him,

res vlakvtēt omēs. Res vlahket licet,
lísala·katí·t ô·mi·s 'lisaláhkit lâycit
and got (home) with him [did] when he had gotten back with him he kept him
he brought him back to his home, and when he had gotten back home with him, he kept him

'culicvtēt omēs. Momen cvrke tatē tat ehocefkv kerrekatēs.
cóleycatí·t ô·mi·s mo·mín cálki tá·ti·ta·t ihocífka kíllíká·ti·s
and raised him then my father his name he didn't know
and raised him. Now my late father didn't know his name.

Ehocefkv kerrekok, Yonv Mvkentase tatēt
ihocífka kílliko·k yownamakintá·si tá·ti·t
his name not knowing Yunah McIntosh
Since he didn't know his name, the late Yunah McIntosh

Felvp Lifvt hocēfvtēt omēs. Momen Arv E. Lifvt
filapléyfat hoci·fatí·t ô·mi·s mo·mín á·la i· léyfat
Philip Raiford named him, that's the way it was [and] Arthur E. Raiford
named him Philip Raiford. And Arthur E. Raiford,

monkat Arthur E. Raiford eppucet okvyēt os cē.
*mónka·t Arthur E. Raiford ippocít o·kayí·t ô·s ci·^*
[or] his son [I am] saying this
his son, is saying this.

Poisoning Fish (Este-Maskoke Rvron 'Makpvccvranen Omat)[i, 5]

A. E. Raiford (Haas I:73–77, corrected VII:57–61)

Hvteceskv	momēcat	ēyetetakēt	omēs.	Hvlonesken	hopohyet
haticíska	*momi·câ·t*	*i·itíta·kí·t*	*ô·mi·s*	*haloniskin*	*hopóhyit*
the first thing	he does	he gets ready [does]		devil's shoestring	he hunts it

The first thing he does is get ready. He hunts for devil's shoestring [hvloneske],

wvnvke	vnvcumēn wvnawihcet,	'cvkotakse,	rē	esyomat	etohkahlet,
wanáki	*anacomí·n wana·wéyhcit*	*'cakotáksi*	*li·*	*isyô·ma·t*	*itohkáhlit*
bunches tied up	several he ties them	bow		arrow together	he puts them

ties up several bundles, gathers his bow and arrows,

uewvn	esakhvtapkēt	omēs.	Estvmvn	'makpvccvranen omat,	er es orat
óywan	*isákhata·pkí·t*	*ô·mi·s*	*ístaman*	*(i)makpáccala·nín o·mâ·t*	*ilisô·la·t*[6]
water	he goes down to [does]		whenever	he's going to poison	when he gets there

and goes down to the water. Whenever he's going to poison, when he gets there,

ue-vfopke	mvn	aknohcet,	hvyatke pokekon	alihket
oyʔafô·pki[7]	*man*	*aknóhcit*	*hayátki*[ii] *pó·kikon*	*a·léyhkit*
near the water	[there]	he stays overnight	just before daylight	he gets up

he stays overnight near the water, gets up just before daylight,

heleswv	hokkolēn	enhahoyēn	sēyvfastēt	omēs.
'hilíswa	*hokkolí·n*	*inha·hoyí·n*	*síyafa·stí·t*	*ô·mi·s*
medicine	two kinds	made for them	he uses it on himself [does]

and uses two prepared medicines on himself.

Sennvrkeshoyēt	ont on omat,
sinnałkishoyí·t	*ônt ó·n o·mâ·t*
(if) someone is pregnant by him	it is in case (it is that)

If someone is pregnant with [his child],

---

[i] Title: *istima·skó·ki lalón (i)makpáccala·nín o·mâ·t* 'if a Muscogee is going to poison fish'.
[ii] Originally: *hayyátki*.

mvn   sēyvfastēt   omēs.   Momen monkat, hvmkan
man   síyafa·stí·t   ô·mi·s   mo·mín   môŋka·t hámka·n
that   he uses on himself [does]   (then)   if not   the other one
he uses that one on himself. And if not, he uses the other one

sēyvfastēt   omēs.   Momen cvkotakse hvtvm rē   esyomat
síyafa·stí·t   ô·mi·s   mo·mín   'cakotáksi hatâm li·   isyô·ma·t
he uses on himself [does]   [then]   bow   and   arrow   all [together]
on himself. And after he uses the medicine on the bow and arrow,

esvfvsitof,   hvlvneske   pvccvranat,
isafasêyto·f   *halaníski*[8]   *páccała·ná·t*
after he uses the medicine [on]   the devil's shoestring   to pound it
he goes into the water

uewvn   esakhvtapkēt   omēs.   Momen   'to-poloke   hvlvneske
óywan   isákhata·pkí·t   ô·mi·s   mo·mín   'topoló·ki   halaníski
water   he goes into   [does]   then   round pole/log devil's shoestring
to pound the devil's shoestring. Then he stands a round log in the water

ohpvccvranat   akhuerihcof   pvccetv   vlicēcēt   omēs.
ohpáccała·ná·t   akhoyłéyhco·f   *paccitá   aléyci·ci·t   ô·mi·s*
to pound it on   after he stands it in the water pounding   he commences [does]
to pound the devil's shoestring on and begins to pound.

Momen   pvccepoyof,   uewv tat   ak-aret,
mo·mín   páccipo·yô·f   *óywata·t   ákka·lít*
then   when he gets through pounding it   the water   he [wades around in]
Then when he's done pounding it, he wades in the water,

ak-eteyamet mehcof,   rvro tat akhacaken   echetv tat
akkitíya·mít míhco·f   *łałóta·t akhá·ca·kín   ichitáta·t*[9]
stirs it up   after he gets through the fish [get] drunk   shooting
and after he stirs it up, the fish start to get drunk, and he begins

vlicēcēt   omēs.   Momen rvro   pvsaten   omat,
aléyci·cí·t   *ô·mi·s*[i]   *mo·mín* *łałó* *pasa·tín*   *o·mâ·t*
he commences [does]   then   fish   he kills any   [if]
to shoot at them. And if he kills any fish,

ehvpo   monkat   'ste   ētv   hvpo tis   es oh-ahyen   norihohcof,
ihapó·   *mónka·t*   *sti*   *í·ta*   *hapó·teys*   *isohháhyin*   *nołeyhóhco·f*
his camp   if not   [person other   camp, even] he takes them [to] after it's cooked
he takes them to his camp or someone else's camp, and after it's cooked,

fvccvlikat   homipof,   fvcēcusekv afvckēt
faccalêyka·t   *homêypo·f*   *facĭ·ⁿcosika* *a·fácki·t*
at noon   after he eats he is full   he is happy
after having eaten at noon, he's happy because he's full

encuko tat   yefulkēpēt   omēs.
incokóta·t   *'yifólki·pí·t*[10]   *ô·mi·s*
his home   he goes to   [does]
and goes back to his home.

About the Customs of Conjurers (Porrvlke Emfulletv)[ii]

A. E. Raiford (Haas IV:86–87)[11]

'Culvke   hokkolet kakvtēs.   Honvnwv   ehiwv   'tepakēt   omvtēs.
'colakí   *hokkô·lit ka·katí·s*   *honánwa*   *ihéywa*   *'tipakí·t*   *ô·mati·s*
old people two   were living   man   (and) his wife together   were
Once upon a time there lived two old people. They were a man and his wife.

Netta   yafkusof   ehute   enkvpahket vhoyet
nittá·[12]   *yăⁿfkoso·f*   *ihóti*   *iŋkapáhkit*   *aho·yít*[13]
day   late in the evening   their home   they left   were going
Late in the evening they left their house,

---

[i] Raiford poisoned some fish once with some Alabamas. The medicine man, John Baker, was an Alabama.

[ii] Title: *po·łâlki imfollitá* 'conjurers' ways'.

toceskvt   likēt   omen   hehcet   efekce taken   acahwet
'tocískat   *léyki·t*   *ô·min*   *híhcit*   *ifíkci tá·kin*   *a·cáhwit*
stump   sitting   was   saw it   their entrails   they took out
found a stump, removed their entrails,

tokeceskvn   oh-vpohyet   hvlwat   fvccvn   vtvmhokvtēs.
'tokicískan   *ohhapóhyit*   *hálwa·t*   *fáccan*   *atámho·katí·s*
the stump   they put them on   [high one]   toward   flew (toward)
put them on the stump, and flew off high into the air.

'Stekene   ēhayat   hēhhahoket
'stikíni   *í·ha·yâ·t*   *hí·hhaho·kít*
horned owl   turning themselves into   they hooted
After they had turned themselves into horned owls, they hooted

hopvyētis   welakēpen   hvyatkewitvtēs.
hopáyi·teys   *wilakĭ·ⁿpin*   *haya·tkiwêytati·s*
even a long ways   they were about   it poss. became day(light)
and maybe traveled far until daylight.

Momen   hvyvtke pokepvtēn   encuko   rvlahokvtēt   omēs.
mo·mín   *hayátki po·kipáti·n*   *incokó*   *'lalá·ho·katí·t*   *ô·mi·s*
Then   after it became day   their home   they came back to   did
As it became daylight, they returned home.

'Ste   hvmket   hēcvtēt   omet
'sti   *hámkit*   *hi·catí·t*   *ô·mit*
person   one   saw it   did
The person who saw it

momēn   vm onayvtēt   ont   omen   okis   cē.
mó·mi·n   *amóna·yatí·t*   *ônt*   *o·mín*   *o·káys*   *ci·^*
that's the way   he told me   did   I say it   (pronounced emphatically)
told it to me exactly this way.

A White Interpreter's Error ('Ste-hvtke Yvtekv)[i]

A. E. Raiford (Haas VII:25–29)

Nvkvftetv ohocēn, este-hvtke yvtekv hahoyen, yvtēkemvts.
nakaftitá ó·ho·ci·n istihátki yatíka[14] ha·hô·yin[15] yati·kimác
court   they were holding white person interpreter they made he interpreted (III)
A meeting was being held, and a white man was made interpreter and interpreted.

Momen 'ste-cate hoktēn akērrv hahoyēn,
mo·mín sticá·ti hoktí·n a·ki·łła ha·hoyí·n[16]
Then an Indian woman a witness had made her
And an Indian woman was made a witness,

fvccēcv ehomv ohliketv ohliken, vpohkv enhahoyen,
faccí·ca ihóma ohleykitá ohlêykin apóhka inhá·ho·yín
the judge before a chair was sitting on questions they were asking her
and sitting on a chair before the judge, was being asked questions.

"Encukopericetskvttē?" kicet, vhakv-hayvt vpohkv enhayet omat,
incokópileycíckatti·^ kaycít aha·kahá·yat apóhka ínha·yít o·mâ·t
did you used to visit him, her? he said the lawyer question [made to her]
"Did you used to visit him?" the lawyer asked her [in English],

yv este-hvtke-yvtekv tat 'stomē yvteketv kerrekat okvtēs.
ya istihátki yatíkata·t stó·mi· yatikitá kíllika·t o·katí·s
this white person- interpreter how to interpret not knowing said
and this white interpreter didn't know how to interpret.

Mv vpohkv enhahoyat yvtekē hat omat,
ma apóhka inha·hô·ya·t yatíki· há·t o·mâ·t[17]
that question that was asked her to interpret did try
He did try to interpret the questions that were asked her,

"Pericetskvttē" kicet em pohen,
piłeycíckatti·^ kaycít ímpo·hín
    he said asking her
and he asked, "Did you used to viss?"[18]

---

[i] Title: *stihátki yatíka* 'the white interpreter'.

"Pericit"   kicet   akērrvtat   akicen,
pileycéyt   kaycít   a·kí·llata·t   á·kaycin
    said   the witness   and he said back to her
"Viss," she said, and the witness said it back to him.

"Ihį"   yvtekv tat   em vyoposkof,
ą̄hą̄   yatíkata·t   imáyopo·skô·f
yes   the interpreter   when he answered her
[Then] the interpreter answered for her "Yes,"

"Estomēn   oketskat   cenkerrepvkot os,"
istó·mi·n   o·kícka·t   ciŋkillipákot ó·s
how   do you mean   I do not understand you
and the Indian woman replied, "I don't understand what you mean."

'ste-cate hoktē tat   akicen   (eskaken   hecakimvts)
sticá·ti hoktí·ta·t   á·kaycín   iskâ·kin   hica·káymac[i]
the Indian woman   replied to him   they 2 were sitting   I saw them (III)
I saw them sitting like that,

estohmen   yvtekv tat   nak   makat   enkeriyet
istóhmin   yatíkata·t   ná·k   ma·kâ·t   iŋkiłêyyit
how   the interpreter   what   he was saying   she understood him
and I don't know if she was somehow able to figure out

'tetayen   em vyoposkvtē   kerraks,   vyēpimvtok.   Mvn vtēkus cē.
*'titá·yin   imáyopo·skatí·   kíłłaks   ayî·peynmató·k   man atî·kos ci·^*
correctly   she answered him   I don't know   for I went away   that's all of it
what the interpreter was saying, because I went away. That's all.

Rabbit and the Tar-Baby

A. E. Raiford, Dec. 1, 193[6] (Haas I:25–41, corrected VII:37–53)

'Ste hvmket   uekiwvn   naket   uewvn em aklewvhēcen   hēcvtēs.
stihámkit   oykéywan   nâ·kit   óywan imakliwahî·cin   hi·catí·s
person one   a spring   something water   had muddied his water   he saw it
A man saw that something had muddied the water in his spring.

---

[i] The one telling the story (i.e., Raiford) says this.

Naket omat,   kerrekatēs.   Naket omat,   kerretv   komvtēs.
nâ·kit o·mâ·t kíłliká·ti·s   nâ·kit o·mâ·t kiłłitá   ko·matí·s
what   it was he didn't know   what   it was   to know   he wanted
He didn't know what it was. He wanted to know what it was.

Momen   nak   vhaken   helokwvn   eshahyet,
mo·mín   nâ·k   ahá·kin   hilókwan   isháhyit
then   something [image]   wax   making it [of]
And he made a figure of pitch

ueki-tempen   yv   nak   vhaken   sakhuericvtēs.
oykeytímpin   ya   nâ·k   ahá·kin   sakhóyłeycatí·s
by the spring   [this] something [image]   he stood it
and stood this figure by the spring.

Momen sakhueren   ohhvyatkvtēs. Momof cufet vrētt omvtet   vlahket,
mo·mín sakhôylin   óhhaya·tkatí·s mo·mô·f cofit ali·tto·matít[19] aláhkit
then   it stood there all night   and   rabbit it had been   came
And it stood there all night. Now it had been Rabbit going about, and he came,

nak   vhake   hehcet   oh-ahyet   "Cenvfkarēs!" kicvtēs.
nâ·k   ahá·ki híhcit   ohháhyit   cináfká·li·s   kaycatí·s
[something image] saw it   went up to it I'll hit you   he told it
saw the figure, went up to it, and said, "I'll hit you!"

Kicof,   a nak makekon   nafkvtēs.   Enke hvmkan esnafkvtēs.
kaycô·f   a·nâ·k má·kikon   na·fkatí·s íŋki hámka·n ísna·fkatí·s
when she told it this back it didn't answer he struck it [hand one] he hit it [with]
When he said that, it didn't say anything, so he hit it. He hit it with one paw.

Nafkaten   enke   'mvlokpvtēs. Momen hvtą   "Cenvfkarēs!"kicvtēs.
nâ·fka·tin   íŋki   málo·kpatí·s mo·mín hatâ·n[20] cináfká·li·s kaycatí·s
when he struck it his hand stuck   [then] again   I will hit you he told it this
When he hit it, his paw stuck to it. And he said again, "I'll hit you!"

Momen   enke   vpvlhvmkan esnvfiken,   mvo   'mvlokpvtēs. Momof,
mo·mín   íŋki   apalhámka·n isnafêykin   maw'   málo·kpatí·s mo·mô·f
[then]   hand   other one   he struck it with [that, too] it stuck   and
And he hit it with his other paw, and that one stuck too. Now

enke   hokkolvt   'mvloklopēpekv, "Cetakkarēs!" kicvtēs.   Momen   takkvtēs.
íŋki   hokkó·lat   'maloklopî·pika   citá·kká·li·s   kaycatí·s   mo·mín   ta·kkatí·s
hands   both   had stuck   I'll kick you   he told it   [then]   he kicked it
both of his paws were stuck, so he said, "I'll kick you!" And he kicked it.

Takkat,   ele   'mvlokpēpvtēs.   Momen hvtvm,   "Cvle   vpvlhvmkan   escetakkarēs!"
tâ·kka·t   ilí   'malókpi·patí·s   mo·mín hatâm   cali   apalhámka·n   iscitá·kká·li·s
kicking it foot   it stuck   [then] again   my foot   other one   I'll kick you with
When he kicked it, his foot stuck to it. And again he said, "I'll kick you with my other foot!"

kicvtēs.   Takkof,   mvo   'mvlokpēpvtēs. Momen ele   omvlkvt
kaycatí·s   ta·kkô·f   maw'   'malókpi·patí·s   mo·mín ilí   omálkat
he told it   when he kicked it [that,too] it stuck   then   feet   all
When he kicked it, that one stuck too. And all his feet

'mvloklopēpekv, estonko tetat   omis,   ekv tvl   'mvhosken   hēcof,
'maloklopî·pika istóŋko· 'titâ·t   o·mêys   iká tâl[i] 'mahô·skin[ii] hi·cô·f
had stuck   couldn't do anything but   head only   was left   when he saw
were stuck to it, and he couldn't do anything, but when he saw he still had his head,

"Ececakharēs!" kicvtēs.   Momen vcakhvtēs.   Vcakhaten,   ekvo
icicákhá·li·s   kaycatí·s   mo·mín aca·khatí·s   acâ·kha·tin[iii]   ikaw'
I'll butt you   he told it   then   he butted it   when he butted it his head, too
he said, "I'll butt you!" And he butted it. When he butted it, his head stuck

'mvlokpēpvtēs. Momof,   estonko tetayvtēs.   Estonko tetayekv,   vlikvtēs.
'malókpi·patí·s mo·mô·f   istóŋko· ('ti)tâ·yatí·s   istóŋko· ('ti)tâ·yika alêykatí·s
stuck   and   he couldn't do anything not doing   he stayed there
to it, too. And he couldn't do anything. Unable to do anything, he stayed there.

Momof,   ueki-pucaset   vlahket   eshēcvtēs. Momen eshēcat
mo·mô·f   oykeypocá·sit   aláhkit   ishi·catí·s mo·mín ishi·câ·t
and then   spring-owner   came   found him [then   finding him]
Then the owner of the spring came and found him. And when he found him,

---

[i] Long way: *iká tálki·t.*

[ii] Also said once: *'mahô·skika.*

[iii] For short: *acâ·kha·n.*

"Cent ontskvt tisē!"   kicvtēs.   Momen   "Celēcvranvyat tvlkēs!" kihcet   ohmof,
cínt ónckatteysi·´   *kaycatí·s mo·mín cili·cała·nayâ·t tâlki·s   kéyhcit   óhmo·f̂*
it has been you   he told it and then I will have to kill you   saying to him after
he said, "So it was <u>you</u>! I'll have to kill you!" he said, and then,

"Estomēn   celēcvyē tetayat   kerrvkot os" kicof,   Cufet   okat,
(i)stó·mi·n   cili·cayi· (´ti)tâ·ya·t   kíłłakot ó·s   kaycô·f   cofít   o·kâ·t
how   [I can] kill you   I don't know saying   Rabbit   said
"I don't know how to kill you," he said, and Rabbit said,

"Cvlēcvranetsket on omat, estomēn   res enholwvkus mahat cvlēcetskē tayat
calí·cala·níckit ó·n o·mâ·t[21] (i)stó·mi·n   ´lisinholwakosmâ·ha·t calí·cícki· tâ·ya·t
if you're going to kill me   how   the worst way   you can kill me
"If you're going to kill me, I'll tell you the very worst way

cem onvyvranis"   kicvtēs.   Estomēn   oketska?"   ueki-pucaset
cimonayáła·néys   kaycatí·s   (i)stó·mi·n o·kícka·˘   oykeypocá·sit
I'm going to tell you he told him   how   do you mean? the spring-owner
you can kill me." "How do you mean?" the spring-owner

kihcet   em pohvtēs. Momen   Cufet   ´mvyoposket   okat
káyhcit   ímpo·hatí·s mo·mín   cofít   máyopo·skít   o·kâ·t
saying   he asked him and   Rabbit answered   and said
asked. And Rabbit answered,

"Estvmin   kvco-rakko-lane vlkat   rakkus mahat esliket   on omat   mvn
istamêyn   kaco·łakkolá·ni âlka·t   łakkosmâ·ha·t islêykit   ó·n o·mâ·t   man
where   greenbrier-patch   the biggest   the patch wherever it is there
"If you go and throw me where the biggest greenbrier patch is,

rvcak-vwiketsken on omat   cvlēcetskvhēs: kvco-lane orēn   cvsekēyvrētok,
´lacakkawêykickin ó·n o·mâ·t cali·cíckahi·s   kaco·lá·ni ołí·n   casikí·yáli·to·k
if you go and throw me in   you will kill me   the briers   awfully   will stick me
you'll kill me: for the greenbriers will stick me terribly

---

[i] For *kéyhcit óhmo·f,* informant said also *kéyhco·f.*

momen	cvhvrpeu	vnretvfvrētok.
mo·mín	*cahálpiw'*	*anlitáfáli·to·k*
and	my skin, too	it will tear it for me

Momof	cvna	hvmkvn
mo·mô·f	*caná·*	*hámkan*
and	my body	whole

and tear my skin too. And the greenbrier's thorns

kvco-lane	em fvskē	cvsekēyekv,	momen	cvhvrpeu	omvl'
kaco·lá·ni	*imfaskí·*	*casikî·yika*	*mo·mín*	*cahálpiw'*	*omál*
the green brier	stickers	will stick me	and	my skin, too	whole

will puncture my whole body, all my skin too

vnletvfepoyekv,	momof	cvstemērkekv,	feknokketv	tetan	vnhayekv,
anlitáfipô·yika	*mo·mô·f*	*castimî·lkika*[22]	*fiknokkitá*	*'titã·ⁿn*	*anhá·yika*
will be torn to pieces	and	I will suffer	heart-ache	[much]	it will cause me

will be torn to pieces, so then I will suffer; it will cause me much heartache,

cvstemerkēt cvlepvrēs"	kicvtēs.	"Tetayē on oks"	ueki-pucaset	enkomof,
castimílki·t calípáli·s	*kaycati·s*	*'titá·yi· ô·n ó·ks*[23]	*oykeypocá·sit*	*ínko·mô·f*
I will suffer I will die	he told him	he was about right	spring-owner	he thought

and I will die pitifully," he told him. "That might be," the spring-owner thought

esayvtēs,	kvco-lane	vlkat	erakwikvranat.	Momen	kvco vlkat	er es ohret
isa·yati·s	*kaco·lá·ni*	*âlka·t*	*ilakwéykala·nâ·t*	*mo·mín*	*kacó· âlka·t*	*ilisóhlit*[24]
he took him	green-brier patch	to throw him in	then	brier-patch	he got there with it

and took him to throw him in the greenbrier patch. And having got to the brier patch,

"Yv oman	oketskisa?"	kicet,	Cufen	em pohvtēs.	"Ihi,	mvn okvyis"
ya ô·ma·n	*o·kíckeysa·^*[i]	*kaycit*	*cofín*	*ímpo·hatí·s*	*eyⁿhéyⁿ*[ii]	*man o·kayêys*
like this	did you mean	he told him	Rabbit	asked it	yes	that is what I meant

he asked Rabbit, "Did you mean like this place?" "Yes, that's what I meant,"

kihcet,	em vyoposkvtēs.	Momof	ele-yopvn	enhvlvthihcet	"Mon omat,
káyhcit	*imáyopo·skatí·s*	*mo·mô·f*	*iliyopán*	*inhalathéyhcit*	*mô·n o·mâ·t*
he told him	he answered	then	hind-legs	got him	well

he replied. Then he held him by the hind legs and told him, "Well then,

---

[i] Or: *o·kíckeyka·^*.

[ii] Phonetically: *ģhẹ* (do re).

ecekwikvranis"   kicof,   esvfvllvtēs,   kvco-lanofvn.
icikwéykała·néys   *keycô·f*   *isáfallati·s*   *kaco·la·nó·fan*
I'm going to throw you in saying   he threw him in   in the green-brier patch
I'm going to throw you in," and threw him in the brier patch.

Mohmen   erlatkat,   "Mvn okēpvyis.   Yv omat   cvhute   mahhet os"
móhmin   *iłła·tkâ·t*   *man oki·payêys*   *ya ô·ma·t*   *cahóti*   *máhhit ô·s*
[then]   when (R.) fell in that's what I meant like this   my home   real [is]
Then when he landed, [Rabbit] said, "That's what I meant. My real home is like this,"

kihcet,   Cufe tat   letiket sumkēpvtēs. Ueki-pucase tat   hēcet   akhuervtēs,
káyhcit *cofíta·t* *litêykit sómki·patí·s* *oykeypocá·sita·t* *hî·cit* *akhôyłati·s*
he saying [Rabbit]   ran   ran away   the spring-owner   seeing it he stood
and Rabbit ran away. The spring-owner stood watching,

estometv   kerrekot.   Cufe tat   momēn   este   em vkerrēpvtēt onkv,
isto·mitá *kíłłikot*   *cofíta·t* *mó·mi·n* *ísti* *imakíłłi·patí·t* *ôŋka*
what to do didn't know Rabbit   [that way] people he deceived   it is
not knowing what to do. Rabbit tricks people that way,

mv es vrahkvn   Cufe-Laksvn   kicet okhoyvtēt omēs.
ma isałáhkan   *cofiłá·ksan*   *kaycít ókho·yatí·t ô·mi·s*
for that reason   Lying-Rabbit   he was called
so for that reason he was called <u>Cufe-Laksv</u> ['Liar Rabbit'].

The Turtle in the Rain

A. E. Raiford, Dec. 16, 1936 (Haas I:66–67, corrected VII:126–127; see also VI:55)

Etot   uewvn   akwakkēt   omen   Lucvt 'mvhvsottat   ohlikvtēs.
itót   *óywan*   *akwákki·t*   *ô·min* *locát* *'máhaso·ttâ·t* *ohlêykati·s*
log   water   lying in (water) was turtle sunning itself was sitting on (it)
A log was lying in the water, and Turtle was sitting on it sunning himself.

Momen   ohlikē   emonken vholocē hahket   oskvtēs.
mo·mín *ohlêyki·*[25]   *imôŋkin* *aholocí·* *háhkit* *o·skati·s*
then   sitting on (it) still   cloudy   it got to be (and) rained
While he was sitting there, it grew cloudy and rained.

Oskē	vlicēcan	vpaken		Lucv tat	"Cvlvcpehce witēs"	kohmet
o·skí·	*aléyci·câ·n*	*apâ·kin*		*locáta·t*	*calacpíhciwêyti·s*	*kóhmit*
raining	it began	[as soon as]		the turtle	"It might get me wet,"	thinking

The moment it began to rain, Turtle thought, "It might get me wet,"

uewvn	yakcēyēpvtēt	omēs.
óywan	*yakcí·yi·patí·t*	*ô·mi·s*
water	went back into	did

and went back into the water.

The Horse Factory (Cerakko Hakvcuko)[i]

A. E. Raiford (Haas II:28–31, corrected VII:81–85)

Cēpvnē	hvmket	ecke	'tepvkēt	tvlof-rakkon	kakvtēt omēs.
ci·pani·	*hámkit*	*ícki*	*'tipaki·t*	*'talo·flákkon*	*ka·katí·t ô·mi·s*[ii]
boy	one	his mother	the 2 together	city	they 2 were living in

A boy and his mother were living in the city.

Momen	netta enhvyvtke	hvmken	mv	cēpanat	sumkvtēs.	Momen
mo·mín	*nittá· inhayátki*	*hámkin*	*ma*	*ci·pâ·na·t*	*somkatí·s*	*mo·mín*
then	morning	one	that	boy	went away	then

And one morning the boy went away. Then

yafkē	encuko	rvlakat,	ecken	hiyomēn	kicet	em onayvtēs:
ya·fkí·	*incokó*	*(i)łála·kâ·t*	*íckin*	*hayyó·mi·n*	*kaycít*	*(i)móna·yati·s*
evening	his home	he came back to	his mother	this way	he said	told her

when he came back to his home in the evening, he told his mother this:

"Estvmin	cerakko	hahoyvtēt omat	eshēcis"	kicvtēs.
istamâyn	*'ciłákko*	*há·ho·yí·t ô·ma·t*	*ishî·ceys*	*kaycatí·s*
where	horses	(where) they make (horses)	I have found out	he said

"I've found out where horses are made," he said.

---

[i] Title: *'ciłákko ha·kacóko* 'horse factory'.

[ii] Or: *ká·ki·t ô·mati·s*; or: *ka·katí·s*.

Momof,   "Estvmimvn?"   kicet   em pohvtēs.
mo·mô·f   *istamâyman˙*   *kaycít*   *impo·hatí·s*
then   where?   she said   his mother asked him
"Where?" his mother asked him.

"Yv 'tehoyvnkv ayvkat   sostat mahe   rorvkat,   kvperv-fvccvayvkat,
ya 'tihoyánka â·yaka·t so·stâ·t mà·hi   lo·lakâ·t   kapiłafácca â·yaka·t
this street   one goes about the fourth when you get there   to the right   if you go
"You go on this street, and when you get to about the fourth [street], you go right,

hvtvm   'tehoyvnkv   esvcahkēpat   mahe   rorvkat,
hatâm   'tihoyánka   isacáhki·pà·t   mà·hi   lo·lakâ·t
again   street   the fifth   about   when one gets there
then when you get to about the fifth street,

kvnvwvn   cukot   likēt omēs. Arit   mvn   ahoyanvyaten
'kanawán   cokót   léyki·t ô·mi·s a·léyt   man   á·hoya·nayâ·tin
corner   house   is there   in my rounds [there] as I was passing by
there's a house on the corner. As I was passing by there,

'ste   hvmket vtotket aren   'Estont omētē?'   kohmit   hēren   hēcvyat
sti   hámkit ato·tkit a·lín   istont o·mi·ti·˙   kóhmeyt   hi·ⁿlin hi·cayâ·t
[person   one]   was working what is he doing   I thought   good   I saw
a man was working. 'What could he be doing?' I thought and looked closely

cerakko   ele   espokē   sostat   'sem vrahricen   hihcis.
'ciłákko   ilí   íspo·kí·   sò·sta·t   'simałáhłeycín   híhceys
horse   foot   last   fourth one   nailing on   I saw it
and saw that he was nailing on the horse's last, fourth foot.

Monkv   cerakkon   hayet omēs   komvyiset okis"   kicet
môŋka   'ciłákkon   ha·yít o·mi·s^i kô·mayeysit o·kéys^ii kaycít
therefore   horse   making   I thought so   he said
So I thought he was making a horse," he said

---

ecken	em onayvtēt	omēs.	
íckin	*imóna·yatí·t*	*ô·mi·s*	
his mother	he told	it's that way	

and told his mother.

The Preacher's Revenge (Herkenvkv Stempvlēcvtē)[i]

A. E. Raiford (Haas II:35–37, corrected VII:87–91)

'Ste-hvtke	herkenvkv	hvmket	herkenakvtēs	kihocvnts.
stihátki	*hiłkináka*	*hámkit*	*hiłkina·katí·s*	*káyho·cánc*
white	preacher	one	preached	it's been said

One white preacher was preaching, it's been said.

Herkenaket	ohtihe	omat	sohhuerof,	'ste	hvmket	vlahket
híłkina·kít	*ohtáyhi*	*ô·ma·t*	*sohhôylo·f*	*sti*	*hámkit*	*aláhkit*
preaching	platform	like	a while standing	person	one	came

While standing on a platform preaching, a man came up

mv	herkenvkvn	raohhvlatvtēs.		Enhomecepētatet
ma	*hiłkinákan*	*la·óhhala·tatí·s*		*inhomicipí·ta·tit*
that	preacher	he took hold of him (preacher)		must have been mad at him

and took hold of the preacher. He was mad at him,

ohhvlatan	vpaken		yvnvwv	'mvtēpkvtēs.	Momen	hvtą
óhhala·tâ·n	*apâ·kin*		*'yanawá*	*máti·pkatí·s*	*mo·mín*	*hatâ·ⁿ*[26]
soon as	he took hold of him		cheek	slapped it	then	again

and as soon as he took hold of him, he slapped him on the cheek. Then

vpvl	hvmkateu		'mvtēpkvtēs.	'Svtuccenvn	'mvtepketvn	kont	omis,
apalhámka·tiw'			*máti·pkatí·s*	*'satóccinan*	*'matipkitán*	*kônt*	*o·mêys*
the other side, too			he slapped	third	to slap	intended to	

he slapped him on the other side too. He tried to slap him a third time,

mv herkenvkv tat	kapvn	kahyet	aetepohyet	tēpket	mēcvtēs.
ma hiłkinákata·t	*ká·pan*	*káhyit*	*a·itipóhyit*	*tĭ·ⁿpkit*	*mi·catí·s*
the preacher	coat	pulled it off	fought him back	whipped him	good/thoroughly

but the preacher pulled off his coat, fought him back, and whipped him good.

---

[i] Title: *hiłkináka stímpali·catí·* 'the preacher's revenge'.

Tepikof, herkenvkvt okat, "Cokv-Rakkot hvmmakēt omēs:
tipêyko·f *hiłkinákat* *o·kâ·t* *co·kalákkot* *hámma·ki·t ô·mi·s*
after he whipped him the preacher said the Bible says this way, thus:
After he whipped him, the preacher said, "The Bible says this:

'Ceyvnvwv hvmken cem vtephoken omat, vpvl hvmkan a stem wiyetskvrēs.'
ciyanawá *hámkin* *cimatípho·kín o·mâ·t*[i] *apalhámka·n* *a·stimwéyyíckáli·s*[ii]
your cheek one if someone slap the other side turn the other side to him
'If someone slaps you on one of your cheeks, you must turn the other [cheek] for him.'

Momis es cem vtuccenihocvranen omat, estometskvrēs maketv sekot omat,
mo·mêys[27] *iscimatoccineyhocála·nín o·mâ·t*[iii] *istó·míckáli·s* *ma·kitá sikó·t ô·ma·t*
but if one slaps you a third time you must doesn't say
But it doesn't say you must do that for him a third time,

esvrahkvn kapv tat kahyit aetohlvtikit
isaláhkan[28] *ká·pata·t* *káhyeyt* *á·itohlatêykeyt*
for that reason coat I pulled it off I fought back at him
and that's why I pulled off [my] coat and fought him back

tēpkit mēc't omis" makvtēt omēs.
tĭ·ⁿpkéyt *mí·ct o·méys*[iv] *ma·katí·t ô·mi·s*
I whipped him I did that that's what he said
and whipped him," he said.

Anecdotes

A. E. Raiford (Haas VII:129–135)

1. Este hvmket 'ste-maskok-punvkv kerrusēt likvtēs.
   (i)sti *hámkit* *stima·sko·kponaká*[29] *kíłłosi·t* *leykatí·s*[30]
   a person [one] Creek language knew a little there was
1. There was a man who knew a little Creek.

---

[i] Shorter form: *cimatípho·k no·mâ·t.*
[ii] Or: *a·istim-.*
[iii] Or: *-łá·n no·mâ·t.*
[iv] Or: *mi·cít o·méys.*

Momen   'ste-maskokvlket   vnvcumēt   encukopericēt
mo·mín   stima·sko·kâlkit   anacomi·t   incokopiłéyci·t[31]
Then   Creek Indians   several   were visiting
And several Creek Indians were visiting

cuko ofvn   tak-vpokvtēs.   Tak-vpoken   vholohcet   tenētkvtēs,
cokó ó·fan   takkapô·kati·s   takkapô·kin   aholóhcit   tini·tkatí·s
in the house   they were sitting   While they were sitting   it clouded up   and thundered
in his home. While they were sitting, it clouded up and thundered

oskvranē omēt   momis   oskekatēs.
óskała·ní· ó·mi·t   mo·mêys   óskiká·ti·s
as if it were going to rain   but   it didn't rain
like it was going to rain, but it didn't rain.

Momen   cuko ofv   tak-vpokvtē   soh-vpēttvn   'yes oh-ossat
mo·mín   cokó ó·fa   takkapó·kati·   sohhapí·ttan   'yisóhho·ssâ·t
Then   in the house   (those) that were   the porch   when they went out on
When those sitting in the house went out on the porch,

mv   este   hvmmakvtēs:
ma   ísti   hámma·katí·s
that   person   said this
that man said this [in Creek]:

"Oskvranis   komvyisan   oskepvkattis   tenētkvyisat."
óskała·néys   kô·mayeysa·n   óskipaká·tteys   tiní·ⁿtkayêysa·t
I'm going to rain   I thought (but)   I didn't rain   I was thundering
"I'm going to rain, I thought, but I didn't rain, I was thundering."

2.   'Ste-maskokvlke   esholwvyēcvkusomēt
     stima·sko·kâlki   isholwayi·cakosô·mi·t[32]
     some Creeks   kinda mean
2.   Some Creeks were kind of mean,

'ste-maskoke   enhayēckv pvnkvn   pvnhoyēn,   yv   estvlke   roricvtēs.
'stima·skó·ki   inha·yi·ckapánkan   pánho·yí·n   ya   istâlki   lóleycatí·s
Creeks'   their fiddle-dance   they were dancing   these   people   got there
and they were dancing the Creeks' fiddle-dances, and these mean people got there.

Hacvkusēt rorihcet tvpocēcet 'stetepoyet fullvtēs.
ha·cakósi·t loléyhcit tapó·ci·cít 'stitípo·yit follatí·s
kinda drunk when they got there were shooting were fighting were about
They were kind of drunk when they got there and were shooting and fighting with people.

Momen nafket pefathuehocvtēt omēs.
mo·mín na·fkít pifa·thóyho·catí·t ò·mi·s
Then they hit them and ran them off did
Then they hit [these drunks] and ran them off.

Pefatkehpof 'ste-hvtke hvmket 'ste-maskok-punvkv kerrusēt omet
pifa·tkíhpo·f 'stihátki hámkit 'stima·sko·kponaká kíłłosi·t ò·mit
after they ran off white person one Creek language knew a little did
After they ran off, a white man who knew a little Creek

hvmmakemvts. Mv este pefatkat
hámma·kimác ma ísti pifâ·tka·t[33]
and said this those people that run off
said this. He called one of the men

hvmken hocēfet okat hiyomēn makemvts:
hámkin hoci·fít o·kâ·t hayyó·mi·n ma·kimác
one he called by name and said this way he said
who ran off by name and spoke like this:

"Mv este cvlēcen omat raharēs kicemvts.
ma ísti cali·cín o·mâ·t łá·há·li·s keycimác
that person killed me if [I will shoot him] he said
"If that man kills me, I'll shoot at him," he said [in Creek].

Mv este cvrahen omat 'lēcarēs maketvn okemvts.
ma ísti cala·hín o·mâ·t li·cá·li·s ma·kitán o·kimác
that person shoots me if I will kill him to say he meant
He meant to say, "If that man shoots at me, I'll kill him."

3. 'Shvyvtketvn rawēt fullēn,
   'shayatkitán ła·wí·t follí·n
   a stompdance we coming back we were about
3. We were coming back from a stompdance,

'shvytvtketv   yvhiketvn   yvhikimvts.
'shayatkitá   yahaykitán   yahaykéymac
stompdance   song   I was singing (III)
and I was singing a stompdance song.

Vnvcumeyēt   tohkvlkēt   ful't omēn,
anacomíyi·t   tohkálki·t   fólto·mi·n
several of us   together   we were about
Several of us were together,

'ste-hvtke   hvmket   'ste-maskok 'punvkv   kerrusēt   epupakemvts.
'stihátki   hámkit   'stima·skó·k 'ponaká   kíllosi·t   ipopâ·kimác
white person   one   Creek language   knew a little   was with us
and a white man who knew a little Creek was with us.

Momen   "Yvhikvs!"   kicēn   yvhiket   okat,
mo·mín   yaháykas   keyci·n   yahaykít   o·kâ·t
Then   Sing!   we said to him   he sang   and said
"Sing!" we told him, and when he sang,

hiyomēn   yvhikemvts: "Hoktvke hokte   welahke   fullen,"
hayyó·mi·n   yahaykimác   hoktaki   hókti   wiláhki   follin
this way   he sang   women   woman   2 are about   several are about
he sang like this: "Women, woman, is about, are about,"

maket   yvhiken   vpelicēmvts.
ma·kít   yahaykín   apíleyci·mac[i]
he said   was singing   we laughed at him
he sang, and we laughed at him.

---

[i] Can't be corrected into a properly constructed stompdance song.

TEXTS BY I. FIELD

A Note on Creek Leaders

I. Field (Haas V:87–89)

Entvstvnvkvlke	entopucen	ohkakvntot
intastanakâlki	*intopócin*	*ohkâ·kántot*[1]
warriors	their benches	used to sit (on their benches) at times

Their warriors used to sit on their benches

vkerrickv	etetakuecet vlket	hvsossv-lecv	sehokēpofv tat,
akiłłéycka	*ititá·koycít álkit*[2]	*haso·ssalíca*	*siho·kî·po·fata·t*
ideas	prepare generally	under the rising sun	while they were there

generally making plans when they lived in the Southeast.

etvlwuce	eslumlohat	wiketv	hakvtēt	omet,
italwocí	*(i)slomlô·ha·t*	*weykitá*	*ha·katí·t*	*ô·mit*
the town	were located	(to quit) office	were given (office)	

Where the little towns were variously located, positions were given,

sehoket omvtēt omēs.	Mv momē	sehokvtē tat
sihô·kit o·matí·t ô·mi·s	*ma mó·mi·*	*siho·katí·ta·t*
at that time where they lived	that way, like that	they used to live

and this is how they lived. Those living that way,

etvlwv	lumlohat	em vkerricvlket	omvtēs cē.
itálwa	*lomlô·ha·t*	*imakiłłeycâlkit*	*ô·mati·s ci·^*
the town	(were located)	their leaders	they were (the leaders)

wherever the towns were located, they were their leaders.

Momis	opunvkv	kocuncokusēn	okvtēt omēs.
mo·mêys	*oponaká*	*koconcokósi·n*	*o·katí·t ô·mi·s*
But	talks	short	they said, made (talks)

But they gave brief talks.

Mv omofv tat	este	hoporrenvkan	encvthokēt	omen,
ma ô·mo·fata·t	*ísti*	*hopołlináka·n*	*incathoki·t³*	*ô·min*
at that time	people	with sense	they picked	did

At that time they picked wise people,

etvlwv	em vkerricvlket	omen,	hahoyēton	ful't omvtēt omēs.
itálwa	*imakiłłeycâlkit*	*ô·min*	*ha·hoyí·ton*	*fólto·matí·t ô·mi·s*[i]
town, nation	their representatives	were	had made	they used to be about

and they were made the towns' representatives and went around for this purpose.

Opunvkv	hiyomakusen	enhoporrēnvlket	omet omvtēs cē.
oponaká	*hayyo·mâ·kosin*⁴	*inhopołli·nâlkit*	*ô·mit o·matí·s ci·*^[ii]
talk, words	like this	their representatives	were

With talks like this, they were their wisemen.

Belief about the *ihosá·*

I. Field (Haas V:59–61)

Ehosa	pihken	on omat,	oskē tis haken
ihosá·	*payhkín*	*ó·n o·mâ·t*	*oskí·teys ha·kín*
	whooping	if it is	even if it begins to rain

If an <u>ehosa</u> is whooping, even if it begins to rain,

es vculvke	em apohicē	fullēpvtēt omēs.
isacolakí	*ima·pohéyci·*	*fólli·patí·t ô·mi·s*
the old-timers	they listened to them	they used to go about listening to them.

the old-timers used to pay attention to them.

---

[i] Short for *follít o·matí·t ô·mi·s*.

[ii] He was aiming to quit and then went back again in telling this story.

Momen ohhvtvlakat   ont okat   este-catvke tat fayēpis
mo·mín ohhatalâ·ka·t   ónt o·kâ·t   istica·takíta·t fá·yi·pêys
Then   further   it says: the Indians   if they are hunting, should be hunting
Moreover they say, even when Indians are hunting,

ehosat   'sakkopanet   ehosvkuecen
ihosá·t   sákkopa·nít   ihósakoycín
           are playing with (the hunters)   making them forget
the <u>ehosa</u> played with them, making them lose their way

fullēpvtēt omēs.   Pihkē tis
fólli·patí·t ò·mi·s   payhkí·teys
they used to be around (making them forget)   (when it's) whooping
as they went about. So when it is going to whoop,

omvhanat,   heleshayvlket   pihkē
omáha·nâ·t[i]   *'hilisha·yâlkit   payhki·*
when they're going to whoop   the doctors   the whooping (the *payhki·*)
the medicine man knows how to make medicine

este hayat   heleshakvn   kerrvkēto
ísti ha·yâ·t   'hilishá·kan   killaki·to·
when they make it a person to make medicine   for they know how
to make someone whoop,

ehosa   pihkēn   em pohet
ihosá·   payhkí·n   impo·hít
the Ihusa   whooping   they ask the Ihusa
and they listen to the <u>ehosa</u> whooping

pihkē tis   em palēn omēn,
payhkí·teys   impa·lí·n o·mí·n
as though its whoop   they were borrowing (its whoop)
as though they were borrowing its whoop.

---

[i] Or: *omála·nâ·t*.

este nak kērrvlket	hvsoss-elecv	sehokēpofv tat,
ísti nâ·kki·ɬâlkit	*haso·ssilíca*	*sihó·ki·pô·fata·t*[5]
the wise people	under the east	when they were there

When kērrvlke ['knowers'] were in the Southeast,

nake kērrvlke	ensukcv	fvcfvkē	omet	sehok't omvtēt	omēs.
nâ·ki ki·ɬâlki	*insókca*	*facfakí·*	*ô·mit*	*siho·kto·matí·t*	*ô·mi·s*
the wise ones	their pockets	were full	were	they were there, then	were.

it was as if their pockets were full [of knowledge].

A Visit of the Shawnee

I. Field (Haas V:63–77)

Tvlofv-cule	kakēpofv tat,	naket	estonkon	este-cate	kakvtēt omēs.
'talo·facóli	*ka·kî·po·fata·t*	*nâ·kit*	*istóŋkon*	*isticá·ti*	*ka·katí·t ô·mi·s*
in the old country	when they stayed	nothing	bothered them	the Indians	lived there

When they lived in the old country, the Indians lived there unmolested.

Momen	vtusvmmvliken	Sawvnokvket	este-maskoken
mo·mín	*atosǎmⁿmaleykin*	*sa·wano·kakít*	*istima·skó·kin*
Then	henceforth	the Shawnee	the Creeks

It was that way for a long time, so the Shawnee visited

encukopericvtēt	omēs,	tvlofv-cule kakēpof.
incokópiłeycatí·t	*ô·mi·s*	*'talo·facóli ka·kî·po·f*
they (Shawnee) visited them (Creeks)	did	when they lived in the old country

the Creeks when they lived in the old country.

Momen	Sawvnokvke	okat	"Ēkvnvn	vnpaletsken		fayēpit
mo·mín	*sa·wano·kaki*	*o·kâ·t*	*i·kanán*	*anpâ·líckin*		*fá·yi·péyt*
Then	the Shawnee	said	land	loan me (i.e., us)		we'll hunt

Then the Shawnee [here portrayed as a single person] said, "Lend me land, and I will hunt,

tvco-hvtken	hayēpit	likēpvyvtet
tacohátkin	*ha·yî·peyt*	*leykî·payátit*
buskground	(I) we'll make (a buskground)	(I) we'll stay for awhile, temporarily

make a dance-ring [tvco-hvtke 'white ring'], and stay awhile,

mv	tvco	hayēpvyat	Sakeyv-pvnkvn	'pvnēpit
ma	*tacó*	*ha·yî·paya·t*	*sa·kiyapánkan*	*páni·péyt*
that	buskground	that I have made	[Sac and Fox dance]	(I) we'll dance

and at the dance-ring I have made, I'll dance the Sac and Fox dance,

taklikēpvyvtet	yefulkeparēs	kicen
takleykî·payátit[6]	*yifolkipá·li·s*[7]	*keycín*
we'll stay temporarily	and then we'll return	he said

stay awhile, and return home," he said,

herakusen	'tem punahoyvtēs.	Momen	okat,
hilă·ⁿkosin	*timponá·ho·yatí·s*[8]	*mo·mín*	*o·kâ·t*
kindly, nice	they talked to each other	Then	he said

and they spoke warmly to each other. Then he said,

"Sakeyv-pvnkv	likēpvyat	fayēpit	'senhvyvtkēpit
sa·kiyapánka[9]	*leykî·paya·t*	*fá·yi·péyt*	*sinhayátki·péyt*
[Sac and Fox]-dance	where I stay	we'll hunt	stay up all night

"Because I dance the Sac and Fox dance, I'll hunt and do all-night rituals

likētt omikv,	centvsekvyv tat	tvco-hvtke
leykî·tto·méyka[10]	*cintasikayáta·t*	*tacohátki*
because I am living there	your citizens	(my) buskground

while living here; your citizens must not come around

yvntakfullekarēs.	Mohmet	vnkaketv	yefulkēpvyof,
yantakfóllliká·li·s	*móhmit*	*aŋka·kitá*	*'yifólki·payô·f*
must not be about on (my buskground)	Then	our staying-place	when we go back

on my white dance-ring. Then when I go back to my home,

erorhoyēpin omat,	ēkvnvt	nekēyvrēs.	Momof	vntvco-hvtke	heleswvt
iłółhoyi·péyn o·mâ·t[i]	*i·kanát*	*nikí·yáli·s*	*mo·mô·f*	*antacohátki*	*'hilíswat*
when I, we 2 get there	the earth	will shake	Then	my buskground-medicine	

when we get there, the earth will shake. Then my white dance-ring medicine

vnyvmahkvrēs	cē.	Momen	tvsekvyvt	on omat,	cem apohicen
anyamáhkáli·s	*ci·^*	*mo·mín*	*tasikayát*	*ô·n o·mâ·t*	*cimá·poheycín*
will be wasted		Then	citizens	if they are	they will listen to you

will be destroyed. Then the citizens, let them pay attention to you

---

[i] Raiford notes Field's mixture of numbers [plural verb in first person singular].

em punayet   etvlwv tat vtehtēcet   ometskvrēs cē"
ímpona·yít   *itálwata·t atihtî·cit*   *omíckáli·s   ci·^*
when you talk to them in their nation, country keep them   you shall
as you speak, and you shall keep them in the nation,"

kicen,   herakusen   'tem punahoyvtēs.   Momen   Sawvnokvke tat
keycín   *hiłă·ⁿkosin timponá·ho·yatí·s*   *mo·mín   sa·wano·kakíta·t*
he told him   kindly   they talked to each other   the Shawnee
he told him, and they spoke warmly with each other. The Shawnee

enkaketvn   rvthoyēpvtēt   os.   Fayēpet   takliket
iŋka·kitán   *láthoyi·patí·t ô·s.   fá·yi·pít   taklêykit*
then staying-place returned to   hunting   he had been staying (and hunting)
returned to their home. They had been staying and hunting

omvtētot momen   mv momof tat   entvco-hvtke   vslvhanēt on
o·matí·tot mo·mín   ma mò·mo·fta·t *intacohátki*   *áslaha·ní·t ô·n*[i]
had been   after doing that way his buskground would go out (of fire)
there, and even then, he knew his white dance-ring

kerrvkētot okvtēs.   Mv rvthoyēpof,   mv tvco likan
kiłłakí·tot o·katí·s   *ma lathoyî·po·f*[11]   *ma tacó lêyka·n*
they knew it   when they said it   when they came back where the buskground is
would be extinguished. When they came back,

Hopēryvholv   entvsekvyv tat mv   ēkvnv   nekēyeko   monken
hopi·łyahóla *intasikayáta·t ma   i·kaná   nikí·yiko·*   *môŋkin*
H.'s   citizens   that ground   (before) it shook before
before the ground shook, some of Hopuethlyahola's citizens were going to the grounds

pvnkv   'sestvhayet   ra takfullvtēt   omēs.
pánka[12] *sistaha·yít*   *la·tákfollatí·t*   *ô·mi·s*
a dance   they mocked (the others) they were three about (mocking)
and imitating the dances [of the Sac and Fox].

---

[i] Or: *áslala·ní·t ô·n* 'would go out (of fire)'.

Mv	tvco-hvtke		likat	mv	oketv tat	heleswv	yvmahkekatēs.
ma	*tacohátki*		*lêykaˑt*	*ma*	*okítataˑt*	*'hilíswa*	*yamáˑhkikáˑtiˑs*
there	where the buskground		is	at that	time	medicine	wasn't destroyed

At this time the medicine at this white dance-ring had not been destroyed.

Em punahoyvtēn		tvsekvyvt	mv		ra takfullat	
imponáˑhoˑyatíˑn		*tasikayát*	*ma*		*laˑtákfollâˑt*	
where they did the talking		the citizens	over that		that they were going about (over)	

Where they did the talking, because the citizens were there [mocking the Shawnee],

omēcicēn	ēcatēcvlket		hacohakēpet	
omiˑcéyciˑn	*iˑcaˑtiˑcâlkit*		*haˑcohaˑkîˑpit*	
because	those that painted themselves		crazy became (crazy)	

the Red Sticks [ēcatēcvlke 'those who painted themselves red'] became enraged,

tvsekvyvt	kak't omvtēs.
tasikayát	*kăⁿktoˑmatíˑs*[13]
the citizens	that had been staying there

and the citizens had been staying there.

Momen	omēcican,	tvlofv-cule	ēkvnvn	'stem wihket
moˑmín	*omíˑceycâˑn*	*'taloˑfacóli*	*iˑkanán*	*stimwéyhkit*
Then	for that reason	the old country	land	they left it to someone else

Then for that reason, they gave up the land of the old country to someone else

awet	omvtēt omēs.	Mv omof,
aˑwít	*oˑmatíˑt ôˑmiˑs*	*ma ôˑmoˑf*
left there	did	at that time

and came here. At that time

vhakv-culen	'sēyvfastet		kak't omvtēt omēs.
ahaˑkacólin	*siˑyafaˑstít*		*kăⁿktoˑmatíˑt ôˑmiˑs*
the old law	they guided themselves by (the old law)		they had been staying there

they had been observing the old laws.

Vhakv tat	hvfvpē ofvn	ra hvlatet	'sēyvfastet,
ahá·kata·t	hafapí· ó·fan	ła·halâ·tit	sí·yafa·stít[i]
the law	(the law) in the woods	got it from	they were guided by

They were guided by the law they had retrieved from the weeds [of time][14]

vhakv	vyēcicet	kak't omvtēt	omēs.
ahá·ka	ayí·ceycít	kă·ⁿkto·matí·t	ô·mi·s
the law	enforcing	had been living there	

and had been enforcing that law.

Yv	ēkvntvcke-rakkon	enwihohken	acunechoyen,
ya	i·kantackiłákkon[ii]	inweyhóhkin	a·conícho·yín[15]
this	district	they let them have it	they were moving them

They assigned them this big territory and were moving them here,

ēme	komat tis	vwēpat	omēcicēn,
í·mi	kô·ma·tteys	awi·pâ·t	omi·céyci·n
they (some)	of their own will	were coming	because

and some came of their own free will

ēhompicvlke tis	eshayet	omvtēt os.
i·hompeycâlkiteys	ísha·yít	o·matí·t ô·s
self-supporting ones	made out (claims)	

and were considered self-supporting.

Yekaken	vyēcicesymmvliken
yikâ·kin	ayi·céycisămⁿmaleykin
they came and stayed	and continued so.

They came and settled here and after a time,

Wvcenvt	lekothv,	kvsappvn	tohyorkof,
wacínat	likó·tha	kasá·ppan	tóhyo·lkô·f
the U.S.	South	North	when they came in contact, had a struggle

when the U.S. South and North were fighting,

---

[i] Or: *'siyáfa·stít*.

[ii] Original: *yeykantackiłákkon*.

momof Hopēryvholv tat 'temfvccetvn ētvpoksvlahtet
mo·mô·f hopi·łyahólata·t timfaccitán i·tapo·ksaláhtit
Then H. an agreement carried it under his arm (had it in his possession)
Hopuethlyahola carried the treaty under his arm

Ēli-hvccen 'sayvtēt os. Ervlvkekot ennettv espoyēpvtēt os.
i·leyháccin sa·yatí·t ô·s iłalakíkot innitta ispó·yi·patí·t ô·s
Eli Creek he took it to before he came back his days he finished did
and took it to Eli Creek. Before he came back, he ended his days.

Momis Ēli-hvcce tat erorhohyofv tat,
mo·mêys i·layháccita·t iłołhóhyo·fata·t[i]
Then Eli Creek after they got there
But after they got to Eli Creek,

suletawv-caten cokperakko hvmken Hopēryvholv pahlen,
solita·wacá·tin cokpiłákko hámkin hopi·łyahóla páhlin
soldiers red (Ind.) one thousand H loaned
Hopuethlyahola lent one thousand Indian soldiers,

momen horre-rakko tat este tohyorket omvtēs cē.
*mo·mín hołłiłákkota·t ísti tóhyo·łkít o·matí·s ci·^*
Then (in) the big war they fought did
and they fought in the Great War.

Momen herkv hakēpofv tat, Tohopkuce maketvn
mo·mín hílka ha·kî·po·fata·t 'toho·pkocí ma·kitán
Then peace after they made (peace) Ft. Gibson they called it
Then when peace came, the few soldiers remaining

estomuset ervhoskat mv suletawv tat cokv-lane maketvn
istô·mosit iłáho·skâ·t ma solitá·wata·t co·kalá·ni ma·kitán
how many were left the soldiers yellow paper they called them
in what was called Ft. Gibson were given a so-called

---

[i] Original: *iłołhô·yo·fata·t.*

emhoyvtēt	os	cē.	Mvt	nake	vfvstetv
ímho·yatí·t	*ô·s*	*ci·^*	*mat*	*ná·ki*	*afastitá*
they gave them	did		that	thing	not to try, determined

yellow paper [discharge papers]. That never has been

seko	monkvtos.	Mvn	vtēkusen	cem ohkērkuecvkis cē.
siko·	*môŋkato·s*	*man*	*atí·kosin*	*cimohki·lkoycakéys ci·^*
not	never has been	that	is all of it	I'm stating to you-all.

taken care of. That is all I'm stating to you all.[16]

How a Chief Used to Talk to his Citizens

I. Field (Haas V:79–85)

Momen	hofonē	hvsoss-elecv	esvculvke	kakēpofv tat,
mo·mín	*hofóni·*	*hasossilíca*	*isacoláki*[17]	*ka·kì·po·fata·t*[i]
Then	a long time ago	in the [southeast]	the old people	while they were living there

Then a long time ago, when the old people lived in the Southeast,

tvsekvyv	oponvkv	etetakvkēn		enpunayet
tasikayá	*oponaká*[18]	*itita·kakí·n*[ii]		*ínpona·yít*
members, citizens	(with) the talk	(that) was prepared for the citizens		talked to them

they prepared a lecture for the citizens and talked to them

kaket	entvco-hvtken	enlumlohicet
kâ·kit	*intacohátkin*	*inlómloheycít*
they lived, sat	the white buskground	they select them (buskground)

and selected their white dance-ring

efēke	hvsvthvkēn	omet
ifî·ki	*hasathaki·n*	*ô·mit*
hearts	clean	they had (clean hearts)

with clean hearts [a clear conscience]

---

[i] Or perhaps: *ká·ki·pô·fata·t.*
[ii] Raiford: *itita·kati·n.*

mēkkvke | em elecvn | | fullicet | omvtēt | omēs.
mi·kkakí | imilicán | | fólleycít | o·matí·t | ô·mi·s
the king | under (the command of (the king)) | | they were about | that's the way | it was

and were under the leadership of the chiefs.

Momen | okat | "Em vliketv tis | kerkvkēn | entopv | ohtehtēcet"
mo·mín | o·kâ·t | imaleykitáteys | kiłkakí·n | intopá | ohtihtî·cit[19]
Then | he said | his clan, even | they knew | on their benches | they put them

Then they would say, "Put each recognized clan in its own arbor."

em opunvye | hēret | estakkak't | | omvtēt | omēs.
imoponáyi[20] | hǐ·ⁿlit | istakkâ·kt | | o·matí·t[21] | ô·mi·s
to talk to | good | sat that way (usually) | | that's the way | they used to do.

and would sit and speak for the benefit of all.

Momen | okat | herahēken | em punayet
mo·mín | o·kâ·t | hiłǎ·ⁿhi·kin | ímpona·yít
Then | he, they said | in a good way | talked to them

They spoke in a nice way to them

tvsekvyv | vnokecē hēret | | omvtēt omēs.
tasikayá | anokicí· hǐ·ⁿli·t | | o·matí·t ô·mi·s
(of) the citizens | did think a lot of (their members) | | it was that way

and would have much respect for the citizens.

"Nettv | estofvto 'stomis | naket | vm estonkon | kakēpeyatē"
nítta | istô·fatostô·meys | nâ·kit | amistónkon | ka·kî·piya·ti·^[22]
day | at any time, day | anything | (not) with me (to happen) | and that we will live

"I hope nothing happens to me and that we will live today and always,"

komet | es takkakvtēt | omēs.
kô·mit | istákka·katí·t | ô·mi·s
they thought | they live in that way |

they thought as they lived in that way.

<u>Em vliketv</u> | maketv | etekerrē | | hēret | mv oketv | omof,
imaleykitá | ma·kitá | itikílli· | | hǐ·ⁿlit | ma okíta | ô·mo·f
the clans | as it is called | knew each other | | well | at that time, | during (that time)

At that time <u>em vliketv</u> ['clans'], as they're called, knew each other well,

em etecakkeyvte vlke   etekerrēt ont   kaket omvtēt   omēs.
imiticâ·kkiyati·[23] *âlki*   *itikílli·t ônt*   *kâ·kit o·matí·t*   *ô·mi·s*
all of his brothers   they did know each other   they lived that way   did.
they knew all of their brothers, and lived that way.

Vheles-kvsvppe   encakcvhēcet
ahiliskasáppi   *incakcahî·cit*
the cold medicine (medicine that had been used)[24]   they stood them up (the medicine)
They stood the cold medicine

kaket   omvtēt omēs.   Mv omofv tat   cukolice   opunvkv
kâ·kit   o·matí·t ô·mi·s   *ma ô·mo·fata·t* *cokolêyci*[25]   *oponaká*
[live]   that's the way they did.   at that time   [women]   talk
up for them. At that time he aimed a talk

nak vhecēn   sehoyet omvtēt omēs.
nâ·k ahíci·n   *siho·yít o·matí·t ô·mi·s*
that meant something towards   that's the way they kept them (citizens) at that time
toward the women.

Mont   oken   em opunayofv tat,
mónt[26]   *o·kín*   *imópona·yô·fata·t*
Then   he meant: while he was talking to them
This he said, when he was talking to them,

"Cenkaketv   yohfulhokatsken omat,
ciŋka·kitá   *yohfólho·ká·ckin*[27] *o·mâ·t*
you-all's place of sitting, living   when you-all do go back (if)
"When you all go back to your homes,

cenkaketv   rorhoyēt   kakatsken omat,
ciŋka·kitá   *łołhoyí·t*   *kâ·ká·ckin*[28] *o·mâ·t*
your place of living   when you get there to (it)   you are living there (if)
when you get to your homes, in your everyday living,

hopuetaken   enpapvkē   tvlkusen   em vhecvkē
hopoytá·kin   *ínpa·pakí·*   *tâlkosin*   *imahicáki·*
the children   to eat with   only   they looked after them
you must eat with the children

hęret   takkaketon   ontskvrēs"   kicet
hĭ·ⁿlit   takkâ·kiton   ónckáłi·s   keycít
well   in that way you must live   they, he said to them
and be a good example for them,"

em opunayet   okvtēt omēs.
imópona·yít[i]   *o·katí·t ô·mi·s*
they talked to them   (meaning) that way.
he said as he talked to them.

Momen   mēkkvken   enpunvkvn   em pohetsken omat
mo·mín   mi·kkakín   inponákan   ímpo·híckin o·mâ·t
Then   the chiefs   their talk   if you should hear them
If you should hear the talk from the chiefs,

momakusen 'punvkv   enlumlohicetv omvtēs   ce.
*mo·mâ·kosin*²⁹ *'ponaká*   *inlómloheycít o·matí·s   ci^*
that's about all, that was the kind of a talk   that he usually gave them.
those were the kinds of words laid before them.

Old-Time Creek Activities

I. Field (Haas V:113–133)

Momen   este-maskoke   yvmv   ēkvntvcke-rakko   yihcofv tat,
mo·mín   istima·skó·ki   yamá   i·kantackiłákko[ii]   *yéyhco·fata·t*
Now   the Creek people   here   (in) this district   after they came here
Now when the Creek people came here to this territory,

punvttv tis   tạyet   omēpekv,
ponáttateys   tă·ⁿyi·t   omî·pika
animals, even   were plentiful   it was
animals were plentiful,

---

[i] Original: *imópana·yít.*

[ii] Raiford says *i·kantackałákko*. According to Hill, both terms are used.

este-maskoke tat afvckēt kakvtēt omēs. Momen etvlwuce esvrahrvkvt
istima·skó·kita·t a·fácki·t ka·kati·t ó·mi·s mo·mín italwocí isalahlakát[30]
the Creeks happily were living it was Then the towns separate

and the Creeks lived happily. Then the separate towns,

fakvto 'stomis em vkerricēpat meskē hakat
fá·kato stô·meys imakiłléyci·pâ·t miskí· ha·kâ·t
hunting even they had taken into consideration summer when it would come

when they considered hunting or whatever, when summer came,

heles-kvsvppe tat encakcvhēcet hesvhoyet
'hiliskasáppita·t[31] *incákcahi·cít hisáho·yít*
the cold, (stale?) medicine they put it in vessels they continued

they put the cold medicine in vessels

meskē nvrkvpv em vculvke entvcako-rakko enhoyanen omat
miskí· nałkapá imacoláki intaca·kołákko[32] *ínhoya·nín o·mâ·t*
summer mid-(summer) the old folks (their) Christmas (if) it passed if

and in mid-summer and also when the old folks' Christmas[i] was over;

ohhvtvlaken em vkerricat rvro em akpaccvlke tis
ohhatalâ·kin imakíłleycâ·t laló imakpa·ccâlkiteys
(they) continued, further on they thought for fish even those that poisoned (fish)

they made plans, and if the fish poisoners'

vkerrickv etetakvten omat em makvlken hayaket omvtēs.
akilléycka ititâ·kat(i)n o·mâ·t[ii] *imma·kâlkin há·ya·kít o·matí·s*
the thought, plan is ready their spokesman they appointed

plans were ready, they appointed their spokesmen.

Momof nettan enhuericakvtēs.
mo·mô·f nittá·n inhoyléyca·katí·s
Then a day they set

Then they set a day.

---

[i] Old-time Christmas, "old Christmas," comes two weeks after Christmas (this year it was Jan. 8th, 1938).

[ii] Raiford would read: *ititâ·kin o·mâ·t*.

Momof   tvsekvyv   sulkat   pohofvt
mo·mô·f   tasikayá   sòlka·t   po·hô·fat
Then   the citizens   a majority (of them)   when they heard it
Then when a majority of citizens had heard of it,

ennvkaften   estomēt   omvhanat   em makvket   em onvyaken
ínnaka·ftín   istó·mi·t   omáha·nâ·t   imma·kakít   imónaya·kin
they met for (that)   whatever way   it's going to be   the spokesmen   would tell them
they met, and their spokesmen would tell them how it was going to be,

etenkerrē   hĕret   sehok't omvtēt omēs.
itiŋkiłli·[i]   *hĭ·ⁿłit   sihó·kto·matí·t ô·mi·s*[ii]
understand one another   well   that was their custom it was
and they used to understand one another well.

Nake   em vcakv   ocvkēn omet   em ohhvyayicof
nâ·ki   imacá·ka   o·caki·n ô·mit imohhayá·yeycó·f
something   that they forbid, (taboo)   they had   when they explained it to them
If there was something forbidden when they explained it to them,

mvn   kerrvkēt   onkv,   hvloneske tat
man   kiłłaki·t   ôŋka   halonískita·t[iii]
that   (for) they knew (that)   for the reason that   devil's shoe-string
they understood the reason,

este   vrahkv   nvcont   omvhanat   kerrvkētok
ísti   ałáhka   nacônt   omáha·nâ·t   kiłłaki·to·k
person   each one   how many   going to be (to each one)   they know
and they knew how much devil's shoestring was needed for each person:

mvn   hopoyet   uewv tat   eshecvkēpet   welak't okekv
man   hopo·yít   óywata·t   ishicáki·pit   wilá·kto·kiká[iv]
that   they hunt (that)   the water   they have found   two are about saying
they hunted for that and went around hunting for water,

---

[i] Long way: *itiŋkiłłaki·.*

[ii] Long way: *siho·kít o·matí·t ò·mi·s.*

[iii] Field said *hanolískita·t,* showing metathesis.

[iv] Long way: *wila·kít o·kiká.*

hopoyvkēn   omat   mvn   esoh-vpēyet
hopóyaki·n   *o·mâ·t*   *man*   *isóhhapi·yít*
(if) they hunt them   (if)   that   they take them to (that)
and if they hunted [devil's shoestring], they took them to it.

eto-cvpcvkēn   wocotepicet   'teyakpusēn   cakcvhēn   omet
itocapcaki·n   *wocótipeycít*   *'tiyákposi·n*   *cakcahí·n*   *ô·mit*
long timbers   make them cut (long timbers)   (kinda) forked   standing   it is
They had them cut long timbers, standing kind of forked,

mv   ohpaccvtēt   hvnoleske   hopoyakat tat
ma   *óhpa·ccatí·t*   *hanolíski*   *hopoyâ·ka·tta·t*
that   (that) they had been beating it on   devil's shoe-string   that they have found
that they used for crushing the devil's shoestring that they found,

uewvn   'sakkvfokuecaket   ohmof   em vcohkvlke   ocēn omet
óywan   *sakkafo·kóyca·kít*   *óhmo·f*   *imaco·hkâlki*   *ó·ci·n ô·mit*
water (in)   (when) they have stirred it up   chaperones   they have
and after they had stirred it up in the water, they had chaperones[i] [to tell the others].

momof   este-catvke tat   es afvckē   hēret   fayaket   momvtēt omēs.
mo·mô·f   *istica·takíta·t*   *isa·fácki·*   *hĭ·ⁿlit*   *fá·ya·kít*   *mo·matí·t ô·mi·s*
after that   the Indians   pleased   very much   (of) hunting   that was their way.
At that time the Indians enjoyed hunting, that was their way.

Momen   hoktvlvke   vce-hocke tat   em etetakēt
mo·mín   *hoktaláki*   *acihóckita·t*   *imitita·kakí·t*
Then   the old women   the pounded corn   they were ready with (the pounded corn)
Then the old women were ready

omēpekv, ennake rakkot omat   kerrēt   ful't omvtēt omēs.
omî·pika   *innâ·ki ɫákkot ô·ma·t*   *kiɫɫi·t*   *fólto·matí·t ô·mi·s*[ii]
they are   it was a big thing to them   knowing that   they were about, that was their custom
with pounded corn, so they would know it was a big thing.

---

[i] The ones that tell them, give them the word, that things are ready.

[ii] Long way: *follít o·matí·t ô·mi·s.*

Mvn momet fullet   em etehoyanen omat
man mo·mít follít   *imitihóya·nín o·mâ·t*
they go about that way   and it is over with them
They went about that way, and when it was over with them,

hvtvm   eto-kvrpe tis   es afvckēpvyēs   komē
hatâm   *itokáłpiteys*   *isa·fácki·payí·s*   *kó·mi·*
again   ball-sticks   I can enjoy myself with   thinking
a town thought, "I can enjoy myself with

etvlwv   vkerricen   omat   em mēkkvket   "Momepekvs!" kon omat
itálwa   *akíłłeyc(i)n*   *o·mâ·t*   *immi·kkakít*   *mo·mipíkas*   *kó·n o·mâ·t*[i]
the town   when they think that   when   their chiefs   let it be so!   if they think that
ball sticks again." Their chiefs, if they thought, "Let it be so!"

etvlwv   pihketvn   oh-ayen omat
itálwa   *payhkitán*   *óhha·yín o·mâ·t*
town   whoop   when the time is approaching
when the time approached for a town to whoop,

aem vkvsamvcok'n omat   mēkkvket
ä·imákasa·macókno·mâ·t   *mi·kkakít*
whenever it has been approved (by the other side)   the chiefs
and if [the other side] approved, when the chiefs

wiketvn   hayofvn,   etetenpunahoyet
weykitán   *ha·yô·fan*   *ititinponá·ho·yít*
appointments of officers   when they have made   they go and talk with them
had appointed the officers, they have an understanding that they talk with one another;

etenkerraket   estomēn   omvhanat
itiŋkíłła·kít   *istó·mi·n*   *omáha·nâ·t*
they have an understanding   whatever way   it's going to be
and however it's going to be,

---

[i] Or: *kô·n o·mâ·t* (same word).

vkerrickv   honhoyē   hēren   etem punahokv tat   etenhayet
akiłłéycka   *honhoyi·*   *hiⁿlin* *itimpona·hokáta·t* *itínha·yít*
ideas, thoughts   (very) heavy   very   talks   (that) they have with each other
they discussed serious thoughts with each other,

retem ohsehok'n omat   em etetaketvn   vtēkusen
'łitimóhsiho·kno·mâ·t   *imitita·kitán*   *atî·kosin*
whenever they come to one understanding   to get ready   only
and whenever they came to an understanding, when the only thing to do was to get ready,

esoh-ayet   em etetakēpen   omat
isóhha·yit   *imititá·ki·pín*   *o·mâ·t*
advance on, going towards   whenever they're ready   when
they went, and whenever they were ready,

momusen   tvsekvyv tat   hopinohēctonkv
mô·mosin   *tasikayáta·t*   *hopǎyⁿnohi·ctoŋká*[133][i]
Then   the townsmen   they see afar distant
then they saw the townsmen far off;

eto-lanofv tat   eshokkolahket   pokkvnockvn   hayet
itola·nó·fata·t   *ishokkoláhkit*[34]   *pokkanóckan*   *ha·yit*
in the green woods   the (two towns) go into   ball-dance   they dance
[both towns] went into the green woods and had a ball-dance,

hoktvke tis   yvhikvkē   hērat   enhopoyet   omet
hoktakiteys   *yaheykaki·*   *hiⁿla·t*   *ínhopo·yít*   *o·mít*
women, even   (who) sing   very well   they select them   do
and they selected women too, who could sing well,

'mvyvhikepicet   omvtēt   omēs.
'mayahéykipeycít[35]   *o·matí·t*   *ô·mi·s*
they used to make them sing   used to   did
and they would make them sing.

---

[i] Or: *hopa·n-.*

Yahket osticen omat afackvlke tat nocicēpvtēs.
ya·hkít *ósteycin* *o·mâ·t* *a·fa·ckâlkita·t*[i] *nocéyci·patí·s*
(when) whooped the fourth time when the fun-makers (the players) would go to sleep
When they whooped for the fourth time, the revelers [players] would go to sleep.

Momen hvyatken omat ēhvlwēckvn em etehoyanen omat
mo·mín *hayâ·tkin* *o·mâ·t* *i·halwí·ckan* *imitihóya·nín o·mâ·t*
Then when day came when (after) lunching after they have had (lunch)
Then when it was day, after lunch,

rakko tat vwvnawicvkēpvtē rahvlvthicahken
lákkota·t *awana·weycakî·pati·* *la·halatheycáhkin*
the horse that they had tied they went and caught them
they went and caught the horses that they had tied,

mēkkvke "Ohpvticepaks!" kic'n omat
mi·kkakí *ohpateycipáks* *keycno·mâ·t*
the chiefs saddle up! when he told them
and when the chiefs told them, "Saddle up!"

momen em etetahket yvhiket rakko oh-vpohket vpēyet
mo·mín *imititáhkit* *yaheykít* *lakko ohhapóhkit* *api·yít*
Then they get ready they sing they get on their horses they go
then they got ready and sang, got on their horses and went,

em wiketv hakat ēkvnv likan roricen omat
imweykitá[36] *ha·kâ·t* *i·kaná* *lêyka·n* *lóleyc(í)n o·mâ·t*
officers those that are ground where it is when they get there
and when the officers arrived at the ground,

em makvke tat homvn vpeyēpatētok
imma·kakíta·t *hóman* *apíyi·patí·to·k*[37]
their spokesmen in front ahead they had gone on
their spokesmen had gone on ahead of them:

---

[i] *a·fa·ckâlkita·t* 'the fun-makers, joy-makers' (refers to the participants of the ball game).

mv   ēroricof   rayicvtēs.
ma   i·łółeycô·f   łá·yeycatí·s
      when they get there   (the other side) they came there.
when they arrived, [the other side] returned.

Mohmen   etem punahoyen   "'Estomusekon   akuekē
móhmin   itimponá·ho·yín   istó·mosíkon   á·koykí·
Then   they talked to each other   without any hindrance   moving this way
Then they had a talk: "They tell me that [the two sides] are moving along well

hēret   welak't omeyisos'   cvkicen
hǐ·ⁿlit   wila·kto·miyêyso·s   cakaycín
very well   we (the 2 sides) are about, all right   they tell me
without interruption and are all right,

era rakpvlikit   rvthot omēs   ce."
*iła·lakpalêykeyt   łátho·to·mí·s   ci^*
they turn right around   we are coming back
and we are turning around and coming back."

Momen   "Nake   'svholwahokat   etennahoyekot
mo·mín   nâ·ki   'saholwa·hô·ka·t   itinna·hoyí·kot[i]
Then   anything   that is dirty (i.e., that is not right)   we didn't talk to each other
Then they said, "We did not use foul language with each other,

herahikusat   vtēkusen   etem punahoyēt   omeyis ce   kicet
hiłǎ·ⁿhikosa·t   atî·kosin   itimponá·ho·yí·t   o·miyêys ci^   keycít
(only) the good   just only   we talked to each other   we did   (they) said
we spoke with virtuous words only,"

em mēkkvke tat   em onayet   omvtēt   omēs.
immi·kkakita·t   imóna·yít   o·matí·t   ô·mi·s
the chiefs (said)   they told them   they used to do   did
and would tell their chiefs.

---

[i] Raiford doesn't understand this word. Might be read *itimpona·hoyí·kot.*

Momen	afackvlke tat	ēhvlwēckv tat	em etehoyanen	omat
mo·mín	*a·fa·ckâlkita·t*	*i·halwí·ckata·t*	*imitihóya·nín*	*o·mâ·t*
Then	the fun-makers	lunches	after they have had	

Then after the revelers had had their lunch,

hvtvm	em makvke tat	reh hecvhanat	vhoyet
hatâm	*imma·kakíta·t*	*łihhicáha·nâ·t*	*aho·yít*
again	the (2) spokesmen	they go to see	the two go

again the two spokesmen went to see,

este	em vhvnkvtktv	nvcomen	etem vkvsamen omat
ísti	*imahaŋkátka*	*nacô·min*	*itimakása·mín o·mâ·t*
people	(just) how many	just	if they agree on how many it shall be

and if they agreed on the number of people,

hvtvm	ra fulhokat	rvlvhohken	em wiketvtaken	hayvtēs.
hatâm	*ła·folhô·ka·t*	*'łala·hóhkin*[38]	*imweykitáta·kin*[i]	*ha·yatí·s*
again	they start back	they come back	officers	they appointed

after the spokesmen had returned, they appointed officers.

Momen	esnehickv tat		hahyet,	"Hiyomē
mo·mín	*isnihéyckata·t*		*háhyit*	*hayyô·mi·*
Then	paraphernalia (paint, costumes, etc.)		they put on	like this

Then they put on their paraphernalia: "In this way

nehickv	cenhahyvyē	em wiketv	es ecohfvcficvyat	ont omat
nihéycka	*cinháhyayí·*	*imweykitá*[ii]	*isicohfacfêycaya·t*	*on(t) o·mâ·t*
style	I made for you	officers	that I have filled in, appointed	that I have

I have made paraphernalia for you officers that I have appointed;

yv	mucvnettv tat	mēkkvke	cem enhoniret
ya	*mocaníttata·t*	*mi·kkakí*	*ciminhonêylit*
this	day	chiefs	have confidence in you

today the chiefs have confidence in you;

---

[i] Originally: *iwweykitáta·kin.*

[ii] Originally: *iwweykitá.*

hvyakpo-hvtke	ecetehvranet	kepayv	enhessvket	omet
hayakpohátki	*icitihála·nít*	*kipá·ya*[i]	*inhissakít*[ii]	*ô·mit*
in white prairie	to put you in	? opposing sides	friends	are

I will put you in the stickball field, the opposite sides are friends [?].

hiyomē	ecetehhē	cem vculvke	enhvyakpo-hvtke	ecetehhvyofv tat
hayyô·mi·	*icitíhhi·*	*cimacoláki*	*inhayakpohátki*	*icitíhhayo·fata·t*
like this	? put in	your old-timers	their white prairie	after I have put you in

now when I put you in your elders' stickball field,

etvlwvn	vnhessetake	renakv	ecokwvcokticen
itálwan	*anhissitá·ki*	*liná·ka*	*icokwacoktêycin*[iii]
(my) town	my friends	sight	frowned on, made a face on you

my town and my friends frown on the sight of you,

vlesketvn	vnhakepvhanen omē estomis	esvculvketon	omat
aliskitán	*anha·kipáhanno·mí·stô·meys*	*isacolakíton*	*o·mâ·t*
a shame	being if it will fall on me	the old-timers	if

even if it brings shame on me, nevertheless as far as the elders are concerned,

yvmv	etvlwv	este	svmomēt	esakpv	honnēt
yamá	*itálwa*	*ísti*	*'samó·mi·t*	*isákpa*	*hónni·t*
this	town, country	person	important	with arms, force	heavy

important people with power occupied this country,

vtēhkvnkis	ensomketv	ocēt	omis
ati·hkáŋkeys	*insomkitá*[iv]	*ó·ci·t*	*ô·meys*
occupied (their country)	its disappearance	will be, have	though, but

and though it may disappear one day,

sehoket omvtētok	vcvnahepohiken	pohyvketv
sihô·kit o·matí·to·k	*acana·hipohêykin*	*pohyakíta*
they were about doing this	it has all disappeared with me	lonesomeness

they were there:

---

[i] Cf. Loughridge and Hodge (1890): *kepáyv* 'the war clan'.

[ii] Original *hissakít* (without prefix).

[iii] Hill would read: *icokwokichô·yin* 'looking at you, watching; having their eyes on you'.

[iv] Original: *i·soŋkitá*.

momen   takkakēt   momat   omēcicēn
mó·min   takkâ·ki·t[i]   *mo·mâ·t   omi·céyci·n*
is   we are living   for that reason
I have lost everything, we are living in lonesomeness, and for that reason,

pohyvketv   etehosickv
pohyakíta   itihoséycka[ii]
lonesomeness   something to make you forget (troubles)
to get the mind off lonesomeness,

makomusēt   etem punahoyvnts   ce.
*ma·kô·mosi·t   itimponá·ho·yánc   ci^*
kinda saying   they talked to each other   did
they made small talk with each other.

Momēpvntvs cē,   hofonof tat.
*mó·mi·pántas ci^*   *hofô·no·fta·t*
that's the way they used to do   long time ago
That's the way it happened, a long time ago.

Ēkvn-lvtketv tis   honnē   hēret   momēpvntvs cē.
*i·kanlatkitáteys   hónni·   hĭ·ⁿlit   mó·mi·pántas ci^*
wrestling, throwing on the ground   severe (heavy, strong)   very was   they used to do
Wrestling [while playing] too, was very severe, as it happened long ago.

Hepokkvnvttēckv   honnē   hēret   momēpvntvs ce.
hipokkanattí·cka[iii]   *hónni·   hĭ·ⁿlit   mó·mi·pántas ci^*
interference with ball-throwing, hindrance   severe   very   That's the way it used to be
Medicine to interfere with the game was very severe, as it happened long ago.

Momen   rē-sehokv   pale-hokkolusēn
mo·mín   li·sihó·ka   pa·lihokkô·losi·n
               scores, tally sticks   just twenty
And the pegs for counting scores were just twenty in number,

---

[i] *Original: takkâ·keyt.*

[ii] Possibly *itihosicéycka.*

[iii] Hill says *pokkanattí·cka.* Hill says Field seems to have two different kinds of ball-games mixed up—i.e., the match-game with the opposite side-of-the-creek game within the same town.

es etohyorkēt	omeyvnts ce.
isitóhyo·łki·t[39]	*o·miyánc ci*^
we scuffled over those (twenty sticks)	that's the way we did (long time ago)
but we would scuffle over those.	

The Boy Who Turned Into a Snake

I. Field (Haas V:97–111)

Fayvlket	vpēyvtēs.	Este	tuccēnet	hvpo	res hayakvtēs.
fa·yâlkit	*api·yatí·s*	*ísti*	*toccî·nit*	*hapó·*	*lishá·ya·katí·s*
hunters	went	people	three	camp	went and made

Hunters once went out. Three people went and made camp.

Momen	fayet	fullvtēs.	Momen	yvt	hvnkat
mo·mín	*fa·yít*	*follatí·s*	*mo·mín*	*yat*	*háŋka·t*[i]
Then	hunting	there were about	Then	this	is one of them

Then they went out hunting. And one of these

cēpanat	erke,	ecke	tepakat	ocēt	omvtēs.
ci·pâ·na·t	*iłki*	*ícki*	*'tipâ·ka·t*	*ó·ci·t*	*ô·mati·s*
the boy	father	and mother	both	he had	did

was a boy who had a father and mother.

Mont	omat	fayē	fullē	oketv ofv tat,
mónt	*o·mâ·t*[40]	*fa·yi·*	*folli·*	*okíta ó·fata·t*
But	at that time	hunting	being about	within that time (while they were hunting)

Now while they were out hunting,

yv	este	cēpanat	custake	tuccēnen	eshēcvtēs.
ya	*ísti*	*ci·pâ·na·t*	*costá·ki*	*toccî·nin*	*ishi·catí·s*
this	person	boy	eggs	three	he found

this boy found three eggs.

Ehvpon	cvwehpet	res vlvkēpvtēs.	Momat	pvpēpvtēs.
ihapó·n	*cawíhpit*	*'lisálaki·patí·s*	*mo·mâ·t*	*papi·patí·s*
to his camp	took them	and brought them back	Then	he ate them

He picked them up and brought them to his camp. Then he ate them.

---

[i] Or: *hámka·t* [*háŋka·t* is an informal way of pronouncing *hámka·t*].

Papet	taklikvtēs.		Momen	hokkolat	rvlahokvtēs.
pâ·pit[41]	*taklêykati·s*		*mo·mín*	*hokkô·la·t*	*'lalá·ho·katí·s*
had eaten them	and was sitting down		Then	the other two	came back

He had eaten them and was sitting down. Then the other two came back.

"Naken	momēt	vnheciken	papit	omis"	kicet	'monayvtēs.
nâ·kin	*mó·mi·t*	*anhicêykin*	*pâ·peyt*[42]	*o·méys*	*keycít*	*móna·yatí·s*
something	like that	I found	I ate it	I have	he told them	he told them

"I found something like that and ate it," he told them.

"Mohmēskotan ontskes"	kicakvtēs.
móhmí·sko·ta·n ónckis	*kéyca·katí·s*
you shouldn't have done that	they told him

"You shouldn't have done that," they told him.

"Nake	ēhoneckē tis	omēpēs"	kitt[43] em onvyaken,
nâ·ki	*i·honícki·teys*[i]	*omî·pi·s*[44]	*kéytt imónaya·kín*
something	scary, fearful, awful	it might be	that's what they were telling him

"It might be something dangerous [or not normal]," they were telling him,

tak-vpoken	yvfiket	yomockvtēs.
takkapô·kin	*yafêykit*	*yomo·ckatí·s*
they 3 were sitting	it got evening	it got dark

and they sat, and it became evening and got dark.

"Naken	momēs"	'culvket ompekv	vketēcvkētatēs.
nâ·kin	*mo·mi·s*	*'colakít ômpika*[45]	*akiti·cakí·tá·ti·s*
something	might happen	for the old people	they watched him

"Something might happen," the old people [thought], so they watched him.

Mv	nerē tat	fekherekot	yomockvtēn	nerē-nvrkvpv	orat tat
ma	*nilí·ta·t*	*fikhiłíkot*	*yomóckati·n*	*nili·nałkapá*	*o·lâ·tta·t*
that	night	restless	after dark	about midnight	when it was

He was restless that night, after dark, when it was about midnight;

---

[i] Original: *i·honíckipeys.*

mv   este cēpanat   fekherekot   nekēyet   takwakkvtēs.
ma   ísti ci·pâ·na·t   fikhilíkot   nikī·ⁿyit   takwâ·kkati·s
that   person, boy   restless got   was moving   was lying down.
the boy was restless, and he lay there moving.

Takwakket omen   vketēcvkēt,   pvnrvnken
takwâ·kkit o·mín   akiti·cakí·t   panlâŋkin[46]
he was lying down   they were watching him   on the other side
The two men lay there on the other side,

mv   este   hokkolat   atakwakhokvtēs.
ma   ísti   hokkô·la·t   a·takwakhô·kati·s
those   people   two   were lying (on the other side of) him
watching him as he lay there.

Ont omen   hvyvtke   oh-vyēpattat   cetto   herakat   hakē vyēpet
ônt o·mín   hayátki[47]   *óhhayi·pâ·tta·t   cítto   hiłâ·ⁿka·t   há·ki· ayi·pít*
it was   day   getting to be   snake   big kind   becoming, getting to be dawn
By daylight when they saw he was turning into a great snake

takwakken   hecakofvt   "Nake   momēs   mahokvnton,
takwâ·kkin   hica·kô·fat   nâ·ki   mo·mí·s   má·ho·kánton
lying down   when they saw him   like that   would happen   that's what has been said
and was lying there, [they told him,] "They said things like that would happen,

'sēyohfvcēcet   ontskes   ce."
si·yohfaci·cit[48]   *ónckis   ci^*
you have proven that on yourself   you have
and you have proven that on yourself."

"Cvmomēpet on   oketskes"   kicen,
camo·mî·pit ó·n[49]   *o·kíckis   keycín*
I am that way   you were right   he said
"I am that way, you're right," he told them,

opunvkv	kocuknusēn	'tem punahoyvtēs	ont omat,
oponaká	*kocóknosi·n*[i]	*timponá·ho·yati·s*	*ônt o·má·t*
talk	short	they talked to each other	they did

and they talked a little while and asked,

"Ceckvlke tat	naken	kicēt cem em onvyvrētē?"	kicof,
cickâlkita·t	*nâ·kin*	*keyci·t cimimonéyáli·ti·*[ii]	*keycô·f*
your parents	what	shall we tell (your parents)?	when he, they said

"What shall we tell your parents?"

"Akhvsuce	mvn	akhvtvpkvhanikv,	cvhecvkvrēs	ce.
akhasóci	*man*	*akhatápkaha·néyka*	*cahicakáli·s*[iii]	*ci*^
little pond	there	I'm going down (to that pond)	they will see me	

"I'm going down into that little pond there, so they will see me.

Momis	cvhocefkv	tatēn	vnhuehkaket	omvrēs"	kicet	'mvyeposkvtēs.
mo·mêys	*cahocífka*	*tá·ti·n*	*anhóyhka·kít*	*omáli·s*	*keycít*	*'mayípo·skatí·s*
But	[my] name	used-to-be	they must call me	they must	he said	in answer.

But they must call me by my former name," he answered.

"Momen	mv	akhvsucen	raklikehpin	yofulhohket,
mo·mín	*ma*	*akhasócin*	*łakleykíhpeyn*	*yofolhóhkit*[50]
Then	that	little pond	when I went and got in there	you 2 go back

"When I'm down in that little pond, you two must go back

cvckvlke tat	em onvyvhvntskat	tvlkēs"	kicvtēs.
cackâlkita·t	*imoneyáháncka·t*[51]	*tâlki·s*	*keycatí·s*
my parents	you tell them	(you) must	he said

and tell my parents," he said.

Efulhohket	enkaketv	rorhohyet
ifolhóhkit	*iŋka·kitá*[iv]	*lołhóhyit*[v]
they 2 went back	to where they stayed	getting there, when they got there

They went back to their home

---

[i] *oponaká kocóknosi·n* = a short talk *or* a few words.

[ii] Could also have said *nâ·kin keyci·t imonayíyali·ti·*^.

[iii] *-l-* or *-h-*.

[iv] Raiford would say *iŋka·kitá*.

[v] Originally: *lółho·yit*.

eckvlken   em onvyakvtēs.
ickâlkin   *imónaya·katí·s*
his parents   they told them
and told his parents.

Nake   'stomahēt   momēpet omen,   'Cvhecetv   'yacaket   omat,
nâ·ki   *stó·ma·hi·t*   *mo·mî·pit o·mín*   *cahicitá*   *ya·câ·kit*   *o·mâ·t*
something   peculiar, mysterious   has happened   to see me   (if) they want if
"Something strange has happened, [and your son] said, 'If they want to see me,

cvhocēfet   vnhuehkaken   omat,   'teheceyvrēs'   maket,
cahóci·fít   *anhóyhka·kín*   *o·mâ·t*   *'tihicíyáli·s*   *ma·kít*
by my name   (if) they call me   if   we will see each other   saying
if they call me by name, we will see each other,'

akhvtvpkehpen   rvthot omēs   kicet,
akhatapkíhpin   *látho·t o·mí·s*[52]   *keycít*
and went down into (the pond)   (and) we 2 came back   they said
and he went down into the water, and we came here," they said.

eckvlke tat   em onvyaken   omof,
ickâlkita·t   *imónaya·kín*   *o·mô·f*
his parents   (when) they told   when, after
And when they told his parents

"Estvmvn   on omat   pum onvyvhvntskat   tvlkēs"   kicvkēpen,
ístaman   *ô·n o·mâ·t*   *pomoneyáháncka·t*   *tâlki·s*   *kéycaki·pín*
wherever   it was   you will have to tell us   have to   they told them
they said, "You will have to tell us where it was,"

vhoyen   yvcakkvfulhokvtēs.
aho·yín   *'yacakkafólho·kati·s*[53]
they 2 went   and (his parents) followed them back
and they both went, and [the parents] followed them back.

Momen   akhvsuce   cọtkusē   akhvtapkvtet   onkot
mo·mín   *akhasocí*   *cǒ·ⁿtkosi·*   *akhatâ·pkatit*   *óŋkot*
Then   pond   very little   he had gotten down into   it didn't seem
Then it was not the little pond he had gone down into [anymore];

uewv tat ēhoneckē hḛret liken eroricvtēs.
óywata·t i·honícki· hĭ·ⁿłit lêykin iłółeycatí·s
the water scary, mysterious very (lying) they got there (to it)
the water was really hazardous when they reached it.

"Yvn omvnks" kicet 'monvyakvtēs.
yan ô·máŋks keycít mónaya·katí·s
this is where it was they said they told them
"This is where it was," they told them.

Momof hocefaket enhuehkakvtēs. Enhuehkē 'svhokkolican
mo·mô·f hocífa·kít inhóyhka·katí·s ínhoyhkí· 'sahókkoleycâ·n
Then by his name they called him (after) calling him the second time
Then they called him by name. When they called him a second time,

mv ue-nvrkvpvn afvnket omat,
ma oynałkapán á·fankít⁵⁴ o·mâ·t⁵⁵
there middle of the water (when) he peeped out
he came up in the middle of the water;

cetto herakv hakepēt omet afvnket omvtēs.
cítto hilá·ka ha·kipí·t ô·mit á·fankít⁵⁶ o·matí·s
snake big, fine kind had become and had peeped out
[it was clear] he had become a fine snake, and he came up.

Enhuehkē monken ạtet vlaken
ínhoyhkí· môŋkin ă·ⁿtit alâ·kin
calling him they kept (calling him) kept coming till he came
They kept calling him till he came,

uewv 'mvtēkēn eckvlke tat ohkakvtēs.
óywa 'mati·kí·n ickâlkita·t óhka·katí·s⁵⁷
(to where) water's edge his parents they sitting (at the water's edge).
and his parents sat on the edge of the water.

Momen enhuehkē monken vwọlusen yvfvnkvtēs.
mo·mín ínhoyhkí· môŋkin awŏ·ⁿlosin yáfankatí·s
Then calling him kept on very close peeped out (from close by)
Then they kept calling, and he came up very close.

"Momēn   cvmomehpet   ēlvpvtkuecit,
mo·mî·n   camo·míhpit   i·lapatkôyceyt
that way   I became, got (that way)   strayed away
"This happened to me, and I strayed away

hoyērvhanvyat   tvlkēs   komit   okit,
hoyì·ⁿlaha·nayâ·t[58]   *tâlki·s*   *kô·meyt*   *o·kéyt*
I to remain that way   have to   I think   I say, mean
and must remain that way, I think,

cenhuehkvkit   okvyvnks"   kicof,
cínhoyhkakéyt   *ô·kayáŋks*   *keycô·f*
(that's the reason) I called you-all   I did   when he said
and [that's why] I called you," he told them,

eckvlke tat   'stomahet os   komaket,
ickâlkita·t   stŏ·ⁿmà·hit ó·s[59]   *ko·mâ·kit*
his parents   very mysterious   they thought it was
and his parents thought it was very mysterious

enkaketv   rvthoyēpvtēt   omēs.
inka·kitá   *láthoyi·pati·t*   *ô·mi·s*
to their staying-place   they came back to (their home)   did
and went back to their home.

Rvlahoket   momēt   os.   'Culakusēt onkv,
'łala·hô·kit   *mo·mî·t*[60]   *ô·s*   *'colă·ⁿkosi·t ôŋka*
they came back   and like this   it was   for they were very old
They got back, and so it was. They were very old,

hvkihhoket   welakvtēs   ce.
hakayhhŏ·ⁿkit   *wila·kati·s*   *ci^*
they kept crying   they were about
so they went about crying and crying.

The Orphan Boy Who Became Thunder

I. Field (Haas V:91–95)

Fayvlket fullvtēs.	Vpēyvtet
faˑyâlkit follatiˑs	*apĭˑⁿyátit*
Hunters were about.	they had been going

Hunters were once about. They had been going a while

hvcce rakkēn	onvpvn	hvpo tat	hayvtēs.
hácci łákkiˑn	*onápan*	*hapóˑtaˑt*	*haˑyatíˑs*
a big creek, stream	on top	their camp	they made

and made camp above a big stream.

Fayvlke tat	lvpvtken	es osset	fullvtēs.	Punvttv tat	pvsvtakvtēs.
faˑyâlkitaˑt	*lapátkin*[61]	*isôˑssit*	*follatiˑs*	*ponáttataˑt*	*pasátaˑkatíˑs*
the hunters	away out	they went	were about	The game	they killed

The hunters were way out in the woods. They killed game.

Momen	entvlkvhoskucet	estehvpo	vhecicē	tatēs.
moˑmín	*intâlkahoskocít*[62]	*istihapóˑ*	*ahicéyciˑ*	*táˑtiˑs*[i]
Then	a motherless child	the camp	watching it	was

Then a little orphan was a caretaker for the camp.

Mv oketv	omof	sumecephon	taklikvtēs.
ma okíta	*ôˑmoˑf*	*somicíphôˑn*[63]	*taklêykatiˑs*
(at) that time	when it was	everybody gone away	and it was there.

At that time, when everybody had gone away, he stayed there.

Naket	hvcce	rakkan	ʼtepoyēpvcoken	ayvtēs	res hēcvtēs.
nâˑkit	*hácci*	*łákkaˑn*	*ʼtipoyĭˑⁿpacókin*	*aˑyatíˑs*	*łíshiˑcatíˑs*
something	creek	big	(smthg.) was fighting	it (child) went	and saw it

[He heard] something fighting in the big stream and went to look.

Res hēcet oman,	Tenētkēn	cetto	herakvn	ʼtepoyen	eshēcvtēs.
łíshiˑcít oˑmâˑn	*tiniˑtkíˑn*	*cítto*	*hiłáˑkan*	*típoˑyín*	*íshiˑcatíˑs*
when it saw it	the thunder	(and) snake	a fine one	were fighting	it saw them

When he looked, he discovered a fine snake fighting Thunder.

---

[i] Also all right: *ahicéyca táˑtiˑs* 'was a watcher'.

Mv omof   cvkotaksen   cvwētatēs.
ma ô·mo·f   *'cakotáksin*   *cawi·tá·ti·s*
At that time   bow   it had
He had his bow at that time.

Mv   este   entvlkvhoskuce tat   cetto-yēkcvt   oket   mv   entvlkvhoskucen
ma   *ísti*   *intâlkahoskocíta·t*   *cittoyí·kcat*[64]   *o·kít* *ma*   *intâlkahoskocín*
that   person   the orphan   snake strong   said: that   little orphan
The strong snake said to the little orphan boy:

"Vm vnicetsken omat,   uewv   estofis   vkvrkvpekot omvrēs.
amáneycíckin   *o·mâ·t*   *óywa*   *istô·feys*   *akałkapíko·t*   *ô·máli·s*[65]
if you help me   if do   water   forever   not go dry   will
"If you help me, the water will never go dry.

Hvcce   tihokvkēs"   kicof,   hvtvm   Tenētkēt   okat
hácci   *teyhokáki·s*[66]   *keycô·f*   *hatâm*   *tini·tki·t*   *o·kâ·t*
stream   let's go across   when he said   again   the thunder   said
Let's cross the stream," he said, and again Thunder said,

"Oskē tat   cenpoyafkē tat   onkv,   vne min   vm vnicvs   cē"   kicof,
oski·ta·t   *cinpoyá·fki·tâ·t*   *oŋká*[67]   *animêyn*   *amanéycas*   *ci·^*   *keycô·f*
the rain   you might not have   me, instead   help me   when he told him
"You might be short of rain, so help me instead!"

cvkotaksen   ocēpekv   cetto-yēkcvn   rahvtēs.
'cakotáksin   *o·cî·pika*   *cittoyí·kcan*   *ła·hatí·s*
bow   for he had   the strong snake   he shot
and [the boy] had his bow, so he shot the strong snake.

Momen   'lēcahken   ratat   ehvpon   rvlaket   entvlkvhoskuce tat
mo·mín   *li·cáhkin*   *łâ·ta·t*   *ihapó·n*   *'lalâ·kit*[68]   *intâlkahoskocíta·t*
Then   [they] killed it started   (to) camp   came back to   the orphan
And they killed it, and the little orphan came back to the camp

taklikvtēs.   Momof   fayvlke tat   eryicvtēs.
taklêykati·s   *mo·mô·f*   *fa·yâlkita·t*   *íłyeycati·s*
was there.   Then   the hunters   came back
and stayed there. Then the hunters came back.

"Naken   onahyetskvs"   kicen,   'tem punahoyen
nâ·kin   onáhyíckas[69]   *keycín*   *timponá·ho·yín*
something, anything   you mustn't tell   he told him   they were talking to each other
[Thunder had] told him, "Don't tell them anything," and they talked to each other

takliket   omvtēs.   Takliket   omisen
taklêykit   o·matí·s   taklêykit   o·mêysin
it was sitting   was   sitting   it had been
while he sat there. He was sitting there

"Onvyvkat   herekot os"   komat   omēcicēt   onayvtēs.
onáyaka·t   hilíkoto·s   *ko·mâ·t*   *omi·céyci·t* *ona·yatí·s*
if I don't tell   it's not good, right   he thought   and because, so   he told it
but thought, "It's not right if I don't tell," and for that reason he told them.

Momvhanen   okhoyekv   onayet   estakliket
mó·maha·nín[70]   *okhô·yika*[71] *ona·yít*   *istaklêykit*
it was to be that way   they meant   were telling   were sitting down
It was meant to be that way, and he sat and was telling it,

res poyat   tenētiket   hvlwēcēpvtēt   omēs   cē.
łíspo·yâ·t   *tini·têykit*   *halwí·ci·patí·t*   *ô·mi·s ci·^*
when he was finishing   it thundered   and he went up high   did
and when he finished, it thundered, and he went up high.

TEXTS BY D. STARR

The Origin of Corn

D. Starr (Haas VII:93–95)

Vce-estet   hoktvlēt   omēs.   Momen   mv   hoktalat
ací ístit   hoktalí·t   ô·mi·s   mo·mín   ma   hoktâ·la·t
corn-person   an old woman   [is]   [Then]   that   old woman
Corn-person is an old woman. And that old woman

cvtvhakvn   hayen,   emosuswvt   hompēt   omvtēs.
catahá·kan   ha·yín   imosóswat   hompí·t   ô·mati·s
blue dumplings made   [her] grandchild   ate   [did]
would make blue dumplings, and her grandson would eat them.

Lehayvn   'staklihcet   uewv   vcvnkēn   ohsvyvkilet,   ohsvyvsayen,
lihá·yan   stakléyhcit   óywa   acánki·n   ohsayakâylit   ohsayása·yín
pot   set it down   water in it   straddled it   wiggling about
She set a kettle down, and she straddled it with water in it, and was wiggling about,

cvtvhakvt   a akpvlatkvtēs.
catahá·kat   a·ákpala·tkatí·s
blue dumplings   fell in
and blue dumplings fell in.

Mv   cēpanat   hehcet   hompetv   eyacekatēs.   Em eyacekon
ma   ci·pâ·na·t híhcit   hompitá   iyá·cikáti·s   imiyá·cikon
that   boy   observing it to eat it   didn't want   not wanting it
The boy saw it and didn't want to eat it. As he didn't want it,

"Cvhēcet ontskēt o.   Cukon vcohnokrihcet,   vyepvs" kihcen,
cahî·cit   ónckí·t ó·   *cokón acohnokłéyhcit   ayípas kéyhcin*
seeing me you did is the reason   house   burn it down on me and leave told him
she said, "You saw me. Burn the house down on me and leave,"

cuko tat   'moh-etehcet,   vyēpvtēs.
cokóta·t   mohhitíhcit   ayi·patí·s
house   set it afire   and left
and he set fire to her house and left.

"Netta   osten   'rvlahket   cvhecetskvrēs."
nittá·   ô·stin   'laláhkit   cahícíckáli·s
[day   four]   return   and you will see me
"Come back in four days, and you will see me."

Mv   cuko   nokrvtēn   'rvlahket,
ma   cokó   no·kłatí·n[1]   *'laláhkit*
the   house   where it was burned   he returned to
He came back to the burnt hous

vce tat   holattuset   esliken   hēcvtes.
acíta·t   holă·ⁿttosit   islêykin   hi·catí·s
the corn   very blue   sitting   he saw
and saw the corn [patch] sitting bright blue.

Monkv   "Vce tat hoktvlēt   omēs"   este-cat-vculvke tat maken,
mônka   acíta·t   hoktalí·t   ô·mi·s   istica·tacolakíta·t   ma·kín
Therefore the corn   an old woman   is   the old Indians   said that
So corn is an old woman," old Indian men say.

"Vce tat   estet   omēs"   maket,   vcayēcēt   fullet omvtēt os.
acíta·t   ístit   ô·mi·s   ma·kít   aca·yi·ci·t   follít o·matí·t ô·s
the corn   a person   is   said   preserved it   being around
"Corn is a person," they said, and they treated it with respect.

The Origin of Tobacco

D. Starr (Haas VII:97–99)

Hece tat   "Hiskvt   hece   hakvtēs,"   'culvke   maket   omen,
hicíta·t   héyskat   hicí   ha·katí·s   'colakí   ma·kít   ô·min
tobacco   copulation tobacco became   the old people say
"Tobacco came from copulation," the old people said.

hoktē   honvnwv   etepvkēt welaket,   mv   ēkvnv tat vtotkakvtēs.
hoktí·   honánwa   itipakí·t wila·kít   ma   i·kanáta·t atótka·katí·s[2]
a woman   and a man together they 2 had been around that ground   they worked
A woman and a man were around together working the land.

Mv mạhusat   hece tat   hontē   hẹret   hueren,
ma mǎ·ⁿhosa·t hicíta·t   hónti·   hĭ·ⁿłit   hôylin
right there   tobacco came up very good was standing
Right there a tobacco plant came up good and was standing,

mvn   vcayehcet,   em ēttē mvn   porwvn   hahyet,
man   aca·yíhcit·   imi·ttí· man   pó·łwan   háhyit
that   they preserved   its fruit that seed to plant made it
and they preserved it, saved its seed for planting,

mvt   hece   hakvtēt   os   maket,
mat   hicí   ha·katí·t   ô·ⁿs   ma·kít
that   tobacco it became   did they say
and that became tobacco, they say;

monkv   hece tat   hiskvt   omēs   makaket omvnts cē.
*môŋka   hicíta·t   héyskat   ô·mi·s   má·ka·kít o·mánc ci·^*
Therefore tobacco copulation is   that's what they say
so tobacco is copulation, they used to say.

Flood Story

D. Starr (Haas VII:101–103)

Uelvokē-rakko	hahkof		hvcce	uewv	vkarpvtēn
oylawki·lákko	*háhko·f*		*hácci*	*óywa*	*aka·lpati·n*[3]
flood	[after it became]		a river	[water]	dried up

After the flood people found fire

estet	totkvn	'shēcvtēs.	Mvn	totkv tat	escawet
ístit	*tó·tkan*	*shi·catí·s*[4]	*man*	*tó·tkata·t*	*isca·wít*[5]
people	fire	found	there	the fire	taking it from

in a dried up stream. They gathered the fire [in containers]

'svpeyēpvtēs.		Mvn	totkv	heckvtēt	omēs	maket
sápiyi·patí·s		*man*	*tó·tka*	*híckati·t*[6]	*ô·mi·s*	*ma·kít*
they went away with it		there	fire	was found		saying

and took it away. That's when fire was found,

'culvke	onvyaken	pohvyvtēt	os.
'colakí	*onáya·kín*	*po·hayáti·t*	*ô·*[n]*s.*
the old people	telling	I heard it	did

I used to hear the old people tell.

Mv	uelvokē-rakko	hakof,		sutv	uewv	vcvtakkēpvtēs.
ma	*oylawki·lákko*	*ha·kô·f*		*sotá*	*óywa*	*acatákki·patí·s*[7]
[that	flood	when it became]		sky	the water	reached to

At the time of the flood, the water reached to the sky.

Momof	toskuce	mvn	vlumhen,
mo·mô·f	*toskocí*	*man*	*alômhin*
Then	woodpeckers	there	lying up against

Then woodpeckers were lying up against it,

uewvn	ehvcet	aktekkētēkvtēs.
óywan	*ihácit*	*aktikkí·ti·katí·s*[8]
water	their tails	were extending into the water

and their tails extended into the water.

Mv   uewv   aktekkētēkatē   monkv,
ma   óywa   aktikkí·ti·ka·tí·   mônka
that   water   where they were extending into   is the reason why
Because they extended into the water,

ehvce   rosrukusēt   ont os   maket   onvyakvnts cē,   'culvke.
iháci   ło·slokósi·t   ònt ô·s   ma·kít   onáya·kánc ci·^   'colakí
their tails   kinda mangy   are   saying   that's what they tell the old people
their tails are kind of mangy, the old people used to tell.

TEXTS BY J. BELL

The Last Ball Game of the Kasihtas

J. Bell, Kasihta (Haas XI:1–7)

Espokē	Kvsehtv,	Kvwetv	'tem afackof,	Kvnkakuce	entakhvyakpon	omen,
ispo·kí·	*kasíhta*	*kawíta*	*'timá·fa·côf*	*kanka·koci*[1]	*intakhayakpó·n*	*o·mín*[2]
Last (game)	Kasihta	Coweta	played together	Ball Hill	prairie near	it was

The last time Kasihta and Coweta played together was on Ball Hill prairie,

Kvwetvn	em pohoyvtēs.	Kvwetv	em paskofv	likē	monkof,
kawítan	*impó·ho·yatí·s*	*kawíta*	*impa·skó·fa*	*lêyki·*	*móŋko·f*
Coweta	lost (the game)	Coweta's	square ground	still in	while there

and Coweta lost. When Coweta still had their square ground,

Kvsehtv Fekseko	enheleshayvtēs.	Momen	pokkvnockv	oh-ayof,
kasihtafíksiko	*inhilísha·yatí·s*	*mo·mín*	*pokkanócka*	*óhha·yôf*
Kastihtafiksiko	was their medicine man	Then	ball camp	while they were going to

Cussetah Fixico made the medicine. When they were going to their [last] ball-camp,

ēkvn-kvrpet	oman	pvne	wakketayat	uewvt	fvcfakēpen,
i·kankálpit	*ô·ma·n*	*paní*	*wakkitâ·ya·t*[3]	*óywat*	*facfakî·pin*
dry weather	it was	hollows	lying	water	were filled up

it was dry weather, [but seeing] the hollows were filled with water,

heleshayvt   okat,   "Epupvlhvmkes"   maken   omis,
'hilishá·yat   o·ká·t   ipopalhámkis⁴   ma·kín   o·mêy·s^i
the medicine man   said   we are beaten   he said   did
the medicine man said, "We are beaten,"

afackvlke mit   afvcketvn   eyacvkēton,   pokko   homahlof,
a·fa·ckâlki mêyt   a·fackitán   iya·cakí·ton   pókko   homáhlo·f⁵
the ball-players⁶   to play the game   wanted to   ball   after it went up in the air
but the ball-players wanted to play anyhow, and after the ball was thrown up,

empoyet omhoyvtēs.   Momen   Kvsehtv Fekseko,
impo·yít ómho·yatí·s   mo·mín   kasihtafíksiko
(game) was won from them   And then   Kasihtafiksiko
they were defeated. And Cussetah Fixico,

Kvwetv   enheleshayvt   okat,   "Kvsehtv tat   vcofvphayet   os.
kawíta   inhilishá·yat   o·ká·t   kasíhtata·t   aco·faphâ·yit⁷   ó·ⁿs
the Coweta   medicine man   said   Kasihta   has overpowered me   it is
Coweta's medicine man said, "Kasihta has overpowered me.

Monkv   Noyakv   min   em afvckarēs."
môŋka⁸   no·yá·ka   mêyn   ima·fackcá·li·s
Therefore   Nuyaka   I'll play them
So I will play Nuyaka [town] instead."

Ohrolopē   cokpe-rakko   hvmken   cokpe-cenvpaken
ohlolopí·   cokpiłákko   hámkin   cokpicinapâ·kin
[year   thousand   one   eight hundred
It was in the summer of the year eighteen hundred

pale-kolvpaken   ēpohkakat   em meskēn   omakvtēs.
pá·li kolapâ·kin   i·pohkâ·ka·t   immiskí·n   oma·katí·s
seventy   six]   in the summer of   it was then
and seventy-six [1876].

---

^i "When he saw the water, he knew he was overpowered. The Kasihta medicine man,
mi·kkohá·co, made the creeks full of water so that the Cowetas would be delayed in arriving.
That is one of the schemes to beat the other side.

They agree on a certain time for the ball go to up—the Cowetas were late getting
there—though the ball did not go up till they got there." (XI:2)

Mv vtēkat	Kvsehtv	etvlwv tat	afvcketv		em pohohekon	aten
ma atî·ka·t	*kasíhta*	*itálwata·t*	*a·fackitá*		*impo·hohíkon*	*à·ⁿtin*
Since then	Kasihta	Tribal Town	(to play) ball game		no-one asked them	until

Since then no one has asked Kasihta to play ball,

momen	ēmeu	vpohekon,		ohrolopē	cokpe-rakko	hvmken
mo·mín	*í·miw*	*apóhikon*		*ohłolopí·*	*cokpiłákko*	*hámkin*
and then	him, too	they didn't ask		year	[thousand	one

and [Kasihta] too, didn't ask, until in the year eighteen

cokpe-cenvpaken	pale-ostvpaken	ostohkakat	omof,
cokpicinapâ·kin	*pá·li ostapâ·kin*	*ostohkâ·ka·t*	*ô·mo·f*
eight hundred	ninety	four]	when it was

hundred and ninety-four [1894],

Pētv Kocmv	hocefkēt	afvcketv	opunvyēcet,
pi·takó·cma	*hocífki·t*	*a·fackitá*	*opónayi·cít*
Peter Coachman	named	ball-game	talked about

[a man] named Peter Coachman talked about a ball-game,

Raprakkon	etem punvyvrē	em vkvsamet	omis,	'tem punvkv	ēkvnv
ła·płákkon[9]	*itimponáyáli·*	*imakasâ·mit*[10]	*o·mêys*	*timponáka*	*i·kaná*
Laplakko town	talked with them	they agreed	did	to talk	(land) place

and they agreed to talk to Thlopthlocco, but there was an error

'tehecvranvtēt		'tehosiken	ohhoyanvtēt	os ce.
'tihicála·nati·t[11]		*'tihosêykin*	*óhhoya·natí·t*	*ô·ⁿs ci^*
that was appointed for the talk		they missed	the day passed	did

in the place appointed for the talk, and the day passed.

The Kasihtas Mock the Shawnees

J. Bell (Haas XI:9–13)

Kvsehtvlke	tvlofv-cule	vpokof,	Sawvnokvlken	'tencukopericēt	omvtēs.
kasihtâlki	*'talo·facóli*	*apó·ko·f*	*sa·wano·kâlkin*	*tincokópiłeycí·t*[12]	*ô·mati·s*
The Kasihtas	old town	were living at	the Shawnees	visited them	did

When the Kasihtas were living in the old country, the Shawnee visited with them.

Posketv tis   encakkakof,
poskitáteys   *incákka·kô·f*
at the Green Corn ceremony   when they have them
When [the Kasihta's] Green Corn ['Fast'] was approaching,

oketv   hvmken   Sawvnokvlket   Kvsehtvn   encukopericvtēs.
okíta   *hámkin*   *sa·wano·kâlkit* *kasíhtan*   *incokópiɫeycatí·s*[13]
(one) time   one   the Shawnees   the Kasihta (obj.) visited
the Shawnees visited the Kasihta one time.

Mv omof,   Ēcatēckv-pvnkvn   Sawvnoket   opanvtēs.
ma ô·mo·f *i·ca·ti·ckapánkan* *sa·wanó·kit* *opa·natí·s*
at that time   Red Paint Dance   the Shawnee   danced
At that time the Shawnee danced the Red Paint dance.

Oketv   'tehoyahnof,   Sawvnoke   ehvpon   vyepvranof   okat
okíta   *'tihoyáhno·f*   *sa·wanó·ki* *ihapó·n*   *ayípaɫa·nô·f*   *o·kâ·t*
(time)   after they (danced) Shawnee   camp (at) getting ready to leave said
After time had passed, as the Shawnee were getting ready to leave camp, one said,

"Este-mvnette   esvcvhayekarēs.   Ayit   cvhapo   rorin   omat,
istimanítti   *isacahá·yiká·li·s* *ă·ⁿyeyt* *cahapó·* *ɫo·ɫéyn*   *o·mâ·t*
the young [people]   don't mock me   I'll go   my camp   I reaching   if I do
"The young people should not mock me. When I reach my camp,

kērretskvrēs.   Ēkvnvn   ohrēfkvyof,   fvnokkvrēs."
kî·ɫíckáɫi·s   *i·kanán* *óhli·fkayô·f*   *fanó·kkáɫi·s*
you'll know (when) the ground when I stomp it   will quiver
you will know. When I stomp on the ground, it will shake."

Em vsēhohat senfvyvtvkekatēs. Opanof,   hiyomaket   omis   maket
imasi·hô·ha·t si·nfayatakíká·ti·s[14] *opa·nô·f* *hayyó·ma·kít* *o·mêys*[i] *ma·kít*
[his warning] they disobeyed   when they danced they did this way did   they [said]
They didn't heed the warning. When they danced, they were doing it this way, they said

---

[i] Or: *oma·kêys*.

oh-afvckakvtēs.   Mohmof,   etvlwv   etekvpakvtēs.   Mvt   omēcicen
ohha·fácka·katí·s   *móhmo·f* *itálwa* *itíkapa·katí·s* *mat* *omí·ceycín*
they rejoiced over it   Then   the town divided   that's   the reason why
and were amused by it. Then the town divided. Because of that,

este-Maskoke   etekvpvkēt   mucv-nettvn   yicēt os ce.
istima·skó·ki *itikapáki·t* *mocaníttan* *yéyci·t ô·ⁿs ci^*
the Creeks   divided   up till today they have reached
the Muscogees are divided to this day.

Rabbit Deceives His Mother-in-Law

J. Bell (Haas XI:85–93)

Pasokolvyv   enhoktvlwvn   aenwakketvn yacēt   arvtēs.   Enhoktvlwvt
pa·soko·layá *inhoktálwan* *a·inwakkitán yá·ci·t*[15] *a·latí·s* *inhoktálwat*
Rabbit   his mother-in-law to lie with he wanting was about his mother-in-law
Pasokolaya [Rabbit] once wanted to sleep with his mother-in-law. His mother-in-law said,

"Ocētis   ocvyatē!   Ocē-akliken   hahyvyēs"   makēt   ont   on.
ocí·teys   *ô·caya·ti^* *oci·akléykin* *háhyayi·s* *má·ki·t* *ônt* *ó·n*[16]
hickory-nuts some if I had   hickory-nut sofkee I'd make   she said
"I wish I had some hickory nuts! I'd make hickory-nut sofkee."

Pasokolvyv   fayē   arvtē   ervlaket,   enhoktvlwvn   'monayet,
pa·soko·layá *fa·yí·*   *a·latí·* *iła̱lâ·kit* *inhoktálwan*   *móna·yít*
Rabbit   hunting   been out came back his mother-in-law told her
Pasokolaya came back from hunting and told his mother-in-law,

"Ocē   maketskvnkē   asin   ocis."
ocí·   *má·kickaŋki·*[17] *asêyn*   *ô·ceys*
hickory-nuts   you talked about yonder   there were some
"The hickory nuts you were talking about were over there."

Enhoktvlwvt   oket   "Estvn?"
inhoktálwat   *o·kít*   *ístan*[i]
his mother-in-law   said   where?
His mother-in-law said, "Where?"

---

[i] "kinda anxious"

"Cvnaksat ravfolotkusvkatē!"
canáksa·t ła·afoló·tkosáka·ti^[18]
ridge   just right around
"Just right around the ridge!"

Pasoko okat, "Mi fvccvn fakv vyvranikv, cem meliyin, hopoyētskēs."
pa·sokó· o·kâ·t mêy fáccan fá·ka ayáła·néyka cimmilêyyeyn hopóyí·cki·s[19]
Rabbit said that way hunting I'm going I'll show you you can gather them
Pasoko said, "I'm going hunting that way, so I'll show you, and you can look for them."

"Enka" enhoktvlwvt kihcen, vhoyvtēs.
iŋka^ inhoktálwat kéyhcin aho·yatí·s
all right his mother-in-law said they went off
"All right," his mother-in-law told him, and they went.

Ocē-rakkot eshueren rem mellet,
oci·lákkot ishôylin[20] łímmillít
big hickory tree standing up he pointed out
He went and pointed out a big hickory tree standing with [nuts] on it,

"Heyvn oceko?" kicvtēs. "Encemikit, cenwvsikin vyocetskēs"
hiyán ó·ciko·[21] keycatí·s incimêykeyt cinwasêykeyn ayo·cícki·s[22]
here it is, here's some he said I'll climb up I'll thrash it you can pick them up
"Here it is," he said. "I'll climb it, thrash it for you, and you can gather them,"

mahket, encemket elvcce talusēt vcakhvten sēhvlahtet, kvciken,
máhkit incimkít ilácci tá·losi·t acâ·khatin si·haláhtit kacêykin
he said climbing it limb dry sticking out he held to it it broke off
he said. He was climbing it and held on to a dry limb sticking out, and it broke,

astaklvtiket, orēn ēennokkice okēt hihhaket
a·staklatêykit olí·n i·innokkêyci[23] ó·ki·t háyhha·kit
he fell to the ground awful bad he hurt himself he pretended he groaned
and he fell to the ground. He pretended he hurt himself really badly and groaned

pvlpakvtēs. Enhoktvlwvt 'svfeksomkēt "Renhuehkvyv?" kicen,
pálpa·katí·s inhoktálwat 'safiksómki·t łinhoyhkaya' keycín
he rolled over and over his mother-in-law excitedly must I call her she said
and rolled over and over. His mother-in-law asked excitedly, "Should I go call for [help]?"

"Huehket aretskof, cvlepvr't os" maken,
hoyhkít   a·licko·f   calípáltó·s[24]   *ma·kín*
calling   you are around   I may die   said
"While you are calling, I may die," he said.

"Naken cem estomēcvyēte?" kicof,
ná·kin   cimístomi·cayi·ti[^25]   *keycô·f*
what   can I do for you   when she said
"What can I do for you?" she asked.

"Acenwakkin   omat,   vnlopicēs   komis" Pasoko maken,
a·cinwâ·kkeyn[26]   *o·mâ·t   ánlopeycí·s   kô·meys   pa·sokó·   ma·kín*
[I lie with you]   if   it will sure help me   I believe   R.   said
"If I lie with you, I think it will help me," Pasoko said,

enhoktvlwvt   "Moman no"   kihcen   aenwakkvtēs.   Mehcof,
inhoktálwat   mô·ma·n nô·   kéyhcin   a·ínwa·kkatí·s   míhco·f
his mother-in-law   all right   she said   he lay with her   After he did
and his mother-in-law said, "All right," and he lay with her. After he did it,

fakv   ayvtēs.   Fayvtē   rvlakof,   sohhvpēttvn svpeknvckēt
fá·ka   a·yatí·s   fa·yati·   lála·kô·f   sohhapí·ttan   sapiknácki·t
hunting   he went off   hunting   after returning   porch   reared back on
he went hunting. When he came back from hunting, he reared back on the porch

ele   tohwikēt   liket   "Ho, ho"   makvtēs.
ilí   tohwéyki·t   lêykit[27]   *ho· ho*[i,28]   *ma·katí·s*
legs crossed   sat   he said
and sat with his legs crossed. "Oh, oh," he said.

"Enokkēpis   okhoyēs ce. Erhecvs" ehiwvn   kicen,
inokki·peys[29]   *ókho·yí·s cî   iłhicás   ihéywan   keycín*
might be sick   causing   go see!   to his wife   said
"He might be sick. Go see," [the mother-in-law] told his wife,

---

[i] Uttered slowly.

rem pohof,   "Opunvkvn   vcohhahos"   makvtēs.
límpo·hô·f   *oponakán*   *acohha·hô·s*[30]   *ma·katí·s*
went and asked him   talk   created about me   he said
and when she went to ask him, he said, "There's talk about me."

Ecken   rem onayen,   "Naken   maket?"   kicof,
íckin   *'limóna·yín*[31]   *nâ·kin*   *ma·kít*   *keycô·f*
her mother   told to her   what   was said   when she said
She went and told her mother who asked, "What was said?"

hvtvm   rem pohen,   "Enhoktvlwvn   aenwakkes"   maket   kicen,
hatâm   *límpo·hín*   *inhoktálwan*   *a·inwâ·kkis*[32]   *ma·kít*   *keycín*
again   asked him   with his mother-in-law   he laid   they said   he said
Again she went and asked him: "They're saying, 'He lay with his mother-in-law,'" he said.

yem onayof,   "Momephoyis   estonhkos,   herhoyētok"   makof,
yímona·yô·f   *mo·mípho·yêys*   *istóŋhko·s*   *hiłhoyí·tok*   *ma·kô·f*
when she told   if they do   it's all right   it's good   when she said
When she returned and told her, she said, "It's all right, it's good,"

Pasokot   "hha"   makvtēs.
pa·sokó·t   *xâ*[i]   *ma·katí·s*
Rabbit   he said
and Pasoko said, "Ahhh."

---

[i] Guttural.

TEXTS BY W. TANYAN

Rabbit Deceives Wolf

W. Tanyan (Haas XI:173–177)

Vrēpvtēs	mahokvnts cē.	Konepehacot	vrętt oman,
ałi·patí·s	*má·ho·kánc ciⁿ?·¹*	*konipihá·cot*[i]	*ałĭ·ⁿt o·mâ·n*
he's going around	they have said	Rabbit	as he was going around

He was once going around, it was told. As Konipiharjo [Rabbit] was going around,

cerakkot	wakken	hehcet,	'tehoyahnet	ayvtēs.
'ciłákkot	*wâ·kkin*	*híhcit*	*'tihoyáhnit*	*a·yatí·s*
horse	lying down	he saw it	he passed by	and went on

he saw a horse lying down and passed by.

Mont	ayē	arof,		enhessen	res vfaccvtēs,	'Ste-puca-rakko.
mónt	*a·yi·*	*a·lô·f*		*inhíssin*	*'lisáfa·ccatí·s²*	*stipoca·łákko*[ii]
Then	going on	after he was around		his friend	he met him	wolf (it was)

And when he went on, he ran into his friend, Big Grandfather [Wolf].

Mont,	"Vnhessē!	Nake	cencvmpvnton	hehcis.
mónt	*anhissi^*	*nâ·ki*	*cincámpantó·n*	*híhceys*
Then	my friend!	something	you like (the best)	I saw it

"My friend! I saw something you like.

---

[i] *konipihá·co* = myth name for Rabbit.

[ii] *stipoca·łákko* = wolf

"Naken?"   "Cerakko   ēlv!"
nâ·kin   *'cilákko*   *i·la^*
something   horse   dead (said Rab.)
"What?" "A dead horse!"

"Mon omat   vhoyvkēts."
mô·n o·mâ·t   *ahóyaki·c*
                  let's go, then (said Wolf)
"Well then, let's go," [said Wolf.]

Mont   rohhoyof,   rakko   ēlv tat   wakken   hecakvtēs.
mónt   *łóhho·yô·f*   *lákko*   *i·lata·t*   *wâ·kkin*   *hica·katí·s*
Then   when they got there horse   dead   lying   they saw it
And when they got there, they saw the dead horse lying there.

"Hvfe-rakkon   mvtan   enhompetsken omat, hēˌrēs"   kicvtēs.
hafiłákkon   *matá·n*   *ínhompíckin³ o·mâ·t* *hi·ⁿli·s*   *keycatí·s*
hind leg   starting in on   you will eat   that's good   he said (Rab.)
"If you eat the thigh first it will be good," [Rabbit] said.

Mohmen   'Ste-puca-rakko tat   hompvranof,
móhmin   *stipoca·łákkota·t*   *hómpała·nô·f*
Then   Wolf   as he began to eat
Then as Big Grandfather was about to eat,

"Hvteccē!   Vm ehakvs.   Hvcet   nekēyēt   omis,   hotalof,   monkv
hatí·cci·⁴   *amihá·kas*   *hácit*   *niki·yí·t*   *ô·meys* *hota·lô·f*   *mónka*
hold on   wait for me   tail   moving   is   when the wind blows therefore
[Rabbit said,] "Hold on! Wait for me. Its tail was moving

cetorofv tis   cenrokvffētok: 'secewvnahyin   hompēt omvccvs."
citoló·fateys   *cinlokáffi·tok*   *'siciwanáhyeyn*   *hompi·t omáccas*
your face, even   might whip you on   I'll tie you up   so you can eat
when the wind was blowing, and it might whip your face; I'll tie you to it so you can eat."

Momen   'Ste-puca-rakko tat   hueren   'svrētt   'svwvnayvtēs.
mo·mín   *stipoca·łákkota·t*   *hóylin*   *'sałĭ·ⁿt⁵*   *'sawána·yatí·s⁶*
Then   Wolf   standing   (taking his time) he tied him up
And as Big Grandfather stood, [Rabbit] took his time tying him to it.

"Hvfe-rakkon hompetskof, vnet hvckon enhompares. Tokvs. Hompvkēts"
hafilákkon hompícko·f anít háckon inhómpá·li·s tókas hómpakí·c
hind leg if you eat I ears I'll eat on Now! Eat!
"While you eat its thigh, I'll eat its ears. Now. Let's eat,"

kihcen, 'Ste-puca-rakko tat hvfen em akkof, cerakko tat atasiket
kéyhcin stipoca·lákkota·t háfin ima·kkò·f 'cilákkota·t a·ta·sèykit[7]
he said Wolf leg as he was biting horse jumped up
he told him, and when Big Grandfather bit into its thigh, the horse jumped up

eslētkvtēs. Momen Konepehaco tat vpelicēpvtēs mahokvnts cē.
ísli·tkatí·s mo·mín konipihá·cota·t apileycĭ·ⁿpati·s má·ho·kánc cĭ·ⁿ?·
ran off with him Then Rabbit was laughing at him That's what they say
and ran off with him. And Konipharjo was laughing at him, it was told.

The Bungling Host

W. Tanyan, Seminole (Haas XI:179–187)[i]

Vrēpvtēs mahokvnts cē. Nokoset enhesse Konepehacon 'svfaccet,
ali·patí·s má·ho·kánc cĭ·ⁿ?· nokósit inhíssi konipihá·con 'safâ·ccit
[was around it was told] Bear his friend Rabbit he (B.) met (Rab.)
He was once going around, it was told. Bear met his friend Konipiharjo [Rabbit]:

"Vnhessē! Vncukopericepvc. Hompetv-rakkon hayvranvyēt ont os" kicvtēs.
anhíssi^ ancokopileycipác hompitalákkon há·ɣaɫa·nayí·t ônt ó·s keycatí·s
my friend come and visit me big feast I'll make it is he (B.) said
"My friend! Come and visit me. I'll make you a big feast," he said.

Momen Konepehacot em pohet okat,
mo·mín konipihá·cot impo·hít o·kâ·t
Then Rabbit heard him and said
And Konipiharjo asked him,

---

[i] "In former times, they told stories only a[t] nighttime. You had to tell four stories—if not, you would get to be humped over. Told them any time of year. Tell little stories when the children get restless at night—but when you tell them stories they'll begin to doze." (XI:178)

"'Stvmin   liketskēt omv?"   kicvtēs.   Momen Nokoset em vyoposket,
stamêyn   lêykícki·t[8] ô·ma[·9]   keycatí·s mo·mín nokósit   imáyopo·skít
where   do you live?   he said   Then   Bear   answered him

"Where do you live?" And Bear replied,

"Vsv mahen   likvyēt os,   cvto-cukon.   Monkv   rorvccvs"   kicvtēs.
asamă·[n]hin[10]   léykayi·t ô·s   catocokón   môŋka[11]   'łołáccas[12]   keycatí·s
way over there I live   at the rock-house   now   come over!   he said

"I live right about over there, at the rock house. So come over," he said.

Mohmen   roh-vcēwusen   Konephaco tat   rorvtēs.
móhmin   łohhacĭ·[n]wosin   konipihá·cota·t   ło·łatí·s
Then   a little later on   Rab.   got there

Then a little later Konipharjo went to [Bear's home].

Mohmen "Likepvs cē,   vnhessē!"   kicvtēs.   Mohmen Nokose tat vrḛtt   omisat,
móhmin leykipás ci·^   anhíssi^   keycatí·s   móhmin nokósita·t ałĭ·[n]t o·mêysa·t
Then   sit down!   my friend   he said   Then   Bear   around while he was

Then [Bear] said, "Have a seat, my friend!" Then as Bear had been going about,

hompetvn   'tetakuecvtēs.   Momis   ḛ 'sem elvokēt   omvtēs.
hompitán   'titá·koycatí·s   mo·mêys   í·[n] similáwki·t[13]   ô·mati·s
food   he had prepared   But   he was just about out of was

he had prepared food. But he was just about out of [food].

Mont ont   "Nake   cencvmpvnton   hopoyvranis"   kihcet,
móntónt   nâ·ki   cincámpantó·[n][14]   hopóyała·néys   kéyhcit
Then   something you like the best   I'll get it   he said

And he said, "I'm going to look for what you like best,"

'slafkv tat   eraehset   fvsēcet,   fvsēcet   mehcet,
slá·fkata·t   iła·íhsit[15]   fasi·cít   fasi·cít   míhcit
knife   he went and got   sharpened   sharpened   he did

and went and took out a knife, sharpened it and sharpened it,

cukon   vfoklotiket   ē-em vsahpet,   neha tat   acahwet,
cokón   afoklotêykit[16]   i·masáhpit   nihá·ta·t   a·cáhwit
house   he went around   he cut himself grease   he took out

circled the house, cut himself, took out grease,

Konepehaco tat   hompicvtēs.   Momen
konipihá·cota·t   *hómpeycatí·s*   *mo·mín*
Rab.   ate   Then
and fed it to Konipiharjo. Then [Konipharjo] said,

"Tipvtēs.   Vnhessē!   Tą   cenhomipis"   kicvtēs.
taypáti·s   *anhíssi^*   *tá·n*[i]   *cinhomêypeys*   *keycatí·s*
that's all right   my friend   a whole lot, plenty   I've eaten from you   he said
"That's good enough. My friend! I have eaten plenty from you," he said.

"Monkv   vneu   rvm orepvccvs.   Matvpon   hompetv-rakko   ocarēs"   kicvtēs.
mônka[17]   *aníw*   *'lamolipáccas*   *ma·tapô·n*   *hompitalákko*   *ó·cá·li·s*   *keycatí·s*
Now   I, too   come over (to my place)   same thing   big feast   I'll have   he said
"So you must come over to my [place] too. I will have a big feast in the same way," he said.

Momen   Nokoset   em pohet   okat,
mo·mín   *nokósit*   *ímpo·hít*   *o·kâ·t*
Then   Bear   heard him   and asked
And Bear asked him,

"'Stvmin   likcēt oma?"   kicvtēs.   Konephacot   okat,
stamêyn   *léykci·t*[ii] *ô·ma·*[18]   *keycatí·s*   *konipihá·cot*   *o·kâ·t*
Where   do you live?   said   Rabbit   said
"Where do you live?" Konipharjo said,

"Vsv mąhē   hvyakpvtēkusan   likvyēt   os."
asamă·ⁿhi·[19]   *hayakpatî·kosa·n*   *léykayi·t*   *ô·ⁿs*
way over there   right on the end of the meadow   I live
"I live right about over there at the edge of the meadow."

Cuko-hvtket   pvhe   mąhēt   eslikēt on   okvtēs.
cokohátkit[20]   *pahí*   *mă·ⁿhi·t*   *isleykí·t ô·n*   *o·katí·s*
white house   grass   very tall   that's where (tall grass) is
He meant a white house sitting over there in the tall grass.

---

[i] = *tă·ⁿyin.*

[ii] = *leykícki·t.*

Momen   Nokose tat   vrēpvtet   Konepehaco tat   rem orvtēs.
mo·mín   *nokósita·t*   *ali·ⁿpatit*   *konipihá·cota·t*   *límo·latí·s*
Then   Bear   kept going around   Rabbit's (place)   he arrived at
Then Bear kept going around and reached Konipiharjo's [place].

Mohmen   "Liks ce"   kicvtēs.   Mohmen   Konepehaco tat   enlētkuset
móhmin   *léyks ciᶺⁱ*   *keycatí·s*   *móhmin*   *konipihá·cota·t*   *í·ⁿli·tkosít*[21]
Then   have a seat! he said   Then   Rabbit   running around
Then [Konipiharjo] said, "Sit down!" Then Konipiharjo tried

lvpkusēn   kont   hompetv tat   'metetakuecvtēs.   Mont   omis,
lápkosi·n[22]   *kônt*   *hompitáta·t*   *'mititá·koycatí·s*   *mônt*   *o·mêys*
fast   tried to be   food   had prepared   Then   it was, but
to run around fast and got food ready for him. But

'sem elvokētatēs.   Momet   "Hompvs ce"   kicvtēs.
'similáwki·tá·ti·s   *mo·mít*   *hómpas ciᶺ*   *keycatí·s*
he was about out of food (enough) Then   Eat!   he said
he was about out of food. Then he said, "Eat!"

Nokose tat   hompetv   oh-vfvnnaket   on   hēcof,
nokósita·t   *hompitá*   *ohhafánna·kít*   *ó·n*   *hi·cô·f*
Bear   food   looked on (table)   when he saw
When he saw Bear looking on the table at the food,

"Yvn   vfoklotikit,   nake   cencvmpvnton   res cem vlvkarēs"
yan   *afoklotêykeyt*[23]   *nâ·ki*   *cincámpantó·n*   *liscimalaká·li·s*
there   around the (house)   something   you like best   I will bring back for you
he told him, "I'll circle around here and bring you something you really like,"

kihcet,   'slafkv-rakko tat   eraehset,   fvsehcet,   cukon   vfoklotkat,
kéyhcit   *sla·fkalákkota·t*   *ila·íhsit*[24]   *fasíhcit*   *cokón*   *afóklo·tkâ·t*
he said   big knife   he went and got   he sharpened it   house   he went around and
and took out a knife, sharpened it, and as he went around the house,

---

ⁱ = *léykas ciᶺ*.

ē-em vsapvtēs.　Momis　"Cenk"　makof,
i·mása·patí·s　mo·mêys　cíŋk　ma·kô·f
cut himself　Then　Exclam.　when he said
he cut himself. But when he said, "Chink,"

"Vnhessē! 'Stomv?"　Nokoset　kicvtēs.　"Tayen　ēyvnvttēcets ce.
*anhíssi^　stó·ma^[25]　nokósit　keycatí·s　tà·ⁿyin[26]　i·yanattí·cíc ci^*
my friend　what's the matter　Bear　said　much　you have hurt yourself
Bear said, "My friend! What's the matter? You've hurt yourself badly.

Vnt omvyvnk'n os"　kicvtēs.　Mahokvnts ce.
ánto·mayáŋknó·s[27]　keycatí·s　má·ho·kánc ciⁿ?ˇ
I was the one that did that　he said
I was the one who did that," he said. It was told.

Ritual Speech[i]

W. Tanyan (Haas XII:15–25)[28]

Ta, hentokis cē. Hiyomatē!
tà·?, hĭntŏkà.ĭsci?^[29]　hăyyŏ·mă·ti·?
[Ritualistic introduction] Now!

Momet vm momvrēs enkomit, tvsekvyv tatē
mŏ·mit ămmŏ·mălĭ·s ĭnkŏ·mĕyt, tăsĭkăyà tă·ti·
And it will happen for me, I believe; I have gone around to the citizens

nettv-kvckv em vrēcit omvyvnken,
nĭttăkăckà ĭmàlĭ·cĕyt ŏ·măyáŋkĭn,
announcing the broken days [i.e., the days leading up to the Green Corn];

tvsekvyv, cukolice, elkvhoske em vhonkvtkv hiyomvtēkēt,
tăsĭkăyà cŏkŏlĕycĭ ĭlkăhŏskĭ ĭmàhŏŋkătkă[30] hăyyŏ·mătĭ·kĭ·t,
the citizens, wives, and orphans are great in number,

---

[i] "This speech is for the dance. The conventionalized speeches for match-games are higher in pitch. Falsetto with slight wavering in voice."

vm punvkvn okvtētis os vnkohmet, takfettv tate vntakcukolaken hēcvyofv,
ămpŏnăkăn ŏkătĭ·tĕysŏ·s ănkŏhmĭt tăkfĭttătă·tĭ·[31] *ăntăkcŏkŏlă·kĭn hĭ·căyŏ·fă?*
they believed my message was from them, and when I saw them enter my yard

"Mont os" kohmit esvmahlvpvtke 'stvmahet os makit omis ce.
mŏntŏ·s kŏhmĕyt ĭsămăhlăpătkĭ stămă·hĭt ŏ·s, mă·kĕyt ŏ·mĕys cĭ?
I thought, "It is happening," and it gives me great comfort, I have said.

Momen hiyomatē, puncukopericvlke fullvranēt omēs.
mŏ·mĭn hăyyŏ·mă·tĭ? pŏncŏkŏpĭlĕycălkĭ fŏllălă·nĭ·t ŏ·mĭ·s
And now we are going to have visitors.

Momen omēto estomis, mvnettvlke afvcketv ētvn hayē omēt
mŏ·mĭn ŏ·mĭ·tŏ(ĭ)stŏ·mĕys mănĭttălkĭ ă·făckĭtă ĭ·tăn hă·yĭ· ŏ·mĭ·t
And even if they pretend to be young ball players

etepelicē omis momē ocēt omēs. Mv tat momen vm momekarēs.
ĭtĭpĭlĕycĭ· ŏ·mĕys mŏ·mĭ· ŏ·cĭ·t ŏ·mĭ·s mătă·t mŏ·mĭn[32] *ămmŏ·mĭkă·lĭ·s*
and make fun of others, it happens sometimes. I do not want that to happen.

"Vnen okhoyis omēs," komvranat ocēt omēt omekv,
"ănĭn ŏkhŏ·yĕys ŏ·mĭ·s," kŏ·mălă·nă·t ŏ·cĭ·t ŏ·mĭ·t ŏ·mĭkă
There is a time when someone may think, "They may mean me,"

mvt momen vm momekarēs makit omis cē.
măt mŏ·mĭn ămmŏmĭkă·lĭ·s[33] *mă·kăyt ŏ·mĕys cĭ?^*
so that is what I do not want to happen; I have spoken.

Monkv este ēyvhēricet takkaket omvrēs.
mŏŋkă ĭstĭ ĭyăhĭ·ⁿlĕycĭt tăkkă·kĭt ŏmălĭ·s
So the two people sitting there should be prepared.

Momen enhessetake em vlaket ont on omat, hompetv holwakusat enkvlēpet,
mŏ·mĭn ĭnhĭssĭtă·kĭ imălă·kĭt ŏnt ŏ·n ŏ·mă·t hŏmpĭtăhŏlwă·kŏsă·t ĭnkălĭ·pĭt
And when their friends come, even food that is not the best should be shared;

vm momvranēt omēs komis maket omēs cē.
*ămmŏ·mălă·nĭ·t ŏ·mĭ·s kŏ·mĕys mă·kĭt ŏ·mĭ·s cĭ?^*
I believe it will happen, I have said.

Momen hiyomatē, este enhessetake hopvye estvmahen sēhokvtēto estohmis,

mŏ·mĭn hăyyŏ·mă·tĭ·[34] *ĭstĭ ĭnhĭssĭtă·kĭ hŏpăyĭ ĭstămă·hĭn sĭ·hŏ·kătĭ·tŏĭstŏhmĕys*

And now friends who live a great distance away,

hiyomat em vcukopērket enfullet ont on omat, vhēricet vsēket em vpēlet,

hăyyŏ·mă·t ĭmăcŏkŏpĭ·lkĭt ĭnfŏllĭt ŏnt ŏ·n ŏ·mă·t[35] *ăhĭ·ⁿlĕycĭt ăsĭ·kĭt ĭmăpĭ·lĭt*

now when they come to visit, show respect, shake hands, smile,

ētem punahoyet omvrēs makit omis cē. Momen hiyomatē,

i·tĭmpŏnă·hŏ·yĭt ŏmălĭ·s mă·kĕyt ŏ·mĕys ci^ mŏ·mĭn hăyyŏ·mă·tĭ·[36]

and talk with one another, I have said. And now,

vm vculvke sehokof, heyvt em afvcketvt omvtētis

ămăcŏlăkĭ sĭhŏ·kŏ·f hĭyăt ĭmă·făckĭtăt ŏ·mătĭ·tĕys

when the old ones were still here, this was their form of enjoyment,

vntatehkvn escvhosē omē hakvtēt ont omis.

ăntă·tĭhkăn[37] *ĭscăhŏsĭ· ŏ·mĭ· hă·kătĭ·t ŏnt ŏ·mĕys*

but for my part, I have kind of forgotten.

Hiyomat vhockvpkusē tetayē afvcketv hayit, hiyomatē takkakin,

hăyyŏ·mă·t ăhŏckăpkŏsĭ·[38] *tĭtă·yĭ· ă·făckĭtă hă·yĕyt hăyyŏ·mă·tĭ· tăkkă·kĕyn*

Now, even though we played ball well enough for some to be envious, we sit here;

vm estomvranēt omēs komis makit omis cē.

*ămĭstŏ·mălă·nĭ·t ŏ·mĭ·s kŏ·mĕys mă·kĕyt ŏ·mĕys ci^*

I believe that something will happen for me, I have said.

Momen cukolice tatē afvcketv tat enhayvranit omis makēt os.

mŏ·mĭn cŏkŏlĕycĭtă·tĭ· ă·făckĭtătă·t ĭnhă·yălă·nĕyt ŏ·mĕys mă·kĭ·t ŏ·s

The women are going to play ball; we will have a game, they said.

Monkv cukolice awet estomēt em vculvke tatē em vfvcketvt omvtē

mŏŋkă cŏkŏlĕycĭ ă·wĭt ĭstŏ·mĭ·t ĭmăcŏlăkĭ tă·tĭ· ĭmăfăckĭtăt ŏ·mătĭ·

So the women will come, and whatever the elders' way of playing ball was

enkerkvkēt omētokv, a-awet vsehoket omvrēs makit omis cē.

*ĭŋkĭlkăkĭ·t ŏ·mĭ·tŏ·kă ă·ă·wĭt ăsĭhŏ·kĭt ŏmălĭ·s mă·kĕyt ŏ·mĕys ci^*

they have an idea, so they will come forward and stand here, I have said.

TEXTS BY E. GOUGE

A Note on Hilabi Town

E. Gouge (Haas XV:179–191)

Helvpe etvlwv tat mahlvpatkus onkot omvtēs.
hilápi itálwata·t mahlapă·ⁿtkos óŋko·t o·matí·s[i]
Hilabi town was not very serious-minded.

"Etvlwv tat afvcketv vm pohēt on omat, aohfolotkusiyēt omarēs.
itálwata·t a·fackitá ámpo·hí·t ô·n[1] *o·mâ·t a·ohfolô·tkosâyyi·t ô·ma·li·s*
"If a town asks me for a game, I will turn around.

Etvlwv estomepēto stomis em afackvyēt omvrēs" maket kaket okat,
itálwa isto·mipí·to· stô·meys imá·fa·ckayí·t omáli·s[2] *ma·kít kâ·kit o·kâ·t*
I will play with any sort of town," they said when they sat down.

"Etvlwv fvccvsekot omarēs" maket kakē ocvtēs. Mv momē makat,
itálwa faccasíkot ô·má·li·s ma·kít ka·kí· o·catí·s ma mó·mi· ma·kâ·t
Saying, "I am not a proper town," they sat down. Talking like that

"Etvlwv estomepēto stomis em afackvyēt omvrēs" makēt omēpekv,
itálwa isto·mipí·to· stô·meys imá·fa·ckayí·t omáli·s[3] *ma·kí·t omî·pika*[4]
they said, "I will play with any sort of town,"

ēmēta tis etem pokkechē tayet etvlwvt omvtēs, maketvt omvnts.
i·mi·tá·teys[5] *itimpokkíchi· tà·yit*[6] *itálwat o·matí·s*[7] *ma·kitát ô·mánc*
and they could even play themselves, they were that kind of town; that was the saying.

---

[i] (didn't do things according to rules).

Ball Game Agreement

E. Gouge (Haas XV:167–169)

Etvlwv 'tem pokkēchat "'Osten etem afvckeyvrēs' maketvn 'temfvccetv" makvtēs.
itálwa timpókki·châ·t[8] *ô·stin itima·fáckiyáli·s ma·kitán timfaccitá*[9] *ma·katí·s*
The towns that played together said the agreement is to play four times.

Monkv afvcketv ostat afackē vtēkat estvmin em pohoyē to stomis,
môŋka a·fackitá ô·sta·t á·fa·ckí· atî·ka·t ístamêyn impó·ho·yí·to· stô·meys[10]
Then every time they played four games, whichever one was beat,

mv afvcketv ostē makē 'tem fvccakvtē etem afacket
ma a·fackitá ô·sti· ma·kí· timfácca·katí· itimá·fa·ckít
agreeing with each other to those four games, they played

esvpēt afvcketv ostat afvckaken omat, estvmi hvmken em pohoyē to stomis,
isapi·ⁿt[11] *a·fackitá ô·sta·t a·fácka·kín o·mâ·t istamêy hámkin impó·ho·yí·to· stô·meys*[12]
and went on, and if they play four games, whichever one was beat,

etohhvhohyet etvlwv "Etenhesset omeyvrēs" mahket
itohhahóhyit itálwa itinhíssit ô·miyáli·s[13] *máhkit*[i]
the [two] came together, and the towns said, "We will be friends with each other,"

temfvccaket omvtēs. Mv momē temfvccakat svnvcomvn etem afvckekot
tímfacca·kít o·matí·s[14] *ma mó·mi· timfácca·kâ·t 'sanácoman*[15] *itima·fáckiko·t*
and they agreed. Agreeing that way, they didn't play together ever again;

este tis etecakkusat welakēs. Mv omēt etvlwv tat kakēpet omvtēs.
ístiteys iticâ·kkosa·t wila·kí·s ma ó·mi·t itálwata·t ká·ki·pít o·matí·s[16]
they went about like brothers. That's the way towns were set up.

Svnvcomvn 'tem afvckekatēs.
'sanácoman 'tima·fáckiká·ti·s[17]
They didn't play against each other ever again.

---

[i] Doesn't know which side first offered to agree to be friends. (This in case of Okchai and other towns.) Didn't become *into·tkí·tka hámki* because that means something like offspring—*into·tkí·tka hámki* never played against each other.

An Okchai Ball Game

E. Gouge (Haas XV:171–177)[i,18]

Etvlwv Okcaye etvlwv ētimvn estem afackē ocvtēs.
itálwa okcá·yi itálwa i·téyman istimá·fa·ckí· o·catí·s
Okchai town had a game with another town.

Mv afvcketv ostē maketv ocat Okcayet etvlwv hvmken em afackvtēs.
ma a·fackitá ô·sti· ma·kitá ô·ca·t okcá·yit itálwa hámkin imá·fa·ckatí·s
They had an understanding that Okchai would play four games with the other town.

Mohmet etem pokkechakvtēs.
móhmit itimpokkícha·katí·s
Then they played ball together.

Hvteceskv etem pokkēchat hvmken em pohoyvtēs.
haticíska itimpókki·châ·t[19] hámkin impó·ho·yatí·s
The first time they played ball together, one of them got beat.

Momof temfvccetv cakkvyē tat afvcketv tuccēnet em vhoskētatēs.
mo·mô·f timfaccitá cakkayí·ta·t a·fackitá toccî·nit imahóski·tá·ti·s
Then, according to the agreement, three games remained.

Monkv hvtvm etem pokkēchvtēs. Mohmen mvo hvmkan em poyvtēs.
móŋka hatâm itimpókki·chatí·s móhmin maw' hámka·n ímpo·yatí·s
So again they played ball together. Then that [time] too, the [same] one got beat.

Momis temfvccetv cakkvyē tat afvcketv hokkolet em vhoskētatēs.
mo·mêys[20] timfaccitá cakkayí·ta·t a·fackitá hokkô·lit imahó·ski·tá·ti·s
Then, according to their agreement, two games remained.

Mohmen hvtvm etem afackvtēs. Mvo hvmken em pohoyvtēs.
móhmin hatâm itimá·fa·ckatí·s maw' hámkin impó·ho·yatí·s
Then they played together again. That [time] too, [the same] one got beat.

---

[i] There are probably no old Okchai left who might know anything about the old ball games. Didn't talk about it to the women and girls so Mrs. G. doesn't know.

Momis temfaccvtē vcakkvyē tat afvcketv hvmket vhoskē monkvtēs.
mo·mâys tímfa·ccatí· acakkayí·ta·t a·fackitá hámkit ahóski· môŋkati·s[21]
Then, according to the agreement, one game still remained.

Mohmen hvtvm etem afvckvtēs. Momen mv espokēt temafackat,
móhmin hatâm itimá·fa·ckatí·s mo·mín ma ispó·ki·t[22] *'timá·fa·ckâ·t*
Once more they played together. Then that last time they played together,

afvcketv yekcēn etem afackvtēs. Mvt espokē afvcketvt omvtēs,
a·fackitá yikci·n itimá·fa·ckatí·s mat íspo·ki· a·fackitát o·mati·s
they played a tough game. That was the last game,

temfvccetv cakkvyē tat.
timfaccitá cakkayí·ta·t
according to the agreement.

Momof mv afvcketv espokē tem afackat, rē-sehokv hvmkuse vlket em vhosken,
mo·mô·f ma a·fackitá íspo·ki· timá·fa·ckâ·t li·sihó·ka hámkosiâlkit imahô·skin
In that last game that they played, each side was just one point short,

hvmket 'svfvliyen afvcketv fekhonnvtēs.
hámkit 'safalèyyin a·fackitá fíkhonnatí·s
and one side threw, and the game ended.

Mohmen mvn okvtētok, etohhvhohyet okakat,
móhmin man o·katí·to·k itohhahóhyit oka·kâ·t
Then as they had discussed, they came together, saying,

"Punyekcē tat momvlkust omekv, etenhesse etehayvkēts," hvmket kicen,
ponyikcí·ta·t[23] *mô·mǎlⁿkost o·miká itinhíssi itihá·yakí·c hámkit keycín*
"Our strength is almost the same, so let's become friends," one said,

etem vkvsahmet etenhesse hakvtēs. Maketv omvnts ce.
*itimakasáhmit itinhíssi ha·katí·s ma·kitá ô·mánc ci^*
and they agreed and became friends. That's the saying.

TEXTS BY A. SULPHUR

A Ball Game Challenge

Alex Sulphur, Eufaula town (Haas XV:185–187)

Yofalv mēkkot ont omis. Mont vntvsekvyv afvcketvn eyacet omen
yofá·la mí·kkot ônt o·méys mónt antasikayá a·fackitán iyá·cit[1] o·mín
I am the chief of Eufaula. My citizens want enjoyment,

ecohhvlakvyēt os. Momen heyv 'tokonhet asfvccēckvt os.
icóhhala·kayi·t[2] ô·s mo·mín hiyá 'tokónhit a·sfaccí·ckat ô·s
and I have come to you. Here is a ball-stick as proof.

Monkv 'ponvkv tat vyoposkē cem pohares ce."
*môŋka[3] 'ponakáta·t ayoposkí· cimpohá·lis ci^*
Therefore, in talk, I will hear an answer from you
Answer of challenged chief:

Mon omat 'tetiyepvtēs, faccusen oketskētok. Vyoposkē tat vnpohet vnhecetskvrēs.
mô·n o·mâ·t 'titaypáti·s[4] fa·ⁿccosin o·kícki·to·k ayoposkí·ta·t ánpo·hít anhicickáli·s
Well, it's all right; what you say is true. You will hear an answer from me.
Challenged chief returning stick:

Yv nake 'tokonhe yvn wvkēcetskvnkē cem ohhvkerricit omosymmvliken,
ya nâ·ki 'tokónhi yan waki·cíckaŋkí· cimohhakillěyⁿceyt omosǎmⁿmaléykin
I have been thinking over the ball-stick of yours that you laid down for some time,

vnfaccat momepekvs ce. Mon omat netta 'tehecvraneyat huerichvnt omēs ce.
*ánfa·ccâ·t mo·mipíkas ci^ mó·n o·mâ·t nittá· 'tihícala·niyâ·t⁵ hoyléychánt^i o·mí·s ci^*
and my decision is to do it. So then we will set the day when we see each other.

Note on the Ball-Game

Alex Sulphur (Haas XV:189)

Etvlwv enkepayv em poyet osticat vtēkat eyohhvpvkē hayet omvtēs.
itálwa iŋkipá·ya ímpo·yít ósteycâ·t atî·ka·t iyohhapakí· ha·yít⁶ ô·mati·s
When a town's enemy beats them four times, they make them members.

Totkētkv em esēt omēs.
to·tkí·tka imísi·t o·mí·s⁷
They take the fire from them.

Oyokofki Town

Alex Sulphur, Eufaula town (Haas XV:191–192)

Horre-rakko omof, cvpucaculet okvntvs oket okat
hoɫłiɫákko ô·mo·f capoca·colít o·kántas o·kít o·kâ·t^ii
During the Civil War, my great grandfather used to say,

horre omēcicēn este etekvpakat horre fullvtē eryihcof,
hóɫłi omi·céyci·n ísti itíkapa·kâ·t hóɫłi follatí· iɫyéyhco·f⁸
after people who were separated because of the war returned from the war,

hvpo hayusēt hvcce wakkosē vpofken yvpoket cuko vnvcomicvseko
hapó· ha·yósi·t⁹ hácci wákkosi· apô·fkin yápo·kít¹⁰ cokó anacoméycasíko^iii
they just made camps and lived where a river lay and lived in

yvpoket omet, hoktvke empokkēchet eshvyatket vpoket ont omatet,
'yapô·kit¹¹ o·mít hoktakí impókki·chít íshaya·tkít apô·kit ónt o·mâ·tit¹²
several houses. The women played ball until morning, and they lived [like that].

---

^i Long way: *hoyłéyc[a]há·nít.*
^ii FS says *o·kít o·kâ·t* is superfluous.
^iii Better: *anacoméycakósi·t.*

etvlwv mvhocefkv ocekot vpoket omen, vculvket esfullet
itálwa 'mahocífka ó·ciko·t apô·kit o·mín acolakít ísfollít
Their town had no name, and they were living [there]. The old people were with them

hocefkv enhayetv komet fvllet omet hocefakvtēt omēs.
hocífka inha·yitá kô·mit fŏl^{n}lit o·mít hocífa·katí·t ô·mi·s
and kept going about wanting to make a name for them, and they named it.

Momat hvcce wakkat, estofis okofkē ont omen,
mo·mâ·t^{13} hácci wâ·kka·t^{14} istô·feys okófki·^{15} ônt o·mín
Then where the river lay, it was always muddy.

"Mvn esvhocēfvkēs" makakvtēs.
man isáhoci·fakí·s^{16} má·ka·katí·s
"We will name it after that," they said.

Mahket "Ue-okofke etvlwv omvrēs" makakvtēs.
máhkit oy?okófki itálwa ô·máli·s^{17} má·ka·katí·s
"It will be Oyokofki ['muddy water'] town," they said.

TEXTS BY D. COOK

[Square Ground Rules]

Daniel Cook (Haas XVI:75–77)

Cukorakko ocat vtēkat vhakv ocēt omvtēs.
cokołákko ô·ca·t atî·ka·t ahá·ka ó·ci·t ô·mati·s
Each square ground had rules.

Semēfvyvtkv mvtvlkusēn omakusēn omakvtēs. Mont mv vhakv yekcvkēn omakvtēs.
'simi·fayátka matálkosi·n omá·kosi·n[1] omâ·kati·s. mônt ma ahá·ka yikcakí·n omâ·kati·s.
These were all they had to direct their affairs. And these rules were very strict.

Tvsekvyv vtēkat omvlkvt mvn sēyenfvyvtakē omvtēs.
tasikayá ati·ka·t omálkat man si·yinfayáta·ki· ô·mati·s
All citizens followed these rules.

Hoktvke tat monkat hopuetake lopocke omvlkvt mvt semēenfvyvtkvt omvtēs.
hoktakíta·t[2] móŋka·t hopoytá·ki lopócki omálkat mat 'simi·infayátkat ô·mati·s.
All the women or small children, those were their rules.

Vhakv 'remēti ocekot omvtēs.
ahá·ka 'limi·têy[3] ó·ciko·t o·mati·s.
There were no other rules.

Bat and the Ball Game

Daniel Cook (Haas XVI:81–85)

Celokke hvthakv tempokkēccvtēs.
ciló·kki hathá·ka timpókki·ccatí·s.
The celokke ['speakers of another language'] and hvthakv ['white ones'] had a ball game.

Tempokkeccvhanē temfaccof, nake tvmēcat vtēkat hvthakvt omvtēs.
timpokkíccaha·ni· tímfa·ccô·f nâ·ki tami·câ·t atì·ka·t hathá·kat ô·mati·s
When they agreed to play ball, anything that flew would be hvthakv.

Momen nake ponvttv ele ostv vtēkat celokket omvtēs.
mo·mín nâ·ki ponátta ili ô·sta atì·ka·t ciló·kkit ô·mati·s.
And the four-legged animals would be celokke.

Momof hvmket arvtēs. Takfvlelēskvt hocefkēt celokke fullan arvtēs.
mo·mô·f hámkit a·latí·s takfalilî·skat hocífki·t ciló·kki follâ·n a·latí·s.
Now there was one among them; one named Bat was among the celokke.

"Hvthakv ontskes. Min hvthakv fullan vyepvs" kihocvtēs.
"hathá·ka ónckis mêyn hathá·ka follâ·n ayípas" kéyho·catí·s.
"You're hvthakv. Go where the hvthakv are," he was told.

Ayet rorof, "Mvtoyecceks. Celokke toyets.
â·yit lo·lô·f "mató·yiccíks ciló·kki tô·yíc[4]
When he went [they said], "You're not one [of us]. You're celokke.

Ponvttv toccekv, ceyacēkot os. Yefulkvs" kihocen, yefulkvtēs.
ponátta tô·ccika ciyá·cí·kot ó·s 'yifólkas "kéyho·cín yifolkatí·s
You're a wild animal, so we don't want you. Go back," he was told, and he went back.

Rorof "Mvtoccekan okhos. Cetvrpvn ocetskētok tvmketskēt onkv,
lo·lô·f "mató·ccíka·n[5] ókhó·s citálpan ô·cicki·to·k tamkícki·t ôŋka
When he got there, [they said,] "You're not one [of us]. You have wings and can fly,

hvthakv toyetskēs. Yefulkepvs" kihocen, yefolkvtēs.
hathá·ka tô·yícki·s 'yifolkipás "kéyho·cín 'yifolkatí·s
so you're hvthakv. Go back," he was told and went back.

Hvthakv vpokan rorof, aeshoyvtēs.
hathá·ka apô·ka·n ło·lô·f a·isho·yatí·s
When he got to where the <u>hvthakv</u> were, they took him in.

Momen wvsketvn huerihocvtēs. Mvt pokkēccv 'svmomemahat omēpvtēs.
mo·mín waskitán hoyłéyho·catí·s mat pokkí·cca 'samo·mimá·ha·t omî·pati·s.
And he was put in the position of guard. He was one of the best ball players.

Rē-sehokv omvlkvn hayet epoyvtēs.
łi·sihó·ka omálkan ha·yít ipo·yatí·s.
He won all the points.

TEXTS BY J. BULLET

About the Loyal Creeks

J. Bullet, Hilabi (Haas VII:105–123)

Hompēt   'svpokeyvtēt on   okis.
hompí·t   sápo·kiyáti·t ô·n[1]   *o·kéys*
we eating   we sitting   we were
We were sitting eating, I recall.

Momen   hompeyvtē tat   wihkēt   sosseyvtēt os cē.
*mo·mín   hompiyáti·ta·t   wéyhki·t   so·ssiyáti·t ô·s ci·^*
Then   eating   we quit   and went out
Then we quit eating and went out.

Hacvlke   omis   fullat   pefathokvtēt omēs.
ha·câlki   ô·meys follâ·t   pifá·tho·katí·t ô·mi·s
when drunkards   like   were around   they would run away
When drunks and such were about, they would run away.

Hompetv   soh-ocēpē   monken,   pefathokvtēt   omēs.
hompitá   sohho·cî·pi·[2]   *mônkin   pifá·tho·katí·t   ô·mi·s*
food   on the table   leaving it   and ran away
With the food still on [the table], they would run away.

Mvn   'stvpahkit   pefathokat,   ayvyvtēt omēs.
man   stapáhkeyt[3]   *pifá·tho·kâ·t   a·yayáti·t ô·mi·s*
them   I got with them   where they were running   and I went
I joined some who were running away and went where they were running.

Momof   horret   hakēpekv   etepohoyat,
mô·mo·f   *hóllit*   *ha·kî·pika*   *itipó·ho·yâ·t*
At that time war   they had made   fighting
At that time, because war had broken out, when they were fighting,

eccv   tvpockat   'mvheremahēt   omvtēt   os.
ícca   *tapo·ckâ·t*   *'mahilimá·hi·t* *o·matí·t* *ô·s*
and guns   shooting   terrible   it was
the shooting of guns was terrible.

Momen   Hopueryvholv   em estvlke   esyomat
mo·mín   *hopoylyahóla*   *imistâlki*   *isyô·ma·t*
Then   [Hopuethlyahola]   his people   together with
And since I was with

momen   vpvkētoyikv,   vneu   letkēpvyvtēt os.
mo·mín   *apáki·tô·yeyka*   *aníw*   *lítki·payáti·t ô·s*
and   I belonged with them, too me, too   I ran, too
Hopuethlyahola's people, I ran too.

Momen   Hopueryvholv   kvsvppof-fvccvn   ayet   vpēyeyvtēt os.
mo·mín   *hopoylyahóla*   *kasappo·ffáccan* *a·yín*   *api·yiyáti·t ô·s*
[and]   [Hopuethlyahola]   northward   going   we went
And Hopuethlyahola was headed north, so we went that way.

Momen   vpēyeyat
mo·mín   *api·yiya·t*
Then   we went
As we went

tvlofuce   Okcvnhakuce   hocefkēt   liken   eroriceyvtēt   os.
'talo·focí   *okcanha·kocí*   *hocífki·t*   *lâykin*   *ilóleyciyáti·t*   *ô·s*
little town   "little salt-maker"   named   was there   we got there   did
we reached a little town called Little Salt-Maker.

Momen   mv   oketv tat   rvfot   omvtēs.   Orē   kvsvppēt   omvtēt os.
mo·mín   *ma*   *okítata·t*   *lafót*   *ô·mati·s* *olí·*   *kasáppi·t*   *ô·mati·t ô·s*
Then   that   time   winter   it was   awful   cold   it was
It was winter at that time. It was awfully cold.

Momen tvcako hvmkis hompēkot fulleyvtēt os.
mo·mín tacá·ko hámkeys hómpi·kot folliyáti·t ô·s
[and] week [one, even] we without eating we were about [were]
Sometimes we went a week without eating.

Vneu 'stelvpikv vtehvkot mv oketv arvyvtēt os.
aníw stilapéyka atíhako·t ma okita a·layáti·t ô·s
[I, too] shoes without that time I was about [was]
I also went around without shoes at that time.

Momen netta vnvcume mahusekon vpokēn
mo·mín nittá· anacomi má·hosikon apò·ki·n
Then days many not very were there
We weren't there many days

hompetv tis, 'stelvpikv tis, accvkē tis, wvcenv-mēkko atotēn
hompitá teys stilapéyka teys a·ccakí· teys wacinamí·kko a·totí·n[4]
food even shoes even clothes even [the president] had sent
when we received food and shoes and clothes

nake momakat caweyvtēt os cē.
*nâ·ki mo·má·ka·t ca·wiyáti·t ô·s ci·^*
things like that we got them did
and such things from the President [of the U.S.].

Momen 'stelvpikv accvkē omakat vchoyepēkv,
mo·mín stilapéyka a·ccakí· o·mâ·ka·t achoyî·pi·ka[5]
[and] shoes clothing like that we had on
And because we had shoes and clothes we were wearing,

momen hompetvo hompēkv, pufvcficēt hvtvm vpēyeyvtēt os cē.
*mo·mín hompitáw hô·mpi·ka pofacféyci·t hatâm api·yiyáti·t ô·s ci·^*
[and] food, too we had eaten we were full again we went (on)
and because we'd eaten food too, we were full and went on again.

Momen vpēyeyat 'stvmv tvlofvt os mahokvtēt ont omis
mo·mín apí·yiya·t[6] *stamá 'taló·fat ô·s má·ho·katí·t ônt o·mêys*
Then we went what town it is they have said but
And they said where we went, which town it was,

cvhosētt   omēt os.
cahosîˑtt   *oˑmíˑt ôˑs*
I have forgotten
but I have forgotten.

Momis   Kansas City   kihocat   enhvsaklatkvt   omvtēs.
moˑmêys   *keynsís síti* *kéyhoˑcâˑt*   *inhasakláˑtkat* *ôˑmatiˑs*
But   Kansas City   (called it)   west of   it was
But it was west of what is called Kansas City.

Momen   mvn   vpokēn   "Abraham Lincoln   rēyvpvyaks"   kihcet,
moˑmín   *man* *apôˑkiˑn* *eyplihéym línkan*   *liˑyapáyaks*   *kéyhcit*
Then   there we were   Abraham Lincoln   go and get him (H.) told
And while we were there, Abraham Lincoln told his soldiers

suletawv   atotēn   Hopueryaholv tat   yvnvs-hvrpe tat   'svpvllahyet,
solitáˑwa *aˑtotíˑn*[7] *hopoyłyahóla taˑt* *yanasháłpi taˑt*   *'sapalláhyit*
soldiers   had sent   [Hopuethlyahola]   buffalo hide   they wrapped him with
to get [Hopuethlyahola], so they wrapped him in a buffalo hide

res awvtēt   os.   Momen   Kansas City   asyicvtēt   omēs.
lísaˑwatíˑt   *ôˑs*   *moˑmín* *keynsissíti* *áˑsyeycatíˑt*   *ôˑmiˑs*
and brought him back did   [and]   Kansas City   got back with him   [did]
and brought him back. And they brought him back to Kansas City.

Momen   asyihohcof,
moˑmín   *aˑsyeyhóhcoˑf*
[and]   after they got back with him
And after they brought him back,

"Hokvs.   Vlakis.   Estomvranin   okatsken   omat"
hókas   *alâˑkeys*   *istóˑmalaˑnéyn*   *oˑkáˑckin*   *oˑmâˑt*
Now   I have come   for me to do   you-all intend   do
Hopuethlyahola told them, "Now. I have come.

Hopueryvholv   'stekicof,   Abraham Lincoln't   okat,
hopoyłyahóla   *stikeycôˑf*   *eypliheymlínkant*   *oˑkâˑt*
[Hopuethlyahola]   when he told them that   Abraham Lincoln   said
If you all intend for me to do something." Abraham Lincoln [sent word back],

"Tvlwv-hvtke min vlvketskvrēn okvyvnks" kihcen,
talwahátki *mêyn* *alákickáłi·n* *ô·kayánks* *kéyhcin*
Washington, instead for you to come to I meant [he told him]
"I meant for you to come to Washington, instead,"

hvta Hopueryvholv tat Tvlwv-hvtken suletawvt 'svpēyvtēt omēs.
hatâ·[8] *hopoyłyahóla ta·t* *talwahátkin* *solitá·wat* *sápi·yatí·t* *ô·mi·s*
then [Hopuethlyahola] Washington the soldiers took him [did]
and then the soldiers took Hopuethlyahola to Washington.

Res orihohcen Abraham Lincoln etehēcvtēs.
'lisołeyhóhcin *eyplihéym línkan* *itíhi·catí·s*
They got there with him Abraham Lincoln saw each other
After they got there, he and Abraham Lincoln met.

Momen "Hokvs cē. Vlakis. Momen tą cvstemerricet ontskes.
mo·mín *hókas* *ci·^* *alâ·keys* *mo·mín* *tă·ⁿ castimiłłêycit*[9] *ônckis,*
[and] Now, then I have come [and] punished me much [you have]
And [Hopuethlyahola said,] "Now. I have come. You have caused me great hardship.

Momēt 'temfvccetvt omekatēs. Hvfvpofvn tąskit hueris.
mó·mi·t *timfaccitát*[10] *omiká·ti·s* *hafapó·fan* *tă·ⁿskeyt* *hôyłeys*
like that our treaty, agreement was not in the woods jumping about I stand, am
Our agreement was not like that. I have been jumping about in the woods.

Cvstemęrket ąrit yv oketv vlak't omis.
castimĭ·ⁿłkit *ă·ⁿłeyt* *ya* *okíta* *alâ·kto·méys*
suffering going about this time I have come (up to)
I have suffered great hardship up to this time.

Momen "Momēt 'temfvccetvt omekatēs," Abraham Lincoln kicvtēt omēs.
mo·mín *mó·mi·t* *timfaccitát* *omiká·ti·s* *eyplihéym línkan* *kaycatí·t ô·mi·s*
[and] like that our agreement was not Abraham Lincoln he told
Our agreement was not like that," he told Abraham Lincoln.

Momen "Tą cvstemerricet ontskes. Cuko tis vnnokricet,
mo·mín *tă·ⁿ castimiłłêycit* *ônckis* *cokó teys* *annókłeycít*
[and] greatly punished me you have] houses, even you have burnt for me
[Continuing, he said,] "You have caused me great hardship. You have burnt my houses,

vm enak ockv   omvlkvn   vnyvmahkuecet   ometskēt os.
aminá·kʔó·cka   *omálkan*   *anyamá·hkoycít*   *omícki·t ô·s*
my belongings   all   destroyed for me   you have
you have destroyed all my belongings.

Momen   vm pētake,   vm estvlkeu   lumhetayēt   a vyepēt os.
mo·mín   *ampi·tá·ki*[11]   *amistâlkiw'*   *lómhitâ·ⁿyi·t*   *a·ʔayípi·t ô·s*
[and]   my children   my people, too   are lying   clear around, everywhere
And my children, my people too, are lying everywhere.

Momēcetskat   'temfvccetv   'tenhayeyvtē
momî·cicka·t   *timfaccitá*   *tínha·yiyáti·*
like you've done   the agreement   we made with each other
What you have done is not in accordance

vcakkvyē   tokot os."
acakkayí·   *tó·ko·t ô·s*
in accordance with   it's not
with the agreement we made."

Momof   Abraham Lincoln tat   hvkihkvtēt   omēs.
mo·mô·f   *eyplihéym línkanta·t*   *hakayhkatí·t*   *ô·mi·s*
Now   Abraham Lincoln   cried   he did
Then Abraham Lincoln cried.

Momen   "Fạccusen   oketskes.   Nanvke   cenyvmahkvyvtē   enrahkv
mo·mín   *fà·ⁿccosin*   *o·kíckis*   *nâ·naki*   *cinyamâ·hkayáti·*   *inłáhka*
[and]   the truth   you speak   what all   I've damaged for you   the price
And he said, "You speak the truth. Tell me whatever the price is

'stomusen   maketsken   omēs   'stomis   cem fēkarēs."
stô·mosin   *ma·kíckin*   *o·mí·s*   *stô·meys*   *cimfi·ká·li·s*
whatever   you say   it is   [whatever]   I will pay you
of the things I have destroyed, and I will pay you."

"Nene-hvtke   ostat   catv   vm vfesakkuecet   ontskes.
ninihátki   *ò·sta·t*   *cá·ta*   *amafìsa·kkôycit*   *ónckis*
peace roads   four   blood   you have splattered over   you have
"You have spattered my blood on the four paths of peace.

Momen 'temfvccetv etenhayeyvtē cent kacet ontskes,
mo·mín timfaccitá itínha·yiyáti· cínt kâ·cit ónckis
[Then] the agreement we made with each other [you] have broken you have
And it is you who has broken the agreement we made,

vnt kvcvkon. Momen vhakv tat cent kvcētt omeccekv,
ánt kacáko·n mo·mín ahá·kata·t cínt kacì·tt o·míccika
[I] have not [broken it] [and] the law you violated you have
not I. And because you have violated the treaty,

vcvnaorketskat, vm fēkvrvntskat tvlkēpvrēs" kicvtēt omēs.
acana·ô·łkícka·t amfi·kaláncka·t talkí·páli·s keycatí·t ô·mi·s
where you have wronged me you to pay me will have to he told him
as you have wronged me, you will have to pay me," he said.

Abraham Lincoln't okat, "Suletawv cokpe-rakkuce hvmken vm pahletsken,
eyplihéym línkant o·kâ·t[12] solitá·wa cokpilakkocí hámkin ampáhlíckin
Abraham Lincoln said soldiers thousand one loan to me
Then Abraham Lincoln said, "Lend me one thousand soldiers,

'stetepoyvkēts" kicof, "Mometis os" kihcet,
stitipoyáki·c keycô·f mo·mí·teys ó·s kéyhcit
let's fight (them) when he told him that will be all right told him
and let's fight them," and Hopuethlyahola said,

Hopueryvholv rvtēpvtēt omēs. Ehvpo ervlakat,
hopoyłyahóla láti·patí·t ô·mi·s[13] ihapó· ilalâ·ka·t
[Hopuethlyahola] and he came back his camp when he returned to
"That will be all right," and came back. When he returned to his camp,

em estvlke tat ensatiket, heleswv enhayen,
imistâlkita·t insa·tèykit[14] 'hilíswa ínha·yín
his people he selected from them medicine he made for them
he selected from his people, he made medicine for them,

mvn 'seyvfastet, ostv 'shvyvtecihcet,
man síyafa·stít ósta 'shayaticéyhcit[15]
that they used on themselves four times they stayed up all night (using it)
and they used that on themselves, staying up for four nights.

Abraham Lincoln ʼmvnicvranat horre es encēyvtēt omēs cē.
eyplihéym línkan ʼmanéycaɫa·nâ·t hólli isínci·yatí·t ô·mi·s ci·^16
[Abraham Lincoln] were going to help him the war did go into
So to help Abraham Lincoln, they entered the war.

Momen etepoyet sehoke monket, horre ʼmeyokseko monken,
mo·mín itípo·yít sihô·ki mônkit hólli ʼmiyóksiko· mônkin
Then fighting still remained the war ended
And while they were still fighting, before the end of the war,

Hopueryvholv elēpvtēt omēs cē.
*hopoyɫyahóla ili·patí·t ô·mi·s ci·^*
[Hopuethlyahola] died
Hopuethlyahola died.

TEXTS BY PASKOFA

[Origin of the Spokokaki]

Paskofa (Haas XVI:71, 93–105)

Ohfvnkv hvlwē likat etvlwv Spokokvke 'tetakuecvtēt os.
ohfánka hálwi· léyka·t itálwa spoko·kakí 'titá·koycatí·t ô·s
The one above who lives on high prepared the tribal town Spokokaki.

'Tetakuehcof, vyvhiket folotēcet fǫllet ēkvnv yohsvpaklet omvtēt os.
*'tita·kóyhco·f ayáhaykít folóti·cít fǒl*ⁿ*lit i·kaná yóhsapa·klít*[1] *o·matí·t ô·s*
After he prepared it, [the people] sang and circled around until they settled on the land.

Este kolvpaket yv etvlwv etetakuecēt os.
ísti kolapâ·kit ya itálwa ititá·koycí·t[2] *ô·s*
Seven people prepared this tribal town.

Mv etvlwv Spokokvke ohhvpo este remētv sekatēt os.
ma itálwa spoko·kakí ohhapó· ísti 'limí·ta[3] *siká·ti·t ô·s*
There were no other camps but the tribal town Spokokaki.

Ēkvnv yvpokvtēs. Mohmen fullekot vpǫkvtēs.
i·kaná yápo·katí·s[4] *móhmin fóllikot apǒ·*ⁿ*kati·s*
They settled on the land. They stayed and didn't go anywhere.

"Vwahet ... fullvkēs" etekicakvtēt os.
awa·hít[5] *...*[6] *fóllaki·s itikéyca·katí·t ô·s*
"Let us separate," they said to one another.

Momet "Vfvnnaket vwahet fullvkēs" etekicakvtēt os.
mo·mít afánna·kít[7] awa·hít[8] follaki·s itikéyca·kati·t ô·s
"Let us look around and separate," they said to one another.

Momen hokkolet hvcce rakkēt wakkēt omen mvn ohpicēcet vhoyvtēs.
mo·mín hokkô·lit hácci łákki·t wákki·t ô·min man ohpéyci·cít aho·yati·s
And two of them went along the bank of a great river.

Momen cetto ueofv akfullat yefvnkvtēs. Yefvnikof,
mo·mín cítto oyó·fa ákfollâ·t yífankati·s[9] yifanêyko·f[10]
And a snake in the water surfaced. After he surfaced,

este hokkolat yossehokvtēs. Momen mv cetto aetempunayvtēs.
ísti hokkô·la·t yóssiho·katí·s mo·mín ma cítto a·itímpona·yatí·s[11]
the two men came and stood [on the bank]. And the snake talked to them.

"Heyvn aakhvtvphoketvn ceyacakhaks?" kicvtēs.
hiyán a·akhataphokítan[12] ciyâ·cákhá·ks[13] keycati·s
"Would you two like to come down here?" he asked them.

Hvmket okat, "Akhvtvpkvkotas" kicvtēs. Momen hvmket okat,
hámkit o·kâ·t akhatápkáko·tâ·s keycati·s mo·mín hámkit o·kâ·t
One said, "I cannot come down." And one said,

"Vnt akhvtvpkarēs" kicvtēs. Momen uewv tat akhvtvpiket ayvtēs.
ánt akhatápká·li·s keycati·s mo·mín óywata·t akhatapêykit[14] a·yati·s
"I will come down." And he descended into the water and went [toward the snake].

Momen mv cetto ēyvpahyet 'svyēpvtēs.
mo·mín ma cítto i·yapáhyit sáyi·patí·s
And the snake joined him and took him away.

Mont ēyvpahyet sayat Cetto-Mēkko likan 'resorvtēs.
mónt i·yapáhyit sâ·ya·t cittomí·kko lêyka·n líso·lati·s
And he took him to where Snake King [or Rattlesnake] lived.

Momen Cetto-Mēkkot resoran okat,
mo·mín cittomí·kkot liso·lâ·n o·kâ·t
And when they arrived, Snake King addressed [the man]:

"Hiyomat yekcetvn cemhoyēt os" kicvtēs.
hayyô·ma·t yikcitán cimhoyi·t[15] *ô·s keycatí·s*
"You have been given power," he said to him.

Estofv tis etvlwv vlke enhomahtv omvrvntsken yekcetv cemhoyēt os" kicvtēs.
istó·fateys itálwa álki inhomá·hta ô·małánckin[16] *yikcitá cimhoyi·t ô·s keycati·s*
You have been given the power to be the leader of the tribal towns always," he told him.

Ohliketv hvtke likvtēs. Mēkko tempen likvtēs.
ohleykitá hátki lêykati·s mí·kko tímpin lêykati·s[17]
There was a white chair nearby. It was near the King.

"Ohlikvs" kihcen, "Hvsossvfvccv vhēcet likvs" kicvtēs.
ohléykas kéyhcin haso·ssafácca ahî·cit[18] *léykas keycati·s*
"Sit," he told him, "Sit facing east," he told him.

"Momen estet vpoket onkv, em etetakvhanet vpoket os" kicvtēs.
mo·mín ístit apô·kit oŋká imititâ·kaha·nít apô·kit ó·s keycatí·s
"Now there are people here, so they are going to get ready," he told him.

"Vhēcet liketsken, yicvrēs" kicvtēs.
ahî·cit lêykickin yéycáłi·s keycatí·s
"Keep looking [east], and they will come," he said to him.

Momen sulkēt omēpen awen hēcvtēs. Nehickvn hayepēt ont yicvtēs.
mo·mín sólki·t omî·pin a·win hi·catí·s nihéyckan ha·yipí·t ònt yeycatí·s.
And there were many, and he saw them coming. They arrived having decorated themselves.

Cetto-Mēkkot ... okat, aempunayet okat, "Vhopvyusēn taktakhvkaks" kicvtēs.
cittomí·kkot ...[19] *o·kâ·t a·impona·yít o·kâ·t ahopayósi·n*[20] *taktakhakáks keycati·s.*
Snake King spoke with them saying, "Line up a little ways from here."

Momen "Hiyomat 'tetaket os" Cetto-Mēkkot kicvtēs.
mo·mín hayyô·ma·t 'titâ·kit ó·s cittomí·kkot keycati·s.
And Snake King told him, "Now it is ready."

Cetto-mēkkot aempunayet okat, ohliketv-hvtke ohlikan
cittomí·kkot a·impona·yít o·kâ·t ohleykitahátki ohléyka·n
Snake King spoke to him, to the one in the white chair;

"Yekcetvn cemhoyēt os" kicvtēs. "Tokvs. 'Tetaket os" kican,
yikcitán cimhoyí·t ô·s keycatí·s tókas 'titâ·kit ó·s keycâ·n
"You have been given the power," he said. "Now. It is ready," and as he said this,

ahuyiret ehomvn erhuervtēs.
a·hoyêɫit ihóman íɫhoyɫatí·s.
[the man] rose and stood before him.

Momen "'Tetaket os" Cetto-Mēkkot kican, "Vpeyaks."
mo·mín 'titâ·kit ó·s cittomi·kkot keycâ·n apíyáks
"It is ready," Snake King said to them, "Go."

Momusen uewvt omekv vpēyet lvpvtken resossvtēs.
mô·mosin óywat ô·mika api·yít lapátkin ɫíso·ssatí·s
Then they went through the water coming out on shore.

Momusen 'resosiyof etowakke tis hayet vpoket omvtēs.
mô·mosin 'lisosêyyo·f itowákkiteys hâ·yit apô·kit o·matí·s
When they came out, they made benches and were seated.

Momen yekcetv emhoyvtē tvlwv vlkēn em mēkkot omvranen yekcetv emhoyvtēt os.
mo·mín yikcitá imhô·yáti· tálwa álki·n immi·kkot ô·maɫa·nín yikcitá ímho·yatí·t ô·s
And the one who had been given power was given power to be king of all the tribal towns.

Momen etvlwv vhvnkateyisē 'tetakuecet omvtēt ont os. Mv em mēkkot
mo·mín itálwa ahaŋkǎ·ⁿtiyeysi· 'titá·koycít o·matí·t ônt ó·s ma immi·kkot
And he prepared those towns we counted awhile ago. That king said,

"Vwahet etvlwv tat fullvkēs. Em vliketvn hahicēt omvrēs" makvtēs.
awa·hít[21] itálwata·t fóllakí·s imaleykitán ha·héyci·t ô·máɫi·s ma·katí·s.
"Let us separate and go about in our tribal town groups. We will form clans," [the king] said.

Encukorakkon ocvkusēt omvranen kittokvtēs.
incokoɫákkon o·cakósi·t ô·maɫa·nín keytto·katí·s.
He told them [each town] would have a square ground.

Em vliketv hayat entopv hayat eskerkēt omvtēs.
imaleykitá ha·yâ·t intopá ha·yâ·t iskíɫki·t ô·mati·s.
In establishing clans, each could be identified by the arbor they made.

TEXTS BY A. GRAYSON

The Wise Old Dog

A. Grayson (Haas XIX:9–13)[1]

Yvhvt ēnvkvftehcet, "Afvcketvn hayvkēts. Afvcketvn hayēn omat,
yahát i·nakaftíhcit a·fackitán há·yakí·c[2] a·fackitán ha·yí·n o·mâ·t
The wolves had a meeting: "Let's celebrate. If we celebrate,

yepohsēcakē fullvnkē em vkeriyet omvlkvn cawēn omat,
'yipohsí·ca·kí· folláŋki· imakilêyyit omálkan câ·wi·n o·mâ·t
we can trick those who chased us back [home], and if we catch all of them,

hompetv tat hompēpēt etefullēpeyē tayēt omēs.
hompitáta·t hómpi·pí·t itifólli·piyí· tâ·yi·t[3] ô·mi·s
then we'll have activities and food to eat.

Ēkvnkorken koriyēt omvlkvn mvn aktēhēn omat, epofvckvkēt fulleyē tayēt omēs.
i·kankólkin kolêyyi·t omálkan man aktî·hi·n o·mâ·t ipo·fáckaki·t fólliyi· tâ·yi·t[4] ô·mi·s
We'll dig a ditch, and if we put them all in it, we can really celebrate.

Sukhuce estencvwēpeyat puletecicvkepvntot sepupenkvlēcak omētvnks.
sokhocí istíncawi·piyâ·t politicéycaki·pántot 'sipopiŋkalí·ca·kít o·mí·táŋks
When we took people's little pigs, they would run us off and take them away from us.

Efv-cule-mahēt Oktasas Mēkko hocefkēt eleyopv kvckēt
ifacolimá·hi·t okta·sa·smi·kko hocífki·t iliyopá kácki·t[5]
A very old dog with a broken hind leg named Oktasas Micco

yvhvn ohcukopericvtēs. Yvhvn kicet okat,
yahán ohcokopíleycati·s[6] *yahán keycít o·kâ·t*[7]
visited the wolves. He told the wolves,

"Cēpvnvke fullicvyvnkē omvlkvn vnsvlvfkuec't omatskes.
ci·panáki fólleycayáŋki· omálkan ansalafkòyct o·má·ckis[8]
"You have made prisoners of all the sons I have.

Monkv 'svm ohsicatskekon omat, horren cenhayvkarēs.
môŋka 'samohséycá·ckikon o·mâ·t[9] *hóllin cinhá·yaká·li·s*
If you do not release them, I will make war on you.

Cepefathueceyat, cenhesaketv tat cem esēkvnks.
cipifá·thoyciyâ·t cinhisa·kitáta·t[10] *cimísi·kánks*
When we made you run, we did not take your lives.

Momis hiyomat cēpvnvken sohsicatskekon omat, omvlkatskaten cepvsvteyvrēs."
mo·mêys hayyô·ma·t ci·panákin sohséycá·ckikon o·mâ·t omálká·cka·tin cipasatíyáli·s
But this time, if you do not free the boys, we will kill all of you."

Monkv yvhv tat penkvlvkehpet esossicvtēs.
môŋka yaháta·t piŋkalakíhpit isósseycatí·s[11]
So the wolves got scared and released them.

TEXTS COLLECTED BY V. RISTE

Curing the Back-ache

John Toney (Braggs) (Riste IV:12–15; Haas VIII:85–91)

Momen	enokketv tat	vnhēckvtēt os.		Ohrolopē	cokperakko	hvmken
mo·mín	*inokkitáta·t*	*ánhi·ckatí·t ô·ⁿs*		*ohlolopí·*	*cokpilákko*	*hámkin*[1]
Now	sickness	I got		year	[thousand	one

Now I have a sickness. In the year nineteen hundred

cokpe	ostvpaken	pale-hokkolen kolvpohkakē	em ofv	cvrat	vnnokkvtēs.
cókpi	*ostapâ·kin*	*pá·li hokkò·lin kolapohkâ·ki·*	*imó·fa*	*caɫá·t*	*ánno·kkatí·s*
hundred	nine	twenty-seven	in]	my back	hurt me

and twenty-seven [1927], my back began to hurt me.

Este-cate	heles-hayvn	vtohtin	vm vlēkcvtēs.		Cvkv-homvn	vncefiket
isticá·ti[2]	*'hilishá·yan*	*atóhteyn*	*amáli·kcati·s*[1]		*cakahomán*	*ancifêykit*
Indian	doctor	I got	and he doctored me		my forehead	he stuck me on

I got an Indian doctor, and he doctored me. He pricked my forehead

vncatehcen,	momen	enokketv	vnwikeko tayen,
anca·tíhcin	*mo·mín*	*inokkitá*	*anwéykiko·tá·yin*
he bled me	and	the sickness	wouldn't quit

and bled me, and my sickness wouldn't quit,

---

[1] Hill says: *amáli·kcatí·t ô·ⁿs* or *amáli·kcatí·t ò·mi·s* is better. The same pattern would have been better in the previous sentence. (VIII:84)

momen   cvra min   catvn   vncvohoyvtēs.
mo·mín   *cała·mêyn*   *cá·tan* *ancáwho·yatí·s*
and then   my back, instead   blood   he took from me
and he took blood from my back instead.

Momen   ehomvn   nokketv   vlikan   heleswvn   vnsiyet,
mo·mín   *ihóman*   *nokkitá* *alêyka·n*   *'hilíswan* *ánseyyít*[3]
Then   the first disease   [where it was]   medicine   he put on it
And where the first sickness was, he put on medicine

momen   poloksēt   vm ensatet,   nokke   vlikat
mo·mín   *polóksi·t* *amínsa·tít*[4]   *nókki*   *alêyka·t*
and   circle   he marked around   the sore [where it was]
and marked a circle around it, and where the sore was,

wakv yvpuce   vm ohtekkehyet   pohkusekon   yvhikvtēs.
wá·ka 'yapocí *amohtikkíhyit*   *póhkosiko·n*   *yaheykatí·s*
cow-horn   he pressed in on it   not quite heard he sang
he pressed the small end of a cow's horn on it and sang almost inaudibly.

Momen   wakv yvpuce   cokpikvtēs.   Momen   yulkvtēs.
mo·mín   *wá·ka 'yapocí*[i] *cókpeykatí·s*   *mo·mín*   *yolkatí·s*
Then   cow-horn   he put in his mouth   [Then]   he sucked it
Then he put the cow's horn in his mouth. And he sucked it.

Catvn   cawvtēs.   Momen   catv   cawat,   uewvn   tvmhluce   uewvt
cá·tan   *ca·watí·s*   *mo·mín*   *cá·ta* *ca·wâ·t*   *óywan*   *tamhlocí*   *óywat*
blood   he took   Then   blood   he had taken   water   a little glass water
He took blood out. And the blood that he took, he put the blood that he took

cvpvtēken   vcvnkēn   mv   catv   cawat   aktēhvtēs.
capatî·kin[5] *acánki·n* *ma*   *cá·ta* *ca·wâ·t*   *ákti·hatí·s*
half-full   put it in   that   blood   he had taken   put it in
in a glass half-full of water.

---

[i] *wa·ka 'yapocí* 'small end of cow's horn'.

Tvmhlucen	uewvn	'setepvyēcet,	catv	remhicat,
tamhlocín	*óywan*	*'sitipáyi·cít*[6]	*cá·ta*	*límheycá·t*
a little tumbler	water	together	blood	that was thinned

He added water to it in the tumbler, and when he had made the blood clear,

cokv-svnorv-cetakke	vncvohoyat		mv	catvn	vpakvtēs.
co·kasano·lacitákki	*ancawhô·ya·t*		*ma*	*cá·tan*	*apa·katí·s*[7]
newspaper crumpled up	that he had taken from me		that	blood	it was with

some crumpled up newspaper that he had taken out of me was with the blood.

Momen	enokketv tat	vfekhonnvtēs.	Catvt	vncvohohyen
mo·mín	*inokkitáta·t*	*afíkhonnatí·s*[i]	*cá·tat*	*ancawhóhyin*
Then	the sickness	stopped.	The blood	he took from me

Then the sickness stopped. The blood was taken from me,

momen	enokketv tat	vncvyayakvtēs.	Mv	vtēkat
mo·mín	*inokkitáta·t*	*ancayá·ya·katí·s*	*ma*	*atî·ka·t*
and	the sickness	got eased (quiet) for me	that	time

and my sickness was eased. Since then

vnnokvtē sekot	os.
annókkati· siko·t	*ô·ⁿs*
it never has hurt me	it is

I have been free from pain.

The Singing River (Hvcce Yvhikv)[ii]

Peter Ewing (Riste I:22–27; Haas VIII:71–83)[iii]

Hvcce	Yvhikv	oh-onvkv	ocēt omēs.
hácci	*yahéyka*	*ohhonáka*	*ó·ci·t ô·mi·s*
River, stream	singing	a story on	there is

There is a story about the Singing River.

---

[i] Could also say: *anfíkhonnatí·s*.

[ii] Title: *hácci yahéyka* 'singing river'.

[iii] "[This] story told by Peter Ewing (real name: Peter Rabbit), *hicíti* town; belonged to Wind clan. His father was a 'raccoon.' Ewing, now dead, was R's brother-in-law." (VIII:70)

Momis   mv   hvccen   okhoyvtē   kerrēskot os.
mo·mêys   ma   háccin   ókho·yati·   kíłłi·sko·t ô·ⁿs
But   that   stream   they meant   is not known
But the river that is meant is not known.

Hvcce   hocefkv   kerrēskot   ont os.   Momis   este-Maskoke
hácci   hocífka   kíłłi·sko·t   ônt ó·ⁿs   mo·mêys   istima·skó·ki
stream   name   no-one knows   it is   But   the Creeks
The name of the river is not known. But it is an old-time Creek

ennak onvkv-vculet omēs.   Tvlofv-cule   vpokof,
innâ·k ʔonakaʔacólit ô·mi·s   'talo·facóli   apô·ko·f
an old-time (Creek) story   old country   when they were living
story. When they were living in the old country,

onvkv   kerkēn   'sawvtēt omēs.
onáka   kíłki·n   sa·watí·t ô·mi·s
story   known   and it was brought out here
the story was known, and they brought it out.

Onvkv   hiyomēn   vlicēcēt   os.
onáka   hayyô·mi·n[8]   aléyci·ci·t   ô·ⁿs
story   like this   it starts   does
The story begins like this.

Hofonof   estet   fullvtēs   makēt os.
hofô·no·f[i]   ístit   follatí·s   ma·kí·t ô·ⁿs
Long time ago   people   were about   it says
A long time ago there were some people, [the story] goes.

Hocefkv   Yvmasvlke   makēt   omēs.   Este   sulkemahēt   omvtēs.
hocífka   yama·sâlki[ii]   ma·kí·t   ô·mi·s   ísti   solkimá·hi·t   o·matí·s[9]
name   peaceful   it says   does   People a lot of them   there were
Their name was Yamasalki ['humble/peaceful ones']. There were very many of them.

---

[i] According to Hill, *hofô·no·f, hofóno·f,* and *hofô·ⁿno·f* are all about the same.
[ii] Or (alternative forms): *yamasâlki, yamasakí·t, yamasakí·.*

Momet	ēyaskvkēt		horre	etvlwv	ētv	enhayetv	yacekot
mo·mít	*i·ya·skakí·t*		*hólli*	*itálwa*	*i·ta*	*inha·yitá*	*yá·ciko·t*[10]
Then	they were humble		war	nation, people	[other]	to make	not wanting

And they were meek and did not wish to make war

omakvtēs.		Este	elēcetv	yacvkekot		omet
omâ·kati·s		*ísti*	*ili·citá*	*ya·cakíko·t*		*ô·mit*
they did		a person	to kill	they not wanting		it was

on other tribes [etvlwv]. They did not want to kill people

hērkusēt	omakvtēs.	Mv momat	omēcicēn,
hĭ·ⁿlkosi·t	*oma·katí·s*[11]	*ma mò·ma·t*	*omi·céyci·n*
very friendly	they were	that way being	[because]

and were very peaceful. For that reason,

etvlwv	ētv	sasat	assēcet	pvsatvtēs.
itálwa	*i·ta*	*sâ·sa·t*	*á·ssi·cít*	*pasa·tatí·s*
nations, tribes	other	that there were	chased them	and killed them

there was another tribe that chased them and killed them.

Momen	vwahēhocen		fullvtētot,		hvtvm	etoh-vtelohket
mo·mín	*awa·hi·hô·cin*		*follatí·tot*		*hatâm*	*itohhatilóhkit*
Then	had been scattered		they had been about		again	they got together

And they were scattered about and again

fullet omvtēs.		Momen	pvsvthoyen		ayen
follít o·matí·s		*mo·mín*	*pasátho·yín*		*a·yín*
and were about		Then	they were being killed		and it went on

came back together. And they kept being killed

nvcumusē	hakvtēs.		Momet	fullet
nacómosi·	*ha·katí·s*		*mo·mít*	*follít*
just a few of them	there got to be		Then	being around

until only a few remained. Then going about,

hvcce rakkē	onvpvn		nvkafvtēs.	Estomēt	ohhvtvlakat	fullvranat
hácci lákki·	*onápan*		*naka·ftatí·s*	*istó·mi·t*	*ohhatalâ·ka·t*	*fóllala·nâ·t*
a big stream	on the banks of		they gathered	How	to continue	to be about

they met on the banks of a big river. They all talked about how they would

monkat   eyoksicvranat   omvlkvt   etem punahoyet   fvccēcvranet omvtēs.
móŋka·t   iyokséycała·nâ·t   omálkat   itimponá·ho·yít   faccí·cała·nít o·matí·s[12]
or   what the end will be   all of them   talked about it   they were to decide
go about increasing or come to an end and were to decide.

Monkv   honvntake,   hoktvkeu,   momen   hopuetakuce
móŋka[13]   *honantá·ki   hoktakíw   mo·mín   hopoyta·kocí*
Therefore   the men   women, too   and   children
So the men, women too, and little children

omvlkvt   nvkaftet omvtēs.   Ennvcumkv   omēcicēn
omálkat   naka·ftít o·matí·s   innacómka   omi·céyci·n
all of them   gathered   their being a few   on account of
all met. Because of their small number,

ēyvniceko   tayet   omekv, enhorret   em vfuloten
i·yanéyciko·   tâ·yit   o·miká inhółłit   imafolô·tin
help themselves not   they could   it was   their enemies   surrounded by
they could not help themselves, and they knew that if they went back

pvlkēn   fulēcen   omis,   pvsvthoyvranat   tvlken   kerraket,
pálki·n   foli·cín   o·mêys   pasathoyáła·nâ·t   tâlkin   kiłłâ·kit
back   they started   being if   to be killed   bound to be   they knew
with their enemies surrounding them, they were sure to be killed.

hvcce   tvyecetvn   hopuetakucet   akpvsatkētok:
hácci   tayicitán   hopoyta·kocít   ákpasa·tkí·to·k
and stream   to cross   the children   for they would get drowned
If they crossed the river, the little children would drown:

estometv   kerrvkekatēs.   Momen   espokē   fvccēcakat   okaket
isto·mitá   kiłłakíká·ti·s   mo·mín   íspo·ki·   faccí·ca·kâ·t   oka·kít
what to do   they didn't know   Then   at last   they decided   and said
they didn't know what to do. Then they decided at last, saying,

"Omvlkvkat   etehvlvthayet,   yvhiket   uewv   enlvokē   ofv   min
omálkaka·t[14]   *itihalathâ·yit*[15]   *yahaykít   óywa   inlawkí·   ó·fa   mêyn*
all of us   let us hold hands   and sing   water-   depths   in   therein
"Let all of us hold hands and enter the depths of the water

esakcēyēpvkēs" mahket honvntake, hoktvke, hopuetakuce omvlkvt
isakcí·yi·pakí·s máhkit honantá·ki hoktaki hopoyta·kocí omálkat
let's go into they said men women children all of them
singing, instead," and all the men, women, and children

etehvlvthayet yvhiket uewv sakcēyvtēs. Yvhikakat pohken
itihalathâ·yit yahăyⁿkit óywa sákci·yatí·s yaháyka·kâ·t pô·hkin
holding hands and singing water they went into they singing it was heard
entered the water holding hands and singing. They could be heard singing

ayen cvyayakvtēs maketvt oh-onvkvt omēs.
ă·ⁿyin cayá·ya·katí·s ma·kitát ohhonákat ô·mi·s
continuing on and it ceased that saying story [is]
and then, after a time, they grew quiet, the story relates.

Estvmv hvccen maketvo sekon, yvhiketv estomēn yvhikahket omvtē
ístama háccin ma·kitáw sikó·n yaheykitá istó·mi·n yaheykáhkit o·matí·
What stream it is not said song what they sang did
What river it is is not said; which song they sang

kerretv sekot omēs.
kiłłitá sikó·t ô·mi·s
to be known not is
is not known.

Momis yvhiketv hērēn yvhikaket omvtē tvlkēs komhoyet omvtēs,
mo·mêys yaheykitá hĭ·ⁿłi·n yahéyka·kít o·matí· tâlki·s kómho·yít o·matí·s
but song good they sang it's bound to have been (others) thought
But it's bound to have been a good song that they sang, it's thought,

este heraket omat 'stelēcetv yacekot omakvtētok.
ísti hiłă·ⁿkit o·mâ·t[16] stili·citá yá·cikot oma·katí·to·k
people good they were to kill anybody not wanting that's the reason
for they were fine people who didn't wish to kill people.

Momet ehocefkv Yvmasvlke maket omekv,
mo·mít ihocífka yama·sâlki ma·kít o·miká[17]
Then their name friendly/humble people it says
And their name was Yamasalki ['humble/peaceful ones'],

mont	est' vkvsvmepuecēt omēs.		Mv	estvlke	akhvtvpēcvtētis
mônt	*istakasamipóyci·t ô·mi·s*		*ma*	*istâlki*	*akhatápi·catí·teys*
and	it leads anyone to believe it		those	people	if they did go into the water

so [that] leads anyone to believe it. The thought is that those people

yvhikakan	pohket	omis,	okhohyēs	kometv	omēs.
yahéyka·kâ·n	*pô·hkit*	*o·mêys*	*okhóhyi·s*	*ko·mitát*	*ô·mi·s*
they singing	were heard	but	it might	the thought	is

who went down into the water might have been heard singing.

Rabbit Deceives Alligator (Cufe momen Hvlpvtv)[i]

(Riste III:2–4; Haas VIII:93–97)

Cufet	arvtēs.	Momen	hvlpvtvn	etehēcvtēs.
cofit	*a·latí·s*	*mo·mín*	*halpatán*	*itíhi·catí·s*
Rabbit	was about	and	alligator	they met, saw each other

There once was a rabbit. And he and Alligator saw each other.

Cufet	okat,	"Estenekricv	hecetskvtē	oca?"	kicof,
cofít	*o·kâ·t*	*istinikléyca*	*hicíckati·*[18]	*ô·ca·ⁿˇ*	*keycô·f*
Rabbit	said:	the devil	you see	did you ever	when he told him

Rabbit asked, "Have you ever seen the Devil?"

Hvlpvtvt	em vyoposkat,	"Momvtēsekot	os"	kicvtēs.
halpatát	*imayópo·skâ·t*[19]	*mó·mati·siko·t*	*ó·ⁿs*[20]	*keycatí·s*
alligator	he answered him	no, I never did		he told him

and Alligator replied, "I never have."

Momen	Cufet	okat,	"Hēcetskis	ehomvn	huyiretskekos"	kicvtēs.
mo·mín	*cofít*	*o·kâ·t*	*hi·cíckeys*	*ihóman*	*hoyêylíckiko·s*	*keycatí·s*
Then	Rabbit	said	if you did see him	before him	you couldn't stand	he told him

Then Rabbit said, "If you did see him, you could not stand before him."

"Momvyēs"	Hvlpvtvt	makvtēs.
mo·mayí·s	*halpatát*	*ma·katí·s*
I can	alligator	he said

"I could," Alligator said.

---

[i] Title: *cofí mo·mín halpatá* 'rabbit and alligator'.

Momof,	Culet	"Este-nekricv	paksen	acentotarēs"		kicvtēs.
mo·mô·f	*cofit*	*istiniklêyca*	*páksin*	*a·cintotá·li·s*[21]		*keycati·s*
after that	[rabbit]	the devil	tomorrow	I'll send him to you		he told him

After that, Rabbit told him, "I'll send the Devil to you tomorrow."

Pakse	omof,	pahce	vhetēcen,	hotvlē	vtohkat,
páksi	*ô·mo·f*	*pá·hci*[22]	*ahiti·cin*[23]	*hotali·*	*ato·hkâ·t*
tomorrow	when it came	big tall grass	he set it afire	wind	driving it

The next day he lit the tall grass on fire, and where the wind drove it,

fenkē	rakkēt	hakvtēs.	Momen	Hvlpvtv	ohhecēt	fenkē-rakkot	ayvtēs.
fiŋkí·[24]	*lákki·t*	*ha·kati·s*	*mo·mín*	*halpatá*	*ohhicí·t*	*fiŋki·lákkot*[25]	*a·yatí·s*
blaze	big	it made	Then	alligator	toward	the big blaze	went

it became a big blaze. Then the big blaze moved toward Alligator.

Momen	Hvlpvtv	enkvsvmket	akhvse uewvn	a akcēyvtēs.
mo·mín	*halpatá*	*inkásamkit*[26]	*akhasí óywan*	*a·ʔákci·yatí·s*
Then	Alligator	got leery	pond of water	he went into

And Alligator grew leery of it and entered a pond of water.

Mont	era ak-ossof,	ekkucē	yopo-hvoken	fenenētken	hēcof,
mônt	*ila·ʔákko·ssô·f*	*ikkocí·*	*'yopo·háwkin*	*finini·ⁿtkin*	*hi·cô·f*
Then	when he came up out of it	smoke	nostrils	was glimmering	when he saw

And when he came up out of it, when he saw smoke glimmering in his nostrils,

cufe	afackvtēs.
cofi	*á·fa·ckatí·s*
Rabbit	got happy

Rabbit got happy.

Rabbit and the Tie-Snakes (Cufe momen 'Stakwvnayv)[i]

(Riste III:21–28; Haas VIII:101–111)

Cufet	arvtēs.	Momet	uewvn	eskvranet	hvcce	rakkēn	oh-ayvtēs.
cofit	*a·latí·s*	*mo·mít*	*óywan*	*iskala·nít*	*hácci*	*lákki·n*	*óhha·yatí·s*
Rabbit	was about	Then	water	going to drink	stream	big	he went to

There once was a rabbit. And he went to a big river to drink water.

---

[i] Title: *cofi mo·mín stakwaná·ya* 'rabbit and tie-snake'.

Momen   rohrofvn,   estakwvnayv uewvn   akkaken   etehēcvtēs.
mo·mín   lóhlo·fan[27]   *istakwaná·ya óywan   akkâ·kin   itíhi·catí·s*
Then   when he got there   tie-snakes   water   (2) living in saw each other
And when he got there, he met two tie-snakes sitting in the water.

Estakwvnayv   hvmkat   hvccemvpe   kolokat
istakwaná·ya   hámka·t   haccimápi   kololô·ka·t
tie-snake   one of them   the stream-bed, -bank (where) it makes a bend
One tie-snake was living on one side where the riverbed

empvlhvmke liket on,   hvmkateu   matvpomēn   akliket on,
impalhámki lêykit ó·n   hámka·tiw   ma·tapó·mi·n[28] *aklêykit ó·n*
on one side was living   the other one[, too]   the same way   was staying
made a bend, and the other one was living the same way [on the other side],

estvmi vlkis   etehehcof,   Cufet   em ēkvsamvtēs.
ístamêy âlkeys[29] *itihíhco·f*   *cofit*   *imi·kása·matí·s*[30]
either one of them when he saw it   Rabbit   he bragged about himself
and when he saw each of them, Rabbit bragged about himself to them.

Momen   okat,   "Cvyekcemahēt   os.   Momen cēmeu   ceyekcēt ont   omis,
mo·mít   o·kâ·t   cayikcimá·hi·t   ô·ⁿs   mo·mín cí·miw ciyíkci·t ônt o·mêys
Then   he said: I am very strong   it is [Then] you, too you are strong but
He said, "I am very strong. And you too are strong,

etenceyvlhoyēn   omat,   cemontalvyēs.   A ecossicvyēs"   kicvtēs.
itinciyálho·yi·n   *o·mâ·t   cimónta·layi·s   a·ʔicósseycayi·s*   *keycatí·s*
we struggle with each other if   I can outdo you   I can get you out he told him
but if we compete together, I can outdo you. I can drive you out," he said.

Momof   estakwvnayv   em vyoposket,   "Estofvn   vmontahletskekos" kicen,
mo·mô·f   istakwaná·ya   imayópo·skít[31] *istó·fan   amontáhlíckiko·s*   *keycín*
whereupon the tie-snake answered him   never   can you outdo me   said
Whereupon the tie-snake answered, "You could never outdo me."

"Momen omat,   nettvn   cenhuericarēs.   Etenceyvlhoyeyvrēs"
mo·mín o·mâ·t   níttan   cinhoyléycá·li·s   itinciyalhoyíyáli·s[32]
If that's the case day   I will set for you   and we will have a struggle
"Well then, I'll set a date for you. We'll have a contest,"

Cufet	kicofvt,		ayvtēs.	Estakwvnayv	hvmkan	matvpomēn
cofit	*keycô·fat*		*a·yatí·s*	*istakwaná·ya*	*hámka·n*	*ma·tapó·mi·n*[33]
Rabbit	when he told him that		he went	tie-snake	other one	the same way

Rabbit said and went. He said the same thing to the other tie-snake,

kicet,	etem punayvtēs.	Momen	estakwvnayv	enhvtecesk
keycít	*itimpóna·yatí·s*[34]	*mo·mín*	*istakwaná·ya*	*inhaticíska*
he told him	he talked with it	[then]	the tie-snake	first one

talking with it. And when the first tie-snake responded

ētvpomēn	kicof,	a vyoposkat	Cufet	"Mon omat
i·tapó·mi·n	*keycô·f*	*a·ayópo·skâ·t*	*cofit*	*mó·n o·mâ·t*
the same way	when he told him	he answered back	[Rabbit	well, then

in the same way, Rabbit answered, "Well then,

nettvn	cenhuericis.	Etenceyvlhoyeyvrēs"	kicofvt,	vyēpvtēs.
níttan	*cinhóyłeycéys*[35]	*itinciyalhoyíyáłi·s*[36]	*keycô·fat*	*ayi·patí·s*
day	I am setting	and we will have a contest	he told him	and left]

I'll set a day. We will compete together," he said and left.

Nettv	kerkē	Cufe	huericvtē	vlakof,
nítta	*kíłki·*	*cofi*	*hóyłeycatí·*	*ala·kô·f*
the day	known	(that) Rabbit	had set	when it came

When the announced day that Rabbit had set had come,

hvcce	kololokat	ennvrkvpvn	huervtētot	pvrkofvkvn	tahcet
hácci	*kololô·ka·t*	*innałkapán*	*hóyłati·tot*[37]	*pałkofákan*	*táhcit*
stream	where it bends	half-way	had been standing	grapevine	he cut

he cut a grapevine standing between the bends of the river

eyoksvn	estvmi vlkis	estakwvnayv	akkakan	rem ohtekkēyvtēs.
iyóksan	*ístamêy âlkeys*	*istakwaná·ya*	*akkâ·ka·n*	*'limohtíkki·yatí·s*[38]
the end	either one	tie-snakes	where they were	he extended

and extended the ends to where each tie-snake was sitting.

Momēcofvt,	pihket	momen	tasket	pvrko-fvkvn	hvlathicvtēs,
momî·co·fat[39]	*payhkít*	*mo·mín*	*ta·skít*	*pałkofákan*	*halá·theycatí·s*
after he did that	he whooped	and	jumped	grapevine	he jerked

After he did that, he whooped and jumped and jerked the grapevine,

vlaket   estenceyvllvranet   omat   eskērkvn.
alâ·kit   *istinciyállala·nit*[40]   *o·mâ·t*   *iskí·lkan*
he had come   to have the struggle with   signal, notice
a signal that he had come to have the contest.

Momen   estakwvnayv   ceyvlletv   vlicēcat,
mo·mín   *istakwaná·ya*   *ciyallitá*   *aléyci·câ·t*
Then   the tie-snakes   to struggle   when they began
Then when the tie-snakes began to struggle,

"Cufen   omis"   komēt   momis   Cufe tokon,
cofìn   *o·méys*[41] *kó·mi·t*   *mo·mêys*   *cofitó·ko·n*
rabbit   I am   he thought   [but]   rabbit it wasn't
they thought, "I have Rabbit," but it wasn't Rabbit,

estakwvnayv   hvmkate min   omvtēs.   Estakwvnayvlket welaket   etehēcof,
istakwaná·ya   *hámka·ti mèyn*   *o·matí·s* *istakwana·yâlkit wila·kít* *itíhi·cô·f*
tie-snake   [other one instead   it was   tie-snakes   were there saw each other]
it was the other tie-snake instead. When the tie-snakes saw each other there,

'tem onvyakat   ēme mit   etenceyvlhoyvtet   omat   kerrakvtēs.
'timonáya·kà·t[42] *i·mi mêyt*   *itinciyalhô·yatit*   *o·mâ·t*   *kiłła·katí·s*
[they talked   he instead   they were struggling being   they found out]
they talked and found out it was the other one instead they were competing with.

Estakwvnayvlket   em vkerhoyvten   kerrakof,
istakwana·yâlkit *imakíłho·yatín*   *kíłła·kô·f*
[tie-snakes   had been tricked   when they found out]
When the tie-snakes found out they had been tricked,

tayen   Cufe   enhomecakvtēs.   Monkv   hvcce   uewvn   catvn   hayakvtēs.
tă·ⁿyin *cofí*   *inhomíca·katí·s*   *mônka*[43]   *hácci*   *óywan* *cá·tan* *há·ya·katí·s*
[very   rabbit   they were angry at   so   river   water   blood   they made]
they were very angry at Rabbit. So they turned the river water to blood.

Momen Cufet   ewvnhket   uewvn   esketvn   eyacis,
mo·mín cofít *iwanhkít*[44]   *óywan* *iskitán* *iya·cèys*[45]
[and   rabbit   was thirsty   water   to drink   wanted, but]
And Rabbit was thirsty and wanted to drink the water,

eskeko   tayet   oyọkusē   hakēpvtēs.
ískiko·   tá·yit   oyǒ·ⁿkosi·   há·ki·pati·s
[not drink he could   scrawny   he became]
but he couldn't drink and grew scrawny.

Mv   omēcicēn   hiyomis   vpessekot   aret   ont   ọs.
ma   omi·céyci·n   hayyǒ·meys   apíssiko·t   a·lí·t   ònt   ó·ⁿs
[that because of   now   not fat   goes about does   it is]
Because of that, now he has no meat on him.

Editors' Endnotes

Introduction, pp. xv–xxx

[1] Mary R. Haas. Birth certificate. Mary R. Haas Papers, American Philosophical Society. Philadelphia, Pennsylvania. Haas's middle name is usually listed as "Rosamond," but her birth certificate and passport show "Rosa."

A number of articles and obituaries have appeared about Haas. Among these are a commemorative volume of *Anthropological Linguistics*, vol. 39(4), 1997, with articles on teaching, anthropology, descriptive linguistics, southeastern languages, Asian languages, and historical linguistics. The article by Sally McLendon in that work has been especially helpful.

[2] Mary R. Haas. Vita. Mary R. Haas Papers, American Philosophical Society.

[3] Haas. Vita. Mary R. Haas Papers.

[4] Mary R. Haas to Morris Opler, 3 May 1941. Mary R. Haas Papers, American Philosophical Society.

[5] Mary R. Haas to Morris Opler, 3 May 1941. Mary R. Haas Papers.

[6] Haas. Vita. Mary R. Haas Papers.

[7] Haas. Vita. Mary R. Haas Papers.

[8] Letter from Franz Boas to Mary R. Haas (Mrs. Morris Swadesh), 21 March 1934. Mary R. Haas Papers, American Philosophical Society.

[9] Harry Hoijer to Mary R. Haas (Mrs. Morris Swadesh), 26 April 1934. Mary R. Haas Papers, American Philosophical Society.

[10] Haas. Vita. Mary R. Haas Papers.

[11] Haas. Vita. Mary R. Haas Papers.

[12] Haas typically received $500 per year to pay for consultants and travel expenses.

[13] Mary R. Haas to Morris Swadesh, 10 May 1937. Mary R. Haas Papers, American Philosophical Society.

[14] Morris Swadesh to Mary R. Haas, 27 June 1937. Mary R. Haas Papers, American Philosophical Society. Haas and Swadesh were not officially divorced until 1940.

[15] Mary R. Haas to Morris Swadesh, 8 October 1939. Mary R. Haas Papers, American Philosophical Society.

[16] Mary R. Haas. "Natchez and Chitimacha Clans and Kinship Terminology." *American Anthropologist* 41 (1939): 597–610.

[17] Mary R. Haas. "Ablaut and Its Function in Muskogee." *Language* 16 (1940): 141–50.

[18] Mary R. Haas. "Tunica," in *Handbook of American Indian Languages*, vol. 4, ed. Franz Boas. (New York: J. J. Augustin, 1940), 1–143.

[19] Mary R. Haas. "The Classification of the Muskogean Languages," in *Language, Culture, and Personality: Essays in Memory of Edward Sapir*, eds. Leslie Spier et al. (Menasha, Wisc.: Banta Publishing Company, 1941), 41–56.

[20] Mary R. Haas to Alexander Spoehr, 18 August 1940. Mary R. Haas Papers, American Philosophical Society.

[21] Mary R. Haas to Morris Swadesh, 26 February 1939. Mary R. Haas Papers, American Philosophical Society.

[22] Franklin Edgerton to Mary R. Haas, 25 August 1941. Mary R. Haas Papers, American Philosophical Society.

[23] See, e.g., Lorene Davis, Susannah Factor, and Mary Haas. *Nak-cokv Yvlunkv Enhake (Seminole Phonics I)*. (Ada: Seminole Bilingual Education Project), ca. 1977.

[24] The proceedings of this conference were later published: William Shipley, ed. *In Honor of Mary R. Haas*. (Berlin: Mouton de Gruyter, 1988).

[25] For her work on Tunica, see: Mary R. Haas. "Tunica," in *Handbook of American Indian Languages*, vol. 4, ed. Franz Boas. (New York: J. J. Augustin, 1940), 1–143.; Mary R. Haas. *Tunica Texts. University of California Publications in Linguistics* 6. (Berkeley: University of California Press, 1950).; Mary R. Haas. *Tunica Dictionary. University of California Publications in Linguistics* 6. (Berkeley: University of California Press, 1953).

For Thai, see: Mary R. Haas and Heng R. Subhanka. *Spoken Thai*. 2 vols. (New York: H. Hold and Co., 1945); Mary R. Haas. *The Thai System of Writing*. (Washington: American Council of Learned Societies, 1954).; Mary R. Haas. *Thai Reader*. (Washington: American Council of Learned Societies, 1954).; Mary R. Haas. *Thai-English Student's Dictionary*. (Stanford: Stanford University Press, 1964).

For more general topics, see: Mary R. Haas. *The Prehistory of Languages*. Janua Linguarum, Series Minor 57. (The Hague: Mouton, 1969); Mary R. Haas. *Language, Culture, and History: Essays*, ed. Anwar S. Dil. (Stanford: Stanford University Press, 1978).

Haas also edited works by others: Edward S. Sapir and Morris Swadesh. *Yana Dictionary*, ed. Mary R. Haas. (Berkeley: University of California Press, 1960).

[26] According to Robyn York (interview with Jack Martin, 31 July 2004), a house fire burnt most of his pictures, personal things, and writings.

[27] Mary R. Haas. Creek Notebook III:158. Mary R. Haas Papers, American Philosophical Society.

[28] Haas. Creek Notebook III:158. Mary R. Haas Papers.

[29] Haas. Creek Notebook XVII:1–79. Mary R. Haas Papers.

[30] The election went to Alec Noon. Haas records the candidates in 1938 as Rollie Canard, A. E. Raiford, Jim Hill, John Jacobs, and Alec Noon.

[31] Robyn York (Hill's great-granddaughter), interview with Jack Martin, 31 July 2004. Robyn was only two when James Hill died, but she remembers sitting on his lap, his suspenders, mustache, and white hair, the smell of ointment and the sound of church songs.

[32] Haas. Creek Notebook III:158. Mary R. Haas Papers.

[33] Dawes Final Rolls, roll No. 6374; 1900 Creek Nation Census; 1910 Federal Census, McIntosh County; 1920 Federal Census, McIntosh County; Haas. Creek Notebook III:158. Mary R. Haas Papers.

[34] Haas. Creek Notebook III:120. Mary R. Haas Papers.

[35] Haas. Creek Notebook V:134. Mary R. Haas Papers.

[36] Haas. Creek Notebook XI:6. Mary R. Haas Papers.; Interview with Mr. Jasper Bell. Indian-Pioneer Papers, vol. 7, interview 7077, 3 August 1937. University of Oklahoma Western History Collections. Norman, Oklahoma.

[37] Mary R. Haas to Catherine Opler, 18 November 1938. Mary R. Haas Papers, American Philosophical Society.; Mary R. Haas to Sigmund Sameth, 29 January 1940. Mary R. Haas Papers, American Philosophical Society.

[38] Jefferson Berryhill, "Interview with Mr. Jasper Bell," Indian-Pioneer Papers, vol. 7, interview 7077. University of Oklahoma Western History Collections, Norman, Oklahoma, 3 August 1937.

[39] Jefferson Berryhill, "Interview with Mr. Jasper Bell," Indian-Pioneer Papers, vol. 7, interview 7077. University of Oklahoma Western History Collections, Norman, Oklahoma, 3 August 1937.; Haas. Creek Notebook X:64. Mary R. Haas Papers. He told Haas, "All Bears are Kings. This is a praising name."

[40] Haas. Creek Notebook X:64, XI:6. Mary R. Haas Papers.; Jefferson Berryhill, "Interview with Mr. Jasper Bell."

[41] Haas. Creek Notebook X:65. Mary R. Haas Papers.

[42] Haas. Creek Notebook XI:6. Mary R. Haas Papers.

[43] Haas. Creek Notebook X:65. Mary R. Haas Papers.

[44] Mary R. Haas to Catherine Opler, 18 November 1938. Mary R. Haas Papers.

[45] Haas. Creek Notebook XVI:72. Mary R. Haas Papers. Haas's notes on informants indicate that Mr. Cook's mother had belonged to Thlewahle tribal town, from which Thlopthucco branched.

[46] Haas. Notes on informants. Mary R. Haas Papers.; Haas. Creek Notebook XVI:79. Mary R. Haas Papers.

[47] Haas. Creek Notebook XV:166. Mary R. Haas Papers.

[48] Haas. Notes on informants. Mary R. Haas Papers.

[49] Big Jack (*lahtamá·ha*) is referred to in Hill's text, "A Match-Game Between Hilabi and Pakantalahasi (1905)" and again in "The Town of Hilabi."

[50] Earnest Gouge. *Totkv Mocvse / New Fire: Creek Folktales*, ed. and trans. Jack B. Martin, Margaret McKane Mauldin, and Juanita McGirt. (Norman: University of Oklahoma Press, 2004). Additional information about Gouge can be found in the introduction of this work.

[51] Sigmund Sameth, "Creek Negroes: A Study of Race Relations." (MA thesis, University of Oklahoma, 1940).

[52] Billie Byrd, "Interview with Adam Grayson," Indian-Pioneer Papers, vol. 35, interview 7812, 10 October 1937. University of Oklahoma Western History Collections.

[53] Haas. Creek Notebook IV:169. Mary R. Haas Papers.

[54] Haas. Creek Notebook V:151. Mary R. Haas Papers.

[55] Riletta Marshall, personal communication to Jack Martin, 2004.

[56] "Tuskegee Indian Baptist Church," last accessed 17 May 2004, http://www.rootsweb.com/~okmcinto/TuskHist.htm.

[57] "Kelley Funeral Home Records 1 Aug 1937 - 31 Dec 1984," last accessed 17 May 2004, http://www.rootsweb.com/~okmcinto/Kelley.txt.

[58] Haas. Creek Notebook XVI:65. Mary R. Haas Papers.

[59] Haas. Notes on informants. Mary R. Haas Papers.

[60] Haas. Notes on informants. Mary R. Haas Papers.

[61] Haas. Creek Notebook I:36. Mary R. Haas Papers.

[62] Haas. Creek Notebook II:67. Mary R. Haas Papers.

[63] 1930 Federal Census, McIntosh County; Felix E. Raiford, personal communication to Jack Martin, 2004.

[64] Haas. Notes on informants. Mary R. Haas Papers.

[65] Interview with Daniel Starr. Indian-Pioneer Papers, vol. 87, interview 6781, 20 July 1937. University of Oklahoma Western History Collections.

[66] Jerome M. Emmons, "Interview with Daniel Starr." Indian-Pioneer Papers, vol. 87, interview 7850, 18 October 1937. University of Oklahoma Western History Collections.; Haas. Notes on informants. Mary R. Haas Papers.

[67] Jerome M. Emmons, "Interview with Daniel Starr."

[68] Haas. Notes on informants. Mary R. Haas Papers.

[69] Haas. Notes on informants. Mary R. Haas Papers. Mr. Sulphur's mother had been a member of Little Tullahassee.

[70] Haas. Notes on informants. Mary R. Haas Papers.

[71] Haas. Creek Notebook XV:185. Mary R. Haas Papers.; Mr. and Mrs. Alex Sulphur to Mary R. Haas, 15 July 1944. Mary R. Haas Papers.

[72] Haas. Creek Notebook XI:129, XI:96. Mary R. Haas Papers.

[73] Alexander Spoehr to Mary R. Haas, 20 November [1939]. Mary R. Haas Papers.

[74] Haas. Creek Notebook XI:132. Mary R. Haas Papers.

[75] Billie Byrd, "Interview with Wesley Tanyan." Indian-Pioneer Papers, vol. 89, interview 1247, 22 December 1937. University of Oklahoma Western History Collections.

[76] Daniel D. Shutt (great nephew of Victor Riste), personal communication to Jack Martin, 1 December 2004.

[77] Fay-Cooper Cole, R. B. Dixon, and A.V. Kidder, "Anthropological Notes and News: Anthropological Scholarships," *American Anthropologist, New Series*, 31.3 (July–Sep 1929), 571–572.

[78] Volumes 2–5 of his Natchez notebooks include Natchez texts with Creek and English word-for-word glosses. This was because, as Haas found, the last speakers of Natchez could speak Creek but not English.

[79] Daniel D. Shutt (great nephew of Victor Riste), personal communication to Jack Martin, 1 December 2004.

[80] Daniel D. Shutt (great nephew of Victor Riste), personal communication to Jack Martin, 1 December 2004.

[81] Harry F. and Edward S. O'Beirne, The Indian Territory: Its Chiefs, Legislators, and Leading Men. (St. Louis, 1898).

[82] These proposed steps are from a typed manuscript (apparently a grant proposal) written about 1941 and found among Haas's papers at the American Philosophical Society.

[83] Lyda Averill Paz to Mary R. Haas, 12 July 1937. Mary R. Haas Papers.

[84] Haas. Creek Notebook VII:31. Mary R. Haas Papers.

[85] Mary R. Haas to C. A. Border, 14 August 1941 Mary R. Haas Papers.

[86] Phonetic transcription attempts to record details of pronunciation, while phonemic transcription records only those contrasts that are important for distinguishing words in a language. The use of phonemic transcription was controversial in Haas's day.

[87] Mary R. Haas. "Nasals and Nasalization in Creek," in *Proceedings of the Third Annual Meeting of the Berkeley Linguistics Society*. eds. Kenneth Whistler et al. (Berkeley: Berkeley Linguistics Society, University of California, Berkeley, 1977), 194–203.; Mary R. Haas. "Tonal Accent in Creek," in *Studies in Stress and Accent*. ed. Larry M. Hyman. *Southern California Occasional Papers in Linguistics* 4. (Los Angeles: University of Southern California, 1977), 195–208.

[88] Many details of Creek phonology and orthography are discussed in Jack B. Martin, *A Grammar of Creek (Muskogee)*. (Lincoln: University of Nebraska Press, 2011.)

[89] Haas, "Nasals and Nasalization in Creek."

[90] See, e.g., Robert N. Loughridge and David M. Hodge. *English and Muskokee Dictionary Collected from Various Sources and Revised* and *Dictionary of the Muskokee or Creek Language in Creek and English*. (St. Louis: J. T. Smith, 1890).

[91] Haas, "Ablaut and its function in Muskogee."; Haas, "Nasals and nasalization in Creek."; Haas, "Tonal accent in Creek."

[92]George Herzog, Stanley S. Newman, Edward Sapir, Mary Haas Swadesh, Morris Swadesh and Charles F. Voegelin. "Some Orthographic Recommendations," *American Anthropologist*, 1934.

[93] When Haas recorded pitch phonetically, she used a grave accent (ˋ) for low pitch, an acute accent (ˊ) for high, a vertical mark (ˈ) for mid, a grave accent + vertical mark (ˋˈ) for mid rising, and a grave accent + acute accent (ˋˊ) for extra high or high rising.

Texts by J. Hill, pp. 1–565

[1] Corrected from *apo·kâ·ka·t* to match Hill ms.

[2] Corrected from *hilí* based on Hill ms.

[3] Corrected (Mauldin) from *api·yít*.

[4] Corrected from *i·yapáhyi·t* to match Hill ms.

[5] Corrected from *apâ·ki* based on Hill ms.

[6] Corrected from *hilí* based on Hill ms.

[7] Corrected from *teynisán* based on Hill ms.

[8] Corrected (Mauldin) from *apo·kiyâ·ti·*.

[9] Portion beginning here was inserted later.

[10] End of insert.

[11] Corrected from *simhoyánosi·n* to match Hill ms.

[12] Corrected from *kanéyti* here and below to match Hill ms. The older pronunciation is *kaní·ti*.

[13] Mauldin: *iláwkata·t*.

[14] Order corrected from *ní·lka íŋkin* to match Hill ms. (either way is fine).

[15] Order corrected from *capósitá·ti·t ha·yít* to match Hill ms.

[16] Corrected to *kéyho·ci·n* to match Hill ms.

[17] This sentence was inserted later.

[18] Corrected (Mauldin) from *o·cî·patin*.

[19] Corrected from *aho·céyn* based on Hill ms.

[20] Corrected (Mauldin) from *isfólho·yâ·ti·*.

[21] Corrected from *hocífki·t istima·skó·ki* based on Hill ms.

[22] Haas notebook has *impa·tá·ka*.

[23] Corrected from *apô·kit* based on Hill ms.

[24] Added *sólka·t* based on Hill ms.

[25] Corrected from *omálka* based on Hill ms.

[26] Corrected from *a·yi·n* to match Hill ms. (better without *n*).

[27] Corrected from *impiŋkalâ·ka·tiw* to match Hill ms. (either way).

[28] Corrected (Mauldin) from *loká·fola·ni·*.

[29] Corrected from *ohhatalakósi·n* based on Hill ms.

[30] Corrected from *ma·ki·* based on Hill ms.

[31] Corrected from *imhóyhho·kín* based on Hill ms.

[32] Haas notebook has *follèyyá·ckas*.

[33] The Hill ms. has the order *oyhomi· iskitá ha·yi·ckapánka*, but Mauldin prefers the order Haas has.

[34] Corrected from *hĭ·ⁿłi·* based on Hill ms.

[35] Mauldin: *pokkiccitá*.

[36] Corrected (Mauldin) from *ánhi·ckiká*.

[37] Corrected from *krayst* based on Hill ms.

[38] Corrected from *oyaksomi·câlki* based on Hill ms. (either way is possible).

[39] Corrected (Mauldin) from *sacaksomicéyhsin*.

[40] Corrected from *há·yati·* based on Hill ms.

[41] Corrected (Mauldin) from *pá·li*.

[42] Corrected from *acapa·hò·yi·* based on Hill ms.

[43] Corrected from *ó·mi·* based on Hill ms.

[44] Haas interpreted the first phrase of this text as a title: *isticá·ti imi·kaná ó·fa* 'in the land of the Indian'. The editors interpret this phrase as being part of the first sentence of the text.

[45] Mauldin: *wayhoyí·n*.

[46] Or could be read: *wáyya·kâ·t*.

[47] Haas's intended corrections here are uncertain. Mauldin has restructured the text from here to the end of the sentence.

[48] Mauldin: *apo·hí·*.

[49] Haas notebook has *áti·n*.

[50] Mauldin: *atì·hkati·s*.

[51] Mauldin: *hónni·n*.

[52] Haas notebook has: *haláki·pâ·t*.

[53] Haas notebook has: *i·yiná·koycít*.

[54] Haas notebook has *po·hoyáti·t*.

[55] Haas notebook has *a·tá·t*.

[56] Or (Mauldin) *iyà·ⁿcisikon*.

[57] Or (Mauldin) *ô·łit*.

[58] McGirt: *iná· inhícka*.

[59] McGirt: *ô·mati·s*.

[60] McGirt: *awí·t*.

[61] Corrected (McGirt) from *òŋkot*.

[62] Corrected (McGirt) from *'tipackalá·noseys*.

[63] McGirt: *ô·mati·s*.

[64] McGirt: *apáki·t.*

[65] McGirt reads these three words as *a·istími·skâ·t sá·si· hâ·kati·s.*

[66] McGirt reads these two words as *cahkî·paŋki· mâ·hi.*

[67] McGirt: *ô·mati·t.*

[68] McGirt: *apa·kít.*

[69] Haas notebook has *mi·kkâ·lki tá·ti.*

[70] I.e., Hotalk Emathla's English name was Edward Bullette.

[71] Haas notebook uses "1000 800" as an abbreviation here and in the next sentence.

[72] Mauldin would delete *ô·mo·f* here.

[73] Mauldin: *atô·kin.*

[74] Mauldin: *iláwkan.*

[75] Mauldin: *itícca·kín.*

[76] Meaning of this word is uncertain.

[77] Haas notebook has *naka·ftí·t.*

[78] This is probably "Big Jack" Gouge, referred to in "A Match-Game Between Hilabi and Pakantalahasi (1905)." His name there is transcribed *lahtamá·ha.*

[79] The word *lakápa* is not known to Mauldin.

[80] The word *cokolákko* 'big house' originally referred to a tribal town's council house, but by the twentieth century had come to mean ceremonial grounds used for dancing and fasting ("busking"). Working with Raiford, Haas translated *cokolákko* as 'buskground', but Hill's intent was to describe Hilabi's council house.

[81] Haas notebook has: *iti·hop-.*

[82] Literally "sharp big house". Haas notes that this is "a round buskground house with a sharp tip". In his travels through the Creek country in 1776, William Bartram described towns as having a public square with four rectangular buildings, a rotunda, and an area for games. One of the four rectangular buildings was used as the summer council house. The rotunda was a circular structure containing a fireplace and used as the winter council house (Waselkov and Braund 1995:168–174). We have used the expression 'round house' here.

[83] Or possibly (Mauldin): *ila·taklêycit.*

[84] Or possibly (Mauldin): *ô·mit.*

[85] Haas notebook has *ina·hátki·t.*

[86] Haas notebook has *aho·pakáti·t.*

[87] Mauldin: *iti·cít.*

[88] Mauldin: *mo·matí·t ôn.*

[89] Haas notebook has *iticántot.*

[90] Mauldin: *ísfollít.*

[91] Haas notebook has *opáŋka* in this text, which was checked in 1937. By 1939, Haas had discovered a limited contrast between *nk* and *ŋk* (at least for some speakers). She then began

transcribing this word as *opánka*. Mauldin pronounces it as *opáŋka* (and consistently pronounces *ŋk* where Haas in her later work distinguishes *nk* and *ŋk*). We have corrected these early forms to *nk* to match Haas's later practices (as we feel Haas would have done).

[92] Mauldin: *ha·yít*.

[93] Mauldin: *ka·kî·pati·*.

[94] Mauldin: *hoya·nín*.

[95] Mauldin: *há·ho·yatí·t*.

[96] Haas notebook has *tiktaŋkí·*. We've changed it to match Haas's later usage.

[97] Mauldin: *kâ·ko·f*.

[98] The phrase *tasikayá ippocitá·ki* is ambiguous, meaning either 'citizens' sons' or 'citizens [and] their sons'. Haas's gloss reflects the first reading, but we feel the second meaning is intended here.

[99] This word is not known to Mauldin.

[100] Haas notebook has *ponsâ·sa·tow*.

[101] Mauldin: *'satothô·yin*.

[102] Mauldin: *noceycín*.

[103] Mauldin: *ahopanhokípi·teys ó·n o·mâ·t*.

[104] Mauldin: *o·kí·s*.

[105] The brush arbors described above are also referred to as *topá*. The word *topá* may have referred to a raised platform originally, but in the twentieth century was used for both 'bed' and 'arbor'.

[106] Haas notebook has *inhopo·hoyí·*.

[107] Haas notebook first had *omalkałâ·nosit*, then changed to *omalkałă·ⁿnosit*. Mauldin reads it the first way.

[108] Mauldin: *áklo·pít*.

[109] Mauldin: *apô·ko·f*.

[110] Haas notebook first had *yomockí·*, but then changed it to *yomócki*. Mauldin reads it the first way.

[111] Mauldin: *itihiłĕyⁿcit*. The pattern in *itihĭ·ⁿłêycit* seems to be older and more expressive.

[112] Mauldin: *hayyó·mosi·n*.

[113] Haas notebook has *kolapâ·kołi·n*.

[114] Shortened from *poskitát omáła·nâ·t*. Haas notebook has *poskitá tá·la·nâ·t*.

[115] Mauldin: *itohkálki·pít*.

[116] Haas notebook has *-asíceycí·*.

[117] Mauldin: *noceycín*.

[118] Mauldin: *si·wana·wêycit*.

[119] Mauldin: *apô·ko·f*.

[120] Mauldin: *inhomâ·htit*.

[121] Haas notebook has *ohhapô·kali·n*.

[122] Mauldin: *iscákcahi·cít*.

[123] Mauldin: *apô·ka·t*.

[124] Mauldin: *apô·kit*.

[125] Haas notebook has *ôŋka*. Shortened from *o·miká*.

[126] The verb *i·lawicitá* is literally 'to make oneself hungry'. The term *poskitá* means 'to fast'. In her word-for-word translations, Haas followed earlier sources in borrowing the Creek term as *busk* in English to describe this form of fasting.

[127] Pronounced *okta·hácci* or more properly *okta·hhácci*, from *oktá·ha* 'sand' + *hácci* 'stream'.

[128] Corrected from *itálwa* based on Hill ms.

[129] A long section has been inserted here after *hayyó·mi·n*.

[130] Another line here: *okta·hácci a·píhkat hocifho·yatí·t ô·mi·s*.

[131] Corrected from *apo·kâ·kin* based on Hill ms. (-*â·k*- is unnecessary).

[132] Corrected from *apo·kâ·kin* based on Hill ms. (with *apo·kâ·kin* indicating distance between the people).

[133] Corrected from *hayyô·man* based on Hill ms.

[134] Haas notebook has *ocâ·ka·t*.

[135] Corrected from *istilásti* to match Hill ms.

[136] These are the names for these towns used in English in the 1800s.

[137] Haas has *cila·yitá ipoca·sitá*. We have deleted the second word to make it consistent with Hill ms.

[138] Corrected (Mauldin) from *hi·ⁿli·t*.

[139] The meaning of *'simanacíci·t* is not clear, but seems related to *anackitá* 'luck' and *'simanácki·* 'handsome'.

[140] End of long insert.

[141] Corrected (Mauldin) from *í·ma·kít*.

[142] Corrected from *o·câ·kit* to match Hill ms. (either is fine).

[143] Corrected from *ó·fa* to match Hill ms.

[144] Mauldin: *afolóti·cít*.

[145] Long insert begins at *pankahá·co*.

[146] Corrected from *halpitakácwat* to match Hill ms.

[147] Corrected from *halpitakácwan* to match Hill ms.

[148] Corrected from *ha·ckowá* to match Hill ms. (-*n* is more specific, telling someone who doesn't know).

[149] Corrected from *iyá·ca·kín* to match Hill ms. (Mauldin feels *iyá·ca·kín* sounds "spur of the moment").

[150] Haas notebook has *opankahá·ca*.

[151] Mauldin: *icca·spánka*.

[152] Corrected (Mauldin) from *a·ssihóhkin*.

[153] This sentence was modified (made more specific) in Haas's notebook.

[154] Corrected from *sinhomá·htat* to match Hill ms.

[155] Beginning of insert.

[156] Corrected from *ałakkóyci·* to match Hill ms.

[157] Corrected from *sósteycô·f* to match Hill ms.

[158] End of insert.

[159] Corrected from *intaphí·* to match Hill ms.

[160] This sentence was added later.

[161] Perhaps *hoktakpá·na* should be *hoktakpánka* (Mauldin).

[162] Corrected from *hilishá·yat* to match Hill ms.

[163] Mauldin: em vtēkē.

[164] Corrected (Mauldin) from *sá·pala·nâ·n*.

[165] Corrected from *mo·mít* to match Hill ms. (either is fine).

[166] Corrected from *nítta* to match Hill ms. (either is fine).

[167] Inserted here later: *po·skâlki pánala·nâ·t sita·hayapánka*.

[168] Corrected from *ta·fahátka* to match Hill ms.

[169] Haas notebook has *sî·si*.

[170] Corrected (Mauldin) from *sálala·nâ·t*.

[171] Corrected (Mauldin) from *ipocá·si·sít*.

[172] Corrected from *'maleykitá* to match Hill ms.

[173] Hill has *Momen* (*mo·mín*) here, but we follow Haas.

[174] Haas notebook has *ałà·ⁿkosi·*.

[175] Insert begins here.

[176] End of insert.

[177] Corrected from *inki·łkoyhô·cin* to match Hill ms.

[178] Corrected from *po·skít* to match Hill ms.

[179] Corrected from *hocífi·* to match Hill ms.

[180] Corrected from *inhoyhkô·f* to match Hill ms.

[181] Corrected from *kéyho·cin* to match Hill ms.

[182] Insert begins after *hicí*.

[183] Corrected from *inho·yô·f* to match Hill ms.

[184] Corrected from *hoci·fyapô·ka·t* to match Hill ms.

[185] Corrected from *sosiko·t* based on Hill ms.

[186] Corrected (Mauldin) *ponhôylatin*.

[187] Corrected from *inhá·yi·tí·t* based on Hill ms.

[188] End of insert.

[189] Corrected from *nakáfho·tâ·n* based on Hill ms.

[190] Haas notebook has *osséyhsit*.

[191] Haas notebook has *aháŋkatâ·t*.

[192] Corrected (Mauldin) from *ipoca·ci·cáhkit*.

[193] Corrected (Mauldin) from *poca·líhcit*.

[194] Corrected (Mauldin) from *'liní·ta*.

[195] Corrected (Mauldin) from *wa·cínta*.

[196] Corrected (Mauldin) from *ina·lástitat*.

[197] Corrected (Mauldin) from *ha·yoyíko·*.

[198] Corrected (Mauldin) from *há·kati*.

[199] McGirt: *hâmkosin palhâmkit*.

[200] McGirt: *hâmka·t*.

[201] McGirt: *hâmkosin*.

[202] McGirt: *apô·ki·*.

[203] McGirt: *lêyka·n*.

[204] McGirt: *pokkíccaha·nâ·t, pokkíccala·nâ·t*.

[205] Haas notebook has *itíma·s̲ín*.

[206] Haas notebook has: *tokons̲ilá·kateys*.

[207] Haas notebook has: *kíłłák̲k̲iko·tot*.

[208] Haas notebook has *cim̲i·ʔa·hô·cakit*.

[209] Haas notebook has: *nakafêykit*.

[210] McGirt: *hiłakimâ·ha·n*.

[211] McGirt: *itihicákała·nâ·t*.

[212] McGirt would say *hiłakimâ·ha·tin*.

[213] McGirt: *nítta*.

[214] McGirt: *hálwała·nâ·tiw'*.

[215] McGirt: *hayakpó·ta·tiw'*.

[216] Haas notebook has *i·imahopółliŋkít*.

[217] Haas notebook has *omálkat*.

[218] McGirt: *ahaŋkathóhyin*.

[219] Haas notebook has *itínwa·lín*.

[220] McGirt: *apâ·kin*.

[221] McGirt reads these two words as *itimá·fa·ckít follín*.

[222] Perhaps this should be *impóhhá·ckin*. McGirt: *impo·há·ckin*.

[223] McGirt: *awă·ⁿhosi·t*.

[224] McGirt: *iyâ·cit*.

[225] McGirt: *yahóla i·má·łan*.

[226] McGirt: *naka·ftít*.

[227] McGirt: *iŋki·łkoyhcit.*

[228] Corrected (McGirt) from *haléywi·.*

[229] Corrected (McGirt) from *halwáła·nít.*

[230] McGirt: *ahaŋkă·ⁿtkosi·.*

[231] Corrected (McGirt) from *takka·kí·pała·nícki·t.*

[232] McGirt: *apatatapáki·t.*

[233] Corrected (McGirt) from *hoyłá·łi·s.*

[234] McGirt: *i·niki·yeycatí·.*

[235] McGirt: *hiłĕyⁿcit.*

[236] Corrected (McGirt) from *awa·hi·cántas.*

[237] Martin would transcribe this as *pokkanóckatá·ła·nâ·t,* from *pokkanóckat omála·nâ·t(i).*

[238] McGirt: *ohhapô·ka·n.*

[239] Corrected from *ayoposhoycít.*

[240] McGirt: *yikcitá simpóna·yâ·t.*

[241] McGirt: *hayyô·ma·ti.*

[242] McGirt: *atî·hko·fa.*

[243] McGirt: *łŏⁿkcosi·.*

[244] McGirt: *ahaŋkă·ⁿtkosi·.*

[245] McGirt: *ayosămmalêykin.*

[246] McGirt: *ístimi·séyt.*

[247] McGirt reads this as *iskâ·kayáti·.* It's not clear why a dual verb is used with a first person singular subject here.

[248] McGirt: *okáko·tis.*

[249] This passage is quite difficult.

[250] McGirt: *'simanacicí·.*

[251] Corrected (McGirt) from *áccipohéykin.*

[252] McGirt: *sihô·ko·fa.*

[253] Corrected from *atihéyko·fa.*

[254] Corrected from *ima·łó·fa.*

[255] Corrected from *hoyłí·peys.*

[256] McGirt: *omi·pí·s.*

[257] McGirt: *itíwala·pkín.*

[258] McGirt: *hâmkosi·.*

[259] Corrected (McGirt) from *ansihô·káłi·n.*

[260] Corrected (McGirt) from *iŋkô·méyka.*

[261] McGirt: *yá·hkikas.*

[262] Corrected (McGirt) from *a·pohéycit.*

[263] Corrected (McGirt) from *inho·hêykit.*

[264] Corrected (McGirt) from *impohathó·yin*. Could also be *impohathô·yin*.

[265] Haas has *ínyaheykín hoktakíw yaheykín*.

[266] Or (McGirt): *imópona·yín*.

[267] McGirt: *o·mâ·t*.

[268] Corrected (McGirt) from *lómhit*. Could also be *lômhit*.

[269] McGirt: *api·yâ·t*.

[270] McGirt: *i·pâ·ki·*.

[271] McGirt reads these three words as *imíto sihô·ka·n ohhapíhyít 'łołéyhcit*. The third word might also be *'lołêycit*.

[272] Haas has *itohhapí·ho·yín*.

[273] McGirt: *yeycít*.

[274] McGirt: *afóloti·cít*.

[275] Or (more common): *i·halíwa*.

[276] Haas has *i·yana·koycapáks*.

[277] Haas notebook has *intokálpin*.

[278] McGirt suggests <vpoket omēs>.

[279] In the modern language, *hasí* means 'sun', but expressions like *nítta hasí* 'day sun' in the text hint that *hasí* originally referred to either the sun or moon.

[280] Haas notebook has: *a·sákko·sít*.

[281] McGirt: *i·halíwa*.

[282] Haas notebook has *a·sosséysíckali·s*.

[283] Haas notebook has *isho·hêykin*.

[284] Haas notebook has: *i·ná·kayyít*.

[285] Haas notebook has *pa·lâ·tkit*.

[286] Haas notebook has *opanaká*.

[287] Haas notebook has *waksâlko*.

[288] Haas notebook has *'kapiccâlka*.

[289] Corrected from *alpatâlki* based on Hill ms. Most speakers say *alpatá* 'alligator', but Hill said *alipatá*.

[290] Corrected from *stô·meys* (short way) based on Hill ms.

[291] Corrected from *ma·kitáw* based on Hill ms.

[292] Corrected from *hámkosi·n* based on Hill ms.

[293] In Creek, men have <ēppucetake> 'sons', while women have <echustake cēpvnvke> 'boy children'. The Creek sentence could be translated more literally this way: "The names of an Alligator clan woman's boy children and a Bear clan man's sons [are]".

[294] Last word appears in Hill's ms, but not in Haas.

[295] Kaccv-yvholv accidentally listed twice in Hill ms.

[296] Corrected from *hoktí·* based on Hill ms.

[297] Corrected from *pinwâlki* based on Hill ms.

[298] Corrected from *konipyahóla* based on Hill ms.

[299] Corrected from *konipi·mála* based on Hill ms.

[300] Corrected from *waksâlki* based on Hill ms.

[301] This was Hill's own name at Kaylaychi and Arbeka tribal towns.

[302] Corrected from *hoktí·* based on Hill ms.

[303] Added *mo·mèys* based on Hill ms.

[304] Corrected from *alpatâlki* based on Hill ms.

[305] Corrected from *alpatâlki* based on Hill ms.

[306] Corrected from *ina·hámki* based on Hill ms.

[307] This text is separated in Haas's notes, but runs together with the preceding and following in Hill ms.

[308] Corrected from *lissawála·nit* based on Hill ms.

[309] Corrected from *oykéywan* based on Hill ms.

[310] Haas notebook has *cahkî·pi·t*

[311] Haas notebook has *atíhhin.*

[312] Mauldin: *nikléycakatí·.*

[313] *nokłeycakáti·* and *nikłeycakáti·* are both commonly used. Edna Gouge says really black corn doesn't need ashes.

[314] Mauldin: *'sitiyáhmit.*

[315] Mauldin: *akti·hô·hin.*

[316] Or (Edna Gouge): *poyafikcawanáki* 'wrapped ghost'.

[317] Mauldin has not heard this word.

[318] Haas originally had *ô·mati·s*, but noted Raiford's preference for *o·mati·s*. Mauldin also reads it as *o·mati·s.*

[319] Haas notebook has *acihátki·n.*

[320] Haas notebook has *inca·wót* here for *inca·wit*, and *ákca·wót* below for *ákca·wit.*

[321] Haas notebook has: *ákca·wót.*

[322] Mauldin: *imahitî·cit.*

[323] Mauldin: *imahitî·cin.*

[324] Mauldin: *ohcâ·nin.*

[325] Mauldin has not heard this word, but cf. *sakkonipitá* 'to make corn stew'.

[326] Haas notebook has *óhho·yanc.*

[327] Haas notebook has *há·ka·ta·n.*

[328] Haas notebook has *ho·cít.*

[329] Haas notebook has *lopocicáhsit*, but notes Raiford's form *lopocicéyhcit.*

[330] Mauldin: *aktî·hit*. The form *aktî·hit* seems to imply that it was done once, so that *aktî·hit* could be translated as 'put it in (liquid)' and *ákti·hít* could be translated as 'would put it in (liquid)'.

[331] Haas notebook has *capkonípkin*, which we take to be an error.

[332] Mauldin: *sohlêycit*.

[333] Haas notebook has *íska·kí·t*.

[334] Haas notebook has *ínca·wót*, but notes Raiford's form *ínca·wít*.

[335] Interpreted May 27, 1937.

[336] Haas notebook has *apisakí·*.

[337] Haas notebook has *siláhsit*.

[338] McGirt: *incáhwit*.

[339] Haas notebook has: *itisilcíhcit*.

[340] McGirt: *kéyca·katí·t*.

[341] McGirt: *ha·ckowán*.

[342] McGirt: *hólki·t*.

[343] This word means 'it boils' rather than 'they boiled it'.

[344] McGirt: *papa·kí·t ô·mati·s*.

[345] McGirt: *hómpa·kí·t o·mati·s*.

[346] McGirt: *há·ya·kí·t o·mati·s*.

[347] I.e., the alligator snapping turtle (*Macroclemys temminckii*).

[348] McGirt: *pa·pít omâ·kati·s*.

[349] McGirt reads these two words as *i·tî·hít oma·kí·s*.

[350] Haas notebook has: *innitłéyhcit*.

[351] Corrected from *ohłá·nin*.

[352] McGirt: *inwaná·weycít*.

[353] McGirt: *ismo·líhcit*.

[354] McGirt: *aktíhhit*.

[355] Haas notebook has *fakki·talá·swa*.

[356] Changed from *ishá·yakáti·t* to match Hill ms.

[357] "(vrkvcuce)" inserted based on Hill ms. This word is not known to Mauldin.

[358] Changed from *há·yipo·yô·f* to match Hill ms.

[359] Changed from *ísfo·yít* 'sawed' to match Hill ms. (*isfó·fo·yít* = 'sawed repeatedly').

[360] Changed from *hómpa·kati·t* 'they would eat' to match Hill ms. (*hómhopati·t* = 'they (people in general) would eat').

[361] *o·mi·s* added to match Hill ms.

[362] Haas notebook has *tá·ti*.

[363] Hill uses the term *natarv* here for potter, a term restricted to 'dirtdauber' for most speakers.

[364] Mauldin: *ałkaswocí*?

[365] Corrected from *pô·fki·s* to match Hill ms.

[366] Corrected from *inłapkí·* to match Hill ms.

[367] Changed from *nakâ·ftit* to match Hill ms.

[368] Changed from *istó·mi·* to match Hill ms.

[369] *itó* added based on Hill ms.

[370] Or also (Mauldin): *siní·pi·cít*.

[371] Haas notebook has *iŋká·lala·nâ·t*.

[372] Corrected from *atalikcéyhci<t>* to match Hill ms.

[373] Haas notebook has *inłapkí·*.

[374] Corrected from *ahóllit* to match Hill ms.

[375] McGirt: *câ·wit*.

[376] McGirt: *sî·sit*.

[377] McGirt: *ô·mati·s*.

[378] Corrected (McGirt) from *'tikapá·ka·kít*.

[379] McGirt: *itínła·pít*.

[380] McGirt: *fikhónneycántot*.

[381] Corrected (McGirt) from *nacó·mosin*.

[382] Corrected (McGirt) from *itimpokkichała·ní·*.

[383] Corrected (McGirt) from *nacó·mosin*.

[384] McGirt: *ístamat*.

[385] Corrected (McGirt) from *omá·ki·s*.

[386] McGirt: *ahaŋkátka*. Speakers are known to vary in the pronunciation of this word.

[387] McGirt: *ô·mati·s*.

[388] McGirt: *ô·mati·s*.

[389] McGirt: *iyâ·cin*.

[390] McGirt: *inhomáhtat*.

[391] These two words corrected (McGirt) from *ha·hó·yin hóylin*.

[392] McGirt: *inhomáhtat*.

[393] Corrected (McGirt) from *inhóylit*.

[394] McGirt: *omâ·kati·s*.

[395] McGirt: *ô·mati·s*.

[396] Corrected (McGirt) from *hoyléycit*. *hoylêycit* is also possible.

[397] McGirt: *afólotkí·*.

[398] McGirt: *omâ·kati·s*.

[399] McGirt: *ahaŋkátka*.

[400] McGirt: *omâ·kati·s*.

[401] McGirt pronounces these two words as *aháŋka·tít omâ·kati·s*.

[402] McGirt pronounces these two words as *aháŋka·tít omâ·kati·s.*

[403] McGirt: *mítita·kô·f.*

[404] McGirt pronounces these two words as *insá·tho·yí·t ô·mati·s.*

[405] McGirt: *ô·mati·s.*

[406] McGirt: *insa·thô·ya·t.*

[407] McGirt: *ò·mati·s.*

[408] McGirt: *ô·mati·s.*

[409] McGirt: *ahaŋkátka.*

[410] McGirt: *ishá·yaki·pít.*

[411] Corrected (McGirt) from *a·yamíski·pi·t.*

[412] McGirt: *iya·cî·pa·t.*

[413] McGirt reads these two words as *cinhopoyakí·t ôŋka.*

[414] McGirt: *imítita·kit.*

[415] Corrected (McGirt) from *'tita·kín.*

[416] McGirt: *istakkapo·hô·yin.*

[417] McGirt: *facfèy^{n}cosit.*

[418] McGirt: *keyci·t.*

[419] McGirt: *mô·meys.*

[420] McGirt: *ô·mati·s.*

[421] McGirt: *hâmkosi·.*

[422] McGirt: *ô·mati·s.*

[423] McGirt: *ko·mâ·kit.*

[424] McGirt: *imititâ·ka·t.*

[425] McGirt: *sapa·klín.*

[426] Corrected (McGirt) from *itínhalâ·tit.*

[427] McGirt: *itohtalhoyeycitán.*

[428] Corrected (McGirt) from *'sapí·ho·yín.*

[429] Corrected (McGirt) from *ihopoyíta.*

[430] Haas notebook has *imititiktáŋki·t.*

[431] Haas notebook has *kowá·kki·.*

[432] Mauldin: *'taláswa·n.*

[433] Haas notebook has *wanâyyit.*

[434] Haas notebook has *ohhapaló·ficeycít.*

[435] Corrected from *ni·kłí·n* to match Hill ms.

[436] Haas's title for this text is: *wacína hółłi itínha·yô·f isticá·ti awa·hatí· hiłka háhki· imi·kaná yohtihêyko·f* 'when the United States Made War on the Creeks', but that is not what the text is about.

[437] Haas notebook has *kíłłako·s.*

[438] Haas notebook has *a·ta·lêykit.*

[439] Or (Mauldin) *si·ccaya·t.*

[440] Mauldin: *i·ccayi·.*

[441] Mauldin: okvyē.

[442] Mauldin: pohken.

[443] Haas notebook has *icêyheyn.*

[444] The word *pinacá·* is not known to Mauldin.

[445] Mauldin: *î·ccaya·t.*

[446] Translation based on Haas VI:44–52.

[447] Haas has *ínho·vín.*

[448] McGirt: *imanhili·t.*

[449] McGirt: *ca·skít.*

[450] McGirt: *imahopayí·ci·t.*

[451] McGirt: *wákki·pín.*

[452] McGirt reads these three words as *acolêycayi· 'sahókko·li·t ô·(ⁿ)s.*

[453] This line inserted later.

[454] *nâ·ki hilíka·tiw* added based on Hill ms.

[455] Corrected from *oponayítateys* based on Hill ms.

[456] Corrected (Mauldin) from *ihóseysít.*

[457] Corrected from *innókkeycít* based on Hill ms. (*innókkeycít* means 'hurt them' instead of 'make them sick').

[458] Haas notebook has *inhoykitá.*

[459] Corrected from *hilishá·ka* based on Hill ms.

[460] Corrected from *hómpiko·* based on Hill ms.

[461] Changed from *yápi* (shorter form) based on Hill ms.

[462] Corrected from *imaha·yitán* to match Hill ms.

[463] Corrected from *opona·yâlkit* to match Hill ms.

[464] Corrected (Mauldin) from *o·caki·t.*

[465] Corrected from *kawapkacókon* to match Hill ms.

[466] Changed from *ayo·pkit* to match Hill ms.

[467] Corrected from *itálwa* to match Hill ms.

[468] Corrected (Mauldin) from *ikkoci·.*

[469] Corrected (Mauldin) from *á·sapa·klin hi·cin.*

[470] *kastimála·nít* is not known to Mauldin.

[471] Mauldin: *impó·fho·kâ·tin.*

[472] A traditional medicine maker blows through a hollow reed into medicine.

[473] Or also (Mauldin): *hòylit* (same meaning here).

[474] Corrected (Mauldin) from *hoktakito·.*

[475] Haas notebook has *wila·ki ʔǒ·f*.

[476] Corrected (Mauldin) from *hi·cí·t*.

[477] Corrected (Mauldin) from *sistóhmit*.

[478] Haas has *pa·lihokkô·li·t* written as another option.

[479] Corrected (Mauldin) from *oski·ta·t istǒ·ⁿmosa·t pô·fkin* 'she blew a little for the rain'.

[480] Haas notebook has *lawkín*.

[481] Corrected (Mauldin) from *ma·kít*.

[482] Or also: *itina·kǒyⁿcosi·*.

[483] *toccî·ni·* 'three' or *toccini·* 'group of three'.

[484] I.e., Orion's Belt. Mauldin is not sure about *-siní·can*.

[485] Haas notebook has *oysaksáwkateys*.

[486] I.e., the Pleiades or Seven Little Sisters.

[487] Corrected from *'kola·ssokló·fkan*.

[488] Corrected from *hǐ·ⁿłosin*.

[489] Corrected (Mauldin) from *ya 'tilo·kâ·t*.

[490] Haas notebook has *somêycatit*.

[491] I.e., the Milky Way.

[492] Corrected (Mauldin) by deleting *atóklika·ppí·* after this word.

[493] *immóŋka* means 'permanent'.

[494] Corrected from *híckati·t* to match Hill ms.

[495] Haas notebook has *iya·cót*.

[496] Corrected from *po·hit* to match Hill ms.

[497] *yópa* added based on Hill ms.

[498] Haas notebook has *acalakí*.

[499] Mauldin: *ka·lô·nit*.

[500] Haas notebook has *citeycít*.

[501] Haas notebook has *citéycikot*.

[502] Haas notebook has *akhotêycit*.

[503] Haas notebook has *otô·kit*.

[504] Or perhaps (Mauldin): *a·yati·ton*.

[505] Haas notebook has *ini·líski·*.

[506] Mauldin: *kǐ·ⁿłlisiko·t*.

[507] Haas notebook has *o·sícka·t*.

[508] MAll of this prediction refers to family and the old homeplace.

[509] Mauldin: *kǐ·ⁿłlisikô·t*.

[510] Haas notebook has *sicifa·skít*.

[511] Mauldin suggests this a condition caused by being around a woman during her period. It's literally "a little menstruation-killed".

[512] *hopvnkv ocof* 'when there's destruction' and *hopvnkof* 'when it breaks down' are old expressions meaning 'in time of war' (see earlier vol.).

[513] Mauldin: *ishóyli·t*.

[514] This is a euphemism for 'bite'.

[515] Haas notebook has *píŋkalí·s*.

[516] Haas notebook has *pa·pí·cka·t*, with rising tone marked out on the first syllable.

[517] Haas notebook has *siła·hóhhali·s*.

[518] Haas notebook has *opanaká*.

[519] Haas notebook has *'lisołéyhsit*.

[520] The meaning of *intákca·yít imóni·pít* is not known to Mauldin.

[521] Mauldin: *ó·misiko·*.

[522] Haas notebook has *ciháhpit*.

[523] Mauldin: *cinníttat*.

[524] Haas notebook has *ciháhko*.

[525] The term *innapá·* 'anyone' and the term *napá* 'no one' are not known to modern speakers.

[526] Haas notebook has *ciháhpin*.

[527] Haas notebook has *iciyakkô·fkin*.

[528] Meaning of *imayamáhki·t omáka·n* not clear to Mauldin.

[529] Haas notebook has *ałă·ⁿkkosi·*.

[530] The meaning here of *nittahátkin* 'white day' is not clear. Mauldin suggests *nittahóyłin* 'someday'.

[531] Haas notebook has *fólla·tí·t*.

[532] Mauldin: *wa·lkín*.

[533] Haas notebook has *simanítti·*.

[534] Haas notebook has *hickoycíka·t*.

[535] Haas notebook has *icó hokêycali·s*.

[536] Haas notebook has *cihohta·li·hókcali·s*.

[537] Haas notebook has *sipisí·teys*.

[538] The word *ohweykocí* is not known to Mauldin.

[539] Haas notebook has *hakeykatí·*.

[540] This section is part of Hill's description of games in Haas's notes. We have separated it out.

[541] Haas notebook has *tikalêykatot*.

[542] Haas notebook has *icfóswa*.

[543] Meaning of *'capakán* is uncertain.

[544] Changed from *'tipá·kan* based on Hill ms.

[545] Haas notebook possibly has *'loka·flóyca·kít*.

[546] Hill sometimes inexplicably writes soksv for yoksv.

[547] Mauldin: *ahá·ka i·tá·n.*

[548] Corrected from *innâ·kit ó·keys* based on Hill ms.

[549] Haas notebook has *sóhha·yô·fa.*

[550] Mauldin: *i·yalêycit.*

[551] Mauldin: *í·yaleycí·.*

[552] Haas notes that the remaining section was dictated without being written first.

[553] Mauldin: *hofóno·f* 'long ago'.

[554] Mauldin does not know this word.

[555] Or also (Mauldin): *o·matí·s.*

[556] Or also (Mauldin): *kô·miyi·.*

[557] Hill here and below describes the Comanche practice of using Plains Sign Language.

[558] Or also (Mauldin): *cinwêyki·ka.*

[559] Haas notebook has *akasâ·má·cka·n.*

[560] Haas notebook has *simano·lâlki.*

[561] Haas notebook has *leykî·pin.* Mauldin feels *leyki·ⁿpin*, implying casualness, is more natural.

[562] Haas notebook has *simano·lâlkita·t.*

[563] Haas notebook has *hoyanipô·kin.*

[564] Or also (Mauldin): *itimó·ci·t.*

[565] Haas notebook has *istima·skó·ka.*

[566] Haas varies between spelling *calá·kki* and *calákki.* Hill's spelling suggests *calákki,* but Mauldin says *calá·kki.* Since there is variation, we have left Haas's spelling unchanged.

[567] Haas notebook has *iya·cít,* but Mauldin prefers *iyá·ci·t,* saying *iya·cít* "sounds odd, like a one-time thing."

[568] Haas notebook has *acahôycíckali·s.*

[569] Haas notebook has *o·hayáti·s.*

[570] Haas notebook has *tó·yako·f.*

[571] Haas notebook has *cacoffánkosit.*

[572] Haas notebook has *acakasami·póyhcit.*

[573] Haas notebook has *hónho·yósin.*

[574] Haas notebook has *'samohwitinkí·.*

[575] Haas notebook has *anhĭ·ⁿlan ô·ⁿs.*

[576] Haas notebook has *tá·ti.*

[577] Mauldin would say *sikó·.*

[578] Mauldin says instead *'łimi·homán.*

[579] Or also (Mauldin): *há·ho·yati·t.*

[580] To be consistent, this should be 'my older brother'.

[581] Haas notebook has *ciho·katí·.*

[582] Literally, "I stood [in this predicament]..."

[583] Haas notebook has *táti·*.

[584] Haas notebook has *oponayi·ci·ma*.

[585] Or also (Mauldin): *ó·cin*.

[586] Haas notebook has *amoyopo·skíckati·t*.

[587] Haas notebook has *amoyópo·skít*.

[588] Mauldin would say *istó·feys* (but *istô·feys* is okay).

[589] Haas notebook has *itimohsihô·k*.

[590] Haas notebook has *killatí·n*.

[591] Mauldin would say *sikón*.

[592] Mauldin would say *sikó·t*.

[593] Haas notebook has *anopícka*.

[594] Haas notebook has *itimó·c*.

[595] Haas notebook has *'tipâ·ki·t*.

[596] Haas notebook has *ha·yi·kâ·ko·f*.

[597] Haas notebook has *makintá·si*.

[598] Haas notebook has *cilí makintá·si*.

[599] Haas notebook has *téyfi*.

[600] Haas notebook has *ská·ti*.

[601] The names appearing in the list above appear to be from Senate Files S-417, Creek Indians, 33rd Congress—1st Session, Memorial of the Muscogee or Creek Nation to the Congress of the United States. A copy of this memorial was found among Mary R. Haas's papers. The English spelling used here follows that list, except that "Hokus Emathla" is changed to "Nokus Emathla" to match Hill's interpretation.

[602] Haas notebook has *siko·* instead of *há·kiko·*, but we follow Hill.

[603] This clause could go with the previous sentence.

[604] Haas notebook has *pocifhoká*.

[605] Haas notebook has *intín-*.

[606] Corrected (Mauldin) from *cahkihohkâ·ka·t*.

[607] Mauldin says *'limi·homán*.

[608] [Originally included with games, but Haas directed to separate (VIII:65)]

[609] McGirt reads these two words as *haya·tkí·t ò·mati·s*.

[610] McGirt: *ô·mati·s*.

[611] McGirt: *ò·mati·s*.

[612] Corrected (McGirt) from *ohłolopí·mocásiw*.

[613] McGirt: *isa·fá·cka·kâ·t*.

[614] McGirt: *acolakíta·tí·*.

[615] McGirt: *o·makí·t*.

[616] McGirt: *hâ·yit.*

[617] McGirt: *ahicéycan.*

[618] McGirt: *tâlkit.*

[619] McGirt: *fo·tkít.*

[620] McGirt: *óhkit.*

[621] McGirt: *o·kít.*

[622] McGirt reads these three words as *istónt a·líckit o·ma·^* 'what are you doing around [here]?'

[623] McGirt: *ałáko·t ô·s.*

[624] McGirt: *omiko'.*

[625] Literally, "'If someone I don't know comes, I might kill him,' you think, don't you?"

[626] McGirt: *omiko'.*

[627] McGirt: *mô·ma·n.*

[628] McGirt: *pô·ha·t.*

[629] McGirt: *la·wáhłit.*

[630] McGirt: *takcáhwit.*

[631] McGirt pronounces these two words as *cínt o·mícki·táŋka'.*

[632] McGirt: *móŋko·táŋks.*

[633] McGirt pronounces these two words as *takkasiksî·ci·t o·mín.*

[634] McGirt: *ha·kô·fan.*

[635] McGirt: *hî·cit.*

[636] McGirt: *ci·yêyt.*

[637] McGirt: *íshoya·nô·f.*

[638] Or perhaps *oskéy^n oskéy^n*. McGirt: *o·skin o·skin.*

[639] McGirt: *'yisohfólo·tkit.*

[640] McGirt: *hôylit.*

[641] McGirt: *sa·lícka·ˇ.*

[642] McGirt: *keycín.*

[643] McGirt reads these two words as *wo·hkâ·n ci·yít.*

[644] McGirt: *kô·mit.*

[645] McGirt: *hoya·nâ·n.*

[646] McGirt: *tóhwala·pkakín.*

[647] McGirt: *ha·kít.*

[648] McGirt: *ô·mati·to·.*

[649] McGirt: *ha·kakî·pin.*

[650] Corrected (McGirt) from *tâ·yi.*

[651] This section is from Haas X:1–23 (continued from VIII).

[652] McGirt: *ha·yít.*

653 McGirt: *ayí·ceycít.*

654 McGirt: *apáki·.*

655 Corrected from *itincokopiłeycâ·t.*

656 McGirt is uncertain about this word.

657 McGirt: *a·acímkas.*

658 McGirt: *ansomicíhpin.*

659 McGirt reads these two words as *cahopołłini·t ô·meys.*

660 McGirt reads these two words as *ciyâ·cit o·ma'.*

661 McGirt reads these two words as *cahopołłini·t ô·ma·t.*

662 McGirt reads these two words as *cahopołłinípi·t ô·ma·t.*

663 McGirt: *canŏⁿkkosi·t.*

664 McGirt reads these three words as *'lo·lícki· tâ·yi·t ô·ma'.*

665 McGirt: *aláhkit.*

666 McGirt reads these two words as *ciyâ·cit o·ma'.*

667 McGirt: *cayâ·cit ó·s.*

668 McGirt: *ó·ci·n ô·ma·t.*

669 McGirt: *omă̆ⁿlkocan.*

670 This word is not known to McGirt.

671 McGirt: *akta·skántot.*

672 McGirt: *imomă̆ⁿlkat.*

673 Corrected (McGirt) from *akká·si·pakátit.* It might also represent *a·ákkisi·pakáti·t* 'take out of water'.

674 Corrected (McGirt) from *ahoyakáłi·s.*

675 McGirt: *a·ákkisi·pâ·t.* The *a·*- prefix here means 'out' or 'from'.

676 McGirt: *a·akkisíka·n.*

677 McGirt: *a·akkisíhpit.*

678 McGirt: *a·akkisípakáłi·s* 'we will take from the water'.

679 McGirt: *hofŏnikantón.*

680 McGirt: *lêykin.*

681 McGirt: *sinhomahá·ki·sko·.*

682 McGirt: *momí·ci·pít.*

683 Corrected (McGirt) from *okí·ckis.*

684 McGirt: *ínli·tkayánc.*

685 Haas notebook has *óŋcki·s.*

686 Mauldin: *ili·cít ô·mi·s.*

687 Haas notebook has *isfoláyacóka·t.*

688 Haas notebook has *híhcac.*

689 Haas notebook has *ahíca·n.*

[690] Haas notebook has *hoktalósi·t*.

[691] This ending was added on later to the original version.

[692] This version reflects III:97–105, which differs in wording from II:143–147.

[693] Haas notebook has 'herb' as the gloss here and in the next sentence (evidently a misunderstanding).

[694] Haas notebook has *ínha·yí·s*.

[695] Haas notebook has *aca·yí·ci·t*.

[696] *ó·ⁿs* is contracted from *o·mís* 'it is'. Mauldin and McGirt pronounce this word as *ó·s* (without nasalization).

[697] McGirt: *ici·yít*.

[698] McGirt: *'laláhkit*.

[699] McGirt: *máhkicka'*.

[700] McGirt: *ta·skíhpeyt*.

[701] McGirt reads this as *tohtâ·lka·n*.

[702] Haas notebook has *sitakhoyáti·t*.

[703] Mauldin suggests *mi·cáhkin*.

[704] McGirt: *itimpokkiccakála·nít*.

[705] Haas notebook has *hálli·câ·t*.

[706] Haas notebook has *takfalilî·skat*.

[707] McGirt prefers *ilí ostâ·kí*.

[708] Haas notebook has *itinfáccí·t*.

[709] McGirt: *achoyí·*.

[710] McGirt reads these last three words as *isfolliyáti·n ácci·t ônt*.

[711] Haas notebook has *inhoyíhkipi·yi·t*.

[712] Haas notebook has *a·líkas*.

[713] Mauldin: *eyciwéyka·ki·s*

[714] Haas notebook has *folá·sko*.

[715] Haas notebook has *ákweykayâ·t*.

[716] Haas records that this is "very funny toward the last."

[717] Or (Mauldin) *ô·ca·tin*.

[718] Or (Mauldin) *kô·mit*.

[719] Haas notebook has *ákweykín*.

[720] Haas notebook has *imi·hâ·kit*.

[721] Haas notebook has *locatokócki·*.

[722] Haas sometimes has *ná·ki* for *nâ·ki*, which we have corrected. The falling tone on the first syllable of *nâ·ki* can be spread over two syllables but sounds different from, e.g., *wá·ka* 'bovine'.

[723] Musical transcription of song at V:178.

[724] Haas indicates that this section is funny.

[725] Haas notebook has *yopǫ́n*.

[726] Haas notebook has: *łá·o·sâ·n*.

[727] McGirt: *límo·lít ó·n*.

[728] McGirt: *łisô·lin*.

[729] McGirt: *kéyhcin*.

[730] McGirt: *'sicíhyeyn.*

[731] McGirt: *keyhô·cin*.

[732] McGirt: *hopóhyít áhyit iló·lin*.

[733] Haas notebook has *fà·cki·s*.

[734] McGirt reads this as *'sapô·kin*.

[735] Haas notebook has *hopołlíŋka* here and in the next clause.

[736] These two words are normally pronounced together: *wa·kahokti·t*.

[737] McGirt: *cayâ·cit ó·s*.

[738] Haas notebook has *impífa·tkít*.

[739] Haas notebook has *sinhonícki·*.

[740] Haas notebook has *isohfáŋkita*.

[741] McGirt: *hĭ·ⁿckosin*.

[742] Haas notebook has *hĭ·li·n*.

[743] Haas notebook has *álki·*.

[744] Haas notebook has *pô·hickaŋka·*.

[745] McGirt reads these three words as *isto·maki·n ha·yít ómho·yati·*.

[746] Haas notebook has *itimakílli·*. McGirt read it this way first and then corrected it to be parallel with the following verbs.

[747] McGirt: *má·ho·kí·t*.

[748] Haas records that this is a "funny story."

[749] McGirt: *hî·cit*.

[750] McGirt: *haláhteyn*.

[751] McGirt: *kô·ma·n hónni·ton.*

[752] McGirt: *cihopołłǐ·ⁿnosikot o·mâ·t*.

[753] McGirt: *nâ·ki istó·mi·*.

[754] As with the word *opánka* 'dance', Haas transcribes this word with *ŋk* in her early work. She later discovered a contrast and began writing it *nk*. We have corrected it to *nk* to reflect her later work.

[755] McGirt: *saláfki·n*.

[756] McGirt: *istihá·ho·yí· tâ·yi·t ô·ma·t*.

[757] McGirt: *ô·míka*. If McGirt is correct, the translation should be, 'so the old crow teaches us,' instead of, 'the old crow teaches us, doesn't he?'

[758] Or (McGirt) *itihî·cit.*

[759] McGirt: *mô·mati·ta·n.*

[760] McGirt: *ha·kî·pit.*

[761] McGirt: *ha·kî·pit.*

[762] McGirt: *'yifolhokípaɫa·ní·s.*

[763] Haas notebook has *hilimá·hin.*

[764] McGirt: *óhhaya·tkít.*

[765] McGirt: *'ɫalâ·kin.*

[766] Haas notebook has *acanɫa·pkâlkita·t.*

[767] Haas notebook has *iscahícaɫa·ní·t.*

[768] Haas notebook has *cistimíɫeyci·teys.*

[769] Haas notebook has *istó·mi·s.*

[770] Haas notebook has *acanɫâ·kota·t.*

[771] Haas notebook has *aho·yakêys.*

[772] McGirt: *lêykati·s.*

[773] Haas notebook has *akossêylit.*

[774] McGirt: *mo·matí·ta·n.*

[775] McGirt: *istinhisá·ki·payáŋks.*

[776] McGirt: *incikci·kitát.*

[777] McGirt: *ancíkci·cín.*

[778] Haas notebook has *acapi·lî·pa·t.*

[779] Haas records that this is a "funny story."

[780] This word is not known to McGirt.

[781] McGirt: *tolpokósi·t.*

[782] McGirt: *â·yit.*

[783] McGirt: *hóhɫit.*

[784] McGirt: *áhyit.*

[785] McGirt: *hoɫhóhyin.*

[786] McGirt: *'masáhtit.*

[787] McGirt: *imása·tâ·n.*

[788] Haas notebook has *i·istimíɫɫéyhsíckis.*

[789] McGirt reads these two words as as *ma·kít ayíhpin.*

[790] McGirt: *ishíhcit.*

[791] McGirt: *ishíhcit.*

[792] Haas notebook has *cokó onápa* 'on top of the house'. It should probably be *cokoʔonápa* (pronounced as one word to mean 'roof').

[793] McGirt: *ɫa·isinwakichóhyin.*

[794] McGirt: *tâ·cka·n.*

[795] Haas notebook has *apa·pít.*

[796] McGirt: *ossíhpit.*

[797] McGirt: *iya·hô·cati·s.*

[798] McGirt: *hofóni· ha·kî·pin.*

[799] McGirt: *lapóti·poséys.*

[800] This word is not known to McGirt.

[801] Haas: *'towáhłit.*

[802] This word is not known to McGirt.

[803] McGirt: *ca·tatolókfit.*

[804] Haas recorded once as *łíso·kolín.*

[805] Or more literally, "Were you thinking, 'This will be enough for my many sons?'"

[806] McGirt: *akcá·ta·katí·t.*

[807] Haas notebook has *iscimi·yapâ·yan.*

[808] McGirt: *acakkapî·yit.*

[809] McGirt: *hicâ·kit.*

[810] Haas originally transcribes this as *ĭ·ⁿyahaykít.*

[811] McGirt: *'sitihóhlit.*

[812] McGirt: *lêyka'.*

[813] Haas notebook has *hopóhkatá·łi·s.*

[814] Haas notebook has *hopóhka.*

[815] Haas has *cinhoyhhô·k[êy] î·.* The square brackets may indicate a deletion.

[816] Haas notebook has *łohhô·yit.*

[817] McGirt: *yáta·t.*

[818] Haas notebook has *nâ·kiccikos.*

[819] McGirt: *hî·cit.*

[820] McGirt: *wâ·kkati·s.*

[821] McGirt: *o·mí·ti·ˇ.*

[822] McGirt: *ili·pín.*

[823] McGirt: *ilí·ho·câ·n.*

[824] McGirt: *pô·hit.*

[825] McGirt: *wéyci·cí· tâ·ya·t.*

[826] McGirt: *cicafíkni·.*

[827] McGirt: *â·yeymac.*

[828] Haas records that this is a "very funny story."

[829] McGirt: *alpatát.*

[830] McGirt: *capâ·kkit* 'got mad'.

[831] McGirt: *hokti·manítti.*

[832] McGirt: *pohâ·katit.*

[833] McGirt: *'mitita·kíhpit.*

[834] McGirt: *lô·lit.*

[835] The value of the musical notes here is based on Haas's transcription of them: do la sol, do la sol, re ti la.

[836] Corrected from *'liso·lín.* McGirt: *'lisô·lin.*

[837] McGirt: *ma·kít.*

[838] McGirt: *a·yatí·ton.*

[839] McGirt: *ca·tî·cakati·n.* .

[840] McGirt: *kohcakhíhcit.*

[841] This word not known to McGirt.

[842] McGirt reads this as *apo·kiphoyíka.*

[843] McGirt reads these two words as *ihéyhsit lêykati·s.*

[844] McGirt: *istiŋkapákho·yâ·t.*

[845] McGirt: *holwakí·s.*

[846] McGirt: *máta·t.*

[847] McGirt: *'taheykícki·.*

[848] McGirt: *ístimi·łkit.*

[849] McGirt: *ma·kít.*

[850] McGirt: *a·yô·fan* 'when she went'. *áhyo·fan* is 'after she went'.

[851] McGirt: *imá·poheycít.*

[852] Corrected from *acitothô·yin.*

[853] McGirt: *a·lopo·ttéyhcit.*

[854] McGirt: *incokpéyhkit* 'put it in his mouth'. *incokpâykit* is 'had it in his mouth'.

[855] McGirt: *imahĭ·ⁿla·t.*

[856] McGirt: *ma·kít.*

[857] McGirt: *ma·kín.*

[858] McGirt: *yifolkít.*

[859] McGirt: *ma·kípho·yín.*

[860] McGirt: *keycín.*

[861] Both Rabbit and his mother use impersonal *-ho-* in speaking about the old woman. This may be a sign of politeness.

[862] McGirt: *láhtit.*

[863] McGirt: *á·yahaykín.*

[864] McGirt: *keycín.*

[865] McGirt: *áhyit.*

[866] McGirt reads these three words as *líhsit 'lisaláhkit tolóhfín.*

[867] McGirt reads these two words as *amóntalkánc amóntalkánc.*

[868] McGirt: *kô·mit.*

[869] McGirt: *imititáhkit.*

[870] McGirt: *inhoyhèykit.* Some speakers pronounce *oy* as [u·].

[871] McGirt: *hi·cít.*

[872] McGirt: *iłanłáhpit.*

[873] McGirt: *áhtit.*

[874] Corrected (McGirt) from *atêyyi·t.*

[875] McGirt: *a·tayáŋks.*

[876] McGirt: *háhyeyt.*

[877] Corrected (McGirt) from *atêyyi·t.*

[878] McGirt: *a·tayáŋks.*

[879] Perhaps this should be *tintakhâ·kosit.* McGirt: *tintakhakósi·t.*

[880] Corrected (McGirt) from *amitita·kò·f.*

[881] McGirt: *tókas.*

[882] McGirt: *lèykati·t.*

[883] McGirt: *tókas.*

[884] McGirt: *lèykati·ta·t.*

[885] McGirt: *annitta awolêycacoksci·^* 'my day has drawn near'.

[886] McGirt: *lèykati·n.*

[887] McGirt: *cino·cánti·ʼ.*

[888] McGirt: *ha·kín.*

[889] McGirt: *fikhonnáhkit.*

[890] McGirt: *ha·kín.*

[891] McGirt: *tíhcit.*

[892] McGirt: *ohpaláhtin.*

[893] Corrected (McGirt) from *hopó·yit.*

[894] McGirt: *wakhóhkin.* In many instances like this, Haas records the falling tone grade (*wakhô·k-*), where McGirt seems to prefer the aspirated grade (*wakhóhk-*).

[895] McGirt: *o·mícki·s.*

[896] McGirt: *la·ʔɬohtá·ski·pín.*

[897] McGirt: *ła·téykiko·mâ·hit.*

[898] Corrected (McGirt) from *imohhoyleyhó·cin.*

[899] McGirt: *na·fkâ·n.*

[900] McGirt: *isna·fkâ·n.*

[901] McGirt: *íŋkita·t.*

[902] McGirt: *óhłi·fkâ·n.*

[903] McGirt: *aca·khâ·n.*

[904] McGirt: *ohkáhlit.*

[905] McGirt: *awanáhyit.*

[906] McGirt reads these two words as *mó·łkała·ní· hâ·kin*.

[907] McGirt: *atî·hka·n*.

[908] McGirt: *lokî·píckeys*.

[909] McGirt: *iciwanáhyeyn*.

[910] McGirt: *mo·łkít*.

[911] McGirt: *i·imałahkóyhcit*.

[912] McGirt: *íhsit*.

[913] McGirt reads this quotation as *cínt ámaki·łlít o·máŋkit a·lít o·mícki·s*.

[914] Corrected (McGirt) from *amahicêycickin*.

[915] McGirt: *opát*.

[916] Corrected (McGirt) from *ahicéycit*.

[917] McGirt: *a·áhtit*.

[918] McGirt: *a·amanatáksas*.

[919] McGirt: *ohháhyit*.

[920] McGirt: *tofáhpit*.

[921] McGirt: *haláhteyn*.

[922] McGirt: *innókłeycéyn*.

[923] McGirt reads these three words as *a·łíckin ayî·pi·n o·kícka´*. The *-ist* suffix appearing here is archaic.

[924] This word is not known to McGirt or Mauldin.

[925] McGirt: *pónlika·fít*.

[926] Haas's marks here (‖‖) may indicate emphasis on the part of the narrator.

[927] McGirt: *óŋkomâ·ⁿhin*.

[928] McGirt: *mó·n o·mâ·t*.

[929] Haas notebook has *hiłă·ⁿki*.

[930] McGirt: *omî·pis*.

[931] McGirt: *opáyhyit*.

[932] McGirt: *'ticokcóhlit*.

[933] McGirt: *ímpona·yít*.

[934] McGirt: *halá·ttoycít*.

[935] McGirt: *halá·ttoycí·* here and below.

[936] McGirt: *i·kanayóksa*.

[937] Corrected (McGirt) from *'yawoléycacóks*.

[938] McGirt: *istônt*.

[939] McGirt: *pomohhałípaccas*.

[940] McGirt: *ohhákkopa·nít*.

[941] McGirt: *ałi·pí·t ô·mi·s*.

[942] McGirt: *lókci·t*.

943 McGirt: *pa·paká´.*

944 McGirt: *pa·pít.*

945 McGirt reads these two words as *asêy ahálwosa·n.*

946 McGirt reads these two words as *li·tkít ła·akta·sêykit.*

947 McGirt: *móŋki·ta·n.*

948 McGirt: *ísla·hakâ·n.*

949 McGirt reads these two words as *sólkihi·li·t.*

950 McGirt: *papí·t.*

951 McGirt: *hâlwa·n.*

952 Corrected (McGirt) from *ła·hohhôylatit.*

953 Haas notebook has *wonanô·tkosit.*

954 McGirt reads these two words as *incínki·pakâ·t ła·paláti·posâ·t.*

955 Corrected (McGirt) from *o·makéysin.*

956 McGirt: *cíyyeyt.*

957 McGirt: *ayi·pâ·n.*

958 Corrected (McGirt) from *ilí·caki·.*

959 McGirt: *ahicêycit.*

960 McGirt: *ma·kít.*

961 McGirt: *'mahitíhcit.*

962 Corrected (McGirt) from *tółní·lt.*

963 McGirt: *iyâ·cit.*

964 McGirt: *kô·mit.*

965 McGirt: *nakáftala·nít.*

966 Corrected (McGirt) from *má·ka·kít.*

967 Corrected (McGirt) from *'limonayákas.*

968 Corrected (McGirt) from *cakeycá·kit.*

969 McGirt: *itíki·łít.*

970 McGirt: *fóllíkot.*

971 McGirt: *ayi·patí·ton.*

972 McGirt: *cinhoyhkâ·kis.*

973 McGirt: *pokeycáŋks.* Perhaps Haas heard *pokêycáŋks.*

974 Haas notebook has *fa 'acóli.*

975 Corrected (McGirt) from *okhó·yáŋks.*

976 McGirt: *a·yâ·n.*

977 Corrected (McGirt) from *o·mayí·taŋks.*

978 McGirt: *yáta·t.*

979 Corrected from *alpatáw* based on Hill ms.

980 Haas notebook has *i·chá·swat.*

[981] Corrected from *stô·feys* (shorter way) based on Hill ms.

[982] *alípa* is not known to Mauldin.

[983] Haas notebook has *ca·nâ·kin*.

[984] Haas notebook has *pomitiktanêycickin*.

[985] Haas notebook has *tô·yeyt* 'I can be'.

[986] Haas notebook has *kó·miyeyt*.

[987] Corrected from *iŋka·lpín* based on Hill ms.

[988] Haas notebook has *akalpi·má·hi·pín*.

[989] Haas notebook has *osêyyat*.

[990] Changed from *hilóŋka* (casual form) based on Hill ms.

[991] Changed from *opónayíckati·* (longer form) based on Hill ms.

[992] Haas notebook has *pónayayi·cayáti·*.

[993] Haas notebook has *kíłłako·n*.

[994] Corrected from *ma·kíckti·* based on Hill ms.

[995] Literally, "But if you say I've never said the things we tell".

[996] Corrected (Mauldin) from *pomi·hâ·kíckin*.

[997] Haas notebook has *onánaks*.

[998] Mauldin feels *fîhki·* is odd.

[999] Corrected (Mauldin) from *lêykati·n*.

[1000] Changed from *sa·fácki·t* (shorter form) based on Hill ms.

[1001] Beginning of a section.

[1002] McGirt: *sakkopánała·nâ·n*.

[1003] McGirt: *mô·ma·t*.

[1004] Corrected (McGirt) from *a·inhatapicéycin*.

[1005] McGirt: *'sahokkô·la·t*.

[1006] Corrected (McGirt) from *a·inhatapicéycin*.

[1007] McGirt: *awáhhin*.

[1008] McGirt: *'satocci·na·t*.

[1009] Corrected (McGirt) from *a·inhatapicéycin*.

[1010] McGirt: *awáhhin*.

[1011] McGirt: *isô·sta·t*.

[1012] Corrected (McGirt) from *a·inhatapicéycin*.

[1013] McGirt: *'sacahkî·pa·n*.

[1014] Corrected (McGirt) from *a·inhatapicéycin*.

[1015] McGirt: *awáhhin*.

[1016] McGirt: *istô·feys*.

[1017] Corrected (McGirt) from *sihô·káłi·s*.

[1018] Corrected from *itimatihéyki·*.

[1019] McGirt: *isa·fachokí·*.

[1020] McGirt: *atî·koseys*.

[1021] McGirt: *isă·ⁿfa·cká·kosit*.

[1022] McGirt: *lêykin*.

[1023] McGirt: *ha·yatí·t*.

[1024] McGirt: *iyâ·cin*.

[1025] McGirt: *i·ilawíhci·t*.

[1026] McGirt: *hómpí·ko·k*.

[1027] McGirt: *ha·yickati·*.

[1028] McGirt: *fiksomêykit*.

[1029] McGirt: *mó·mi·*.

[1030] McGirt: *lóhłit*.

[1031] McGirt: *fóllali·to·k*.

[1032] McGirt doesn't know *kólhin*.

[1033] McGirt: *ahópa·nís*.

[1034] McGirt: *'sacáhyit*.

[1035] McGirt: *'łacaléyhcit*.

[1036] McGirt: *lóhłit*.

[1037] McGirt: *ahópa·nacóks*.

[1038] McGirt: *łisléyhcit*.

[1039] Corrected (McGirt) from *hôyłíckáłi·s*.

[1040] McGirt: *ísmoŋkati·t*.

[1041] McGirt: *innakafhô·tin*.

[1042] McGirt: *mô·n*.

[1043] McGirt: *ma·kati·t*.

[1044] Corrected (McGirt) from *istikiníta·t*.

[1045] McGirt: *himo·khihŏ·ⁿkit*.

[1046] McGirt reads these two words as *mó·mihiłi·t*.

[1047] McGirt: *ô·matí·s*.

[1048] McGirt: *wâ·kka·n*.

[1049] Corrected (McGirt) from *a·ohyo·pkít*.

[1050] McGirt: *inŏ·ⁿkka*.

[1051] McGirt: *iláleykit*.

[1052] McGirt: *inŏ·ⁿkka*.

[1053] Corrected (McGirt) from *'lisolipô·fat*.

[1054] McGirt: *imóhpo·fkín*.

[1055] Haas notebook has *illi·tâ·yi·n*.

[1056] McGirt: *a·łatít*.

¹⁰⁵⁷ McGirt: *mó·mala·nín.*

¹⁰⁵⁸ Corrected (McGirt) from *issafali·nâyyin.*

¹⁰⁵⁹ Corrected (McGirt) from *ha·ki·pacókin.*

¹⁰⁶⁰ Corrected (McGirt) from *pó·heyt.*

¹⁰⁶¹ McGirt: *ónt.*

¹⁰⁶² Corrected (McGirt) from *isfali·nêyyin.*

¹⁰⁶³ Corrected (McGirt) from *pó·hi·t.*

¹⁰⁶⁴ Corrected (McGirt) from *isfali·nêyyin.*

¹⁰⁶⁵ McGirt: *yákla·tkâ·t.*

¹⁰⁶⁶ McGirt: *a·acóhkoykín.*

¹⁰⁶⁷ McGirt: *inniki·yâ·t.*

¹⁰⁶⁸ McGirt reads these two words as *'tiná·koycí· hâ·kin.*

¹⁰⁶⁹ Perhaps this should be *kô·maki istô·meys.*

¹⁰⁷⁰ McGirt: *a·acosséyhcit.*

¹⁰⁷¹ McGirt: *a·osséyhcit.*

¹⁰⁷² McGirt: *'titá·koycít.*

¹⁰⁷³ Corrected (Mauldin) from *hámkin.*

¹⁰⁷⁴ Haas notebook has *killiko·.*

¹⁰⁷⁵ Corrected (Mauldin) from *sila·yít.*

¹⁰⁷⁶ Corrected (Mauldin) from *kĭ·ⁿłli·.*

¹⁰⁷⁷ Corrected (Mauldin) from *cifáhli.*

¹⁰⁷⁸ Haas notebook has *óhhit.*

¹⁰⁷⁹ Haas notebook has *o·mâ·.*

¹⁰⁸⁰ Haas notebook has *yaka·kót.*

¹⁰⁸¹ Corrected (Mauldin) from *mă·ⁿhosin.*

¹⁰⁸² Corrected (Mauldin) from *'ma nácki hĭ··ⁿli mâ·hi·.*

¹⁰⁸³ Haas notebook has *hĭ·li·s.*

¹⁰⁸⁴ Mauldin: *omálkan.*

¹⁰⁸⁵ Haas notebook has *potimponêykot.*

¹⁰⁸⁶ Haas notebook has *holwaycí·.*

¹⁰⁸⁷ Mauldin: *holwayi·cimá·ha·t.*

¹⁰⁸⁸ Corrected (Mauldin) from *impiŋkaláki.*

¹⁰⁸⁹ Haas notebook has *follít.*

¹⁰⁹⁰ Haas notebook has *caweykakípiko·t â·yit.*

¹⁰⁹¹ Corrected (Mauldin) from *iswanákan.*

¹⁰⁹² Haas notebook has *ci·yohhawanâ·yeyt.*

¹⁰⁹³ Corrected (Mauldin) from *á·weykayí·t os.*

¹⁰⁹⁴ Haas notebook has *lî·pkeyn.*

[1095] Haas notebook has *casolo·ttêykit*.

[1096] Haas notebook has *a·calápkikon*.

[1097] Haas notebook has *a·ta·sêyyit*.

[1098] Haas notebook has *akiłłéyhcit*.

[1099] Haas notebook has *hâ·keyn*.

[1100] Haas notebook has *łiswéyhwayyí·*.

[1101] Mauldin has never heard this word.

[1102] Mauldin is not sure of the meaning of this word: 'sensitive'?

[1103] Haas notebook has *oponayí· o·câ·t*.

[1104] Haas notebook has *stón-*.

[1105] This line is in Hill's original but was not included in Haas's texts.

[1106] This is hymn #100 (pp. 111–113) in Loughridge and Winslett (1937). In the 1990's it was sung to the tune "How Happy Are They".

[1107] The suffix *-hkan* appears twice in this hymn and seems to add emphasis. It was not used much after about 1900.

[1108] Haas notebook has *hatóci*.

[1109] Haas notebook has *tolá·łwa*.

[1110] Haas notebook has *aca·fă·ⁿckosamkís*.

[1111] Mauldin: *immi·kosápa·káŋkis*.

[1112] Haas notebook has *omálkí·ła·ti^*.

[1113] Haas notebook has *amístin i·łatí·s*.

[1114] Haas notebook has *leykántis*.

[1115] Haas notebook has *ô·mi*.

[1116] Mauldin: *ônt*.

[1117] Haas notebook has *mi·kosapkocóko*.

[1118] This is hymn #179 (pp. 198–199) in Loughridge and Winslett (1937). There are two ways to sing it, long and short.

[1119] Mauldin: *cimmi·kosă·ⁿpiyáti·*. This would be *cimmi·kosă·ⁿpiyátit* if spoken.

[1120] Haas notebook has *mô·mosi·*.

[1121] Corrected (Mauldin) from *si·powa·hí·cas*.

[1122] Haas notebook has *inkapáka·ki·yô·fat*.

[1123] Haas notebook has *hoyá·ci·s*.

[1124] Mauldin: *cimmi·kosápała·nít*.

[1125] Mauldin feels *poha·yíckati·* 'you who created us' would be more natural.

[1126] Haas notebook has *pona·píswa*.

[1127] Haas notebook has *ona· ?apíswa*.

[1128] Haas notebook has *półkit tô·yícka*.

[1129] Haas notebook has *kî·łli·*.

[1130] Or (M): *pompoyafikca*.

[1131] Or (M): *isyomăl^nkosin*; Haas notebook has *isomă·^nkosin*.

[1132] Corrected (M) from *ó·mi·t*.

[1133] Haas notebook has *iyă·^nskâ·kosi·t*.

[1134] Haas notebook has *cimimátticeycíyatin*.

[1135] Mauldin feels *isponweykipás* would be usual here (more humble).

[1136] Haas notebook has *omanéycas*.

[1137] Mauldin would say *akiłłêy^nciyisikot*.

[1138] Mauldin: *cimmi·kkosa·pí·s*.

[1139] Haas notebook has *ohmacáski*.

[1140] Haas notebook has *oháła·ni·t*.

[1141] Haas notebook has *naka·fti·yô·f*.

[1142] Haas notebook has *o·hyâ·t*.

[1143] Corrected (Mauldin) from *ponhickáli·^ns*.

[1144] Haas notebook has *omíkan*.

[1145] Mauldin feels *ohmocáski·n* would be better here.

[1146] Haas notebook has *cimhá·ka*.

[1147] Haas notebook has *i·wéyki·t*, but Mauldin feels *i·wêyki·t* is better. The former means 'continually let go', while *i·wêyki·t* means 'let go once'.

[1148] Corrected (Mauldin) from *nâ·k afêyki·*.

[1149] Corrected (Mauldin) from *sólki·to·k*.

[1150] Haas notebook has *iscahalâ·kíckin*.

[1151] Haas notebook has *kĭ·^nłayi·sikot*.

[1152] Haas notebook has *hôyłeys*.

[1153] Corrected (Mauldin) from *akiłłéycas*.

[1154] Or also (Mauldin): *ishicî·peyt*.

[1155] Or also (Mauldin): *kô·mayeys*.

[1156] Corrected (Mauldin) from *ałî·^npayeyt ô·mi·s*.

[1157] Mauldin has a short final o in this pattern: *isicínła·payáti·to*.

[1158] Haas notebook has *omálkat*.

[1159] Haas notebook has *cimpoyifíkca*.

[1160] Corrected (Mauldin) from *acá·ka*.

[1161] Haas notebook has *ma·kéyt*.

[1162] Corrected (Mauldin) from *i·hóci·féyt facci·cayáli·s*.

[1163] Mauldin: *immi·kosà·^npeyt*.

[1164] Or (Hill): *Emen* 'amen'.

[1165] Haas notebook has *hĭ·^nlosi·*.

[1166] Corrected (Mauldin) from *amiticakkitâlki*.

[1167] Haas notebook has *ohtotho·yaki·*.

[1168] Or also (Mauldin): *'sahókko·lâ·t*.

[1169] Corrected (Mauldin) from *incolâlki*.

[1170] English translation here reflects the King James version.

[1171] Or also (Mauldin): *tó·ka·t*.

[1172] Corrected (Mauldin) from *mo·matí·ka·n*.

[1173] For Mauldin, this word means 'shall we create an obstacle' rather than 'shall we escape'.

[1174] Translation here is from Acts 5:20, King James Version.

[1175] Acts 7:52–53.

[1176] Haas notebook has *ci·mi eyncalâlki*.

[1177] Haas notebook has *cinhíckakáti·t*.

[1178] Mauldin feels *hâlwa·t i·kanáw* would be clearer.

[1179] Corrected (Mauldin) from *hocífkit*.

[1180] Corrected (Mauldin) from *impapáki·*.

[1181] Haas notebook has *imitita·wéyhcit*.

[1182] Haas notebook has *tàlⁿkosita*.

[1183] Haas notebook has *ohtahéykaki·t*. Should either be *ohtahéykáli·t* 'will be cursed' or *ohtahéykati·t* 'was cursed'.

[1184] Haas notebook has *keycatí·s*, but Hill's ms. suggests *kéyho·cati·t ô·ⁿs*.

[1185] Haas has *halwi· ísti*, but this is usually pronounced as one word.

[1186] Haas notebook has *ka·cín*.

[1187] Corrected (M) from *sólki·n*.

[1188] Or (Mauldin) *hâ·kin*.

[1189] Corrected (Mauldin) from *cahki·pi*.

[1190] Genesis 5:32.

[1191] In this quotation Hill paraphrases Genesis chapter 6, sometimes quite closely.

[1192] Genesis 6:17.

[1193] Mauldin feels *ili ʔósti* is odd.

[1194] Haas notebook has *atî·kat*.

[1195] Or better (Mauldin): *akíłeyci· atî·ka·t*.

[1196] Corrected (Mauldin) from *innô·ⁿkéycosit*.

[1197] Haas notebook has *á·heycayáti·t*.

[1198] Genesis 6:7.

[1199] Genesis 6:7.

[1200] Or also (Mauldin) *akasâ·mi·t*.

[1201] Haas notebook has *oha·kâ·t*.

[1202] Corrected (Mauldin) from *i·yina·kóycaki·patín*.

[1203] Corrected (Mauldin) from *ispomaláhki*.

[1204] Corrected (Mauldin) from *ci·yistimiłłéyci*.

[1205] Corrected (Mauldin) from *iscí·kiyáli·s*.

[1206] Corrected (Mauldin) from *cahiłimă·ⁿhi·n*.

[1207] Corrected (Mauldin) from *'simató·tka*.

[1208] Haas notebook has *ayátkikas*.

[1209] Genesis 19:2.

[1210] Corrected (Mauldin) from *so·ssít*.

[1211] Or also (Mauldin): *mŏ·ⁿmatî·kin*.

[1212] Haas notebook has *na·ʔołéyká·ckas*.

[1213] Corrected (Mauldin) from *móhmo·f*.

[1214] Old word. Mauldin would say *sohhóskeycatí·s*.

[1215] Haas notebook has *atałłêycit*.

[1216] Corrected (Mauldin) from *'tipâ·kat*.

[1217] Haas notebook has *ó·ci·t*.

[1218] Mauldin feels this is out of order.

[1219] Haas left out *ó·ci· mônkit cihó·fa lêykin* (from Hill ms.).

[1220] Second occurrence of *nítta* left out in Haas notebook.

[1221] Corrected (Mauldin) from *istó·má·ha·t*.

[1222] Corrected (Mauldin) from *ó·ciko·t*.

[1223] Corrected (Mauldin) from *onayáti·t*.

[1224] Corrected (Mauldin) from *kacíta folliyáti*.

[1225] Haas has *aka·hi·ciyátit*. Mauldin has corrected this to the more expressive *haka·hi·ⁿciyátit*.

[1226] Or also (Mauldin): *oná·hoyatí·*.

[1227] Corrected (Mauldin) from *anokicki·^*.

[1228] Haas notebook has *pómmi·lkín*.

[1229] Corrected (Mauldin) from *apo·kiyáli·*.

[1230] Corrected (Mauldin) from *ipofă·ⁿckâ·kosit*.

[1231] Haas notebook has *i·yaca·yeycipíta*.

[1232] Haas notebook has *imi·kósa·pí·t*.

[1233] Haas notebook has *hi·rot*. Hill's spelling (Helot) here and below shows less English influence.

[1234] Haas notebook has *co·tkosmâ·ha·t*.

[1235] Haas notebook has *iméyncilat*.

[1236] Haas notebook has "*(ístat o·cít)*" here, but also "este vtotet" at the side.

[1237] Haas notebook has *hokkolêyci*.

[1238] Mauldin would not say *nítta tá·ki* for 'days'.

[1239] Haas notebook has *istô·min*.

[1240] Corrected (Mauldin) from Haas *nokkít* to *nókki·t ot*.

[1241] M"hard to say *ow*".

[1242] Haas notebook has *imona·yitá*.

[1243] Haas has *ceyms*, but we follow Hill.

[1244] Haas notebook has *ísli·catí·s*.

[1245] M"today we say *ákpeykatí·s*."

[1246] M "*catotilá·ca* would be better for 'chain'."

[1247] Acts 12:6.

[1248] Corrected (Mauldin) from *akití·cipo·yâ·t*.

[1249] Haas notebook *ahá·ka afa·stâlki*.

[1250] Corrected (Mauldin) from *capa·kkít*.

[1251] Or also (Mauldin): *ohhatalâ·kit*.

[1252] Corrected (Mauldin) from *leykitâ·ya·t*.

[1253] Corrected (Mauldin) from *iyohhakása·mâ·t*.

[1254] Corrected (Mauldin) from *ocî·piya·t*.

[1255] Corrected (Mauldin) from *hǐ·ⁿli·n*.

[1256] Corrected (Mauldin) from *inhapílkosi·*.

[1257] Haas notebook has *ami·há·kas*.

[1258] Haas notebook has *hicáli·s*.

Texts by T. Marshall, pp. 567–606

[1] McGirt: *lêykati·s*.

[2] McGirt: *ha·yít*.

[3] McGirt: *ko·mâ·kati·s*.

[4] McGirt reads these two words as: *kiłłakítan ko·mâ·kati·s*.

[5] Haas has *kíllikâ·li·s*.

[6] Mauldin pronounces these words as compounds: *stipa·pahoktí·* 'female lion', *istipa·pahonánwa* 'male lion'.

[7] Haas notebook has *ła·íssit*.

[8] Haas in her "Creek Vocabulary" identified *motáka* as a chunkey stone (a stone disk used in a game). The game was forgotten by the 19th century, though the word survived in stories like this. In Florida Seminole Creek, *motáka* has come to refer to marbles.

[9] Mauldin: *ô·mika*.

[10] Haas notebook has *istó·mosit*.

[11] Haas notebook has *ipâ·ka·n*.

[12] Haas notebook has *issi·pit*.

[13] Mauldin: *'sanacomán*.

[14] Haas notebook has *poha·kít*.

[15] The spelling in Haas's notebook suggests *'laláki·pí·t*.

[16] Haas notebook: *'timoponayyi·-*.

[17] *ohfáccata·t* is circled in Haas notebook with arrow before *ná·ki*.

[18] This word can be read as *icó yápin* 'Deer's horns' or as *icoyapín* 'deer horns'.

[19] Haas notebook: *mi·ya·cî·tot*.

[20] Haas notebook: *hi·cáki·s*.

[21] Mauldin: *sáyi·pít*.

[22] Haas's notebook may suggest instead: *islítkosi· ha·yít*.

[23] Haas first recorded the bird names here as *sânlacókwa* 'hummingbird' and *akcâwhka* 'crane', but corrected them to *lânlacókwa* and *akcâwhko*.

[24] McGirt: *'lolî·pit*.

[25] McGirt: *samokhá·ki·t*.

[26] Based on Haas's translation: V:142.

[27] Translation based on Haas's translation in V:144, 146.

[28] McGirt: *hâmkosin*.

[29] McGirt: *'hilíswa*.

[30] McGirt: *istó·mi·*.

[31] McGirt: *wa·lít*.

[32] McGirt: *ímpoha·kín*.

[33] Haas notebook has this as two words: *si·sayyá·cki· taŋki·n*.

[34] McGirt: *annokkeycî·tt ó·s < annokkeycî·pit ó·s*.

[35] Haas notebook has *lakpálḟeycít*.

[36] Haas notebook has *ahâlwat*.

[37] McGirt: *a·óhtolomkín*.

[38] Haas notebook has *ohhopóllíŋkít*. McGirt reads this as *ohhopollínki·t*.

[39] McGirt: *wa·kkô·f*.

[40] McGirt: *ahopáhyit*.

[41] Haas notebook has *sika·lô·nit*. McGirt reads it as *si·ka·lóhnit*.

[42] McGirt pronounces this as *'takoca·cá·ti*.

[43] McGirt: *niha·cámpa*.

[44] Haas notebook has *lo·ká·ckin*.

[45] Haas notebook has *saláhtit*.

[46] The placement of *man* here is odd. McGirt reads it as *halpatá mêyn* 'an alligator instead'.

[47] Haas notebook has *yákkafaŋkatí·s*.

[48] McGirt: *mô·mo·f*.

[49] McGirt: *háhyit*.

[50] McGirt: *o·mati·s*.

[51] McGirt: *iha·nayáŋks*.

[52] McGirt: *tintakháhkit*.

[53] Haas notebook has *hopołłiŋkata·t*.

[54] McGirt: *tincihálho·yati·s* (different speakers say the word differently).

[55] McGirt: *apa·láŋkiw'*.

[56] McGirt: *akká·ki·*.

[57] McGirt: *tinhalatákala·ná·t*.

[58] McGirt: *lô·li·n*.

[59] McGirt: *âlkit*.

[60] McGirt: *tinhalátipeycati·s* (different speakers say it different ways).

[61] McGirt: *akíti·câ·t*.

[62] McGirt: *tinhaláta·kít*.

[63] McGirt: *'sanacomán*.

[64] McGirt: *nacô·min*.

[65] Haas notebook has: *api·yitán*.

[66] McGirt: *atihtíhcit*.

[67] McGirt: *'simohcakcahíhcit*. In examples like this, *'simohcákcahi·cít* could be translated as 'was nailing them in', and *'simohcakcahíhcit* could be translated as 'nailed them in' (roughly, ongoing vs. perfective aspect).

[68] Haas notebook has: *ohfâŋki·t*.

Texts by A. E. Raiford, pp. 607–629

[1] Contracted from *li·tkí·ha·yít*.

[2] Haas notebook has *íssit*.

[3] Haas notebook has *acoleysakí·*.

[4] This is presumably Colonel Daniel Newnan McIntosh (1822–1896), youngest son of William McIntosh.

[5] This is stated to be the title, but it seems to run into the text.

[6] Mauldin: *ilíso·lâ·t*.

[7] Haas notebook has *oyyafó·pki*.

[8] Mauldin: *haloníski*.

[9] Mauldin: *iccitáta·t*.

[10] Haas notebook has *yofólki·pi·t*.

[11] Translation based on free translation, IV:84.

[12] Or (Mauldin) *nítta*.

[13] Haas notebook has *aho·yi·t*.

[14] Haas notebook has *istihatkiyatíka*.

[15] McGirt: *há·ho·yí·n.*

[16] McGirt: *ha·hô·yin.*

[17] McGirt: *inhá·ho·yâ·t yati·ki· há·t o·mâ·t.*

[18] The white interpreter invents a word <pericetv> in Creek (instead of <encukopericetv> 'to visit'). We have translated his error by making up the word *viss* in English (instead of *visit*).

[19] Mauldin: *ali·ttô·matit,* contracted from *ali·pít ô·matit.*

[20] Haas notebook has *hatâ·.*

[21] Haas notebook has *cali·calánckit ô·n o·mâ·t.*

[22] Haas notebook has *iccastimî·lkika.*

[23] Haas notebook has *'titâ·yiyô·nó·ks* and a shorter form *'titâ·yô·nó·ks.*

[24] Haas notebook has *ilisóllit.*

[25] Haas notebook has *ohlêyki·t.*

[26] Haas notebook has *hatâ·.*

[27] Or (Mauldin) *mô·meys.*

[28] Haas notebook has *isalákkan.*

[29] McGirt: *stima·skó·ki 'ponaká.*

[30] McGirt: *lêykati·s.*

[31] McGirt: *incokopíleycít.*

[32] McGirt: *isholwayi·cakóso·mi·t.*

[33] McGirt: *pifa·tkâ·t.*

Texts by I. Field, pp. 631–663

[1] Haas's notebook suggests *óhka·kántot.*

[2] Mauldin reads this as *ititá·koycâlkit.*

[3] Mauldin: *incátho·kí·t.*

[4] Mauldin: *hayyo·makósi·n.*

[5] Haas's notebook suggests *siho·kî·po·fata·t.*

[6] Mauldin: *takleykĭ·ⁿpayátit.*

[7] Haas writes *yo-* here but then questions whether it should be *yi-.*

[8] Haas notebook has *timpan-.*

[9] Haas notebook has *sapiyapáŋka* here. Hill seems to have preferred *sa·kiyá* for Sac and Fox, while Raiford guessed it might be *sapiyá.*

[10] Contracted from *leykî·pit o·méyka.* These contractions are not usually written in the traditional Creek spelling, but we suggest <likētt omikv>.

[11] Mauldin: *lathóyi·pô·f.*

[12] Haas would normally write *pánka* here.

[13] Mauldin: *kâ·kto·mati·s.*

[14] Margaret Mauldin: "Old people used to refer to neglected things as being lost in the weeds, and it clearly meant the weeds of time!"

[15] Mauldin: *a·conichô·yin.*

[16] Haas added the following note, written phonetically: "H. says that this story is all mixed up. He never did tell the story because he himself can't tell it straight."

[17] Mauldin: *isacolakí.*

[18] Haas notebook has *hoponaká.*

[19] Mauldin: *ohtíhti·cít.*

[20] Mauldin: *imoponayí·.*

[21] Haas notebook has *istákka·k to·matí·t.*

[22] Haas notebook appears to have: *ka·kî·paya·ti·^.*

[23] Haas notebook appears to have *imiticakkiyatí.* The word would seem to mean 'our brothers'.

[24] Raiford interpreted *ahiliskasáppi* 'cold medicine' as a medicine that had been used. For McGirt, it's a medicine containing an herb that keeps the medicine cold even in hot weather.

[25] Haas has *coholéyci,* evidently intending *cokolêyci.* Raiford also suggests this, translating *cokolêyci* literally as 'a house standing'.

[26] Haas notebook has *mônt.*

[27] Haas notebook has *yoffólhokí·ckin.*

[28] Haas notebook appears to have *ka·kíckin.*

[29] Mauldin: *mo·makósi·n.*

[30] Haas notebook has *issałahłakát.*

[31] Haas notebook has *hiliskasápkita·t,* but also records the more usual *hiliskasáppita·t* for Raiford.

[32] Haas notebook has *intaca·kałákko.*

[33] McGirt reads this as *hopáyi·n ohhî·ctoŋká.*

[34] Haas notebook has *issokoláhkit.*

[35] Haas notebook has *'mayiheykípeycít.*

[36] Haas notebook has *iwweykitá* as the original form, changed to *imweykitá.* The prefix *im-* generally has the shape *im-,* but some speakers use *iw-* before *w* (Haas 1977a).

[37] Haas has *api·pi·tá·ti·to·k.*

[38] Haas notebook has *'łalahóhkin.*

[39] Haas notebook has *isitó·yo·łkí·t.*

[40] Haas notebook records these two words as *mônt o·mâ·t.* We have changed it to *mónt o·mâ·t.* A better transcription might be *mónto·mâ·t* (as there is a downstep after the first syllable).

[41] Mauldin: *pa·pít.*

[42] Mauldin: *pa·péyt.*

[43] <kitt> is a very casual contraction of <kicet> that may seem improper to some as a written form.

[44] Mauldin: *omi·pi·s*.

[45] A very casual contraction of *omî·pika*. Jim Hill wrote his texts in Creek, and they have a more formal feel. This text was presumably dictated to Haas and sometimes captures less formal speech.

[46] Haas notebook has *panlánkin*. Mauldin reads it as *panłámkin*.

[47] Mauldin: *hayatkí·*.

[48] Haas notebook also writes this as *si·yohfacci·cit*.

[49] Haas notebook has *ó·n*.

[50] Haas originally had *yifolhóhkit* but then changed it to *yofolhóhkit*. She has *ifolhóhkit* in the next sentence. Perhaps she has captured the speech of two consultants.

[51] Contracted from *imonayáha·nícka·t*.

[52] Contracted from *łátho·yít o·mí·s*.

[53] Mauldin: *'yacakfólho·katí·s*.

[54] Haas notebook has *á·faŋkít*, but we have changed *ŋk* to *nk* in this and related forms to match her later usage.

[55] Haas notebook originally had *a·fâŋkit o·mâ·t* 'as he was [in the state of] peeping out [of the water]'. This is how Mauldin reads it. Haas then changed it to *á·faŋkít o·mâ·t* 'as he was [in the process of] peeping out [of the water].

[56] Mauldin: *a·fáŋkit*.

[57] Mauldin: *ohkâ·katí·s*.

[58] Mauldin: *hóyłaha·nayâ·t*. The stem *hoyĭ·ⁿł-* appears to be a previously undescribed grade form of *hoył-* 'stand'.

[59] Haas notebook has *sto·mâ·hit ó·s*.

[60] Perhaps this should be *mo·mî·tt*, contracted from *mo·mî·pit*.

[61] Mauldin: *lapátki·n*.

[62] Mauldin: *intalkahoskocít*.

[63] Contracted from *somiciphô·yin*.

[64] Haas notebook has *cítto yi·kcat*. This expression evidently refers to a type of snake, but we haven't heard the term.

[65] Mauldin: *akalkapikot omáli·s*.

[66] Haas notebook first had *téyho·katí·s* 'they went across'. This was then partially changed to *teyho·kakí·s* 'let's go across'. We've corrected the latter to *teyhokáki·s*.

[67] Haas notebook has *ôŋka*. The last two words are contracted from *cinpoyá·fki· tâ·yit oŋká*.

[68] Haas notebook has *'łałâ·kit*.

[69] Haas also records a shorter version of this word: *onáhckas*.

[70] Mauldin: *mó·mała·nín*.

[71] Mauldin: *ókho·yiká.*

Texts by D. Starr, pp. 665–669

[1] McGirt: *nò·kłati·n.*

[2] Here 'working the land' seems to be a euphemism for having sex.

[3] McGirt: *aka·łpatín.*

[4] Haas notebook has: *si·cati·s.*

[5] McGirt: *iscáhwit.*

[6] McGirt: *hi·ckati·t.*

[7] Haas notebook has: *acatá·kki·pati·s.*

[8] McGirt: *aktikki·tî·kati·s.*

Texts by J. Bell, pp. 671–678

[1] This word not known to McGirt.

[2] McGirt: *ô·min.*

[3] McGirt: *wákki· tâ·ya·t.*

[4] McGirt: *ipopalhámki·s.*

[5] Haas notebook has *hamáhlo·f.* McGirt: *homa·lô·f.*

[6] The use of *a·fa·ckâlki* for 'ball-players' is not known to McGirt. She would say *pokkiccâlki.*

[7] This word is uncertain.

[8] Corrected (McGirt) from *móŋka.*

[9] Corrected (McGirt) from *laplákkon.*

[10] McGirt: *imákasa·mít.*

[11] McGirt: *'tihícala·nati·t.*

[12] McGirt: *tincokopíleyci·t.*

[13] McGirt: *incokopíleycati·s.*

[14] McGirt: *sinfayatakiká·ti·s.*

[15] McGirt: *yá·cit.*

[16] McGirt reads the four words as *ha·yayí·s   ma·kít ónt ó·n.*

[17] McGirt: *ma·kíckaŋkí·.*

[18] McGirt: *'lafolô·tkosáka·ti^.*

[19] McGirt: *hopo·yícki·s.*

[20] Corrected (McGirt) from *ishóylin.*

[21] Corrected (McGirt) from *ò·ciko·.*

[22] Corrected (McGirt) from *ayó·ci·cki·s.*

[23] McGirt: *i·innokkéyci·*.

[24] Corrected (McGirt) from *calipáłtó·s*.

[25] McGirt: *cimístomi·cayi·ti·ˇ*.

[26] McGirt: *eycinwâ·kkeyn*.

[27] Corrected from *léykit*.

[28] Haas's symbol ['] here probably represents aspiration.

[29] Corrected (McGirt) from *inokkí·peys*.

[30] Corrected (McGirt) from *acóhha·hô·s*.

[31] McGirt: *łímona·yín*.

[32] McGirt: *a·inwâ·kki·s*.

Texts by W. Tanyan, pp. 679–687

[1] McGirt: *ci·^*.

[2] McGirt: *łisafa·ccatí·s*.

[3] Corrected (McGirt) from *inhompíckin*.

[4] McGirt: *hatícci·*.

[5] From *'sałĭⁿpit*.

[6] McGirt: *sáwana·yatí·s*.

[7] Haas has *a·ta·sêykin*.

[8] Corrected (McGirt) from *leykícki·t*.

[9] McGirt: *ô·ma·ˇ*. McGirt and Mauldin consistently use long final vowels for information questions (asking 'where', 'what', 'who', etc.).

[10] McGirt: *asêy mâ·hin*.

[11] Corrected (McGirt) from *móŋka*. This word can be pronounced *móŋka* or *moŋká* with different senses.

[12] Corrected from *łółaccás*.

[13] Haas has *similáwki·*.

[14] Corrected (McGirt) from *cincampantó·n*.

[15] Haas has *iła·íssit*.

[16] McGirt: *afolotêykit*.

[17] Corrected (McGirt) from *móŋka*.

[18] McGirt: *lêykícki·t ô·ma·ˇ*.

[19] McGirt: *asêy mâ·hi*.

[20] Haas notebook has *cokohátkin*.

[21] McGirt: *ínli·tkosít*.

[22] Haas notebook has *lápki·n*.

[23] McGirt: *afolotêykeyt*.

[24] Haas has *ila·íssit*.

[25] McGirt: *sto·má·^*.

[26] McGirt: *tâ·yin*. Both *tâ·yin* 'much' and *tǎ·ⁿyin* 'very much' make sense here and are usually spelled the same way.

[27] *ánto·mayáŋknó·s* is from *anít o·mayáŋkin ó·s*.

[28] Line breaks, apparently reflecting phrasing, are as in original. Grave accent indicates "do appr. a below mid. c." ^ indicates sol with fall. First line is "Ritualistic intro." Vowel of first word is [ɔ].

[29] Haas does not analyze this introduction, but it might come from *ínt o·kêys ci·^* 'he [the chief] was saying'.

[30] McGirt: *imahaŋkátka*.

[31] McGirt: *takfíttata·ti*.

[32] McGirt: *mo·mí·n*.

[33] McGirt: *ammo·miká·li·s*.

[34] McGirt: *heyyô·ma·ti*.

[35] Haas has *ŏ·mǎtĭ·kĭn*.

[36] McGirt: *heyyô·ma·ti*.

[37] McGirt: *ánta·tíhkan*. The ending *-hkan* was not used much after about 1900.

[38] We are not sure what this word is.

Texts by E. Gouge, pp. 689–692

[1] McGirt: *ámpo·hít ó·n*.

[2] McGirt: *ô·máli·s*.

[3] McGirt: *ô·máli·s*.

[4] Corrected (McGirt) from *omí·pika*.

[5] Haas notebook also has *i·mi·tá·leys*, but Fannie Sulphur offered this form.

[6] McGirt reads these two words as *itimpókki·ccí· tâ·yi·t*.

[7] McGirt: *ô·mati·s*.

[8] McGirt: *timpókki·ccâ·t*.

[9] McGirt: *tinfaccitá*.

[10] Corrected from *impó·ho·yí·t o·s stô·meys*.

[11] McGirt: *isápi·t*, from *isápi·yít*.

[12] Corrected from *impó·ho·yí·t o·s stô·meys*.

[13] McGirt: *omíyáli·s*.

[14] McGirt reads these two words as *tinfácca·kí·t ô·mati·s*.

[15] McGirt: *'sanacomá*.

[16] McGirt: *ô·mati·s*.

[17] Corrected (McGirt) from *'timafáckiká·ti·s.*

[18] Translation based in part on XV:172.

[19] McGirt: *itimpokkícca·kâ·t.*

[20] McGirt: *mô·meys.*

[21] Corrected (McGirt) from *ahò·ski· móŋkati·s.*

[22] McGirt: *ispo·kí·t.*

[23] Haas notebook has this for FS, *poyyikcí·ta·t* for EG.

Texts by A. Sulphur, pp. 693–695

[1] Corrected (McGirt) from *iyá·cit.*

[2] McGirt: *icohhalâ·kayi·t.*

[3] Corrected (McGirt) from *móŋka.*

[4] McGirt: *'titayyipáti·s.*

[5] McGirt: *'tihicáɫa·niyâ·t.*

[6] McGirt reads these two words as *i·yohhapáki· ha·yí·t.*

[7] Add notes, p. 189?

[8] McGirt: *íɫyeycô·f.*

[9] McGirt: *ha·yosít.*

[10] Corrected (McGirt) from *apó·ʃkin yapo·kit.*

[11] Corrected from *yapô·kit.* Or (McGirt): *yápo·kít.*

[12] McGirt: *o·matí·t.*

[13] McGirt: *mô·ma·t.*

[14] McGirt: *wákka·t.*

[15] McGirt: *okófki·t.*

[16] McGirt: *isahocífaki·s.*

[17] McGirt: *omáli·s.*

Texts by D. Cook, pp. 696–698

[1] Corrected (Mauldin) from *amá·kosi·n.* The word *omá·kosi·n* could be omitted.

[2] Haas notebook has *hoktakitat.*

[3] Corrected (Mauldin) from *'limi·ⁿtêy.*

[4] Corrected (Mauldin) from *ciló·kkit ô·yí·c.*

[5] Corrected from *mató·cciko·n.*

[1] McGirt: *'sapô·kiyáti·t ó·n.*

[2] McGirt: *sohho·cipí·.*

[3] McGirt: *stapâ·keyt.*

[4] McGirt: *a·tô·tin.*

[5] Haas notebook has: *achoyî·pika.*

[6] McGirt: api·yiyâ·t.

[7] McGirt: *a·tô·tin.*

[8] McGirt: *hatâ·ⁿ.*

[9] Haas notebook has: *tà·ⁿcastimiłêycit.*

[10] McGirt: *tinfaccitát.*

[11] McGirt: *ampoytá·ki* (shortened from *anhopoytá·ki*)

[12] Haas has *eyplihéym linkan to·kâ·t.*

[13] McGirt: *'łatipáti·t ô·mi·s.*

[14] Haas notebook has: *insatêykit.*

[15] Haas notebook has: *'sayaticéyhcit.*

[16] Haas notebook has: *isinciyáti·t ô·mi·s ci·^.*

Texts by Paskofa, pp. 707–710

[1] Corrected (Mauldin) from *yóhsapaklít.*

[2] Or also (Mauldin): *itá·koyci·t.*

[3] Corrected (Mauldin) from *istilimí·ta.*

[4] Corrected (Mauldin) from *'yapô·kati·s.*

[5] Or also (Mauldin): *awâ·hit.*

[6] Line is in original notebook.

[7] Corrected from *afónna·kit.*

[8] Or also (Mauldin): *awâ·hit.*

[9] Corrected (Mauldin) from *iyáfankati·s: iyáfankati·s* would mean 'kissed himself'.

[10] Corrected (Mauldin) from *iyafanêyko·f.*

[11] Corrected (Mauldin) from *a·yatímpona·yatí·s.*

[12] Corrected (Mauldin) from *akhataphokitan.*

[13] Corrected (Mauldin) from *ciyâ·cákhaks.*

[14] Haas notebook has *okhatapéykit.*

[15] Or also (Mauldin): *címho·yí·t.*

[16] Mauldin: *ô·malá·nckin.*

[17] Haas notebook has *leykatí·s.*

[18] Or also (Mauldin): *ahíci·t.*

[19] Line is in original notebook.

[20] Corrected (Mauldin) from *oho·payósi·n.*

[21] Or also (Mauldin): *awâ·hit.*

Texts by A. Grayson, pp. 711–712

[1] Adam Grayson was a Creek freedman. There are a few peculiarities in transcription here that we take to be mistakes on Haas's part rather than features of Mr. Grayson's speech.

[2] Haas notebook has *á·yakí·c*.

[3] Haas notebook has *itifólli·yít â·yi·t*.

[4] Haas notebook has *fólli·t â·yi·t*.

[5] Haas notebook has *iliyo·pokkácki·t*.

[6] Haas notebook has *ohsokopíleycatí·s*.

[7] Haas notebook has *o·kêyt*.

[8] Haas notebook has *ancalafkóyt o·mác*. Grayson may have pronounced *ct* here as *tt*.

[9] Haas notebook has *amohseytá·cikono·mâ·t* (but see a similar form below).

[10] Haas notebook has *cinhissa·kitáta·t*.

[11] Haas notebook has *isóhseycatí·s* (perhaps the way he spoke?). Mauldin feels it is odd that this verb is singular: "maybe he's talking about the wolf population."

Texts Collected by V. Riste, pp. 713–725

[1] McGirt: *hâmkin*.

[2] A portion of text here (*isticá·ti 'hilishá·yan atóhteyn amáli·kcatí·s. cakahomán ancifêykit anca·tíhcin*) is bracketed in Haas's notes, perhaps indicating they were to be deleted.

[3] McGirt: *anséyhyit*.

[4] McGirt: *aminsáhtit*.

[5] Corrected (McGirt) from *capatí·kin*.

[6] McGirt: *'sitipayíhcit*.

[7] McGirt: *apâ·kati·s*.

[8] McGirt: *hayyó·mi·n*.

[9] McGirt: *ô·mati·s*.

[10] McGirt: *ya·cakiko·t*.

[11] McGirt: *omâ·kati·s*.

[12] McGirt: *ô·mati·s*.

[13] Corrected (McGirt) from *móŋka*.

[14] Corrected (McGirt) from *omálkakat*.

[15] McGirt: *itihalatháhyit*.

[16] Corrected (McGirt) from *o·má·t*.

[17] McGirt reads these two words as *ma·kí·t ô·mika*.

[18] McGirt: *hi·cíckati·t*.

[19] McGirt: *imáyopo·skâ·t*.

[20] McGirt: *ôꞏs.*

[21] McGirt: *eycintotáꞏliꞏs.*

[22] This word is not known to McGirt or Mauldin.

[23] McGirt: *ahítiꞏcín.*

[24] This may be an error for *finkiꞏ.*

[25] This may be an error for *finkiꞏlákkoꞇ*

[26] This word is uncertain.

[27] McGirt: *loꞏlôꞏfan.*

[28] Corrected (McGirt) from *maꞏtapóꞏmin.*

[29] Corrected (McGirt) from *ístamey âlkeys.*

[30] McGirt: *imíꞏkasaꞏmatíꞏs.*

[31] McGirt: *imáyopoꞏskít.*

[32] McGirt: *itincihalhoyíyáliꞏs.*

[33] Corrected (McGirt) from *maꞏtapóꞏmin.*

[34] McGirt: *itímponaꞏyatíꞏs.*

[35] McGirt: *cinhoyłéycáꞏliꞏs* 'I will set'.

[36] McGirt: *itincihalhoyíyáliꞏs.*

[37] McGirt: *hôyłatiꞏtoꞇ.*

[38] Corrected (McGirt) from *'limoktíkkiꞏyatíꞏs.*

[39] McGirt *momiꞏcôꞏfaꞇ.*

[40] McGirt: *istincihállałaꞏnít.*

[41] McGirt: *ôꞏmeys.*

[42] McGirt: *'timónayaꞏkâꞏt.*

[43] Corrected (McGirt) from *móŋka.*

[44] Corrected (McGirt) from *iwánhkiꞇ.*

[45] McGirt: *iyâꞏceys.*

CPSIA information can be obtained
at www.ICGtesting.com
Printed in the USA
LVOW09*1752030118
561660LV00018B/266/P

9 780520 286429